Best Practices

for Hospital & Health-System Pharmacy

Position & Guidance Documents of ASHP

2004-2005 Edition

American Society of Health-System Pharmacists®

Bethesda, Maryland

The ASHP policies in this book, positions and guidance documents, are intended to foster improvements in pharmacy practice and patient care. The content of individual positions and guidance documents should be assessed in the context of your own health system, its policies and procedures, as well as applicable federal and state laws and regulations.

Guidance documents, in particular, evolve because of advances in technology, new knowledge from research, and lessons from experience. Additionally, medication information is constantly evolving because of ongoing research and clinical experience, and it is often subject to interpretation and unique clinical situations. The American Society of Health-System Pharmacists (ASHP) endeavors to ensure the completeness and timeliness of the information presented. However, the reader is advised that the publisher, contributors, editors, and reviewers make no representations concerning the suitability of the information for any purpose, and are not responsible for the immediate currency of the information, for any errors or omissions, or for any consequences arising from the use of these materials. All decisions made within the context of pharmacy practice should be based on the independent judgment of the practitioner.

For more than 60 years, ASHP has helped pharmacists who practice in hospitals and health systems improve medication use and enhance patient safety. The Society's 30,000 members include pharmacists and pharmacy technicians who practice in inpatient, outpatient, home-care, and long-term-care settings, as well as pharmacy students. For more information about the wide array of ASHP activities and the many ways in which pharmacists help people make the best use of medicines, visit ASHP's Web site, www.ashp.org, or its consumer Web site, www.SafeMedication.com.

Editor: Bruce Hawkins

Published by the American Society of Health-System Pharmacists, 7272 Wisconsin Avenue, Bethesda, MD 20814.

ASHP® is a service mark of the American Society of Health-System Pharmacists™, Inc.; registered in the U.S. Patent and Trademark Office.

ISBN: 1-58528-110-7

To Joseph H. Deffenbaugh, Jr., R.Ph., M.P.H., CAPT (Pharmacist Director), USPHS (Ret.), in grateful recognition of a lifetime of service dedicated to promoting public health

American Society of Health-System Pharmacists, 1996–2004
- Director, Public Health and Quality
- Editor, *Best Practices for Health-System Pharmacy*

United States Public Health Service, Indian Health Service, 1963–1995
- Public Health Service Distinguished Service Medal, 1993
- Public Health Service Meritorious Service Medal, 1992
- Indian Health Service Outstanding Service Plaque, 1991
- Public Health Service Outstanding Service Medal, 1989
- Nashville Area Tribes, Tribal Chiefs' Award, 1988
- Public Health Service Commendation Medal, 1987
- Public Health Service Hazardous Duty Service Award, 1983
- Public Health Service Isolated Hardship Service Award, 1981

Reason's whole pleasure, all the joys of sense,
Lie in three words,—health, peace, and competence.
—Alexander Pope, *Essay on Man*

Contents

* Indicates content that has been added or revised since the 2003–2004 edition.

Drug Distribution and Control—continued

DISTRIBUTION

Education and Training

_____

* Indicates content that has been added or revised since the 2003–2004 edition.

Ethics

Formulary Management (Medication-Use Policy Development)

Government, Law, and Regulation

---

* Indicates content that has been added or revised since the 2003–2004 edition.

Government, Law, and Regulation—continued

Medication Misadventures

Medication Therapy and Patient Care

ORGANIZATION AND DELIVERY OF SERVICES

* Indicates content that has been added or revised since the 2003–2004 edition.

Medication Therapy and Patient Care—continued

SPECIFIC PRACTICE AREAS

Pharmaceutical Industry

DRUG PRODUCTS, LABELING, AND PACKAGING

---

* Indicates content that has been added or revised since the 2003–2004 edition.

Pharmaceutical Industry—continued

MARKETING

Pharmacy Management

COMPENSATION AND REIMBURSEMENT

HUMAN RESOURCES

* Indicates content that has been added or revised since the 2003–2004 edition.

* Indicates content that has been added or revised since the 2003–2004 edition.

ASHP Therapeutic Guidelines—continued

Page Locator for Guidance Documents by Type and Title

ASHP Technical Assistance Bulletins

Acknowledgments

ASHP gratefully acknowledges the following persons who donated their expertise in drafting the new and revised guidance documents added to this edition and those who reviewed and submitted comments on interim drafts of the documents.

ASHP Statement on the Use of Dietary Supplements

Drafter: David J. Kroll, Ph.D.

Reviewers: American Dietetic Association (ADA)
             American Medical Association (AMA)
             American Nurses Association (ANA)
             National Consumers League
             Public Citizen (PC)
             Ron Barnes, M.S.
             Carol J. Bickford, Ph.D., RN, BC (ANA)
             Lisa Boothby, Pharm.D.
             Cindi Brennan, Pharm.D., M.H.A.
             Sian Carr-Lopez, Pharm.D.
             Steven Chen, Pharm.D.
             Kevin J. Colgan, M.A.
             David Copelan, Pharm.D.
             Joseph Cranston, Ph.D. (AMA)
             Denise E. Daly, Pharm.D.
             Peter A.G. M. De Smet, Pharm.D., Ph.D.
             Joseph Deffenbaugh (CAPT., USPHS, Ret.), M.P.H.
             Kim H. DeRhodes
             Paul Doering, M.S.
             Deanna Dreher, Pharm.D.
             Christine F. Edie, Pharm.D.
             Steven Eggleston, Pharm.D.
             Carla B. Frye, Pharm.D., BCPS, FASHP
             Bill J. Gurley, Ph.D.
             Guy Hasegawa, Pharm.D.
             Col. W. Mike Heath, M.B.A.
             Roxanne Homar, Pharm.D.
             Marianne F. Ivey, Pharm.D., M.P.H., FASHP
             Cherry Jackson, Pharm.D.
             Roger Klotz
             Cynthia L. LaCivita, Pharm.D.
             Alan H. Mutnick, Pharm.D.
             Brian M. Meyer, M.B.A.
             Charlie Myers, Pharm.D.
             Keith Olsen, Pharm.D.
             Roland Patry, M.S.
             Marjorie S. Phillips, M.S., FASHP
             Steven C. Piscitelli, Pharm.D.
             Darryl S. Rich, Pharm.D., M.B.A., FASHP
             Larry D. Sasich, Pharm.D., M.P.H., FASHP (PC)
             Douglas Scheckelhoff, M.S.
             Gayle N. Scott, Pharm.D., FASCP, BCPS, ELS, CGP
             Kelly M. Shields, Pharm.D.
             Susan C. Smolinske, Pharm.D., BCPS, DABAT
             Sharm Steadman, Pharm.D., BCPS, FASHP, CDE
             Gary Stein, Ph.D.
             Jennifer Strickland, Pharm.D.
             Cynthia Thompson, Ph.D., RD, FADA (ADA)
             Kasey K. Thompson, Pharm.D.
             Candy Tsourounis, Pharm.D.
             Sherry Umhoeffer, M.B.A.
             Paul C. Walker, Pharm.D.
             Dennis M. Williams, Pharm.D.
             David R. Witmer, Pharm.D.
             Raymond Woosley, Ph.D.
             William A. Zellmer, M.P.H.

ASHP Guidelines on the Pharmacist's Role in the Development, Implementation, and Assessment of Critical Pathways

Expert Panel: Diane M. Cappelletty, Pharm.D.
             Greg Gousse, M.S., FASHP
             William R. Martin, M.S., FASHP
             Mary Lynn McPherson, Pharm.D., BCPS, CDE, FASHP
             Antonio Petitta, M.B.A.

Reviewers: Patricia Grunwald, Pharm.D.
             Thomas G. Hall, Pharm.D., FASHP
             Maureen Knell, Pharm.D., BCPS/ Cardiology
             Calvin H. Knowlton, Ph.D., M.Div.
             Kristen A. Perkerson, Pharm.D.
             David S. Roffman, Pharm.D., BCPS
             Linda S. Tyler, Pharm.D., FASHP
             Elizabeth Udeh, Pharm.D.
             Doug Weschules, Pharm.D.
             Chris Zimmerman, Pharm.D.

ASHP Therapeutic Position Statement on the Use of Low Molecular Weight Heparin for Adult Outpatient Treatment of Acute Deep Vein Thrombosis

Drafters: Donald J. Tillman, Pharm.D.
             Daniel M. Witt, Pharm.D.

Reviewers: Academy of Managed Care Pharmacy
             Aventis
             American Academy of Nurse Practitioners
             American Pharmacists Association

American College of Chest Physicians
Patricia M. Jenkins, Pharm.D., C.A.C.P.
Stuart T. Haines, Pharm.D., BCPS
Joseph F. Steiner, Pharm.D.
R. Donald Harvey, III, Pharm.D., BCPS,
  BCOP
Lee Green M.D., MPH
William L. Greene, Pharm.D., BCPS,
  FASHP
Richard Hinkle, R.Ph., J.D.

ASHP Therapeutic Position Statement on Strategies for Identifying and Preventing Pneumococcal Resistance

Drafter: Marianne Billeter, Pharm.D., BCPS

Reviewers: Academy of Managed Care Pharmacy
              American Geriatrics Society
              American Pharmacists Association
              Cardinal Health Pharmacy Management
              American College of Clinical Pharmacy

Introduction

The American Society of Health-System Pharmacists (ASHP) is the 30,000-member national professional association that represents pharmacists who practice in hospitals, health maintenance organizations, long-term care facilities, home care agencies, and other components of health systems. The ASHP has extensive publishing and educational programs designed to help members improve their delivery of pharmaceutical care, and it is a national accrediting organization for pharmacy residency and pharmacy technician training programs.

The Compendium

ASHP, since its founding, has developed official professional policies in the form of policy positions and guidance documents about pharmacy practice, first for hospitals, and then for the continuum of practice settings in integrated health systems. Since 1984, these policies have been compiled annually in *Best Practices for Hospital & Health-System Pharmacy,* a compendium of ASHP policy positions, statements, guidelines, technical assistance bulletins, therapeutic position statements, therapeutic guidelines, and selected ASHP-endorsed documents. *Best Practices* reflects the intent of ASHP's professional policies to foster improvements in pharmacy practice and patient care.

The compendium is organized by topic to help readers quickly locate related documents. The table of contents is structured by topic, and under each topic the relevant ASHP policy positions, statements, guidelines, technical assistance bulletins, and endorsed documents are listed. The therapeutic documents are listed by type. Following the table of contents is a page locator for documents by type and title, and the index lists each document, to assist readers who are accustomed to searching for a specific document by its title.

Origins and Purposes of ASHP's Policy Positions and Guidance Documents

Policy positions generally originate with an ASHP council and are approved by the ASHP Board of Directors and ASHP House of Delegates. Some policy positions originate as House of Delegate resolutions. Statements, guidelines, and technical assistance bulletins originate with an ASHP council or commission. Statements are approved by the Board of Directors and the House of Delegates, because of their broad philosophical nature. Other types of documents are approved by the Board of Directors only. Therapeutic position statements and therapeutic guidelines originate with the ASHP Commission on Therapeutics and are approved by the Board of Directors.

There is a gradation in detail among the guidance documents. Policy positions are short pronouncements, intended to address professional practice. Often, principles established in policy positions are elaborated on in statements and guidelines. Statements express basic philosophy, guidelines offer programmatic advice, and technical assistance bulletins offer more detailed programmatic advice. Of the two types of therapeutic documents, therapeutic guidelines are thorough discussions of drug use and therapeutic position statements are concise responses to specific therapeutic issues.

The guidance documents of ASHP represent a consensus of professional judgment, expert opinion, and documented evidence. They provide guidance and direction to ASHP members and pharmacy practitioners and to other audiences who affect pharmacy practice. Their use may help to comply with federal and state laws and regulations, to meet accreditation requirements, and to improve pharmacy practice and patient care. They are written to establish reasonable goals, to be progressive and challenging, yet attainable as "best practices" in applicable health-system settings. They generally do not represent minimum levels of practice, unless titled as such, and should not be viewed as ASHP requirements.

The use of ASHP's guidance documents by members and other practitioners is strictly voluntary. Their content should be assessed and adapted based on independent judgment to meet the needs of local health-system settings.

The need for authoritative guidance in pharmacy practice has grown with changes in health care and with the shifting influences from regulatory, accrediting, risk-management, financing, and other bodies. Because of the complex nature of ASHP guidance documents, ASHP does not typically undertake immediate development of new documents or expedited revisions to existing documents in response to environmental changes. Other ASHP activities and services, such as educational sessions at national meetings and *American Journal of Health-System Pharmacy (AJHP)* articles, provide more timely information that may be helpful, until sufficient experience is gained to serve as the basis for a document.

Definitions

The types of guidance documents included in this compendium are defined as follows:

ASHP Policy Position: A pronouncement on an issue related to pharmacy professional practice, as approved by the Board of Directors and House of Delegates.

ASHP Statement: A declaration and explanation of basic philosophy or principle, as approved by the Board of Directors and the House of Delegates.

ASHP Guideline: Advice on the implementation or operation of pharmacy practice programs, as approved by the Board of Directors.

ASHP Technical Assistance Bulletin: Specific, detailed advice on pharmacy programs or functions as developed by an ASHP staff division in consultation with experts, as approved by the Board of Directors.*

ASHP Therapeutic Guideline: Thorough, systematically developed advice for health-care professionals on appropriate use of medications for specific clinical circumstances, as approved by the Board of Directors.

ASHP Therapeutic Position Statement: Concise statements that respond to specific therapeutic issues of concern to health care consumers and pharmacists, as approved by the Board of Directors.

ASHP-Endorsed Document: Professional policy developed by another organization that offers guidance on some aspect of pharmacy practice or medication use, as approved by the Board of Directors.

---

*The ASHP Board of Directors voted in November 1997 to discontinue the title "Technical Assistance Bulletin" in ASHP guidance documents, assigning the title "Guidelines" in its place. Over time, the title "Guidelines" will replace the title "Technical Assistance Bulletin" on existing documents when they are revised.

Development of Guidance Documents

The responsible ASHP council or commission recommends the development of a guidance document after considering whether the topic: a) has generated a need among practitioners for authoritative advice; b) has achieved some stability and there is sufficient experience upon which to base a statement or guideline; c) is relevant to the practice of a significant portion of ASHP's members; d) is within the purview of pharmacy practice in health systems; e) is without other sufficient guidance; and f) does not pose significant legal risks to ASHP. Another consideration is whether ASHP leadership believes that there is room for improvements in practice and that an ASHP document would foster that improvement. The Board of Directors must support the recommendations before developmental processes begin.

The processes used to draft and review new or revised documents vary depending on the body responsible for their development and on the type of document. These processes are described below. Once approved, the document draft becomes an official ASHP policy and is published in *AJHP*, added to ASHP's Web site, and incorporated into the next edition of *Best Practices for Hospital & Health-System Pharmacy*. Therapeutic documents are reviewed and revised as needed every three years, and policy positions and practice documents every five years.

ASHP Statements and Guidelines

Any of the ASHP policy-recommending bodies (councils and commissions) may initiate and oversee the development of ASHP statements and guidelines; however, most of them are initiated by the Council on Professional Affairs. The development of these documents generally includes the following steps:

1. A group of experts on a given topic volunteers to develop a preliminary draft. Drafters are selected based on demonstrated knowledge of the topic and their practice settings. Most often, the drafters are ASHP members.
2. The draft is sent by ASHP to reviewers who have interest and expertise in the given topic. Reviewers consist of members and selected individuals knowledgeable in the content area, representatives of various ASHP bodies, and other professional organizations. A draft of particular interest to ASHP's membership may be published in *AJHP*, posted on ASHP's Web site, or discussed at an open hearing or in a network forum during an ASHP Annual or Midyear Clinical meeting to solicit comments.
3. Based on the comments, a revised draft is submitted to the appropriate ASHP policy-recommending body for action. When the draft meets the established criteria for

content and quality, that body recommends that the Board of Directors approve the document.

ASHP Therapeutic Guidelines and Therapeutic Position Statements

The Commission on Therapeutics has responsibility for the development of ASHP therapeutic guidelines and ASHP therapeutic position statements.

Therapeutic Guidelines—The development of these documents generally includes the following steps:

1. When the Commission on Therapeutics (COT) identifies a topic for therapeutic guideline development, ASHP formally solicits proposals for a contractual arrangement with an individual, group, or organization to draft the guidelines document and coordinate its review. The contractor will work with a panel of 6–10 experts appointed by ASHP who have diverse backgrounds relevant to the topic.
2. A systematic analysis of the literature is performed, and scientific evidence is evaluated based on predetermined criteria. Recommendations in the document are based on scientific evidence or expert consensus. When expert judgment must be used, the document indicates the scientific reasoning that influenced the decision. Scientific evidence takes precedence over expert judgement. Each recommendation is accompanied by projections of the relevant health and cost outcomes that could result.
3. The expert panel and COT review each draft of the guidelines document and provide comments. This process is repeated until the expert panel and COT are satisfied with the content.
4. ASHP solicits multidisciplinary expert input on the draft. Reviewers consist of members and selected individuals knowledgeable in the content area, representatives of various ASHP bodies, and other professional organizations.
5. Once the above processes are completed, COT recommends that the ASHP Board of Directors approve it.

ASHP Therapeutic Position Statements (TPS)—The development of these documents generally includes the following steps:

1. One or more experts on a given topic are assigned to draft the TPS. Drafters are selected based on demonstrated knowledge of the topic and their practice setting. Most often, the drafters are ASHP members.
2. The proposed draft document is reviewed by COT, which may suggest modifications. This process is repeated until COT is satisfied with the content.
3. ASHP solicits multidisciplinary expert input on the draft. Reviewers consist of members and selected individuals knowledgeable in the content area, representatives of various ASHP bodies, and other professional organizations.
4. Once the above processes are completed, COT finalizes the draft and recommends that the ASHP Board of Directors approve it.

Access to ASHP Positions and Guidance Documents

Besides publishing in *AJHP* and *Best Practices for Hospital & Health-System Pharmacy*, policy positions and guidance documents are available through ASHP's Web site at **www.ashp.org**. They are located at the ASHP Policy Positions, Statements, and Guidelines heading under "Resources." A chronological compendium of policy positions is also available at *ASHP Policy Positions (1982–2004)* under "About ASHP" and "Policy and Governance."

Opportunities to Be a Part of Guidance Document Development

ASHP members determine the needs for policy guidance documents. They write and review the drafts. And, as members of policy-recommending bodies, the Board of Directors, and House of Delegates, they approve the documents.

ASHP members are encouraged to take an active role in the development of documents by suggesting topic ideas for new documents or modifications to current ones, volunteering to be drafters or reviewers, and completing survey and evaluation forms. Members may comment on or express their interests in participating in the development of documents by contacting the editor at (301) 657-3000 or by e-mail at ppsad@ashp.org.

Mission Statement of the American Society of Health-System Pharmacists (ASHP)

ASHP believes that the **mission of pharmacists** is to help people make the best use of medications.

The **mission of ASHP** is to advance and support the professional practice of pharmacists in hospitals and health systems and serve as their collective voice on issues related to medication use and public health.

Approved by the ASHP House of Delegates, June 4, 2001.

The bibliographic citation for this document is as follows: American Society of Health-System Pharmacists. Mission statement of the American Society of Health-System Pharmacists (ASHP). *Am J Health-Syst Pharm.* 2001; 58:1524.

ASHP Vision Statement for Pharmacy Practice in Hospitals and Health Systems

ASHP dedicates itself to achieving a vision for pharmacy practice in hospitals and health systems in which pharmacists:

1. Will significantly enhance patients' health-related quality of life by exercising leadership in improving both the use of medications by individuals and the overall process of medication use.
2. Will manage patient medication therapy and provide related patient care and public health services.
3. Will be the primary individuals responsible for medication use and drug distribution systems.
4. Will be recognized as patient care providers and sought out by patients to help them achieve the most benefit from their therapy.
5. Will take a leadership role to continuously improve and redesign the medication-use process with the goal of achieving significant advances in (a) patient safety, (b) health-related outcomes, (c) prudent use of human resources, and (d) efficiency.
6. Will lead evidence-based medication-use programs to implement best practices.
7. Will have an image among patients, health professionals, administrators, and public policy makers as caring and compassionate medication-use experts.

Approved by the ASHP House of Delegates, June 4, 2001.

The bibliographic citation for this document is as follows: American Society of Health-System Pharmacists. ASHP vision statement for pharmacy practice in hospitals and health systems. *Am J Health-Syst Pharm.* 2001; 58:1524.

ASHP Policy Positions, Statements, Guidelines, and Technical Assistance Bulletins

Automation and Information Technology

Automation and Information Technology

Electronic Information Systems (0405)

Source: Council on Administrative Affairs

To advocate the use of electronic information systems, with appropriate security controls, that enable the integration of patient-specific data that are accessible in all components of a health system; further,

To urge computer software vendors and pharmaceutical suppliers to provide standards for definition, collection, coding, and exchange of clinical data used in the medication-use process; further,

To pursue formal and informal liaisons with appropriate health care associations to ensure that the interests of patient care and safety in the medication-use process are fully represented in the standardization, integration, and implementation of electronic information systems; further,

To strongly encourage health-system administrators, regulatory bodies, and other appropriate groups to provide health-system pharmacists with full access to patient-specific clinical data.

This policy supersedes ASHP policy 9909.

Machine-Readable Coding and Related Technology (0308)

Source: Council on Administrative Affairs

To declare that the identity of all medications should be verifiable through machine-readable coding technology and to support the goal that all medications be electronically verified before they are administered to patients in health systems; further,

To urge the Food and Drug Administration, other regulatory agencies, contracting entities, and others to mandate that pharmaceutical manufacturers place standardized machine-readable coding that includes National Drug Code, lot number, and expiration date on all manufacturers' unit dose, unit of use, and injectable drug packaging; further,

To strongly encourage health systems to adopt machine-readable coding and point-of-care technology to (1) improve the accuracy of medication administration and documentation, (2) improve efficiencies within the medication-use process, and (3) improve patient safety; these systems should be planned, implemented, and managed with pharmacist involvement and should be in all areas of the health system where drugs are used.

This policy supersedes ASHP policy 0204.

Pharmacist's Role in Electronic Patient Information and Prescribing Systems (0203)

Source: Council on Administrative Affairs

To strongly advocate key decision roles of pharmacists in the planning, selection, implementation, and maintenance of electronic patient information systems (including computerized prescriber order-entry systems) to facilitate clinical decision support, data analysis, and education of users for the purpose of ensuring the safe and effective use of medications.

This policy supersedes ASHP policy 9807.

Electronic Health and Business Technology and Services (0233)

Source: Council on Professional Affairs

To encourage pharmacists to assume a leadership role in their health systems with respect to strategic planning for and implementation of electronic health and business technology and services; further,

To advocate the inclusion of e-health technology and telepharmacy issues and applications in pharmacy school curricula.

This policy supersedes ASHP policy 0015.

Computerized Prescriber Order Entry (0105)

Source: Council on Administrative Affairs

To advocate the use of computerized entry of medication orders or prescriptions by the prescriber when (1) it is planned, implemented, and managed with pharmacists' involvement, (2) such orders are part of a single, shared database that is fully integrated with the pharmacy information system and other key information system components, especially the patient's medication administration record, (3) such computerized order entry improves the safety, efficiency, and accuracy of the medication-use process, and (4) it includes provisions for the pharmacist to review and verify the order's appropriateness before medication administration, except in those instances when review would cause a medically unacceptable delay.

This policy supersedes ASHP policy 9806.

Online Pharmacy and Internet Prescribing (0009)

Source: Council on Legal and Public Affairs

To support collaborative efforts of the Food and Drug Administration, the National Association of Boards of Pharmacy, and the Federation of State Medical Boards, as stated in the Principles of Understanding on the Sale of Drugs on the Internet, to regulate prescribing and dispensing of medications via the Internet; further,

To support legislation or regulation that requires pharmacy World Wide Web sites to list the states in which the pharmacy and pharmacists are licensed, and, if prescribing services are offered, requires that the sites (a) ensure that a legitimate patient-prescriber relationship exists (consistent with professional practice standards) and (b) list the states in which the prescribers are licensed; further,

To support the concept of voluntary accreditation of pharmacy Web sites and appropriate consumer education about the risks and benefits of using Internet pharmacies; further,

To support the principle that any medication distribution or drug therapy management system must provide timely access to, and interaction with, appropriate professional pharmacist patient care services.

Management of Blood Products and Derivatives (9919)
Source: Council on Legal and Public Affairs
To strongly encourage the computer software industry to provide data fields for lot number, expiration date, and other necessary and appropriate information for blood products and derivatives and biologicals, in order to facilitate compliance with regulatory requirements concerning the use of these products, particularly with respect to recalls or withdrawals.

This policy was reviewed in 2003 by the Council on Legal and Public Affairs and by the Board of Directors and was found to still be appropriate.

Telepharmacy (9920)
Source: Council on Professional Affairs
To foster among health-system pharmacists and leaders of the telecommunications industry a common vision for the integration of telecommunication technology into the delivery of pharmaceutical care.

This policy was reviewed in 2003 by the Council on Professional Affairs and by the Board of Directors and was found to still be appropriate.

Regulation of Automated Drug Distribution Systems (9813)
Source: Council on Legal and Public Affairs
To work with the Drug Enforcement Administration and other agencies to seek regulatory and policy changes to accommodate automated drug distribution in health systems.

This policy was reviewed in 2002 by the Council on Legal and Public Affairs and by the Board of Directors and was found to still be appropriate.

Automated Systems (9205)
Source: Council on Legal and Public Affairs
To support the use of current and emerging technology in the advancement of pharmaceutical care; further,

To encourage a review and evaluation of the state and federal legal and regulatory status of new technologies as they apply to pharmacy practice.

This policy was reviewed in 2001 by the Council on Legal and Public Affairs and by the Board of Directors and was found to still be appropriate.

ASHP Statement on the Pharmacist's Role with Respect to Drug Delivery Systems and Administration Devices

Technological advances in drug delivery systems and administration devices frequently enable improved control of drug administration. Such advances may offer numerous potential benefits to patients, including improved therapeutic outcomes in disease management, improved patient compliance with drug regimens, and greater efficiency and economy in disease therapy. These advances constitute an important aspect of pharmaceutical knowledge and are routinely incorporated into pharmacy practice as they occur.

A drug delivery system is defined as one in which a drug (one component of the system) is integrated with another chemical, a drug administration device, or a drug administration process to control the rate of drug release, the tissue site of drug release, or both. A drug administration device is an apparatus that is used for introducing a drug to the body or controlling its rate of introduction. Drug delivery systems include (but are not limited to) osmotic pumps, thermal isolation, transdermal patches, liposomal encapsulation, iontophoresis, phonophoresis, magnetic migration, and implantation. Drug administration devices include (but are not limited to) mechanical (e.g., balloon-driven), gravity-driven, and electromechanical pumps. Some of the latter are portable, implantable, computer controlled, or patient controlled. Some enable the simultaneous infusion of multiple drugs. Drug administration control devices include plasma concentration monitoring and administration rate monitoring devices, which incorporate computers.

Pharmacists bear a substantial responsibility for ensuring optimal clinical outcomes from drug therapy and are suited by education, training, clinical expertise, and practice activities to assume responsibility for the professional supervision of drug delivery systems and administration devices. As a natural extension of efforts to optimize drug use, pharmacists should participate in organizational and clinical decisions with regard to these systems and devices. Some decisions and activities in which pharmacists should participate follow. Others may be appropriate as well.

1. Research and development of innovative drug delivery systems and administration devices.
2. Evaluation and research to determine the direct and comparative efficacy, safety, and cost-effectiveness of specific drug delivery systems and administration devices.
3. In conjunction with pharmacy and therapeutics committees (or other appropriate medical staff committees), decisions to choose or exclude particular drug delivery systems and administration devices for use in specific organizational settings.
4. Development of organization-specific policies and procedures regarding the acquisition, storage, distribution, use, maintenance, and ongoing product quality control of drug delivery systems and administration devices.
5. Choice of a particular drug delivery system or administration device for use in a specific patient's drug therapy.
6. Direct communication with patients to instruct them in the use of such systems and devices and to gather information necessary to monitor the outcome of their therapy.
7. Monitoring of the ongoing clinical effectiveness and suitability of specific drug delivery systems or administration devices with respect to specific patients and the communication of clinically relevant observations and recommendations to prescribers and other health professionals involved in the patients' care.

Failures or malfunctions of drug administration devices may lead to patient harm. Reports of such problems should be made in accordance with the provisions of the Safe Medical Devices Act of 1990 (PL 101–629).

Recommendations for Additional Reading

Acevedo ML. Electronic flow control. *NITA*. 1983; 6:105–6.

Akers MJ. Current problems and innovations in intravenous drug delivery. Considerations in using the i.v. route for drug delivery. *Am J Hosp Pharm*. 1987; 44:2528–30.

Alexander MR. Current problems and innovations in intravenous drug delivery. Developing and implementing a contract for electronic infusion devices. *Am J Hosp Pharm*. 1987; 44:2553–6.

Anderson RW, Cohen JE, Cohen MR, et al. Hospital pharmacy symposium on new concepts in parenteral drug delivery. *Hosp Pharm*. 1986; 21:1033–55.

Baharloo M. Iontophoresis and phonophoresis: a role for the pharmacist. *Hosp Pharm*. 1987; 22:730–1.

Block LH, Shukla AJ. Drug delivery in the 1990s. *US Pharm*. 1986; 11(Oct):51–6, 58.

Boothe CD, Talley JR. Mechanical and electronic intravenous infusion devices. Part 1. *Infusion*. 1986; 10:6–8.

Chandrasekaran SK, Benson H, Urquhart J. Methods to achieve controlled drug delivery, the biomedical engineering approach. In: Robinson JR, ed. Sustained and controlled release drug delivery systems. New York: Marcel Dekker; 1978:557–93.

Colangelo A. Current problems and innovations in intravenous drug delivery. Drug preparation techniques for i.v. drug delivery systems. *Am J Hosp Pharm*. 1987; 44:2550–3.

Davis SR. Latest developments in drug delivery systems—abstracts. *Hosp Pharm*. 1987; 22:890–908.

Goodman MS, Wickham R. Venous access devices: oncology nurse overview. *Hosp Pharm*. 1985; 20:495–511.

Holm A, Campbell N. Role of institutional review boards in facilitating research, marketing of drugs and devices, and protecting human subjects. *Drug Dev Ind Pharm*. 1985; 11:1–12.

Juliano RL. Drug delivery systems. New York: Oxford University Press; 1980.

Kelly WN, Christensen LA. Selective patient criteria for the use of electronic infusion devices. *Am J IV Ther Clin Nutr*. 1983; 10(Mar):18, 19, 21, 25, 26, 29.

Kirschenbaum B, Klein S. Pharmacy-coordinated infusion device evaluation. *Am J Hosp Pharm*. 1984; 41:1181–3.

Leff RD. Current problems and innovations in intravenous drug delivery. Features of i.v. devices and equipment that affect i.v. drug delivery. *Am J Hosp Pharm*. 1987; 44:2530–3.

Longer MA, Robinson JR. Sustained-release drug delivery systems. In: Gennaro AR, ed. Remington's pharmaceutical sciences. Easton, PA: Mack Publishing Company; 1985:1644–61.

McFarlane AE. Role for pharmacists in the provision of medical devices. *Aust J Hosp Pharm*. 1986; 16:78.

Mutschler E. Now and future of drug delivery systems. *Pharm Tech*. 1983(Suppl); 7:13–5.

Nahata MC. Current problems and innovations in intravenous drug delivery. Effect of i.v. drug delivery systems on pharmacokinetic monitoring. *Am J Hosp Pharm*. 1987; 44:2538–42.

Piecoro JJ Jr. Current problems and innovations in intravenous drug delivery. Development of an institutional i.v. drug delivery policy. *Am J Hosp Pharm*. 1987; 44:2557–9.

Polack AE, Roberts MS. Drug delivery systems. *Med J Aust*. 1986; 144:311–4.

Rapp RP. Current problems and innovations in intravenous drug delivery. Considering product features and costs in selecting a system for intermittent i.v. drug delivery. *Am J Hosp Pharm*. 1987; 44:2533–8.

Reilly KM. Current problems and innovations in intravenous drug delivery. Problems in administration techniques and dose measurement that influence accuracy of i.v. drug delivery. *Am J Hosp Pharm*. 1987; 44:2545–50.

Reiss RE. Volumetric IV pumps. *Pharm Tech*. 1983(Suppl); 7:46–9.

Self TH, Brooks JB, Lieberman P, et al. The value of demonstration and role of the pharmacist in teaching the correct use of pressurized bronchodilators. *Can Med Assoc J*. 1983; 128:129–31.

Selton MV. Implantable pumps. *CRC Crit Rev Biomed Eng*. 1987; 14:201–40.

Smith KL. Developments in drug delivery systems. *Hosp Pharm*. 1987; 22:905–6.

Talley JR. Mechanical and electronic intravenous infusion devices. Part 2. *Infusion*. 1986; 10:31–4.

Talley JR. Mechanical and electronic intravenous infusion devices. Part 3. *Infusion*. 1986; 10:58–62.

Talsma H, Crommelin DJA. Liposomes as drug delivery systems, part I: preparation. *Pharm Tech*. 1992(Oct); 16:98, 100, 102, 104, 106.

Urquhart J. Implantable pumps in drug delivery. *Pharm Tech*. 1983(Suppl); 7:53–4.

Zenk KE. Current problems and innovations in intravenous drug delivery. Intravenous drug delivery in infants with limited i.v. access and fluid restriction. *Am J Hosp Pharm*. 1987; 44:2542–5.

This statement was reviewed in 1998 by the Council on Professional Affairs and by the ASHP Board of Directors and was found to still be appropriate.

Approved by the ASHP Board of Directors, November 18, 1992, and the ASHP House of Delegates, June 9, 1993. Revised by the ASHP Council on Professional Affairs. Supersedes a previous version approved by the ASHP House of Delegates on June 5, 1989, and the ASHP Board of Directors on November 16, 1988.

The bibliographic citation for this document is as follows: American Society of Hospital Pharmacists. ASHP statement on the pharmacist's role with respect to drug delivery systems and administration devices. *Am J Hosp Pharm*. 1993; 50:1724–5.

ASHP Guidelines on the Safe Use of Automated Compounding Devices for the Preparation of Parenteral Nutrition Admixtures

Purpose

Automated compounding devices are frequently used by pharmacists for the extemporaneous preparation of parenteral nutrition admixtures. This continuing shift from manual compounding procedures comes as a result of significant advances in automated technology, as well as in response to changing health care demands to provide admixture compounding in a safer, more efficient, and more accurate manner. Approximately 65% of the hospitals in the United States currently use automated compounding devices for parenteral nutrition admixtures on a daily basis.[a] Compounders are also used for other types of intravenous admixtures and in other settings, including home care and long-term-care facilities; therefore, the overall magnitude of their use may be substantial. As with other automated systems or devices, the benefits can be realized only when the technology is used appropriately. Significant patient harm may occur when safety and quality assurance measures are overlooked or circumvented.[1]

The purpose of these guidelines is to outline the key issues that should be considered to safely and cost-effectively incorporate this technology into the pharmacy operations of health care organizations. The guidelines focus on parenteral nutrition admixtures, but the safety issues are also applicable to the use of compounders for other types of i.v. admixtures. The term "health care organization" is used throughout the guidelines as a general descriptor and is intended to be inclusive of any of the practice settings and types of facilities in which compounders are used, including, for example, home infusion companies. These guidelines should be used in conjunction with the ASHP Guidelines on Quality Assurance for Pharmacy-Prepared Sterile Products and device manufacturers' instruction manuals and training materials. Pharmacists should use professional judgment in assessing their health care organization's needs for automated compounding devices and in adapting these guidelines to meet those needs.

Background

The act of extemporaneously compounding any parenteral formulation is complex and not without inherent risks; therefore, compounding tasks are best performed by personnel most qualified to do so. An incompatible, unstable, or contaminated i.v. infusion may induce significant patient morbidity and even mortality.[1] Pharmacists are specifically educated and legally responsible for performing these tasks safely. Pharmacists are also responsible for training other personnel to perform relatively simple tasks with the least risk possible.

The extemporaneous preparation of multiadditive products, such as parenteral nutrition admixture compounding, should be performed under the direct supervision of a pharmacist and in the appropriate environment.[2] The historical method of compounding these multicomponent admixtures has been to manually use gravity-driven transfers for large-volume additives, such as amino acids, dextrose, lipids, and sterile water. Small-volume additives, such as electrolytes, trace minerals, multivitamins, and drugs, have often been added manually and separately with a syringe. Thus, this compounding method is limited by the visual inspection of volumes transferred between stock containers, as well as by the precision of the calibrations marked on the stock containers or transfer devices.

The manual method of parenteral nutrition admixture compounding is labor-intensive and requires multiple manipulations of infusion containers, sets, syringes, needles, and so forth, which can lead to the extrinsic contamination of the final admixture with sterile and nonsterile contaminants. A sterile contaminant can be particulate matter from elastomeric vial enclosures (needle cores), and nonsterile contaminants can be bacteria and other infectious materials. Minimizing the number of extemporaneous manipulations of the parenteral infusion containers and supplies improves compounding efficiency and reduces the risk of extrinsic contamination and associated sequelae.[3]

The emergence of automated technology as an alternative approach to parenteral nutrition admixture compounding has led to potentially improved compounding accuracy with the use of fluid pump technology and software that controls the compounder pump. Fluid can be delivered from the source container to the final container by using either a volumetric or a gravimetric fluid pumping system. Volumetric systems transfer a specified volume of fluid from a source container to a final container via a rotary peristaltic pump. The tubing is stretched around a rotor and, as the rotor turns, solution is pulled from the source container and pushed toward the final container. Measurements are based on the theory that each rotor movement advances a constant amount of fluid through the system. The total volume delivered is calculated by the volume pulled into the tubing by each rotor movement multiplied by the number of movements. These systems usually incorporate a final check of the *actual* total bag weight by comparing it with a calculated *expected* weight.

In gravimetric systems, measurement of fluid volume delivered from the source container to the final container is determined by weighing the fluid transferred and dividing the weight by the solution's known specific gravity, thereby converting weight to volume. Two types of gravimetric pumps are available: additive and subtractive. With an additive pump, a single load cell is positioned to measure each fluid as it is delivered to the final container. With a subtractive pump, load cells are positioned beneath the source containers to measure each fluid as it is being pumped from its source container. Weight is determined by subtracting the posttransfer weight from the pretransfer weight of the container for each source solution. When all transfers are completed, the system compares the *actual* total bag weight with a calculated *expected* weight.

In addition to the compounder, dedicated software may be used to electronically transfer information to the compounding device. Automated compounding software has additional features that can enhance the management of the parenteral nutrition program. Software issues and their integrity are additional critical components unique to compounder methods and require continuous monitoring to ensure that the operations are correct.[4]

Justification for the Use of Automated Compounding Devices

When is it appropriate to use compounders, and how will decisions affect others within and outside the pharmacy department? It is incumbent upon the pharmacist to ensure that the department is fully knowledgeable about the operation of the compounder and that a minimum acceptable standard of pharmacy practice is met. First, internal decisions need to be made to justify the expenses associated with this technology. Second, policies and procedures should be in place to assess workflow, establish training programs, and standardize compounder use in the specific pharmacy practice setting. Third, changing current compounder contracts may result in more cost than the savings that might appear in the new contracts. Specifically, the initial incorporation of an automated compounder into daily pharmacy practice is a labor-intensive effort, and such transitions can be disruptive and can even increase the risk of errors. This may be particularly true during staff orientation to new devices. Such changes must be carefully reviewed; if they are determined to be worthwhile, a well-coordinated transition plan should be devised beforehand. Whether transition costs (including the potential for unused sets and supplies) can be deferred to the new contract is another factor for consideration.

The principal emphasis associated with using automated compounding devices in health care organizations should be improving patient care and enhancing efficiency while remaining cost-effective. "Cost-effectiveness" is, therefore, a relative term with respect to personnel, as the labor saved is often redirected to other aspects of pharmaceutical care that could also improve patient safety. Time that was previously spent on operations associated with parenteral nutrition admixture compounding can now be aimed at other issues, such as optimization of drug and nutritional therapies, reorganization of product utilization, quality assurance programs, and augmentation of other core pharmaceutical services. Specific objectives related to cost justification of automated compounding devices may include the following:

1. Enhanced efficiency and worker safety during the parenteral nutrition compounding process and patient safety with parenteral use.
2. Reduction in labor associated with manually compounded parenteral nutrition admixtures. Assessment of the overall labor and material costs associated with the current manual compounding methods should include hidden costs such as pharmacists' time to perform calculations, quality assurance checks, and compounder set-up, as well as staff training (initial and ongoing).
3. Reduction in waste through more efficient use of base solutions and additives. Inventory can often be reduced by consolidating source solutions to a few high-concentration, large-volume additives.

In some cases in which the cost of implementing automated compounding technology in one facility is prohibitive, health care organizations have opted to explore regional compounding centers or outsourcing to contractors.

Performance Requirements and Responsibilities

The use of automated devices for compounding parenteral nutrition admixtures should be clearly defined by the health care organization and the manufacturer. This includes the ongoing responsibilities of the pharmacy department and those of the manufacturer during and after implementation of the compounder in the pharmacy practice setting.

Three areas need to be clearly defined before choosing an automated compounding system: (1) the system's performance requirements, (2) the manufacturer's responsibilities, and (3) the pharmacy department's responsibilities. The performance requirements of the automated compounding system should ensure that

1. The compounder exceeds the level of accuracy achieved with manual compounding. The automated compounding device should be accurate to within 5% of the amount programmed, with verification of the amount pumped versus the programmed amount for each ingredient.
2. The automated compounding device has inherent safeguards, including the ability to detect inadvertent source-solution mixups; the ability to detect situations that could result in inaccurate deliveries, such as occluded transfer-set tubing and empty source containers; and the ability to keep incompatible source solutions separate.
3. The automated compounding software alerts the user when formulation issues arise.
4. The automated compounding software meets the standards of the American Society for Parenteral and Enteral Nutrition for parenteral nutrition label formats.[5]
5. The automated compounding software assists the pharmacist in producing physicochemically compatible parenteral nutrition formulations.
6. The automated compounding software provides useful clinical information.
7. The automated compounding software integrates with existing pharmacy programs wherever possible to optimize patient care and avoid therapeutic duplications.

The contractual agreement with the manufacturer should provide continuous support of the compounder and software, including information updates, problem solving, and emergency coverage. FDA considers all automated compounding devices class II devices,[6] and as such they must comply with federal regulations. The manufacturer's responsibilities are as follows:

1. The manufacturer should supply, and the pharmacist should verify, that the device is 510K cleared as evidence of compliance with regulatory requirements; that the device meets the fire and safety standards established by Underwriters Laboratories (i.e., is UL-

approved); that the operator's manual and other documentation support recommendations for use; and that accuracy statements and manufacturer claims are valid.

2. The manufacturer should provide 24-hour support for the compounder and its software throughout the life of the contract.
3. The manufacturer should routinely provide the latest version of the compounder software in a timely manner.
4. The manufacturer should ensure adequate availability of compounding supplies.
5. The manufacturer should provide detailed information and instructions on the appropriate use of the compounder and its software. References should be provided when appropriate.
6. The manufacturer should comply with FDA requirements for reporting adverse events.

Within the pharmacy department, specific policies and procedures should be developed that address responsibilities for compounder operations and maintenance, staff training, and monitoring compounder performance at all times. Before selecting and implementing an automated compounder, the pharmacy department should

1. Define and agree on automated compounding system needs and performance requirements.
2. Develop an implementation team with a lead person.
3. Develop a set of policies and procedures.

Control of the Automated Compounding Device in Daily Operations

The pharmacy department is responsible for the use, maintenance, and performance of the automated compounding device, including decisions about who has access to the compounder and its operations. Specific consideration should be given to the following:

1. Only designated pharmacy department personnel should have access to the compounder and its software. The level of access should correspond to the level of authority and expertise of the personnel.
2. Before being granted access to a compounder, pharmacy personnel should pass established competency-standard testing.
3. Access to and use of the compounder by pharmacy support personnel (i.e., pharmacy technicians, students, and other designated support staff) should be directly supervised by an authorized pharmacist.
4. The additive configuration or sequence of the compounder for compounding parenteral nutrition admixtures should not be altered from the established format without the authorization of a designated pharmacist.
5. The compounder should not be used for any purpose other than parenteral nutrition admixture compounding without authorization from a designated pharmacist. If the compounder is used for other extemporaneous drug preparation, this should be done separately from the schedule for parenteral nutrition admixtures. The use of the compounder in this manner will likely require the use of new compounding sets and admixture configurations.

Safety and Efficacy Features

The complexity of automated compounding device functions makes it imperative that the pharmacy department develop a specific plan for ensuring safe and efficacious use at all times. The safety and efficacy features should outline the core principles necessary for carrying out the complex tasks of parenteral nutrition compounding. The plan should identify the minimum standards that are routinely assessed through an established monitoring and surveillance program. Automated compounding devices on the market differ in hardware design, mechanisms of fluid transfer, and software applications. Consequently, sterility and quality assurance testing procedures and measures are also different, including routine assessments of accuracy in the delivery of correct amounts of nutrients. Consideration should be given to the following in accordance with the device manufacturer's specific instructions:

1. Establishing minimum competency standards for all personnel who have access to and operate the compounder. Competency standards should ensure that the compounder user has sufficient expertise to identify errors that may inadvertently bypass quality assurance systems. The competency standards should be reviewed and validated on a routine basis for all personnel operating the compounder.
2. Establishing specific procedures for the operation of the compounder that standardize its use, irrespective of the individual operator. Changes in compounder operations should occur only when authorized and should be communicated to all staff involved in compounding.
3. Including sterility and quality assurance measures to avoid extrinsic contamination and to ensure accurate delivery of parenteral nutrition additives.
4. Ensuring that compounder tubing changes occur at appropriate specified time intervals in accordance with the manufacturer's recommendations.
5. Devising methods for assessing and calibrating the accuracy of the compounder in delivering precise levels of substrates and additives.
6. Developing a contingency plan and a readily available backup system or method for providing uninterrupted parenteral nutrition therapy to patients in the event of compounder failure.
7. Ensuring that adequate amounts of solutions and supplies for automated compounding are on hand.

Quality Assurance Monitoring and Documentation

Automated compounding devices are intended to provide a higher margin of accuracy and to streamline the labor-intensive tasks associated with the manual extemporaneous preparation of large-volume, multiadditive parenteral nutrition admixtures and other admixtures. The compounders are not designed to replace oversight functions, which require the expertise of a pharmacist.

In theory, automated compounding devices provide compounding accuracy superior to that of traditional methods of manual compounding. However, the performance of compounders must be critically challenged by the pharmacist to ensure that their manufacturing specifications are equal to the task. In the pharmaceutical industry, that process is called validation. Ongoing quality assurance measures specified by the device manufacturer for assessing the performance of the compounder, as well as corrective actions, should be clearly delineated in policies separate from those dedicated to operational tasks. "Ongoing" means daily, and whatever measures are determined to be essential should be performed each day because random checks may not detect a more insidious, intermittent flaw that could assume major clinical significance.[7,8]

The pharmacy department may work with other departments to assess the compounder's performance if such expertise is not available within the pharmacy department. For example, portions of parenteral nutrition admixtures may be sent to the health care organization's laboratory to determine dextrose content. However, laboratory methods are usually designed for biological rather than pharmaceutical systems and should be validated to meet USP requirements for the components being tested. If outside departments participate in the quality assurance program, their methods should be appropriately validated in accordance with USP specifications and the results documented within the pharmacy department records on the compounder's performance.

The pharmacy department should develop a monitoring and surveillance plan with output reports that encompasses the principles outlined under the section on safety and efficacy features. The plan should detail specific policies and procedures that will ensure the continuing operation of the automated compounding device at optimum performance levels at all times. The data generated by the monitoring procedures should be reported to the pharmacy director and other appropriate oversight personnel and kept as a permanent record of the compounder's operations. These reports should be regularly reviewed in the assessment of trends and other long-term measures of performance. Specific consideration should be given to

1. Establishing performance standards and continuous quality assurance measures for assessing the compounder's performance and product quality during setup and in-process (during compounding) and end-process testing.
2. Establishing quality assurance testing of user-defined software variables validating that the correct responses to user commands occur.
3. Validating all quality assurance testing before implementation.
4. Establishing a minimum performance standard for each quality assurance test. For example, deviations in the accuracy of delivering a single additive cannot exceed a predetermined percent error without immediate corrective actions.
5. Documenting all quality assurance data on a daily basis. A comprehensive review of the data and documentation of performance trends should be performed at scheduled intervals as necessitated by aseptic conditions. The compounder should have scheduled, routine cleaning and maintenance according to the manufacturer's recommendations to ensure proper operation.

Storage and Inventory

The pharmacy department is responsible for housing the automated compounding device, related disposable supplies, and admixture ingredients. Other departments, such as materials management, may order and store additional supplies for the compounder yet defer to the pharmacy for the selection of the components necessary for proper compounder operation. Specific consideration should be given to

1. Maintaining an adequate inventory of supplies necessary for compounder operation and patient needs.
2. Procuring all large-volume parenteral nutrition components (amino acids, dextrose, and lipids) from one manufacturer unless such combinations have adequate physicochemical data that ensure the stability, compatibility, and safety of the final formulations commensurate with the data for single-source products.[5] Any proposed substitute products should be assessed for compatibility and approved by designated pharmacy personnel qualified to do so and possibly by the pharmacy and therapeutics committee if clinical issues are identified.
3. If a health care organization's contract requires a change in the brand of parenteral products, designated pharmacy personnel should verify that the new products are compatible. If a new product is approved, designated pharmacy personnel should verify that the new product is compatible, add it to the compounder formulary, and revise the admixture requirements and instructions relevant to the compounder's operations.

Education and Training

Pharmacists, by education and training, are competent to safely compound pharmaceuticals, including parenteral nutrition admixtures. Nevertheless, the introduction of automated compounding devices requires specific training of pharmacists as well as other pharmacy personnel in the operation, maintenance, and quality assurance of compounders. Specific consideration should be given to ensuring that

1. Pharmacy administration determines the individuals who will be responsible for education and training in the use of the compounders.
2. All education and training are documented in a permanent record maintained in the pharmacy department and in personnel files.
3. All pharmacy personnel using or supervising compounder operations are tested at regular intervals to ensure that individuals meet the department's minimum competency standards.
4. Retraining, competency assessment, and appropriate documentation accompany upgrades and new versions of the compounder to ensure the continued proficiency of personnel, safety of compounder operations, and adequacy of oversight.

Device Variability

Automated compounding devices are marketed by several manufacturers. Even though there are similarities among compounders, there may be significant differences in the design, accuracy, operation, maintenance, software, and manufacturing support, among other things. The safe operation and supervision of any given compounder depend on adherence to the manufacturer's specific instructions and continuous quality assurance monitoring of compounder performance. The safe and efficient operation of an automated compounding system depends on defined responsibilities for the pharmacy and manufacturer, as well as on strict adherence to policies, procedures, and quality assurance programs.

References

1. Food and Drug Administration. Safety alert: hazards of precipitation associated with parenteral nutrition. *Am J Hosp Pharm.* 1994; 51:1427–8.
2. American Society of Hospital Pharmacists. ASHP technical assistance bulletin on quality assurance for pharmacy-prepared sterile products. *Am J Hosp Pharm.* 1993; 50:2386–98.
3. McClendon RR. A comparative evaluation of methods used to compound parenteral nutrition solutions. *Nutr Support Serv.* 1983; 3:46–9.
4. Driscoll DF. Clinical delivery of nutritional therapy: automated compounders and patient-specific feeding. *Nutrition.* 1996; 12:461–2. Editorial.
5. American Society for Parenteral and Enteral Nutrition National Advisory Group on Standards and Practice Guidelines for Parenteral Nutrition. Safe practices for parenteral nutrition formulations. *JPEN J Parenter Enteral Nutr.* 1998; 22:49–66.
6. Trautman KA. The FDA and worldwide quality system requirements guidebook for medical devices. Milwaukee, WI: ASQ Quality Press; 1997.
7. Driscoll DF. Delivery of nutritional therapy: quality assurance of automated compounding devices. *Nutrition.* 1996; 12:651–2. Editorial.
8. Fields HS. Establishing core performance requirements for automated TPN compounders. *Am J Health-Syst Pharm.* 1996; 53:1607. Letter.

---

[a]Mihalski T, Clintec Nutrition Division, Baxter Healthcare. Personal communication. 1999 Mar 15.

Approved by the ASHP Board of Directors on April 27, 2000. Developed through the ASHP Council on Professional Affairs.

The bibliographic citation for this document is as follows: American Society of Health-System Pharmacists. ASHP Guidelines on the Safe Use of Automated Compounding Devices for the Preparation of Parenteral Nutrition Admixtures. *Am J Health-Syst Pharm.* 2000; 57:1343–8.

ASHP Guidelines on the Safe Use of Automated Medication Storage and Distribution Devices

Purpose

Automated medication storage and distribution devices are an increasingly prevalent component of the medication-use process in health care organizations. The pharmacy profession's transition to pharmaceutical care, changes in health care systems, and pressures to reduce costs have created interest in availability of and use of automated devices. ASHP supports the use of automated devices when it frees pharmacists from labor-intensive distributive functions, helps pharmacists provide pharmaceutical care, and improves the accuracy and timeliness of distributive functions. Experience with automated devices suggests that when they are used appropriately these benefits can be realized.[1-4] When automated devices are not used appropriately, their complexity, design and function variations, maintenance requirements, staff-training requirements, and other factors can have undesirable effects and compromise patient safety.[5,6] The National Association of Boards of Pharmacy (NABP) has adopted language on automation for incorporation into the NABP Model State Pharmacy Act and Model Rules. The Model Act uses the term "automated pharmacy systems" and defines them as "including, but not limited to, mechanical systems that perform operations or activities, other than compounding or administration, relative to the storage, packaging, dispensing, or distribution of medications, and which collect, control, and maintain all transaction information."[7] Data-processing and bar-code technologies, although incorporated as integral components of some of these systems, are not considered in the Model Act definition of automated drug distribution technology. The Model Rules suggest specific requirements and options for helping individual states determine which are appropriate.[8] These ASHP guidelines reflect and expand upon the requirements of the Model Rules.

Automated pharmacy systems are designed for centralized filling of individual patient prescriptions and unit dose medication orders, for decentralized dispensing cabinets, and for other purposes. This document addresses primarily computer-controlled decentralized medication-dispensing cabinets, which ASHP prefers to call automated medication storage and distribution devices. Since many of the concepts may be applicable to related technologies, the term "automated system" will be used generally and the term "automated device" will be used specifically. Automated pharmacy devices are located in hospital patient care units, surgical suites, emergency rooms, long-term-care facilities, physicians' offices, and other settings. Several manufacturers produce automated devices with a variety of configurations and software capabilities that may interface with the pharmacy's and the health care organization's information systems.[9,10]

The purposes of these guidelines are to (1) propose goals and objectives for the safe use of automated medication storage and distribution devices in the medication-use process, (2) provide guidance on the safe use of automated devices to pharmacists and others involved in the medication-use process, and (3) advise vendors of automated devices about the safety needs of those in health care who use their systems.

Background

The appropriate, accurate, and timely distribution of medications to patients is a well-established responsibility of pharmacists. In acute care settings in particular, distribution systems have been developed that enable pharmacists to review medication orders and to oversee the preparation and packaging or selection of medication doses, as well as the delivery of doses to patient care units. Automation has evolved to ease fulfillment of pharmacists' distributive responsibilities, expand distribution-system capabilities, and improve efficiencies.

The use of automated medication storage and distribution devices continues to evolve. Some health care organizations deploy one or several devices in selected areas, such as emergency rooms, that are floor-stock intensive and where lost charges can be substantial; or for selected categories of medications, such as controlled substances, that have time-consuming tracking and documentation requirements. Some organizations deploy devices throughout patient care areas to cover nearly all medications used.

The rapid development of technology applications in health care, including automated devices, and pressures to expand their use have raised concerns about patient safety, access to medications, and possible legislative and regulatory barriers. Several pharmacy organizations, in cooperation with NABP, launched the Automation in Pharmacy Initiative, which produced draft language for inclusion in the NABP Model State Pharmacy Act and Model Rules and a white paper on automation in pharmacy.[11,12] The white paper noted that there were no national standards for automated pharmacy systems and reminded pharmacists that they have professional responsibility for ensuring that appropriate policies and procedures and quality assurance programs are in place to ensure safety, accuracy, security, and patient confidentiality.

Goals and Objectives

Goals for the use of automated devices in the medication-use process should focus on improving patient care and resource use. Specific objectives related to these goals may include the following:

1. Information necessary for appropriate medication management and patient care is accurate, accessible, and timely.
2. Appropriate medications are readily available and accessible to meet patient needs within safety and security controls.
3. Vulnerabilities to medication errors are minimized, and those that remain are identified, documented, and modified.
4. Staff members involved in the medication-use process are safety conscious, accurate, and productive.
5. Patients are satisfied with the quality and delivery of care.
6. Medication distribution services are facilitated across the continuum of practice settings in health care systems.

7. Resource management is improved by linking supply-reordering channels to the medication distribution system.

Requirements

Automated medication storage and distribution devices should be thought of by users as tools for improving the medication-use process, rather than as inherent solutions to problems in that process. Consideration should be given to how the technology can be adapted to meet the goals and objectives of the user rather than to how the user's systems should be redesigned to fit the automated device.

Before deciding to deploy automated devices in the medication-use process, an organization should assess its circumstances; the safety, patient care, and resource benefits it hopes to gain; and how the benefits would be observed and measured. It should also determine if the automated devices being considered are capable of producing the desired benefits. Specific consideration should be given to

1. Incorporating the use of automated devices into the organization's strategic planning (i.e., ensuring that automation is compatible with the vision and mission of the organization).
2. Assessing the use of automation from a complete systems standpoint. Automated devices should integrate well with other systems and processes, both manual and automated. Interfaces with overall patient-care computer systems especially must be considered.
3. Establishing performance standards for safety, accuracy (including medication error rates), timeliness, and costs.
4. Determining the responsibilities of the automated device vendor and the organization for installation, maintenance, training, operations, and troubleshooting.
5. Ensuring effective training for the organization's employees who have automated device involvement and user responsibilities.

Since the medication-use process involves multiple health care disciplines, selection of automated devices and establishment of rules for their use will require decisions that meet the needs of the disciplines involved. However, since pharmacists have professional and legal responsibility for the safety and integrity of the entire medication-use process, they should provide leadership in the development and maintenance of policies and procedures for the safe use of automated systems. Any system or device adopted for drug distribution and control should meet the intent of established professional standards and guidelines regarding patient safety. The automated system or device should

1. Provide the following inherent safety features of unit dose drug distribution systems
    *   Medications are contained in, and administered from, single unit or unit dose packages,
    *   Medications are dispensed in ready-to-administer form to the extent possible,
    *   Medication is available for administration to the patient only at the time at which it is to be administered, and
    *   A patient medication profile is concurrently maintained in the pharmacy for each patient.
2. Provide for prospective, timely review of medication

orders by a pharmacist at all appropriate decision points in the medication-use process, especially before administration of the first dose; and provide for the independent interpretation of the medication order by a pharmacist and a nurse.
3. Ensure safe medication storage, distribution, access, and use wherever the devices are deployed in the organization's practice settings. Safety includes meeting required environmental conditions for the storage and handling of medications.
4. Comply with applicable federal and state consumer protection laws and regulations. State boards of pharmacy may have different requirements for the use of automated devices in various practice settings and for obtaining approval for their use.

Access to Medications through Automated Systems

All medication distribution systems, both automated and nonautomated, have features that give nurses and other caregivers access to some medications before order review and approval by a pharmacist, especially in patient emergencies. Clearly stated organizational policies should be developed that limit access to medications before orders have been reviewed and approved by a pharmacist. Access to medications should be limited to the following cases:

1. The order has been reviewed and approved by a pharmacist.
2. The drug product has been approved by a multidisciplinary committee of physicians, pharmacists, and nurses who agree that it has minimal risk for misadventures.
3. There is a clinically urgent need for the medication that outweighs the potential risk.
4. Medication retrieval and administration are supervised by an identifiable, responsible physician (in the emergency department, catheterization laboratory, etc.).

Provision should be made for the retrospective review and reconciliation by a pharmacist of orders that were initiated without a pharmacist's review and approval.

Safety Checks

The pharmacy is responsible for ensuring that the automated system operates as designed and is well maintained to prevent errors and system interruptions. All elements of the automated system require periodic checking, including, as applicable, patient information and medication profiles, computer controls for access, operations of drawers and bins, and transaction records.

1. Each organization that uses an automated system should have a written plan for safe and effective use of the system. The plan should be developed by the pharmacy in that organization, with input from nursing, medicine, and other disciplines that may be affected by the system. The plan should address
    *   Potential sources of medication errors and the procedures to be followed to avoid such errors,
    *   Limits on access to medications,
    *   How medications will be packaged and labeled,

- Procedures for ensuring the security of controlled substances,
- Procedures for auditing all system transactions,
- Procedures for avoiding drug product cross-contamination, and
- Procedures for ensuring operator safety.

2. Each organization should have a written plan for ensuring the accuracy of (a) medications stored and accessed through an automated system and (b) machine-readable identification on medications. This plan should provide
   - A thorough review of the automated system to identify potential sources of error that may be introduced in operating that system,
   - Policies and procedures designed to preclude errors, and
   - A quality assurance program for reviewing medication error data and identifying opportunities for improvement.

3. Any organization that allows external suppliers to replenish medications in automated systems should have a written plan for ensuring medication accuracy.[13] When appropriate, the plan should address medications tagged with machine-readable identification.

4. Each organization should have a written contingency plan for maintaining timely medication distribution, security, and documentation when system interruptions occur.

Monitoring and Surveillance

Pharmacists are responsible legally and organizationally for ensuring that drug supplies are adequately controlled and that medication use is documented within the health care organization. Automated systems usually provide options for tracking and accounting for medication use. These options often include freestanding computer-controlled access and record keeping for each device, computer-controlled access and record keeping linked to the pharmacy information system, and computer linkages among the pharmacy, patient record, or billing information systems. Appropriate interfaces with pharmacy and overall patient-care computer systems are critical. Each of these options may require a different level of oversight.

1. The organization should have a written plan for the monitoring and surveillance of medications accessed through automated systems. The plan should be developed by the pharmacy with input from nursing and communicated to staff members responsible for its implementation.

2. The plan should include
   - Identification of the data to be captured and the reports generated that are used to monitor medication use (data and reports may vary by drug categories and requirements for control and accountability),
   - Assignment of responsibility for reviewing the reports, for scheduling the frequency of report reviews, and for reporting discrepancies,
   - Assignment of responsibility for resolving discrepancies, scheduling the resolution of discrepancies, following up on unresolved discrepancies, and taking action if the discrepancy is not resolved on schedule, and

- A description of the process for investigating trends in discrepancies and assigning responsibility for this.

3. Compliance with the plan should be monitored through the organization's quality assurance program.

Storage and Inventory

The drawer and bin configurations of automated devices vary from multidrug and multidose matrix drawers to individual patient drawers and single drug and unit dose bins within drawers. Controls may vary from allowing access to multiple medications and multiple doses to allowing access to only a single medication and single dose for a specific patient. Matrix drawers and similar configurations may allow access to medications other than those approved by a pharmacist for a specific patient. Location lights, bin lids, and locking bin lids are available on some matrix drawers to reduce vulnerability to errors.

The pharmacy should develop criteria for determining the drug products and quantities that will be stored under different levels of access control in specific configurations of drawers and bins. Patient safety should be the primary concern in establishing criteria. These criteria should address

1. The frequency and appropriateness of individual medication use.

2. The effective use of reports available through the automated system related to safe, accurate, and timely withdrawal of medications.

3. The identification of drug products that are considered inappropriate for inclusion in automated devices (e.g., products with short expiration dates, those that require special storage conditions, those with special preparation requirements, those that present cross-contamination problems, and those that pose high risks to patients and employees).

4. The need for ongoing monitoring by a pharmacist of the contents of the automated device, considering such points as evolving therapeutic trends, the differing needs of individual patient care areas, and the capabilities and safety features of the automated system.

5. Policies addressing drug product integrity, including
   - The importance of accuracy and integrity of product labels,
   - How medications removed from an automated device, but not used, should be handled,
   - How medication waste is accounted for,
   - Checking of products for expiration and beyond-use dates,
   - Identification of and follow-up on tampered products,
   - Storage of products, and
   - Procedures for delivering medications to patient care units and individual patients.

6. Controls that ensure accurate restocking of devices, such as access controls on drawers and bins, including location lights and bin lids that support safe access.

Security and Responsibility

Among pharmacy's responsibilities for the medication-use process is preventing threats to patient and employee safety and economic loss through medication misuse, pilferage, and diversion.

1. Each organization that uses an automated medication distribution system should have a written plan that assigns responsibility and addresses issues of security. The plan should be developed by the pharmacy in that organization, with input from nursing, medicine, and other disciplines that may be affected by the system. The plan should clearly identify that the pharmacist in charge has general responsibility for the automated system. The plan should specify who in the pharmacy and elsewhere in the organization has responsibility for computer-interface issues; operational problems; the accuracy of medications contained in the system; maintenance of access codes, magnetic cards, and other more positive identification methods; and training and retraining of users and what skills those individuals must have.

2. The specific responsibilities of all personnel involved in operating or using the automated system should be set forth in written policies and procedures.

Education and Training

Automated systems bring together information systems, machines, and humans in highly complex, interdependent relationships. Involved individuals must possess the knowledge and skills required by their responsibilities.

1. The organization using automated systems should have procedures for ensuring that all staff members involved receive adequate education and training, both initially and on an ongoing basis.

2. The organization should ensure that there are adequate resources for providing effective education and training.

3. The organization should ensure that the content of education and training programs is continually updated.

4. The organization should evaluate staff members to ensure competency in the use of the automated system; the evaluations should be documented.

References

1. Ray MD, Aldrich LT, Lew PJ. Experience with an automated point-of-use drug distribution system. *Hosp Pharm.* 1995; 30:18,20–3,27–30.

2. Borel JM, Karen LR. Effect of an automated, nursing unit-based drug-dispensing device on medication errors. *Am J Health-Syst Pharm.* 1995; 52:1875–9.

3. Guerrero RM, Nickman NA, Jorgenson JA. Work activities before and after implementation of an automated dispensing system. *Am J Health-Syst Pharm.* 1996; 53:548–54.

4. Schwarz HO, Brodowy BA. Implementation and evaluation of an automated dispensing system. *Am J Health-Syst Pharm.* 1995; 52:823–8.

5. Barker KN. Ensuring safety in the use of automated medication dispensing systems. *Am J Health-Syst Pharm.* 1995; 52:2445–7.

6. Tribble DA. How automated systems can (and do) fail. *Am J Health-Syst Pharm.* 1996; 53:2622–7.

7. National Association of Boards of Pharmacy Model State Pharmacy Act, article 1, section 105(b), p.12.

8. National Association of Boards of Pharmacy Model Rules for Pharmaceutical Care, section2(2) (e, f, and m), p 9.2, and section 3L, pp 9.13–9.14.

9. Perini VJ, Vermeulen LC. Comparison of automated medication-management systems. *Am J Hosp Pharm.* 1994; 51:1883–91.

10. ECRI. Automated decentralized pharmacy dispensing systems. *Health Devices.* 1996; 25:436–73.

11. Riley KY. Staying ahead of the curve, automation in pharmacy initiative works toward real-world solutions. *Consult Pharm.* 1997; 12:757–8,761–3,765.

12. Barker KN, Felkey BG, Flynn EA, et al. White paper on automation in pharmacy. *Consult. Pharm.* 1998; 13:256–93.

13. Louie C, Brethauer B, Dong D, et al. Use of a drug wholesaler to process refills for automated medication dispensing machines. *Hosp Pharm.* 1997; 32:367–75.

Approved by the ASHP Board of Directors, April 22, 1998. Developed by the ASHP Council on Professional Affairs.

The bibliographic citation for this document is as follows: American Society of Health-System Pharmacists. ASHP Guidelines on the Safe Use of Automated Medication Storage and Distribution Devices. *Am J Health-Syst Pharm.* 1998; 55:1403–7.

Drug Distribution and Control

Drug Distribution and Control

Pharmaceutical Counterfeiting (0401)

Source: Council on Professional Affairs

To foster increased pharmacist and public awareness of drug product counterfeiting; further,

To encourage pharmacists to purchase and handle medications in ways that enhance the transparency and integrity of the drug product supply chain; further,

To encourage pharmacists to identify instances of drug product counterfeiting and to respond by assisting the patient in receiving appropriate treatment and monitoring, documenting patient outcomes, and notifying the patient, prescriber, and appropriate state and federal regulatory bodies (e.g., the Food and Drug Administration's MedWatch system); further,

To provide consumers and health professionals with information on how to avoid counterfeit drug products and how to recognize, respond to, and report encounters with suspicious drug products; further,

To foster research and education on the extent, methods, and impact of drug product counterfeiting and on strategies for preventing and responding to drug product counterfeiting.

Pharmacy Drug Theft (0303)

Source: House of Delegates Resolution

To support the development of policies and guidelines for health-system pharmacists designed to deter drug product theft and thereby enhance both the integrity of the drug distribution chain and the safety of the workplace; further,

To encourage the development of systems that limit the diversion and abuse potential of medications, including high-cost drugs and controlled substances, and thereby reduce the likelihood that these products will be targets of theft.

Pharmacist's Role in Drug Procurement, Distribution, Surveillance, and Control (0232)

Source: Council on Professional Affairs

To affirm the pharmacist's expertise and responsibility in the procurement, distribution, surveillance, and control of all drugs used within health systems; further,

To encourage the Joint Commission on Accreditation of Healthcare Organizations, other accreditation bodies, and governmental entities to enhance patient safety by supporting the pharmacist's role in drug procurement, distribution, surveillance, and control.

(*Note*: For purposes of this policy, drugs include those used by inpatients and outpatients, large- and small-volume injectables, radiopharmaceuticals, diagnostic agents including radiopaque contrast media, anesthetic gases, blood-fraction drugs, dialysis fluids, respiratory therapy drugs, biotechnologically produced drugs, investigational drugs, drug samples, drugs brought to the setting by patients or family, and other chemicals and biological substances administered to patients to evoke or enhance pharmacologic responses.)

This policy supersedes ASHP policy 9908.

Optimizing the Medication-Use Process (9903)

Source: Council on Administrative Affairs

To urge health-system pharmacists to assume leadership, responsibility, and accountability for the quality, effectiveness, and efficiency of the entire medication-use process (including prescribing, dispensing, administration, monitoring, and education) across the continuum of care; further,

To urge health-system pharmacists to work in collaboration with patients, prescribers, nurses, and other health care providers in improving the medication-use process.

This policy was reviewed in 2003 by the Council on Administrative Affairs and by the Board of Directors and was found to still be appropriate.

Procurement

Prudent Purchasing of Pharmaceuticals (0014)
Source: Council on Legal and Public Affairs
To support existing laws and legitimate practices that allow organized health care settings to purchase drug products and related supplies at prices that minimize health care costs; further,

To support the principle of prudent purchase of pharmaceutical products and related supplies by public and private entities using appropriate professional practices to achieve that end; further,

To encourage government support of existing local professional activities (e.g., drug-use review, formulary systems, pharmacy and therapeutics committees, and patient counseling) already practiced in organized health care settings that are methods of promoting quality and cost-effective pharmaceutical care for patients.

This policy supersedes ASHP policies 9003 and 9105.

ASHP Guidelines for Selecting Pharmaceutical Manufacturers and Suppliers

Pharmacists are responsible for selecting, from hundreds of manufacturers and suppliers of drugs, those that will enable them to fulfill an important obligation: ensuring that patients receive pharmaceuticals and related supplies of the highest quality and at the lowest cost. These guidelines are offered as an aid to the pharmacist in achieving this goal.

Obligations of the Supplier

Pharmacists may purchase with confidence the products of those suppliers meeting the criteria presented here. Other factors such as credit policies, delivery times, and the breadth of a supplier's product line also must be considered when selecting a supplier.

Technical Considerations

1. On request of the pharmacist (an instrument such as the ASHP Drug Product Information Request Form[a] is useful in this regard), the supplier should furnish
   a. Analytical control data.
   b. Sterility testing data.
   c. Bioavailability data.
   d. Bioequivalency data.
   e. Descriptions of testing procedures for raw materials and finished products.
   f. Any other information that may be indicative of the quality of a given finished drug product.
   Testing data developed by independent laboratories should be identified by the supplier. All information should be supplied at no charge.
2. There should be no history of recurring product recalls indicative of deficient quality control procedures.
3. The supplier should permit visits (during normal business hours) by the pharmacist to inspect its manufacturing and control procedures.
4. All drug products should conform to the requirements of *The United States Pharmacopeia–The National Formulary (USP–NF)* (the most recent edition) unless otherwise specified by the pharmacist. Items not recognized by *USP–NF* should meet the specifications set forth by the pharmacist.
5. To the extent possible, all products should be available in single unit or unit dose packages. These packages should conform to the "ASHP Technical Assistance Bulletin on Single Unit and Unit Dose Packages of Drugs."[1]
6. The name and address of the manufacturer of the final dosage form and the packager or distributor should be present on the product labeling.
7. Expiration dates should be clearly indicated on the package label and, unless stability properties warrant otherwise, should occur in January or July.
8. Therapeutic, biopharmaceutic, and toxicologic information should be available to the pharmacist on request. Toxicity information should be available around the clock.
9. Patient/staff educational materials that are important for proper use of the product should be routinely available.

10. On request, the supplier should furnish proof of any claims made with respect to the efficacy, safety, and superiority of its products.
11. On request, the supplier should furnish, at no charge, a reasonable quantity of its products to enable the pharmacist to evaluate the products' physical traits, including pharmaceutical elegance (appearance and absence of physical deterioration or flaws), packaging, and labeling.

Distribution Policies

1. Whenever possible, delivery of a drug product should be confined to a single lot number.
2. Unless otherwise specified or required by stability considerations, not less than a 12-month interval between a product's time of delivery and its expiration date should be present.
3. The supplier should accept for full credit (based on purchase price), without prior authorization, any unopened packages of goods returned within 12 months of the expiration date. Credits should be in cash or applied to the institution's account.
4. The supplier should ship all goods in a timely manner, freight prepaid, and enclose a packing list with each shipment. All items "out of stock" should be noted, and the anticipated availability of the item should be clearly indicated. There should be no extensive recurrence of back orders.
5. The supplier should warrant title to commodities supplied, warrant them to be free from defects and imperfections and fit for any rational use of the product, and indemnify and hold the purchaser harmless against any and all suits, claims, and expenses, including attorneys' fees, damages, and injuries or any claims by third parties relating to the products.

Marketing and Sales Policies

1. The supplier should not, without written consent, use the pharmacist's or his or her organization's name in any advertising or other promotional materials or activities.
2. The supplier should honor formulary decisions made by the organization's pharmacy and therapeutics committee, and the supplier's sales representatives should comply with the organization's regulations governing their activities.
3. The supplier should not offer cash, equipment, or merchandise to the organization or its staff as an inducement to purchase its products.
4. Discounts should be in cash or cash credit, not merchandise, and should be clearly indicated on invoices and bills rather than consisting of end-of-year rebates or similar discount practices.
5. In entering into a contract to supply goods, the supplier should guarantee to furnish, at the price specified, any minimum amount of products so stated. If the supplier is unable to meet the supply commitment, the supplier

should reimburse the organization for any excess costs incurred in obtaining the product from other sources. If, during the life of the contract, a price reduction occurs, the lower price should prevail.

6. All parties to the bidding process should respect the integrity of the process and the contracts awarded thereby.

Responsibilities of the Purchaser

It may be desirable to purchase drugs or other commodities on a competitive bid basis. The pharmacist should ensure that competitive bidding procedures conform to the guidelines below:

1. Invitations to bid should be mailed to the suppliers' home offices with copies to their local representatives (if any), unless suppliers specify otherwise.
2. Potential bidders should be given no less than 3 weeks to submit a bid.
3. The opening date for bids should be specified and honored by the purchaser.
4. The language of the invitation to bid should be clear and should indicate the person (and organization address and telephone number) the bidder should contact in the event of questions or problems. Specifications should be complete with respect to products, packagings, and quantities desired.
5. If bidding forms are used, they should contain adequate space for the bidder to enter the information requested.
6. The winning bidder should be notified in writing. Unsuccessful bidders may be informed of who won the award at what price, if they so request.

7. The quantities specified in the invitation to bid should be a reasonable estimate of requirements.
8. If the invitation to bid is offered on behalf of a group of purchasers, the individual members of the group should not engage in bidding procedures of their own and should purchase the goods in question from the winning bidder.

Reference

1. American Society of Hospital Pharmacists. ASHP technical assistance bulletin on single unit and unit dose packages of drugs. *Am J Hosp Pharm.* 1985; 42:378–9.

ᵃAvailable from ASHP, 7272 Wisconsin Avenue, Bethesda, MD 20814.

Approved by the ASHP Board of Directors, November 14, 1990. Revised by the ASHP Council on Professional Affairs. Supersedes previous versions approved November 17–18, 1983, and September 22, 1989.

The bibliographic citation for this document is as follows: American Society of Hospital Pharmacists. ASHP guidelines for selecting pharmaceutical manufacturers and suppliers. *Am J Hosp Pharm.* 1991; 48:523–4.

ASHP Guidelines on Managing Drug Product Shortages

Purpose

Short-term back orders and long-term unavailability of drug products have been a challenge to pharmacy managers for many years.[1] Nevertheless, these drug product shortages have been increasing in frequency and severity since the late 1990s.[2–4] The causes are varied and involve all segments of the "supply chain." Changes in policies and practices among these segments individually and collectively contribute to drug product shortages. The challenge for pharmacy managers is to enable the provision of seamless equivalent drug therapy at comparable costs.

Managing drug product inventories and supply situations is particularly complex for health care organizations because of the large number of monotherapies and monoproducts available. Drug product shortages can delay and compromise patient care and increase total costs, including those of alternative therapies, delivery devices, and staff training. The department of pharmacy should take a leadership role in managing shortages by developing appropriate strategies and an awareness campaign.[5]

Strategies for dealing with drug product shortages are similar to disaster planning and risk management contingencies for major snowstorms, mass casualty events, temporary wholesaler shutdowns, and preparations made for the Year 2000.[6]

This guideline describes the factors contributing to drug product shortages and recommends a general process for inventory management in preparing for and working through shortage situations. Included are strategies for identifying alternative therapies, working with suppliers, and collaborating with physicians. Because of the differences and complexities in health care organizational arrangements and practice settings, some aspects of these guidelines may not be applicable. Pharmacy managers should use their professional judgment in assessing and adapting this guideline to meet the needs of their own settings and to comply with the health care organization's policies and procedures.

Background

Managing drug product shortages has become routine, forcing health care organizations to expend more personnel time and other resources identifying, tracking, and resolving shortage problems. Pharmacy managers, when confronted with the unavailability of a drug product, want information to make decisions about meeting patient needs for the product. They want to know the reason for the product's unavailability, when supplies of the product will be available, options for obtaining the product from alternative sources, alternative therapies and related information for health services staff, and the cost consequences of alternative sources or therapies. Segments of the supply chain, especially manufacturers, have been inconsistent in providing information and assistance to health care organizations. The difficulty in obtaining information is exacerbated by the many players, complexities, and uncertainties in the supply chain.

Shortages can be the result of one, several, or any combination of factors throughout the supply chain. For the purposes of this guideline, the supply chain includes sources of raw materials, manufacturers, regulators, wholesalers, prime vendors, buying groups, and end-user health care organizations. The "just-in-time" approach to procurement and inventory management among manufacturers, distributors, and end-users has reduced the ability of the supply chain to maintain drug product availability during disruptions. Many end-user health care organizations have reduced on-hand inventories to the extent that they are dependent on daily replenishments from suppliers. Inventories no longer provide an adequate buffer and, under some circumstances, a temporary back order becomes a critical drug product shortage for the end-user. The factors that follow contribute to disruptions in the availability of drug products.

Raw and Bulk Material Unavailability. Disruptions can occur in the availability of raw and bulk materials to manufacturers of finished drug products. This is especially problematic when multiple manufacturers make a drug product with material available from only one source (e.g., the sole source for bulk penicillin G sodium) that discontinues production. Availability problems arise when raw materials come from undeveloped parts of the world or where there are hostilities, animal diseases contaminate tissue used to extract raw material, climatic and other environmental changes depress the growth of plants used to extract raw material, or raw materials are degraded or contaminated during harvesting, storage, or transport.

For example, the dexamethasone shortage was caused by one manufacturer's change from beef protein to a plant source when the European precautions to prevent bovine spongiform encephalopathy were enacted. Other examples of drugs involved in shortages caused by the unavailability of raw and bulk materials include prochlorperazine, metoclopramide, phenobarbital, isoproterenol, and bretylium.

Manufacturing Difficulties. Shortages can occur when the primary or only manufacturer of a drug product halts production in response to a Food and Drug Administration (FDA) enforcement action concerning noncompliance with Current Good Manufacturing Practices (CGMPs). FDA actions are intended to protect the public from potentially unsafe drug products. These actions are evaluated by the FDA Center for Drug Evaluation and Research (CDER) drug shortage coordinator to determine if the action might cause a medical necessity problem. If necessary, FDA will assist the manufacturer's return to compliance.

Manufacturing difficulties have been the leading cause of injectable drug product shortages. Immune globulin intravenous pentelate was in short supply for years because numerous manufacturers experienced manufacturing difficulties and related regulatory problems that suspended production. One of several manufacturers of naloxone and tetanus toxoid discontinued production as a result of such difficulties. The remaining manufacturers were unable to meet the demand.

Voluntary Recalls. Voluntary recalls can cause shortages, especially when a sole manufacturer's drug product dominates the market supply. Voluntary recalls usually affect specific lots and are conducted because of a lack of assurance that the recalled product is safe and for nonsafety related reasons, such as technical deficiencies in the drug's labeling. An ethical dilemma could arise when complying with the voluntary recall that may knowingly cause a shortage in a given health care organization.

Manufacturer Production Decisions. Manufacturer production decisions can cause shortages. Occasionally, manufacturers temporarily or permanently reduce production amounts of certain drug products as they shift production or reallocate resources to other products. An apparent practice among some manufacturers has been the halt of production when annual quotas are met.

A manufacturer's reasoned, sound business decision to discontinue production of a drug product because of insufficient financial return can cause a shortage. A shortage of diptheria and tetanus toxoids and acellular pertussis vaccine absorbed was precipitated when one of the manufacturers, claiming low revenues, discontinued its product. Under this circumstance, FDA might perform a medical necessity evaluation and, if the unavailability of the product puts the public at risk, encourage other manufacturers to produce the product.

Orphan Drug Products. Drug products used to treat rare disorders for a relatively small patient population might be difficult to obtain. The federal Orphan Drugs Program provides incentives for manufacturers who are willing to produce them. In addition, the National Organization for Rare Disorders may become involved through lobbying and other actions.

Restricted Drug Product Distribution. An increase in the number of drug products available only through restricted distribution methods has caused artificial shortages for some health care organizations. As the result of either market approval requirements or postmarketing surveillance, manufacturers limit the availability of specific drug products with known adverse effects, e.g., Propulsid (cisapride) and Tikosyn (dofetilide). Only selected suppliers and end-users that comply with manufacturer agreements are able to obtain the product. A manufacturer can also place restrictions on a drug product that cannot be manufactured in sufficient quantities to meet demand (e.g., Enbrel [etanerept]).

Industry Consolidations. Manufacturer mergers often result in decisions to narrow the focus of product lines, resulting in the discontinuation of drug products. In addition, merged manufacturers of competing products may consolidate production, making product supply more vulnerable should problems arise.

Market Shifts. The addition of a generic product to the market can precipitate a decrease in the production of the innovator product, causing reductions in overall availability. Procurement decisions, such as "closed categories" by large health care organizations, can also shift the market for a given drug product. Military action can also cause an unexpected market shift, as seen during "Desert Storm" when large quantities of albumin were diverted to the conflict.

Unexpected Increases in Demand. Occasionally, an unexpected increase in demand for a drug product exceeds production capacity. This may occur as a result of a product's popularity for new unlabeled uses, a substantial disease outbreak, or unpredictable factors of demand. Shortages could be prolonged when the raw materials are limited or manufacturing processes are complex and are dependent on a long lead time. Succinylcholine was in short supply because of an increase in demand and delays in shipping raw materials. The Enbrel Enrollment program was established to ensure a continued supply for enrolled patients when demand exceeded capacity.

Nontraditional Distributors. The shortage of drug products has attracted several nontraditional distributors who have been able to obtain certain products (e.g., immune globulin, influenza virus vaccine, and dexamethasone injection). When demand exceeded supply through normal channels, these distributors announced the availability of these products at substantially higher prices. How they obtain these products and whether their activities contribute to shortages in unknown.

Compounding pharmacies also have announced the availability of drugs that are in short supply (e.g., dexamethasone injection and hyaluronidase injection). Caution is warranted because preparations from these pharmacies may not have FDA-approved labeling and their sources of raw materials have been questioned.

Natural Disasters. Natural disasters cause drug product shortages when they affect manufacturing facilities, particularly those of manufacturers that are the sole source for a drug product or category of products. For example, hurricane damage to manufacturing facilities in the Caribbean in 1997 caused shortages of several drugs, including gentamicin and the combination of piperacillin and tazobactam.

Process

Health care organizations should develop a contingency planning strategy to prepare for the possibility of a prolonged drug product shortage.[5] Although it is often not possible to predict when shortages will occur, the process for dealing with them can be defined beforehand. A point person should be identified to implement and monitor this process and establish an organizational approach to decision-making and communication. Committee structures and responsibilities should be determined to assist decision-making during each phase of the process, e.g., pharmacy and therapeutics committee, medical executive committee.

Contingency planning can be divided into three key areas: the assessment phase, the preparation phase, and the contingency phase. Assessment requires a critical evaluation of the current situation and the potential impact of the shortage on the health care organization. An effective evaluation examines the reason for the shortage and the manufacturer's estimated release date and encompasses both internal supply availability and external availability.

The preparation phase focuses on all the activities that can be performed before the actual effects of the shortage are felt. Depending on the health care organization's inventory when a back order or other notice is received, there is often lead time before actual stock depletions. All diseases that are dependent or interdependent on the unavailable drug product and alternative therapies are identified. Since many drug products have limited therapeutic alternatives, outages can have significant patient care and cost consequences. Preparation should also focus on developing methodologies for implementation and communication.

The contingency phase involves operations and circumstances for which preparation is limited because of incomplete information, financial constraints, or circumstances beyond the health care organization's control. For example, biological products are available only in increments and at a very high cost when no therapeutic alternatives are readily available or when shortages are longer than anticipated. Since direct control over availability is not possible, health care organizations must prepare for the product's unavailability.

Assessment Phase

For each shortage, an assessment is conducted to evaluate its impact. The potential impact is determined by using the shortage's expected duration to conduct a threat analysis and inventory assessment.

Duration of Shortage. Product manufacturers, distributors, FDA, and other sources can be contacted to determine the reason for the shortage and its expected duration. Predictions of when the product will be available help to determine the health care organization's ability to endure and guide short- and long-term strategies.

Although the end result is the same, the time to impact and duration of impact will vary depending on the reason for the shortage and where problems occur along the supply chain, from raw materials to manufacturer, manufacturer to wholesaler, and wholesaler to health care organization. The lack of raw material may affect several manufacturers of the finished drug product. A manufacturer's problems may affect only its product. Effects on distributors are dependent on their inventory levels.

Threat to Patient Care and Costs. A threat analysis evaluates all relevant factors of the shortage, such as duration, current inventory, medical necessity, and alternative sources or therapies, to determine the shortage's potential impact on patient care and costs. Health care organizations will not be equally affected by a given shortage depending on the scope and level of services and service population.

Inventory on Hand. Once a shortage is confirmed, the inventory on hand is counted and the time period it will cover is estimated. Available inventory includes all supplies of the drug product within the health care organization, including the pharmacies, inpatient units and ambulatory care clinics, automated medication storage and distribution devices, floor stock, code carts, and preprepared trays.

Based on available quantities and historical usage, an estimate can be made as to how long the health care organization can endure a shortage. Usage history can be obtained from procurement and issue records held by distributors, the purchasing department, and the pharmacy department. Inventory counts of all alternative drug products should be converted into common measurement units to augment estimates of usage. The assessment of how long the available inventory of the shortage drug product and possible alternative products would last should include both the current usage rates and reduced rates after conservation measures are implemented.

Preparation Phase

Once an imminent shortage has been confirmed, steps should be taken to prepare for known and potential problems in maintaining patient care and controlling costs.

Therapeutic Alternatives. The first step in the preparation phase is to identify therapeutic alternatives to the unavailable drug product. The health care organization should have a formal process for identifying and approving therapeutic alternatives. The point person in the pharmacy who is responsible for managing drug product shortages should initiate this process. Decisions about alternative therapies with other drug products should be made in collaboration with medical, nursing, and pharmacy representatives and approved by the appropriate medical committee(s).

Communication and Patient Safety. Information about the drug product shortage, alternative therapies, temporary therapeutic guidelines, and implementation plans should be communicated to the medical and nursing staffs by the most effective means available within the health care organization. This is essential for patient safety and preventing medication errors caused by confusion over different drug products' dosages, onset, duration, and other factors. Pharmacy department staff responsible for assisting prescribers with medication orders and aiding nursing staff with administration should be thoroughly informed about the alternative therapy decisions and implementation plans. In addition, sustained communication is necessary to reach medical, nursing, and pharmacy staffs working varied shifts or services.

External Relationships with Other Health Care Organizations and Health Systems. The preparation phase includes, where applicable, establishing collaborative arrangements with other health care organizations within a regional network or system. Available supplies of a potentially unavailable product and information about alternative therapies could be shared among the facilities.

Patient Prioritization. In the event of prolonged shortages of drug products, especially when alternative therapies are limited, a patient priority plan may be needed. A multidisciplinary team should develop criteria for the use of the product. Prescribing could be limited to select patients or services within the health care organization. For drug products with defined durations of therapy, prescribers and pharmacists may have to consult each other to ensure that adequate supplies are available for a patient's entire course of therapy. Carefully written guidelines should be provided to assist frontline pharmacists to appropriately assess and respond to medication orders for drug products under a patient priority limitation.

The health care organization's risk management and ethics staffs or committees should be consulted when developing criteria that would limit a drug product's use and force a prescriber to decide whom should receive a drug product.

Other Supply Sources. Other potential sources of the drug product should be investigated during the preparation phase as early as possible to minimize supply disruptions. Alternative manufacturers and distributors should be contacted to determine availability, contract arrangements, item numbers, and payment terms.

Stockpiling Restraint. Pharmacy managers are cognizant of a drug product shortage's potential impact on patient care and concerns for litigation when optimal care could be compromised without use of the drug product. Nevertheless, they are also challenged by the pressure to control inventory and the pressure to increase inventory in preparation for stock outages.

One of the greatest challenges associated with preparation for shortages concerns inventory management. Despite pressures to do otherwise, good citizenship requires restraint from ordering quantities in excess of normal use that could contribute to the shortage and divert unneeded supplies away from other health care organizations with patients in need.[7] Health care organizations should refrain from stockpiling (hoarding), which causes two distinct problems:

1. Stockpiling can cause artificial shortages when health care organizations drain the supply chain and exceed manufacturing capacities, and
2. Increased inventory is costly and may not be absorbed by normal usage if shortages do not occur as anticipated.

Speculative purchases in response to a potential shortage also have drawbacks, depending on the likely cause for the shortage and where it might occur in the supply chain. Problems may arise that pose threats to, but do not reach, end-users. This happens when the supply chain, from raw material to finished product, contains several months' supply. With long lead times, many problems are corrected before a shortage actually occurs.

In the event that administration mandates acquisition and maintenance of an emergency supply, quantities should be kept to a minimum and reviewed judiciously, similar to preparations made for a distributor's temporary shutdown. Under real or potential shortage situations, manufacturers and distributors have placed caps on quantities exceeding the health care organization's normal purchasing patterns.

Contingency Phase

The final, or last resort, phase of the process is devising a contingency plan that encompasses those aspects of preparation involving circumstances beyond direct control. When a drug product is only available from a nontraditional, off-contract source, is not available from any source, or does not have acceptable alternative therapies, thought and action are required to minimize the consequences of potential compromises in patient care and budget deficits.

Risk Management and Liability. One potential complication of a shortage is litigation by patients who feel that they have received improper care as a result of delays, prioritization, or alternative therapy. Even though risk management and legal representatives may have participated in earlier phases of the process, they should be notified immediately when all options for obtaining either the drug product or acceptable alternatives have been exhausted.

Budget Considerations. In the event that the drug product is available only from nontraditional distributors, estimates of the costs of using these sources should be prepared. The financial implications are subsequently presented through budget channels with a request and justification for contin-gency funds. Additional expenditures caused by drug shortages should be well documented to explain budget variances and to support future budget proposals.

Information Coordination and Communication. The appropriate health care organizational departments and committees should collaborate in preparing a communications strategy to keep staff, patients, and external interests informed of potential drug product shortages. Patients or family members should be counseled when a drug shortage will delay or compromise care, especially when patients have been stabilized on the drug product and alternatives may not be as effective, e.g., antiepileptics or antiarrhythmics.

Communication with the media, national professional or patient organizations, and government agencies may help to raise awareness of the shortage and its potential consequences. Attention may encourage production by other manufacturers, collaborative efforts to develop alternative therapies, and ad hoc training opportunities on the safe and effective use of alternatives.

Government Intervention. FDA is responsible for assisting with drug product shortages to the extent of its authorities. These responsibilities are dispersed among several components of CDER. Limits on FDA's activities are dependent on whether a shortage meets "medical necessity" criteria. FDA will attempt to prevent or alleviate shortages of medically necessary products.

"A product is considered to be medically necessary, or a medical necessity, if it is used to treat or prevent a serious disease or medical condition, and there is no other available source of that product or alternative drug that is judged by medical staff to be an adequate substitute."[8] Patient inconvenience and cost to the patient, institution, and manufacturer are insufficient bases to classify a product as a medical necessity.

A medical necessity determination involves a risk-benefit evaluation of the compromising issue with the product and the medical need for the product. In drug product shortage situations where FDA has determined that the product is medically necessary, FDA will act within its authorities. Actions may include discussions with pharmaceutical manufacturers to encourage additional sources, technical assistance to manufacturers experiencing CGMP difficulties, or expedited reviews of drug product marketing applications or manufacturer CGMP-related improvements. The FDA may take these actions whether the cause of the shortage involves business decisions to stop manufacturing the product, voluntary recalls, FDA enforcement actions, etc. Information on the availability of medically necessary products is posted on the FDA/CDER Web site (www.fda.gov/cder/drug/shortages).

The FDA encourages consumers and health care professionals and organizations to report drug product shortages. Reports should be made to FDA's CDER Drug Information Branch by calling 1-888-463-6332. Even though a drug product is not medically necessary, the FDA does obtain information about its availability.

CDER is not responsible for biologicals, such as immune globulin and vaccines. These products are the responsibility of the FDA Center for Biological Evaluation and Research, which does not have a comparable shortage program.

Conclusion

Drug product supply issues are becoming more frequent,

whether they are the result of manufacturing difficulties or natural disasters that affect production, reductions in the supply of raw materials, voluntary recalls, manufacturer business decisions, FDA enforcement actions to ensure public safety, or artificial shortages due to stockpiling. Although it is impractical to prepare for every potential shortage, proper planning can minimize adverse effects on patient care and health care organization costs and prevent problems from escalating into crises. The key to success will undoubtedly be found in the effectiveness of information gathering, teamwork to assess options, and communication with providers, patients, and administrators.

References

1.   Schwartz MA. Prescription drugs in short supply: case histories. New York: Marcel Dekker; 1980.
2.   Nordenberg T. When a drug is in short supply. *FDA Consum*. 1997; 31:30–2.
3.   Vecchione A. Drug shortages: industry copes as it waits for supplies. *Hosp Pharm Rep*. 1997; 11:1,7.
4.   Nelson RE, Biderdorf RI. Nationwide drug shortages: it's time to take the lead. *Nutr Clin Pract*. 1998; 13:295–7.
5.   Schrand LM, Troester TS, Ballas ZK, et al. Preparing for drug shortages: one teaching hospital's approach to the IVIG shortage. *Formulary*. 2001; 36:52,56–9.
6.   Wechsler J. Pharmacists, health organizations map plans to ensure systems, supplies are ready for Y2K. *Formulary*. 1999; 34:620–1.
7.   Myers CE. Artificial shortages of drug supplies. *Am J Health-Syst Pharm*. 1999; 56:727.
8.   Food and Drug Administration. CDER Manual of policies and procedures: drug shortage management. www.fda.gov/cder/drug/shortages.

Developed through the ASHP Council on Administrative Affairs and approved by the ASHP Board of Directors on March 28, 2001.

The bibliographic citation for this document is as follows: American Society of Health-System Pharmacists. ASHP guidelines on managing drug product shortages. *Am J Health-Syst Pharm*. 2001; 58:1445–50.

Preparation and Handling

Compounding Versus Manufacturing (0225)

Source: Council on Legal and Public Affairs

To support the principle that compounding, when done to meet anticipatory patient needs, is part of the practice of pharmacy and is not manufacturing; further,

To foster educational efforts relating to pharmacy compounding in health systems.

This policy supersedes ASHP policy 9107.

Pharmaceutical Waste (0231)

Source: Council on Professional Affairs

To work closely with regulatory bodies and appropriate organizations to develop standards that address pharmaceu-

tical hazardous waste as defined in the Resource Conservation and Recovery Act, for the purpose of simplifying the disposal of these substances in health systems; further,

To encourage pharmaceutical manufacturers and the Environmental Protection Agency to provide guidance and assistance to health systems in their pharmaceutical waste-destruction and waste-recycling efforts; further,

To promote awareness of pharmaceutical waste regulations within health systems; further,

To encourage pharmaceutical manufacturers to streamline packaging of drug products to reduce waste materials.

This policy supersedes ASHP policy 9110.

ASHP Guidelines on
Pharmacy-Prepared Ophthalmic Products

Pharmacists are frequently called on to prepare sterile products intended for ophthalmic administration when a suitable sterile ophthalmic product is not available from a licensed manufacturer. These products may be administered topically or by subconjunctival or intraocular (e.g., intravitreal and intracameral) injection and may be in the form of solutions, suspensions, or ointments.

The sterility of these products, as well as accuracy in the calculation and preparation of doses, is of great importance. Ocular infections and loss of vision caused by contamination of extemporaneously prepared ophthalmic products have been reported.[1,2] Drugs administered by subconjunctival or intraocular injection often have narrow therapeutic indices. In practice, serious errors in technique have occurred in the preparation of intravitreal solutions, which resulted in concentrations up to double the intended amounts.[3] To ensure adequate stability, uniformity, and sterility, ophthalmic products from licensed manufacturers should be used whenever possible.

The following guidelines are intended to assist pharmacists when extemporaneous preparation of ophthalmic products is necessary. These guidelines do not apply to the manufacturing of sterile pharmaceuticals as defined in state and federal laws and regulations. Other guidelines on extemporaneous compounding of ophthalmic products also have been published.[4,5]

1. Before compounding any product for ophthalmic use, the pharmacist should review documentation that substantiates the safety and benefit of the product when administered into the eye. If no such documentation is available, the pharmacist must employ professional judgment in determining suitability of the product for ophthalmic administration.

2. Important factors to be considered in preparing an ophthalmic medication include the following:[6]
   a. Sterility.
   b. Tonicity.
   c. pH, buffering.
   d. Inherent toxicity of the drug.
   e. Need for a preservative.
   f. Solubility.
   g. Stability in an appropriate vehicle.
   h. Viscosity.
   i. Packaging and storage of the finished product.

3. A written procedure for each ophthalmic product compounded should be established and kept on file and should be easily retrievable. The procedure should specify appropriate steps in compounding, including aseptic methods, and whether microbiologic filtration or terminal sterilization (e.g., autoclaving) of the finished product is appropriate.

4. Before preparation of the product is begun, mathematical calculations should be reviewed by another person or by an alternative method of calculation in order to minimize error. This approach is especially important for products, such as intraocular injections, for which extremely small doses are frequently ordered, necessitating multiple dilutions. Decimal errors

in the preparation of these products may have serious consequences.

5. Accuracy in compounding ophthalmic products is further enhanced by the use of larger volumes, which tends to diminish the effect of errors in measurement caused by the inherent inaccuracy of measuring devices. Larger volumes, however, also necessitate special attention to adequate mixing procedures, especially for ointments.

6. Strict adherence to aseptic technique and proper sterilization procedures are crucial in the preparation of ophthalmic products. All extemporaneous compounding of ophthalmic products should be performed in a certified laminar airflow hood (or, for preparing cytotoxic or hazardous agents, a biological safety cabinet).[5] Only personnel trained and proficient in the techniques and procedures should prepare ophthalmic products. Quality-assurance principles for compounding sterile products should be followed, and methods should be established to validate all procedures and processes related to sterile product preparation. In addition, the following should be considered:
   a. Ingredients should be mixed in sterile empty containers. Individual ingredients often can first be drawn into separate syringes and then injected into a larger syringe by insertion of the needles into the needle-free tip of the larger syringe. The larger syringe should be of sufficient size to allow for proper mixing of ingredients.
   b. To maximize measurement accuracy, the smallest syringe appropriate for measuring the required volume should be used. When the use of a single syringe would require estimation of the volume (e.g., measuring 4.5 ml in a 5-ml syringe with no mark at the 4.5-ml level), the use of two syringes of appropriate capacities (or two separate syringe "loads") should be considered in order to provide a more accurate measurement.
   c. A fresh disposable needle and syringe should be used at each step to avoid contamination and prevent error due to residual contents.
   d. When multiple dilutions are required, the containers of interim concentrations should be labeled to avoid confusion.
   e. In the preparation of an ophthalmic product from either (1) a sterile powder that has been reconstituted or (2) a liquid from a glass ampul, the ingredients should be filtered through a 5-μm filter to remove any particulate matter.

7. For ophthalmic preparations that must be sterilized, an appropriate and validated method of sterilization should be determined on the basis of the characteristics of the particular product and container. Filtration of the preparation through a 0.22-μm filter into a sterile final container is a commonly used method; however, this method is not suitable for sterilizing ophthalmic suspensions and ointments.[7] When an ophthalmic preparation is compounded from a nonsterile ingredient, the

final product must be sterilized before it is dispensed. Sterilization by autoclaving in the final container may be possible, provided that product stability is not adversely affected and appropriate quality control procedures are followed.[6]

8. Preservative-free ingredients should be used in the preparation of intraocular injections, since some preservatives are known to be toxic to many of the internal structures of the eye.[6]

9. In the preparation of ophthalmic products from cytotoxic or other hazardous agents, the pharmacist should adhere to established safety guidelines for handling such agents.[8,9]

10. The final container should be appropriate for the ophthalmic product and its intended use and should not interfere with the stability and efficacy of the preparation.[10] Many ophthalmic liquids can be packaged in sterile plastic bottles with self-contained dropper tips or in glass bottles with separate droppers. Ophthalmic ointments should be packaged in sterilized ophthalmic tubes. Injectables that are not for immediate use should be packaged in sterile vials rather than in syringes, and appropriate overfill should be included. All containers should be adequately sealed to prevent contamination.

11. The pharmacist should assign appropriate expiration dates to extemporaneously prepared ophthalmic products; these dates should be based on documented stability data as well as the potential for microbial contamination of the product.[11] The chemical stability of the active ingredient, the preservative, and packaging material should be considered in determining the overall stability of the final ophthalmic product.[12]

12. Ophthalmic products should be clearly and accurately labeled. In some cases, it may be appropriate to label the products with both the weight and concentration of active ingredients and preservatives. Labels should also specify storage and handling requirements and expiration dates. Extemporaneously prepared ophthalmic products dispensed for outpatient use should be labeled in accordance with applicable state regulations for prescription labeling.

References

1. Associated Press. Pittsburgh woman loses eye to tainted drugs; 12 hurt. *Baltimore Sun.* 1990; Nov 9:3A.

2. Associated Press. Eye drop injuries prompt an FDA warning. *N Y Times.* 1990; 140(Dec 9):39I.

3. Jeglum EL, Rosenberg SB, Benson WE. Preparation of intravitreal drug doses. *Ophthalmic Surg.* 1981; 12:355–9.

4. Reynolds LA. Guidelines for preparation of sterile ophthalmic products. *Am J Hosp Pharm.* 1991; 48:2438–9.

5. Reynolds LA, Closson R. Ophthalmic drug formulations. A handbook of extemporaneous products. Vancouver, WA: Applied Therapeutics; (in press).

6. The United States Pharmacopeia, 22nd rev., and The National Formulary, 17th ed. Rockville, MD: The United States Pharmacopeial Convention; 1989:1692–3.

7. Allen LV. Indomethacin 1% ophthalmic suspension. *US Pharm.* 1991; 16(May):82–3.

8. American Society of Hospital Pharmacists. ASHP technical assistance bulletin on handling cytotoxic and hazardous drugs. *Am J Hosp Pharm.* 1990; 47:1033–49.

9. OSHA work-practice guidelines for personnel dealing with cytotoxic (antineoplastic) drugs. *Am J Hosp Pharm.* 1986; 43:1193–204.

10. Ansel HC, Popovich NG. Pharmaceutical dosage forms and drug delivery systems. 5th ed. Philadelphia: Lea & Febiger; 1990:354–7.

11. Stolar MH. Expiration dates of repackaged drug products. *Am J Hosp Pharm.* 1979; 36:170. Editorial.

12. Remington's pharmaceutical sciences. 19th ed. Gennaro AR, ed. Easton, PA: Mack Publishing; 1990:1581–959.

These guidelines were reviewed in 2003 by the Council on Professional Affairs and by the Board of Directors and were found to still be appropriate.

Approved by the ASHP Board of Directors, April 21, 1993. Developed by the ASHP Council on Professional Affairs.

The bibliographic citation for this document is as follows: American Society of Hospital Pharmacists. ASHP technical assistance bulletin on pharmacy-prepared ophthalmic products. *Am J Hosp Pharm.* 1993; 50:1462–3.

ASHP Guidelines on Quality Assurance for Pharmacy-Prepared Sterile Products

Patient morbidity and mortality have resulted from incorrectly prepared or contaminated pharmacy-prepared products.[1-7] Pharmacists seldom know that inaccurate or contaminated products are dispensed when pharmacy quality monitors are inadequate.[8-10] In contemporary health care organizations, more patients are receiving compounded sterile products that are stored for extended periods before use (allowing the growth of a pathological bioload of microorganisms[11]), more patients are seriously ill, and more patients are immunocompromised than ever before.

These ASHP guidelines are intended to help pharmacists and pharmacy technicians prepare sterile products of high quality.[a] The pharmacist is responsible for compounding and dispensing sterile products of correct ingredient identity, purity (freedom from physical contaminants, such as precipitates,[12] and chemical contaminants), strength (including stability[13] and compatibility), and sterility and for dispensing them in appropriate containers, labeled accurately and appropriately for the end user.

Other professional organizations have published useful guidelines on compounding and dispensing sterile products. The United States Pharmacopeia (USP) publishes the official compendium *The United States Pharmacopeia and The National Formulary* (*USP*) and its supplements, all of which may have legal implications for pharmacists.[14,15] The reader would especially benefit from studying the *USP* general information chapter on sterile drug products for home use,[13] which is referred to often in this ASHP guideline. The National Association of Boards of Pharmacy (NABP) has published less detailed model regulations for use by state boards of pharmacy.[16,17] The American Society for Parenteral and Enteral Nutrition (A.S.P.E.N.) recently published a special report on safe practices for parenteral nutrition formulations.[18]

Other governmental and accreditation sources are more general. The Joint Commission on Accreditation of Healthcare Organizations (JCAHO) publishes at least four sets of standards that mention pharmacy compounding. The hospital accreditation standards simply state that the organization adheres to laws, professional licensure, and practice standards governing the safe operation of pharmaceutical services.[19] The JCAHO home care standards require that medications be safely prepared, including "using appropriate techniques for preparing sterile and nonsterile medications and products." For example, the home care standards state that "appropriate quality-control techniques are used to check for preparation accuracy and absence of microbial contamination. Techniques for preparing sterile products follow guidelines established by the American Society of Health-System Pharmacists."[20] The JCAHO standards for long-term-care pharmacies list important conditions for product preparation, such as separate areas for sterile product preparation, use of a laminar-airflow workbench or class 100 cleanroom, and quality control systems to ensure the accuracy and sterility of final products.[21] The JCAHO standard for ambulatory care infusion centers states, among other things, several facility-related standards, for example the use of biological safety cabinets to protect personnel preparing cytotoxic or hazardous medications; work surfaces free of

equipment, supplies, records, and labels unrelated to the medication being prepared; and a separate area for preparing sterile products that is constructed to minimize opportunities for particulate and microbial contamination.[22]

The Food and Drug Administration (FDA) publishes regulations on current good manufacturing practices that apply to sterile products made by pharmaceutical manufacturers for shipment in interstate commerce. Pursuant to the FDA Modernization Act of 1997 (FDAMA), Section 503A of the Food, Drug, and Cosmetic Act states that pharmacy compounding must comply with an applicable *USP* monograph, if one exists, and the *USP* chapter on pharmacy compounding[14] or be a component of an FDA-approved drug product; or, if neither of these apply to the ingredient being compounded, the substance must appear on a list of bulk drug substances developed by FDA and must be accompanied by a valid certificate of analysis and be manufactured in an FDA-registered establishment.[23] Inactive ingredients compounded by licensed pharmacies must comply with applicable *USP* monographs, if they exist, and the *USP* chapter on pharmacy compounding.[14] FDAMA prohibits pharmacists from compounding drug products that appear on a list of products that have been withdrawn or removed from the market because they have been found unsafe or ineffective. FDAMA also says that pharmacists may not compound, regularly or in inordinate amounts, drug products that are essentially copies of commercially available drug products; nor may they compound drug products identified by regulation as presenting demonstrable difficulties for compounding that reasonably demonstrate an adverse effect on safety or effectiveness.

The Centers for Disease Control and Prevention (CDC) has published guidelines for hand washing, prevention of intravascular infections, and hospital environmental control.[24,25]

The ASHP Guidelines on Quality Assurance for Pharmacy-Prepared Sterile Products are applicable to pharmaceutical services in various practice settings, including, but not limited to, hospitals, community pharmacies, nursing homes, ambulatory care infusion centers, and home care organizations. ASHP has also published practice standards on handling cytotoxic and hazardous drugs[26] and on pharmacy-prepared ophthalmic products.[27] These ASHP guidelines *do not* apply to the *manufacture* of sterile pharmaceuticals as defined in state and federal laws and regulations, *nor* do they apply to the preparation of medications by pharmacists, nurses, or physicians in emergency situations for *immediate* administration to patients (e.g., cardiopulmonary resuscitation). All guidelines may not be applicable to the preparation of radiopharmaceuticals.

These guidelines are referenced with supporting scientific data when such data exist. In the absence of published supporting data, guidelines are based on expert opinion or generally accepted pharmacy procedures. Pharmacists are urged to use professional judgment in interpreting these guidelines and applying them in practice. It is recognized that, in certain emergency situations, a pharmacist may be requested to compound products under conditions that do not meet these guidelines. In such situations, it is incumbent upon the pharmacist to employ professional judgment in weighing the potential patient risks and benefits associated with the compounding procedure in question.

Objectives. The objectives of these guidelines are to provide

1. Information on quality assurance and quality control activities that should be applied to the preparation of sterile products in pharmacies and
2. A method to match quality assurance and quality control activities with the potential risks to patients posed by various types of products.

Multidisciplinary Input. Pharmacists are urged to participate in the quality or performance improvement, risk management, and infection control programs of their health care organizations, including developing optimal sterile product procedures.

Definitions. Definitions of selected terms, as used in this document, are provided in Appendix A. For brevity in this document, the term *quality assurance* will be used to refer to both quality assurance and quality control (as defined in Appendix A), as befits the circumstances.

Risk-Level Classification

In this document, sterile products are grouped into three levels of risk to the patient, increasing from least (level 1) to greatest (level 3) potential risk based on the danger of exposing multiple patients to inaccurate ingredients or pathogens and based on microbial growth factors influenced by product storage time, temperature and product ability to support microbial growth, surface and time exposure of critical sites, and microbial bioload in the environment. When circumstances make risk-level assignment unclear, guidelines for the higher risk level should prevail. Consideration should be given to factors that increase potential risk to the patient such as high-risk administration sites and immunocompromised status of the patient. A comparison of risk-level attributes appears in Appendix B.

Risk Level 1. Risk level 1 applies to compounded sterile products that exhibit characteristics 1, 2, *and* 3, stated below. All risk level 1 products should be prepared with sterile equipment (e.g., syringes and vials), sterile ingredients and solutions, and sterile contact surfaces for the final product. Risk level 1 includes the following:

1. Products
   a. Stored at room temperature (see Appendix A for temperature definitions) and completely administered within 28 hours after preparation or
   b. Stored under refrigeration for 7 days or less before complete administration to a patient over a period not to exceed 24 hours (Table 1) or
   c. Frozen for 30 days or less before complete administration to a patient over a period not to exceed 24 hours.
2. Unpreserved sterile products prepared for administration to one patient or batch-prepared products containing suitable preservatives prepared for administration to more than one patient.
3. Products prepared by closed-system aseptic transfer of

sterile, nonpyrogenic, finished pharmaceuticals (e.g., from vials or ampuls)[b] obtained from licensed manufacturers into sterile final containers (e.g., syringes, minibags, elastomeric containers, portable infusion-device cassettes) obtained from licensed manufacturers.

Examples of risk level 1 processes include transferring a sterile drug product from a vial into a commercially produced i.v. bag; compounding total parenteral nutrient (TPN) solutions by combining dextrose injection and amino acids injection via gravity transfer into a sterile empty container, with or without the subsequent addition of sterile drug products to the final container with a sterile needle and syringe; and transferring a sterile, preserved drug product into sterile syringes with the aid of a mechanical pump and appropriate sterile transfer tubing device.

Risk Level 2. Risk level 2 sterile products exhibit characteristic 1, 2, *or* 3, stated below. All risk level 2 products should be prepared with sterile equipment, sterile ingredients and solutions, and sterile contact surfaces for the final product and with closed-system transfer methods. Risk level 2 includes the following:

1. Products stored beyond 7 days under refrigeration, stored beyond 30 days frozen, or administered beyond 28 hours after preparation and storage at room temperature (Table 1).
2. Batch-prepared products *without preservatives* (e.g., epidural products) that are intended for use by more than one patient. (Note: Batch-prepared products without preservatives that will be administered to multiple patients carry a greater risk to the patients than products prepared for a single patient because of the potential effect of inaccurate ingredients or product contamination on the health and well-being of a larger patient group.)
3. Products compounded by complex or numerous manipulations of sterile ingredients obtained from licensed manufacturers in a sterile container or reservoir obtained from a licensed manufacturer by using closed-system aseptic transfer; for example, TPN solutions prepared with an automated compounder. (Note: So many risks have been associated with automated compounding of TPN solutions that its complexity requires risk level 2 procedures.[18])

Examples of risk level 2 processes include preparing portable-pump reservoirs for multiday (i.e., ambient temperature) administration; subdividing the contents of a bulk, sterile injectable (without preservatives) into single-dose syringes; and compounding TPN solutions with an automated compounding device involving repeated attachment of fluid containers to proximal openings of the compounder tubing set and of empty final containers to the distal opening, the process concluding with the transfer of additives into the filled final container from individual drug product containers or from a pooled additive solution.

Risk Level 3. Risk level 3 products exhibit either characteristic 1 *or* 2:

1. Products compounded from nonsterile ingredients or compounded with nonsterile components, containers, or equipment before terminal sterilization.

Table 1.

Assignment of Products to Risk Level 1 or 2 according to Time and Temperature before Completion of Administration

Risk Level	Room Temperature (15–30 °C)	No. Days Storage	
		Refrigerator (2–8 °C)	Freezer (−20 to −10 °C)
1	Completely administered within 28 hr	≤7	≤30
2	Storage and administration exceed 28 hr	>7	>30

2. Products prepared by combining multiple ingredients—sterile or nonsterile—by using an open-system transfer or open reservoir before terminal sterilization.

Examples of risk level 3 products are calcium levulinate injection, estradiol in oil injection, and morphine sulfate 50-mg/mL injection.[32]

Quality Assurance for Risk Level 1

RL 1.1: Policies and Procedures.[33] Up-to-date policies and procedures for compounding sterile products should be written and available to all personnel involved in these activities. When policies and procedures are changed they should be updated, as necessary, to reflect current standards of practice and quality. Additions, revisions, and deletions should be communicated to all personnel involved in sterile compounding and related activities. These policies and procedures should address personnel education and training requirements, competency evaluation, product acquisition, storage and handling of products and supplies, storage and delivery of final products, use and maintenance of facilities and equipment,[34] appropriate garb and conduct for personnel working in the controlled area, process validation, preparation technique,[35] labeling, documentation, and quality control.[36] Further, written policies and procedures should address personnel access and movement of materials into and near the controlled area. Policies and procedures for monitoring environmental conditions in the controlled area should take into consideration the amount of exposure of the product to the environment during compounding and the environmental control devices used to create the critical area. Sources of information include vendor-supplied inservice programs and multimedia training programs, such as videotapes and Internet-site information. Before compounding sterile products, all personnel involved should read the policies and procedures. Written policies and procedures are required for all environmental control devices used to create the critical area for manipulation of sterile products. Examples of such devices are laminar-airflow workstations, biological safety cabinets, class 100 cleanrooms, and barrier isolator workstations (see Appendix A).[c]

RL 1.2: Personnel Education, Training, and Evaluation.
Training is the most important factor in ensuring the quality of sterile products. Pharmacy personnel preparing or dispensing sterile products must receive suitable didactic and experiential training and competency evaluation through demonstration, testing (written or practical), or both. Some aspects that should be included in training programs include aseptic technique; critical-area contamination factors; environmental monitoring; facilities, equipment, and supplies; sterile product calculations and terminology; sterile product compounding documentation; quality assurance procedures; aseptic preparation procedures; proper gowning and gloving

technique; and general conduct in the controlled area. In addition to knowledge of chemical, pharmaceutical, and clinical properties of drugs, pharmacists should be knowledgeable about the principles of pharmacy compounding.[14] Videotapes[37,38] and additional information on the essential components of a training, orientation, and evaluation program are described elsewhere.[39,40] All pharmacy and nonpharmacy personnel (e.g., environmental services staff) who work in the controlled area should receive documented training on cleaning, sanitizing, and maintaining equipment used in the controlled area. Training should be specific to the environmental control device and equipment present in the controlled area and should be based on current procedures.

The aseptic technique of each person preparing sterile products should be observed and evaluated as satisfactory during orientation and training and at least annually thereafter.[41] In addition to observation, methods of evaluating the knowledge of personnel include written or practical tests and process validation.[42,43]

RL 1.3: Storage and Handling within the Pharmacy.[44]
Solutions, drugs, supplies, and equipment used to prepare or administer sterile products should be stored in accordance with manufacturer or *USP* requirements. Temperatures in refrigerators and freezers used to store ingredients and finished sterile preparations should be monitored and documented daily to ensure that compendial storage requirements are met. Warehouse and other pharmacy storage areas where ingredients are stored should be monitored to ensure that temperature, light, moisture, and ventilation remain within manufacturer and compendial requirements. To permit adequate floor cleaning, drugs, supplies, and compounding equipment should be stored on shelving, cabinets, and carts above the floor. Products that have exceeded their expiration dates should be removed from active storage areas. Before use, each drug, ingredient, and container should be visually inspected for damage, defects, and expiration date.[45]

Unnecessary personnel traffic in the controlled area should be minimized. Particle-generating activities, such as removal of intravenous solutions, drugs, and supplies from cardboard boxes, should not be performed in the controlled area. Products and supplies used in preparing sterile products should be removed from shipping containers outside the controlled area before aseptic processing is begun. Packaging materials and items generating unacceptable amounts of particles (e.g., cardboard boxes, paper towels [unless lint-free], reference books) should not be permitted in the controlled area or critical area. The removal of immediate packaging designed to retain the sterility or stability of a product (e.g., syringe packaging, light-resistant pouches) is an exception; obviously, this type of packaging should not be removed outside the controlled area. Disposal of packaging materials, used syringes, containers, and needles should be performed at least daily, and more often if needed, to enhance sanitation and avoid accumulation in the controlled area. Trash cans should be below the level of the laminar-airflow workbench and should be removed from the controlled area before being emptied. Sharps containers should be safely placed into the waste stream, according to policies developed by the institution to comply with regulations of the Occupational Safety and Health Administration (OSHA).

In the event of a product recall, there should be a mechanism for tracking and retrieving affected products from specific patients to whom the products were dispensed.

RL 1.4: Facilities[46] and Equipment.[47] The controlled area should be a limited-access area sufficiently separated from other pharmacy operations to minimize the potential for contamination that could result from the unnecessary flow of materials and personnel into and out of the area. The controlled area is a buffer from outside air that is needed because strong air currents from briefly opened doors, personnel walking past the laminar-airflow workbench, or the air stream from the heating, ventilating, and air conditioning system can easily exceed the velocity of air from the laminar-airflow workbench. Also, operators introducing supplies into the laminar-airflow workbench or reaching in with their arms can drag contaminants from the environment surrounding the workbench.[15] Cleanliness of the controlled area can be enhanced by (1) limiting access to those personnel assigned to work in the controlled area, (2) having those personnel wear the appropriate garb, (3) donning and removing garb outside the controlled area, (4) keeping doors to the controlled area closed, (5) limiting storage in the controlled area to items in constant use, (6) using low-particulate shelving, counters, and carts (e.g., stainless steel) in the controlled area, (7) not allowing cardboard and other particle-generating materials in the controlled area, (8) controlling the temperature and humidity inside the room, and (9) implementing a regular cleaning (e.g., nightly floor disinfection) and maintenance schedule.[48]

Barrier isolator workstations are closed systems and are not as sensitive to their external environment as laminar-airflow equipment. It is good practice to (1) place barrier isolator workstations in limited-access areas, (2) control the temperature and humidity of the surrounding area, and (3) clean and sanitize the surrounding area on a routine basis.[49]

Special precautions should be taken to clean equipment and compounding areas meticulously after preparing products that contain allergenic ingredients (e.g., sulfonamides and penicillins). Equipment should be of appropriate design and size for compounding and suitable for the intended uses. Equipment and accessories used in compounding should be inspected, maintained, and cleaned at appropriate intervals to ensure the accuracy and reliability of their performance.[14]

Computer entry, order processing, label generation, and record keeping should be performed outside the critical area. The controlled area should be well organized[50] and lighted[51] and of sufficient size to support sterile compounding activities. For hand washing, a sink with hot and cold running water should be in close proximity to but outside the controlled area. Refrigeration, freezing, ventilation, and room temperature control capabilities appropriate for storage of ingredients, supplies, and pharmacy-prepared sterile products in accordance with manufacturer, USP, and state or federal requirements should exist. The controlled area should be cleaned and disinfected at regular intervals with appropriate agents, according to written policies and procedures.[52]

Disinfectants should be alternated periodically to prevent development of resistant microorganisms.[d] The floors of the controlled area should be nonporous and washable to enable regular disinfection. Active work surfaces in the controlled area (e.g., carts, compounding devices, counter surfaces) should be disinfected, in accordance with written procedures. Refrigerators, freezers, shelves, and other areas where pharmacy-prepared sterile products are stored should be kept clean.

Sterile products must be prepared in a class 100 environment (i.e., the critical area).[29] Such an environment exists inside a certified horizontal- or vertical-laminar-airflow workbench, a class 100 cleanroom, or a barrier isolator.[53] Cytotoxic and other hazardous products should be prepared in a vented class II biological safety cabinet or a barrier isolator of appropriate design to meet the personnel exposure limits described in product material safety data sheets (MSDS).[54] Barrier isolators are gaining favor as clean environments, especially for cytotoxic drug compounding.[55–57] Properly maintained barrier isolators provide suitable environments for the preparation of risk level 1, 2, and 3 sterile products.[58]

Laminar-airflow workbenches are designed to be operated continuously. If a laminar-airflow workbench is turned off between aseptic processes, it should be operated long enough to allow complete purging of room air from the critical area (e.g., at least 30 minutes), then disinfected before use. Barrier isolators, because of their closed nature, require less start-up time. If the barrier isolator has been turned off for less than 24 hours, a two-minute start-up time is sufficient. For periods greater than 24 hours, the chamber should be sanitized and the isolator should not be used for a minimum of 10 minutes after application of the sanitizing agent. The critical-area work surface and all accessible interior surfaces of the workbench should be disinfected with an appropriate agent before work begins and periodically thereafter, in accordance with written policies and procedures.[52] The exterior surfaces of the laminar-airflow workbench should be cleaned periodically with a mild detergent or suitable disinfectant; 70% isopropyl alcohol may damage the workbench's clear plastic surfaces. The laminar-airflow workbench should be certified by a qualified contractor[59] every six months[53] or when it is relocated to ensure operational efficiency and integrity. Prefilters in the laminar-airflow workbench should be changed (or cleaned, if they are washable) periodically (e.g., monthly), in accordance with written policies and procedures.

A method should be established for calibrating and verifying the accuracy of automated compounding devices used in aseptic processing (e.g., routine reconstitution of bulk or individual vials, transferring of doses from a bulk container to a minibag, syringe, or other single-dose container).

RL 1.5: Garb.[60] Procedures should require that personnel wear clean gowns or coveralls that generate few particles in the controlled area.[53] Scrub attire by itself is not acceptable (but can, like street clothes, be covered by a gown or coverall). Hand, finger, and wrist jewelry should be minimized or eliminated. Fingernails should be kept clean and trimmed. Head and facial hair should be covered. Masks are recommended because most personnel talk[61] or may cough or sneeze. Gloves are recommended. Personnel who have demonstrated sensitivity to latex should use either powder-free, low-latex protein gloves or, in the case of severe allergy, latex-free (synthetic) gloves.[62,63]

RL 1.6: Aseptic Technique[64,65] and Product Preparation.[66] Sterile products must be prepared with aseptic technique in a class 100 environment. Personnel should scrub their hands and forearms for an appropriate length of time with a suitable antimicrobial skin cleanser at the beginning of each aseptic compounding process and when reentering the controlled area, in accordance with written procedures. Personnel should wear appropriate attire (see RL 1.5: Garb). Eating, drinking, and smoking are prohibited in the controlled area. Talking should be minimized in the critical area during aseptic preparation (even when masks are worn).

Ingredients used to compound sterile products should be determined to be stable, compatible, and appropriate for the product to be prepared, according to manufacturer or USP guidelines or appropriate scientific references. The ingredients of the preparation should be predetermined to result in a final product that meets physiological norms for solution osmolality and pH, as appropriate for the intended route of administration. Each ingredient and container should be inspected for defects, expiration date, and product integrity before use. Expired, inappropriately stored, or defective products must not be used in preparing sterile products. Defective products should be promptly reported to the FDA MedWatch Program.[67]

Only materials essential for preparing the sterile product should be placed in the laminar-airflow workbench or barrier isolator. The surfaces of ampuls, vials, and container closures (e.g., vial stoppers) should be disinfected by swabbing or spraying with an appropriate disinfectant solution (e.g., 70% isopropyl alcohol or 70% ethanol) before placement in the workbench. Materials used in aseptic preparation should be arranged in the critical area (within the laminar-airflow workbench or barrier isolator) in a manner that prevents interruption of the unidirectional airflow between the high-efficiency particulate air (HEPA) filter and critical sites of needles, vials, ampuls, containers, and transfer sets. All aseptic procedures should be performed at least 6 inches inside the front edge of the laminar-airflow workbench, in a clear path of unidirectional airflow between the HEPA filter and work materials (e.g., needles, closures). The number of personnel preparing sterile products in the workbench at one time should be minimized. Overcrowding of the critical work area may interfere with unidirectional airflow and increase the potential for compounding errors. Likewise, the number of units being prepared in the workbench at one time should allow unobstructed airflow over critical areas. Automated compounding devices and other equipment placed in or adjacent to the critical area should be cleaned, disinfected, and placed to avoid contamination or disruption of the unidirectional airflow between the HEPA filter and sterile surfaces. Closed systems like barrier isolators require less stringent placement of sterile units and equipment because the critical area encompasses the entire work surface. Hand and arm movements are not critical because the walls of the barrier isolator provide protection from the outside environment.[50]

Aseptic technique should be used to avoid touch contamination of sterile needles, syringe parts (e.g., plunger, syringe tip), and other critical sites. Solutions from ampuls should be properly filtered to remove particles. Solutions of reconstituted powders should be mixed carefully, ensuring complete dissolution of the drug with the appropriate diluent. Needle entry into vials should be performed in such a manner as to avoid coring of the vial closure. Some patients may require a latex-free admixture to avoid severe allergic reac-

tions.[68] Latex-related policies and procedures should be developed by each institution, given the paucity of evidence that latex closures and syringe plungers are implicated in patient reactions to latex.[69,70] Before, during, and after the preparation of sterile products, the pharmacist should carefully check the identity and verify the amounts and sequence of the additives in sterile preparations against the original prescription, medication order, or other appropriate documentation (e.g., computerized patient profile, label generated from a pharmacist-verified order) before the product is released or dispensed.

RL 1.7: Process Validation.[71] Validation of aseptic processing procedures provides a mechanism for ensuring that processes consistently result in sterile products of acceptable quality.[10] In risk level 1, process validation (or process simulation) of compounding procedures is actually a method of assessing the adequacy of an operator's aseptic technique. Each individual involved in the preparation of sterile products should successfully complete a validation process on technique before being allowed to prepare sterile products. The validation process should follow written procedures.[42,43,45] Commercial kits are available for process validation; however, their ability to support microbial growth should be tested by challenging the intended kit with an indicator organism (e.g., *Bacillus stearothermophilus*) that can be purchased in known concentrations, is known not to be pathogenic, and grows only at relatively high temperatures.

Process simulation allows for the evaluation of opportunities for microbial contamination during all steps of sterile product preparation. The sterility of the final product is a cumulative function of all processes involved in its preparation and is ultimately determined by the processing step providing the lowest probability of sterility.[31] Process simulation testing is carried out in the same manner as normal production, except that an appropriate microbiological growth medium is used in place of the actual product used during sterile preparation. The same personnel, procedures, equipment, and materials are involved. Completed medium samples are incubated. If no microbial growth is detected, this provides evidence that adequate aseptic technique was used. If growth is detected, the entire sterile preparation process must be evaluated, corrective action taken, and the process simulation test performed again. No products intended for patient use should be prepared by an individual until the process simulation test indicates that the individual can competently perform aseptic procedures. It is recommended that personnel competency be revalidated at least annually, whenever the quality assurance program yields an unacceptable result, and whenever unacceptable techniques are observed; this revalidation should be documented.

RL 1.8: Expiration Dating.[72] All pharmacy-prepared sterile products should bear an appropriate expiration date. The expiration date assigned should be based on currently available drug stability information and sterility considerations. Sources of drug stability information include references (e.g., *AHFS Drug Information,[73] Extended Stability for Parenteral Drugs,[74] Handbook on Injectable Drugs,[75] King Guide to Parenteral Admixtures[76]*), manufacturer recommendations, and reliable, published research. When interpreting published drug stability information, the pharmacist should consider all aspects of the final sterile product being prepared (e.g., drug reservoir, drug concentration, storage conditions). Methods used for establishing expiration dates should be documented.

Appropriate inhouse (or contract service) stability testing may be used to determine expiration dates when drug stability data are not readily available. Home care pharmacies are often required to assign extended beyond-use dates to sterile products, so ASHP has published guidelines for home care pharmacies that address beyond-use dating.[74,77]

RL 1.9: Labeling.[78] Sterile products should be labeled with at least the following information:

1. For patient-specific products: the patient's name and any other appropriate patient identification (e.g., location, identification number); for batch-prepared products: control or lot number,
2. All solution and ingredient names, amounts, strengths, and concentrations (when applicable),
3. Expiration date and time, when applicable,
4. Prescribed administration regimen, when appropriate (including rate and route of administration),
5. Appropriate auxiliary labeling (including precautions),
6. Storage requirements,
7. Identification (e.g., initials) of the responsible pharmacist (and technician),
8. Device-specific instructions (when appropriate), and
9. Any additional information, in accordance with state or federal requirements; for example, a prescription number for products dispensed to ambulatory care, long-term-care, and home care patients.

The label should be legible and affixed to the final container in a manner enabling it to be read while the sterile product is being administered (when possible). Written policies and procedures should address proper placement of labels on containers.[79]

RL 1.10: End-Product Evaluation.[80] The final product should be inspected when preparation is completed and again when the product is dispensed. This inspection includes an evaluation for container leaks, container integrity, solution cloudiness or phase separation, particulates in the solution, appropriate solution color, and solution volume. The responsible pharmacist should verify that the product was compounded accurately with the correct ingredients, quantities of each ingredient, containers, and reservoirs; different methods may be used for end-product verification (e.g., observation, calculation checks, documented records). Refractive index measurement may also be used to verify the addition of dextrose, for example in parenteral nutrient solutions.[81]

RL 1.11: Handling of Sterile Products Outside the Pharmacy.[82] Pharmacists should participate in developing procedures for the safe use (e.g., stability, sterility) of sterile products once they are distributed outside the pharmacy. How the product is transported from the pharmacy, how it is stored outside the pharmacy, and methods for return, recycling, and disposal should be addressed in written policies and procedures.[15,83] Sterile products should be transported so as to be protected from extremes of temperature outside their range of stability and from light if they are photosensitive. Storage containers and packaging verified as suitable for protection during transport should be specified. Transit time and conditions should also be specified and controlled. Delivery personnel should be instructed on special handling procedures. Once delivered to the end user, sterile products should be appropriately stored before use. Pharmacists should

ascertain that the user has appropriate locations and equipment for storage (e.g., a refrigerator with a suitable thermometer). Special instructions for storage should be a part of the label or a separate information sheet (e.g., instructions for cleanliness, proper storage, interpretation of the expiration date and how to look for signs of product deterioration). The pharmacist should be notified if storage conditions do not remain suitable so that the pharmacist can give advice as to the disposition of the sterile products and remedies for storage problems. Pharmacists should participate in training end users on the proper care and storage of sterile products, either directly or through written instructional materials.

RL 1.12: Documentation.[84] The following should be documented and maintained on file for an adequate period of time, according to organizational policies and state regulatory requirements: (1) the training and competency evaluation of employees in sterile product procedures, (2) refrigerator and freezer temperatures, (3) certification of laminar-airflow workbenches, and (4) other facility quality control logs specific to the pharmacy's policies and procedures (e.g., cleaning logs for facilities and equipment). Pharmacists should also maintain appropriate dispensing records for sterile products, in accordance with state regulatory requirements.

Quality Assurance for Risk Level 2

Because the risks of inaccurate products are associated with more complex procedures and because instability and contamination are more likely with long-term storage and administration, more stringent requirements are appropriate for risk level 2 preparations. These requirements may be viewed as more important in circumstances where the medical need is *routine*. In circumstances where the medical need for a product is immediate (and there is not a suitable alternative) or when the preparation of such a product is rare, professional judgment should be applied to the extent to which some guidelines (e.g., cleanroom design and final product testing before product dispensing) must be applied.

RL 2.1: Policies and Procedures. In addition to all guidelines for risk level 1, a written quality assurance program should define and identify necessary environmental monitoring devices and techniques to be used to ensure an adequate environment for risk level 2 sterile product preparation. Examples include the use of airborne particle counters, air velocity and temperature meters, viable particle samplers (e.g., slit samplers), agar plates, and swab sampling of surfaces and potential contamination sites. All aspects of risk level 2 sterile product preparation, storage, and distribution, including such details as the choice of cleaning materials and disinfectants and the monitoring of equipment accuracy, should be addressed in written policies and procedures. Limits of acceptability (threshold or action levels) for environmental monitoring and process validation and actions to be implemented when thresholds are exceeded should be defined in written policies. For sterile batch compounding, written policies and procedures should be established for the use of master formulas and work sheets and for appropriate documentation. Policies and procedures should also address personnel attire in the controlled area, lot number determination and documentation, and any other quality assurance procedures unique to compounding risk level 2 sterile products.

RL 2.2: Personnel Education, Training, and Evaluation.
All guidelines for risk level 1 should be met. In addition to guidelines for risk level 1, assessment of the competency of personnel preparing risk level 2 sterile products should include appropriate process validation (as described in RL 1.7: Process validation). However, process simulation procedures for assessing the preparation of risk level 2 sterile products should be representative of all types of manipulations, products, and batch sizes personnel preparing risk level 2 products are likely to encounter.[15] Personnel should also be taught which products are to undergo end-product quantitative analysis (see RL 2.10).

RL 2.3: Storage and Handling. All storage and handling guidelines for risk level 1 should be met.

RL 2.4: Facilities and Equipment. In addition to all guidelines for risk level 1, the following guidelines should be followed for risk level 2 sterile product preparation:

1. The controlled area should meet the standards of a class 10,000 cleanroom,[e] as defined by Federal Standard 209E.[85,f] A positive air pressure relative to adjacent pharmacy areas is required, as are an appropriate number of air exchanges per hour and appropriate humidity and temperature levels.[86] For open-architecture cleanrooms, it is appropriate to measure the volume of air entering the cleanroom versus the volume of air entering adjacent rooms, so as to ensure a positive pressure gradient for the cleanroom. To allow proper cleaning and disinfection, walls, floors, and ceilings in the controlled area should be nonporous. To help reduce the number of particles in the controlled area, an adjacent support area (e.g., anteroom) should be provided. A properly maintained barrier isolator also provides an acceptable environment.[57] A barrier isolator provides a class 100 environment for product preparation; therefore, the isolator itself can be in a separate area of the pharmacy but need not actually be in a cleanroom.

2. Cleaning materials (e.g., mops, sponges, and germicidal disinfectants) for use in the cleanroom should be carefully selected. They should be made of materials that generate a low amount of particles. If reused, cleaning materials should be cleaned and disinfected between uses.

3. The critical-area work surfaces (e.g., interior of the laminar-airflow workbench) should be disinfected frequently and before and after each batch-preparation process with an appropriate agent, according to written policies and procedures. Floors should be disinfected at least daily. Carpet or porous floors, porous walls, and porous ceiling tiles are not suitable in the controlled area because these surfaces cannot be properly cleaned and disinfected. Exterior workbench surfaces and other hard surfaces in the controlled area, such as shelves, carts, tables, and stools, should be disinfected weekly and after any unanticipated event that could increase the risk of contamination. Walls should be cleaned at least monthly.

4. To ensure that an appropriate environment is maintained for risk level 2 sterile product preparation, an effective written environmental monitoring program is recommended.[87] Sampling of air and surfaces according to a written plan and schedule is recommended.[31] The plan and frequency should be adequate to document that the controlled area is suitable and that the laminar-airflow workbench or biological safety cabinet meets class 100 requirements. Limits of acceptability (thresholds or action levels) and appropriate actions to be taken in the event thresholds are exceeded should be specified. *USP* presents examples of environmental monitoring.[15] Settle plates or wipe samples can provide a simple but effective means of routinely monitoring airborne microbial contamination in controlled and critical areas.[45,88,89]

5. To help reduce the number of particles in the controlled area, an adjacent support area (e.g., anteroom) of high cleanliness, separated from the controlled area by a barrier (e.g., plastic curtain, partition, wall), is recommended. Appropriate activities for the support area include, but are not limited to, hand washing, gowning and gloving, removal of packaging and cardboard items, and cleaning and disinfecting hard-surface containers and supplies before placing these items into the controlled area.

6. Methods should be established for calibrating and verifying the accuracy and sterility of automated compounding methods used in aseptic processing.[90–96]

RL 2.5: Garb. All guidelines for risk level 1 should be met. Gloves, gowns, and masks are required for the preparation of all risk level 2 sterile products. Even when sterile gloves are used, they do not remain sterile during aseptic compounding; however, they do assist in containing bacteria, skin, and other particles that may be shed even from scrubbed hands. Clean gowns, coveralls, or closed jackets with sleeves having elastic binding at the cuff are recommended; these garments should be made of low-shedding materials. Shoe covers may be helpful in maintaining the cleanliness of the controlled area. Barrier isolators do not require the same level of gowning as laminar-airflow workstations as long as they operate as closed systems with HEPA filtration of air entering and leaving the barrier isolator and a separate area for entrance, such as an air lock for product transfers.

During sterile product preparation, gloves should be rinsed frequently with a suitable agent (e.g., 70% isopropyl alcohol) and changed when their integrity is compromised (i.e., when they are punctured or torn). Personnel should discard gloves upon leaving the cleanroom and don new gloves upon reentering the cleanroom.

RL 2.6: Aseptic Technique and Product Preparation.[97–99]
All guidelines for risk level 1 sterile product preparation should be met. Relative to batch-prepared products, a master work sheet should be developed for a batch of each discrete identity and concentration of sterile product to be prepared. The master work sheet should consist of the formula, components, compounding directions or procedures, a sample label, and evaluation and testing requirements. Once the original master work sheet is approved by the designated pharmacist, a verified duplicate (e.g., a photocopy) of the master work sheet should be used as the preparation work sheet from which each batch is prepared and on which all documentation for each batch occurs. (For small-formula, frequently prepared batches, it may be more efficient to have multiple lines on the preparation work sheet for documenting more than one batch.) The preparation work sheet should be used to document the following:

1. Identity of all solutions and ingredients and their corresponding amounts, concentrations, or volumes,

2. Manufacturer lot number and expiration date for each component,
3. Component manufacturer or suitable manufacturer identification number,
4. Container specifications (e.g., syringe, pump cassette),
5. Lot or control number assigned to batch,
6. Expiration date of batch-prepared products,
7. Date of preparation,
8. Identity (e.g., initials, codes, signatures) of personnel involved in preparation,
9. End-product evaluation and testing specifications and results,
10. Storage requirements,
11. Specific equipment used during aseptic preparation (e.g., a specific automated compounding device), and
12. Comparison of actual yield with anticipated yield, when appropriate.

However documentation is done, a procedure should exist for easy retrieval of all records pertaining to a particular batch. Each batch of sterile products should bear a unique lot number. Identical lot numbers must never be assigned to different products or different batches of the same product. Lot numbers may be alphabetic, numeric, or alphanumeric.

The process of combining multiple sterile ingredients into a single sterile reservoir for subdivision into multiple units for dispensing may necessitate additional quality control procedures. A second pharmacist should verify calculations associated with this process, when possible; this verification should be documented. Because this process often involves making multiple entries into the intermediate sterile reservoir, the likelihood of contamination may be greater than that associated with the preparation of other risk level 2 sterile products.

For preparation involving automated compounding devices, a pharmacist should verify data entered into the compounding device before compounding begins. End-product checks should be performed to verify accuracy of ingredient delivery. These checks may include weighing and visually verifying the final product. For example, the expected weight (in grams) of the final product, based on the specific gravities of the ingredients and their respective volumes, can be documented on the compounding formula sheet, dated, and initialed by the responsible pharmacist. Once compounding is completed, each final product can be weighed and its weight compared with the expected weight. The product's actual weight should fall within a preestablished threshold for variance. Visual verification may be aided by marking the beginning level of each bulk container before starting the automated mixing process and checking each container after completing the mixing process to determine whether the final levels appear reasonable in comparison with expected volumes. The operator should also periodically observe the device during the mixing process to ensure that the device is operating properly (e.g., check to see that all stations are operating). If there are doubts whether a product or component has been properly prepared or stored, the product should not be used.

RL 2.7: Process Validation. Each individual involved in the preparation of risk level 2 sterile products should successfully complete a validation process, as recommended for risk level 1. Process simulation for compounding risk level 2 sterile products should be representative of all types of manipulations, products, and batch sizes that personnel preparing risk level 2 sterile products are likely to encounter.

RL 2.8: Expiration Dating. All guidelines for risk level 1 should be met.

RL 2.9: Labeling. All guidelines for risk level 1 should be met.

RL 2.10: End-Product Evaluation. All guidelines for risk level 1 should be met. For complex or toxic products, it is appropriate, when possible, to obtain quantitative testing of the accuracy of sterile additives, for example, the dextrose concentration in pediatric parenteral nutrient solutions or the potassium concentration in cardioplegia solutions.[g]

RL 2.11: Handling of Sterile Products Outside the Pharmacy. All guidelines for risk level 1 should be met.

RL 2.12: Documentation. All guidelines for risk level 1 should be met. Additionally, documentation of end-product sampling and batch-preparation records should be maintained for an adequate period, in accordance with organizational policies and procedures and state regulatory requirements.[100] Documentation for sterile batch-prepared products should include the

1. Master work sheet,
2. Preparation work sheet, and
3. End-product evaluation and testing results.

Quality Assurance for Risk Level 3

Risk level 3 addresses the preparation of products that pose the greatest potential risk to patients. The quality assurance activities described in this section are clearly more demanding—in terms of processes, facilities, and final product assessment—than for risk levels 1 and 2. Ideally, the activities described for risk level 3 would be used for all high-risk products. However, the activities may be viewed as most important in circumstances where the medical need for such high-risk products is *routine*. In circumstances where the medical need for such a product is immediate (and there is not a suitable alternative) or when the preparation of such a product is rare, professional judgment must be applied as to the extent to which some activities (e.g., strict facility design, quarantine, and final product testing before product dispensing) should be applied.

RL 3.1: Policies and Procedures. There should be written policies and procedures related to every aspect of preparation of risk level 3 sterile products. These policies and procedures should be detailed enough to ensure that all products have the identity, strength, quality, and purity purported for the product.[14,101] All policies and procedures should be reviewed and approved by the designated pharmacist. There should be a mechanism designed to ensure that policies and procedures are communicated, understood, and adhered to by personnel cleaning or working in the controlled area or support area. Written policies and procedures should define and identify the environmental monitoring activities necessary to ensure an adequate environment for risk level 3 sterile product preparation.

In addition to the policies and procedures required for risk levels 1 and 2, there should be written policies and procedures for the following:

1. Component selection, handling, and storage,
2. Any additional personnel qualifications commensurate with the preparation of risk level 3 sterile products,
3. Personnel responsibilities in the controlled area (e.g., sterilization, cleaning, maintenance, access to controlled area),
4. Equipment use, maintenance, calibration, and testing,
5. Sterilization and expiration dating,
6. Master formula and master work sheet development and use,
7. End-product evaluation and testing,
8. Appropriate documentation for preparation of risk level 3 sterile products,
9. Use, control, and monitoring of environmentally controlled areas and calibration of monitoring equipment,
10. Process simulation for each risk level 3 sterile product,
11. Quarantine of products and release from quarantine, if applicable,
12. A mechanism for recalling products from patients in the event that end-product testing procedures yield unacceptable results, and
13. Any other quality control procedures unique to the preparation of risk level 3 sterile products.

RL 3.2: Personnel Education, Training, and Evaluation.

Persons preparing sterile products at risk level 3 must have specific education, training, and experience to perform all functions required for the preparation of risk level 3 sterile products. However, final responsibility should lie with the pharmacist, who should be knowledgeable in pharmacy compounding practice[14] and proficient in quality assurance requirements, equipment used in the preparation of risk level 3 sterile products, and other aspects of sterile product preparation. The pharmacist should have sufficient education, training, experience, and demonstrated competency to ensure that all sterile products prepared from sterile or nonsterile components have the identity, strength, quality, and purity purported for the products.[101] In addition to the body of knowledge required for risk levels 1 and 2, the pharmacist should possess sufficient knowledge in the following areas:

1. Aseptic processing,
2. Quality control and quality assurance as related to environmental, component, and end-product testing,
3. Sterilization techniques,[98] and
4. Container, equipment, and closure system selection.

All pharmacy personnel involved in the cleaning and maintenance of the controlled area should be specially trained and thoroughly knowledgeable in the special requirements of class 100 critical-area technology and design. There should be documented, ongoing training for all employees to enable retention of expertise.

RL 3.3: Storage and Handling.

In addition to guidelines for risk levels 1 and 2, risk level 3 policies and procedures for storage and handling should include procurement, identification, storage, handling, testing, and recall of nonsterile components.[14,101]

Components and finished products ready to undergo end-product testing should be stored in a manner that prevents their use before release by a pharmacist, minimizes the risk of contamination, and enables identification. There should be identified storage areas that can be used to quarantine products, if necessary, before they are released.[15]

RL 3.4: Facilities and Equipment.

Preparation of risk level 3 sterile products should occur in a class 100 horizontal- or vertical-laminar-airflow workbench that is properly situated in a class 10,000 cleanroom *or* in a properly maintained and monitored class 100 cleanroom (without the workbench).[102] The cleanroom area should have a positive pressure differential relative to adjacent, less clean areas of at least 0.05 inch of water. A properly designed and maintained barrier isolator provides an aseptic environment for risk level 3 products.

To allow proper cleaning and disinfection, walls, floors, and ceilings in the controlled area should be nonporous. To help reduce the number of particles in the controlled area, an adjacent support area (e.g., anteroom) should be provided.

During the preparation of risk level 3 sterile products, access to the controlled area or cleanroom should be limited to those individuals who are required to be in the area and are properly attired. The environment of the main access areas directly adjacent to the controlled area (e.g., anteroom) should meet at least Federal Standard 209E class 100,000 requirements. To help maintain a class 100 critical-area environment during compounding, the adjacent support area (e.g., anteroom) should be separated from the controlled area by a barrier (e.g., plastic curtain, partition, wall). Written policies and procedures for monitoring the environment of the controlled area and adjacent areas should be developed.

No sterile products should be prepared in the controlled area if it fails to meet established criteria specified in the policies and procedures. A calibrated particle counter capable of measuring air particles 0.5 mm and larger should be used to monitor airborne particulate matter.[103] Before product preparation begins, the positive-pressure air status should meet or exceed the requirements. Air samples should be taken at several places in the controlled area with the appropriate environmental monitoring devices (e.g., nutrient agar plates). Surfaces on which work actually occurs, including laminar-airflow workbench surfaces and tabletops, should be monitored by using surface contact plates, the swab-rinse technique, or other appropriate methods.[104]

Test results should be reviewed and criteria should be preestablished to determine the point at which the preparation of risk level 3 sterile products will be disallowed until corrective measures are taken. When the environment does not meet the criteria specified in the policies and procedures, sterile product processing should immediately cease and corrective action should be taken. In the event that this occurs, written policies and procedures should delineate alternative methods of sterile product preparation to enable timely fulfillment of prescription orders.

Equipment should be adequate to prevent microbiological contamination. Methods should be established for the cleaning, preparation, sterilization, calibration, and documented use of all equipment.

Critical-area work surfaces should be disinfected with an appropriate agent before the preparation of each product. Floors in the controlled area should be disinfected at least daily. Exterior workbench surfaces and other hard surfaces in the controlled area, such as shelves, tables, and stools, should be disinfected weekly and after any unanticipated event that could increase the risk of contamination. Walls and ceilings in the controlled area or cleanroom should be disinfected at least weekly.

Large pieces of equipment, such as tanks, carts, and tables, used in the controlled area or cleanroom should be made of a material that can be easily cleaned and disinfected; stainless steel is recommended. Stools and chairs should be cleanroom quality. Equipment that does not come in direct contact with the finished product should be properly cleaned, rinsed, and disinfected before being placed in the controlled area. All nonsterile equipment that will come in contact with the sterilized final product should be properly sterilized before introduction into the controlled area; this precaution includes such items as tubing, filters, containers, and other processing equipment. The sterilization process should be monitored and documented.[101]

RL 3.5: Garb. All guidelines for risk levels 1 and 2 should be met. Additionally, cleanroom garb should be worn inside the controlled area at all times during the preparation of risk level 3 sterile products. Attire should consist of a low-shedding coverall, head cover, face mask, and shoe covers. These garments may be either disposable or reusable. Head and facial hair should be covered. Before donning these garments over street clothes, personnel should thoroughly wash their hands and forearms with a suitable antimicrobial skin cleanser.[25] Sterile disposable gloves should be worn and rinsed frequently with an appropriate agent (e.g., 70% isopropyl alcohol) during processing. The gloves should be changed if their integrity is compromised. If persons leave the controlled area *or* support area during processing, they should regown with clean garments before reentering.

RL 3.6: Aseptic Technique and Product Preparation. All guidelines for risk levels 1 and 2 should be met. Methods should ensure that components and containers remain free from contamination and are easily identified as to the product, lot number, and expiration date. If components are not finished sterile pharmaceuticals obtained from licensed manufacturers, pharmacists should ensure that these components meet USP and FDA standards. Products prepared from nonsterile ingredients should be tested to ensure that they do not exceed specified endotoxin limits, unless the ingredient will denature all proteins (e.g., concentrated hydrochloric acid).[105] As each new lot of components and containers is received, the components should be quarantined until properly identified, tested, or verified by a pharmacist.[101]

The methods for preparing sterile products and using process controls should be designed to ensure that finished products have the identity, strength, quality, and purity they are intended to have. Any deviations from established methods should be documented and appropriately justified.

A master work sheet should be developed for the preparation of each risk level 3 sterile product. Once the pharmacist approves the master work sheet, a verified duplicate of the master work sheet should be used as the controlling document from which each sterile end product or batch of prepared products is compounded and on which all documentation for that product or batch occurs. The preparation work sheet should document all the requirements for risk level 2 plus the following:

1. Comparison of actual with anticipated yield,
2. Sterilization methods,[106,107]
3. Pyrogen testing,[108] and
4. Quarantine specifications.

The preparation work sheet should serve as the batch record for each time a risk level 3 sterile product is prepared. Each batch of pharmacy-prepared sterile products should bear a unique lot number, as described in risk level 2.

There should be documentation on the preparation work sheet of all additions of individual components plus the signatures or initials of those individuals involved in the measuring or weighing and addition of these components.

The selection of the final packaging system (including container and closure) for the sterile product is crucial to maintaining product integrity.[109] To the extent possible, presterilized containers obtained from licensed manufacturers should be used. If an aseptic filling operation is used, the container should be sterile at the time of the filling operation. If nonsterile containers are used, methods for sterilizing these containers should be established. Final containers selected should be capable of maintaining product integrity (i.e., identity, strength, quality, and purity) throughout the shelf life of the product.[110]

For products requiring sterilization, selection of an appropriate method of sterilization is of prime importance. Methods of product sterilization include sterile filtration, autoclaving, dry heat sterilization, chemical sterilization, and irradiation.[111,112] The pharmacist must ensure that the sterilization method used is appropriate for the product components and does not alter the pharmaceutical properties of the final product. A method of sterilization often used by pharmacists is sterile filtration.[113] In sterile filtration, the filter should be chosen to fit the chemical nature of the product, and the product should be filtered into presterilized containers under aseptic conditions. Sterilizing filters of 0.22-μm or smaller porosity should be used in this process. Colloidal or viscous products may require a 0.45-μm filter; however, extreme caution should be exercised in these circumstances, and more stringent end-product sterility testing is essential.[114]

To ensure that a bacteria-retentive filter did not rupture during filtration of a product, an integrity test should be performed on all filters immediately after filtration. This test may be accomplished by performing a bubble point test, in which pressurized gas (e.g., air in a syringe attached to the used filter) is applied to the upstream side of the filter with the downstream outlet immersed in water and the pressure at which a steady stream of bubbles begins to appear is noted.[98] The observed pressure is then compared with the manufacturer's specification for the filter. To compare the used filter with the manufacturer's specifications, which would be based on the filtration of water through the filter, it is necessary to first rinse the filter with sterile water for injection. An observed value lower than the manufacturer's specification indicates that the filter was defective or ruptured during the sterilization process. Methods should be established for handling, testing, and resterilizing any product processed with a filter that fails the integrity test.

RL 3.7: Process Validation. In addition to risk level 1 and 2 guidelines, written policies and procedures should be established to validate all processes involved in the preparation of risk level 3 sterile products (including all procedures, equipment, and techniques) from sterile or nonsterile components. In addition to evaluating personnel technique, process validation provides a mechanism for determining whether a particular process will, when performed by qualified personnel, consistently produce the intended results.[115]

RL 3.8: Expiration Dating. In addition to risk level 2 guidelines, there should be reliable methods for establishing all expiration dates, including laboratory testing of products for sterility, nonpyrogenicity, and chemical content, when necessary. These tests should be conducted in a manner based on appropriate statistical criteria, and the results documented.

RL 3.9: Labeling. All guidelines for risk levels 1 and 2 should be met.

RL 3.10: End-Product Evaluation. For each preparation of a sterile product or a batch of sterile products, there should be appropriate laboratory determination of conformity (i.e., purity, accuracy, sterility, and nonpyrogenicity) to established written specifications and policies. Any reprocessed material should undergo complete final product testing. Additionally, process validation should be supplemented with a program of end-product sterility testing, according to a formal sampling plan.[116–127] Written policies and procedures should specify measurements and methods of testing. Policies and procedures should include a statistically valid sampling plan and acceptance criteria for the sampling and testing. The criteria should be statistically adequate to reasonably ensure that the entire batch meets all specifications. Products not meeting all specifications should be rejected and discarded. There should be a mechanism for recalling all products of a specific batch if end-product-testing procedures yield unacceptable results. On completion of final testing, products should be stored in a manner that ensures their identity, strength, quality, and purity.

It is advisable to quarantine sterile products compounded from nonsterile components, pending the results of end-product testing. If products prepared from nonsterile components must be dispensed before satisfactory completion of end-product testing, there must be a procedure to allow for immediate recall of the products from patients to whom they were dispensed.

RL 3.11: Handling of Sterile Products Outside the Pharmacy. All guidelines for risk levels 1 and 2 should be met.

RL 3.12: Documentation. In addition to the guidelines for risk levels 1 and 2, documentation for risk level 3 sterile products should include

1. Preparation work sheet,
2. Sterilization records of final products (if applicable),
3. Quarantine records (if applicable), and
4. End-product evaluation and testing results.

References

1. Hughes CF, Grant AF, Lick BD, et al. Cardioplegic solution: a contamination crisis. *J Thorac Cardiovasc Surg.* 1986; 91:296–302.
2. Pittsburgh woman loses eye to tainted drugs; 12 hurt. *Baltimore Sun.* 1990; Nov 9:3A.
3. ASHP gears up multistep action plan regarding sterile drug products. *Am J Hosp Pharm.* 1991; 48:386–90.
4. Dugleaux G, Coutour XL, Hecquard C, et al. Septicemia caused by contaminated parenteral nutrition pouches: the refrigerator as an unusual cause. *JPEN J Parenter Enteral Nutr.* 1991; 15:474–5.
5. Solomon SL, Khabbaz RF, Parker RH, et al. An outbreak of *Candida parapsilosis* bloodstream infections in patients receiving parenteral nutrition. *J Infect Dis.* 1984; 149:98–102.
6. Food and Drug Administration. Hazards of precipitation with parenteral nutrition. *Am J Hosp Pharm.* 1994; 51:427–8.
7. Pierce LR, Gaines A, Varricchio R, et al. Hemolysis and renal failure associated with use of sterile water for injection to dilute 25% human albumin solution. *Am J Health-Syst Pharm.* 1998; 55:1057,1062,1070.
8. Flynn EA, Pearson RE, Barker KN. Observational study of accuracy in compounding i.v. admixtures at five hospitals. *Am J Health-Syst Pharm.* 1997; 54:904–12.
9. Santell JP, Kamalich RF. National survey of quality assurance activities for pharmacy-prepared sterile products in hospitals and home infusion facilities—1995. *Am J Health-Syst Pharm.* 1996; 53:2591–605.
10. Kastango ES, Douglass K. Improving the management, operations and cost effectiveness of sterile-product compounding. *Int J Pharm Compd.* 1999; 3:253–8.
11. Guynn JB Jr, Poretz DM, Duma RJ. Growth of various bacteria in a variety of intravenous fluids. *Am J Hosp Pharm.* 1973; 30:321–5.
12. Hasegawa GR. Caring about stability and compatibility. *Am J Hosp Pharm.* 1994; 51:1533–4. Editorial.
13. Stability considerations in dispensing practice (general information chapter 1191). In: The United States pharmacopeia, 24th rev., and The national formulary, 19th ed. Rockville, MD: The United States Pharmacopeial Convention; 1999:2128–30.
14. Pharmacy compounding practices (general information chapter 1161). In: The United States pharmacopeia, 24th rev., and The national formulary, 19th ed. Rockville, MD: The United States Pharmacopeial Convention; 1999:2118–22.
15. Sterile drug products for home use (general information chapter 1206). In: The United States pharmacopeia, 24th rev., and The national formulary, 19th ed. Rockville, MD: The United States Pharmacopeial Convention; 1999:2130–43.
16. Good compounding practices applicable to state licensed pharmacies. *Natl Pharm Compliance News.* 1993; May:2–3, Oct:2–3.
17. Model rules for sterile pharmaceuticals. Chicago: National Association of Boards of Pharmacy; 1993:12.1–3.
18. National Advisory Group on Standards and Practice Guidelines for Parenteral Nutrition. Safe practices for parenteral nutrition formulations. *JPEN J Parenter Enteral Nutr.* 1998; 22:49–66.
19. Standard 3.3. Policies and procedures support safe medication prescription or ordering. In: 1999 Hospital accreditation standards. Chicago: Joint Commission on Accreditation of Healthcare Organizations; 1999:88.
20. Standard TX 5.1. Medications are prepared safely. In: 1999–2000 Comprehensive accreditation manual for home care. Chicago: Joint Commission on Accreditation of Healthcare Organizations; 1999:182.
21. Standard TX 2.3. The pharmacy organization maintains proper conditions of sanitation, temperature, light, moisture, ventilation, segregation, safety, and security for preparing medications. 1996–1998 Standards for long term care pharmacies. Chicago: Joint Commission on Accreditation of Healthcare Organizations; 1996:70–1.
22. Standard TX 3.3. Prescribing and ordering of medications follow established procedures. 1998–99 Comprehensive accreditation manual for ambulatory care. Chicago: Joint Commission on Accreditation of

Healthcare Organizations; 1998:211.

23. Food and Drug Modernization Act of 1997, Pub. L. No. 105–115, 111 Stat. 2296.

24. Centers for Disease Control. Guideline for prevention of intravascular infections. *Am J Infect Control.* 1983; 11(5):183–93.

25. Centers for Disease Control. Guideline for handwashing and hospital environmental control. *Am J Infect Control.* 1986; 4(8):110–29.

26. American Society of Hospital Pharmacists. ASHP technical assistance bulletin on handling cytotoxic and hazardous drugs. *Am J Hosp Pharm.* 1990; 47:1033–49.

27. American Society of Hospital Pharmacists. ASHP technical assistance bulletin on pharmacy-prepared ophthalmic products. *Am J Hosp Pharm.* 1993; 50:1462–3.

28. Cleanrooms and associated controlled environments—part 1: classification of air cleanliness. International standard ISO 14644-1. 1st ed. New York: American National Standards Institute; 1999.

29. Federal standard no. 209E. Airborne particulate cleanliness classes in cleanrooms and clean zones. Washington, DC: General Services Administration; 1992.

30. Microbiological evaluation of clean rooms and other controlled environments (general information chapter 1116). In: The United States Pharmacopeia, 24th rev., and The national formulary, 19th ed. Rockville, MD: The United States Pharmacopeial Convention; 1999:2009–106.

31. Validation of aseptic filling for solution drug products. Technical monograph no. 22. Philadelphia: Parenteral Drug Association; 1996.

32. Formulations: *Int J Pharm Compd.* 1999; 2:297–307.

33. Buchanan EC. Policies and procedures for sterile product preparation. In: Principles of sterile product preparation. Bethesda, MD: American Society of Health-System Pharmacists; 1995:133–8.

34. Standard operating procedure of a horizontal laminar air flow hood. *Int J Pharm Compd.* 1997(Sep/Oct); 1:344–5.

35. Standard operating procedure for general aseptic procedures carried out at a laminar air flow workbench. *Int J Pharm Compd.* 1998(May/Jun); 2:242.

36. Standard operating procedure for particulate testing for sterile products. *Int J Pharm Compd.* 1997(Jan/Feb); 2:78.

37. Quality assurance of pharmacy-prepared sterile products. Bethesda, MD: American Society of Hospital Pharmacists; 1994. Videotape and workbook.

38. Safe handling of cytotoxic and hazardous drugs. Bethesda, MD: American Society of Health-System Pharmacists; 1990. Videotape and study guide.

39. Schneider PJ, Buchanan EC. Personnel education, training and evaluation. In: Principles of sterile product preparation. Bethesda, MD: American Society of Health-System Pharmacists; 1995:9–15.

40. Hunt ML. Training manual for intravenous admixture personnel. 5th ed. Chicago: Precept; 1995.

41. Gallagher M. Home care pharmacist competency assessment program. *Am J Health-Syst Pharm.* 1999; 56:1549–53.

42. Dirks I, Smith FM, Furtado D, et al. Method for testing aseptic technique of intravenous admixture personnel. *Am J Hosp Pharm.* 1982; 39:457–9.

43. Brier KL. Evaluating aseptic technique of pharmacy personnel. *Am J Hosp Pharm.* 1983; 40:400–3.

44. McKinnon BT. Handling of sterile products within the pharmacy. In: Principles of sterile product preparation. Bethesda, MD: American Society of Health-System Pharmacists; 1995:111–6.

45. Morris BG, Avis KE. Quality-control plan for intravenous admixture programs. 1: Visual inspection of solutions and environmental testing. *Am J Hosp Pharm.* 1980; 37:189–95.

46. Buchanan EC. Sterile compounding facilities. In: Principles of sterile product preparation. Bethesda, MD: American Society of Health-System Pharmacists; 1995:25–35.

47. Schneider PJ. Equipment for sterile product preparation. In: Principles of sterile product preparation. Bethesda, MD: American Society of Health-System Pharmacists; 1995:37–43.

48. Lau D, Shane R, Yen J. Quality assurance for sterile products: simple changes can help. *Am J Hosp Pharm.* 1994; 51:1353. Letter.

49. Rahe H. Containment Technologies Group, Inc. Personal communication. 1999 Oct.

50. Hunt ML. Training manual for intravenous admixture personnel. 5th ed. Chicago: Precept; 1995:67–70.

51. Buchanan TL, Barker KN, Gibson JT, et al. Illumination and errors in dispensing. *Am J Hosp Pharm.* 1991; 48:2137–45.

52. Denny VF, Kopis EM, Marsik FJ. Elements for a successful disinfection program in the pharmaceutical environment. *PDA J Pharm Sci Technol.* 1999; 53:115–24.

53. Frieben WR. Control of the aseptic processing environment. *Am J Hosp Pharm.* 1983; 40:1928–35.

54. Scheckelhoff DJ. Handling, preparation and disposal of cytotoxic and hazardous agents. In: Principles of sterile product preparation. Bethesda, MD: American Society of Health-System Pharmacists; 1995:63–9.

55. Favier M, Hansel S, Bressole F. Preparing cytotoxic agents in an isolator. *Am J Hosp Pharm.* 1993; 50: 2335–9.

56. Mosko P, Rahe H. Barrier isolation technology: a labor-efficient alternative to cleanrooms. *Hosp Pharm.* 1999; 34:834–8.

57. Pilong A, Moore M. Conversion to isolators in a sterile preparation area. *Am J Health-Syst Pharm.* 1999; 56:1978–80.

58. Tillett L. Barrier isolators as an alternative to a cleanroom. *Am J Health-Syst Pharm.* 1999; 56:1433–6.

59. Bryan D, Marback RC. Laminar air flow equipment certification: what the pharmacist needs to know. *Am J Hosp Pharm.* 1984; 41:1343–9.

60. McKinnon BT. Personnel behavior and garb use. In: Principles of sterile product preparation. Bethesda, MD: American Society of Health-System Pharmacists; 1995:57–62.

61. Coriell LL, McGarrity GJ, Horneff J. Medical applications of dust-free rooms: I. Elimination of airborne bacteria in a research laboratory. *Am J Public Health.* 1967; 57:1824–36.

62. NIOSH recommends steps for reducing work-related exposure to latex. *Am J Health-Syst Pharm.* 1997; 54:1688,1691.

63. Dasher G, Dasher T. The growing problem of latex allergies. *Infusion.* 1996; 2(Jan):23–7.

64. Hunt ML. Techniques used in preparing intravenous admixtures. In: Training manual for intravenous ad-

mixture personnel. Chicago: Precept; 1995:87–103.

65. Scheckelhoff DJ. Use of aseptic technique. In: Principles of sterile product preparation. Bethesda, MD: American Society of Health-System Pharmacists; 1995:49–56.

66. Buchanan EC. Sterile product formulation and compounding. In: Principles of sterile product preparation. Bethesda, MD: American Society of Health-System Pharmacists; 1995:17–24.

67. Kessler DA. MedWatch: The new FDA medical products reporting program. *Am J Hosp Pharm.* 1993; 50:1921–36.

68. Rice SP, Gutfeld MB. Preparation of latex-safe products. *Am J Health-Syst Pharm.* 1998; 55:1462–7.

69. Holzman RS. Latex allergy: an emerging operating room problem. *Anesth Analg.* 1993; 76:635–41.

70. McDermott JS, Gura KM. Procedures for preparing injectable medications for latex-sensitive patients. *Am J Health-Syst Pharm.* 1997; 54:2516–7.

71. Schneider PJ. Process validation. In: Principles of sterile product preparation. Bethesda, MD: American Society of Health-System Pharmacists; 1995:121–4.

72. McKinnon BT. Factors influencing expiration dates. In: Principles of sterile product preparation. Bethesda, MD: American Society of Health-System Pharmacists; 1995:95–103.

73. McEvoy GK, ed. AHFS drug information 99. Bethesda, MD: American Society of Health-System Pharmacists; 1999.

74. Bing C, ed. Extended stability for parenteral drugs. Bethesda, MD: American Society of Health-System Pharmacists; in press.

75. Trissel LA. Handbook on injectable drugs. 10th ed. Bethesda, MD: American Society of Health-System Pharmacists; 1998.

76. Catania PN, ed. King guide to parenteral admixtures. St. Louis, MO: King Guide; 1999.

77. American Society of Health-System Pharmacists. ASHP guidelines: minimum standard for home care pharmacies. *Am J Health-Syst Pharm.* 1999; 56:629–38.

78. Scheckelhoff DJ. Labeling of sterile products. In: Principles of sterile product preparation. Bethesda, MD: American Society of Health-System Pharmacists; 1995:105–9.

79. Davis NM. Optimal checking of pharmacy-prepared sterile products. *Hosp Pharm.* 1996; 31:102. Editorial.

80. Schneider PJ. End-product evaluation. In: Principles of sterile product preparation. Bethesda, MD: American Society of Health-System Pharmacists; 1995:125–8.

81. Meyer GE, Novielli KA, Smith JE. Use of refractive index measurement for quality assurance of pediatric parenteral nutrition solutions. *Am J Hosp Pharm.* 1987; 44:1617–20.

82. Scheckelhoff DJ. Handling of sterile products outside the pharmacy. In: Principles of sterile product preparation. Bethesda, MD: American Society of Health-System Pharmacists; 1995:117–20.

83. Chamallas SN, Fishwick JJ, Riesenberg M. Special delivery, keeping the product stable during shipping. *Infusion.* 1997; 4(3):30–2.

84. McKinnon BT. Documentation of sterile product preparations. In: Principles of sterile product preparation. Bethesda, MD: American Society of Health-System Pharmacists; 1995:129–31.

85. Schumock GT, Kafka PS, Tormo VJ. Design, con-

struction, implementation, and cost of a hospital pharmacy cleanroom. *Am J Health-Syst Pharm.* 1998; 55:458–63.

86. Gianino RR. Misconceptions about cleanrooms. *Am J Hosp Pharm.* 1994; 51:239–40. Letter.

87. Fundamentals of a microbiological environmental monitoring program. Technical report no. 13. Philadelphia: Parenteral Drug Association; 1990.

88. Whyte W. In support of settle plates. *PDA J Pharm Sci Technol.* 1996; 50:201–4.

89. Hyde HA. Origin of bacteria in the clean room and their growth requirements. *PDA J Pharm Sci Technol.* 1998; 52:154–8.

90. American Society of Health-System Pharmacists. ASHP guidelines on the safe use of automated compounding devices for the preparation of parenteral nutrition admixtures. *Am J Health-Syst Pharm.* 2000; 57:1343–8.

91. Davis NM. Unprecedented procedural safeguards needed with the use of automated iv compounders. *Hosp Pharm.* 1992; 27:488. Editorial.

92. Murphy C. Ensuring accuracy in the use of automatic compounders. *Am J Hosp Pharm.* 1993; 50:60. Letter.

93. Dickson LB, Somani SM, Herrmann G, et al. Automated compounder for adding ingredients to parenteral nutrient base solutions. *Am J Hosp Pharm.* 1993; 50:678–82.

94. Fishwick JJ, Murphy CC, Riesenberg MC, et al. Weight-based accuracy of parenteral nutrient solutions prepared with an automated compounder. *Am J Health-Syst Pharm.* 1997; 54:678–9.

95. Johnson R, Coles BJ, Tribble DA. Accuracy of three automated compounding systems determined by end-product laboratory testing and comparison with manual preparation. *Am J Health-Syst Pharm.* 1998; 55:1503–7.

96. Combeau D, Rey JB, Rieutord A, et al. Accuracy of two filling systems for parenteral nutrient solutions. *Am J Health-Syst Pharm.* 1998; 55:1606–10.

97. Boylan JC. Essential elements of quality control. *Am J Hosp Pharm.* 1983; 40:1936–9.

98. McKinnon BT. Preparation and sterilization of batch compounds. In: Principles of sterile product preparation. Bethesda, MD: American Society of Health-System Pharmacists; 1995:71–7.

99. McKinnon BT. Batch preparation documentation. In: Principles of sterile product preparation. Bethesda, MD: American Society of Health-System Pharmacists; 1995:79–94.

100. Lima HA. Required documentation for home infusion pharmacies—compounding records. *Int J Pharm Compd.* 1998; 2:354–9.

101. Avis KE. Assuring the quality of pharmacy-prepared sterile products. *Pharmacopeial Forum.* 1997; 23:3567–76.

102. Fontan JE, Arnaud P, Brion F. Laminar-airflow ceiling in a hospital pharmacy cleanroom. *Am J Health-Syst Pharm.* 1998; 55:182–3. Letter.

103. Chandler SW, Trissel LA, Wamsley LM, et al. Evaluation of air quality in a sterile-drug preparation area with an electronic particle counter. *Am J Hosp Pharm.* 1993; 50:2330–4.

104. Schneider PJ. Environmental monitoring. In: Principles of sterile product preparation. Bethesda, MD: American Society of Health-System Pharmacists; 1995:45–8.

105. Bacterial endotoxins test (general tests and assays chapter 85). In: The United States pharmacopeia, 24th rev., and The national formulary, 19th ed. Rockville, MD: The United States Pharmacopeial Convention; 1999:1829–31.

106. Roberts JH, Wilson JD. Technical report no. 26: sterilizing filtration of liquids. *PDA J Pharm Sci Technol.* 1998; 52(suppl S1):1–31.

107. Akers MJ. Sterilization and depyrogenation: principles and methods. *Int J Pharm Compd.* 1999; 3:263–9.

108. Pyrogen test (general tests and assays chapter 151). In: The United States pharmacopeia, 24th rev., and The national formulary, 19th ed. Rockville, MD: The United States Pharmacopeial Convention; 1999:1850–1.

109. Aspects of container/closure integrity. Technical information bulletin no. 4. Philadelphia: Parenteral Drug Association; 1983.

110. Neidich RL. Selection of containers and closure systems for injectable products. *Am J Hosp Pharm.* 1983; 40:1924–7.

111. Validation of steam sterilization cycles. Technical information bulletin no. 1. Philadelphia: Parenteral Drug Association; 1978.

112. Turco S, ed. Sterile dosage forms: their preparation and clinical application. Philadelphia: Lea & Febiger; 1994:57–78.

113. McKinnon BT, Avis KE. Membrane filtration of pharmaceutical solutions. *Am J Hosp Pharm.* 1993; 50:1921–36.

114. Eudailey WA. Membrane filters and membrane filtration processes for health care. *Am J Hosp Pharm.* 1983; 40:1921–3.

115. Wilson JD. Aseptic process monitoring—a better strategy. *PDA J Pharm Sci Technol.* 1999; 53:111–4.

116. Sterility tests (general tests and assays chapter 71). In: The United States pharmacopeia, 24th rev., and The national formulary, 19th ed. Rockville, MD: The United States Pharmacopeial Convention; 1999:1818–23.

117. Choy FN, Lamy PP, Burkhart VD, et al. Sterility-testing program for antibiotics and other intravenous admixtures. *Am J Hosp Pharm.* 1982; 39:452–6.

118. Doss HL, James JD, Killough DM, et al. Microbiologic quality assurance for intravenous admixtures in a small hospital. *Am J Hosp Pharm.* 1982; 39:832–5.

119. Posey LM, Nutt RE, Thompson PD. Comparison of two methods for detecting microbial contamination in intravenous fluids. *Am J Hosp Pharm.* 1981; 38:659–62.

120. Akers MJ. Progress toward a preferred method of monitoring the sterility of intravenous admixtures. *Am J Hosp Pharm.* 1982; 39:1297. Editorial.

121. Hoffman KH, Smith FM, Godwin HN, et al. Evaluation of three methods for detecting bacterial contamination in intravenous solutions. *Am J Hosp Pharm.* 1982; 39:1299–302.

122. Miller CM, Furtado D, Smith FM, et al. Evaluation of three methods for detecting low-level bacterial contamination in intravenous solutions. *Am J Hosp Pharm.* 1982; 39:1302–5.

123. DeChant RL, Furtado D, Smith FH, et al. Determining a time frame for sterility testing of intravenous admixtures. *Am J Hosp Pharm.* 1982; 39:1305–8.

124. Bronson MH, Stennett DJ, Egging PK. Sterility testing of home and inpatient parenteral nutrition solutions. *JPEN J Parenter Enteral Nutr.* 1988; 12:25–8.

125. Levchuk JW, Nolly RJ, Lander N. Method for testing the sterility of total nutrient admixtures. *Am J Hosp Pharm.* 1988; 45:1311–21.

126. Akers MJ, Wright GE, Carlson KA. Sterility testing of antimicrobial-containing injectable solutions prepared in the pharmacy. *Am J Hosp Pharm.* 1991; 48:2414–8.

127. Murray PR, Sandrock MJ. Sterility testing of a total nutrient admixture with a biphasic blood-culture system. *Am J Hosp Pharm.* 1991; 48:2419–21.

---

[a]Unless otherwise stated in this document, the term sterile products refers to sterile drugs or nutritional substances that are prepared (e.g., compounded or repackaged) by pharmacy personnel.

[b]Ampuls, swabbed and opened appropriately with contents filtered upon removal, should be considered part of a "closed" system.

[c]Isolator guidelines appear under risk level 1 sections because their greatest use is likely to be in the preparation of cytotoxic sterile products, most of which are risk level 1 processes.

[d]The need to alternate germicides is controversial. According to Akers and Moore (Microbiological monitoring of pharmaceutical cleanrooms: the need for pragmatism, *J Adv Appl Contam Control.* 1998; 1[1]:23–4,26,28,30), the data do not support alternating germicides. A literature search (Kopis EM. *Cleanrooms.* 1996; 10[10]:48–50) found little evidence for periodic alternation of disinfectants; the search did find that alternating use of acidic and alkaline phenolic disinfectants reduces resistance arising in pseudomonads adhering to hard surfaces. If ethanol 70% or isopropyl alcohol 70% is used as the primary disinfectant, it should be sterile filtered through a 0.22-mm filter before use.

[e]According to Trissel and Chandler (*Am J Hosp Pharm.* 1993; 50:1858–61), pharmacy air is nearly class 10,000 cleanroom quality already. However, true cleanrooms add HEPA air filtering and designate room air changes and room air pressure differentials to ensure cleanliness (*Am J Hosp Pharm.* 1994; 51:239–40. Letter).

[f]Note that the International Organization for Sanitation (ISO) is preparing documents that should replace Federal Standard 209E. The ISO documents (numbered 14644-1 through 14644-7 and 14698-1 through 14698-3) are being prepared by a technical committee consisting of members from six countries, including the United States. Document 14644-1 is published in final form and classifies the air cleanliness of cleanrooms and associated controlled environments. In 14644-1 ISO cleanroom class 5 is equivalent to Federal Standard 209E class 100, and ISO class 7 is equivalent to Federal Standard 209E class 10,000.

[g]As in general information chapter 1206 in *USP*, which does not require sterility testing until the third risk level, this assumes that sterile components remain sterile throughout preparation. Many sterile products are prepared in batches too small or used too quickly after preparation to make sterility testing meaningful. Also, one of the purposes of process validation is to determine that personnel and processes can produce a sterile product.

Supersedes the ASHP Technical Assistance Bulletin on Quality Assurance for Pharmacy-Prepared Sterile Products, dated September 24, 1993.

Approved by the ASHP Board of Directors, on April 27, 2000 Developed through the ASHP Council on Professional Affairs

The bibliographic citation for this document is as follows: American Society of Health-System Pharmacists. ASHP Guidelines on Quality Assurance for Pharmacy-Prepared Sterile Products. *Am J Health-Syst Pharm.* 2000; 57:1150–69.

Appendix A—Glossary

Action Level: Established particulate or microbial counts or results that require corrective action when exceeded.

Aseptic Preparation or Aseptic Processing: The technique involving procedures designed to preclude contamination (of drugs, packaging, equipment, or supplies) by microorganisms during processing.

Batch Preparation: Compounding of multiple sterile product units, in a single discrete process, by the same individuals, carried out during one limited time period.

Cleanroom: A room (1) in which the concentration of airborne particles is controlled, (2) that is constructed and used in a manner to minimize the introduction, generation, and retention of particles inside the room, and (3) in which other relevant variables (e.g., temperature, humidity, and pressure) are controlled as necessary.[28] For example, the air particle count in a class 100 cleanroom cannot exceed a total of 100 particles 0.5 µm or larger per cubic foot of air.[29]

Clean Zone: Dedicated space (1) in which the concentration of airborne particles is controlled, (2) that is constructed and used in a manner that minimizes the introduction, generation, and retention of particles inside the zone, and (3) in which other relevant variables (e.g., temperature, humidity, and pressure) are controlled as necessary. This zone may be open or enclosed and may or may not be located within a cleanroom.[28] For example, an open-architecture controlled area should be a clean zone.

Closed-System Transfer: The movement of sterile products from one container to another in which the containers–closure system and transfer devices remain intact throughout the entire transfer process, compromised only by the penetration of a sterile, pyrogen-free needle or cannula through a designated closure or port to effect transfer, withdrawal, or delivery. Withdrawal of a sterile solution from an ampul through a particulate filter in a class 100 environment would generally be considered acceptable; however, the use of a flexible closure vial, when available, would be preferable.

Compounding: For purposes of these guidelines, compounding simply means the mixing of ingredients to prepare a medication for patient use. This activity would include dilution, admixture, repackaging, reconstitution, and other manipulations of sterile products.

Controlled Area: For purposes of these guidelines, a controlled area is the area designated for preparing sterile products. This is referred to as the buffer zone (i.e., the cleanroom in which the laminar-airflow workbench is located) by USP.[15]

Corrective Action: Action to be taken when the results of monitoring indicate a loss of control or when action levels are exceeded.

Critical Area: Any area in the controlled area where products or containers are exposed to the environment.

Critical Site: An opening providing a direct pathway between a sterile product and the environment or any surface coming into contact with the product or environment.

Critical Surface: Any surface that comes into contact with previously sterilized products or containers.

Designated Pharmacist: The pharmacist chosen by experience and training to be in charge of a sterile product preparation area or unit in a licensed pharmacy.

Expiration Date: The date (and time, when applicable) beyond which a product should not be used (i.e., the product should be discarded beyond this date and time). Expiration date and time should be assigned on the basis of both stability and risk level, whichever is the shorter period. **Note:** Circumstances may occur in which the expiration date and time arrive while an infusion is in progress. When this occurs, judgment should be applied in determining whether it is appropriate to discontinue that infusion and replace the product. Organizational policies on this should be clear.[15]

High-Efficiency Particulate Air (HEPA) Filter: A filter composed of pleats of filter medium separated by rigid sheets of corrugated paper or aluminum foil that direct the flow of air forced through the filter in a uniform parallel flow. HEPA filters remove 99.97% of all air particles 0.3 µm or larger. When HEPA filters are used as a component of a horizontal- or vertical-laminar-airflow workbench, an environment can be created consistent with standards for a class 100 cleanroom.

Isolator (or Barrier Isolator): A closed system made up of four solid walls, an air-handling system, and transfer and interaction devices. The walls are constructed so as to provide surfaces that are cleanable with coving between wall junctures. The air-handling system provides HEPA filtration of both inlet and exhaust air. Transfer of materials is accomplished through air locks, glove rings, or ports. Transfers are designed to minimize the entry of contamination. Manipulations can take place through either glove ports or half-suits.

Media Fill: See process validation or simulation.

Preservatives: For purposes of these guidelines, preservatives refer to any additive intended to extend the content, stability, or sterility of active ingredients (e.g., antioxidants, emulsifiers, bacteriocides).

Process Validation or Simulation: Microbiological simulation of an aseptic process with growth medium processed in a manner similar to the processing of the product and with the same container or closure system.[30] Process simulation tests are synonymous with medium fills, simulated product fills, broth trials, and broth fills.

Quality Assurance: For purposes of these guidelines, quality assurance is the set of activities used to ensure that the processes used in the preparation of sterile drug products lead to products that meet predetermined standards of quality.

Quality Control: For purposes of these guidelines, quality control is the set of testing activities used to determine that the ingredients, components (e.g., containers), and final sterile products prepared meet predetermined requirements with respect to identity, purity, nonpyrogenicity, and sterility.

Repackaging: The subdivision or transfer of a compounded product from one container or device to a different container or device, such as a syringe or an ophthalmic container.

Sterilization: A validated process used to render a product free of viable organisms.

Sterilizing Filter: A filter that, when challenged with a solution containing the microorganism *Pseudomonas diminuta* at a minimum concentration of 10^{12} organisms per square centimeter of filter surface, will produce a sterile effluent.

Temperatures (USP): Frozen means temperatures between

–20 and –10 °C (–4 and 14 °F). Refrigerated means temperatures between 2 and 8 °C (36 and 46 °F). Room temperature means temperatures between 15 and 30 °C (59 and 86 °F).

Validation: Documented evidence providing a high degree of assurance that a specific process will consistently produce a product meeting its predetermined specifications and quality attributes.

Worst Case: A set of conditions encompassing upper and lower processing limits and circumstances, including those within standard operating procedures, that pose the greatest chance of process or product failure when compared with ideal conditions. Such conditions do not necessarily induce product or process failure.[31]

Appendix B—Comparison of Risk-Level Attributes

This appendix does not show all details of the guidelines, nor does it tell whether an aspect of the sterile compounding process is "required" (must be) or "advisable" (should be). Regardless of the examples given, each compounding pharmacist must decide, according to the circumstances at the time, what conditions are appropriate for compounding a sterile product. In an emergency, it may be of more benefit to a patient to receive a sterile drug prepared under lower risk-level conditions. For the immunocompro-mised patient, even simple, single-patient admixtures may need to be compounded under higher risk-level conditions.

Definition of Products by Risk Level

Risk Level 1	Risk Level 2	Risk Level 3
Products that are (1) stored at room temperature and completely administered within 28 hours from preparation, (2) unpreserved and sterile and prepared for administration to one patient, or batch prepared for administration to more than one patient and contain suitable preservatives, and (3) prepared by closed-system aseptic transfer of sterile, nonpyrogenic, finished pharmaceuticals obtained from licensed manufacturers into sterile final containers obtained from licensed manufacturers.	Products that are (1) administered beyond 28 hours after preparation and storage at room temperature, (2) batch prepared without preservatives and intended for use by more than one patient, or (3) compounded by complex or numerous manipulations of sterile ingredients obtained from licensed manufacturers in a sterile container obtained from a licensed manufacturer by using closed-system, aseptic transfer.	Products that are (1) compounded from nonsterile ingredients or with nonsterile components, containers, or equipment before terminal sterilization or (2) prepared by combining multiple ingredients (sterile or nonsterile) by using an open-system transfer or open reservoir before terminal sterilization.

Examples of Sterile Products by Risk Level

Risk Level 1	Risk Level 2	Risk Level 3
Single-patient admixture Single-patient ophthalmic, preserved Single-patient syringes without preservatives used in 28 hours Batch-prefilled syringes with preservatives Total parenteral nutrient (TPN) solution made by gravity transfer of carbohydrate and amino acids into an empty container with the addition of sterile additives with a syringe and needle	Injections for use in portable pump or reservoir over multiple days Batch-reconstituted antibiotics without preservatives Batch-prefilled syringes without preservatives TPN solutions mixed with an automatic compounding device	Alum bladder irrigation Morphine injection made from powder or tablets TPN solutions made from dry amino acids TPN solutions sterilized by final filtration Autoclaved i.v. solutions

Policies and Procedures

Risk Level 1	Risk Level 2	Risk Level 3
Up-to-date policies and procedures for compounding sterile products should be available to all involved personnel. When policies are changed, they should be updated. Procedures should address personnel education and training, competency evaluation, product acquisition, storage and handling of products and supplies, storage and delivery of final products, use and maintenance of facilities and equipment, appropriate garb and conduct of personnel working in the controlled area, process validation, preparation technique, labeling, documentation, quality control, and material movement.	In addition to risk level 1 guidelines, procedures describe environmental monitoring devices and techniques, cleaning materials and disinfectants, equipment accuracy monitoring, limits of acceptability and corrective actions for environmental monitoring and process validation, master formula and work sheets, personnel garb, lot numbers, and other quality control methods.	Procedures cover every aspect of preparation of level 3 sterile products, so that all products have the identity, strength, quality, and purity purported for the product. Thirteen general policies and procedures, in addition to those in levels 1 and 2, are required.

Personnel Education, Training, and Evaluation

Risk Level 1	Risk Level 2	Risk Level 3
All pharmacy personnel preparing sterile products should receive suitable didactic and experiential training and competency evaluation through demonstration or testing (written or practical). In addition to the policies and procedures listed above, education includes chemical, pharmaceutical, and clinical properties of drugs and current good compounding practices.	In addition to guidelines in risk level 1, training includes assessment of competency in all types of risk level 2 procedures via process simulation. Personnel show competency in end-product testing as well.	Operators have specific education, training, and experience to prepare risk level 3 products. Pharmacist knows principles of good compounding practice for risk level 3 products, including aseptic processing; quality assurance of environmental, component, and end-product testing; sterilization; and selection and use of containers, equipment, and closures.

Storage and Handling in the Pharmacy

Risk Level 1	Risk Level 2	Risk Level 3
Solutions, drugs, supplies, and equipment must be stored according to manufacturer or USP requirements. Refrigerator and freezer temperatures should be documented daily. Other storage areas should be inspected regularly to ensure that temperature, light, moisture, and ventilation meet requirements. Drugs and supplies should be shelved above the floor. Expired products must be removed from active product storage areas. Personnel traffic in storage areas should be minimized. Removal of products from boxes should be done outside controlled areas. Disposal of used supplies should be done at least daily. Product-recall procedures must permit retrieving affected products from specific involved patients.	All guidelines for risk level 1 apply.	In addition to risk level 1 guidelines, procedures include procurement, identification, storage, handling, testing, and recall of components and finished products. Finished but untested products must be quarantined under minimal risk for contamination or loss of identity in an identified quarantine area.

Facilities and Equipment

Risk Level 1	Risk Level 2	Risk Level 3
The controlled area should be separated from other operations to minimize unnecessary flow of materials and personnel through the area. The controlled area must be clean, well lighted, and of sufficient size for sterile compounding. A sink with hot and cold water should be near, but not in, the controlled area. The controlled area and inside equipment must be cleaned and disinfected regularly. Sterile products must be prepared in a class 100 environment (the critical area), such as within a horizontal- or vertical-laminar-airflow workbench or barrier isolator. Computer entry, order processing, label generation, and record keeping should be performed outside the critical area. The critical area must be disinfected periodically. A workbench should be recertified every six months or when it is moved; prefilters should be changed periodically. Pumps should be recalibrated according to procedure.	In addition to risk level 1 guidelines, the following are recommended for risk level 2 products: controlled area must meet class 10,000 cleanroom standards; cleaning supplies should be selected to meet cleanroom standards; critical-area work surface must be cleaned between batches; floors should be disinfected daily, equipment surfaces weekly, and walls monthly; and there should be environmental monitoring of air and surfaces. An anteroom of high cleanliness is desirable. Automated compounding devices must be calibrated and verified as to accuracy, according to procedure.	Products must be prepared in a class 100 workbench in a class 10,000 cleanroom, in a class 100 cleanroom, or in a suitable barrier isolator. Access to the cleanroom must be limited to those preparing the products who are in appropriate garb. Methods are needed for cleaning, preparing, sterilizing, calibrating, and documenting the use of all equipment. Walls and ceilings should be disinfected weekly. All nonsterile equipment that is to come in contact with the sterilized final product should be sterilized before introduction into the cleanroom. An anteroom of high cleanliness (i.e., class 100,000) should be provided. Appropriate cleaning and disinfection of the environment and equipment are required.

Garb

Risk Level 1	Risk Level 2	Risk Level 3
In the controlled area, personnel wear low-particulate, clean clothing covers such as clean gowns or coverall with sleeves having elastic cuffs. Hand, finger, and wrist jewelry is minimized or eliminated. Nails are clean and trimmed. Gloves are recommended; those allergic to latex rubber must wear gloves made of a suitable alternative. Head and facial hair is covered. Masks are recommended during aseptic preparation. Personnel preparing sterile products scrub their hands and arms with an appropriate antimicrobial skin cleanser.	In addition to risk level 1 guidelines, gloves, gowns, and masks are required. During sterile preparation, gloves should be rinsed frequently with a suitable agent (e.g., 70% isopropyl alcohol) and changed when their integrity is compromised. Shoe covers are helpful in maintaining the cleanliness of the controlled area.	In addition to risk level 1 and 2 guidelines, cleanroom garb must be worn inside the controlled area at all times during the preparation of risk level 3 sterile products. Attire consists of a low-shedding coverall, head cover, face mask, and shoe covers. Before donning this garb, personnel must thoroughly wash their hands and arms. Upon return to the controlled area or support area during processing, personnel should regown with clean garb.

Aseptic Technique and Product Preparation

Risk Level 1	Risk Level 2	Risk Level 3
Sterile products must be prepared in a class 100 environment. Personnel scrub their hands and forearms for an appropriate period at the beginning of each aseptic compounding process. Eating, drinking, and smoking are prohibited in the controlled area. Talking is minimized to reduce airborne particles. Ingredients are determined to be stable, compatible, and appropriate for the product to be prepared, according to manufacturer, USP, or scientific references. Ingredients result in final products that meet physiological norms as to osmolality and pH for the intended route of administration. Ingredients and containers are inspected for defects, expiration, and integrity before use. Only materials essential for aseptic compounding are placed in the workbench. Surfaces of ampuls and vials are disinfected before placement in the workbench. Sterile components are arranged in the workbench to allow uninterrupted laminar airflow over critical surfaces of needles, vials, ampuls, etc. Usually only one person and one preparation are in the workbench at a time. Automated devices and equipment are cleaned, disinfected, and placed in the workbench to enable laminar airflow. Aseptic technique is used to avoid touch contamination of critical sites of containers and ingredients. Sterile powders are completely reconstituted. Particles are filtered from solutions. Needle cores are avoided. The pharmacist checks before, during, and after preparation to verify the identity and amount of ingredients before release.	In addition to risk level 1 guidelines, a master work sheet containing formula, components, procedures, sample label, final evaluation, and testing is made for each product batch. A separate work sheet and lot number are used for each batch. When combining multiple sterile ingredients, a second pharmacist should verify calculations. The pharmacist should verify data entered into an automatic compounder before processing and check the end product for accuracy.	In addition to risk level 1 and 2 guidelines, non-sterile components must meet USP standards for identity, purity, and endotoxin levels, as verified by a pharmacist. Batch master work sheets should also include comparisons of actual with anticipated yields, sterilization methods, and quarantine specifications. Presterilized containers should be used if feasible. Final containers must be sterile and capable of maintaining product integrity through-out shelf life. Sterilization method is based on properties of the product. Final filtration methods require attention to many elements of product, filter, and filter integrity.

Process Validation

Risk Level 1	Risk Level 2	Risk Level 3
All persons who prepare sterile products should pass a process validation of their aseptic technique before they prepare sterile products for patient use. Personnel competency should be reevaluated by process validation at least annually, whenever the quality assurance program yields an unacceptable result, and whenever unacceptable techniques are observed. If microbial growth is detected, the entire sterile process must be evaluated, corrective action taken, and the process simulation test performed again.	All risk level 1 guidelines apply, and process-simulation procedures should cover all types of manipulations, products, and batch sizes that are encountered in risk level 2.	In addition to risk level 1 and 2 guidelines, written policies should be made to validate all processes (including all procedures, components, equipment, and techniques) for each risk level 3 product.

Handling Sterile Products Outside the Pharmacy

Risk Level 1	Risk Level 2	Risk Level 3
Sterile products are transported so as to be protected from excesses of temperatures and light. Transit time and condition should be specified. Delivery personnel should be trained as appropriate. Pharmacists ascertain that the end user knows how to properly store products. End users notify pharmacists when storage conditions are exceeded or when products expire so that pharmacists can arrange safe disposal or return.	All guidelines for risk level 1 should be met.	All guidelines for risk level 1 should be met.

Documentation

Risk Level 1	Risk Level 2	Risk Level 3
The following must be documented according to policy, laws, and regulations: (1) training and competency evaluation of employees, (2) refrigerator and freezer temperature logs, (3) certification of workbenches, and (4) other facility quality control logs as appropriate. Pharmacists maintain appropriate records for the compounding and dispensing of sterile products.	In addition to the guidelines in risk level 1, documentation of end-product testing and batch-preparation records must be maintained according to policies, laws, and regulations.	In addition to the guidelines in risk levels 1 and 2, documentation for risk level 3 products must include (1) preparation work sheet, (2) sterilization records if applicable, (3) quarantine records if applicable, and (4) end-product evaluation and testing records.

Expiration Dating

Risk Level 1	Risk Level 2	Risk Level 3
All sterile products must bear an appropriate expiration date. Expiration dates are assigned based on current drug stability information and sterility considerations. The pharmacist considers all aspects of the final product, including drug reservoir, drug concentration, and storage conditions.	All guidelines for risk level 1 should be met.	In addition to risk level 1 and 2 guidelines, there must be a reliable method for establishing all expiration dates, including laboratory testing of product stability, pyrogenicity, and chemical content when necessary.

Labeling

Risk Level 1	Risk Level 2	Risk Level 3
Sterile products should be labeled with at least the following information: (1) for patient-specific products, the patient's name and other appropriate patient identification; for batch-prepared products, control or lot numbers, (2) all solution and ingredient names, amounts, strengths, and concentrations, (3) expiration date (and time when applicable), (4) prescribed administration regimen, (5) appropriate auxiliary labeling, (6) storage requirements, (7) identification of the responsible pharmacist, (8) any device-specific instructions, and (9) any additional information, in accordance with state and federal regulations. A reference number for the prescription or order may also be helpful. The label should be legible and affixed to the product so that it can be read while being administered.	All guidelines for risk level 1 must be met.	All guidelines for risk levels 1 and 2 must be met.

End-Product Evaluation

Risk Level 1	Risk Level 2	Risk Level 3
The final product must be inspected for container leaks, integrity, solution cloudiness or phase separation, particulates in solution, appropriate solution color, and solution volume. The pharmacist must verify that the product was compounded accurately as to ingredients, quantities, containers, and reservoirs.	In addition to risk level 1 guidelines, toxic products, like concentrated glucose and potassium chloride, should be tested for accuracy of concentration.	In addition to risk level 1 and 2 guidelines, the medium-fill procedure should be supplemented with a program of end-product sterility testing according to a formal sampling plan. Samples should be statistically adequate to reasonably ensure that batches are sterile. A method for recalling batch products should be established if end-product testing yields unacceptable results. Each sterile preparation or batch must be laboratory tested for conformity to written specifications (e.g., concentration, pyrogenicity). It is advisable to quarantine sterile products compounded from nonsterile components pending the results of end-product testing.

ASHP Technical Assistance Bulletin on Handling Cytotoxic and Hazardous Drugs

In 1985, the "ASHP Technical Assistance Bulletin on Handling Cytotoxic Drugs in Hospitals"[1] summarized published information on handling hazardous drugs, referred to as cytotoxics, as of July 1984. As more information became available on the types of hazardous agents that may represent a health risk to the occupationally exposed population, and as the handling of such substances became routine in hospitals, community pharmacies, home care settings, clinics, and physicians' offices, the need to revise the Technical Assistance Bulletin became apparent.

Early concerns regarding occupational exposure to hazardous agents involved primarily drugs used in cancer therapy. Therefore, the terms "antineoplastics" (drugs used to treat neoplasms) and "chemotherapy" were used in early reports and guidelines. Although any chemical used therapeutically may be referred to as chemotherapy, this term is currently used, both in the medical and lay communities, to mean drug therapy of cancer. In an attempt to be more precise, many professionals adopted the term "cytotoxic" or "cell killer." Not all antineoplastics, however, are cytotoxic, nor are all cytotoxics used exclusively in the treatment of cancer. "Cytotoxic" is often used to refer to any agent that may be genotoxic, oncogenic, mutagenic, teratogenic, or hazardous in any way. As our knowledge of the hazardous nature of many agents grows and as new hazardous agents (e.g., genotoxic biologicals and some biotechnological agents) continue to be developed, cytotoxic is a less appropriate term. In deference to the original Technical Assistance Bulletin, cytotoxic remains in the title of this revision. The remainder of the document, however, will refer exclusively to hazardous drugs or agents, except in very specific instances.

In January 1986, the Federal Occupational Safety and Health Administration (OSHA) released recommendations on safe handling of cytotoxic drugs by health-care personnel.[2] This revised Technical Assistance Bulletin includes information from these recommendations, modified by subsequent discussions with OSHA, and from published reports by the National Institutes of Health,[3] the National Study Commission on Cytotoxic Exposure,[4] and the American Medical Association's (AMA) Council on Scientific Affairs,[5] along with other published information on this issue as of June 1988.

The safe handling of hazardous drugs is an issue that must be addressed in health-care settings and one that may even affect, in a home care environment, persons other than the patient. Inasmuch as possible, the pharmacist should take the lead in establishing policies and procedures to ensure the proper handling of all hazardous drugs in any health-care setting. The recommendations contained in this Technical Assistance Bulletin should be applied to any area where hazardous drugs are handled. Procedures specific to noninstitutional care settings have been included where available.[6–8] Because of the many questions about implementing the recommendations in the original Technical Assistance Bulletin, this revision contains detailed information in those areas of greatest concern. The recommendations contained here should be supplemented with the professional judgments of qualified staff and with newer information as it develops.

Hazardous Drug Dangers

The danger to health-care personnel from handling a hazardous drug stems from a combination of its inherent toxicity and the extent to which workers are exposed to the drug in the course of carrying out their duties. This exposure may be through inadvertent ingestion of the drug on foodstuffs (e.g., workers' lunches), inhalation of drug dusts or droplets, or direct skin contact. Drugs that may represent occupational hazards include any that exhibit the following characteristics:

1. Genotoxicity [i.e., mutagenicity and clastogenicity (see Appendix A) in short-term test systems].
2. Carcinogenicity in animal models, in the patient population, or both, as reported by the International Agency for Research on Cancer (IARC).
3. Teratogenicity or fertility impairment in animal studies or treated patients.
4. Evidence of serious organ or other toxicity at low doses in animal models or treated patients.

The oncogenic and teratogenic effects of therapeutic doses of several antineoplastic agents are well established.[9–13] The mutagenic properties of some cytotoxics, immunosuppressants, antiviral agents, and biological response modifiers have also been documented.[14] The long-term effects (e.g., cancer, impaired fertility, and organ damage) of continued exposure to small amounts of one or more of such drugs remain undetermined.

For example, it is known that long-term use of potent immunosuppressive agents may result in the development of lymphoma. It is not known, however, at what drug level or over what period of time this may occur and how this correlates with possible drug levels achieved through occupational exposure during preparation and administration of hundreds or thousands of injectable and oral doses of these agents.

Studies have attempted to assess indirectly the potential exposure of hospital pharmacists and nurses to some hazardous drugs in several health-care settings including physicians' offices.[15–21] These studies examined the urine mutagenicity or evidence of chromosome damage in subjects who prepared or administered primarily antineoplastic injections. The mutagenicity and chromosome damage that were found were thought to document exposure to and absorption of the drugs that had been handled. An association may exist between carcinogenicity and chromosome breakage or mutagenicity. Therefore, one might conclude that handling hazardous drugs entails some danger to health-care personnel. These studies, although not conclusive, support the postulated occupational risks.

However, several reports make the situation slightly more ominous. Palmer and coworkers[22] measured chromosome damage in 10 patients receiving chlorambucil. They found that the damage was cumulative and was related to both the daily dose and the duration of therapy. Another report[23] described permanent liver damage in three nurses who had worked 6, 8, and 16 years, respectively, on an oncology ward. On the basis of histories, the investigators suggested that the liver injuries may have been related to the intensity and duration of exposure to certain toxic agents. The chlorambucil study involved therapeutic doses of drug, and three cases of liver damage is a small base for drawing any final conclusions. Nevertheless, this information is disturbing in view of the fact that many health-care workers prepare or administer hundreds or even thousands of doses of hazardous drugs during their careers. If low-dose exposure to these agents is cumulative, this exposure should be minimized by strict compliance with safe handling procedures.

The value of chromosome and mutagenicity studies as indicators of the occupational risks of exposure to hazardous drugs has been questioned.[24–28] However, several researchers have employed more direct methods of determining whether or not workers have been exposed to and absorbed hazardous drugs handled in the customary manner. Demonstration that absorption has occurred would be strong support for the imposition of safety measures. (The absorption of hazardous drug is presumed to be a health risk.)

A letter[29] described a study that used the presence of thioethers in the urine as an indicator of exposure to alkylating agents (i.e., certain antineoplastic drugs). The mean urinary thioether concentration (UTC) was higher in a group of 15 oncology nurses after a 5-day rotation than it was when they returned to work after a 3-day leave ($p < 0.01$). There was no difference between the mean pre-exposure UTC and that of a group of 20 nurses who never handled antineoplastic drugs. Twelve of the 15 nurses wore gloves when handling the drugs; none wore any other form of protective apparel. Drug preparation procedures were not reported.

Using gas chromatography, Hirst's group[30] found cyclophosphamide in the urine of two nurses working in a cancer clinic who took no special precautions when handling the drug. They also demonstrated that cyclophosphamide can be absorbed through intact skin. On the other hand, another group of researchers[31] looked for (but could not detect) platinum in the urine of 10 pharmacists and nurses who frequently prepared or administered cisplatin and other platinum-containing antineoplastic agents. However, these subjects employed several protective measures when working with the drugs; this may have influenced the results (and demonstrated the effectiveness of the safety precautions employed). Also, the assay method may not have been sensitive enough.

With a different type of approach, Neal et al.[32] detected fluorouracil in the air of a drug preparation room and nearby office (where the drug was not prepared). A similar study[33] showed that routine drug manipulations in a horizontal laminar airflow hood contaminated the air in an intravenous admixture preparation room. Fluorouracil and cefazolin sodium were the test drugs employed.

Certain antineoplastic drugs have also been implicated in reproductive risks in humans. There have been reports of fetal loss or malformation occurring in pregnancies of women receiving drug therapy for cancer during the first trimester.[34] Two controlled, retrospective Finnish studies[35,36] attempted to examine the relationship between occupational exposure to antineoplastics and reproductive risks in nurses. One study of nurses reported a statistically significant correlation between the birth of children with malformations and the nurses' preparation and administration of antineoplastics more than once a week during the first trimester of pregnancy. At the time of these nurses' exposure, few protective mechanisms were used.

The second study was done in cooperation with the U.S. National Institute for Occupational Safety and Health (NIOSH); it examined only the incidence of fetal loss and did not investigate the condition of live births. The study showed a significant association between fetal loss and occupational exposure to antineoplastic drugs during the first trimester. Both studies are subject to criticism regarding recall bias and determination of exposure data. Concern about exposure of pregnant workers to hazardous drugs, at least in the first trimester, is, however, valid in light of the reproductive risk reported with therapeutic exposure to certain antineoplastics. At therapeutic doses, these drugs have also been shown to suppress testicular function and spermatogenesis.[37–39] While the relationship between occupational exposure to hazardous drugs and testicular dysfunction has not been assessed, this potential complication should be considered in light of the effects on treated patients.

To date, these reports provide the primary evidence that health-care workers exposed to hazardous drugs during the course of their work may be absorbing these drugs and may be at risk for adverse outcomes.

Additional research in this area is needed, but awareness of the problem has led to overall reduction of exposures, either by improved drug handling techniques or through the implementation of safety programs,[40,41] and thus fewer exposed health-care workers are available for study. Definitive knowledge of the occupational dangers of handling hazardous drugs may someday be available through epidemiologic studies of health-care workers.

In theory, correct and perfect preparation and handling techniques will prevent drug particles or droplets from escaping from their containers while they are being manipulated. Our opinion is that near-perfect technique is uncommon; therefore, contamination of the workplace is likely and worker exposure may increase without protective equipment and other safety measures. This is particularly true, we think, in the absence of any structured training and quality-assurance programs covering the proper handling of hazardous drugs. (Such programs are most likely to be found in health-care settings where the preparation of hazardous drugs is centralized.) Beyond problems in technique, however, contamination also will occur from inevitable spills and from the breakage of hazardous drug containers. ASHP believes that the occupational dangers of exposure to hazardous drugs can be summarized as follows:

1. If hazardous drugs are handled in the same way as other less hazardous substances (e.g., potassium chloride solutions and multivitamin tablets), contamination of the work environment is almost certain to occur.
2. The limited data available suggest that this contamination may result in exposure to and absorption of the drugs by health-care personnel and others. The amount of drug absorbed by any one individual on any given day probably is very small, except for instances of excessive exposure.
3. However, if experience with the therapeutic use of hazardous drugs indicates that the damage is cumulative, individuals whose job responsibilities require them to prepare or administer large numbers of hazardous drug doses for long periods of time (e.g., oncology or transplant nurses and pharmacy intravenous service staff) are at greater risk.
4. Considering the above, the use of procedures, equipment, and materials that demonstrably or theoretically

reduce exposure to hazardous drugs in the health-care workplace is necessary.

The question remains: What safety precautions should be employed?

Safety Precautions

Ideally, the safety precautions employed to protect health-care workers handling hazardous drugs would be those whose efficacy and cost-effectiveness have been documented. Since these drugs have many different physical and chemical properties, research studies into environmental contamination and safety-garment penetration for all questionable drugs are problematic. However, several studies have attempted to demonstrate the effectiveness of certain recommended interventions. Hoy and Stump[42] concluded that a commercial air-venting device, when used with appropriate technique, effectively reduced the release of drug aerosols during reconstitution of drugs packaged in vials. A study by Anderson et al.[16] provides support for preparing hazardous drugs in a vertical laminar airflow biological safety cabinet (BSC) (NSF Class II;[43] see Appendix B) rather than a horizontal airflow clean air work station.

A more recent air-sampling study,[44] carried out in a hospital pharmacy work area where a Class II BSC was used to prepare cytotoxic drugs, detected no fluorouracil during the study period. The study was limited to one drug and two short study periods; the results indicate that a Class II BSC, in conjunction with stringent aseptic technique and recommended procedures for handling hazardous drugs, may reduce environmental contamination by these drugs.

While common sense suggests that the airflow characteristics of containment cabinets would provide greater worker protection than open airflow workstations, it should also suggest that the front opening of the Class II BSC might present potential for environmental contamination and increased worker exposure to hazardous agents. Indeed, as demonstrated by an industrial hygiene experiment,[45] a Class II BSC may cause occasional leakage toward the operator and into the environment if it is placed in an area of strong air drafts or frequent personnel traffic. The containment characteristics of the Class II BSC are compromised whenever the intake or exhaust grilles are blocked (e.g., by placing equipment or supplies on the front grille or too near the back exhaust) or by too much movement on the part of the operator.

Gloves are a major source of protection, whether the work is performed with or without a Class II BSC. The permeability of various glove materials to selected drugs has been examined.[46-49] By using various methods to determine and quantitate penetration, researchers found that permeability of the glove material varied with the drug, contact time, and glove thickness. None of the glove materials tested was impervious to all drugs, and no material was statistically superior except as related to thickness. A thicker glove material is optimal. In addition, several glove materials showed variation in permeability within a manufacturer's lot. These studies do establish that gloves can provide protection against skin contact with the tested drugs, although the degree of protection has not been substantiated. Protection from skin contact is important since many of the problem drugs are skin irritants or even vesicants and, as Hirst et al.[30] showed, at least one (cyclophosphamide) is absorbed through the skin.

Only one study[50] looked at the permeability of gown materials to drugs. Lab coats and disposable isolation gowns were penetrated immediately and were therefore inappropriate for study. Of the four other gown materials studied, Kaycel and nonporous Tyvek had greater permeability than the coated fabrics (Saranex-laminated Tyvek and polyethylene-coated Tyvek). As with gloves, permeability was drug specific. The investigators concluded that users of garments made of Kaycel and nonporous Tyvek should be aware of the potential of these materials for permeability to certain drugs. An earlier report[51] supports the wearing of gloves and gowns. Additional research is needed in the area of protective garments and equipment. Since substantive data are still lacking, health-care professionals should choose protective measures on the basis of expert recommendations, professional judgment, and common sense as well as scientifically established facts.

Recommended Safe Handling Methods

The balance of this article presents our recommendations for policies, procedures, and safety materials for controlling, preparing, administering, containing, and disposing of hazardous drugs. The recommendations are given in a format that can be used either as a base for establishing safe handling methods or for evaluating existing procedures as part of a quality-assurance program. ASHP believes these recommendations represent a conservative but reasonable approach to the precautions that should be taken.

The recommendations are in the format of evaluation criteria organized into four groups. This format should be useful in establishing a quality-assurance system for all nontherapeutic aspects of hazardous drug use. Each group begins with a broad goal, followed by a set of specific criteria and recommendations for achieving the goal. The four goals reflect the following axioms for handling hazardous drugs:

1. Protect and secure packages of hazardous drugs.
2. Inform and educate all involved personnel about hazardous drugs and train them in the safe handling procedures relevant to their responsibilities.
3. Do not let the drugs escape from containers when they are manipulated (i.e., dissolved, transferred, administered, or discarded).
4. Eliminate the possibility of inadvertent ingestion or inhalation and direct skin or eye contact with the drugs.

The handling of hazardous drugs is a complex issue, and the advice of medical experts, occupational physicians, industrial hygienists, legal counsel, and others should be obtained when organizational policy is being established.

Goal I. Accidental contamination of the health-care environment, resulting in exposure of personnel, patients, visitors, and family members to hazardous substances, is prevented by maintaining the physical integrity and security of packages of hazardous drugs.

1. *Access to all areas where hazardous drugs are stored is limited to specified authorized staff.*
2. *A method should be present for identifying to personnel those drugs that require special precautions (e.g., cytotoxics).[52] One way to accomplish this is to apply appropriate warning labels (see Figure 1) to all hazardous drug containers, shelves, and bins where the drug products are stored.*

3. *A method of identifying, for patients and family members, those drugs that require special precautions in the home should be in place.* This may be accomplished in the health-care setting by providing specific labeling for discharge medications, along with counseling and written instructions. Providers of home care and supplies should develop similar labeling and instructional material for the protection of patients and their families.

4. *Methods for identifying shipping cartons of hazardous drugs should be required from manufacturers and distributors of these drugs.*

5. *Written procedures for handling damaged packages of hazardous drugs should be maintained.* Personnel involved in shipping and receiving hazardous drugs should be trained in these procedures, including the proper use of protective garments and equipment. Damaged shipping cartons of hazardous drugs should be received and opened in an isolated area (e.g., in a laboratory fume hood, if available, not in a BSC used for preparing sterile products). Protective apparel—disposable closed-front gown or coveralls, disposable utility gloves over disposable latex gloves, NIOSH-approved[53] air-purifying half-mask respirator (may be disposable) equipped with a high-efficiency filter, and eye protection—should be worn. Broken containers and contaminated packaging materials should be placed in the designated receptacles as described in this article.

6. *Facilities (e.g., shelves, carts, counters, and trays) for storing hazardous drugs are designed to prevent breakage and to limit contamination in the event of leakage.* Bins, shelves with barriers at the front, or other design features that reduce the chance of drug containers falling to the floor should be used. Hazardous drugs requiring refrigeration should be stored separately from nonhazardous drugs in individual bins designed to prevent breakage and contain leakage.

7. *Methods for transporting hazardous drugs to the health-care setting should be consistent with environmental protection and national or local regulations for transporting hazardous substances.* When hazardous drugs are being transported to the home care setting, appropriate containers (e.g., lined cardboard boxes) and procedures should be used to prevent breakage and contain leakage. Hazardous drug containers should be secured to prevent handling by unauthorized persons. Transportation vehicles should be kept locked at all times.

Figure 1. One example of a suitable warning label for cytotoxic and hazardous drugs. Other labels may be used.

For transporting hazardous drugs within the health-care setting, methods that do not cause breakage of or leakage from drug containers should be used. Conveyances that produce severe mechanical stress on their contents (e.g., pneumatic tubes) must not be used to transport hazardous drugs. The drugs must be securely capped or sealed and properly packaged and protected during transport to reduce further the chance of breakage and spillage in a public area such as a corridor or elevator. Adequate instruction and appropriate containers should be provided to patients for transporting discharge and home care medications that require special precautions.

Goal II. The preparation of hazardous drugs does not result in contamination of the health-care work environment or excessive exposure of personnel, patients, or family members to hazardous drug powders, dusts, liquids, or mists.

1. *Written policies and standard procedures for preparing hazardous drugs are maintained.*
    a. They should include a method for identifying for health-care personnel the particular drugs covered by these policies.
    b. Policies and procedures should be consistent with applicable government regulations, professional practice standards, and the recommendations of pharmaceutical manufacturers, hospital safety officers, and other knowledgeable parties.
    c. Since several departments, such as pharmacy, nursing, transportation, maintenance, housekeeping, and medical staff, will be involved with some aspect of the hazardous drug handling issue, preparation of safe handling policies and procedures must be a collaborative effort. Pharmacy should take the lead in this effort.
    d. All personnel who handle cytotoxic and other hazardous agents should have access to the procedures pertaining to their responsibilities. Deviations from the standard procedures must not be permitted except under defined circumstances.

2. *A method for orienting all involved personnel to the special nature of the hazardous drugs in question and the policies and procedures that govern their handling is present.*
    a. The orientation should include, as appropriate, a discussion of the known and potential hazards of the drugs and explanation of all relevant policies. Training done in association with the orientation should cover all relevant techniques and procedures and the proper use of protective equipment and materials. The contents of the orientation program and attendance should be well documented and sufficient to meet "worker right to know" statutes and regulations.
    b. While implementation of a safety program should reduce the risk of personnel exposure to hazardous drugs, the efficacy of such a program in protecting personnel during preparation or administration of these drugs has yet to be demonstrated. The limitations of such a program should be made known to hazardous drug handlers.
    c. Until the reproductive risks (or lack thereof) associated with handling hazardous drugs within

a safety program have been substantiated, staff who are pregnant or breast-feeding should be allowed to avoid contact with these drugs. Policies should be in effect that provide these individuals with alternative tasks or responsibilities if they so desire. In general, these policies should encourage personnel to solicit recommendations from their personal physicians regarding the need for restricted duties. In the case of personnel actively trying to conceive or father a child, a similar policy should be considered, and a specific time period (e.g., 3 months) should be agreed on. Legal counsel should be sought when establishing policies.

d. Prospective temporary and permanent employees who may be required to work with hazardous drugs should be so notified and should receive adequate information about the policies and procedures pertaining to their use. This notification should be documented during the interview process and retained as part of the employment record for all employees.

e. All individuals handling hazardous drugs who do not have employee status (e.g., contract workers, students, residents, medical staff, and volunteers) should be informed through proper channels of the special nature of the drugs. If they choose to handle the hazardous drugs, then they will be expected to comply with established policies and procedures for preparing, administering, and containing hazardous drugs and their associated waste.

3. *A system for verifying and documenting acceptable staff performance of and conformance with established procedures is maintained.*

a. Methods of determining adherence to departmental safety program policies and procedures should be in place. Proper technique is essential to maintain the sterility of the product being manipulated and to reduce the generation of hazardous drug contaminants. Therefore, after initial training and at regular intervals, the knowledge and competence of personnel preparing and administering these drugs should be evaluated and documented. This evaluation should include written examinations and an observed demonstration of competence in the preparation and simulated administration of practice solutions. The monitoring of staff performance and the control of hazardous drugs usually are best achieved if the storage and preparation of the drugs are centralized within one area or department.

b. All personnel involved with the transportation, preparation, administration, and disposal of cytotoxic and hazardous substances should continually be updated on new or revised information on safe handling of cytotoxic and hazardous substances. Policies and procedures should be updated accordingly.

4. *Sufficient information is maintained on safe use of the hazardous drugs in the work area.*

a. The pharmacy should provide access to information on toxicity, treatment of acute exposure (if available), chemical inactivators, solubility, and

stability of hazardous drugs (including investigational agents) used in the workplace. This information should be in addition to information required to ensure patient safety during therapy with these drugs and to be in compliance with all applicable laws and regulations. The information must be easily and readily accessible to all employees where these drugs are routinely handled.

b. Currently, a large number of investigational agents that are potentially hazardous are under clinical study. Staff members should not prepare or administer any investigational agent unless they have received adequate information and instruction about the safe and correct use of the drug. The clinical protocol should include appropriate handling and disposal techniques, if available. When information is limited, pre-clinical data should be used to assess the health risk of the agent.

5. *Appropriate engineering controls should be in place to protect the drug product from microbial contamination and to protect personnel and the environment from the potential hazards of the product.* These engineering controls should be maintained according to applicable regulations and standards.

a. Class 100 clean air work stations,[54] both horizontal and vertical airflow (with no containment characteristics), are inappropriate engineering controls for handling hazardous drugs because they provide no personnel protection and permit environmental contamination. Although there are no engineering controls designed specifically for the safe handling of hazardous chemicals as sterile products, Class II[43] contained vertical flow BSCs (biohazard cabinets) have been adopted for this use. Biohazard cabinetry is, however, designed for the handling of infectious agents, not hazardous chemicals. Therefore, the limitations of such cabinetry must be understood by purchaser and operator. Manufacturers, vendors, the National Sanitation Foundation (NSF), and some certifying agencies are appropriate sources of information regarding BSCs.

b. BSCs are available in three classes (Appendix B). Based on design, ease of use, and cost considerations, Class II contained vertical flow biohazard cabinetry is currently recommended for use in preparing sterile doses of hazardous drugs. Class II cabinetry design and performance specifications are defined in NSF Standard 49.[43] BSCs selected for use with hazardous drugs should meet NSF Standard 49 specifications to ensure the maximum protection from these engineering controls. NSF Standard 49 defines four types of Class II cabinetry, depending on the amount of contaminated air that is recirculated through high-efficiency particulate air (HEPA) filters within the cabinet (see Appendix B).

Selection criteria for Class II cabinetry should include the types and amounts of hazardous drugs prepared, the available location and amount of space, NSF Standard 49, any local requirements for handling hazardous materials and ducting contaminated air, and the cost of the cabinet and related ventilation. Minimum recommendations are a Class II, Type A cabinet (recirculating a major portion of contaminated air through a HEPA filter and back into the cabinet and exhausting a minor portion, through a HEPA filter, to the workroom). In light of the continued development of hazardous drugs having differing physical properties, selection of a Type A cabinet that can be converted to a Type B3 (greater inflow velocity, contaminated ducts and plenums under negative pressure and vented to the outside) may be a prudent investment. There are currently no data to indicate that the use of an auxiliary charcoal filter is more effective in retaining hazardous drugs than the mandatory exhaust HEPA filter of the Type A cabinet.

Type B BSCs are designed to provide more personnel protection than Type A through their greater inflow velocities and required external exhaust of contaminated air. Types B1 (exhausting approximately 70% of the contaminated air to the outside through a HEPA filter) and B2 (exhausting 100% of the contaminated air to the outside through a HEPA filter) require outside exhaust ducts with auxiliary blowers. The Type B2 cabinet is preferred, but unavailability of adequate "makeup" air may eliminate it in favor of the Type B1. All exhaust ducting of any type of BSC must meet applicable codes and ordinances. Ducting into the "dead space" in the ceiling is inappropriate and may be illegal, because it may contaminate ventilation systems and promote contamination of the environment and personnel not directly involved in hazardous drug handling.

In the selection of any BSC, ceiling height should also be considered. Several manufacturers' models have top-load HEPA filters. In workrooms with standard-height ceilings, the filters are difficult to access for certification, which may require that the entire BSC be moved when the filter must be replaced. Because of restrictions of space and cost, the 2-foot wide, Class II, Type A BSC may seem to be the only choice for smaller institutions, outpatient centers, and physician offices. There are, however, many limitations to the smaller cabinet. Because NSF testing facilities are not currently adaptable to 2-foot BSC models, no 2-foot BSC is NSF approved. Selection of a 2-foot cabinet should, therefore, include thorough investigation of cabinet design and knowledge of the reliability of the manufacturer. In all cases, the manufacturer's 2-foot cabinet should not differ extensively from designs used for its NSF-approved larger models.

c.   All Class II BSCs have an open front with inward airflow forming a "curtain" or barrier to protect the operator and the environment from contaminants released in the BSC work area. Because BSCs are subject to breaks in their containment properties if there is interference with the inward airflow through the work area access opening, placement of the BSC and operator training are critical. The placement of a BSC in an area with drafts or in close proximity to other airflow

devices (e.g., horizontal flow hoods, air conditioners, air vents, fans, and doors) may interfere with the inward airflow through the opening and may release contaminants into the workroom.

The horizontal motion of an operator's arms in the opening may also result in similar workroom contamination. Because smaller BSCs are more sensitive to disruption of the inward airflow barrier, the use of a 2- to 3-foot BSC is associated with a greater risk of releasing contaminants than are larger cabinets and requires that the operator be more carefully trained and monitored. It is critical that all operators know the proper method for preparing hazardous drugs in a BSC and that they understand the limitations of BSCs.

d.   Class II BSCs should be certified according to specifications of NSF Standard 49 and Class 100 specifications of Federal Standard 209C.[54] Certification should take place on initial installation, whenever the cabinet is moved or repaired, and every 6 months thereafter. At present, there are no licensing requirements for individuals who certify Class II BSCs. It is, therefore, imperative that the pharmacist responsible for the intravenous preparation area be familiar with the certification requirements for Class II BSCs and the test procedures that should be performed.[55]

All BSCs should be tested for the integrity of the HEPA filter, velocity of the work access airflow and supply airflow, airflow smoke patterns, and integrity of external surfaces of the cabinet and filter housings. Testing of the integrity of the HEPA filter generally ensures that the particulate count in the work area is less than that required to meet Class 100 conditions of Federal Standard 209C.[54] Class II, Type B1 BSCs may be prone to exceed Class 100 particle counts and should have routine particulate testing as part of the certification process. Individuals certifying the BSC should be informed of the hazardous nature of the drugs being prepared in the BSC and should wear appropriate protective apparel (see section 5g).

e.   BSCs should be cleaned and disinfected regularly to ensure a proper environment for preparation of sterile products. For routine cleanups of surfaces between decontaminations, water should be used (for injection or irrigation) with or without a small amount of cleaner. If the contamination is soluble only in alcohol, then 70% isopropyl or ethyl alcohol may be used in addition to the cleaner. In general, alcohol is not a good cleaner, only a disinfectant, and its use in a BSC should be limited. The BSC should be disinfected with 70% alcohol before any aseptic manipulation is begun. The excessive use of alcohol should be avoided in BSCs where air is recirculated (i.e., Class II, Type A, B3, and, to a lesser extent, B1) because alcohol vapors may build up in the cabinet.

A lint-free, plastic-backed disposable liner may be used in the BSC to facilitate spill cleanup. Problems with the use of such a liner include introduction of particulates into the work area, "lumping" of a wet liner that causes unsteady placement of drug containers, poor visibility of spills, and creation of additional contaminated disposables. If used, the liner should be changed frequently and whenever it is overtly contaminated.

f.   The BSC should be operated with the blower turned on continuously, 24 hours a day, 7 days a week. Hazardous drug aerosols and spills generated in the work area of the BSC routinely accumulate in the deposits of room dust and particles under the work tray. These contaminants are too heavy to be transported to the HEPA filter located at the top of the cabinet. In addition, the plenums in all of the BSCs currently available in the United States become contaminated during use; these plenums cannot be accessed for washing. Turning off the blower may allow contaminated dust to recirculate back into the workroom, especially if other sources of air turbulence, such as horizontal hoods, air intakes, air conditioners, and fans, are located near the BSC. Whether or not the BSC is vented to the outside, the downward airflow velocity is insufficient to move and "trap" room dust, spill debris, and other contaminants on the HEPA filter. If it is necessary to turn off a BSC, first the entire cabinet, including all parts that can be reached, should be thoroughly cleaned with a detergent that will remove surface contamination and then rinsed (see section 5g). Once the BSC is clean, the blower may be turned off and the work access opening of the BSC and the HEPA exhaust area may be covered with impermeable plastic and sealed with tape to prevent any contamination from inadvertently escaping from the BSC. The BSC must be sealed with plastic whenever it is moved or left inoperative for any period of time.

g.   The BSC should be decontaminated on a regular basis (ideally at least weekly) and whenever there is a spill or the BSC is moved or serviced, including for certification. While NSF Standard 49 recommends decontamination with formaldehyde to remove biohazard contamination, chemical (drug) contamination is not removed by such treatment. Currently, no single reagent will deactivate all known hazardous drugs; therefore, decontamination of a BSC used for such drugs is limited to removal of contamination from a nondisposable surface (the cabinet) to a disposable surface (e.g., gauze or towels) by use of a good cleaning agent that removes chemicals from stainless steel.

The cleaning agent selected should have a pH approximating that of soap and be appropriate for stainless steel. Cleaners containing chemicals such as quaternary ammonium compounds should be used with caution, because they may be hazardous to humans and their vapors may build up in any BSC where air is recirculated (see section 5e). Similar caution should be used with any pressurized aerosol cleaner; spraying a pressurized aerosol into a BSC may disrupt the protective containment airflow, damage the HEPA filter, and cause an accumulation of the propellant within a BSC where air is recirculated, resulting in a fire and explosion hazard.

During decontamination, the operator should wear a disposable closed-front gown, disposable latex gloves covered by disposable utility gloves, safety glasses or goggles, a hair covering, and a disposable respirator, because the glass shield of the BSC occasionally must be lifted (see 5j). The blower must be left on, and only heavy toweling or gauze should be used in the BSC to prevent it from being "sucked" up the plenum and into the HEPA filter.

Decontamination should be done from top to bottom (areas of lesser contamination to greater) by applying the cleaner, scrubbing, and rinsing thoroughly with distilled or deionized water. All contaminated disposables should be contained in sealable bags for transfer to larger waste containers. The HEPA filter must not become wet during cleaning of the protective covering (e.g., grille front). This covering, therefore, should not be cleaned with spray cleaners while it is in place. Removable parts of the BSC should be cleaned within the containment area of the BSC and should not be removed from the cabinet. The work tray usually can be lifted and placed against the back wall for cleaning of the undersurface of the tray and exposure of the very bottom (or sump) of the BSC.

The drain spillage trough area collects room dust and all spills, so it is the most heavily contaminated area and must be thoroughly cleaned (at least twice with the cleaning agent). The trough provides limited access to the side and back plenums; surfaces should be cleaned as high as possible. BSCs have sharp metal edges, so disposable utility gloves are more durable and appropriate than surgical latex gloves for decontamination. Gloves should be changed immediately if torn. All plenum surfaces must be rinsed well, with frequent changes of water and gauze. If the BSC is equipped with a drainpipe and valve, it may be used to collect rinse water. The collection vessel used must fit well around the drain valve and not allow splashing. Gauze may be used around the connection to prevent aerosol from escaping. The collection vessel must have a tight-fitting cover, and all rinse water (and gauze, if used) must be disposed of as contaminated waste. The outside of the BSC should be wiped down with cleaner to remove any drip or touch contamination.

Cleaner and rinse containers are generally contaminated during the procedure and should remain in the BSC during cleaning or be placed on a plastic-backed, absorbent liner outside the BSC. All bottles must be discarded as contaminated waste after decontamination of the BSC. All protective apparel (e.g., gown, gloves, goggles, and respirator) should be discarded as contaminated waste. Work area surfaces should be disinfected with 70% alcohol before any aseptic operation is begun. With good planning, decontamination of a 4-foot BSC should take about 1 hour.

h. Because of its design and decontamination limitations, the BSC should be considered a contaminated environment and treated as such. The use of the BSC should be restricted to the preparation of sterile dosage forms of hazardous drugs. Access to the BSC should be limited to authorized personnel wearing appropriate protective clothing.

i. If a BSC previously used for biologicals will be adopted for use with hazardous drugs, the BSC should be completely decontaminated of biohazardous agents by use of NSF Standard 49 decontamination techniques. Both HEPA filters should be replaced and the cabinet tested against the *complete* requirements of NSF Standard 49 Appendix B and the particulate limitations of Class 100 conditions of Federal Standard 209C. A BSC used for hazardous drugs that will be recycled for use with hazardous drugs in another section of the institution or in another institution must be surface decontaminated (as described in section 5g), sealed (as in section 5f), and carefully transported to its new location before the filters are replaced (as in section 5j). Once in its new location, the BSC must be recertified.

j. The HEPA filters of the BSC must be replaced whenever they restrict required airflow velocity or if they are overtly contaminated (e.g., by a breach in technique that causes hazardous drug to be introduced onto the clean side of the supply HEPA filter). Personnel and environmental protection must be maintained during replacement of a contaminated HEPA filter. Because replacement of a HEPA filter generally requires breaking the integrity of the containment aspect of the cabinet, this procedure may release contamination from the filter into the pharmacy or intravenous preparation area if carried out in an inappropriate manner.

Before replacement of a HEPA filter contaminated with hazardous drugs, the BSC service agent should be consulted for a mutually acceptable procedure for replacing and subsequently disposing of a contaminated HEPA filter. One procedure would include moving the BSC to a secluded area or using plastic barriers to segregate the contaminated area. Protective clothing and equipment must be used by the servicer. The BSC should be decontaminated before filter replacement (see section 5g). The contaminated filters must be removed, bagged in thick plastic, and prepared for disposal in a hazardous waste dump site or incinerator licensed by the Environmental Protection Agency (EPA).

When arranging for disposal, precise terms should be used to describe the hazard (e.g., "toxic chemicals" or "chemical carcinogens," not "cytotoxic" or "chemotherapy") to ensure that contractors are not inadvertently misled in the classification of the hazard. Disposal of an entire contaminated BSC should be approached in the same manner. The filters should be removed, bagged, and disposed of separately from the BSC. If no available service company will arrange for removal of the filter (or entire BSC) and its ultimate disposal, a licensed hazardous waste contractor should be used. The use of triple layers of thick plastic (e.g., 2-mil low-linear or 4-mil plastic) for initial covering of the filter or cabinet and then the construction of a plywood crate for transport to an EPA-licensed hazardous waste dump site or incinerator is suggested.

6. *Engineering controls should be supplemented with personal protective apparel and other safety materials.* Policies and procedures should be in place to ensure that these materials are used properly and consistently.

a. Workers should wear powder-free, disposable surgical latex gloves of good quality when preparing hazardous drugs. Selection criteria for gloves should include thickness (especially at the fingertips where stress is the greatest), fit, length, and tactile sensation. While no glove material has been shown to be impervious to all hazardous drugs or to be statistically superior in limiting drug penetration, thickness and time in contact with drug are crucial factors affecting permeability.[47–49]

The practice of double gloving is supported by research that indicates that many glove materials vary in drug permeability even within lots;[48,49] therefore, double gloving is recommended. This recommendation is based on currently available research findings. Evidence to show that single gloves are sufficiently protective might make this recommendation unnecessary. In general, surgical latex gloves fit better, have appropriate elasticity for double gloving and maintaining the integrity of the glove-gown interface, and have sufficient tactile sensation (even during double gloving) for stringent aseptic procedures.

b. Powdered gloves increase the particulate level in the filtered air environment of the BSC and leave a powder residue on the surfaces of supplies, final product, and the hands that may absorb contamination generated in the BSC; therefore, powdered gloves should be avoided. The use of sterile gloves is unnecessary during operations involving nonsterile surfaces. Hands must be thoroughly washed and dried before gloves are donned and when a task or batch is completed. If only powdered gloves are available, all powder must be washed off the outside of the outer glove before any operation is begun, and hands should be washed once gloves have been removed.

c. Two pairs of fresh gloves should be put on when beginning any task or batch. The outer glove should be changed immediately if contaminated. Both gloves should be changed if the outer glove is torn, punctured, or overtly contaminated with drug (as in a spill) and every hour during batch operations. During removal of gloves, care should be taken to avoid touching the inside of the glove or the skin with the contaminated glove fingers. To limit transfer of contamination from the BSC into the work area, outer gloves should be removed after each batch and should be placed in "zipper"-closure plastic bags or other sealable containers for disposal.

d. The worker should wear a protective disposable gown made of lint-free, low-permeability fabric with a solid front, long sleeves, and tight-fitting elastic or knit cuffs when preparing hazardous drugs. Washable garments are immediately penetrated by liquids and therefore provide little, if any, protection. In addition, washable garments require laundering and thus potentially expose other personnel to contamination.

e. When double gloving, one glove should be placed under the gown cuff and one over. The glove-gown interface should be such that no skin on the arm or wrist is exposed. Gloves and gowns should not be worn outside the immediate preparation area. On completion of each task or batch, the worker should, while wearing outer gloves, wipe all final products with gauze. The outer gloves should then be removed and placed, along with the gauze, in a sealable container (e.g., a zipper-closure plastic bag) within the BSC. All waste bags in the BSC should be sealed and removed for disposal. The gown should be removed and placed in a sealable container before removal of the inner gloves. The inner gloves should be removed last and placed in the container with the gown.

f. Workers who are not protected by the containment environment of a BSC should use respiratory protection when handling hazardous drugs. Respiratory protection should be an adjunct to and not a substitute for engineering controls.

g. Surgical masks of all types provide no respiratory protection against powdered or liquid aerosols of hazardous drugs.

h. In situations where workers may be exposed to potential eye contact with hazardous drugs, an appropriate plastic face shield or splash goggles should be worn. Eyewash fountains should be available in areas where hazardous drugs are routinely handled. Inexpensive alternatives include an intravenous bag of 0.9% sodium chloride solution (normal saline) or irrigation bottle of water or saline with appropriate tubing.

7. *Proper manipulative technique to maintain the sterility of injectable drugs and to prevent generation of hazardous drug contaminants is used consistently.*

a. Proper manipulative technique must be taught to all workers who will be required to prepare hazardous drugs.[56] Preparers should demonstrate competence in these techniques once training has been completed and at least annually thereafter.

b. Systems to ensure that these techniques are adhered to should exist, along with systems to ensure patient safety by providing that drugs are properly selected, calculated, measured, and delivered.

c. The work area should be designed to provide easy access to those items necessary to prepare, label, and transport final products; contain all related waste; and avoid inadvertent contamination of the work area.

d. Maintenance of proper technique requires an organized approach to the preparation of sterile doses of hazardous drugs in a BSC. All drug and nondrug items required for completing a dose or batch and for containing the waste should be assembled and placed in the BSC; care should be

taken not to overload the BSC work area. All calculations and any label preparation should be completed at this time. Appropriate gowning, hand washing and gloving (or glove changing), and glove washing should be completed before any manipulations are begun. Unnecessary moving in and out of the BSC should be avoided during aseptic manipulations.

e. Syringes and intravenous sets with Luer-lock type fittings should be used for preparing and administering hazardous drug solutions, since they are less prone to accidental separation than friction fittings. Care must be taken to ensure that all connections are secure. Syringes should be large enough so that they are not full when containing the total drug dose. This is to ensure that the plunger does not separate from the syringe barrel. Doses should be dispensed in several syringes when this problem arises.

f. The contents of an ampul should be gently tapped down from the neck and top portion of the ampul before it is opened. The ampul should be wiped with alcohol before being opened. A sterile gauze pad should be wrapped around the neck of the ampul when it is opened.

g. Substantial positive or negative deviations from atmospheric pressure within drug vials and syringes should be avoided.

h. For additional worker protection, equipment such as venting devices with 0.2-μm hydrophobic filters and 5-μm filter needles or "straws" may be used. It is critical that the worker be proficient with these devices before using them with hazardous drugs. Improper use of these devices may result in increased, rather than decreased, risk of exposure.

i. Final products should be dispensed in ready-to-administer form. If possible, intravenous administration sets should be attached to the bag or bottle in the BSC and primed with plain fluid before the hazardous drug is added. However, if total volume is a concern, intravenous sets may be primed with diluted drug solution, which is discarded into an appropriate container within the BSC. Potential disadvantages to this approach include difficulty in selecting the appropriate administration set when several methods of administering hazardous drugs exist, potential contamination of the outside of the intravenous set, and the risk of the intravenous set becoming dislodged from the bag or bottle during transport.

j. The outside of bags or bottles and intravenous sets (if used) should be wiped with moist gauze to remove any inadvertent contamination. Entry ports should be wiped with sterile, alcohol-dampened gauze pads and covered with appropriate seals or caps.

k. Final products should be placed in sealable containers (e.g., zipper-closure plastic bags) to reduce the risk of exposing ancillary personnel or contaminating the environment. Containers should be designed such that damage incurred during storage or transport is immediately visible and any leakage is fully contained. For offsite transport, appropriate storage conditions (e.g., refrigerated, padded, and locked carriers) should also be used.

l. Excess drug should be returned to the drug vial whenever possible or discarded into a closed container (empty sterile vial). Placing excess drug in any type of open container, even while working in the BSC, is inappropriate. Discarding excess drug into the drainage trough of the BSC is also inappropriate. These practices unnecessarily increase the risk of exposure to large amounts of hazardous drug.

m. All contaminated materials should be placed in leakproof, puncture-resistant containers within the contained environment of the BSC and then placed in larger containers outside the BSC for disposal. To minimize aerosolization, needles should be discarded in puncture-resistant containers without being clipped.

8. *Procedures for the preparation and dispensing of noninjectable dosage forms of hazardous drugs are established and followed.*

a. Although noninjectable dosage forms of hazardous drugs contain varying proportions of drug to nondrug (nonhazardous) components, there is potential for personnel exposure and environmental contamination with the hazardous components. Procedures should be developed to avoid the release of aerosolized powder or liquid into the environment during manipulation of these drugs.

b. Drugs designated as hazardous should be labeled or otherwise identified as such to prevent their improper handling.

c. Tablet and capsule forms of these drugs should not be placed in automated counting machines, which subject them to stress and may introduce powdered contaminants into the work area.

d. During *routine handling* of hazardous drugs and contaminated equipment, workers should wear one pair of gloves of good quality and thickness.

e. The counting and pouring of hazardous drugs should be done carefully, and clean equipment dedicated for use with these drugs should be used. Contaminated equipment should be cleaned initially with water-saturated gauze and then further cleaned with detergent and rinsed. The gauze and rinse should be disposed of as contaminated waste.

f. During *compounding* of hazardous drugs (e.g., crushing, dissolving, and preparing an ointment), workers should wear low-permeability gowns and double gloves. Compounding should take place in a protective area such as a disposable glove box. If compounding must be done in the open, an area away from drafts and traffic must be selected, and the worker should use appropriate respiratory protection.

g. When hazardous drug tablets in unit-of-use packaging are being crushed, the package should be placed in a small sealable plastic bag and crushed with a spoon or pestle; caution should be used not to break the plastic bag.

h. Disposal of unused or unusable oral or topical dosage forms of hazardous drugs should be performed in the same manner as for hazardous injectable dosage forms and waste.

9. *Personnel know the procedures to be followed in case of accidental skin or eye contact with hazardous drugs.*

a. Each health-care setting should have an established first aid protocol for treating cases of direct contact with hazardous drugs, many of which are irritating or caustic and can cause tissue destruction. Medical care providers in each setting should be contacted for input into this protocol. The protocol should include immediate treatment measures and should specify the type and location of medical followup and work-injury reporting. Copies of the protocol, highlighting emergency measures, should be posted wherever hazardous drugs are routinely handled.

b. Hazardous drug work areas should have a sink (preferably with an eyewash fountain) and appropriate first aid equipment to treat accidental skin or eye contact according to the protocol.

c. In settings where hazardous drug handlers are offsite (e.g., home use), protocols must be part of orientation programs, and copies of the procedures should be immediately accessible to handlers, along with appropriate first aid equipment and emergency phone numbers to call for followup and reporting.

10. *All hazardous drugs are labeled with a warning label stating the need for special handling.*

a. A distinctive warning label with an appropriate CAUTION statement should be attached to all hazardous drug materials, consistent with state laws and regulations. This would include, for example, syringes, intravenous containers, containers of unit-dose tablets and liquids, prescription vials and bottles, waste containers, and patient specimens that contain hazardous drugs.

b. The hazardous drugs discussed in this Technical Assistance Bulletin are chemical hazards and *not* infectious hazards. Because the term "biohazard" refers to an infectious hazard, the use of this term or the biohazard symbol (in any variation) on the label of drugs that are chemical hazards is inappropriate and may be misleading to staff and contract workers who are familiar with the biohazard symbol. An example of a suitable label is shown in Figure 1.

c. All staff and contract workers should be informed about the meaning of the label and the special handling procedures that have been established.

d. In settings where patients or their families will be responsible for manipulating these drugs, they should be made aware of the need for special handling and the reasons behind it.

Goal III. Procedures for administering hazardous drugs prevent the accidental exposure of patients and staff and contamination of the work environment.

1. *A method for informing and training health-care professionals in these procedures is maintained.*

a. Only individuals trained to administer hazardous drugs should be allowed to perform this function. Training programs should contain information on the therapeutic and adverse effects of these drugs and the potential, long-term health risk to personnel handling them. Each individual's knowledge and technique should be evaluated before administration of these drugs. This should be done by written examination and direct observation of the individual's performance.

2. *Standard procedures for the safe administration of hazardous drugs are established and followed.* These procedures ensure the safety of both the patient and health-care personnel.

   a. Intravenous administration sets (e.g., vented, nonvented, and minidrip) and infusion devices appropriate for use with the final product should be selected.

   b. Syringes and intravenous sets with Luer-lock fittings should be used whenever possible.

   c. Preparation of the final product for administration should take place in a clean, uncluttered area separate from other activities and excessive traffic. A plastic-backed absorbent liner should be used to cover the work area to absorb accidental spills. A single pair of disposable latex gloves and a disposable gown should be worn. The glove and gown cuffs should be worn in a manner that produces a tight fit (e.g., loose glove tucked under gown cuff; tight glove fitted over gown cuff). Hands must be thoroughly washed before gloves are donned.

   Administration sets should be attached with care (if not attached during drug preparation). Administration sets and devices should be monitored for leakage.

   d. Priming of intravenous sets should not allow any drug to be released into the environment. Hazardous drug solutions may be "piggybacked" into primary intravenous solutions and primed by retrograde flow of the primary solution into the secondary tubing. All Y-site connections should be taped securely. Alternatively, the intravenous set may be primed with plain solution before the hazardous drug solution bag or bottle is connected. Some intravenous sets can be primed so that the fluid enters the medication port of the intravenous bag. The priming fluid may also be discarded into a sealable plastic bag containing absorbent material if care is taken not to contaminate the sterile needle tip. Likewise, a sterile gauze pad should be placed close to the sterile needle tip when air is expelled from a syringe. The syringe plunger should first be drawn back to withdraw liquid from the needle before air is expelled. Care should be taken not to contaminate the sterile needle with gauze fibers or microorganisms.

   e. Intravenous containers designed with venting tubes should not be used. If such containers must be used, gauze should be placed over the tube when the container is inverted to catch any hazardous drug solution trapped in the tube. If containers with solid stoppers are used, any vacuum present should be eliminated before the container is attached to a primary intravenous or to a manifold. If a series of bags or bottles is used to deliver the drug, the intravenous set should be discarded with each container because removing the spike from the container is associated with a greater risk of environmental contamination than priming an intravenous set. (Use of secondary sets for administration of hazardous drugs reduces the cost of this recommendation and the risk of priming.)

   f. A plastic-backed absorbent liner should be placed under the intravenous tubing during administration to absorb any leakage and prevent the solution from spilling onto the patient's skin. The use of sterile gauze around any "push" sites will reduce the likelihood of releasing drug into the environment.

   g. The use of eye protection (safety glasses or goggles) during work with hazardous drugs, especially vesicants, should be considered. Work at your waist level, if possible; avoid working above the head or reaching up for connections or ports.

   h. All contaminated gauze, syringes, intravenous sets, bags, bottles, etc., should be placed in sealable plastic bags and placed in a puncture-resistant container for removal from the patient-care area.

   i. Gloves should be discarded after each use and immediately if contaminated. Gowns should be discarded on leaving the patient-care area and immediately if contaminated. Hands must be washed thoroughly after hazardous drugs are handled.

   j. Gloves should be worn when urine and other excreta from patients receiving hazardous drugs are being handled. Skin contact and splattering should be avoided during disposal. While it may be useful to post a list of drugs that are excreted in urine and feces and the length of time after drug administration during which precautions are necessary, an alternative is to select a standard duration (e.g., 48 hours) that covers most of the drugs and is more easily remembered.

   k. Disposable linen or protective pads should be used for incontinent or vomiting patients. Nondisposable linen contaminated with hazardous drug should be handled with gloves and treated similarly to that for linen contaminated with infectious material. One procedure is to place the linen in specially marked water-soluble laundry bags. These bags (with the contents) should be prewashed; then the linens should be added to other laundry for an additional wash. Items contaminated with hazardous drugs should not be autoclaved unless they are also contaminated with infectious material.

3. *Appropriate apparel and materials needed to protect staff and patients from exposure and to protect the work environment from contamination are readily available.* Supplies of disposable gloves and gowns, safety glasses, disposable plastic-backed absorbent liners, gauze pads, hazardous waste disposal bags, hazardous drug warning labels, and puncture-resistant containers for disposal of needles and ampuls should be conveniently located for all areas where hazardous drugs are handled. Assembling a "hazardous drug preparation and administration kit" is one way to furnish nursing and medical personnel with the mate-

rials needed to reduce the risk of preparing and administering a hazardous drug.

4. *Personnel know the procedures to be followed in case of accidental skin or eye contact with hazardous drugs. (See Goal II9.)*

Goal IV. The health-care setting, its staff, patients, contract workers, visitors, and the outside environment are not exposed to or contaminated with hazardous drug waste materials produced in the course of using these drugs. (See Figure 2 for proposed flow chart for handling contaminated items.)

1. *Written policies and procedures governing the identification, containment, collection, segregation, and disposal of hazardous drug waste materials are established and maintained.* All health-care workers who handle hazardous drugs or waste must be oriented to and must follow these procedures.

2. *Throughout institutional health-care facilities and in alternative health-care settings, hazardous drug waste materials are identified, contained, and segregated from all other trash.*

   a. Hazardous drug waste should be placed in specially marked (specifically labeled CAUTION: HAZARDOUS CHEMICAL WASTE) thick plastic bags or leakproof containers. These receptacles should be kept in all areas where the drugs are commonly used. All and only hazardous drug waste should be placed in them. Receptacles used for glass fragments, needles, and syringes should be puncture resistant. Hazardous drug waste should not be mixed with any other waste. Waste containers should be handled with uncontaminated gloves.

   b. Health-care personnel providing care in a patient's home should have with them all the equipment and supplies necessary to contain properly any hazardous drug waste that is generated during the visit. Contaminated needles and syringes, intravenous containers, intravenous sets, and any

broken ampuls should be placed in leakproof, puncture-resistant containers. Gloves, gowns, drug vials, etc., should be sealed in specially labeled (CAUTION: HAZARDOUS CHEMICAL WASTE) thick plastic bags or leakproof containers. All waste should be removed from the patient's home and transported to a designated area. Additional precautions should be taken during transport, including temporary storage in a spill-resistant container and ensuring that the vehicle is locked at all times. Hazardous waste should be securely stored at a designated area until it is picked up for appropriate disposal. Patients or their caregivers should be instructed on methods for the proper handling of excreta from patients receiving hazardous drugs.

   c. Unless restricted by state or local regulations, hazardous drug waste may be further divided into trace and bulk-contaminated waste, if desired, to reduce costs of disposal. As defined by the EPA, bulk-contaminated materials are solutions or containers whose contents weigh more than 3% of the capacity of the container.[57,58] For example, empty intravenous containers and intravenous administration sets usually are considered trace waste; half-empty vials of hazardous drugs and unused final doses in syringes or intravenous containers are considered bulk-contaminated waste. If trace and bulk-contaminated waste are handled separately, bulk-contaminated waste should be segregated into more secure receptacles for containment and disposal as toxic waste. While this may allow for less expensive overall disposal of hazardous waste, it also requires close monitoring of the containment and segregation process to prevent the accidental discarding of a bulk-contaminated container into a trace-waste receptacle.

   d. All hazardous waste collected from drug preparation and patient-care areas should be held in a secure place in labeled, leakproof drums or cartons (as required by state or local regulation or disposal contractor) until disposal. This waste should be disposed of as hazardous or toxic waste in an EPA-permitted, state-licensed hazardous waste incinerator. Transport to an offsite incinerator should be done by a contractor licensed to handle and transport hazardous waste. (While licenses are generally required to transport infectious waste as well as hazardous waste, these are different classes of contractors and may not be interchanged. Verification of possession and type of license should be documented before a contractor is engaged.)

   e. If access to an appropriately licensed incinerator is not available, transport to and burial in an EPA-licensed hazardous waste dump site is an acceptable alternative. While there are concerns that destruction of carcinogens by incineration may be incomplete, newer technologies and stringent licensing criteria have improved this disposal method. (Again, the existence and type of license should be verified before use of a contract incinerator.)

   f. Chemical deactivation of hazardous drugs should

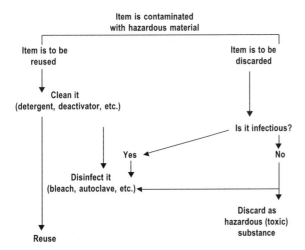

Figure 2. Proposed flow chart for handling chemical hazards versus biohazards. Disinfection of a disposable item contaminated with both infectious and hazardous material may not be necessary, depending on the degree of infectious hazard (e.g., human immunodeficiency virus versus *Escherichia coli*) and depending on the method of disposal (e.g., burial versus incineration).

be undertaken only by individuals who are thoroughly familiar with the chemicals and the procedures required to complete such a task. The IARC recently published a monograph describing methods for chemical destruction of some cytotoxic (antineoplastic) drugs in the laboratory setting.[59] The chemicals and equipment described, however, are not generally found in the clinical setting, and many of the deactivating chemicals are toxic and hazardous. Most procedures require the use of a chemical fume hood. The procedures are generally difficult, and the deactivation is not always complete. Serious consideration should be given to the negative aspects of chemical deactivation before one commits to such a course of action.

3. *Materials to clean up spills of hazardous drugs are readily available and personnel are trained in their proper use.* A standard cleanup protocol is established and followed.

   a. "Spill kits" containing all materials needed to clean up spills of hazardous drugs should be assembled or purchased. These kits should be readily available in all areas where hazardous drugs are routinely handled. If hazardous drugs are being prepared or administered in a nonroutine area (home setting or unusual patient-care area), a spill kit should be obtained by the drug handler. The kit should include two pairs of disposable gloves (one outer pair of utility gloves and one inner latex pair); low permeability, disposable protective garments (coveralls or gown and shoe covers); safety glasses or splash goggles; respirator; absorbent, plastic-backed sheets or spill pads; disposable toweling; at least two sealable thick plastic hazardous waste disposal bags (prelabeled with an appropriate warning label); a disposable scoop for collecting glass fragments; and a puncture-resistant container for glass fragments.

   b. All individuals who routinely handle hazardous drugs must be trained in proper spill management and cleanup procedures. Spills and breakages must be cleaned up immediately according to the following procedures. If the spill is not located in a confined space, the spill area should be identified and other people should be prevented from approaching and spreading the contamination. Wearing protective apparel from the spill kit, workers should remove any broken glass fragments and place them in the puncture-resistant container. Liquids should be absorbed with a spill pad; powder should be removed with damp disposable gauze pads or soft toweling. The hazardous material should be completely removed and the area rinsed with water and then cleaned with detergent. The spill cleanup should proceed progressively from areas of lesser to greater contamination. The detergent should be thoroughly rinsed and removed. All contaminated materials should be placed in the disposal bags provided and sealed and transported to a designated containment receptacle.

   c. Spills occurring in the BSC should be cleaned up immediately; a spill kit should be used if the volume exceeds 150 ml or the contents of one drug vial or ampul. If there is broken glass, utility gloves should be worn to remove it and place it in the puncture-resistant container located in the BSC. The BSC, including the drain spillage trough, should be thoroughly cleaned. If the spill is not easily and thoroughly contained, the BSC should be decontaminated after cleanup. If the spill contaminates the HEPA filter, use of the BSC should be suspended until the cabinet has been decontaminated and the HEPA filter replaced. (See Goal II 5j.)

   d. If hazardous drugs are routinely prepared or administered in carpeted areas, special equipment is necessary to remove the spill. Absorbent powder should be substituted for pads or sheets and left in place on the spill for the time recommended by the manufacturer. The powder should then be picked up with a small vacuum unit reserved for hazardous drug cleanup. The carpet should then be cleaned according to usual procedures. The vacuum bag should be removed and discarded or cleaned, and the exterior of the vacuum cleaner should be washed with detergent and rinsed before being covered and stored. The contaminated powder should be discarded into a sealable plastic bag and segregated with other contaminated waste materials. Alternatively, inexpensive wet or dry vacuum units may be purchased for this express use and used with appropriate cleaners. All such units are contaminated, once used, and must be cleaned, stored, and ultimately discarded appropriately (i.e., like BSCs).

   e. The circumstances and handling of spills should be documented. Health-care personnel exposed during spill management should also complete an incident report or exposure form.

4. *Hazardous drug waste is disposed of in accordance with all applicable state, federal, and local regulations for the handling of hazardous and toxic waste.*

   a. Regulatory agencies such as the EPA and state solid and hazardous waste agencies and local air and water quality control boards must be consulted regarding the classification and appropriate disposal of drugs that are defined as hazardous or toxic chemicals. EPA categorizes several of the antineoplastic agents (including cyclophosphamide and daunorubicin) as toxic wastes, while many states are more stringent and include as carcinogens certain cytotoxic drugs (azathioprine) and hormonal preparations (diethylstilbestrol and conjugated estrogens). EPA also allows exemptions from toxic waste regulations for "small quantity generators,"[57] whereas certain states do not. It is critical to research these regulations when disposal procedures are being established.

Other Hazardous Drug Issues

The handling of hazardous drugs, some of which are defined by the EPA as toxic chemicals, has implications that go beyond the health-care setting. Disposal of hazardous materials and toxic chemicals continues to be a controversial issue of which the disposal of hazardous drugs is but a small part. The EPA currently issues permits for both burial and incineration of hazardous waste. Some such facilities may purport to possess permits to handle these types of hazardous agents when, in fact, they do not meet the requirements or are only in the initial stages of obtaining permits. It is imperative that health-care facilities verify the license or permit status of any contractor used to remove or dispose of infectious or hazardous waste. In addition, many hazardous drugs are excreted unchanged or as equally toxic metabolites. The amount of hazardous drug transferred to the environment (primarily through the water supply) from this source may exceed that resulting from the hospital trash pathway. No good methods for reducing this source of contamination are currently known.

Definitive risks of handling these drugs may never be fully determined without epidemiologic data from a national registry of handlers of hazardous drugs (and chemicals). There is no method available for routine monitoring of personnel for evidence of hazardous drug exposure. Tests for the presence of mutagens or chromosomal damage are not drug specific and are of value only in controlled studies. Chemical analysis of urine for the presence of hazardous drugs at the sensitivity level needed to detect occupational exposure is limited to a few drugs and is not yet commercially available.

This document is designed to identify areas of risk in the handling of hazardous drugs and to provide recommendations for reducing that risk. A safety program should be coupled with a strong quality-assurance program that periodically evaluates and verifies staff adherence to and performance of the established safe handling policies and procedures. Until some type of external monitoring of exposure levels from handling hazardous drugs is commercially available, development of and compliance with a safety program remain the most logical means for minimizing occupational risk.

References

1. American Society of Hospital Pharmacists. ASHP technical assistance bulletin on handling cytotoxic drugs in hospitals. *Am J Hosp Pharm.* 1985; 42:131–7.
2. Yodaiken R. Safe handling of cytotoxic drugs by health care personnel. Washington, DC: Occupational Safety and Health Administration; 1986 Jan 29. (Instructional publication 8-1.1).
3. U.S. Public Health Service, National Institutes of Health. Recommendations for the safe handling of parenteral antineoplastic drugs. Washington, DC: U.S. Department of Health and Human Services; 1983. (NIH publication 83-2621).
4. Recommendations for handling cytotoxic agents. Providence, RI: National Study Commission on Cytotoxic Exposure; 1987 Sep.
5. AMA Council on Scientific Affairs. Guidelines for handling parenteral antineoplastics. *JAMA.* 1985; 253:1590–2.
6. Scott SA. Antineoplastic drug information and handling guidelines for office-based physicians. *Am J Hosp Pharm.* 1984; 41:2402–3.
7. Barstow J. Safe handling of cytotoxic agents in the home. *Home Healthc Nurse.* 1986; 3:46–7.
8. Barry LK, Booher RB. Promoting the responsible handling of antineoplastic agents in the community. *Oncol Nurs Forum.* 1985; 12:40–6.
9. Berk PD, Goldberg JD, Silverstein MN, et al. In-creased incidence of leukemia in polycythemia vera associated with chlorambucil therapy. *N Engl J Med.* 1981; 304:441–7.
10. Penn I. Occurrence of cancer in immune deficiencies. *Cancer.* 1974; 34:858–66.
11. Schafer AI. Teratogenic effects of antileukemic therapy. *Arch Intern Med.* 1981; 141:514–5.
12. Stephens JD, Golbus MS, Miller TR, et al. Multiple congenital abnormalities in a fetus exposed to 5-fluo-rouracil during the first trimester. *Am J Obstet Gynecol.* 1980; 137:747–9.
13. IARC monographs on the evaluation of the carcinogenic risk of chemicals to humans. Geneva, Switzerland: World Health Organization; 1981.
14. Benedict WF, Baker MS, Haroun L, et al. Mutagenicity of cancer chemotherapeutic agents in the *Salmonella/microsome* test. *Cancer Res.* 1977; 37:2209–13.
15. Falck K, Grohn P, Sorsa M, et al. Mutagenicity in urine of nurses handling cytostatic drugs. *Lancet.* 1979; 1:1250–1.
16. Anderson RW, Puckett WH, Dana WJ, et al. Risk of handling injectable antineoplastic agents. *Am J Hosp Pharm.* 1982; 39:1881–7.
17. Norppa H, Sorsa M, Vainio H, et al. Increased sister chromatid exchange frequencies in lymphocytes of nurses handling cytostatic drugs. *Scand J Work Environ Health.* 1980; 6:299–301.
18. Waksvik H, Klepp O, Brogger A. Chromosome analyses of nurses handling cytostatic agents. *Cancer Treat Rep.* 1981; 65:607–10.
19. Nikula E, Kiviniitty K, Leisti J, et al. Chromosome aberrations in lymphocytes of nurses handling cytostatic agents. *Scand J Work Environ Health.* 1984; 10:71–4.
20. Chrysostomou A, Morley AA, Sehadri R. Mutation frequency in nurses and pharmacists working with cytotoxic drugs. *Aust N Z J Med.* 1984; 14:831–4.
21. Rogers B, Emmett EA. Handling antineoplastic agents: urine mutagenicity in nurses. *Image J Nurs Sch.* 1987; 19:108–13.
22. Palmer RG, Dore CJ, Denman AM. Chlorambucil-induced chromosome damage to human lymphocytes is dose-dependent and cumulative. *Lancet.* 1984; 1:246–9.
23. Sotaniemi EA, Sutinen S, Arranto AJ, et al. Liver damage in nurses handling cytostatic agents. *Acta Med Scand.* 1983; 214:181–9.
24. How real is the hazard? *Lancet.* 1984; 1:203.
25. Tuffnell PG, Gannon MT, Dong A, et al. Limitations of urinary mutagen assays for monitoring occupational exposure to antineoplastic drugs. *Am J Hosp Pharm.* 1986; 43:344–8.
26. Cloak MM, Connor TH, Stevens KR, et al. Occupational exposure of nursing personnel to antineoplastic agents. *Oncol Nurs Forum.* 1985; 12:33–9.
27. Connor TH, Anderson RW. Demonstrating mutagenicity testing using the Ames test. *Am J Hosp Pharm.* 1985; 42:783–4.
28. Connor TH, Theiss JC, Anderson RW, et al. Re-evaluation of urine mutagenicity of pharmacy personnel exposed to antineoplastic agents. *Am J Hosp Pharm.* 1986; 43:1236–9.
29. Jagun O, Ryan M, Waldrom HA. Urinary thioether excretion in nurses handling cytotoxic drugs. *Lancet.* 1982; 2:443–4.
30. Hirst M, Tse S, Mills DG, et al. Occupational exposure

to cyclophosphamide. *Lancet*. 1984; 1:186–8.

31. Venitt S, Crofton-Sleigh C, Hunt J, et al. Monitoring exposure of nursing and pharmacy personnel to cytotoxic drugs: urinary mutation assays and urinary platinum as markers of absorption. *Lancet*. 1984; 1:74–6.

32. Neal A deW, Wadden RA, Chiou WL. Exposure of hospital workers to airborne antineoplastic agents. *Am J Hosp Pharm*. 1983; 40:597–601.

33. Kleinberg ML, Quinn MJ. Airborne drug levels in a laminar flow hood. *Am J Hosp Pharm*. 1981; 38:1301–3.

34. Gililland J, Weinstein L. The effects of chemotherapeutic agents on the developing fetus. *Obstet Gynecol Surv*. 1983; 38:6–13.

35. Hemminki K, Kyyronen P, Lindbohm ML. Spontaneous abortions and malformations in the offspring of nurses exposed to anesthetic gases, cytostatic drugs and other potential hazards in hospitals, based on registered information of outcome. *J Epidemiol Community Health*. 1985; 39:141–7.

36. Selevan SH, Lindbohm ML, Hornung RW, et al. A study of occupational exposure to antineoplastic drugs and fetal loss in nurses. *N Engl J Med*. 1985; 333:1173–8.

37. Richter P, Calamera JC, Morgenfeld MC, et al. Effect of chlorambucil on spermatogenesis in the human with malignant lymphoma. *Cancer*. 1970; 25:1026–30.

38. Maguire LC. Fertility and cancer therapy. *Postgrad Med*. 1979; 65:293–5.

39. Sherins JJ, DeVita VT Jr. Effect of drug treatment for lymphoma on male reproductive capacity. *Ann Intern Med*. 1973; 79:216–20.

40. Gregoire RE, Segal R, Hale KM. Handling antineoplastic-drug admixtures at cancer centers: practices and pharmacist attitudes. *Am J Hosp Pharm*. 1987; 44:1090–5.

41. Cohen IA, Newland SJ, Kirking DM. Injectable-antineoplastic-drug practices in Michigan hospitals. *Am J Hosp Pharm*. 1987; 44:1096–105.

42. Hoy RH, Stump LM. Effect of an air-venting filter device on aerosol production from vials. *Am J Hosp Pharm*. 1984; 41:324–6.

43. National Sanitation Foundation Standard: Class II (laminar flow) Biohazard Cabinetry. Standard 49. Ann Arbor, MI: National Sanitation Foundation; 1987 Jun.

44. McDiarmid MA, Egan T, Furio M, et al. Sampling for airborne fluorouracil in a hospital drug preparation area. *Am J Hosp Pharm*. 1986; 43:1942–5.

45. Clark RP, Goff MR. The potassium iodide method for determining protection factors in open-fronted microbiological safety cabinets. *J Appl Biol*. 1981; 51:461–73.

46. Connor TH, Laidlaw JL, Theiss JC, et al. Permeability of latex and polyvinyl chloride gloves to carmustine. *Am J Hosp Pharm*. 1984; 41:676–9.

47. Laidlaw JL, Connor TH, Theiss JC, et al. Permeability of latex and polyvinyl chloride gloves to 20 antineoplastic drugs. *Am J Hosp Pharm*. 1984; 41:2618–23.

48. Slevin ML, Ang LM, Johnston A, et al. The efficiency of protective gloves used in the handling of cytotoxic drugs. *Cancer Chemother Pharmacol*. 1984; 12:151–3.

49. Stoikes ME, Carlson JD, Farris FF, et al. Permeability of latex and polyvinyl chloride gloves to fluorouracil and methotrexate. *Am J Hosp Pharm*. 1987; 44:1341–6.

50. Laidlaw JL, Connor TH, Theiss JC, et al. Permeability of four disposable protective-clothing materials to seven antineoplastic drugs. *Am J Hosp Pharm*. 1985; 42:2449–54.

51. Falck K, Sorsa M, Vainio H. Use of the bacterial fluctuation test to detect mutagenicity in urine of nurses handling cytostatic drugs. *Mutat Res*. 1981; 85:236–7.

52. Myers CE. Preparing a list of cytotoxic agents. *Am J Hosp Pharm*. 1987; 44:1296, 1298. Questions and Answers.

53. National Institute of Occupational Safety and Health. Respirator decision logic. Washington, DC: U.S. Department of Health and Human Services; 1987. (DHHS, NIOSH publication 87–108).

54. Commissioner, Federal Supply Service, General Services Administration. Federal Standard 209C. Clean room and work station requirements, controlled environments. Washington, DC: U.S. Government Printing Office; 1988.

55. Bryan D, Marback MA. Laminar-airflow equipment certification: what the pharmacist needs to know. *Am J Hosp Pharm*. 1984; 41:1343–9.

56. Wilson JP, Solimando DA. Aseptic technique as a safety precaution in the preparation of antineoplastic agents. *Hosp Pharm*. 1981; 15:575–81.

57. F40 CFR 261.5.

58. Vaccari PL, Tonat K, DeChristoforo R, et al. Disposal of antineoplastic wastes at the National Institutes of Health. *Am J Hosp Pharm*. 1984; 41:87–93.

59. Castegnaro M, Adams J, Armour MA, et al., eds. Laboratory decontamination and destruction of carcinogens in laboratory wastes: some antineoplastic agents. International Agency for Research on Cancer Scientific Publication 73. Fair Lawn, NJ: Oxford University Press; 1985.

Appendix A—Glossary

Biohazard: An infectious agent presenting a real or potential risk to humans and the environment.

Carcinogen: Any cancer-producing substance.

Chemotherapy: The treatment of disease by chemical means; first applied to use of chemicals that affect the causative organism unfavorably but do not harm the patient; currently used to describe drug (chemical) therapy of neoplastic diseases (cancer).

Clastogenic: Giving rise to or inducing disruption or breakage, as of chromosomes.

Contamination: The deposition of potentially dangerous material where it is not desired, particularly where its presence may be harmful or constitute a hazard.

Cytotoxic: Possessing a specific destructive action on certain cells; used commonly in referring to antineoplastic drugs that selectively kill dividing cells.

Decontamination: Removal, neutralization, or destruction of a toxic (harmful) agent.

Exposure: The condition of being subjected to something, as to chemicals, that may have a harmful effect. Acute exposure is exposure of short duration, usually exposure of heavy intensity; chronic exposure is long-term exposure, either continuous or intermittent, usually referring to exposure of low intensity.

Genotoxic: Damaging to DNA; pertaining to agents (radiation or chemical substances) known to damage DNA, thereby causing mutations or cancer.

Hazardous: Dangerous; risky; representing a health risk.

Mutagen: Chemical or physical agent that induces or increases genetic mutations by causing changes in DNA.

Plenum: Space within a biohazard cabinet where air flows;

plenums may either be under positive (greater than atmospheric pressure) or negative pressure, depending on whether the air is "blown" or "sucked" through the space.

Respirator: A National Institute of Occupational Safety and Health (NIOSH) approved, air-purifying half-mask respirator equipped with a high-efficiency filter; may be disposable (discarded after the end of its recommended period of use).

Trough: Drain spillage trough; an area below the biological safety cabinet's work surface, provided to retain spillage from the work area.

Utility Gloves: Heavy, disposable gloves, similar to household latex gloves.

Appendix B—Classification of Biohazard Cabinetry (Biological Safety Cabinets)[43]

Class I: A ventilated cabinet for personnel and environmental protection, with an unrecirculated inward airflow away from the operator.
Note: The cabinet exhaust air is treated to protect the environment before it is discharged to the outside atmos-phere. This cabinet is suitable for work with low- and moderate-risk biological agents when no product protection is required.

Class II: A ventilated cabinet for personnel, product, and environmental protection, having an open front with inward airflow for personnel protection, high-efficiency particulate air (HEPA) filtered laminar airflow for product protection, and HEPA-filtered exhausted air for environmental protection.
Note: When toxic chemicals or radionuclides are used as adjuncts to biological studies or pharmaceutical work, Class II cabinets designed and constructed for this purpose should be used.

- *Type A (formerly designated Type 1)*: Cabinets that (1) maintain minimum calculated average inflow velocity of 75 feet per minute (fpm) through the work area access opening; (2) have HEPA-filtered downflow air from a common plenum (i.e., plenum from which a portion of the air is exhausted from the cabinet and the remainder is supplied to the work area); (3) may exhaust HEPA-filtered air back into the laboratory; and (4) may have positive-pressure-contaminated ducts and plenums. Type A cabinets are suitable for work with low- to moderate-risk biological agents in the absence of volatile toxic chemicals and volatile radionuclides.

- *Type B1 (formerly designated Type 2)*: Cabinets that (1) maintain a minimum (calculated or measured) average inflow velocity of 100 fpm through the work area access opening; (2) have HEPA-filtered downflow air composed largely of uncontaminated recirculated inflow air; (3) exhaust most of the contaminated downflow air through a dedicated duct exhausted to the atmosphere after it passes through a HEPA filter; and (4) have all biologically contaminated ducts and plenums under negative pressure or surrounded by negative-pressure ducts and plenums. Type B1 cabinets are suitable for work with low- to moderate-risk biological agents. They may also be used with biological agents treated with minute quantities of toxic chemicals and trace amounts of radionuclides required as an adjunct to microbiological studies if work is done in the directly exhausted portion of the cabinet or if the chemicals or radionuclides will not interfere with the work when recirculated in the downflow air.

- *Type B2 (sometimes referred to as "total exhaust")*: Cabinets that (1) maintain a minimum (calculated or measured) average inflow velocity of 100 fpm through the work area access opening; (2) have HEPA-filtered downflow air drawn from the laboratory or the outside air (i.e., downflow air is not recirculated from the cabinet exhaust air); (3) exhaust all inflow and down-flow air to the atmosphere after filtration through a HEPA filter without recirculation in the cabinet or return to the laboratory room air; and (4) have all contaminated ducts and plenums under negative pressure or surrounded by directly exhausted (nonrecirc-ulated through the work area) negative-pressure ducts and plenums. Type B2 cabinets are suitable for work with low- to moderate-risk biological agents. They may also be used with biological agents treated with toxic chemicals and radionuclides required as an adjunct to microbiological studies.

- *Type B3 (sometimes referred to as "convertible cabinets")*: Cabinets that (1) maintain a minimum (calculated or measured) average inflow velocity of 100 fpm through the work access opening; (2) have HEPA-filtered downflow air that is a portion of the mixed downflow and inflow air from a common exhaust plenum; (3) discharge all exhaust air to the outdoor atmosphere after HEPA filtration; and (4) have all biologically contaminated ducts and plenums under negative pressure or surrounded by negative-pressure ducts and plenums. Type B3 cabinets are suitable for work with low- to moderate-risk biological agents treated with minute quantities of toxic chemicals and trace quantities of radionuclides that will not interfere with the work if recirculated in the downflow air.

- *Other Types*: Other cabinets may be considered Class II if they meet these requirements for performance, durability, reliability, safety, operational integrity, and cleanability.

Class III: A totally enclosed, ventilated cabinet of gas-tight construction. Operations in the cabinet are conducted through attached rubber gloves. The cabinet is maintained under negative air pressure of at least 0.5 inch (12.7 mm) water gauge (wg). Supply air is drawn into the cabinet through HEPA filters. The exhaust air is treated by double HEPA filtration or by HEPA filtration and incineration.

This Technical Assistance Bulletin was reviewed in 1996 by the Council on Professional Affairs and by the ASHP Board of Directors and was found to still be appropriate.

Revised by ASHP's Clinical Affairs Department in collaboration with Luci A. Power, M.S., Senior Consultant, Power Enterprises, San Francisco, CA. Reviewed by the officers of the ASHP Special Interest Group (SIG) on Oncology Pharmacy Practice and approved by the ASHP Council on Professional Affairs, September 20, 1989. Approved by the ASHP Board of Directors, November 15–16, 1989. Supersedes a previous version approved by the Board of Directors on November 14, 1984.

The bibliographic citation for this document is as follows: American Society of Hospital Pharmacists. ASHP technical assistance bulletin on handling cytotoxic and hazardous drugs. *Am J Hosp Pharm.* 1990; 47:1033–49.

ASHP Technical Assistance Bulletin on Compounding Nonsterile Products in Pharmacies

Introduction

Pharmacists are the only health care providers formally trained in the art and science of compounding medications.[1,2] Therefore, pharmacists are expected, by the medical community and the public, to possess the knowledge and skills necessary to compound extemporaneous preparations. Pharmacists have a responsibility to provide compounding services for patients with unique drug product needs.

This Technical Assistance Bulletin is intended to assist pharmacists in the extemporaneous compounding of nonsterile drug products for individual patients. Included in this document is information on facilities and equipment, ingredient selection, training, documentation and record keeping, stability and beyond-use dating, packaging and labeling, and limited batch compounding. This document is not intended for manufacturers or licensed repackagers.

Facilities and Equipment

Facilities. It is not necessary that compounding activities be located in a separate facility; however, the compounding area should be located sufficiently away from routine dispensing and counseling functions and high traffic areas. The area should be isolated from potential interruptions, chemical contaminants, and sources of dust and particulate matter. To minimize chemical contaminants, the immediate area and work counter should be free of previously used drugs and chemicals. To minimize dust and particulate matter, cartons and boxes should not be stored or opened in the compounding area. The compounding area should not contain dust-collecting overhangs (e.g., ceiling utility pipes, hanging light fixtures) and ledges (e.g., windowsills). Additionally, at least one sink should be located in or near the compounding area for hand washing before compounding operations. Proper temperature and humidity control within the compounding area or facility is desirable.

Work areas should be well lighted, and work surfaces should be level and clean. The work surface should be smooth, impervious, free of cracks and crevices (preferably seamless), and nonshedding. Surfaces should be cleaned at both the beginning and the end of each distinct compounding operation with an appropriate cleaner or solvent. The entire compounding facility should be cleaned daily or weekly (as needed) but not during the actual process of compounding.

Equipment. The equipment needed to compound a drug product depends upon the particular dosage form requested. Although boards of pharmacy publish lists of required equipment and accessories, these lists are not intended to limit the equipment available to pharmacists for compounding.[2] Equipment should be maintained in good working order. Pharmacists are responsible for obtaining the required equipment and accessories and ensuring that equipment is properly maintained and maintenance is documented.

Weighing Equipment. In addition to a torsion balance, pharmacists who routinely compound may need to use a top-loading electronic balance that has a capacity of at least 300 g, a sensitivity of ±1 mg (or 0.1 mg), and 1-mg, 100-mg, 1-g, and 100-g weights for checking. Balances should be maintained in areas of low humidity and should be stored on flat, nonvibrating surfaces away from drafts. At least annually, the performance of balances should be checked according to the guidelines found in *Remington's Pharmaceutical Sciences,*[3] *USP XXII NF XVII: The United States Pharmacopeia–The National Formulary (USP–NF),*[4] or *USP DI Volume III: Approved Drug Products and Legal Requirements*[5] or the instructions of the balance manufacturer. Performance should be documented.

Weights should be stored in rigid, compartmentalized boxes and handled with metal, plastic, or plastic-tipped forceps—not fingers—to avoid scratching or soiling. Since most Class III prescription balances are only accurate to ±5 or 10 mg, Class P weights may be used for compounding purposes.[4] The *USP–NF* recommends that the class of weights used be chosen to limit the error to 0.1%. In practical terms this means that Class P weights can be used for weighing quantities greater than 100 mg.

The minimum weighable quantity must be determined for any balance being used for compounding. To avoid errors of 5% or more on a Class III balance with a sensitivity requirement of 6 mg, quantities of less than 120 mg of any substance should not be weighed. Smaller quantities may be weighed on more sensitive balances. If an amount is needed that is less than the minimum weighable quantity determined for a balance, an aliquot method of measurement should be used.

Measuring Equipment. The pharmacist should use judgment in selecting measuring equipment. The recommendations given in the *USP–NF* General Information section on volumetric apparatus should be followed. For maximum accuracy in measuring liquids, a pharmacist should select a graduate with a capacity equal to or slightly larger than the volume to be measured. The general rule is to measure no less than 20% of the capacity of a graduate. Calibrated syringes of the appropriate size may be preferred over graduated cylinders for measuring viscous liquids such as glycerin or mineral oil, since these liquids drain slowly and incompletely from graduated cylinders. Viscous liquids may also be weighed if this is more convenient, provided that the appropriate conversions from volume to weight are made by using the specific gravity of the liquid. Thick, opaque liquids should be weighed. For example, if a formulation specifies 1.5 mL of a liquid, it is better to use a 3-mL syringe with appropriate graduations to measure 1.5 mL than to use a 10-mL graduated cylinder, since quantities of less than 2.0 mL cannot be accurately measured in a 10-mL graduate. Also, if an opaque, viscous chemical, such as Coal Tar, USP, must be measured, it is more accurate to weigh the substance than to try to read a meniscus on a graduated cylinder or a fill line on a syringe.

For volumes smaller than 1 mL, micropipettes are recommended, in sizes to cover the range of volumes measured. Two or three variable pipettes can usually cover the range from about 50 µL to 1 mL.

Although conical graduates are convenient for mixing

solutions, the error in reading the bottom of the meniscus increases as the sides flare toward the top of the graduate. Therefore, for accurate measurements, cylindrical graduates are preferred. Conical graduates having a capacity of less than 25 mL should not be used in prescription compounding.[4]

Compounding Equipment. Pharmacists need at least two types of mortars and pestles—one glass and one Wedgwood or porcelain. The sizes of each will depend on the drug products being compounded. Glass mortars should be used for liquid preparations (solutions and suspensions) and for mixing chemicals that stain or are oily. Generally, glass mortars should be used for antineoplastic agents. Because of their rough surface, Wedgwood mortars are preferred for reducing the size of dry crystals and hard powder particles and for preparing emulsions. Porcelain mortars have a smoother surface than Wedgwood mortars and are ideal for blending powders and pulverizing soft aggregates or crystals. When Wedgwood mortars are used for small amounts of crystals or powders, the inside surface may first be lightly dusted with lactose to fill any crevices in which the crystals or powders might lodge. If the contact surfaces of the mortar and pestle become smooth with use, rubbing them with a small amount of sand or emery powder may adequately roughen them. Over extended use, a pestle and a mortar become shaped to each other's curvature. Thus, to ensure maximum contact between the surface of the head of each pestle and the interior of its corresponding mortar, pestles and mortars should not be interchanged.[3]

The compounding area should be stocked with appropriate supplies. Although supply selection depends on the types of products compounded, all areas should have weighing papers, weighing cups, or both to protect balance pans and spatulas. Glassine weighing papers (as opposed to bond weighing paper) should be used for products such as ointments, creams, and some dry chemicals. Disposable weighing dishes should also be stocked for substances like Coal Tar, USP.

Each compounding area should have stainless steel and plastic spatulas for mixing ointments and creams and handling dry chemicals. The pharmacist should exercise judgment in selecting the size and type of spatula. Small spatula blades (6 inches long or less) are preferred for handling dry chemicals, but larger spatula blades (>6 inches) are preferred for large amounts of ointments or creams and for preparing compactible powder blends for capsules. Plastic spatulas should be used for chemicals that may react with stainless steel blades. A variety of spatulas should be stocked in the compounding area, including 4-, 6-, and 8-inch stainless steel spatulas (one each) and 4- and 6-inch plastic spatulas (one each). Imprinted spatulas should not be used in compounding, since the imprinted ink on the spatula blade may contaminate the product.

The compounding area should contain an ointment slab, pill tile, or parchment ointment pad. Although parchment ointment pads are convenient and reduce cleanup time, parchment paper cannot be used for the preparation of creams because it will absorb water. Therefore, an ointment slab or pill tile is necessary. If suppositories are compounded, appropriate suppository molds, either reusable or disposable, should be available.

Other useful equipment and supplies may include funnels, filter paper, beakers, glass stirring rods, a source of heat (hot plate or microwave oven), a refrigerator, and a freezer—in some cases, an ultrafreezer capable of maintaining temperatures as low as –80 °C.

Ingredients

Ideally, only USP or NF chemicals manufactured by FDA-inspected manufacturers should be used for compounding. Although chemicals labeled USP or NF meet *USP–NF* standards for strength, quality, and purity for human drug products, the facilities in which the chemicals were manufactured may not meet FDA Good Manufacturing Practice (GMP) standards. In the event that a needed chemical is not available from an FDA-inspected facility, the pharmacist should, by next best preference, obtain a USP or NF product. If that is not available, the pharmacist should use professional judgment and may have to obtain the highest-grade chemical possible. Chemical grades that may be considered in this situation are ACS grade (meeting or exceeding specifications listed for reagent chemicals by the American Chemical Society) and FCC grade (meeting or exceeding requirements defined by the Food Chemicals Codex). Additional professional judgment is especially necessary in cases of chemical substances that have not been approved for *any* medical use. Particularly in these cases, but also in others as needed, the pharmacist, prescriber, and patient should be well informed of the risks involved.

Selection of ingredients may also depend on the dosage form to be compounded. In most cases, the prescriber specifies a particular dosage form, such as a topical ointment, oral solution or rectal suppository. Sometimes, however, the prescriber relies on the pharmacist to decide on an appropriate form. Irrespective of how the drug order is written, the pharmacist should evaluate the appropriateness of ingredients and the drug delivery system recommended. Factors to consider in selecting the dosage form include (1) physical and chemical characteristics of the active ingredient, (2) possible routes of administration that will produce the desired therapeutic effect (e.g., oral or topical), (3) patient characteristics (e.g., age, level of consciousness, ability to swallow a solid dosage form), (4) specific characteristics of the disease being treated, (5) comfort for the patient, and (6) ease or convenience of administration.

In checking the physical form of each ingredient, the pharmacist should not confuse drug substances that are available in more than one form. For example, coal tar is available as Coal Tar, USP, or Coal Tar Topical Solution, USP; phenol is available as Liquified Phenol, USP, or Phenol, USP; sulfur is available as Precipitated Sulfur, USP, or Sublimed Sulfur, USP. If ingredients are liquids, the pharmacist should consider compounding liquid dosage forms such as solutions, syrups, or elixirs for the final product. If ingredients are crystals or powders and the final dosage form is intended to be a dry dosage form, options such as divided powders (powder papers) or capsules should be considered. If ingredients are both liquids and dry forms, liquid formulations such as solutions, suspensions, elixirs, syrups, and emulsions should be considered.

Care must be exercised when using commercial drug products as a source of active ingredients. For example, extended-release or delayed-release products should not be crushed. Also, since chemicals such as preservatives and excipients in commercial products may affect the overall stability and bioavailability of the compounded product, their presence should not be ignored. Information on preservatives and excipients in specific commercial products can be found in package inserts and also in the dosage form section of selected product monographs in *USP DI Volume I*.[6]

If an injectable drug product is a possible source of active ingredient, the pharmacist should check the salt form of the injectable product to make sure it is the same salt form ordered. If it is necessary to use a different salt because of physical or chemical compatibility considerations or product availability, the pharmacist should consult with the prescriber. Some injectable products contain active constituents in the form of prodrugs that may not be active when administered by other routes. For example, if an injectable solution is a possible source of active ingredient for an oral product, the pharmacist must consider the stability of the drug in gastric fluids, the first-pass effect, and palatability. Also, if injectable powders for reconstitution are used, expiration dating may have to be quite short.

Storage

All chemicals and drug products must be stored according to *USP–NF* and manufacturer specifications. Most chemicals and drug products marketed for compounding use are packaged by the manufacturer in tight, light-resistant containers. Chemicals intended for compounding should be purchased in small quantities and stored in the manufacturer's original container, which is labeled with product and storage information. This practice fosters the use of fresh chemicals and ensures that the manufacturer's label remains with the lot of chemical on hand. Certificates of purity for chemical ingredients should be filed for a period of time no less than the state's time requirement for retention of dispensing records.

The manufacturer's label instructions for storage should be followed explicitly to ensure the integrity of chemicals and drug products and to protect employees. Most chemicals and commercial drug products may be stored at controlled room temperature, between 15 and 30 °C (59 and 86 °F); however, the pharmacist should always check the manufacturer's label for any special storage requirements. Storage information provided for specific commercial drug products in *USP DI Volume I* and on product labels follows the definitions for storage temperatures found in the General Notices and Requirements section of *USP–NF*. An acceptable refrigerator maintains temperatures between 2 and 8 °C (36 and 46 °F); an acceptable freezer maintains temperatures between –20 and –10 °C (–4 to +14 °F).

To protect pharmacy employees and property, hazardous products such as acetone and flexible collodion must be stored appropriately. Safety storage cabinets in various sizes are available from laboratory suppliers.

Personnel

Compounding personnel include pharmacists and supportive personnel engaged in any aspect of the compounding procedures.

Training. The pharmacist—who is responsible for ensuring that the best technical knowledge and skill, most careful and accurate procedures, and prudent professional judgment are consistently applied in the compounding of pharmaceuticals—must supervise all compounding activities and ensure that supportive personnel are adequately trained to perform assigned functions. Both pharmacists and the compounding personnel they supervise should participate in programs designed to enhance and maintain competence in compounding. Training programs should include instruction in the following areas:

- Proper use of compounding equipment such as balances and measuring devices—including guidelines for selecting proper measuring devices, limitations of weighing equipment and measuring apparatus, and the importance of accuracy in measuring.
- Pharmaceutical techniques needed for preparing compounded dosage forms (e.g., levigation, trituration, methods to increase dissolution, geometric dilution).
- Properties of dosage forms (see Pharmaceutical Dosage Forms in *USP–NF*) to be compounded and related factors such as stability, storage considerations, and handling procedures.
- Literature in which information on stability, solubility, and related material can be found (see suggested references at the end of this document).
- Handling of nonhazardous and hazardous materials in the work area, including protective measures for avoiding exposure, emergency procedures to follow in the event of exposure, and the location of Material Safety Data Sheets (MSDSs) in the facility.[7–10]
- Use and interpretation of chemical and pharmaceutical symbols and abbreviations in medication orders and in product formulation directions.
- Pharmaceutical calculations.

Procedures should be established to verify the ability of staff to meet established competencies. These procedures may include observation, written tests, or quality control testing of finished products.

Attire. Personnel engaged in compounding should wear clean clothing appropriate for the duties they perform. Protective apparel, such as head, face, hand, and arm coverings, should be worn as necessary to preclude contamination of products and to protect workers.

Generally, a clean laboratory jacket is considered appropriate attire for most personnel performing nonsterile compounding activities. Personnel involved in compounding hazardous materials should wear safety goggles, gloves, a mask or respirator, double gowns, and foot covers as required, depending on the substance being handled. To avoid microbial contamination of compounded drug products, written policies should be established that address appropriate precautions to be observed if an employee has an open lesion or an illness. Depending on the situation, an affected employee may be required to wear special protective apparel, such as a mask or gloves, or may be directed to avoid all contact with compounding procedures.

Reference Materials

Pharmacists and supportive personnel must have ready access to reference materials on all aspects of compounding (see suggested references at the end of this document). Earlier editions of some references, such as *Remington's Pharmaceutical Sciences,* provide more comprehensive compounding information than do the later editions. Information on compounding extemporaneous dosage forms from commercially available products can sometimes be obtained from the product's FDA-approved labeling (package insert), the manufacturer, a local pharmacy college, or a drug information center. It is essential that the stability and proper storage conditions for extemporaneous products be thoroughly researched. Therefore, the availability of adequate references and appropriate training in the use of the references is important.

Documentation and Record Keeping

Each step of the compounding process should be documented. Pharmacists should maintain at least four sets of records in the compounding area: (1) compounding formulas and procedures, (2) a log of all compounded items, including batch records and sample batch labels (see section on packaging and labeling), (3) equipment-maintenance records, including documentation of checks of balances, refrigerators, and freezers, and (4) a record of ingredients purchased, including certificates of purity for chemicals (see section on ingredient selection) and MSDSs.

Compounding procedures should be documented in enough detail that preparations can be replicated and the history of each ingredient can be traced. Documentation should include a record of who prepared the product (if the compounder is not a pharmacist, the supervising pharmacist should also sign the compounding record); all names, lot numbers, and quantities of ingredients used; the order of mixing, including any interim procedures used (such as preparing a solution and using an aliquot); the assigned beyond-use date; and any special storage requirements (see section on stability and expiration dating). Compounding formulas and procedures should be written in a typeface that can be read easily. If formulas originate from published articles, copies of the articles should be attached to or filed with the written procedures.

Equipment maintenance and calibrations should be documented and the record maintained in an equipment-maintenance record file. Refrigerator and freezer thermometers should be checked and documented routinely, as should alarm systems indicating that temperatures are outside of acceptable limits.

Follow-up contact with patients who have received extemporaneously compounded products is recommended to ascertain that the product is physically stable and that no adverse effects have occurred from use of the product. Documentation of the contact and the findings is recommended.

Stability, Expiration, and Beyond-Use Dating

The *USP–NF*[4] defines stability as the extent to which a dosage form retains, within specified limits and throughout its period of storage and use, the same properties and characteristics that it possessed at the time of its preparation. The *USP–NF* lists the following five types of stability:

- Chemical
- Physical
- Microbiological
- Therapeutic
- Toxicological

Factors affecting stability include the properties of each ingredient, whether therapeutically active or inactive. Environmental factors such as temperature, radiation, light, humidity, and air can also affect stability. Similarly, such factors as particle size, pH, the properties of water and other solvents

employed, the nature of the container, and the presence of other substances resulting from contamination or from the intentional mixing of products can influence stability.[4]

Since compounded drug products are intended for consumption immediately or storage for a very limited time, stability evaluation and expiration dating are different for these products than for manufactured drug products. According to criteria for assigning dating in the *USP–NF*[4] General Notices and Requirements section and the Code of Federal Regulations,[11] the pharmacist labeling extemporaneously compounded drug products should be concerned with the beyond-use date as used by *USP–NF* or the expiration date as used by the Code of Federal Regulations. For uniformity, the term *beyond-use date* will be used in the remainder of this bulletin. The beyond-use date is defined as that date after which a dispensed product should no longer be used by a patient.

Determination of the period during which a compounded product may be usable after dispensing should be based on available stability information and reasonable patient needs with respect to the intended drug therapy. When a commercial drug product is used as a source of active ingredient, its expiration date can often be used as a factor in determining a beyond-use date. For stability or expiration information on commercial drug products, the pharmacist can refer to *USP DI Volume I*.[6] If no information is available, the manufacturer should be contacted. When the active ingredient is a USP or NF product, the pharmacist may be able to use the expiration dating of similar commercial products for guidance in assigning a beyond-use date. In addition, the pharmacist can often refer to published literature to obtain stability data on the same active ingredient under varying conditions and in different formulations.[12]

The pharmacist must assess the potential for instability that may result from the new environment for the active ingredients—from the combination of ingredients and the packaging materials. According to *USP–NF*,[4] hydrolysis, oxidation-reduction, and photolysis are the most common chemical reactions that cause instability. When the possibility of such reactions exists, the pharmacist should seek additional stability data or consider other approaches. These could, in extreme cases, include the preparation and dispensing of more than one compounded drug product or the use of alternative methods of dosing. For some drugs, the latter methods might include, for example, crushing a tablet or emptying the contents of a hard gelatin capsule into an appropriate food substance at each dosing time.

In assigning a beyond-use date for compounded drug products, the pharmacist should use all available stability information, plus education and experience in deciding how factors affecting product stability should be weighted. In the absence of stability data to the contrary or any indication of a stability problem, the following general criteria for assigning maximum beyond-use dates are recommended. It must be emphasized that these are *general* criteria. Professional judgment as discussed elsewhere in this section must be used in deciding when these general criteria may not be appropriate.

- When a manufactured final-dosage-form product is used as a source of active ingredient, use no more than 25% of the manufacturer's remaining expiration dating or six months, whichever is less;
- When a USP or NF chemical not from a manufactured final-dosage-form product is used, use no more than six months;

- In other cases, use the intended period of therapy or no more than 30 days, whichever is less.

All compounded products should be observed for signs of instability. Observations should be performed during preparation of the drug product and any storage period that may occur before the compounded drug product is dispensed. A list of observable indications of instability for solid, liquid, and semisolid dosage forms appears in *USP–NF*.

Packaging and Labeling

The packaging of extemporaneously compounded products for ambulatory patients should comply with regulations pertaining to the Poison Prevention Packaging Act of 1970. These regulations can be found in *USP–NF*.[4]

Containers for compounded products should be appropriate for the dosage form compounded. For example, to minimize administration errors, oral liquids should never be packaged in syringes intended to be used for injection.

The drug product container should not interact physically or chemically with the product so as to alter the strength, quality, or purity of the compounded product. Glass and plastic are commonly used in containers for compounded products. To ensure container inertness, visibility, strength, rigidity, moisture protection, ease of reclosure, and economy of packaging, glass containers have been the most widely used for compounded products.[3] Amber glass and some plastic containers may be used to protect light-sensitive products from degradation; however, glass that transmits ultraviolet or violet light rays (this includes green, blue, and clear ["flint"] glass) should not be used to protect light-sensitive products.

The use of plastic containers for compounded products has increased because plastic is less expensive and lighter in weight than glass. Since compounded products are intended for immediate use, most capsules, ointments, and creams should be stable in high-density plastic vials or ointment jars. Only plastic containers meeting *USP–NF* standards should be used.[4] Reclosable plastic bags may be acceptable for selected divided powders that are intended to be used within a short period of time.

Each compounded product should be appropriately labeled according to state and federal regulations. Labels should include the generic or chemical name of active ingredients, strength or quantity, pharmacy lot number, beyond-use date, and any special storage requirements. If a commercial product has been used as a source of drug, the generic name of the product should be used on the label. The trade name should not be used because, once the commercial drug product has been altered, it no longer exists as the approved commercial product. Listing the names and quantities of inactive ingredients on labels is also encouraged. The coining of short names for convenience (e.g., "Johnson's solution") is strongly discouraged; these names provide no assistance to others who may need to identify ingredients (e.g., in emergency circumstances).

Capsules should be labeled with the quantity (micrograms or milligrams) of active ingredient(s) per capsule. Oral liquids should be labeled with the strength or concentration per dose (e.g., 125 mg/5 mL or 10 meq/15 mL). If the quantity of an active ingredient is a whole number, the number should not be typed with a decimal point followed by a zero. For example, the strength of a capsule containing 25 mg of active ingredient should be labeled as 25 mg and not 25.0 mg. In cases where the dosage strength is less than a whole number, a zero should precede the decimal point (e.g., 0.25 µg).[13]

In expressing salt forms of chemicals on a label, it is permissible to use atomic abbreviations. For example, HCl may be used for hydrochloride, HBr for hydrobromide, Na for sodium, and K for potassium.

Vehicles should also be stated on labels, especially if similar products are prepared with different vehicles. For example, if a pharmacist prepares two potassium syrups, one using Syrup, USP, as the vehicle and one using a sugar-free syrup as the vehicle, the name of the vehicle should be included on the labels.

Liquids and semisolid concentrations may be expressed in terms of percentages. When the term "percent" or the symbol "%" is used without qualification for solids and semisolids, percent refers to weight in weight; for solutions or suspensions, percent refers to weight in volume; for solutions of liquids in liquids, percent refers to volume in volume.[4]

Labels for compounded products that are prepared in batches should include a pharmacy-assigned lot number. Assignment of a pharmacy lot number must enable the history of the compounded product to be traced, including the person compounding the product and the product's formula, ingredients, and procedures. Being able to trace the history of a batch is essential in cases of a drug product recall or withdrawal.

In the preparation of labels for batches of compounded products, all extra labels should be destroyed, since pharmacy lot numbers change with each batch. If computers, memory typewriters, or label machines are used to print batch labels, care must be taken to ensure that the memory and printing mechanism have been cleared and the correct information is programmed before any additional labels are made. It is a good practice to run a blank label between each batch of labels to ensure that the memory has been erased or cleared. To document the information printed on each set of labels, a sample label printed for the batch should be attached to the compounded-product log. If labels are sequentially prepared for different drug products, procedures should exist to minimize the risk of mislabeling the compounded products. These procedures should ensure, for example, that labels for one drug product are physically well separated from labels for any other drug product.

Auxiliary labels are convenient for conveying special storage or use information. Auxiliary labels should be attached conspicuously to containers, if possible. If the container is too small for both a general label and an auxiliary label, special storage and use instructions should appear on the label in a format that will emphasize the instructions.

Limited Batch Compounding

The purpose of extemporaneously compounding products is to provide individualized drug therapy for a particular patient. When a pharmacist is repeatedly asked to prepare identical compounded products, it may be reasonable and more efficient for the pharmacist to prepare small batches of the compounded product.

Batch sizes should be consistent with the volume of drug orders or prescriptions the pharmacist receives for the compounded product and the stability of the compounded product. The pharmacist should use judgment in deciding reasonable batch sizes. Product assays should be performed by a chemical analysis laboratory on a regular basis to ensure product consistency among various lots, product uniformity, and stability. Analyses should be repeated every time an ingredient (active or inert) or procedure is changed. Documentation of assay findings should be filed for a period no less than the state's time requirement for the retention of dispensing records.

General Compounding Considerations

To provide the patient with the most stable drug product, the pharmacist should take the following steps upon receiving a prescription order that requires compounding.

First, the pharmacist should determine if a similar commercial product is available. A pharmacist can refer to various reference texts to check the availability of identical or similar products. Package inserts from commercially available products also contain information on inactive ingredients that can be compared with the requested formulation. If there is a commercially manufactured identical product, the local availability of the product should be determined.

When a similar product is commercially available, the pharmacist should determine which ingredients are different from the requested formulation to decide whether or not the commercial product can be used. At this stage, the pharmacist should seek answers to the following questions:

- Are all of the ingredients appropriate for the condition being treated?
- Are the concentrations of the ingredients in the drug order reasonable?
- Are the physical, chemical, and therapeutic properties of the individual ingredients consistent with the expected properties of the ordered drug product?

If the answers to these questions are positive, the pharmacist should consult the prescriber about the possibility of dispensing the commercial product. (In some states, pharmacists may not be required to obtain permission from the prescriber to dispense a commercial product if the formulation is identical to the drug order.) Dispensing a commercial product is preferable to extemporaneously compounding a drug product because commercial products carry the manufacturer's guarantee of labeled potency and stability.

If there is not a commercial product available with the same or similar formulation, the pharmacist should consider asking the prescriber the following questions:

- What is the purpose of the order? There may be another way to achieve the purpose without compounding a product.
- Where did the formula originate (article, meeting, colleague)?
- How will the drug product be used?
- Does the patient have other conditions that must be considered?
- For how long will the drug product be used?

If possible, the pharmacist should obtain a copy of the original formula to determine the extent to which the formulation has been tested for stability. When documentation is not available, the pharmacist should review the ingredients for appropriateness and reasonable concentrations.

For drug products that must be compounded, the pharmacist should closely observe the compounded drug product for any signs of instability. Such observations should be performed during preparation of the drug product and during any storage period that may occur before the compounded drug product is dispensed.

If specific packaging information is not available, a light-resistant, tight container, such as an amber vial or bottle, should be used to maximize stability (see section on packaging and labeling).

The pharmacist should label the compounded drug product, including an appropriate beyond-use date and storage instructions for the patient.

Specific Compounding Considerations

Accepted, proven compounding procedures for products including solutions, suspensions, creams, ointments, capsules, suppositories, troches, emulsions, and powders may be found in reference sources or the pharmacy literature. For additional information, pharmacists should check references cited in this document or consult colleagues or colleges of pharmacy with known expertise in compounding.

Glossary

For the purposes of this document, the following terms are used with the meanings shown.

Active Ingredient: Any chemical that is intended to furnish pharmacologic activity in the diagnosis, cure, mitigation, treatment, or prevention of disease or to affect the structure or function of the body of man or other animals.[4]

Batch: Multiple containers of a drug product or other material with uniform character and quality, within specified limits, that are prepared in anticipation of prescription drug orders based on routine, regularly observed prescribing patterns.

Cold: Any temperature not exceeding 8 °C (46 °F).[4]

Commercially Available Product: Any drug product manufactured by a producer registered with the Department of Health and Human Services as a pharmaceutical manufacturer.

Compounding: The mixing of substances to prepare a drug product.

Container: A device that holds a drug product and is or may be in direct contact with the product.[3]

Cool: Any temperature between 8 and 15 °C (46 and 59 °F).[4]

Drug Product: A finished dosage form that contains an active drug ingredient usually, but not necessarily (in the case of a placebo), in combination with inactive ingredients.[4]

Extemporaneous: Impromptu; prepared without a standard formula from an official compendium; prepared as required for a specific patient.

Inactive Ingredient: Any chemical other than the active ingredients in a drug product.[4]

Manufacturer: Anyone registered with the Department of Health and Human Services as a producer of drug products.[14]

Sensitivity Requirements: The maximal load that will cause one subdivision of change on the index plate in the position of rest of the indicator of the balance.[4]

Stability: The chemical and physical integrity of a drug product over time.[4]

Trituration: The reducing of substances to fine particles by rubbing them in a mortar with a pestle.[3]

Warm: Any temperature between 30 and 40 °C (86 and 104 °F).[4]

Suggested References

Product Availability

American Drug Index
Drug Facts & Comparisons
Physicians' Desk Reference
The Extra Pharmacopoeia (Martindale)
CHEMSOURCES
AHFS Drug Information

Compounding Techniques

Compounding Companion PC-Based Software
King's *Dispensing of Medications*
Remington's Pharmaceutical Sciences
Contemporary Compounding column in *U.S. Pharmacist*

Pharmaceutical Calculations

Stoklosa and Ansel's *Pharmaceutical Calculations*
Math—Use It or Lose It column in *Hospital Pharmacy*
Calculations in Pharmacy column in *U.S. Pharmacist*

Drug Stability and Compatibility

American Journal of Hospital Pharmacy
ASHP's *Handbook on Extemporaneous Formulations*
ASHP's *Handbook on Injectable Drugs*
International Pharmaceutical Abstracts
Journal of the Parenteral Drug Association (now *Journal of Pharmaceutical Science and Technology*)
Canadian Society of Hospital Pharmacists *Extemporaneous Oral Liquid Dosage Preparations*
Pediatric Drug Formulations
Physicians' Desk Reference
Contemporary Compounding column in *U.S. Pharmacist*
AHFS Drug Information
The Merck Index

References

1. Pancorbo SA, Campagna KD, Devenport JK, et al. Task force report of competency statements for pharmacy practice. *Am J Pharm Educ.* 1987; 51:196–206.
2. Allen LV Jr. Establishing and marketing your extemporaneous compounding service. *US Pharm.* 1990; 15(Dec):74–7.
3. Remington's pharmaceutical sciences. 18th ed. Gennaro AR, ed. Easton, PA: Mack Publishing; 1990; 1630–1, 1658, 1660.
4. The United States Pharmacopeia, 22nd rev., and The National Formulary, 17th ed. Rockville, MD: The United States Pharmacopeial Convention; 1989.
5. USP DI Volume III: Approved drug products and legal requirements. 14th ed. Rockville, MD: The United States Pharmacopeial Convention; 1994.
6. USP DI Volume I: Drug information for the health care professional. 14th ed. Rockville, MD: The United States Pharmacopeial Convention; 1994.
7. 29 §C.F.R. 1910. 1200(1990).
8. ASHP technical assistance bulletin on handling cytotoxic and hazardous drugs. *Am J Hosp Pharm.* 1990; 47:1033–49.
9. Feinberg JL. Complying with OSHA's Hazard Communication Standard. *Consult Pharm.* 1991; 6:444, 446, 448.
10. Myers CE. Applicability of OSHA Hazard Communication Standard to drug products. *Am J Hosp Pharm.* 1990; 47:1960–1.
11. 21 C.F.R. §211.137.
12. Connors KA, Amidon GL, Stella VJ. Chemical stability of pharmaceuticals: a handbook for pharmacists. 2nd ed. New York: Wiley; 1986.
13. American Society of Hospital Pharmacists. ASHP guidelines on preventing medication errors in hospitals. *Am J Hosp Pharm.* 1993; 50:305–14.
14. Fitzgerald WL Jr. The legal authority to compound in pharmacy practice. *Tenn Pharm.* 1990; 26(Mar): 21–2.

Approved by the ASHP Board of Directors, April 27, 1994. Developed by the Council on Professional Affairs.

The bibliographic citation for this document is as follows: American Society of Hospital Pharmacists. ASHP technical assistance bulletin on compounding nonsterile products in pharmacies. *Am J Hosp Pharm.* 1994; 51:1441–8.

Safe Practices for Parenteral Nutrition Formulations

NOTICE: These A.S.P.E.N. Practice Guidelines for Safe Practices for Parenteral Nutrition Formulations are based upon general conclusions of health professionals who, in developing such guidelines, have balanced potential benefits to be derived from a particular mode of providing parenteral nutrition against certain risks inherent with parenteral nutrition feeding formulations. The underlying judgment regarding the propriety of any specific practice guideline or procedure must be made by the attending health professional in light of all circumstances presented by the individual patient and the needs and resources particular to the locality. These guidelines are not a substitute for the exercise of judgment by the health professional, but rather are a tool to be used by the health professional in the exercise of such judgment. These guidelines are voluntary and should not be deemed inclusive of all proper methods of care of exclusive methods of care reasonably directed toward obtaining the same result.

Preface

The members of the American Society for Parenteral and Enteral Nutrition (A.S.P.E.N.) are health care professionals representing medicine, nursing, pharmacy, and dietetics dedicated to assuring that every patient receives optimal nutrition care. The mission of A.S.P.E.N. is to serve as a preeminent, interdisciplinary, research-based, patient-centered clinical nutrition society throughout the world.

Patients may be treated with parenteral nutrition in any of several care settings including hospitals, long-term care or rehabilitation facilities, or at home. Because patients transfer from one health care environment to another, it is the opinion of the A.S.P.E.N. Board of Directors that the practice guidelines in the "Safe Practices for Parenteral Nutrition Feeding Formulations" document become the standard of practice for the provision of parenteral nutrition.

"Safe Practices for Parenteral Nutrition Formulations" is organized into six sections. Each section includes an introduction to the problem area addressed, with examples of cases in which harm or data support the need for practice guidelines to ensure patient safety; specific practice guidelines based on consensus of the National Advisory Group (NAG) members; summary of areas requiring further work; and a list of supporting references. The introduction summarizes the process A.S.P.E.N. used to develop this document. The members of the NAG on Standards and Practice Guidelines for Parenteral Nutrition are as follows:

Chairman:
Jay Mirtallo, MS, RPh, BCNSP
Ohio State University
Columbus, Ohio

David Driscoll, PhD, BCNSP
Beth Israel Deaconess Medical Center
Boston, Massachusetts

Richard Helms, PharmD, BCNSP
University of Tennessee
Memphis, Tennessee

Vanessa Kumpf, PharmD, BCNSP
Clarian Hospital
Indianapolis, Indiana

Barbara McKinnon, PharmD, BCNSP
Nova Factor
Memphis, Tennessee

This document was internally reviewed by the A.S.P.E.N. Pharmacists, Standards and Public Policy committees and approved by the A.S.P.E.N. Board of Directors after external review by individuals and other organizations of health care professionals. An important outcome of preparing these practice guidelines is the recognition that more research and information is needed in several of the areas covered. A.S.P.E.N. and the NAG recognize that the practice guidelines will have broad ramifications in changing clinical practice in many health care settings for pharmacists, physicians, nurses, dietitians, and technical support personnel. It is the hope of the NAG that these guidelines will be accepted and used to prevent future patient harm and will serve as a catalyst for future research.

Section I. Introduction

Over the past 3 decades, parenteral nutrition (PN) has become an important adjunctive therapy in a variety of disease states. Parenteral nutrition formulations are extremely complex admixtures containing amino acids, dextrose, lipids, water, electrolytes, trace elements, and vitamins—40 or more components. Parenteral nutrition refers to all PN formulations; total nutrient admixtures (TNAs) are PN formulations that include intravenous fat emulsions (IFEs); and 2-in-1 formulations are PN formulations that do not include IFEs. Early PN programs focused on minimizing the frequency, severity, and type of complications that could result from this therapy. The interdisciplinary approach was found to improve efficacy, reduce complications, and facilitate efficient, cost-effective PN therapy. Despite the highly successful use of PN for many years, the following adverse events demonstrate that errors in managing this complicated therapy can result in serious harm and even death:

- Two deaths related to errors in PN compounding led to a Safety Alert being issued by the US Food and Drug Administration (FDA).[1] Autopsy of the patients involved found diffuse microvascular pulmonary emboli. There were also at least two other cases of respiratory distress occurring in patients at the same institution. These patients had received TNAs thought to contain a precipitate of calcium phosphate that resulted from improper admixture practices in the pharmacy.

- Hospital personnel misinterpreted the dextrose content on the label of a PN formulation used in home care, which resulted in a pediatric patient's death.[2] The home care label read: "300 mL of 50% dextrose." The hospital pharmacy interpreted this as a final concentration of dextrose 50% (more than twice the maximum concentration normally or typically used in PN therapy). The patient died after 2 days of receiving infusion of the incorrect formula.

- Two other fatal incidents have been reported involving pharmacy compounding operations for pediatric solutions.[3] One infant was overdosed with dextrose when the PN was prepared with amino acids and two bags of 50% dextrose in place of one bag of 50% dextrose and one bag of sterile water. The other infant was underdosed with dextrose while receiving a 1.75% final concentration of dextrose solution rather than a 17.5% concentration.
- Another PN formulation was compounded with no dextrose, resulting in irreversible brain damage when administered to a neonate.[4]
- An incident involving the misinterpretation of a label resulted in iron overload and liver toxicity in a child receiving PN with iron dextran.[5] In this case, the PN label read, "iron dextran 1 mL," the intention being to use a 1-mg/mL concentration prediluted by the pharmacy. However, the solution containing the undiluted, 50-mg/mL concentration was used in compounding and resulted in a 50-fold error in the dose administered.
- Four children were infected, two of whom died, as a result of receiving contaminated PN admixtures.[6] *Enterobacter cloacae* was cultured from disposable tubing that was used in the automated compounding of these PN admixtures.

As a result of these events, in 1995 A.S.P.E.N. established the National Advisory Group (NAG) on Standards and Practice Guidelines for Parenteral Nutrition. The purpose of this group was to identify problem areas in PN therapy specifically related to pharmacy practice and to make recommendations and guidelines that foster safe practices based on experience and the literature. It is realized that these recommendations may result in significant changes in practice related to prescribing, compounding, labeling, and administering PN, but these examples prove that inconsistent practices within hospitals and other health care environments have the potential to cause harm. Pharmaceutical problem areas identified by the group were as follows: PN labeling, compounding, formulas, stability, and filtering. Guidelines are presented in a format similar to the A.S.P.E.N. *Guidelines for the Use of Parenteral and Enteral Nutrition in Adult and Pediatric Patients,*[7] beginning with a background of the issue, then rationales of various methods to address the issue, followed by a list of practice guidelines based on consensus of the NAG members, and concluding with a summary of areas in which further research is needed and references supporting the evidence presented.

References

1. Food and Drug Administration. Safety Alert. Hazards of precipitation associated with parenteral nutrition. *Am J Hosp Pharm* 51:1427–8, 1994.
2. Carey LC, Haffey M. Incident: Home TPN formula order misinterpreted after hospital admission. *Home Care Highlights* Spring: 7, 1995.
3. Cobel MR. Compounding pediatric dextrose solutions. Medication error alert. *ASHP Newsletter* August: 3, 1995.
4. Gebbart F. Test hyperal solutions? Florida mom says yes. *Hosp Pharm Report* February: 35, 1992.
5. Iron overdose due to miscommunication of TPN order.

Error alert. *Pharmacy Today* September, 1995.
6. Two children die after receiving infected TPN solutions. *Pharm J* August: 3, 1994.
7. A.S.P.E.N. Board of Directors: Guidelines for the use of parenteral and enteral nutrition in adult and pediatric patients. *JPEN* 17 (Suppl): 4SA, 1993.

Section II. Labeling Parenteral Nutrition Formulations

Background. The manner in which PN ingredients are labeled varies considerably. PN base components (dextrose, amino acids, and IFEs) are labeled as:

- the volume of the percent of original concentration added (250 mL of 50% dextrose),
- the percent of final concentration after admixture (25% dextrose), and
- the grams per liter or grams in the total volume of PN admixed (250 g per liter or 375 g per total volume).

Additives, especially electrolytes, are labeled as millimoles or millequivalents per liter or per volume. For example, sodium chloride (NaCl) in a dose of 80 mEq/L admixed in a PN formulation with a volume of 2 L may be labeled as follows:

NaCl 80 mEq/L
NaCl 160 mEq per total volume
Na 80 mEq/L, Cl 80 mEq/L
Na 160 mEq and Cl 160 mEq per total volume.

This lack of standardization causes a great deal of confusion when patients are transferred between health care environments. Thus an essential component of a patient transfer between health care environments is a pharmacist-to-pharmacist interaction to resolve potential problems with transfer of the prescription. Misinterpretation of a PN label that led to a patient's death[1] exemplifies what may happen if this interaction does not occur. To avoid misinterpretation, the labels for PN admixtures should be standardized. All PN labels in any health care environment must express clearly and accurately what the patient is receiving at any time.

Each method of labeling has distinct advantages and disadvantages. The use of the percent of original dextrose or amino acid concentration is specific for the product used by the pharmacy in compounding the PN admixture. However, interpretation of this label requires a knowledge of pharmaceutical calculations in order to determine the nutrient value of the PN admixture. This necessitates training professionals in several health care disciplines to determine the nutrient value of the PN admixture being administered. Using the percent of final concentration of dextrose, amino acids, or fat still requires calculations to determine the caloric value or dose being administered, but it is traditionally the most accepted type of label because it is consistent with the label of the original products as shipped from the manufacturer. To minimize calculation errors and provide a label more consistent with dispensing a PN admixture as a nutrient, some programs have used grams of base components per liter. This simplifies the conversion of the nutrients to calorie and gram doses being provided, but still must be converted to daily doses. This label also supports those programs that compound PN admixtures in only liter quantities so that prescriptions may be written as quantity per liter and thus are consistent with the additive as it appears on the label.

Finally, grams per total volume, with use of a 24-hour nutrient infusion system, is most consistent with that of a nutrient label, requiring the least number of calculations to determine the calorie or gram dose per day. It also supports the most cost-effective system of PN compounding and delivery, which is the 24-hour nutrient infusion system.[2] This system has been determined to decrease PN wastage and to reduce personnel time in compounding and administering PN. Conceptually, this system is successful when acute electrolyte disorders are managed separately from the PN until the time that electrolyte changes in the PN go into effect. This system also requires the use of automated compounding devices, which have been shown to be more accurate and faster than gravity-fill PN admixture systems.

PN Label Template. The sample PN label templates provide a format to standardize labels for adult, pediatric, and neonatal patients. A supplemental label template for IFE is also provided for those instances when IFEs are administered separately from the PN admixture. Because of the complex nature of the label, several points should be clarified:

- The amount per day is the only column required on the label, but some programs accustomed to amounts per liter may supplement the label by adding a second column reflecting quantities per liter in parentheses. The components are labeled as amount per day to facilitate review of the order for appropriate nutrient doses. However, certain additives expressed as quantity per liter and as labeled in parentheses in the PN label template may be useful to the clinician in determining whether the PN may be infused via peripheral or central vein. Those familiar with ordering PN electrolytes (similar to other intravenous fluids) as mEq/L, will be able to interpret the mEq/L electrolyte content more easily if provided in this format on the PN label. Finally, many programs order additives as quantity per liter. Labeling as such allows for the final check of the PN by the nurse against the physician's order prior to its administration. This final check to confirm that the PN content is the same as the physician's order is an essential component of the PN system. Care should be taken to develop a label that is clear and concise and of a size that fits neatly on the PN admixture. Accordingly, some may choose to dispense the PN formulation with a supplemental form providing these optional details that may also be used for documenting PN administration in the patient's chart.
- The PN label specifies the route of administration.
- The administration date and time and expiration date and time are expressed clearly on the label. The administration date, as the term denotes, is the date and time the PN formulation is scheduled to be administered to the patient. This may be the same day that it was compounded and is different from the date and time of admixture, which should be included on the compounding worksheet but is not necessary on the label.
- The dosing weight is provided so that anyone evaluating the contents of the label may determine whether the doses of nutrients are appropriate. Dosing weight refers to the weight used in calculating nutrient doses and

may be the patient's actual, ideal, dry, or adjusted body weight.

- The phosphorus content is provided as both the millimole quantity of phosphorus as well as the milliequivalent quantity of the additive salt's cation, potassium or sodium.
- If the PN admixture includes overfill, it is clearly stated on the label.
- Rate is expressed in mL/hr over 24 hours. If the PN admixture is cycled, the infusion duration and rates are to be expressed on the label.
- For home care, additives to be admixed at home are labeled as Patient Additives.
- An auxillary label may also be desired that would list the individual electrolytes as milliequivalents and the phosphorus content as millimoles provided per day. The auxillary label could also express the amount of total and nonprotein calories provided per day, as well as the percent of total and nonprotein calories provided by carbohydrate and fat.
- Notation of who prepared and checked the PN admixture is not required on the label if this is noted on a compounding worksheet maintained in the pharmacy.
- If IFEs are not included in the PN admixture, this line may be omitted from the label.

Practice Guidelines: Labeling.

1. The labels for PN admixtures should be standardized.

    - The amount per day is the only column required on the label for the base formula, electrolyte additives, micronutrients, and medications. This method supports the use of the 24-hour nutrient infusion system.
    - Using the quantity per liter option in parentheses supports those programs that continue to admix PN in 1-L volumes.
    - The dosing weight is required on the label.

2. Auxillary labels or information may be used, especially when PN orders are written in a different format than the label.
3. Patient transfer between health care environments requires pharmacist-to-pharmacist communication regarding the accurate transfer to the PN prescription.
4. The PN label is compared with the physician's order and for expiration date prior to administration.

Areas Requiring Further Work. The concepts used in developing the practice guidelines were developed for hospitalized patients and for institutions and organizations having a consistent number of patients receiving PN therapy. It is assumed that these concepts apply to alternative health care settings, as well as those hospitals having only a few patients receiving PN. It may be that the cost of implementing a once-per-day nutrient infusion system that includes automated compounding would be excessive for pharmacies with small numbers of patients receiving PN. Various alternatives to achieving the concepts for labeling in these circumstances may be successful but have not yet been determined objectively.

References

1. Carey LC, Haffey M. Incident: Home TPN formula

order misinterpreted after hospital admission. *Home Care Highlights* Spring: 7, 1995.

2. Mirtallo JM, Jozefzcyck KG, Hale KM, et al. Providing 24-hour nutrient infusions to critically ill patients. *Am J Hosp Pharm* 43: 2205–8, 1986.

Section III. Standard Nutrient Ranges and Sample PN Formulations

Background. PN formulations should be designed to meet the estimated nutrition requirements for each individual

Standard PN Label Template
Adult Patient

Institution/Pharmacy Name, Address and Pharmacy Phone Number		
Name Dosing Weight	Location	
Administration Date/Time	Expiration Date/time	
Base Formula Amount/day	(Amount/L)	
Dextrose g	(g/L)	
Amino acids[a] g	(g/L)	
Lipid[a] g	(g/L)	
Electrolytes		
Sodium chloride mEq	(mEq/L)	
Sodium acetate mEq	(mEq/L)	
Potassium chloride mEq	(mEq/L)	
Potassium acetate mEq	(mEq/L)	
Potassium phosphate mmol of P	(mmol/L)	
(mEq of K)	(mEq/L)	
Sodium phosphate mmol of P	(mmol/L)	
(mEq of Na)	(mEq/L)	
Calcium gluconate mEq	(mEq/L)	
Magnesium sulfate mEq	(mEq/L)	
Vitamins, trace elements and medications		
Multiple vitamins[a] mL		
Multiple trace elements[a] mL		
Insulin Units	(Units/L)	
H$_2$ - antagonists[a] mg		
Rate____mL/hr Volume____mL	Infuse over 24 hours	
Admixture contains____mL plus ____mL overfill		
Central Line Use Only		

[a] Specify product name.
g = gram.

Standard IFE Label Template
Adult, Neonate or Pediatric Patient

Institution/Pharmacy Name, Address and Pharmacy Phone Number			
Name Dosing Weight	Location		
Administration Date/Time	Expiration Date/time		
	Volume	Amount/kg/day	Amount/day
Intravenous fat emulsion(%)	____mL	g/kg	g
Infusion rate ____mL/hr Infuse over ____hours			
Contains overfill - Discard any unused volume after 24 hours			
For peripheral or central line administration			

Standard PN Label Template
Neonate or Pediatric Patient

Institution/Pharmacy Name, Address and Pharmacy Phone Number		
Name Dosing Weight	Location	
Administration Date/Time	Expiration Date/time	
Base Formula	**Amount/kg/day**	**Amount/day**
Dextrose	**g/kg**	**g**
Amino acids[a]	**g/kg**	**g**
Electrolytes		
Sodium chloride[b]	**mEq/kg**	**mEq**
Sodium acetate[b]	mEq/kg	mEq
Potassium chloride[b]	mEq/kg	mEq
Potassium acetate[b]	mEq/kg	mEq
Potassium phosphate[b]	mmol of P/kg	mmol of P
	(mEq of K)/kg	(mEq of K)
Sodium phosphate[b]	**mmol of P/kg**	**mmol of P**
	(mEq of Na)/kg	**(mEq of Na)**
Calcium gluconate	**mEq/kg**	**mEq**
Magnesium sulfate	**mEq/kg**	**mEq**
Vitamins, trace elements and medications		
Multiple vitamins[a]	**mL/kg**	**mL**
Multiple trace elements[a]	**mL/kg**	**mL**
L-cysteine	**mg/g protein**	**mg**
H₂ antagonists[a]	**mg/kg**	**mg**

Rate____mL/hr   Volume_____mL   Infuse over 24 hours

Admixture contains_____mL plus____mL overfill

Central Line Use Only

[a] Specify product name.

[b] Since the admixture usually contains multiple sources of sodium, potassium, chloride, acetate, and phosphorus, the amount of each electrolyte/kg provided by the PN admixture is determined by adding the amount of electrolyte provided by each salt.

patient. However, the pharmacist needs to be able to recognize when the amount of nutrient ordered for a patient is not within an acceptable standard range. The ordered quantity of protein, carbohydrate, fat, electrolytes, fluid, vitamins, and trace elements should all be assessed for appropriateness before they are compounded. Acceptable ranges for each of these nutrients should be based on compatibility, stability, and normal clinical requirements. It is not the intent of this document to provide guidelines on the nutrient requirements in various disease states and conditions. Rather, the purpose of providing standard nutrient ranges is to serve as a reference point and to guide the pharmacist in safe practice. The standard nutrient ranges apply to adult and pediatric patients with normal organ function.

Sample PN formulations are provided to illustrate use of the standard PN label template in the adult and pediatric patient. The sample formulations have been designed to provide nutrients within the standard ranges established. Some institutions may find it helpful to develop order forms for standard PN formulations that apply to specific patient populations with normal organ function. This may aid the prescriber in designing a complete, balanced, and physically compatible PN formulation that adequately meets the estimated daily nutritional requirements in that patient population.

Standard Nutrient Ranges. Standard ranges for protein and

calories for adults should be based on actual body weight, or an estimated dosing weight if actual weight is >120% or ideal body weight. Various published guidelines are available that attempt to estimate dosing weight in obese patients.[1] See Table I for general guidelines for protein, calorie, and fluid requirements in adult patients. The standard distribution of nonprotein calories is 70% to 85% as carbohydrate and 15% to 30% as fat. This distribution may be adjusted on the basis of tolerance; however, there is limited clinical benefit when fat content exceeds 30% of nonprotein calories.[2] In adult patients, it is recommended that the fat content of the PN formulation not exceed 2.5 g/kg/day and carbohydrate content not exceed approximately 7 g/kg/day.

Standards ranges for electrolytes, vitamins, and trace elements in adult patients with normal organ function are provided in Tables II through IV. Sodium and potassium requirements for a given patient are highly variable and generally not limited by compatibility restraints. In general, sodium and potassium requirements in the PN formulation are 1 to 2 mEq/kg/day but should be customized to meet individual patient needs. Chloride and acetate content should be adjusted to maintain acid-base balance. In general, acid-base balance can be maintained by use of approximately equal amounts of chloride and acetate, but it may require adjustment on the basis of the clinical situation. Amino acid solutions themselves contain various amounts of chloride

TABLE I
Daily protein and calorie requirements for the adult*

Protein	
Maintenance	0.8–1.0 g/kg
Catabolic patients	1.2–2 g/kg
Energy	
Total Calories	25–30 kcal/kg
Volume	20–40 mL/kg

*Assumes normal organ function.

TABLE II
Daily electrolyte additions to adult PN formulations*

Electrolyte	Parenteral equivalent of recommended dietary allowance	Standard intake
Calcium	10 mEq	10–15 mEq†
Magnesium	10 mEq	8–20 mEq
Phosphate	30 mmol	20–40 mmol†
Sodium	N/A	1–2 mEq/kg + replacement
Potassium	N/A	1–2 mEq/kg
Acetate	N/A	As needed to maintain acid-base balance
Chloride	N/A	As needed to maintain acid-base balance

*Assumes normal organ function.
†See Section V for compatibility guidelines.
N/A = nonapplicable.

TABLE III
Daily vitamin supplementation to adult PN formulations*†

Vitamin	Intake
Thiamin (B_1)	3 mg
Riboflavin (B_2)	3.6 mg
Niacin (B_3)	40 mg
Folic acid	400 µg
Pantothenic acid	15 mg
Pyridoxine (B_6)	4 mg
Cyanocobalmin (B_{12})	5 µg
Biotin	60 µg
Ascorbic Acid (C)	100 mg
Vitamin A	3300 IU
Vitamin D	200 IU
Vitamin E	10 IU

*Assumes normal organ function.
†Vitamin K supplementation 2–4 mg/week in PN patients not receiving oral anticoagulation therapy.

TABLE IV
Daily trace element supplementation to adult PN formulations*

Trace element	Intake[5,6]
Chromium	10–15 µg
Copper	0.3–0.5 mg
Manganese	60–100 µg
Zinc	2.5–5 mg

*Assumes normal organ function.

TABLE V
Daily fluid requirements for pediatric patients[7]

Body weight	Amount
<1500 g	130–150 mL/kg
1500–2000 g	110–130 mL/kg
2.5–10 kg	100 mL/kg
>10 kg–20 kg	1000 mL for 10 kg + 50 mL/kg for each kg >10
>20 kg	1500 mL for 20 kg + 20 mL/kg for each kg >20

TABLE VI
Daily protein requirements (g/kg) for pediatric patients*

Neonates	2.5–3.0
Infants	2.0–2.5
Children	1.5–2.0
Adolescents	0.8–2.0

*Assume normal age-related organ function.

TABLE VII
Daily energy requirements (nonprotein kcal/kg) for pediatric patients

Preterm neonate	120–140
<6 months	90–120
6–12 months	80–100
1–7 yr	75–90
7–12 yr	60–75
>12–18 yr	30–60

and acetate, depending on the individual product, for buffering purposes.[3] For this reason, it is necessary to state on the PN label the specific amino acid product name used in compounding. It is not necessary, however, to list the amount of chloride, phosphorus, and acetate from the amino acid solution on the PN label, as this may lead to confusion.

Guidelines for parenteral vitamin requirements in adults have been established by the Nutrition Advisory Group (NAG) of the Department of Foods and Nutrition, American Medical Association (AMA).[4] The AMA-NAG does not include vitamin K as part of the multivitamin formulation in order to avoid interactions in patients receiving oral anticoagulants. However, patients receiving PN, especially those also receiving antibiotic therapy, may need vitamin K supplementation. The AMA-NAG recommendations for patients receiving PN include vitamin K supplementation of 2 to 4 mg/week in patients not receiving oral anticoagulation therapy. The patient's prothrombin time (PT) or international normalized ratio (INR) should be monitored for signs of vitamin K deficiency to determine the need for vitamin K supplementation.

The AMA-NAG also published recommendations for the parenteral administration of chromium, copper, manganese, and zinc.[5] The guidelines should be considered approximations, and it should be recognized that variations among individual patients may exist. For example, supplementation of selenium 20 to 60 µg/day is recommended for patients receiving long-term PN. Routine iron supplementation to PN formulations is not recommended.

Standard nutrient ranges for infants and children receiving PN have been established. Rapidly changing organ function, metabolic, immaturity, and normal but rapid weight gain, particularly in neonates and infants, are age-related descriptors of nutrient need.

Therefore, each table characterizes ranges for neonates, infants, children, and occasionally, adolescents (Tables V through VII). As can be readily appreciated, requirements for fluids, protein, and energy are substantially higher on a unit-of-weight basis for children than for adults. The addition of L-cysteine HCl as an admixture just prior to PN administration is recommended by manufacturers of neonatal and infant amino acid formulations. The most commonly recommended dose is 40 mg of L-cysteine HCl per gram of amino acids. Current practice suggests supplementation with L-cysteine HCl for the first year of life, although practice varies widely. The distribution of PN nonprotein calories for pediatric patients does not vary significantly from that for the adult receiving PN; however, it is worth noting that the typical enteral diet of the neonate or infant derives approximately 50% of nonprotein calories from fat. Therefore, a PN solution appears less physiologically similar to standard enteral feedings in the neonate or infant than in the older child and adult. For the purposes of this document, calories will be nonprotein calories when the pediatric population is referred to, particularly the neonatal or infant population. Because of rapid growth with associated increase in lean body mass, it is desirable to consider protein for its protein synthetic role and not merely as a calorie source. Ranges for calories and protein for adults should be used for an individual >18 years of age.

There is growing evidence that a 20% IFE is the preferred product for use in the neonate and infant. In addition to its greater calorie content per unit volume, the lower content of surface active agents (egg phosphatides) per gram of fat results in a more normal concentration of

Sample PN Formulation
Adult Patient

Institution/Pharmacy Name, Address and Pharmacy Phone Number		
Name Administration Date/Time	Dosing weight: 70 kg	Location Expiration Date/Time
Base Formula	Amount/day	(Amount/L)
Dextrose	400 g	(166.7 g/L)
Amino acids[a]	100 g	(41.7 g/L)
Lipid[a]	65 g	(27.1 g/L)
Electrolytes		
Sodium chloride	80 mEq	(33.3 mEq/L)
Sodium acetate	80 mEq	(33.3 mEq/L)
Potassium chloride	40 mEq	(16.7 mEq/L)
Potassium phosphate	30 mmol of P	(12.5 mmol/L)
	(45 mEq of K)	(18.8 mEq/L)
Calcium gluconate	10 mEq	(4.2 mEq/L)
Magnesium sulfate	10 mEq	(4.2 mEq/L)
Vitamins, trace elements and medications		
Multiple vitamins[a]	10 mL	
Multiple trace elements[a]	1-3 mL[b]	
Infusion rate 100 mL/hr	Volume 2400 mL	Infuse over 24 hours
Admixture contains 2400 mL plus 100 mL overfill		
Central Line Use Only		

[a] Specify product name.
[b] Volume dependent on specific product used.

Sample PN Formulation
Pediatric Patient

Institution Name, Address and Pharmacy Phone Number		
Patient Name Administration Date/Time	Dosing Weight 15 kg	Location Expiration Date/Time
Base Formula	Amount/kg/day	Amount/day
Dextrose	20 g	300 g
Amino acids[a]	2 g	30 g
Electrolytes		
Sodium chloride	3 mEq	45 mEq
Sodium phosphate	0.7 mmol	10.5 mmol
	(0.9 mEq of Na)	(14 mEq of Na)
Potassium chloride	1 mEq	15 mEq
Potassium acetate	0.7 mEq	10 mEq
Calcium gluconate	1 mEq	15 mEq
Magnesium sulfate	0.3 mEq	4.5 mEq
Vitamins, trace elements and medications		
Pediatric multivitamins[b]	5 mL	
Pediatric multiple trace[c]	0.1 mL	1.5 mL
Infusion rate 50 mL/hr	Volume 1200 mL	Infuse over 24 hours
Admixture contains 1200 mL plus 100 mL overfill		
Central Line Use Only		

[a] Specify product name.
[b] MVI-Pediatric®.
[c] PTE-5®.

Sample PN Formulation
Pediatric Patient

Institution/Pharmacy Name, Address and Pharmacy Phone Number			
Patient Name			Location
Administration Date/Time		Dosing Weight 15 kg	
		Expiration date/time	
	Volume	Amount/kg/day	Amount/day
IFE 20%	144 mL	1.9 g	28.8 g[a]
Infusion rate 6 mL/hr		Infuse over 24 hours	
For peripheral or central line administration			

[a]Combines with Pediatric PN formulation to provide 90 mL/kg/day and 87 kcal/kg/day.

Sample PN Formulation
Infant Patient

Institution Name, Address and Pharmacy Phone Number		
Patient Name	Dosing Weight 5 kg	Location
Administration Date/time	Expiration Date/Time	
Base Formula	Amount/kg/day	Amount/day
Dextrose	25 g	125 g
Amino acids[a]	2.5 g	12.5 g
Electrolytes		
Sodium chloride	2.5mEq	12.5 mEq
Sodium phosphate	1.0 mmol	5.3 mmol
	(1.4 mEq of Na)	(7 mEq of Na)
Potassium chloride	1 mEq	5 mEq
Potassium acetate	1 mEq	5 mEq
Calcium gluconate	2 mEq	10 mEq
Magnesium sulfate	0.4 mEq	2 mEq
Vitamins, trace elements and medications		
Pediatric multivitamins[b]		5 mL
Pediatric multiple trace[c]	0.25 mL	1.25 mL
L-cysteine HCl	100 mg	500 mg
Infusion rate 21 mL/hr[a]	Volume 504 mL	Infuse over 24 hours
Admixture contains 504 mL plus 50 mL overfill		
Central Line Use Only		

[a]Specify product name.
[b]MVI-Pediatric®.
[c]PTE-5®.

TABLE VIII
*Daily electrolyte and mineral requirements for pediatric patients**

Electrolyte	Neonates	Infants/children	Adolescents
Sodium	2–5 mEq/kg	2–6 mEq/kg	Individualized
Chloride	1–5 mEq/kg	2–5 mEq/kg	Individualized
Potassium	1–4 mEq/kg	2–3 mEq/kg	Individualized
Calcium	3–4 mEq/kg	1–2.5 mEq/kg	10–20 mEq
Phosphorus	1–2 mmol/kg	0.5–1 mmol/kg	10–40 mmol
Magnesium	0.3–0.5 mEq/kg	0.3–0.5 mEq/kg	10–30 mEq

*Assumes normal age-related organ function.

TABLE IX
*Daily dose recommendation for pediatric multiple vitamins**†

Manufacturer		AMA-NAG	
Weight (kg)	Dose (mL)	Weight (kg)	Dose
<1	1.5	<2.5	2 mL/kg
1–3	3.25	>2.5	5 mL
>3	5	—	—

*Asumes normal age-related organ function.
†Pediatric multiple vitamin formulation (5 mL): A (IU) 2300, D (IU) 400, E (IU) 7, K (μg) 200, C (mg) 80, B_1 (mg) 1.2, B_2 (mg) 1.4, B_3 (mg) 17, B_5 (mg) 1, B_6 (mg) 1, B_{12} (μg) 1, Biotin (μg) 20, Folic acid (μg) 140.

TABLE X
*Trace element daily requirements for pediatrics**†

Trace element	Preterm neonates (μg/kg)	Term neonates (μg/kg)	<5 years old (μg/kg)	Older children and adolescents
Zinc	400	300	100	2–5 mg
Copper	20	20	20	200–500 μg
Manganese	1	1	2–10	50–150 μg
Chromium	0.2	0.2	0.14–0.2	5–15 μg
Selenium	2–3	2–3	2–3*	30–40 μg
Iodide	1**	1**	1**	—

*Limit = 40 μg/kg.
**Percutaneous absorption from protein-bound iodine may be adequate.

*Assumes normal age-related organ function.
†Recommended intakes of trace elements cannot be achieved through the use of a single pediatric multitrace product. Only through the use of individualized trace element products can recommended intakes of trace elements be achieved.[6]

components of circulating lipoproteins, especially density lipoproteins.[8] In the very low birth weight infant, the use of a 20% IFE does require accurate and low-flow pump delivery systems. Currently, the American Academy of Pediatrics (AAP) recommends the delivery of IFE over 20 to 24 hours per day with a limit of 4 g/kg/day.[9] In general, 3 g/kg/day is the accepted limit for IFE administration in the small-for-gestational-age neonates and preterm neonates less than 32 weeks of gestational age.

Standard ranges for electrolytes, minerals, vitamins, and trace elements for infants and children with normal organ function are found in Tables VIII through X. Calcium and phosphate requirements of the neonate and infant are substantially different from those of the older child and are

dramatically different from the requirements for the adult (Table VIII). These differences in mineral needs are reflected in the composition of neonatal and infant formulas and human milk. When one attempts to meet these increased requirements in pediatric PN solutions, problems can arise because calcium and phosphate salts are incompatible in aqueous solution (addressed in greater detail in Section V). In general, adult doses of electrolytes should be used for a child who weighs more than 50 kg.

Guidelines have been established for vitamin and trace element additions to PN solutions for pediatric patients up to age 11.[10] As for adults, the guidelines should be considered approximations of need, with individual patient variation to be expected. The long-term use (home PN) of multi-trace element products at recommended doses is associated with excessive blood concentrations of chromium.[11] The ratio of trace elements in commercially available products for pediatric use results in excessive intake of manganese if recommended doses of zinc are given. It is clear that micronutrient requirements for children receiving PN is a fertile area for research and an area in which further commercial product development is required.

Practice Guidelines: Nutrient Ranges.

1. The development of order forms for standard adult and pediatric PN formulations may aid the prescriber in designing a complete, balanced, and physically compatible formulation that meets the estimated daily nutritional requirements of patients with normal organ function.

2. The pharmacist should access the PN formulation to determine whether its contents are within an acceptable standard range based on the specific patient population (ie, adult or pediatric patient) or whether a clinical disease state or condition warrants a dose outside the standard range.

Areas Requiring Further Work. Further work is needed to determine optimal parenteral trace element requirements in adult and pediatric patients and to develop commercially available multi-trace element solutions that better meet these requirements. The use of currently available multi-trace element solutions may result in toxicity of certain trace elements in patients with certain diseases. This problem may

Sample Supplemental IFE Label
Infant Patient

Institution/Pharmacy Name, Address and Pharmacy Phone Number			
Name		Dosing Weight 5 kg	Location
Administration date/time		Expiration date/time	
	Volume	Amount/kg/day	Amount/day[a]
IFE 20%	48 mL	1.9 g	9 g
Infusion rate 2 mL/hr		Infuse over 24 hours	
For peripheral or central line administration			

[a]Combines with infant PN formulation to provide 110 mL/kg/day and 104 kcal/kg/day.

be compounded by trace element contamination, particularly aluminum, found in large-volume parenteral formulations and additives.

References

1. Ireton-Jones CS, Francis C. Obesity: nutrition support practice and application to critical care. *Nutr Clin Pract.* 10:144–9, 1995.

2. Delafosse B, Viale JP, Tissot S, et al. Effects of glucose-to-lipid ratio and type of lipid on substrate oxidation rate in patients. *Am J Physiol.* 267 (5 Part 1): E775-E780, 1994.

3. McEvoy GK (ed). American Hospital Formulary Service (AHFS) Drug Information. American Society of Health-System Pharmacists Inc., Bethesda, MD, 1996.

4. American Medical Association Department of Foods and Nutrition, 1975. Multivitamin preparations for parenteral use: a statement by the Nutrition Advisory Group. *JPEN.* 3:258–62, 1979.

5. American Medical Association Department of Foods and Nutrition. Guidelines for essential trace element preparations for parenteral use. A statement by an expert panel. *JAMA.* 241:2051–4, 1979.

6. Shils ME. Parenteral nutrition. IN Shils ME, Olson JA, Shike M (eds). Modern Nutrition in Health and Disease, 8th ed, Lea and Febiger, Philadelphia, 1988, pp 1444–7.

7. Holliday MA, Seger WE. The maintenance need for water in parenteral fluid therapy. *Pediatrics.* 19:823–32, 1957.

8. Haumont D, Deckelbaum RJ, Richelle M, et al. Plasma lipid concentration in low birth weight infants given parenteral nutrition with twenty or ten percent lipid emulsion. *J Pediatr.* 115:787–93, 1989.

9. Committee on Nutrition, American Acadamy of Pediatrics. Commentary on parenteral nutrition. *Pediatrics.* 71:547–52, 1983.

10. Green HL, Hambidge KM, Schanler R, et al. Guidelines for the use of vitamins, trace elements, calcium, magnesium, and phosphorus in infants and children receiving total parenteral nutrition: Report of the Subcommittee on Pediatric Parenteral Nutrition Requirements from the Committee on Clinical Practice Issues of the American Society for Clinical Nutrition. *Am J Clin Nutr.* 48:1324–42, 1988.

11. Moukarel AA, Song MK, Buchman AL, et al. Excessive chromium intake in children receiving total parenteral nutrition. *Lancet.* 339:385–8, 1992.

Section IV. Extemporaneous Compounding of Parenteral Nutrient Formulations: Screening The Nutrient Prescription

Background. Serious disorders and death have been attributed to PN formulations having inappropriate nutrient compositions. Deficiencies of trace elements and essential fatty acids have been reported in both pediatric and adult patient populations.[1,2] The most dramatic, yet insidious, example of the dangers associated with the omission of micronutrients occurred during the national parenteral multivitamin shortage during the summer of 1988[3] and throughout 1997.[4] In 1988, omission of parenteral multivitamins resulted in three deaths of patients predisposed to vitamin deficiencies. Specifically, three patients died as a result of refractory lactic acidosis associated with thiamin deficiency that was accentuated by the administration of dextrose in the PN mixture. Similarly, a death related to the omission of dextrose from a neonatal PN formulation caused irreversible brain damage. Finally, life-threatening deficiencies have resulted when patients have received phosphate-free PN.[5] Overdoses of nutrients included in PN formulations may also be harmful. As explained in Section I, the incorrect admixture of a PN formulation resulting in excessive dextrose infusions led to a patient's death, and a 50-fold error in an iron dextran admixture caused serious liver damage in a child. In all these cases, there was inadequate review of the PN prescription for appropriateness of dose and adequacy of nutrient composition. It is the responsibility of the pharmacist to review each prescription for appropriate indication, dose, and route of administration, and the potential for drug-drug, drug-nutrient and drug-laboratory interactions.[5]

For those systems requiring that the PN prescription be rewritten each day, the potential exists for transcription errors that omit or significantly increase nutrient doses. In this regard, it is important when refilling the day's order for PN therapy that the pharmacist review the contents of the PN formulation for consistency with the previous day's prescription. Major deviations should be questioned to avoid nutrition-related complications. For example, the pharmacist should clarify with the prescribing physician a prescription for a patient if insulin was present in the previous day's order at a dose of 20 units and the present order is for 100 units without a change in the quantity of dextrose received between the two days. In this case, it is both appropriate and reasonable to question the order. Other orders that might be appropriately questioned are drug and nutrient quantities; other large-scale changes including omissions, dramatic increases, or decreases; and other types of extreme day-to-day fluctuations.

Practice Guidelines: Nutrient Prescription.

1.   The energy, protein, fluid, electrolyte, vitamin, trace element, and medication content should be reviewed for all PN prescriptions to assure that a complete and balanced nutrient formulation is provided. *Balanced* is defined as the presence of the proper proportion of calories, protein, electrolytes, trace elements, and vitamins to assure adequate use by and assimilation into the body.

2.   Each of the PN components should be assessed for adequacy of dose and for the potential of a compatibility or stability problem. Any dose of a nutrient outside a normal range that is *not* explained by an unusual patient condition or history should be questioned and clarified before the PN is compounded.

Areas Requiring Further Work. Traditionally, the pharmacist is assigned the responsibility of verifying the indication, dose, and use of a drug or nutrient, as is the case with PN. It is recognized that because of the variety in the organization of nutrition support teams, this responsibility may be reassigned to other team members instead of the pharmacist. Also, some computer software for PN admixture may be programmed to cue the pharmacist that the PN admixture is inappropriate when nutrient doses are outside an acceptable range.

PN Compounding

Background. The 1994 FDA Safety Alert (referred to in Section I) highlights the serious consequences that are possible when quality compounding practices are not in place. The responsibility of the dispensing pharmacist is to ensure that the PN formulation is prepared, labeled, controlled, stored, dispensed, and distributed properly.[6] PN formulations are sometimes considered high-risk sterile products because of the large number of chemical entities found in the admixture process and the complex nature of PN admixing, whether with gravimetric or automated compounding.[7-9] Serious harm may come to patients receiving a PN formulation that has precipitates resulting from a chemical interaction between nutrients that are present in too high a dose, exposed to extremes of temperature, or admixed in an improper sequence. Automated or manual methods of PN compounding are available. The compounding of the PN admixture can be accomplished manually through the separate addition of nutrients via syringe or needle delivery or with the aid of sterile solution transfer sets. The manual method allows the pharmacist to decide the order of mixing and should be carefully undertaken to avoid potentially lethal incompatibilities. Alternatively, automated compounding devices are widely available that admix PN formulations under computed-assisted commands connected to special hardware housed with sterile, disposable compounding sets. Assistance in optimizing the compounding order for automated compounding devices should be obtained through consultation with the manufacturer of macronutrients currently used at the institution because brand-specific issues might influence compatibility of the final formulation, as well as the manufacturer of the compounding device. Finally, there are premixed PN products that come in a variety of forms that include, for example, crystalline amino acids with electrolytes, amino acid or dextrose kits as either separate entities or in the same container separated by a divider that can be released or activated to produce the final admixture, or even an empty container as a dual-chamber bag. However, even these preassembled units require some level of pharmaceutical compounding in an aseptic environment prior to use.

Observing the physical appearance of the final admixture is one of the most fundamental quality assurance measures that pharmacists routinely apply. Although it represents a crude measure of compatibility, it does identify gross particulate matter that likely represents the greatest clinical risk of embolic syndrome if infused into the patient. The process generally includes a detailed assessment of the final formulation against a dark background under high-intensity illumination. For translucent intravenous solutions, the highly trained eye is searching for the presence of insoluble particulate matter, such as "cores" from elastomeric vial enclosures, cotton fibers from alcohol wipes, etc, as well as characteristic indicators of incompatible formulation such as gas formation, turbidity or haziness, or crystal formation. It is important to remember that in the absence of any obvious physical signs of incompatibility, visual clarity does not equate with safety. Subvisible particulate matter may exist and may still be capable of inducing an embolic syndrome that originates at the level of the capillaries. However, visual assessments are valuable and necessary in the routine quality assurance process; they should be supplemented with other safety-enhancing measures that include sufficient documentation of the concentrations of nutrients prepared, use of filters in

the manufacturing process or during the infusion, and possibly particle-size analysis when available. Documentation of the daily compounding activities for PN formulations, irrespective of the products or procedures used, should exist. Such documentation should include batch records for all formulations prepared and should be consistent with institutional policies and procedures.

Opaque parenteral dispersions such as TNAs can still be visually assessed. The principal aim of this assessment is to identify signs of phase separation, in which the instability of the emulsion is manifested by the presence of free oil either as individually discernible fat droplets or a continuous layer at the surface of the formulation. In general, creaming is a common occurrence and not a significant determinant of infusion safety except in extreme cases.

Practice Guidelines: Compounding.

1. The additive sequence in compounding should be optimized and validated as a safe and efficacious method.

2. If the manual method currently in use at an institution has not been recently reviewed, or if the contract with a particular manufacturer of macronutrients is about to change, then a review of the compounding method is strongly recommended. This review should include an evaluation of the most current literature as well as consultation with the manufacturer when necessary.

3. Manufacturers of automated methods of PN compounding should provide an additive sequence that ensures the safety of the compounding device. This compounding sequence should be reviewed with the manufacturer of the parenteral nutrient products used by institution. As most institutions in the United States are represented by buying groups with many participants, such buying groups should not only ensure the safety and support of the automated compounding device, but should avoid splitting PN contracts (mixing brands of amino acids, dextrose and IFEs) unless such combinations have adequate physicochemical data that ensure the stability, compatibility, and safety of the final formulations commensurate with the data for single-source PN products.

4. Each PN formulation compounded should be visually inspected for signs of gross particulate contamination, particulate formation, and/or phase separation of TNAs.

Quality Assurance of the Compounding Process

Background. Numerous cases have been reported of adverse events associated with erroneous final concentrations of dextrose in parenteral fluids. Also infections events have occurred from microbial contamination of pharmacy-prepared PN formulations.[10]

In-process or end-product testing of PN formulations should be performed in accordance with US Pharmacopeia (USP) standards and American Society of Health System Pharmacists (ASHP) recommendations for sterile-product admixture.[7-9] Because of the complex nature of PN formulations, these processes may be modified to accommodate the special physicochemical characteristics of PN with use of the methodologies for gravimetric, chemical, or refractometric analysis and in-process testing.

Gravimetric Analysis. Weight-based delivery of PN additives is the principal method by which automated compounders prepare PN admixtures. These devices provide a high degree of accuracy and compound the admixture in a fraction of the time it takes with the use of manual, gravity-fed compounding techniques. In general, as a final check of the admixture, the PN formulation is weighed and is expected to be within an acceptable margin of error. However, this process evaluates only the accuracy of the total contents and not individual additives. To ensure that certain additives having a narrow margin of safety are assessed individually, pharmacists can apply gravimetric techniques similar to those used by the compounding device. This is particularly important for additives such as potassium chloride and highly interactive salts such as phosphates. In the case of potassium chloride, a 2000-mL final PN volume with a 5% compounding error acceptance means that a 100-mL overfill would be tolerated. If the entire overfill came from the potassium chloride container(s), it could be lethal. Thus individual monitoring of certain PN additives is recommended, and this monitoring can be simply accomplished within the sterile compounding facility each day. The gravimetric method is preferred, with use of the analytical balance associated with the automated compounder.

Chemical Analysis. A random, but continuously applied assessment of the final glucose concentration is reasonable. One approach is through the use of glucose measuring devices that allow for *direct* assessment of the dextrose concentration. Although these instruments have a limited effective range of detection, appropriate dilutions may be made from a PN aliquot to measure the final concentrations of dextrose and to assure that they are in accordance with the prescribed quantities intended for the patient. When this quality assurance method is devised, it is important to outline a stepwise procedure, validate the findings against appropriate control glucose solutions, and apply the appropriate error analysis that gauges an acceptable margin of error.

Refractometric Analysis. Refractometers have been used in pharmacy practice for determining dextrose content. However, pharmacists may need training and experience in order to obtain consistent and reliable results. In addition, because refractometry measures a physical characteristic of dextrose (ie, refractive index), it is an *indirect* determinant of dextrose concentration and is subject to interference by other components, as well as to variation in technique from one operator to another and in subsequent interpretation of the final results. As with direct measurement techniques of dextrose concentration, the procedures should be validated in a similar manner to ensure the integrity of the results. Refractometers are rendered inoperable with TNAs, and therefore are of no use for these formulations.

In-Process Testing. There are three ways to test the integrity of the extemporaneous compounding process of PN formulations, and all three can be accomplished at any time before, during, or after the hours of operation for PN manufacturing. For purposes of this summary, "in-process" can include any one of the aforementioned periods. The amount of potassium chloride used after each stock bottle exchange, along with the appropriate density conversion for the additive tested, can be determined gravimetrically at multiple points during the day within the compounding facility. As long as the number of patients who received a portion of the stock from a container is properly recorded, the pharmacist can determine whether the delivery is accurate by analyzing a subset of the PN formulations and can take appropriate action for only those formulations affected, thereby reducing the costs associated with waste if they need to be remade. Similarly, individual PN containers can be analyzed for dextrose content during chemical or refractometric analysis, which can be applied in a cost-effective manner.

In addition to these assessments of hardware function, the software can be similarly challenged to see whether the response is appropriate to the command. For example, if extraordinary amounts of calcium and phosphorus are entered into the compounding program, does the software recognize a potential incompatibility? Such challenges to the software program are best performed either before or after the PN admixtures are formulated, rather than during the time of operation. This is because such tests run the risk of an inadvertent compounding command that may be overlooked and could result in dispensing an incompatible and potentially dangerous formulation.

Practice Guidelines: Quality Assurance.

1. Gravimetric analyses that indirectly assess the accuracy of the individual additives delivered or the final contents of the PN can be readily applied in the pharmacy practice setting. Particular attention should be focused on the most dangerous additives that tolerate the least margin of error such as the potassium salts.

2. Chemical analyses that directly measure the final content of the individual additives can be easily incorporated into the PN compounding operations of the pharmacy. The accuracy of the PN dextrose content is an example of an additive that may be associated with significant morbidity and mortality.

3. Refractometric analysis is an alternative, as well as an indirect measure of the final additive concentration. For example, dextrose concentration is frequently assessed by this technique. However, this method is limited to PN formulations that do not contain an IFE.

4. In-process or end-product testing of PN formulations is recommended daily so as to ensure that a safe final formulation is dispensed to the patient.

5. The aseptic extemporaneous preparation of intravenous admixtures intended for patient administration should adhere to the ASHP Technical Assistance Bulletin on Quality Assurance for Sterile Products.[9]

References

1. Heller RM, Kirchner SA, O'Neill JA, et al. Skeletal changes of copper deficiency in infants receiving prolonged parenteral nutrition. *J Pediatr.* 93:847–51, 1978.

2. Riella MC, Broviac JW, Wells M, et al. Essential fatty acid deficiency in human adults during total parenteral nutrition. *Ann Intern Med.* 83:786–9, 1975.

3. Anonymous. Death associated with thiamine deficient total parenteral nutrition. *MMWR.* 38:43, 1987.

4. Alliou M, Ehrinpreis MN. Storage of intravenous

multivitamin solution in the United States [Letter]. *N Engl J Med.* 337(1):54–5, 1997.

5.   Travis SF, Sugarman HJ, Ruberg RL, et al. Alterations of red-cell glycolytic intermediates and oxygen transport as a consequence of hypophosphaternia in patients receiving intravenous hyperalimentation. *N Engl J Med.* 285:763–8, 1971.

6.   A.S.P.E.N. Board of Directors. Standard of Practice: Nutrition support pharmacists. *Nutr Clin Pract.* 8:124–7, 1993.

7.   Sterile Drug Products for Home Use (1206). USP23/NF18. United States Pharmacopeial Convention Inc., Rockville MD, 1995, pp 1963–75.

8.   Total parenteral nutrition/total nutrient admixture. USP DI Update, vol I and II. United States Pharmacopeial Convention Inc., Rockville, MD, 1996, pp 66–71.

9.   ASHP Technical Assistance Bulletin on quality assurance for pharmacy-prepared sterile products. *Am J Hosp Pharm.* 50:2386–98, 1993.

10. Bozetti F, Bonfanti G, Regalia E, et al. Catheter sepsis from infusate contamination. *Nutr Clin Pract.* 5:156–9, 1990.

Section V. Stability and Compatibility of Parenteral Nutrition Formulations: PN Stability

Background. The stability of PN formulations principally focuses on the degradation of nutritional components over time. The Maillard reaction ("the browning reaction") is well-known and involves the decomposition of carbohydrates by certain amino acids such as glycine, which is facilitated by temperatures used for sterilization of commercial products. Thus the combination of amino acids and dextrose must be compounded by the pharmacist rather than provided in a single commercial package. It is generally recognized that the extemporaneous compounding of any PN formulation accelerates the rate of physicochemical destabilization. Presently, certain amino acids, multivitamins, and lipids are most susceptible to instability. Except for an isolated case report, the discoloration of commercial amino acid products forming a bluish hue is not associated with adverse effects. However, the oxidation reaction involving tryptophan that produces the discoloration should be prevented by storage away from light and, preferably, keeping the manufacturer's protective packaging intact until the time of use.

From a clinical perspective, the physicochemical stability of PN formulations is largely focused on multivitamins, several of which are known to deteriorate substantially over time. For the most part, despite their degradation, very few produce clinically significant disturbances in the acute-care setting. They tend to be more important in patients who have marginal body stores and who are dependent on long-term PN support. The clearest example of this was demonstrated in a case report of a home patient who received weekly batches of PN formulations prepared by a hospital pharmacy in which the vitamins were added for a period of up to 7 days. Within 6 months, the patient had night blindness, was treated with a large intra-muscular dose of vitamin A, and the symptoms resolved. Six months later, the patient had a relapse in symptoms, prompting an investigation into why the multivitamin supplement was insufficient in meeting the patient's needs. Because the vitamins were added up to a week before the solution was administered, substantial amounts of vitamin A were lost to degradation and adsorption into the plastic matrix of the infusion container. Adding the vitamins to the PN formulation daily just prior to infusion resolved the problem.[1]

Similarly, when ascorbic acid was added in a batch fashion, it degraded and resulted in the formation of a large, discernible precipitate in the PN admixture. Careful analysis revealed that the precipitate was calcium oxalate. Oxalic acid is a degradation product of vitamin C that readily reacts with free calcium. Significant degradation can be avoided by adding vitamins just prior to infusion.[2]

The extemporaneous preparation of L-glutamine for addition to a PN admixture poses several concerns. L-glutamine has limited stability in PN formulations, and it requires special parenteral manufacturing techniques not routinely available in most institutional pharmacies. The formulation needs to be evaluated to ensure that its final contents meet the desired concentration and that it is sterile and free of pyrogens. Assuming the sterile compounding facility is qualified to make such a product, it is the pharmacist's responsibility to quarantine the product and ensure that it passes the aforementioned tests prior to its infusion. In most cases, the quarantine period is at least 7 days in order to complete the microbiologic analyses for the appearance of slow-growing pathogens. For products with limited stability, however, USP guidelines do allow for release of the product prior to the end of the quarantine period. Therefore, although less than ideal, quality control issues arising after quarantine can be dealt with retrospectively.

In addition to the above concerns for PN formulations, the stability of submicron lipid droplets must also be maintained in TNA dispersions during the period of infusion. Because the TNA dispersion is stabilized by an anionic emulsifier and numerous destabilizing cations are routinely included in the admixture, there is a risk of infusing an unstable and potentially dangerous admixture. Generally, when producing a TNA, the pharmacist is guided by the manufacturer of the lipid emulsion product as to its physicochemical limitations. The pharmacist is urged to use this brand-specific information and not to extrapolate to other products.

The use of dual-chamber bags, whereby for example, the lipid is physically separated from the remaining admixture components, can enhance the shelf-life of extemporaneously prepared TNAs. Its greatest utility appears to be in the home care setting, where batch preparation of PN formulations is most common.

Although TNAs have been formulated for use in the neonate and infant, stability of lipid particles within the admixture must be established for each combination of additives before use. The higher content of divalent cations can reduce particle zeta potential (negative surface charge), resulting in coalescence. Additionally, higher content of calcium and phosphate in neonatal and infant PN admixtures increases the risk of precipitation, which can go undetected because of TNA opacity.

PN Compatibility. The compexity typical of PN formulations poses several possible physicochemical incompatibilities. Degradation of drugs or nutrients is always a possibility, yet little evidence exists that such reactions cause clinical harm. The most serious risk of incompatibility in PN formulations and thus the most imminent threat to the patient arises when macroprecipitates exceeding 5 to 7 μ form in the admixture and pass into the central circulation. Two forms of precipitates—solid and liquid—may appear in an extemporaneously prepared admixture. Commonly, the existence of crystalline matter is most frequently cited in PN formulations, yet with the use of TNA emulsions, phase separation with the liberation of free oil constitutes the lipid precipitate.

Solid precipitates can develop when an incompatible combination of various salts is added to a PN formulation; this results in the formation of insoluble product. Calcium salts are reactive compounds and readily form insoluble products with a number of additives. Dibasic calcium phosphate ($CaHPO_4$) is an example of one of the most dangerous incompatible combinations and has resulted in embolic deaths when infused in the clinical setting. This can be avoided through a variety of measures. First, calcium gluconate is the preferred form of calcium used in multicomponent PN formulations. Calcium chloride is far more reactive than an equivalent amount of calcium gluconate salt. Second, the order of compounding is extremely important in order to avoid the formulation of an insoluble precipitate that would otherwise be soluble if added in the correct sequence. Generally, phosphate should be added first, and calcium should be added near the end of the compounding sequence to take advantage of the maximum volume of the PN formulation. Other risks of forming solid precipitates include using bicarbonate salts when indicated to correct a base deficit through the PN formulation. Again, bicarbonate reacts with calcium to form the insoluble product calcium carbonate. If an alkalinizing salt is indicated, then sodium or potassium acetate should be used. The dose of alkalinizing salt is the same for either bicarbonate or acetate (1 mEq of bicarbonate has the same alkalinizing power as 1 mEq of acetate). Finally, ascorbic acid is a highly unstable vitamin that has been suggested to be added in supraphysiologic quantities (up to 2000 mg per day) in the PN formulation for its antioxidant effects. However, because of its unstable characteristics, it readily degrades to form oxalic acid, which is also highly reactive with calcium, forming the insoluble product calcium oxalate. Thus the use of this vitamin in supraphysiologic quantities should be given via separate infusion, not in the PN formulation.

Phase separation and the liberation of free oil from the destablization of TNAs can result when an excess of cations is added to a given admixture. The higher the cation valence, the greater the destablizing power; thus trivalent cations such as Fe^{+3} (from iron dextran) are more disruptive than divalent cations such as calcium and magnesium. Monovalent cations such as sodium and potassium are least disruptive to the emulsifier, yet when given in sufficiently high concentrations, they may also produce instability. There is no safe concentration of iron dextran in any TNA.[3] Of the divalent and monovalent cations, adult patients' clinical needs can usually be met without significant concern of producing an unstable and potentially dangerous formulation. Even the order of compounding can cause instability of TNAs, and the compounding sequence must not place destabilizing additives such as the cations or hypertonic dextrose in close sequence with a minimally diluted intravenous fat emulsion. In general, the pharmacist should be guided by the instructions of the manufacturer for the macronutrients and the automated compounder in use to ensure that all parenteral nutrients are compounded optimally, and that they are safe and compatible.

The presence of enlarged lipid globules can be successfully identified if the proper techniques are used. There are only two stages of emulsion destabilization that are detectable by the naked eye, namely creaming and coalescence. As visual observation is the most routinely applied quality assurance method used by practicing pharmacists, an appreciation of the physical signs of TNA integrity is essential. The initial stage in emulsion breakdown is creaming, which occurs most immediately upon standing once fat emulsion has been mixed with the other chemical constituents (nutrients, electrolytes, vitamins, etc). The presence of a cream layer is visible at the surface of the emulsion as a translucent band separate from the remaining TNA dispersion. Although the lipid particles in the cream layer are destabilized, their individual droplet identities are generally preserved; pharmacists should expect creaming of TNA emulsions but this is safe for patient administration.

The terminal stage of emulsion destabilization is the coalescence of small lipid particles forming large droplets that may vary in size from 5 to 50+ μ that pose potential clinical danger, yet escape visual detection. The existence of coalesced lipid particles in a TNA is characterized by the variable presence of yellow-brown oil droplets at or near the TNA surface. In its usual presentation, the free oil may exist as individual spherical droplets or as segmented (discontinuous) oil layers. Careful observation of each TNA is required to detect the subtle appearance of coalescence. In its most extreme form, the oil forms a continuous layer of yellow-brown liquid at the surface that is readily discernible from the remaining dispersion and can be accompanied by marbling or streaking of the oil throughout the admixture. In either case, the presence of free oil in any form in a TNA should be considered unsafe for parenteral administration.[4] The danger associated with the infusion of unstable lipid droplets enlarged through electromechanical destabilization is unclear. However, the existence of fat globules >5 μ in diameter comprising >0.4% of the total fat present has been shown to be pharmaceutically unstable, and such admixtures are considered unfit for intravenous administration.[3]

The manufacturers of lipid emulsions use a variety of stability assessment techniques; however, laser assessment is the most reliable and sensitive to the subtle, yet important physicochemical changes in emulsion stability that serve as a harbinger of possible dangers. There are currently three methods of laser analysis frequently used in the assessment of lipid emulsion stability—laser diffraction, photon correlation spectroscopy, and light obscuration or extinction. The first two techniques principally focus on the submicron globules and provide information about mean particle size. They are relatively insensitive to the remote, yet potentially significant, droplets that have been enlarged through electromechanical destabilization. Laser diffraction and photon correlation spectroscopy do not count individual particles, but through a variety of mathematical correlations, they construct the typical particle size distribution around the mean globule size. The principal benefit of these techniques is to the manufacturer during the homogenization of lipid droplets in the production of the commercial emulsion.

Finally, standard PN formulations have been useful to organizations whereby the physicochemical stability and compatibility are assured via adequate documentation by the institution or the manufacturer of parenteral nutrient products. Such standardization limits the risk of compounding and dispensing potentially unstable or incompatible PN formulations. However, any change in the composition of standard formulations needs to be applied cautiously and with adequate assurance that the new or revised formula is stable and compatible.

Practice Guidelines: Stability and Compatibility.

1. The dose, admixture preparation, packaging, delivery process, and storage and administration method should be confirmed to ensure that the PN is stable and all components are compatible.

2. The responsible pharmacist should verify that the coinfusion of drugs with PN either admixed in the PN formulation or coinfused through the same intravenous tubing is safe, stable, and free from incompatibilities.

3. Decisions related to stability and compatibility should be made according to the most reliable information available from the literature or manufacturer of intravenous nutrients. If no information exists, stability and compatibility of the PN must be determined in consultation with the manufacturer before it is dispensed to the patient.

4. Given the limited amount of published stability information available, the use of a 2-in-1 formulation with separate administration of an IFE is recommended for neonatal and infant patients.

References

1. Howard L, Chu R, Feman S, et al. Vitamin A deficiency from long-term parenteral nutrition. *Ann Intern Med.* 93:576–7, 1980.
2. Gupta VD. Stability of vitamins in total parenteral nutrient solutions. *Am J Hosp Pharm.* 43:2132, 1986.
3. Driscoll DF, Bhargava HN, Li L, et al. Physicochemical stability of total nutrient admixtures. *Am J Hosp Pharm.* 52:623–34, 1995.
4. Driscoll DF. Total nutrient admixtures: Theory and practice. *Nutr Clin Pract.* 10:114–9, 1995.

Section VI. In-Line Filtration of PN Admixtures

Background. Use of an in-line filter with PN can prevent the administration of particulate matter, air, and microorganisms to patients. The National Coordinating Committee on Large Volume Parenterals,[1] the Intravenous Nurses Society,[2] and the Food and Drug Administration[3] have recommended that in-line filters be used during the administration of intravenous products such as PN formulations.

Rationale for the Use of In-Line Filters. *Particulates.* It is known that both large-volume injectables and their containers have minute amounts of particulate matter and that additional particulates may be introduced to solutions with multiple additives, such as PN formulations. The entry of large numbers of particles of diverse sizes and composition into pulmonary capillaries and their dissemination into other organs, such as the renal medulla, brain, lungs, spleen, and liver, may lead to blockage of these vessels and harmful effects on the surrounding tissues. Particles of 5 to 20 μ and larger are capable of obstructing blood flow through the pulmonary capillaries, which could lead to complications such as pulmonary embolism.[4,5]

Phlebitis. Foreign particles can produce phlebitis at the injection site.[6] Although phlebitis is not a consideration when PN is administered through a central vein, phlebitis can be a therapy-limiting problem when it is administered peripherally. Use of an in-line filter has been shown to delay the development and reduce the incidence of phlebitis, and even reduced the length of hospital stay in one study.[7,8,9] However, other studies have reported no benefit.[10,11]

Reasons for these mixed results may be related to differences in the pH and composition of the infused solutions, the compounding techniques used in their preparation, and study design differences. If pharmacists use a filter needle for incorporation of reconstituted solutions into large-volume fluids or incorporate a final filtration step during compounding, the clinical benefit of a second filtration through an in-line filter in reducing phlebitis may be negligible.

Microprecipitates. Formation of microprecipitates in intravenous admixtures is principally dependent on concentration, pH, and temperature. If no filter is used, microprecipitates can be infused, potentially causing catheter occlusion and loss of intravenous access, as well as patient harm. Formation of microprecipitates due to concentrations of calcium and phosphate in excess of their solubility is a potentially harmful source of particulate matter. Factors that affect the solubility of calcium and phosphate in PN have been described.[12,13] Precipitation is more likely to occur at higher temperatures because the more insoluble dibasic calcium phosphate predominates at higher temperatures.[13] This is of particular concern with TNAs because the opacity of the emulsion prevents effective visual inspection. Precipitation may occur inside the catheter at body temperature even though a precipitate was not visible in the admixture on inspection.[14] Two deaths and at least two other cases of respiratory distress have been attributed to microprecipitates of calcium and phosphate in TNAs.[15] Drug precipitates may also cause a crystalline occlusion similar to calcium phosphate. In-line filters are recommended as a means of removing these crystals and avoiding catheter occlusion.[16,17]

Initial visual inspection cannot be relied upon to detect formation of a precipitate. Unless a formulation is grossly incompatible, it is unlikely that a precipitate will form instantaneously.[5] In most situations, precipitates may take hours to develop, thus visual inspection at the time of compounding or dispensing may not detect a precipitate. Additionally, the limitations of visual detection should be recognized. The highly trained unaided eye is capable of distinguishing particulate matter as small as 50 μ.[12] However, because of variations in visual acuity and the difficulty of paying close attention when large numbers of PN formulations are inspected on a daily basis, precipitates may escape detection by inspection. Even at best, visual detection is limited to particles with a diameter ≥50 μ, but particles in the range of 5 to 20 μ may lodge in the pulmonary capillaries and cause complications.[6,8] By the time a precipitate can be detected by visual inspection, the formulation is grossly incompatible and unsafe for administration.[18]

Filters have sometimes been criticized because they may clog, causing infusion pumps to sound their alarm and requiring nursing intervention. It should be recognized that a clogged filter is a potential sign of a precipitate. It is never appropriate to remove a clogged filter and allow the admixture to infuse without a filter.

Infection. A PN formulation can become contaminated during compounding or during setup for administration. PN formulations are at risk for contamination because of the multiple manipulations required for compounding and the ability of these solutions to support the growth of fungal and Gram-negative microorganisms.[19] Contaminated PN formulations have been linked to patient infections, and episodes of contamination have been reported with PN formulations without IFEs, TNAs, and even in-use manufacturer's bottles of lipid emulsion.[20-23] Use of a 0.2-μ filter can remove microorganisms, either as a final step in the compounding process or in-line during solution administration; however, this is limited to use with 2-in-1 formulations.

Use of a 0.2-μ filter is a reliable method of sterilization, but contamination can occur from exposure of solutions to the environment after filtration or from touch contamination distal to the filter. Additionally, manipulation of the filter itself may provide an opportunity for contamination.[13]

Pyrogens. Once bacteria are trapped on the surface of a membrane filter, it is possible for pyrogen, or Gram-negative endotoxin, to leak through the pores in the filter. Bacterial endotoxin can pass through standard membranes such as cellulose acetate or polysulfone.[24] However, filters are available with a positive charge on their surface that can retain the pyrogens by electomagnetic forces. A positively charged nylon membrane has been shown to produce a pyrogen-free effluent for 96 hours when used with 2-in-1 formulations.[24]

Air Emboli. Air emboli can be prevented by the use of air-venting in-line filters to prevent air from being introduced into the patient. Although the chance of patient harm from air emboli is relatively remote in adults, it is much greater in infants.[13]

Limitations to the Use of Filters. A 0.22-μ filter is not appropriate for use with lipid emulsions. Stable lipid emulsions usually contain lipid droplets ranging in size from less than 0.1 μ to approximately 1.0 μ. Even though these particles are readily deformed and can be pumped through a 0.22-μ filter, it is not advisable to do so because the particles will shear, altering the emulsion's stability.[13] The manufacturers of lipid emulsions advise against passing them through a 0.22-μ filter either alone or in a TNA. Lipids or TNAs can be safely filtered through a pore size of 1.2 μ or greater.[25] A 1.2-μ filter is not a sterilizing filter, and it will not reliably remove common bacterial contaminants such as *Staphylococcus epidermidis or Escherichia coli*.[26] However, use of a 1.2-μ filter will remove large organisms such as *Canadian albicans* that are approximately 3 to 6 μ in diameter.[27] Additionally, a 1.2-μ filter will remove particulate matter from the administration line.[28] Since particles 5 μ and greater can lodge in the pulmonary capillaries, use of a 1.2-μ in-line filter has been recommended as a standard.

Use of in-line filters can cause decreased flow rates, clogs, or air locks. These problems can lead to increased manipulation of the intravenous administration set, creating a potential for the introduction of contamination. Many current pumps and controllers are equipped with air-in-line alarms that decrease the need for the air-eliminating filters. Although filters can dependably remove particulates that are present in the line proximal to the filter, it is unclear whether this is true for those that form or are introduced distal to the filter. In one case, a patient developed pulmonary deposition of calcium phosphate crystals while receiving a 2-in-1 formulation at home administered through intravenous tubing that used a 0.22-μ filter. The patient

denied observing crystals in the solution, and solution bags stored in the refrigerator appeared clear. However, when the patient's solution bags were placed in a 37°C water bath, rapid precipitation and crystal formation occurred within 1 hour.[29]

Finally, in the current cost-conscious health care environment, the high cost of filters cannot be ignored.

Filter Selection. A number of types of filter membranes may be acceptable for use with PN formulations. Membrane filters composed of mixed esters of cellulose can be used for most PN formulations, but they should not be used for fluids with a pH outside the range of 4.0 or 7.5. Polysulfone filters are chemically inert, and they are acceptable for a wider range of pH values. Specially processed nylon 66 filters are available with a positively charged surface that is used to adsorb negatively charges substances such as pyrogens, bacteria, and viruses.[13]

Most in-line filters should be used for no more than 24 hours because of the build-up of trapped bacteria and subsequent potential for leakage of pyrogens through the filter membrane. Filter membranes made of positively charged nylon may be used for up to 96 hours for 2-in-1 formulations because of their ability to retain bacteria and pyrogens more reliably.[30] By use of a positively charged nylon filter, the tubing change period can be extended to 72 to 96 hours, which can offset the additional cost of using an in-line filter.[31]

Consensus. In the current cost-constrained health care environment, it is difficult to assure complete control of the prescribing, compounding, delivery, and administration of PN formulations. The solubility of calcium and phosphate is not entirely predictable. Even when the best compounding practices are followed, some risk of solution contamination exists. Use of a filter provides an additional safety check to prevent patient harm.

It should be noted that use of filters is not a complete cure for the potential problems of contamination or precipitation of PN formulations. Skill in prescribing and formulation and careful aseptic technique during compounding and handling of solutions are required to minimize the risk of patient harm.

Practice Guidelines: In-Line Filtration.

1. A 0.2-μ filter should be used for 2-in-1 formulations. A 1.2- to 5-μ filter should be used for TNAs. Alternatively, a 1.2-μ filter may be used for all PN formulations.
2. A filter that clogs during administration of PN is indicative of a problem and may be replaced but should never be removed entirely.

Areas Requiring Further Work. Further work is needed to more clearly define the appropriate use of filters in clinical practice. For example:

- What patient and environmental factors lead to development of microprecipitates distal to the filter?
- Would use of an in-line filter with an automated compounder be beneficial in removing contaminants and microprecipitates, and if so, could the filter be used for multiple patient containers, reducing the overall cost? Or would filtration during compounding be of little benefit because these products are initially sterile, and development of microprecipitates might occur after

the filtration step?

- Is use of a one-piece tubing and in-line filter unit advantageous compared with a separate add-on filter unit in reducing manipulation and potential contamination?
- What is the most appropriate replacement interval for filters, given the trend toward extending the duration of tubing use?
- Do pyrogen-retentive filters have a role for TNAs, or is the positively charged filter membrane's performance affected by the negatively charged exterior of lipid droplets?

All these questions need to be answered.

References

1. National Coordinating Committee on Large Volume Parenterals. Recommendations to pharmacists for solving problems with large volume parenterals. *Am J Hosp Pharm.* 37:663–7, 1980.

2. Anonymous. Intravenous nursing standards of practice. *J Intraven Nurs suppl.* S56–7, 1990.

3. Food and Drug Administration. Safety alert: Hazards of precipitation associated with parenteral nutrition. *Am J Hosp Pharm.* 51:1427–8142, 1994.

4. Turco S, Davis NM. Clinical significance of particulate matter: A review of the literature. *Hosp Pharm.* 8:137–40, 1973.

5. Driscoll DF. Total nutrient admixtures: Theory and practice. *Nutr Clin Pract.* 10:114–9, 1995.

6. DeLuca D, Rapp RP, Bivins B, et al. Filtration and infusion phlebitis: A double-blind prospective clinical study. *Am J Hosp Pharm.* 32:1001–7, 1975.

7. Falchuk KH, Peterson L, McNeil BJ. Microparticulate-induced phlebitis. Its prevention by in-line filtration. *N Engl J Med.* 312:78–82, 1985.

8. Allcutt DA, Lort D, McCollum CN. Final inline filtration for intravenous infusions: Prospective hospital study. *Br J Surg.* 70:111–3, 1983.

9. Rusho WJ, Bair JN. Effect of filtration on complications of postoperative intravenous therapy. *Am J Hosp Pharm.* 36:1355–6, 1979.

10. Rypins EB, Johnson BH, Reder B, et al. Three-phase study of phlebitis in patients receiving peripheral intravenous hyperalimentation. *Am J Surg.* 159:222–5, 1990.

11. Maddox RR, John JF Jr, Brown LL, et al. Effect of inline filtration on postinfusion phlebitis. *Clin Pharm.* 3:58–61, 1983.

12. Driscoll DG, Newton DW, Bistrian BR. Precipitation of calcium phosphate from parenteral nutrition fluids. *Am J Hosp Pharm.* 51:2834–6, 1994.

13. McKinnon BT, Avis KE. Membrane filtration of pharmaceutical solutions. *Am J Hosp Pharm.* 50:1921–36, 1993.

14. Robinson LA, Wright BT. Central venous catheter occlusion caused by body-heat-mediated calcium-phosphorus precipitation. *Am J Hosp Pharm.* 39:120–1, 1982.

15. Carey LC, Haffey M. Incident: Home TPN formula order misinterpreted after hospital admission. *Home Care Highlights.* Spring:7, 1995.

16. Rubin M, Bilik R, Aserin A, et al. Catheter obstruction; analysis of filter content of total nutrient admixture. *JPEN.* 13:641–3, 1989.

17. Rubin M. Response to Dr Pennington's letter [Letter]. *JPEN.* 14:551, 1990.

18. McKinnon BT. FDA safety alert: Hazards of precipitation associated with parenteral nutrition. *Nutr Clin Pract.* 11:59–65, 1996.

19. Thompson B, Robinson LA. Infection control of parenteral nutrition solutions. *Nutr Clin Pract.* 6:49–54, 1991.

20. Bozetti F, Bonfanti G, Regalia E, et al. Catheter sepsis from infusate contamination. *Nutr Clin Pract.* 5:156–9, 1990.

21. DeCicco M, Chiardaia V, Veronese A, et al. Source and route of microbial colonization of parenteral nutrition catheters. *Lancet.* 2:1258–61, 1989.

22. Dolvin BJ, Davis PD, Holland TA. Contamination rates of 3-in-1 total parenteral nutrition in a clinical setting. *JPEN.* 11:403–5, 1987.

23. Ebbert ML, Farraj M, Hwang LT. The incidence and clinical significance of intravenous fat emulsion during infusion. *JPEN.* 11:42–5, 1987.

24. Baumgartner TG, Schmidt GL, Thakker KM, et al. Bacterial endotoxin retention by inline intravenous filters. *Am J Hosp Pharm.* 43:681–4, 1986.

25. Wells P. A guide to total nutrient admixtures. *Precept,* Chicago, 1992.

26. Mershon J, Nogami W, Williams JM, et al. Bacterial/fungal growth in a combined parenteral nutrition solution. *JPEN.* 10:498–502, 1986.

27. Warshawsky KY. Intravenous fat emulsions in clinical practice. *Nutr Clin Pract.* 7:187–96, 1992.

28. Driscoll DF, Bacon MN, Bistrian BR. Effects of in-line filtration on particle size distribution in total nutrient admixtures. *JPEN.* 20:296–301, 1996.

29. Knowles JB, Cusson G, Smith M, et al. Pulmonary deposition of calcium phosphate crystals as a complication of home total parenteral nutrition. *JPEN.* 13:209–13, 1989.

30. Clarke R. A cost-effective system for TPN. *Nursing Times.* 86:65–7, 1990.

31. Robathan G, Woodger S, Meranta D. A prospective study evaluating the effects of extending total parenteral nutrition line changes to 72 hours. *J Intraven Nurs.* 18:84–7, 1995.

This document was reviewed in 2003 by the Council on Professional Affairs and by the Board of Directors and was found to still be appropriate.

Prepared by the National Advisory Group on Standards and Practice Guidelines for Parenteral Nutrition.

Approved by A.S.P.E.N. Board of Directors, January 17, 1997.

Distribution

Technician-Checking-Technician Programs (0310)

Source: Council on Administrative Affairs

To advocate technician-checking-technician programs (with appropriate quality control measures) in order to permit redirection of pharmacist resources to patient care activities; further,

To advocate state board of pharmacy approval of these programs.

Intermediate Category of Drugs (0220)

Source: Council on Legal and Public Affairs

To support, with appropriate changes in federal statutes and regulations, the establishment of an intermediate category of drug products that do not require a prescription but are available only from pharmacists and licensed health care professionals who are authorized to prescribe medications; further,

To base such support on the following facts:

1. Some drug products that are potential candidates for switching from prescription-only to nonprescription status raise concerns about patient safety as nonprescription products; these products could be better controlled, monitored, and evaluated by making them available only from pharmacists and licensed health care professionals who are authorized to prescribe medications; and
2. Pharmacists have the education, training, and expertise to help patients make appropriate therapeutic decisions associated with the use of such drug products; further,

To support that the regulatory system for this intermediate category of drug products contain the following features:

1. Drug products appropriate for this intermediate category would be identified through the advice of pharmacists, physicians, and other licensed health professionals who are authorized to prescribe medications, on the basis of the medical conditions to be treated and potential adverse effects (as indicated in FDA-approved labeling);

2. Pharmacists would be able to provide drugs in this intermediate category directly to patients without a prescription, on the basis of appropriate assessment and professional consultation;
3. Licensed health professionals who currently have prescribing authority would continue to have the ability to prescribe medications in this intermediate category; and
4. Data from postmarketing surveillance, epidemiologic studies, and adverse-drug-reaction reporting would be collected to help determine a drug product's eventual movement to nonprescription status, return to prescription-only status, or continuation in the intermediate category.

This policy supersedes ASHP policy 8511.

New and Emerging Pharmacy Systems (0008)

Source: Council on Legal and Public Affairs

To support the use of new and emerging medication ordering and distribution systems (e.g., via the World Wide Web) when such systems (a) provide the elements of pharmaceutical care, (b) ensure that patients will not receive improperly labeled and packaged, deteriorated, outdated, counterfeit, or non-FDA-approved drug products, (c) provide appropriate relationships between an authorized prescriber and patient, (d) enhance the continuity of patient care, and (e) support the pharmacist's role as a patient care advocate.

Dispensing by Nonpharmacists and Nonprescribers (0010)

Source: Council on Legal and Public Affairs

To reaffirm the position that all medication dispensing functions must be performed by, or under the supervision of, a pharmacist; further,

To reaffirm the position that any relationships that are established between a pharmacist and other individuals in order to carry out the dispensing function should preserve the role of the pharmacist in (a) maintaining appropriate patient protection and safety, (b) complying with regulatory and legal requirements, and (c) providing individualized patient care.

ASHP Statement on Unit Dose Drug Distribution

The unit dose system of medication distribution is a pharmacy-coordinated method of dispensing and controlling medications in organized health-care settings.

The unit dose system may differ in form, depending on the specific needs of the organization. However, the following distinctive elements are basic to all unit dose systems: medications are contained in single unit packages; they are dispensed in as ready-to-administer form as possible; and for most medications, not more than a 24-hour supply[a] of doses is delivered to or available at the patient-care area at any time.[1,2]

Numerous studies concerning unit dose drug distribution systems have been published over the past several decades. These studies indicate categorically that unit dose systems, with respect to other drug distribution methods, are (1) safer for the patient, (2) more efficient and economical for the organization, and (3) a more effective method of utilizing professional resources.

More specifically, the inherent advantages of unit dose systems over alternative distribution procedures are

1. A reduction in the incidence of medication errors.
2. A decrease in the total cost of medication-related activities.
3. A more efficient usage of pharmacy and nursing personnel, allowing for more direct patient-care involvement by pharmacists and nurses.
4. Improved overall drug control and drug use monitoring.
5. More accurate patient billings for drugs.
6. The elimination or minimization of drug credits.
7. Greater control by the pharmacist over pharmacy workload patterns and staff scheduling.
8. A reduction in the size of drug inventories located in patient-care areas.

9. Greater adaptability to computerized and automated procedures.

In view of these demonstrated benefits, the American Society of Hospital Pharmacists considers the unit dose system to be an essential part of drug distribution and control in organized health-care settings in which drug therapy is an integral component of health-care delivery.

References

1. Summerfield MR. Unit dose primer. Bethesda, MD: American Society of Hospital Pharmacists; 1983.
2. American Society of Hospital Pharmacists. ASHP technical assistance bulletin on hospital drug distribution and control. *Am J Hosp Pharm.* 1980; 37:1097–1103.

---

[a]In long-term care facilities, a larger supply of medication (e.g., 48 or 72 hours) may be acceptable.

Approved by the ASHP Board of Directors, November 16, 1988, and by the ASHP House of Delegates, June 5, 1989. Supersedes previous versions approved by the House of Delegates on June 8, 1981, and by the Board of Directors on April 19, 1975, and November 13–14, 1980.

The bibliographic citation for this document is as follows: American Society of Hospital Pharmacists. ASHP statement on unit dose drug distribution. *Am J Hosp Pharm.* 1989; 46:2346.

ASHP Statement on Pharmacist's Responsibility for Distribution and Control of Drug Products

A fundamental purpose of pharmaceutical services in any setting is to ensure the safe and appropriate use of drug products and drug-related devices. Fulfillment of this responsibility is enhanced through the pharmacist's involvement in all aspects of the use of drugs.[1]

This involvement should include decisions and actions with respect to the evaluation, procurement, storage, distribution, and administration of all drug products. The pharmacist is responsible for development, in consultation with appropriate other professionals, departments, and interdisciplinary committees in the setting, of all drug-use control policies. The pharmacist should be directly responsible for the control and distribution of all stocks of drugs.

The Federal Food, Drug, and Cosmetic Act defines the term *drug* as "(A) articles recognized in the official United States Pharmacopeia, official Homeopathic Pharmacopeia of the United States, or official National Formulary, or any supplement to any of them; and (B) articles intended for use in the diagnosis, cure, mitigation, treatment, or prevention of disease in man or other animals; and (C) articles (other than food) intended to affect the structure or any function of the body of man or other animals; and (D) articles intended for use as a component of any article specified in clauses (A), (B), or (C) of this paragraph; but does not include devices or their components, parts, or accessories."[2]

For purposes of this document, drugs include those used by inpatients and outpatients, large- and small-volume injections, radiopharmaceuticals, diagnostic agents including radiopaque contrast media, anesthetic gases, blood-fraction drugs, dialysis fluids, respiratory therapy drugs, biotechnologically produced drugs, investigational drugs, drug samples, drugs brought to the setting by patients or family, and other chemicals and biological substances administered to patients to evoke or enhance pharmacologic responses.

The pharmacist's responsibility for drug-use control extends throughout the setting served. This purview extends to all pharmacy satellite locations (inpatient and outpatient, including those serving the general public), emergency rooms, surgical and labor and delivery suites (and related areas such as recovery rooms), anesthesiology, nuclear medicine, radiology, dialysis areas, ambulatory care clinics and treatment (including surgery) areas, respiratory therapy areas, central sterile supply centers, blood banks, intensive care areas, cardiac catheterization suites, research areas, and all other areas in which drugs are handled and used. The pharmacist should be responsible for drug-use policies and routine inspection of all drug stocks, even if direct custody and distribution are not possible.

The pharmacist also has an advocacy responsibility with respect to decisions and policies about the use of drug-related devices as they affect drug therapy. As appropriate, the pharmacist may also be assigned direct responsibility for control and distribution of drug-related devices.[3] Drug-related devices include electromechanical pumps, devices for administration of injectable drugs, devices for monitoring plasma drug concentration, and devices for monitoring drug administration rate.

References

1. American Society of Hospital Pharmacists. ASHP guidelines: minimum standard for pharmacies in institutions. *Am J Hosp Pharm.* 1985; 42:372–5.
2. 21 U.S.C. §321 (g) (1).
3. American Society of Hospital Pharmacists. ASHP statement on the pharmacist's role with respect to drug delivery systems and administration devices. *Am J Hosp Pharm.* 1989; 46:802–4.

This statement was reviewed in 2001 by the Council on Administrative Affairs and by the Board of Directors and was found to still be appropriate.

Approved by the ASHP Board of Directors, November 16, 1994, and by the ASHP House of Delegates, June 5, 1995. Revised by the ASHP Council on Professional Affairs. Supersedes a previous version dated June 3, 1992.

The bibliographic citation for this document is as follows: ASHP statement on the pharmacist's responsibility for distribution and control of drug products. In: *Practice Standards of ASHP 1996–97.* Deffenbaugh JH, ed. Bethesda, MD: American Society of Health-System Pharmacists; 1996.

ASHP Technical Assistance Bulletin on Hospital Drug Distribution and Control

Drug control (of which drug distribution is an important part) is among the pharmacist's most important responsibilities. Therefore, adequate methods to assure that these responsibilities are met must be developed and implemented. These guidelines will assist the pharmacist in preparing drug control procedures for all medication-related activities. The guidelines are based on the premise that the pharmacy is responsible for the procurement, distribution, and control of *all* drugs used within the institution. In a sense, the entire hospital is the pharmacy, and the pharmacy service is simply a functional service extending throughout the institution's physical and organizational structures.

It should be noted that, although this document is directed toward hospitals, much of it is relevant to other types of health-care facilities.

Pharmacy Policies, Procedures, and Communications

Policy and Procedure Manuals.[1] The effectiveness of the drug control system depends on adherence to policies (broad, general statements of philosophy) and procedures (detailed guidelines for implementing policy). The importance of an up-to-date policy and procedure manual for drug control cannot be overestimated. All pharmacy staff must be familiar with the manual; it is an important part of orientation for new staff and crucial to the pharmacy's internal communication mechanism. In addition, preparing written policies and procedures requires a thorough analysis of control operations; this review might go undone otherwise.

Drug control begins with the setting of policy. The authority to enforce drug control policy and procedures must come from the administration of the institution, with the endorsement of the medical staff, via the pharmacy and therapeutics (P&T) committee and/or other appropriate committee(s). Because the drug control system interfaces with numerous departments and professions, the P&T committee should be the focal point for communications relating to drug control in the institution. The pharmacist, with the cooperation of the P&T committee, should develop media such as newsletters, bulletins, and seminars to communicate with persons functioning within the framework of the control system.

Inservice Training and Education. Intra- and interdepartmental education and training programs are important to the effective implementation of policies and procedures and the institution's drug control system in general. They are part of effective communication and help establish and maintain professional relationships among the pharmacy staff and between it and other hospital departments. Drug control policies and procedures should be included in the pharmacy's educational programs.

Standards, Laws, and Regulations

The pharmacist must be aware of and comply with the laws, regulations, and standards governing the profession. Many of these standards and regulations deal with aspects of drug control. Among the agencies and organizations affecting institutional pharmacy practice are those described below.

Regulatory Agencies and Organizations. The U.S. government, through its Food and Drug Administration (FDA), is responsible for implementing and enforcing the federal Food, Drug, and Cosmetic Act. The FDA is responsible for the control and prevention of misbranding and of adulteration of food, drugs, and cosmetics moving in interstate commerce. The FDA also sets label requirements for food, drugs, and cosmetics; sets standards for investigational drug studies and for marketing of new drug products; and compiles data on adverse drug reactions.

The U.S. Department of the Treasury influences pharmacy operation by regulating the use of tax-free alcohol through the Bureau of Alcohol, Tobacco and Firearms. The U.S. Department of Justice affects pharmacy practice through its Drug Enforcement Agency (DEA) by enforcing the Controlled Substances Act of 1970 and other federal laws and regulations for controlled drugs.

Another federal agency, the Health Care Financing Administration, has established Conditions of Participation for hospitals and skilled nursing facilities to assist these institutions to qualify for reimbursement under the health insurance program for the aged (Medicare) and for Medicaid.

The state board of pharmacy is the agency of state government responsible for regulating pharmacy practice within the state. Practitioners, institutions, and community pharmacies must obtain licenses from the board to practice pharmacy or provide pharmacy services in the state. State boards of pharmacy promulgate numerous regulations pertaining to drug dispensing and control. (In some states, the state board of health licenses the hospital pharmacy separately or through a license that includes all departments of the hospital.)

Standards and guidelines for pharmaceutical services have been established by the Joint Commission on Accreditation of Hospitals (JCAH)[2] and the American Society of Hospital Pharmacists (ASHP).[3] The United States Pharmacopeial Convention also promulgates certain pharmacy practice procedures as well as official standards for drugs and drug testing. Professional practice guidelines and standards generally do not have the force of law but rather are intended to assist pharmacists in achieving the highest level of practice. They may, however, be employed in legal proceedings as evidence of what constitutes acceptable practice as determined by the profession itself.

In some instances, both federal and state laws may deal with a specific activity; in such cases, the more stringent law will apply.

The Medication System

Procurement: Drug Selection, Purchasing Authority, Responsibility, and Control.[4–6] The selection of pharmaceuticals is a basic and extremely important professional function of the hospital pharmacist who is charged with making decisions regarding products, quantities, product specifications, and sources of supply. It is the pharmacist's obligation to establish and maintain standards assuring the quality, proper storage, control, and safe use of all pharmaceuticals and related supplies (e.g., fluid administration sets); this responsibility must not be delegated to another individual. Although the actual purchasing of drugs and supplies may be performed by a nonpharmacist, the setting of quality standards and specifications requires professional knowledge and judgment and must be performed only by the pharmacist.

Economic and therapeutic considerations make it necessary for hospitals to have a well-controlled, continuously updated formulary. It is the pharmacist's responsibility to develop and maintain adequate product specifications to aid in the purchase of drugs and related supplies under the formulary system. The *USP–NF* is a good base for drug product specifications; there also should be criteria to evaluate the acceptability of manufacturers and distributors. In establishing the formulary, the P&T committee recommends guidelines for drug selection. However, when his knowledge indicates, the pharmacist must have the authority to reject a particular drug product or supplier.

Although the pharmacist has the authority to select a brand or source of supply, he must make economic considerations subordinate to those of quality. Competitive bid purchasing is an important method for achieving a proper balance between quality and cost when two or more acceptable suppliers market a particular product meeting the pharmacist's specifications. In selecting a vendor, the pharmacist must consider price, terms, shipping times, dependability, quality of service, returned goods policy, and packaging; however, prime importance always must be placed on drug quality and the manufacturer's reputation. It should be noted that the pharmacist is responsible for the quality of all drugs dispensed by the pharmacy.

Records. The pharmacist must establish and maintain adequate recordkeeping systems. Various records must be retained (and be retrievable) by the pharmacy because of governmental regulations; some are advisable for legal protection, others are needed for JCAH accreditation, and still others are necessary for sound management (evaluation of productivity, workloads, and expenses and assessment of departmental growth and progress) of the pharmacy department. Records must be retained for at least the length of time prescribed by law (where such requirements apply).

It is important that the pharmacist study federal, state, and local laws to become familiar with their requirements for permits, tax stamps, storage of alcohol and controlled substances, records, and reports.

Among the records needed in the drug distribution and control system are

- Controlled substances inventory and dispensing records.
- Records of medication orders and their processing.
- Manufacturing and packaging production records.
- Pharmacy workload records.
- Purchase and inventory records.
- Records of equipment maintenance.
- Records of results and actions taken in quality-assurance and drug audit programs.

Receiving Drugs. Receiving control should be under the auspices of a responsible individual, and the pharmacist must ensure that records and forms provide proper control upon receipt of drugs. Complete accountability from purchase

order initiation to drug administration must be provided.

Personnel involved in the purchase, receipt, and control of drugs should be well trained in their responsibilities and duties and must understand the serious nature of drugs. All nonprofessional personnel employed by the pharmacy should be selected and supervised by the pharmacist.

Delivery of drugs directly to the pharmacy or other pharmacy receiving area is highly desirable; it should be considered mandatory for controlled drugs. Orders for controlled substances must be checked against the official order blank (when applicable) and against hospital purchase order forms. All drugs should be placed into stock promptly upon receipt, and controlled substances must be directly transferred to safes or other secure areas.

Drug Storage and Inventory Control. Storage is an important aspect of the total drug control system. Proper environmental control (i.e., proper temperature, light, humidity, conditions of sanitation, ventilation, and segregation) must be maintained wherever drugs and supplies are stored in the institution. Storage areas must be secure; fixtures and equipment used to store drugs should be constructed so that drugs are accessible only to designated and authorized personnel. Such personnel must be carefully selected and supervised. Safety also is an important factor, and proper consideration should be given to the safe storage of poisons and flammable compounds. Externals should be stored separately from internal medications. Medications stored in a refrigerator containing items other than drugs should be kept in a secured, separate compartment.

Proper control is important wherever medications are kept, whether in general storage in the institution or the pharmacy or patient-care areas (including satellite pharmacies, nursing units, clinics, emergency rooms, operating rooms, recovery rooms, and treatment rooms). Expiration dates of perishable drugs must be considered in all of these locations, and stock must be rotated as required. A method to detect and properly dispose of outdated, deteriorated, recalled, or obsolete drugs and supplies should be established. This should include monthly audits of all medication storage areas in the institution. (The results of these audits should be documented in writing.)

Since the pharmacist must justify and account for the expenditure of pharmacy funds, he must maintain an adequate inventory management system. Such a system should enable the pharmacist to analyze and interpret prescribing trends and their economic impacts and appropriately minimize inventory levels. It is essential that a system to indicate subminimum inventory levels be developed to avoid "outages," along with procedures to procure emergency supplies of drugs when necessary.

In-House Manufacturing, Bulk Compounding, Packaging, and Labeling.[7,8] As with commercially marketed drug products, those produced by the pharmacy must be accurate in identity, strength, purity, and quality. Therefore, there must be adequate process and finished product controls for all manufacturing/bulk compounding and packaging operations. Written master formulas and batch records (including product test results) must be maintained. All technical personnel must be adequately trained and supervised.

Packaging and labeling operations must have controls sufficient to prevent product/package/label mixups. A lot number to identify each finished product with its production and control history must be assigned to each batch.

The Good Manufacturing Practices of the FDA is a useful model for developing a comprehensive control system.

The pharmacist is encouraged to prepare those drug dosage forms, strengths, and packagings that are needed for optimal drug therapy but that are commercially unavailable. Adequate attention must be given to the stability, palatability, packaging, and labeling requirements of these products.

Medication Distribution (Unit Dose System).[9–11] Medication distribution is the responsibility of the pharmacy. The pharmacist, with the assistance of the P&T committee and the department of nursing, must develop comprehensive policies and procedures that provide for the safe distribution of all medications and related supplies to inpatients and outpatients.

For reasons of safety and economy, the preferred method to distribute drugs in institutions is the *unit dose* system. Although the unit dose system may differ in form depending on the specific needs, resources, and characteristics of each institution, four elements are common to all: (1) medications are contained in, and administered from, single unit or unit dose packages; (2) medications are dispensed in ready-to-administer form to the extent possible; (3) for most medications, not more than a 24-hour supply of doses is provided to or available at the patient-care area at any time; and (4) a patient medication profile is concurrently maintained in the pharmacy for each patient. Floor stocks of drugs are minimized and limited to drugs for emergency use and routinely used "safe" items such as mouthwash and antiseptic solutions.

(1) Physician's drug order: writing the order. Medications should be given (with certain specified exceptions) only on the *written* order of a qualified physician or other authorized prescriber. Allowable exceptions to this rule (i.e., telephone or verbal orders) should be put in written form immediately and the prescriber should countersign the nurse's or pharmacist's signed record of these orders within 48 (preferably 24) hours. Only a pharmacist or registered nurse should accept such orders. Provision should be made to place physician's orders in the patient's chart, and a method for sending this information to the pharmacy should be developed.

Prescribers should specify the date and time medication orders are written.

Medication orders should be written legibly in ink and should include

- Patient's name and location (unless clearly indicated on the order sheet).
- Name (generic) of medication.
- Dosage expressed in the metric system, except in instances where dosage must be expressed otherwise (i.e., units, etc.).
- Frequency of administration.
- Route of administration.
- Signature of the physician.
- Date and hour the order was written.

Any abbreviations used in medication orders should be agreed to and jointly adopted by the medical, nursing, pharmacy, and medical records staff of the institution.

Any questions arising from a medication order, including the interpretation of an illegible order, should be referred to the ordering physician by the pharmacist. It is desirable for the pharmacist to make (appropriate) entries in the patient's medical chart pertinent to the patient's drug therapy. (Proper authorization for this must be obtained.[12]) Also, a duplicate record of the entry can be maintained in the pharmacy profile.

In computerized patient data systems, each prescriber should be assigned a unique identifier; this number should be included in all medication orders. Unauthorized personnel should not be able to gain access to the system.

(2) Physician's drug order: medication order sheets. The pharmacist (except in emergency situations) must receive the physician's original order or a direct copy of the order before the drug is dispensed. This permits the pharmacist to resolve questions or problems with drug orders before the drug is dispensed and administered. It also eliminates errors which may arise when drug orders are transcribed onto another form for use by the pharmacy. Several methods by which the pharmacy may receive physicians' original orders or direct copies are

1. Self-copying order forms. The physician's order form is designed to make a direct copy (carbon or NCR) which is sent to the pharmacy. This method provides the pharmacist with a duplicate copy of the order and does not require special equipment. There are two basic formats:
   a. Orders for medications included among treatment orders. Use of this form allows the physician to continue writing his orders on the chart as he has been accustomed in the past, leaving all other details to hospital personnel.
   b. Medication orders separated from other treatment orders on the order form. The separation of drug orders makes it easier for the pharmacist to review the order sheet.
2. Electromechanical. Copying machines or similar devices may be used to produce an exact copy of the physician's order. Provision should be made to transmit physicians' orders to the pharmacy in the event of mechanical failure.
3. Computerized. Computer systems, in which the physician enters orders into a computer which then stores and prints out the orders in the pharmacy or elsewhere, are used in some institutions. Any such system should provide for the pharmacist's verification of any drug orders entered into the system by anyone other than an authorized prescriber.

(3) Physician's drug order: time limits and changes. Medication orders should be reviewed automatically when the patient goes to the delivery room, operating room, or a different service. In addition, a method to protect patients from indefinite, open-ended drug orders must be provided. This may be accomplished through one or more of the following: (1) routine monitoring of patients' drug therapy by a pharmacist; (2) drug class-specific, automatic stop-order policies covering those drug orders not specifying a number of doses or duration of therapy; and (3) automatic cancellation of all drug orders after a predetermined (by the P&T committee) time interval unless rewritten by the prescriber. Whatever the method used, it must protect the patient, as well as provide for a timely notification to the prescriber that the order will be stopped *before* such action takes place.

(4) Physician's drug order: receipt of order and drug profiles. A pharmacist must review and interpret every medication order and resolve any problems or uncertainties

with it before the drug is entered into the dispensing system. This means that he must be satisfied that each questionable medication order is, in fact, acceptable. This may occur through study of the patient's medical record, research of the professional literature, or discussion with the prescriber or other medical, nursing, or pharmacy staff. Procedures to handle a drug order the pharmacist still believes is unacceptable (e.g., very high dose or a use beyond that contained in the package insert) should be prepared (and reviewed by the hospital's legal counsel). In general, the physician must be able to support the use of the drug in these situations. It is generally advisable for the pharmacist to document actions (e.g., verbal notice to the physician that a less toxic drug was available and should be used) relative to a questionable medication order on the pharmacy's patient medication profile form or other pharmacy document (not in the medical record).

Once the order has been approved, it is entered into the *patient's medication profile*. A medication profile must be maintained in the pharmacy for all inpatients and those outpatients routinely receiving care at the institution. (Note: Equivalent records also should be available at the patient-care unit.) This essential item, which is continuously updated, may be a written copy or computer maintained. It serves two purposes. First, it enables the pharmacist to become familiar with the patient's total drug regimen, enabling him to detect quickly potential interactions, unintended dosage changes, drug duplications and overlapping therapies, and drugs contraindicated because of patient allergies or other reasons. Second, it is required in unit dose systems in order for the individual medication doses to be scheduled, prepared, distributed, and administered on a timely basis. The profile information must be reviewed by the pharmacist *before* dispensing the patient's drug(s). (It also may be useful in retrospective review of drug use.)

Patient profile information should include

- Patient's full name, date hospitalized, age, sex, weight, hospital I.D. number, and provisional diagnosis or reason for admission (the format for this information will vary from one hospital to another).
- Laboratory test results.
- Other medical data relevant to the patient's drug therapy (e.g., information from drug history interviews).
- Sensitivities, allergies, and other significant contraindications.
- Drug products dispensed, dates of original orders, strengths, dosage forms, quantities, dosage frequency or directions, and automatic stop dates.
- Intravenous therapy data (this information may be kept on a separate profile form, but there should be a method for the pharmacist to review both concomitantly).
- Blood products administered.
- Pharmacist's or technician's initials.
- Number of doses or amounts dispensed.
- Items relevant or related to the patient's drug therapy (e.g., blood products) not provided by the pharmacy.

(5) Physician's drug order: records. Appropriate records of each medication order and its processing in the pharmacy must be maintained. Such records must be retained in accordance with applicable state laws and regulations. Any changes or clarifications in the order should be written in the chart. The signature(s) or initials of the person(s) verifying the transcription of medication orders into the

medication profile should be noted. A way should be provided to determine, for all doses dispensed, who prepared the dose, its date of dispensing, the source of the drug, and the person who checked it. Other information, such as the time of receipt of the order and management data (number of orders per patient day and the like) should be kept as desired. Medication profiles also may be useful for retrospective drug use review studies.

(6) Physician's drug order: special orders.[5,6,13,14] Special orders (i.e., "stat" and emergency orders and those for nonformulary drugs, investigational drugs, restricted use drugs, or controlled substances) should be processed according to specific written procedures meeting all applicable regulations and requirements.

(7) Physician's drug order: other considerations. The pharmacy, nursing, and medical staffs, through the P&T committee, should develop a schedule of standard drug administration times. The nurse should notify the pharmacist whenever it is necessary to deviate from the standard medication schedule.

A mechanism to continually inform the pharmacy of patient admissions, discharges, and transfers should be established.

(8) Intravenous admixture services.[15] The preparation of sterile products (e.g., intravenous admixtures, "piggybacks," and irrigations) is an important part of the drug control system. The pharmacy is responsible for assuring that all such products used in the institution are (1) therapeutically and pharmaceutically appropriate (i.e., are rational and free of incompatibilities or similar problems) to the patient; (2) free from microbial and pyrogenic contaminants; (3) free from unacceptable levels of particulate and other toxic contaminants; (4) correctly prepared (i.e., contain the correct amounts of the correct drugs); and (5) properly labeled, stored, and distributed. Centralizing all sterile compounding procedures within the pharmacy department is the best way to achieve these goals.

Parenteral admixtures and related solutions are subject to the same considerations presented in the preceding sections on "physician's drug order." However, their special characteristics (e.g., complex preparation or need for sterility assurance) also mandate certain additional requirements concerning their preparation, labeling, handling, and quality control. These are described in Reference 15.

It is important that the pharmacy is notified of any problems that arise within the institution pertaining to the use of intravenous drugs and fluids (infections, phlebitis, and product defects).

(9) Medication containers, labeling, and dispensing: stock containers. The pharmacist is responsible for labeling medication containers. Medication labels should be typed or machine printed. Labeling with pen or pencil and the use of adhesive tape or china marking pencils should be prohibited. A label should not be superimposed on another label. The label should be legible and free from erasures and strikeovers. It should be firmly affixed to the container. The labels for stock containers should be protected from chemical action or abrasion and bear the name, address, and telephone number of the hospital. Medication containers and labels should not be altered by anyone other than pharmacy personnel. Prescription labels should not be distributed outside the pharmacy. Accessory labels and statements (shake well, may not be refilled, and the like) should be used as required. Any container to be used outside the institution should bear its name, address, and phone number.

Important labeling considerations are

1. The metric system should be given prominence on all labels when both metric and apothecary measurement units are given.
2. The names of all therapeutically active ingredients should be indicated in compound mixtures.
3. Labels for medications should indicate the amount of drug or drugs in each dosage unit (e.g., per 5 ml and per capsule).
4. Drugs and chemicals in forms intended for dilution or reconstitution should carry appropriate directions.
5. The expiration date of the contents, as well as proper storage conditions, should be clearly indicated.
6. The acceptable route(s) of administration should be indicated for parenteral medications.
7. Labels for large volume sterile solutions should permit visual inspection of the container contents.
8. Numbers, letters, coined names, unofficial synonyms, and abbreviations should not be used to identify medications, with the exception of approved letter or number codes for investigational drugs (or drugs being used in blinded clinical studies).
9. Containers presenting difficulty in labeling, such as small tubes, should be labeled with no less than the prescription serial number, name of drug, strength, and name of the patient. The container should then be placed in a larger carton bearing a label with all necessary information.
10. The label should conform to all applicable federal, state, and local laws and regulations.
11. Medication labels of stock containers and repackaged or prepackaged drugs should carry codes to identify the source and lot number of medication.
12. Nonproprietary name(s) should be given prominence over proprietary names.
13. Amount dispensed (e.g., number of tablets) should be indicated.
14. Drug strengths, volumes, and amounts should be given as recommended in References 11 and 16.

(10) Medication containers, labeling, and dispensing: inpatient medications.[11,16] Drug products should be as ready for administration to the patient as the current status of pharmaceutical technology permits. Inpatient medication containers and packages should conform to applicable *USP* requirements and the guidelines in References 11 and 16.

Inpatient self-care and "discharge" medications should be labeled as outpatient prescriptions (see below).

(11) Medication containers, labeling, and dispensing: outpatient medications.[17] Outpatient medications must be labeled in accordance with state board of pharmacy and federal regulations. As noted, medications given to patients as "discharge medication" must be labeled in the pharmacy (not by nursing personnel) as outpatient prescriptions.

The source of the medication and initials of the dispenser should be noted on the prescription form at the time of dispensing. If feasible, the lot number also should be recorded.

An identifying check system to ensure proper identification of outpatients should be established.

Outpatient prescriptions should be packaged in accordance with the provisions of the Poison Prevention Packaging Act of 1970 and any regulations thereunder. They must also meet any applicable requirements of the *USP*.

Any special instructions to or procedures required of the patient relative to the drug's preparation, storage, and administration should be either a part of the label or accompany the medication container received by the patient. Counseling of the patient sufficient to ensure understanding and compliance (to the extent possible) with his medication regimen must be conducted. Nonprescription drugs, if used in the institution, should be labeled as any other medication.

(12) Delivery of medications. Couriers used to deliver medications should be reliable and carefully chosen.

Pneumatic tubes, dumbwaiters, medication carts, and the like should protect drug products from breakage and theft. In those institutions having automatic delivery equipment, such as a pneumatic tube system, provision must be made for an alternative delivery method in case of breakdown.

All parts of the transportation system must protect medications from pilferage. Locks and other security devices should be used where necessary. Procedures for the orderly transfer of medications to the nurse should be instituted; i.e., drug carts or pneumatic tube carriers should not arrive at the patient-care area without the nurse or her designee acknowledging their arrival.

Medications must always be properly secured. Storage areas and equipment should meet the requirements presented in other sections of these guidelines.

(13) Administration of medications. The institution should develop detailed written procedures governing medication administration. In doing so, the following guidelines should be considered:

1. All medications should be administered by appropriately trained and authorized personnel in accordance with the laws, regulations, and institutional policies governing drug administration. It is particularly important that there are written policies and procedures defining responsibility for starting parenteral infusions, administering all intravenous medications, and adding medications to flowing parenteral fluids. Procedures for drug administration by respiratory therapists and during emergency situations also should be established. Exceptions to any of these policies should be provided in writing.
2. All medications should be administered directly from the medication cart (or equivalent) at the patient's room. The use of unit dose packaged drugs eliminates the need for medication cups and cards (and their associated trays), and they should not be used. A medication should not be removed from the unit dose package until it is to be administered.
3. Medications prepared for administration but not used must be returned to the pharmacy.
4. Medications should be given as near the specified time as possible.
5. The patient for whom the medication is intended should be positively identified by checking the patient's identification band or hospital number or by other means as specified by hospital policy.
6. The person administering the medication should stay with the patient until the dose has been taken. Exceptions to this rule are specific medications which may be left at the patient's bedside upon the physician's written order for self-administration.
7. Parenteral medications that are not to be mixed together in a syringe should be given in different injection sites on the patient or separately injected into the

administration site of the administration set of a compatible intravenous fluid.

8. The pharmacy should receive copies of all medication error reports or other medication-related incidents.

9. A system to assure that patients permitted to self-medicate do so correctly should be established.

(14) Return of unused medication. All medications that have not been administered to the patient must remain in the medication cart and be returned to the pharmacy. Only those medications returned in unopened sealed packages may be reissued. Medications returned by outpatients should not be reused. Procedures for crediting and returning drugs to stock should be instituted. A mechanism to reconcile doses not given with nursing and pharmacy records should be provided.

(15) Recording of medication administration. All administered, refused, or omitted medication doses should be recorded in the patient's medical record according to an established procedure. Disposition of doses should occur immediately after administering medications to each patient and before proceeding to the next patient. Information to be recorded should include the drug name, dose and route of administration, date and time of administration, and initials of the person administering the dose.

Drug Samples and Medical Sales Representatives.[18] The use of drug samples within the institution is strongly discouraged and should be eliminated to the extent possible. They should never be used for inpatients (unless, for some reason, no other source of supply is available to the pharmacy). Any samples used must be controlled and dispensed through the pharmacy.

Written regulations governing the activities of medical sales representatives within the institution should be established. Sales representatives should receive a copy of these rules and their activities should be monitored.

Investigational Drugs.[13] Policies and procedures governing the use and control of investigational drugs within the institution are necessary. Detailed procedural guidelines are given in Reference 13.

Radiopharmaceuticals. The basic principles of compounding, packaging, sterilizing, testing, and controlling drugs in institutions apply to radiopharmaceuticals. Therefore, even if the pharmacy department is not directly involved with the preparation and dispensing of these agents, the pharmacist must ensure that their use conforms to the drug control principles set forth in this document.

"Bring-In" Medications. The use of a patient's own medications within the hospital should be avoided to the extent possible. They should be used only if the drugs are not obtainable by the pharmacy. If they are used, the physician must write an appropriate order in the patient's medical chart. The drugs should be sent to the pharmacy for verification of their identity; if not identifiable, they must not be used. They should be dispensed as part of the unit dose system, not separate from it.

Drug Control in Operating and Recovery Rooms.[19] The institution's drug control system must extend to its operating room complex. The pharmacist should ensure that all drugs used within this area are properly ordered, stored, prepared, and accounted for.

Emergency Medication Supplies. A policy to supply emergency drugs when the pharmacist is off the premises or when there is insufficient time to get to the pharmacy should exist. Emergency drugs should be limited in number to include only those whose prompt use and immediate availability are generally regarded by physicians as essential in the proper treatment of sudden and unforeseen patient emergencies. The emergency drug supply should not be a source for normal "stat" or "p.r.n." drug orders. The medications included should be primarily for the treatment of cardiac arrest, circulatory collapse, allergic reactions, convulsions, and bronchospasm. The P&T committee should specify the drugs and supplies to be included in emergency stocks.

Emergency drug supplies should be inspected by pharmacy personnel on a routine basis to determine if contents have become outdated and are maintained at adequate levels. Emergency kits should have a seal which visually indicates when they have been opened. The expiration date of the kit should be clearly indicated.

Pharmacy Service When the Pharmacy Is Closed. Hospitals provide services to patients 24 hours a day. Pharmaceutical services are an integral part of the total care provided by the hospital, and the services of a pharmacist should be available at all times. Where around the clock operation of the pharmacy is not feasible, a pharmacist should be available on an "on call" basis. The use of "night cabinets" and drug dispensing by nonpharmacists should be minimized and eliminated wherever possible.

Drugs must not be dispensed to outpatients or hospital staff by anyone other than a pharmacist while the pharmacy is open. If it is necessary for nurses to obtain drugs when the pharmacy is closed and the pharmacist is unavailable, written procedures covering this practice should be developed. They generally should provide for a limited supply of the drugs most commonly needed in these situations; the drugs should be in proper single dose packages and a log should be kept of all doses removed. This log must contain the date and time the drugs were removed, a complete description of the drug product(s), name of the (authorized) nurse involved, and the patient's name.

Drugs should not be dispensed to emergency room patients by nonpharmacist personnel if the pharmacy is open. When no pharmacist is available, emergency room patients should receive drugs packaged, to the extent possible, in single unit packages; no more than a day's supply of doses should be dispensed. The use of an emergency room "formulary" is recommended.[20]

Adverse Drug Reactions. The medical, nursing, and pharmacy staffs must always be alert to the potential for, or presence of, adverse drug reactions. A written procedure to record clinically significant adverse drug reactions should be established. They should be reported to the FDA, the involved drug manufacturer, and the institution's P&T committee (or its equivalent). Adverse drug reaction reports should contain

- Patient's age, sex, and race.
- Description of the drug reaction and the suspected cause.
- Name of drug(s) suspected of causing the reaction.
- Administration route and dose.
- Name(s) of other drugs received by patient.
- Treatment of the reaction, if any.

These reports, along with other significant reports from the literature, should be reviewed and evaluated by the P&T committee. Steps necessary to minimize the incidence of adverse drug reactions in the facility should be taken.

Medication Errors. If a medication error is detected, the patient's physician must be informed immediately. A written report should be prepared describing any medication errors of clinical import observed in the prescribing, dispensing, or administration of a medication. This report, in accordance with hospital policy, should be prepared and sent to the appropriate hospital officials (including the pharmacy) within 24 hours.

These reports should be analyzed, and any necessary action taken, to minimize the possibility of recurrence of such errors. Properly utilized, these incident reports will help to assure optimum drug use control. Medication error reports should be reviewed periodically by the P&T committee. (It should be kept in mind that, in the absence of an organized, independent error detection system, most medication errors will go unnoticed.)

The following definitions of medication errors are suggested. A *medication error* is broadly defined as a dose of medication that deviates from the physician's order as written in the patient's chart or from standard hospital policy and procedures. Except for errors of omission, the medication dose must actually reach the patient; i.e., a wrong dose that is detected and corrected before administration to the patient is not a medication error. Prescribing errors (e.g., therapeutically inappropriate drugs or doses) are excluded from this definition.

Following are the nine categories of medication errors:

1. *Omission error*: the failure to administer an ordered dose. However, if the patient refuses to take the medication, no error has occurred. Likewise, if the dose is not administered because of recognized contraindications, no error has occurred.

2. *Unauthorized drug error*: administration to the patient of a medication dose not authorized for the patient. This category includes a dose given to the wrong patient, duplicate doses, administration of an unordered drug, and a dose given outside a stated set of clinical parameters (e.g., medication order to administer only if the patient's blood pressure falls below a predetermined level).

3. *Wrong dose error*: any dose that is the wrong number of preformed units (e.g., tablets) or any dose above or below the ordered dose by a predetermined amount (e.g., 20%). In the case of ointments, topical solutions, and sprays, an error occurs only if the medication order expresses the dosage quantitatively, e.g., 1 inch of ointment or two 1-second sprays.

4. *Wrong route error*: administration of a drug by a route other than that ordered by the physician. Also included are doses given via the correct route but at the wrong site (e.g., left eye instead of right).

5. *Wrong rate error*: administration of a drug at the wrong rate, the correct rate being that given in the physician's order or as established by hospital policy.

6. *Wrong dosage form error*: administration of a drug by the correct route but in a different dosage form than that specified or implied by the physician. Examples of this error type include use of an ophthalmic ointment when a solution was ordered. Purposeful alteration (e.g.,

crushing of a tablet) or substitution (e.g., substituting liquid for a tablet) of an oral dosage form to facilitate administration is generally not an error.

7. *Wrong time error*: administration of a dose of drug greater than ± *X* hours from its scheduled administration time, *X* being as set by hospital policy.

8. *Wrong preparation of a dose*: incorrect preparation of the medication dose. Examples are incorrect dilution or reconstitution, not shaking a suspension, using an expired drug, not keeping a light-sensitive drug protected from light, and mixing drugs that are physically/chemically incompatible.

9. *Incorrect administration technique*: situations when the drug is given via the correct route, site, and so forth, but improper technique is used. Examples are not using Z-track injection technique when indicated for a drug, incorrect instillation of an ophthalmic ointment, and incorrect use of an administration device.

Special Considerations Contributing to Drug Control

Pharmacy Personnel and Management.[21–24] Adequate numbers of competent personnel and a well-managed pharmacy are the keys to an effective drug control system. References 21–24 provide guidance on the competencies required of the pharmacy staff and on administrative requirements of a well-run pharmacy department.

Assuring Rational Drug Therapy: Clinical Services.[21,25] Maximizing rational drug use is an important part of the drug control system. Although all pharmacy services contribute to this goal in a sense, the provision of drug information to the institution's patients and staff and the pharmacy's clinical services are those that most directly contribute to rational drug therapy. They are, in fact, institutional pharmacists' most important contributions to patient care.

Facilities. Space and equipment requirements relative to drug storage have been discussed previously. In addition to these considerations, space and equipment must be sufficient to provide for safe and efficient drug preparation and distribution, patient education and consultation, drug information services, and proper management of the department.

Hospital Committees Important to Drug Control.[26,27] Several hospital committees deal with matters of drug control, and the pharmacist must actively participate in their activities. Among these committees (whose names may vary among institutions) are the P&T committee, infection control committee, use review committee, product evaluation committee, patient care committee, and the committee for protection of human subjects. Of particular importance to the drug control system are the formulary and drug use review (DUR) functions of the P&T committee (although DUR in many institutions may be under a use review or quality-assurance committee).

Drug Use Review.[28] Review of how drugs are prescribed and used is an important part of institutional quality-assurance and drug control systems. DUR programs may be performed retrospectively or, preferably, concurrently or prospectively. They may utilize patient outcomes or therapeutic processes as the basis for judgments about the appropriateness of drug prescribing and use. Depending on the review methodology, the pharmacist should be involved in

1. Preparing, in cooperation with the medical staff, drug use criteria and standards.
2. Obtaining quantitative data on drug use, i.e., information on the amounts and types of drugs used, prescribing patterns by medical service, type of patient, and so forth. These data will be useful in setting priorities for the review program. They also may serve as a measure of the effectiveness of DUR programs, assist in analyzing nosocomial infection and culture and sensitivity data, and help in preparing drug budgets.
3. Reviewing medication orders against the drug use criteria and standards.
4. Consulting with prescribers concerning the results of 3 above.
5. Participating in the followup activities of the review program, i.e., educational programs directed at prescribers, development of recommendations for the formulary, and changes in drug control procedures in response to the results of the review process.

It should be noted that the overall DUR program is a joint responsibility of the pharmacy and the organized medical staff; it is not unilaterally a pharmacy or medical staff function.

Quality Assurance for Pharmaceutical Services.[29] To ensure that the drug control system is functioning as intended, there should be a formalized method to (1) set precise objectives (in terms of outcome and process criteria and standards) for the system; (2) measure and verify the degree of compliance with these standards, i.e., the extent to which the objectives have been realized; and (3) eliminate any noncompliance situations. Such a *quality-assurance program* will be distinct from, though related to, the DUR activities of the department.

Drug Recalls. A written procedure to handle drug product recalls should be developed. Any such system should have the following elements:

1. Whenever feasible, notation of the drug manufacturer's name and drug lot number should appear on outpatient prescriptions, inpatient drug orders or profiles, packaging control records, and stock requisitions and their associated labels.
2. Review of these documents (prescriptions, drug orders, and so forth) to determine the recipients (patients and nursing stations) of the recalled lots. Optimally, this would be done by automated means.
3. In the case of product recalls of substantial clinical significance, a notice should go to the recipients that they have a recalled product. The course of action they should take should be included. In the case of outpatients, caution should be exercised not to cause undue alarm. The uninterrupted therapy of the patients must be assured; i.e., replacement of the recalled drugs generally will be required. The hospital's administration and nursing and medical staffs should be informed of any recalls having significant therapeutic implications. Some situations also may require notifying the physicians of patients receiving drugs that have been recalled.

4. Personal inspection of all patient-care areas should be made to determine if recalled products are present.
5. Quarantine of all recalled products obtained (marked "Quarantined—Do Not Use") until they are picked up by or returned to the manufacturer.
6. Maintenance of a written log of all recalls, the actions taken, and their results.

Computerization.[30] Many information handling tasks in the drug control system (e.g., collecting, recording, storing, retrieving, summarizing, transmitting, and displaying drug use information) may be done more efficiently by computers than by manual systems. Before the drug control system can be computerized, however, a comprehensive, thorough study of the existing manual system must be conducted. This study should identify the data flow within the system and define the functions to be done and their interrelationships. This information is then used as the basis to design or prospectively evaluate a computer system; any other considerations, such as those of the hospital accounting department, are subordinate.

The computer system must include adequate safeguards to maintain the confidentiality of patient records.

A backup system must be available to continue the computerized functions during equipment failure. All transactions occurring while the computer system is inoperable should be entered into the system as soon as possible.

Data on controlled substances must be readily retrievable in written form from the system.

Defective Drug Products, Equipment, and Supplies. The pharmacist should be notified of any defective drug products (or related supplies and equipment) encountered by the nursing or medical staffs. All drug product defects should be reported to the USP–FDA–ASHP Drug Product Defect Reporting Program.

Disposal of Hazardous Substances. Hazardous substances (e.g., toxic or flammable solvents and carcinogenic agents) must be disposed of properly in accordance with the requirements of the Environmental Protection Agency or other applicable regulations. The substances should not be poured indiscriminately down the drain or mixed in with the usual trash.

Unreconstituted vials or ampuls and unopened bottles of oral medications supplied by the National Cancer Institute (NCI) should be returned to the NCI's contract storage and distribution facility.

Other intact products should be returned to the original source for disposition.

Units of anticancer drugs no longer intact, such as reconstituted vials, opened ampuls, and bottles of oral medications, and any equipment (e.g., needles and syringes) used in their preparation require a degree of caution greater than with less toxic compounds to safeguard personnel from accidental exposure. The National Institutes of Health recommends that all such materials be segregated for special destruction procedures. The items should be kept in special containers marked *"Danger—Chemical Carcinogens."* Needles and syringes first should be rendered unusable and then placed in specially marked plastic bags. Care should be taken to prevent penetration and leakage of the bags. Excess liquids should be placed in sealed containers; the original vial is satisfactory. Disposal of all of the above materials should be by incineration to destroy organic material.

Alternate disposal for BCG vaccine products has been recommended by the Bureau of Biologics (BOB). The BOB suggests that all containers and equipment used with BCG vaccines be sterilized prior to disposal. Autoclaving at 121 °C for 30 minutes will sterilize the equipment.

At all steps in the handling of anticancer drugs and other hazardous substances, care should be taken to safeguard professional and support services personnel from accidental exposure to these agents.

References

1. Ginnow WK, King CM Jr. Revision and reorganization of a hospital pharmacy policy and procedure manual. *Am J Hosp Pharm.* 1978; 35:698–704.

2. Accreditation manual for hospitals 1980. Chicago: Joint Commission on Accreditation of Hospitals; 1979.

3. Publications, reprints and services. Washington, DC: American Society of Hospital Pharmacists; current edition.

4. American Society of Hospital Pharmacists. ASHP guidelines for selecting pharmaceutical manufacturers and distributors. *Am J Hosp Pharm.* 1976; 33:645–6.

5. American Society of Hospital Pharmacists. ASHP guidelines for hospital formularies. *Am J Hosp Pharm.* 1978; 35:326–8.

6. American Society of Hospital Pharmacists. ASHP statement of guiding principles on the operation of the hospital formulary system. *Am J Hosp Pharm.* 1964; 21:40–1.

7. American Society of Hospital Pharmacists. ASHP guidelines for repackaging oral solids and liquids in single unit and unit dose packages. *Am J Hosp Pharm.* 1979; 36:223–4.

8. 21 CFR Parts 210 and 211. Current good manufacturing practices in manufacturing, processing, packing or holding of drugs. April 1979.

9. Sourcebook on unit dose drug distribution systems. Washington, DC: American Society of Hospital Pharmacists; 1978.

10. American Society of Hospital Pharmacists. ASHP statement on unit dose drug distribution. *Am J Hosp Pharm.* 1975; 32:835.

11. American Society of Hospital Pharmacists. ASHP guidelines for single unit and unit dose packages of drugs. *Am J Hosp Pharm.* 1977; 34:613–4.

12. American Society of Hospital Pharmacists. ASHP guidelines for obtaining authorization for pharmacists' notations in the patient medical record. *Am J Hosp Pharm.* 1979; 36:222–3.

13. American Society of Hospital Pharmacists. ASHP guidelines for the use of investigational drugs in institutions. *Am J Hosp Pharm.* 1979; 36:221–2.

14. American Society of Hospital Pharmacists. ASHP guidelines for institutional use of controlled substances. *Am J Hosp Pharm.* 1974; 31:582–8.

15. Recommendations of the National Coordinating Committee on Large Volume Parenterals. Washington, DC: American Society of Hospital Pharmacists; 1980.

16. National Coordinating Committee on Large Volume Parenterals. Recommendations for the labeling of large volume parenterals. *Am J Hosp Pharm.* 1978; 35:49–51.

17. American Society of Hospital Pharmacists. ASHP guidelines on pharmacist-conducted patient counseling. *Am J Hosp Pharm.* 1976; 33:644–5.

18. Lipman AG, Mullen HF. Quality control of medical service representative activities in the hospital. *Am J Hosp Pharm.* 1974; 31:167–70.

19. Evans DM, Guenther AM, Keith TD, et al. Pharmacy practice in an operating room complex. *Am J Hosp Pharm.* 1979; 36:1342–7.

20. Mar DD, Hanan ZI, LaFontaine R. Improved emergency room medication distribution. *Am J Hosp Pharm.* 1978; 35:70–3.

21. American Society of Hospital Pharmacists. ASHP minimum standard for pharmacies in institutions. *Am J Hosp Pharm.* 1977; 34:1356–8.

22. American Society of Hospital Pharmacists. ASHP guidelines on the competencies required in institutional pharmacy practice. *Am J Hosp Pharm.* 1975; 32:917–9.

23. American Society of Hospital Pharmacists. ASHP training guidelines for hospital pharmacy supportive personnel. *Am J Hosp Pharm.* 1976; 33:646–8.

24. American Society of Hospital Pharmacists. ASHP competency standard for pharmacy supportive personnel in organized health care settings. *Am J Hosp Pharm.* 1978; 35:449–51.

25. American Society of Hospital Pharmacists. ASHP statement on clinical functions in institutional pharmacy practice. *Am J Hosp Pharm.* 1978; 35:813.

26. American Society of Hospital Pharmacists. ASHP statement on the pharmacy and therapeutics committee. *Am J Hosp Pharm.* 1978; 35:813–4.

27. American Society of Hospital Pharmacists. ASHP statement on the hospital pharmacist's role in infection control. *Am J Hosp Pharm.* 1978; 35:814–5.

28. Antibiotic use review and infection control: evaluating drug use through patient care audit. Chicago: InterQual, Inc.; 1978.

29. Model quality assurance program for hospital pharmacies, revised. Washington, DC: American Society of Hospital Pharmacists; 1980.

30. Sourcebook on computers in pharmacy. Washington, DC: American Society of Hospitals Pharmacists; 1978.

Developed by the ASHP Council on Professional Affairs. Approved by the ASHP Board of Directors, March 20, 1980. Revised November 1981.

The bibliographic citation for this document is as follows: American Society of Hospital Pharmacists. ASHP technical assistance bulletin on hospital drug distribution and control. *Am J Hosp Pharm.* 1980; 37:1097–103.

ASHP Technical Assistance Bulletin on Single Unit and Unit Dose Packages of Drugs

Drug packages must fulfill four basic functions:

1. Identify their contents completely and precisely.
2. Protect their contents from deleterious environmental effects (e.g., photodecomposition).
3. Protect their contents from deterioration due to handling (e.g., breakage and contamination).
4. Permit their contents to be used quickly, easily, and safely.

Modern drug distribution systems use single unit packages to a great extent and, in fact, such packages are central to the operation of unit dose systems, intravenous admixture services, and other important aspects of pharmacy practice. These guidelines have been prepared to assist pharmaceutical manufacturers and pharmacists in the development and production of single unit and unit dose packages, the use of which has been shown to have substantial benefits.

A *single unit* package is one that contains one discrete pharmaceutical dosage form, i.e., one tablet, one 2-ml volume of liquid, one 2-g mass of ointment, etc. A *unit dose* package is one that contains the particular dose of the drug ordered for the patient. A single unit package is also a *unit dose* or *single dose* package if it contains the particular dose of the drug ordered for the patient. A unit dose package could, for example, contain two tablets of a drug product.

General Considerations

Packaging Materials. Packaging materials (and the package itself) must possess the physical characteristics required to protect the contents from (as required) light, moisture, temperature, air, and handling. The material should not deteriorate during the shelf life of the contents. Packages should be of lightweight, nonbulky materials that do not produce toxic fumes when incinerated. Materials that may be recycled or are biodegradable, or both, are to be preferred over those that are not. Packaging materials should not absorb, adsorb, or otherwise deleteriously affect their contents. Information should be available to practitioners indicating the stability and compatibility of drugs with various packaging materials.

Shape and Form. Packages should be constructed so that they do not deteriorate with normal handling. They should be easy to open and use, and their use should require little or no special training or experience. Unless the package contains a drug to be added to a parenteral fluid or otherwise used in compounding a finished dosage form, it should allow the contents to be administered directly to the patient (or IPPB apparatus or fluid administration set) without any need for repackaging into another container or device (except for ampuls).

Label Copy. Current federal labeling requirements must be adhered to, with attention also given to the items at right. The desired copy and format are as follows:

Nonproprietary Name
(and proprietary name if to be shown)
Dosage Form (if special or other than oral)
Strength
Strength of Dose and Total Contents Delivered
(e.g., number of tablets and their total dose)
Special Notes (e.g., refrigerate)
Expiration Date
Control Number

1. *Nonproprietary and proprietary names.* The nonproprietary name and the strength should be the most prominent part of the package label. It is not necessary to include the proprietary name, if any, on the package. The name of the manufacturer or distributor should appear on the package. In addition, the name of the manufacturer of the finished dosage form should be included in the product labeling. The style of type should be chosen to provide maximum legibility, contrast, and permanence.
2. *Dosage form.* Special characteristics of the dosage form should be a part of the label, e.g., extended release. Packages should be labeled as to the route of administration if other than oral, e.g., topical use. In a package containing an injection, the acceptable injectable route(s) of administration should be stated on both outer and inner packages, i.e., both on the syringe unit and carton (if any).
3. *Strength.* Strength should be stated in accordance with terminology in the *American Hospital Formulary Service*. The metric system should be used, with dosage forms formulated to provide the rounded-off figures in the *USP* table of approximate equivalents and expressed in the smallest whole number. Micrograms should be used through 999, then milligrams through 999, then grams. Thus, 300 mg, *not* 5 gr, nor 325 mg, nor 0.3 g; 60 mg, *not* 1 gr, nor 0.06 g, nor 64.5 mg, nor 65 mg; 400 mcg, *not* 1/150 gr, nor 0.4 mg, nor 0.0004 g; ml (milliliters) should be used instead of cc (cubic centimeters).
4. *Strength of dose and total contents delivered.* The total contents and total dose of the package should be indicated. Thus, a unit dose package containing a 600-mg dose as two 300-mg tablets should be labeled "600 mg (as two 300-mg tablets)." Likewise, a 500-mg dose of a drug in a liquid containing 100 mg/ml should be labeled "Delivers 500 mg (as 5 ml of 100 mg/ml)."
5. *Special notes.* Special notes such as conditions of storage (e.g., refrigerate), preparation (e.g., shake well or moisten), and administration (e.g., not to be chewed) that are not obvious from the dosage form designation are to be included on the label.
6. *Expiration date.* The expiration date should be prominently visible on the package. If the contents must be reconstituted prior to use, the shelf life of the final product should be indicated. Unless stability data warrant otherwise, expiration dates should fall during

January and July to simplify recall procedures.

7. *Control number (lot number).* The control number should appear on the package.

Product Identification Codes. The use of product identification codes, appearing directly on the dosage form, is encouraged.

Evidence of Entry. The package should be so designed that it is evident, when the package is still intact, that it has never been entered or opened.

Specific Considerations

Oral Solids

1. *Blister package.* A blister package should
   a. Have an opaque and nonreflective backing (flat upper surface of package) for printing.
   b. Have a blister (dome or bubble) of a transparent material that is, preferably, flat bottomed.
   c. Be easily peelable.
   d. If it contains a controlled substance, be numbered sequentially for accountability purposes.
2. *Pouch package.* A pouch package should
   a. Have one side opaque and nonreflective for printing.
   b. Be easily deliverable, i.e., large tablets in large pouches, small tablets in small pouches.
   c. Tear from any point or from multiple locations.
   d. If it contains a controlled substance, be numbered sequentially for accountability purposes.
3. The packages should be such that contents can be delivered directly to the patient's mouth or hand.

Oral Liquids

1. The packages should be filled to deliver the labeled contents. It is recognized that overfilling will be necessary, depending on the shape of the container, the container material, and the formulation of the dosage form.
2. The label should state the contents as follows: Delivers ____mg (or g or mcg) in ____ml.
3. If reconstitution is required, the amount of vehicle to be added should be indicated. These directions may take the form of "fill to mark on container" in lieu of stating a specific volume.
4. Syringe-type containers for oral administration should not accept a needle and should be labeled "For Oral Use Only."
5. Containers should be designed to permit administration of contents directly from the package.

Injectables

1. The device should be appropriately calibrated in milliliters and scaled from the tip to the fill line. Calibrated space may be built into the device to permit addition of other drugs. The label should state the contents as follows: Delivers ____mg (or g or mcg) in ____ml.
2. An appropriate size needle may be an integral part of the device. The needle sheath should not be the plunger. The plunger should be mechanically stable in the barrel of the syringe.
3. The device should be of such a design that it is patient ready and assembly instructions are not necessary.
4. The sheath protecting the needle should be a nonpenetrable, preferably rigid material, to protect personnel from injury. The size of the needle should be indicated.
5. The device should be of such a design that easy and visible aspiration is possible. It should be as compact as possible and of such a size that it can be easily handled.

Parenteral Solutions and Additives

1. The approximate pH and osmolarity of parenteral solutions should be stated on the label. The amount of overfill also should be noted. Electrolyte solutions should be labeled in both mEq (or millimole) and mg concentrations. Solutions commonly labeled in terms of percent concentration, e.g., dextrose, should also be labeled in w/v terms.
2. Parenteral fluid container labels should be readable when hanging and when upright or in the normal manipulative position.
3. Drugs to be mixed with parenteral infusion solutions should be packaged into convenient sizes that minimize the need for solution transfers and other manipulations.
4. Partially filled piggyback-type containers should
   a. Be recappable with a tamperproof closure.
   b. Have a hanger.
   c. Have volume markings.
   d. Be designed to minimize the potential for contamination during use.
   e. Contain a partial vacuum for ease of reconstitution.
5. If an administration set is included with the container, it should be compatible with all large volume parenteral delivery systems.

Other Dosage Forms—Ophthalmics, Suppositories, Ointments, etc. Dosage forms other than those specifically discussed above should be adequately labeled to indicate their use and route of administration and should adhere to the above and other required package labeling and design criteria.

Approved by the ASHP Board of Directors, November 14–15, 1984. Revised by the ASHP Council on Clinical Affairs. Supersedes the previous version, which was approved on March 31–April 1, 1977.

The bibliographic citation for this document is as follows: American Society of Hospital Pharmacists. ASHP technical assistance bulletin on single unit and unit dose packages of drugs. *Am J Hosp Pharm.* 1985; 42:378–9.

ASHP Technical Assistance Bulletin on Repackaging Oral Solids and Liquids in Single Unit and Unit Dose Packages

To maximize the benefits of a unit dose drug distribution system, all drugs must be packaged in single unit or unit dose packages.[a] However, not all drugs are commercially available in single unit (or unit dose) packages. Therefore, the institutional pharmacist must often repackage drugs obtained in bulk containers (e.g., bottles of 500 tablets) into single unit packages so that they may be used in a unit dose system.

Certain precautions must be taken if the quality of drugs repackaged by the pharmacist is to be maintained. The guidelines presented herein will assist the pharmacist in developing procedures for repackaging drugs in a safe and acceptable manner:

1. The packaging operation should be isolated, to the extent possible, from other pharmacy activities.
2. Only one drug product at a time should be repackaged in a specific work area. No drug products other than the one being repackaged should be present in the immediate packaging area. Also, no labels other than those for the product being repackaged should be present in the area.
3. Upon completion of the packaging run, all unused stocks of drugs and all finished packages should be removed from the packaging area. The packaging machinery and related equipment should then be completely emptied, cleaned, and inspected before commencing the next packaging operation.
4. All unused labels (if separate labels are used) should be removed from the immediate packaging area. The operator should verify that none remains in the packaging machine(s). If labels are prepared as part of the packaging operation, the label plate (or analogous part of the printing apparatus) should be removed or adjusted to "blank" upon completion of the run. This will help assure that the correct label is printed during any subsequent run. There should be a procedure to reconcile the number of packages produced with the number of labels used (if any) and destroyed (if any) and the number of units or volume of drug set forth to be packaged.
5. Before beginning a packaging run, an organoleptic evaluation (color, odor, appearance, and markings) of the drug product being repackaged should be made. The bulk container should also be examined for evidence of water damage, contamination, or other deleterious effects.
6. All packaging equipment and systems should be operated and used in accordance with the manufacturer's or other established instructions. There should be valid justification and authorization by the supervisor for any deviation from those instructions on the part of the operator.
7. The pharmacist should obtain data on the characteristics of all packaging materials used. This information should include data on the chemical composition, light transmission, moisture permeability, size, thickness

(alone or in laminate), recommended sealing temperature, and storage requirements.

8. Unit dose packages and labels should, to the extent possible, comply with the "ASHP Guidelines for Single Unit and Unit Dose Packages of Drugs."[1]
9. Whenever feasible, a responsible individual, other than the packaging operator, should verify that (a) the packaging system (drug, materials, and machines) is set up correctly and (b) all procedures have been performed properly. Ultimate responsibility for all packaging operations rests with the pharmacist.
10. Control records of all packaging runs must be kept. These records should include the following information: (1) complete description of the product, i.e., name, strength, dosage form, route of administration, etc.; (2) the product's manufacturer or supplier; (3) control number; (4) the pharmacy's control number if different from the manufacturer's; (5) expiration dates of the original container and the repackaged product; (6) number of units packaged and the date(s) they were packaged; (7) initials of the operator and checker (if any); (8) a sample of the label and, if feasible, a sample of the finished package, which should not be discarded until after the expiration date and which should be examined periodically for signs of deterioration; and (9) description (including lot number) of the packaging materials and equipment used.
11. It is the responsibility of the pharmacist to determine the expiration date to be placed on the package, taking into account the nature of the drug repackaged, the characteristics of the package, and the storage conditions to which the drug may be subjected. This date must not be beyond that of the original package.[b]
12. All drugs should be packaged and stored in a temperature- and humidity-controlled environment to minimize degradation caused by heat and moisture. A relative humidity of 75% at 23°C should not be exceeded. Packaging materials should be stored in accordance with the manufacturer's instructions and any applicable regulations.
13. Written procedures (both general and product specific) governing repackaging operations should be prepared and updated as required. Any deviation from these procedures should be noted and explained on the control record. Operators must understand the procedures (and operation of all packaging equipment) before commencing the run.
14. Applicable FDA and USP requirements concerning the type of package required for specific drug products must be followed.
15. Drugs and chemicals with high vapor pressures should be stored separately from other products to minimize cross contamination.

References

1. American Society of Hospital Pharmacists. ASHP

guidelines for single unit and unit dose packages of drugs. *Am J Hosp Pharm.* 1977; 34:613–4.

2.   Stolar MH. Expiration dates of repackaged drug products. *Am J Hosp Pharm.* 1979; 36:170. Editorial.

---

[a]A *single unit* package is one which contains one discrete pharmaceutical dosage form, e.g., one tablet or one 5-ml volume of liquid. A *unit dose* package is one which contains the particular dose of drug ordered for the patient. A *single unit* package is a *unit dose (or single dose)* package if it contains that particular dose of drug ordered for the patient.

[b]For specific recommendations on expiration date policy, see Reference 2.

Revised by the ASHP Board of Directors, November 16–17, 1978.

Developed originally by a joint working group of the American Society of Hospital Pharmacists and the American Society of Consultant Pharmacists and representatives of the drug packaging industry. The original document subsequently was approved officially by the Boards of Directors of ASHP and ASCP. FDA reviewed the original document and commended ASHP and ASCP for developing the guidelines.

The bibliographic citation for this document is as follows: American Society of Hospital Pharmacists. ASHP technical assistance bulletin on repackaging oral solids and liquids in single unit and unit dose packages. *Am J Hosp Pharm.* 1983; 40:451–2.

Education and Training

Education and Training

Continuing Professional Development (0408)
Source: Council on Educational Affairs
To endorse the concept of continuing professional development (CPD), which involves personal self-appraisal, educational plan development, plan implementation, documentation, and evaluation; further,

To strongly encourage the development of a variety of mechanisms and tools that pharmacists can use to assess their CPD needs; further,

To support the efforts of individual pharmacists to understand CPD (including the fact that various options are available for self-assessment) and to implement CPD; further,

To collaborate with other pharmacy organizations in the development of effective strategies for piloting the implementation of CPD; further,

To strongly support objective assessment of the outcomes of implementation of CPD; further,

To encourage colleges of pharmacy and accredited pharmacy residency programs to teach the principles, concepts, and skills of CPD.

Skills Needed to Provide Interdisciplinary and Interprofessional Patient Care (0311)
Source: Council on Educational Affairs
To encourage colleges of pharmacy and other health professions schools to focus on the need to teach students the skills necessary for working with other health care professionals to provide patient care; further,

To encourage the American Council on Pharmaceutical Education to include standards for teaching the provision of interprofessional patient care throughout the curriculum; further,

To encourage and support pharmacists' collaboration with other health professionals in the development of purposeful, deliberative interprofessional practice models.

(*Note: Interdisciplinary* refers to communication between disciplines *within* a profession; *interprofessional* refers to communication *across* the health care professions.)
This policy supersedes ASHP policy 9914.

Interdisciplinary and Interprofessional Instruction on Performance Improvement and Patient Safety (0312)
Source: Council on Educational Affairs
To urge colleges of pharmacy and other health professions schools to include instruction, in an interdisciplinary and interprofessional fashion, on the principles of performance improvement and patient safety and train students in how to apply these principles in practice.

(*Note: Interdisciplinary* refers to communication between disciplines *within* a profession; *interprofessional* refers to communication *across* the health care professions.)
This policy supersedes ASHP policy 0208.

Patient-Centered Care (0313)
Source: Council on Educational Affairs
To encourage that the principles of patient-centered care be integrated throughout the college of pharmacy curriculum.

Cultural Competence (0314)
Source: Council on Educational Affairs
To foster cultural competence among pharmacy students, residents, and practitioners and within health systems for the purpose of achieving optimal therapeutic outcomes in diverse patient populations.

Practice Sites for Colleges of Pharmacy (0315)
Source: Council on Educational Affairs
To encourage practitioner input in pharmacy education; further,

To encourage that institutional and health-system environments be used as sites for experiential training of pharmacy students; further,

To encourage colleges of pharmacy and health systems to define and develop appropriate organizational relationships that permit a balance of patient care and service, as well as educational and research objectives, in a mutually beneficial manner; further,

To include the administrative interests of both the health system and the college of pharmacy in defining these organizational relationships to ensure compatibility of institutional (i.e., health system or university) and departmental (i.e., pharmacy department and department in the college) objectives; further,

To encourage pharmacists and pharmacy leaders to recognize that part of their professional responsibility is the development of new pharmacy practitioners.
This proposed policy supersedes ASHP policy 9810.

Licensure for Pharmacy Graduates of Foreign Schools (0323)
Source: Council on Legal and Public Affairs
To support state licensure eligibility of a pharmacist who has graduated from a pharmacy program accredited by the American Council on Pharmaceutical Education (ACPE) or accredited by an ACPE-recognized accreditation program.

Public Funding for Pharmacy Residency Training (0325)
Source: Council on Legal and Public Affairs
To support legislation and regulation that ensures public funding for accredited pharmacy residency programs consistent with the needs of the public and the profession; further,

To oppose legislation or regulation involving reimbursement levels for graduate medical education that adversely affects pharmacy residencies at a rate disproportionate to other residency programs.
This policy supersedes ASHP policy 9811.

Substance Abuse and Chemical Dependency (0209)
Source: Council on Educational Affairs
To collaborate with appropriate professional and academic organizations in fostering adequate education on substance abuse and chemical dependency at all levels of pharmacy education (i.e., schools of pharmacy, residency programs, and continuing-education providers); further,

To support federal, state, and local initiatives that promote pharmacy education on substance abuse and chemical dependency; further,

To advocate the incorporation of education on substance abuse and chemical dependency into the accreditation standards for Doctor of Pharmacy degree programs and pharmacy technician training programs.

Health Literacy (0210)
Source: Council on Educational Affairs
To encourage the development of educational programs for pharmacy students, residents, and practitioners on assessing the level of general literacy and health literacy of patients; further,

To encourage pharmacists, when communicating medication information to patients, to use techniques that take into account the patient's level of general literacy and health literacy; further,

To seek opportunities to support research on health literacy as it relates to the appropriate use of medicines.

Pharmacy Technician Training (0212)
Source: Council on Educational Affairs
To support the goal that technicians entering the pharmacy work force have completed an accredited program of training; further,

To encourage expansion of accredited pharmacy technician training programs.
This policy supersedes ASHP policy 0109.

Residency Programs (0216)
Source: Council on Educational Affairs
To strongly advocate that all pharmacy residency programs become accredited as a means of ensuring and conveying program quality.
This policy supersedes ASHP policy 8715.

Nonaccredited Pharm.D. Programs (0107)
Source: Council on Educational Affairs
To support the position that every educational program that offers a pharmacy degree must be accredited by the American Council on Pharmaceutical Education (ACPE), regardless of licensure status of students enrolled.

Nontraditional Pharm.D. Accessibility (0108)
Source: Council on Educational Affairs
To encourage colleges of pharmacy to continue to develop innovative ACPE-accredited programs that meet the professional advancement needs of practitioners, using distance learning and other advanced technologies where appropriate; further,

To identify and publicize mechanisms available to baccalaureate-degree pharmacists for overcoming barriers to the attainment of the Pharm.D. degree.

Residency Training for Pharmacists Who Provide Direct Patient Care (0005)
Source: Council on Educational Affairs
To recognize that optimal direct patient care by a pharmacist requires the development of clinical judgment, which can be acquired only through experience and reflection on that experience; further,

To establish as a goal that pharmacists who provide direct patient care should have completed an ASHP-accredited residency or have attained comparable skills through practice experience.

Fostering Pharmacy Leadership (9901)
Source: Council on Administrative Affairs
To encourage pharmacy managers to serve as mentors to their staff, pharmacy students, pharmacy residents, and peers in a manner that fosters the development of future pharmacy leaders.

This policy was reviewed in 2003 by the Council on Administrative Affairs and by the Board of Directors and was found to still be appropriate.

Pharmacy Residency Training (9911)
Source: Council on Education Affairs
To continue efforts to increase the number of pharmacy residency training programs and positions available; further,

To expand efforts to make pharmacy students aware early in their education of the career choices available to them and the importance health-system employers attach to the completion of a residency.

This policy was reviewed in 2003 by the Council on Educational Affairs and by the Board of Directors and was found to still be appropriate.

Leadership Development in Colleges of Pharmacy (9913)
Source: Council on Educational Affairs
To encourage colleges of pharmacy to include leadership skills in professional curricula; further,

To encourage colleges of pharmacy to offer combined residency-degree programs to develop pharmacy leaders; further,

To encourage colleges of pharmacy to develop more opportunities for students to pursue combined degree programs (e.g., Pharm.D.-M.B.A.) that develop administrative, management, and leadership skills in addition to pharmacy education.

This policy was reviewed in 2003 by the Council on Educational Affairs and by the Board of Directors and was found to still be appropriate.

Position on the Entry-Level Doctor of Pharmacy Degree (9809)
Source: Council on Educational Affairs
To reaffirm the official policy of ASHP to support the Doctor of Pharmacy degree as the single entry-level degree for professional pharmacy practice; further,

To strongly encourage the development of viable and widely available external and nontraditional Doctor of Pharmacy degree programs; further,

To be an active participant in the American Council on Pharmaceutical Education (ACPE) process for the revision of accreditation standards for entry-level education in pharmacy; further,

To provide the ACPE with appropriate documents and background materials in order to demonstrate the ASHP position and support for ACPE's intent on this important issue; further,

To actively monitor the long-range impact that the single entry-level degree will have on residency education, availability of experiential training sites, graduate education, and continuing education programs, and the resulting health-system pharmacist applicant pool.

This policy supersedes ASHP policy 9101.

Career Counseling (8507)
Source: Council on Educational Affairs
To urge colleges of pharmacy to develop career counseling programs to make students aware of postgraduate career options, including residency training and career paths in various types of practice; further,

To urge that career counseling occur in a structured manner early in the curriculum and be continued throughout the curriculum; further,

To urge practitioners in various organized health care settings to make themselves available to colleges of pharmacy for participation in both structured and unstructured career counseling.

This policy was reviewed in 2001 by the Council on Educational Affairs and by the Board of Directors and was found to still be appropriate.

External Degree Programs and Initiatives for Helping Practitioners Upgrade Skills (8508)
Source: Council on Educational Affairs
To encourage the broadest possible consortial approach to developing viable and widely available external degree programs within the shortest possible time; further,

To urge schools of pharmacy to develop flexible mechanisms that permit full-time practitioners to participate in courses in the contemporary curriculum and to urge directors of pharmacy to encourage staff participation in part-time academic work and to develop appropriate and flexible work hours to permit full-time staff to become part-time students; further,

To urge educational consortia, colleges of pharmacy, and other organizations to evaluate options in addition to a formal external degree program that can assist practitioners in upgrading their skills and to encourage these groups to develop a curricular approach to continuing education aimed at improving practice competence; further,

To urge these groups to develop measurable performance criteria for competence.

This policy was reviewed in 2001 by the Council on Educational Affairs and by the Board of Directors and was found to still be appropriate.

ASHP Practice Standards as an Integral Part of Educational Process (8407)
Source: Council on Educational Affairs
To encourage faculties in schools of pharmacy and preceptors of ASHP-accredited residency training programs to use the ASHP standards of practice as an integral part of training programs and courses.

This policy was reviewed in 2001 by the Council on Educational Affairs and by the Board of Directors and was found to still be appropriate.

ASHP Statement on Continuing Education

Next to integrity, competence is the first and most fundamental moral responsibility of all the health professions....Each of our professions must insist that competence will be reinforced through the years of practice. After the degree is conferred, continuing education is society's only real guarantee of the optimal quality of health care.

—Edmund D. Pellegrino

In an era of rapidly accelerating change in health-care delivery, the roles of pharmacy practitioners are being constantly redefined. As roles change, competency requirements change; and as pharmacy practitioners assume the increased responsibilities demanded in these new roles, they must make a corresponding commitment to improve their professional competence. Continuing education is a means by which practitioners can gain the knowledge and skills necessary to develop, maintain, and improve their professional competence.

In keeping with the mission of the American Society of Health-System Pharmacists (ASHP), the purpose of continuing education for health professionals is the improvement of patient care and health maintenance and the enrichment of health careers. Every practitioner should assume personal responsibility for maintaining and improving professional competence through lifelong, self-directed education. Every pharmacist should set personal educational objectives based on individual needs and career goals. One way to achieve these objectives is through continuing education experiences judiciously selected from among area, regional, and national resources. It should be the role of ASHP to facilitate the efforts of the pharmacist in self-directed education.

Objectives

The objectives for the continuing education services of ASHP shall be

1. To help pharmacists develop a more complete understanding of the importance and methods of lifelong, self-directed education and to encourage and assist them toward this goal.
2. To help practitioners evaluate their professional performance, identify areas where improvement is needed, and set realistic and attainable educational goals.
3. To provide to practitioners information on available area, regional, and national educational resources which will help them achieve their personal educational objectives.
4. To assist pharmacists in selecting educational resources that most effectively fulfill their individual needs.
5. To provide to pharmacists continuing education re-

sources in a variety of formats and media best suited for the subject matter and needs of the greater number of learners.

Authority

Matters relating to continuing education services will be considered by the Council on Educational Affairs and will be submitted to the Board of Directors for review.

Guidelines

The following guidelines are used in the development and conduct of continuing education programs and activities of ASHP:

1. Continuing education programs will be planned and conducted in accordance with the Criteria for Quality of the Continuing Education Provider Approval Program of the Accreditation Council for Pharmacy Education.
2. ASHP will collaborate, when appropriate, with other professional organizations, agencies, and educational institutions in the planning and conduct of continuing education activities.
3. When appropriate, due consideration will be given to the curricular approach in the planning and implementation of continuing education activities.
4. ASHP may limit or restrict the enrollment for any continuing education program, depending on the nature and requirements of the particular program.
5. ASHP's overall continuing education activity is intended to be self-supporting; however, the benefit versus cost value to members of a specific educational program must also be considered.

This statement was reviewed in 2003 by the Council on Educational Affairs and by the ASHP Board of Directors and was found to still be appropriate.

Approved by the ASHP Board of Directors, November 15, 1989. Developed by the Council on Educational Affairs. Supersedes a previous version approved by the ASHP House of Delegates on May 15, 1978.

The bibliographic citation for this document is as follows: American Society of Hospital Pharmacists. ASHP statement on continuing education. *Am J Hosp Pharm.* 1990; 47:1855.

Definitions of Pharmacy Residencies and Fellowships

Pharmacy residencies (originally termed "internships") began in the early 1930s, primarily for the purpose of training pharmacists for the management of pharmacy services in hospitals. The first nonacademic residency program is believed to have been conducted by Harvey A. K. Whitney at the University of Michigan Hospital.[1] Approximately 10 years later, the first residency program combined with formal graduate studies was created.[2] Developments in these programs eventually led the American Society of Hospital Pharmacists to establish, in 1948, standards for pharmacy internships in hospitals.[3] Those standards defined an internship as "a period of organized training in an accredited hospital pharmacy under the direction and supervision of personnel qualified to offer such training."

Two types of internships were recognized, nonacademic and academic. The nonacademic internship consisted of a period of training in a hospital pharmacy. The academic internship consisted of training in a hospital pharmacy and study in an accredited graduate school associated with a school of pharmacy and leading to a Master of Science degree.

In 1962, following several revisions in the standards, ASHP established an accreditation process and accreditation standards for residencies in hospital pharmacy.[4,5] In this action, the term "internship" was replaced by "residency." A residency was defined as "a postgraduate program of organized training . . ." (and further detailed within the various standards). In 1985, the concept that a resident's training should be *directed* was incorporated into the definition.[6–9] It was also acknowledged that a residency is practice oriented and that it is possible for a residency to focus on a defined (specialized) area.

During the early 1970s, numerous residencies developed in *clinical* practice, leading to the establishment, in 1980, of accreditation standards for clinical pharmacy and specialized residency training.[10,11] In 1986, the American Pharmaceutical Association published a compilation of programmatic essentials for community pharmacy residencies.[12] In that same year, the American College of Apothecaries published specific guidelines for the accreditation of community pharmacy residencies.[13]

Paralleling these developments and fostered by a growing sophistication and clinical thrust in institutional pharmacy practice, postgraduate research-oriented programs (generally termed "fellowships") developed in the 1970s. These programs were conducted primarily in colleges of pharmacy and in academically based health centers to educate and train individuals to conduct pharmacy research. A 1981 survey of fellowship programs reported the existence of 58 fellowships in 19 topic areas.[14] Two-thirds of these fellowships had existed for 3 years or less. The oldest program had existed for less than 9 years. The ASHP Research and Education Foundation initiated clinical fellowships in 1978 and defined a pharmacy fellowship as "a directed, but highly individualized program [that] emphasizes research. The focus of a pharmacy fellowship is to develop the participant's (the fellow's) ability to conduct research in his or her area of specialization."[15,16]

ASHP publishes an annual directory of ASHP-accredited residency programs. In 1985, there were 184 accredited programs.[17] The American College of Clinical Pharmacy publishes an annual listing of residencies and fellowships conducted by its members. In 1985, ACCP reported the availability of 51 such residencies and 83 such fellowships.[18] Another source reported 115 known fellowships in 1986.[19] In that year, there were 12 clinical fellowships sponsored by the ASHP Research and Education Foundation in nine areas of specialization.

By 1986, a lack of conformity had arisen in the use of the terms "residency" and "fellowship," and considerable potential existed for program applicants to be misinformed or misled regarding program purposes and content. In 1986, at the recommendation of the ASHP Commission on Credentialing, ASHP invited six other national pharmacy organizations to discuss the issue and develop consensus definitions for the terms. The definitions and interpretations that follow resulted from that conference. These definitions and interpretations are viewed as accurate for current residencies and fellowships yet sufficiently broad and flexible to allow the development of new types of programs. Education, practice, and research developments may generate changes in residencies and fellowships and ultimately stimulate revisions in the definitions and interpretations.

Residency

Definition. A pharmacy residency is an organized, directed, postgraduate training program in a defined area of pharmacy practice.

Interpretation. Residencies exist primarily to train pharmacists in professional practice and management activities. Residencies provide experience in integrating pharmacy services with the comprehensive needs of individual practice settings and provide indepth experiences leading to advanced practice skills and knowledge. Residencies foster an ability to conceptualize new and improved pharmacy services. Within a given residency program, there is considerable consistency in content for each resident. In addition, accreditation standards and program guidelines produced by national pharmacy associations provide considerable program content detail and foster consistency among programs.

A residency is typically 12 months or longer in duration, and the resident's practice experiences are closely directed and evaluated by a qualified practitioner–preceptor. A residency may occur at any career point following an entry-level degree in pharmacy. Individuals planning practice-oriented careers are encouraged to complete all formal academic education before entry into a residency.

Fellowship

Definition. A pharmacy fellowship is a directed, highly individualized, postgraduate program designed to prepare the participant to become an independent researcher.

Interpretation. Fellowships exist primarily to develop competency in the scientific research process, including conceptualizing, planning, conducting, and reporting research. Under the close direction and instruction of a qualified researcher–preceptor, the participant (the fellow) receives a highly individualized learning experience that utilizes research interests and knowledge needs as a focus for his or her education and training. A fellowship graduate should be capable of conducting collaborative research or functioning as a principal investigator.

Fellowships are typically offered through colleges of pharmacy, academic health centers, or specialized healthcare institutions. Fellowships are usually offered for predetermined, finite periods of time, often exceeding 12 or even 24 months. Individuals planning research-oriented careers should expect to complete formal education in research design and statistics either before or during a fellowship. A fellowship candidate is expected to possess basic practice skills relevant to the knowledge area of the fellowship. Such skills may be obtained through practice experience or through an appropriate residency and should be maintained during the program.

References

1. Niemeyer G. Ten years of the American Society of Hospital Pharmacists, 1942–1952: education and training. *Bull Am Soc Hosp Pharm.* 1952; 9:363–75.

2. American Society of Hospital Pharmacists. Approval program for internships in hospital pharmacy. *Bull Am Soc Hosp Pharm.* 1955; 12:309–13.

3. American Society of Hospital Pharmacists. Standards for internships in hospital pharmacies. *Bull Am Soc Hosp Pharm.* 1948; 5:233–4.

4. American Society of Hospital Pharmacists. Minimum standard for pharmacy internship in hospitals. *Bull Am Soc Hosp Pharm.* 1955; 12:288–90.

5. American Society of Hospital Pharmacists. Accreditation standard for residency in hospital pharmacy. *Am J Hosp Pharm.* 1963; 20:378–80.

6. American Society of Hospital Pharmacists. Accreditation standard for pharmacy residency in a hospital. *Am J Hosp Pharm.* 1971; 28:189–90.

7. American Society of Hospital Pharmacists. Accreditation standard for pharmacy residency in a hospital. *Am J Hosp Pharm.* 1973; 30:1129.

8. American Society of Hospital Pharmacists. ASHP accreditation standard for pharmacy residency in a hospital (with guide to interpretation). *Am J Hosp Pharm.* 1979; 36:74–80.

9. American Society of Hospital Pharmacists. ASHP accreditation standard for hospital pharmacy training (with guide to interpretation). *Am J Hosp Pharm.* 1985; 42:2008–18.

10. American Society of Hospital Pharmacists. ASHP accreditation standard for residency training in clinical pharmacy (with guide to interpretation). *Am J Hosp Pharm.* 1980; 37:1223–8.

11. American Society of Hospital Pharmacists. ASHP accreditation standard for specialized residency training (with guide to interpretation). *Am J Hosp Pharm.* 1980; 37:1229–32.

12. American Pharmaceutical Association, Academy of Pharmacy Practice. APhA community pharmacy residency program: programmatic essentials. *Am Pharm.* 1986; NS26:35–43.

13. American College of Apothecaries. Guidelines for accreditation of community pharmacy residencies. Memphis, TN: American College of Apothecaries; 1986.

14. Kaul AF, Powell SH, Cyr DA. Postgraduate pharmacy fellowships. *Drug Intell Clin Pharm.* 1981; 15:981–5.

15. ASHP Commission on Credentialing. Statement of definition of pharmacy fellowships and residency. Bethesda, MD: American Society of Hospital Pharmacists; 1981.

16. McConnell W. Fellowship program in critical care pharmacy. In: Majerus TC, Dasta JF, eds. Practice of critical care pharmacy. Rockville, MD: Aspen Systems; 1985:59–68.

17. American Society of Hospital Pharmacists. Residency directory. Accredited pharmacy residency programs and programs participating in the 1986 ASHP resident matching program. Bethesda, MD: American Society of Hospital Pharmacists; 1985.

18. American College of Clinical Pharmacy. Residency and fellowship programs offered by members of the American College of Clinical Pharmacy, 1986–87. Kansas City, MO: American College of Clinical Pharmacy; 1986.

19. Kaul AF, Janosik JE, Powell SH. Postgraduate pharmacy fellowships (1985–86). *Drug Intell Clin Pharm.* 1986; 20:203–8.

Developed by an ad hoc consortium made up of representatives from the American Association of Colleges of Pharmacy (AACP), the American College of Apothecaries (ACA), the American College of Clinical Pharmacy (ACCP), the American Pharmaceutical Association (APhA), the American Society of Consultant Pharmacists (ASCP), the American Society of Hospital Pharmacists (ASHP), and the National Association of Retail Druggists (NARD); the consortium was convened by ASHP and met on August 4, 1986. Approved by the ASHP Board of Directors, November 20, 1986, and subsequently approved by ACCP, APhA, ASCP, ACA, and AACP.

The bibliographic citation for this document is as follows: American Society of Hospital Pharmacists. Definitions of pharmacy residencies and fellowships. *Am J Hosp Pharm.* 1987; 44:1142–4.

Ethics

Ethics

"P.D." (Pharmacy Doctor) Designation for Pharmacists (0217)
Source: Council on Educational Affairs
To oppose the use of "P.D." or any other designation that implies an academically conferred degree where none exists.
This policy supersedes ASHP policy 8308.

Patient's Right to Choose (0013)
Source: Council on Legal and Public Affairs
To support the right of the patient or his or her representative as allowed under state law to develop, implement, and make informed decisions regarding his or her plan of care; further,

To acknowledge that the patient's rights include being informed of his or her health status, being involved in care planning and treatment, and being able to request or refuse treatment; further,

To support the right of the patient in accord with state law to (a) formulate advance directives and (b) have health care practitioners who comply with those directives.
This policy supersedes ASHP policy 9406.

ASHP Position on Assisted Suicide (9915)
Source: Council on Legal and Public Affairs
To remain neutral on the issue of health professional participation in assisted suicide of patients who are terminally ill; further,

To affirm that the decision to participate in the use of medications in assisted suicide is one of individual conscience; further,

To offer guidance to health-system pharmacists who practice in states in which assisted suicide is legal.
This policy was reviewed in 2003 by the Council on Legal and Public Affairs and by the Board of Directors and was found to still be appropriate.

Conscientious Objection by Pharmacists to Morally, Religiously, or Ethically Troubling Therapies (9802)
Source: House of Delegates Resolution
ASHP recognizes a pharmacist's right to conscientious objection to morally, religiously, or ethically troubling therapies and supports the establishment of systems that protect the patient's right to obtain legally prescribed and medically indicated treatments while reasonably accommodating the pharmacist's right of conscientious objection.
This policy was reviewed in 2002 by the Council on Professional Affairs and by the Board of Directors and was found to still be appropriate.

Nondiscriminatory Pharmaceutical Care (9006)
Source: Council on Professional Affairs
To adopt the following positions in regard to nondiscriminatory pharmaceutical care:

- All patients have the right to privacy, respect, confidentiality, and high-quality pharmaceutical care.
- No patient should be refused pharmaceutical care or denied these rights based solely on diagnosis.
- Pharmacists must always act in the best interest of individual patients while not placing society as a whole at risk.

This policy was reviewed in 2001 by the Council on Professional Affairs and by the Board of Directors and was found to still be appropriate.

Use of Drugs in Capital Punishment (8410)
Source: Council on Legal and Public Affairs
To support the following concepts:

1. The decision by a pharmacist to participate in the use of drugs in capital punishment is one of individual conscience.
2. Pharmacists, regardless of who employs them, should not be put at risk of any disciplinary action, including loss of their jobs, because of refusal to participate in capital punishment.

This policy was reviewed in 2001 by the Council on Legal and Public Affairs and by the Board of Directors and was found to still be appropriate.

ASHP Statement on Pharmacist's Decision-making on Assisted Suicide

Preamble

Consistent with the intent of the Code of Ethics for Pharmacists "to state publicly the principles that form the fundamental basis of the roles and responsibilities of pharmacists," the American Society of Health-System Pharmacists issues this Statement on Pharmacist Decision-making on Assisted Suicide. The practice of providing competent patients with pharmaceutical means of ending their lives raises issues of professional obligations to patients and to other professionals involved in patient care. We affirm the ASHP policy (9802) that supports the right of a pharmacist to participate or not in morally, religiously, or ethically troubling therapies.

This Statement establishes a framework for pharmacist participation in the legal and ethical debate about the appropriate care of patients at the end of life. This Statement will help pharmacists resolve the growing questions about the ethical obligations of health care professionals to provide care and alleviate suffering. It is hoped that this framework and its use by pharmacists will virtually eliminate a patient's request for assisted suicide.

When asked to evaluate and comment on legislative, regulatory, or judicial actions or on organizational policies of health systems regarding pharmaceutical care, pharmacists should use the principles expressed in this Statement in developing their responses.

Guiding Principles

Professional Tradition. The basic tenet of the profession is to provide care and affirm life. The pharmacy profession is founded on a tradition of patient trust. The trust developed between each patient and members of the health care team makes it important for each professional to examine the moral and ethical issues of patients' requests for assistance in dying. Pharmacists should serve as advocates for the patient throughout the continuum of care.

Respect for Patients. *Patient autonomy.* Pharmacists should ensure the rights of competent patients to know about all legally available treatment options while communicating to patients and their caregivers (including family members if appropriate) the overall duty of health care professionals to preserve life.

Confidentiality. Pharmacists should maintain the confidentiality of all patient information, regardless of whether they agree with the values underlying the patient's choice of treatment or decision to forgo any particular treatment.

Decision-making. Patients' ability to exercise their ethical and legal right to choose or decline treatment is dependent upon pharmacists informing patients and their health care providers about the nature of pharmaceutical options. Those options are constantly changing, given the dynamic aspect of the pharmaceutical marketplace and the evolving nature of hospice care and available palliative treatments.

Health Care Systems. *Collaboration.* Collaboration among members of the health care team must occur at both the patient care and the public policy levels. It is the pharmacist's responsibility to educate members of the health care team about the pharmacotherapeutic options available in treating the patient's condition. Health care team members include the patient, members of the patient's family, and caregivers.

Confidentiality. The patient's right of confidentiality and right to determine his or her therapy, including end-of-life decisions, shall be respected, included, and considered in the decision process in health care systems. Pharmacists should maintain the confidentiality of all patient information, regardless of whether they agree with the values underlying the patient's choice of treatment or decision to forgo any particular treatment.

Covenant with Society. Health care is delivered in a system in which each profession makes a contribution on the patient's behalf. An act in one part of the system has consequences in other parts of that system. Each profession has a covenant with society, founded on a relationship of trust with the patient. The trust developed between each patient and members of the health care team makes it important for each professional to examine the moral and ethical issues of patients' requests for assistance in dying.

Barriers to Care. Health care professionals must address the following barriers to adequate end-of-life care:

1. Inadequate knowledge and use of pain- and symptom-management therapies.
2. The paucity of published data related to the ingestion of lethal drugs and the outcomes thereof.
3. Insufficient education of health care professionals about end-of-life and palliative care issues.
4. Inadequate recognition that end-of-life care is the responsibility of the entire health care team.
5. Legal and regulatory issues that deter appropriate provision of pain and symptom management.

Professional Obligations. *Conscientious Objection.* Pharmacists must retain their right to participate or not in morally, religiously, or ethically troubling therapies. Procedures should be in place to ensure that employers are able to provide care to the patient and provide adequate services to the patient and caregiver. The employer has specific responsibilities, and the employee cannot be a barrier to the employer's ability to fulfill those obligations. Employers must reasonably accommodate the employee pharmacist's right to not participate in morally, religiously, or ethically troubling therapies.

Obligation to the Patient. Pharmacists should support appropriate drug therapy to ensure that palliative care and aggressive pain management are available for all patients in need. Pharmacists, as part of their professional responsibility, must offer to provide counseling services to the patient and caregivers and be prepared to provide pharmaceutical care to the patient until the end of life.

Obligation to Team Members. The pharmacist, as a member of a health care team responsible for the care of a patient, is accountable for providing the team members with detailed information concerning efficacious use of pharmaceutical and other therapies available that may affect the options open to the patient.

As active members of an interdisciplinary team caring for patients, pharmacists must be central participants in all decisions relating to medication management of the patient. Pharmacists should respect the opinions and specific areas of expertise of the other members of the health care team.

Pharmacist Education. Pharmacists are often inadequately trained in the care of dying patients. Therefore, pharmacists' education at all levels (undergraduate, graduate, continuing education) should be sensitive to these issues and offer the development of skills and knowledge concerning care of the dying. Pharmacists should make a personal, professional commitment to learn more about end-of-life care.

Recommended Readings

Supreme Court Decisions

1. *Washington v. Glucksberg,* decided June 26, 1997.
2. *Vacco v. Quill,* decided June 26, 1997.
3. Angell M. The Supreme Court and physician-assisted suicide—the ultimate right. *N Engl J Med.* 1997; 336:50-3.
4. Annas GJ. The bell tolls for a constitutional right to physician-assisted suicide. *N Engl J Med.* 1997; 337:1098-103.
5. Burt RA. The Supreme Court speaks: not assisted suicide but a constitutional right to palliative care. *N Engl J Med.* 1997; 337:1234-6.
6. Gostin LO. Deciding life and death in the courtroom: from *Quinlan* to *Cruzan, Glucksberg,* and *Vacco*—a brief history and analysis of constitutional protection of the "right to die." *JAMA.* 1997; 278:1523-8.
7. Orentlicher D. The Supreme Court and physician-assisted suicide: rejecting assisted suicide but embracing euthanasia. *N Engl J Med.* 1997; 337:1236-9.
8. Palmer LI. Institutional analysis and physicians' rights after *Vacco v. Quill. Cornell J Law Public Policy.* 1998; 7:415-30.

Professional Organization Position Statements/Policies

1. American Bar Association house of delegates. Report of action taken at 1997 annual meeting.
2. American Pharmaceutical Association. Code of Ethics for Pharmacists.
3. American Pain Society. Treatment of pain at the end of life.
4. National League for Nursing. Life-terminating choices: a framework for nursing decision-making.
5. American Medical Association Policy on Physician-Assisted Suicide, 1996.
6. American Nurses Association. Position statement on assisted suicide.
7. American Geriatrics Society. Position statement on the care of dying patients.
8. National Hospice Organization.

Assisted Suicide

1. Dixon KM, Kier KL. Longing for mercy, requesting death: pharmaceutical care and pharmaceutically assisted death. *Am J Health-Syst Pharm.* 1998; 55:578-85.
2. Hamerly JP. Views on assisted suicide: perspectives of the AMA and the NHO. *Am J Health-Syst Pharm.* 1998; 55:543-7.
3. Lee BC. Views on assisted suicide: the aid-in-dying perspective. *Am J Health-Syst Pharm.* 1998; 55:547-50.
4. Meier DE, Emmons CA, Wallenstein S et al. A national survey of physician-assisted suicide and euthanasia in the United States. *N Engl J Med.* 1998; 338:1193-201.
5. Mullan K, Allen WL, Brushwood DB. Conscientious objection to assisted death: can pharmacy address this in a systematic fashion? *Ann Pharmacother.* 1996; 30:1185-91.
6. Rupp MT. Issues for pharmacists in assisted patient death. In: Battin MP, Lipman AG, eds. Drug use in assisted suicide and euthanasia. Binghamton, NY: Haworth; 1996.
7. Rupp MT. Physician-assisted suicide and the issues it raises for pharmacists. *Am J Health-Syst Pharm.* 1995; 52:1455-60.
8. Rupp MT, Isenhower HL. Pharmacists' attitudes toward physician-assisted suicide. *Am J Hosp Pharm.* 1994; 51:69-74.
9. Stein GC. Assisted suicide: an issue for pharmacists. *Am J Health-Syst Pharm.* 1998; 55:539. Editorial.
10. Van der Maas PJ, van der Wal G, Haverkate I et al. Euthanasia, physician-assisted suicide, and other medical practices involving the end of life in the Netherlands, 1990–1995. *N Engl J Med.* 1996; 335:1699-705.
11. Van der Wal G, van der Maas PJ, Bosma JM et al. Evaluation of the notification procedure for physician-assisted death in the Netherlands. *N Engl J Med.* 1996; 335:1706-11.
12. Vaux KL. Views on assisted suicide: an ethicist's perspective. *Am J Health-Syst Pharm.* 1998; 55:551-3.

End-of-Life Care

1. Foley KM. Competent care for the dying instead of physician-assisted suicide. *N Engl J Med.* 1997; 336:54-8.
2. Quill TE, Lo B, Brock DW. Palliative options of last resort: a comparison of voluntarily stopping eating and drinking, terminal sedation, physician-assisted suicide, and voluntary active euthanasia. *JAMA.* 1997; 278:2099-104.
3. Suicide prevention: efforts to increase research and education in palliative care. Washington, DC: General Accounting Office, 1998 Apr; report HEHS-98-128.

Miscellaneous

1. Board of Directors report on the Council on Legal and Public Affairs, ASHP House of Delegates Session—1994.
2. Board of Directors report on the Council on Professional Affairs, ASHP House of Delegates Session—1998.

3. Board of Directors report on the Council on Legal and Public Affairs, ASHP House of Delegates Session—1998.
4. Statement of Attorney General Reno on Oregon's Death with Dignity Act. June 5, 1998.
5. Schnabel J, Schnabel G. Pharmacy information. In: Haley K, Lee M, eds. The Oregon Death With Dignity Act: A Guidebook for Health Care Providers. Portland: Oregon Health Sciences University, Center for Ethics in Health Care; 1998 Mar.

This statement was reviewed in 2003 by the Council on Legal and Public Affairs and by the Board of Directors and was found to still be appropriate.

Approved by the ASHP Board of Directors, April 21, 1999, and by the ASHP House of Delegates, June 7, 1999. Developed by the Council on Legal and Professional Affairs.

Copyright © 1999, American Society of Health-System Pharmacists, Inc. All rights reserved.

The bibliographic citation for this document is as follows: American Society of Health-System Pharmacists. ASHP statement on pharmacist's decision-making on assisted suicide. *Am J Health-Syst. Pharm.* 1999; 56:1661–4.

Relevant ASHP Policies

Pharmacist Support for Dying Patients (0307)
Source: Council on Professional Affairs
To support the position that care for dying patients is part of the continuum of care that pharmacists should provide to patients; further,

To support the position that pharmacists have a professional obligation to work in a collaborative and compassionate manner with patients, family members, caregivers, and other professionals to help fulfill the patient care needs, especially the quality-of-life needs, of dying patients of all ages; further,

To support research on the needs of dying patients; further,

To provide education to pharmacists on caring for dying patients, including education on clinical, managerial, professional, and legal issues; further,

To urge the inclusion of such topics in the curricula of colleges of pharmacy.

This policy supersedes ASHP policies 9814 and 9816.

Conscientious Objection by Pharmacists to Morally, Religiously, or Ethically Troubling Therapies (9802)
ASHP recognizes a pharmacist's right to conscientious objection to morally, religiously, or ethically troubling therapies and supports the establishment of systems that protect the patient's right to obtain legally prescribed and medically indicated treatments while reasonably accommodating the pharmacist's right of conscientious objection.

This policy was reviewed in 2002 by the Council on Professional Affairs and by the Board of Directors and was found to still be appropriate.

Use of Drugs in Capital Punishment (8410)
To support the following concepts:

1. The decision by a pharmacist to participate in the use of drugs in capital punishment is one of individual conscience.
2. Pharmacists, regardless of who employs them, should not be put at risk of any disciplinary action, including loss of their jobs, because of refusal to participate in capital punishment.

This policy was reviewed in 2001 by the Council on Legal and Public Affairs and by the Board of Directors and was found to still be appropriate.

ASHP Guidelines on Pharmacists' Relationships with Industry

In the practice of their profession, pharmacists should be guided only by the consideration of patient care. Pharmacists should neither accept nor retain anything of value that has the potential to affect materially their ability to exercise judgments solely in the interests of patients. A useful criterion in determining acceptable activities and relationships is this: Would the pharmacist be willing to have these relationships generally known? Notwithstanding this responsibility, pharmacists may benefit from guidance in their relationships with industry. To this end, the following suggestions are offered.

Gifts and Hospitality

Gifts, hospitality, or subsidies offered to pharmacists by industry should not be accepted if acceptance might influence, or appear to others to influence, the objectivity of clinical judgment or drug product selection and procurement.

Continuing Education

Providers of continuing education that accept industry funding for programs should develop and enforce policies to maintain complete control of program content.

Subsidies to underwrite the costs of continuing-education conferences, professional meetings, or staff development programs can contribute to the improvement of patient care and are permissible. Payments to defray the costs of a conference should not be accepted directly or indirectly from industry by pharmacists attending the conference or program. Contributions to special or educational funds for staff development are permissible as long as the selection of staff members who will receive the funds is made by the department of pharmacy.

It is appropriate for faculty at conferences or meetings to accept reasonable honoraria and reimbursement for reasonable travel, lodging, and meal expenses. However, direct subsidies from industry should not be accepted to pay the costs of travel, lodging, or other personal expenses of pharmacists attending conferences or meetings, nor should subsidies be accepted to compensate for the pharmacists' time.

Scholarships or other special funds to permit pharmacy students, residents, and fellows to attend carefully selected educational conferences may be permissible as long as the selection of students, residents, or fellows who will receive the funds is made by the academic or training institution.

Consultants and Advisory Arrangements

Consultants who provide genuine services for industry may receive reasonable compensation and accept reimbursement for travel, lodging, and meal expenses. Token consulting or advisory arrangements cannot be used to justify compensating pharmacists for their time, travel, lodging, and other out-of-pocket expenses.

Clinical Research

Pharmacists who participate in practice-based research of pharmaceuticals, devices, or other programs should conduct their activities in accord with basic precepts of accepted scientific methodology. Practice-based drug studies that are, in effect, promotional schemes to entice the use of a product or program are unacceptable.

Disclosure of Information

To avoid conflicts of interest or appearances of impropriety, pharmacists should disclose consultant or speaker arrangements or substantial personal financial holdings with companies under consideration for formulary inclusion or related decisions. To inform audiences fully, speakers and authors should disclose, when pertinent, consultant or speaker and research funding arrangements with companies.

Additional Issues

The advice in this document is noninclusive and is not intended to limit the legitimate exchange of prudent scientific information.

This guideline was reviewed in 2001 by the Council on Legal and Public Affairs and by the ASHP Board of Directors and was found to still be appropriate.

Approved by the ASHP Board of Directors, November 20, 1991. Developed by the ASHP Council on Legal and Public Affairs.

The language used in many of the guidance issues contained in this document was adapted, with permission, from documents developed by the American Medical Association (*JAMA.* 1991; 265:501) and the American College of Physicians (*Ann Intern Med.* 1990; 112:624–6).

The bibliographic citation for this document is as follows: American Society of Hospital Pharmacists. ASHP guidelines on pharmacists' relationships with industry. *Am J Hosp Pharm.* 1992; 49:154.

Code of Ethics for Pharmacists

Preamble

Pharmacists are health professionals who assist individuals in making the best use of medications. This Code, prepared and supported by pharmacists, is intended to state publicly the principles that form the fundamental basis of the roles and responsibilities of pharmacists. These principles, based on moral obligations and virtues, are established to guide pharmacists in relationships with patients, health professionals, and society.

Principles

I. *A pharmacist respects the covenantal relationship between the patient and pharmacist.*
   Interpretation: Considering the patient–pharmacist relationship as a covenant means that a pharmacist has moral obligations in response to the gift of trust received from society. In return for this gift, a pharmacist promises to help individuals achieve optimum benefit from their medications, to be committed to their welfare, and to maintain their trust.

II. *A pharmacist promotes the good of every patient in a caring, compassionate, and confidential manner.*
   Interpretation: A pharmacist places concern for the well-being of the patient at the center of professional practice. In doing so, a pharmacist considers needs stated by the patient as well as those defined by health science. A pharmacist is dedicated to protecting the dignity of the patient. With a caring attitude and a compassionate spirit, a pharmacist focuses on serving the patient in a private and confidential manner.

III. *A pharmacist respects the autonomy and dignity of each patient.*
   Interpretation: A pharmacist promotes the right of self-determination and recognizes individual self-worth by encouraging patients to participate in decisions about their health. A pharmacist communicates with patients in terms that are understandable. In all cases, a pharmacist respects personal and cultural differences among patients.

IV. *A pharmacist acts with honesty and integrity in professional relationships.*
   Interpretation: A pharmacist has a duty to tell the truth and to act with conviction of conscience. A pharmacist avoids discriminatory practices, behavior or work conditions that impair professional judgment, and actions that compromise dedication to the best interests of patients.

V. *A pharmacist maintains professional competence.*
   Interpretation: A pharmacist has a duty to maintain knowledge and abilities as new medications, devices, and technologies become available and as health information advances.

VI. *A pharmacist respects the values and abilities of colleagues and other health professionals.*
   Interpretation: When appropriate, a pharmacist asks for the consultation of colleagues or other health professionals or refers the patient. A pharmacist acknowledges that colleagues and other health professionals may differ in the beliefs and values they apply to the care of the patient.

VII. *A pharmacist serves individual, community, and societal needs.*
   Interpretation: The primary obligation of a pharmacist is to individual patients. However, the obligations of a pharmacist may at times extend beyond the individual to the community and society. In these situations, the pharmacist recognizes the responsibilities that accompany these obligations and acts accordingly.

VIII. *A pharmacist seeks justice in the distribution of health resources.*
   Interpretation: When health resources are allocated, a pharmacist is fair and equitable, balancing the needs of patients and society.

This endorsed document was reviewed in 2002 by the Council on Legal and Public Affairs and by the Board of Directors and was found to still be appropriate.

Formulary Management

(Medication-Use Policy Development)

Formulary Management

Expression of Therapeutic Purpose of Prescribing (0305)

Source: Council on Professional Affairs

To advocate that the prescriber provide or pharmacists have immediate access to the intended therapeutic purpose of prescribed medications in order to ensure safe and effective medication use.

This policy supersedes ASHP policy 9708.

Biological Drugs (0316)

Source: Council on Professional Affairs

To encourage pharmacists to take a leadership role in their health systems for all aspects of the proper use of biologic therapies, including preparation, storage, control, distribution, administration procedures, safe handling, and therapeutic applications; further,

To facilitate education of pharmacists about the proper use of biologic therapies.

This proposed policy supersedes ASHP policy 0017.

Appropriate Dosing of Medications in Patient Populations with Unique Needs (0228)

Source: Council on Professional Affairs

To advocate reforms in medication-use systems, including electronic systems, and health care provider education and training that facilitate optimal patient-specific dosing in populations of patients (e.g., pediatrics, geriatrics) with altered pharmacokinetics and pharmacodynamics.

Medication Formulary System Management (0102)

Source: Council on Administrative Affairs

To declare that decisions on the management of a medication formulary system (1) should be based on clinical, ethical, legal, social, philosophical, quality-of-life, safety, and pharmacoeconomic factors that result in optimal patient care, and (2) must include the active and direct involvement of physicians, pharmacists, and other appropriate health care professionals; further,

To declare that decisions on the management of a medication formulary system should not be based solely on economic factors.

This policy supersedes ASHP policy 9803.

Gene Therapy (0103)

Source: Council on Administrative Affairs

To declare that health-system decisions on the selection, use, and management of gene therapy agents should be based on the same principles as a medication formulary system in that (1) decisions are based on clinical, ethical, legal, social, philosophical, quality-of-life, safety, and pharmacoeconomic factors that result in optimal patient care and (2) such decisions must include the active and direct involvement of physicians, pharmacists, and other appropriate health care professionals.

Pharmacogenomics (0016)

Source: The Council on Professional Affairs

To encourage pharmacists to take a leadership role in the therapeutic applications of pharmacogenomics; further,

To advocate the inclusion of pharmacogenomics and its application to therapeutic decision-making in school of pharmacy curricula.

Inline Filters (0018)

Source: The Council on Professional Affairs

To support the principle that pharmacists be involved in the development of policies in their practice settings on the use of inline filtration for intravenous administration of fluids, nutrients, and medications.

Role of Pharmacists and Business Leaders in Health Care Services and Policies (9819)

Source: Council on Professional Affairs

To support the principle that business leaders and health professionals must share responsibility and accountability for providing optimal health care services to patients; further,

To support the principle that business leaders should expect practicing pharmacists to formulate policies that affect the prerogative of pharmacists to make optimal care decisions on behalf of patients.

Standardization of Drug Medication Formulary Systems (9601)

Source: Council on Administrative Affairs

To support the concept of a standardized medication formulary system among components of integrated health systems when standardization leads to improved patient outcomes; further,

To include in the formulary-standardization process the direct involvement of the health system's physicians, pharmacists, and other appropriate health care professionals.

Medical Devices (9106)

Source: Council on Legal and Public Affairs

To support public and private initiatives to clarify and define the relationship among drugs, devices, and new technologies in order to promote safety and effectiveness as well as better delivery of patient care.

This policy was reviewed in 2001 by the Council on Legal and Public Affairs and by the Board of Directors and was found to still be appropriate.

Generic Drug Products (9005)

Source: Council on Legal and Public Affairs

To encourage pharmacists in organized health care settings to assume a greater leadership role in legislative and other arenas relating to drug product selection and evaluation.

This policy was reviewed in 2001 by the Council on Legal and Public Affairs and by the Board of Directors and was found to still be appropriate.

Therapeutic Interchange (8708)

Source: Council on Legal and Public Affairs

To support the concept of therapeutic interchange of various drug products by pharmacists under arrangements where pharmacists and authorized prescribers interrelate on the behalf of patient care.

This policy was reviewed in 2003 by the Council on Legal and Public Affairs and by the Board of Directors and was found to still be appropriate.

ASHP Statement on the Pharmacy and Therapeutics Committee

The multiplicity of drugs available and the complexities surrounding their safe and effective use make it necessary for organized health-care settings to have a sound program for maximizing rational drug use. The pharmacy and therapeutics (P&T) committee, or its equivalent, is the organizational keystone to this program.

The P&T committee evaluates the clinical use of drugs, develops policies for managing drug use and drug administration, and manages the formulary system. This committee is composed of physicians, pharmacists, and other health professionals selected with the guidance of the medical staff. It is a policy-recommending body to the medical staff and the administration of the organization on matters related to the therapeutic use of drugs.

Purposes

The primary purposes of the P&T committee are

1. *Policy Development.* The committee formulates policies regarding evaluation, selection, and therapeutic use of drugs and related devices.[a]
2. *Education.* The committee recommends or assists in the formulation of programs designed to meet the needs of the professional staff (physicians, nurses, pharmacists, and other health-care practitioners) for complete current knowledge on matters related to drugs and drug use.

Organization and Operation

While the composition and operation of the P&T committee might vary among specific practice sites, the following generally will apply:

1. The P&T committee should be composed of at least the following voting members: physicians, pharmacists, nurses, administrators, quality-assurance coordinators, and others as appropriate. The size of the committee may vary depending on the scope of services provided by the organization. Committee members should be appointed by a governing unit or authorized official of the organized medical staff.
2. A chairperson from among the physician representatives should be appointed. A pharmacist should be designated as secretary.
3. They should meet regularly, at least six times per year, and more often when necessary.
4. The committee should invite to its meetings persons within or outside the organization who can contribute specialized or unique knowledge, skills, and judgments.
5. An agenda and supplementary materials (including minutes of the previous meeting) should be prepared by the secretary and submitted to committee members in sufficient time before each meeting for them to review the material properly.
6. The minutes of committee meetings should be prepared by the secretary and maintained in the perma-

nent records of the organization.
7. Recommendations of the committee should be presented to the medical staff or its appropriate committee for adoption or recommendation.
8. Liaison with other organizational committees concerned with drug use should be maintained.
9. Actions of the committee should be routinely communicated to the various health-care personnel involved in the care of the patient.
10. The committee should be organized and operated in a manner that ensures the objectivity and credibility of its recommendations. The committee should establish a conflict of interest policy with respect to committee recommendations and actions.
11. In formulating drug use policies for the organization, the committee should be attentive to the content and changes in pertinent guidelines and policies of professional organizations and standards-setting bodies such as the American Society of Hospital Pharmacists, the American Hospital Association, medical and nursing associations, the Joint Commission on Accreditation of Healthcare Organizations, governmental agencies, and others as appropriate.

Functions and Scope

The basic organization of each health-care setting and its medical staff may influence the specific functions and scope of the P&T committee. The following list of committee functions is offered as a guide:

1. To serve in an evaluative, educational, and advisory capacity to the medical staff and organizational administration in all matters pertaining to the use of drugs (including investigational drugs).
2. To develop a formulary of drugs accepted for use in the organization and provide for its constant revision. The selection of items to be included in the formulary should be based on objective evaluation of their relative therapeutic merits, safety, and cost. The committee should minimize duplication of the same basic drug type, drug entity, or drug product.[b]
3. To establish programs and procedures that help ensure safe and effective drug therapy.
4. To establish programs and procedures that help ensure cost-effective drug therapy.
5. To establish or plan suitable educational programs for the organization's professional staff on matters related to drug use.
6. To participate in quality-assurance activities related to distribution, administration, and use of medications.
7. To monitor and evaluate adverse drug (including, but not limited to, biologics and vaccines) reactions in the health-care setting and to make appropriate recommendations to prevent their occurrence.
8. To initiate or direct (or both) drug use evaluation programs and studies, review the results of such activities, and make appropriate recommendations to optimize drug use.

9. To advise the pharmacy department in the implementation of effective drug distribution and control procedures.
10. To disseminate information on its actions and approved recommendations to all organizational health-care staff.

---

^aFor additional information, see the "ASHP Statement on the Formulary System" (*Am J Hosp Pharm.* 1983; 40:1384–5) and the "ASHP Technical Assistance Bulletin on the Evaluation of Drugs for Formularies" (*Am J Hosp Pharm.* 1988; 45:386–7).

^bFor additional information, see the "ASHP Technical Assistance Bulletin on Drug Formularies" (*Am J Hosp Pharm.* 1991; 48:791–3).

Approved by the ASHP Board of Directors, November 20, 1991, and by the ASHP House of Delegates, June 1, 1992. Revised by the ASHP Council on Professional Affairs. Supersedes previous versions approved by the House of Delegates, May 15, 1978, and June 6, 1984.

The bibliographic citation for this document is as follows: American Society of Hospital Pharmacists. ASHP statement on the pharm-acy and therapeutics committee. *Am J Hosp Pharm.* 1992; 49:2008–9.

ASHP Statement on the Formulary System

Preamble

The care of patients in hospitals and other health-care facilities is often dependent on the effective use of drugs. The multiplicity of drugs available makes it mandatory that a sound program of drug usage be developed within the institution to ensure that patients receive the best possible care.

In the interest of better patient care, the institution should have a program of objective evaluation, selection, and use of medicinal agents in the facility. This program is the basis of appropriate, economical drug therapy. The formulary concept[a] is a method for providing such a program and has been utilized as such for many years.

To be effective, the formulary system must have the approval of the organized medical staff, the concurrence of individual staff members, and the functioning of a properly organized pharmacy and therapeutics (P&T) committee[b] of the medical staff. The basic policies and procedures governing the formulary system should be incorporated in the medical staff bylaws or in the medical staff rules and regulations.

The P&T committee represents the official organizational line of communication and liaison between the medical and pharmacy staffs. The committee is responsible to the medical staff as a whole, and its recommendations are subject to approval by the organized medical staff as well as to the normal administrative approval process.

This committee assists in the formulation of broad professional policies relating to drugs in institutions, including their evaluation or appraisal, selection, procurement, storage, distribution, and safe use.

Definition of Formulary and Formulary System

The *formulary* is a continually revised compilation of pharmaceuticals (plus important ancillary information) that reflects the current clinical judgment of the medical staff.[c]

The *formulary system* is a method whereby the medical staff of an institution, working through the P&T committee, evaluates, appraises, and selects from among the numerous available drug entities and drug products those that are considered most useful in patient care. Only those so selected are routinely available from the pharmacy. The formulary system is thus an important tool for assuring the quality of drug use and controlling its cost. The formulary system provides for the procuring, prescribing, dispensing, and administering of drugs under either their nonproprietary or proprietary names in instances where drugs have both names.

Guiding Principles

The following principles will serve as a guide to physicians, pharmacists, nurses, and administrators in hospitals and other facilities utilizing the formulary system:

1. The medical staff shall appoint a multidisciplinary P&T committee and outline its purposes, organization, function, and scope.
2. The formulary system shall be sponsored by the medical staff based on the recommendations of the P&T committee. The medical staff should adapt the principles of the system to the needs of the particular institution.
3. The medical staff shall adopt written policies and procedures governing the formulary system as developed by the P&T committee. Action of the medical staff is subject to the normal administrative approval process. These policies and procedures shall afford guidance in the evaluation or appraisal, selection, procurement, storage, distribution, safe use, and other matters relating to drugs and shall be published in the institution's formulary or other media available to all members of the medical staff.
4. Drugs should be included in the formulary by their nonproprietary names, even though proprietary names may be in common use in the institution. Prescribers should be strongly encouraged to prescribe drugs by their nonproprietary names.
5. Limiting the number of drug entities and drug products routinely available from the pharmacy can produce substantial patient-care and (particularly) financial benefits. These benefits are greatly increased through the use of *generic equivalents* (drug products considered to be identical with respect to their active components; e.g., two brands of tetracycline hydrochloride capsules) and *therapeutic equivalents* (drug products differing in composition or in their basic drug entity that are considered to have very similar pharmacologic and therapeutic activities; e.g., two different antacid products or two different alkylamine antihistamines). The P&T committee must set forth policies and procedures governing the dispensing of generics and therapeutic equivalents. These policies and procedures should include the following points:
   - That the pharmacist is responsible for selecting, from available generic equivalents, those drugs to be dispensed pursuant to a physician's order for a particular drug product.
   - That the prescriber has the option, at the time of prescribing, to specify the brand or supplier of drug to be dispensed for that particular medication order/prescription. The prescriber's decision should be based on pharmacologic or therapeutic considerations (or both) relative to that patient.
   - That the P&T committee is responsible for determining those drug products and entities (if any) that shall be considered therapeutic equivalents. The conditions and procedures for dispensing a therapeutic alternative in place of the prescribed drug shall be clearly delineated.
6. The institution shall make certain that its medical and nursing staffs are informed about the existence of the formulary system, the procedures governing its operation, and any changes in those procedures. Copies of the formulary must be readily available and accessible at all times.
7. Provision shall be made for appraisal and use of drugs not included in the formulary by the medical staff.
8. The pharmacist shall be responsible for specifications as to the quality, quantity, and source of supply of all

drugs, chemicals, biologicals, and pharmaceutical preparations used in the diagnosis and treatment of patients. When applicable, such products should meet the standards of the *United States Pharmacopeia*.

Recommendation

A formulary system, based on these guiding principles, is important in drug therapy in institutions. In the interest of better and more economical patient care, its adoption by medical staffs is strongly recommended.

The policy of the American Medical Association on drug formularies and therapeutic interchange is consistent with this practice standard of ASHP (see *Am J Hosp Pharm.* 1994; 51:1808–10).

[a]The formulary system is adaptable for use in any type of health-care facility and is not limited to hospitals.

[b]For additional information, see the "ASHP Statement on the Pharmacy and Therapeutics Committee" (*Am J Hosp Pharm.* 1992; 49:2008–9).
[c]For additional information, see the "ASHP Guidelines on Formulary System Management" (*Am J Hosp Pharm.* 1992; 49:648–52).

Approved by the ASHP Board of Directors, November 18, 1982, and by the ASHP House of Delegates, June 7, 1983. Developed by the ASHP Council on Clinical Affairs. Supersedes the "ASHP Statement of Guiding Principles on the Operation of the Hospital Formulary System" approved by the Board of Directors, January 10, 1964.

The bibliographic citation for this document is as follows: American Society of Hospital Pharmacists. ASHP statement on the formulary system. *Am J Hosp Pharm.* 1983; 40:1384–5.

ASHP Statement on the
Use of Medications for Unlabeled Uses

The freedom and responsibility to make drug therapy decisions that are consistent with patient-care needs is a fundamental precept supported by ASHP. This activity is a professional duty of pharmacists not limited by language in Food and Drug Administration (FDA)-approved product labeling.

The prescribing, dispensing, and administration of FDA-approved drugs for uses, treatment regimens, or patient populations that are not reflected in FDA-approved product labeling often represent a therapeutic approach that has been extensively studied and reported in medical literature. Such uses are *not* indicative of inappropriate usage. Health-care professionals should appreciate the critical need for freedom in making drug therapy decisions and understand the implications of unlabeled uses. ASHP supports third-party reimbursement for FDA-approved drug products appropriately prescribed for unlabeled uses.

Definition of Unlabeled Use

The FDA approves drug products for marketing in the United States. Such a product approved for marketing is often termed an "FDA-approved drug." FDA also approves each drug product's labeling (container label, package insert, and certain advertising); the term "FDA-approved labeling" applies here. Drug uses that are not included in the indications or dosage regimens listed in the FDA-approved labeling are defined as "unlabeled uses." For purposes of this document, unlabeled use includes the use of a drug product in (1) doses, (2) patient populations, (3) indications, or (4) routes of administration that are not reflected in FDA-approved product labeling.

It is important to recognize that FDA cannot approve or disapprove physician prescribing practices of legally marketed drugs. FDA does regulate what manufacturers may recommend about uses in their products' labeling and what manufacturers can include in advertising and promotion.

The sometimes-used term "unapproved use" is a misnomer, implying that FDA regulates prescribing and dispensing activities. This term should be avoided.[1] Other terminology that is sometimes used to describe unlabeled use includes "off-label use," "out-of-label use," and "usage outside of labeling."

According to FDA, unlabeled use encompasses a range of situations that extend from inadequate to carefully conceived investigations, from hazardous to salutary uses, and from infrequent to widespread medical practice. Accepted medical practice often involves drug use that is not reflected in FDA-approved drug-product labeling.[2]

Health-Care Issues Related to Unlabeled Use

Access to Drug Therapies. The prescribing and dispensing of drugs for unlabeled uses are increasing.[3,4] In many clinical situations, unlabeled use represents the most appropriate therapy for patients. Failure to recognize this or, more importantly, regarding such use as "unapproved" or "experimental" may restrict access to necessary drug therapies.

Lack of Practice Standards. Well-defined medical practice standards that differentiate between experimental therapies and established practice will probably always be somewhat lacking, owing to the advancement of medical science and the dynamic nature of medical practice. Standards of practice for certain drug therapies, particularly biotechnologically produced drugs, cancer chemotherapy, and AIDS treatments, are continually evolving. The dynamic nature of these drug therapies makes it difficult for professional societies to review scientific data expediently and to develop standards that remain absolutely current.

Failure of Package Insert and FDA-Approved Labeling to Reflect Current Practice. For FDA-approved product labeling to be modified, scientific data must be submitted by a product's manufacturer to FDA to support any additional indication(s) and dosage regimen(s). Once they are submitted, FDA must review the data and make a decision to permit alteration of the package insert.

Knowing that unlabeled uses are permitted, and knowing that the accumulation and submission of scientific data to FDA to modify labeling is a time-consuming and often expensive process, some pharmaceutical manufacturers elect not to pursue labeling changes. Therefore, a product's labeling sometimes fails to represent the most current therapeutic information for a drug, and situations naturally occur when it is appropriate to prescribe drugs for unlabeled uses.

Pharmacist's Role

ASHP believes that pharmacists in organized health-care settings bear a significant responsibility for ensuring optimal outcomes from all drug therapy. With respect to unlabeled uses, the role of the pharmacist should be to

1. Fulfill the roles of patient advocate and drug information specialist.
2. Develop policies and procedures for evaluating drug orders (prescriptions) and dispensing drugs for unlabeled uses in their own work settings. Such policies and procedures might address the documentation of scientific support, adherence to accepted medical practice standards, or a description of medical necessity.
3. Develop proactive approaches to promote informed decisionmaking by third-party payers for health-care services.

Role of Drug Information Compendia

The Medicare Catastrophic Coverage Act of 1988 (now repealed) included the statements that "in carrying out the legislation, the Secretary [of Health and Human Services] shall establish standards for drug coverage. In establishing such standards, which are based on accepted medical practice, the Secretary shall incorporate standards from such current authoritative compendia as the Secretary may select."[5] Specific compendia recommended were the *AHFS*

Drug Information, *AMA Drug Evaluations*, and *USP Dispensing Information, Volume I*. Despite the repeal of the Act, some third-party payers have adopted guidelines that endorse these three compendia as authoritative information sources with respect to unlabeled uses for drug products.

Positions on Unlabeled Use

FDA Position. A statement entitled "Use of Approved Drugs for Unlabeled Indications" was published in the *FDA Drug Bulletin* in April 1982 to address the issues of appropriateness and legality of prescribing approved drugs for uses not included in FDA's approved labeling. This statement included the following:

> The Food, Drug and Cosmetic Act does not limit the manner in which a physician may use an approved drug. Once a product has been approved for marketing, a physician may prescribe it for uses or in treatment regimens or patient populations that are not included in approved labeling. Such "unapproved" or, more precisely, "unlabeled" uses may be appropriate and rational in certain circumstances, and may, in fact, reflect approaches to drug therapy that have been extensively reported in medical literature.[1]

Other Organizations. Other organizations that have published positions on the issue of unlabeled uses of drug products are the Health Care Financing Administration (HCFA),[6] the Blue Cross and Blue Shield Association of America (BC/BS),[7] and the Health Insurance Association of America (HIAA).[8]

The American Medical Association, American Society of Clinical Oncology, Association of American Cancer Institutes, Association of Community Cancer Centers, Candlelighters Childhood Cancer Foundation, Memorial Sloan Kettering Cancer Center, National Cancer Institute, and the National Institute of Allergy and Infectious Diseases jointly developed a consensus statement and recommendations regarding use and reimbursement of unlabeled uses of drug products.[9]

These statements are consistent with the ASHP position.

Reimbursement Issues

As a cost-containment measure, most third-party payers exclude coverage for experimental therapies. Drug therapy coverage decisions are complicated, because often it is difficult to differentiate among an accepted standard of practice, an evolving standard of practice, and investigational therapies. Data demonstrating medical necessity and improved patient outcome are often difficult to retrieve. Consequently, insurance carriers and managed care provid-

ers have sometimes elected to cover only those indications included in FDA-approved drug-product labeling and have frequently denied coverage for unlabeled uses of drug products.

ASHP believes that such coverage denials restrict patients from receiving medically necessary therapies that represent the best available treatment options. A growing number of insurance carriers are following the BC/BS and HIAA guidelines that encourage the use of the three authoritative drug compendia, peer-reviewed literature, and consultation with experts in research and clinical practice to make specific coverage decisions. ASHP supports informed decisionmaking that promotes third-party reimbursement for FDA-approved drug products appropriately prescribed for unlabeled uses.

References

1. Use of approved drugs for unlabeled indications. *FDA Drug Bull.* 1982; 12:4–5.
2. Nightingale SL. Use of drugs for unlabeled indications. *FDA Q Rep.* 1986(Sep); 269.
3. Mortenson LE. Audit indicates many uses of combination therapy are unlabeled. *J Cancer Program Manage.* 1988; 3:21–5.
4. Off-label drugs: initial results of a national survey. Washington, DC: U.S. General Accounting Office. 1991:1–27.
5. PL 100-360, 1988.
6. Health Care Financing Administration. Medicare carriers' manual. Section 2050.5. Washington, DC: U.S. Department of Health and Human Services; 1987 Aug.
7. Statement on coverage recommendation for FDA-approved drugs. Chicago: Blue Cross and Blue Shield Association; 1989 Oct 25.
8. Statement of the Health Insurance Association of America (HIAA) on coverage for unapproved drugs and drug-related costs. Presented to the National Committee to Review Current Procedures for Approval of New Drugs for Cancer and AIDS. 1989 Oct 25.
9. Cancer economics. *Cancer Lett.* 1989; Suppl(Jun):2–3.

Approved by the ASHP Board of Directors, November 20, 1991, and by the ASHP House of Delegates, June 1, 1992. Developed by the Council on Professional Affairs.

The bibliographic citation for this document is as follows: American Society of Hospital Pharmacists. ASHP statement on the use of medications for unlabeled uses. *Am J Hosp Pharm.* 1992; 49:2006–8.

ASHP Guidelines on
Formulary System Management

Preamble

The purposes of these guidelines are to

- Provide an outline of recommended techniques and processes for formulary system management.
- Define terms associated with formulary system management.
- Provide guidance and direction to pharmacists on how to apply the concepts of formulary system management within the context of the "ASHP Statement on the Formulary System."[1]
- Describe the pharmacist's responsibility and leadership role, in partnership with the medical staff, in the management of the formulary system.

The formulary system, as defined in the "ASHP Statement on the Formulary System," is a method for evaluating and selecting suitable drug products for the formulary of an organized health-care setting.[1] Formulary system management is the application of various techniques to ensure high quality and cost-effective drug therapy through the formulary system.

The formulary of an organized health-care setting (e.g., a given hospital, managed care, or home-care operation) is a list of drugs (and associated information) that are considered by the professional staff in that setting to be the most useful in patient care.[1]

Development, maintenance, and approval of the formulary are the responsibilities of the pharmacy and therapeutics (P&T) committee, or its equivalent, which exists as a committee of the medical staff.[2] These responsibilities include oversight of the procedures used to carry out these formulary functions. The information a formulary should contain and the way a formulary should be organized are described in the "ASHP Technical Assistance Bulletin on Drug Formularies."[3]

Three key elements are important for the establishment and maintenance of a credible formulary. They are

1. A collaborative work relationship among health-care professionals, such as occurs in an organized health-care setting.
2. A defined medical staff (or physician-provider network) that practices within that health-care setting.
3. An interdisciplinary P&T committee as a committee of the medical staff.

Principles of
Formulary System Management

The purpose for ongoing management of the formulary system is to optimize patient care through rational selection and use of drugs and drug products within the health-care setting. Pharmacists play a primary role in assessing the relative safety and efficacy of pharmaceuticals nominated for addition to or deletion from the formulary. Through the application of techniques of formulary system management and through reevaluation and improvement of these techniques as necessary, the effectiveness of the formulary system is continuously assessed, resulting in quality improvement of the overall drug use process. Both therapeutic outcomes and costs related to the drug use process can thus be optimized.

Prescriber acceptance of the formulary management process is essential to effect quality improvements through formulary system management. Pharmacists play a key leadership role in fostering this acceptance by clarifying and supporting the goals and processes of formulary system management. Restated, the goal of formulary system management should be sound therapeutics. To achieve this goal successfully, prescribers should be actively involved in developing the techniques used to manage the formulary system. Communication and understanding among pharmacists, prescribers, other health-care providers, and the P&T committee members should be timely and routine. Pharmacists should ensure that a balanced presentation of drug information is provided to prescribers.

Techniques of formulary system management fall into three general categories: (1) drug use evaluation, (2) formulary maintenance, and (3) drug product selection.

Drug Use Evaluation

Drug use evaluation is an ongoing, structured, organizationally authorized process designed to ensure that drugs are used appropriately, safely, and effectively. A well-designed drug use evaluation program applies continuous quality improvement methods to the drug use process. Drug use evaluation should be a part of the hospital's overall quality-assurance program.[4] The role and responsibilities of pharmacists in drug use evaluation are identified in the "ASHP Guidelines on the Pharmacist's Role in Drug Use Evaluation."[5] Drug use evaluation is a quality-assurance activity, but it may also be considered a formulary system management technique. The P&T committee should be involved in the drug use evaluation process.

Effective drug use evaluation begins with drug use criteria or treatment guidelines approved by the P&T committee on behalf of the medical staff. Drug use evaluation should measure and compare the outcomes of patients whose treatment did, or did not, comply with approved criteria or guidelines. Based on this comparative information, criteria or guidelines can be revised, compliance can be encouraged, educational programs can be initiated, or changes can be made to the formulary system. Drug use evaluation programs should include provisions for periodic review of all components of the system.

Drug Use Criteria. In cases where a drug poses potential efficacy, toxicity, or utilization problems for the health-care setting, criteria may be established by the P&T committee to promote appropriate use. Drug use criteria are approved guidelines regarding how, or under what conditions, a drug is recommended for use. Preliminary drug use criteria should be developed at the time that a drug is proposed for addition to the formulary. Drug use criteria should be updated as needed over time. There are three general types of criteria:

diagnosis criteria, prescriber criteria, and drug-specific criteria. Criteria of any type can be used independently or in combination.

Diagnosis criteria identify indications that constitute acceptable uses for a formulary drug within the health-care setting. Protocols, if any, for restricting the use of a formulary drug to specific diagnoses or medical conditions should be established by the P&T committee. For instance, a particular colony-stimulating factor might be approved for use only as an adjunct to cancer chemotherapy. Use of this drug for other indications would then fall outside the approved diagnosis criteria.

Prescriber criteria identify prescribers approved to use specific formulary drugs or drug classes. Examples include limiting the use of specific injectable antibiotics to infectious disease specialists or establishing cardiologists or emergency room physicians as the only approved prescribers for thrombolytic drugs.

Drug-specific criteria identify approved doses, frequency of administration, duration of therapy, or other aspects that are specific to the use of a formulary drug. An example would be limiting the dosing of a long-acting injectable antibiotic to once every 24 hours. More frequent dosing regimens might require approval by an infectious disease specialist.

Treatment Guidelines. Treatment guidelines are similar to drug use criteria, except that treatment guidelines focus on disease-based drug therapy. Whereas drug use criteria relate to a specific drug, treatment guidelines outline a recommended therapeutic approach to specific diseases. This approach generally identifies the use of several different drugs, depending on disease severity or specific patient characteristics. A treatment guideline, for example, may outline a recommended approach to treating community-acquired pneumonia, reflux esophagitis, or otitis media, or it may list drugs to be used in bone marrow transplantation.

Treatment guidelines are typically developed and approved by P&T committees for high risk, high volume, or problem-prone diseases encountered in the health-care setting.

Formulary Maintenance

Formulary maintenance techniques include

- Therapeutic drug class review.
- Processes by which drug products are added to or deleted from the formulary.
- Use of nonformulary drugs in unique patient situations.

To be effective in improving the drug use process, pharmacists and medical staff must work collaboratively. The pharmacist should assume responsibility and a leadership role in the development and presentation of information required by the P&T committee for decisionmaking. The medical staff must understand and support the processes by which these techniques are applied, as well as participate in the development and review of information.

Therapeutic Drug Class Review. It is useful for the P&T committee to review the use and therapeutic effects of several classes of drug products every year. Examples of drug classes suitable for review are nonsteroidal anti-inflammatory agents, injectable cephalosporins, antihistamines, β-blockers, and neuromuscular blockers. These reviews can be prompted by criteria set by the P&T committee itself. For example, based on the number of adverse drug reaction reports, new information in the medical literature, or drug class expenditures, the committee can determine which classes of formulary drugs are worthy of reassessment.

The goal is to identify preferred agents based on effectiveness, toxicity, or cost differences within the same class. It is important that appropriate medical staff input, outside the committee, be solicited during these reviews. Outcomes of therapeutic class reviews can include development of new drug use criteria, new treatment guidelines, or changes to the formulary.

Formulary Addition or Deletion. To strengthen the ability of the P&T committee to make sound decisions on changes to the formulary, it is recommended that there be an approved policy and procedure for requesting changes to the formulary. This process typically involves submission of a request to the P&T committee by pharmacists or members of the medical staff.[2]

Consideration of a drug for addition to the formulary should include a review of an evaluation report (monograph) prepared by the pharmacy. A recommendation on how to prepare and organize an evaluation report can be found in the "ASHP Technical Assistance Bulletin on the Evaluation of Drugs for Formularies."[6] In addition to monograph information, an impact statement describing the effects of the proposed change on the quality and cost of patient care and drug therapy should accompany each request for addition to or deletion from the formulary.

The use of predetermined decision-reassessment dates is advised (e.g., the drug is placed on the formulary for a 6-month evaluation) to allow the committee to review the actual impact of certain formulary decisions. Reassessment dates are especially useful in situations where the expected impact of the formulary decision on the quality or cost of drug therapy may be significant or uncertain.

Use of Nonformulary Drugs. In general, only formulary drugs are endorsed as appropriate for *routine* use within the organized health-care setting. The underlying principle for the existence of a process for approval of nonformulary drugs is that individual or unique patient needs can exist that may not be satisfied by the use of formulary drugs.

There should be an approved policy and procedure for obtaining approval for use of nonformulary drugs. This process should include the generation of information on the use of nonformulary drugs to enable the P&T committee to review trends in nonformulary drug use, which may influence formulary addition or deletion decisions. There should also be a process in place for obtaining nonformulary drugs in a timely manner.

In managed care settings, the decision to approve the use of nonformulary drugs is separate from the decision to grant payment coverage for a drug. Coverage decisions are governed by the patient's contract with a specific health plan.

Drug Product Selection

Pharmacists and prescribers must understand the concept of therapeutic equivalence to ensure proper application of generic substitution and therapeutic interchange principles.

Pharmacists should assume a leadership role in drug product selection by proposing opportunities for drug product selection. This includes evaluation and assessment of bioequivalence data; storage, dispensing, and administration characteristics; cost; and other relevant product information. Pharmacists must also ensure that products of adequate quality are procured.

The application of generic substitution and therapeutic interchange principles may result in a drug product being dispensed to the patient that is different from the product originally prescribed. To ensure high quality drug therapy, therapeutic equivalence between the product dispensed and that prescribed must be ensured.

Therapeutic Equivalence. The 1991 edition of the *Approved Drug Products with Therapeutic Equivalence Evaluations* (FDA Orange Book) describes therapeutic equivalence as a guideline to assist in drug substitution between chemically identical products.[7] Both generic substitution and therapeutic interchange, however, should be safe and effective if the therapeutic equivalence of products to be exchanged has been established. For the purpose of this document, drugs are considered therapeutically equivalent if they can be expected to produce essentially the same therapeutic outcome and toxicity.

The use of therapeutically equivalent products can contribute to improvement in the drug use process by maintaining a high quality of drug therapy in the most cost-effective manner.

Generic Substitution. For the purpose of this document, generic substitution is defined as the substitution of drug products that contain the same active ingredient(s) and are chemically identical in strength, concentration, dosage form, and route of administration to the drug product prescribed (i.e., these are "pharmaceutical equivalents" as defined in the FDA Orange Book[7]). These products can also be termed "generic equivalents." Logically, these products should display therapeutic equivalence.

The key word in this definition is "identical." For example, the substitution of one brand of propranolol tablets for another represents the application of generic substitution if the strength of the active ingredients and the dosage form are identical. To ensure quality patient care, the two propranolol products must also be shown to achieve therapeutic equivalence as defined above. The substitution of purified pork insulin for human insulin is not generic substitution, because the products are not chemically identical. However, the interchangeability of these products may be acceptable under the principle of therapeutic interchange (discussed below), provided that therapeutic equivalence can be ensured.

Prescribers have the prerogative to override a generic substitution. In some cases, a patient preference may negate an otherwise acceptable generic substitution. The P&T committee is responsible for determining which drugs are acceptable for generic substitution and for developing guidelines for pharmacists who carry out this formulary system management activity. Typically, pharmacists determine which products are purchased and dispensed as generic substitutes. In most health-care settings, prescribers prospectively authorize generic substitution during their credentialing process. Notification of generic substitution is generally not provided to the prescriber at the time that a generic equivalent is dispensed.

Therapeutic Interchange. Therapeutic interchange is de-fined, for the purpose of this document, as the interchange of various therapeutically equivalent drug products by pharmacists under arrangements between pharmacist(s) and authorized prescriber(s) who have previously established and jointly agreed on conditions for interchanges.

Therapeutic interchange occurs pursuant to development of agreements between pharmacists and prescribers and implies that there is appropriate and timely communication between them. Therapeutic interchange agreements can vary from simple understandings to complex protocols. For example, a therapeutic interchange agreement permitting interchange between cephradine and cephalexin may be a simple arrangement; the dose and dosage form of the two drugs are equivalent, and the drugs typically can be interchanged in the treatment of any disease for which the drugs are indicated. A therapeutic interchange arrangement that permits the interchangeability of different colony-stimulating factors in treating a specific diagnosis pursuant to specific protocols might be more complex. In either case, the P&T committee acts on behalf of the medical staff to develop and approve these arrangements.

The approval of a therapeutic interchange arrangement is typically a separate decision by a P&T committee, unrelated to adding or deleting drugs from the formulary. In some settings, all drugs that may be therapeutically interchanged are acceptable to the formulary, and the pharmacy is authorized to purchase and dispense the most cost-effective products. In other settings, certain drug products are deemed interchangeable, but the P&T committee designates a preferred product and approves it for formulary addition. Then the other equivalent drugs or products are deleted from the formulary.

To remain effective over time, therapeutic interchange decisions should be routinely reviewed and revised as appropriate. Therapeutic interchange may not be appropriate for all patients. Professional judgment must be exercised by the pharmacist and the prescriber. Consultation with the prescriber and the patient may be necessary. Prescribers have the prerogative to override a therapeutic interchange. In some cases, a patient preference may negate an otherwise acceptable therapeutic interchange.

Pharmacists should strive for consistency of product use to avoid unnecessary switching of products dispensed to patients. When a change is made, the pharmacist should ensure that appropriate monitoring and followup are undertaken to identify and prevent any unexpected or untoward patient response. The pharmacist should provide appropriate notification and educational materials to prescribers, patients, and other health-care providers as needed regarding therapeutic interchange decisions.

References

1. American Society of Hospital Pharmacists. ASHP statement on the formulary system. *Am J Hosp Pharm.* 1983; 40:1384–5.
2. American Society of Hospital Pharmacists. ASHP statement on the pharmacy and therapeutics committee. *Am J Hosp Pharm.* 1984; 41:1621.
3. American Society of Hospital Pharmacists. ASHP technical assistance bulletin on drug formularies. *Am J Hosp Pharm.* 1991; 48:791–3.
4. Joint Commission on Accreditation of Healthcare Organizations. Accreditation manual for hospitals. Chicago: Joint Commission on Accreditation of

Healthcare Organizations; 1992:140.

5.   American Society of Hospital Pharmacists. ASHP guidelines on the pharmacist's role in drug-use evaluation. *Am J Hosp Pharm.* 1988; 45:385–6.

6.   American Society of Hospital Pharmacists. ASHP technical assistance bulletin on the evaluation of drugs for formularies. *Am J Hosp Pharm.* 1988; 45:386–7.

7.   U.S. Department of Health and Human Services. Approved drug products with therapeutic equivalence evaluations. 11th ed. Washington, DC: U.S. Government Printing Office; 1991:1–3.

Approved by the ASHP Board of Directors, November 20, 1991. Developed by the ASHP Council on Professional Affairs. Marvin A. Chamberlain developed the initial draft for council review.

The bibliographic citation for this document is as follows: American Society of Hospital Pharmacists. ASHP guidelines on formulary system management. *Am J Hosp Pharm.* 1992; 49:648–52.

ASHP Guidelines on Medication-Use Evaluation

Medication-use evaluation (MUE) is a performance improvement method that focuses on evaluating and improving medication-use processes with the goal of optimal patient outcomes. MUE may be applied to a medication or therapeutic class, disease state or condition, a medication-use process (prescribing, preparing and dispensing, administering, and monitoring), or specific outcomes.[1] Further, it may be applied in and among the various practice settings of organized health systems.

MUE encompasses the goals and objectives of drug-use evaluation (DUE) in its broadest application, with an emphasis on improving patient outcomes. Use of "MUE," rather than "DUE,"[2] emphasizes the need for a more multifaceted approach to improving medication use. MUE has a common goal with the pharmaceutical care it supports: to improve an individual patient's quality of life through achievement of predefined, medication-related therapeutic outcomes.[3,4] Through its focus on the system of medication use, the MUE process helps to identify actual and potential medication-related problems, resolve actual medication-related problems, and prevent potential medication-related problems that could interfere with achieving optimum outcomes from medication therapy.

In organized health systems, MUE must be conducted as an organizationally authorized program or process that is proactive, criteria based, designed and managed by an interdisciplinary team, and systematically carried out. It is conducted as a collaborative effort of prescribers, pharmacists, nurses, administrators, and other health care professionals on behalf of their patients.

MUE Objectives

Some typical objectives of MUE include

- Promoting optimal medication therapy.
- Preventing medication-related problems.
- Evaluating the effectiveness of medication therapy.
- Improving patient safety.
- Establishing interdisciplinary consensus on medication-use processes.
- Stimulating improvements in medication-use processes.
- Stimulating standardization in medication-use processes.
- Enhancing opportunities, through standardization, to assess the value of innovative medication-use practices from both patient-outcome and resource-utilization perspectives.
- Minimizing procedural variations that contribute to suboptimal outcomes of medication use.
- Identifying areas in which further information and education for health care professionals may be needed.
- Minimizing costs of medication therapy. These costs may be only partly related to the direct cost of medications themselves. When medications are selected and managed optimally from the outset, the costs of complications and wasted resources are minimized, and overall costs are decreased.
- Meeting or exceeding internal and external quality standards (e.g., professional practice standards, accreditation standards, or government laws and regulations).

Steps of the MUE Process

While the specific approach varies with the practice setting and patient population being served, the following common steps occur in the ongoing MUE process:

- Establish organizational authority for the MUE process and identify responsible individuals and groups.
- Develop screening mechanisms (indicators) for comprehensive surveillance of the medication-use system.
- Set priorities for in-depth analysis of important aspects of medication use.
- Inform health care professionals (and others as necessary) in the practice setting(s) about the objectives and expected benefits of the MUE process.
- Establish criteria, guidelines, treatment protocols, and standards of care for specific medications and medication-use processes. These should be based on sound scientific evidence from the medical and pharmaceutical literature.
- Educate health care professionals to promote the use of criteria, guidelines, treatment protocols, and standards of care.
- Establish mechanisms for timely communication among health care professionals.
- Initiate the use of MUE criteria, guidelines, treatment protocols, and standards of care in the medication-use process.
- Collect data and evaluate care.
- Develop and implement plans for improvement of the medication-use process based on MUE findings (if indicated).
- Assess the effectiveness of actions taken, and document improvements.
- Incorporate improvements into criteria, guidelines, treatment protocols, and standards of care, when indicated.
- Repeat the cycle of planning, evaluating, and taking action for ongoing improvement in medication-use processes.
- Regularly assess the effectiveness of the MUE process itself and make needed improvements.

Selecting Medications and Medication-Use Processes for Evaluation

Medications or medication-use processes should be selected for evaluation for one or more of the following reasons:

1. The medication is known or suspected to cause adverse reactions, or it interacts with another medication, food, or diagnostic procedure in a way that presents a significant health risk.
2. The medication is used in the treatment of patients who may be at high risk for adverse reactions.
3. The medication-use process affects a large number of patients or the medication is frequently prescribed.
4. The medication or medication-use process is a critical component of care for a specific disease, condition, or procedure.

5. The medication is potentially toxic or causes discomfort at normal doses.

6. The medication is most effective when used in a specific way.

7. The medication is under consideration for formulary retention, addition, or deletion.

8. The medication or medication-use process is one for which suboptimal use would have a negative effect on patient outcomes or system costs.

9. Use of the medication is expensive.

Indicators Suggesting a Need for MUE Analysis

Certain events (indicators) serve as "flags" of potential opportunities to improve medication use. Some are

- Adverse medication events, including medication errors, preventable adverse drug reactions, and toxicity.
- Signs of treatment failures, such as unexpected re-admissions and bacterial resistance to anti-infective therapy.
- Pharmacist interventions to improve medication therapy, categorized by medication and type of intervention.
- Nonformulary medications used or requested.
- Patient dissatisfaction or deterioration in quality of life.

Roles and Responsibilities in the MUE Process

The roles of individual health care professionals in MUE may vary according to practice setting, organizational goals, and available resources. The organizational body (e.g., quality management committee, pharmacy and therapeutics committee) responsible for the MUE process should have, at a minimum, prescriber, pharmacist, nurse, and administrator representation. Other health care professionals should contribute their unique perspectives when the evaluation and improvement process addresses their areas of expertise and responsibility. Temporary working groups may be used for specific improvement efforts.

Pharmacist's Responsibilities in MUE

Pharmacists, by virtue of their expertise and their mission of ensuring proper medication use, should exert leadership and work collaboratively with other members of the health care team in the ongoing process of medication-use evaluation and improvement.[5] Responsibilities of pharmacists in the MUE process include

- Developing an operational plan for MUE programs and processes that are consistent with the health system's overall goals and resource capabilities.
- Working collaboratively with prescribers and others to develop criteria for specific medications and to design effective medication-use processes.
- Reviewing individual medication orders against medication-use criteria and consulting with prescribers and others in the process as needed.
- Managing MUE programs and processes.
- Collecting, analyzing, and evaluating patient-specific data to identify, resolve, and prevent medication-related problems.

- Interpreting and reporting MUE findings and recommending changes in medication-use processes.
- Providing information and education based on MUE findings.

Resources

Some resources helpful in designing and managing an MUE process are listed here.

- The primary professional literature and up-to-date reference texts are key resources necessary for the development of MUE criteria. In general, local consensus should be based on medical and pharmaceutical literature recommendations.
- Published criteria, such as found in *AJHP* and ASHP's *Criteria for Drug Use Evaluation* (volumes 1–4), provide medication-specific criteria that may be adapted for local use.
- Computer software programs, including proprietary programs designed specifically for MUE functions, may be helpful in managing data and reporting.
- External standards-setting bodies, such as the Joint Commission on Accreditation of Healthcare Organizations, publish medication-use indicators that can help to identify portions of the medication-use system that require improvement.

Follow-up Actions in an MUE Process

The MUE process itself should be reviewed regularly to identify opportunities for its improvement. The success of an MUE process should be assessed in terms of improved patient outcomes. Medication-use system changes that evolve from MUE findings should be developed by the departments and medical services with responsibility for providing care, rather than solely through a committee having oversight for MUE (e.g., a pharmacy and therapeutics committee). Typical follow-up actions based on MUE findings include contact with individual prescribers and other health care professionals, information and education (newsletters, seminars, clinical care guidelines) for health care professionals, changes in medication-use systems, and changes in medication-therapy monitoring processes. MUE should be conducted as an ongoing interdisciplinary and collaborative improvement process. Punitive reactions to quality concerns are often counterproductive. It is important to communicate and commend positive achievements (care that meets or exceeds expectations) and improvements.

Pitfalls

Some common pitfalls to avoid in performing MUE activities include the following[6]:

1. Lack of authority. An MUE process that does not involve the medical staff is likely to be ineffective. Authoritative medical staff support and formal organizational recognition of the MUE process are necessary.

2. Lack of organization. Without a clear definition of the roles and responsibilities of individuals involved (e.g., who will develop criteria, who will communicate with other departments, who will collect and summarize data, and who will evaluate data), an MUE process may not succeed.

3. Poor communication. Everyone affected by the MUE process should understand its importance to the health system, its goals, and its procedures. The pharmacist should manage the MUE process and have the responsibility and authority to ensure timely communication among all professionals involved in the medication-use process. Criteria for medication use should be communicated to all affected professionals prior to the evaluation of care. MUE activity should be a standing agenda item for appropriate quality-of-care committees responsible for aspects of medication use.

4. Poor documentation. MUE activities should be well documented, including summaries of MUE actions with respect to individual medication orders and the findings and conclusions from collective evaluations. Documentation should address recommendations made and follow-up actions.

5. Lack of involvement. The MUE process is not a one-person task, nor is it the responsibility of a single department or professional group. Medication-use criteria should be developed through an interdisciplinary consensus process. Lack of administrative support can severely limit the effectiveness of MUE. The benefits of MUE should be conveyed in terms of improving patient outcomes and minimizing health-system costs.

6. Lack of follow-through. A one-time study or evaluation independent of the overall MUE process will have limited success in improving patient outcomes. The effectiveness of initial actions must be assessed and the action plan adjusted if necessary. It is important not to lose sight of the improvement goals.

7. Evaluation methodology that impedes patient care. Data collection should not consume so much time that patient care activities suffer. Interventions that can improve care for an individual patient should not be withheld because of the sampling technique or evaluation methodology.

8. Lack of readily retrievable data and information management. Existing data capabilities need to be assessed and maximum benefit obtained from available computerized information management resources. Deficiencies in information gathering and analysis should be identified and priorities for upgrading information support established.

References

1. Nadzam DM. Development of medication-use indicators by the Joint Commission on Accreditation of Healthcare Organizations. *Am J Hosp Pharm.* 1991; 48:1925–30.

2. American Society of Hospital Pharmacists. ASHP guidelines on the pharmacist's role in drug-use evaluation. *Am J Hosp Pharm.* 1988; 45:385–6.

3. Hepler CD, Strand LM. Opportunities and responsibilities in pharmaceutical care. *Am J Hosp Pharm.* 1990; 47:533–43.

4. American Society of Hospital Pharmacists. ASHP statement on pharmaceutical care. *Am J Hosp Pharm.* 1993; 50:1720–3.

5. Angaran DM. Quality assurance to quality improvement: measuring and monitoring pharmaceutical care. *Am J Hosp Pharm.* 1991; 48:1901–7.

6. Todd MW. Drug use evaluation. In: Brown TR, ed. Handbook of institutional pharmacy practice. 3rd ed. Bethesda, MD: American Society of Hospital Pharmacists; 1992.

Approved by the ASHP Board of Directors, April 24, 1996. Developed by the ASHP Council on Professional Affairs. Supersedes the ASHP Guidelines on the Pharmacist's Role in Drug-Use Evaluation, dated November 19, 1987.

The bibliographic citation for this document is as follows: American Society of Health-System Pharmacists. ASHP guidelines on medication-use evaluation. *Am J Health-Syst Pharm.* 1996; 53:1953–5.

ASHP Technical Assistance Bulletin on Drug Formularies

The formulary system is an ongoing process whereby an organization's pharmacy and medical staffs, working through a pharmacy and therapeutics (P&T) committee (or its equivalent), evaluate and select from among the drug products available those considered to be most useful in patient care. These products then are routinely available for use within the organization. The formulary system is a powerful tool for improving the quality and controlling the cost of drug therapy, and its use is strongly encouraged.

Formulary systems are applicable in any health-care setting including inpatient facilities, ambulatory care, and managed care organizations. Central to the operation of the formulary system is the formulary, a continually revised compilation of selected drug products plus important ancillary information about the use of the drugs and relevant organizational policies and procedures.

Since the formulary is the vehicle by which the medical staff and others make use of the formulary system, it is important that it be complete, concise, and easy to use. These guidelines are offered as an aid to pharmacists preparing a formulary or improving an existing one. They do not deal with the specific drug products that might be included in a formulary or with the selection process but, rather, with the formulary's format, organization, and content.

This document is complementary to the "ASHP Statement on the Formulary System,"[1] which should be consulted for further information on the formulary system.

Formulary Content and Organization

The primary objectives of the formulary are to provide (1) information on the drug products[a] approved for use, (2) basic therapeutic information about each item, (3) information on organizational policies and procedures governing the use of drugs, and (4) special information about drugs such as dosing guidelines and nomograms, abbreviations approved for prescribing, and sodium content of various formulary items. In accordance with these objectives, the formulary should consist of three main parts:

1. Information on organizational policies and procedures concerning drugs.
2. Drug products list.
3. Special information.

A more detailed look at each section follows.

Information on Organizational Policies and Procedures Concerning Drugs. Material to be included in this section will vary from organization to organization. Generally, the following items may be included:

1. Formulary policies and procedures, including such items as restrictions on drug use (if any) and procedures for requesting that a drug be added to the formulary.
2. Brief description of the P&T committee, including its membership, responsibilities, and operation.
3. Organizational regulations governing the prescribing, dispensing, and administration of drugs, including the

writing of drug orders and prescriptions, approved abbreviations for prescribing drugs, controlled substances considerations, generic and therapeutic equivalency policies and procedures, automatic stop orders, verbal drug orders, investigational drug policies, patients' use of their own medications, self-administration of drugs by patients, use of drug samples, policies relative to "stat" and "emergency" drug orders, use of emergency carts and kits, use of floor stock items, use of drug administration devices, prescribing by staff of medications for their own use, rules to be followed by drug manufacturers' representatives, standard drug administration times, and the reporting of adverse drug reactions and medication errors. Other topics should be included as deemed appropriate.

4. Pharmacy operating procedures such as hours of service, prescription policies, pharmacy charging policies, prescription labeling and packaging practices, drug distribution procedures, handling of drug information requests, and other services of the pharmacy (e.g., patient education programs and pharmacy bulletins).
5. Information on using the formulary, including how the formulary entries are arranged, the information contained in each entry, and the procedure for looking up a given drug product. Reference to sources of detailed information on formulary drugs [e.g., *AHFS Drug Information (AHFS-DI)* or the pharmacy's drug information service] should be included.

Drug Products List. This section is the heart of the formulary and consists of one or more descriptive entries for each drug item plus one or more indexes to facilitate use of the formulary.

Drug item entries. The entries can be arranged in several ways: (1) alphabetically by generic name, with entries for synonyms and brand names containing only a "see (generic name)" notation; (2) alphabetically within therapeutic class, usually following the *AHFS-DI* classification scheme; (3) a combination of the two systems whereby the bulk of the drugs are contained (alphabetically) in a "general" section that is supplemented by several "special" sections such as ophthalmic and otic drugs, dermatologicals, and diagnostic agents.

The type of information to be included in each entry will vary. At a minimum, each entry must include the following:

1. Generic name of the primary active drug entity or product; combination products may be listed by generic, common, or trade names.
2. Common synonym(s) and brand name(s); there should be a note in the "directions for use" section of the formulary explaining that inclusion or omission of a given brand name does not imply that it is or is not stocked by the pharmacy.
3. Dosage form(s), strength(s), packaging(s), and size(s) stocked by the pharmacy.
4. Formulation (active ingredients) of a combination product.

5. *AHFS-DI* category number.

Additional information that may be part of the drug entries includes

1. Usual adult or pediatric dosage ranges, or both.
2. Special cautions and notes such as "do not administer intravenously" or "refrigerate."
3. Controlled substances class (schedule).
4. Cost information; this information generally will be most useful where a therapeutic classification system is used or, alternatively, lists of similar drugs can be presented showing relative cost data.

Indexes to the drug products list. Two indexes will facilitate the use of the formulary:

1. Generic name–brand name/synonym cross index. The proper page number reference should be included in each entry. An example of this type of index is:

   Ophthaine: brand of proparacaine HCl, p 114
   Ophthetic: brand of proparacaine HCl, p 114
   Opium tincture, camphorated; synonym for paregoric, p 103
   Paregoric: p 103
   Proparacaine HCl: p 114

   This index can be integrated into the drug products list rather than being a separate entity. The list, in this event, must be arranged alphabetically.
2. Therapeutic/pharmacologic index. This index lists all formulary items within each therapeutic category. It is useful for ascertaining what therapeutic alternatives exist for a given situation such as patient allergy to a particular drug. An example of this type of index, beginning with the *AHFS-DI* classification code, is:

4:00	Antihistamine drugs
	Brompheniramine maleate, p 14
	Chlorpheniramine maleate, p 14
	Diphenhydramine HCl, p 14
	Promethazine HCl, p 20
8:00	Anti-infective agents
8:04	Amebicides
	Emetine HCl, p 33
	Iodoquinol, p 22

Special Information. The material to be included in this section will vary from organization to organization. However, what is included should be of general interest to the professional staff. Typically, it contains information not readily available from other sources. Examples of the type of items often found in the special information section are

1. Nutritional products list.
2. Tables of equivalent dosages of similar drugs (e.g., corticosteroids).
3. Standard parenteral nutrition formulas.
4. Guidelines for calculating pediatric dosages.
5. Table of the sodium content of drug products.
6. List of sugar-free drug products.
7. List of items (e.g., moisturizing lotion and toothpaste) typically supplied to all new inpatients.
8. Contents of emergency carts.

9. Lists of dialyzable drugs.
10. Pharmacokinetic dosing and monitoring information.
11. Metric conversion tables.
12. Examples of blank or completed organizational forms such as prescription blanks, requests for nonformulary drugs, and adverse drug reaction report forms.
13. Tables of drug interactions, drug interferences with diagnostic tests, and injectable drug incompatibilities.
14. Poison control information, including telephone numbers of poison control centers.
15. Dosages, concentrations, and standard dilutions of common emergency drugs.
16. Standard vehicles and dilutions for pediatric injections.
17. Electrolyte content of large-volume parentcrals.

Format and Appearance of the Formulary

The physical appearance and structure of a printed formulary have an important influence on its use. Although elaborate and expensive artwork and materials are unnecessary, the formulary should be visually pleasing, easily readable, and professional in appearance. The need for proper grammar, correct spelling and punctuation, and neatness is obvious.

There is no single format or arrangement that all formularies must follow. A typical formulary might have the following composition:

1. Title page.
2. Table of contents.
3. Information on policies and procedures concerning drugs.
   a. Disciplines and specialties represented on the P&T committee.
   b. Objectives and operation of the formulary system.
   c. Regulations and procedures for prescribing and dispensing drugs.
   d. Pharmacy services and procedures.
   e. Instructions on use of the formulary.
4. Products accepted for use in the organization.
   a. Items added and deleted since the previous edition.
   b. Generic–brand name cross-reference list.
   c. Pharmacologic/therapeutic index with relative cost codes.
   d. Descriptions of drug products by pharmacologic/therapeutic class.
5. Appendix.
   a. Guidelines for calculating pediatric doses.
   b. Nomograms (e.g., for estimating body surface area).
   c. Schedule of standard drug administration times.

Several techniques can be used to improve the appearance and ease of use of the formulary such as

1. Using a different color paper for each section of the formulary.
2. Using an edge index.
3. Making the formulary pocket size.
4. Printing the generic name heading of each drug entry in boldface type or using some other method for making it stand out from the rest of the entry.

Distribution of the Formulary

When printed formularies are used, copies should be placed at each patient care location, including clinics, other outpatient care areas, and emergency rooms. Each pharmacist and division of the pharmacy should receive a copy. Heads of departments providing direct patient care should receive a copy, as should hospital administration. Each member of the medical staff should receive a copy. Enough copies should be printed to allow for replacement of lost or worn copies. An alternative to a printed formulary is an online formulary accessible by computer terminals.

Necessary steps should be taken to ensure that the nursing and medical staffs are familiar with the formulary and know how to use it.

Keeping the Formulary Current

Generally, the formulary will need to be revised annually. Additions and deletions to the formulary, changes in drug products, removal of drugs from the market, and changes in hospital policies and procedures all will necessitate periodic revision of the formulary.

There should be a system for including "between revision" changes in the current edition of the formulary. One method is to attach formulary supplement sheets inside the covers of the formulary books. Lists of changes can also be distributed to the medical staff. Newsletters to the medical staff may be useful as vehicles for transmitting the information. Changes to online, computer-accessible formularies can be made as they occur.

Using a different color for the cover of each printed edition of the formulary will help reduce confusion between current and past editions.

Reference

1. American Society of Hospital Pharmacists. ASHP statement on the formulary system. *Am J Hosp Pharm.* 1983; 40:1384–5.

---

a"Drug product" refers to a specific drug entity/dosage form/strength/packaging/package size combination. Only certain dosage forms or strengths, for example, of a given drug entity might be included in a formulary.

Approved by the ASHP Board of Directors, November 14, 1990. Revised by the ASHP Council on Professional Affairs. Supersedes previous versions approved November 15, 1977, and November 14–15, 1984.

The bibliographic citation for this document is as follows: American Society of Hospital Pharmacists. ASHP technical assistance bulletin on drug formularies. *Am J Hosp Pharm.* 1991; 48:791–3.

ASHP Technical Assistance Bulletin on the Evaluation of Drugs for Formularies

Preamble

One of the major responsibilities of a pharmacy and therapeutics (P&T) committee is to develop and maintain a drug formulary system. The formulary can be used as the basis for promoting optimal pharmacotherapy because it contains only those drugs judged by the P&T committee to be in the best interest of the patient's health needs in terms of efficacy and cost. The pharmacist is a key member of the drug evaluation team because of his or her knowledge of pharmacology, pharmacokinetics, toxicology, therapeutics, and drug purchasing.

A thorough, critical review of the pharmaceutical and medical literature is necessary for evaluating drugs proposed for admission to a formulary. Comparative data associated with a drug's efficacy, adverse effects, and cost and the determination of its potential therapeutic advantages and deficiencies require critical evaluation by the pharmacist. Drugs may be added to or deleted from a formulary based on evaluation by the P&T committee. Alternative actions might include either conditional approval for a specific time period (with subsequent reevaluation) or temporary limitation of a drug's use to an individual medical service specialty with future reassessment.

Evaluation Report Considerations

A standardized evaluation report should be developed by the pharmacy for use in the evaluation process. It is recommended that each report include the following information:

1. Generic name.
   - List the officially approved name of all chemical entities in the drug product.
2. Trade name(s).
   - List the most common trade name(s) of the drug product.
3. Source(s) of supply.
   - Identify the pharmaceutical vendors from which the drug product can be procured.
   - For a generic drug product, identify the actual manufacturer; if applicable, identify the vendors distributing the product.
4. *American Hospital Formulary Service Drug Information* classification number.
   - List the number for quick access and retrieval of information.
5. Pharmacologic classification.
   - State the pharmacologic class to which the drug belongs and any similar properties it possesses compared with existing drugs.
   - State the mechanism of action; if the mechanism of action is unknown, state this. If applicable, the mechanism of action may be compared with that of another drug or class of drugs.
6. Therapeutic indications.
   - State the uses of the drug as approved by the Food and Drug Administration; indicate whether the use is prophylactic, therapeutic, palliative, curative, adjunctive, or supportive.
   - Evaluate uses of the drug in comparison with other established forms of therapy, using, if possible, human studies for comparison. Comparisons should emphasize therapeutics (efficacy, incidence of treatment success, remission, sensitivity, ease of monitoring, and treatment periods required) and include a critical analysis of clinical studies in such areas as patient population, methodology, statistics, and conclusions.
   - Identify non-FDA-labeled uses for the drug and those uses that show promise in investigational studies.
7. Dosage forms.
   - List all dosage forms available as approved by FDA; list unit cost.
8. Bioavailability and pharmacokinetics.
   - List bioavailability data for the most common route of administration and dosage of the drug. Other bioavailability data should be available on request by the P&T committee.
   - List pharmacokinetic data for absorption, distribution, metabolism, and excretion of the drug. For absorption, include information on the extent and rate of absorption of the drug by the usual routes of administration; the factors that might affect the rate or extent of absorption; the therapeutic, toxic, and lethal blood levels; the period of time required for onset, peak, and duration of therapeutic effect; and the half-life and factors affecting it. For distribution, include information on the usual distribution of the drug in body tissues and fluids, the drug's propensity to cross the blood–brain barrier or placenta or to appear in human milk, the drug's propensity for protein binding, and the drug's volume of distribution. For metabolism, include information on sites of metabolism, extent of biotransformation, and metabolic products and their activity. For excretion, include information on routes of elimination from the body, factors affecting elimination, and the form in which the drug is eliminated.
9. Dosage range.
   - List the dosage range for different routes of administration of the drug.
   - List initial, maintenance, maximal, geriatric, and pediatric doses for the drug.
10. Known adverse effects and toxicities.
    - Discuss adverse effects of the drug and their frequency of occurrence from research data of human studies.
    - Discuss means or methods of preventing or treating adverse effects and toxicities. Benefits of disease treatment and risks of adverse effects should be emphasized.
11. Special precautions.
    - List precautions and contraindications for certain disease states or other conditions.
    - Compare all of the preceding data with existing similar agents, where applicable.

- List potential drug interactions if deemed clinically important.
12. Comparisons.
    - List therapeutic comparisons with other drugs or treatment regimens.
    - List cost comparison data of a standard treatment regimen with the new drug versus currently used drugs.
    - List unusual monitoring or drug administration requirements for the drug.
13. Recommendations.
    - Formulate recommendations from analysis of all of the preceding data and consideration of other factors such as medical staff preference, distribution problems, and availability of the drug. Recommend action to be taken with regard to the drug's formulary status, as follows:
      Uncontrolled: To be available for use by all medical staff.
      Monitored: To be available for use by all medical staff, but its use is to be monitored.
      Restricted: To be available for use by the medical staff of a specific service or department.
      Conditional: To be available for use by all medical staff for a specific time period.
      Deletion: To be deleted from the current formulary.

Recommended Reference Materials

This list of recommended references includes those sources that commonly provide useful information in drug evaluation; however, review of additional specialty journals or other sources may be required.

- Texts.
    1. *American Hospital Formulary Service Drug Information.*
    2. *Drug Topics Redbook Annual Pharmacists' Reference.*
    3. *Facts and Comparisons.*
    4. *Martindale—The Extra Pharmacopoeia.*
    5. *Physicians' Desk Reference.*
    6. *The Pharmacological Basis of Therapeutics.*
- Periodicals and abstracting systems.
    1. *American Journal of Hospital Pharmacy.*
    2. *Annals of Internal Medicine.*
    3. *Archives of Internal Medicine.*
    4. *Antimicrobial Agents and Chemotherapy.*

5. *Clinical Pharmacology and Therapeutics.*
6. *Clinical Pharmacy.*
7. *Drug Therapy.*
8. Drugdex.
9. Drugs.
10. *Drug Intelligence and Clinical Pharmacy.*
11. *Hospital Formulary.*
12. *Hospital Therapy.*
13. Iowa Drug Information System.
14. *International Pharmaceutical Abstracts.*
15. *Journal of the American Medical Association.*
16. *The Lancet.*
17. *Medical Letter on Drugs and Therapeutics.*
18. *New England Journal of Medicine.*
19. Paul de Haen Information Systems.
20. *Pharmacotherapy.*

This technical assistance bulletin is supplementary to the "ASHP Statement on the Pharmacy and Therapeutics Committee,"[1] "ASHP Statement on the Formulary System,"[2] and "ASHP Technical Assistance Bulletin on Hospital Formularies,"[3] which should be consulted for further information on the formulary system.

References

1. American Society of Hospital Pharmacists. ASHP statement on the pharmacy and therapeutics committee. *Am J Hosp Pharm.* 1984; 41:1621.
2. American Society of Hospital Pharmacists. ASHP statement on the formulary system. *Am J Hosp Pharm.* 1983; 40:1384–5.
3. American Society of Hospital Pharmacists. ASHP technical assistance bulletin on hospital formularies. *Am J Hosp Pharm.* 1985; 42:375–7.

Developed by the ASHP Council on Professional Affairs. Approved by the ASHP Board of Directors, November 19, 1987. Supersedes an earlier version approved by the Board of Directors, April 30, 1981.

The bibliographic citation for this document is as follows: American Society of Hospital Pharmacists. ASHP technical assistance bulletin on the evaluation of drugs for formularies. *Am J Hosp Pharm.* 1988; 45:386–7.

Principles of a Sound Drug Formulary System

These principles have been endorsed by the following organizations:

- Academy of Managed Care Pharmacy
- Alliance of Community Health Plans
- American Medical Association
- American Society of Health-System Pharmacists
- Department of Veterans Affairs, Pharmacy Benefits Management Strategic Healthcare Group
- National Business Coalition on Health
- U.S. Pharmacopeia

Preamble

A coalition of national organizations representing health care professionals, government, and business leaders formed a working group (see Appendix III) to develop a set of principles specifying the essential components that contribute to a sound drug formulary system. The Coalition was formed in September 1999 in response to the widespread use of drug formularies in both inpatient and outpatient settings and the lack of understanding about formularies among the public. Also, proposed federal legislation that would provide a prescription drug benefit for Medicare beneficiaries has brought increased attention to the appropriate role and management of drug formulary systems within drug benefit programs.

The formulary system, when properly designed and implemented, can promote rational, clinically appropriate, safe, and cost-effective drug therapy. The Coalition has enumerated these principles, however, because it recognizes that patient care may be compromised if a formulary system is not optimally developed, organized, and administered. This document contains "Guiding Principles" that the Coalition believes must be present for a drug formulary system to appropriately serve the patients it covers. The absence of one or more of these "Guiding Principles" should be cause for careful scrutiny of a formulary system. A glossary (see Appendix I) and bibliography (see Appendix II) are included with the "Guiding Principles" to clarify terminology and to provide additional resources, respectively.

The Coalition believes that the presence of consensus-based Formulary System Principles can assist decision-makers who must balance the health care quality and cost equation. Further, the Guiding Principles will be a valuable educational tool for national, state, and local public policy makers, health care system administrators, purchasers and third-party payers, practitioners, and consumers and patient advocates. These parties all have an interest in designing formulary systems that ensure patients have access to rational, clinically appropriate, safe, and cost-effective therapy and which supports an affordable and sustainable drug benefit program.

Definitions

Drug Formulary System. An ongoing process whereby a health care organization, through its physicians, pharmacists, and other health care professionals, establishes policies on the use of drug products and therapies, and identifies drug products and therapies that are the most medically appropriate and cost-effective to best serve the health interests of a given patient population.

Drug Formulary. A continually updated list of medications and related information, representing the clinical judgement of physicians, pharmacists, and other experts in the diagnosis and/or treatment of disease and promotion of health.

Guiding Principles

Formulary system decisions are based on scientific and economic considerations that achieve appropriate, safe, and cost-effective drug therapy.

- Clinical decisions are based on the strength of scientific evidence and standards of practice that include, but are not limited, to the following:
  - Assessing peer-reviewed medical literature, including randomized clinical trials (especially drug comparison studies), pharmacoeconomic studies, and outcomes research data.
  - Employing published practice guidelines, developed by an acceptable evidence-based process.
  - Comparing the efficacy as well as the type and frequency of side effects and potential drug interactions among alternative drug products.
  - Assessing the likely impact of a drug product on patient compliance when compared to alternative products.
  - Basing formulary system decisions on a thorough evaluation of the benefits, risks, and potential outcomes for patients; risks encompass adverse drug events (adverse drug reactions and medication errors, such as those caused by confusing product names or labels).
- Economic considerations include, but are not limited, to the following:
  - Basing formulary system decisions on cost factors only after the safety, efficacy, and therapeutic need have been established.
  - Evaluating drug products and therapies in terms of their impact on total health care costs.
  - Permitting financial incentives only when they promote cost management as part of the delivery of quality medical care. Financial incentives or pressures on practitioners that may interfere with the delivery of medically necessary care are unacceptable.

The formulary system encompasses drug selection, drug utilization review, and other tools to foster best practices in prescribing, dispensing, administration, and monitoring of outcomes.

- The formulary system:
  - Provides drug product selection and formulary maintenance (see above).
  - Provides drug use evaluation (also called drug utilization review) to enhance quality of care for patients by assuring appropriate drug therapy.
  - Provides for the periodic evaluation and analysis of

treatment protocols and procedures to ensure that they are up-to-date and are consistent with optimum therapeutics.

- Provides for the monitoring, reporting, and analysis of adverse results of drug therapy (e.g., adverse drug reactions, medication errors) to continuously improve the quality of care.

The Pharmacy and Therapeutics (P&T) Committee, or equivalent body, comprised of actively practicing physicians, pharmacists, and other health care professionals, is the mechanism for administering the formulary system, which includes developing and maintaining the formulary and establishing and implementing policies on the use of drug products.

- The Pharmacy and Therapeutics Committee:
  - Objectively appraises, evaluates, and selects drugs for the formulary.
  - Meets as frequently as is necessary to review and update the appropriateness of the formulary system in light of new drugs and new indications, uses, or warnings affecting existing drugs.
  - Establishes policies and procedures to educate and inform health care providers about drug products, usage, and committee decisions.
  - Oversees quality improvement programs that employ drug use evaluation.
  - Implements generic substitution and therapeutic interchange programs that authorize exchange of therapeutic alternatives based upon written guidelines or protocols within a formulary system. (Note: Therapeutic substitution, the dispensing of therapeutic alternates without the prescriber's approval, is illegal and should not be allowed—see Glossary.)
  - Develops protocols and procedures for the use of and access to non-formulary drug products.

Physicians, pharmacists, and other health care professionals provide oversight of the formulary system.

- Health care organization policies should ensure appropriate oversight of the P&T Committee and its decisions by the medical staff or equivalent body.

The formulary system must have its own policies, or adhere to other organizational policies, that address conflicts of interest and disclosure by P&T committee members.

- Formulary system policies should:
  - Require P&T committee members to reveal, by signing a conflict of interest statement, economic and other relationships with pharmaceutical entities that could influence Committee decisions.
  - Exclude product sponsor representatives from P&T committee membership and from attending P&T committee meetings.
  - Require P&T committee members to adhere to the formulary system's policy on disclosure and participation in discussion as it relates to conflict of interest.

The formulary system should include educational programs for payers, practitioners, and patients concerning their roles and responsibilities.

- The formulary system should:
  - Inform physicians, pharmacists, other health care professionals, patients, and payers about the factors that affect formulary system decisions, including cost containment measures; the procedures for obtaining non-formulary drugs; and the importance of formulary compliance to improving quality of care and restraining health care costs.
  - Proactively inform practitioners about changes to the formulary or to other pharmaceutical management procedures.
  - Provide patient education programs that explain how formulary decisions are made and the roles and responsibilities of the patient, especially the importance of patient compliance with drug therapy to assure the success of that therapy.
  - Disclose the existence of formularies and have copies of the formulary readily available and accessible.
  - Provide rationale for specific formulary decisions when requested.

The formulary system should include a well-defined process for the physician or other prescriber to use a non-formulary drug when medically indicated.

- The formulary system should:
  - Enable individual patient needs to be met with non-formulary drug products when demonstrated to be clinically justified by the physician or other prescriber.
  - Institute an efficient process for the timely procurement of non-formulary drug products and impose minimal administrative burdens.
  - Provide access to a formal appeal process if a request for a non-formulary drug is denied.
  - Include policies that state that practitioners should not be penalized for prescribing non-formulary drug products that are medically necessary.

Appendix I—Glossary

Drug Formulary System: An ongoing process whereby a health care organization, through its physicians, pharmacists, and other health care professionals, establishes policies on the use of drug products and therapies, and identifies drug products and therapies that are the most medically appropriate and cost effective to best serve the health interests of a given patient population.

Drug Formulary: A continually updated list of medications and related information, representing the clinical judgement of physicians, pharmacists, and other experts in the diagnosis and/or treatment of disease and promotion of health.

Pharmacy & Therapeutics (P&T) Committee: An advisory committee that is responsible for developing, managing, updating, and administering the drug formulary system.

Generic Substitution: The substitution of drug products that contain the same active ingredient(s) and are chemically identical in strength, concentration, dosage form, and route of administration to the drug product prescribed.

Therapeutic Alternates: Drug products with different chemical structures but which are of the same pharmacological and/or therapeutic class, and usually can be expected to have similar therapeutic effects and adverse reaction profiles when administered to patients in therapeutically equivalent doses.

Therapeutic Interchange: Authorized exchange of therapeutic alternates in accordance with previously established and approved written guidelines or protocols within a formulary system.

Therapeutic Substitution: The act of dispensing a therapeutic alternate for the drug product prescribed without prior authorization of the prescriber. This is an illegal act because only the prescriber may authorize an exchange of therapeutic alternates.

Drug Utilization Review (Drug Use Review, DUR, and Drug Use Evaluation): Process used to assess the appropriateness of drug therapy by engaging in the evaluation of data on drug use in a given health care environment against predetermined criteria and standards.

Appendix II—Bibliography

1. Academy of Managed Care Pharmacy, Concepts in Managed Care Pharmacy Series—Formulary Management (Alexandria, VA: 1998).

2. American Medical Association. Board of Trustees Report PPP, Principles of Drug Utilization Review. In, American Medical Association House of Delegates Proceedings, 140th Annual Meeting. Chicago: American Medical Association; June 1991; 225–7.

3. American Medical Association. Board of Trustees Report 45, Drug Formularies and Therapeutic Interchange. In, American Medical Association House of Delegates Proceedings, 47th Interim Meeting. New Orleans: American Medical Association; December 1993; 155–8.

4. American Medical Association. Council on Ethical and Judicial Affairs Report 2, Managed Care Cost Containment Involving Prescription Drugs. In, American Medical Association House of Delegates Proceedings, 144th Annual Meeting. Chicago: American Medical Association; June 1995; 207–13.

5. American Medical Association. Board of Trustees Report 9, Pharmaceutical Benefits Management Companies. In, American Medical Association House of Delegates Proceedings, 51st Interim Meeting. Dallas: American Medical Association; December 1997; 33–44.

6. American Society of Consultant Pharmacists. Guidelines for the Development of Formulary Systems in Nursing Facilities; July 1996.

7. American Society of Hospital Pharmacists. ASHP Statement on the Formulary System. *Am J Hosp Pharm.* 1983; 40:1384–5.

8. American Society of Hospital Pharmacists. ASHP Guidelines on Formulary System Management. *Am J Hosp Pharm.* 1992; 49:648–52.

9. American Society of Hospital Pharmacists. ASHP Statement on the Pharmacy and Therapeutics Committee. *Am J Hosp Pharm.* 1992; 49:2008–9.

10. American Society of Health-System Pharmacists. ASHP Guidelines on Medication-Use Evaluation. *Am J Health-Syst Pharm.* 1996; 53:1953–5.

11. American Society of Hospital Pharmacists. ASHP Technical Assistance Bulletin on Drug Formularies. *Am J Hosp Pharm.* 1991; 48:791–3.

12. American Society of Hospital Pharmacists. ASHP Technical Assistance Bulletin on the Evaluation of Drugs for Formularies. *Am J Hosp Pharm.* 1988; 45:386–7.

13. Covington TR and Thornton JL. The formulary system: A cornerstone of drug benefit management, in A Pharmacist's Guide to Principles and Practices of Managed Care Pharmacy. Ito S and Blackburn S, eds. Foundation for Managed Care Pharmacy, Alexandria VA. 1995:35–49.

14. Dillon MJ. Drug Formulary Management, in Managed Care Pharmacy Practice. Navarro RP ed. Aspen Publishers, Inc., Gaithersburg, MD. 1999:145–65.

15. Hejna CS and Shepherd MD. Pharmacy and therapeutics committee and formulary development, in A Pharmacist's Guide to Principles and Practices of Managed Care Pharmacy. Ito S and Blackburn S, eds. Foundation for Managed Care Pharmacy, Alexandria VA. 1995:27–34.

16. National Committee for Quality Assurance. UM 10 procedures for pharmaceutical management. 2000 Standards for Accreditation of MCOs. 1999:58–60.

17. National Committee for Quality Assurance. UM 10 procedures for pharmaceutical management. 2000 Surveyor Guidelines for the Accreditation of MCOs. 1999:173–82.

18. PCMA Response to American Medical Association Report, I-97, "Pharmaceutical Benefits Management Companies." September 1998.

19. Rucker TD and Schiff GD. Drug formularies: myths-in-formation. *Medical Care.* 1990; 28:928–42. Reprinted in *Hospital Pharmacy.* 1991; 26:507–14.

Appendix III—Coalition Working Group

Academy of Managed Care Pharmacy
Judith A. Cahill, C.E.B.S., Executive Director

Richard Fry, Senior Director, Pharmacy Affairs

American Medical Association
Joseph W. Cranston, Ph.D., Director-Science, Research and Technology

American Society of Health-System Pharmacists
William A. Zellmer, M.P.H., Deputy Executive Vice President

Department of Veterans Affairs
John E. Ogden, Director, Pharmacy Services

Michael A. Valentino, Associate Chief Consultant for Pharmacy Benefits Management

National Business Coalition on Health
Catherine Kunkle, Vice President

U.S. Pharmacopeia
Jacqueline L. Eng, Senior Vice President, Program Development

Keith W. Johnson, Vice President and Director, New and Off-Label Uses

Thomas R. Fulda, Program Director, Drug Utilization Review Programs

Nancy B. Mabie, Assistant Director, Pharmacy Affairs

Observer
AARP
David Gross, Senior Policy Advisor, Public Policy Institute

Public Comment Requested

To ensure that knowledgeable and interested parties beyond the Coalition Working Group had an opportunity to contribute to the Principles development process, a preliminary set of principles was distributed for public comment to 50-plus organizations in February 2000. Comments received were thoroughly reviewed and considered by the Coalition Working Group.

These principles were endorsed by the ASHP Board of Directors on June 4, 2000.

Government, Law, and Regulation

Government, Law, and Regulation

0410 Medicare Prescription Drug Benefit
Source: Council on Legal and Public Affairs
To strongly advocate a fully funded prescription drug program for eligible Medicare beneficiaries that maintains the continuity of patient care and ensures the best use of medications; further,

To recommend that the program should at a minimum contain the following: (1) appropriate product reimbursement based on transparency of drug costs; (2) payment for indirect costs and practice expenses related to the provision of pharmacy services, based on a study of those costs; (3) appropriate coverage and payment for patient care services provided by pharmacists; and (4) open access to the pharmacy provider of the patient's choice.

(*Note: Fully funded* means the federal government will make adequate funds available to fully cover the Medicare program's share of prescription drug program costs; *eligible* means the federal government may establish criteria by which Medicare beneficiaries qualify for the prescription drug program.)
This policy supersedes ASHP policy 0317.

Compounding by Health Professionals (0411)
Source: Council on Legal and Public Affairs
To advocate the adoption, in all applicable state laws and regulations governing health care practice, of the intent of the requirements and the outcomes for patient safety as described in *United States Pharmacopeia* Chapter 797 ("Pharmaceutical Compounding—-Sterile Preparations'').

Uniform State Laws and Regulations Regarding Pharmacy Technicians (0412)
Source: Council on Legal and Public Affairs
To advocate that pharmacy move toward the following model with respect to technicians as the optimal approach to protecting public health and safety: (1) development and adoption of uniform state laws and regulations regarding pharmacy technicians; (2) mandatory completion of a nationally accredited standardized program of education and training as a prerequisite to pharmacy technician certification; and (3) mandatory certification by the Pharmacy Technician Certification Board (or another comparable nationally validated, psychometrically sound certification program approved by the state board of pharmacy) as a prerequisite to the state board of pharmacy granting the technician permission to engage in the full scope of responsibilities authorized by the state; further,

To advocate registration of pharmacy technicians by state boards of pharmacy; further,

To advocate, with respect to certification, as an interim measure until the optimal model is fully implemented, that individuals be required either (1) to have completed a nationally accredited standardized program of education and training or (2) to have at least one year of full-time equivalent experience as pharmacy technicians before they are eligible to become certified; further,

To advocate that licensed pharmacists be held accountable for the quality of pharmacy services provided and the actions of pharmacy technicians under their charge.

(*Note: Certification* is the process by which a nongovernmental agency or association grants recognition to an individual who has met certain predetermined qualifications specified by that agency or association. *Registration* is the process of making a list or being enrolled in an existing list; registration should be used to help safeguard the public through interstate and intrastate tracking of the technician work force and preventing individuals with documented problems from serving as pharmacy technicians.)
This policy supersedes ASHP policy 0322.

Importation of Pharmaceuticals (0413)
Source: Council on Legal and Public Affairs
To advocate for the continuation and application of laws and regulations enforced by the Food and Drug Administration and state boards of pharmacy with respect to the importation of pharmaceuticals in order to (1) maintain the integrity of the pharmaceutical supply chain and avoid the introduction of counterfeit products into the United States; (2) provide for continued patient access to pharmacist review of all medications and preserve the patient-pharmacist-prescriber relationship; and (3) provide adequate patient counseling and education, particularly to patients taking multiple high-risk medications; further,

To urge the FDA and state boards of pharmacy to vigorously enforce federal and state laws in relation to importation of pharmaceuticals by individuals, distributors (including wholesalers), and pharmacies that bypass a safe and secure regulatory framework.
This policy supersedes ASHP policy 0320.

Dietary Supplements Containing Ephedrine Alkaloids (0302)
Source: Commission on Therapeutics
To support a ban on the manufacture and sale of dietary supplements containing ephedrine alkaloids because (1) ephedrine alkaloids pose a significant risk of illness and injury, (2) changes in product labeling are not adequate to protect the public from these dangers, (3) the use of these products represents significant expenditures for a health-related remedy of unsubstantiated value, and (4) other safe and effective interventions are available for all common uses of these products.

Drug Product Shortages (0319)
Source: Council on Legal and Public Affairs
To strongly encourage the Food and Drug Administration to consider, in its definition of "medically necessary" drug products, the impact of medication-use factors, taking into account that if an unfamiliar product is introduced in a clinical setting because the customary product is unavailable, there is increased risk to patient safety; further,

To support government-sponsored incentives for manufacturers to maintain an adequate supply of medically necessary pharmaceutical products; further,

To advocate laws and regulations that would (1) require pharmaceutical manufacturers to notify the appropriate government body at least 12 months in advance of voluntarily discontinuing a medically necessary product, (2) provide effective sanctions for manufacturers that do not comply with this mandate, and (3) require prompt public disclosure of a notification to voluntarily discontinue a medically necessary product; further,

To encourage the appropriate government body to seek the cooperation of manufacturers in maintaining the supply of a medically necessary product after being informed of a voluntary decision to discontinue that product.

This policy supersedes ASHP policy 0221.

Counterfeit Drugs (0321)

Source: Council on Legal and Public Affairs

To encourage the Food and Drug Administration (FDA) to take the steps necessary to ensure that (1) all drug products entering the country are thoroughly inspected and tested to establish that they have not been adulterated or misbranded and (2) patients will not receive improperly labeled and packaged, deteriorated, outdated, counterfeit, or non-FDA-approved drug products; further,

To encourage the FDA to develop and implement regulations to (1) restrict or prohibit licensed drug distributors (drug wholesalers, repackagers and manufacturers) from purchasing legend drugs from unlicensed entities and (2) to accurately document at any given point in the distribution chain the original source of drugs and chain of custody from the manufacturer to the pharmacy; further,

To urge Congress to provide adequate funding or authority to impose user fees to accomplish these objectives.

This policy supersedes ASHP policy 8609.

Greater Access to Less Expensive Generic Drugs (0222)

Source: Council on Legal and Public Affairs

To support legislation and regulations that promote greater patient access to less expensive generic drug products.

FDA's Public Health Mission (0012)

Source: Council on Legal and Public Affairs

To support the Food and Drug Administration's public health mission of ensuring the safety and effectiveness of drugs, biologics, and medical devices through risk assessment, appropriate product approval, labeling approval, manufacturing oversight, and consultation with health professionals, while deferring to state regulation and professional self-regulation on matters related to the use of drugs, biologics, and medical devices; further,

To support the allocation of sufficient federal resources to allow FDA to meet its defined public health mission; further,

To support the appointment of practicing pharmacists to FDA advisory committees as one mechanism of ensuring that decisions made by the agency incorporate the unique knowledge of the profession of pharmacy for the further benefit of the patient; further,

To support an ongoing dialogue between FDA and ASHP for the purpose of exploring ways to advocate the best use of FDA-regulated products by consumers and health care professionals.

This policy supersedes ASHP policy 9606.

Compliance with Governmental Payment Policies (9902)

Source: Council on Administrative Affairs

To encourage pharmacy managers to identify and resolve medication-related billing issues in government health care programs that could cause challenges under fraud and abuse laws; further,

To encourage pharmacy managers to establish an internal audit system for medication-related services, in conjunction with their corporate compliance programs, in order to meet the requirements of government health care payment policies.

This policy was reviewed in 2003 by the Council on Administrative Affairs and by the Board of Directors and was found to still be appropriate.

Generic Pharmaceutical Testing (9010)

Source: House of Delegates Resolution

To support and foster legislative and regulatory initiatives designed to improve and restore public and professional confidence in the drug approval and regulatory process in which all relevant data are subject to public scrutiny.

This policy was reviewed in 2004 by the House of Delegates and was found to still be appropriate.

ASHP Statement on Principles for Including Medications and Pharmaceutical Care in Health Care Systems

Introduction

The United States government, individual state governments, and private health care systems are moving toward reforming the way that they provide health care to their citizens or beneficiaries. As they do so, policy makers must improve their medication-use systems to address problems of access, quality, and cost of medicines and pharmaceutical care services. This document offers principles for achieving maximum value from the services of the nation's pharmacists.

Although pharmaceuticals and pharmaceutical care are among the most cost-effective methods of health care available, there is evidence that the public is not currently realizing the full potential benefit from these resources. Illnesses related to improper medication use are costing the health care systems in the United States billions of dollars per year in patient morbidity and mortality. Pharmacists are prepared and eager to help other health providers and patients prevent and resolve medication-related problems, and health care systems should facilitate and take advantage of pharmacists' expertise.

These principles are offered to guide health policy makers in their deliberations concerning the inclusion of medications and pharmacists' services in health care systems.

Principles

Principle I. Health care systems must make medications available to patients and provide for pharmaceutical care, which encompasses pharmacists' health care services and health promotional activities that ensure that medications are used safely, effectively, and efficiently for optimal patient outcomes.

Principle II. Careful distinction must be made between policies that affect pharmacist reimbursement and policies that affect pharmacist compensation. Health care systems must reimburse pharmacists for the medications they provide patients (including the costs of drug products, the costs associated with dispensing, and related administrative costs). Health care systems also must compensate pharmacists for the services and care that they provide to patients, which result in improved medication use and which may not necessarily be associated with dispensing.

Principle III. Patients differ in their needs for pharmaceutical care services. The method of compensating pharmacists for their services must recognize the value of the different levels and types of services that pharmacists provide to patients based on pharmacists' professional assessments of patients' needs.

Principle IV. Pharmacists must be enabled and encouraged to use their professional expertise in making medication-related judgments in collaboration with patients and health care colleagues. Health care systems must not erect barriers to pharmacists' exercising professional judgments; nor should health care systems prescribe specific services or therapies for defined types of patients.

Principle V. Pharmacists should have access to relevant patient information to support their professional judgments and activities. Pharmacists should be encouraged and permitted to make additions to medical records for the purpose of adding their findings, conclusions, and recommendations. Pharmacists will respect the confidential nature of all patient information.

Principle VI. Health care systems must be designed to enable, foster, and facilitate communication and collaboration among pharmacists and other care providers to ensure proper coordination of patients' medication therapies.

Principle VII. Quality assessment and assurance programs related to individual patient care should be implemented at local levels through collaborative efforts of health care practitioners rather than through centralized bureaucracies. Quality assessment and assurance procedures for medication use (such as pharmacy and therapeutics committees, formulary systems, drug-use evaluation programs, and patient outcomes analyses) are most effective when the professionals who care for covered patients are involved in the design and implementation of the procedures. Moreover, such programs must recognize local variations in epidemiology, demography, and practice standards. Information related to quality assessment and assurance activities must be held in confidence by all parties.

Principle VIII. Demonstration projects and evaluation studies in the delivery of pharmaceutical care must be enabled, fostered, and implemented. New services, quality assessment and assurance techniques, and innovative medication delivery systems are needed to improve the access to and quality of medication therapy and pharmaceutical care while containing costs.

Principle IX. Health care policies that are intended to influence practices of those associated with pharmacy, such as the pharmaceutical industry or prescribers, should address those audiences directly rather than through policies that affect reimbursement, compensation, or other activities of pharmacists.

This statement was reviewed in 2002 by the Council on Legal and Public Affairs and by the ASHP Board of Directors and was found to still be appropriate.

Approved by the ASHP Board of Directors, November 18, 1992, and by the ASHP House of Delegates, June 7, 1993. Developed by a committee of the Joint Commission of Pharmacy Practitioners and subsequently reviewed and approved by the ASHP Council on Legal and Public Affairs.

The bibliographic citation for this document is as follows: American Society of Hospital Pharmacists. ASHP statement on principles for including medications and pharmaceutical care in health care systems. *Am J Hosp Pharm.* 1993; 50:756–7.

Medication Misadventures

Medication Misadventures

Pharmacist's Responsibility for Patient Safety (0227)
Source: Council on Professional Affairs
To affirm that individual pharmacists have a professional responsibility to ensure patient safety through the use of proven interventions and best practices; further,

To affirm that employee performance measurement and evaluation systems should incorporate measures that support and encourage a focus on patient safety by pharmacists.

Statutory Protection for Medication-Error Reporting (0011)
Source: Council on Legal and Public Affairs
To collaborate with other health care providers, professions, and stakeholders to advocate and support federal legislative and regulatory initiatives that provide liability protection for the reporting of actual and potential medication errors by individuals and health care providers; further,

To seek federal liability protection for medication-error reporting that is similar in concept to that which applies to reporting safety incidents and accidents in the aviation industry.

Drug Names, Labeling, and Packaging Associated with Medication Errors (0020)
Source: The Council on Professional Affairs
To urge drug manufacturers and FDA to involve practicing pharmacists, nurses, and physicians in decisions about drug names, labeling, and packaging to help eliminate (a) look-alike and sound-alike drug names, and (b) labeling and packaging characteristics that contribute to medication errors; further,

To inform pharmacists and others, as appropriate, about specific drug names, labeling, and packaging that have documented association with medication errors.
This policy supersedes ASHP policy 9007.

Medication Errors and Risk Management (0021)
Source: The Council on Professional Affairs
To urge that pharmacists be included in health care organizations' risk management processes for the purpose of (a) assessing medication-use systems for vulnerabilities to medication errors, (b) implementing medication-error prevention strategies, and (c) reviewing occurrences of medication errors and developing corrective actions.
This policy supersedes ASHP policy 8614.

Reporting Medication Errors and Adverse Drug Reactions (9918)
Source: Council on Legal and Public Affairs
To encourage pharmacists to exert leadership in establishing a nonthreatening, confidential atmosphere in their work places to encourage pharmacy staff and others to report actual and suspected medication errors and adverse drug reactions in a timely manner; further,

To provide leadership in supporting a single, comprehensive medication error reporting program that:
a) fosters a confidential, non-threatening, and non-punitive environment for the submission of medication error reports;
b) receives and analyzes these confidential reports to identify system-based causes of medication errors or potential errors; and
c) recommends and disseminates error prevention strategies; further,

To provide leadership in encouraging the participation of all stakeholders in the reporting of medication errors to this program.
This policy was reviewed in 2003 by the Council on Legal and Public Affairs and by the Board of Directors and was found to still be appropriate.

Medication Misadventures (9805)
Source: Council on Administrative Affairs
To affirm that pharmacists must assume a leadership role in preventing, investigating, and eliminating medication misadventures across the continuum of care.
This policy was reviewed in 2002 by the Council on Administrative Affairs and by the Board of Directors and was found to still be appropriate.

Human Factors Concepts (9609)
Source: Council on Professional Affairs
To encourage pharmacists to apply human factors concepts (human errors related to inadequate systems or environment) in the prevention, analysis, and reporting of medication errors; further,

To encourage research (in conjunction with other groups, as appropriate) to identify human factors causes of medication errors and opportunities for their prevention.

ASHP Statement on Reporting Medical Errors

Position

The incidence of death and serious harm caused by mistakes and accidents in health care is unacceptable.[1] This serious public health problem merits top-priority national attention. Addressing this issue will require major reforms and sizable investment of resources throughout the health care system, including the medication use process, which is a particular focus of the American Society of Health-System Pharmacists (ASHP).

ASHP believes that the following steps should be taken as part of a comprehensive national solution to the problem: (1) The establishment of a standardized, uniform nationwide system (with the characteristics noted below) of mandatory reporting of adverse medical events that cause death or serious harm, (2) continued development and strengthening of systems for voluntary reporting of medical errors, and (3) strengthening efforts to implement process changes that reduce the risk of future errors and improve patient care.

The fundamental purpose of reporting systems for medical errors is to learn how to improve the health care delivery process to prevent these errors. Reporting of medical errors must become culturally accepted throughout health care. A major investment of resources will be required in the health care system to apply the lessons derived from the reporting of medical errors. Marshaling those resources is an urgent issue for the governing boards of health care institutions, health care administrators, health professionals, purchasers of health care (including federal and state governments), third party payers, public policy makers, credentialing organizations, the legal profession, and consumers.

Requirements

The primary goal of *mandatory reporting* of adverse medical events that cause death or serious harm should be to foster accountability for health care delivery process changes to prevent errors or adverse medical events. If a patient dies or is seriously harmed because of a mistake or accident in the health care system, the practitioner or institution responsible for the patient's care should report the incident to a designated state health body. Further, states should be obligated to share information based on these reports promptly with a national coordinating body and with national programs that are designed to improve the quality and enhance the safety of patient care.

ASHP's support of a mandatory reporting system is contingent upon the system having the following characteristics:

1. An overall focus on improving the processes used in health care, with the proper application of technical expertise to analyze and learn from reports,
2. Legal protection of confidentiality of patients, health care workers, and the information submitted to the extent feasible while preserving the interest of public accountability,
3. Nonpunitive in the sense that the submission of a report, per se, does not engender a penalty on the reporting institution or practitioner or others involved in the incident,
4. A definition of "serious harm" that concentrates on long-term or irreversible patient harm, so as not to overburden the reporting system,
5. National coordination and strong federal efforts to ensure compliance with standardized methods of reporting, analysis, and follow up, that emphasize process improvement and avoid a culture of blame,
6. Adequate resources devoted to report analysis, timely dissemination of advisories based on report analysis, and development of appropriate quality improvement efforts, and
7. Periodic assessment of the system to ensure that it is meeting its intent and not having serious undesired consequences.

Experience associated with current mandatory state reporting of adverse medical events and mandatory public health reporting of certain infectious diseases should be assessed, and the best practices of such programs should be applied to the new system of mandatory reporting of adverse medical events that cause death or serious harm.

The primary goals of *voluntary reporting* of medical errors should be quality improvement and enhancement of patient safety. Reports by frontline practitioners of errors and "near misses" are a strength of such programs when report analysis and communication lead to prevention of similar occurrences. The public interest will be served if protection is granted to individuals who submit reports to voluntary reporting programs. The Medication Errors Reporting Program operated by the United States Pharmacopeia in cooperation with the Institute for Safe Medication Practices is an important initiative that merits strengthening; this program may be a model for voluntary reporting of other types of medical error.

Reference

1. Institute of Medicine Division of Health Care Services Committee on Quality of Health Care in America. To err is human: building a safer health system. Washington, DC: National Academy Press; 1999.

Approved by the ASHP House of Delegates, June 5, 2000.

The bibliographic citation for this document is as follows: American Society of Health-System Pharmacists. ASHP statement on reporting medical errors. *Am J Health-Syst Pharm.* 2000; 57:1531–2.

[*Editor's note*: Other relevant ASHP policies are contained in the ASHP Guidelines on Preventing Medication Errors in Hospitals, the ASHP Guidelines on Preventing Medication Errors with Antineoplastic Agents, and policy positions 9609, 9805, 9918, 0011, 0020, and 0021.]

ASHP Guidelines on Adverse Drug Reaction Monitoring and Reporting

Pharmacists in organized health care systems should develop comprehensive, ongoing programs for monitoring and reporting adverse drug reactions (ADRs).[1] It is the pharmacist's responsibility and professional obligation to report any suspected ADRs. ADR-monitoring and reporting programs encourage ADR surveillance, facilitate ADR documentation, promote the reporting of ADRs, provide a mechanism for monitoring the safety of drug use in high-risk patient populations, and stimulate the education of health professionals regarding potential ADRs. A comprehensive, ongoing ADR program should include mechanisms for monitoring, detecting, evaluating, documenting, and reporting ADRs as well as intervening and providing educational feedback to prescribers, other health care professionals, and patients. Additionally, ADR programs should focus on identifying problems leading to ADRs, planning for positive changes, and measuring the results of these changes. Positive outcomes resulting from an ADR program should be emphasized to support program growth and development.

ASHP does not suggest that there is a predictable rate of incidence or severity of ADRs. The number and severity of ADRs reported in a given organization or setting would vary with the organization's size, type, patient mix, drugs used, and the ADR definition used.

Definitions

ASHP defines a significant ADR as any unexpected, unintended, undesired, or excessive response to a drug that

1. Requires discontinuing the drug (therapeutic or diagnostic),
2. Requires changing the drug therapy,
3. Requires modifying the dose (except for minor dosage adjustments),
4. Necessitates admission to a hospital,
5. Prolongs stay in a health care facility,
6. Necessitates supportive treatment,
7. Significantly complicates diagnosis,
8. Negatively affects prognosis, or
9. Results in temporary or permanent harm, disability, or death.

Consistent with this definition, an *allergic reaction* (an immunologic hypersensitivity, occurring as the result of unusual sensitivity to a drug) and an *idiosyncratic reaction* (an abnormal susceptibility to a drug that is peculiar to the individual) are also considered ADRs.

Several other definitions of ADRs exist, including those of the World Health Organization (WHO),[2] Karch and Lasagna,[3] and the Food and Drug Administration (FDA).[4]

WHO: "Any response to a drug which is noxious and unintended, and which occurs at doses normally used in man for prophylaxis, diagnosis, or therapy of disease, or for the modification of physiological function."

Karch and Lasagna: "Any response to a drug that is noxious and unintended, and that occurs at doses used in humans for prophylaxis, diagnosis, or therapy, excluding failure to accomplish the intended purpose."

FDA: For reporting purposes, FDA categorizes a *serious adverse event* (events relating to drugs or devices) as one in which "the patient outcome is death, life-threatening (real risk of dying), hospitalization (initial or prolonged), disability (significant, persistent, or permanent), congenital anomaly, or required intervention to prevent permanent impairment or damage."

For perspective, it may be helpful to note events that are not classified as ADRs. A *side effect* is defined by ASHP as an expected, well-known reaction resulting in little or no change in patient management (e.g., drowsiness or dry mouth due to administration of certain antihistamines or nausea associated with the use of antineoplastics). ASHP further defines a side effect as an effect with a predictable frequency and an effect whose intensity and occurrence are related to the size of the dose. Additionally, drug withdrawal, drug-abuse syndromes, accidental poisoning, and drug-overdose complications should not be defined as ADRs.

While individual health care organizations may need to apply ADR surveillance to different degrees for different groups of patients, ASHP believes it would be greatly beneficial if a common definition of ADRs were used in all settings to facilitate reporting, collective surveillance, and ADR-trend research.

Program Features

A comprehensive ADR-monitoring and reporting program should be an integral part of an organization's overall drug-use system. An ADR-monitoring and reporting program should include the following features:

1. The program should establish
   a. An ongoing and concurrent (during drug therapy) surveillance system based on the reporting of suspected ADRs by pharmacists, physicians, nurses, or patients.[5]
   b. A prospective (before drug therapy) surveillance system for high-risk drugs or patients with a high risk for ADRs.
   c. A concurrent surveillance system for monitoring alerting orders. Alerting orders include the use of "tracer" drugs that are used to treat common ADRs (e.g., orders for immediate doses of antihistamines, epinephrine, and corticosteroids), abrupt discontinuation or decreases in dosage of a drug, or stat orders for laboratory assessment of therapeutic drug levels.[6,7]
2. Prescribers, caregivers, and patients should be notified regarding suspected ADRs.
3. Information regarding suspected ADRs should be reported to the pharmacy for complete data collection

and analysis, including the patient's name, the patient's medical and medication history, a description of the suspected ADR, the temporal sequence of the event, any remedial treatment required, and sequelae.

4. High-risk patients should be identified and monitored. High-risk patients include but are not limited to pediatric patients, geriatric patients, patients with organ failure (e.g., hepatic or renal failure), and patients receiving multiple drugs.[6]

5. Drugs likely to cause ADRs ("high-risk" drugs) should be identified, and their use should be monitored. Examples of drugs that may be considered as high risk include aminoglycosides, amphotericin, antineoplastics, corticosteroids, digoxin, heparin, lidocaine, phenytoin, theophylline, thrombolytic agents, and warfarin.[6]

6. The cause(s) of each suspected ADR should be evaluated on the basis of the patient's medical and medication history, the circumstances of the adverse event, the results of dechallenge and rechallenge (if any), alternative etiologies, and a literature review.

7. A method for assigning the probability of a reported or suspected ADR (e.g., confirmed or definite, likely, possible, and unlikely) should be developed to categorize each ADR. Algorithms[8–10] may be useful in establishing the causes of suspected ADRs. Subjective questions and the professional judgment of a pharmacist can be used as additional tools to determine the probability of an ADR. Questions might include the following:

   a. Was there a temporal relationship between the onset of drug therapy and the adverse reaction?

   b. Was there a dechallenge; i.e., did the signs and symptoms of the adverse reaction subside when the drug was withdrawn?

   c. Can signs and symptoms of the adverse reaction be explained by the patient's disease state?

   d. Were there any laboratory tests that provide evidence for the reaction being an ADR?

   e. What was the patient's previous general experience with the drug?

   f. Did symptoms return when the agent was readministered?

8. A method for ranking ADRs by severity should be established.[11]

9. A description of each suspected ADR and the outcomes from the event should be documented in the patient's medical record.

10. Serious or unexpected ADRs should be reported to the Food and Drug Administration (FDA) or the drug's manufacturer (or both).[a]

11. All ADR reports should be reviewed and evaluated by a designated multidisciplinary committee (e.g., a pharmacy and therapeutics committee).

12. ADR-report information should be disseminated to health care professional staff members for educational purposes. Good topics for medical staff education include preventing ADRs and appropriate and effective care for patients who experience ADRs. Educational programs can be conducted as morning "report" discussions, newsletters, "grand rounds" presentations, algorithms for treatment, and multidisciplinary reviews of drug-use evaluations. Patient confidentiality should be preserved.

13. In settings where it is possible, a pharmacy-coordinated ADR team or committee, consisting of a physician, nurse, quality improvement leader, an administrator, and a pharmacist is recommended.[12–15] The team should be charged with adopting a definition for the organization, promoting awareness of the consequences of ADRs, establishing mechanisms for identifying and reporting ADRs, reviewing ADR patterns or trends, and developing preventive and corrective interventions.

14. Continuous monitoring of patient outcomes and patterns of ADRs is imperative. Findings from an ADR-monitoring and reporting program should be incorporated into the organization's ongoing quality improvement activities. The process should include the following:

    a. Feedback to all appropriate health care staff,

    b. Continuous monitoring for trends, clusters, or significant individual ADRs,

    c. Educational efforts for prevention of ADRs, and

    d. Evaluation of prescribing patterns, patient monitoring practices, patient outcomes, and the ADR program's effect on overall and individual patient outcomes.

An overall goal of the ADR process should be the achievement of positive patient outcomes.

Benefits

An ongoing ADR-monitoring and reporting program can provide benefits to the organization, pharmacists, other health care professionals, and patients. These benefits include (but are not limited to) the following:

1. Providing an indirect measure of the quality of pharmaceutical care through identification of preventable ADRs and anticipatory surveillance for high-risk drugs or patients.

2. Complementing organizational risk-management activities and efforts to minimize liability.

3. Assessing the safety of drug therapies, especially recently approved drugs.

4. Measuring ADR incidence.

5. Educating health care professionals and patients about drug effects and increasing their level of awareness regarding ADRs.

6. Providing quality-assurance screening findings for use in drug-use evaluation programs.

7. Measuring the economic impact of ADR prevention as manifested through reduced hospitalization, optimal and economical drug use, and minimized organizational liability.

Role of the Pharmacist

Pharmacists should exert leadership in the development, maintenance, and ongoing evaluation of ADR programs. They should obtain formal endorsement or approval of such programs through appropriate committees (e.g., a pharmacy and therapeutics committee and the executive committee of the medical staff) and the organization's administration. In settings where applicable, input into the design of the program should be obtained from the medical staff, nursing staff, quality improvement staff, medical records department, and risk managers.[8,16–18] The pharmacist should facilitate

1. Analysis of each reported ADR,
2. Identification of drugs and patients at high risk for being involved in ADRs,
3. The development of policies and procedures for the ADR-monitoring and reporting program,
4. A description of the responsibilities and interactions of pharmacists, physicians, nurses, risk managers, and other health professionals in the ADR program,
5. Use of the ADR program for educational purposes,
6. Development, maintenance, and evaluation of ADR records within the organization,
7. The organizational dissemination and use of information obtained through the ADR program,
8. Reporting of serious ADRs to the FDA or the manufacturer (or both), and
9. Publication and presentation of important ADRs to the medical community.

Direct patient care roles for pharmacists should include patient counseling on ADRs, identification and documentation in the patient's medical record of high-risk patients, monitoring to ensure that serum drug concentrations remain within acceptable therapeutic ranges, and adjusting doses in appropriate patients (e.g., patients with impaired renal or hepatic function).

References

1. American Society of Hospital Pharmacists. ASHP technical assistance bulletin on hospital drug distribution and control. *Am J Hosp Pharm.* 1980; 37:1097–103.
2. Requirements for adverse reaction reporting. Geneva, Switzerland: World Health Organization; 1975.
3. Karch FE, Lasagna L. Adverse drug reactions—a critical review. *JAMA.* 1975; 234:1236–41.
4. Kessler DA. Introducing MedWatch, using FDA form 3500, a new approach to reporting medication and device adverse effects and product problems. *JAMA.* 1993; 269:2765–8.
5. Prosser TR, Kamysz PL. Multidisciplinary adverse drug reaction surveillance program. *Am J Hosp Pharm.* 1990; 47:1334–9.
6. Koch KE. Adverse drug reactions. In: Brown TR, ed. Handbook of institutional pharmacy practice. 3rd ed. Bethesda, MD: American Society of Hospital Pharmacists; 1992.
7. Koch KE. Use of standard screening procedures to identify adverse drug reactions. *Am J Hosp Pharm.* 1990; 47:1314–20.
8. Karch FE, Lasagna L. Toward the operational identification of adverse drug reactions. *Clin Pharmacol Ther.* 1977; 21:247–54.
9. Kramer MS, Leventhal JM, Hutchinson TA, et al. An algorithm for the operational assessment of adverse drug reactions. I. Background, description, and instructions for use. *JAMA.* 1979; 242:623–32.
10. Naranjo CA, Busto U, Sellers EM, et al. A method for estimating the probability of adverse drug reactions. *Clin Pharmacol Ther.* 1981; 30:239–45.
11. Hartwig SC, Siegel J, Schneider PJ. Preventability and severity assessment in reporting adverse drug reactions. *Am J Hosp Pharm.* 1992; 49:2229–32.
12. Accreditation Manual for Hospitals. Chicago: Joint Commission on Accreditation of Healthcare Organizations; 1989:121, 180.
13. Keith MR, Bellanger-McCleery RA, Fuchs JE. Multidisciplinary program for detecting and evaluating adverse drug reactions. *Am J Hosp Pharm.* 1989; 46:1809–12.
14. Kimelblatt BJ, Young SH, Heywood PM, et al. Improved reporting of adverse drug reactions. *Am J Hosp Pharm.* 1988; 45:1086–9.
15. Nelson RW, Shane R. Developing an adverse drug reaction reporting program. *Am J Hosp Pharm.* 1983; 40:445–6.
16. Swanson KM, Landry JP, Anderson RP. Pharmacy-coordinated, multidisciplinary adverse drug reaction program. *Top Hosp Pharm Manage.* 1992; 12(Jul):49–59.
17. Flowers P, Dzierba S, Baker O. A continuous quality improvement team approach to adverse drug reaction reporting. *Top Hosp Pharm Manage.* 1992; 12(Jul):60–7.
18. Guharoy SR. A pharmacy-coordinated, multidisciplinary approach for successful implementation of an adverse drug reaction reporting program. *Top Hosp Pharm Manage.* 1992; 12(Jul):68–74.

---

[a]To report an adverse drug event to the FDA, use the MedWatch program. Reports can be mailed (MedWatch, 5600 Fishers Lane, Rockville, MD 20852-9787), faxed (800-FDA-0178), called in (800-FDA-1088), or reported by modem (800-FDA-7737). An easy-to-use FDA form 3500 can be used. This form should be available from a pharmacy.

Approved by the ASHP Board of Directors, November 16, 1994. Revised by the ASHP Council on Professional Affairs. Supersedes a previous version dated November 16, 1988.

The bibliographic citation for this document is as follows: American Society of Health-System Pharmacists. ASHP guidelines on adverse drug reaction monitoring and reporting. *Am J Health-Syst Pharm.* 1995; 52:417–9.

ASHP Guidelines on Preventing Medication Errors in Hospitals

The goal of drug therapy is the achievement of defined therapeutic outcomes that improve a patient's quality of life while minimizing patient risk.[1] There are inherent risks, both known and unknown, associated with the therapeutic use of drugs (prescription and nonprescription) and drug administration devices. The incidents or hazards that result from such risk have been defined as drug misadventuring, which includes both adverse drug reactions (ADRs) and medication errors.[2] This document addresses medication errors—episodes in drug misadventuring that should be preventable through effective systems controls involving pharmacists, physicians and other prescribers, nurses, risk management personnel, legal counsel, administrators, patients, and others in the organizational setting, as well as regulatory agencies and the pharmaceutical industry.

This document suggests medication error prevention approaches that should be considered in the development of organizational systems and discusses methods of managing medication errors once they have occurred. These guidelines are primarily intended to apply to the inpatient hospital setting because of the special collaborative processes established in the setting [e.g., formulary system, pharmacy and therapeutics (P&T) committee, and opportunity for increased interaction among health-care providers].

Recommendations for practice settings other than hospitals are beyond the scope of this document, although many of the ideas and principles may be applicable.

Medication errors compromise patient confidence in the health-care system and increase health-care costs. The problems and sources of medication errors are multidisciplinary and multifactorial. Errors occur from lack of knowledge, substandard performance and mental lapses, or defects or failures in systems.[3,4] Medication errors may be committed by both experienced and inexperienced staff, including pharmacists, physicians, nurses, supportive personnel (e.g., pharmacy technicians), students, clerical staff (e.g., ward clerks), administrators, pharmaceutical manufacturers, patients and their caregivers, and others. The incidence of medication errors is indeterminate; valid comparisons of different studies on medication errors are extremely difficult because of differences in variables, measurements, populations, and methods.[2]

Many medication errors are probably undetected. The outcome(s) or clinical significance of many medication errors may be minimal, with few or no consequences that adversely affect a patient. Tragically, however, some medication errors result in serious patient morbidity or mortality.[3] Thus, medication errors must not be taken lightly, and effective systems for ordering, dispensing, and administering medications should be established with safeguards to prevent the occurrence of errors. These systems should involve adequately trained and supervised personnel, adequate communications, reasonable workloads, effective drug handling systems, multiple procedural and final product checks by separate individuals, quality management, and adequate facilities, equipment, and supplies.

The pharmacist's mission is to help ensure that patients make the best use of medications.[5] This applies to all drugs used by inpatients or ambulatory patients, including oral or injectable products, radiopharmaceuticals, radiopaque contrast media, anesthetic gases, blood-fraction drugs, dialysis fluids, respiratory therapy agents, investigational drugs, drug samples, drugs brought into the hospital setting by patients, and other chemical or biological substances administered to patients to evoke a pharmacological response.[6]

Through a systems-oriented approach, the pharmacist should lead collaborative, multidisciplinary efforts to prevent, detect, and resolve drug-related problems that can result in patient harm.[1] An understanding of the risk factors associated with medication errors should enable improved monitoring of patients and medications associated with increased risk for serious errors and should enable the development of organizational systems designed to minimize risk.[7] The pharmacist should participate in appropriate organizational committees and work with physicians, nurses, administrators, and others to examine and improve systems to ensure that medication processes are safe.

Types of Medication Errors

Medication errors include prescribing errors, dispensing errors, medication administration errors, and patient compliance errors. Specific types of medication errors are categorized in Table 1, based on a compilation of the literature.[3,7–18]

A *potential error* is a mistake in prescribing, dispensing, or planned medication administration that is detected and corrected through intervention (by another health-care provider or patient) before actual medication administration. Potential errors should be reviewed and tabulated as separate events from errors of occurrence (errors that actually reach patients) to identify opportunities to correct problems in the medication use system even before they occur. Detection of potential errors should be a component of the hospital's routine quality improvement process. Documentation of instances in which an individual has prevented the occurrence of a medication error will help identify system weaknesses and will reinforce the importance of multiple checks in the medication use system.

Recommendations for Preventing Medication Errors

Organizational systems for ordering, dispensing, and administering medications should be designed to minimize error. Medication errors may involve process breakdowns in more than one aspect of a system. This section provides recommendations to the management staff (general and departmental) of hospitals, as well as to individual prescribers, pharmacists, nurses, patients, pharmaceutical manufacturers, and others.

Organizational and Departmental Recommendations. Organizational policies and procedures should be established to prevent medication errors. Development of the policies and procedures should involve multiple departments, including pharmacy, medicine, nursing, risk management, legal counsel, and organizational administration. The following recommendations are offered for organizational management and clinical staff:[3,8,11–14,16,19–29]

Table 1.
Types of Medication Errors[3,7-18,a]

Type	Definition
Prescribing error	Incorrect drug selection (based on indications, contraindications, known allergies, existing drug therapy, and other factors), dose, dosage form, quantity, route, concentration, rate of administration, or instructions for use of a drug product ordered or authorized by physician (or other legitimate prescriber); illegible prescriptions or medication orders that lead to errors that reach the patient
Omission error[b]	The failure to administer an ordered dose to a patient before the next scheduled dose, if any
Wrong time error	Administration of medication outside a predefined time interval from its scheduled administration time (this interval should be established by each individual health care facility)
Unauthorized drug error[c]	Administration to the patient of medication not authorized by a legitimate prescriber for the patient
Improper dose error[d]	Administration to the patient of a dose that is greater than or less than the amount ordered by the prescriber or administration of duplicate doses to the patient, i.e., one or more dosage units in addition to those that were ordered
Wrong dosage-form error[e]	Administration to the patient of a drug product in a different dosage form than ordered by the prescriber
Wrong drug-preparation error[f]	Drug product incorrectly formulated or manipulated before administration
Wrong administration-technique error[g]	Inappropriate procedure or improper technique in the administration of a drug
Deteriorated drug error[h]	Administration of a drug that has expired or for which the physical or chemical dosage-form integrity has been compromised
Monitoring error	Failure to review a prescribed regimen for appropriateness and detection of problems, or failure to use appropriate clinical or laboratory data for adequate assessment of patient response to prescribed therapy
Compliance error	Inappropriate patient behavior regarding adherence to a prescribed medication regimen
Other medication error	Any medication error that does not fall into one of the above predefined categories

[a] The categories may not be mutually exclusive because of the multidisciplinary and multifactorial nature of medication errors.

[b] Assumes no prescribing error. Excluded would be (1) a patient's refusal to take the medication or (2) a decision not to administer the dose because of recognized contraindications. If an explanation for the omission is apparent (e.g., patient was away from nursing unit for tests or medication was not available), that reason should be documented in the appropriate records.

[c] This would include, for example, a wrong drug, a dose given to the wrong patient, unordered drugs, and doses given outside a stated set of clinical guidelines or protocols.

[d] Excluded would be (1) allowable deviations based on preset ranges established by individual health care organizations in consideration of measuring devices routinely provided to those who administer drugs to patients (e.g., not administering a dose based on a patient's measured temperature or blood glucose level) or other factors such as conversion of doses expressed in the apothecary system to the metric system and (2) topical dosage forms for which medication orders are not expressed quantitatively.

[e] Excluded would be accepted protocols (established by the pharmacy and therapeutics committee or its equivalent) that authorize pharmacists to dispense alternate dosage forms for patients with special needs (e.g., liquid formulations for patients with nasogastric tubes or those who have difficulty swallowing), as allowed by state regulations

[f] This would include, for example, incorrect dilution or reconstitution, mixing drugs that are physically or chemically incompatible, and inadequate product packaging.

[g] This would include doses administered (1) via the wrong route (different from the route prescribed), (2) via the correct route but at the wrong site (e.g., left eye instead of right), and (3) at the wrong rate of administration.

[h] This would include, for example, administration of expired drugs and improperly stored drugs.

1. Using the principles of the formulary system, the P&T committee (or its equivalent)—composed of pharmacists, physicians, nurses, and other health professionals—should be responsible for formulating policies regarding the evaluation, selection, and therapeutic use of drugs in organized health-care settings.

2. Care and consideration must be given in hiring and assigning personnel involved in medication ordering, preparation, dispensing, administration, and patient education. Policies and procedures should be developed that ensure adequate personnel selection, training, supervision, and evaluation. This would include the need to ensure proper interviewing, orientation, evaluation of competency, supervision, and opportunities for continuing professional and technical education.

3. Sufficient personnel must be available to perform tasks adequately. Policies and procedures should ensure that reasonable workload levels and working hours are established and rarely exceeded.

4. Suitable work environments should exist for the preparation of drug products. Potential error sources within the work environment, such as frequent interruptions, should be identified and minimized.

5. Lines of authority and areas of responsibility within the hospital should be clearly defined for medication or-

dering, dispensing, and administration. The system should ensure adequate written and oral communications among personnel involved in the medication use process to optimize therapeutic appropriateness and to enable medications to be prescribed, dispensed, and administered in a timely fashion. All systems should provide for review and verification of the prescriber's original order (except in emergency situations) before a drug product is dispensed by a pharmacist. Any necessary clarifications or changes in a medication order must be resolved with the prescriber before a medication is administered to the patient. Written documentation of such consultations should be made in the patient's medical record or other appropriate record. Nursing staff should be informed of any changes made in the medication order. Changes required to correct incorrect orders should be regarded as potential errors, assuming the changes occurred in time to prevent the error from reaching the patient.

6. There should be an ongoing, systematic program of quality improvement and peer review with respect to the safe use of medications. A formal drug use evaluation (DUE) program, developed and conducted through collaborative efforts among medicine, pharmacy, and nursing, should be integrated and coordinated with the

overall hospital quality improvement program. To prevent medication errors, a portion of the DUE program should focus on monitoring the appropriate use of any drugs associated with a high frequency of adverse events, including specific drug classes (such as antimicrobials, antineoplastic agents, and cardiovascular drugs) and injectable dosage forms (e.g., potassium products, narcotic substances, heparin, lidocaine, procainamide, magnesium sulfate, and insulin). The quality improvement program should include a system for monitoring, reviewing, and reporting medication errors to assist in identifying and eliminating causes of errors (system breakdowns) and preventing their recurrence. Table 2 lists common causes of medication errors, i.e., areas where there may be system breakdowns.

7. Pharmacists and others responsible for processing drug orders should have routine access to appropriate clinical information about patients (including medication, allergy, and hypersensitivity profiles; diagnoses; pregnancy status; and laboratory values) to help evaluate the appropriateness of medication orders.

8. Pharmacists should maintain medication profiles for all patients, both inpatients and ambulatory patients, who receive care at the hospital. This profile should include adequate information to allow monitoring of medication histories, allergies, diagnoses, potential drug interactions and ADRs, duplicate drug therapies, pertinent laboratory data, and other information.

9. The pharmacy department must be responsible for the procurement, distribution, and control of all drugs used within the organization. Adequate hours for the provision of pharmaceutical services must be maintained; 24-hour pharmaceutical service is strongly recommended in hospital settings. In the absence of 24-hour pharmaceutical service, access to a limited supply of medications should be available to authorized nonpharmacists for use in initiating urgent medication orders. The list of medications to be supplied and the policies and procedures to be used (including subsequent review of all activity by a pharmacist) should be developed by the P&T committee (or its equivalent). Items should be chosen with safety in mind, limiting wherever possible medications, quantities, dosage forms, and container sizes that might endanger patients. The use of well-designed night cabinets, after-hours drug carts, and other methods would preclude the need for non-pharmacists to enter the pharmacy. Access to the pharmacy by nonpharmacists (e.g., nurses)

for removal of doses is strongly discouraged; this practice should be minimized and eliminated to the fullest extent possible. When 24-hour pharmacy service is not feasible, a pharmacist must be available on an "on-call" basis.

10. The pharmacy manager (or designee), with the assistance of the P&T committee (or its equivalent) and the department of nursing, should develop comprehensive policies and procedures that provide for efficient and safe distribution of all medications and related supplies to patients. For safety, the recommended method of distribution within the organized health-care setting is the unit dose drug distribution and control system.

11. Except in emergency situations, all sterile and nonsterile drug products should be dispensed from the pharmacy department for individual patients. The storage of nonemergency floor stock medications on the nursing units or in patient-care areas should be minimized. Particular caution should be exercised with respect to drug products that have commonly been involved in serious medication errors or whose margin of safety is narrow, such as concentrated forms of drug products that are intended to be diluted into larger volumes (e.g., concentrated lidocaine and potassium chloride for injection concentrate). All drug storage areas should be routinely inspected by pharmacy personnel to ensure adequate product integrity and appropriate packaging, labeling, and storage. It is important that drug products and other products for external use be stored separately from drug products for internal use.

12. The pharmacy director and staff must ensure that all drug products used in the organizational setting are of high quality and integrity. This would include, for example, (1) selecting multisource products supported by adequate bioavailability data and adequate product packaging and labeling, (2) maintaining an unexpired product inventory, and (3) keeping abreast of compendial requirements.

13. The use of a patient's own or "home" medications should be avoided to the fullest extent possible. Use of such medications should be allowed only if there is a need for the patient to receive the therapy, the drug product is not obtainable by the pharmacy, and no alternative therapy can be prescribed. If such medications are used, the prescribing physician must write an appropriate order in the patient's medical record. Before use, a pharmacist should inspect and identify the medication. If there are any unresolved questions with respect to product identity or integrity, the medication must not be used.

14. All discontinued or unused drugs should be returned to the department of pharmacy immediately on discontinuation or at patient discharge. Discharged patients must not be given unlabeled drug products to take home, unless they are labeled for outpatient use by the pharmacy in accordance with state and federal regulations. Discharged patients should be counseled about use of any medications to be used after discharge.

15. It is recommended that there be computerized pharmacy systems in place that enable automated checking for doses, duplicate therapies, allergies, drug interactions, and other aspects of use. Where possible, the use of technological innovations such as bar coding is recommended to help identify patients, products, and

Table 2.
Common Causes of Medication Errors

Ambiguous strength designation on labels or in packaging
Drug product nomenclature (look-alike or sound-alike names, use of lettered or numbered prefixes and suffixes in drug names)
Equipment failure or malfunction
Illegible handwriting
Improper transcription
Inaccurate dosage calculation
Inadequately trained personnel
Inappropriate abbreviations used in prescribing
Labeling errors
Excessive workload
Lapses in individual performance
Medication unavailable

care providers. Pharmacy-generated medication administration records or labels are recommended to assist nurses in interpreting and documenting medication activities.

16. Adequate drug information resources should be available for all health-care providers involved in the drug use process.

17. Standard drug administration times should be established for the hospital by the P&T committee (or its equivalent), with input from the departments of nursing and pharmacy. Policies and procedures should allow for deviations from the standard times when necessary. Further, standard drug concentrations and dosage charts should be developed to minimize the need for dosage calculations by staff.

18. The P&T committee (or its equivalent) should develop a list of standard abbreviations approved for use in medication ordering. There should be efforts to prohibit or discourage the use of other abbreviations in medication ordering.

19. A review mechanism should be established through the P&T committee specifying those responsible for data collection and evaluation of medication error reports. The review group should investigate causes of errors and develop programs for decreasing their occurrence. The review group should be composed of representatives from pharmacy, nursing, medicine, quality assurance, staff education, risk management, and legal counsel.

20. The pharmacy department, in conjunction with nursing, risk management, and the medical staff, should conduct ongoing educational programs to discuss medication errors, their causes, and methods to prevent their occurrence. Such programs might involve seminars, newsletters, or other methods of information dissemination.

Recommendations for Prescribers. Prescribing is an early point at which medication errors can arise. It has been estimated that 1% of hospitalized patients suffer adverse events as the result of medical mismanagement[30] and that drug-related complications are the most common type of adverse event.[7] The following recommendations for preventing medication errors are suggested for physicians and other prescribers[3,7,11–16,31]:

1. To determine appropriate drug therapy, prescribers should stay abreast of the current state of knowledge through literature review, consultation with pharmacists, consultation with other physicians, participation in continuing professional education programs, and other means. It is especially crucial to seek information when prescribing for conditions and diseases not typically experienced in the prescriber's practice.

2. Prescribers should evaluate the patient's total status and review all existing drug therapy before prescribing new or additional medications to ascertain possible antagonistic or complementary drug interactions. To evaluate and optimize patient response to prescribed drug therapy, appropriate monitoring of clinical signs and symptoms and of relevant laboratory data is necessary.

3. In hospitals, prescribers should be familiar with the medication ordering system (e.g., the formulary system, participation in DUE programs, allowable delega-

tion of authority, procedures to alert nurses and others to new drug orders that need to be processed, standard medication administration times, and approved abbreviations).

4. Drug orders should be complete. They should include patient name, generic drug name, trademarked name (if a specific product is required), route and site of administration, dosage form, dose, strength, quantity, frequency of administration, and prescriber's name. In some cases, a dilution, rate, and time of administration should be specified. The desired therapeutic outcome for each drug should be expressed when the drug is prescribed. Prescribers should review all drug orders for accuracy and legibility immediately after they have prescribed them.

5. Care should be taken to ensure that the intent of medication orders is clear and unambiguous. Prescribers should

   a. Write out instructions rather than using nonstandard or ambiguous abbreviations. For example, write "daily" rather than "q.d.," which could be misinterpreted as q.i.d. (causing a drug to be given four times a day instead of once) or as o.d. (for right eye).

   b. Do not use vague instructions, such as "take as directed," because specific instructions can help differentiate among intended drugs.

   c. Specify exact dosage strengths (such as milligrams) rather than dosage form units (such as one tablet or one vial). An exception would be combination drug products, for which the number of dosage form units should be specified.

   d. Prescribe by standard nomenclature, using the drug's generic name (United States Adopted Name or USAN), official name, or trademarked name (if deemed medically necessary). Avoid the following: locally coined names (e.g., Dr. Doe's syrup); chemical names [e.g., 6-mercaptopurine (instead of mercaptopurine) could result in a sixfold overdose if misinterpreted]; unestablished abbreviated drug names (e.g., "AZT" could stand for zidovudine, azathioprine, or aztreonam); acronyms; and apothecary or chemical symbols.

   e. Always use a leading zero before a decimal expression of less than one (e.g., 0.5 ml). Conversely, a terminal zero should never be used (e.g., 5.0 ml), since failure to see the decimal could result in a 10-fold overdose. When possible, avoid the use of decimals (e.g., prescribe 500 mg instead of 0.5 g).

   f. Spell out the word "units" (e.g., 10 units regular insulin) rather than writing "u," which could be misinterpreted as a zero.

   g. Use the metric system.

6. Written drug or prescription orders (including signatures) should be legible. Prescribers with poor handwriting should print or type medication or prescription orders if direct order entry capabilities for computerized systems are unavailable. A handwritten order should be completely readable (not merely recognizable through familiarity). An illegible handwritten order should be regarded as a potential error. If it leads to an error of occurrence (that is, the error actually reaches the patient), it should be regarded as a prescribing error.

7. Verbal drug or prescription orders (that is, orders that

are orally communicated) should be reserved only for those situations in which it is impossible or impractical for the prescriber to write the order or enter it in the computer. The prescriber should dictate verbal orders slowly, clearly, and articulately to avoid confusion. Special caution is urged in the prescribing of drug dosages in the teens (e.g., a 15-mEq dose of potassium chloride could be misheard as a 50-mEq dose). The order should be read back to the prescriber by the recipient (i.e., the nurse or pharmacist, according to institutional policies). When read back, the drug name should be spelled to the prescriber and, when directions are repeated, no abbreviations should be used (e.g., say "three times daily" rather than "t.i.d."). A written copy of the verbal order should be placed in the patient's medical record and later confirmed by the prescriber in accordance with applicable state regulations and hospital policies.

8. When possible, drugs should be prescribed for administration by the oral route rather than by injection.

9. When possible, the prescriber should talk with the patient or caregiver to explain the medication prescribed and any special precautions or observations that might be indicated, including any allergic or hypersensitivity reactions that might occur.

10. Prescribers should follow up and periodically evaluate the need for continued drug therapy for individual patients.

11. Instructions with respect to "hold" orders for medications should be clear.

Recommendations for Pharmacists. The pharmacist is expected to play a pivotal role in preventing medication misuse. The value of pharmacists' interventions to prevent medication errors that would have resulted from inappropriate prescribing has been documented.[7,32,33] Ideally, the pharmacist should collaborate with the prescriber in developing, implementing, and monitoring a therapeutic plan to produce defined therapeutic outcomes for the patient.[1] It is also vital that the pharmacist devote careful attention to dispensing processes to ensure that errors are not introduced at that point in the medication process. The following recommendations are suggested for pharmacists[3,4,8–10,14,16,18–20,28,29]:

1. Pharmacists should participate in drug therapy monitoring (including the following, when indicated: the assessment of therapeutic appropriateness, medication administration appropriateness, and possible duplicate therapies; review for possible interactions; and evaluation of pertinent clinical and laboratory data) and DUE activities to help achieve safe, effective, and rational use of drugs.

2. To recommend and recognize appropriate drug therapy, pharmacists should stay abreast of the current state of knowledge through familiarity with literature, consultation with colleagues and other health-care providers, participation in continuing professional education programs, and other means.

3. Pharmacists should make themselves available to prescribers and nurses to offer information and advice about therapeutic drug regimens and the correct use of medications.

4. Pharmacists should be familiar with the medication ordering system and drug distribution policies and procedures established for the organizational setting to provide for the safe distribution of all medications and related supplies to inpatients and ambulatory patients. In particular, pharmacists should be familiar with all elements that are designed into the system to prevent or detect errors. Actions by any staff that would (even unintentionally) defeat or compromise those elements should serve as "alerts" to the pharmacist that safety may be affected. Any necessary followup action (e.g., education or reeducation of staff) should ensue promptly. Policies and procedures to be followed for "hold" orders should be clear and understood by pharmacy, medical, and nursing staffs.

5. Pharmacists should never assume or guess the intent of confusing medication orders. If there are any questions, the prescriber should be contacted prior to dispensing.

6. When preparing drugs, pharmacists should maintain orderliness and cleanliness in the work area and perform one procedure at a time with as few interruptions as possible.

7. Before dispensing a medication in nonemergency situations, the pharmacist should review an original copy of the written medication order. The pharmacist should ensure that all work performed by supportive personnel or through the use of automated devices is checked by manual or technological means. All processes must conform with applicable state and federal laws and regulations. Pharmacists should participate in, at a minimum, a self-checking process in reading prescriptions, labeling (drug or ingredients and pharmacist-generated labeling), and dosage calculations. For high risk drug products, when possible, all work should be checked by a second individual (preferably, another pharmacist). Pharmacists must make certain that the following are accurate: drug, labeling, packaging, quantity, dose, and instructions.

8. Pharmacists should dispense medications in ready-to-administer dosage forms whenever possible. The unit dose system is strongly recommended as the preferred method of drug distribution. The need for nurses to manipulate drugs (e.g., measure, repackage, and calculate) prior to their administration should be minimized.

9. Pharmacists should review the use of auxiliary labels and use the labels prudently when it is clear that such use may prevent errors (e.g., "shake well," "for external use only," and "not for injection").

10. Pharmacists should ensure that medications are delivered to the patient-care area in a timely fashion after receipt of orders, according to hospital policies and procedures. If medication doses are not delivered or if therapy is delayed for any reason pending resolution of a detected problem (e.g., allergy or contraindications), the pharmacist should notify the nursing staff of the delay and the reason.

11. Pharmacists should observe how medications are actually being used in patient-care areas to ensure that dispensing and storage procedures are followed and to assist nurses in optimizing patient safety.

12. Pharmacy staff should review medications that are returned to the department. Such review processes may reveal system breakdowns or problems that resulted in medication errors (e.g., omitted doses and unauthorized drugs).

13. When dispensing medications to ambulatory patients

(e.g., at discharge), pharmacists should counsel patients or caregivers and verify that they understand why a medication was prescribed and dispensed, its intended use, any special precautions that might be observed, and other needed information. For inpatients, pharmacists should make their services available to counsel patients, families, or other caregivers when appropriate.

14. Pharmacists should preview and provide advice on the content and design of preprinted medication order forms or sheets if they are used.

15. Pharmacists should maintain records sufficient to enable identification of patients receiving an erroneous product.

Recommendations for Nurses. By virtue of their direct patient-care activities and administration of medications to patients, nurses—perhaps more than any other health-care providers—are in an excellent position to detect and report medication errors. Nurses often serve as the final point in the checks-and-balances triad (physicians and other prescribers, pharmacists, and nurses) for the medication use process; thus, they play an important role in risk reduction. The following recommendations for preventing medication administration errors are suggested[3,14,16,17,34]:

1. Nurses who practice in organized health-care settings should be familiar with the medication ordering and use system (e.g., participation in DUE activities, order processing, and standard medication administration times).

2. Nurses should review patients' medications with respect to desired patient outcomes, therapeutic duplications, and possible drug interactions. Adequate drug information (including information on medication administration and product compatibilities) should be obtained from pharmacists, nurses, other health-care providers, the literature, and other means when there are questions. There should be appropriate followup communication with the prescriber when this is indicated.

3. All drug orders should be verified before medication administration. Nurses should carefully review original medication orders before administration of the first dose and compare them with medications dispensed. Transcriptions of orders should be avoided to the extent possible and should be recognized as prime opportunities for errors. Doses should not be administered unless the meaning of the original order is clear and unambiguous and there are no questions with respect to the correctness of the prescribed regimen. Nurses should check the identity and integrity (e.g., expiration date and general appearance) of the medications dispensed before administering them. When there are discrepancies, the nurse should contact the pharmacy department and determine the appropriate action.

4. Patient identity should be verified before the administration of each prescribed dose. When appropriate, the patient should be observed after administration of the drug product to ensure that the doses were administered as prescribed and have the intended effect.

5. All doses should be administered at scheduled times unless there are questions or problems to be resolved. Medication doses should not be removed from packaging or labeling until immediately before administra-

tion. The administration of medication should be documented as soon as it is completed.

6. When standard drug concentrations or dosage charts are not available, dosage calculations, flow rates, and other mathematical calculations should be checked by a second individual (e.g., another nurse or a pharmacist).

7. The drug distribution system should not be circumvented by "borrowing" medications from one patient (or another hospital area) to give to a different patient or by stockpiling unused medications. If there are apparent missing doses, it is important that the pharmacy be contacted for explanation or correction. There may be an important reason why the dose was not sent to the patient-care area (e.g., allergy, contraindication, and questionable dose), and resolution of the potential question or problem may be pending.

8. If there are questions when a large volume or number of dosage units (e.g., more than two tablets, capsules, vials, or ampuls) is needed for a single patient dose, the medication order should be verified. Consult with the pharmacist and prescriber as appropriate.

9. All personnel using medication administration devices (e.g., infusion pumps) should understand their operation and the opportunities for error that might occur with the use of such devices.

10. Nurses should talk with patients or caregivers to ascertain that they understand the use of their medications and any special precautions or observations that might be indicated. Any counseling needed should be provided before the first dose is administered, when possible.

11. When a patient objects to or questions whether a particular drug should be administered, the nurse should listen, answer questions, and (if appropriate) double check the medication order and product dispensed before administering it to ensure that no preventable error is made (e.g., wrong patient, wrong route, and dose already administered). If a patient refuses to take a prescribed medication, that decision should be documented in the appropriate patient records.

Recommendations for Patients and Personal Caregivers. Patients (or their authorized caregivers or designees) have the right to know about all aspects of their care, including drug therapy. When patient status allows, health-care providers should encourage patients to take an active role in their drug use by questioning and learning about their treatment regimens. Generally, if patients are more knowledgeable, anxieties about the uncertainty of treatments can be alleviated and errors in treatment may be prevented. The following suggestions are offered to help patients whose health status allows, and their caregivers, make the best use of medications[3]:

1. Patients should inform appropriate direct health-care providers (e.g., physicians, nurses, and pharmacists) about all known symptoms, allergies, sensitivities, and current medication use. Patients should communicate their actual self-medication practices, even if they differ from the prescribed directions.

2. Patients should feel free to ask questions about any procedures and treatments received.

3. Patients should learn the names of the drug products that are prescribed and administered to them, as well as dosage strengths and schedules. It is suggested that

patients keep a personal list of all drug therapy, including prescribed drugs, nonprescription drugs, home remedies, and medical foods. Patients should also maintain lists of medications that they cannot take and the reasons why. This information should be shared with health-care providers. Patients should be assertive in communicating with health-care providers when anything seems incorrect or different from the norm.

4. After counseling from an authorized health-care provider about the appropriateness of the medication, patients should take all medications as directed.

Recommendations for Pharmaceutical Manufacturers and Approval Organizations. Poor designs with respect to drug product packaging and labeling, as well as selection of inappropriate or confusing nomenclature, have been identified as factors that contribute to serious medication errors by practitioners.[4,35–37] Pharmaceutical manufacturers and approval agencies should be responsive to efforts of practitioners to minimize errors. The following guidelines are recommended for the pharmaceutical industry and regulatory authorities[3,4,16,38]:

1. Drug manufacturers and the Food and Drug Administration are urged to involve pharmacists, nurses, and physicians in decisions about drug names, labeling, and packaging.
2. Look-alike or sound-alike trademarked names and generic names should be avoided.
3. Similar proprietary appearances of packaging and labeling should be avoided, because look-alike products contribute to medication errors.
4. The use of lettered or numbered prefixes and suffixes in trademarked names is generally discouraged. Lettered prefixes or suffixes could be mistaken for instructions or strength. Commonly used medical abbreviations should never be used in trademarked names (e.g., "HS" could stand for half-strength or a bedtime dose). Numbers as part of trademarked names could be mistaken for quantities to be administered. Coined abbreviations that could be misinterpreted (e.g., MTX, U, and HCTZ) should not be used in trademarked names.
5. Special instructions should be highlighted on labeling, such as the need for dilution before administration.
6. The most prominent items on the product label should be information in the best interest of safety (e.g., product name and strength). Less prominence should be given to company names or logos.
7. Drug manufacturers are encouraged to make dosage forms available commercially in unit dose and unit-of-dispensing containers, as well as bulk packaging, to facilitate their appropriate use in all practice settings.
8. Drug manufacturers must communicate with health-care providers (i.e., pharmacists, physicians, and nurses) when changes are made in product formulations or dosage forms.

Monitoring and Managing Medication Errors

Monitoring Medication Errors. Ongoing quality improvement programs for monitoring medication errors are needed. The difficulty in detecting errors has long been recognized as one of the barriers to studying the problem effectively.[39] Medication errors should be identified and documented and their causes studied in order to develop systems that minimize recurrence.[3,4,7,10,11,14,16,22,40] Several error monitoring techniques exist (e.g., anonymous self-reports, incident reports, critical incident technique, and disguised observation technique) and may be applied as appropriate to determine the rates of errors.[9,40,41] There are differences in the validity of data obtained by the various error monitoring techniques or combined techniques. Program managers should determine the best method for use in their organizations in consideration of utility, feasibility, and cost. Monitoring programs for medication errors should consider the following risk factors[6,10,11,22,40,41]:

1. Work shift (higher error rates typically occur during the day shift).
2. Inexperienced and inadequately trained staff.
3. Medical service (e.g., special needs for certain patient populations, including geriatrics, pediatrics, and oncology).
4. Increased number or quantity of medications per patient.
5. Environmental factors (lighting, noise, and frequent interruptions).
6. Staff workload and fatigue.
7. Poor communication among health-care providers.
8. Dosage form (e.g., injectable drugs are associated with more serious errors).
9. Type of distribution system (unit dose distribution is preferred; floor stock should be minimized).
10. Improper drug storage.
11. Extent of measurements or calculations required.
12. Confusing drug product nomenclature, packaging, or labeling.
13. Drug category (e.g., antimicrobials).
14. Poor handwriting.
15. Verbal (orally communicated) orders.
16. Lack of effective policies and procedures.
17. Poorly functioning oversight committees.

Managing Medication Errors. Medication errors result from problematic processes, but the outcomes of medication errors could range from minimal (or no) patient risk to life-threatening risk. Classification of the potential seriousness and clinical significance of detected medication errors should be based on predefined criteria established by the P&T committee (or its equivalent). The error classification should be based on the original order, standard medication dispensing and administration procedures, dosage forms available, acceptable deviation ranges, potential for adverse consequences and patient harm, and other factors.[6,32,41]

Classification of medication errors should allow for better management of followup activities upon medication error detection. A simple classification of medication errors is the following: (1) clinically significant (includes potentially fatal or severe, potentially serious, and potentially significant errors) or (2) minor.[7,33] Hartwig, Denger, and Schneider defined seven medication error severity levels, as follows[41]:

Level 0—Nonmedication error occurred (potential errors would be classified here).
Level 1—An error occurred that did not result in patient harm.
Level 2—An error occurred that resulted in the need for increased patient monitoring but no change in vital signs and no patient harm.
Level 3—An error occurred that resulted in the need for

increased patient monitoring with a change in vital signs but no ultimate patient harm, or any error that resulted in the need for increased laboratory monitoring.

Level 4—An error occurred that resulted in the need for treatment with another drug or an increased length of stay or that affected patient participation in an investigational drug study.[a]

Level 5—An error occurred that resulted in permanent patient harm.

Level 6—An error occurred that resulted in patient death.

Medication error classifications could also be based on probability and severity scales analogous to those used in ADR reporting programs.[42,43]

Determination of the causes of medication errors should be coupled with assessment of the severity of the error. While quality management processes should include programs to decrease the incidence of all medication errors, effort should be concentrated on eliminating the causes of errors associated with greater levels of severity. There should be established mechanisms for tracking drugs or drug classes that are involved in medication errors. Correlations between errors and the method of drug distribution should also be reviewed (e.g., unit dose, floor stock, or bulk medications; premixed or extemporaneously compounded products; and oral or injectable products). These processes will help identify system problems and stimulate changes to minimize the recurrence of errors.

Quality improvement programs should provide guidance for patient support, staff counseling and education, and risk management processes when a medication error is detected. Incident reporting policies and procedures and appropriate counseling, education, and intervention programs should be established in all hospitals. Risk management processes for medication errors should include pharmacists, physicians, and nurses, in addition to risk management specialists, legal counsel, and others as appropriate. The following actions are recommended upon error detection[3,7,10,11,16,17,27,43]:

1. Any necessary corrective and supportive therapy should be provided to the patient.

2. The error should be documented and reported immediately after discovery, in accordance with written procedures. For clinically significant errors, an immediate oral notice should be provided to physicians, nurses, and pharmacy managers. A written medication error report should follow promptly.

3. For clinically significant errors, fact gathering and investigation should be initiated immediately. Facts that should be determined and documented include what happened, where the incident occurred, why the incident occurred, how the incident occurred, and who was involved. Appropriate product evidence (e.g., packaging and labeling) should be retrieved and retained for future reference until causative factors are eliminated or resolved.

4. Reports of clinically significant errors and the associated corrective activities should be reviewed by the supervisor and department head of the area(s) involved, the appropriate organizational administrator, the organizational safety committee (or its equivalent), and legal counsel (as appropriate).

5. When appropriate, the supervisor and the staff members who were involved in the error should confer on

how the error occurred and how its recurrence can be prevented. Medication errors often result from problems in systems rather than exclusively from staff performance or environmental factors[2,3,44]; thus, error reports should not be used for punitive purposes but to achieve correction or change.

6. Information gained from medication error reports and other means that demonstrates continued failure of individual professionals to avoid preventable medication errors should serve as an effective management and educational tool in staff development or, if necessary, modification of job functions or staff disciplinary action.

7. Supervisors, department managers, and appropriate committees should periodically review error reports and determine causes of errors and develop actions to prevent their recurrence (e.g., conduct organizational staff education, alter staff levels, revise policies and procedures, or change facilities, equipment, or supplies).

8. Medication errors should be reported to a national monitoring program so that the shared experiences of pharmacists, nurses, physicians, and patients can contribute to improved patient safety and to the development of valuable educational services for the prevention of future errors. Reports of medication errors can be made by telephone to the United States Pharmacopeial Convention, Inc. (USP) Medication Errors Reporting Program (1-800-23ERROR). Reports can be submitted to USP on a confidential basis if the reporter so chooses. Other reporting programs may also be in existence or under development. Reporting programs are intended to track trends and inform practitioners, regulators, and the pharmaceutical industry of potential product and system hazards that have a documented association with medication errors.

References

1. Hepler CD, Strand LM. Opportunities and responsibilities in pharmaceutical care. *Am J Hosp Pharm.* 1990; 47:533–43.

2. Manasse HR Jr. Medication use in an imperfect world: drug misadventuring as an issue of public policy, part 1. *Am J Hosp Pharm.* 1989; 46:929–44.

3. Davis NM, Cohen MR. Medication errors: causes and prevention. Huntingdon Valley, PA: Neil M. Davis Associates; 1981.

4. Zellmer WA. Preventing medication errors. *Am J Hosp Pharm.* 1990; 47:1755–6. Editorial.

5. Zellmer WA. ASHP plans for the future. *Am J Hosp Pharm.* 1986; 43:1921. Editorial.

6. American Society of Hospital Pharmacists. ASHP statement on the pharmacist's responsibility for distribution and control of drugs. *Am J Hosp Pharm.* 1991; 48:1782.

7. Lesar RS, Briceland LL, Delcoure K, et al. Medication prescribing errors in a teaching hospital. *JAMA.* 1990; 263:2329–34.

8. American Society of Hospital Pharmacists. ASHP technical assistance bulletin on hospital drug distribution and control. *Am J Hosp Pharm.* 1980; 37:1097–103.

9. Allan EL, Barker KN. Fundamentals of medication error research. *Am J Hosp Pharm.* 1990; 47:555–71.

10. Betz RP, Levy HB. An interdisciplinary method of

classifying and monitoring medication errors. *Am J Hosp Pharm.* 1985; 42:1724–32.

11. Leape LL, Brennan TA, Laird N, et al. The nature of adverse events in hospitalized patients—results of the Harvard medical practice study II. *N Engl J Med.* 1991; 324:377–84.

12. Ingrim NB, Hokanson JA, Guernsey BG, et al. Physician noncompliance with prescription-writing requirements. *Am J Hosp Pharm.* 1983; 40:414–7.

13. Anderson RD. The physician's contribution to hospital medication errors. *Am J Hosp Pharm.* 1971; 28:18–25.

14. Cooper JW. Consulting to long-term care patients. In: Brown TR, Smith MC, eds. Handbook of institutional pharmacy practice. 2nd ed. Baltimore, MD: Williams & Wilkins; 1986:649–61.

15. Bedell SE, Dertz DC, Leeman D, et al. Incidence and characteristics of preventable iatrogenic cardiac arrest. *JAMA.* 1991; 265:2815–20.

16. Fuqua RA, Stevens KR. What we know about medication errors: a literature review. *J Nurs Qual Assur.* 1988; 3:1–17.

17. Intravenous Nurses Society. Intravenous nursing standards of practice. *J Intraven Nurs.* 1990; 13(Apr):Suppl.

18. American Society of Hospital Pharmacists. ASHP statement on the pharmacist's clinical role in organized health care settings. *Am J Hosp Pharm.* 1989; 46:2345–6.

19. American Society of Hospital Pharmacists. ASHP guidelines on the pharmacist's role in drug-use evaluation. *Am J Hosp Pharm.* 1988; 45:385–6.

20. American Society of Hospital Pharmacists. ASHP guidelines: minimum standard for pharmacies in institutions. *Am J Hosp Pharm.* 1985; 42:372–5.

21. American Society of Hospital Pharmacists. ASHP guidelines for obtaining authorization for documenting pharmaceutical care in patient medical records. *Am J Hosp Pharm.* 1989; 46:338–9.

22. Barker KN, Pearson RE. Medication distribution systems. In: Brown TR, Smith MC, eds. Handbook of institutional pharmacy practice. 2nd ed. Baltimore, MD: Williams & Wilkins; 1986:325–51.

23. Cohen MR, Davis NM. Assuring safe use of parenteral dosage forms in hospitals. *Hosp Pharm.* 1990; 25:913–5. Editorial.

24. American Society of Hospital Pharmacists. ASHP statement on the pharmacy and therapeutics committee. *Am J Hosp Pharm.* 1992; 49:2008–9.

25. Barker KN, Pearson RE, Hepler CD, et al. Effect of an automated bedside dispensing machine on medication errors. *Am J Hosp Pharm.* 1984; 41:1352–8.

26. American Society of Hospital Pharmacists. ASHP guidelines for selecting pharmaceutical manufacturers and suppliers. *Am J Hosp Pharm.* 1991; 48:523–4.

27. Joint Commission on Accreditation of Healthcare Organizations. 1992 Accreditation manual for hospitals, vol. 1: standards. Oakbrook Terrace, IL: Joint Commission on Accreditation of Healthcare Organizations; 1991.

28. American Society of Hospital Pharmacists. ASHP guidelines on pharmacist-conducted patient counseling. *Am J Hosp Pharm.* 1984; 41:331.

29. American Society of Hospital Pharmacists. ASHP statement on unit dose drug distribution. *Am J Hosp Pharm.* 1989; 46:2346.

30. Brennan TA, Leape LL, Laird NM, et al. Incidence of adverse events and negligence in hospitalized patients—results of the Harvard medical practice study I. *N Engl J Med.* 1991; 324:370–6.

31. American Society of Hospital Pharmacists. Medication errors: a closer look (videocassette). Bethesda, MD: American Society of Hospital Pharmacists; 1988. 20 min.

32. Folli HL, Poole RL, Benitz WE, et al. Medication error prevention by clinical pharmacists in two children's hospitals. *Pediatrics.* 1987; 19:718–22.

33. Blum KV, Abel SA, Urbanski CJ, et al. Medication error prevention by pharmacists. *Am J Hosp Pharm.* 1988; 45:1902–3.

34. American Society of Hospital Pharmacists and American Nurses Association. ASHP and ANA guidelines for collaboration of pharmacists and nurses in institutional care settings. *Am J Hosp Pharm.* 1980; 37:253–4.

35. Derewicz HJ. Color-coded packaging and medication errors. *Am J Hosp Pharm.* 1978; 35:1344–6. Letter.

36. Myers CE. Color-coding of drug product labels and packages. *Am J Hosp Pharm.* 1988; 45:1660.

37. Clifton GD, Record KE. Color coding of multisource products should be standardized or eliminated. *Am J Hosp Pharm.* 1988; 45:1066. Letter.

38. Proceedings of the 41st annual session of the ASHP House of Delegates. Report of the House of Delegates. *Am J Hosp Pharm.* 1990; 47:1807–17.

39. Barker KN, McConnell WE. The problems of detecting medication errors in hospitals. *Am J Hosp Pharm.* 1962; 19:361–9.

40. McClure ML. Human error—a professional dilemma. *J Prof Nurs.* 1991; 7:207.

41. Hartwig SC, Denger SD, Schneider PJ. A severity-indexed, incident-report based medication-error reporting program. *Am J Hosp Pharm.* 1991; 48:2611–6.

42. Maliekal J, Thornton J. A description of a successful computerized adverse drug reaction tracking program. *Hosp Formul.* 1990; 25:436–42.

43. Miwa LJ, Fandall RJ. Adverse drug reaction program using pharmacist and nurse monitors. *Hosp Formul.* 1986:1140–6.

44. Anderson ER Jr. Disciplinary action after a serious medication error. *Am J Hosp Pharm.* 1987; 44:2690, 2692.

---

[a]The mention of investigational drugs in the definition of level 4 errors (and nowhere else in the levels) may lead some to believe that any error involving an investigational drug should automatically be classified as a level 4 error. However, in discussing this issue at its September 1992 meeting, the ASHP Council on Professional Affairs noted that it is the effect on the patient (for a medication of any type) that really should determine what level of error is involved.

Approved by the ASHP Board of Directors, June 23, 1993, reaffirming the version approved November 18, 1992. Developed by the ASHP Council on Professional Affairs.

The bibliographic citation for this document is as follows: American Society of Hospital Pharmacists. ASHP guidelines on preventing medication errors in hospitals. *Am J Hosp Pharm.* 1993; 50:305–14.

ASHP Guidelines on Preventing Medication Errors with Antineoplastic Agents

Purpose

The purpose of these guidelines is to assist practitioners in improving their antineoplastic medication-use system and error-prevention programs. They supplement ASHP's Guidelines on Preventing Medication Errors in Hospitals and address error prevention within diverse health care settings.[1] Further, these guidelines provide updated general guidance to include a standard definition of a "medication error" and applicable aspects of recommendations from the National Coordinating Council on Medication Error Reporting and Prevention (NCCMERP).

NCCMERP's definition of a medication error is "any preventable event that may cause or lead to inappropriate medication use or patient harm while the medication is in the control of the health care provider, patient, or consumer. Such events may be related to professional practice, health care products, procedures, and systems, including prescribing; order communication; product labeling, packaging, and nomenclature; compounding; dispensing; distribution; administration; education; monitoring; and use."[2]

Comprehensive recommendations are provided in these guidelines for preventing errors with antineoplastic agents in health care organizations, with an emphasis on hospitals and ambulatory care clinics that offer direct pharmacy services. Nevertheless, it is strongly recommended that the guidance also be adopted by other settings, including physician office practices and home care. The recommendations cover known procedural, technical, and behavioral elements that could systematically reduce a health care organization's vulnerabilities to errors. However, strict adherence to good practice recommendations is not sufficient. Since the complexities of antineoplastic therapy afford unlimited opportunities for system failures, continuous diligence to verify accuracy is critical by all persons responsible for medication-use functions.

These guidelines focus on the medication-use responsibilities shared by and unique to specific professional health care disciplines, progressing from general to specific applications. The structure of the guidelines, by necessity, includes the repetition of some material, repeated and enhanced in specific sections and recommendations for different health care disciplines.

The guidelines contain the following major sections:

1. Recommendations for health care organizations,
2. Recommendations for multidisciplinary monitoring of medication use and verification,
3. Recommendations for prescribing systems and prescribers,
4. Recommendations for medication preparation and dispensing systems and roles for pharmacists,
5. Recommendations for medication administration systems and roles for nurses,
6. Recommendations for patients,
7. Recommendations for manufacturers and regulatory agencies, and
8. Managing medication errors.

Because of the complexity of and differences in practice settings and organizational arrangements, aspects of these guidelines may be more applicable to some practice settings than others. Pharmacists, physicians, nurses, and other health care providers should use their professional judgment in assessing and adapting the guidance to their own setting. These guidelines address a specific aspect of the medication-use process and should be augmented as appropriate by other ASHP practice statements and guidelines.

Background

The prevalence of medication errors associated with antineoplastic agents, as with other drug categories, is not precisely known, but it may be surmised that incorrect use of antineoplastic agents consistently produces serious adverse effects in patients. Antineoplastics are drug products that cause serious toxicities at FDA-approved dosages and with FDA-approved administration schedules. Extra precautions are therefore necessary to prevent antineoplastic-related medication errors. Advocates for safe medication use and oncology pharmacy specialists have recommended that health care organizations improve their medication-use systems specifically to prevent medication errors with antineoplastics.[3–6] Antineoplastic-related medication-error prevention has become a priority, especially in hospitals. However, many antineoplastic therapies are also administered outside the inpatient setting. An increasing number of patients receive treatment for cancer in ambulatory care settings. Thus, error-prevention strategies should be applicable to the diverse settings in which antineoplastic agents are used.

Recommendations for Health Care Organizations

Optimal and comprehensive patient care, especially for patients receiving antineoplastic agents, requires the participation of multiple health care disciplines. Systems are necessary to coordinate the functions throughout the medication-use process of prescribing, preparing, dispensing, and administering drugs, and to educate and counsel patients.

Health care organizations in which multiple disciplines are represented should establish committees with representatives from each discipline to develop policies and procedures for the medication-use process and to oversee its operation. These should include educational and competency requirements for persons with medication-use responsibilities, general system requirements that minimize vulnerabilities to errors, and periodic auditing of physicians', pharmacists', and nurses' proficiency with the system. Further, near misses and errors should be analyzed, and problems in the procedures that place patients and staff at risk should be resolved.

Education, Competency, and Credentialing. All practice settings should establish policies and procedures ensuring that health care providers who prescribe, prepare, dispense, and administer antineoplastic medications and monitor patients receiving those medications are competent to perform those functions. For pharmacists and nurses, specific education and experience or board certification in a practice specialty may be included in the credentialing process.

Employers should evaluate prospective employees' training and previous practice experiences for knowledge and mastery of the skills that are essential prerequisites for the new position. Prerequisites for employment should include discipline-appropriate training in how to safely handle antineoplastic drug products. Deficiencies in applicants' training and experience must be identified and remedied before new employees assume patient care responsibilities. Training for new and current employees should emphasize collaboration among health care providers to ensure optimal patient care and outcomes and worker safety.

All health care providers who prescribe, prepare, dispense, and administer antineoplastic medications and monitor patients receiving those medications should be oriented in their practice setting before commencing patient care responsibilities. Orientation should introduce to new employees all of the departments, service providers, and functions that affect patient care. Each provider's roles and responsibilities should be identified, and it should be clarified how health care providers from different disciplines are expected to interact.

Further, health care organizations should require that all personnel who prescribe, prepare, dispense, administer, and handle hazardous drugs and materials that are contaminated with hazardous drugs and that all persons who may be exposed to hazardous-drug-contaminated materials during their job performance complete job-appropriate training and evaluation. They should demonstrate competence, knowledge, and proficiency in techniques and procedures for safely handling (preventing exposure to oneself, other persons, and the environment, and managing accidental exposure) hazardous drugs. Those competencies should be reassessed annually or more frequently if performance problems occur. It is the responsibility of medication-use system administrators and supervisory personnel to know the current government restrictions that limit or prohibit some health care providers from preparing and administering antineoplastic medications.

Health care providers who participate in an antineoplastic medication-use process and those who monitor patients receiving antineoplastics should be knowledgeable and have current information available about each of the following factors on the antineoplastic drug products used in their practice setting:

1. Names of antineoplastic drug formulations,
2. Indications and whether those indications comply with the FDA-approved labeling or are part of an investigational protocol,
3. Routes of administration,
4. Administration schedules,
5. Appropriate dosages and, when applicable, constraints for the maximum dose of medication that can be safely given during a single administration,
6. Appropriate handling conditions,
7. Potential adverse effects, and
8. Potential drug interactions.

Every practice setting where cancer patients receive antineoplastic therapy should provide opportunities for continuing professional and technical education related to antineo-

plastic drug use. A portion of the annual continuing-education programs for health care providers specializing in oncology should be related to antineoplastic agents and their uses.

Providers who use drug-delivery devices, such as i.v. pumps and infusion controllers, to administer antineoplastic medications should be required to demonstrate competencies related to the clinical application, function (general use, operational limits, alarms), and care of these devices; problems that may occur with the devices; and troubleshooting.

Communication and Access to Information. Many errors occurring in the medication-use process are caused or promulgated by inadequate patient-specific information. Patients' medical records should be organized and made readily accessible for use by all providers who prescribe, dispense, and administer antineoplastic medications to enable independent confirmation that all prerequisite criteria have been met before commencing antineoplastic treatment. In some cases, individual disciplines may keep additional patient records that supplement the patient's primary medical record. For example, it has historically been the responsibility of pharmacists and pharmacies to maintain patient-specific medication profiles, records of medications that were prescribed and dispensed for each patient.

Providers who practice at sites where pharmacists do not participate in patient care also should document and maintain medication profiles for their patients. Medication profiles for antineoplastic therapies should include at least the following information:

1. Patient's name and a unique identifying code or number,
2. A brief medical history that identifies a patient's cancer diagnosis,
3. Known drug-related adverse events, allergies, and medication-, nutrient-, and food-related sensitivities,
4. Vital statistics that may affect treatment intensity, particularly those needed to calculate medication doses, including height, weight, body surface area (BSA), age, sex, and pertinent laboratory values (e.g., serum creatinine, creatinine clearance, liver transaminases),
5. Data about all medications used by a patient, including the date the medications were prescribed if it differs from the date they were prepared and administered, the date the medications were prepared and dispensed if it differs from the date the medications were administered, drug identity, drug dosage, total drug dosage administered per unit interval (e.g., day, week, treatment cycle), administration route, administration schedule as a function of the treatment plan (e.g., every three hours; days 1, 8, and 15), rate of administration (when relevant), prescribed duration of use (e.g., number of doses to administer; number of treatment hours, days, or weeks), and the product manufacturer's identity and product lot numbers and expiration dates for drugs dispensed from that facility,
6. Additional ingredients and diluting agents and the amounts used in extemporaneously compounded medications,
7. Primary references that describe the treatment regimen, and
8. An up-to-date treatment history, including the treatment cycle or course number for each treatment repetition, the dates on which a patient last received treatment, how previous treatment was tolerated, and the

cumulative amount of drug previously administered for medications with established absolute cumulative dosage limits (e.g., anthracyclines, bleomycin) or constraints against repeated administration as a function of time.

Ambulatory care, home care, and managed care organizations are vulnerable to the same communication and interpretation errors that occur in hospitals. These settings and organizational arrangements, however, introduce additional opportunities for errors of omission and duplication when treatments and other services are provided at multiple locations and by more than one participating provider or group of providers. In hospitals and integrated health systems, patient-specific medical information has traditionally been communicated through a single comprehensive medical record. In contrast, providers in private practice, home care, and managed care organizations generally cannot rely on the availability of a comprehensive medical record, because medication prescribing, preparing, and administering may occur at geographically separate facilities.

Local policies should be developed to ensure that orders for a patient's antineoplastic medications are transmitted accurately and completely, simultaneously protecting patient confidentiality. Electronic means of communication are recommended to transmit up-to-date, accurate, and comprehensive patient-specific medical information among providers. Thus, data entered into this electronic system by any one provider are immediately available to all. Until a single unifying network becomes available for all health care providers, portable printed and electronic records that ensure patient safety and confidentiality must be devised.

Schedule Coordination. Since oncology patients often receive care from more than one health care provider, their primary provider should coordinate patient care with other providers and facilities. Efficient organizational systems should have someone to coordinate a patient's health care needs with the providers' schedules. Administrative coordinators are an interface between a patient's primary provider and other providers and services. They plan and document scheduling for patients' treatments, laboratory tests, follow-up visits, consultations, supportive care, and assistance from home health care contractors, hospice facilities, and social services.

Standardize Medication Ordering. To the extent possible, medication prescribing, preparation, dispensing, and administration should be standardized. Patient care facilities should develop and use standardized preprinted medication-order forms or forms that are retrievable from a computerized database for requesting frequently used antineoplastic treatments and treatment-related services. Well-designed standardized medication-order forms decrease potential errors by organizing treatment information in a clear, consistent, and uniform format.

Standardized forms should be developed collaboratively with all local health care providers who prescribe, prepare, and administer antineoplastic medications. Forms should be preprinted with treatment-specific information, such as generic drug names, specifications for drug dosage and dosage modifications as a function of patient-specific variables, and administration routes and schedules. They should also include space for prescribers to note laboratory test results that affect dosages, administration rates, and

treatment duration. These forms may also permit prescribers to schedule laboratory tests and request other services for comprehensive patient care.

Standardized medication-order forms simplify and expedite ordering medications by requiring prescribers to supply only patient-specific information, such as

1. Patient's name and unique identifying code or number,
2. Date the order was generated,
3. Time and date treatments are to be administered,
4. Patient-specific laboratory values (e.g., height, body weight, BSA, pertinent laboratory values) from which dosages and administration rates are calculated,
5. Planned medication dosages and administration rates as a function of patient-specific factors and the calculated doses and rates to be administered,
6. Patient's allergies and medication and nutrient sensitivities,
7. Prescriber's name and signature, and
8. Prescriber's telephone, pager, or fax number (or another means to communicate with the prescriber).

Preprinted forms should specify, by protocol number or publication reference, the treatment that is to be administered.[3,7]

For investigational antineoplastic treatments, standardized forms should also include the study name and protocol number. Color-coded forms, for example, may be used to designate different types of treatment, such as commercially marketed antineoplastic and investigational medications.

Standardized order forms eliminate many of the problems related to misinterpreting medication orders that are commonly associated with nonstandardized orders; however, health care providers must be aware that interpretation errors may still result from illegible handwriting. Multipurpose preprinted forms that list antineoplastic medications alphabetically may also contribute to prescribing errors when two similar drug names appear in close proximity. Since lined paper can obscure the details of a prescriber's orders, preprinted forms should be printed on unlined paper.

Self-replicating forms (e.g., carbon copies, no-carbon-required paper) can produce copies that are difficult to read. Providers who prepare and administer medications on the basis of a copy of a prescriber's order should be wary of ambiguous notations, artifact markings, and omissions on the copy. Each facility should restrict antineoplastic ordering (e.g., access to medication-order forms) to providers with the appropriate clinical privileges. Health care organizations that depend on standardized forms must also ensure that only the most current versions of standardized forms are available and that obsolete forms are recalled and destroyed.

Computerized Prescriber Order Entry. Computerized prescriber order-entry (CPOE) systems provide many of the same safety and convenience features as preprinted order forms with several important advantages, including an efficient means for simultaneously disseminating orders to various providers. CPOE simplifies prescribing and eliminates the potential for introducing errors into a medication-use system when intermediaries are required to accurately interpret and transcribe orders into a manual database.

CPOE can also provide online information about drug dosages and administration schedules, both of which can be updated from a central location. Computer software can also provide additional safety and convenience features, such as automated scheduling of multiple-day treatments, repeated treatment cycles, and laboratory tests and automated calculation of mathematically derived patient-specific data (e.g., BSA, lean body weight, drug dosages). In addition, software can decrease the likelihood of errors by incorporating features that detect drug dosages and administration schedules greater than and less than predetermined limits and by alerting system users when potentially interacting medications are prescribed.[8]

Safeguards are also required for CPOE systems. Access privileges should be limited to authorized health care providers. The system should electronically record when users enter, change, and discontinue orders. Providers should review and verify orders before treatment is started.

Oral Orders for Antineoplastic Medications. Except for discontinuing treatment, medication-use systems should not permit health care providers to transmit or accept orders to commence or modify antineoplastic medication that are communicated orally.[3,4,9] Oral orders for medications, spoken face-to-face or by telephone, circumvent an essential checkpoint in the order-verification process, whether they are communicated directly to persons who prepare medications or received and reported by one or more intermediaries.[10]

Stat Orders for Antineoplastic Medications. It is rarely necessary to begin antineoplastic treatment as quickly as possible. In general, Stat orders for antineoplastic medications potentially compromise essential order-verification safeguards and are almost never appropriate. Except for urgently required treatments, antineoplastic medication preparation and administration should be scheduled when staffing is adequate to ensure that appropriate safety checks are performed and to implement treatment. It is essential that patient care is not compromised under any circumstances. Persons who design medication-use systems are challenged to incorporate antineoplastic medication-order-verification systems that cannot be circumvented and do not introduce unnecessary delays in processing the orders.

Standardize Dosage Calculation. Medication-use systems should establish whether drug dosages should be routinely calculated as a function of actual or ideal (lean) body weight and develop standardized criteria that direct dosage calculation as a function of this weight. Treatment plans and medication orders should indicate whether patients' actual or ideal body weight was used in calculating drug dosages and identify the equation from which dosages were calculated.

Methods should be standardized for calculating BSA and ideal body weight, rounding calculated results (e.g., drug dosages and administration rates), and changing dosages and administration rates in response to changes in patients' weight and stature. For dosage and administration rates calculated from pharmacokinetic data, the mathematical equations that describe how calculated values were derived should appear in the treatment plans and medication orders.

Standardize Medication Orders. Standards should be established for the content of an acceptable medication order, requirements for patient-specific measurements, and data that must be included on medication-order forms.[11,12] The following standards are recommended:

1. All orders for patient care services should be clearly dated;

2. When ordering antineoplastic medications, the generic drug name should be used; use generic drug names approved by the United States Adopted Names (USAN) program. Brand names are not acceptable unless they aid in identifying combination drug products or a particular drug formulation (e.g., to distinguish between liposomal and nonliposomal product formulations);

3. Specify the dosage form;

4. Orders for medications should include the patient-specific data from which drug doses are calculated (height, weight, BSA, laboratory test results). When drug dosages and schedules are modified for current or anticipated pathologies, treatment plans and medication orders should explicitly identify the factors on which treatment modifications are based;

5. Drug dosages and calculated doses should be expressed in metric notation whenever possible. The word *units* should never be abbreviated in medication orders where drug dosages and administration rates are expressed in biological activity units (e.g., aldesleukin, asparaginase, bleomycin);

6. Medication orders should specify the drug dosage, calculated dose, and append the total cycle or course dosage;

7. Administration vehicle solutions and volumes should be specified, unless standard solutions and volumes have been established;

8. Specify the administration route;

9. Specify the administration rate;

10. Specify the administration schedule and the duration of treatment. Treatment plans and medication orders should specify the interval between repeated doses, the days on which each dose is to be given within a treatment cycle or course, and the total length of a treatment cycle or course;

11. Specify the dates and times when drug administration is to commence, or identify the temporal sequence in which each medication is to be administered. When 1200 is written as 12 a.m. or 12 p.m., it may be incorrectly interpreted. Directions indicating events for 1200 should be written as 12:00 noon, or 12:00 midnight, or expressed in the 24-hour system.

A medication order that complies with these recommendations would appear as follows for a patient with a BSA of 2 m^2: Azorhubarb injection 100 mg/m^2/dose = 200 mg in 100 mL 5% dextrose injection/dose, administer by continuous intravenous infusion over 24 hours, every 48 hours for three doses days 1, 3, and 5. Start at 8:00 a.m. on April 1, 2001 (total dose/cycle = 600 mg).

Although health care providers have traditionally used abbreviations, acronyms, and nicknames to describe antineoplastic medications and treatment regimens (e.g., ADR [doxorubicin], MTX [methotrexate], VBL [vinblastine], "platinum" [carboplatin or cisplatin], ICE [ifosfamide, carboplatin, and etoposide], MOPP [mechlorethamine, vincristine, procarbazine, and prednisone], ProMACE [prednisone, methotrexate, doxorubicin, cyclophosphamide, and epipodophyllotoxicin], and Cy-TBI [cyclophosphamide and total body irradiation]), the practice is potentially dangerous and should be avoided. Abbreviations for drug names, scheduling information, and directions for medication use should be prohibited in medication orders. Nonstandard abbreviations, Latin abbreviations, and apothecaries' weights and measures should not be used in orders for antineoplastic medications. Whenever possible, measurement units should be expressed in metric notation.

Establish Dosage Limits and Acceptable Routes of Administration. Medication-use systems should include utilization limits for antineoplastic medications. Constraints should be developed to limit maximum antineoplastic drug dosages and administration routes and schedules. Multidisciplinary peer review should be completed before established drug administration limits are exceeded.[3,4] These constraints should include the maximum amount of an antineoplastic drug that may be administered as a single dose, the maximum amount that may be administered during a defined time interval (including maximum administration rates for parenterally administered medications), and the routes by which each drug should be administered.

Constraints for dosage and administration rate may be defined by treatment regimens and protocols and may vary among protocols. In contrast, the types of treatments administered in some practice settings may be consistently similar, permitting the establishment of absolute maximum dose limits within that practice setting.

Limits should also be established for the maximum amount of an antineoplastic drug that may be administered during one treatment course or cycle and, when appropriate, the maximum amount of drug that may be administered to a single patient within his or her lifetime.[3] In addition, dosage limits should be established for antineoplastic medications used in specific combination regimens (defined for each drug) in which clinical toxicities may be exacerbated by combining agents with overlapping adverse-effect profiles.

Antineoplastic drug-use limits should appear prominently in printed treatment descriptions (e.g., protocol summaries, "care maps," schematic treatment diagrams) and on printed medication-order forms and computer-based medication-order templates. Computer software that alerts health care providers whenever an order for antineoplastic medications exceeds defined limits would be ideal.[13] For patients who receive antineoplastic medications for which cumulative dosage limits have been established, cumulative dosage data should be constantly updated in their permanent medical records and in any supplementary records. Patients' cumulative dosage data should be audited and independently confirmed by health care providers when verifying orders for antineoplastic medications.[3,14]

In each health care organization, the medication-use system should include a multidisciplinary committee that oversees matters related to medication-use limits. The committee should proactively develop and establish policies and procedures for resolving disagreements related to patient treatment among providers; whether medications should be prepared, dispensed, and administered if a discrepancy cannot be resolved; and how medication-use-related disputes are to be resolved. Committee membership should comprise all providers who have responsibilities in the medication-use process in the organization.[3]

Investigational Antineoplastic Medications. Cancer patients often receive investigational (i.e., experimental) anticancer treatments at facilities participating in clinical trials. Consideration must be given to ensure that the same safety precautions and checks that are used for FDA-approved antineoplastic therapies apply similarly to prescribing, preparing, dispensing, and administering investigational medications and monitoring patients who receive those therapies.

Facility administrators should ensure that adequate staff is maintained to support an investigational drug program.[10] Ideally, nurses and pharmacists should be involved early in the process of developing clinical protocols involving the use of commercially marketed and investigational antineoplastic medications.[15] This helps to ensure that investigational medications are prepared and administered in accordance with local policies and procedures. Nurses and pharmacists should be voting members on regulatory and review committees that evaluate the scientific and ethical treatment of patients receiving antineoplastic medications and monitor investigational therapies (e.g., institutional review boards).[3]

Because a protocol governs and supplies the rules for drug use in clinical trials, an up-to-date copy of the study protocol should be available for review at all sites where medications are prepared and administered. All staff should be informed through inservice education programs before new protocols are implemented. Inservice programs and study-related information should be provided by persons associated with the investigational study (e.g., principal investigator, associate investigators, protocol chairperson, study-coordinating personnel). If an investigational protocol is to be conducted at more than one site within a health care system, procedures should be developed to ensure that up-to-date information is available at all study sites where patients receive protocol-directed care.

Procedures for supplying health care providers with information about patients' dose assignments, drug dosage, and schedule modifications should also be devised. A separate procedure should be established allowing independent dose-checking activity among all disciplines involved in the medication-use process for investigational drugs.

Recommendations for Multidisciplinary Monitoring of Medication Use and Verification

Independent medication-order verification is an essential safeguard that ensures the accuracy and appropriateness of medical treatment. It is imperative that health care providers resolve any questions related to medication orders before treatment commences. Providers should recognize that medication-order verification and other system safeguards ensure patients' safety.[3,7,14]

Lack of information about patients and their medications has been described as the most frequent cause of medication errors.[9,16] In order to independently verify prescribers' orders for medications, all persons who prepare and administer antineoplastic medications and those who monitor patients who have received antineoplastics should also have access to complete, up-to-date copies of treatment protocols and patient-specific data.[3,9,14] Drug information and reference materials should be readily available to all persons who provide patient care.

Each health care provider has a responsibility to share information with other providers and consultants to ensure patient safety and an optimal treatment outcome. Policies that regulate treatment verification standards should describe how prescribers, medically responsible and senior authorizing physicians, pharmacists and pharmacy technicians, persons responsible for administering medications, and other persons who are responsible for transcribing and transmitting medication orders should interact.

Providers who prescribe, prepare, dispense, and administer antineoplastic medications should perform as many independent manual checks as possible. Treatment-verification systems may incorporate computerized medication-order safety checks but should also include as many independent manual checks as possible.[3,10] Ideally, computerized systems are used to calculate and verify dosages and the rate and route of administration for antineoplastic drug orders and to screen medication orders for compliance with dosage limits. In addition to facilitating chemotherapy-order processing, computer software can also serve as a double check on prescribers' orders. Systems requiring pharmacists to transcribe prescribers' medication orders into a computerized or manual drug-ordering system should have a second pharmacist recheck all order-processing documents and product labeling before a drug product is dispensed.

Providing medications to patients includes four discreet steps: prescribing, preparation, dispensing, and administration. The ideal verification system has nine established checkpoints to ensure that an antineoplastic drug is accurately prescribed, prepared, dispensed, and administered to the patient for whom it was intended (Figure 1). Different individuals should complete each check so that no single person bears responsibility for checking his or her own work.

Prescribing antineoplastic medications (checkpoint 1). Health care providers who prescribe, prepare, and administer antineoplastic drugs should be familiar with the entire treatment regimen. A prescriber should complete as many orders as possible comprising a patient's antineoplastic treatment regimen and include orders for preparative and supportive care medications. This practice ensures that orders can be checked for completeness and accuracy and compliance with planned treatment.

When orders for antineoplastic drugs must be countersigned by a second medically responsible individual, the person who countersigns the medication orders should critically evaluate each order for an antineoplastic treatment. This is checkpoint 1. The orders should be compared with patient-specific data and verified against original reference sources that describe the treatment regimen (e.g., a published article, validated standard reference text, investigational protocol).

Preparing antineoplastic medications (checkpoints 2–4). Checkpoint 2 requires persons receiving a prescriber's order for antineoplastic medications to review the original written medication orders and independently verify them against published standards (e.g., product package labeling, reports published in professional journals, treatment protocols, standard reference textbooks).

Because erroneous information sometimes appears in published information, orders for noninvestigational antineoplastic medications should be verified against the primary reference in which the specific treatment was described (e.g., published reports, study protocols, meeting proceedings). If a primary reference is not available, the treatment regimen should be confirmed with a resource that previously had been validated as accurately describing the planned treatment (locally compiled handbooks, guides, and compendia) or at least two alternative publications, including reviews and reference textbooks.[3,12] Investigational drug doses and administration schedules must be verified against a study protocol that was approved by all relevant regulatory agencies and study sponsors (e.g., institutional review board, National Cancer Institute, FDA).

Although preprinted order forms preclude the necessity of repeatedly verifying drug names, dosages, routes, and schedules each time a preprinted form is used, all medication orders should be evaluated for completeness, compliance with the planned regimen, and, during repeated courses, deviations from previous treatments by following these requirements:

1. Measurements from which a patient's medication dosage and administration rate are calculated should be confirmed (e.g., height, weight, BSA);
2. The date a patient was last treated and the next planned treatment date should be compared to ensure that an appropriate interval has elapsed since treatment was last administered;
3. Patient-specific data (e.g., height, weight, BSA) should be remeasured and, when applicable, recalculated to determine whether changes from previous measurements indicate corresponding changes in dosage or administration rates;
4. Appropriate laboratory test and physical assessment values should be evaluated, and primary treatment references should be consulted to determine whether they are within acceptable ranges or if treatment modifications are indicated; and
5. A patient's allergy, drug sensitivity, and adverse drug effect histories and his or her current medication profile should be evaluated for potential drug interactions with planned antineoplastic treatment.

Orders prescribed by physicians-in-training and nonphysician health care providers with prescribing privileges (e.g., nurse practitioners, physician assistants)

Figure 1. Medication-order verification system. These nine established checkpoints ensure that an antineoplastic drug is accurately prescribed, prepared, dispensed, and administered to the patient for whom it was intended.

Prescribing
Order Generated ⟶ Order Authorization
(*If Required*) (Checkpoint 1)

Preparing
Order Evaluated (Checkpoint 2)
↓
Product Evaluated (Checkpoint 3)
↓
Worksheet Setup (Checkpoint 4)

Dispensing
Product Dispensed to Patient   Product Dispensed to Caregiver
Product Evaluated   Order Evaluated
with Patient (Checkpoint 5)   (Checkpoint 6)
                                                            ↓
                                                    Product Evaluated
                                                    (Checkpoint 7)

Administering
Patient Examines Product   Product Checked with Patient
and Labeled Instructions (Checkpoint 8)   (Checkpoint 9)

should be verified with at least one medically responsible person, other than the prescriber, who is knowledgeable about medical oncology. Verification includes confirming correct treatment before commencing the initial cycle, dosage and administration schedule modifications, and deviations from planned or expected treatment.

For patients who receive treatment in clinical studies in which more than one primary or ancillary treatments are prescribed (e.g., dose- and duration-escalating studies), treatment assignment and dosage and administration schedule modifications should be confirmed with at least one person directly associated with the clinical trial, other than the prescriber (e.g., the principal investigator, an associate investigator, research nurses or pharmacists, a study coordinator or chairperson). Consult with the prescriber when expected treatment modifications were not ordered or when nonstandard modifications were prescribed.

Instructions for diluents, drug administration sequence and duration, number of doses, and starting date and time should be checked. Review and confirm that appropriate ancillary and supportive medications that facilitate antineoplastic drug delivery and those required by protocol have been prescribed and are complete and accurate (e.g., premedications, hydration, cytoprotectant and "rescue" medications, antiemetics, hematopoietic growth factors). Discrepancies between prescribed medications and planned treatment should be brought to the prescriber's attention and resolved before medication preparation proceeds.

At checkpoint 3, after treatment orders have been verified, all work related to medication-order processing and preparation accuracy should be routinely documented in a standardized format. Drug preparation work sheets (sometimes referred to as work cards or admixture or compounding logs, sheets, and cards) identify the drug products prepared for each patient and the persons who prepared and checked the medications. Although layout and design may vary among work sheets, and data may be organized as a continuous log in which each drug product appears on separate consecutive lines or as a separate record for each patient, all work sheets should detail the techniques used in preparing the drug products. They should also identify special preparation and dispensing information, such as the indication of special product containers, requirements for filtration, the need for special diluents, intermediate dilution steps, and how and when administration sets should be attached to the drug product container. Order processing, drug preparation, and processing records should be confirmed by a second individual (preferably a pharmacist).[3,4] The calculations written on preparation work sheets should be independently verified by a second health care provider who did not prepare the work sheet. Independent verification should include checking the work sheet for completeness and accuracy of content, with particular attention given to special preparation instructions. A checklist identifying the necessary elements in a drug preparation work sheet may be helpful for this step (Figure 2).[3]

At checkpoint 4, drug products should be checked, after preparation, against both the preparation work sheet and the original order by an individual who was not involved in preparing the work sheet. Checklists may also be helpful for this step.[3]

Dispensing antineoplastic medications (checkpoint 5). Checkpoint 5 requires persons dispensing medications to patients or caregivers for outpatient use to verify a patient's identity when a medication is dispensed. Patients who self-

administer their medications or personal caregivers should visually examine the medication, confirm whether its appearance meets their expectations, and compare its instructions with information they received from their health care providers (e.g., a chemotherapy calendar).

Dispensing and administering antineoplastic medications (checkpoints 6–9). At checkpoint 6, before starting treatment, each antineoplastic medication should be checked against the prescriber's orders by at least two individuals who are trained and competent to administer antineoplastic medications. All dosage- and administration rate-related calculations should be independently confirmed. Health care providers should routinely confirm that the medication will be administered to the intended patient by comparing a patient's name and unique identifying code or number with medication labels (e.g., alpha–numeric characters or bar codes) and that a drug product's identity, ancillary components (e.g., additional medications, diluent, and vehicle solutions), route of administration, and schedule are correct.

At checkpoint 7, health care providers should examine the medication container and note whether the content's general appearance is what was expected. Many chemotherapeutic parenteral products have distinctive colors, and product coloration should be confirmed before administration.

At checkpoint 8, patients who self-administer their medications (or receive it from personal caregivers) should carefully read the container's label to confirm the product's identity and review its instructions for use each time they take a medication.

At checkpoint 9, patients should be encouraged to ask questions about their treatment before its administration and compare its appearance and medication label with information they received about the treatment.

In ambulatory care practice, it is common for patients to receive parenteral antineoplastic medications in a setting where a physician and a nurse complete all tasks related to prescribing, preparing, administering, and monitoring treatment without a pharmacist's participation. Under these circumstances, the two health care providers involved should check the other's work. Both providers should be involved in the entire process. The person preparing antineoplastic medications should work from written orders.

Recommendations for Prescribing Systems and Prescribers

Antineoplastic prescribing is complicated by numerous medical publications that report indications, dosages, and administration schedules inconsistent with FDA-approved product labeling. Antineoplastic treatments are frequently based on preliminary reports, meta-analyses, and promising, albeit anecdotal, information. Prescribers must exercise great care in correctly interpreting this information and clearly communicating orders for antineoplastic medications with other health care providers.

System administrators should weigh the merits of requiring orders for all antineoplastic medications and other high-risk drugs prescribed by physicians-in-training to be countersigned by a senior physician with expertise in the specialty to safeguard against errors in interpretation and prescribing.

Health care providers with privileges of prescribing antineoplastic drugs should complete an orientation of local policies and procedures related to prescribing antineoplastics

Figure 2. Antineoplastic drug preparation checklists.

Checklist for Initial Setup of Antineoplastic Drug Work Card

This form should be completed by the pharmacist checking the work card. Place check mark (or N/A) in each space after each check is completed. Your check marks and initials at the bottom of this work sheet are your personal assurance that you checked all these items for accuracy in the setup and transcription of information onto the work card. Each drug requires a separate checklist.

Patient _____ Drug _____

Start date _____

Administration time _____

Stop date _____

Duration _____

Correct drug name _____

Number of doses _____

Dose _____

Drug concentration _____

Drug volume _____

Diluent _____

Volume of diluent _____ Overfill _____ Drug in overfill ____

Expiration time _____

Special delivery devices (tubing, cassette, container, etc.) _____

Correct route of administration _____

Correct mixing instructions (special directions, e.g., "Do Not Filter") _____

Auxiliary label information (e.g., "Do Not Refrigerate," "Use In-line Filter," "For Intrathecal Use Only") _____

Correct total volume _____

Pharmacist's initials _____ Date _____

This record should remain with the work card for the duration of the order and be saved for the supervisor for review after discontinuation of the order.

Supervisor's initials _____ Date _____

Checklist for Preparing and Labeling Antineoplastic Drugs

For each order you check, verify that each element is correct with a check mark.

Patient _____ Drug _____

Date _____

Label check

Patient name is same as on front of work card _____

Drug name on label matches drug name written on back of work card _____

Dose on label matches dose written on back of work card _____

Diluent on label matches diluent written on back of work card _____

Volume of diluent on label matches volume of diluent on back of work card _____

Correct date to prepare _____

Expiration date and time _____

Correct time (expiration date not greater than administration time) _____

For each drug/additive

Correct drug used _____ Proper protocol supply ____

Drug concentration in each vial _____

Additives, such as sodium bicarbonate solution, for which large stock bottles are used (which remain in hood) are visually checked, lot number is verified, and technician is asked to verify volume used _____

Syringe plunger is pulled back to volume required for dose _____

Drug lot number on each vial matches lot number written on work card _____

Calculations are checked _____

Drug has not expired _____

For each diluent

Correct diluent _____ Volume of diluent _____

Diluent has not expired _____

Special instructions followed

Air purged from bag ____

Tubing affixed/primed to end of line _____

Diluent for reconstitution _____

Correct container _____ Proper overfill ___ Drug in overfill ___

Final miscellaneous steps

Chemotherapy work card checklist is in card pocket _____

Solution is inspected for impurities/floaters_____

Label is initialed (on left-hand side of label just below last additive or drug) **after** being affixed to correct admixture _____

Total volume to be infused _____ Red chemo i.v. seal _____

"Caution chemo" label _____ Other auxiliary labeling ____

Zip-lock bag _____

Work card is initialed _____

Pharmacist's initials _____ Date _____

Supervisor's initials _____ Date _____

---

before they are permitted to order them for patient care.

Health care providers should locally develop standardized dosage and administration schedule modifications for each antineoplastic medication. Treatment modifications may be appropriate for patients with the following characteristics: (1) preexisting pathologies and whose health may be compromised by treatment with particular antineoplastics (e.g., withholding or decreasing bleomycin dosages in patients with preexisting pulmonary dysfunction or cardiotoxic agents in patients with congestive heart failure), (2) a history of severe, prolonged, or cumulative adverse effects after previous antineoplastic treatments, (3) impaired physiological function that predisposes patients to altered pharmacodynamic responses (e.g., renal or hepatic impairment), and (4) low or decreased performance status.

Health care providers should also establish standardized guidelines for prescribing drugs that are routinely administered concomitantly with antineoplastic medications. Medication-use guidelines for supportive care and ancillary agents (e.g., antiemetics, hydration, chemoprotectants) should be made accessible to all health care providers who prescribe, prepare, and administer antineoplastic drugs and for persons who perform clinical monitoring.

When generating medication orders in a setting where preprinted ordering forms, CPOE, and other electronic and mechanical means (e.g., a typewriter) are not available, prescribers should legibly print the names of medications, dosages, routes of administration, and administration schedules in plain block letters and Arabic numerals. Unless it is considered inappropriate by the prescriber, handwritten medication orders should include the indications for which they are prescribed (e.g., for sore mouth, for nausea, for chronic lymphocytic leukemia).

When antineoplastic treatment (ordering, preparing, and administering) is coordinated at a single location, it is the prescriber's responsibility, or in the conduct of clinical trials, it is the principal investigator's responsibility, to provide information about the treatment (e.g., protocols, publication reprints) to those who prepare and administer medications and monitor patient outcomes. It remains the prescriber's responsibility to answer questions and provide information to other health care providers when treatment is implemented in a place that is geographically separate from the prescriber's location. Prescribers, clinical investigators, and medically responsible staff are strongly urged to provide to healthcare providers who prepare and administer antineoplastic medications a complete printed (or electronically reproduced) copy of the treatment regimen.

General Guidelines for Prescribing Antineoplastic Medications.[3,5,7,17] The following are general guidelines for prescribing antineoplastic drugs:

1. Instructions for medication regimens should be explicit, complete, clear, and easy to follow. Treatment regimens should be described accurately and consistently in all written and published materials in which antineoplastic medication use is described;
2. Medication-use systems should require health care providers to use standardized vocabulary and nomenclature for describing treatment with antineoplastic medications;
3. Use uniform and consistent notations to express quantifiable amounts (dosage, concentration, volume, and time);
4. Never trail a whole number with a decimal point followed by a zero (e.g., write "5 mg," not "5.0 mg");
5. When writing amounts less than one, the expression should be written with a leading zero, which precedes the decimal point (e.g., "0.125 mg");
6. In all treatment plans and medication orders, identify the dosage, the calculated dose, and, parenthetically, the total dosage (the amount of drug as a function of body weight, BSA, or other factors) that patients are to receive during a treatment cycle; and
7. When treatment day enumeration is arbitrary, day 1 typically describes the day treatment commences. In contrast, hematopoietic progenitor-cell transplantation regimens often include day 0, and significant treatment-related events both before and after a progenitor-cell graft is administered are distinguished by negative (minus) and positive (plus) prefixes, respectively.

Specific Recommendations for Parenterally Administered Medications.[7] Health care providers should adhere to the following guidelines for parenteral antineoplastic drugs:

1. In treatment plans and orders, doses should be expressed as the total amount of medication to be administered from a single container (i.e., the total amount of medication per syringe, bag, or other container);
2. For medication admixtures that can be prepared in more than one way, practitioners should institute a priori, standard, and consistent methods directing how each medication will be prepared and administered; and
3. For drug products with extended stability and when a medication is administered from a single container for more than 24 hours, a prescriber's order for treatment should specify the amount of medication to be administered during each 24-hour interval.[7] A drug order for a patient with a BSA of 2 m² should read: "Drug XYZ" (8 mg/m²/day × 3 days) 48 mg in 150 mL 0.9% sodium chloride injection by continuous intravenous infusion over 72 hours, days 1–3. Start on 04/01/2001 at 0800 (total dose/cycle = 48 mg).

Specific Recommendations for Orally Administered Medications.[7] Health care providers should adhere to the following guidelines when oral medications are the prescribed antineoplastic treatment:

1. In treatment plans and medication orders, describe drug doses and schedules as the amount of medication to be taken per dose, not as a total daily dose that is to be taken in divided doses;
2. In treatment plans, medication orders, and instructions to a patient, identify the number of doses to be administered or taken;
3. When doses for a solid orally administered dosage form are greater or less than available dose strengths, specify whether and how doses are to be rounded to the nearest capsule or tablet strength (e.g., Should tablet formulations be broken to deliver a calculated dose? Should high and low doses be administered on alternating days to deliver an average dose?);
4. Whenever possible, include instructions about how medications are to be taken with respect to food ingestion and whether particular types of food may affect medication activity; and
5. Explicitly identify essential ancillary medications and supportive care that should accompany an antineoplastic treatment regimen.

Recommendations for Medication Preparation and Dispensing Systems and Roles for Pharmacists

For each practice setting, persons representing the various health care disciplines that prescribe, prepare, and administer antineoplastic medications should participate in planning and managing local medication-use systems.

Standardize Medication Preparation Guidelines. Health care providers should establish standardized guidelines for reconstituting, diluting, admixing, packaging, and labeling commonly used antineoplastics and other medications that are routinely administered with antineoplastics. Each practice facility should also establish a standardized method for labeling multidose vials and reconstituted drug products. Standardized medication preparation guidelines should be prominently displayed (e.g., as a chart) for easy accessibility in areas where orders are processed and medications prepared.

Policies and procedures should be developed for situations in which medications are prepared at facilities that are geographically removed from where treatment is administered. Procedural protocols should describe requirements for medication packaging, storage conditions during transportation, duration of transport, and handling after delivery. Medication couriers should receive training in organizational policies for handling medications and should immediately report when conditions and handling practices deviate from procedural standards. In addition, handling procedures should ensure patient confidentiality and provide guidelines for emergency situations, such as hazardous-drug spills.

Persons who prepare and dispense antineoplastic medications should ensure timely drug delivery to patients and patient care areas after receiving written orders. If dispensing is delayed for any reason, health care providers awaiting the medications should be notified.[3]

Quality Assurance. In collaboration with health care providers who prescribe and administer medications, pharmacists and persons who prepare and dispense medications should take the initiative in developing and managing quality-assurance programs for their medication-use systems. These programs should preeminently include surveillance and reporting systems that track potential and actual medication errors and evaluate the proximal causes of errors among processes and systems and preventive measures.[3,18] The major advantage of multidisciplinary participation is that each discipline's perspectives and methods for conceptualizing system flaws and solutions can be incorporated in designing strategies for preventing medication errors. Confidential reporting is essential to the success of a medication-error surveillance and reporting system. Only by understanding what causes and contributes to errors can the number of errors be reduced. In designing a medication-error surveillance and reporting system, strategic emphasis should be placed on understanding why errors occur and not on blaming or censuring personnel.[19]

Orientation on Medication-Error Reduction. Pharmacy supervisors and managers should develop an orientation program about medication errors commonly associated with antineoplastic drugs to train pharmacy personnel who prepare and dispense antineoplastic medications. Pharmacists should develop ongoing interdisciplinary educational programs that focus awareness on potential medication errors with antineoplastic medications, strategies for preventing errors, and local and national medication-error reporting and evaluation systems for all practitioners who have direct patient contact.

Pharmacists should engage the support of medical and nursing administrators and supervisors to encourage their staff (particularly those in professional training programs) to complete antineoplastic medication-error awareness programs.[9] Educational programs should be discipline specific. Program content should include medication-error case scenarios and discussion about the effects that medication errors have on patients' quality of life and the health system.[3,10]

Standardize Drug Procurement and Storage. Pharmacists who select and procure drugs should strive to minimize or eliminate look-alike drug product containers and limit the availability of different vial sizes for parenteral medications whenever possible.[4] Frequent additions to the variety of available drug products and changes among alternative manufacturers' drug products can contribute to medication-use errors and should be avoided. When practicable, drug products with similar names and packaging should not be stored next to each other. Medication-use systems that involve a formulary should separate nonformulary products from those that are on the formulary. Health care providers should familiarize themselves with antineoplastic drugs that are not on their formulary before prescribing, preparing, and administering them.

Standardize Medication Preparation and Dispensing. Antineoplastic medications should be dispensed in ready-to-administer dosage forms whenever possible. Generally, antineoplastics for intermittent parenteral administration should be prepared so that each medication container has only one dose. The risk of incorrect medication use is increased when the amount of drug dispensed in a single container exceeds the amount to be administered during a 24-hour period. It is essential that individuals and committees responsible for developing and overseeing medication-use systems establish guidelines on whether prescribers may order antineoplastic preparations to be administered from a single container for more than 24 hours. In all practices where parenteral drugs with extended stability (more than 24 hours) are sanctioned, it is imperative that the duration of their use is clearly labeled and that health care providers are trained to correctly prescribe, prepare, and administer them.[7]

When preparing an antineoplastic admixture, a quantity of medication that most closely approximates the prescribed dose should be segregated from other drug supplies. For treatment regimens that include two or more drugs, especially when medications are to be administered by different routes, the medications should be physically segregated during preparation and when administered. Compounded medications should be prepared one at a time, using standardized techniques whenever possible. When measuring diluent solutions used to reconstitute medications and drugs to be added to a secondary container, a person other than the individual who measured the volume should visually confirm the measurement before the solutions are transferred from the measuring device to the secondary container. This may be accomplished by visual inspection or by weighing syringes, other transfer devices, and intermediate product containers before fluid transfer is completed. Alternatively, post hoc methods for checking medication preparation include "pulling back" syringe plungers and marking syringe barrels to demonstrate the volume of fluid that was injected into the secondary container. In any medication-checking system, the person who confirms the technical accuracy of the person who prepares the admixture should examine all containers used during preparation.

Antineoplastic agents are administered parenterally by many routes other than the intravenous route (e.g., intrathecally, intrahepatically, intrapleurally, intraarterially). Inadvertent administration by the wrong route (e.g., giving vincristine intrathecally) can result in serious or fatal consequences. Medication-use systems should include policies and procedures that distinguish medications administered by the intravenous route from those intended for administration by other routes.

Standardize Medication Labeling. Strict procedures should be established for standardizing medication labeling. A uniform, systematic labeling method should be used, especially when multiple drugs are prepared for a single patient.

Medication labels should be mechanically printed (not handwritten). Extemporaneously compounded antineoplastic medications should be labeled immediately after preparation. Oral medications should also be sealed with childproof or poisoning-prevention closures. Auxiliary labels may facilitate distinguishing among medications that are administered by particular delivery methods.

Labels for oral dosage forms, rectal suppositories, and topically applied unit-dose products should include all of the following information:

1. Patient's name and unique identifying code or number and patient's location within a treatment facility (when applicable),
2. Date (with or without specifying time) the medication was dispensed,
3. Generic drug name,
4. Dosage form and strength,
5. Amount of medication per dose (when the container dispensed holds more than one dose),
6. Administration route,
7. Detailed instructions to the patient for self-administering the medication,
8. Supplemental administration instructions, such as the starting and completion dates and times, number of doses to administer, cautionary information about when medications are to be taken in relation to food ingestion and other medications, and instructions and warnings regarding administration route, storage conditions, and container closures, and
9. The number of drug product units dispensed within each container (the number of tablets, capsules, or suppositories, packaged in a single container).

Labels for injectable dosage form containers should include all of the following information:

1. Patient's name and unique identifying code or number and patient's location within a treatment facility (when applicable);
2. Generic drug name;
3. The amount of medication per container and the amount of medication per dose when a product container holds more than one dose, as drug product containers may hold more medication than is intended for a single administration (e.g., multiple doses for intermittent administration). Identify how much overfill is added to a container when excess medication and fluid volumes are added to displace air from the tubing lumen ("dead space") in administration sets;
4. Route of administration; for example, medications prescribed for administration other than by the intravenous route—especially those for intrathecal administration—should bear ancillary labels that distinctively identify the intended administration route;
5. The name and either the amount or concentration of all drug additives in a drug product;
6. Diluent (vehicle fluid) name;
7. The volume of fluid to be administered. Volume to be administered should be specified, especially when it differs from the total volume within a medication container (i.e., when the product contains an amount of fluid in excess of the volume to be delivered);
8. Administration rate and duration. Ideally, both administration rate and duration should be specified. Because administration rates can be calculated from the volume to be administered and duration of administration, duration is the essential component;
9. Supplemental administration instructions, such as starting and completion dates and times, prohibitions about when medications are not to be administered in relation to other medications, instructions and warnings regarding administration route, handling, and storage conditions (e.g., information about special requirements for administration sets including inline filtration, warnings to avoid intrathecal administration with vinca alkaloid drugs, and hazardous-drug warning labels);
10. When it is necessary to prepare more than one medication intended for sequential administration, the container labels should be numbered. Indicate the sequence in which each container is to be used plus the total number of containers (e.g., bag 1 of 3, bottle 3 of 7);
11. Date (with or without specifying time) the medication was ordered or prepared. Investigational compounds, in particular, should be labeled with the date and time they were prepared;
12. Date (with or without specifying time) after which a medication should no longer be used (expiration information);
13. Cautionary warnings as required for hazardous-drug products;[20]
14. Storage specifications; and
15. The name (with or without specifying location or telephone number) of the institution, pharmacy, or practice from which a medication was dispensed and the prescriber's identity.

Credentialing Pharmacists for Antineoplastic Medication-Use Programs. Pharmacy managers and supervisors should require pharmacist employees to complete training and demonstrate competencies related to antineoplastic medication use, evaluating medication orders, preparing antineoplastic medications, safe handling procedures, error surveillance and reporting programs, and local policies as a prerequisite to pharmacist credentialing. Health care organizations should periodically reassess pharmacist employees' competencies related to their responsibilities, increasing the frequency of reassessment if performance problems occur.[6]

Roles for Pharmacists. Among primary health care providers, pharmacists generally are best positioned to ensure that medications are used rationally and safely and increase others' awareness about medication errors and how to prevent them. Pharmacists should participate in all aspects of patient care related to antineoplastic treatment, including developing rational policies for safe and appropriate medication use and other services consistent with pharmaceutical care.[3,9] Pharmacists should participate with other primary health care providers in multidisciplinary groups that develop, implement, and periodically reevaluate practice-specific procedures and processes for verifying antineoplastic medication orders, resolving procedural questions related to confirming and processing medication orders, and evaluating and resolving disputes among health care providers.

Each organization should establish a minimum acceptable level of pharmacist participation in the error-prevention elements of patient care, such as proactively reviewing medication orders, screening laboratory results, providing drug information and patient counseling, and reviewing drug storage conditions.[3,21]

The following areas are recommended for pharmacist participation:

1. Educate health care providers about medication errors,
2. Independently verify medication dosages, routes of administration, and schedules,
3. Participate in multidisciplinary efforts to establish drug-specific utilization constraints that limit maximum doses, administration rates, and administration schedules for antineoplastic medications,
4. Participate in multidisciplinary efforts to standardize the prescribing vocabulary,
5. Participate in multidisciplinary efforts to educate patients, their families, and personal caregivers,
6. Improve communication among health care providers and among health care providers, patients, and caregivers, and
7. Work with drug manufacturers.

Drug information resources and education for providers. Pharmacists should help ensure the availability of up-to-date references on the appropriate use of antineoplastic drugs for all health care providers involved in medication use.[3,10] Drug information resources should provide information about drug products' FDA-approved labeling and investigational uses. Information should be developed or selected, including drug-specific precautionary warnings and information about adverse effects, particularly dosage- and schedule-limiting effects; potential interactions with other drugs, disease states, and foods; administration methods, including drug admixture stability and compatibility data; usual adult and pediatric dosages; dosage recommendations for single- and multiple-treatment courses; treatment modifications for persons with concurrent pathologies or end-organ impairment; and pharmacokinetically based dosing and monitoring guidelines.

Pharmacists should develop and provide discipline-specific educational materials about antineoplastic medication use to health care providers who prescribe, prepare, and administer antineoplastic medications. The instructional tools developed for each professional health care discipline should complement the materials developed for the other disciplines.[3] Whenever new antineoplastics, treatment regimens, and treatment protocols are introduced into their practice setting, pharmacists should assume a continuous, proactive leadership role in developing educational programs and materials for health care providers, patients, and caregivers.[3,10]

For patients whose care is transferred from oncologists to nonspecialist practitioners, oncology pharmacy specialists should develop and provide drug monographs, medication-use summaries, and other treatment-related materials describing how antineoplastic medications and treatment regimens are to be accomplished.[4,9] The need is especially acute among organizations and practitioners who provide local care for patients enrolled in clinical trials or receiving investigational antineoplastic treatments.

Treatment protocols. Oncology pharmacy specialists should participate in developing treatment protocols for standard treatments and clinical investigations. In practice settings where antineoplastic agents and treatment regimens are used routinely, pharmacists should initiate the development of tools that standardize the way medications are ordered, thereby facilitating accurate and appropriate prescribing, order interpretation and verification, and medication

processing and dispensing.[10,22] Pharmacists should lead initiatives to standardize drug preparation procedures, including reconstitution, dilution, and drug admixture methods for commonly used parenteral antineoplastic medications.[4]

CPOE. When circumstances and resources permit, pharmacists should work with information systems personnel, computer programmers, and software vendors to develop CPOE systems. System requirements should include mechanisms for standardizing medication orders, decreasing opportunities for error by minimizing data entry, and screening orders for medication doses and administration schedules that exceed established limits. Pharmacists should advocate for and participate in establishing maximum safe antineoplastic dosage and scheduling limits with physicians, nurses, and other primary health care providers.

Vocabulary and nomenclature. Pharmacists are uniquely qualified to lead multidisciplinary efforts toward developing and implementing clear, detailed, standardized vocabulary and nomenclature for antineoplastic treatment regimens, medication orders, and administration instructions. Pharmacists should participate in the early stages of protocol development for standard treatments and clinical investigations to ensure that pharmacotherapeutic regimens are clearly described, easily understood, and incorporate standardized language, content, abbreviations, and units of measure.[3,7,9]

Patient education and counseling. When meeting or interviewing patients, their family members, or other home-based caregivers (e.g., completing medication-use and allergy histories, screening blood pressure, performing ongoing treatment response assessment, dispensing medications), pharmacists should provide medication education and counseling. They should verify that patients and their caregivers understand the following:

1. The purpose of the medication and its intended use,
2. The appropriate use and safe handling of medications and administration devices,
3. Appropriate temperature and safe storage conditions,
4. Special precautions to prevent exposure to hazardous materials that may be present in patients' clothing, linens, body fluids, and excreta during and after treatment,
5. The potential interactions with other medications and foods,
6. Common and possible adverse effects associated with the medication,
7. Methods for preventing and managing adverse effects, and
8. What to do if potentially serious adverse effects occur.[3,13]

Pharmacists should provide educational materials to patients and suggest supplemental and alternative information resources, such as the National Cancer Institute information services department (1-800-4-CANCER or 1-800-422-6237 and www.nci.nih.gov), the American Cancer Society, libraries, and bookstores.[3]

Advocates for patients' rights. Pharmacists should encourage patients and their caregivers to participate in their own care and advise patients how to protect themselves from medication errors. Pharmacists should advise patients that they are entitled to satisfactory answers from their health care providers. Pharmacists should encourage patients to double-check the details of their treatment, including drug names and dosages, and to request dosage recalculation if their biological measurements change. Pharmacists who participate in developing treatment plans and protocols should ensure that consent-for-treatment forms truly secure patients' informed consent. Pharmacists should help to prepare treatment consent forms; provide patients with an accurate and detailed description of their treatment plan in clear, unambiguous, and easily understood language and answers to their questions about the treatment and alternative treatment options; and assess patients' understanding of expected and possible outcomes. Pharmacists should also describe their role as primary care providers and the care they provide.[3,4]

Clinical intervention, analysis, and performance improvement. In addition to dispensing medications, pharmacists in various settings can provide a vital service toward improving the quality of patient care by implementing a proactive clinical intervention program and documenting health care providers' deviations from planned antineoplastic treatments. Longitudinal data collection, analysis, and reporting can reveal system flaws that failed to prevent or facilitated prescribing errors, suggest targets for quality improvement, and validate pharmacists' interventions.

Pharmacists should proactively work with other primary care providers to establish medication-use reporting and surveillance programs. Committees established for this purpose should comprise representatives from medical, nursing, pharmacy, and risk-management disciplines. Programs should continually evaluate local medication-use systems to identify potential problems and solutions related to medication use and prevent medication errors.[3,18] Such programs in institutions should seek endorsement from appropriate local multidisciplinary committees (e.g., pharmacy and therapeutics, medical executive, and clinical practice committees).

Feedback for pharmaceutical manufacturers and regulators. Pharmacists should work with pharmaceutical manufacturers and FDA to eliminate ambiguous, confusing, and potentially misleading drug product and treatment information from published resources (e.g., product packaging, package inserts, official compendia, and promotional information). Pharmacists working in the pharmaceutical manufacturing industry should proactively identify preventable causes of product-user errors and adverse effects associated with product labeling, packaging, and promotion.[23] Pharmacists' voluntary participation in national reporting programs can increase the awareness of medication errors and promote error prevention throughout the nation's health care system. These aggregate data promote changes in product identity, packaging, labeling, commercial information, and marketing practices that are subject to manufacturers' control and governmental regulation.[3,17]

Recommendations for Medication Administration Systems and Roles for Nurses

Nurses are often the last link in the chain of health care providers who provide treatment with antineoplastic medications. To safeguard patients from mistakes that have potentially lethal consequences, elaborate systems have evolved that include

- Requirements for credentialing persons who administer antineoplastic medications,
- Tools and methods to facilitate documentation and identification of correct medication use,

- Independent verification of medication orders,
- Accurate documentation of medication use and effects and patient care,
- Strict compliance with regulations and practice standards, and
- Patient education regarding medication safety.

Credentialing Nurses for Antineoplastic Medication-Use Programs. Nursing managers and supervisors should require nurse employees to complete training and demonstrate nursing care-related competencies, such as administering antineoplastic medications, caring for patients who have received antineoplastic medications, and knowing about local policies. Specialty certification is encouraged. Nurses may be required to complete additional training and competency assessments before they are permitted to administer experimental medications. Training usually combines didactic and supervised practical instruction. Didactic instruction generally includes training about specific antineoplastic agents, appropriate dosages and dosage ranges, adverse effects and clinical toxicities, administration techniques, and safe handling. Technical experience in administering antineoplastic medications commonly starts with role-playing exercises and practicing technical skills on nonhuman models and proceeds through clinical interactions under the supervision of an experienced mentor. Performance evaluations test trainees for satisfactory cognitive and motor competencies. Health care organizations should periodically (annually or more frequently if performance problems occur) reassess nurses' competencies related to their responsibilities.

Standardized Tools for Recording Medication Administration. Nurses with a variety of experiences have devised and contributed to designing tools to facilitate the prevention of drug administration errors, such as standardized work sheets used to calculate medication dosages and administration rates and checklists of pertinent laboratory results and physiological measurements. Treatment flow sheets provide easily interpretable information about when a patient's previous treatments were administered, whether dosages and medication delivery deviated from planned treatment, and the cumulative amount of medication administered. Thoughtfully designed treatment flow sheets may become part of a patient's permanent medical record and can be an invaluable resource for patient care.

Checking Orders and Equipment for Administering Antineoplastic Medications. Medication orders for antineoplastics are commonly checked by two nurses working independently. As has been discussed previously, double checks by two licensed health care providers help to ensure that medications are prescribed and administered appropriately. In addition, nurses should evaluate and confirm the functional integrity of vascular access devices (and devices for other administration routes), medication pumps, and other devices that control medication delivery. For adjustable and programmable mechanical and electronic devices, mechanical adjustments or electronic programming for delivering the correct dose at the appropriate rate should be verified with another health care provider who is knowledgeable about the delivery device before it is used to administer medications. Another individual who checks adjustments and programming should independently examine the adjustments made to the device and review the programming.

Recording and Tracking Antineoplastic Use. After medications have been administered, it is a nurse's responsibility to manually or electronically record the activity. The documentation should include the patient's name, the names of all medications administered, dosages, administration routes, rates of administration, the date and time administration began, the duration of administration or time that treatment was completed, and whether adverse effects were observed or reported by the patient during or after administration. Communications with patients, other health care providers, and personal caregivers should be documented in an objective, chronological narrative style, reporting the dates and times the events occurred, the names of involved persons, and how questions and problems were resolved.

Nurses and other personnel should immediately report to medically responsible personnel and their supervisors any instance in which medications were used incorrectly and the events attributable to the error. In response to discovering a medication-use error, a provider's primary responsibility is to ensure the patient's safety. Subsequently, the error and related circumstances should be recorded as is indicated by specific policies and procedures. Medication-use error reports (also called occurrence or incident reports) should be written in an objective, chronological, narrative style without editorial remarks and speculative comments. Comprehensive incident reports are useful in discovering and evaluating system flaws and may provide the impetus for improving medication-use systems.

To prevent medication errors, nurses and other personnel who administer antineoplastic medications must comply with policies and procedures that define standards of practice. It is important, however, to periodically reevaluate practice standards in order to assess how well a medication-use system functions, make appropriate changes, and, ultimately, improve patient safety and the quality of care.

Health care providers administering antineoplastic medications should not deviate from previously stated guidelines for ordering, preparing, and administering antineoplastic agents. Examples of inappropriate practice include borrowing medications from a patient's drug supply to give to another patient and preparing agents without the proper facilities or staff. Medication administration schedules should be followed as closely as possible; providers and caregivers should strive to comply with treatment plans. Drug administration should be documented promptly after it is completed, and providers administering antineoplastic medications should rigorously comply with local requirements for documenting treatment. To prevent the inadvertent duplication of treatment, it is recommended that one individual assumes the primary responsibility for each patient during a work period (shift or tour of duty).

Nurses and Patient Education. Nurses and other personnel who administer antineoplastic medications should encourage patients and their personal caregivers to ask questions about their treatment. Patient education guidelines may be included in treatment maps and clinical care plans.

Recommendations for Patient Education

Well-informed patients (and their authorized caregivers) are the vital last link in the safety chain to prevent errors related to antineoplastic medications. Patients are entitled to know all pertinent facts about the medications they receive during their treatment. Health care providers have an obligation to encourage patients to ask questions and to provide answers.

The following suggestions are offered to help patients and their caregivers ensure optimal outcomes from the cancer therapy medications.

Multifocal Medication Education. Patients need multifocal education about the purpose, adverse effects, schedules, routes of administration, and descriptions (e.g., colors, shapes) for all the medications they will receive during their treatment. This includes the primary antineoplastic regimen and all ancillary and supportive medications, such as anti-emetics and medications that hasten bone marrow recovery. When patients are well informed and the information they receive is reinforced by nurses, pharmacists, and other caregivers, they are better prepared to detect a misinterpreted medication order and assertively question conflicting information.[74] Health care professionals should be sensitive to the emotional aspects of patients with cancer when planning medication education. Education should take place at a time when a patient is able to listen and understand. Medication education should not be attempted when patients are sedated or confused as a result of medications or immediately after receiving their cancer diagnosis.

Patients should participate in their care by asking questions about their cancer treatment and related medications and by confirming the regimen with their nurse before receiving treatment. Health care providers should make educational materials available in counseling and treatment areas to encourage patients to learn more about their cancer therapies.

Health-System Procedures Education. Patients should understand the health system's plan for antineoplastic medication-error prevention. They should become familiar with their providers' routine procedures for checking medication orders so that they can understand the safeguards that have been established and why delays may occur before their treatment can be started. For example, patients can remind the person administering chemotherapy to compare medication labels with a patient's identity and can verify their height and weight each time they are measured.

Patient Participation in a Medication-Use System. Patients (or their caregivers) should be knowledgeable about their medications and the ways in which the medications are to be administered according to their treatment plan. In some circumstances, patients should be encouraged to take responsibility for some of their care to help improve their quality of life. Examples include self-administering medications, maintaining the patency of vascular access devices, giving themselves a subcutaneous injection, and troubleshooting a problem with the portable infusion pump. Patients should demonstrate their abilities to perform these functions if they are included in the therapy plan.

Patients should be given a detailed treatment calendar that identifies all of the medication events that are expected to occur throughout their treatment. Patients should be encouraged to keep their calendar with them to compare the expected treatment with what is being dispensed and administered.

Patients' Responsibilities. Patients should be taught to detect and to seek help in managing adverse effects that may occur during their cancer treatment. Patients should promptly inform their health care providers about adverse effects experienced during a chemotherapy cycle before the next cycle commences. Patients should keep a list of the medications that they self-administered to treat these adverse effects.

It is important for health care providers to be able to determine a potential for interactions between a patient's nonantineoplastic medications and the chemotherapy they are to receive. Therefore, patients should provide to their providers a list of all medications they are using, including over-the-counter preparations, natural products and dietary supplements, and other complementary and alternative medicines.

Recommendations for Manufacturers and Regulatory Agencies

Pharmaceutical manufacturers have a responsibility to exercise care in designing product packaging and labeling and in promoting their products, as these features may contribute to errors in prescription, product selection, preparation, and administration. Companies that market antineoplastic agents should develop and support educational programs that encourage safe and accurate prescribing, preparation, administration, and handling of their products. The following guidelines address some of the major areas.

Product Naming, Packaging, and Labeling. Companies should avoid trademarking drug names that look or sound similar to those of other drug products. Proprietary drug names for new products and product formulations should be dissimilar from other generic and proprietary names. Manufacturers should avoid appending letters and numbers to drug names as this practice can result in potential confusion with dosage strengths, medication quantities, and the amount of medication to be administered.

Product packaging and labeling should provide clear, easily distinguished features to identify a drug and the amount of drug per dosage unit (e.g., tablet, capsule, wafer) and within a product container (e.g., vials, bags, bottles, prefilled syringes). It is particularly important that a drug product's USAN-approved generic name appear more prominently than other information on the product label. Drug names should be printed on both the front and back of the containers and packaging of parenteral drugs; "TALL man" characters should be used to distinguish between similar drug names. Container labels for drugs that are in solution and for those that require reconstitution or dilution before they are used should identify the total drug content in mass units (or biological activity units) rather than concentration.[24] Product packaging and labeling that include both mass and concentration values should be designed to display mass units more prominently.

Labels should be unique and well designed. Distinguishing colors and contrasting hues facilitate identifying and distinguishing drug products and products in different strengths and concentrations. Warnings and special or unique instructions should be prominently displayed on product packaging and labeling. Unique labeling and packaging techniques should be used to prevent product misidentification and to warn about dosing errors and unique characteristics that predispose medication users to potentially serious or life-threatening toxicities. Examples include the unique way that the Platinol-AQ brand of cisplatin injection (Bristol-Myers Squibb, Princeton, NJ) is packaged to prevent misidentification with carboplatin and the cautionary statements on vials containing vincristine sulfate injection that warn against using the entire contents of a vial for a single patient (on bulk packages) and that intrathecal administration may be fatal.

A statement that declares a drug's approved routes of administration is optional and may or may not appear on product packaging. If the agent is approved for administration by only one route, it must be clearly indicated.

Appropriate storage temperatures or conditions should be clearly visible on drug labeling and packaging.

Drug labeling and packaging must identify the manufacturer's product lot or control number.

Drugs that must be reconstituted and diluted before clinical use should include reconstitution instructions that identify appropriate diluents and volumes.

A manufacturer's drug product preparation date (for experimental drugs) or an expiration date should be clearly visible on the product label.

Special instructions, such as "Shake Well," "Do Not Shake," "Albumin Required," and instructions for dilution, should appear on product labeling. In cases where important information will not fit on a product label, a package insert may be required as part of the labeling and packaging.

Product changes should be widely communicated to prescribers, pharmacists, nurses, and other health care providers involved in drug prescribing, preparation, and administration.

Package inserts and product information that describe medical indications, medication doses, administration schedules, and product use should not include abbreviations. This is especially important for drugs used in complex treatment regimens.

Educational Materials and Programs. Pharmaceutical manufacturers and drug product sponsors should be encouraged to provide educational materials and programs that promote and encourage safe use of their drug products. Programs should clearly explain the indications appearing on FDA-approved labeling, dosages, methods for preparation, and administration routes and schedules. Treatment descriptions should be standardized and consistent with guidelines designed to prevent medication-use errors.[7] Medication names and administration information should not be abbreviated in educational and promotional materials.

Regulatory Oversight. Regulatory agencies have a responsibility to review product packaging, labeling, and advertising to ensure that their content accurately reflects safety and efficacy data and conforms with language that has been approved by the FDA. A key component in those reviews should be that the product packaging and labeling facilitate safe and appropriate use and prevent users from making errors in selecting, preparing, and administering a drug product. Pharmacists should be consulted in screening proprietary drug names, product packaging, and labeling before drug products are approved for commercial use.

Managing Medication Errors

Medication-use errors with antineoplastics are distinguished from errors with other types of drugs in two important ways, both of which relate to antineoplastics' inherent toxicity. Individually and categorically, the therapeutic index for antineoplastic drugs is less than that for any other class of drugs. Adverse effects are an expected pharmacodynamic consequence attendant with antineoplastic use, and clinical toxicities may occur and persist at substantially lower dosages and schedules than are therapeutically used. The second characteristic distinguishing between antineoplastics and other types of drugs is that with the latter, subtherapeutic doses may not produce adverse effects that delay retreatment. In contrast, antineoplastic medications given in error at subtherapeutic doses (or underdoses) may not provide a therapeutic benefit, but they may compromise patients' ultimate response to therapy by delaying effective treatment until adverse effects are resolved. Underdoses may also cause or contribute to cumulative long-term patient harm as a result of adverse effects, delayed treatment, or both. It should be noted that antineoplastic treatments are almost always repeated, and the effect of a medication-use error may not be apparent until long after the error occurred. Consequently, if treatment plans and medication orders are not verified during each treatment cycle, errors may be compounded during repeated cycles and go undetected throughout an entire treatment course.

In addition to the actions already set forth in the "ASHP Guidelines on Preventing Medication Errors in Hospitals,"[1] the following are recommended after detecting a medication error[6]:

1. Implement monitoring and interventions for controlling injurious effects and ensuring patient safety;
2. Determine if an error could have previously occurred during prior treatment in the same patient and in other patients. Medication preparation work sheets or logs and drug administration records should be evaluated. Unexpected toxicities and an apparent or unaccountable lack of therapeutic and adverse effects should be investigated when it is suspected that a medication error occurred;
3. Seek the advice of health care professionals from various disciplines. The perspective of providers in other disciplines may facilitate discovering and understanding the circumstances that allowed a medication error to occur;
4. Determine whether an immediate temporizing or "stop-gap" change in policy or procedure is necessary to prevent recurrence of an error while the proximal cause is being analyzed;
5. Provide immediate professional counseling and support for employees implicated in causing or contributing to an error resulting in serious patient harm. Counseling and support should be offered to all personnel who learn that they have been involved in a medication error without regard for how recently the error occurred;
6. Establish procedures to inform and follow up with patients and their families about a medication error;
7. Understand that reporting medication errors and adverse drug reactions is a responsibility that should be shared by all health care providers. However, health systems may designate a person or committee specifically responsible for reporting and investigating medication errors and adverse drug reactions. In investigational drug studies, a study's principal investigator must report serious adverse events to the trial's sponsors (the drug manufacturer and the investigational new drug application holder) and to the institutional review board that oversees study conduct. Investigational drug sponsors are required to report to the FDA serious adverse effects associated with investigational agents, even if they are caused by a medication-use error; and
8. Encourage practitioners to report medication errors to a national medication-error tracking program. This

allows other providers to learn how medication errors occur and how they can be prevented. Reporting mechanisms for medication-use systems should be standardized by policy. Mechanisms must be developed for ongoing, interdisciplinary analysis and use of information that is reported to medication-error databases.[25]

Categorizing Medication Errors. In practice settings where a variety of disciplines provide patient care, serious potential and actual errors should be reported to an oversight committee composed of representatives of all the disciplines that provide care. By standardizing the way medication errors are reported, comparisons between reports and databases are facilitated, error trends are more easily identified, and system-based solutions can be developed.[26] Continuous oversight by a multidisciplinary quality-assurance committee promotes continuity and permits all primary patient care providers to evaluate system flaws and develop and improve the quality of processes and systems that safeguard patient care.[18] Medication-use oversight committees are advised to review medication-error reports from systems other than their own and evaluate their local medication-use system for design characteristics that may permit similar errors.[9,15]

"ASHP Guidelines on Preventing Medication Errors in Hospitals"[1] recommend adopting a system for categorizing medication-error severity such as the one developed by Myers and Hartwig et al.[25,26] Although this system is generally applicable to errors of occurrence with antineoplastic drugs, it categorizes errors by severity and prioritizes them without consideration for the frequency at which repeated errors occur. Accordingly, errors with the highest severity ranking receive the greatest efforts toward remediation. In contrast, potential errors are assigned a "zero" ranking, the lowest severity level, as they do not reach patients. By relegating potential errors to the lowest priority category, this outcome severity-based system risks trivializing system-design flaws. Errors discovered before they reach patients could cause devastating consequences, yet serious nascent errors are often transformed into potential errors only by serendipitous discovery. Therefore, potential errors should be distinguished from errors of occurrence and subcategorized based on their potential to cause harm.[25,26] However, potential errors should not be taken less seriously than errors of occurrence. When serious potential errors are discovered, the systems and processes that contributed to the errors should be evaluated and their proximal causes identified. The greatest efforts toward remediation of potential errors and errors of occurrence should be concentrated on eliminating the causes of errors that could have and had, respectively, the greatest adverse effects on patients' health.

NCCMERP's definition for medication errors includes any event that may cause or lead to inappropriate medication use.[2] The definition is complemented by the *NCCMERP Taxonomy of Medication Errors*, a comprehensive expandable tool intended for use in developing databases and analyzing medication-error reports. The *Taxonomy* provides standardized language and structure for recording and tracking medication-error-related data for errors of occurrence and potential errors. NCCMERP permits interested persons to adopt it as it is presented or adapt it for use in a particular practice setting.

References

1. American Society of Hospital Pharmacists. ASHP

guidelines on preventing medication errors in hospitals. *Am J Hosp Pharm.* 1993; 50:305–14.

2. National Coordinating Council on Medication Error Reporting and Prevention. About medication errors. www.nccmerp. org (accessed 2001 Jun 4).

3. Cohen MR, Anderson RW, Attilio RM, et al. Preventing medication errors in cancer chemotherapy. *Am J Health-Syst Pharm.* 1996; 53:737–46.

4. Attilio RM. Caring enough to understand: the road to oncology medication error prevention. *Hosp Pharm.* 1996; 31:17–26.

5. Beckwith MC, Tyler LS. Preventing medication errors with antineoplastic agents, part 1. *Hosp Pharm.* 2000; 35:511–23.

6. Beckwith MC, Tyler LS. Preventing medication errors with antineoplastic agents, part 2. *Hosp Pharm.* 2000; 35:732–47.

7. Kohler DR, Montello MJ, Green L, et al. Standardizing the expression and nomenclature of cancer treatment regimens. *Am J Health-Syst Pharm.* 1998; 55:137–44.

8. Berard CM, Mahoney CD, Welch DW, et al. Computer software for pharmacy oncology services. *Am J Health-Syst Pharm.* 1996; 53:733,752–6.

9. Kloth DD. Assuring safe care for cancer patients through an organized multidisciplinary team effort. *Hosp Pharm.* 1997; 32(suppl 1):S21–5.

10. Fischer DS, Alfano S, Knobf MT, et al. Improving the cancer chemotherapy use process. *J Clin Oncol.* 1996; 14:3148–55.

11. Lajeunesse JD. Quality assurance methods in chemotherapy production. *Hosp Pharm.* 1997; 32(suppl 1): S8–13.

12. Attilio RM. Strategies for reducing chemotherapy-related medication errors: improving the chemotherapy prescribing, dispensing, and administration process, and the patient's role in ensuring safety. *Hosp Pharm.* 1997; 32(suppl 1):S14–20.

13. Hutcherson DA, Gammon DC. Preventing errors with antineoplastic agents: a pharmacist's approach. *Hosp Pharm.* 1997; 32:194–202,209.

14. United Kingdom Joint Council for Clinical Oncology. Quality control in cancer chemotherapy. Managerial and procedural aspects. Oxford, England: Royal College of Physicians of London, 1994.

15. Cohen MR. Enhancing chemotherapy safety through medication system improvements. *Hosp Pharm.* 1997; 32(suppl 1):S1–7.

16. Leape LL, Bates DW, Cullen DJ, et al. Systems analysis of adverse drug events. *JAMA.* 1995; 274:35–43.

17. USP Quality Review. National council focuses on coordinating error reduction efforts. Rockville, MD: United States Pharmacopeial Convention, 1997 Jan.

18. Top-priority actions for preventing adverse drug events in hospitals. Recommendations of an expert panel. *Am J Health-Syst Pharm.* 1996; 53:747–51.

19. Pepper GA. Errors in drug administration by nurses. *Am J Health-Syst Pharm.* 1995; 52:390–5.

20. OSHA Training and Education Directive 1.15—Controlling exposure to hazardous drugs. Section V. Chap. 3. Washington, D.C.: U.S. Department of Labor, 1995 Sep 22.

21. Waddell JA, Solimando DA Jr, Strickland WR, et al. Pharmacy staff interventions in a medical center hematology–oncology service. *J Am Pharm Assoc.* 1998; 38:451–6.

22. Thorn DB, Sexton MG, Lemay AP, et al. Effect of a cancer chemotherapy prescription form on prescription completeness. *Am J Hosp Pharm.* 1989; 46:1802–6.

23. Lesar TS, Lomaestro BM, Pohl H. Medication-prescribing errors in a teaching hospital. A 9-year experience. *Arch Intern Med.* 1997; 157:1569–76.

24. Cohen MR. Drug product characteristics that foster drug-use-system errors. *Am J Health-Syst Pharm.* 1995; 52:395–9.

25. Myers CE. Needed: an interdisciplinary approach to drug misadventures. *Am J Health-Syst Pharm.* 1995; 52:367. Editorial.

26. Hartwig SC, Denger SD, Schneider PJ. Severity-indexed, incident report-based medication error-reporting program. *Am J Hosp Pharm.* 1991; 48:2611–6.

Developed through the ASHP Council on Professional Affairs and approved by the ASHP Board of Directors on April 19, 2002.

The bibliographic citation for this document is as follows: American Society of Health-System Pharmacists. ASHP guidelines on preventing medication errors with antineoplastic agents. *Am J Health-Syst Pharm.* 2002; 59:1648–68.

Recommendations from the National Coordinating Council for Medication Error Reporting and Prevention

Recommendations to Correct Error-Prone Aspects of Prescription Writing

The National Coordinating Council for Medication Error Reporting and Prevention emphasizes that illegibility of prescriptions and medication orders has resulted in injuries to, or deaths of patients. The Council, therefore, has made the following recommendations to help minimize errors.

- *All prescription documents must be legible. Prescribers should move to a direct, computerized, order entry system.*
- *Prescription orders should include a brief notation of purpose (e.g., for cough), unless considered inappropriate by the prescriber.* Notation of purpose can help further assure that the proper medication is dispensed and creates an extra safety check in the process of prescribing and dispensing a medication. The Council does recognize, however, that certain medications and disease states may warrant maintaining confidentiality.
- *All prescription orders should be written in the metric system except for therapies that use standard units such as insulin, vitamins, etc.* Units should be spelled out rather than writing "U." The change to the use of the metric system from the archaic apothecary and avoirdupois systems will help avoid misinterpretations of these abbreviations and symbols, and miscalculations when converting to metric, which is used in product labeling and package inserts.
- *Prescribers should include age, and when appropriate, weight of the patient on the prescription or medication order.* The most common errors in dosage result in pediatric and geriatric populations in which low body weight is common. The age (and weight) of a patient can help dispensing health care professionals in their double check of the appropriate drug and dose.
- *The medication order should include drug name, exact metric weight or concentration, and dosage form.* Strength should be expressed in metric amounts and concentration should be specified. Each order for a medication should be complete. The pharmacist should check with the prescriber if any information is missing or questionable.
- *A leading zero should always precede a decimal expression of less than one.* A terminal or trailing zero should never be used after a decimal. Ten-fold errors in drug strength and dosage have occurred with decimals due to the use of a trailing zero or the absence of a leading zero.
- *Prescribers should avoid use of abbreviations including those for drug names (e.g., MOM, HCTZ) and Latin directions for use.* The abbreviations in the chart below are found to be particularly dangerous because they have been consistently misunderstood and therefore, should never be used. The Council reviewed the uses for many abbreviations and determined that any attempt at standardization of abbreviations would not adequately address the problems of illegibility and misuse.
- *Prescribers should not use vague instructions such as "Take as directed" or "Take/Use as needed" as the sole direction for use.* Specific directions to the patient are useful to help reinforce proper medication use, particularly if therapy is to be interrupted for a time. Clear directions are a necessity for the dispenser to: (1) check the proper dose for the patient; and, (2) enable effective patient counseling.

Dangerous Abbreviations

Abbreviation	Intended Meaning	Common Error
U	Units	Mistaken as a zero or a four (4) resulting in overdose. Also mistaken for "cc" (cubic centimeters) when poorly written.
µg	Micrograms	Mistaken for "mg" (milligrams) resulting in a ten-fold overdose.
Q.D.	Latin abbreviation for every day	The period after the "Q" has sometimes been mistaken for an " I, " and the drug has been given "QID" (four times daily) rather than daily.
Q.O.D.	Latin abbreviation for every other day	Misinterpreted as "QD" (daily) or "QID" (four times daily). If the "O" is poorly written, it looks like a period or " I ."
SC or SQ	Subcutaneous	Mistaken as "SL" (sublingual) when poorly written.
T I W	Three times a week	Misinterpreted as "three times a day" or "twice a week."
D/C	Discharge; also discontinue	Patient's medications have been prematurely discontinued when D/C, (intended to mean "discharge") was misinterpreted as "discontinue," because it was followed by a list of drugs.
HS	Half strength	Misinterpreted as the Latin abbreviation "HS" (hour of sleep).
cc	Cubic centimeters	Mistaken as "U" (units) when poorly written.
AU, AS, AD	Latin abbreviation for both ears; left ear; right ear	Misinterpreted as the Latin abbreviation "OU" (both eyes); "OS" (left eye); "OD" (right eye)

In summary, the Council recommends:

Don't Wait . . . Automate!
When In Doubt, Write It Out!
When In Doubt, Check It Out!
Lead, Don't Trail!

Recommendations on Labeling and Packaging to Industry (Manufacturers of Pharmaceuticals and Devices)

The Council recommends that industry not use any printing on the cap and ferrule of injectables except to convey warnings.

The Council encourages industry to employ failure mode and effects analysis in its design of devices, and the packaging and labeling of medications and related devices.

The Council encourages industry to employ machine-readable coding (e.g. bar coding) in its labeling of drug products. The Council recognizes the importance of standardization of these codes for this use.

The Council encourages printing the drug name (brand and generic) and the strength on both sides of injectables, and IV bags, containers, and overwraps. For large volume parenterals and IV piggybacks (minibags), the name of the drug should be readable in both the upright and inverted positions.

The Council encourages industry to support the development of continuing education programs focusing on proper preparation and administration of its products.

The Council encourages industry to use innovative labeling to aid practitioners in distinguishing between products with very similar names, for example, the use of tall letters such as VinBLAStine and VinCRIStine.

The Council encourages industry to avoid printing company logos and company names that are larger than the type size of the drug name.

The Council encourages collaboration among industry, regulators, standards-setters, health care professionals, and patients to facilitate design of packaging and labeling to help minimize errors.

Adopted May 12, 1997 by the National Coordinating Council for Medication Error Reporting and Prevention.

Recommendations on Labeling and Packaging to Regulators and Standards-Setters

The Council recommends that FDA restrict the use of any printing on the cap and ferrule of injectables except to convey warnings.

The Council recommends the use of innovative labeling to aid practitioners in distinguishing between products with very similar names, for example, the use of tall letters such as VinBLAStine and VinCRIStine.

The Council recommends that FDA discourage industry from printing company logos and company names that are larger than the type size of the drug name.

The Council supports the recommendations of the USP-FDA Advisory Panel on Simplification of Injection

Labeling. Furthermore, the Council encourages USP/FDA to consider expansion of the concepts of simplification to apply to:

- Package inserts
- Labeling of other pharmaceutical dosage forms

The Council encourages further development of FDA's error prevention analysis efforts to provide consistent regulatory review of product labeling and packaging relative to the error-prone aspects of their design.

The Council encourages collaboration among regulators, standards-setters, industry, health care professionals, and patients to facilitate design of packaging and labeling to help minimize errors.

The Council encourages USP/FDA to examine feasibility and advisability of use of tactile cues in container design and on critical drugs. Such cues may be in the design of the container or embedded in the label.

The Council encourages the printing of the drug name (brand and generic) and the strength on both sides of injectables and IV bags, containers, and overwraps. For large volume parenterals and IV piggybacks (minibags), the name of the drug should be readable in both the upright and inverted positions.

Adopted May 12, 1997 by the National Coordinating Council for Medication Error Reporting and Prevention.

Recommendations to Health Care Organizations to Reduce Errors Due to Labeling and Packaging of Drug Products and Related Devices

The Council recommends the establishment of a systems approach to reporting, understanding, and prevention of medication errors in health care organizations. The organization's leaders should foster a culture and systems that include the following key elements:

a.   An environment that is conducive to medication error reporting through the FDA MedWatch Program and/or the USP Practitioners' Reporting Network.

b.   An environment which focuses on improvement of the medication use process.

c.   Mechanisms for internal reporting of actual and potential errors including strategies that encourage reporting.

d.   Systematic approaches within the health care organization to identify and evaluate actual and potential causes of errors including Failure Mode and Effects Analysis (FMEA)[1] and root cause analysis.

e.   Processes for taking appropriate action to prevent future errors through improving both systems and individual performance.

In addition, the Council makes the following recommendations to health care organizations to reduce errors due to labeling and packaging of drug products and related devices:

1.   The Council recommends that health care organizations employ machine readable coding (e.g., bar cod-

ing) in the management of the medication use process.

2. The Council recommends reevaluation of existing storage systems for pharmaceuticals by health care organizations and establishment of mechanisms to insure appropriate storage and location throughout the organization from bulk delivery to point of use. The following issues should be considered when applicable:

- Storage and location that will help distinguish similar products from one another
- Storage and location of certain drugs, (e.g., concentrates, paralyzing agents) that have a high risk potential
- Scope, access, and accountability for floor stock medications
- Safety and accountability of access to pharmaceuticals in the absence of a pharmacist (e.g., floor stock, eliminate access to pharmacy after hours)
- Labeling and packaging of patient-supplied medications.

3. The Council recommends the development of policies and procedures for repackaging of medications that will clarify labeling to help avoid errors.
4. The Council encourages collaboration among health care organizations, health care professionals, patients, industry, standard-setters, and regulators to facilitate design of packaging and labeling to help minimize errors.
5. The Council recommends that health care organizations develop and implement (or provide access to) education and training programs for health care professionals, technical support personnel, patients, and caregivers that address methods for reducing and preventing medication errors.

Adopted March 30, 1998 by the National Coordinating Council for Medication Error Reporting and Prevention.

Recommendations to Health Care Professionals to Reduce Errors Due to Labeling and Packaging of Drug Products and Related Devices

The Council encourages health care professionals to routinely educate patients and caregivers to enhance understanding and proper use of their medications and related devices. Furthermore, the Council encourages health care professionals to regularly participate in error prevention training programs and, when medication errors do occur, to actively participate in the investigation.

In addition, the Council makes the following recommendations to health care professionals to reduce errors due to labeling and packaging of drug products and related devices:

1. The Council encourages health care professionals to use only properly labeled and stored drug products and to read labels carefully (at least three times—before, during, and after use).
2. The Council encourages collaboration among health care professionals, health care organizations, patients, industry, standard-setters, and regulators to facilitate design of packaging and labeling to help minimize errors.
3. The Council encourages health care professionals to

take an active role in reviewing and commenting on proposed regulations and standards that relate to labeling and packaging (i.e., *Federal Register* and *Pharmacopeial Forum*).
4. The Council encourages health care professionals to report actual and potential medication errors to national (e.g., FDA MedWatch Program and/or the USP Practitioners' Reporting Network), internal, and local reporting programs.
5. The Council encourages health care professionals to share error-related experiences, case studies, etc., with their colleagues through newsletters, journals, bulletin boards, and the Internet.

Adopted March 30, 1998 by the National Coordinating Council for Medication Error Reporting and Prevention.

Recommendations to Reduce Errors Related to Administration of Drugs
Adopted June 29, 1999

1. The Council recommends that any order that is incomplete, illegible, or of any other concern should be clarified prior to administration using an established process for resolving questions.
2. The Council recommends that as one aspect of the overall medication use system, the following checks be performed immediately prior to medication administration: the right medication, in the right dose, to the right person, by the right route, at the right time.
3. The Council recommends that users of medication administration devices be knowledgeable about the device function and limitations.
4. The Council recommends that when electronic infusion control devices are employed, only those that prevent free-flow upon removal of the administration set should be used.
5. The Council encourages the use of linked automated systems (e.g., direct order entry, computerized medication administration record, bar coding) to facilitate review of prescriptions, increase the accuracy of administration, and reduce transcription errors.
6. The Council recommends that all persons who administer medications have adequate access to patient information, as close to the point of use as possible, including medical history, known allergies, prognosis, and treatment plan, to assess the appropriateness of administering the medication.
7. The Council recommends that all persons who administer medications have easily accessible product information as close to the point of use as possible, and are:

- Knowledgeable about indications for use of the medication as well as precautions and contraindications;
- Knowledgeable of the expected outcome from its use;
- Knowledgeable about potential adverse reactions and interactions with food or other medication;
- Knowledgeable of actions to take when adverse reactions or interactions occur; and,
- Knowledgeable about storage requirements.

8. The Council recommends that health care profession-

als administer only medications that are properly labeled and that during the administration process, labels be read three times: when reaching for or preparing the medication, immediately prior to administering the medication, and when discarding the container or replacing it into its storage location.

9. The Council recommends that at the time of administration, the name, purpose and effects of the medication be discussed with the patient and/or caregiver.

10. The Council recommends ongoing patient monitoring for desired and/or unexpected medication effects.

11. The Council recommends that the role of the work environment be considered when assessing safety of the drug administration process. Factors such as lighting, temperature control, noise-level, occurrence of distractions (e.g., telephone and personal interruptions, performance of unrelated tasks, etc.) should be examined. Sufficient resources must be provided for the given workload. The science of ergonomics (use dictionary definition) should be employed in the design of safe systems.

12. The Council recommends that data be collected regarding the actual and potential errors of administration for the purpose of continuous quality improvement.

Recommendations for Avoiding Error-Prone Aspects of Dispensing Medications

1. The Council recommends that prescriptions/orders always be reviewed by a pharmacist prior to dispensing. Any orders that are incomplete, illegible, or of any other concern should be clarified using an established process for resolving questions.

2. The Council recommends that patient profiles be current and contain adequate information that allows the pharmacist to assess the appropriateness of a prescription/order.

3. The Council recommends design of the dispensing area to prevent errors. Design should address fatigue-reducing environmental conditions (e.g., lighting, air conditioning, noise level, ergonomic fixtures); minimize distractions (e.g., telephone and personnel interruptions, clutter, unrelated tasks); and provide sufficient resources for workload.

4. The Council recommends that product inventory be arranged to help differentiate medications from one another. This may include the use of visual discriminators such as signs or markers. This is particularly important when confusion exists between or among strengths, similar looking labels, and similar sounding names.

5. The Council recommends that a series of checks be established to assess the accuracy of the dispensing process prior to the medication being provided to the patient. Whenever possible, an independent check by a second individual should be used. Other methods of checking include the use of automation, computer systems, and patient profiles.

6. The Council recommends that labels be read at least three times, for example, when selecting the product, when packaging the product, and when returning the product to the shelf.

7. The Council recommends that pharmacists counsel patients. Counseling should be viewed as an opportunity to verify the accuracy of dispensing and the patient's understanding of proper medication use.

8. The Council recommends that pharmacies collect data regarding actual and potential errors for the purpose of continuous quality improvement.

[1]Lieberman, P. Design failure mode and effects analysis and the industry. Automotive Engineering (AUTE). 1990; 31.

Approved by the National Coordinating Council for Medication Error Reporting and Prevention, March 19, 1999.

Medication Therapy and Patient Care

Organization and Delivery of Services

Scope and Hours of Pharmacy Services (0403)
Source: Council on Administrative Affairs
To support the principle that all patients should have 24-hour access to a pharmacist responsible for their care.

To advocate alternative methods of pharmacist review of medication orders (such as remote review) before drug administration when onsite pharmacist review is not available; further,

To support the use of remote medication order review systems that communicate pharmacist approval of orders electronically to the hospital's automated medication distribution system; further,

To promote the importance of pharmacist access to pertinent patient information, regardless of proximity to patient.
This policy supersedes ASHP policy 9706.

Documentation of Pharmacist Patient Care Services (0407)
Source: Council on Administrative Affairs
To encourage the documentation of pharmacist patient care services in order to validate their impact on patient outcomes and total cost of care.
This policy supersedes ASHP policy 9910.

Continuity of Care (0301)
Source: Section of Home, Ambulatory, and Chronic Care Practitioners
To recognize that continuity of patient care is a vital requirement in the appropriate use of medications; further,

To strongly encourage pharmacists to assume professional responsibility for ensuring the continuity of pharmaceutical care as patients move from one setting to another (e.g., ambulatory care to inpatient care to home care); further,

To encourage the development of strategies to address the gaps in continuity of pharmaceutical care.

Performance Improvement (0202)
Source: Council on Administrative Affairs
To encourage pharmacists to establish performance improvement processes within their practice settings that measure both operational and patient outcomes; further,

To encourage pharmacists to use contemporary performance improvement techniques and methods for ongoing improvement in their services; further,

To support pharmacists in their development and implementation of performance-improvement processes.
This policy supersedes ASHP policy 9808.

Pharmacy Benefits for the Uninsured (0101)
Source: Council on Administrative Affairs
To support the principle that all patients have the right to receive care from pharmacists; further,

To declare that health system pharmacists should play a leadership role in ensuring access to pharmacists' services for indigent or low-income patients who lack insurance coverage and for patients who are underinsured; further,

To advocate better collaboration among health systems, community health centers, state and county health departments, and the federal Health Resources and Services Administration (HRSA) in identifying and addressing the needs of indigent and low-income patients who lack insurance coverage and of patients who are underinsured.

Patient Satisfaction (0104)
Source: Council on Administrative Affairs
To encourage pharmacists to establish mechanisms within their practice settings that measure the level of satisfaction patients have with pharmacy services and with the outcomes of their drug therapy; further,

To construct such mechanisms in a manner that will (1) provide a system for monitoring trends in the quality of pharmacy services to patients, (2) increase recognition of the value of pharmacy services, and (3) provide a basis for making improvements in the process and outcomes of pharmacy services; further,

To facilitate a dialogue with and education of national patient satisfaction database vendors on the role and value of clinical pharmacy services.

Patient Adherence Programs as Part of Health Insurance Coverage (0116)
Source: Council on Legal and Public Affairs
To support the pharmacist's role in patient medication adherence programs that are part of health insurance plans; further,

To support those programs that (1) maintain the direct patient-pharmacist relationship; (2) are based on the pharmacist's knowledge of the patient's medical history, indication for the prescribed medication, and expected therapeutic outcome; (3) use a communication method desired by the patient; (4) are consistent with federal and state regulations for patient confidentiality; and (5) are consistent with ASHP policy on confidentiality of patient health care information.

Pharmacist Validation of Information Related to Medications (9921)
Source: Council on Professional Affairs
To support consultation with a pharmacist as a primary means for consumers to validate publicly available information related to medications.
This policy was reviewed in 2003 by the Council on Professional Affairs and by the Board of Directors and was found to still be appropriate.

Collaborative Drug Therapy Management Activities (9801)
Source: House of Delegates Resolution
To support the participation of pharmacists in collaborative drug therapy management, which is defined as a multidisciplinary process for selecting appropriate drug therapies, educating patients, monitoring patients, and continually assessing outcomes of therapy; further,

To recognize that pharmacists participate in collaborative drug therapy management for a patient who has a confirmed diagnosis by an authorized prescriber; further,

To recognize that the activities of a pharmacist in collaborative drug therapy management may include, but not be limited to, initiating, modifying, and monitoring a patient's drug therapy; ordering and performing laboratory and related tests; assessing patient response to therapy; counseling and educating a patient on medications; and administering medications.

This policy was reviewed in 2002 by the Council on Professional Affairs and by the Board of Directors and was found to still be appropriate.

Multidisciplinary Action Plans for Patient Care (9804)
Source: Council on Administrative Affairs
To support pharmacists as integral participants in the development of multidisciplinary action plans for patient care (care MAPs), disease-management plans, and health-management plans.

This policy was reviewed in 2002 by the Council on Administrative Affairs and by the Board of Directors and was found to still be appropriate.

Collaborative Drug Therapy Management (9812)
Source: Council on Legal and Public Affairs
To pursue the development of federal and state legislative and regulatory provisions that authorize collaborative drug therapy management by the pharmacist as a component of pharmaceutical care; further,

To actively support affiliated state societies in the pursuit of state-level collaborative drug therapy management authority for pharmacists.

This policy was reviewed in 2002 by the Council on Legal and Public Affairs and by the Board of Directors and was found to still be appropriate.

Medication Administration by Pharmacists (9820)
Source: Council on Professional Affairs
To support the position that the administration of medicines is part of the routine scope of pharmacy practice; further,

To support the position that pharmacists who administer medicines should be skilled to do so; further,

To support the position that pharmacists should be participants in establishing procedures in their own work settings with respect to the administration of medicines (by anyone) and monitoring the outcomes of medication administration.

This policy was reviewed in 2002 by the Council on Professional Affairs and by the Board of Directors and was found to still be appropriate.

Patient-Focused Care (9401)
Source: Council on Administrative Affairs
To support the concept of patient-focused care when it (a) is planned and implemented with pharmacists' involvement; (b) fosters the provision of pharmaceutical care; and (c) is motivated by a goal of improved patient care.

ASHP Statement on Confidentiality of Patient Health Care Information

ASHP believes patients should have the right to access and review their medical records and the ability to correct factual errors in those records. Patients should also have the right to know who has access to their medical records and to authorize how their medical information will be used. ASHP recognizes that patients consider certain medical information to be particularly sensitive. Nevertheless, ASHP believes all medical information is sensitive and should be given the utmost protection.

ASHP believes that pharmacists must have access to patient health records in order to provide quality care and ensure the safe use of medications. ASHP also believes that with access to the patient's health record comes the pharmacist's professional responsibility to safeguard the patient's rights to privacy and confidentiality. Within health systems, all authorized practitioners should be encouraged to communicate freely with each other but to maintain patient confidentiality and privacy. Uniquely identifiable patient information should not be exchanged without the patient's authorization for any reason not directly related to the provision of health care services.

ASHP believes there is no potential for a breach of patient confidentiality when patient information is aggregated for use in legitimate research and statistical measurement and is not uniquely identifiable. Therefore, specific authorization by individual patients for access to this information is not needed.

Pharmacists participate extensively in clinical trials of drugs. ASHP believes all clinical trial data must be recorded and stored in such a way that the subjects' rights of privacy and confidentiality are protected. The current process for storage and retrieval of clinical trial data contains adequate safeguards to protect patient information. As part of the established procedure for obtaining informed consent, patients receive a statement describing the parties that will have access to patient-identifiable information. These parties include institutional personnel who audit the information for quality or financial integrity and personnel from the study sponsor or FDA who monitor compliance with regulations.

ASHP believes pharmacy residency programs and other training programs must implement policies and procedures to ensure the confidentiality of patient medical records while allowing pharmacy students and residents access to these records in the course of their training.

ASHP believes a minimum standard for protection of patient health information should be adopted as federal law. States should retain the ability to adopt standards that are more stringent than federal law.

ASHP believes that strict governmental protections, with appropriate penalties for violations, must be in place to preclude dissemination of patient-identifiable information outside the health system (i.e., to an unauthorized third party) for any purposes that do not involve the direct provision of patient care or administration of health benefits. Health systems must have written policies and procedures in place to guard against the unauthorized collection, use, or disclosure of protected health information. Strict governmental penalties, including criminal sanctions for egregious violations, should be considered. However, inadvertent infractions with no intent to harm should be subject to the health care organization's disciplinary process or civil penalties.

Approved by the ASHP Board of Directors, April 21, 1999, and by the ASHP House of Delegates, June 7, 1999. Developed by the Council on Legal and Public Affairs.

The bibliographic citation for this document is as follows: American Society of Health-System Pharmacists. ASHP statement on the confidentiality of patient health care information. *Am J Health-Syst Pharm.* 1999; 56:1664.

ASHP Statement on Pharmaceutical Care

The purpose of this statement is to assist pharmacists in understanding pharmaceutical care. Such understanding must precede efforts to implement pharmaceutical care, which ASHP believes merit the highest priority in all practice settings.

Possibly the earliest published use of the term pharmaceutical care was by Brodie in the context of thoughts about drug use control and medication-related services.[1,2] It is a term that has been widely used and a concept about which much has been written and discussed in the pharmacy profession, especially since the publication of a paper by Hepler and Strand in 1990.[3-5] ASHP has formally endorsed the concept.[6] With varying terminology and nuances, the concept has also been acknowledged by other national pharmacy organizations.[7,8] Implementation of pharmaceutical care was the focus of a major ASHP conference in March 1993.

Many pharmacists have expressed enthusiasm for the concept of pharmaceutical care, but there has been substantial inconsistency in its description. Some have characterized it as merely a new name for clinical pharmacy; others have described it as anything that pharmacists do that may lead to beneficial results for patients.

ASHP believes that pharmaceutical care is an important new concept that represents growth in the profession beyond clinical pharmacy as often practiced and beyond other activities of pharmacists, including medication preparation and dispensing. All of these professional activities are important, however, and ASHP continues to be a strong proponent of the necessity for pharmacists' involvement in them. In practice, these activities should be integrated with and culminate in pharmaceutical care provided by individual pharmacists to individual patients.

In 1992, ASHP's members urged the development of an officially recognized ASHP definition of pharmaceutical care.[9] This statement provides a definition and elucidates some of the elements and implications of that definition. The definition that follows is an adaptation of a definition developed by Hepler and Strand.[3]

Definition

The mission of the pharmacist is to provide pharmaceutical care. Pharmaceutical care is the direct, responsible provision of medication-related care for the purpose of achieving definite outcomes that improve a patient's quality of life.

Principal Elements

The principal elements of pharmaceutical care are that it is *medication related*; it is *care* that is *directly provided* to the patient; it is provided to produce *definite outcomes*; these outcomes are intended to improve the patient's *quality of life*; and the provider accepts personal *responsibility* for the outcomes.

Medication Related. Pharmaceutical care involves not only medication therapy (the actual provision of medication) but also decisions about medication use for individual patients. As appropriate, this includes decisions *not* to use medication therapy as well as judgments about medication selection, dosages, routes and methods of administration, medication

therapy monitoring, and the provision of medication-related information and counseling to individual patients.

Care. Central to the concept of care is caring, a personal concern for the well-being of another person. Overall patient care consists of integrated domains of care including (among others) medical care, nursing care, and pharmaceutical care. Health professionals in each of these disciplines possess unique expertise and must cooperate in the patient's overall care. At times, they share in the execution of the various types of care (including pharmaceutical care). To pharmaceutical care, however, the pharmacist contributes unique knowledge and skills to ensure optimal outcomes from the use of medications.

At the heart of any type of patient care, there exists a one-to-one relationship between a caregiver and a patient. In pharmaceutical care, the irreducible "unit" of care is one pharmacist in a direct professional relationship with one patient. In this relationship, the pharmacist provides care directly to the patient and for the benefit of the patient.

The health and well-being of the patient are paramount. The pharmacist makes a direct, personal, caring commitment to the individual patient and acts in the patient's best interest. The pharmacist cooperates directly with other professionals and the patient in designing, implementing, and monitoring a therapeutic plan intended to produce definite therapeutic outcomes that improve the patient's quality of life.

Outcomes. It is the goal of pharmaceutical care to improve an individual patient's quality of life through achievement of definite (predefined), medication-related therapeutic outcomes. The outcomes sought are

1. Cure of a patient's disease.
2. Elimination or reduction of a patient's symptomatology.
3. Arresting or slowing of a disease process.
4. Prevention of a disease or symptomatology.

This, in turn, involves three major functions: (1) identifying potential and actual medication-related problems, (2) resolving actual medication-related problems, and (3) preventing potential medication-related problems. A medication-related problem is an event or circumstance involving medication therapy that actually or potentially interferes with an optimum outcome for a specific patient. There are at least the following categories of medication-related problems[3]:

- *Untreated indications.* The patient has a medical problem that requires medication therapy (an indication for medication use) but is not receiving a medication for that indication.
- *Improper drug selection.* The patient has a medication indication but is taking the wrong medication.
- *Subtherapeutic dosage.* The patient has a medical problem that is being treated with too little of the correct medication.
- *Failure to receive medication.* The patient has a medical problem that is the result of not receiving a medication (e.g., for pharmaceutical, psychological, sociological, or economic reasons).
- *Overdosage.* The patient has a medical problem that is

being treated with too much of the correct medication (toxicity).

- *Adverse drug reactions.* The patient has a medical problem that is the result of an adverse drug reaction or adverse effect.
- *Drug interactions.* The patient has a medical problem that is the result of a drug–drug, drug–food, or drug–laboratory test interaction.
- *Medication use without indication.* The patient is taking a medication for no medically valid indication.

Patients may possess characteristics that interfere with the achievement of desired therapeutic outcomes. Patients may be noncompliant with prescribed medication use regimens, or there may be unpredictable variations in patients' biological responses. Thus, in an imperfect world, intended outcomes from medication-related therapy are not always achievable.

Patients bear a responsibility to help achieve the desired outcomes by engaging in behaviors that will contribute to—and not interfere with—the achievement of desired outcomes. Pharmacists and other health professionals have an obligation to educate patients about behaviors that will contribute to achieving desired outcomes.

Quality of Life. Some tools exist now for assessing a patient's quality of life. These tools are still evolving, and pharmacists should maintain familiarity with the literature on this subject.[10,11] A complete assessment of a patient's quality of life should include both objective and subjective (e.g., the patient's own) assessments. Patients should be involved, in an informed way, in establishing quality-of-life goals for their therapies.

Responsibility. The fundamental relationship in any type of patient care is a mutually beneficial exchange in which the patient grants authority to the provider and the provider gives competence and commitment to the patient (accepts responsibility).[3] Responsibility involves both moral trustworthiness and accountability.

In pharmaceutical care, the direct relationship between an individual pharmacist and an individual patient is that of a professional covenant in which the patient's safety and well-being are entrusted to the pharmacist, who commits to honoring that trust through competent professional actions that are in the patient's best interest. As an accountable member of the health-care team, the pharmacist must document the care provided.[4,7,12,13] The pharmacist is personally accountable for patient outcomes (the quality of care) that ensue from the pharmacist's actions and decisions.[1]

Implications

The idea that pharmacists should commit themselves to the achievement of definite outcomes for individual patients is an especially important element in the concept of pharmaceutical care. The expectation that pharmacists personally accept responsibility for individual patients' outcomes that result from the pharmacists' actions represents a significant advance in pharmacy's continuing professionalization. The provision of pharmaceutical care represents a maturation of pharmacy as a clinical profession and is a natural evolution of more mature clinical pharmacy activities of pharmacists.[14]

ASHP believes that pharmaceutical care is fundamental to the profession's purpose of helping people make the best use of medications.[15] It is a unifying concept that transcends all types of patients and all categories of pharmacists and pharmacy organizations. Pharmaceutical care is applicable and achievable by pharmacists in all practice settings. The provision of pharmaceutical care is not limited to pharmacists in inpatient, outpatient, or community settings, nor to pharmacists with certain degrees, specialty certifications, residencies, or other credentials. It is not limited to those in academic or teaching settings. Pharmaceutical care is not a matter of formal credentials or place of work. Rather, it is a matter of a direct personal, professional, responsible relationship with a patient to ensure that the patient's use of medication is optimal and leads to improvements in the patient's quality of life.

Pharmacists should commit themselves to continuous care on behalf of individual patients. They bear responsibility for ensuring that the patient's care is ongoing despite work-shift changes, weekends, and holidays. An important implication is that a pharmacist providing pharmaceutical care may need to work as a member of a team of pharmacists who provide backup care when the primary responsible pharmacist is not available. Another is that the responsible pharmacist should work to ensure that continuity of care is maintained when a patient moves from one component of a health-care system to another (e.g., when a patient is hospitalized or discharged from a hospital to return to an ambulatory, community status). In the provision of pharmaceutical care, professional communication about the patient's needs between responsible pharmacists in each area of practice is, therefore, essential. ASHP believes that the development of recognized methods of practicing pharmaceutical care that will enhance such communication is an important priority for the profession.

Pharmaceutical care can be conceived as both a purpose for pharmacy practice and a purpose of medication use processes. That is, a fundamental professional reason that pharmacists engage in pharmacy practice should be to deliver pharmaceutical care. Furthermore, the medication use systems that pharmacists (and others) operate should be designed to support and enable the delivery of pharmaceutical care by individual pharmacists. ASHP believes that, in organized health-care settings, pharmaceutical care can be most successfully provided when it is part of the pharmacy department's central mission and when management activity is focused on facilitating the provision of pharmaceutical care by individual pharmacists. This approach, in which empowered frontline staff provide direct care to individual patients and are supported by managers, other pharmacists, and support systems, is new for many pharmacists and managers.

An important corollary to this approach is that pharmacists providing pharmaceutical care in organized health-care settings cannot provide such care alone. They must work in an interdependent fashion with colleagues in pharmacy and other disciplines, support systems and staff, and managers.[7] It is incumbent on pharmacists to design work systems and practices that appropriately focus the efforts of all activities and support systems on meeting the needs of patients. Some patients will require different levels of care, and it may be useful to structure work systems in light of those differences.[16,17] ASHP believes that the provision of pharmaceutical care and the development of effective work systems to document and support it are major priorities for the profession.

In the provision of pharmaceutical care, pharmacists use their unique perspective and knowledge of medication therapy to evaluate patients' actual and potential medication-related problems. To do this, they require direct access to clinical information about individual patients. They make judgments regarding medication use and then advocate optimal medication use for individual patients in cooperation with other professionals and in consideration of their unique professional knowledge and evaluations. Pharmaceutical care includes the active participation of the patient (and designated caregivers such as family members) in matters pertinent to medication use.

The acknowledgment of pharmacists' responsibility for therapeutic outcomes resulting from their actions does not contend that pharmacists have exclusive authority for matters related to medication use. Other health-care professionals, including physicians and nurses, have valuable and well-established, well-recognized roles in the medication use process. The pharmaceutical care concept does not diminish the roles or responsibilities of other health professionals, nor does it imply any usurping of authority by pharmacists. Pharmacists' actions in pharmaceutical care should be conducted and viewed as collaborative. The knowledge, skills, and traditions of pharmacists, however, make them legitimate leaders of efforts by health-care teams to improve patients' medication use.

Pharmaceutical care requires a direct relationship between a pharmacist and an individual patient. Some pharmacists and other pharmacy personnel engage in clinical and product-related pharmacy activities that do not involve a direct relationship with the patient. Properly designed, these activities can be supportive of pharmaceutical care, but ASHP believes it would be confusing and counterproductive to characterize such activities as pharmaceutical care. ASHP believes that clinical and product-related pharmacy activities are essential, however, and are as important as the actions of pharmacists interacting directly with patients.

Pharmaceutical educators must teach pharmaceutical care to students.[18] Providers of continuing education should help practicing pharmacists and other pharmacy personnel to understand pharmaceutical care. Students and pharmacists should be taught to conceptualize and execute responsible medication-related problem-solving on behalf of individual patients. Curricula should be designed to produce graduates with sufficient knowledge and skills to provide pharmaceutical care competently.[8,18] Initiatives are under way to bring about these changes.[8] Practicing pharmacists must commit their time as preceptors and their workplaces as teaching laboratories for the undergraduate and postgraduate education and training necessary to produce pharmacists who can provide pharmaceutical care.[8]

Research is needed to evaluate various methods and systems for the delivery of pharmaceutical care.

Pharmaceutical care represents an exciting new vision for pharmacy. ASHP hopes that all pharmacists in all practice settings share in this vision and that the pharmaceutical care concept will serve as a stimulus for them to work toward transforming the profession to actualize that vision.

References

1. Brodie DC. Is pharmaceutical education prepared to lead its profession? The Ninth Annual Rho Chi Lecture. *Rep Rho Chi.* 1973; 39:6–12.
2. Brodie DC, Parish PA, Poston JW. Societal needs for drugs and drug-related services. *Am J Pharm Educ.* 1980; 44:276–8.
3. Hepler CD, Strand LM. Opportunities and responsibilities in pharmaceutical care. *Am J Hosp Pharm.* 1990; 47:533–43.
4. Penna RP. Pharmaceutical care: pharmacy's mission for the 1990s. *Am J Hosp Pharm.* 1990; 47:543–9.
5. Pierpaoli PG, Hethcox JM. Pharmaceutical care: new management and leadership imperatives. *Top Hosp Pharm Manage.* 1992; 12:1–18.
6. Oddis JA. Report of the House of Delegates: June 3 and 5, 1991. *Am J Hosp Pharm.* 1991; 48:1739–48.
7. American Pharmaceutical Association. An APhA white paper on the role of the pharmacist in comprehensive medication use management; the delivery of pharmaceutical care. Washington, DC: American Pharmaceutical Association; 1992 Mar.
8. Commission to Implement Change in Pharmaceutical Education. A position paper. Entry-level education in pharmacy: a commitment to change. *AACP News.* 1991; Nov (Suppl):14
9. Oddis JA. Report of the House of Delegates: June 1 and 3, 1992. *Am J Hosp Pharm.* 1992; 49:1962–73.
10. Gouveia WA. Measuring and managing patient outcomes. *Am J Hosp Pharm.* 1992; 49:2157–8.
11. MacKeigan LD, Pathak DS. Overview of health-related quality-of-life measures. *Am J Hosp Pharm.* 1992; 49:2236–45.
12. Galinsky RE, Nickman NA. Pharmacists and the mandate of pharmaceutical care. *DICP Ann Pharmacother.* 1991; 21:431–4.
13. Angaran DM. Quality assurance to quality improvement: measuring and monitoring pharmaceutical care. *Am J Hosp Pharm.* 1991; 48:1901–7.
14. Hepler CD. Pharmaceutical care and specialty practice. *Pharmacotherapy.* 1993; 13:64S–9S.
15. Zellmer WA. Expressing the mission of pharmacy practice. *Am J Hosp Pharm.* 1991; 48:1195. Editorial.
16. Smith WE, Benderev K. Levels of pharmaceutical care: a theoretical model. *Am J Hosp Pharm.* 1991; 48:540–6.
17. Strand LM, Cipole RJ, Morley PC, et al. Levels of pharmaceutical care: a needs-based approach. *Am J Hosp Pharm.* 1991; 48:547–50.
18. O'Neil EH. Health professions education for the future: schools in service to the nation. San Francisco, CA: Pew Health Profession Commission; 1993.

This statement was reviewed in 1998 by the Council on Professional Affairs and the ASHP Board of Directors and was found to still be appropriate.

Approved by the ASHP Board of Directors, April 21, 1993, and by the ASHP House of Delegates, June 9, 1993. Developed by the ASHP Council on Professional Affairs.

The bibliographic citation for this document is as follows: American Society of Hospital Pharmacists. ASHP statement on pharmaceutical care. *Am J Hosp Pharm.* 1993; 50:1720–3.

ASHP Guidelines on Pharmacist-Conducted Patient Education and Counseling

Purpose

Providing pharmaceutical care entails accepting responsibility for patients' pharmacotherapeutic outcomes. Pharmacists can contribute to positive outcomes by educating and counseling patients to prepare and motivate them to follow their pharmacotherapeutic regimens and monitoring plans. The purpose of this document is to help pharmacists provide effective patient education and counseling.

In working with individual patients, patient groups, families, and caregivers, pharmacists should approach education and counseling as interrelated activities. ASHP believes pharmacists should educate and counsel all patients to the extent possible, going beyond the minimum requirements of laws and regulations; simply offering to counsel is inconsistent with pharmacists' responsibilities. In pharmaceutical care, pharmacists should encourage patients to seek education and counseling and should eliminate barriers to providing it.

Pharmacists should also seek opportunities to participate in health-system patient-education programs and to support the educational efforts of other health care team members. Pharmacists should collaborate with other health care team members, as appropriate, to determine what specific information and counseling are required in each patient care situation. A coordinated effort among health care team members will enhance patients' adherence to pharmacotherapeutic regimens, monitoring of drug effects, and feedback to the health system.

ASHP believes these patient education and counseling guidelines are applicable in all practice settings—including acute inpatient care, ambulatory care, home care, and long-term care—whether these settings are associated with integrated health systems or managed care organizations or are freestanding. The guidelines may need to be adapted; for example, for use in telephone counseling or for counseling family members or caregivers instead of patients. Patient education and counseling usually occur at the time prescriptions are dispensed but may also be provided as a separate service. The techniques and the content should be adjusted to meet the specific needs of the patient and to comply with the policies and procedures of the practice setting. In health systems, other health care team members share in the responsibility to educate and counsel patients as specified in the patients' care plans.

Background

The human and economic consequences of inappropriate medication use have been the subject of professional, public, and congressional discourse for more than two decades.[1–5] Lack of sufficient knowledge about their health problems and medications is one cause of patients' nonadherence to their pharmacotherapeutic regimens and monitoring plans; without adequate knowledge, patients cannot be effective partners in managing their own care. The pharmacy profession has accepted responsibility for providing patient education and counseling in the context of pharmaceutical care to improve patient adherence and reduce medication-related problems.[6–9]

Concerns about improper medication use contributed to the provision in the Omnibus Budget Reconciliation Act of 1990 (OBRA '90) that mandated an offer to counsel Medicaid outpatients about prescription medications. Subsequently, states enacted legislation that generally extends the offer-to-counsel requirement to outpatients not covered by Medicaid. Future court cases may establish that pharmacists, in part because of changing laws, have a public duty to warn patients of adverse effects and potential interactions of medications. The result could be increased liability for pharmacists who fail to educate and counsel their patients or who do so incorrectly or incompletely.[10]

Pharmacists' Knowledge and Skills

In addition to a current knowledge of pharmacotherapy, pharmacists need to have the knowledge and skills to provide effective and accurate patient education and counseling. They should know about their patients' cultures, especially health and illness beliefs, attitudes, and practices. They should be aware of patients' feelings toward the health system and views of their own roles and responsibilities for decision-making and for managing their care.[11]

Effective, open-ended questioning and active listening are essential skills for obtaining information from and sharing information with patients. Pharmacists have to adapt messages to fit patients' language skills and primary languages, through the use of teaching aids, interpreters, or cultural guides if necessary. Pharmacists also need to observe and interpret the nonverbal messages (e.g., eye contact, facial expressions, body movements, vocal characteristics) patients give during education and counseling sessions.[12]

Assessing a patient's cognitive abilities, learning style, and sensory and physical status enables the pharmacist to adapt information and educational methods to meet the patient's needs. A patient may learn best by hearing spoken instructions; by seeing a diagram, picture, or model; or by directly handling medications and administration devices. A patient may lack the visual acuity to read labels on prescription containers, markings on syringes, or written handout material. A patient may be unable to hear oral instructions or may lack sufficient motor skills to open a child-resistant container.

In addition to assessing whether patients know *how* to use their medications, pharmacists should attempt to understand patients' attitudes and potential behaviors concerning medication use. The pharmacist needs to determine whether a patient is willing to use a medication and whether he or she intends to do so.[13,14]

Environment

Education and counseling should take place in an environment conducive to patient involvement, learning, and acceptance—one that supports pharmacists' efforts to establish caring relationships with patients. Individual patients, groups, families, or caregivers should perceive the counseling environment as comfortable, confidential, and safe.

Education and counseling are most effective when

conducted in a room or space that ensures privacy and opportunity to engage in confidential communication. If such an isolated space is not available, a common area can be restructured to maximize visual and auditory privacy from other patients or staff. Patients, including those who are disabled, should have easy access and seating. Space and seating should be adequate for family members or caregivers. The design and placement of desks and counters should minimize barriers to communication. Distractions and interruptions should be few, so that patients and pharmacists can have each other's undivided attention.

The environment should be equipped with appropriate learning aids, e.g., graphics, anatomical models, medication administration devices, memory aids, written material, and audiovisual resources.

Pharmacist and Patient Roles

Pharmacists and patients bring to education and counseling sessions their own perceptions of their roles and responsibilities. For the experience to be effective, the pharmacist and patient need to come to a common understanding about their respective roles and responsibilities. It may be necessary to clarify for patients that pharmacists have an appropriate and important role in providing education and counseling. Patients should be encouraged to be active participants.

The pharmacist's role is to verify that patients have sufficient understanding, knowledge, and skill to follow their pharmacotherapeutic regimens and monitoring plans. Pharmacists should also seek ways to motivate patients to learn about their treatment and to be active partners in their care. Patients' role is to adhere to their pharmacotherapeutic regimens, monitor for drug effects, and report their experiences to pharmacists or other members of their health care teams.[12,15] Optimally, the patient's role should include seeking information and presenting concerns that may make adherence difficult.

Depending on the health system's policies and procedures, its use of protocols or clinical care plans, and its credentialing of providers, pharmacists may also have disease management roles and responsibilities for specified categories of patients. This expands pharmacists' relationships with patients and the content of education and counseling sessions.

Process Steps

Steps in the patient education and counseling process will vary according to the health system's policies and procedures, environment, and practice setting. Generally, the following steps are appropriate for patients receiving new medications or returning for refills[12–21]:

1. Establish caring relationships with patients as appropriate to the practice setting and stage in the patient's health care management. Introduce yourself as a pharmacist, explain the purpose and expected length of the sessions, and obtain the patient's agreement to participate. Determine the patient's primary spoken language.
2. Assess the patient's knowledge about his or her health problems and medications, physical and mental capability to use the medications appropriately, and attitude toward the health problems and medications. Ask open-ended questions about each medication's purpose and

what the patient expects, and ask the patient to describe or show how he or she will use the medication.

Patients returning for refill medications should be asked to describe or show how they have been using their medications. They should also be asked to describe any problems, concerns, or uncertainties they are experiencing with their medications.

3. Provide information orally and use visual aids or demonstrations to fill patients' gaps in knowledge and understanding. Open the medication containers to show patients the colors, sizes, shapes, and markings on oral solids. For oral liquids and injectables, show patients the dosage marks on measuring devices. Demonstrate the assembly and use of administration devices such as nasal and oral inhalers. As a supplement to face-to-face oral communication, provide written handouts to help the patient recall the information.

    If a patient is experiencing problems with his or her medications, gather appropriate data and assess the problems. Then adjust the pharmacotherapeutic regimens according to protocols or notify the prescribers.
4. Verify patients' knowledge and understanding of medication use. Ask patients to describe or show how they will use their medications and identify their effects. Observe patients' medication-use capability and accuracy and attitudes toward following their pharmacotherapeutic regimens and monitoring plans.

Content

The content of an education and counseling session may include the information listed below, as appropriate for each patient's pharmacotherapeutic regimen and monitoring plan.[8,9,20] The decision to discuss specific pharmacotherapeutic information with an individual patient must be based on the pharmacist's professional judgment.

1. The medication's trade name, generic name, common synonym, or other descriptive name(s) and, when appropriate, its therapeutic class and efficacy.
2. The medication's use and expected benefits and action. This may include whether the medication is intended to cure a disease, eliminate or reduce symptoms, arrest or slow the disease process, or prevent the disease or a symptom.
3. The medication's expected onset of action and what to do if the action does not occur.
4. The medication's route, dosage form, dosage, and administration schedule (including duration of therapy).
5. Directions for preparing and using or administering the medication. This may include adaptation to fit patients' lifestyles or work environments.
6. Action to be taken in case of a missed dose.
7. Precautions to be observed during the medication's use or administration and the medication's potential risks in relation to benefits. For injectable medications and administration devices, concern about latex allergy may be discussed.
8. Potential common and severe adverse effects that may occur, actions to prevent or minimize their occurrence, and actions to take if they occur, including notifying the prescriber, pharmacist, or other health care provider.
9. Techniques for self-monitoring of the pharmacotherapy.

10. Potential drug–drug (including nonprescription), drug–food, and drug–disease interactions or contraindications.
11. The medication's relationships to radiologic and laboratory procedures (e.g., timing of doses and potential interferences with interpretation of results).
12. Prescription refill authorizations and the process for obtaining refills.
13. Instructions for 24-hour access to a pharmacist.
14. Proper storage of the medication.
15. Proper disposal of contaminated or discontinued medications and used administration devices.
16. Any other information unique to an individual patient or medication.

These points are applicable to both prescription and nonprescription medications. Pharmacists should counsel patients in the proper selection of nonprescription medications.

Additional content may be appropriate when pharmacists have authorized responsibilities in collaborative disease management for specified categories of patients. Depending on the patient's disease management or clinical care plan, the following may be covered:

1. The disease state: whether it is acute or chronic and its prevention, transmission, progression, and recurrence.
2. Expected effects of the disease on the patient's normal daily living.
3. Recognition and monitoring of disease complications.

Documentation

Pharmacists should document education and counseling in patients' permanent medical records as consistent with the patients' care plans, the health system's policies and procedures, and applicable state and federal laws. When pharmacists do not have access to patients' medical records, education and counseling may be documented in the pharmacy's patient profiles, on the medication order or prescription form, or on a specially designed counseling record.

The pharmacist should record (1) that counseling was offered and was accepted and provided or refused and (2) the pharmacist's perceived level of the patient's understanding.[9] As appropriate, the content should be documented (for example, counseling about food–drug interactions). All documentation should be safeguarded to respect patient confidentiality and privacy and to comply with applicable state and federal laws.[10]

References

1. Smith MC. Social barriers to rational drug therapy. *Am J Hosp Pharm.* 1972; 29:121–7.
2. Priorities and approaches for improving prescription medicine use by older Americans. Washington, DC: National Council on Patient Information and Education; 1987.
3. Manasse HR Jr. Medication use in an imperfect world: drug misadventuring as an issue of public policy, part 1. *Am J Hosp Pharm.* 1989; 46:929–44.
4. Manasse HR Jr. Medication use in an imperfect world: drug misadventuring as an issue of public policy, part 2. *Am J Hosp Pharm.* 1989; 46:1141–52.
5. Johnson JA, Bootman JL. Drug-related morbidity and mortality: a cost-of-illness model. *Arch Intern Med.* 1995; 155:1949–56.
6. Summary of the final report of the Scope of Pharmacy Practice Project. *Am J Hosp Pharm.* 1994; 51:2179–82.
7. Hepler CD, Strand LM. Opportunities and responsibilities in pharmaceutical care. *Am J Hosp Pharm.* 1990; 47:533–42.
8. Hatoum HT, Hutchinson RA, Lambert BL. OBRA 90: patient counseling—enhancing patient outcomes. *US Pharm.* 1993; 18(Jan):76–86.
9. OBRA '90: a practical guide to effecting pharmaceutical care. Washington, DC: American Pharmaceutical Association; 1994.
10. Lynn NJ, Kamm RE. Avoiding liability problems. *Am Pharm.* 1995; NS35(Dec):14–22.
11. Herrier RN, Boyce RW. Does counseling improve compliance? *Am Pharm.* 1995; NS35(Sep):11–2.
12. Foster SL, Smith EB, Seybold MR. Advanced counseling techniques: integrating assessment and intervention. *Am Pharm.* 1995; NS35(Oct):40–8.
13. Bond WS, Hussar DA. Detection methods and strategies for improving medication compliance. *Am J Hosp Pharm.* 1991; 48:1978–88.
14. Felkey BG. Adherence screening and monitoring. *Am Pharm.* 1995; NS35(Jul):42–51.
15. Herrier RN, Boyce RW. Establishing an active patient partnership. *Am Pharm.* 1995; NS35(Apr):48–57.
16. Boyce RW, Herrier RN, Gardner M. Pharmacist-patient consultation program, unit I: an interactive approach to verify patient understanding. New York: Pfizer Inc.; 1991.
17. Pharmacist-patient consultation program, unit II: counseling patients in challenging situations. New York: Pfizer Inc.; 1993.
18. Pharmacist-patient consultation program, unit III: counseling to enhance compliance. New York: Pfizer Inc.; 1995.
19. Boyce RW, Herrier RN. Obtaining and using patient data. *Am Pharm.* 1991; NS31(Jul):65–70.
20. Herrier RN, Boyce RW. Communicating risk to patients. *Am Pharm.* 1995; NS35(Jun):12–4.
21. APhA special report: medication administration problem solving in ambulatory care. Washington, DC: American Pharmaceutical Association; 1994.

This guideline was reviewed in 2001 by the Council on Professional Affairs and by the ASHP Board of Directors and was found to still be appropriate.

Approved by the ASHP Board of Directors, November 11, 1996. Revised by the ASHP Council on Professional Affairs. Supersedes the ASHP Statement on the Pharmacist's Role in Patient-Education Programs dated June 3, 1991, and ASHP Guidelines on Pharmacist-Conducted Patient Counseling dated November 18, 1992.

The bibliographic citation for this document is as follows: American Society of Health-System Pharmacists. ASHP guidelines on pharmacist-conducted patient education and counseling. *Am J Health-Syst Pharm.* 1997; 54:431–4.

ASHP Guidelines on a Standardized Method for Pharmaceutical Care

Need for a Standardized Method

The purpose of this document is to provide pharmacists with a standardized method for the provision of pharmaceutical care in component settings of organized health systems. Since the introduction of the pharmaceutical care concept[1] and the development of the ASHP Statement on Pharmaceutical Care,[2] considerable variation in pharmacists' provision of pharmaceutical care has been noted. ASHP believes pharmacists need a standardized method for providing pharmaceutical care.

This document describes a standardized method based on functions that all pharmacists should perform for individual patients in organized health systems. The use of this method would foster consistency in the provision of pharmaceutical care in all practice settings. It would support continuity of care both within a practice setting (e.g., among pharmacists on different work shifts caring for an acutely ill inpatient) and when a patient moves among practice settings (e.g., when an inpatient is discharged to home or ambulatory care). Further, a standardized method would establish consistent documentation so that patient-specific and medication-related information could be shared from pharmacist to pharmacist and among health professionals.

The need to identify the functions involved in pharmaceutical care and the critical skills necessary to provide it was discussed at the San Antonio consensus conference in 1993.[3] Functions for the provision of pharmaceutical care were identified by the practitioner task force of the Scope of Pharmacy Practice Project.[4] Those functions have been defined in more detail in the pharmacotherapy series of the ASHP Clinical Skills Program.[5–9]

These Guidelines are not specific to any practice setting. ASHP believes this standardized method can be used in acute care (hospitals), ambulatory care, home care, long-term care, and other practice settings. Functions can be tailored as appropriate for a given practice setting. It is recognized that the degree of standardization and tailoring appropriate for a given work site will depend on the practice environment, the organization of services (e.g., patient-focused or department-focused), working relationships with other health professionals, the health system's and patient's financial arrangements, and the health system's policies and procedures. ASHP believes the use of the systematic approaches encouraged by these guidelines will assist pharmacists in implementing and providing pharmaceutical care in their work sites.

Functions of Pharmaceutical Care

ASHP believes that a standardized method for the provision of pharmaceutical care should include the following:

- Collecting and organizing patient-specific information,
- Determining the presence of medication-therapy problems,
- Summarizing patients' health care needs,
- Specifying pharmacotherapeutic goals,
- Designing a pharmacotherapeutic regimen,
- Designing a monitoring plan,

- Developing a pharmacotherapeutic regimen and corresponding monitoring plan in collaboration with the patient and other health professionals,
- Initiating the pharmacotherapeutic regimen,
- Monitoring the effects of the pharmacotherapeutic regimen, *and*
- Redesigning the pharmacotherapeutic regimen and monitoring plan.

These major functions have been adapted, in part, from the pharmacotherapy series of the ASHP Clinical Skills Program and the final report of the ASHP Model for Pharmacy Practice Residency Learning Demonstration Project.

Collecting and Organizing Pertinent Patient-Specific Information. Information should be collected and used as a patient-specific database to prevent, detect, and resolve the patient's medication-related problems and to make appropriate medication-therapy recommendations. The database should include the following sections, each containing specific types of information to the extent that it is relevant to medication therapy:

Demographic
  Name
  Address
  Date of birth
  Sex
  Religion and religious affiliation
  Occupation

Administrative
  Physicians and prescribers
  Pharmacy
  Room/bed numbers
  Consent forms
  Patient identification number

Medical
  Weight and height
  Acute and chronic medical problems
  Current symptoms
  Vital signs and other monitoring information
  Allergies and intolerances
  Past medical history
  Laboratory information
  Diagnostic and surgical procedures

Medication therapy
  Prescribed medications
  Nonprescription medications
  Medications used prior to admission
  Home remedies and other types of health products used
  Medication regimen
  Compliance with therapy
  Medication allergies and intolerances
  Concerns or questions about therapy
  Assessment of understanding of therapy
  Pertinent health beliefs

Behavioral/lifestyle
> Diet
> Exercise/recreation
> Tobacco/alcohol/caffeine/other substance use or abuse
> Sexual history
> Personality type
> Daily activities

Social/economic
> Living arrangement
> Ethnic background
> Financial/insurance/health plan

Objective and subjective information should be obtained directly from patients (and family members, other caregivers, and other health professionals as needed). A physical assessment should be performed as needed. In addition, information can be obtained by reviewing the patient's health record and other information sources.

Information in the patient's health record should be understood, interpreted, and verified for accuracy before decisions are made about the patient's medication therapy. With access to the patient's health record comes the professional responsibility to safeguard the patient's rights to privacy and confidentiality. The Privacy Act of 1974,[10] professional practice policies,[11,12] and policies and procedures of organized health systems provide guidance for the pharmacist in judging the appropriate use of patient-specific information.

The patient (as well as family members, caregivers, and other members of the health care team as needed) should be interviewed. This is necessary for the pharmacist to establish a direct relationship with the patient, to understand the patient's needs and desired outcome, to obtain medication-related information, and to clarify and augment other available information. Pharmacists in many practice settings, including ambulatory care, may need to perform physical assessments to collect data for assessing and monitoring medication therapy.

Information, including clinical laboratory test results, gathered or developed by other members of the health care team may not be in the patient's health record. Therefore, to ensure that the patient information is current and complete, other sources should be checked. Other sources may include medication profiles from other pharmacies used by the patient.

Although it is ideal to have a comprehensive database for all patients, time and staffing limitations may necessitate choices regarding the quantity of information and the number of patients to follow. Choices could be determined by the health system's policies and procedures, by clinical care plans, or by disease management criteria in the patient's third-party health plan.

Systems for recording patient-specific data will vary, depending on pharmacists' preferences and practice settings. Electronic documentation is recommended. Some information may already be in the patient's health record. Therefore, when authorized, the additional information gathered by the pharmacist should be recorded in the patient's health record so that it can be shared with other health professionals. Abstracted summaries and work sheets may also be useful.

Determining the Presence of Medication-Therapy Problems. Conclusions should be drawn from the integration of medication-, disease-, laboratory test-, and patient-specific information. The patient's database should be assessed for any of the following medication-therapy problems:

- Medications with no medical indication,
- Medical conditions for which there is no medication prescribed,
- Medications prescribed inappropriately for a particular medical condition,
- Inappropriate medication dose, dosage form, schedule, route of administration, or method of administration,
- Therapeutic duplication,
- Prescribing of medications to which the patient is allergic,
- Actual and potential adverse drug events,
- Actual and potential clinically significant drug–drug, drug–disease, drug–nutrient, and drug–laboratory test interactions,
- Interference with medical therapy by social or recreational drug use,
- Failure to receive the full benefit of prescribed medication therapy,
- Problems arising from the financial impact of medication therapy on the patient,
- Lack of understanding of the medication therapy by the patient, and
- Failure of the patient to adhere to the medication regimen.

The relative importance of problems must be assessed on the basis of specific characteristics of the patient or the medication. Checklists, work sheets, and other methods may be used to determine and document the presence of medication-therapy problems. The method should be proactive and should be used consistently from patient to patient.

Summarizing Patients' Health Care Needs. The patient's overall needs and desired outcomes and other health professionals' assessments, goals, and therapy plans should be considered in determining and documenting the medication-related elements of care that are needed to improve or prevent deterioration of the patient's health or well-being.

Specifying Pharmacotherapeutic Goals. Pharmacotherapeutic goals should reflect the integration of medication-, disease-, laboratory test-, and patient-specific information, as well as ethical and quality-of-life considerations. The goals should be realistic and consistent with goals specified by the patient and other members of the patient's health care team. The therapy should be designed to achieve definite medication-related outcomes and improve the patient's quality of life.

Designing a Pharmacotherapeutic Regimen. The regimen should meet the pharmacotherapeutic goals established with the patient and reflect the integration of medication-, disease-, laboratory test-, and patient-specific information; ethical and quality-of-life considerations; and pharmacoeconomic principles. It should comply with the health system's medication-use policies, such as clinical care plans and disease management plans. The regimen should be designed for optimal medication use within both the health system's and the patient's capabilities and financial resources.

Designing a Monitoring Plan for the Pharmacotherapeutic Regimen. The monitoring plan should effectively evaluate achievement of the patient-specific pharmacotherapeutic goals and detect real and potential adverse effects. Measurable, observable parameters should be determined for each goal. Endpoints should be established for assessing whether the goal has been achieved. The needs of the patient, characteristics of the medication, needs of other health care team members, and policies and procedures of the health care setting will influence the monitoring plan.

Developing a Pharmacotherapeutic Regimen and Corresponding Monitoring Plan. The regimen and plan developed in collaboration with the patient and other health professionals should be systematic and logical and should represent a consensus among the patient, prescriber, and pharmacist. The approach selected should be based on consideration of the type of practice setting, its policies and procedures, practice standards, and good professional relations with the prescriber and patient. The regimen and monitoring plan should be documented in the patient's health record to ensure that all members of the health care team have this information.

Initiating the Pharmacotherapeutic Regimen. Depending on the regimen and plan, the pharmacist could, as appropriate, implement all or portions of the pharmacotherapeutic regimen. Actions should comply with the health system's policies and procedures (e.g., prescribing protocols) and correspond to the regimen and plan. Orders for medications, laboratory tests, and other interventions should be clear and concise. All actions should be documented in the patient's health record.

Monitoring the Effects of the Pharmacotherapeutic Regimen. Data collected according to the monitoring plan should be sufficient, reliable, and valid so that judgments can be made about the effects of the pharmacotherapeutic regimen. Changes in patient status, condition, medication therapy, or nonmedication therapy since the monitoring plan was developed should be considered. Missing or additional data should be identified. Achievement of the desired endpoints should be assessed for each parameter in the monitoring plan. A judgment should be made about whether the pharmacotherapeutic goals were met. Before the pharmacotherapeutic regimen is adjusted, the cause for failure to achieve any of the pharmacotherapeutic goals should be determined.

Redesigning the Pharmacotherapeutic Regimen and Monitoring Plan. Decisions to change the regimen and plan should be based on the patient's outcome. When clinical circumstances permit, one aspect of the regimen at a time should be changed and reassessed. Recommendations for pharmacotherapeutic changes should be documented in the same manner used to document the original recommendations.

Pharmacist's Responsibility

An essential element of pharmaceutical care is that the pharmacist accepts responsibility for the patient's pharmacotherapeutic outcomes. The same commitment that is applied to designing the pharmacotherapeutic regimen and monitoring plan for the patient should be applied to its implementation. The provision of pharmaceutical care requires monitoring the regimen's effects, revising the regimen as the patient's condition changes, documenting the results, and assuming responsibility for the pharmacotherapeutic effects.

References

1. Hepler CD, Strand LM. Opportunities and responsibilities in pharmaceutical care. *Am J Hosp Pharm.* 1990; 47:533–43.
2. American Society of Hospital Pharmacists. ASHP statement on pharmaceutical care. *Am J Hosp Pharm.* 1993; 50:1720–3.
3. Implementing pharmaceutical care. Proceedings of an invitational conference conducted by the American Society of Hospital Pharmacists and the ASHP Research Foundation. *Am J Hosp Pharm.* 1993; 50: 1585–656.
4. Summary of the final report of the Scope of Pharmacy Practice Project. *Am J Hosp Pharm.* 1994; 51:2179–82.
5. Shepherd MF. Clinical skills program pharmacotherapy series module 1. Reviewing patient medical charts. Bethesda, MD: American Society of Hospital Pharmacists; 1992.
6. Mason N, Shimp LA. Clinical skills program pharmacotherapy series module 2. Building a pharmacist's patient data base. Bethesda, MD: American Society of Hospital Pharmacists; 1993.
7. Mason N, Shimp LA. Clinical skills program—module 3. Constructing a patient's drug therapy problem list. Bethesda, MD: American Society of Hospital Pharmacists; 1993.
8. Jones WN, Campbell S. Clinical skills program pharmacotherapy series module 4. Designing and recommending a pharmacist's care plan. Bethesda, MD: American Society of Hospital Pharmacists; 1994.
9. Frye CB. Clinical skills program pharmacotherapy series module 5. Monitoring the pharmacist's care plan. Bethesda, MD: American Society of Hospital Pharmacists; 1994.
10. PL 93-579. 5 U.S.C.A. 552a (88 Stat. 1896).
11. ASHP guidelines for obtaining authorization for documenting pharmaceutical care in patient medical records. *Am J Hosp Pharm.* 1989; 46:338–9.
12. Principles of practice for pharmaceutical care. Washington, DC: American Pharmaceutical Association; 1995.

Approved by the ASHP Board of Directors, April 24, 1996. Developed by the ASHP Council on Professional Affairs.

The bibliographic citation for this document is as follows: American Society of Health-System Pharmacists. ASHP guidelines on a standardized method for pharmaceutical care. *Am J Health-Syst Pharm.* 1996; 53:1713–6.

ASHP Guidelines on the Pharmacist's Role in the Development, Implementation, and Assessment of Critical Pathways

Purpose

The purpose of these guidelines is (1) to describe the pharmacist's role in the development, implementation, and assessment of critical pathways (CPs) and (2) to help pharmacists prepare for that responsibility. Because pharmacotherapy is a central component of many CPs, pharmacists should take leadership roles in the development, implementation, and assessment of CPs. By assuming leadership roles, pharmacists can help improve patient outcomes, contribute to cost-effective patient care, and promote multidisciplinary approaches to patient care and performance improvement. Although pharmacist involvement in the early stages of CP development is crucial to success, CP development is generally cyclical, and pharmacists should seek opportunities to become involved at any stage in the cycle of CP development, implementation, and assessment.

Background

The development of CPs has been stimulated by the desire to improve patient outcomes by applying evidence-based clinical practice guidelines; increased interest in measuring and improving the quality of health care, including continuous-quality-improvement (CQI) initiatives; and managed care and other market-driven health care reforms. CPs can be defined as patient care management plans that delineate key steps along an optimal treatment timeline to achieve a set of predetermined intermediate and ultimate goals for patients who have clearly defined diagnoses or require certain procedures.[1] CPs have also been called care guides, clinical pathways, clinical care plans, and care maps.[2] CPs derive from the industrial engineering concept of critical paths[3] and were originally associated with inpatient acute care and used primarily by nurses. CPs have evolved to incorporate the spectrum of patient care providers and settings and to include CQI concepts.[4] CPs and similar tools are developed in many facilities for many purposes.[5–20] Although dismissed by some critics as "cookbook medicine," CPs have in some cases been shown to improve patient outcomes[21–26] and to reduce health care expenses.[27–36] ASHP believes that carefully developed and skillfully managed CPs can improve the care of patients across the spectrum of health-system settings, as well as improve the allocation of scarce health care resources.

Typical CP Process

Each health system will use a process of CP development, implementation, and assessment that meets its own needs within its own structure, culture, practice settings, and policies and procedures, but these processes do share common elements. Typically, once a disease or procedure is selected for CP development, a multidisciplinary team analyzes its current management (including process variances, costs, and outcomes), evaluates the scientific literature, and develops a plan of care. The planned actions for each discipline on the health care team are mapped on a timeline for the specific

---

Summary of guidelines. Because pharmacotherapy is a central component of many critical pathways, pharmacists should take leadership roles in their development, implementation, and assessment.

Pharmacists can improve the development of critical pathways by ensuring the evidence-based selection of medications, establishing measures for monitoring patients for drug efficacy and adverse effects, and evaluating the proposed critical pathway for patient safety.

Pharmacists can improve the implementation of critical pathways by documenting processes and outcomes, ensuring proper patient selection and medication use, monitoring patients for drug efficacy and adverse effects, and providing for continuity of care.

Pharmacists can improve the assessment of critical pathways by measuring and analyzing processes and outcomes, disseminating the results of those analyses, and reviewing the critical pathways' pharmacotherapy to keep pace with changes in best practices.

---

disease or procedure.[37] Pharmacists perform the following functions in a typical CP: oversee the selection of medications by using an evidence-based approach, develop the criteria for medication selection or dosages, monitor patients for drug efficacy and adverse effects (or establish parameters for monitoring), and ensure continuity of care across the health system. The following describes common steps in the development, implementation, and assessment of CPs.[3]

1. *Select diagnoses and procedures.* Diagnoses and procedures selected for CP development usually include those with high process variability, high cost, high patient volume, and high risk. CPs can be developed for common or specialized diagnoses (e.g., myocardial infarction, diabetes mellitus) or procedures (e.g., transurethral prostatectomy, coronary artery bypass grafting), for diagnoses that are likely to cause changes in health status (e.g., uncontrolled asthma), and for diseases requiring complicated pharmacotherapeutic regimens (e.g., AIDS). The criteria for selection should be developed with input from administrative and clinical leaders to ensure institutionwide acceptance and should be based on scientific evidence.

2. *Appoint a development team.* The development team should include key health care providers from all organizational components involved in the CP. The importance of a multidisciplinary approach to CP development cannot be overemphasized. If possible, consideration should be given to including a patient representative on the CP development team. Although insurance carriers and managed care providers may not have representatives on the development team, their protocols or guidelines should be evaluated by the

team for inclusion in the CP as appropriate.

3. *Conduct a search of the scientific literature.* A literature and database search conducted early in the process will help identify measures for assessing current processes and outcomes and will help ensure an evidence-based approach to the CP.

4. *Document current processes and outcomes.* The current processes, costs, variances, and outcomes need to be documented, usually through flow charting of the current process, retrospective chart review, and benchmarking. Benchmarking may be internal or external to the health system. Depending on the health system's resources, benchmarking may rely on chart review or may use computerized databases that compare physicians' use of resources, health-system costs, and outcomes for specific diagnosis-related groups. This step identifies the health system's practice and compares it with published clinical guidelines that are preferably consensus based (e.g., guidelines from the Agency for Healthcare Research and Quality or the American Heart Association). The team developing the CP should use an evidence-based approach to identify, discuss, and resolve the gaps between clinical guidelines and current local practice. Input from the practitioners who will be involved in the CP is crucial to the success of this process evaluation and CP development in general.

5. *Develop the CP.* Multidisciplinary, standardized development of the CP ensures integration of care and elimination of duplication and oversights. The CP should state its goals, define actions essential to achieving those goals, provide for patient education, outline assessment of patient safety, identify measures of conformance and outcomes, and describe required documentation. The actions and resources required for implementation should be discussed and agreed upon by all disciplines involved.
   a. Goals and outcomes
      - Define the specific goals or measurable outcomes of the CP (e.g., decreased length of stay, decreased ventilator time, reduced overall patient cost, decreased pain scores, early ambulation).
      - Select the areas of focus or categories of actions essential to achieving the goals and outcomes. To ensure consistency and continuity, these areas of focus should be standardized for all CPs developed within a health system; examples of focus areas are treatments, medications, and patient education and counseling.
      - Determine the appropriate time frame. This will vary according to the disease or procedure being addressed and the practice setting (e.g., emergency room, ambulatory care clinic, acute care hospital). The time frame may be specified in minutes, hours, days, or phases. A workload assessment may be required to develop appropriate time frames.
      - Define the activity for the focus area under the appropriate time frame (e.g., "pharmacist provides medication-use education and counseling on discharge day").
   b. Patient education
      - Modify the CP, using lay terms in the patient's primary language, to educate the patient about

activities to be performed, time frames, and expected outcomes. In some practice settings, the patient may be an active partner in CP decision-making and implementation.
   c. Patient safety
      - Identify potential risks to the patient that may arise from use of the CP. For example, the CP could be subjected to the institution's failure-mode and effects analysis, or the medication safety self-assessment tool of the Institute for Safe Medication Practices could be used to assess the safety of the practices outlined in the CP.[38]
   d. Monitoring
      - Identify measures of conformance and variance so that the CP and the resulting outcomes can be continuously improved. Variances are deviations from the CP that may be positive or negative, avoidable or unavoidable, consequential or inconsequential. Sources of variances include patient responses to medications, physician decisions, and system breakdowns.
   e. Documentation
      - Develop a single, multidisciplinary work sheet or other tool that describes the CP's actions and time frames and provides spaces for documenting that actions were performed.[12] Describe how this tool will be used and how data will be collected.

6. *Obtain approval for the CP and educate participants.* To ensure global acceptance among all health care provider groups, the CP should be approved by appropriate committees, especially those of the medical staff. The impact of CP implementation on practitioner workloads will require careful consideration, and departmental policies or procedures may need to be modified. The pharmacy and therapeutics (P&T) committee should review pharmacotherapeutic issues associated with the CP early enough during development that therapeutic concerns can be addressed as they arise rather than after the CP is implemented. After the CP is approved, all health care team members involved in the care of the patients affected by the CP should be educated about the anticipated outcomes, specific actions and time frames, and professional responsibilities associated with the CP.

7. *Implement the CP.* After the necessary education and training of providers, the CP is available for use. Starting the CP as a pilot project for a small number of patients may provide valuable initial assessments that will facilitate wider implementation. Staff members should be designated to identify patients suitable for the CP and to guide their enrollment and the CP's use. Patients enrolled in a CP are assigned to a health care team whose members have specific responsibilities for actions and time frames.

8. *Assess the CP.* Because not all consequences of a CP are foreseeable, CPs require periodic assessment. Assessments after a few days or weeks of use may gauge only the feasibility of the CP and not its success in achieving desired goals, but they should identify unexpected problems that may require modifications to the CP. Surveys of health care practitioners may be useful in such initial assessments. Assessments after a few months of use may provide an initial perspective on the CP's success but may not be sufficient to fully evaluate

outcomes. Assessments after longer periods should produce evidence supporting the CP's original goals. Regular analysis of the results and variances, as well as new information (e.g., new indications for medications) and technologies (e.g., new pharmacotherapy), provides data for a root-cause analysis and continuous improvement of the CP.

9. *Disseminate the results of the assessment.* The results of the assessment should be shared not just with health-system managers or members of the CP development or oversight committees but with all staff involved in the CP. Widespread dissemination allows for more suggestions for improvement from all members of the health care team and encourages acceptance of any alterations in the CP required by the assessment. Publishing the results in a journal, sharing the experience with a practice network, or presenting the results at a meeting expands the general pool of knowledge concerning CPs.

Pharmacist Involvement

These guidelines suggest actions to help prepare pharmacists and pharmacy departments for involvement in the development, implementation, and assessment of CPs at various levels of care and in different practice settings. The applicability of these guidelines depends on a pharmacist's or pharmacy department's current level of involvement in patient care and CPs. Pharmacists should focus on incorporating contemporary pharmaceutical care principles (e.g., assessing medication orders, developing pharmacotherapeutic regimens and monitoring plans, educating and counseling patients, calculating doses according to pharmacokinetic principles, conducting medication-use evaluations [MUEs], and managing anticoagulation therapy) in the development, implementation, and assessment of CPs.[39–42]

Preparing for Involvement in CP Development. Pharmacists should learn about their health system's approach to CP development and assess their readiness for involvement. They should

1. Review the health system's current strategic plan with respect to CPs. Because CPs are inherently collaborative, pharmacists should try to understand this strategic plan from the perspective of other health care providers, seeking advice from them when necessary. When reviewing the strategic plan, pharmacists should also consider the needs of specific patient populations served by their institutions.

2. Educate the pharmacy staff on the purposes and processes of CP development and the contents of CPs. The patient care decisions required in CPs demand clinical knowledge, and the pharmacotherapy involved should be based on evidence in the scientific literature. This clinical knowledge is fundamental to the CP. An effective contributor to the CP process needs to first acquire the clinical knowledge on which the CP is based and then use CQI, teamwork, negotiation, and administrative skills to develop, implement, and assess the CP.

3. Discuss CP experiences with pharmacy colleagues within and outside the health system. Pharmacists should create a forum within the health system for ongoing dialogue about CPs; for example, CPs could be made a regular agenda item for the P&T committee

meeting and for other multidisciplinary clinical and departmental meetings.

4. Monitor pharmacy, nursing, quality management, health-system, health care, and management literature for ideas on CP development, implementation, and assessment. CPs from other institutions may be used as examples of and frameworks for mapping care, but they should not be adopted directly, because acceptance and use are greater when CPs are developed or adapted by their users.

5. Identify opportunities for contributing, through the provision of pharmaceutical care, to the health system's patient care delivery and improvement efforts.

Initiating Involvement. Pharmacists should begin their involvement in the CP process in ways most appropriate to their health system's structure, culture, practice settings, and policies and procedures. Involvement may vary substantially from one health system to another, but in general pharmacists should

1. Develop relationships with nursing, medical, dietary, laboratory, quality management, risk management, respiratory care, and other personnel through routine meetings, nursing and medical forums, and other multidisciplinary opportunities. These relationships should be used to promote pharmacists' contributions to collaborative patient care. The pharmacy department should support the use of CPs as an effective way to integrate and align services, processes, and costs.

2. Support or initiate the implementation of a multidisciplinary team for CP development and oversight and ensure that the pharmacy department and the P&T committee are represented on the oversight committee.

3. Seek leadership roles on the health system's CP oversight committee and development teams but be willing to accept subordinate roles. For example, pharmacists should be willing to lead or assist with literature evaluation for the health system's CP development teams.

4. Identify qualities required for the pharmacist's role and develop a consistent process for selecting the most appropriate pharmacists to participate on the various CP development teams.

5. Ensure the ongoing involvement of the P&T committee in the CP process. The P&T committee can facilitate the process by

   • Reviewing and endorsing the pharmacotherapy proposed for inclusion in each CP.

   • Establishing a standing P&T subcommittee or liaison position to assist CP development teams. The subcommittee or liaison would have the opportunity to educate the CP team about the formulary process, the process for MUE, the appropriate use of restricted medications, and other critical medication-use issues.

   • Publishing CPs and information about the health system's experiences with CPs in the P&T committee newsletter.

   • Developing the drug therapy portion of the CP assessment into an MUE.

6. Emphasize to pharmacists, other health care providers, and health-system administrators pharmacists' responsibility for implementing CP steps that involve pharmacotherapeutic regimens and monitoring, medication distribution, and patient education and counseling.

7. Initiate, after appropriate approvals, the development of the pharmacotherapeutic components of CPs.

8. Offer to evaluate and adapt the pharmacotherapeutic components of existing protocols and guidelines for CPs under development. Maintain a pharmacotherapy database to facilitate CP updates when new medications and pharmacotherapeutic alternatives become available.

9. Develop patient education and counseling materials for the pharmacotherapeutic components of CPs and develop plans for pharmacists or other members of the health care team to provide education and counseling to patients.

10. Advocate the development and use of preprinted medication orders (hard copy or electronic) and consistent use of terminology (e.g., generic drug names, decimals and units of measurement, and standardized terms and abbreviations) within the CP.

11. Be proactive in anticipating alternative processes or drug regimens that may be required in unusual circumstances, such as drug shortages.

Maintaining Involvement. Pharmacists' continued involvement in CPs will depend on their ability to demonstrate their contributions to patient care delivery and improvement to the CP oversight committee and development teams and to the health system's administration. To accomplish this, pharmacists can

1. Monitor the literature of pharmacy, nursing, quality management, health systems, health care, and management for ideas on CP development, implementation, and assessment.

2. Identify new areas for CP development on the basis of medication-use data (e.g., medication error data and MUE findings).

3. Incorporate CPs into the pharmacy department's culture by building responsibilities and performance expectations for CP development, implementation, and assessment into pharmacists' job descriptions.

4. Identify and train pharmacy staff on their roles and responsibilities for implementing the pharmaceutical care components of CPs.

5. Provide objective clinical input that is based on scientific evidence.

6. Ensure consistent use of terminology (e.g., generic drug names, decimals and units of measurement, and standardized terms and abbreviations), rational medication use, and appropriate monitoring. This could be done by the P&T committee or by a pharmacist who coordinates and reviews the pharmacotherapeutic efforts of all CPs.

7. Maintain good working relationships with CP development teams. The pharmacist member should be confident, assertive, cooperative, and effective in communicating with other health care providers.

8. Develop and maintain clinical and management skills through ongoing self-education.

Contributing to the CQI Aspects of CPs. The pharmacist should ensure that the pharmaceutical care actions of the CP contribute to patient satisfaction, desired clinical outcomes, and financial goals by

1. Monitoring the literature for best-practice results relat-

ing to specific disease states (as defined by federal diagnosis-related-group classification) and comparing these results with the health system's experience.

2. Ensuring that an internal system of CP tracking and therapeutic review is in place for the rapid insertion of new, more effective therapies into the CP and that CPs are integrated into the institution's CQI processes.

3. Assisting the development of patient satisfaction surveys.

4. Monitoring the results of the CPs and using them to perform MUEs.[42] Since patients enrolled in CPs are receiving predetermined pharmacotherapeutic regimens and monitoring, this is an excellent opportunity to perform disease- and outcome-oriented MUEs. The pharmacist should review the variances and outcomes associated with the CP, determine the effects of pharmacotherapy, and use this analysis to modify the CP. The pharmacotherapeutic component must be specific enough (e.g., specifying the medication and dosage) that its influence on the outcomes can be determined with confidence.

5. Ensuring that CPs are updated when there are changes in institutional practices (e.g., formulary changes) or when external practices change (e.g., guidelines are revised, dosage or monitoring recommendations are revised).

Ensuring the Continuity of a CP. Many CPs require continuity of care across various levels of care and practice settings. Such CPs should specify referral patterns among the levels of care and practice settings. To help accomplish this, pharmacists can

1. Ensure that members of all organizational components are included in the development and assessment of the CP as appropriate for the particular disease or procedure. Included might be personnel in the emergency department, the operating room, the intensive care unit, the step-down unit, the general nursing unit, the rehabilitation unit, the long-term-care facility, the ambulatory care clinic, the laboratory, and the home care service.

2. Develop relationships with ambulatory care, home care, and long-term-care pharmacists and other health care providers to foster the seamless provision of pharmaceutical care by inviting pharmacist members of managed care organizations to participate in CP development, exchanging CPs with the managed care organizations, and creating work teams to ensure the continuity of care.

3. Organize interdisciplinary sharing of information (e.g., recent laboratory test results) and documentation that are useful to all health care providers.

4. Develop a plan to communicate and monitor both internal and external CPs so that pharmacists have a full understanding of the CP process and can evaluate and adjust the CP as necessary when new therapeutic modalities emerge. Optimize this by using electronic and Internet technology to rapidly insert new pharmacotherapies into CPs when appropriate and evaluate which pharmacotherapies are included in which CPs to ensure consistency in medication management.

5. Initiate dialogue among pharmacists to ensure the continuity of the individual patient's CP. For example, when a patient is admitted, the hospital pharmacist

should, if necessary and with the patient's permission, contact the patient's community pharmacist or managed care company to obtain information as allowed under local, state, and federal laws (e.g., the Health Insurance Portability and Accessibility Act). The pharmacist should document an accurate medication history (prescription and nonprescription products, dietary supplements, and home remedies), the patient's history of adverse drug reactions and allergies, the patient's medication-taking behaviors (adherence, health beliefs, and social and cultural issues), and any self-monitoring. This does not obviate the requirement for the pharmacist to establish a professional relationship with the patient and to obtain information directly. When the patient is discharged, the hospital pharmacist could (in accordance with the institution's policies and procedures and with the patient's permission) prepare an original discharge summary or append to the physician's discharge summary any necessary notes regarding medications. An appropriate member of the discharge team should forward the discharge summary to relevant health care providers (e.g., physicians, home care nurses, and community or home care pharmacists). The summary should include the patient's chief complaint, the patient's height and weight, a history of the present illness (including the hospital course), pregnancy and lactation status, prescription and nonprescription medications on admission and at discharge, patient education and counseling, the monitoring plan (including patient self-monitoring and a plan for long-term monitoring of the patient's pharmacotherapeutic regimen), and a person to contact if the patient has questions. The pharmacist should check any discharge prescriptions against the indications listed in the discharge summary.

The Pharmacist's Responsibility

Carefully developed and skillfully managed CPs can improve the quality of care and the allocation of health care resources. Because pharmacotherapy is a central component of many CPs, pharmacists can help improve patient outcomes, contribute to cost-effective patient care, and promote team approaches to patient care and performance improvement by incorporating contemporary pharmaceutical care principles, activities, and services into the development, implementation, and assessment of CPs. Health systems will develop CPs in ways that are most appropriate to their patient populations, organizational structure, culture, and environment, so it is the responsibility of health-system pharmacists to identify opportunities to become involved in and improve the CPs in their institutions.

References

1. Darer J, Pronovost P, Bass E. Use and evaluation of critical pathways in hospitals. *Eff Clin Pract.* 2002; 5:114–9.
2. Lumsdon K, Hagland M. Mapping care. *Hosp Health Netw.* 1993; 67:34–40.
3. Coffey RJ, Richards JS, Remmert CS, et al. An introduction to critical paths. *Qual Manag Health Care.* 1992; 1:45–54.
4. Jaggers LD. Differentiation of critical pathways from other health care management tools. *Am J Health-Syst Pharm.* 1996; 53:311–3.
5. Koch KE. Opportunities for pharmaceutical care with critical pathways. *Top Hosp Pharm Manag.* 1995; 14:1–7.
6. Stevenson LL. Critical pathway experience at Sarasota Memorial Hospital. *Am J Health-Syst Pharm.* 1995; 52:1071–3.
7. Gousse GC, Rousseau MR. Critical pathways at Hartford Hospital. *Am J Health-Syst Pharm.* 1995; 52:1060–3.
8. Shane R, Vinson B. Use of critical pathways and indicators in pharmacy practice. *Top Hosp Pharm Manag.* 1995; 14:55–67.
9. Gouveia WA, Massaro FJ. Critical pathway experience at New England Medical Center. *Am J Health-Syst Pharm.* 1995; 52:1068–70.
10. Saltiel E. Critical pathway experience at Cedars-Sinai Medical Center. *Am J Health-Syst Pharm.* 1995; 52:1063–8.
11. Nelson SP. Critical pathways at University of Iowa Hospitals and Clinics. *Am J Health-Syst Pharm.* 1995; 52:1058–60.
12. Marrie TJ, Lau CY, Wheeler SL, et al. A controlled trial of a critical pathway for treatment of community-acquired pneumonia. CAPITAL Study Investigators. Community-Acquired Pneumonia Intervention Trial Assessing Levofloxacin. *JAMA.* 2000; 283:749–55.
13. Cannon CP, Hand MH, Bahr R, et al. Critical pathways for management of patients with acute coronary syndromes: an assessment by the National Heart Attack Alert Program. *Am Heart J.* 2002; 143:777–89.
14. Jones S. A clinical pathway for pediatric gastroenteritis. *Gastroenterol Nurs.* 2003; 26:7–18.
15. Nierman DM. A structure of care for the chronically critically ill. *Crit Care Clin.* 2002; 18:477–91.
16. Kercsmar CM, Myers TR. Clinical pathways in treatment of asthma. *Curr Opin Allergy Clin Immunol.* 2002; 2:183–7.
17. Mavroukakis SA, Muehlbauer PM, White RL Jr, et al. Clinical pathways for managing patients receiving interleukin 2. *Clin J Oncol Nurs.* 2001; 5:207–17.
18. Zevola DR, Raffa M, Brown K. Using clinical pathways in patients undergoing cardiac valve surgery. *Crit Care Nurse.* 2002; 22:31–9,44–50.
19. Rymer MM, Summers D, Soper P. Development of clinical pathways for stroke management: an example from Saint Luke's Hospital, Kansas City. *Clin Geriatr Med.* 1999; 15:741–64.
20. Bisanz A, DeJesus Y, Saddler DA. Development, implementation, and ongoing monitoring of pathways for the treatment of gastrointestinal cancer at a comprehensive cancer center. *Gastroenterol Nurs.* 1999; 22:107–14.
21. Sesperez J, Wilson S, Jalaludin B, et al. Trauma case management and clinical pathways: prospective evaluation of their effect on selected patient outcomes in five key trauma conditions. *J Trauma.* 2001; 50:643–9.
22. Mamolen NL, Brenner PS. The impact of a burn wound education program and implementation of a clinical pathway on patient outcomes. *J Burn Care Rehabil.* 2000; 21:440–5.
23. Crane M, Werber B. Critical pathway approach to diabetic pedal infections in a multidisciplinary setting. *J Foot Ankle Surg.* 1999; 38:30–3.
24. Baker CM, Miller I, Sitterding M, et al. Acute stroke

patients comparing outcomes with and without case management. *Nurs Case Manag.* 1998; 3:196–203.

25. Holtzman J, Bjerke T, Kane R. The effects of clinical pathways for renal transplant on patient outcomes and length of stay. *Med Care.* 1998; 36:826–34.

26. Petitta A, Kaatz S, Estrada C, et al. The transition to medication system performance indicators. *Top Hosp Pharm Manag.* 1995; 14:20–6.

27. Johnson KB, Blaisdell CJ, Walker A, et al. Effectiveness of a clinical pathway for inpatient asthma management. *Pediatrics.* 2000; 106:1006–12.

28. Philbin EF, Rocco TA, Lindenmuth NW, et al. The results of a randomized trial of a quality improvement intervention in the care of patients with heart failure. The MISCHF Study Investigators. *Am J Med.* 2000; 109:443–9.

29. Murphy M, Noetscher C, Lagoe R. A multihospital effort to reduce inpatient lengths of stay for pneumonia. *J Nurs Care Qual.* 1999; 13:11–23.

30. Dzwierzynski WW, Spitz K, Hartz A, et al. Improvement in resource utilization after development of a clinical pathway for patients with pressure ulcers. *Plast Reconstr Surg.* 1998; 102:2006–11.

31. Boykin JV Jr, Crossland MC, Cole LM. Wound healing management: enhancing patient outcomes and reducing costs. *J Healthc Resour Manag.* 1997; 15:22,24–6.

32. Leibman BD, Dillioglugil O, Abbas F, et al. Impact of a clinical pathway for radical retropubic prostatectomy. *Urology.* 1998; 52:94–9.

33. Bailey R, Weingarten S, Lewis M, et al. Impact of clinical pathways and practice guidelines on the management of acute exacerbations of bronchial asthma. *Chest.* 1998; 113:28–33.

34. Uchiyama K, Takifuji K, Tani M, et al. Effectiveness of the clinical pathway to decrease length of stay and cost for laparoscopic surgery. *Surg Endosc.* 2002; 16:1594–7.

35. Wilson SD, Dahl BB, Wells RD. An evidence-based clinical pathway for bronchiolitis safely reduces antibiotic overuse. *Am J Med Qual.* 2002; 17:195–9.

36. Smith DM, Gow P. Towards excellence in quality patient care: a clinical pathway for myocardial infarction. *J Qual Clin Pract.* 1999; 19:103–5.

37. Kirk JK, Michael KA, Markowsky SJ, et al. Critical pathways: the time is here for pharmacist involvement. *Pharmacotherapy.* 1996; 16:723–33.

38. Institute for Safe Medication Practices. Medication safety self-assessment. www.ismp.org/pages/mssacaprdf.html (accessed 2003 May 16).

39. American Society of Hospital Pharmacists. ASHP statement on pharmaceutical care. *Am J Hosp Pharm.* 1993; 50:1720–3.

40. American Society of Hospital Pharmacists. ASHP statement on principles for including medications and pharmaceutical care in health care systems. *Am J Hosp Pharm.* 1993; 50:756–7.

41. American Society of Health-System Pharmacists. ASHP guidelines on a standardized method for pharmaceutical care. *Am J Health-Syst Pharm.* 1996; 53: 1713–6.

42. American Society of Health-System Pharmacists. ASHP guidelines on medication-use evaluation. *Am J Health-Syst Pharm.* 1996; 53:1953–5.

Approved by the ASHP Board of Directors on April 15, 2004. Developed by the ASHP Council on Professional Affairs. Supersedes the "ASHP guidelines on the pharmacists' role in the development of clinical care plans" dated November 16, 1996.

The bibliographic citation for this document is as follows: American Society of Health-System Pharmacists. ASHP guidelines on the pharmacist's role in the development, implementation, and assessment of critical pathways. *Am J Health-Syst Pharm.* 2004; 61:939–45.

ASHP Guidelines on Documenting Pharmaceutical Care in Patient Medical Records

Purpose

The professional actions of pharmacists that are intended to ensure safe and effective use of drugs and that may affect patient outcomes should be documented in the patient medical record (PMR). These guidelines describe the kinds of information pharmacists should document in the PMR, how that information should be documented, methods for obtaining authorization for pharmacist documentation, and the important role of training and continuous quality improvement (CQI) in documentation.

Background

Pharmaceutical care is the direct, responsible provision of medication-related care for the purpose of achieving definite outcomes that improve a patient's quality of life.[1] A core principle of pharmaceutical care is that the pharmacist accepts professional responsibility for patient outcomes.[2] Integrating pharmaceutical care into a patient's overall health care plan requires effective and efficient communication among health care professionals. As an integral member of the health care team, the pharmacist must document the care provided. Such documentation is vital to a patient's continuity of care and demonstrates both the accountability of the pharmacist and the value of the pharmacist's services. Moreover, because clinical services (e.g., those incident to a physician's services) are generally considered reimbursable only when they are necessary for the medical management of a patient and when the service provided and the patient's response are carefully documented, thorough documentation may increase the likelihood of reimbursement. Early implementation of such documentation practices may help health-system pharmacies cope with documentation requirements in the event pharmacists' clinical services become reimbursable.

The PMR's primary purpose is to convey information for use in patient care; it serves as a tool for communication among health care professionals. Information in the PMR may also be used in legal proceedings (e.g., as evidence), education (e.g., for training students), research (e.g., for evaluating clinical drug use), and quality assurance evaluations (e.g., to ascertain adherence to practice standards).[3]

Clinical recommendations made by a pharmacist on behalf of the patient, as well as actions taken in accordance with these recommendations, should be documented in a permanent manner that makes the information available to all the health care professionals caring for the patient. ASHP believes that, to ensure proper coordination of patients' medication therapies, health care systems must be designed to enable, foster, and facilitate communication and collaboration among health care providers.[2] Health care systems must not erect barriers to that communication or to the exercise of the professional judgment of health care providers.

Although telephone calls and other oral communication may be necessary for immediate interventions, they do not allow for the dissemination of information to care providers who are not a part of the conversation. Such interventions should be documented in the PMR as soon as possible after the acute situation has settled. For less urgent and routine recommendations, timely documentation is also preferred, because delays in response to telephone calls or pager messages may lead to miscommunicated or undocumented recommendations. Unofficial, temporary, or removable notes placed in the PMR do not provide a standard of acceptable communication or documentation and therefore are discouraged. Documentation that is not a part of the PMR (e.g., documentation in pharmacy records) may provide a degree of risk reduction; however, such documentation does not provide important information to other care providers and can interrupt continuity of care when the patient is discharged or transferred.

Documenting Pharmaceutical Care

Pharmacists should be authorized and encouraged to make notations in the PMR for the purpose of documenting their findings, assessments, conclusions, and recommendations.[2] ASHP believes that all significant clinical recommendations and resulting actions should be documented in the appropriate section of the PMR. The pharmacy department should establish policies and procedures for documenting information in the PMR. Such policies and procedures will help pharmacists exercise good judgment in determining what information to document in the PMR and how to present it.

Examples of information a pharmacist may need to document in the PMR include, but are not limited to, the following:

1. A summary of the patient's medication history on admission, including medication allergies and their manifestations.
2. Oral and written consultations provided to other health care professionals regarding the patient's drug therapy selection and management.
3. Physicians' oral orders received directly by the pharmacist.
4. Clarification of drug orders.
5. Adjustments made to drug dosage, dosage frequency, dosage form, or route of administration.
6. Drugs, including investigational drugs, administered.
7. Actual and potential drug-related problems that warrant surveillance.
8. Drug therapy-monitoring findings, including
   a. The therapeutic appropriateness of the patient's drug regimen, including the route and method of administration.
   b. Therapeutic duplication in the patient's drug regimen.
   c. The degree of patient compliance with the prescribed drug regimen.
   d. Actual and potential drug–drug, drug–food, drug–laboratory test, and drug–disease interactions.
   e. Clinical and pharmacokinetic laboratory data pertinent to the drug regimen.
   f. Actual and potential drug toxicity and adverse effects.
   g. Physical signs and clinical symptoms relevant to the patient's drug therapy.

9. Drug-related patient education and counseling provided.

Documentation by pharmacists should meet established criteria for legibility, clarity, lack of judgmental language, completeness, need for inclusion in the PMR (versus an alternative form of communication), appropriate use of a standard format (e.g., SOAP [subjective, objective, assessment, and plan] or TITRS [title, introduction, text, recommendation, and signature]), and how to contact the pharmacist (e.g., a telephone or pager number).[4]

The authority to document pharmaceutical care in the PMR comes with a responsibility to ensure that patient privacy and confidentiality are safeguarded and the communication is concise and accurate. Local, state, and federal guidelines and laws (including the Health Insurance Portability and Accountability Act of 1996 [HIPAA]) and risk management sensitivities should be considered. Nonjudgmental language should be used, with care taken to avoid words that imply blame (e.g., *error, mistake, misadventure,* and *inadvertent*) or substandard care (e.g., *bad, defective, inadequate, inappropriate, incorrect, insufficient, poor, problem,* and *unsatisfactory*).[3] Facts should be documented accurately, concisely, and objectively; such documentation should reflect the goals established by the medical team.

Documentation of a formal consultation solicited by a physician or other health care provider may include direct recommendations or suggestions as appropriate. However, unsolicited informal consultations, clinical impressions, findings, suggestions, and recommendations should generally be documented more subtly, with indirect recommendations presented in a way that allows the provider to decline the suggestion without incurring a liability. For example, the phrase "may want to consider" creates an opportunity for the suggestion to be acted upon or not, depending on presenting clinical factors.

Obtaining Authorization to Document Pharmaceutical Care

The authority to document pharmaceutical care in the PMR is granted by the health care organization in accordance with organizational and medical staff policies. Although documenting pharmaceutical care in the PMR is a pharmacist's professional responsibility, physicians and other health care professionals may not be accustomed to or open to this practice.

The following steps are recommended for obtaining authorization to document pharmaceutical care in the PMR:

1. Determine the existing organizational and medical staff policies regarding authority for documentation in the PMR. These policies may provide specific guidance on how to proceed.
2. Ascertain whether other nonphysician and nonnurse providers in the organization or affiliated organizations have been granted authority to document patient care activities in the PMR. If so, consult them regarding the process used to establish the authority.
3. Identify physicians in the organization who are willing to support documentation of pharmaceutical care in the PMR.
4. Identify the committees in the organization whose recommendations or decisions will be required to establish authority for pharmacists to document pharmaceu-

tical care in the PMR. Determine the necessary sequence of these approvals. Committees typically involved include the pharmacy and therapeutics (P&T) committee, the executive committee of the medical staff, a quality-assurance committee (e.g., the CQI committee), and the medical records committee.
5. Determine the accepted method and format for submitting a proposal requesting authority to document pharmaceutical care in the PMR. In some organizations, a written proposal may be required. If so, determine the desired format (length, style, and necessary justification) and deadlines for proposal submission. An oral presentation to the deciding bodies may be required. If so, determine in advance the desired presentation format and supporting materials desired by these bodies.
6. Draft a written plan describing
   a. Examples of information to be documented in the PMR. It may be helpful to describe how this important information may be lost or miscommunicated if it is not documented in the PMR.
   b. The locations within the PMR where documentation will be made and any special format or forms proposed. New forms will have to comply with HIPAA regulations and will require review and approval by specific organizational or medical staff committees. To achieve the goal of effective communication among all the members of the health care team, compartmentalization of the PMR should be avoided.
   c. The persons who will be documenting pharmaceutical care in the PMR (i.e., pharmacists, residents, or students). If pharmacy residents or students will be making notations in the PMR, procedures regarding authority and cosignatures will also have to be described.
7. Review the draft plan with the chair of the P&T committee, the director of nursing, the director of medical records, and other appropriate administrative personnel, such as the organization's risk management officer and legal counsel.
8. Seek the endorsement and recommendation of the P&T committee.
9. In appropriate sequence, seek the endorsement or decision of any other committees necessary for ultimate approval. Monitor the proposal's course through the various committees and provide assistance, clarification, or additional data as necessary.
10. When the final approving body grants PMR documentation authority, participate in the required policy development and the communication of the new policy to the individuals or departments in the organization that will be affected by the change (e.g., nurses, the medical staff, the quality-assurance staff, and the medical records department).

Training and CQI

Pharmacist documentation in the PMR is a skill that requires ongoing training and evaluation.[4] A temporary committee may be formed to manage the initial training required to implement pharmacist documentation in the PMR. That committee may consider offering presentations by physicians or other members of the health care team to provide their perspective on how to effectively communicate using the PMR. The information in those presentations may be reinforced by workshops on documentation skills. Presentation and workshop topics may include the choice of communication method (i.e., when documentation in the PMR is preferred to other means of communication), the documentation format (e.g., SOAP or TITRS), documentation etiquette, and legal requirements.[4] Documentation skills should be demonstrated before a pharmacist is allowed to make notations in the PMR.[4] The ASHP Clinical Skills Program is another tool for training pharmacists to use the PMR.[3]

Documentation of pharmaceutical care should also be one of the many functions addressed in CQI efforts. Pharmacy department CQI efforts should include the development of quality indicators that can be used to evaluate pharmacist documentation in the PMR.[4] Other CQI efforts might analyze and improve systemwide policies and procedures for documenting medication use.[5] Periodic review of organizational policies and procedures will allow for their revision in response to changes in health care and advances in technology, including the availability of an electronic PMR.[6,7]

References

1. Hepler CD, Strand LM. Opportunities and responsibilities in pharmaceutical care. *Am J Hosp Pharm.* 1990; 47:533–43.
2. American Society of Hospital Pharmacists. ASHP statement on pharmaceutical care. *Am J Hosp Pharm.* 1993; 50:1720–3.
3. Shepherd MF. Professional conduct and use of patient medical records. In: ASHP Clinical Skills Program, module 1: reviewing patient medical charts. Bethesda, MD: American Society of Hospital Pharmacists; 1992:38–41.
4. Lacy CF, Saya FG, Shane RR. Quality of pharmacists' documentations in patients' medical records. *Am J Health-Syst Pharm.* 1996; 53:2171–5.
5. Matuschka P. Improving documentation of preoperative antimicrobial prophylaxis. *Am J Health-Syst Pharm.* 1998; 55:993–4.
6. Lau A, Balen RM, Lam R, et al. Using a personal digital assistant to document clinical pharmacy services in an intensive care unit. *Am J Health-Syst Pharm.* 2001; 58:1229–32.
7. Gordon W, Malyuk D, Taki J. Use of health-record abstracting to document pharmaceutical care activities. *Can J Hosp Pharm.* 2000; 53:199–205.

Approved by the ASHP Board of Directors, February 20, 2003. Revised by the ASHP Council on Professional Affairs. Supercedes the ASHP Guidelines for Obtaining Authorization for Documenting Pharmaceutical Care in Patient Medical Records dated November 16, 1988.

The bibliographic citation for this document is as follows: American Society of Health-System Pharmacists. ASHP guidelines on documenting pharmaceutical care in patient medical records. *Am J Health-Syst Pharm.* 2003; 60:705–7.

Specific Practice Areas

Pain Management (0306)
Source: Council on Professional Affairs
To advocate fully informed patient and caregiver participation in pain management decisions as an integral aspect of patient care; further,

To advocate that pharmacists actively participate in the development and implementation of health-system pain management policies and protocols; further,

To support the participation of pharmacists in pain management, which is a multidisciplinary, collaborative process for selecting appropriate drug therapies, educating patients, monitoring patients, and continually assessing outcomes of therapy; further,

To encourage the education of pharmacists, pharmacy students, and other health care providers regarding the principles of pain management.
This policy supersedes ASHP policy 9815.

Pharmacist Support for Dying Patients (0307)
Source: Council on Professional Affairs
To support the position that care for dying patients is part of the continuum of care that pharmacists should provide to patients; further,

To support the position that pharmacists have a professional obligation to work in a collaborative and compassionate manner with patients, family members, caregivers, and other professionals to help fulfill the patient care needs, especially the quality-of-life needs, of dying patients of all ages; further,

To support research on the needs of dying patients; further,

To provide education to pharmacists on caring for dying patients, including education on clinical, managerial, professional, and legal issues; further,

To urge the inclusion of such topics in the curricula of colleges of pharmacy.
This policy supersedes ASHP policies 9814 and 9816.

Pharmacists' Role in Immunization and Vaccines (0213)
Source: Council on Educational Affairs
To affirm that pharmacists have a role in promoting and administering proper immunizations to patients and employees in all settings; further,

To encourage pharmacists to seek opportunities for involvement in disease prevention through community immunization programs; further,

To advocate the inclusion of the pharmacist's role in immunization in school of pharmacy curricula; further,

To strongly encourage pharmacists to use available opportunities and materials to educate at-risk patients, their caregivers, parents, guardians, and health care providers about the importance of immunizations.
This policy supersedes ASHP policies 0019 and 0111.

Interventions to Reduce HIV Risk Behavior in Intravenous Drug Users (9711)
Source: House of Delegates Resolution
ASHP supports the use of needle and syringe exchange programs, drug abuse treatment, and community outreach programs for substance abusers to reduce the risk of transmission of the human immunodeficiency virus (HIV), hepatitis B virus, and hepatitis C virus in intravenous drug users.
This policy was reviewed in 2001 by the Council on Professional Affairs and by the Board of Directors and was found to still be appropriate.

Primary and Preventive Care (9407)
Source: Council on Professional Affairs
To support primary and preventive care roles for pharmacists in the provision of pharmaceutical care; further,

To collaborate with physician, nursing, and health-system administrator groups in pursuit of these goals.
This policy was reviewed in 2001 by the Council on Professional Affairs and by the Board of Directors and was found to still be appropriate.

ASHP Statement on the Pharmacist's Role in Clinical Pharmacokinetic Monitoring

The American Society of Health-System Pharmacists (ASHP) believes that clinical pharmacokinetic monitoring is a fundamental responsibility of all pharmacists providing pharmaceutical care. Clinical pharmacokinetic monitoring is an integral component of pharmaceutical care for selected patients based on their specific pharmacotherapy, disease states and related factors, and treatment goals. ASHP believes that clinical pharmacokinetic monitoring is essential to achieving positive outcomes for these patients across the continuum of care and in all practice settings of health systems. Examples of such outcomes include decreased mortality, decreased length of treatment, decreased length of hospital stay, decreased morbidity (either improved symptoms of disease or improved recuperation), and decreased adverse effects from drug therapy.

Background

Clinical pharmacokinetics is the process of applying pharmacokinetic principles to determine the dosage regimens of specific drug products for specific patients to maximize pharmacotherapeutic effects and minimize toxic effects. Application of these principles requires an understanding of the absorption, distribution, metabolism, and excretion characteristics of specific drug products in specific diseases and patient populations. The influence of factors such as age, sex, diet, pathophysiologic conditions, and concomitant use of other drug products must also be understood. The development of patients' individualized dosage regimens should be based on integrated findings from monitoring both the drug concentration-versus-time profiles in biological fluids and the pharmacologic responses to these drug products.

Within the pharmaceutical care process, pharmacists' clinical functions include appropriate and cost-conscious therapeutic drug monitoring and provision of clinical pharmacokinetic assessments. Clinical pharmacokinetic monitoring is necessary when the range between minimal effectiveness and toxicity is narrow and the results of the drug assay provide significant information for clinical decision-making. In the absence of drug concentration measurements, patient-specific characteristics and physiological markers should be used to provide clinical pharmacokinetic assessments and make dosage-regimen recommendations.

Responsibilities

The following responsibilities should be part of clinical pharmacokinetic services or monitoring conducted by pharmacists:

1. Designing patient-specific drug dosage regimens based on the pharmacokinetic and pharmacologic characteristics of the drug products used, the objectives of drug therapy, concurrent diseases and drug therapy, and other pertinent patient factors (e.g., demographics, laboratory data) that improve the safety and effectiveness of drug therapy and promote positive patient outcomes.

2. Recommending or scheduling measurements of drug concentrations in biological fluids (e.g., plasma, serum, blood, cerebrospinal fluid) or tissues in order to facilitate the evaluation of dosage regimens.

3. Monitoring and adjusting dosage regimens on the basis of pharmacologic responses and biological fluid and tissue drug concentrations in conjunction with clinical signs and symptoms or other biochemical variables.

4. Evaluating unusual patient responses to drug therapy for possible pharmacokinetic and pharmacologic explanations.

5. Communicating patient-specific drug therapy information to physicians, nurses, and other clinical practitioners and to patients orally and in writing, and including documentation of this in the patient's health record.

6. Educating pharmacists, physicians, nurses, and other clinical practitioners about pharmacokinetic principles and appropriate indications for clinical pharmacokinetic monitoring, including the cost-effective use of drug concentration measurements.

7. Developing quality assurance programs for documenting improved patient outcomes and economic benefits resulting from clinical pharmacokinetic monitoring.

8. Promoting collaborative relationships with other individuals and departments involved in drug therapy monitoring to encourage the development and appropriate use of pharmacokinetic principles in pharmaceutical care.

Pharmacists with specialized education, training, or experience may have the opportunity to assume the following additional responsibilities:

1. Designing and conducting research to expand clinical pharmacokinetic knowledge and its relationship to pharmacologic responses, exploring concentration-response relationships for specific drugs, and contributing to the evaluation and expansion of clinical pharmacokinetic monitoring as an integral part of pharmaceutical care.

2. Developing and applying computer programs and point-of-care information systems to enhance the accuracy and sophistication of pharmacokinetic modeling and applications to pharmaceutical care.

3. Serving as an expert consultant to pharmacists with a general background in clinical pharmacokinetic monitoring.

Readers are referred to ASHP's more thorough publications on the subject of clinical pharmacokinetic monitoring, including *Clinical Pharmacokinetics Pocket Reference* and *Concepts in Clinical Pharmacokinetics: A Self-Instructional Course.*

This statement was reviewed in 2003 by the Council on Professional Affairs and by the Board of Directors and was found to still be appropriate.

Approved by the ASHP Board of Directors, November 15, 1997, and by the ASHP House of Delegates, June 3, 1998. Revised by the ASHP Council on Professional Affairs. Supersedes a previous version approved by the House of Delegates on June 5, 1989.

The bibliographic citation for this document is as follows: American Society of Health-System Pharmacists. ASHP statement on the pharmacist's role in clinical pharmacokinetic monitoring. *Am J Health-Syst Pharm*. 1998; 55:1726–7.

ASHP Statement on the Pharmacist's Role in Hospice and Palliative Care

Position

The American Society of Health-System Pharmacists (ASHP) believes that pharmacists have a pivotal role in the provision of hospice and palliative care and that pharmacists should be integral members of all hospice interdisciplinary teams. Pharmacists practicing in U.S. health systems have been active in defining and providing palliative care since the introduction of hospice through a demonstration project supported by the National Cancer Institute and conducted in New Haven, Connecticut, between 1974 and 1977.[1]

Palliative care has been defined by the World Health Organization (WHO) as "the active total care of patients whose disease is not responsive to curative treatment."[2] WHO notes that control of pain, other symptoms, and psychological, social, and spiritual problems is paramount. The goal of palliative care is achievement of the best quality of life for patients and their families.

Pharmaceutical care is defined as the direct, responsible provision of medication-related care for the purpose of achieving definite outcomes that improve a patient's quality of life.[3] Medication therapy is the cornerstone of most—but not all—symptom control in palliative care. The goals of palliative care and pharmaceutical care are consistent, with the latter being a necessary component of good palliative care.

Hospice is a philosophy and program that delivers palliative care. Hospice care is provided by an interdisciplinary team, which provides expert medical care, pain management, and emotional and spiritual support expressly tailored to the patient's wishes. Emotional and spiritual support are also extended to the family of the patient. In U.S. hospice programs, care is usually provided in the patient's home or in a home-like setting operated by a hospice program. Hospice and palliative care share the same core values and philosophies.

The purpose of this statement is to describe pharmacist's responsibilities and to promote understanding of the various ways in which pharmacists provide or contribute to the provision of care to patients who might be nearing the end of life.

Background

Currently, there are over 3100 operational or planned hospice programs in the 50 states, the District of Columbia, Puerto Rico, and Guam.[4] According to the National Hospice and Palliative Care Organization, 42% of hospices were freestanding in 2000 and 33% were affiliated with hospitals, 22% with home health agencies, and 9% with hospital systems. Over 700,000 patients were served in 2000, and that number is growing annually. In that same year, 73% of hospices were nonprofit, 20% were for-profit institutions, and 7% were run by government.

In 2000, 2.4 million Americans died from all causes. Hospices admitted approximately 700,000 patients. Of those, 600,000 died while under hospice care. Patients are discharged from hospices typically because of stabilization of disease, moving to an area or facility not served by a hospice, and patient and family preference. Over half of patients who die of cancer in the United States are cared for by a hospice. Hospices across the country are caring for increasing numbers of patients with cardiac disease, AIDS, renal disease, end-stage pulmonary disease, dementia, amyotrophic lateral sclerosis, Parkinson's disease, and other degenerative neurologic diseases.

Hospice care is covered by Medicare Part A, private health insurance, and Medicaid in most states for patients who meet certain criteria. Any Medicare beneficiary who has a terminal illness with a prognosis of less than six months is, if the disease runs its normal course as certified by the attending physician and the hospice medical director, eligible for the hospice Medicare benefit.[5] Ninety-one percent of U.S. hospices have met Medicare certification requirements to provide this benefit to Medicare beneficiaries at no cost to the beneficiaries. Many hospices receive charitable contributions to cover the cost of care for terminally ill patients who cannot afford to pay for their care.

Palliative care should be provided in conjunction with curative care at the time of diagnosis of a potentially terminal illness. Palliative care alone may be indicated when attempts at a cure are judged to be futile. Admissions to hospice and palliative care programs often come too late for optimal services to be provided.[6] The mean length of stay is 50 days, and the median is 25 days.[4] Many hospice patients die within days to a week after admission to a program.

A nationwide Gallup survey conducted in 1996 indicated that 9 out of 10 adults, if terminally ill and with six months or less to live, would prefer to be cared for at home. A majority of adults would be interested in a comprehensive program of care, such as hospice. When asked to name their greatest fear associated with death, most respondents cited being a burden to family and friends. Pain was the second most common fear. Effective hospice programs address these concerns.

Pharmaceutical services provided by pharmacists in U.S. hospices were surveyed qualitatively and quantitatively in 1979 and 1991.[7,8]

While many pharmacists continue to serve hospice programs as volunteer consultants to the interdisciplinary team, a growing number of those who work with hospice programs are now considered integral staff and are paid for their services. Inhouse pharmacies have increased since the mid-1990s, and the number continues to grow. A hospice that can support its own pharmacy typically has an average daily census of 200 patients. Most pharmacists who provide pharmaceutical services to hospice programs are not employed directly by the hospices but by a provider of pharmaceutical services, such as a home health pharmacy or hospital. Many are employees of pharmacies that have contracts with hospices to provide drug products and services. In recent years, specialized hospice pharmacy services have been developed in several parts of the United States, and such programs are growing rapidly.

The Hospice Interdisciplinary Team. According to Medicare hospice regulations, a hospice interdisciplinary team should include a doctor of medicine or osteopathy, a registered nurse, a social worker, and a pastoral or other counselor. Many other professionals and support persons often serve on such teams. In addition, Medicare regulations state that the hospice must "employ a licensed pharmacist; or have a formal agreement with a licensed pharmacist to advise the hospice on ordering, storage, administration, disposal, and recordkeeping of drugs and biologicals." According to the two published surveys of pharmacist activities in hospices, the hospice pharmacist typically is a full member of the interdisciplinary team.[7,8]

By regulation, a patient's plan of care must be reviewed and updated at specified intervals. If a hospice has more than one team, then it must designate the team by which a particular patient will be cared for. Hospice teams typically meet for one or two hours two to four times a month to review patients' care, status, and needs. Treatment plan modifications, determinations of need for additional services, and planning for consultations with specialists, changes in care settings, imminent death, and other important events are discussed. Education and training are often provided at these meetings as well.

The hospice medical director is a doctor of medicine or osteopathy who is responsible for the medical component of the patient's care. The director also serves as a consultant to the patient's primary care physicians and the hospice program staff. Pharmacists coordinate pharmacotherapy by making recommendations for appropriate therapy, educating patients and the hospice team about medications, monitoring therapeutic responses, and performing other medication-related functions. Adjusting drug therapy in accordance with treatment algorithms is a new role for pharmacists in some hospice and palliative care settings.

A registered nurse coordinates the implementation of each patient's plan of care. After certified nursing assistants, who may provide personal care on a daily basis, nurses make the largest number of home visits. Social workers are responsible for the psychosocial care of patients and their families, and they arrange bereavement care for families after patients die. The volunteer director recruits, trains, and coordinates volunteers—another essential component of hospice care. Volunteers provide needed relief for family caregivers and a broad range of services to patients and their families.

Chaplains address spiritual and existential issues. Hospice chaplaincy is typically nondenominational and is often provided in coordination with patients' own clergy. Other frequent participants in team meetings include nursing assistants, home health aides, dietitians, physical therapists, occupational therapists, speech therapists, and hospice administrative personnel. Students and postgraduate trainees from a variety of professions, including pharmacy, often attend as well.

Value of the Pharmacist's Care. Most hospice and palliative care is reimbursed through a capitation plan. Therefore, fees for service generally do not apply. Pharmacists can improve the cost-effectiveness of pharmacotherapy for symptom control in hospice care through patient-specific monitoring for drug therapy outcomes, recommending alternative drug products and dosage forms, minimizing duplicative and interacting medications, compounding medications extemporaneously, improving drug storage and transportation, and educating staff, patients, and families about the most efficient ways of handling and using medications. Systems for documenting these activities and determining cost-effectiveness and the cost–benefit and cost–utility ratios of medications used in the care of terminally ill patients are needed.

Avoidance of admissions to hospitals or long-term-care facilities through improved symptom control is a highly desirable and cost-effective outcome of pharmaceutical care for hospice and palliative care patients.

The Pharmacist's Responsibilities

High-quality hospice and palliative care requires both traditional and expanded pharmacist activities, including a variety of clinical, educational, administrative, and support responsibilities:

1. *Assessing the appropriateness of medication orders and ensuring the timely provision of effective medications for symptom control.* Pharmacists maintain patient medication profiles and monitor all prescription and nonprescription medication use for safety and effectiveness. Pharmacists provide patients with essential medications within a time frame that ensures continuous symptom control (especially pain relief) and avoids the need for emergency medical services.

2. *Counseling and educating the hospice team about medication therapy.* Pharmacists attend hospice team meetings to advise other team members about medication therapy, including dosage forms, routes of administration, costs, and availability of various drug products. This is done through regularly scheduled educational sessions. Pharmacists develop and maintain a library of contemporary references about medications, dietary supplements, and alternative and complementary therapies. Pharmacists advise members of the hospice team about the potential for toxicity from and interactions with dietary supplements and alternative and complementary therapies.

3. *Ensuring that patients and caregivers understand and follow the directions provided with medications.* Pharmacists ensure that all medication labeling is complete and understandable by patients and their caregivers. Hospice pharmacists communicate with patients, either through the team or in person, about the importance of adhering to the prescribed drug regimen. Pharmacists explain the differences among addiction, dependence, and tolerance and dispel patient and caregiver misconceptions about addiction to opiate agonists. Pharmacists ensure the availability of devices and equipment to permit accurate measurement of liquid dosage forms by patients and their caregivers. Pharmacists counsel patients about the role and potential toxicity of alternative and complementary therapies. When needed, hospice pharmacists visit patients' homes to communicate directly with patients and their caregivers and to make necessary assessments.

4. *Providing efficient mechanisms for extemporaneous compounding of nonstandard dosage forms.* Hospice pharmacists communicate with pharmaceutical manufacturers to determine the availability of nonstandard dosage forms. Medication-compounding needs in hospice care include the preparation of dosage forms to ease administration (e.g., concentrated sublingual solutions, topical medications), flavoring medications to promote compliance, eliminating or adjusting ingredients that patients cannot tolerate, and preparing or changing drug concentrations. Whenever possible, pharmacists compound formulations for which stability and bioavailability data are available.

5. *Addressing financial concerns.* Hospice benefits usually cover medications. However, patients may lack insurance coverage or benefits may not cover medications that are not considered strictly palliative. Pharmacists communicate with pharmaceutical manufacturers to obtain medications through patient assistance programs.

6. *Ensuring safe and legal disposal of all medications after death.* Medications dispensed to patients are "owned" by the patients and, in most states, cannot be used for other patients. Medications remaining in patients' homes fall under a variety of hazard categories. Pharmacists are able to assist families with the removal of the medications from the home in compliance with federal and state drug control and environmental protection laws and regulations.

7. *Establishing and maintaining effective communication with regulatory and licensing agencies.* Because hospice patients often require large quantities of controlled substances, open communication with both state and federal controlled-substance agencies is important. Pharmacists ensure compliance with laws and regulations pertaining to medications.

Pharmacists' Scope of Practice

The pharmacist may have a range of practice privileges that vary in their level of authority and responsibility. Pharmacists who participate in hospice and palliative care should meet the health care organization's competency requirements to ensure that they provide appropriate quality and continuity of patient care. They should demonstrate required knowledge and skills, which may be obtained through practice-intensive continuing education and pharmacy practice and specialty residencies.

The specific practice of pharmacists should be defined within a scope-of-practice document or a similar tool or protocol developed by the health care organization. The scope-of-practice document defines activities that pharmacists would provide within the context of collaborative practice as a member of the interdisciplinary team, as well as limitations where appropriate. The document should indicate referral and communication guidelines, including the documentation of patient encounters and methods for sharing patient information with collaborating medical providers.

Also included in the scope-of-practice document should be references to activities that will review the quality of care provided and the methods by which the pharmacist will maintain continuing professional competency for functions encompassed by the scope-of-practice document. A process should be in place, and responsible parties identified, to review and update the scope-of-practice document as appropriate.

Documentation of Services

As members of the interdisciplinary health care team, pharmacists should have access to patients' health records and authority to make entries necessary for the team's coordinated care of the patient. With access to the patient's health record comes the pharmacist's professional responsibility to safeguard the patient's rights to privacy and confidentiality. Patients should be informed that pharmacists, as well as other members of the team, have access to their records.

Pharmacists should routinely sign patient-review records at interdisciplinary team meetings. Pharmacist documentation in patient records should include drug therapy recommendations, monitoring of medication effects, patient and family education and counseling activities, and other activities as indicated. Medication profiles should be maintained and should include information about prescription and nonprescription drug products, dietary supplements, and alternative and complementary therapies. Pharmacists also should maintain detailed formulation files for all extemporaneously compounded dosage forms. Other records should be maintained in compliance with applicable federal and state laws and regulations.

References

1. Lipman AG. Drug therapy in terminally ill patients. *Am J Hosp Pharm.* 1975; 32:270–6.

2. World Health Organization Expert Committee. Cancer pain relief and palliative care. Technical report series 804. Geneva, Switzerland: World Health Organization; 1990.

3. American Society of Hospital Pharmacists. ASHP statement on pharmaceutical care. *Am J Hosp Pharm.* 1993; 50:1720–3.

4. National Hospice and Palliative Care Organization. NHPCO facts and figures on hospice care in America. www.nhpco.org (accessed 2002 Apr 11).

5. Gage B, Miller SC, Coppola K et al. Important questions for hospice in the next century. www.aspe.hhs.gov/daltcp/Reports/impques.htm#execsum (accessed 2001 Nov 27).

6. Lipman AG. Evidence-based palliative care. *J Pharm Care Pain Symptom Control.* 1999; 7(4):1–9.

7. Berry JI, Pulliam CC, Caiola SM et al. Pharmaceutical services in hospices. *Am J Hosp Pharm.* 1981; 38:1010–4.

8. Arter SG, Berry JI. The provision of pharmaceutical care to hospice patients: results of the National Hospice Pharmacist Survey. *J Pharm Care Pain Symptom Control.* 1993; 1(1):25–42.

Suggested Readings

1. Lipman AG, Berry JI. Pharmaceutical care of terminally ill patients. *J Pharm Care Pain Symptom Control.* 1995; 3(2):31–56.

2. Arter SG, Lipman AG. Hospice care: a new opportunity for pharmacists. *J Pharm Pract.* 1990; 3:28–33.

3. Lipman AG. Pain management in the home care and hospice patient. *J Pharm Pract.* 1990; 3:1–11.

4. Wilkins C. Pharmacy and hospice: a personal experience. *Consult Pharm.* 1988; 3:462–5.

5. Arter SG, DuBe J, Mahoney J. Hospice care and the pharmacist. *Am Pharm.* 1987; NS27:616–24.

6. Murphy DH. The delicate art of caring: treating the whole person. *Am Pharm.* 1984; NS24:388–90.

7. Quigley JL, Quigley MA, Gumbhir AK. Pharmacy and hospice: partners in patient care. *Am Pharm.* 1982; NS22:420–3.

8. Berry JI. Pharmacy services in hospice organizations. *Hosp Formul.* 1982; 17:1333–8.

9. Mullan PA. Pharmacy and hospice: opportunities for service. *Am Pharm.* 1982; NS22:424–6.

10. Oliver CH. Pharmacy and hospice: talk with the dying patient. *Am Pharm.* 1982; NS22:429–33.

11. DuBe JE. Hospice care and the pharmacist. *US Pharm.* 1981; Apr:25–38.
12. Gable FB. Death with dignity: the pharmacist's role in hospice care. *Apothecary.* 1980; Sep/Oct:62–7.
13. Hammel MI, Trinca CE. Patient needs come first at Hillhaven hospice: pharmacy services essential for pain control. *Am Pharm.* 1978; NS18:655–7.
14. Nee D. Pharmacy practice in a hospice setting. *Fla Pharm Today.* 1995; Apr:19–23.

Approved by the ASHP Board of Directors in April 2002 and ASHP House of Delegates in June 2002. Developed through the ASHP Council on Professional Affairs.

The bibliographic citation for this document is as follows: American Society of Health-System Pharmacists. ASHP statement on the pharmacist's role in hospice and palliative care. *Am J Health-Syst Pharm.* 2002; 59:1770–3.

ASHP Statement on the Pharmacist's Role in Infection Control

The American Society of Health-System Pharmacists (ASHP) believes that pharmacists have a responsibility to participate in the infection control programs of health systems. This responsibility arises, in part, from pharmacists' understanding of and influence over antimicrobial use within the health system. Further, ASHP believes that the pharmacist's ability to effectively participate in infection control programs and to assist in the appropriate use of antimicrobials throughout the health system can be best realized through membership on multidisciplinary work groups and committees within the health system. These efforts should minimize the misuse of antimicrobials, ultimately resulting in successful therapeutic outcomes for patients with infectious diseases, and reduce the risk of infections for other patients and employees.

Background

Identifying and reducing the risks of acquiring and transmitting infections among patients, health care workers, and others is an essential part of improving patient outcomes in the various practice settings of health systems. Most health systems maintain an infection control program that is directed by a multidisciplinary infection control committee. The specific program and responsibilities of the infection control committee (or its equivalent) may differ among health systems.

Typically, the infection control committee develops organizational policies and procedures addressing

1. The management and provision of patient care and employee-health services.
2. The education of staff, patients, family members, and other caregivers in the prevention and control of infections.
3. Surveillance systems to track the occurrence and transmission of infections.
4. Surveillance systems to track the use of antimicrobials and the development of resistance.

Responsibilities of Pharmacists

Pharmacists' responsibilities for infection control include reducing the transmission of infections, promoting the rational use of antimicrobial agents, and educating health professionals, patients, and the public.

Reducing the Transmission of Infections. Pharmacists should participate in efforts to prevent or reduce the transmission of infections among patients, health care workers, and others within all of the health system's applicable practice settings. This may be accomplished through

1. Participating in the infection control committee (or its equivalent).
2. Advising the health system on the selection and use of appropriate antiseptics, disinfectants, and sterilants.
3. Establishing internal pharmacy policies, procedures,

and quality control programs to prevent contamination of drug products prepared in or dispensed by the pharmacy department. This is of paramount importance in the preparation and handling of sterile products.[1] Other considerations include (but are not limited to) provisions for cleaning pharmaceutical equipment (e.g., laminar-airflow hoods and bulk-compounding equipment) and establishment of appropriate personnel policies (e.g., limiting the activities of staff members who exhibit symptoms of a cold, flu, or other infectious condition).

4. Encouraging the use of single-dose packages of sterile drug products instead of multiple-dose containers, except in sterile environments.
5. Recommending policies for the frequency of changing intravenous administration sets or monitoring equipment, other invasive devices, and dressings. In addition, working with the individuals and health-system committees responsible for selecting and controlling equipment and devices for intravenous medication administration.
6. Recommending proper labeling, dating, and storage of sterile products and multiple-dose sterile-product containers (if used).
7. Encouraging routine immunization of appropriate individuals and periodic screening for selected transmissible diseases (e.g., tuberculosis).
8. Advocating the uniform use of universal precautions by all health care workers and patients.[2]
9. Recommending policies for the frequency of changing ventilator tubing and other noninvasive patient devices that may serve as sources of infection.
10. Developing guidelines for risk assessment, treatment, and monitoring of patients and health care workers who have been in contact with persons with a transmissible infectious disease.

Promoting Rational Use of Antimicrobial Agents. An important clinical responsibility of the pharmacist is to ensure the rational use of antimicrobial agents throughout the health system. In the context of infection control, this responsibility extends to the establishment of strategies for minimizing the development of resistant strains of microorganisms as well as for optimizing therapeutic outcomes in individual patients. Functions related to this responsibility may include

1. Working within the pharmacy and therapeutics committee (or equivalent) structure, which may include infectious disease-related subcommittees, to ensure that the number and types of antimicrobial agents available are appropriate for the patient population served. Such decisions should be based on the needs of special patient populations and microbiological trends within the health system. High priority should be given to developing antimicrobial-use policies that result in optimal therapeutic outcomes while minimizing the risk of the emergence of resistant strains of microorganisms.

2. Encouraging multidisciplinary collaboration within the health system to ensure that the prophylactic, empirical, and therapeutic uses of antimicrobial agents result in optimal patient outcomes. This may include restricted antimicrobial-use procedures, therapeutic interchange, treatment guidelines, and clinical care plans.[3]

3. Establishing and operating a multidisciplinary, concurrent antimicrobial-monitoring program that uses patient outcomes to assess the effectiveness of antimicrobial-use policies throughout the health system.

4. Generating and analyzing quantitative data on antimicrobial-drug use to perform pharmacoeconomic analysis.

5. Working with the microbiology laboratory to ensure that appropriate microbial susceptibility tests are reported on individual patients in a timely manner, and assisting the laboratory in compiling susceptibility reports (at least annually) for distribution to prescribers within the health system to guide empirical therapy. These reports may be most effective if categorized by infection site (e.g., urinary pathogens, respiratory pathogens, blood pathogens) or by patient care area (e.g., intensive care unit, oncology, pediatric, ambulatory clinic, long-term care).

Educational Activities. The pharmacist's role includes providing education and information about infection control to health professionals, patients, and members of the public who come in contact with the health system's practice settings. Specific activities may include

1. Providing clinical conferences, newsletters, and other types of educational forums for health professionals on topics such as antimicrobial use and resistance, decontaminating agents (disinfectants, antiseptics, and sterilants), aseptic technique and procedures, and sterilization methods.

2. Educating and counseling inpatients, ambulatory care patients, and home care patients in the following areas: adherence to prescribed directions for antimicrobial use, storing and handling medications and administration devices, and other infection control procedures (e.g., medical waste disposal).

3. Participating in public health education and awareness programs aimed at controlling the spread of infectious diseases:
   a. Promoting prudent use of antimicrobials,
   b. Providing immunization access for children and adults, and
   c. Promoting appropriate infection control measures (e.g., proper hand-washing techniques).

References

1. American Society of Hospital Pharmacists. ASHP technical assistance bulletin on quality assurance for pharmacy-prepared sterile products. *Am J Hosp Pharm.* 1993; 50:2386–98.

2. Garner JS, and the Hospital Infection Control Practices Advisory Committee. Guideline for isolation precautions in hospitals. *Infect Control Hosp Epidemiol.* 1996; 17:54–80.

3. American Society of Health System Pharmacists. ASHP guidelines on the pharmacist's role in the development of clinical care plans. *Am J Health-Syst Pharm.* 1997; 54:314–8.

Suggested Readings

Centers for Disease Control and Prevention. Draft guideline for infection control in health care personnel, 1997. *Fed Regist.* 1997; 62:47276–327.

Centers for Disease Control and Prevention. Update: vaccine side effects, adverse reactions, contraindications, and precautions. *MMWR.* 1996; 45(RR-12):1–35.

Diekema DJ, Doebbeling BN. Employee health and infection control. *Infect Control Hosp Epidemiol.* 1995; 16:292–301.

Gardner P, Schaffner W. Immunization of adults. *N Engl J Med.* 1993; 328:1252–8.

Goldmann DA, Weinstein RA, Wenzel RP, et al. Strategies to prevent and control the emergence and spread of antimicrobial-resistant microorganisms in hospitals. A challenge to hospital leadership. *JAMA.* 1996; 275:234–40.

Kollef M, Shapiro S, Fraser V, et al. A randomized trial of ventilator circuit changes. *Ann Intern Med.* 1995; 123:168–74.

Rutala WA. APIC guideline for selection and use of disinfectants. 1994, 1995, and 1996 APIC Guidelines Committee. Association for Professionals in Infection Control and Epidemiology, Inc. *Am J Infect Control.* 1996; 24:313–42.

Sepkowitz KA. Occupationally acquired infections in health care workers. *Ann Intern Med.* 1996; 125:826-34, 917–28.

Centers for Disease Control and Prevention, National Center for Infectious Diseases, Hospital Infections Program. [World Wide Web site] http:\\www.cdc.gov/ncidod/hip/hip.htm (accessed August 12, 1997.) Draft Guideline for Infection Control in Health Care Personnel, 1997 Information for Health-Care Workers: Occupational Exposure to HIV Vancomycin Intermediate-resistant *Staphylococcus aureus* (VISA).

This statement was reviewed in 2003 by the Council on Professional Affairs and by the Board of Directors and was found to still be appropriate.

Approved by the ASHP Board of Directors, November 15, 1997, and by the ASHP House of Delegates, June 3, 1998. Revised by the ASHP Council on Professional Affairs. Supersedes a previous version approved by the House of Delegates on June 4, 1986.

The bibliographic citation for this document is as follows: American Society of Health-System Pharmacists. ASHP statement on the pharmacist's role in infection control. *Am J Health-Syst Pharm.* 1998; 55:1724–6.

ASHP Statement on the Pharmacist's Role in Primary Care

Position

The American Society of Health System Pharmacists (ASHP) believes that pharmacists have a role in meeting the primary care needs of patients by fulfilling their responsibilities to provide pharmaceutical care and, in states where it is authorized, through their expanded responsibilities in collaborative drug therapy management.

Pharmaceutical care is the direct, responsible provision of medication-related care for the purpose of achieving definite outcomes that improve a patient's quality of life.[1] Pharmacists establish relationships with patients to ensure the appropriateness of medication therapy and patients' understanding of their therapy, and to monitor the effects of that therapy. In collaborative drug therapy management, pharmacists enter agreements with physicians and other prescribers that may authorize pharmacists, for patients who have a confirmed diagnosis, to select appropriate medication therapies and regimens and adjust them on the basis of patients' responses.

National and international organizations, states, and health care organizations, among others, may have differing or overlapping definitions of primary care. Primary care is a concept intended to improve the quality of care received by everyone in the United States.[2] For the purposes of this document, primary care is defined as the provision of integrated, accessible health care services by clinicians who are accountable for addressing a majority of personal health care needs, developing a sustained partnership with patients, and practicing in the context of family and community. Primary care services should be comprehensive, coordinated, and continuously provided over time by individuals or a team of health care professionals according to the patient's needs. Services should be accessible to patients by telephone or at sites of care provision. Clinicians who provide these services are responsible for the quality of care, the satisfaction of patients, and the efficient use of resources, as well as for their own ethical behavior.[3]

Practice elements of pharmaceutical care and collaborative drug therapy management are consistent with the intents and evolving forms of primary care. ASHP supports the development of definitions and working models of primary care that recognize and incorporate the services of pharmacists for meeting primary care needs of patients. In general, pharmacists contribute to the provision of primary care through the delivery of pharmaceutical care and in collaboration with other health care providers.[4-9] Furthermore, pharmacists may directly provide a limited range of primary care functions in addition to those encompassed by pharmaceutical care, either independently or in collaboration with other members of a primary care team.[10,11] High-quality, coordinated, and continuous medication management for patients should be measurable as a result of the provision of pharmaceutical care within a primary care delivery model. The benefits to patients are valuable access to medication information, the prevention and resolution of medication-related problems, improved outcomes, and increased satisfaction.[12] Pharmacists are able to use medication-related encounters with patients to provide information and either resolve or make a referral for other health care needs.

The purposes of this statement are to promote understanding of the various ways in which pharmacists provide or contribute to the provision of primary care in integrated health systems and to clarify future directions for pharmacists in efforts to expand patient care services in primary care.

Background

Changes in the nation's health care system, especially the growth of managed care and integrated health systems, are stimulating adoption of primary care as a way of meeting basic health care needs and managing access to specialty services. Integrated health systems are organized to deliver acute, intermediate, long-term, home, and ambulatory care. They are intended to seamlessly provide care across practice settings through appropriate use of individual health professionals and teams.[13] Integrated systems offer opportunities for pharmacists and other health care providers to detect and respond to the medication-related needs of patients in transition between settings (e.g., from inpatient to ambulatory care). As integrated systems expand to offer more intensive ambulatory care services and cover broader geographic areas, primary care will become more prominent. Improving patients' access to and continuity of care, implementing disease management, and focusing on quality-related outcomes contribute to optimizing drug costs within the total costs of patient care.[14] Pharmacists involved in primary care contribute to all of these.

Pharmacists participate in primary care services in a variety of practice settings within integrated health systems, including the acute (inpatient), physician office, clinic, pharmacy, long-term, and home settings. A growing number of acute care hospitals have pharmacists participating in patient care activities in ambulatory care clinics and hospital-based home health care services.[15] Along with other providers, pharmacists are expanding and further defining practice models to meet the pharmaceutical and primary care needs of patients throughout the continuum of care.

Responsibilities

Pharmacists involved in primary care participate with other team members in the management of patients for whom medications are a focus of therapy. Pharmacists' responsibility is to optimize patients' medication therapy. Primary care pharmaceutical services should be designed to support the various components of the medication-use process (ordering, dispensing, administering, monitoring, and educating) as individual steps or as they relate to one another in the continuum of care. Pharmacists should evaluate all components of the medication-use process to optimize the potential for positive patient outcomes.

Functions. In general, pharmacists who participate in providing primary care to individual patients perform the following functions in collaboration with physicians and other members of the primary care team:

- Perform patient assessment for medication-related factors.

- Order laboratory tests necessary for monitoring outcomes of medication therapy.
- Interpret data related to medication safety and effectiveness.
- Initiate or modify medication therapy care plans on the basis of patient responses.
- Provide information, education, and counseling to patients about medication-related care.
- Document the care provided in patients' records.
- Identify any barriers to patient compliance.
- Participate in multidisciplinary reviews of patients' progress.
- Communicate with payers to resolve issues that may impede access to medication therapies.
- Communicate relevant issues to physicians and other team members.

Expanded Functions. Expanded primary care functions of pharmacists include all the functions previously described as well as:

- Provide individualized health promotion and disease prevention, including administration of immunizations where this is legally and organizationally authorized.
- Perform limited physical assessment and supervise medication therapy with appropriate collaborative drug therapy management authority.

Pharmacists' Scope of Practice. The pharmacist may have a range of practice privileges that vary in their extent of authority and responsibility. Pharmacists who participate in collaborative primary care practice should meet the health care organization's competency requirements to ensure that they provide appropriate quality and continuity of patient care. They should demonstrate required knowledge and skills that may be obtained through practice-intensive continuing education and pharmacy practice and specialty residencies. The specific practice of pharmacists who participate in collaborative primary care should be defined within a scope-of-practice document or a similar tool developed by the health care organization. The scope-of-practice document defines activities that pharmacists would provide within the context of collaborative primary care practice, as well as limitations where appropriate. The document should indicate referral and communication guidelines, including the documentation of patient encounters and methods for sharing patient information with collaborating medical providers. Also included should be references to activities that will review the quality of care provided and the methods by which the pharmacist will maintain continuing professional competency for functions within the scope-of-practice document. A process should be in place to review and update the scope-of-practice document as appropriate.

Description of Services Provided. The services offered by the pharmacist range from consulting with the health care team to providing direct support of the patient while working in collaboration with the health care team. The pharmacist provides medication therapy outcomes management as part of the patient's ongoing care. The level of intensity of services varies as the patient's needs change. For chronic illnesses, services may range from health maintenance care to active management of treatment; for acute illnesses, services may range from facilitating access to medical care to providing initial management. In this context, health maintenance may include counseling (e.g., abuse of alcohol, tobacco, and other drugs; use of seat belts) and ordering screening procedures (e.g., blood lipids and glucose, fecal occult blood). The complexity of services provided varies according to patient need and support from within the integrated health system.

Areas of primary care pharmacy practice that have previously been demonstrated to be cost-effective and to improve outcomes include participation on primary care teams and primary care clinics for medication monitoring and refill in the management of general or specific pharmacotherapy (e.g., for asthma, hypertension, dyslipidemia, anticoagulation, dermatologic diseases, diabetes, and psychotherapeutics).[16-23]

Documentation of Pharmacists' Care. Pharmacists in each setting should routinely document the quantity and quality of services provided and the estimated effect on patient outcomes. Pharmacists must safeguard patients' rights to privacy and confidentiality. Patient information should be shared only with members of the health care team and others with authorized access as needed for the care of patients.

Methods for referral to other health care providers and documentation of care provided should be defined and must occur as a routine part of the daily functions of a pharmacist's practice. When more than one pharmacist is involved in delivering care, practice standards for the group should be adopted and should serve as a guide for all. Pharmacists must also establish methods of communication among themselves in order to provide and ensure continuity of pharmaceutical care on behalf of patients served.

Value of Pharmacist's Care. Methods for obtaining compensation or economic and professional credit for value-added services must continue to be addressed. Structures designed to measure the practitioner's effectiveness as part of an innovative team should be instituted. The pharmacy profession should embrace these activities in the form of well-structured research. Integrated health systems will need to receive adequate support to expand the availability of pharmacists to provide pharmaceutical care as an essential component of primary care.

References

1. American Society of Health System Pharmacists. ASHP statement on pharmaceutical care. *Am J Hosp Pharm.* 1993; 50:1720–3.
2. Rubin E. Beyond the rhetoric: ensuring the availability of primary care. Report of an AHC/FASHP retreat. *Am J Pharm Educ.* 1993; 57:191–3.
3. Donaldson MS, Yordy KD, Lohr KN, et al., eds. Primary care: America's health in a new era. Committee on the Future of Primary Care, Division of Health Services, Institute of Medicine. Washington, DC: National Academy Press; 1996.
4. Koecheler JA, Abramowitz PW, Swim SE, et al. Indicators for the selection of ambulatory patients who warrant pharmacist monitoring. *Am J Hosp Pharm.* 1989; 46:729–32.
5. Lobas LH, Lepinski PW, Abramowitz PW. Effects of pharmaceutical care on medication cost and quality of patient care in an ambulatory-care clinic. *Am J Hosp Pharm.* 1992; 49:1681–8.
6. Chrischelles EQ, Helling DK, Aschoff CR. Effect of clinical pharmacy services on the quality of family

practice physician prescribing and medication costs. *Drug Intell Clin Pharm.* 1989; 23:417–21.

7.   Monson R, Bond CA, Schuna A. Role of the clinical pharmacist in improving drug therapy: clinical pharmacists in outpatient therapy. *Arch Intern Med.* 1981; 141:1441–4.

8.   Bond CA, Monson R. Sustained improvement in drug documentation, compliance, and disease control: a four-year analysis of an ambulatory care model. *Arch Intern Med.* 1984; 114:1159–62.

9.   Jameson J, VanNoord G, Vanderwoud K. The impact of a pharmacotherapy consultation on the cost and outcome of medical therapy. *J Fam Pract.* 1995; 41:469–72.

10.   Dong BJ, Echaves SA, Brody RV, et al. Pharmacist provision of preventive health services in a hypertension clinic. *Am J Health-Syst Pharm.* 1997; 54:564–6.

11.   Furmaga EM. Pharmacist management of a hyperlipidemia clinic. *Am J Hosp Pharm.* 1993; 50:91–5.

12.   Galt KA, Skrabal MA, Abdouch I, et al. Using patient expectations and satisfaction data to design a new pharmacy service model in a primary care clinic. *J Manage Care Pharm.* 1997; 3:531–40.

13.   American Society of Health-System Pharmacists. Vision statement. American Society of Health-System Pharmacists. *Am J Health-Syst Pharm.* 1996; 53:174.

14.   Chamberlain MA. The vertically integrated pharmacy department. *Am J Health-Syst Pharm.* 1998; 55:669–75.

15.   Raehl CL, Bond CA, Pitterle ME. Ambulatory pharmacy services affiliated with acute care hospitals. *Pharmacotherapy.* 1993; 13:618–25.

16.   Chandler C, Barriuso P, Rozenberg-Ben-Dror K, et al. Pharmacists on a primary care team at a Veterans Affairs medical center. *Am J Health-Syst Pharm.* 1997; 54:1280–7.

17.   Oke TO. Primary health care services with a functional ambulatory care clinical pharmacy in a low income housing project clinic. *J Natl Med Assoc.* 1994; 86:465–8.

18.   Alsuwaidan S, Malone DC, Billups SJ, et al. Characteristics of ambulatory care clinics and pharmacists in Veterans Affairs medical centers. *Am J Health-Syst Pharm.* 1998; 55:68–72.

19.   Libby EA, Laub JJ. Economic and clinical impact of a pharmacy-based antihypertensive replacement program in primary care. *Am J Health-Syst Pharm.* 1997; 54:2079–83.

20.   Konzem SL, Morreale AP, Kaplan LA. Pharmacist-managed primary care dermatology clinic. *Hosp Pharm.* 1996; 31:823–5,834.

21.   Wilson Norton JL, Gibson DL. Establishing an outpatient anticoagulation clinic in a community hospital. *Am J Health-Syst Pharm.* 1996; 53:1151–7.

22.   Lacro JP, Kodsi A, Dishman B, et al. Primary care role of psychopharmacists in an ambulatory care setting. *Calif J Health-Syst Pharm.* 1995; 7:9–10.

23.   Galt KA. Cost avoidance, acceptance, and outcomes associated with a pharmacotherapy consult clinic in a Veteran's Affairs medical center. *Pharmacotherapy.* 1998; 18:1103–11.

Approved by the ASHP Board of Directors, April 21, 1999, and by the ASHP House of Delegates, June 7, 1999. Developed by the Council on Professional Affairs.

Kimberly A. Galt, Pharm.D., FASHP, Richard F. Demers, and Richard N. Herrier, Pharm.D., are gratefully acknowledged for drafting this document.

The bibliographic citation for this document is as follows: American Society of Health-System Pharmacists. ASHP statement on the pharmacist's role in primary care. *Am J Health-Syst Pharm.* 1999; 56:1665–7.

ASHP Statement on the Pharmacist's Role in Substance Abuse Prevention, Education, and Assistance

Position

The American Society of Health-System Pharmacists (ASHP) believes that pharmacists have the unique knowledge, skills, and responsibilities for assuming an important role in substance abuse prevention, education, and assistance. Pharmacists, as health care providers, should be actively involved in reducing the negative effects that substance abuse has on society, health systems, and the pharmacy profession. Further, ASHP supports efforts to rehabilitate pharmacists and other health-system employees whose mental or physical impairments are caused by dependency on psychoactive drugs.

Background

The term "substance abuse," as used in this Statement, includes those diseases described by the American Psychiatric Association's Diagnostic and Statistical Manual of Mental Disorders, fourth edition, text revision (DSM-IV-TR) criteria as "psychoactive substance use disorders."[1] Psychoactive substances are abused primarily to depress, stimulate, or distort brain activity. Examples include alcohol, tobacco, "street" drugs (e.g., marijuana, lysergic acid diethylamide [LSD], cocaine, methamphetamine, inhalants, methylenedioxymethamphetamine [MDMA], gammahydroxybutyrate [GHB], heroin), and the nonmedical use or the overuse of psychoactive and other prescription and nonprescription drugs (e.g., oxycodone, ketamine, methadone, and dextromethorphan).

Substance abuse is a major societal problem. The 2000 National Household Survey on Drug Abuse, a primary source of statistical information on the use of illegal drugs by the U.S. population, estimated that (a) 4.3 million Americans (or 1.9% of the total population) ages 12 years or older were current illicit drug users, (b) 7.1 million Americans (or 3.2% of the total population) were dependent on illicit drugs or alcohol, and (c) 5.1 million Americans (or 2.3% of the total population) were dependent on alcohol.[2] A study of psychiatric disorders in America suggested a lifetime prevalence of substance abuse disorders of 16.4%, of alcohol abuse or dependency of 13.3%, and of other drug abuse or dependency of 5.9%.[3] Studies suggest that the prevalence of drug abuse among health professionals appears to be similar to that in the general population.[4-6] Given their access, however, health professionals abuse prescription drugs more often and "street" drugs less often than does the general population.

Substance abuse frequently coexists with and complicates other psychiatric disorders, and it is a common and often unrecognized cause of physical morbidity. Intravenous drug abuse is a major factor in the spread of HIV and hepatitis. Alcohol is a major factor in cirrhosis of the liver, and tobacco is a key contributor to emphysema and lung cancer. Collectively, substance abuse contributes significantly to morbidity and mortality in our population and to the cost of health care.

Substance abuse is also a serious workplace problem. The Substance Abuse and Mental Health Services Administration reported that approximately 70% of those reporting illicit drug use within the past month were currently employed full-time and that 1 in 12 full-time employees reports current use of illicit drugs.[7] Substance abuse by employees of health care organizations leads to reduced productivity, increased absenteeism, drug diversion, and, almost certainly, increased accidents and medication misadventures. Consequently, it affects the quality of patient care, liability, and operational and health care costs.

Pharmacists have unique, comprehensive knowledge about the safe and effective use of medications and about the adverse effects of their inappropriate use. The provision of pharmaceutical care to individual patients involves pharmacists assessing the appropriateness of pharmacotherapy, counseling, and monitoring medication-use outcomes. Health-system pharmacists have organizational responsibilities for contributing to the (a) development of the health care organization's medication-use policies, including input into the decisions of the pharmacy and therapeutics committee, (b) development of clinical care plans and other types of protocols, and (c) investigation and prevention of adverse medication events. Furthermore, pharmacists have legal and organizational responsibilities for medication distribution and control across the continuum of practice settings within health care organizations. With this combination of knowledge and organizational responsibilities, pharmacists are prepared to serve in leadership and service roles in substance abuse prevention and education and assist in a variety of patient care, employee health, and community activities.

Responsibilities

The scope of substance abuse responsibilities of pharmacists varies with the health care organization's mission, policies and procedures, patient population, and community. The responsibilities listed below should be adapted to meet local needs and circumstances. Each responsibility is intended to be applicable to any substance of abuse; therefore, specific substances are generally not mentioned. Pharmacists should be involved in substance abuse prevention, education, and assistance by performing the following activities:

Prevention

1. Participating in or contributing to the development of substance abuse prevention and assistance programs within health care organizations. A comprehensive program should consist of (a) a written substance abuse policy, (b) an employee education and awareness program, (c) a supervisor training program, (d) an employee assistance program, (e) peer support systems, such as pharmacist recovery networks, and (f) drug testing.[8]

2. Participating in public substance abuse education and prevention programs (e.g., in primary and secondary schools, colleges, churches, and civic organizations) and stressing the potential adverse health consequences of the misuse of legal and use of illegal drugs.

3. Discouraging pharmacist involvement in the sale of alcohol and tobacco products.
4. Establishing a multidisciplinary controlled-substance inventory system that discourages diversion and enhances accountability that complies with statutory and regulatory requirements. Where helpful, for example, procedures might require the purchase of controlled substances in tamper-evident containers and maintenance of a perpetual inventory and ongoing surveillance system.
5. Working with local, state, and federal authorities in controlling substance abuse (e.g., complying with controlled-substance reporting regulations and cooperating in investigations that involve the misuse of controlled substances, especially diversions from a health care organization).
6. Working with medical laboratories to (a) identify substances of abuse by using drug and poison control information systems, (b) establish proper specimen collection procedures based on knowledge of the pharmacokinetic properties of abused substances, and (c) select proper laboratory tests to detect the suspected substances of abuse and to detect tampering with samples.

Education

1. Providing information and referral to support groups appropriate to the needs of people whose lives are affected by their own or another person's substance abuse or dependency.
2. Providing recommendations about the appropriate use of mood-altering substances to health care providers and the public, including those persons recovering from substance dependency and their caregivers.[9]
3. Fostering the development of undergraduate and graduate pharmacy school curricula and pharmacy technician education on the topic of substance abuse prevention, education, and assistance.[10]
4. Providing substance abuse education to fellow pharmacists, other health care professionals, and other employees of their health care organization.
5. Instructing drug abuse counselors in drug treatment programs about the pharmacology of abused substances and medications used for detoxification.
6. Promoting and providing alcohol risk-reduction education and activities.
7. Maintaining professional competency in substance abuse prevention, education, and assistance through formal and informal continuing education.
8. Conducting research on substance abuse and addiction.

Assistance

1. Assisting in the identification of patients, coworkers, and other individuals who may be having problems related to their substance abuse, and referring them to the appropriate people for evaluation and treatment.
2. Participating in multidisciplinary efforts to support and care for the health care organization's employees and patients who are recovering from substance dependency.
3. Supporting and encouraging the recovery of health professionals with alcoholism or other drug addictions.

Major elements of an employer's support program might include (a) a willingness to hire or retain employees, (b) participating in monitoring and reporting requirements associated with recovery or disciplinary contracts, (c) maintaining an environment supportive of recovery, (d) establishing behavioral standards and norms among all employees that discourage the abuse of psychoactive substances, including alcohol, and (e) participating in peer assistance programs.
4. Collaborating with other health care providers in the development of the pharmacotherapeutic elements of drug detoxification protocols.
5. Providing pharmaceutical care to patients being treated for substance abuse and dependency.
6. Maintaining knowledge of professional support groups (e.g., state- and national-level pharmacist recovery networks) and other local, state, and national organizations, programs, and resources available for preventing and treating substance abuse (see "Other resources").
7. Refusing to allow any student or employee, including health professionals, to work, practice, or be on-site for rotations within the health care organization while his or her ability to safely perform his or her responsibilities is impaired by drugs, including alcohol. The refusal should follow the organization's policies and procedures, the principles of ethical and responsible pharmacy practice, and statutory requirements. Practice should not be precluded after appropriate treatment and monitoring, if approved by the treatment provider or contract monitor (or both, when applicable).

References

1. American Psychiatric Association. Diagnostic and statistical manual of mental disorders. 4th ed. Washington, DC: American Psychiatric Association; 2000:198–9.
2. Epstein JF. Substance dependence, abuse and treatment: findings from the 2000 National Household Survey on Drug Abuse. Rockville, MD: U.S. Department of Health and Human Services, 2002; DHHS publication no. SMA 02-3642 (Series A-16).
3. Robins L, Regier D. Psychiatric disorders in America: the epidemiologic catchment area study. New York: Free Press; 1991:81–154.
4. McAuliffe WE, Santangelo SL, Gingras J, et al. Use and abuse of controlled substances by pharmacists and pharmacy students. *Am J Hosp Pharm.* 1987; 44:311–7.
5. Sullivan E, Bissell L, Williams E. Chemical dependency in nursing: the deadly diversion. Menlo Park, CA: Addison-Wesley; 1988.
6. Bissell L, Haberman PW, Williams RL. Pharmacists recovering from alcohol and other drug addictions: an interview study. *Am Pharm.* 1989; NS29(6):19–30. [Erratum, *Am Pharm.* 1989; NS29(9):11.]
7. Office of Applied Studies, Substance Abuse and Mental Health Services Administration. An analysis of worker drug use and workplace policies and programs. Rockville, MD: U.S. Department of Health and Human Services; 1997.
8. Center for Substance Abuse Prevention, Substance Abuse and Mental Health Services Administration. Making your workplace drug free: a kit for employers. Rockville, MD: U.S. Department of Health and Human Services; 1994.

9. Davis NH. Dispensing and prescribing cautions for medical care during recovery from alcohol and drug addiction. *J Pharm Pract.* 1991; 6:362–8.

10. Baldwin JN, Light K, Stock C, et al. Curricular guidelines for pharmacy education: substance abuse and addictive disease. *Am J Pharm Educ.* 1991; 55:311–6.

Other Resources

1. Hogue MD, McCormick DD, eds. Points of light: a guide for assisting chemically dependent health professional students. Washington, DC: American Pharmaceutical Association; 1996.

2. AACP Special Interest Group on Pharmacy Student and Faculty Impairment. American Association of Colleges of Pharmacy guidelines for the development of psychoactive substance use disorder policies for colleges of pharmacy. *Am J Pharm Educ.* 1999; 63:28S–34S.

3. Tucker DR, Gurnee MC, Sylvestri MF, et al. Psychoactive drug use and impairment markers in pharmacy students. *Am J Pharm Educ.* 1988; 52:42–7.

4. Miederhoff PA, Voight FB, White CE. Chemically impaired pharmacists: an emerging management issue. *Top Hosp Pharm Manage.* 1987; 7(Nov):75–83.

5. Kriegler KA, Baldwin JN, Scott DM. A study of alcohol and other drug use behaviors and risk factors in health profession students. *J Am Coll Health.* 1994; 42:259–65.

6. Haberman P. Alcoholism in the professions. Troy, MI: Performance Resource; 1991.

7. Bissell L, Royce JE. Ethics for addiction professionals. Center City, MN: Hazelden Foundation; 1994.

8. Colvin R. Prescription drug addiction: the hidden epidemic. Omaha, NE: Addicus; 2002.

9. Crosby L, Bissell L. To care enough: intervention with chemically-dependent colleagues. Minneapolis: Johnson Institute; 1989.

10. Johnson VE. Intervention: how to help someone who doesn't want help. A step-by-step guide for families and friends of chemically-dependent persons. Minneapolis: Johnson Institute; 1989.

11. Rinaldi RC, Steindler EM, Wilford BB, et al. Clarification and standardization of substance abuse terminology. *JAMA.* 1988; 259:555–7.

12. Brown ME, Trinkoff AM, Christen AG, et al. Impairment issues for health care professionals: review and recommendations. *Subst Abus.* 2002; 23S:155–65.

13. Dole EJ, Tommasello AC. Recommendations for implementing effective substance abuse education in pharmacy practice. *Subst Abus.* 2002; 23S:263–71.

14. National Clearinghouse for Alcohol and Drug Information (NCADI). The clearinghouse is a federally funded service that assists in finding information on all aspects of substance abuse. Many publications and educational materials are available free of charge from NCADI. Telephone, 800-729-6686; Web site, http://store.health.org/.

15. Center for Substance Abuse Prevention (CSAP) Workplace Helpline (for employers). Telephone, 800-967-5752; e-mail, helpline@samhsa.gov.

16. National Association of State Alcohol and Drug Abuse Directors (NASADAD). The association coordinates and encourages cooperative efforts between the federal government and state agencies on substance abuse. NASADAD serves as a resource on state drug programs and can provide contacts in each state. Web site, www.nasadad.org.

17. Community organizations are available to help with drug or alcohol problems. Treatment counselors may be valuable in developing assistance policies and in providing professional education about treatment and referral systems. Community drug-abuse-prevention organizations may be helpful in prevention efforts, including community drug education. Check your local telephone directory under headings such as Alcoholism Information and Treatment, Drug Abuse Information and Treatment, and Counselors.

18. Twelve-step groups (usually available locally unless otherwise noted; listed telephone numbers and Web sites are for national headquarters):
    a. Adult Children of Alcoholics (ACOA); for adults who, as children, lived with alcoholic parents. Telephone, 310-534-1815; Website, www.adultchildren.org/.
    b. Al-Anon; provides information on alcoholism and alcohol abuse and refers callers to local Al-Anon support groups established to help people affected by others' alcohol misuse. Telephone, 888-425-2666; Web site, www.al-anonorg/.
    c. Alateen; for adolescents affected by alcoholics. Web site, www.al-anon.org/alateen.html.
    d. Alcoholics Anonymous (AA); provides information and support to recovering alcoholics. Telephone, 212-870-3400; Website, www.alcoholicsanonymous.org.
    e. Cocaine Anonymous (CA); for individuals with cocaine dependencies. Telephone, 310-559-5833; Web site, www.ca.org/.
    f. International Pharmacists Anonymous (IPA); for pharmacists in recovery (a national group that often holds support-group meetings at national and regional conferences). Contact IPA List Keeper, 319 East 5th Street, Ogallala, NE 69153-2201; telephone, 308-284-8296; Website, http://mywebpages.comcast.net/ipa/ipapage.htm.
    g. Nar-Anon; for helping people affected by another's drug misuse. Telephone, 310-547-5800.
    h. Narcotics Anonymous (NA); provides information and support to recovering substance abusers. Telephone, 818-773-9999; Web site, www.na.org.

19. Advocacy and professional substance abuse education:
    a. American Pharmacists Association (APhA) Pharmacy Recovery Program; for information sharing, education, and advocacy. Telephone, 800-237-2742. The American Dental Association, American Medical Association, and American Nurses Association have similar programs.
    b. The Pharmacy Section (cosponsored by APhA and APhA Academy of Students of Pharmacy) of the University of Utah School on Alcoholism and Other Drug Dependencies (a one-week seminar each summer); for learning to deal with substance abuse problems as they affect the profession. Telephone, 801-538-4343; Web site, www.med.utah.edu/ads/.

Approved by the ASHP Board of Directors on April 15, 2003, and by the ASHP House of Delegates on June 1, 2003. Developed through the ASHP Council on Professional Affairs. Supersedes the ASHP Statement on the Pharmacist's Role in Substance Abuse Prevention, Education, and Assistance approved by the ASHP Board of Directors, April 22, 1998, and revised and approved by the ASHP House of Delegates and the ASHP Board of Directors, June 3, 1998.

Note: This statement had not been published in *AJHP* when *Best Practices for Health-System Pharmacy 2003–2004* went to press. Some minor editorial differences may exist between this document and the official version that will eventually appear in *AJHP*.

ASHP Statement on the Role of Health-System Pharmacists in Emergency Preparedness

The United States has experienced and remains vulnerable to many events that cause large numbers of casualties. The tragic events of September 11, 2001, and the subsequent anthrax exposures and deaths also awakened the nation to the threat of homeland terrorist attacks.

As the United States began to enhance counterterrorism measures in response to the homeland terrorist attacks of September 11, 2001, it became clear that hospital and health-system pharmacists have an essential role in emergency preparedness.

Position

The American Society of Health-System Pharmacists (ASHP) believes that hospital and health-system pharmacists must assertively exercise their responsibilities in preparing for and responding to disasters, and the leaders of emergency planning at the federal, regional, state, and local levels must call on pharmacists to participate in the full range of issues related to pharmaceuticals. For the purposes of this Statement, disasters include natural disasters (e.g., floods, hurricanes, tornadoes, earthquakes, and forest fires); industrial accidents (e.g., explosions, fires, chemical releases, radiation escape from nuclear power plants, and airplane or train crashes); and terrorist attacks with weapons of mass destruction (WMD), including biological and chemical agents and radiological, nuclear, and explosive devices.

General Principles

1. On the basis of their education, training, experience, and legal responsibilities, pharmacists should have a key role in the planning and execution of (a) pharmaceutical distribution and control and (b) drug therapy management of patients during disasters.
2. The expertise of the pharmacist should be sought in (a) developing guidelines for the diagnosis and treatment of casualties and exposed individuals, (b) selecting pharmaceuticals and related supplies for national and regional stockpiles and local emergency inventories in emergency-preparedness programs, (c) ensuring proper packaging, storage, handling, labeling, and dispensing of emergency supplies of pharmaceuticals, (d) ensuring appropriate deployment of emergency supplies of pharmaceuticals, and (e) ensuring appropriate education and counseling of individuals who receive pharmaceuticals from an emergency supply in response to a disaster.
3. Pharmacists should be in a position to advise public health officials on appropriate messages to convey to the public about the use of essential pharmaceuticals in response to disasters, giving consideration to issues such as adverse effects, contraindications, the effectiveness of alternative pharmaceuticals, and the potential development of drug-resistant infectious agents.
4. In the event of a disaster, pharmacists should be called on to collaborate with physicians and other prescribers in managing the drug therapy of individual victims.

Advice to Hospital and Health-System Pharmacy Directors

Every hospital and health-system pharmacy director (or designee) should

1. Become well informed about the local history of and potential for natural disasters and industrial accidents, as well as the threat of terrorist attacks with WMD, including potential agents that could be used and the related diagnostic and treatment issues;
2. Become thoroughly informed of federal, regional, state, local, and institutional plans for emergency-preparedness, especially those related to the distribution, control, and use of pharmaceuticals;
3. Ensure that the pharmaceutical components of the institution's emergency plans are coordinated with the overall local preparedness plans involving other institutions, community pharmacies, and wholesalers, as well as coordinated with federal, regional, and state plans;
4. Ensure that the appropriate pharmaceuticals and related equipment and supplies are in stock at the institution, consistent with the overall local emergency-preparedness plan, which should account for the interim between the occurrence of a disaster and the receipt of federal or state assistance;
5. Ensure that information about the appropriate use of pharmaceuticals in response to a disaster is available to the health professionals in the institution;
6. Ensure that the institution does not engage in stockpiling of pharmaceuticals without regard to local emergency-preparedness plans that are designed to meet the needs of the whole community; and
7. Ensure that pharmacy personnel are trained to implement the institution's emergency plans.

Advice to Hospital and Health-System Pharmacists

Every hospital and health-system pharmacist should

1. Become well informed about the local history of and potential for natural disasters and industrial accidents, as well as the threat of terrorist attacks with WMD, including potential agents that could be used and the related diagnostic and treatment issues;
2. Become thoroughly informed of local and institutional plans for emergency preparedness, especially those related to the distribution, control, and use of pharmaceuticals;
3. Share with professional colleagues and patients evidence-based information on pharmaceuticals used to respond to disasters;
4. Act assertively to prevent and allay panic and irrational responses to disasters;

5. Strongly discourage individuals from developing personal stockpiles of pharmaceuticals for use in the event of chemical, biological, or nuclear terrorism;

6. Consider volunteering in advance of a disaster to assist in (a) distributing emergency supplies of pharmaceuticals, (b) dispensing and administering medications and immunizations, and (c) managing the drug therapy of individual victims; and

7. Develop and maintain first-aid skills and complete and maintain basic cardiac life support (BCLS) certification. BCLS certification may be required for administering injectable medications, such as vaccines.

Advice to Hospital and Health-System Administrators

Hospital and health-system administrators should

1. Ask the pharmacy director to participate in preparing the institution's emergency-preparedness plan and to consider participating in the development of local, state, regional, and federal emergency-preparedness plans;

2. Consult with the pharmacy director to coordinate the institution's participation in the building of emergency pharmaceutical supplies for use in the community;

3. Refrain from building institutional stockpiles of pharmaceuticals that are not coordinated with the local plan;

4. Encourage local preparedness-planning officials to involve pharmacists in the full range of issues related to pharmaceuticals; and

5. Encourage and enable pharmacy personnel employed by the institution to participate in local, state, regional, and federal emergency-preparedness planning and to volunteer for community service in the event of a disaster.

Advice to Emergency-Preparedness Planners

Emergency-preparedness planners at the federal, regional, state, and local levels should

1. Consult with qualified pharmacists in all areas in which the pharmacist's expertise would contribute to the creation and execution of workable plans;

2. Inform pharmacists, through national and state pharmacy organizations, of plans for deployment of emergency pharmaceutical supplies so that appropriate plans can be made at the local level; and

3. Consult with qualified pharmacists on messages that should be conveyed to the public about the appropriate use of pharmaceuticals in the event of a disaster.

Advice to State Societies of Health-System Pharmacists

State societies of health-system pharmacists should

1. Offer their assistance to state and local emergency-preparedness planning officials, especially in identifying qualified pharmacists to participate in emergency-preparedness planning;

2. Advise their members of information unique to the state regarding pharmacists' participation in emergency-preparedness planning and deployment efforts; and

3. Establish a volunteer network of health-system pharmacists for deployment in the event of a terrorist attack.

Commitments Made by ASHP

In support of the efforts of health-system pharmacists in emergency preparedness and counterterrorism, ASHP will

1. Maintain an electronic communications network of hospital pharmacy department directors that can be used to transmit urgent information related to emergency preparedness and counterterrorism;

2. Disseminate promptly to ASHP members important new information related to pharmacist involvement in emergency preparedness and counterterrorism;

3. Disseminate to ASHP members and others in the health care community timely evidence-based information about pharmaceuticals used when responding to disasters; and

4. Meet with government officials and others when necessary to clarify promptly important issues that affect the involvement of health-system pharmacists in emergency preparedness and counterterrorism.

Approved by the ASHP Board of Directors on February 21, 2003, and by the ASHP House of Delegates on June 1, 2003. Developed through the ASHP Council on Professional Affairs. Supersedes the ASHP Statement on the Role of Health-System Pharmacists in Counterterrorism approved by the ASHP Board of Directors, November 27, 2001, and revised and approved (as the ASHP Statement on the Role of Health-System Pharmacists in Emergency Preparedness) by the ASHP House of Delegates and the ASHP Board of Directors, June 2, 2002.

Note: This statement had not been published in *AJHP* when *Best Practices for Health-System Pharmacy 2003–2004* went to press. Some minor editorial differences may exist between this document and the official version that will eventually appear in *AJHP*.

ASHP Statement on the Pharmacist's Role in the Care of Patients with HIV Infection

Position

The American Society of Health System Pharmacists (ASHP) believes that pharmacists have a role in the care of patients infected with human immunodeficiency virus (HIV). Pharmacists have a responsibility to provide pharmaceutical care to these patients and, in states where it is authorized, can expand on that responsibility through collaborative drug therapy management.

Pharmaceutical care is the direct, responsible provision of medication-related care for the purpose of achieving definite outcomes that improve a patient's quality of life.[1] Pharmacists establish relationships with patients to ensure the appropriateness of medication therapy and patients' understanding of their therapy and to monitor the effects of that therapy. In collaborative drug therapy management, pharmacists enter into agreements with physicians who may authorize pharmacists to select appropriate medication therapies for patients who have a confirmed diagnosis and adjust them on the basis of patients' responses.[2]

Clinicians who provide these services are responsible for the quality of care, the satisfaction of patients, and the efficient use of resources, as well as their own ethical behavior.[3] High-quality, coordinated, and continuous medication management for patients should be measurable as a result of the provision of these services. The potential benefits to patients include access to medication information, the prevention and resolution of medication-related problems, improved outcomes, and increased satisfaction.[4] Pharmacists are able to use medication-related encounters with patients to provide information and either resolve problems or make a referral for health care needs.

The purposes of this statement are to promote an understanding of the various ways in which pharmacists can provide or contribute to the provision of care for patients infected with HIV in integrated health systems and to suggest future directions for pharmacists to expand patient care services.

Background

HIV infection, like many other chronic illnesses, affects nearly every organ system of the body. HIV is pathogenic in some instances, and superinfection by bacteria, other viruses, or fungi is common in the advanced stages of HIV infection. Unlike some other illnesses, HIV infection can be prevented by curbing high-risk behaviors,[5] so the illness still carries a social stigma among some who believe that they are not at risk. Among those at high risk for HIV infection are intravenous drug users and the severely mentally ill,[6] whose conditions may discourage testing for HIV infection or disclosure of HIV status and can also hinder treatment. Discrimination against HIV-infected individuals in housing and employment persists and may impede the delivery of health care by disrupting the stability of home and work life.

Our understanding of the basic pathophysiology and immunology of HIV infection continues to evolve on an almost-daily basis, and drug development occurs at a rapid pace. Since 1990, the Food and Drug Administration (FDA) has averaged one new antiretroviral agent approval per year;

several years have seen the approval of two or three new antiretrovirals.[7] With these rapidly changing and complex therapeutic options, it is a challenge for many primary care providers to keep abreast of state-of-the-art strategies for managing HIV infection and provide comprehensive treatment for a relatively small population of patients. General practitioners know intuitively what has been shown in the literature: patients who are cared for by physician experts in HIV infection have better outcomes.[8–10] The advent of effective antiretroviral therapies has increased the need for clinicians with a broad knowledge of and experience managing HIV infection's concomitant diseases. In addition, important drug–drug interactions exist between antiretroviral agents and drugs used to treat opportunistic infections, between antiretroviral agents and drugs used to treat non-HIV-related comorbidities, and among the antiretroviral agents themselves. Failure to recognize these drug–drug interactions may result in additional or exacerbated adverse effects, nonadherence, therapeutic failure, or irreversible drug resistance. HIV-infected patients require extraordinary counseling and education regarding their treatment, from the importance of adherence to ways to recognize and cope with long-term consequences of therapy. The complexity of pharmacotherapy for patients with HIV infection presents special challenges and opportunities for pharmacists interested in developing a specialized knowledge base about HIV treatment.

There are a range of places within integrated health systems where pharmacists are likely to interact directly with patients infected with HIV: outpatient pharmacies, ambulatory care clinics, inpatient settings, dialysis units, hospices, and home infusion and home health care companies. Pharmacists are often considered the most accessible health professional; they are frequently at the frontline in helping HIV-infected patients deal with barriers to medication access, managing adverse effects and drug interactions, and adhering to medication regimens. Because many HIV-infected patients feel disconnected from the community, compassion on the part of the pharmacist can forge a strong bond with the patient and perhaps enhance patient adherence to antiretroviral treatment.

Patients' ability to adhere to antiretroviral regimens is essential to achieving the goals of drug therapy. Although the exact degree of adherence needed to ensure successful outcomes from drug therapy is not known, one study found that patients must take 95% of their doses to maintain drug levels that will achieve viral suppression, prevent drug resistance, and avert treatment failure.[11] Lack of adherence is often cited as the most common cause of the development of drug resistance and reduced effectiveness or therapeutic failure.[12] Mutations that lead to resistance to one drug may confer resistance to other drugs in the same therapeutic class, severely limiting future treatment options.[13,14]

Causes of nonadherence are multifactorial and differ greatly from patient to patient. In general, adherence has not been related to patient age, race, sex, education level, socioeconomic status, or history of substance abuse.[15] The principal factors associated with nonadherence to antiretroviral therapies appear to be patient-related, and include mental illness (particularly untreated depression), unstable housing, active substance abuse, and major life crises.[16,17] Some patients stop or reduce the dosage of antiretroviral medication because of adverse effects.[17-19] Other factors that have been shown to negatively affect adherence include inconvenient frequency of drug administration, dietary restrictions, and pill burden.[17] A health care professional's assessment of a patient's ability to adhere to a medication regimen is a notoriously poor predictor of actual adherence.[20,21] In one study, the most important predictor of a patient's lack of success with an antiretroviral regimen was the patient's inability to keep appointments with the health care practitioner.[22]

Responsibilities

Pharmacists involved in the care of HIV-infected patients participate with other members of the health care team (e.g., physicians, physician assistants, nurse practitioners, nurses, dietitians, social workers, case managers, and pastoral care providers) in the management of patients for whom medications are a focus of therapy. The pharmacist's responsibility is to optimize the patient's medication therapy. Because of the rapid changes in HIV treatment, pharmacists involved in the care of HIV-infected patients should commit themselves to weekly if not daily education from journals or other sources. Pharmacy services should be designed to support the various components of the medication-use process (ordering, dispensing, administering, monitoring, and educating) as individual steps or as they relate to one another in the continuum of care. Pharmacists should evaluate all components of the medication-use process to optimize the potential for positive patient outcomes.[2] Particular care is needed in the prescribing and dispensing phases because the names of many antiretroviral agents sound and look similar, especially when they are handwritten, and some physicians continue to refer to antiretroviral agents by their chemical or investigational names. Verification of the appropriateness of the antiretroviral cocktail and its dosages is important because dosing recommendations change frequently as more becomes known about individual drug pharmacokinetics and because drug–drug interactions may be used clinically to simplify or increase the efficacy of drug regimens. Pharmacists should screen the medication profile for potential drug–drug and drug–food interactions. A number of antiretroviral drugs cannot be taken with certain foods, and it is the responsibility of the pharmacist to ensure that the patient and caregivers (dietitians, nurses, family members, and friends) are aware of these dietary restrictions.

Pharmacists are responsible for assessing patients' readiness to adhere to drug therapy, assisting in the design of therapeutic plans to increase the likelihood of adherence, assisting the patient in successful implementation of drug therapy, intervening when the patient states or intimates that he or she cannot or will not adhere to treatment, and providing ongoing monitoring of adherence. The public health implications of inconsistent adherence are much greater with antiretroviral agents than with other chronic medications. The pharmacist can promote patient adherence by considering the patient's history of adverse effects when recommending a regimen; helping to develop a daily medication administration schedule that accommodates the patient's sleep, work, and meal schedules; providing memory aids for medication taking; recruiting an adherence coach; and educating and motivating patients and caregivers.[23] To ensure a consistent supply of antiretroviral medications, patients need to be counseled to plan for medication refills so they are never without these medications. Pharmacists, along with other health care professionals, are responsible for postmarketing surveillance of adverse drug events. Suspected adverse drug events should be reported to the patient's primary care provider and to FDA's MedWatch program. Many antiretroviral medications were marketed with scant data about their long-term effects because FDA's accelerated drug approval process allows certain drugs to be approved with only six months of clinical (Phase III) data. Pharmacists should also be aware of the potential for adverse events or drug interactions caused by dietary supplements and should report those as well.

Pharmacists' ability to recognize potential opportunistic infections or other HIV-associated complications and appropriately refer the patient for evaluation and management by a physician is critical. In addition, pharmacists have an obligation and an opportunity to educate members of the community about prevention of HIV infection and may be in a position to recognize persons undertaking high-risk behaviors. The pharmacist should recommend testing of persons at high risk for HIV infection and help educate patients infected with HIV about how to modify their behavior to prevent disease transmission.

The advent of effective antiretroviral therapies has made the treatment of hospitalized patients with acute HIV-related conditions more complex. Pharmacists still need to be prepared to recognize, prevent, and treat the acute opportunistic infections associated with advanced AIDS. The extended survival of those undergoing antiretroviral therapies introduces new comorbidities, such as diseases of the liver, malignancies, hyperlipidemia, and diabetes mellitus, which pharmacists must take into account as they provide pharmaceutical care.

Care for dying patients is also part of the continuum of pharmaceutical care that pharmacists should provide to patients. Pharmacists have a professional obligation to work in a collaborative and compassionate manner with patients, family members, caregivers, and other health care professionals to help fulfill the pharmaceutical care needs—especially nutrition support; the management of diarrhea, electrolyte imbalances, pain, and depression; and other quality-of-life needs—of dying patients.[24,25]

When more than one pharmacist is involved in delivering care, practice standards for the group should be adopted and should serve as a guide for all. Pharmacists should also establish methods of communication among themselves in order to provide and ensure continuity of pharmaceutical care on behalf of the patients served.[2] Methods for referral to other health care providers should also be defined.

Functions. In general, pharmacists perform the following functions in collaboration with physicians and other members of the health care team[2]:

1. Perform patient assessment for medication-related factors.
2. Order or recommend laboratory tests necessary for monitoring outcomes of medication therapy and potential drug toxicities, and cancel unnecessary laboratory tests.
3. Provide drug information to physicians and other members of the health care team.
4. Identify potential and actual drug–drug interactions and make recommendations for dosage modification or alternative therapies, if appropriate.

5. Interpret data related to medication safety and effectiveness.

6. Initiate or modify medication therapy or patient care plans on the basis of patient responses.

7. Provide information, education, and counseling to patients about medication-related care.

8. Document the care provided in patients' records.

9. Identify any barriers to patient adherence to medication regimens.

10. Communicate with prescribers known instances of nonadherence to medication therapy and propose strategies to the prescriber and patient to improve the likelihood of success of subsequent regimens.

11. Communicate relevant issues to physicians and other members of the health care team.

12. Participate in multidisciplinary reviews of patients' progress. Hospice caregivers and volunteer community service organizations should be included in this review as appropriate.

13. Communicate with payers to resolve issues that may impede access to medication therapies.

Expanded Functions. In addition to the aforementioned functions, pharmacists practicing in some settings and with some interdisciplinary relationships may engage in the following activities:

1. Monitoring efficacy of the regimen by tracking $CD4^+$ T lymphocyte counts and viral load and providing input about patients' response to therapy to other members of the health care team.

2. Providing individualized health promotion recommendations and disease prevention advice and activities, including administration of immunizations where authorized by law and institutional policies.

3. Assessing patient knowledge about HIV infection and its treatment and educating patients about the pathophysiology and natural history of HIV infection and progression to AIDS; the goals, mechanism of action, and duration of antiretroviral drug therapy; potential adverse effects from and interactions with antiretroviral drug therapy and ways to manage adverse effects; the concept of drug resistance and the importance of adherence to the therapeutic regimen; laboratory monitoring of therapeutic response to antiretroviral drug therapy; and therapeutic strategies for overcoming therapeutic failure.

4. Recognizing (using accepted guidelines) when patients are at risk for opportunistic infections, recommending initiation or discontinuation of prophylaxis, and intervening to ensure evaluation and management by a physician or other practitioner (e.g., physician assistant, nurse practitioner, or clinical pharmacist).

5. Performing limited physical assessment and supervising medication therapy with appropriate collaborative drug therapy management authority.

6. Assessing the indications for HIV drug-resistance testing, the appropriateness of timing for sample collection, interpreting test results, and designing a new antiretroviral regimen in consultation with an expert in drug resistance.

7. Referring patients to other health care or social service providers, such as psychologists, psychiatrists, social workers, case managers, and chemical dependency providers or support groups (e.g., Alcoholics Anony-

mous or Narcotics Anonymous) in conjunction with the patient's primary care provider.

8. Educating the community about modes of HIV transmission and effective techniques for prevention of transmission.

9. Encouraging public policy decisions that reduce the risk of transmission of HIV, hepatitis B, hepatitis C, and other sexually transmitted diseases.[26]

10. Performing research related to antiretroviral therapy (e.g., adherence, quality of life, pharmacokinetics).

Pharmacists' Scope of Practice. The pharmacist may have a range of practice privileges that varies in its extent of authority and responsibility. Pharmacists who participate in the collaborative care of patients with HIV should meet the health care organization's competency requirements to ensure that they provide appropriate quality and continuity of patient care. They should demonstrate required knowledge and skills that may be obtained through practice-intensive continuing education, pharmacy practice, and specialty residencies. The specific practice of pharmacists who participate in collaborative practice should be defined within a scope-of-practice document or similar tool or protocol developed by the health care organization. The scope-of-practice document should define activities that pharmacists would provide within the context of collaborative practice, as well as limitations when appropriate. The document should indicate referral and communication guidelines, including the documentation of patient encounters and methods for sharing patient information with collaborating medical providers.[2] Pharmacists participating in collaborative practice should remember that, although diagnosing is not within the pharmacist's scope of practice, the pharmacist must be able to recognize the manifestations of opportunistic infections and complications of HIV infection and treatment in order to know when to refer a patient to the appropriate practitioner. Also included in the scope-of-practice document should be references to activities that will review the quality of care provided and the methods by which the pharmacist will maintain continuing professional competency for functions encompassed by the scope-of-practice document. A process should be in place, and responsible parties identified, to review and update the scope-of-practice document as appropriate.

Description of Services Provided. The services offered by the pharmacist range from consulting with the health care team to providing direct support to the patient while working in collaboration with the health care team. The pharmacist provides medication therapy outcomes management as part of the patient's ongoing care. The level of intensity of services varies as the patient's needs change and the disease progresses. For patients who suspect HIV infection, the pharmacist should refer the patient for confidential or anonymous testing (anonymous testing is not available in every state in the United States). Pharmacists also have an important responsibility to ensure the availability of emergency antiretroviral therapy in postexposure prophylaxis and provide counseling and education to the exposed person. For persons who are newly diagnosed with HIV infection, the pharmacist may facilitate access to medical care or refer a patient to a provider who specializes in the care of patients with HIV infection. The pharmacist may be called on to assess the patient's readiness and ability to adhere to antiretroviral therapy, provide initial or follow-up education on HIV-related disease and complications, as well as antiretroviral medications, and evaluate adherence to a therapeutic regimen. The pharmacist should maintain a current knowledge of antiretroviral therapy and may be called on to recommend and monitor the patients' antiretroviral therapy in collaboration with primary care providers or other members of the health care team. When collaborating with HIV specialists, the pharmacist is often asked to conduct follow-up visits with patients whose disease is stable or make an early follow-up telephone call or visit with patients just starting antiretroviral therapy. For patients with known HIV infection of longer duration, the pharmacist may be expected to ensure that the patient is monitored for long-term complications of antiretroviral therapy, such as diabetes mellitus or metabolic, cardiovascular, or hepatic complications. In the absence of a dietitian, the pharmacist may also monitor for changes in the patient's weight and appetite. The complexity of services provided varies according to the patient's needs and support from within the integrated health system, as well as the availability of other health care professionals on the team. In many situations, the pharmacist may play (or supplement) the role of financial counselor or social worker to facilitate access to medications. To deliver uninterrupted antiretroviral drug therapy, the pharmacist will often need to be knowledgeable about financial resources available to patients with HIV infection.

Documentation of Pharmacists' Care. The professional actions of pharmacists that are intended to ensure safe and effective use of drugs and that may affect patient outcomes should be documented in the patients' medical records.[27] Pharmacists in every practice setting should routinely document the quantity and quality of services provided and the estimated effect on patient outcomes.

Confidentiality of medical data is protected by common law and by constitutional rights to privacy. Confidentiality for the HIV-infected person is a critical issue because of the stigma that is sometimes still associated with the illness. Pharmacists should always take extreme care in discussing drug therapy to ensure that confidential medical information is not overheard by other individuals. Information about medications should be disclosed only to appropriate individuals and only with authorized consent from the patient, preferably in writing. Before counseling anyone other then the patient about medications, the pharmacist needs to ascertain that the person with whom he or she is speaking has been authorized by the patient. Pharmacists are urged to explore their local and state laws that may apply to the confidentiality of medical records.

Value of Pharmacists' Care. Methods for obtaining compensation or economic and professional credit for value-added services must continue to be addressed. Structures designed to measure the practitioner's effectiveness as part of an innovative team should be instituted. The pharmacy profession should embrace these activities in the form of well-structured research.[2] Integrated health systems, as well as other treatment settings, will need to receive adequate support to expand the availability of pharmacists to provide pharmaceutical care as an essential component of the care of HIV-infected patients. Therefore, aggressive research must be pursued to demonstrate the importance and effectiveness with respect to outcomes of the pharmacist's role in educating the patient about his or her disease and medications.[2] Because many patients with HIV infection are eventually disabled and disenfranchised, few patients are able to pay out-of-pocket for drug therapy management services, as some patients do for diabetes education or smoking-cessation programs. Third-party payers who cover patients with HIV infection (e.g., private health insurance, state AIDS drug assistance programs, and Medicaid) must begin to cover the cost of patient education and adherence monitoring.

References

1. American Society of Hospital Pharmacists. ASHP statement on pharmaceutical care. *Am J Hosp Pharm.* 1993; 50:1720–3.
2. American Society of Health-System Pharmacists. ASHP statement on the pharmacist's role in primary care. *Am J Health-Syst Pharm.* 1999; 56:1665–7.
3. Donaldson MS, Yordy KD, Lohr KN, et al., eds. Primary care: America's health in a new era. Washington, DC: National Academy Press; 1996:33.
4. Galt KA, Skrabal MA, Abdouch I, et al. Using patient expectations and satisfaction data to design a new pharmacy service model in a primary care clinic. *J Manage Care Pharm.* 1997; 3:531–40.
5. Centers for Disease Control and Prevention. HIV/AIDS surveillance report, 2001; 13(2):14–5.
6. Rosenberg SD, Goodman LA, Osher FC, et al. Prevalence of HIV, hepatitis B, and hepatitis C in people with severe mental illness. *Am J Public Health.* 2001; 91:31–7.
7. Food and Drug Administration. Antiretroviral drugs approved by FDA for HIV. www.fda.gov/oashi/aids/virals.html (accessed 2003 Feb 24).
8. Zuger A, Sharp VL. HIV specialists: the time has come. *JAMA.* 1997; 278:1131–2.
9. Valenti WM. The HIV specialist improves quality of care and outcomes. *AIDS Read.* 2002; 12:202–5.
10. Gardner LI, Holmberg SD, Moore J, et al. Use of highly active antiretroviral therapy in HIV-infected women: impact of HIV specialist care. *J Acquir Immune Defic. Syndr* 2002; 29:69–75.
11. Paterson D, Swindells S, Mohr J, et al. Adherence to protease inhibitor therapy and outcomes in patients with HIV infection. *Ann Intern Med.* 2000; 133:21–30.
12. Deeks SG, Hecht FM, Swanson M, et al. HIV RNA and CD4 cell count response to protease inhibitor therapy in an urban AIDS clinic: response to both initial and salvage therapy. *AIDS.* 1999; 13:F35–43.
13. Report of the NIH Panel to Define Principles of Therapy of HIV Infection. *Ann Intern Med.* 1998; 128(12, pt. 2):1057–78.
14. Dybul M, Fauci AS, Bartlett JG, et al. Guidelines for using antiretroviral agents among HIV-infected adults and adolescents: *Ann Intern Med.* 2002; 137(5, pt. 2):381–433.
15. Sacett DL, Snow JS. The magnitude of compliance and non-compliance. In: Haynes RB, Tayloe DW, Sackett DL, eds. Compliance in health care. Baltimore, MD: Johns Hopkins University Press; 1979:31.
16. Besch CL. Compliance in clinical trials. *AIDS.* 1995; 9:1–10.
17. Chesney MA. Factors affecting adherence to antiretroviral therapy. *Clin Infect Dis.* 2000; 30(suppl 2):S171–6.
18. Ammassari A, Murri R, Pezzotti P, et al. Self-reported symptoms and medication side effects influence adherence to highly active antiretroviral therapy in persons with HIV infection. *J Acquir Immune Defic Syndr.* 2001; 28:445–9.

19. Heath KV, Singer J, O'Shaughnessy MV, et al. Intentional nonadherence due to adverse symptoms associated with antiretroviral therapy. *J Acquir Immune Defic Syndr.* 2002; 31:211–7.

20. Crespo-Fierro M. Compliance/adherence and care management in HIV disease. *J Assoc Nurses AIDS Care.* 1997; 8:43–54.

21. Bangsberg DR, Hecht FM, Clague H, et al. Provider assessment of adherence to HIV antiretroviral therapy. *J Acquir Immune Defic Syndr.* 2001; 26:435–42.

22. Lucas GM, Chaisson RE, Moore RD. Highly active antiretroviral therapy in a large urban clinic: risk factors for virologic failure and adverse drug reactions. *Ann Intern Med.* 1999; 131:81–7.

23. Bartlett JA. Addressing the challenges of adherence. *J Acquir Immune Defic Syndr.* 2002; 29:S2–10.

24. American Society of Health-System Pharmacists. Medication therapy and patient care: specific practice areas: position 9816 (appropriate pharmacy support for dying patients). In: Deffenbaugh JH, ed. Best practices for health-system pharmacy: positions and guidance documents of ASHP. 2002–2003 ed. Bethesda, MD: 2002; 200.

25. Joint Commission on Accreditation of Healthcare Organizations. Pain assessment and management standards—hospitals. www.jcrinc.com (Accessed 2003 Jul 22).

26. American Society of Health-System Pharmacists. ASHP statement on the pharmacist's role in infection control. *Am J Health-Syst Pharm.* 1998; 55:1724–6.

27. American Society of Health-System Pharmacists. ASHP guidelines on documenting pharmaceutical care in patient medical records. *Am J Health-Syst Pharm.* 2003; 60:705–7.

Other Resources

Web Site Resources

General HIV Care and Treatment Information
- Healthcare Communication Group-Clinical Care Options for HIV (www.healthcg.com/hiv)
- U.S. Department of Health and Human Services AIDSinfo Web site (www.aidsinfo.nih.gov)
- Medscape-AIDS(www.hiv.medscape.com/home/topics/aids)

- HIV Insite Home (www.hivinsite.ucsf.edu)
- HIV Insite International AIDS Society (www.hivinsite.ucsf.edu/medical/iasusa)

Clinical Practice Guidelines and Recommendations
- *Morbidity and Mortality Weekly Report* (www.cdc.gov/epo/mmwr)
- U.S. Department of Health and Human Services AIDSinfo Web site (www.aidsinfo.nih.gov)

Drug Interactions
- Clinical Management of HIV–AIDS Drug Interactions (www.healthcg.com/hiv/treatment/interactions)
- Georgetown University Medical Center Division of Clinical Pharmacology (www.dml.georgetown.edu/depts/pharmacology)
- University of California at San Francisco (http://arvdb.ucsf.edu)

Clinical Trials
- U.S. Department of Health and Human Services AIDSinfo Web site (www.aidsinfo.nih.gov)

Hotlines

- University of California at San Francisco Warmline (800) 933-3413

HIV Certificate Programs

- SouthEast AIDS Training and Education Center, Atlanta GA
- Charlotte AHEC, Charlotte NC (800) 874-2417.

Developed through the ASHP Council on Professional Affairs. Approved by the ASHP Board of Directors on April 15, 2003, and by the ASHP House of Delegates on June 1, 2003.

Note: This statement had not been published in *AJHP* when *Best Practices for Health-System Pharmacy 2003–2004* went to press. Some minor editorial differences may exist between this document and the official version that will eventually appear in *AJHP*.

ASHP Statement on the Use of Dietary Supplements

Position

The American Society of Health-System Pharmacists (ASHP) believes that the widespread, indiscriminate use of dietary supplements presents substantial risks to public health and that pharmacists have an opportunity and a professional responsibility to reduce those risks. ASHP recognizes that patients may choose to use legally available dietary supplements, but believes that the decision to use substances that may be pharmacologically active should always be based on reliable information about their safety and efficacy. The current regulatory framework governing dietary supplements does not provide consumers or health care providers with sufficient information on safety and efficacy to make informed decisions. Furthermore, standards for product quality are currently inadequate. ASHP recognizes the concerns raised by the dietary supplement industry regarding regulating dietary supplements as nonprescription drugs because of the industry's inability to patent product ingredients. Still, ASHP urges Congress to amend the Dietary Supplement Health and Education Act of 1994 (DSHEA) to require that the Food and Drug Administration (FDA) develop a regulatory scheme to ensure that dietary supplements are safe and effective. ASHP believes that dietary supplements, at a minimum, should (1) receive FDA approval for evidence of safety and efficacy, (2) meet manufacturing standards for identity, strength, quality, purity, packaging, and labeling, and (3) undergo mandatory postmarketing reporting of adverse events, including drug interactions.

ASHP strongly encourages in vitro and clinical studies of interactions between dietary supplements and medications. Because of the demonstrated risk of these interactions, ASHP discourages the concurrent use of dietary supplements and drug therapy, especially those therapies for which failure may have irreversible consequences (e.g., immunosuppressive therapy, cancer chemotherapy, treatment for human immunodeficiency virus infection, anticoagulation therapy, and hormonal contraceptive therapy).

ASHP believes that the criteria used to evaluate dietary supplements for inclusion in health-system formularies should be as rigorous as those established for nonprescription drugs and that the self-administered use of dietary supplements during a health-system stay may increase risks to patients and liabilities to health care professionals and institutions.

ASHP urges pharmacists and other health care practitioners to integrate awareness of dietary supplement use into everyday practice and encourages pharmacists to increase efforts to prevent interactions between dietary supplements and drugs. ASHP also supports the education of pharmacists and other health care practitioners in the taxonomy, formulation, pharmacology, and pharmacokinetics of dietary supplements and believes that such education should be required in college of pharmacy curricula.

Background

Dietary supplements are defined in DSHEA as products "intended to supplement the diet" that contain vitamins, minerals, herbs or other botanicals, amino acids; "a dietary substance for use by man to supplement the diet by increasing the total daily intake"; or "a concentrate, metabolite, constituent, extract, or combinations of these ingredients."[1]

Evidence of variability in dietary supplement content[2-8] has spurred efforts to standardize products. Current federal regulations regarding the manufacture of dietary supplements are not adequate.[9] Some manufacturers voluntarily follow good manufacturing practices (GMPs) devised by their own trade groups (e.g., the National Nutritional Foods Association GMP Certification Program[10]), and the U.S. Pharmacopeia (USP) has created voluntary standards for a handful of dietary supplements.[11] Manufacturers that wish to carry the "USP approved" seal on their product labels have to subject their products to testing by USP. The creation of these voluntary programs reflects a widespread concern, even on the part of dietary supplement manufacturers, that production processes must be regulated. Although FDA has had the authority to establish dietary supplement GMPs for almost a decade, it issued its first proposed rule on the topic in 2003.[12]

DSHEA does not require FDA to review evidence of the efficacy or safety of dietary supplements, so manufacturers have no burden to prove that their products are effective or safe. Although dietary supplement labeling cannot claim activity in the treatment of a specific disease or condition, claims that suggest an effect on the "structure or function of the body" are allowed.[1] For example, dietary supplements containing echinacea can be labeled as supporting immune health (as a "function") but cannot be labeled as preventing or ameliorating colds (treating a disease). Regardless of this distinction between function and treatment, consumers are bombarded by the lay press (and even some scientific literature) with what can only be described as specific-disease indications for dietary supplements (e.g., glucosamine for osteoarthritis, black cohosh for menopausal symptoms, and St. John's wort for depression).

The health claims allowed in dietary supplement labeling by current interpretation of DSHEA create further confusion for consumers. FDA's attempt to hold these health claims to the same scientific standard required for conventional foods was struck down in *Pearson* v. *Shalala*, so FDA must permit dietary supplement labels to carry "qualified" health claims based on equivocal scientific evidence.[13]

Although DSHEA does require that dietary supplements be safe, it does not require prospective testing to ensure safety. To remove a product from the market, FDA must prove that the product is unsafe. Under DSHEA, some dietary supplements that were banned from the U.S. market because of concerns about their safety have been allowed to return (e.g., sassafras tea, dehydroepiandrosterone). Demonstrably unsafe products have made their way onto the market, and fatal adverse reactions have been reported.[14,15]

Establishing the safety record of dietary supplements has been complicated by the lack of systematically collected data about their adverse reactions. The MedWatch system has been used to a limited extent to report adverse events related to dietary supplement use, but, nine years after the passage of DSHEA, FDA is still developing an adverse-reaction-reporting system for dietary supplements. Despite the limited data, however, the number of case reports of interactions between dietary supplements and medications is growing.[16–21] The safety of dietary supplements for special populations (e.g., children, pregnant women, people with impaired organ or immunologic function) has also not been demonstrated.

Dangers to Public Health

It has been estimated that 40% of the U.S. population uses dietary supplements often and that almost twice as many have used at least 1 of the estimated 29,000 dietary supplements on the market.[22] Out-of-pocket expenditures on dietary supplements total approximately $18 billion annually.[23] Such widespread and indiscriminate use of dietary supplements presents five dangers to the public health:

1. Some dietary supplements are inherently unsafe when ingested orally (e.g., chaparral, ephedra, comfrey, tiractricol, aristolochic acid, pennyroyal).[24–28]
2. Lax regulation of dietary supplement manufacturing presents the risk of contamination or adulteration with harmful substances, including carcinogens,[29–32] and of dangerous variability in active ingredient content among products.[2–8]
3. The use of dietary supplements may compromise, delay, or supplant treatment with therapies of proven efficacy.[16–21,25]
4. Dietary supplements may present dangers to special populations (e.g., children, pregnant women, patients undergoing surgery, patients with impaired organ or immunologic function).
5. Spending on dietary supplements represents an enormous health-related expenditure of unsubstantiated value.[33]

Since the mid-19th century, the federal government has exercised its responsibility to protect Americans from hazardous or adulterated foods and medicines. ASHP believes that, with the passage and implementation of DSHEA, the federal government has abandoned its duty to create a regulatory scheme for dietary supplements that adequately protects the health of consumers. Under DSHEA, consumers and health care practitioners are not provided with the information they need to use dietary supplements safely. To reduce the dangers posed by the current regulatory framework, Congress should amend DSHEA to

1. Require that dietary supplements undergo FDA approval for evidence of safety and efficacy,
2. Mandate FDA-approved dietary supplement labeling that describes safe use in a clear, standardized format, including the potential for interaction with medications and cautions for special populations,
3. Require FDA to promulgate and enforce GMPs for dietary supplements,
4. Require that dietary supplements meet FDA-established standards for identity, strength, purity, and quality, and
5. Empower FDA to establish and maintain an adverse-event-reporting system specifically for dietary supplements, and require dietary supplement manufacturers to report suspected adverse reactions to FDA.

Implications for Practice

Although examples of persons rejecting potentially life-saving medical interventions in favor of alternative therapies can be found in the medical and lay press,[34] the presumption that most users of dietary supplements reject traditional treatments is unfounded. One survey found that most individuals who use alternative therapies for a specific symptom or disease are also receiving care and prescription medications from a physician or surgeon.[35] In a more recent nationwide survey, almost 20% of adults taking prescription drugs reported that they were taking at least one dietary supplement, not including vitamin or mineral supplements.[36]

Pharmacists and other health care practitioners therefore have an opportunity to reduce the risks associated with dietary supplement use. Health care providers face unfamiliar challenges in this effort, however, because much of the information they typically use to establish pharmaceutical treatment regimens is lacking for dietary supplements. Product content is not standardized, therapeutic goals are vague, and evidence of efficacy and safety is absent or ambiguous. ASHP believes that pharmacists, as medication-use experts and accessible members of the health care team, are uniquely qualified and positioned to counsel patients using or considering the use of dietary supplements. Despite their professional responsibility to provide patients with sound advice, pharmacists (like other health care providers) are frustrated by the lack of reliable information about the safety and efficacy of dietary supplements. Pharmacists have shown that they can improve medication safety by identifying and preventing adverse drug events,[37] and they could play a similar role in preventing adverse events due to dietary supplement use if they had sound, evidence-based professional resources.

Incorporate Awareness of Dietary Supplement Use into Practice. ASHP urges pharmacists and other health care practitioners to integrate awareness of dietary supplement use into everyday practice. ASHP believes that all health systems should have an institutional policy regarding the use of dietary supplements. Such policies should allow pharmacists and other health care practitioners to exercise their professional judgment and try to balance patient autonomy and institutional concerns.

Patient Counseling. Although most consumers of alternative therapies also take prescription medications,[35] one survey found that 72% of respondents who used alternative therapies did not report that use to their health care providers.[38] Pharmacists and other health care practitioners must therefore routinely inquire about a patient's current or planned use of dietary supplements, providing examples so that patients understand what is meant (e.g, asking "Do you use dietary supplements, such as St. John's wort or gingko?").[39] This information will allow pharmacists and other health care practitioners to counsel the patient about dietary supplement use and monitor for adverse reactions and drug interactions.

When counseling patients about dietary supplements, the concept of *caveat emptor* (buyer beware) must be emphasized because the content and safety of dietary supplements are not well regulated. ASHP believes that all pharmacists, at a minimum, should be familiar with the pharmacology and pharmacokinetics of common dietary supplements that might contraindicate concurrent use with a therapeutic regimen (i.e., proven and potential pharmacokinetic and pharmacodynamic interactions with prescription and nonprescription medications) to the extent that sound evidence exists. To provide informed counsel to patients using or considering the use of dietary supplements, pharmacists further need to be familiar with the following:

- The typical uses of common dietary supplements and

the scientific literature regarding their efficacy and safety,

- The proven and potential interactions between common dietary supplements and prescription and nonprescription medications,
- The methods of therapeutic monitoring for common dietary supplements, including signs and symptoms of potential adverse effects and toxicities,
- The proven and potential effects of certain disease states on supplement absorption, distribution, and elimination, and
- The safety of using dietary supplements before or after surgery.

Despite the shortcomings of the data on dietary supplements, the limited references on the topic that are available should be consulted.[40–45]

Patients stabilized on a combination of a supplement and medication should be cautioned not to suddenly discontinue the use of either without first consulting with the prescriber. The potential for adverse effects from an interaction exists both when a dietary supplement is discontinued and when it is initiated.

Dietary supplement sales have a very high potential for profit. Despite the expectation that pharmacies should receive a profit from the sale of products, professional ethics mandate that any recommendations or purchasing suggestions be made with the well-being of the customer or patient as the primary concern. Pharmacists should also review promotional and reference materials promulgated in or by their workplaces to ensure that these materials are evidence based and not misleading or deceptive. The scientific literature about the safety and efficacy of dietary supplements is updated continually. Pharmacists have a responsibility to continually monitor that literature and incorporate the evolving knowledge into their care for and advice to patients.

Inclusion in Formularies. ASHP believes that the criteria used to evaluate dietary supplements for inclusion in health-system formularies should be as rigorous as those established for prescription and nonprescription drugs. The Joint Commission on Accreditation of Healthcare Organizations (JCAHO) has recommended that medical staff weigh the patient care implications of dietary supplements with the same rigor applied to prescription and nonprescription medications,[46] and all JCAHO medication management standards apply to dietary supplements, as well as prescription and nonprescription drugs.[47] ASHP believes that the decision to include any product in a health-system formulary should be based on comparative data regarding efficacy, adverse effects, cost, and potential therapeutic advantages and deficiencies.[48] The lack of definitive evidence of efficacy and safety and the demonstrated variability in product content make most dietary supplements unsuitable for inclusion in health-system formularies.[49] More research is needed to determine the relative effectiveness of dietary supplements and their safety for all patient populations, especially drug–supplement interactions.

The shortcomings that make most dietary supplements unsuitable for inclusion in formularies also argue strongly against their self-administered use by patients during a health-system stay. ASHP believes that the use of self-administered medications should be avoided to the extent possible[50] and that pharmacists should identify all drug products before their use.[51] There is currently no way to definitively deter-mine the content of dietary supplements brought into health systems. In addition, discontinuing supplement use may be advisable as part of the diagnostic workup, and the possibility that supplement use may have contributed to hospitalization should be considered.

If an institution decides, as a matter of patient autonomy, to allow the use of dietary supplements, such use should require a prescribed order for the specific dietary supplement in the patient medical record and pharmacist review and verification of the order. Health systems should be aware that the use of dietary supplements may expose patients to risks, and the health system and staff should take steps to reduce potential liability (e.g., require patients to sign a liability waiver for dietary supplement use) and decrease those risks.

Conclusion

Current regulation of the manufacture and labeling of dietary supplements fails to address substantial risks to the public health. As the activity of some dietary supplements has become apparent, so have their dangers and the shortcomings of the current regulatory framework. These laws and regulations should be revised, with the primary goal of providing consumers and health care practitioners with the information they need to use dietary supplements safely and effectively. In short, dietary supplements should be regulated in a manner that ensures that they are safe and effective. Regardless of the shortcomings of the current regulatory framework, pharmacists have an opportunity and a professional responsibility to reduce the risks presented by dietary supplement use.

References

1. Dietary Supplement Health and Education Act of 1994 (SB 784). http://thomas.loc.gov/ (accessed 2003 Apr 1).
2. Gurley BJ, Wang P, Gardner SF. Ephedrine-type alkaloid content of nutritional supplements containing *Ephedra sinica* (Ma-huang) as determined by high performance liquid chromatography. *J Pharm Sci.* 1998; 87:1547–53.
3. Harkey MR, Henderson GL, Gershwin ME, et al. Variability in commercial ginseng products: an analysis of 25 preparations. *Am J Clin Nutr.* 2001; 73:1101–6.
4. Parasrampuria J, Schwartz K, Petesch R. Quality control of dehydroepiandrosterone dietary supplement products. *JAMA.* 1998; 280:1565. Letter.
5. Feifer AH, Fleshner NE, Klotz L. Analytical accuracy and reliability of commonly used nutritional supplements in prostate disease. *J Urol.* 2002; 168:150–4.
6. De los Reyes GC, Koda RT. Determining hyperforin and hypericin content in eight brands of St. John's wort. *Am J Health-Syst Pharm.* 2002; 59:545–7.
7. Glisson JK, Rogers HE, Abourashed EA, et al. Clinic at the health food store? Employee recommendations and product analysis. *Pharmacotherapy.* 2003; 23:64–72.
8. Gurley BJ, Gardner SF, Hubbard MA. Content versus label claims in ephedra-containing dietary supplements. *Am J Health-Syst Pharm.* 2000; 57:963–9.
9. Fontanarosa PB, Rennie D, DeAngelis CD. The need for regulation of dietary supplements—lessons from

ephedra. *JAMA*. 2003; 289:1568–70. Editorial.

10. National Nutritional Foods Association. NNFA GMP certification program overview. www.nnfa.org/services/science/gmp.htm (accessed 2003 Dec 12).

11. U.S. Pharmacopeia. U.S. Pharmacopeia dietary supplement verification program. www.usp-verified.org (accessed 2004 May 13).

12. Food and Drug Administration. Current good manufacturing practice in manufacturing, packing, or holding dietary ingredients and dietary supplements. Proposed rule. *Fed Regist*. 2003; 68:12157–263.

13. *Pearson* v. *Shalala,* 164 F.3d 650 (D.C. Cir. 1999).

14. Food and Drug Administration. Illnesses and injuries associated with the use of selected dietary supplements. www.cfsan.fda.gov/~dms/ds-ill.html (accessed 2003 Feb 14).

15. Palmer ME, Haller C, McKinney PE, et al. Adverse events associated with dietary supplements: an observational study. *Lancet*. 2003; 361:101–6.

16. Williamson EM. Drug interactions between herbal and prescription medicines. *Drug Saf*. 2003; 26:1075–92.

17. Fugh-Berman A. Herb–drug interactions. *Lancet*. 2000; 355:134–8.

18. Yue QY, Bergquist C, Gerdén B. Safety of St. John's wort *(Hypericum perforatum)*. *Lancet*. 2000; 355:576–7. Letter.

19. Brazier NC, Levine MA. Drug–herb interaction among commonly used conventional medicines: a compendium for health care professionals. *Am J Ther*. 2003; 10:163–9.

20. Izzo AA, Ernst E. Interactions between herbal medicines and prescribed drugs: a systematic review. *Drugs*. 2001; 61:2163–75.

21. Piscitelli SC, Burstein AH, Chaitt D, et al. Indinavir concentrations and St. John's wort. *Lancet*. 2000; 355:547–8. Letter. [Erratum, *Lancet*. 2001; 357:1210.]

22. Office of the Inspector General. Dietary supplement labels: key elements. Report OEI-01-01-00120. http://oig.hhs.gov/oei/reports/oei-01-01-00120.pdf (accessed 2004 May 13).

23. Annual overview of the nutrition industry VII. *Nutr Bus J*. 2002; 7(May/Jun):1–11.

24. Food and Drug Administration. Dietary supplements: warnings and safety information. www.cfsan.fda.gov/~dms/ds~warn.html (accessed 2004 May 21).

25. De Smet PA. Herbal remedies. *N Engl J Med*. 2002; 347:2046–56.

26. Blumenthal M, ed. The complete German Commission E monographs—therapeutic guide to herbal medicines. Austin, TX: American Botanical Council; 1998:116,125–6.

27. Nortier JL, Martinez MC, Schmeiser HH, et al. Urothelial carcinoma associated with the use of a Chinese herb *(Aristolochia fangchi)*. *N Engl J Med*. 2000; 342:1686–92.

28. Shekelle PG, Hardy ML, Morton SC, et al. Efficacy and safety of ephedra and ephedrine for weight loss and athletic performance: a meta-analysis. *JAMA*. 2003; 289:1537–45.

29. Slifman NR, Obermeyer WR, Musser SM, et al. Contamination of botanical dietary supplements by *Digitalis lanata*. *N Engl J Med*. 1998; 339:806–11.

30. Food and Drug Administration. Letter to health care professionals: FDA concerned about botanical products, including dietary supplements, containing aristolochic acid. http://vm.cfsan.fda.gov/~dms/ds-botl2.html (accessed 2003 Apr 1).

31. De Smet PA. Toxicological outlook on the quality assurance of herbal remedies. In: De Smet PA, Keller K, Hansel R, et al., eds. Adverse effects of herbal drugs. Vol. 1. Berlin: Springer-Verlag; 1992:1–72.

32. De Smet PA. The safety of herbal products. In: Jonas WB, Levin JS, eds. Essentials of complementary and alternative medicine. Philadelphia: Lippincott Williams & Wilkins; 1999:108–47.

33. De Smet PA. Health risks of herbal remedies. *Drug Saf*. 1995; 13:81–93.

34. Eisenberg DM, Davis RB, Ettner SL, et al. Trends in alternative medicine use in the United States, 1990–1997: results of a follow-up national study. *JAMA*. 1998; 280:1569–75.

35. Astin JA. Why patients use alternative medicine: results of a national study. *JAMA*. 1998; 279:1548–53.

36. Kaufman DW, Kelly JP, Rosenberg L, et al. Recent patterns of medication use in the ambulatory adult population of the United States: the Slone survey. *JAMA*. 2002; 287:337–44.

37. Leape LL, Cullen DJ, Clapp M, et al. Pharmacist participation on physician rounds and adverse drug events in the intensive care unit. *JAMA*. 1999; 282:267–70.

38. Eisenberg DM, Kessler RC, Van Rompay MI, et al. Perceptions about complementary therapies relative to conventional therapies among adults who use both: results from a national survey. *Ann Intern Med*. 2001; 135:344–51.

39. Ang-Lee MK, Moss J, Yuan CS. Herbal medicines and perioperative care. *JAMA*. 2001; 286:208–16.

40. Chambliss WG, Hufford CD, Flagg ML, et al. Assessment of the quality of reference books on botanical dietary supplements. *J Am Pharm Assoc*. 2002; 42:723–34.

41. Haller CA, Anderson IB, Kim SY, et al. An evaluation of selected herbal reference texts and comparison to published reports of adverse herbal events. *Adverse Drug React Toxicol Rev*. 2002; 21:143–50.

42. Kemper KJ, Amata-Kynvi A, Sanghavi D, et al. Randomized trial of an internet curriculum on herbs and other dietary supplements for health care professionals. *Acad Med*. 2002; 77:882–9.

43. Sweet BV, Gay WE, Leady MA, et al. Usefulness of herbal and dietary supplement references. *Ann Pharmacother*. 2003; 37:494-9.

44. Office of Dietary Supplements. International Bibliographic Information on Dietary Supplements (IBIDS) database. http://ods.od.nih.gov/showpage.aspx?pageid=48 (accessed 2003 Dec 11).

45. Memorial Sloan-Kettering Cancer Center. AboutHerbs Web site. www.mskcc.org/mskcc/html/11570.cfm (accessed 2003 Dec 11).

46. Rich DS. Ask the Joint Commission: understanding JCAHO requirements for hospital pharmacies. St. Louis: Facts and Comparisons; 2002:132–3.

47. Medication management standards. In: Comprehensive accreditation manual for hospitals, 2004 update. Oakbrook Terrace, IL: Joint Commission on Accreditation of Healthcare Organizations; 2004:MM1–20.

48. American Society of Hospital Pharmacists. ASHP technical assistance bulletin on the evaluation of drugs for formularies. *Am J Hosp Pharm*. 1988; 45:386–7.

49. Ansani NT, Ciliberto NC, Freedy T. Hospital policies regarding herbal medicines. *Am J Health-Syst Pharm.* 2003; 60:367–70.

50. American Society of Hospital Pharmacists. ASHP technical assistance bulletin on hospital drug distribution and control. *Am J Hosp Pharm.* 1980; 37:1097–1103.

51. American Society of Health-System Pharmacists. ASHP guidelines: minimum standard for pharmacies in hospitals. *Am J Health-Syst Pharm.* 1995; 52:2711–7.

Approved by the ASHP Board of Directors on April 14, 2004, and by the ASHP House of Delegates on June 20, 2004. Developed through the ASHP Council on Professional Affairs. Supersedes ASHP policies 0223, 0304, and 0324.

The bibliographic citation for this document is as follows: American Society of Health-System Pharmacists. ASHP Statement on the Use of Dietary Supplements. *Am J Health-Syst Pharm.* 2004; 61:1707–11.

ASHP Guidelines on the Provision of Medication Information by Pharmacists

Definition of Terms and Basic Concepts

The provision of medication information is among the fundamental professional responsibilities of pharmacists in health systems. The primary focus of this Guidelines document is to help pharmacists in various practice settings develop a systematic approach to providing medication information. Medication information may be patient specific, as an integral part of pharmaceutical care, or population based, to aid in making decisions and evaluating medication use for groups of patients (e.g., medication evaluation for formulary changes, medication-use evaluations). The goal of providing carefully evaluated, literature-supported evidence to justify specific medication-use practices should be to enhance the quality of patient care and improve patient outcomes. To be an effective provider of medication information, the pharmacist must be able to[1]

1. Perceive and evaluate the medication information needs of patients and families, health care professionals, and other personnel, and
2. Use a systematic approach to address medication information needs by effectively searching, retrieving, and evaluating the literature and appropriately communicating and applying the information to the patient care situation.

Medication Information Activities

A variety of medication information activities may be provided, depending on the particular practice setting and need. The following activities, which are often performed in an organized health care setting, are enhanced by using a systematic approach to meeting medication information needs[2–5]:

1. Providing medication information to patients and families, health care professionals, and other personnel.
2. Establishing and maintaining a formulary based on scientific evidence of efficacy and safety, cost, and patient factors.
3. Developing and participating in efforts to prevent medication misadventuring, including adverse drug event and medication error reporting and analysis programs.
4. Developing methods of changing patient and provider behaviors to support optimal medication use.
5. Publishing newsletters to educate patients, families, and health care professionals on medication use.
6. Educating providers about medication-related policies and procedures.
7. Coordinating programs to support population-based medication practices (e.g., development of medication-use evaluation criteria and pharmacotherapeutic guidelines).
8. Coordinating investigational drug services.
9. Providing continuing-education services to the health care professional staff.
10. Educating pharmacy students and residents.
11. Applying health economic and outcome analysis.
12. Developing and maintaining an active research program.

An individual pharmacist may have full or partial responsibility for all or some of these activities. For example, preparing drug monographs for pharmacy and therapeutics committees was once considered almost exclusively the responsibility of the drug information center or drug information specialist. As pharmacy practice has evolved, the expertise and knowledge base of individual pharmacy practitioners have been integrated into this process. The pharmacist may prepare the monograph or, if a medication is adopted for use, may assist in designing the medication-use evaluation (MUE) criteria, collecting data, or educating health care professionals on appropriate use. Any of these activities may contribute to a larger medication policy management program coordinated by a medication information center or specialist. As pharmacists in various organized health care settings have become more involved in providing pharmaceutical care, their activities have become less distributive and more information based, requiring a higher level of competence by all pharmacists in meeting medication information needs.

Systematic Method for Responding to Medication Information Needs

The provision of medication information can be initiated by the pharmacist or requested by other health care professionals, patients and their family members, or the general public. The process is similar, regardless of how a medication information question is generated (e.g., by the pharmacist or by another health professional) or the context in which the information will be used (e.g., in a newsletter or for solving a patient-specific problem). The pharmacist must not only accumulate and organize the literature but also objectively evaluate and apply the information from the literature to a particular patient or situation.[6–8] Consideration should be given to the ethical and legal aspects of responding to medication information requests.[9,10] A systematic method can be outlined as follows:

1. To probe for information and develop a response with the appropriate perspective, consider the education and professional or experiential background of the requester.
2. Identify needs by asking probing questions of the patient, family members, or health care professional or by examining the medical record to identify the true question. This helps in optimizing the search process and assessing the urgency for a response.
3. Classify requests as patient-specific or not and by type of question (e.g., product availability, adverse drug event, compatibility, compounding/formulation, dosage/administration, drug interaction, identification, pharmacokinetics, therapeutic use/efficacy, safety in pregnancy and nursing, toxicity and poisoning) to aid in assessing the situation and selecting resources.

4. Obtain more complete background information, including patient data, if applicable, to individualize the response to meet the patient's, family's, or health care professional's needs.

5. Perform a systematic search of the literature by making appropriate selections from the primary, secondary, and tertiary literature and other types of resources as necessary.

6. Evaluate, interpret, and combine information from the several sources. Other information needs should be anticipated as a result of the information provided.

7. Provide a response by written or oral consultation, or both, as needed by the requester and appropriate to the situation. The information, its urgency, and its purpose may influence the method of response.

8. Perform a follow-up assessment to determine the utility of the information provided and outcomes for the patient (patient-specific request) or changes in medication-use practices and behaviors.

9. Document the request, information sources, response, and follow-up as appropriate for the request and the practice setting.

Resources

It is the responsibility of the pharmacist to ensure that up-to-date resources, including representative primary, secondary, and tertiary literature, are available to assist in answering a variety of types of medication information requests. Pharmacists should be familiar with not only the components of the literature (e.g., primary) but also the features of individual resources in each component; this makes searching more efficient so that time can be used optimally in analyzing, applying, and communicating the information. The drug information modules of the ASHP Clinical Skills Program[6–8] describe the strengths and weaknesses of the different literature components and list frequently used resources and the types of information included in each publication. The following should be considered in purchasing literature resources:

1. Attributes of the literature (e.g., frequency of update, qualifications and affiliations of authors, year of publication, type of information, organization of material, type of medium, and cost).

2. Practice setting of the pharmacist (e.g., type of facility and needs of individuals within the environment).

3. Literature currently available and readily accessible.

4. Funds allocated for literature purchases.

The volume and sophistication of medication information, as well as the demand for it, are increasing, and human memory has limitations. Consideration should be given to using computers as a tool in the decision-making process. There are several areas in which computers can be valuable in the provision of medication information.[11] Databases are available for information management, retrieval, and communication. Information management databases include software for MUE, documentation of questions and responses, and preparation of reports of adverse drug events. Information retrieval sources include bibliographic databases (e.g., International Pharmaceutical Abstracts, Iowa Drug Information Service, MEDLINE) and full-text databases (e.g., Drug Information Fulltext).[12,13] Textbooks (e.g., *AHFS Drug Information*) and journals can also be accessed through computer technology. Some information is available through electronic bulletin boards (e.g., PharmNet) and the Internet.[14–16] Computerized medical records can also be a valuable tool in assessing either individual patient needs or population-based needs.

Documentation and Quality Assessment

Individual practicing pharmacists should base their documentation of medication information requests and responses on the type and purpose of the request and the subsequent use of the documentation. For patient-specific medication information, requests and responses could be documented in the patient's medical record. Documentation may also be considered necessary for quality assessment and other performance improvement and management activities.

Documentation of medication information requests and responses should include, as appropriate for the purposes of the documentation, the following:

1. Date and time received.
2. Requester's name, address, method of contact (e.g., telephone or beeper number), and category (e.g., health care discipline, patient, public).
3. Person assessing medication information needs.
4. Method of delivery (e.g., telephone, personal visit, mail).
5. Classification of request.
6. Question asked.
7. Patient-specific information obtained.
8. Response provided.
9. References used.
10. Date and time answered.
11. Person responding to request.
12. Estimated time in preparation and for communication.
13. Materials sent to requesters.
14. Outcome measures suggested (e.g., impact on patient care, improvements in medication use, and requester satisfaction).

Responses to requests for medication information should be accurate, complete, and timely for maximal clinical usefulness and to establish credibility for pharmacist-provided information. Quality assessment of responses should be included in the medication information process; this could be selective for certain types of patient-specific requests, random by numbers of requests or for certain time periods, or on some other basis appropriate to meet the needs of the health system.

Keeping Current

It is the responsibility of the pharmacist to keep abreast of advancements both in the tools that can be used to systematically address information requests and in the information itself regarding pharmacotherapeutic or other issues affecting the practice of pharmacy.

References

1. Troutman WG. Consensus-derived objectives for drug information education. *Drug Inf J.* 1994; 28:791–6.

2. Rosenberg JM, Ruentes RJ, Starr CH, et al. Pharmacist-operated drug information centers in the United States. *Am J Health Syst-Pharm.* 1995; 52:991–6.

3. ASHP supplemental standard and learning objectives for residency training in drug information practice. In: Practice standards of ASHP 1994–95. Hicks WE, ed. Bethesda, MD: American Society of Hospital Pharmacists; 1994.

4. American Society of Hospital Pharmacists. ASHP accreditation standard for residency in pharmacy practice (with an emphasis on pharmaceutical care). *Am J Hosp Pharm.* 1992; 49:146–53.

5. American Society of Hospital Pharmacists. ASHP statement on the pharmacist's clinical role in organized health care settings. *Am J Hosp Pharm.* 1989; 46:2345–6.

6. Galt KA. Clinical skills program drug information series, module 1. Analyzing and recording a drug information request. Bethesda, MD: American Society of Hospital Pharmacists; 1994.

7. Smith GH, Norton LL, Ferrill MJ. Clinical skills program drug information series, module 2. Evaluating drug literature. Bethesda, MD: American Society of Health-System Pharmacists; 1995.

8. Galt KA, Calis KA, Turcasso NM. Clinical skills program drug information series, module 3. Responding to a drug information request. Bethesda, MD: American Society of Health-System Pharmacists; 1995.

9. Kelly WN, Krause EC, Krowinski WJ, et al. National survey of ethical issues presented to drug information centers. *Am J Hosp Pharm.* 1990; 47:2245–50.

10. Arnold RM, Nissen JC, Campbell NA. Ethical issues in a drug information center. *Drug Intell Clin Pharm.* 1987; 21:1008–11.

11. Dasta JF, Greer ML, Speedie SM. Computers in health care: overview and bibliography. *Ann Pharmacother.* 1992; 26:109–17.

12. Hoffman T. The ninth annual medical hardware and software buyers' guide. *MD Comput.* 1992; 9: 359–500.

13. Baker DE, Smith G, Abate MA. Selected topics in drug information access and practice: an update. *Ann Pharmacother.* 1994; 28:1389–94.

14. Gora-Harper ML. Value of pharmacy-related bulletin board services as a drug information resource. *J Pharm Technol.* 1995; 11:95–8.

15. Glowniak JV, Bushway MK. Computer networks as a medical resource. *JAMA.* 1994; 271:1934–9.

16. McKinney WP, Barnas GP, Golub RM. The medical applications of the Internet: information resources for research, education and patient care. *J Gen Intern Med.* 1994; 9:627–34.

Approved by the ASHP Board of Directors, April 24, 1996. Developed by the ASHP Council on Professional Affairs.

The bibliographic citation for this document is as follows: American Society of Health-System Pharmacists. ASHP guidelines on the provision of medication information by pharmacists. *Am J Health-Syst Pharm.* 1996; 53:1843–5.

ASHP Guidelines for Providing Pediatric Pharmaceutical Services in Organized Health Care Systems

Patient care consists of integrated domains of care, including medical care, nursing care, and pharmaceutical care. The provision of pharmaceutical care involves not only medication therapy but decisions about medication selection, dosages, routes and methods of administration, medication therapy monitoring, and the provision of medication-related information and counseling to individual patients.[1] The pediatric patient population poses some unique challenges to the pharmaceutical care provider in terms of these medication-related activities. These challenges include the lack of published information on the therapeutic uses and monitoring of drugs in pediatric patients; the lack of appropriate commercially available dosage forms and concentrations of many drugs for pediatric patients; and the resulting need to develop innovative ways of ensuring that the patient receives the drug in a manner that allows the intended therapeutic effect to be realized.[2] These guidelines are intended to assist pharmacists in meeting the special needs of the pediatric patient in any organized health care setting.

General Principles

The pharmacy service should be organized in accordance with the principles of good management. It should be under the direction of a pharmacist and be provided with sufficient physical facilities, personnel, and equipment to meet the pharmaceutical care needs of the pediatric population. Resources necessary for compounding and testing alternative doses and dosage forms of commercially available products are essential. The pharmacy should comply with all applicable federal, state, and local laws, codes, statutes, and regulations.[3] The setting should meet applicable accreditation criteria of the Joint Commission on Accreditation of Healthcare Organizations. Organizations such as the National Association of Children's Hospitals and Related Institutions, the American Academy of Pediatrics, and the Pediatric Pharmacy Administrative Group are useful sources of further information on pediatric health care services.

Orientation and Training Programs

Orientation, training, and staff development programs for pharmacists providing services to pediatric patients should emphasize dosage calculations, dosage-form selection appropriate to the patient's age and condition, and specialized drug preparation and administration techniques. Pharmacists should be familiar with the pharmacokinetic and pharmacodynamic changes that occur with age (e.g., in volume of distribution, protein binding, renal elimination, metabolism, muscle mass, and fluid requirements) and with disease-specific conditions that might affect drug choice or administration (e.g., short-gut syndrome, lactose intolerance). A sensitivity to the nature, frequency, and severity of medication-related errors in the pediatric population is important for all pharmacy personnel.[4]

Inpatient Services

A lack of availability of commercially prepared dosage forms, combined with the documented risk of calculation errors, requires the use of comprehensive unit dose drug distribution systems and intravenous (i.v.) admixture services for pediatric patients. Appropriate dosage standardization in both oral and parenteral drug distribution systems may facilitate the provision of these services.

Unit Dose System. The pediatric unit dose system must meet the original intent of these systems, which is to minimize errors and provide drugs to the patient care areas in ready-to-administer form. Multidose containers and stock medications should be avoided. An extemporaneous preparation service should facilitate the preparation and packaging of medications according to sound compounding principles.

I.V. Admixture Service. The drugs provided by the i.v. admixture service should include all i.v. push, i.v. minibag, intramuscular, and subcutaneous doses; large-volume injections; antineoplastic agents; parenteral nutrient fluids; ophthalmic products; peritoneal dialysis solutions; and irrigation fluids. Knowledge of pediatric fluid requirements and limitations, drug administration techniques and devices, and acceptable volumes for intramuscular injection is critical. Care should be taken when making dilutions to maximize concentrations of drug products (when safe to do so) for fluid-sensitive patients, as well as to minimize hyperosmolar solutions that might lead to destruction of vasculature or, in the neonate, intraventricular hemorrhage. Quality controls for both manually prepared and computer-driven preparation should exist to ensure that each product contains the ingredients ordered and that they are properly labeled. Knowledge of products that contain benzyl alcohol and the risks of this substance in neonates is essential in a pediatric i.v. admixture service.

The labels of all products should be evaluated for legibility, clarity of expression, and their potential for leading to a medication error.[5] Labels should include the drug name; the drug concentration; the route of administration; the expiration date or time; appropriate instructions for administration, additional preparation, and storage; and the lot number (if a batch-prepared product).[6]

Ambulatory Care Services

Ambulatory care pharmacy services should be attentive to the unique drug needs of the pediatric patient. These include the need for special dosage forms (e.g., liquids and chewable tablets), measuring devices, and detailed counseling on drug administration. When product stability is a problem, caregivers may have to be taught how to prepare an appropriate dosage form in the home. Consideration must be given to taste and the need for an extra prescription container to be taken to school or daycare. Children should be included whenever possible in discussions concerning their medications. In the ambulatory care setting, the pharmacist is well positioned to play a role in preventive health care, including poison prevention and immunization.[7]

Drug Information

Drug information services should provide the pharmacist practicing in the pediatric setting with information unique to the pediatric population. References should include pediatric medical texts and current information on pediatric dosages, extemporaneous formulations, drug compatibilities and stability, poison control, and drug effects during pregnancy and lactation. Drug information should be available in areas where decisions are being made about drug therapy. Literature supporting the use of drugs for unlabeled uses in pediatric patients should also be available.[8] Pharmacists should provide other health care professionals with information on new and investigational drugs, adverse effects of and contraindications to drug therapy, compatibility and stability information, dosage computations, pharmacokinetics, and drug interactions. This may be accomplished through educational presentations, seeing patients in conjunction with other caregivers ("rounding"), and printed materials (e.g., newsletters).

Therapeutic Drug Monitoring

Therapeutic drug monitoring enables assessment of therapeutic outcomes and recognition at the earliest moment of an undesirable response to a drug. Both desired and undesired effects should be documented. The person performing therapeutic drug monitoring should take into consideration the age-related differences in dosage when recommending or reviewing drug therapy.

Pharmacokinetic Services

For both oral and injectable drugs, pharmacokinetic services should ensure that the drug has been administered appropriately before samples are taken for the measurement of serum drug concentrations. The frequency and timing of sampling should also be monitored to avoid excessive and traumatic sampling in children. Knowledge of age-related differences in absorption, distribution, metabolism, and elimination is essential for the pharmacist who is involved in pharmacokinetic services for pediatric patients. The collection and publication of accurate pharmacokinetic data on the pediatric population are encouraged.

Patient and Caregiver Education

Pharmacists should counsel and educate patients and caregivers about their medications, including the purpose of each medication, dosage instructions, potential drug interactions, potential adverse effects, and any specific age-related issues (e.g., compounding and diluting techniques, measuring and administration instructions). Caregivers should be informed of any drug products for which crushing, chewing, dividing, or diluting should be avoided. Suggestions about masking the taste of an unpleasant medication should also be provided. Administration of products, including ophthalmics, otics, inhalers, and injectables, should be demonstrated. The

prevention of accidental ingestion of medications should also be emphasized. The benefits of educational programs are best realized when a cooperative multidisciplinary approach is used. Sharing of pertinent information by all participants is fundamental to the success of patient education services.[9]

Medication Errors

Systems for the recognition, documentation, and prevention of medication errors are essential for the pediatric population. Pharmacist participation in quality-improvement committees and the participation of pharmacists, nurses, physicians, and risk managers are important in minimizing medication errors in pediatric patients. The development and enforcement of policies and procedures for minimizing medication errors are essential. Pediatric patients are especially vulnerable to errors caused by mistakes in calculations. Pharmacists should recognize that since some commercially available products are available in strengths that can be potentially toxic to a pediatric patient, special scrutiny of these products is necessary.[5]

Adverse Drug Reactions

Pediatric patients frequently have the same kinds of adverse drug reactions that adults have, but adverse reactions in the pediatric population may be harder to recognize or of greater or lesser intensity. The lack of literature on newly introduced therapeutic agents makes it imperative to monitor experience with new drugs initially used in the pediatric population. Comprehensive adverse drug reaction monitoring and reporting programs are important in reducing the occurrence of these reactions in pediatric patients.[10]

Drug-Use Evaluation

Drug-use evaluation should be directed at drugs with a low therapeutic index that require extensive monitoring, those that are responsible for serious medication errors in the institution, and those that are found to be associated with high frequency of preventable adverse drug reactions. Cost-related issues may also become important in the evaluations, since many expensive drugs are not available in package sizes appropriate for the pediatric patient.

Research

Pediatric patients have long been recognized as "therapeutic orphans" because of a relative absence of therapeutic trials in this patient population. The reasons for this are numerous and include ethical issues, potential adverse publicity, possible litigation, methodological hurdles, and an inability to justify such studies for economic reasons. Nonetheless, the need for timely and effective research on medication safety, efficacy, and practical application in the pediatric population is compelling. The paucity of pediatric drug information, the impact of new drug delivery systems, the expansion of adult diseases (such as AIDS) into the pediatric population, and expanded applications of new and established therapeutic agents are all areas warranting additional research. The pediatric pharmacist can be directly involved in collaboration with other health care providers in conducting pediatric research. Examples of pediatric research topics include, but are not limited to, the following:

- Safety and efficacy of drug products in pediatric patients;
- Pharmacokinetics and pharmacodynamics of new medications;
- Stability, safety, and efficacy of extemporaneously compounded sterile and nonsterile drug products;
- Safety and efficacy of administration techniques;
- Comparative evaluations of medications addressing treatment regimens, outcomes of therapy, and their relative costs;
- Behavioral and socioeconomic compliance issues in pediatric pharmaceutical care; and
- New and existing pharmacy drug distribution systems and services for pediatric patients.

Examples of direct involvement include

- Serving as a member of an institutional review board;
- Maintenance, oversight, and dissemination of all information on investigational drug studies and comparative trials involving medications in the pediatric population; and
- Maintenance, coordination, and oversight of policies and procedures involving investigational drug studies and comparative trials involving medications in the pediatric population.

References

1. American Society of Hospital Pharmacists. ASHP statement on pharmaceutical care. *Am J Hosp Pharm.* 1993; 50:1720–3.
2. Pediatric Pharmacy Administration Group Committee on Pediatric Pharmacy Practice. Pediatric pharmacy practice guidelines. *Am J Hosp Pharm.* 1991; 48:2475–7.
3. American Society of Hospital Pharmacists. ASHP guidelines: minimum standard for pharmacies in institutions. *Am J Hosp Pharm.* 1985; 42:372–5.
4. Folli HL, Poole RL, Benitz WE, et al. Medication error prevention by clinical pharmacists in two children's hospitals. *Pediatrics.* 1987; 79:718–22.
5. American Society of Hospital Pharmacists. ASHP guidelines on preventing medication errors in hospitals. *Am J Hosp Pharm.* 1993; 50:305–14.
6. American Society of Hospital Pharmacists. ASHP technical assistance bulletin on single unit and unit dose packages of drugs. *Am J Hosp Pharm.* 1985; 42:378–9.
7. American Society of Hospital Pharmacists. ASHP technical assistance bulletin on the pharmacist's role in immunization. *Am J Hosp Pharm.* 1993; 50:501–5.
8. American Society of Hospital Pharmacists. ASHP statement on the use of medications for unlabeled uses. *Am J Hosp Pharm.* 1992; 49:2006–8.
9. American Society of Hospital Pharmacists. ASHP guidelines on pharmacist-conducted patient counseling. *Am J Hosp Pharm.* 1993; 50:505–6.
10. American Society of Hospital Pharmacists. ASHP guidelines on adverse drug reaction monitoring and reporting. *Am J Hosp Pharm.* 1989; 46:336–7.

Approved by the ASHP Board of Directors, April 27, 1994. Developed by the ASHP Council on Professional Affairs.

The bibliographic citation for this document is as follows: American Society of Hospital Pharmacists. ASHP guidelines for providing pediatric pharmaceutical services in organized health care systems. *Am J Hosp Pharm.* 1994; 51:1690–2.

ASHP Guidelines on Surgery and Anesthesiology Pharmaceutical Services

Purpose

In hospitals, surgery and anesthesiology generally have been without direct pharmacist involvement. Drugs have been available through a stock-distribution system maintained by operating-room (OR) personnel, and documentation of controlled-substance use has often been handled by personnel other than those administering the drugs. More important, without direct pharmacist involvement, patient-related issues that are best addressed by a pharmacist usually have been handled by other health care personnel out of necessity. ASHP believes that pharmaceutical services (including drug-use control) to these areas should be provided by pharmacists, ideally with their direct presence. In many hospitals this is accomplished through an onsite satellite pharmacy.[1–5]

The purpose of these guidelines is to help pharmacists identify services they could provide in the areas of surgery and anesthesiology, decide on the scope of these services, and develop performance improvement plans. In addition, the appendix provides guidance for justifying and implementing a satellite pharmacy. Some topics outlined in these guidelines are the subject of other ASHP practice standards, which should be referred to for additional information and guidance. Pharmacists should use professional judgment in assessing their organization's needs for pharmaceutical services in surgery and anesthesiology. The guidance should be adapted, as applicable, to meet those needs.

The term "surgery and anesthesiology pharmaceutical services" should not be interpreted too literally. Many satellite pharmacies serving surgery and anesthesiology areas also serve other areas. These may include cystoscopy and endoscopy suites, cardiac catheterization laboratories or suites, preoperative holding areas, postanesthesia care units (PACUs), labor and delivery rooms, freestanding surgical centers, and critical care areas. In general, these satellite pharmacies are termed "OR satellite pharmacies" and the pharmacist an "OR pharmacist." The guidelines do not distinguish among terms, because terms may be applied differently in various settings. The terms "satellite pharmacy" and "the pharmacist" are used in their broadest senses.

Pharmaceutical Services

The successful establishment of pharmaceutical services in surgery and anesthesiology will depend to a large extent on the OR pharmacist's ability to positively affect drug-use management, take a leadership role in all aspects of cost containment, and contribute to improving patient care and outcomes.

The performance of many activities and services may be improved in surgery and anesthesiology through the establishment of pharmaceutical services. Often these include the following:

1. Drug preparation and distribution;
2. Drug inventory control;
3. Waste reduction;
4. Drug cost reduction;
5. Improved revenue generation through accurate patient billing;
6. Improved documentation of drugs administered to patients[6];
7. Clinical activities;
8. Formulary management;
9. Drug accountability and control, including adherence to organizational drug-use guidelines;
10. Quality assurance and continuous quality improvement;
11. Compliance with standards of the Joint Commission on Accreditation of Healthcare Organizations (JCAHO);
12. Informational, educational, and research activities;
13. Involvement with the use of drug administration devices; and
14. Enhanced interdisciplinary decision-making.

Drug Preparation and Distribution

In most ORs, the drug preparation and distribution functions can be improved by pharmacy personnel practicing in this setting. These activities should not be so labor-intensive as to exclude cognitive services being provided by the pharmacist. Technicians should be assigned most of the drug preparation and distribution activities, under the supervision of a pharmacist. Drug preparation and distribution can be accomplished in various ways. For non-anesthesiology drugs and drugs that are not case specific, a secure general supply of predetermined medications in limited quantities (e.g., in cart or cassette) can be provided, with the understanding that these drugs may be used for any patient. Anesthesiology medications could be supplied by case or by daily stock replenishment (e.g., an "anesthesia cart"). Increasingly, automated medication storage and distribution devices (e.g., Pyxis Medstation [Cardinal Health]) are being used to supply medications to the anesthesiology, nursing, and surgery staffs. With these devices, automatic and more accurate patient charging is often realized and pharmacy staff spend less time in distribution activities. The methods chosen may depend on the preferences and needs of the anesthesiologists and surgery staff, available resources, and whether there is a satellite pharmacy. The choice should be based on the method that will provide accurate and timely delivery of medications to meet the needs of patients. The common objectives for all methods, however, are reducing the time spent by nursing and anesthesiology staff in gathering and preparing medications and maximizing patient safety by limiting the selection of drugs, quantities, and dosage forms.

Drug Accountability and Control

The pharmacist should be responsible for all drugs and controlled substances dispensed and distributed in the setting. Pharmacy technicians could be assigned most of the responsibility for these daily activities. If there is a satellite pharmacy, all drug inventories, to the extent possible, should be centralized there. Minimal drug stock should be kept in each surgical suite. Ideally, the satellite pharmacy should be staffed whenever the surgery and anesthesiology areas are normally staffed. If the satellite pharmacy is not open 24 hours a day, it may be necessary to establish an after-hours drug supply (e.g., a cart). The pharmacist should decide the drugs and quantities required for this supply and the accountability system to be used. The supply levels should be checked and replenished daily. With an OR pharmacy, trends in drug use or disappearance are more easily identified, noted, and reconciled. Systems to track drugs used, to adjust par levels as needed, and to monitor drug expiration dates should be devised.

Clinical Services

Provision of clinical services should be a major focus of pharmacists practicing in the surgery and anesthesiology areas. These services may be similar to those provided to all other patient care areas. Clinical services can be provided by a pharmacist even without a satellite pharmacy.

To make effective clinical contributions, the pharmacist should be familiar with all drugs used in the setting, including drugs for general and regional anesthesia, neuromuscular blockade, analgesia, preoperative management, hemodynamic control, diagnosis and manipulation during surgery, prevention of infection, treatment of intraoperative emergencies, control of bleeding, and postoperative nausea and vomiting (PONV). Knowledge may be gained by observation of surgery and anesthesia procedures, attendance at anesthesia and surgery conferences, assigned topics to be presented by each pharmacy team member, review of pertinent literature, and direct clinical involvement in patient care. Clinical services may include the following[7]:

Medication-Use Management. The pharmacist is especially suited to taking a leadership role in medication-use management in the OR. This could be accomplished through the development of pharmaceutical practice guidelines and critical pathways for select surgical procedures, including intraoperative drug use. Guidelines are routinely developed for the neuromuscular blocking agents, synthetic opioids, propofol, antiemetic agents, volatile inhalation agents, and anti-infectives for surgical prophylaxis. Additional guidelines could be developed on the basis of organizational needs. It has been demonstrated that pharmaceutical practice guidelines for anesthesia-related medications reduce costs without adversely affecting patient outcomes.[8-10] With or without established guidelines, the presence of an OR satellite pharmacy allows the pharmacist to reinforce the appropriate use of agents dispensed from the pharmacy and to monitor patient outcomes.

Medication-Regimen Review. Whenever possible, medication requests from surgery or anesthesiology staff should be evaluated before the drug is dispensed for appropriateness (e.g., allergies, disease states, adherence to pharmaceutical practice guidelines), dose, route of administration, timing of administration, and cost compared with other therapeutic alternatives. The pharmacist should review the surgery schedule and routinely screen patient profiles or charts before surgery for allergies (e.g., antimicrobials, narcotics, latex) and notify appropriate personnel of pertinent findings. In addition, doses, timing, and choices of prophylactic antimicrobials should be monitored. Profiles or charts should also be reviewed whenever possible for potential perioperative

drug–drug or drug–disease interactions and for proper continuation of maintenance medications and discontinuation of unnecessary medications postoperatively.

Medication-Use Evaluation. The pharmacist should take a leadership role in the performance of medication-use evaluations by establishing criteria, collecting data, analyzing the data, making recommendations, and performing follow-up. Data collection is often more easily accomplished prospectively or concurrently by coordination with surgery and anesthesiology staff. High-cost or high-use medications are good starting places for medication-use evaluations in the OR. Medication-use evaluations are especially useful for assessing compliance with established guidelines. In organizations with automated anesthesia record keepers, collection and manipulation of medication-use information is greatly facilitated.[11]

Drug Information. The pharmacist should provide timely and accurate drug information in response to known needs and random inquiries. Inquiries may originate from any type of staff, including surgery and recovery-room staff, anesthesia staff, residents, nurses, perfusionists, and students. Drug information may be provided in oral or written form, as appropriate. The preparation of responses could require detailed literature searches with accompanying interpretations. The satellite pharmacy should maintain a body of pharmaceutical literature containing current primary, secondary, and tertiary literature sources. Scientific and professional practice journals in pharmacy, anesthesiology, and surgery should be directly available or readily accessible to support clinical decision-making for patients in the OR. Online drug information and access to the Internet should also be readily available to OR pharmacists. Reference texts should be current and should provide detailed information in at least the following areas: drug action, adverse effects, dosages, drugs of choice, efficacy, formulations, incompatibilities, indications for use, drug interactions, laws and regulations, pharmacology, pediatric medication administration (if applicable), nonprescription drugs, drug use during pregnancy and lactation, pathophysiology, pharmacokinetics, toxicology, surgery, and anesthesia. The pharmacist may also develop and distribute a newsletter and make available specific articles of interest to others in the setting. The pharmacist should have access to a formal drug information center.

Formulary System. The pharmacist should continually evaluate the organization's formulary and advise the medical staff and pharmacy and therapeutics (P&T) committee about drug efficacy, adverse-effect experiences, cost, and ongoing need for formulary agents. OR pharmacists can enforce P&T committee-approved restrictions on anesthesiology and surgery drugs and educate OR personnel on these restrictions.

Drug Research. The pharmacist should strive to initiate and participate in research related to drug use in surgery and anesthesia. Pharmacists could be principal investigators or could support the studies of others (e.g., perform randomization, prepare drugs, assist in study design and data collection). Because the OR is one of the most medication-intensive areas of a hospital, it is an excellent setting for pharmacoeconomic analyses and outcome studies.[12-14] These studies are best accomplished when they are collaborative. Given that newer anesthetic agents are often more expensive than older ones, studies are useful for learning whether a higher drug cost will result in a lower total cost for the patient.

Adverse-Drug-Reaction Monitoring and Reporting. The pharmacist should monitor, detect, document, report, and recommend appropriate management of adverse drug reactions that occur in the OR. OR health care providers should be asked to report suspected adverse drug reactions to the OR pharmacist for follow-up.

Education. Educational presentations on drug-related topics should be made regularly by the pharmacist to surgery and anesthesiology residents and staff, nursing staff, pharmacy staff, and other personnel. This could include information on drugs added to the organization's formulary, drug precautions, periodic reviews of drugs used during cardiac and respiratory arrest, pain management, and the management of malignant hyperthermia and latex allergy. The pharmacist should also educate OR personnel about drugs used in the setting, giving special attention to the synthetic opioids neuromuscular blocking agents, anesthetic gases, intravenous anesthetic agents, local anesthetics, antiemetics, and antimicrobials (surgical prophylaxis).

Formal educational rotations in the satellite pharmacy may be conducted for undergraduate and graduate pharmacy students, pharmacy residents, or pharmacy fellows. Specific learning and experiential goals and objectives should be developed. The student should learn about satellite pharmacy services and preoperative, intraoperative, and postoperative medication therapy through didactic instruction, observation, project participation, and selected readings. Rotations should be coordinated with the anesthesiology and nursing departments.

Rounds. When possible, the pharmacist should be an active participant with anesthesia, surgery, and PACU staff in patient care rounds. The pharmacist may limit rounds to specific types of patients (e.g., cardiothoracic surgery, transplant) for whom the pharmacist's preoperative or postoperative involvement may be most beneficial. The pharmacist should participate in anesthesia grand rounds, morbidity and mortality reviews, and other scheduled educational sessions as appropriate. Pharmacy grand rounds could be conducted by pharmacy staff to provide detailed drug information or to supplement anesthesia grand round topics.

Pain Management. The pharmacist should participate actively in epidural anesthesia, patient-controlled analgesia, and other pain-management programs. Participation could include the development of such a program, identification of appropriate patients, patient education, drug preparation, educational presentations to other staff, and participation in rounds with acute-pain-management teams as time permits.

Participation in Emergency Life Support. The pharmacist should be authorized to participate in the medication therapy for cardiac or respiratory arrests that occur in the OR. At a minimum, the pharmacist should have current certification in basic cardiac life support (BCLS) procedures and, preferably, training in advanced cardiac life support (ACLS). The pharmacist should also participate in the treatment of malignant hyperthermia by preparing and maintaining malignant hyperthermia emergency kits and preparing and administering medications used to treat malignant hyperthermia.

Pharmacokinetic Management and Consultation. The pharmacist should participate in the pharmacokinetic management of patients and should serve as a consultant to surgery and anesthesiology staff on pharmacokinetic of medications dosing.

Compliance with JCAHO Standards. The presence of pharmacy personnel in the surgery and anesthesiology areas, especially with an established satellite pharmacy, could help to ensure adherence to Joint Commission standards. Specifically, pharmacy plays a key role in compliance with the standards related to the medication-use process. These include reviewing medication orders; considering patient information when preparing and dispensing medication(s); ensuring pharmaceutical services are available when the pharmacy department is closed or pharmacy personnel are not available; controlling the preparation and dispensing of medication(s) (drugs should be secure from tampering, safe from patient-to-patient contamination, and properly labeled); ensuring that emergency medications are consistently available, controlled, and secure in the pharmacy and patient care areas; and monitoring the effects of medications on patients.

Documentation of Clinical Activities. The pharmacist should document clinical activities and identify activities leading to improved patient outcomes and cost reductions. This type of information is critical in order for the pharmacist to prove his or her value and the ongoing need for the services provided. The pharmacist is responsible for safeguarding the patient's rights to privacy and the confidentiality of the patient's clinical information.

Controlled Substances

All controlled-substance procedures should comply with applicable federal and state laws and regulations as well as the organization's policies and procedures. Procedures for the satellite pharmacy and the surgery and anesthesiology areas served should address the following:

1. Controlled substances (and other drugs) to be monitored;
2. Methods of distribution;
3. Records;
4. Ordering;
5. Storage, access, and inventory control;
6. Reconciliation and disposal;
7. Discrepancy reporting and disciplinary action; and
8. Performance of quality control checks.

The goal of the controlled-substance system is to prevent diversion yet be practical enough that patient care is not adversely affected. The system should limit exposure to controlled substances, be accountable and consistent, and contain an educational component for health care personnel.[15]

Controlled Substances (and Other Drugs) to be Monitored. The pharmacist should be responsible for monitoring the use of all controlled substances. As required (e.g., because of abuse or diversion potential), drugs other than controlled substances (e.g., ketamine) could also be handled according to procedures similar or identical to those used for controlled substances.

Methods of Distribution

One of two primary methods could be used for distribution of controlled substances in the OR: a per-case method or a daily-supply method.

A per-case system is advantageous in that it minimizes the quantity of controlled substances available to the anesthesiologist and the anesthetist at any one time and allows for a good audit trail. Its major disadvantage is that it is very time intensive for an organization that performs many surgeries per day. This time may be better spent by the pharmacist in clinical activities.

Daily distribution of controlled substances is less time intensive and can be accomplished from a central pharmacy or an OR satellite pharmacy. Its disadvantages are that greater amounts of controlled substances are dispensed at one time and that these substances need to be kept secure throughout the day.

The various advantages and disadvantages of each method must be considered and the appropriate system selected on an organization-specific basis.

To the extent possible, controlled substances should be distributed only in response to signed orders or oral requests from prescribers. Given the urgency often present during surgical procedures, the necessity for prescribers to devote undivided attention to anesthesia procedures, and the use of sterility-safeguard procedures during surgery, it may not always be possible to comply with such a requirement. When it is possible, the organization's standard physician-order sheet or a special controlled-substance request form developed specifically for use in the surgical suite could be used. A par level of controlled substances needed per type of case or for the day could be devised; requests for controlled substances beyond this would be treated as special orders. Whatever the methods used, clear documentation that all controlled substances used were administered to the patient should be signed by the responsible prescribers at the end of each surgical procedure. Ideally, unused controlled substances drawn up by the anesthesiologist should be returned to the satellite pharmacy and wasted by the pharmacist. Alternatively, controlled substances could be disposed of by the anesthesiologist in the presence of a witness, with both parties documenting the disposal. No matter the system, disposal of contaminated controlled substances (e.g., with blood or other body fluid) should occur in the OR and be properly documented.

Records

Records should be kept of the following:

1. Controlled substances dispensed;
2. Controlled-substance inventories;
3. Controlled substances returned (including controlled substances drawn up but not used), and records reconciliation;
4. Controlled substances disposed; and
5. Controlled-substance use, categorized by prescriber.

If the satellite pharmacy does not provide 24-hour services, the documentation procedures for after-hours use should be as similar as possible to those used when the satellite pharmacy is staffed. This will help ensure staff efficiency and familiarity with the record-keeping requirements after hours. Forms specific to the setting and to the after-hours circumstance may have to be developed.

Ordering

The pharmacist should be responsible for ordering all controlled substances for the satellite pharmacy. Once received, the controlled substances should be added to the satellite pharmacy's stock and recorded in inventory records. If the satellite pharmacy does not provide 24-hour services, the pharmacist is responsible for ensuring that adequate supplies are available in a secure, specially designated after-hours location. The pharmacist should maintain controlled-substance inventory amounts sufficient only to meet the needs of the OR for a reasonable time. This time should depend on the frequency and timeliness with which controlled substances are available from the central pharmacy. Less inventory is required, for example, if controlled substances are ordered on a daily basis rather than less often. The inventory system should be perpetual in order to provide the most current record of controlled substances on hand.

Shortly after the initial opening of a satellite pharmacy and after drug use has stabilized, stock levels should be reassessed and adjusted as needed. During ordering, the pharmacist should note developing trends in use. Nonformulary controlled substances should be dispensed only by special request.

Storage, Access, and Inventory Control

Controlled substances should be stored in a locked space (e.g., cabinet, drawer, cart) within the satellite pharmacy. These storage spaces should remain locked when controlled substances are not being dispensed. Access to the space should be limited to satellite pharmacy personnel. If 24-hour satellite pharmacy services are not provided, a separate locked after-hours storage space will be required. Kits of after-hours controlled substances may be useful. No matter how they are configured or located, all after-hours supplies should be checked and all records reconciled by satellite pharmacy staff on the first working day after the after-hours supplies are entered.

If possible, one person per shift should be identified as being responsible for controlled substances (and related procedures) when the satellite pharmacy is not open. That person should have access (key or code) to locked after-hours supplies. This approach enables more consistent record keeping, limits the number of people with access to after-hours supplies, and enables more reliable monitoring of controlled-substance use. Individuals often assigned this responsibility include an "in-charge" nurse or the "first-call" anesthesiology resident.

Controlled-substance inventories should be verified by physical count at least once daily. If the satellite pharmacy is open for two shifts, an end-of-shift count by the morning pharmacist is recommended. The use of automated medication storage and distribution devices for controlled substances may be a timesaving benefit for maintaining a perpetual inventory. Unscheduled audits of controlled substances in the satellite pharmacy should be done by staff not normally assigned to this setting. The results should be documented.

Reconciliation and Disposal

A thorough system for reconciling controlled-substance use should be developed and include the following components[16-18]:

1. *Comparison of quantities dispensed with quantities documented as administered.* The quantity of controlled substances returned to the satellite pharmacy should be compared with the quantity dispensed. The amount dispensed should equal the amount returned (unopened and partially filled containers and partially used syringes) plus the amount documented as administered.

2. *Verification of use through review of the anesthesia record.* The anesthesia record should be reviewed to ensure that the amount documented as administered (in records returned to the satellite pharmacy) is identical to the amount documented in the patient's anesthesia record. This verification is ideally done for all cases but may be done by periodic audits of randomly selected cases if anesthesia records are not readily available for every case.

3. *Qualitative testing of returned controlled substances.* To verify that unadulterated drug is contained in partially used containers returned to the satellite pharmacy, a refractometer or other device can be used. It is important to randomly audit controlled-substance returns in order to detect trends in diversion. The organization's legal department should be consulted to make sure such testing is permitted.

The pharmacist should account for all controlled substances dispensed and should report all discrepancies to internal and external authorities as required.

Disposal of controlled substances (e.g., partially used syringes) should be done in the satellite pharmacy by a member of the pharmacy staff in the presence of a witness. This action should be documented in the satellite pharmacy's controlled-substance records.

Communication and Education

It is important that there are open lines of communication among the pharmacist, the chair of anesthesiology (or designee), and the head surgical nurse to allow sharing of information indicative of diversion (e.g., behavioral change). In addition, periodic continuing education for all members of the OR team on the potential for substance abuse may sensitize staff to this problem.[15]

Performance Improvement

The pursuit of continuous improvement in the quality of services provided should be a philosophy of practice of the pharmacist and the satellite pharmacy staff.[19] In that light, many activities may be seen as pertinent to performance improvement efforts. Some of these are the following:

1. Adverse-drug-reaction monitoring and reporting,
2. Medication-error monitoring and reporting,
3. Medication histories,
4. Periodic inspections of all drug storage sites,
5. Drug therapy monitoring related to improved patient outcome (e.g., decreased time in the PACU, decreased frequency of PONV),
6. Medication-use evaluations,
7. Drug-interaction monitoring,
8. Controlled-substance monitoring,
9. Quality control of compounded parenterals (e.g., cardioplegic solutions) and batch-prepared syringes,
10. Medication-waste monitoring, and

11. Allergy and patient demographic monitoring.

Some of these activities should not be difficult to implement in a satellite pharmacy, because ongoing procedures should already be developed for the organization overall. Sometimes, it may be necessary to develop new programs or variations of existing ones tailored to the surgery and anesthesiology areas.

Other Activities

Policies and Procedures. If there is a satellite pharmacy, the pharmacist should develop and maintain policies and procedures for the satellite pharmacy and its services. There should be policies and procedures for the preparation of drug kits (if applicable), medication distribution systems, controlled-substance handling, hours of operation, preparation of parenteral products, expiration-date checking and monthly inspections, recycling of products, monitoring of drug inventory levels, staff training, quality assurance activities, and after-hours drug distribution.

Interdisciplinary Interfaces. The pharmacist should function as a liaison between the pharmacy department and all staff in the setting served, including anesthesiology, nursing, and surgery staff; perfusionists; and management staff. The pharmacist should represent the pharmacy department on appropriate interdisciplinary committees charged with evaluating or making recommendations about services and medication selection and use in the surgery and anesthesiology areas. A committee specifically designed to focus on pharmacy matters may be appropriate.

Financial Analysis. The pharmacist should document drug costs, service costs, revenues, and savings attributable to the satellite pharmacy and the activities (clinical and distributive) of its staff. If there is no OR satellite pharmacy, some of the aforementioned items will not need to be included in the analysis. Financial reports should be prepared periodically (e.g., quarterly, annually) and provided to the hospital administration and the departments of anesthesiology, surgery, and pharmacy.

The Pharmacy Technician's Role

Pharmacy technicians assigned to the satellite pharmacy should be trained to perform their assigned functions. It is critical and appropriate for the technician to do most of the drug distribution-related activities in the satellite pharmacy. Within the total work force of pharmacy technicians in the organization, it is desirable to have some technicians trained as available back-up staff for the satellite pharmacy. Technicians should be trained and certified by the Pharmacy Technician Certification Board or equivalent. In general, technician training and experience should include parenteral drug preparation, drug distribution procedures, physician-order interpretation, anesthesia and OR record interpretation, computer order entry, and controlled-substance record keeping. Specific training should include a review of the following:

1. Procedures unique to surgical suites, including special apparel (e.g., caps, masks, foot covers) and restricted movements and areas within surgical suites;
2. Surgical-suite terms, including abbreviations and acronyms used to name surgical procedures;

3. Drug classes, indications for use, and proper handling of drugs routinely used in surgical suites (e.g., special packaging, preservative requirements for spinal and epidural drugs, infusion concentrations);
4. Controlled-substance procedures;
5. Emergency drugs typically used in surgical suites; and
6. A review of the role of the pharmacy technician in the OR pharmacy area.

Typical activities performed by pharmacy technicians in the satellite pharmacy under the supervision of the pharmacist are drug distribution, controlled-substance handling, sterile drug preparation, drug ordering and restocking, orientation and training of new staff, and quality assurance activities. Each of these will be discussed in greater detail.

Drug Distribution. The technician could distribute medications to storage sites in the setting and prepare per-case or per-prescriber kits of medications and distribute these after they have been checked by the pharmacist. If automated medication storage and distribution devices are used, the technician is responsible for all activities associated with restocking these. Given the nature of surgical procedures and the urgency of the need for the requested medications, distribution would be required in response to oral requests. The pharmacist should screen such requests to ensure proper choices of drugs for specific patients. The technician should be trained to ask about patient allergies and relay this information to the pharmacist before preparing a medication. The technician also should be taught which situations must be handled by the pharmacist (e.g., drug information, dose calculations).

The technician could return unused drugs to stock and charge patients or departments for medications used.

Another technician function could be to check and replenish after-hours drug supplies and charge medications used to appropriate patients or departments.

The technician could be responsible for monthly inspections of drug storage areas and drug supply areas in the satellite pharmacy. Technicians should be assigned their own inspection zone when drugs are stored in many places.

Controlled Substances. Other responsibilities of the technician could be the distribution of controlled substances and the creation of appropriate records according to the distribution procedures of the satellite pharmacy and according to federal and state laws and regulations. Typical activities could include helping with inventory counts, maintaining perpetual inventory records, disposing of controlled substances with the pharmacist, and participating in audits, assays, and preparation of reports.

Sterile Drug Preparation. The technician could aseptically compound, package, and label sterile drugs—for injection and for irrigation—and document all products made. Appropriate records of drug name, diluent, lot numbers, and expiration dates of batch-prepared products should be maintained by the technician.

Drug Ordering and Restocking of the Pharmacy Satellite. In addition, technicians could routinely order replenishment supplies of drugs for the satellite pharmacy, check supplies delivered in response to the orders, and place the stock in appropriate places. Requests for odd medications or unusual trends in medication demand should be reported to the pharmacist for further review.

Orientation and Training of New Staff. Helping with the orientation and training of new staff (including other technicians and pharmacy students) could also be a responsibility of the technician. An orientation checklist, workflow sheets, and task lists are helpful training tools. An OR pharmacy student module would be a helpful teaching tool for students on rotation in the satellite pharmacy.

Quality Assurance. The technician could be involved in quality assurance activities of the satellite pharmacy. Such activities may include regular controlled-substance audits or assays, microbiological monitoring of parenteral drugs prepared, and inspections of drug supplies (e.g., expiration dates).

Summary

Pharmaceutical services in surgery and anesthesiology should be the standard of practice in health care organizations across the United States. Although not essential, an onsite satellite pharmacy would help in the provision of these services. A majority of distribution-related activities should be done by technicians. The availability of automated devices and other technology may lessen, to some extent, the time devoted to drug distribution. It is important for the OR pharmacist to concentrate on the provision of clinical services, such as medication-use management, drug information services, medication-use evaluations, formulary management, and pharmacoeconomic analyses of anesthesia-related medications. These activities provide the best opportunity for the pharmacist to contribute to improving patient care and outcomes and containing costs. Finally, pharmaceutical services in surgery and anesthesiology should be periodically assessed for patient care and financial effectiveness.

References

1. Powell PJ, Maland L, Bair JN et al. Implementing an operating room pharmacy satellite. *Am J Hosp Pharm.* 1983; 40:1192–8.
2. Opoien D. Establishment of surgery satellite pharmacy services in a large community hospital. *Hosp Pharm.* 1984; 19:485–90.
3. Keicher PA, McAllister JC III. Comprehensive pharmaceutical services in the surgical suite and recovery room. *Am J Hosp Pharm.* 1985; 42:2454–62.
4. Buchanan EC, Gaither MW. Development of an operating room pharmacy substation on a restricted budget. *Am J Hosp Pharm.* 1986; 43:1719–22.
5. Vogel DP, Barone J, Penn F et al. Ideas for action: the operating room pharmacy satellite. *Top Hosp Pharm Manag.* 1986; 6:63–80.
6. Donnelly AJ. Multidisciplinary approach to improving documentation of medications used during surgical procedures. *Am J Hosp Pharm.* 1989; 46:724–8.
7. Shafer AS. Clinical pharmacy practice in the operating room. *J Pharm Pract.* 1993; 6:165–70.
8. Gora-Harper ML, Hessel E II, Shadick D. Effect of prescribing guidelines on the use of neuromuscular blocking agents. *Am J Health-Syst Pharm.* 1995; 52:1900–4.
9. Freund PR, Borolle TA, Posner KL, et al. Cost-effective reduction of neuromuscular-block drug expenditures. *Anesthesiology.* 1997; 87:1044–9.
10. Lubarsky DA, Glass PSA, Ginsberg B, et al. The successful implementation of pharmaceutical practice

guidelines. *Anesthesiology.* 1997; 86:1145–60.

11. Lubarsky DA, Sanderson IC, Gilbert WC, et al. Using an anesthesia information management system as a cost containment tool. *Anesthesiology.* 1997; 86:1161–9.

12. Lorighlin KA, Weingarten CM, Nagelhout J, et al. A pharmacoeconomic analysis of neuromuscular blocking agents in the operating room. *Pharmacotherapy.* 1996; 16:942–50.

13. DeMonaco HJ, Shah AS. Economic considerations in the use of neuromuscular blocking drugs. *J Clin Anesth.* 1994; 6:383–7.

14. Tang J, Watcha MF, White PF. A comparison of costs and efficacy of ondansetron and droperidol as prophylactic antiemetic therapy for elective outpatient gynecologic procedures. *Anesth Analg.* 1996; 83:304–13.

15. Castellano FC. Developing methods for preventing and detecting substance abuse in the operating room: a disease approach. *J Pharm Pract.* 1993; 6:159–64.

16. Satterlee GB. System for verifying use of controlled substances in anesthesia. *Am J Hosp Pharm.* 1989; 46:2506–8.

17. Shovick VA, Mattei TJ, Karnack CM. Audit to verify use of controlled substances in anesthesia. *Am J Hosp Pharm.* 1988; 45:1111–3.

18. Gill DL, Goodwin SR, Knudsen AK, et al. Refractometer screening of controlled substances in an operating room satellite pharmacy. *Am J Hosp Pharm.* 1990; 47:817–8.

19. Hawkins PR. Quality improvement: pharmacy involvement in the operating room. *J Pharm Pract.* 1993; 6:171–6.

Appendix—
Justifying and Implementing an Operating-Room Satellite Pharmacy

Justification of the need for a satellite pharmacy is a critical step in establishing pharmaceutical services in surgery and anesthesiology.[1,2]

The pharmacist's ability to positively affect medication-use management, to take a leadership role in all aspects of cost containment, and to contribute to improved patient care and outcomes must be highlighted.

Familiarization with Surgery and Anesthesiology Pharmaceutical Services. As an initial step, the person in charge of the project should become familiar with typical surgery and anesthesiology satellite pharmacy services. Review of pertinent literature, discussions with pharmacists in other organizations, and site visits to established satellite pharmacies are methods of accomplishing this step. The site visit is especially useful, because it can reinforce and further define information gained by other means. At the conclusion of this step, the pharmacist should have a realistic view of the types and scope of services typically provided.

Obtaining Support. If justification is to be successful, the support of key individuals from the major departments affected by the service should be obtained.[1] In most organizations, these are hospital administration, anesthesiology (anesthesiologists and certified registered nurse anesthetists), and surgery, operating-room (OR), and postanesthesia care unit nursing.

The support of the anesthesiology department is necessary because this department represents the major users of medications in the OR and has significant patient care responsibilities in this setting. Support for pharmaceutical services from anesthesiology department administration is important for the success of the project. If the request for satellite pharmacy services originates in the anesthesiology department, the justification process may be simpler and more collaborative. Data gathered during the preliminary review of the site and information obtained from the literature can be used when the project is discussed with anesthesiology administration. It may be valuable to solicit the support of any anesthesiologists who have been especially receptive to pharmacy involvement. Many anesthesiologists have had positive experiences with OR pharmaceutical services at other organizations. The proposal for a satellite pharmacy might then be presented jointly by pharmacy personnel and anesthesiologists. Once formalized, the proposal should be presented to hospital administration. The administration's opinion will provide some guidance on how to facilitate the approval process for the satellite pharmacy.

If conceptual support from these groups is obtained, development of a more formal proposal can begin. If there are still concerns about the benefits gained from OR satellite pharmacy services, it may be helpful to propose an interim step to expose more hospital staff to OR pharmaceutical services in order to keep the process moving forward. One possible approach is to suggest that a pilot project be conducted involving several ORs or one specific surgical specialty. The establishment of a permanent satellite pharmacy would depend on favorable results from the pilot project.

Initial Assessment of Setting. A general review of the surgery and anesthesiology areas to be served by the satellite pharmacy should be done after staff have become familiar with the project. At this time, it is not essential that detailed information be obtained. Useful information to collect includes the following:

1. All locations and quantities of drugs stored in the setting,
2. The location and storage of controlled substances,
3. Controlled-substance accountability systems used,
4. Drug preparation and distribution procedures used in the setting,
5. Billing systems used for all drugs,
6. Stock replenishment and rotation systems used, and
7. The role (or potential role) of automation in the involved areas.

The collection of this information could be speeded by a tour of the area and by inquiries through nurses, anesthesiologists, supply technicians, surgeons, and other OR personnel (e.g., perfusionists).

Formal Proposal. The development of a formal proposal is an important part of the justification process. It is essential that the proposal be well organized and factual. The writers of the proposal should expect the proposal to be examined in great detail by hospital administration and others during the decision-making process. The proposal should expand upon the information obtained in the initial review of the surgery and anesthesiology areas. Information that should be in the proposal includes the following:

1. The dollar value of current drug inventory,

2. The dollar value of drugs used per period (e.g., per year),
3. The dollar value of patient charges currently generated,
4. The estimated dollar value of increased revenue,
5. The average cost of drugs used per surgical case,
6. An estimated cost of drug waste per period,
7. The general quality and completeness of controlled-substance records,
8. The number of controlled-substance discrepancies reported per month,
9. The number of reports of drug-related incidents received per month,
10. The time personnel in the setting currently spend performing pharmacy-related activities,
11. The time pharmacy personnel currently spend performing activities for the setting, and
12. Opportunities for collaborative efforts by pharmacy–anesthesiology, pharmacy–nursing, pharmacy–perfusion, and pharmacy–surgery in drug-use management (e.g., development of pharmaceutical practice guidelines, performance of medication-use evaluations).

Collection of this information could be helped through the formation of a multidisciplinary team. Representatives of the departments of pharmacy, anesthesiology, nursing, and surgery should be included. This approach has several benefits. Data collection can be expedited, because the expertise of each individual can be used. The value of a satellite pharmacy will be continually reinforced to these individuals, and all groups will have input into the decision-making process.

A formal proposal should be prepared once the required information has been collected. Minimally, the proposal should contain the following sections[1]:

1. Introduction;
2. Statement of problems and anticipated benefits (and beneficiaries);
3. Summary of the proposed services;
4. Cost–benefit analysis, including staffing, estimated cost savings, revenue projections, and inventory savings; and
5. Implementation plan.

During preparation of these sections, it is important to be as specific as possible and to assign dollar values whenever these are available. The proposal should be endorsed by the members of the multidisciplinary team and should be submitted to the administration by the director of pharmacy. Careful planning, data collection, analysis, and presentation of the information gathered will make approval more likely.

Implementation. Implementation should begin as soon as possible after administrative approval.[1] Implementation steps should be planned and executed in a clear, concise manner. To guide planning, an implementation time line should be developed (e.g., Gantt chart), listing the steps to be taken, the task force member responsible for each step, and the expected amount of time required for each activity. The amount of time required for each activity may vary from organization to organization, but the order in which the steps should be performed will be reasonably standard.

The major implementation steps and an approximate order in which they should be completed are as follows[1]:

1. Obtain a formal commitment of space,
2. Assign a project leader (who should be responsible for the project's development and need not be the pharmacist who will be assigned to staff the satellite pharmacy; often, it is valuable for the project leader to be a supervisor or assistant director),
3. Identify construction and equipment needs,
4. Oversee construction work,
5. Obtain and install equipment,
6. Draft policies and procedures (e.g., controlled-substance accountability, medication distribution system, inventory control),
7. Develop job descriptions,
8. Select staff (pharmacists and support personnel),
9. Design and print forms,
10. Formalize policies and procedures,
11. Determine satellite pharmacy drug-stock levels,
12. Train staff,
13. Identify back-up and relief staff and orient them to the setting,
14. Educate nursing staff,
15. Educate anesthesiology department staff,
16. Educate surgeons,
17. Open the satellite pharmacy for operation,
18. Determine future goals for service, and
19. Determine systems for periodic analyses of the impact of the program.

Many of these steps can be expedited by a close working relationship with members of the anesthesiology and nursing departments.

The satellite pharmacy's services should be monitored and evaluated on an ongoing basis through workload statistics, data on controlled-substance discrepancies, financial data, and patient outcomes data. In addition, the satisfaction levels of the nursing and anesthesiology staffs should be assessed before the program is implemented, six months after implementation, and yearly after that.

References

1. Vogel DP, Barone J, Penn F, et al. Ideas for action: the operating room pharmacy satellite. *Top Hosp Pharm Manage.* 1986; 6:63–80.
2. Ziter CA, Dennis BW, Shoup LK. Justification of an operating-room satellite pharmacy. *Am J Hosp Pharm.* 1989; 46:1353–61.

These guidelines were reviewed in 2003 by the Council on Professional Affairs and by the Board of Directors and were found to still be appropriate.

Approved by the ASHP Board of Directors November 14, 1998. Developed through the ASHP Council on Professional Affairs. Supersedes the ASHP Technical Assistance Bulletin on Surgery and Anesthesiology Pharmaceutical Services dated November 14, 1990.

The bibliographic citation for this document is as follows: American Society of Health-System Pharmacists. ASHP guidelines on surgery and anesthesiology pharmaceutical services. *Am J Health-Syst Pharm.* 1999; 56:887–95.

ASHP Guidelines on the Pharmacist's Role in Immunization

Purpose

Pharmacists can play an important role in disease prevention by advocating and administering immunizations. Such activities are consistent with the preventive aspects of pharmaceutical care and have been part of pharmacy practice for over a century.[1,2] These guidelines address the pharmacist's role in promoting and conducting proper immunization of patients in all organized health care settings. The pharmacist's role in promoting disease prevention through participation in community efforts is also discussed.

Background

Each year, an average of 90,000 Americans die of vaccine-preventable infections such as influenza, pneumococcal disease, and hepatitis B.[3–5] Most of these people visited health care providers in the year preceding their deaths but were not vaccinated.[6–11] Influenza and pneumonia, considered together, are the fifth leading cause of death for Americans 65 years of age or older.[12] Although vaccination rates for U.S. children at the time they enter school exceed 95%, nearly 25% do not complete their primary series by the age of two years.[13] Most American adults are inadequately vaccinated, particularly against pneumococcal disease, influenza, hepatitis B, tetanus, and diphtheria.[6] Tens of millions of Americans remain susceptible to potentially deadly infections despite the availability of effective vaccines.

This long-standing failure to adequately immunize the U.S population helped prompt the inclusion of immunization as a leading health indicator for Healthy People 2010.[14] The renewed focus on immunization and the potential for increased vaccination needs in response to threats of bioterrorism should stimulate pharmacists, as well as other health care providers, to reassess what they and their institutions can do to improve immunization rates in their communities. Pharmacists can contribute to this effort by administering immunizations where scope of practice allows and by promoting immunization in other ways.

Immunization Administration

As health care providers, pharmacists can administer vaccines or host other health care professionals who can administer vaccines. Pharmacists must understand the legal and professional mechanisms by which authorization to administer vaccines is granted, as well as the additional responsibilities and considerations that accompany this expanded role. The feasibility of vaccine administration by pharmacists within a particular practice site or health care system can be determined by analyzing the issues of legal authority, training, and program structure.

Legal Authority. The pharmacist's authority to administer vaccines is determined by each state's laws and regulations governing pharmacy practice. At least 36 states permit vaccine administration by pharmacists as part of the scope of pharmacy practice.[15] The American College of Physicians–American Society of Internal Medicine supports pharmacists as sources of immunization information, hosts of immunization sites, and immunizers.[16] Vaccine administration may occur pursuant to individual prescription orders or through standing orders or protocols. The Centers for Disease Control and Prevention (CDC) Advisory Committee on Immunization Practices recommends the use of standing orders to improve adult immunization rates.[17] Its recommendations encourage pharmacists, among other providers, to establish standing-order programs in long-term-care facilities, home health care agencies, hospitals, clinics, workplaces, and managed care organizations. The Centers for Medicare and Medicaid Services (CMS) no longer requires a physician order for influenza or pneumoccocal immunizations administered in participating hospitals, long-term-care facilities, or home health care agencies.[18] Development of state-specific protocols or standing-order programs can be facilitated through partnerships with state pharmacy associations, boards of pharmacy, and health departments.

Training. Although legal authority to administer vaccines may be granted through pharmacy practice acts, pharmacists must achieve competency in all aspects of vaccine administration. A comprehensive training program should address the following:

1. The epidemiology of and patient populations at risk for vaccine-preventable diseases,
2. Public health goals for immunization (e.g., local, regional, state, and federal goals),
3. Vaccine safety (e.g., risk–benefit analysis),
4. Screening for contraindications and precautions of vaccination in each patient,
5. Vaccine stability and transportation and storage requirements,
6. Immunologic drug interactions,
7. Vaccine dosing (including interpreting recommended immunization schedules and patient immunization records and determining proper dosing intervals and the feasibility of simultaneous administration of multiple vaccines),
8. Proper dose preparation and injection technique,
9. Signs and symptoms of adverse reactions to vaccines, adverse reaction reporting, and emergency procedures, such as basic and advanced cardiac life support (BCLS and ACLS),
10. Documentation,
11. Reporting to the primary care provider or local health department, and
12. Billing.

Live and videotaped programming is available through some state and national pharmacy associations and offered in many pharmacy school curricula. Information regarding immunizations can change rapidly. To maintain competency, pharmacists must have access to current immunization references (e.g., CDC's National Immunization Program publications, including the "Pink Book"[19]) and continuing-education programs to stay abreast of evolving guidelines and recommendations.

Program Structure. A vaccine administration program requires a solid infrastructure of appropriately trained staff, physical space, and written policies and procedures to ensure appropriate vaccine storage and handling, patient screening and education, and documentation. The structure of a vaccine administration program must also provide for storage and disposal of injection supplies, disposal of and prevention of exposure to biological hazards as dictated by the Occupational Safety and Health Administration (OSHA), and emergency procedures (e.g., BCLS and ACLS). Pharmacists should be fully immunized to protect their health and the health of their patients.[20]

Reimbursement. Immunization has repeatedly been shown to be cost-effective[21-24]; it may be the most cost-effective practice in medicine. However, third-party reimbursement policies often do not provide coverage for recommended vaccines despite this evidence. A major exception is Medicare Part B, which not only covers immunization services for its participants but also recognizes and compensates pharmacists as mass immunization providers. Enrollment as a Medicare provider is required to bill for covered services. Provider status can be obtained through local Medicare offices, which also process CMS claims for reimbursement (CMS-1500 claims). The CMS Web site (www.cms.hhs.gov) is a useful source for billing information. Pharmacists should continue to closely monitor other immunization reimbursement policies and advocate third-party coverage for immunizations as a cost-effective preventive measure. For patients without insurance coverage, requesting out-of-pocket payments from the patient remains a viable option for pharmacists to obtain compensation for their immunization services.

Immunization Promotion

Pharmacists who do not administer vaccines can promote immunization through six types of activities: (1) history and screening, (2) patient counseling, (3) documentation, (4) formulary management, (5) administrative measures, and (6) public education.[25,26] These promotional activities can also be integrated into or accompany a pharmacy-based immunization program.

History and Screening. Pharmacists can promote proper immunization by identifying patients in need of immunization. Tasks that support this objective include gathering immunization histories, encouraging use of vaccine profiles, issuing vaccination records to patients,[27-34] preventing immunologic drug interactions,[35,36] and screening patients for immunization needs.[28-33, 37-39]

Immunization screening should be a component of all clinical routines, regardless of the practice setting. All health care institutions should implement consistent, systematic monitoring systems and quality indicators to ensure that all patients are assessed for immunization adequacy before they leave the facility. The health care provider designated to identify patient immunization needs should have the authority, knowledge, and responsibility to provide or arrange for the immunization service.[40] Clinics that provide treatment for a large number of patients at high risk for contracting vaccine-preventable diseases (e.g., diabetic, asthmatic, heart disease, and geriatric clinics) have a particular obligation to employ immunization screening and ensure appropriate vaccine use.

Screening for immunization needs may be organized in several ways; prototype screening forms are available.[39,41]

Pharmacists should seek out leadership roles in some or all of the following forms of immunization screening.

Occurrence Screening. With this type of screening, vaccine needs are identified at the time of particular events, such as hospital or nursing home admission or discharge, ambulatory care or emergency room visits, mid-decade birthdays (e.g., years 25, 35, and 45),[42,43] and any contact with a health care delivery system for patients under 8 years or over 50 years of age.

Diagnosis Screening. This screening reviews the vaccine needs of patients with conditions that increase their risk of preventable infections. Diagnoses such as diabetes, asthma, heart disease, acute myocardial infarction, congestive heart failure, chronic obstructive pulmonary disease, hemophilia, thalassemia, most types of cancer, sickle cell anemia, chronic alcoholism, cirrhosis, human immunodeficiency virus infection, and certain other disorders should prompt specific attention to the patient's vaccine needs.[12,33,42] The immunization rate for patients diagnosed with community-acquired pneumonia is considered a marker for quality by some accrediting bodies. Incorporating assessment of vaccination status into an institution's critical pathways has been shown to improve vaccination rates.[44]

Procedure Screening. Immunization needs are assessed on the basis of medical or surgical procedures using this type of screening. These procedures include splenectomy, heart or lung surgery, organ transplantation, antineoplastic therapy, radiation therapy, immunosuppression of other types, dialysis, and prescription of certain medications used to treat conditions that increase patients' risk of preventable infections.[45,46] When designing and implementing automated prescription databases, pharmacy managers should consider specifications that allow retrieval of lists of patients receiving drugs that suggest the need for immunization.[33,37]

Periodic Mass Screening. This type of screening is a comprehensive assessment of immunization adequacy in selected populations at a given time. Such screening may be conducted, for example, during autumn influenza programs or outbreaks of certain vaccine-preventable illnesses (e.g., measles and meningococcal disease).[29,32,33] Schools and other institutions can perform mass screening when registering new students or residents. Mass screening may also be appropriate in areas where no comprehensive immunization program has been conducted recently. This type of screening helps improve vaccine coverage rates at a given time, but long-term benefits are much greater when such intermittent programs are combined with ongoing comprehensive screening efforts. Several states, including South Dakota, New Jersey, and Oklahoma, have enacted laws requiring that influenza and pneumococcal vaccines be offered annually to residents of nursing homes.

Occupational Screening. This screening method focuses on the immunization needs of health care personnel whose responsibilities place them at risk of exposure to certain vaccine-preventable diseases or bring them into contact with high-risk patients (i.e., patients with those conditions listed in the *Diagnosis Screening* section above). Health care providers who have contact with these patients should receive an annual influenza vaccination. Health care employers frequently provide immunization screening and vaccination of employees as part of employee health programs. OSHA requires that health care employers provide hepatitis B vaccination at no cost, on a voluntary basis, to all employees at risk for occupational exposure to blood borne pathogens.[47] Depending on their risk of exposure, it may be advisable for members of the pharmacy staff to receive hepatitis B vaccination.

Screening for Contraindications and Precautions. After candidates for immunization have been identified, they should be screened for contraindications and precautions. A CDC-reviewed contraindication screening questionnaire is available.[48]

Patient Counseling. Patients in need of immunization should be advised of their infection risk and encouraged to accept the immunizations they need. Patient concerns about vaccine safety and efficacy should be discussed and addressed.[49,50] Health care providers can influence patients' attitudes regarding immunization.[51,52] Physicians should be informed of their patients' need for vaccination if standing orders or collaborative practice agreements are not in place. Patients who need immunizations should be vaccinated during the current health care contact unless valid contraindications exist. Delaying vaccination until a future appointment increases the risk that the patient will not be vaccinated.

Advising patients of their need for immunization can take several forms. In the ambulatory care setting, individualized or form letters can be mailed to patients, patients can be called by telephone, or an insert can be included with prescriptions informing patients of their infection risk and the availability and efficacy of vaccines.[30,33,53–55] Adhesive reminder labels can also be affixed to prescription containers for drugs used to treat conditions that may indicate the need for vaccination against influenza and pneumococcal disease (e.g., digoxin, warfarin, theophylline, and insulin[33]); these labels would be analogous to labels currently in widespread use (e.g., "Shake well" and "Take with food or milk"). Such labels might read, "You may need flu or pneumonia vaccine: Ask your doctor or pharmacist." Chart notes, consultations, messages to patients, one-on-one conversations, and similar means can be used to communicate with inpatients and institutional patients.[28,31,56]

Federal law requires that health care providers who administer diphtheria, tetanus, pertussis, measles, mumps, rubella, varicella, polio, *Haemophilus influenzae* type B, hepatitis B, and pneumococcal conjugate vaccines give the most recent version of the CDC-developed Vaccine Information Statement (VIS) to the adult or the parent or legal guardian of the child to be vaccinated.[57] VISs are available in many languages from state or local health departments or the CDC.[58] VISs are also available for other commonly used vaccines, such as influenza, pneumococcal polysaccharide, hepatitis A, meningococcal, and anthrax vaccines. Pharmacists should also ensure that informed consent is obtained in a manner that complies with state laws.[20]

Documentation. The National Childhood Vaccine Injury Act of 1986 (NCVIA) requires all health care providers who administer vaccines to maintain permanent vaccination records and to report occurrences of certain adverse events specified in the act.[57,59] The recipient's permanent medical record (or the equivalent) must state the date the vaccine was administered, the vaccine's manufacturer and lot number, and the name, address, and title of the person administering the vaccine. Pharmacists in organized health care settings may encourage compliance with this requirement by providing reminder notices each time doses of vaccines are dispensed.[60] Automated databases that allow for long-term storage of patient immunization information may provide an efficient method for maintaining and retrieving immuniza-

tion records.[39] Efforts to develop electronic vaccination registries, especially for children, are under way by states collaborating with CDC.[61]

NCVIA also mandates that selected adverse effects noted after any inoculation be reported to the Vaccine Adverse Event Reporting System (www.vaers.org).[57,59,62] Because pharmacists have experience with adverse-drug-reaction reporting, they can take the lead in developing and implementing a program to meet this requirement, even if they are not responsible for administering the vaccine.

Patients should maintain personal immunization records that document all immunization experiences and function as a backup if the clinicians' immunization records are lost. Several personal immunization record forms are available. Public Health Service Form 731 (International Certificate of Vaccination), colloquially called the "yellow shot record," is used to document vaccines indicated for international travel but can also serve as a patient's personal record of vaccinations. The Immunization Action Coalition distributes a standard adult immunization record card developed in collaboration with CDC.[63] In addition, each state and the District of Columbia prints its own uniform immunization record form for pediatric immunizations, which may also be a suitable personal patient record. It has been recommended that adults carry personal immunization records in their wallets.[46]

Formulary Management. Formulary systems in organized health care settings should include vaccines, toxoids, and immune globulins available for use in preventing diseases in patients and staff. Decisions by the pharmacy and therapeutics committee (or its equivalent) on immunologic drug choices require consideration of relevant immunologic pharmaceutics, immunopharmacology, and disease epidemiology. Because of their expertise and training, pharmacists are well equipped to provide information and recommendations on which these decisions may be based.

It is the pharmacist's responsibility to develop and maintain product specifications to aid in the purchase of drugs under the formulary system.[64,65] The pharmacist should establish and maintain standards to ensure the quality, proper storage, and proper use of all pharmaceuticals dispensed. Pharmacists must choose between single dose or multidose containers of vaccines on the basis of efficiency, safety, economic, and regulatory considerations. Pharmacists in institutions should develop guidelines on the routine stocking of immunologic drugs in certain high-use patient care areas.

Proper transportation and storage are an important consideration for immunologic drugs, including vaccines, because many require storage at refrigerated or frozen temperatures. Pharmacists have an important responsibility to maintain the "cold chain" in the handling of these drugs. Detailed references on this topic have been published.[66–73] Storage considerations include the conditions in all areas in which immunologic drugs are kept, as well as a method for ensuring that immunologic drugs received by the pharmacy have been transported under suitable conditions.

It is important that methods be established for detecting and properly disposing of outdated and partially administered immunologic agents. Live viral (e.g., varicella, yellow fever, and smallpox) and live bacterial (e.g., bacille Calmette-Guérin) vaccines should be disposed of in the same manner as other infectious biohazardous waste.

Administrative Measures. Pharmacists on key committees (e.g., infection control and risk management) in organized health care settings can promote adequate immunization delivery among staff and patients by encouraging the development of sound organizational policies on immunization. Health care organizations should develop policies and protocols that address the following:

1. Hepatitis B preexposure prophylaxis for health care workers at risk for exposure to blood products and other contaminated items,[45,74–76]
2. Hepatitis B postexposure (e.g., needle stick) prophylaxis for previously unvaccinated patients, health care personnel, and personnel who have been vaccinated but do not have a previously documented serologic response,[45,74–76]
3. Rabies preexposure and postexposure prophylaxis,[77]
4. Wound management guidelines designed to prevent tetanus and diphtheria,[78,79]
5. Valid contraindications to vaccination to ensure patient safety and minimize inappropriate exclusions from vaccination,[78,80,81]
6. Requirements for employee immunization against measles, rubella, influenza, and other diseases,[42,82]
7. Tuberculosis screening of patients and staff,[83,84]
8. Immunization of persons at high risk (e.g., patients with diabetes, asthma, heart disease, and pregnant or immunocompromised patients). Current authoritative guidelines on this subject should be consulted,[42,46,58,85,86] and
9. Emergency measures in the event of vaccine-related adverse reactions. Such measures should address the availability of epinephrine and other emergency drugs, as well as BCLS and ACLS.

Public Education. Pharmacists have ample opportunities to advance the public health through immunization advocacy. Pharmacists can facilitate disease prevention strategies, because many potential victims of influenza and pneumococcal disease visit pharmacies and are seen by pharmacists daily. Pharmacists can lead local activities in observance of National Adult Immunization Week each October.[37] Working with local public health departments, state or national immunization coalitions, and other groups (e.g., state or local parent—teacher, diabetes, heart, lung, or retired persons' associations), pharmacists can promote vaccination among high-risk populations. Newsletters, posters, brochures, and seminars may be used to explain the risk of preventable infections to pharmacy staff, other health care personnel, and patients. Excellent resources are available from the Immunization Action Coalition and the National Coalition for Adult Immunization.

References

1. Hepler CD, Strand LM. Opportunities and responsibilities in pharmaceutical care. *Am J Hosp Pharm.* 1990; 47:533–43.
2. Grabenstein JD. Pharmacists and immunization: increasing involvement over a century. *Pharm Hist.* 1999; 41:137–52.
3. Prevention and control of influenza: recommendations of the Advisory Committee on Immunization Practices. *MMWR Recomm Rep.* 2002; 51(RR-3):1–31.
4. Prevention of pneumococcal disease: recommendations of the Advisory Committee on Immunization Practices (ACIP). *MMWR Recomm Rep.* 1997; 46(RR-8):1–24.
5. Thompson WW, Shay DK, Weintraub E, et al. Mortality associated with influenza and respiratory syncytial virus in the United States. *JAMA.* 2003; 289:179–86.
6. Williams WW, Hickson MA, Kane MA, et al. Immunization policies and vaccine coverage among adults. The risk for missed opportunities. *Ann Intern Med.* 1988; 108:616–25.
7. Fedson DS, Harward MP, Reid RA, et al. Hospital-based pneumococcal immunization. Epidemiologic rationale from the Shenandoah study. *JAMA.* 1990; 264:1117–22.
8. Fedson DS. Influenza and pneumococcal immunization strategies for physicians. *Chest.* 1987; 91:436–43.
9. Fedson DS. Improving the use of pneumococcal vaccine through a strategy of hospital-based immunization: a review of its rationale and implications. *J Am Geriatr Soc.* 1985; 33:142–50.
10. Magnussen CR, Valenti WM, Mushlin AI. Pneumococcal vaccine strategy. Feasibility of a vaccination program directed at hospitalized and ambulatory patients. *Arch Intern Med.* 1984; 144:1755–7.
11. Vondracek TG, Pham TP, Huycke MM. A hospital-based pharmacy intervention program for pneumococcal vaccination. *Arch Intern Med.* 1998; 158:1543–7.
12. Bratzler DW, Houck PM, Jiang H, et al. Failure to vaccinate Medicare inpatients: a missed opportunity. *Arch Intern Med.* 2002; 162:2349–56.
13. Barker L, Luman E, Zhao Z, et al. National, state, and urban area vaccination coverage levels among children aged 19–35 months—United States, 2001. *MMWR. Morb Mortal Wkly Rep.* 2002; 51(30):664–6.
14. Office of Disease Prevention and Health Promotion. Healthy people 2010. www.healthypeople.gov (accessed 2003 Mar 12).
15. American Pharmaceutical Association. States where pharmacists can immunize. www.aphanet.org/pharmcare/immunofact.html (accessed 2003 Mar 6).
16. Keely JL. Pharmacist scope of practice. *Ann Intern Med.* 2002; 136:79–85.
17. Use of standing orders programs to increase adult vaccination rates: recommendations of the Advisory Committee on Immunization Practices (ACIP). *MMWR Recomm Rep.* 2000; 49(RR01):15–26.
18. 42 C.F.R. §482–4.
19. Centers for Disease Control and Prevention. Epidemiology and prevention of vaccine-preventable diseases. 7th ed. Atlanta: U.S. Department of Health and Human Services; 2003.
20. Grabenstein JD. High expectations: standards and guidelines for immunization delivery. *Hosp Pharm.* 2000; 35:841–51.
21. Sisk JE, Moskowitz AJ, Whang W, et al. Cost-effectiveness of vaccination against pneumococcal bacteremia among elderly people. *JAMA.* 1997; 278:1333–9.
22. Van den Oever R, de Graeve D, Hepp B, et al. Pharmacoeconomics of immunisation: a review. *Pharmacoeconomics.* 1993; 3:286–308.
23. Nichol KL, Lind A, Margolis KL, et al. The effectiveness of vaccination against influenza in healthy, working adults. *N Engl J Med.* 1995; 333:889–93.
24. Nichol KL, Margolis KL, Wuorenma J, et al. The efficacy and cost-effectiveness of vaccination against influenza among elderly persons living in the community. *N Engl J Med.* 1994; 331:778–84.
25. Grabenstein JD. Immunizations: what's a health-sys-

tem pharmacy to do? Part 1. *Hosp Pharm.* 1998; 33:742,745–50,753.

26. Grabenstein JD. Immunizations: what's a health-system pharmacy to do? Part 2. *Hosp Pharm.* 1998; 33:870–2,876–80.

27. Huff PS, Hak SH, Caiola SM. Immunizations for international travel as a pharmaceutical service. *Am J Hosp Pharm.* 1982; 39:90–3.

28. Spruill WJ, Cooper JW, Taylor WJR. Pharmacist-coordinated pneumonia and influenza vaccination program. *Am J Hosp Pharm.* 1982; 39:1904–6.

29. Grabenstein JD, Smith LJ, Carter DW, et al. Comprehensive immunization delivery in conjunction with influenza vaccination. *Arch Intern Med.* 1986; 146:1189–92.

30. Williams DM, Daugherty LJ, Aycock DG, et al. Effectiveness of improved targeting efforts for influenza immunization in an ambulatory-care setting. *Hosp Pharm.* 1987; 22:462–4.

31. Morton MR, Spruill WJ, Cooper JW. Pharmacist impact on pneumococcal vaccination rates in long-term-care facilities. *Am J Hosp Pharm.* 1988; 45:73. Letter.

32. Grabenstein JD, Smith LJ, Watson RR, et al. Immunization outreach using individual need assessments of adults at an Army hospital. *Public Health Rep.* 1990; 105:311–6.

33. Grabenstein JD, Hayton BD. Pharmacoepidemiologic program for identifying patients in need of vaccination. *Am J Hosp Pharm.* 1990; 47:1774–81.

34. Grabenstein JD. Get it in writing: documenting immunizations. *Hosp Pharm.* 1991; 26:901–4.

35. Grabenstein JD. Drug interactions involving immunologic agents. Part I. Vaccine—vaccine, vaccine—immunoglobulin, and vaccine—drug interactions. *DICP.* 1990; 24:67–81.

36. Grabenstein JD. Drug interactions involving immunologic agents. Part II. Immunodiagnostic and other immunologic drug interactions. *DICP.* 1990; 24:186–93.

37. Grabenstein JD. Pneumococcal pneumonia: don't wait, vaccinate. *Hosp Pharm.* 1990; 25:866–9.

38. Grabenstein JD, Casto DT. Recommending vaccines to your patients' individual needs. *Am Pharm.* 1991; NS31:58–67.

39. Grabenstein JD. Immunization delivery: a complete guide. St. Louis: Facts and Comparisons; 1997.

40. Fedson DS, Houck P, Bratzler D. Hospital-based influenza and pneumococcal vaccination: Sutton's law applied to prevention. *Infect Control Hosp Epidemiol.* 2000; 21:692–9.

41. Immunization Action Coalition. Do I need any vaccinations today? www.immunize.org/catg.d/4036need.htm (accessed 2003 Mar 12).

42. Guide for adult immunization. 3rd ed. Philadelphia: American College of Physicians; 1994.

43. Slobodkin D, Zielske PG, Kitlas JL, et al. Demonstration of the feasibility of emergency department immunization against influenza and pneumococcus. *Ann Emerg Med.* 1998; 32:537–43.

44. Robke JT, Woods M, Heitz S. Pharmacist impact on pneumococcal vaccination rates through incorporation of immunization assessment into critical pathways in an acute care setting. *Hosp Pharm.* 2002; 37:1050–4.

45. Hepatitis B virus: a comprehensive strategy for eliminating transmission in the United States through uni-versal childhood vaccination. Recommendations of the Immunization Practices Advisory Committee (ACIP). *MMWR Recomm Rep.* 1991; 40(RR-13):1–25.

46. Canadian National Advisory Committee on Immunization. Canadian immunization guide. 5th ed. Ottawa, Ont.: Ministry of National Health and Welfare; 1998.

47. 29 C.F.R. §1910.1030.

48. Immunization Action Coalition. Screening questionnaire for adult immunization. www.immunize.org/catg.d/p4065scr.pdf (accessed 2003 Mar 12).

49. Grabenstein JD, Wilson JP. Are vaccines safe? Risk contamination applied to vaccination. *Hosp Pharm.* 1999; 34:713–4,717–8,721–3,727–9.

50. Kirk JK, Grabenstein JD. Interviewing and counseling patients about immunizations. *Hosp Pharm.* 1991; 26:1006–10.

51. Nichol KL, MacDonald R, Hauge M. Factors associated with influenza and pneumococcal vaccination behavior among high-risk adults. *J Gen Intern Med.* 1996; 11:673–7.

52. Gene J, Espinola A, Cabezas C, et al. Do knowledge and attitudes about influenza and its immunization affect the likelihood of obtaining immunization? *Fam Pract Res J.* 1992; 12:61–73.

53. Grabenstein JD, Hartzema AG, Guess HA, et al. Community pharmacists as immunization advocates: a clinical pharmacoepidemiologic experiment. *Int J Pharm Pract.* 1993; 2:5–10.

54. Grabenstein JD, Guess HA, Hartzema AG. People vaccinated by pharmacists: Descriptive epidemiology. *J Am Pharm Assoc.* 2001; 41:46–52.

55. Grabenstein JD, Guess HA, Hartzema AG, et al. Effect of vaccination by community pharmacists among adult prescription recipients. *Med Care.* 2001; 39:340–8.

56. Casto DT. Prevention, management, and control of influenza: roles for the pharmacist. *Am J Med.* 1987; 82(suppl 6A):64–7.

57. Health Services & Resources Administration. Vaccine injury table. *Fed Regist.* 1997; 62:7685–90.

58. Centers for Disease Control and Prevention. Vaccine Information Statements. www.cdc.gov/nip/publications/vis (accessed 2003 Mar 27).

59. Update on adult immunization. Recommendations of the Immunization Practices Advisory Committee (ACIP). *MMWR Recomm Rep.* 1991; 40(RR-12):1–94.

60. Grabenstein JD. Compensation for vaccine injury: balancing society's need and personal risk. *Hosp Pharm.* 1995; 30:831–2,834–6.

61. Grabenstein JD. Vaccination records must be available to be used. *J Am Pharm Assoc.* 2000; 40:113.

62. Kapit RM, Grabenstein JD. Adverse events after immunization: reports and results. *Hosp Pharm.* 1995; 30:1031–2,1035–6,1038,1041.

63. Immunization Action Coalition. Adult immunization record card. www.immunize.org/adultizcards/index.htm (accessed 2003 Mar 12).

64. American Society of Hospital Pharmacists. ASHP technical assistance bulletin on hospital drug distribution and control. *Am J Hosp Pharm.* 1980; 37:1097–103.

65. ASHP statement on the pharmacist's responsibility for distribution and control of drug products. In: Deffenbaugh JH, ed. Best practices for health-system pharmacy. Positions and guidance documents of ASHP.

2002–2003 ed. Bethesda, MD: American Society of Health-System Pharmacists; 2002:91.

66. Grabenstein JD. ImmunoFacts: vaccines and immunologic drugs. 28th ed. St Louis: Facts and Comparisons; 2002.

67. Centers for Disease Control and Prevention. Vaccine management: recommendations for handling and storage of selected biologicals. www.cdc.gov/nip/publications/vac_mgt_book.htm (accessed 2003 Mar 27).

68. Casto DT, Brunell PA. Safe handling of vaccines. *Pediatrics.* 1990; 87:108–12.

69. Ross MB. Additional stability guidelines for routinely refrigerated drug products. *Am J Hosp Pharm.* 1988; 45:1498–9. Letter.

70. Sterchele JA. Update on stability guidelines for routinely refrigerated drug products. *Am J Hosp Pharm.* 1987; 44:2698, 2701. Letter.

71. Miller LG, Loomis JH Jr. Advice of manufacturers about effects of temperature on biologicals. *Am J Hosp Pharm.* 1985; 42:843–8.

72. Vogenberg FR, Souney PF. Stability guidelines for routinely refrigerated drug products. *Am J Hosp Pharm.* 1983; 40:101–2.

73. Wolfert RR, Cox RM. Room temperature stability of drug products labeled for refrigerated storage. *Am J Hosp Pharm.* 1975; 32:585–7.

74. Update: recommendations to prevent hepatitis B virus transmission—United States. *MMWR Morb Mortal Wkly Rep.* 1995; 44:574–5.

75. Update: recommendations to prevent hepatitis B virus transmission—United States. *MMWR Morb Mortal Wkly Rep.* 1999; 48:33–4.

76. Prevention of hepatitis A through active or passive immunization: recommendations of the Advisory Committee on Immunization Practices (ACIP). *MMWR Recomm Rep.* 1999; 48(RR-12):1–37.

77. Human rabies prevention—United States, 1999. Recommendations of the Advisory Committee on Immunization Practices (ACIP). *MMWR Recomm Rep.* 1999; 48(RR-1):1–21.

78. Diphtheria, tetanus, and pertussis: recommendations for vaccine use and other preventive measures. Recommendations of the Immunization Practices Advisory Committee (ACIP). *MMWR Recomm Rep.* 1991; 40(RR-10):1–28.

79. Grabenstein JD. Stop buying tetanus toxoid (with one exception). *Hosp Pharm.* 1990; 25:361–2.

80. Pertussis vaccination: use of acellular pertussis vaccines among infants and young children. Recommendations of the Advisory Committee on Immunization Practices (ACIP). *MMWR Recomm Rep.* 1997; 46(RR-7):1–25.

81. American Academy of Pediatrics Committee on Infectious Diseases. The relationship between pertussis vaccine and brain damage: reassessment. *Pediatrics.* 1991; 88:397–400.

82. Immunization of health-care workers: recommendations of the Advisory Committee on Immunization Practices (ACIP) and the Hospital Infection Control Practices Advisory Committee (HICPAC). *MMWR Recomm Rep.* 1997; 46(RR-18):1–42.

83. Screening for tuberculosis and tuberculosis infection in high-risk populations: recommendations of the Advisory Council for the Elimination of Tuberculosis. *MMWR Recomm Rep.* 1995; 44(RR-11):19–34.

84. Anergy skin testing and tuberculosis [corrected] preventive therapy for HIV-infected persons: revised recommendations. *MMWR Recomm Rep.* 1997; 46(RR-15):1–10.

85. Health information for international travel, 2001–02. Washington, DC: Government Printing Office; 2001.

86. American College of Obstetricians and Gynecologists committee opinion. Immunization during pregnancy. *Obstet Gynecol.* 2003; 101:207–12.

Developed through the ASHP Council on Professional Affairs and approved by the ASHP Board of Directors on May 31, 2003.

The bibliographic citation for this document is as follows: American Society of Health-System Pharmacists. ASHP Guidelines on the Pharmacist's Role in Immunization. *Am J Health-Syst Pharm.* 2003; 60:1371–7.

Pharmaceutical Industry

Drug Products, Labeling, and Packaging

Ready-to-Use Packaging for All Settings (0402)

Source: Council on Professional Affairs

To advocate that pharmaceutical manufacturers provide all medications used in ambulatory care settings in unit-of-use packages; further,

To urge the Food and Drug Administration to support this goal; further,

To encourage pharmacists to adopt unit-of-use packaging for dispensing prescription medications to ambulatory patients; further,

To support continued research on the safety benefits and patient adherence associated with unit-of-use packaging and other dispensing technologies.

(*Note:* A *unit-of-use* package is a container—closure system designed to hold a specific quantity of a drug product for a specific use and intended to be dispensed to a patient without any modification except for the addition of appropriate labeling.)

Standardization, Automation, and Expansion of Manufacturer-Sponsored Patient-Assistance Programs (0404)

Source: Council on Administrative Affairs

To advocate standardization of application criteria, processes, and forms for manufacturer-sponsored patient assistance programs (PAP); further,

To advocate the automation of PAP application processes through computerized programs, including Web-based models; further,

To advocate expansion of PAPs to include high-cost drugs used in inpatient settings.

Unit Dose Packaging Availability (0309)

Source: Council on Administrative Affairs

To advocate that pharmaceutical manufacturers provide all medications used in health systems in unit dose packages; further,

To urge the Food and Drug Administration to support this goal in the interest of public health and patient safety.

Drug Shortages (0002)

Source: Council on Administrative Affairs

To declare that pharmaceutical manufacturers, distributors, group purchasing organizations, and regulatory bodies, when making decisions that may create drug product shortages, should strive to prevent those decisions from compromising the quality and safety of patient care.

Pediatric Dosage Forms (9707)

Source: Council on Professional Affairs

To support efforts that stimulate development of pediatric dosage forms of drug products.

This policy was reviewed in 2001 by the Council on Professional Affairs and by the Board of Directors and was found to still be appropriate.

Use of Color to Identify Drug Products (9608)

Source: Council on Professional Affairs

To support the reading of drug product labels as the most important means of identifying drug products; further,

To oppose reliance on color by health professionals and others to identify drug products; and further,

To oppose actions by manufacturers of drug products and others to promulgate reliance on color to identify drug products.

This policy was reviewed in 2003 by the Council on Professional Affairs and by the Board of Directors and was found to still be appropriate.

Expiration Dating of Pharmaceutical Products (9309)

Source: House of Delegates Resolution

To support and actively promote the maximal extension of expiration dates of pharmaceutical products as a means of reducing health care costs and to recommend that pharmaceutical manufacturers review their procedures to accomplish this end.

This policy was reviewed in 2001 by the Council on Professional Affairs and by the Board of Directors and was found to still be appropriate.

Needle-Free Drug Preparation and Administration Systems (9202)

Source: Council on Administrative Affairs

To encourage manufacturers' efforts to create cost-effective drug preparation and drug administration systems that do not require needles.

This policy was reviewed in 2001 by the House of Delegates and by the Board of Directors and was found to still be appropriate.

Tamper-Evident Packaging on Topical Products (9211)

Source: House of Delegates Resolution

ASHP should support the standardization and requirement of tamper-evident packaging on all topical products, including all dermatologicals and nonprescription products.

This policy was reviewed in 2001 by the Council on Professional Affairs and by the Board of Directors and was found to still be appropriate.

Drug Names, Labeling, and Packaging (9007)

Source: Council on Professional Affairs

To urge drug manufacturers and FDA to involve practicing pharmacists, nurses, and physicians in decisions about drug names, labeling, and packaging; further,

To inform pharmacists, and others as appropriate, about specific drug names, labeling, and packaging that have documented association with medication errors.

Drug Nomenclature (9011)

Source: House of Delegates Resolution

To work with the FDA, USP, and pharmaceutical industry to assure that drug products are named in a manner that clearly and without confusion permits identification of ingredients' strengths and changes.

This policy was reviewed in 2003 by the Council on Legal and Public Affairs and by the Board of Directors and was found to still be appropriate.

Codes on Solid Dosage Forms of Prescription Drug Products (8709)

Source: Council on Legal and Public Affairs

To support efforts requiring manufacturers of solid dosage form prescription drug products to imprint a readily identifiable code indicating the manufacturer of the drug product and the product's ingredients; further,

To make information on transition of the codes readily available.

This policy was reviewed in 2001 by the Council on Legal and Public Affairs and by the Board of Directors and was found to still be appropriate.

International System of Units (8612)

Source: Council on Professional Affairs

To not advocate, at this time, adoption of the International System of Units (SI units) as the exclusive labeling for drug dosages and concentrations; further,

To urge labelers to include: (1) units of mass, volume, or percentage concentrations and (2) moles or millimoles in labeling until the health professions and the public can be educated and be comfortable with use of SI units in prescribing and labeling drug products.

This policy was reviewed in 2001 by the Council on Professional Affairs and by the Board of Directors and was found to still be appropriate.

Elimination of Apothecary System (8613)

Source: Council on Professional Affairs

To recommend to all health professions and to the Pharmaceutical Manufacturers Association (PMA) [now the Pharmaceutical Research and Manufacturers of America (PhRMA)] that the apothecary system be eliminated in referring to dosage quantities and strengths.

This policy was reviewed in 2001 by the Council on Professional Affairs and by the Board of Directors and was found to still be appropriate.

Size, Color, and Shape of Drug Products (8310)

Source: Council on Legal and Public Affairs

To approve the authority of manufacturers to copy the size, shape, and color of generically equivalent drug products as a means of promoting better patient compliance (rational drug therapy), but only when the source and identity of the product are readily ascertainable from a uniform mark or symbol on the product.

This policy was reviewed in 2001 by the Council on Legal and Public Affairs and by the Board of Directors and was found to still be appropriate.

Marketing

Restricted Distribution Systems (0114)

Source: Council on Legal and Public Affairs

To reiterate support for the current system of drug distribution in which prescribers and pharmacists exercise their professional responsibilities on behalf of patients; further,

To acknowledge that there may be limited circumstances in which constraints on the traditional drug distribution mechanism may be appropriate if the following principles are met: (1) the requirements do not interfere with the continuity of care for the patient; (2) the requirements preserve the pharmacist–patient relationship; (3) the requirements are based on scientific evidence fully disclosed and evaluated by physicians, pharmacists, and others; (4) there is scientific consensus that the requirements are necessary and represent the least restrictive means to achieve safe and effective patient care; (5) the cost of the product and any associated product or services are identified for purposes of reimbursement, mechanisms are provided to compensate providers for special services, and duplicative costs are avoided; (6) all requirements are stated in functional, objective terms so that any provider who meets the criteria may participate in the care of patients; and (7) the requirements do not interfere with the professional practice of pharmacists, physicians, and others; further,

To strongly encourage pharmaceutical manufacturers and the Food and Drug Administration to consult with practicing pharmacists when they contemplate the establishment of a restricted distribution system for a drug product.

This policy supersedes ASHP policy 9104.

Direct-to-Consumer Advertising of Pharmaceuticals (9701)

Source: Council on Legal and Public Affairs and the Board of Directors

To support direct-to-consumer advertising that is educational in nature about prescription drug therapies for certain medical conditions and appropriately includes pharmacists as a source of information; further,

To oppose direct-to-consumer advertising of specific prescription drug products; further,

To support the development of legislation or regulation that would require nonprescription drug advertising to state prominently the benefits and risks associated with product use that should be discussed with the consumer's pharmacist or physician.

This policy was reviewed in 2001 by the Council on Legal and Public Affairs and by the Board of Directors and was found to still be appropriate.

Drug Samples (9702)

Source: Council on Legal and Public Affairs

To oppose drug sampling or similar drug marketing programs that (1) do not provide the elements of pharmaceutical care, (2) result in poor drug control, allowing patients to receive improperly labeled and packaged, deteriorated, outdated, and unrecorded drugs, (3) provide access to prescription drugs by unauthorized, untrained personnel, (4) may encourage inappropriate prescribing habits, or (5) may increase the cost of treatment for all patients.

This policy was reviewed in 2001 by the Council on Legal and Public Affairs and by the Board of Directors and was found to still be appropriate.

Manufacturer-Sponsored Patient-Assistance Programs (9703)

Source: Council on Legal and Public Affairs

To encourage pharmaceutical manufacturers to (1) extend their patient assistance programs to serve the needs of both uninsured and underinsured patients, (2) enhance access to and availability of such programs, and (3) incorporate the elements of pharmaceutical care into these programs.

This policy was reviewed in 2001 by the Council on Legal and Public Affairs and by the Board of Directors and was found to still be appropriate.

ASHP Guidelines for Pharmacists on the Activities of Vendors' Representatives in Organized Health Care Systems

For purposes of this document, vendors' representatives are defined as agents who promote products and provide information and services to health care providers on behalf of manufacturers and suppliers. The narrow focus of this document is on those vendors who serve and interact with settings with respect to drug products, drug-related devices, and other equipment, supplies, and services purchased by pharmacies.

Each individual setting should develop its own specific policies and procedures relating to the activities of vendors' representatives. Such policies and procedures should supplement and complement applicable federal, state, and local laws and regulations (for example, statutes that address prescription drug-product sampling). The ASHP Guidelines on Pharmacists' Relationships with Industry, the ASHP Guidelines for Selecting Pharmaceutical Manufacturers and Suppliers, and setting-specific conflict-of-interest policies may be helpful in the development of policies and procedures.[1,2] The policies and procedures should be developed by the setting's pharmacy and therapeutics committee (or equivalent body) and approved by higher authorities in the setting as required. Depending on the individual setting, policies and procedures may be useful in the following areas.

1. *A defined scope of applicability.* The vendors' representatives to which any policies and procedures apply should be defined by the individual setting. For example, if the policies and procedures are applicable only to drug-product vendors' representatives and not to those promoting medical–surgical supplies, packaging equipment, or drug administration devices, this should be clearly stated.

2. *Orientation of representatives.* In some individual settings, vendors' representatives receive an orientation packet upon their initial visit to the setting. Such a packet might contain a copy of the setting's policies and procedures, a medical staff directory, and the formulary. Some settings provide a formal orientation program that includes meeting key individuals and touring the setting.

3. *Directory.* In some individual settings, a file of current vendor-contact information is maintained in the pharmacy. A form for recording such information might include the following:
   - The vendor's name and address;
   - The name, address, telephone number, and answering service number (if any), and drug-product assignment (purview) of each representative;
   - The name, address, and telephone number of the representative's manager;
   - The names, telephone numbers, and emergency telephone numbers of the vendor's directors of distribution, sales, and product information (titles may vary); and
   - The names and telephone numbers of the vendor's medical director and research director (titles may vary).

4. *Availability of vendor-contact information to professionals in the setting.* In some individual settings, the pharmacy department provides the setting's professional staff with the information in item 3, upon request.

5. *Registration while on premises.* In some individual settings, vendors' representatives register with the pharmacy department or other designated department upon each visit to the setting. At such time, the vendors' representatives document the time, purpose, and location of their appointments. In many settings, during the registration process, the representative is provided with a dated name badge to be prominently worn along with the representative's current vendor-supplied name tag (if any).

6. *Locations permitted.* In some individual settings, restriction (if any) from patient care and pharmacy storage and work areas in the setting are specified in the policies and procedures. Meetings with professional staff are conducted in areas convenient to staff and generally in non-patient-care areas.

7. *Appointments and purposes.* In some individual settings, representatives are encouraged to schedule appointments with appropriate pharmacy department staff to
   - Provide information useful for product evaluation. Representatives might be asked to include balanced scientific literature (journal reprints, for example) on drug-product safety and efficacy, as well as documentation of likely cost benefits.
   - Provide timely information on the vendor's products and services.
   - Facilitate procurement and crediting transactions.
   - Obtain and provide information necessary to support the setting's formulary system.
   - Facilitate informational activities for the pharmacy staff and other health care professionals with respect to the vendor's products.

8. *Exhibits.* In some individual settings, the pharmacy department provides opportunities for vendors' representatives to distribute informational material by arranging for organized, scheduled exhibits. Policies and procedures about the times, places, content, and conduct of such events are established.

9. *Dissemination of promotional materials.* In some individual settings, there are policies and procedures about the dissemination (by vendors' representatives) of information on formulary and nonformulary products, including the designation of appropriate categories of recipients of the information (e.g., attending physicians, department chairmen, house staff physicians). Representatives may be asked to promptly provide the pharmacy department with copies of all informational and promotional materials disseminated in the setting. The Food and Drug Administration (FDA) prohibits the

advertising and promotion of drug products for uses not reflected in FDA-approved product labeling ("unlabeled uses").[3] Pharmacists and other health care professionals should be aware of these laws and regulations when evaluating the content of promotional materials.

10. *Samples.* In some individual settings, there are policies and procedures with respect to product samples. ASHP urges that the use of drug samples within the institution be eliminated to the extent possible.[4,5]

11. *Noncompliance.* In some individual settings, policies and procedures exist to address noncompliance with the policies and procedures by either vendors' representatives or professional staff.

Each setting should have policies and procedures concerning research to be conducted on its premises. Pharmacists and vendors' representatives should clearly differentiate research from sales and promotional activities, applying appropriate policies and procedures accordingly.[6] Generally, scientific research involving drug products is coordinated through research departments of product manufacturers rather than through sales and promotional representatives.

References

1. American Society of Hospital Pharmacists. ASHP guidelines on pharmacists' relationships with industry. *Am J Hosp Pharm.* 1992; 49:154.
2. American Society of Hospital Pharmacists. ASHP guidelines for selecting pharmaceutical manufacturers and suppliers. *Am J Hosp Pharm.* 1991; 48:523–4.
3. American Society of Hospital Pharmacists. ASHP statement on the use of medications for unlabeled uses. *Am J Hosp Pharm.* 1992; 49:927–8.
4. American Society of Hospital Pharmacists. ASHP guidelines: minimum standard for pharmacies in institutions. *Am J Hosp Pharm.* 1985; 42:372–5.
5. Greenberg RB. The Prescription Drug Marketing Act of 1987. *Am J Hosp Pharm.* 1988; 45:2118–26.
6. American Society of Hospital Pharmacists. ASHP guidelines for pharmaceutical research in organized healthcare settings. *Am J Hosp Pharm.* 1989; 46:129–30.

This guideline was reviewed in 1998 by the Council on Professional Affairs and by the ASHP Board of Directors and was found to still be appropriate.

Approved by the ASHP Board of Directors, November 17, 1993. Developed by the Council on Professional Affairs.

The bibliographic citation for this document is as follows: American Society of Hospital Pharmacists. ASHP guidelines for pharmacists on the activities of vendors' representatives in organized health care systems. *Am J Hosp Pharm.* 1994; 51:520–1.

Pharmacy Management

Pharmacy Management

Workload Monitoring and Reporting (0406)
Source: Council on Administrative Affairs
To advocate the development and implementation of a pharmacy workload monitoring system that analyzes the impact of pharmacy services on patient outcomes; further,

To define pharmacy workload as all activities related to providing pharmacy patient care services; further,

To continue communications with health-system administrators, consulting firms, and professional associations on the value of pharmacists' services and on the use of valid and reliable data to assess pharmacy workload and staffing effectiveness; further,

To encourage practitioners and vendors to develop and use a standard protocol for collecting and reporting pharmacy workload data and patient outcomes; further,

To advocate to health-system administrators, consulting firms, and vendors of performance-measurement services firms the use of comprehensive pharmacy workload and staffing effectiveness measurements.

This policy supersedes ASHP policy 9907.

ASHP Guidelines on Outsourcing Pharmaceutical Services

Purpose

Health-system pharmacy, as an essential component in health care organizations, is challenged by changes in the structure and financing of health care to reduce costs and improve performance. One option being used to achieve these goals is outsourcing. Outsourcing is a formal arrangement by which a health care organization contracts with an outside company to obtain selected pharmaceutical services or comprehensive management of the organization's pharmacy. Through this arrangement, the organization negotiates a contract with a company to access its expertise, technologies, and resources.

ASHP believes that the organization's pharmacist-in-charge (e.g., a pharmacy director) must take complete responsibility for patient outcomes from all medication-related activities performed at or for the organization's work sites, whether they are carried out by the organization's or contractor's onsite staff or by the contractor off site. This responsibility should be explicitly stated in all outsourcing contracts.

Health care organizations considering outsourcing pharmaceutical services should have a clear understanding of what they want to accomplish. Consideration should include, at the least, an internal needs assessment, a cost analysis, and a careful review of possible contractors. The organization should examine the potential long-term consequences of outsourcing as well as the short-term outcomes expected during a contract's performance period.

The purpose of these guidelines is to provide an overview of factors and processes for health care organizations to consider when exploring outsourcing. The ideas presented in this document could be used for strategic planning with the organization's decision-makers, for drafting contract provisions, for comparing prospective contractors, for preparing for contract negotiations, or for evaluating a contractor's performance. These guidelines may be applied, for example, to independent and networked acute care hospitals, ambulatory care clinics, and home care providers.

This document includes ideas about reasons for outsourcing and reasons for not outsourcing, services available from contractors, the outsourcing process and outsourcing arrangements, and evaluation of contractor performance. The appendix provides a topical list of contract provisions, some of which relate to specific pharmaceutical services, pharmacy practices, or administrative functions that may be the subject of other ASHP practice standards. Organizations should refer to pertinent ASHP practice standards for additional information on which to base their contract provisions, agreements, and decisions. This document addresses representative outsourcing options and contract agreements and is not intended to cover all situations. Managers of pharmacy and health care organizations should use their professional judgment about applicability to their own needs and circumstances.

Environment

Various environmental influences and market forces that may contribute to outsourcing being considered as an option include the following.

Organizational and Operational

- Re-engineering and downsizing initiatives
- Consolidation and integration of health systems and departments within health systems
- Elimination of or reduction in the size of traditional departments
- Reorganization around patient-focused care
- Implementation of automated pharmacy systems and the attendant need to reorganize medication distribution functions

Staffing

- Shortage of nurses and other health care professionals
- Shortage of pharmacists with specific experience and capabilities

Financial and Cost-Control

- Restricted budgets
- Increased operating costs
- Increased drug costs
- Increased emphasis on measuring performance in terms of staffing and costs instead of clinical outcomes

Quality

- Increased expectations of and pressures from accreditation organizations and consumer groups to improve the quality of patient care

Governmental and Regulatory

- Increased numbers of individuals dependent on federal, state, and local governments for health care
- Reduced ability of federal, state, and local governments to finance health care
- Increased government controls on reimbursement for health care

Competitive

- Increased competition among health care organizations
- Increased competition among suppliers of pharmaceutical products and related services

Purposes of Outsourcing

Health care organizations that conduct in-depth assessments may decide that outsourcing either is or is not a good option for meeting their needs. Reasons for their decision will vary according to a variety of factors.

Reasons Health Care Organizations Outsource Pharmaceutical Services. Organizations tend to outsource pharmaceutical services when guided by a careful assessment of their capabilities of providing services themselves, when unsuccessful in using their own resources to provide services, or, in some cases, when influenced by a consultant. Contracting with an outsourcing firm may produce one or more of the following results.

Organizational and operational
- Ease the consolidation of pharmaceutical services in integrated health systems
- Resolve operational inefficiencies (e.g., by improving medication distribution systems, designing new pharmacy workspaces, reducing medication dispensing and administration errors, and improving computer and information systems)
  - Enable the organization to acquire additional resources and expertise to carry out other changes (e.g., reallocation of existing staff to pharmaceutical care roles in patient care areas)
  - Provide educational programs for patients and their families and for health care staff

Staffing
- Help the organization to staff hard-to-fill pharmacy positions
- Allow the organization to reach optimal staffing levels for achieving productivity targets

Financial and cost-control
- Control or reduce the cost of the organization's services
- Control or reduce labor costs (e.g., by shifting the cost of employees, benefits, and liabilities to a contractor)
- Enable the organization to acquire a contractor who will share the risks associated with operating the pharmaceutical services
- Avoid the cost of purchasing and maintaining pharmacy equipment
- Avoid the cost of physical remodeling (e.g., by using an offsite contractor to provide specific services for which remodeling would be required)
- Increase the organization's financial operating margin (e.g., by allowing the organization to purchase drugs in bulk quantities, use group purchasing contracts, decrease lost charges, improve billing accuracy, decrease drug diversion and pilferage, improve drug formularies, and transfer drug inventory, equipment, and supply activities to a contractor)

Quality
- Enable the organization to maintain or improve the quality of patient care (e.g., by expanding clinical services and pharmaceutical care, establishing new services, and obtaining specialized expertise in pharmaceutical care)
- Provide support for the medical and nursing staffs and improve physician–nursing–pharmacy collaboration

Governmental and regulatory
- Correct regulatory and accreditation problems relating to pharmaceutical services
- Ensure continuing compliance with accreditation and certification standards

Competitive
- Enhance the organization's image
- Allow the organization to gain an edge on competitors

through improvements in service, quality, or price

Reasons Health Care Organizations Do Not Outsource Pharmaceutical Services. An organization's choice to continue providing its own pharmaceutical services may be based on one or more of the following reasons.

Organizational and operational
- A belief that pharmaceutical services are well managed and are provided as effectively as or better than they could be by a contractor
- Negative experiences with outsourcing contractors (pharmacy or nonpharmacy) or awareness of other organizations' negative experiences with such contractors
- Concern that the decision to outsource pharmaceutical services can be reversed only with great difficulty
- A belief that the organization's needs are currently met cost-effectively and that changes are therefore unnecessary
- Concern about losing short-term and long-term control over decisions about pharmaceutical services
- Concern about reduced involvement of pharmacy leadership in organizationwide initiatives (e.g., development and implementation of information systems, clinical care plans or pathways, and disease management)

Staffing
- Concern that staff will be reduced to unacceptable levels
- Concern about potentially alienating relationships between pharmacists and other health care staff

Financial and cost-control
- An assessment that outsourcing would increase rather than decrease costs
- Concern that high-cost drugs might be excluded from contract agreements
- Concern that the organization may not be able to recapitalize pharmaceutical services if outsourcing is unsuccessful

Quality
- Concern that conflicting values and priorities of the outsourcing contractor and the organization will reduce quality
- Concern that clinical quality could be reduced as a result of a loss of continuity of pharmacy staffing and relationships with medical and nursing staffs

Professional responsibility
- Concern that outsourcing will confuse or dilute the onsite pharmacists' ultimate professional authority and responsibility for all medication-related activities and outcomes at the site

Pharmaceutical Services Provided by Contractors

Some contractors manage and provide comprehensive pharmaceutical services. Other contractors focus more on providing specialty services or carrying out specific tasks (e.g., drug information services, offsite preparation of sterile products). The needs of the health care organization should guide the identification of potential contractors with the appropriate expertise and capabilities. Examples of services that may be available from contractors follow. (This list is likely to grow over time.)

Organizational and Operational

- Development of pharmacy policies, procedures, and processes
- Pharmacy record-keeping systems
- Productivity reviews
- Feasibility studies on expanding services (e.g., outpatient dispensing and home infusion)
- Unit dose medication distribution
- Pharmacy-based or offsite preparation of sterile products
- Pharmacokinetic monitoring and dosage determinations
- Medication therapy monitoring (e.g., for appropriate and effective use)
- Investigational drug programs
- Patient profile reviews
- Medication therapy-related consultation with physicians, nurses, and other health care professionals
- Assessment of patients' nutritional needs
- Guidance in purchasing and implementing automated pharmacy equipment
- Educational programs for patients, families, and caregivers
- Drug information services
- Packaging and repackaging of pharmaceuticals

Staffing

- Competency assessment and performance review
- Management, operational, and clinical training
- Recruitment and retention assistance

Financial and Cost-Control

- Billing
- Inventory control
- Formulary management

Quality

- Performance improvement (including improvement of medication use and reduction of medication errors)
- Quality assurance

Outsourcing Process

After the health care organization has completed an internal assessment of its needs and capabilities and decided to explore outsourcing, it should identify and contact reputable and experienced contractors. Some organizations simply identify prospective contractors and ask them to submit a proposal. A more thorough approach is to require prospective contractors to respond to a request for proposals (RFP). Although a formal RFP (and the contractor's formal proposal based on the RFP) may not be necessary, the information found in typical RFPs and proposals may be helpful for making a decision about outsourcing.

Contents of RFPs. RFPs often include the following information.

- A description of the organization (including statistical information)
- The organization's financial status (e.g., a current balance sheet and audited financial statement, the pharmacy's financial status)
- A description of the process the organization will use to select the contractor
- The organization's standard terms and conditions for contracting for services
- The names and telephone numbers of individuals in the organization who are involved in the outsourcing decision (the director of pharmacy should be included)
- A description of the specific outsourced services required of the contractor (e.g., pharmacy workspace design, intravenous admixture preparation, and implementation of an automated pharmacy system) and performance-measurement criteria or targets
- The date(s) on which the contractor can inspect the facility and the pharmacy
- The number of copies of the proposal to submit
- The name and address of the individual to whom the proposal is to be delivered
- Acceptable method(s) for delivery of the proposal (e.g., mail, delivery service, courier)
- A statement that the organization reserves the right to cancel its solicitation for services and reject any and all proposals
- A deadline date and time for receipt of the proposal
- The date on which the contractor would be expected to initiate services
- The date by which the selected contractor must provide a written contract
- Other requirements related to the proposal (e.g., that it be typewritten, that it include reference to an RFP number [if any], that it be signed by an officer of the firm who is authorized to contract)

Contents of Proposals. RFPs often require contractors to submit the following information with their proposals.

- A brief history of the contractor, including its mission, vision, and values
- The location of the contractor's offices and other facilities that would provide services to the organization
- The names, addresses, telephone numbers, and résumés or background information on the individual(s) who will provide the services
- Evidence that the contractor can provide qualified staff who are licensed or eligible for licensure by federal, state, and local agencies and a history of turnover in management, pharmacist, and support staff
- A history of the results of Joint Commission on Accreditation of Healthcare Organizations (JCAHO), Health Care Financing Administration, National Committee for Quality Assurance, state, or other accreditation or regulatory surveys conducted in the contractor's sites
- Proof of professional liability, general liability, and workers'-compensation insurance coverage (including the name, address, and telephone number of the insurance company) and a history of claims filed against the contractor
- Minimum-experience requirements (e.g., years of experience in providing outsourced pharmacy-management services, total number of clients served, current number of clients)

- A list of the requested services that the contractor can provide
- A list of the requested services that the contractor cannot provide and the reasons for the contractor's inability to provide them
- Evidence of organizational and staff experience and competence (including nature and extent) in the services the contractor can provide (e.g., pharmaceutical care, specialty clinical practice, antineoplastic medication preparation, enteral and parenteral nutrition solution preparation), as pertinent
- A copy of a standard or proposed contract
- A list of all fees and charges that would be billed under the contract and the detailed methods for their calculation, as well as a billing schedule
- A description of reports that the contractor will be expected to submit to the organization
- Information relating to the contractor's financial status and stability (e.g., balance sheets and audited financial statements for the past three years, bank references, lists of principal equity owners)
- The names, addresses, and telephone numbers of current clients receiving similar services
- The names, addresses, and telephone numbers of other clients served within the past two years and the reasons for all, if any, terminations of services
- Written references and copies of annual performance-improvement reports from clients of a similar size with similar types of patients

Visits to Contractors and Their Clients. Contractors should allow the organization's representatives to visit their corporate offices and production facilities and to tour pharmacies in the facilities of other clients. The contractor should provide ample opportunity for the organization's representatives to confer with the contractor's corporate and pharmacy staff.

Evaluating Proposals. A decision to outsource pharmaceutical services should be collaborative and should involve, as appropriate, the governing board, the chief executive officer (CEO), the chief financial officer (CFO), the chief operating officer (COO), the chief of the medical staff, the chair of the pharmacy and therapeutics committee, the director of nursing (DON), the director of pharmacy, and department heads, for example. The organization should scrutinize the following factors when evaluating proposals.

- Services offered versus services requested (including the contractor's ability to enhance current services)
- Professional experience (e.g., years of service; number, size, and types of clients; knowledge of the client's business)
- Financial stability (e.g., ability to absorb start-up expenses and to commit the resources needed to effect change)
- References and reputation (e.g., client-satisfaction reports, reputation in the health care industry, commitment to improving patient care)
- Technology or automated pharmacy systems (e.g., up-to-date hardware, proprietary software, the capability to interface with the organization's information systems)
- Education and training (e.g., internal and external continuing-education programs, educational allowances for professional and technical staff)

- Additional qualities (e.g., high employee morale, confidentiality, creativity, sensitivity to minorities and the community, willingness to share risks and rewards)
- Cost aspects of services (e.g., cost-effectiveness, ability to affect economies of scale)

The organization should assign an evaluation rating to each proposal. Ratings should be weighted appropriately with respect to professional services, experience, references, and cost of services. The organization should base its decision to outsource pharmaceutical services on its assessment of the contractor's ability to meet the organization's needs and fulfill the terms of the contract.

Negotiating the Contract. The organization should carefully review the proposal and clarify the provisions of the contract. Assistance from the organization's risk-management and legal counsel may be necessary. Negotiations can ensure a contract that best meets the needs of the organization and the contractor.

Signing the Contract. In some organizations the director of pharmacy may be authorized to sign contracts for outsourced services. If this is not the case, the director of pharmacy should be fully involved in negotiating the contract and advising the authorized signer(s).

Outsourcing Arrangement

The health care organization and the contractor should agree on the outsourcing arrangement that best meets their needs. Several outsourcing options are available to health care organizations. Variations and combinations of these options are common. The contract should clearly describe the outsourcing arrangement. Examples of outsourcing arrangements include the following.

Consulting. The contractor acts as a pharmacy consultant to the organization. Some consulting arrangements are limited to an assessment of all pharmaceutical services or to specific aspects of pharmaceutical services (e.g., clinical pharmacy services, productivity, compliance with JCAHO standards). Other consulting arrangements may include advising the pharmacy and helping it to improve its services.

Onsite Advisor. The contractor provides a full-time onsite advisor to the organization's director of pharmacy. The advisor works with the director of pharmacy and others, as needed, to carry out programs that will fulfill the contract provisions.

Management of Specific Pharmaceutical Services. The contractor provides one or more specific services (e.g., i.v. admixture preparation, drug information, stock replenishment, medication distribution). Services may be provided onsite or at an offsite location.

Comprehensive Management. The contractor assumes complete responsibility for operating the pharmacy and may provide some or all of the pharmacy staff.

Contract Provisions

A contract that meets the needs of the health care organization and of the contractor is the foundation for a successful relationship. Contracts should include provisions of the outsourcing arrangement that describe agreements between the organization and the contractor concerning their respective responsibilities. These provisions will vary depending on the kind and scope of services outsourced. For example, contractors who prepare sterile products at an offsite location will not require onsite pharmacy space and utilities. Also, the assignment of responsibilities may vary. A contract may specify that the organization will purchase all drugs. Conversely, another contract may assign this responsibility to the contractor. See the appendix for examples of contract provisions.

Evaluation of Contractor's Performance

Health care organizations should evaluate and document their contractor's performance and assess their contractor's compliance with the terms of the contract. Objective and subjective evaluations should be regular (e.g., quarterly or annually). Evaluations should address all measurable standards of performance that are specified in the contract. Evaluations should be multidisciplinary and should involve, for example, the CEO, CFO, COO, DON, and medical staff representatives, as appropriate. An evaluation may include an assessment of how well the contractor performed the following functions.

- Improved the quality of patient care
- Responded to the organization's needs
- Helped the organization to achieve its financial and patient-outcome goals
- Evaluated the productivity and performance of pharmacy staff
- Provided continuing education for pharmacy staff
- Implemented and improved pharmacy clinical programs
- Improved pharmacy processes (e.g., medication dispensing and delivery)
- Reduced and controlled pharmacy costs without compromising patient care
- Worked and communicated effectively with the organization's staff and resolved interdepartmental problems
- Participated effectively in the organization's performance-improvement program

Suggested Reading

1. Curtis FR, Stai HC. Contract pharmacy services. In: Brown TR, ed. Handbook of institutional pharmacy practice, 3rd ed. Bethesda, MD: American Society of Hospital Pharmacists; 1992:299–306.
2. Talley CR. Outsourcing drug distribution. *Am J Health-Syst Pharm.* 1997; 54:37. Editorial.
3. Schneider PJ. Outsourcing: a key to professional survival. *Am J Health-Syst Pharm.* 1997; 54:41–3.
4. Lazarus HL. Outsourcing: a success story. *Am J Health-Syst Pharm.* 1997; 54:43–4.
5. Puckett WH. Outsourcing: taking the first step. *Am J Health-Syst Pharm.* 1997; 54:45–8.
6. Kolar GR. Outsourcing: route to a new pharmacy practice model. *Am J Health-Syst Pharm.* 1997; 54:48–52.
7. Eckel FM. Outsourcing: at odds with pharmacy's professional foundation. *Am J Health-Syst Pharm.* 1997; 54:52–5.
8. Gates DM, Smolarek RT, Stevenson JG. Outsourcing the preparation of parenteral nutrient solutions. *Am J Health-Syst Pharm.* 1996; 53:2176–8.
9. Burruss RA, Carroll NV, Schraa C, et al. Outsourcing inpatient IV compounding: expense and medication error implications. *Pharm Pract Manage Q.* 1996; 16(3):52–9.
10. McAllister JC III. Collaborating with re-engineering consultants: maintaining resources for the future. *Am J Health-Syst Pharm.* 1995; 52:2676–80.
11. Anderson RJ. Clinical service contracts between hospital pharmacy departments and colleges of pharmacy. *Am J Hosp Pharm.* 1991; 48:1994–7.
12. Murphy JE, Ward ES, Job ML. Implementing and maintaining a private pharmacokinetics practice. *Am J Hosp Pharm.* 1990; 47:591–7.
13. Souhrada L. Contract management. *Hospitals.* 1990; 64(8):66–8.
14. Wagner M. Basic pitfalls can undermine hospital–service firm relationship. *Mod Healthc.* 1993; 23(8):32.
15. Wagner M. Contract-managed pharmacy departments are just the prescription at some hospitals. *Mod Healthc.* 1988; 18(8):36–40.

Appendix—Contract Provisions

The following are examples of contract provisions that, among others, the organization and contractor might adapt as needed and include in a contract, depending on the scope of services being considered. In addition, a contract would include provisions about the specific pharmaceutical services to be provided by the contractor. The language in contract provisions should be adapted to meet the needs of the health care organization and to comply with the organization's contracting policies and applicable laws and regulations.

Accreditation and Certification: A contract may include a requirement that services meet or exceed applicable accreditation and certification standards. These include, but are not limited to, the standards (or requirements) of the following organizations.

- Joint Commission on Accreditation of Healthcare Organizations
- American Osteopathic Association
- Health Care Financing Administration
- National Committee for Quality Assurance

After-Hours Pharmaceutical Services when 24-Hour Services Are Not Provided: The contractor may agree, for example, to provide an after-hours stock of drug products for authorized staff to use in filling urgent medication orders. In addition, the contractor may agree to ensure that a pharmacist is on call or available to return to the facility to provide pharmaceutical services.

Automation: A contract may outline responsibilities for the purchase or lease and the use of automated medication storage and distribution equipment and software associated with the equipment.

Choice of Law: There may be a statement that the contract is governed by the laws of the state in which patient care is provided.

Compensation for Contractor's Services: There may be compensation arrangements, which vary greatly but are often based on one or more of the following principles.

- Management fee(s)
- Fee per item dispensed or service performed
- Fixed fee per patient per patient day, admission, discharge, adjusted patient day, adjusted admission, or adjusted discharge

Besides agreeing on a compensation arrangement, the organization and the contractor may agree on ways for the contractor to share the financial risk of contract performance with the organization; these might include guarantees or incentives for meeting targets and penalties for underperformance.

Computer Equipment and Information Systems: A contract may outline responsibilities for the purchase, ownership, and maintenance of computer equipment and related software. Agreements might extend to personal computers used by pharmacy staff. There should be clear agreement about access to and use of data generated by the information system.

Confidentiality: There may be a requirement that information not generally available to the public (e.g., financial statements, medical records, market information) be kept confidential. Both parties must agree to safeguard access to computer databases and patient records to ensure that the patient's rights to privacy and confidentiality is protected. Use of the information should be limited solely to purposes specified in the contract.

Contractor Reports: The content and regularity of performance reports that the contractor will submit to the organization may be specified.

Controlled Substances: Responsibilities may be assigned for the procurement and security of controlled substances in compliance with Drug Enforcement Administration (DEA) and state regulations. For example, the organization may be required to

- Register with the DEA and any state equivalent for each site involved
- Assume complete responsibility for record keeping and security of controlled substances throughout the facility
- Ask the contractor to maintain proper records and provide adequate security for controlled substances as required by federal, state, and local laws and regulations and
- Verify that the contractor maintains proper records and provides adequate security for controlled substances

It may be necessary for the organization to grant power of attorney to the contractor to order and purchase controlled substances.

Similarly, the contractor may be required to

- Ensure that all registrations are current
- Order and maintain an adequate stock of controlled substances
- Ensure compliance with record-keeping and security requirements
- Inform the organization of problems with compliance

Cost Control: A contract may include objectives, methods, and performance measures for controlling costs.

Cytotoxic and Hazardous Drug Products: Responsibilities for ensuring the safety of the organization's staff and patients during the preparation and distribution of cytotoxic and hazardous drug products may be assigned. Either the organization or the contractor should provide a hazardous-materials handling program, in-cluding staff training, that meets Occupational Safety and Health Administration (OSHA) requirements.

Drug Inventory Disposition upon Termination of the Contract: A provision for the disposition of the drug inventory is based on inventory ownership. In cases in which the drug inventory may be purchased by either party, a mutually acceptable, independent appraiser could decide the purchase price. Legal advice may be needed to ensure that purchases comply with the Prescription Drug Marketing Act and other applicable laws and regulations.

Drug Inventory Ownership: If the contractor purchases the organization's inventory, a mutually acceptable, independent appraiser could decide the purchase price. Expired and other unusable drugs should be excluded from the purchase. The contractor could agree to obtain credit for the organization for expired and other unusable drugs if credit is obtainable. Legal advice may be needed to ensure that purchases comply with the Prescription Drug Marketing Act and other applicable laws and regulations.

Drug Ordering: A contract may assign responsibilities for selecting vendors and purchasing drug supplies for the organization. The contract should specify that all drugs used must be subject to approval by the organization's pharmacy and therapeutics (P&T) committee or its equivalent. The organization should understand how purchasing discounts are accounted for, recorded, and distributed. The impact of removing pharmacy items from group purchasing programs should be clear also.

Early Termination: There may be conditions for early termination of the contract.

Extension of Period of Performance: Conditions for extending the period of performance may be included in the contract.

Forms: Responsibilities for the design, approval, purchase, and storage of forms may be assigned.

Formulary System: A contract may assign responsibilities for evaluation of medications, collaboration with the P&T committee, and provision of formulary-related information services.

Hours of Pharmacy Operation: A contract may specify hours of operation that meet or exceed legal requirements and that are sufficient to serve patients' needs.

Laws, Rules, and Regulations: Requirements for services to meet or exceed federal, state, and local laws, rules, and regulations may be specified. These include but are not limited to those of FDA, DEA, OSHA, and the state board of pharmacy. The pharmacy should maintain (e.g., display, file) the appropriate licenses, permits, and records of equipment maintenance and certification. Any contractor required to be licensed as a manufacturer must be so licensed. The organization may agree to allow the contractor to act on the organization's behalf in communicating with the state board of pharmacy and other regulatory agencies.

Liability Insurance: Responsibilities for maintaining liability insurance coverage for the acts of employees may be assigned. The contract might specify, for example, that the contractor must maintain adequate liability insurance coverage for the acts of its employees.

Nondiscrimination: There might be a requirement that the contractor abide by all laws and regulations relating to discrimination in appointments, promotions, and terminations.

Ownership of Equipment, Fixtures, and Supplies: A contract may specify ownership of equipment, fixtures, and supplies and responsibilities for ensuring that equipment is maintained and certified according to applicable practice standards, laws, and regulations.

Performance Improvement: Responsibilities for establishing any performance-improvement programs and integrating them with the organization's performance-improvement activities may be included. Performance-improvement programs might be appropriate, for example, for the ordering, dispensing, and administering of medications and for the monitoring of medication effects and misadventures, including adverse drug reactions and adverse drug events.

Period of Performance: The contract might specify the period for which the contractor will provide services to the organization.

Pharmacy Staff Education and Training: Responsibilities for required ongoing staff education and training may be specified. For example, there might be an agreement that the contractor's staff will participate in the organization's education and training programs. In addition, the contractor may agree to provide specific training to ensure that all pharmacy personnel can perform any duties imposed by contractor-implemented functions.

Pharmacy Staff Employment: There may be a provision for the employment of pharmacists and technical and support personnel; this may specify those who will be employed by the organization and those who will be employed by the contractor. Whether employed by the organization or by the contractor, all staff should be competent and legally qualified. The organization should retain the right to assess, accept, or reject the performance of any of the contractor's staff who are used at the organization's work sites.

Pharmacy Staff Expenses: Responsibilities for any personnel expenses may be assigned. A contract might specify, for example, that the organization will be responsible for the salary, wages, and benefits of its employees whereas the contractor will be responsible for such expenses for its own employees. The contract might also allocate expenses for parking, meal discounts, and similar privileges for employees.

Pharmacy Staff Levels: There may be a requirement that the staffing levels for the contracted services be sufficient to meet the organization's needs.

Pharmacy Staff Orientation: A contract may assign responsibilities for orientation of all new pharmacy staff members to the organization and to the pharmacy, according to the organization's requirements.

Pharmacy Staff Performance: Responsibilities for pharmacy staff competency assessments and performance evaluations and for ensuring that assessments and evaluations are based on criteria in the individual's job description may be assigned.

Policies and Procedures: Responsibilities may be assigned for developing policies and procedures covering the outsourced services, all of which should comply with applicable laws, regulations, and accreditation or certification standards. The contract should specify that the policies and procedures must not conflict with those of the organization.

Purchasing and Accounts Payable: Responsibilities for maintaining the pharmacy's purchasing and accounts-payable functions, including ordering drugs, monitoring costs, and authorizing payment to vendors, might be specified.

Record Maintenance: A contract may assign responsibilities for maintaining and storing records. The contract should specify that all pertinent records must be kept for the time required by law and by the organization.

Space: Responsibilities for space required by the contractor to provide onsite services might be outlined. The organization should agree to provide space for the provision of onsite contractor services that is acceptable to the contractor and within the guidelines of the agencies that regulate the practice of pharmacy. Organizations might agree to provide the following facilities, depending on the contract's scope of services.
- Adequate square footage
- Space for preparing, compounding, packaging, and storing drugs under proper conditions
- Space for receiving and storing intravenous fluids and supplies
- Refrigerators and freezers
- Adequate space for maintaining and storing pharmacy records
- Laminar-airflow hoods and biological safety cabinets (if needed)

Sterile Products: A contract might include requirements for the quality of sterile products provided by the contractor. The contractor should ensure that sterile products (e.g., large-volume intravenous admixtures, total parenteral nutrient solutions) are prepared and labeled in a suitable environment by trained and competent employees. The contractor should provide quality-control information periodically and on demand. For services that involve deliveries, the contract should specify order cutoff and delivery times, any penalties for late deliveries, and arrangements for after-hours or emergency services and deliveries.

Successors: The rights of each party in the event that the organization or contractor merges or transfers its business or assets to a successor may be included in a contract.

Utilities: A contract may assign responsibility for utilities required by the contractor to provide onsite services. These utilities may include the following, as appropriate.
- Electrical service
- Water
- Heating and air conditioning
- Plumbing
- Janitorial services
- Internal and external telephone services (allowance might be made for a private external telephone line for the contractor)
- Security
- Waste disposal

This guideline was reviewed in 2002 by the Council on Administrative Affairs and by the Board of Directors and was found to still be appropriate.

Approved by the ASHP Board of Directors, April 22, 1998. Developed through the Council on Administrative Affairs.

The bibliographic citation for this document is as follows: American Society of Health-System Pharmacists. ASHP guidelines on outsourcing pharmaceutical services. *Am J Health-Syst Pharm.* 1998; 55:1611–7.

ASHP Technical Assistance Bulletin on Assessing Cost-Containment Strategies for Pharmacies in Organized Health-Care Settings

Health-care cost-containment efforts continue to exert increased pressure on providers of care to cost justify and improve the quality of their services. As increasingly scarce resources are allocated within an organization, the administrative skills of the pharmacy manager will play a key role in determining whether the level of services offered by the department can be maintained or expanded. Pharmacists in organized health-care settings are faced with constraints on reimbursement and increasing pressure to reduce not only the cost of drug therapy but also the total cost of providing pharmaceutical services.

Pharmacy managers who are evaluating the performance and benefits of existing pharmaceutical services or the addition of new services or personnel should conduct five key analyses: environmental, internal, demand, benefit, and cost. An environmental analysis assesses the external environment of regulatory and demographic changes, payer and competitor activities, and changes in the workforce supply. Internal analyses identify the strengths and weaknesses of the pharmacy in the specific practice site.

A demand analysis uses statistics and data to assess the demand for pharmaceutical services; useful demand information includes the number and types of services, the number and intensity of patients receiving pharmaceutical care, and the use of pharmaceutical services and products per diagnosis-related group (DRG) or per member month. A benefit analysis describes and quantifies benefits that accrue to the organization because of pharmaceutical care; they could include cost savings, improvements in quality of care, reductions in length of stay, and risk management benefits. Finally, the costs of providing pharmaceutical care can be determined in a cost analysis of salaries, supplies, overhead, and other fixed and variable costs.

This document is intended as an instrument for identifying the components of the internal analysis.

In identifying areas for potential cost reductions, it is imperative that pharmacy managers evaluate the benefits and costs of the entire drug use process. Since few analytical tools are currently available for identifying and evaluating components of the drug use process, ASHP's Council on Administrative Affairs designed and recommended a checklist to assist the pharmacy manager in that task.

If the scope of pharmacy cost responsibility extends beyond the product to the entire drug use process, then it is more likely that effective cost reductions can be achieved without compromising quality. The drug use process is defined as a multistage continuum that begins with the perception of a need for a drug and ends with an evaluation of the drug's effectiveness in the patient. This continuum includes the selection of a drug regimen, the delivery of the drug product, its administration to the patient, the monitoring of its effects, and the patient's therapeutic outcome. The ultimate responsibility of the pharmacist is to ensure the safe and appropriate use of drugs at all points along this continuum.

The Council on Administrative Affairs designed the checklist as an audit to assist the pharmacy manager in assessing current cost-containment strategies and in estab-

lishing new ones. The multilevel format of the checklist allows its use by all pharmacy managers, regardless of their experience or the organization's size and level of care. This document is intended to be applicable to all organized health-care settings. Individual questions in the checklist may contain terminology that is specific to a distinct practice. For example, "per member month" and "plan pharmacies" may only be applicable to a managed care setting, and "intravenous fluid waste" may only be applicable to an acute care inpatient setting.

The purpose of the checklist is not to establish standards or to identify what services must be offered; rather, it is to assist in determining optimal services for an individual organization. It is a self-evaluation tool to be used only for internal assessment. The audit checklist examines four critical areas: drug product costs, drug therapy regimen costs, productivity, and information systems.

I. Drug Product Costs

Controlling the drug product and its cost is a primary responsibility of a pharmacy department. The definition of drug product cost includes not only the acquisition cost but the total system cost incurred in delivering the product to the patient. The questions in this section will assist in auditing nonacquisition costs.

A.   *Purchasing and Inventory Control*

1.   Is a single-brand purchasing policy in effect for the pharmacy department?
      a. Has the pharmacy and therapeutics (P&T) committee approved a written generic substitution policy?
      b. Has the P&T committee approved a written therapeutic interchange policy?

For questions 2–5, consider whether prime vendors or competitive bidding is used, either individually or through a group purchasing arrangement, and answer the applicable questions for your pharmacy.

2.   Is competitive bidding or a pharmaceutical rebate used for
      High dollar cost items?
      High dollar volume items?
      a. Is either of these methods used:
          Guaranteed prices?
          Price ceilings for the term of the contract?
      b. Are the following considered when evaluating bids:
          Prompt payment discount?
          Terms of payment?
          Prompt payment of rebates?
          Nonperformance penalties?
          Delivery time limitations?
          Returned and damaged goods policy and service?
          Electronic order entry capabilities?
          Value-added services?

c. Are contracts negotiated when appropriate?

d. Are contracts renegotiated on a regular basis (e.g., annually)?

3. Is group purchasing used when advantageous?

4. If group purchasing is used:

a. Are prices guaranteed?

b. Is there a mechanism for determining that group prices are not higher than those that could be obtained otherwise?

5. Are primary wholesalers or wholesale contracts used for specific drugs when appropriate?

a. Is the wholesaler fee equal to or less than the cost of purchasing drugs directly? (Consider all factors such as increased investment revenues, decreased number of purchase orders, reduced inventory value, and receiving costs.)

b. Have inventories been adequately reduced?

c. Have ordering and receiving costs been adequately reduced?

d. Do outages that require payment of premium prices occur frequently?

e. Are there frequent outages?

6. Are volume discounts and rebate agreements evaluated for net savings (gross savings minus increased carrying or administrative cost) before purchase?

7. Has an inventory turnover rate been calculated for your organization?

a. Is this rate optimal for the facility?

8. Are any of the following used in inventory control: ABC method, minimum and maximum quantities, EOQ/EOV, and just-in-time/stockless inventory arrangements?

9. Do checks occur at regular intervals to verify that appropriate purchasing and inventory control methods are being followed?

a. Are reorder points adjusted as needed?

b. Is outdated stock returned promptly?

10. Are inventories controlled in dispensing areas?

a. Are minimum and maximum inventories maintained?

b. Is the space allotted for each product restricted?

c. Is there a routine check for outdated drugs and excesses?

d. Are exchange systems used when appropriate (e.g., carts, shelf units, and boxes)?

11. Are drug inventories outside the pharmacy controlled (e.g., nursing units and emergency, operating, and recovery rooms)?

a. Is an approved floor stock list used for nondrug items?

b. Are there maximum allowable quantities for each item?

c. Are inventory dollar limits set for each area?

d. Are areas checked monthly for excesses and outdated drugs?

12. Are inventories controlled in plan pharmacies?

a. Are plan pharmacies audited for appropriate drug inventory and dispensing?

B. *Waste and Pilferage*

1. Are bid negotiating, ordering, receiving, and invoice verifying functions separated to the extent feasible?

a. Are packing lists and invoices matched against purchase orders for accuracy of item, quantity, and price?

b. Are purchase or accounts-payable ledgers verified?

c. Is there a periodic audit of all purchasing functions?

2. Are costs of goods sold compared with costs of goods purchased by therapeutic categories?

3. Does the distribution system account for all doses dispensed?

a. Are all unused medications returned to the pharmacy?

b. Is the number of drugs used on a p.r.n. basis reduced to a minimum?

c. Are multiple requests for missing doses investigated?

d. Is there a tracking system to monitor the frequency and number of missing doses?

4. Have diversion and pilferage of controlled substances been reduced to a minimum?

a. Are amounts of controlled substances purchased compared with amounts dispensed?

b. Are amounts of controlled substances dispensed compared with amounts administered and recorded in patient charts?

c. Is there accountability of controlled substances in the operating and recovery suites?

5. Are there controls to minimize waste of intravenous admixtures?

a. Are there written policies for use of infusion pumps, controllers, and other drug delivery devices?

b. Are there lists of drugs approved for use with pumps and controllers?

c. Have policies been established for the use of intravenous administration sets, emphasizing routine changes (with written exceptions)?

d. Are automatic stop orders used to reduce waste?

e. Are there policies restricting oral orders?

f. Does an intravenous therapy team exist?

g. Are audits conducted to determine the dollar amount of intravenous fluid waste?

h. Are there mechanisms for easy, efficient communication of intravenous fluid rate changes and discontinued orders?

i. Are standardized dosages, solutions, and volumes established for intravenous drugs?

j. Are total parenteral nutrition (TPN) solutions standardized?

k. Have manufacturers' premixed solutions been evaluated for their economic advantages?

l. Has the calibrated-drip-chamber method of administration of intravenous drugs been evaluated?

m. Have prefilled syringes been evaluated for cost-effectiveness?

n. Are pharmacy intravenous fluid profiles reconciled regularly with those on the nursing units?

o. Has the period of advance preparation been reduced to decrease waste?

p. Are returned intravenous solutions reused when possible?

q. Has extended use of pump cassettes or tubing been considered?

r. Have the costs and benefits of syringe pumps versus intermittent small volume containers been evaluated?

6.   Is the pharmacy a secure work area?
    a. Are locks in place?
    b. Is the number of keys limited?

II. Drug Therapy Costs

As the pharmacy's influence over the entire drug use process expands, the opportunities for cost control are increased. Significant costs are associated with inappropriate drug choice, adverse drug reactions, and subtherapeutic treatment. Pharmacists can reduce costs and improve outcomes by adopting a patient-centered practice model referred to as pharmaceutical care. Under this model, described by Hepler and Strand (*Am J Hosp Pharm*. 1990; 47:533–43), the pharmacist is responsible for "(1) identifying potential and actual drug-related problems, (2) resolving actual drug-related problems, and (3) preventing potential drug-related problems."

By working with the patient and other professionals, the pharmacist can influence the perceived need for a drug, the selection of the product, and the patient's use of the drug throughout the duration of therapy, regardless of the setting. This integrated approach can reduce the total cost of drug therapy. The questions in this section will assist the manager in the evaluation of cost-reduction strategies.

A.   Formulary Systems

1.   Is there a policy for a single generic equivalent of each drug?
2.   Is there a policy that combination products generally are nonformulary drugs?
3.   Is there a policy that allows the pharmacy to decide which dosage sizes of a formulary drug will be stocked or reimbursed?
4.   Are there procedures to discourage use of nonformulary drugs?
    a. Are physicians required to complete a special form that indicates the reason for use of nonformulary drugs?
    b. Is cosignature by an attending physician required before nonformulary drugs can be dispensed?
    c. Do pharmacists contact prescribers of nonformulary drugs to recommend formulary equivalents?
    d. Is there a policy not to stock nonformulary drugs routinely?
    e. Are prescribers monitored for excessive use of nonformulary drugs?
5.   Does the formulary contain cost information?
6.   Is price information updated at least annually?
7.   Are items in the formulary grouped by therapeutic categories?
8.   Is the formulary evaluated periodically for ineffective or obsolete drugs?

B.   Pharmacy and Therapeutics Committee

These questions were developed to encourage the P&T committee to establish policies for each highlighted area.

1.   Are well-documented drug reviews prepared for all drugs that are being considered for formulary inclusion?
    a. Does each review contain an evaluation of clinical studies?
    b. Does each review contain a list of other drugs in the therapeutic category?

c. Does each review contain a cost comparison of these drugs?
    d. Has the cost impact of each formulary addition been calculated?
    e. Is a formal recommendation made by the pharmacy to the committee?
    f. Are pertinent deletions of similar drugs suggested?
2.   Are automatic stop orders in effect for selected classes of agents such as
    Antibiotics?
    P.R.N. analgesics?
    Blood components?
    Large volume injectable solutions?
3.   Do automatic stop orders take effect when patients have surgery?
    Are transferred to another service?
    Are transferred to and from intensive care units?
4.   Is there a system or P&T committee policy that limits the duration of prophylactic antibiotic therapy?
5.   Are therapeutic categories containing high risk, high volume, or expensive drugs reviewed regularly to reduce therapeutic duplicates and minimize drug therapy problems? (Examples of these categories include antihistamines, broad-spectrum penicillins, cephalosporins, histamine H_2-receptor antagonists, and nonsteroidal anti-inflammatory agents.)
    a. Are drugs removed from the formulary if they provide no unique benefit?
6.   Is there a restricted drug category in the formulary to control expensive agents and highly toxic drugs with limited uses that cannot be removed from the formulary?
7.   Has the number of controlled substances on the formulary been reduced when possible?
8.   Do physicians document their experiences with newly implemented P&T committee actions?
    a. Are these experiences communicated to the committee?
9.   Has the P&T committee established microbial-sensitivity reporting mechanisms that reflect cost-effectiveness criteria?
10. Are there policies in place regarding P&T committee member activities and conflict of interest?
11. Are there policies in place regarding appropriate activities of pharmaceutical manufacturer representatives within the organization?
12. Are there policies in place regarding pharmaceutical industry sponsorship of presentations within the organization?

C.   Clinical Pharmacy Services

Clinical pharmacy services, whose goal is improved patient outcomes, include patient and professional education, drug use evaluations and monitoring, and pharmacokinetic consulting. While documentation of discrete clinical pharmacy services is important, the underlying premise is that improved patient outcomes will result in cost reductions. ASHP's PharmaTrend product identifies the following as measures of clinical services during a given reporting period:

1.   Number of patient-care encounters.
2.   Number of patient chart reviews.
3.   Number of times pharmacists provided drug information to a physician or nurse.
4.   Number of times pharmacists participated in patient-

care rounds.

5. Number of conferences or lectures presented.
6. Number of pharmacokinetic consultations.
7. Number of literature searches with written replies.
8. Number of literature searches with oral replies.
9. Number of times pharmacists participated in cardio-pulmonary resuscitation.
10. Number of drug use evaluations conducted.
11. Number of nutritional support consultations.
12. Number of inservice programs presented.
13. Number of drug information center consultations.
14. Number of pharmacy newsletter issues prepared.

Additionally, PharmaTrend provides pharmacists with six clinical service indicators: clinical service work units per pharmacy patient-day, clinical service work units per admission, clinical service hours as percentage of total personnel hours, clinical service salary cost per pharmacy patient-day, clinical service salary cost per clinical service work unit, and an estimate of clinical services productivity.

The following additional questions are provided to assist pharmacy managers in collecting data for identifying the benefits of providing clinical services.

1. Are drug use evaluations conducted to identify problem areas and determine the cost-effectiveness of drugs in general?
2. Are there criteria for evaluating the benefits of all drugs (e.g., reduction in average length of stay and reduction in cost per member month)?
3. Is there a specific plan for assessing the cost of drug therapies (e.g., a target disease program)?
4. Are physicians educated about the cost of drug therapy?
   a. Are newsletters and memos used as educational tools?
   b. Are medical rounds used?
   c. Are teaching grand rounds used?
   d. Are informal lines of communication developed with the medical staff?
   e. Do physicians hold meetings with pharmacy representatives?
   f. Do prescribers receive regular feedback on their prescribing activity and cost?
5. Is a target drug program in effect that uses pharmacists to control the use of expensive or toxic drugs that cannot be removed from the formulary?
   a. Are criteria for appropriate drug use provided?
   b. Is the target drug program preceded by an educational newsletter?
   c. Do pharmacists review patient profiles daily for use of the target drugs?
   d. Does the pharmacist recommend alternative therapy when drug use is deemed inappropriate?
   e. Is there followup communication with physicians who frequently prescribe specific drugs inappropriately?
6. Do pharmacists provide pharmacokinetic services?
7. Do pharmacists participate in the training of patients for home therapy?
8. Do pharmacists work closely with personnel responsible for intravenous drug and solution administration?
   a. Do they decrease use of intravenous solutions to keep intravenous lines open?
   b. Do they decrease duration of intravenous solution therapy?
   c. Do they decrease duration of intravenous piggyback drug therapy by changing to intramuscular or oral administration when possible?
   d. Do they decrease unnecessary intravenous drug administration?
   e. Do they target areas where waste could be decreased?
9. Are pharmacists used on the TPN team to promote cost-effective activities?
10. Do pharmacists provide any of the following services to the outpatient clinics:
    Dispensing?
    Monitoring?
    Clinical services or consultations?
    Education?
    a. Do they recommend less expensive therapy when appropriate?
    b. Do they help reduce excess medication use in this setting?
11. Do pharmacists use laboratory data to evaluate the efficacy of drug therapy and to anticipate toxicity or adverse effects?
12. Does the pharmacy actively participate in organizational cost-containment studies that address patient-care issues?
13. Do pharmacists participate in discharge planning for patients?
14. Do pharmacists participate in infection control activities within the organization?
15. Do pharmacists routinely evaluate drug therapy to prevent and identify potential adverse drug reactions?
16. Do pharmacists participate in technology assessment activities within the organization?

III. Improving Productivity

A basic definition of productivity is the ratio between goods or services produced (output) and factors that have contributed to their production (input). The PharmaTrend manual defines productivity as the ratio of the amount of time theoretically needed to produce all of the pharmacy's output to the amount of staff time actually available. However, the productivity of employees does not depend entirely on work performance; it is also influenced by technological development, skills and attitudes of supervisors, quality of materials, managerial environment, departmental job and function statements, layout and flow of work within the department, and other factors.

Monitoring departmental productivity is a key element of any cost-containment strategy. The questions in this section can be used in evaluating methods for improving departmental productivity.

A. *Effective Personnel Management Skills*

1. Have job analyses been conducted?
2. Are job descriptions rewritten periodically (e.g., annually)?
3. Have alternative staffing methods been considered such as job sharing, part-time hours, flextime, 10-hour shifts, and use of on-call personnel?
4. Is there an effective performance appraisal system in the department?

5. Are work methods and redistribution of staffing regularly reviewed?
6. Do supportive personnel perform all functions that do not require a pharmacist?
7. Has departmental personnel turnover been evaluated?
8. Are evaluations of performance appraisal, work methods, supportive personnel, and turnover used regularly in designing the department's staffing?
9. Has overtime been analyzed?
10. Have behavioral and motivational factors affecting productivity been assessed?
11. Is there a cost-effective orientation and training program?
12. Is a participative problem-solving program (e.g., quality improvement) used to build productive attitudes?
13. Is improved productivity a pharmacy objective and commitment?
14. Is the organization managed in a way that positively develops productive employee attitudes?

B. Development of Systems to Improve Productivity

1. Have new technologies been evaluated for increasing efficiency or decreasing required personnel hours (e.g., premixed intravenous admixtures, new drug delivery systems, and automation)?
2. Have all systems in the drug use process been evaluated for maximum efficiency (e.g., delivery and transportation, unit dose system, intravenous admixture system, billing, and claims processing system)?
3. Have productivity measurements been established?
4. Have management systems (e.g., total quality management) that support improved productivity been implemented?
5. Is computerization used effectively?
   a. Is the charging system computerized or automated?
   b. Is the drug distribution system computerized?
   c. Is adequate computer support available for clinical services?
6. Does the facility design promote efficient work?
   a. Have optimal workflow patterns been examined for each area of the pharmacy?
7. Are communication devices properly used?
   a. Is the telephone system used efficiently?
   b. Are state-of-the-art communication devices and systems used?
   c. Is communication effective between departmental sections, between shifts, among personnel, and among multiple providers?

IV. Information Management

Providers cannot function under the prospective pricing system without accurate and timely access to internal information. There is a need for identifying and capturing the necessary data in a form that pharmacy managers can use. Changes in health care will create new information needs that can be best met by combining clinical and financial data into a common system.

The success of the information system in addressing managers' needs will depend strongly on the development of an indepth strategy by those who will use this assistem. In general terms, the strategy for developing clinical and financial reporting systems should include the following steps:

1. Evaluate the pharmacy's information needs.
2. Determine the availability of data within the organization.
3. Obtain and use the data currently available in the department and organization.
4. Plan methods for obtaining needed data that are not currently available.

The pharmacy manager must rapidly collect, evaluate, and act on complex information. Adequate information systems support is needed to collect and evaluate data pertinent to pharmacy operations, clinical services, and management functions. The questions in this section will assist the pharmacy manager in evaluating the usefulness and relevance of specific information systems.

1. Does the pharmacy receive adequate and appropriate reports, in a timely manner, from the organization's data processing or management information systems (MIS) department for cost-containment planning?
   a. Are detailed expense, revenue, and cost-of-goods reports received for each accounting period?
   b. Are reports adequate in explanation of detail?
   c. Are variance reports available that show actual versus budgeted use?
   d. Are reports matched with statistics maintained within the pharmacy?
   e. Do the reports detail expenses by drug or by drug category, especially for high cost items?
   f. Does the pharmacy receive regular full-time equivalent (FTE) use reports (e.g., how many FTEs are used and the variance between budget and actual)?
   g. Does the department receive adequately detailed expense reports that itemize products purchased from central warehousing, from wholesalers, and directly from manufacturers?
2. Are appropriate and comprehensive reports regularly prepared by pharmacy management for the organization's administration?
   a. Does the pharmacy prepare evaluative reports of activities and expenditures to include:
      1) A report of drug purchases, detailing actual dollar purchases for the given time period?
      2) A report per drug or drug category?
   b. Are computers used effectively for supporting the following departmental functions:
      1) Purchasing and inventory control?
      2) Drug information service?
      3) Drug preparation and distribution systems?
      4) Clinical pharmacy services?
      5) Drug use evaluation?
      6) Pharmacokinetic services?
      7) Drug therapy monitoring systems?
      8) Outpatient or ambulatory care systems?
      9) Claims processing and benefits design?
   c. Is the pharmacy computer system appropriately connected with the organization's mainframe system?
   d. Are microcomputers available for support of serv-ices that the hospital mainframe cannot support?
3. Have applicable federal and state regulations been reviewed?
4. Is information on national or regional departmental performance data (e.g., Monitrend and PharmaTrend) used for comparison?

Approved by the ASHP Board of Directors, September 27, 1991. Supersedes an April 25, 1985 version which was developed by the ASHP Council on Administrative Affairs. The questions in the checklist sections on drug product costs and drug therapy costs were adapted from the following article: Abramowitz PW. Controlling financial variables—changing prescribing patterns. *Am J Hosp Pharm*. 1984; 41:503–15.

The bibliographic citation for this document is as follows: American Society of Hospital Pharmacists. ASHP technical assistance bulletin on assessing cost-containment strategies for pharmacies in organized health-care settings. *Am J Hosp Pharm*. 1992; 49:155–60.

Compensation and Reimbursement

Reimbursement for Unlabeled Uses of FDA-Approved Drug Products (0206)
Source: Council on Administrative Affairs
To support third-party reimbursement for FDA-approved drug products appropriately prescribed for unlabeled uses.
This policy supersedes ASHP policy 9001.

Product Reimbursement and Pharmacist Compensation (0207)
Source: Council on Administrative Affairs
To pursue, in collaboration with public and private payers, the development of improved methods of reimbursing pharmacies for the cost of drug products dispensed and associated overhead; further,

To educate pharmacists about those methods; further,

To pursue, with federal and state health-benefit programs and other third-party payers, the development of a standard mechanism for compensation of pharmacists for patient care services and compounding and dispensing services; further,

To pursue changes in federal, state, and third-party payment programs to (1) define pharmacists as providers of patient care and (2) issue provider numbers to pharmacists that allow them to bill for patient care services; further,

To educate and assist pharmacists in their efforts to attain provider status and receive compensation for patient care services.
This policy supersedes ASHP policy 0115.

ASHP Statement on Third-Party Compensation for Clinical Services by Pharmacists

Historically, institutional pharmacists have been concerned primarily with dispensing drugs and secondarily with providing drug-related information. With the major increase in the number, potency, and toxicity of drugs in recent years, pharmacists are increasingly providing clinical services. This means that the primary focus of institutional pharmacy practice is shifting from a system of drug distribution to one of drug use control, which includes both drug distribution and provision of information. Therefore, a substantial portion of many pharmacies' total expenses and workload relates to patient service activities. These activities, which are not directly related to drug dispensing, are described in the "ASHP Statement on Clinical Functions in Institutional Pharmacy Practice."[1]

Clinical pharmacy services and rational drug therapy are essential components of total patient care and contributing factors to the reduction of patient-care costs. Federal and state legislation and regulations and numerous private standards[a] recognize the benefits of clinical pharmacy services and strongly encourage, if not require, the provision of these services to patients in organized health-care settings. To maintain clinical pharmacy services in organized health-care settings, the following principles should be noted by health-care administrators, third-party payers, and pharmacy managers:

1. Currently, many types of third-party payment systems are in use, including such diverse payment mechanisms as Medicare prospective pricing (e.g., diagnosis-related groups), capitated payments for health maintenance organizations, and cost-based reimbursement for commercial third-party insurance. Each third-party payer may use different payment or reimbursement mechanisms,[b] and each hospital's reimbursement may vary by its location, its primary third-party payer, and its case mix. Therefore, pharmacy managers must be cognizant of the types of compensation received by their individual hospitals and must structure their pharmaceutical services in a manner that permits identification and monitoring of costs versus benefits under each payment mechanism.

2. Regardless of the payment mechanism, clinical services are generally considered reimbursable or payable items when they are integral to the case management plan for each patient and when the costs and benefits of the service are carefully documented. Payment for clinical services may also be determined by the third-party payer's review and approval of the service. In the case of commercial insurers, those who are insured can direct that payment for clinical services be included in their policies.

3. Pharmacists should take the initiative in proposing clinical programs and documenting the health-care benefits of such programs. They should develop such services and cooperate with provider fiscal officers to document accurately the related costs. Services should also be consistent with regulatory agency, industry, and institutional standards of cost identification and allocation. Likewise, pharmacists should document the cost impact of such services on the entire drug use continuum, which includes the selection of a drug regimen, delivery of the drug product, its administration to the patient, and the monitoring of its effects. Pharmacy administrators must play a central role in identifying the clinical services that should be provided by their institution and ensuring that each service is consistent with professional standards.

4. Methods used to determine costs of clinical pharmacy services should be consistent with the methods used to determine costs of other patient-care services. The costs and charges associated with clinical pharmacy services should reflect the provider's reasonable fiscal needs for providing such services.

5. Mechanisms for charging patients for pharmaceutical services may take one of several forms. A patient charge mechanism for pharmaceutical services should be developed by the provider's fiscal officer and pharmacists, taking into account professional trends, management philosophy, and the implications of that patient charging mechanism for reimbursement or payment.

6. Reimbursement or payment for clinical services will usually be to the provider (i.e., the institution), not directly to the pharmacist. Generally, charges for pharmaceutical services will be rendered as part of the provider's bill to the patient. Pharmacy or pharmacist compensation for services generally should be resolved with the provider and may take any form that is acceptable to both parties.

Reference

1. American Society of Hospital Pharmacists. ASHP statement on clinical functions in institutional pharmacy practice. *Am J Hosp Pharm*. 1978; 35:813.

[a]An example is the "ASHP Statement on Clinical Pharmacy and Its Relationship to the Hospital" (*Am J Hosp Pharm*. 1971; 28:357).
[b]Generally, payment refers to prospective compensation, and reimbursement refers to retrospective compensation.

Approved by the ASHP House of Delegates, June 3, 1985, and by the Board of Directors, April 25, 1985. Developed by the ASHP Council on Administrative Affairs. Supersedes the "ASHP Statement on Reimbursement and Payment for Clinical Pharmacy Services," which was approved June 8, 1981.

The bibliographic citation for this document is as follows: American Society of Hospital Pharmacists. ASHP statement on third-party compensation for clinical services by pharmacists. *Am J Hosp Pharm*. 1985; 42:1580–1.

ASHP Guidelines for Implementing and Obtaining Compensation for Clinical Services by Pharmacists

For some time, pharmacies in organized health-care settings have been moving from a product-centered structure to a more patient-oriented clinical practice. Clinical pharmacy services or patient-oriented pharmaceutical services are now a recognized and necessary component of health care. However, new trends in reimbursement, such as prospective pricing and capitation payments, provide different incentives for hospitals—to manage in terms of product lines instead of patient services.

In such a financial environment, it is essential that the value of any nonproduct-centered service be well documented and that the service be cost-justifiable. Pharmacists planning to initiate new clinical services may have to meet certain administrative requirements, including the following: (1) to provide an accurate accounting of all of the resources required; (2) to delineate the costs of the service and its effect on patient outcomes; (3) to obtain approval from the institution's administration and medical staff for provision of the service on a routine basis; and (4) to identify an appropriate mechanism for patient charging and for obtaining reimbursement or payment[a] from the third-party payer.

Generally, third-party payers do not have formal policies that prohibit their reimbursing and paying providers for clinical pharmacy services. However, payment is predicated on acceptance and endorsement of the service by the involved administrative and medical staffs and by the third-party payer's formal review and approval of the benefit coverage (and, in the case of patients covered by private insurance plans, by the provision of the service as a covered benefit of their plan). Approval of reimbursement for clinical services, however, varies from area to area and from carrier to carrier.

This document presents a set of general guidelines for use in obtaining administrative support and subsequent reimbursement or payment for a new pharmaceutical service. Often, many steps of the process may be omitted. For example, it should not be necessary to conduct a preliminary trial of a widely accepted, though not universally adopted, service (such as use of patient medication profiles). However, a careful review of the literature may be necessary for documenting the direct impact of the new service on expenses and determining whether or not the proposed new service will generate a revenue surplus. With fixed reimbursement, hospital administrators are unlikely to approve any new service unless its benefits are fully documented and unless its result is an overall savings.

When clinical pharmacy services are initially established in the hospital, they should be viewed as an important component of the drug use continuum, not as a separate entity. After establishment of the initial clinical services at the hospital, the approach to obtaining additional clinical services should focus on patient audit results and on the approval of the pharmacy and therapeutics (P&T) committee.

These guidelines are written for use by pharmacy directors in hospitals. However, they can be adapted for use in other situations (e.g., by a pharmacist providing services as part of a medical group practice or a health maintenance organization).

The guidelines are as follows:

1. Prepare, for the provider's administration, a written proposal for short-term (e.g., 3 months) implementation of the proposed service. The proposal should include the following elements:

   a. A clear, concise description of the service.

   b. The rationale for the service, including published references if available.

   c. Written support for the service by the P&T committee and other appropriate parties (e.g., infections committee, department of nursing, and applicable medical services).

   d. The expected benefits of the service to patients and the institution in terms of costs and quality of care, as measured by indices such as decrease in length of stay, decrease in incidence of therapeutic failures, decrease in duration of therapy, and decrease in drug expenditures. *This is the most important section of the document; for the proposal to receive administration approval, the available information and calculations must prove that the benefits exceed the costs of providing the service.*

   e. Estimated startup and operating expenses and revenue[b] of the service, plus its personnel, equipment, and material requirements.

2. Obtain the administration's formal approval of the implementation project.

3. Initiate the project, keeping complete records of all expenses, outputs (e.g., the number of patient consultations), and personnel hours devoted to it. In addition to the indices listed in Item 1d, the following elements should be documented: changes in length of stay, costs of treatment, and changes in levels of personnel productivity. This information will be needed to develop charges for the service and to obtain reimbursement or payment.

4. On completion of the project, prepare a report of its implementation for the administration. This report should focus on fiscal and workload data, including total pharmacy cost per patient, service unit, or diagnosis-related group, and a suggested charge based on these data. Information on acceptance of the program by patients and staff should be included when possible. This report should also project the manpower and financial resources needed to perform the service as a routine pharmacy function.

5. Obtain formal approval from administration to implement the service on an institutionwide basis.

6. Assist the institution's administration and financial manager in developing the information needed to include the costs of the service in its compensation agreements with third-party carriers. To obtain compensation, certain administrative requirements (such as formal approval of the service by the P&T committee) may have to be met.

7. Regularly evaluate the objectives and impact of the new program or service, based on changes in payment

mechanisms, and prepare annual updates on these clinical pharmacy services. For example, it will become important to report annual cost savings or decreased readmissions over a baseline figure.

---

[a]Generally, payment refers to prospective compensation, and reimbursement refers to retrospective compensation.

[b]In cooperation with the provider's fiscal offices, and depending on the acceptance of the service within the health-care system, the pharmacy department should determine whether payment for the service can or should be received.

Approved by the ASHP Board of Directors, April 25, 1985. Developed by the ASHP Council on Administrative Affairs. Supersedes the "ASHP Guidelines for Implementing and Obtaining Reimbursement for Clinical Pharmaceutical Services," approved November 13–14, 1980.

The bibliographic citation for this document is as follows: American Society of Hospital Pharmacists. ASHP guidelines for implementing and obtaining compensation for clinical services by pharmacists. *Am J Hosp Pharm.* 1985; 42:1581–2.

Human Resources

Cultural Diversity Among Health Care Providers (0409)
Source: Council on Educational Affairs
To foster awareness of the cultural diversity of health care providers; further,

To foster recognition of the impact that cultural diversity of health care providers may have on the medication-use process; further,

To develop the cultural competencies of pharmacy practitioners, technicians, students, and educators.

Role of Licensing, Credentialing, and Privileging in Collaborative Drug Therapy Management (0318)
Source: Council on Legal and Public Affairs
To recognize licensure of pharmacists as the only state-imposed legal requirement necessary for pharmacists engaged in providing collaborative drug therapy management services; further,

To support the current practice of pharmacists and prescribers negotiating and establishing collaborative drug therapy management agreements in which the pharmacist receives delegated authority; further,

To support the use of privileging processes in those practice environments where explicit privileging is required to receive delegated authority; any additional training or credentials required of pharmacists engaging in these practices should be determined by the local practice site; further,

To stipulate that privileging should be conducted by an oversight body of the practice site.

(*Note: Privileging* is the process by which an oversight body of a health care organization or other appropriate provider body, having reviewed an individual health care provider's credentials and performance and found them satisfactory, authorizes that individual to perform a specific scope of patient care services within that setting.)
This policy supersedes ASHP policy 0219.

Staffing for Safe and Effective Patient Care (0201)
Source: Council on Administrative Affairs
To encourage pharmacy managers to work in collaboration with physicians, nurses, health-system administrators, and others to outline key pharmacist services that are essential to safe and effective patient care; further,

To encourage pharmacy managers to be innovative in their approach and to factor into their thinking legal requirements, accreditation standards, professional standards of practice, and the resources and technology available in individual settings; further,

To support the following principles:

- Sufficient qualified staff must exist to ensure safe and effective patient care;
- During periods of staff shortages, pharmacists must exert leadership in directing resources to services that are the most essential to safe and effective patient care;
- Within their own organizations, pharmacists should develop contingency plans to be implemented in the event of insufficient staff—actions that will preserve services that are the most essential to safe and effective

patient care and will, as necessary, curtail other services; and

- Among the essential services for safe and effective patient care is pharmacist review of new medication orders before the administration of first doses; in settings where patient acuity requires that reviews of new medication orders be conducted at any hour and similar medication-use decisions be made at any hour, there must be 24-hour access to a pharmacist.

This policy supersedes ASHP policy 0001.

Image of and Career Opportunities for Pharmacy Technicians (0211)
Source: Council on Educational Affairs
To promote the image of pharmacy technicians as valuable contributors to health care delivery; further,

To develop and disseminate information about career opportunities that enhance the recruitment and retention of qualified pharmacy technicians.

Image of and Career Opportunities for Health-System Pharmacists (0214)
Source: Council on Educational Affairs
To expand the public information program promoting the professional image of health-system pharmacists to the general public, public policymakers, other health care professionals, and health-system decision-makers; further,

To provide ASHP informational and recruitment materials identifying opportunities for pharmacy careers in health systems.
This policy supersedes ASHP policy 9710.

Pharmacist Recruitment and Retention (0218)
Source: Council on Legal and Public Affairs
To support federal and state incentive programs for new pharmacy graduates to practice in underserved areas; further,

To provide information and educational programming on strategies used by employers for successful recruitment and retention of pharmacists and pharmacy technicians; further,

To conduct regular surveys on trends in the health-system pharmacy work force, including retention rates for pharmacists and pharmacy technicians.

Professional Socialization (0110)
Source: Council on Educational Affairs
To encourage pharmacists to serve as mentors to students, residents, and colleagues in a manner that fosters the adoption of a) high professional aspirations for pharmacy practice, b) high personal standards of integrity and competence, c) a commitment to serve humanity, d) habits of analytical thinking and ethical reasoning, and e) a commitment to life-long learning.

Professional Development as a Retention Tool (0112)

Source: Council on Educational Affairs

To recognize that pharmacy department staff development is an essential component of staff recruitment and retention as well as quality of work life; further,

To recognize that staff development encompasses more than formal inservice or external programs and includes informal learning among colleagues, mentoring, and other types of learning; further.

To strongly encourage pharmacy directors and health-system administrators to support staff development programs as an important benefit that aids in recruiting and retaining qualified practitioners; further,

To assist pharmacy directors with staff development initiatives by providing a variety of educational programs, services, and resource materials.

This policy supersedes ASHP policy 8706.

Financial Management Skills (0003)

Source: Council on Administrative Affairs

To foster the systematic and ongoing development of management skills for all health-system pharmacists in the areas of (a) health-system economics, (b) business plan development, (c) financial analysis, (d) pharmacoeconomic analysis, (e) diversified pharmacy services, and (f) compensation for pharmaceutical care; further,

To encourage schools of pharmacy to incorporate these management areas in students' course work and clerkships; further,

To integrate these management areas into the practice management requirements in the ASHP Standard for Residency in Pharmacy Practice (with an Emphasis on Pharmaceutical Care).

This policy supersedes ASHP policy 8301.

Pharmacist Credentialing (0006)

Source: Council on Educational Affairs

To support the position that credentialing is a voluntary professional activity distinct and separate from the licensing process; further,

To endorse the goals and the standards-based approach to credentialing being pursued by the Council on Credentialing in Pharmacy (CCP); further,

To support the position that all widely accepted post-licensure pharmacy credentialing programs must meet quality standards that are being established by CCP.

Opposition to Creation of "Pharmacist Assistant" Category of Licensed Pharmacy Personnel (0025)

Source: House of Delegates

To reaffirm the following statement in the "White Paper on Pharmacy Technicians" (April 1996) endorsed by ASHP and the American Pharmaceutical Association:

"Although there is a compelling need for pharmacists to expand the purview of their professional practice, there is also a need for pharmacists to maintain control over all aspects of drug product handling in the patient care arena, including dispensing and compounding. No other discipline is as well qualified to ensure public safety in this important aspect of health care."

Further,

To note that some interest groups in pharmacy have advocated for the creation of a new category of licensed personnel called "Pharmacist Assistant" that would have (a) less education and training than pharmacists and (b) independent legal authority to perform many of the functions that are currently restricted to licensed pharmacists; further,

To support the optimal use of well-trained, certified pharmacy technicians under the supervision of licensed pharmacists; further,

To oppose the creation of a category of licensed personnel in pharmacy such as "Pharmacist Assistant" that would have legal authority to perform independently those professional pharmacy functions that are currently restricted to licensed pharmacists.

Human Immunodeficiency Virus (HIV) Positive Employees (9201)

Source: Council on Administrative Affairs

To adopt the position that mandatory routine testing of health care workers for infection with the human immunodeficiency virus is unnecessary; further,

To support the use of universal precautions for infection control.

This policy was reviewed in 2002 by the Council on Administrative Affairs and by the Board of Directors and was found to still be appropriate.

Drug Testing (9103)

Source: Council on Legal and Public Affairs

To recognize the use of pre-employment drug testing or drug testing for cause during employment based on defined criteria and with appropriate validation procedures; further,

To support employer-sponsored drug programs that include a policy and process that promote the recovery of impaired individuals.

This policy was reviewed in 2001 by the Council on Legal and Public Affairs and by the Board of Directors and was found to still be appropriate.

Employee Testing (9108)

Source: Council on Legal and Public Affairs

To oppose the use of truth-verification testing such as polygraphs as routine employment practices because of the possible interference with the rights of individuals; further,

To recognize the limited use of such testing during employment where such testing may protect the rights of individuals against false witness.

This policy was reviewed in 2001 by the Council on Legal and Public Affairs and by the Board of Directors and was found to still be appropriate.

Tobacco and Tobacco Products (8807)

Source: Council on Professional Affairs

To discourage the use and distribution of tobacco and tobacco products in and by pharmacies; further,

To seek, within the bounds of public law and policy, to eliminate the use and distribution of tobacco and tobacco products in meeting rooms and corridors at ASHP-sponsored continuing education events; further,

To join with other interested organizations in statements and expressions of opposition to the use of tobacco and tobacco products.

This policy was reviewed in 2001 by the Council on Professional Affairs and by the Board of Directors and was found to still be appropriate.

Human Immunodeficiency Virus Infections (8808)
Source: Council on Professional Affairs
To seek input in the decisions of government and other organizations to express the concerns of pharmacists with regard to the handling of drugs and drug-related devices for the treatment and prevention of human immunodeficiency virus (HIV) infections; further,

To continue to inform pharmacists about drug and drug-related developments in the treatment of HIV infections.

This policy was reviewed in 2001 by the Council on Professional Affairs and by the Board of Directors and was found to still be appropriate.

Pharmacy Technicians (8610)
Source: Council on Legal and Public Affairs
To work toward the removal of legislative and regulatory barriers preventing pharmacists from delegating certain technical activities to other trained personnel.

This policy was reviewed in 2001 by the Council on Legal and Public Affairs and by the Board of Directors and was found to still be appropriate.

ASHP Guidelines on the Recruitment, Selection, and Retention of Pharmacy Personnel

Purpose

These guidelines are intended to assist pharmacy managers in the recruitment, selection, and retention of qualified employees. The pharmacy manager working in an organized health care system will usually have to work with the system's human resources department and within the framework of the specific recruitment, selection, and hiring policies of the organization.

Recruitment

Position Descriptions. Well-developed job descriptions are extremely important in addressing many personnel issues. They are often used to establish salary ranges, define performance expectations, and write performance evaluations, but they can also be crucial tools in a successful recruitment effort.[1] The position description should contain detailed information on the knowledge, skills, experience, and abilities that an acceptable candidate should possess. The following information may be included in a position description:

- Position title and position control number (if applicable),
- Duties, essential job functions, and responsibilities of the position,
- Education, training, experience, and licensure required,
- Knowledge, skills, and abilities required to perform assigned duties,
- Reporting relationships,
- Pay grade and salary range (optional),
- Education and training required to maintain competence, and
- Other specifications of the position that may be required to meet legal requirements (e.g., the Americans with Disabilities Act) or the objectives of the organization (e.g., residency or certification requirements).

[*Note:* A variety of sample job descriptions can be found in Section 7.3 of the *Pharmacy Management Toolkit: Tools of the Trade for Pharmacy Managers and Directors* (CD-ROM) and in module 1 of *Competence Assessment Tools for Health-System Pharmacies* (online and print versions), both available from ASHP.]

A revised position description should be reviewed with staff members currently in that position and with the supervisor of that position. In many workplaces, human resources departments maintain a file of position descriptions and may require approval of all position descriptions in the organization. Procedures specific to the workplace should be followed. Staff with legal expertise should review revised position descriptions to determine compliance with organizational and legal requirements.

Recruitment Sources. Recruitment processes will depend on the type of position being filled. Strategies for filling a support staff position may not be appropriate when searching for a management candidate and vice versa. A recruitment plan should be developed for each position being filled. This plan should incorporate strategies that have worked in the past while allowing for innovative ideas. Organizations that recruit frequently or have very limited candidate pools should consider a continuous recruitment plan so that a list of prospective candidates is available even before an opening occurs.

Recruitment of individuals from within the department or the organization (e.g., from another department) creates internal growth opportunities and may result in greater employee retention and staff loyalty. Internal recruitment may also be less disruptive and expensive. To facilitate internal recruitment, notice of a vacant position can be posted within the organization before the information is made available to outsiders. Posting can be accomplished by various means, including memoranda, e-mail, voice mail, newsletters, announcements at staff meetings, and bulletin boards.

Recruitment of outside candidates expands the number of potential candidates and the experience available to the organization. It brings in new talent and discourages a reliance on seniority as the primary basis for promotion. Budgetary constraints and the urgency to fill a position may affect the recruitment method selected for external candidates. When recruitment of individuals outside the organization becomes necessary, the following methods should be considered:

- Advertisements in professional journals, newspapers, state professional society newsletters, and electronic bulletin boards,
- Personnel placement services provided by national or state professional societies,
- Oral and written recommendations from colleagues. Some organizations offer a "finder's fee" for hires that result from an employee referral,
- Personal discussion or correspondence with potential candidates,
- Recruitment visits to colleges of pharmacy or to facilities that conduct technician-training programs,
- Professional recruiting firms, which typically charge the organization a percentage of the position's annual salary. In addition, recruitment advertising companies offer access to a list of job seekers for a fee,
- Familiarizing students with the organization by offering summer jobs or participating in college of pharmacy experiential rotations,
- Tuition assistance programs for students in exchange for future work commitments,
- A "prospect list" of individuals applying for previous job openings, which can often be supplied by the human resources department,
- Internet-job-site postings,
- Community job fairs and local or state welfare-to-work programs, and
- Organization-sponsored events such as continuing-education sessions, award presentations, or community outreach programs.

The ability to recruit qualified candidates will depend on a multitude of factors, including the financial stability and location of the organization, the area's cost of living, the organization's compensation program (including salary, fringe benefits, and raise structure), the position's schedule and reporting structure, opportunities for professional growth and advancement, and the reputation and scope of pharmaceutical services offered. Only some of these factors are within the pharmacy manager's control.

Preinterview Information. The applicant's correspondence, resumé or curriculum vitae, letters of recommendation, academic records, and completed application form (if any) should be carefully evaluated on the basis of the position description to determine the suitability of the candidate for an interview.

There are certain legal restrictions on the type of information that may be requested from candidates on an application form. In general, an application form may request only information that relates directly to the evaluation of the applicant's ability to perform the job for which he or she is applying. If an application form different from that of the organization is used, it is advisable to have the human resources and legal departments review it before distribution to potential candidates.

Selection

Initial Screening Interview. An initial screening interview may be necessary if several qualified candidates have been identified. The screening interview is generally a brief interview conducted by the human resources department or the direct supervisor for the position; it offers a quick assessment of the suitability of the candidate for the position. This interview is often conducted by telephone, especially if the candidate lives far away. The screening interview should be documented and included in the applicant's file.

The Interview Process. A successful interview process is one that matches the best available candidate with a specific position. The process should allow the interviewers to predict the future performance of candidates as accurately as possible. One style of interview is the individual interview—one interviewer and one interviewee. Individual interviews offer the advantages of simplicity, ease of scheduling, and consistency of perspective. Because they are less intimidating to the candidate than group interviews, individual interviews may allow the interviewer to more accurately evaluate the applicant and provide the applicant with more opportunities to ask questions. The disadvantage of an individual interview is that it does not allow for multiple viewpoints and therefore increases the chance that something will be overlooked.

Another style, team interviewing, involves a group of interviewers. Members of the team may interview the candidate individually and then pool their results or they may interview the candidate as a group. The well-prepared team approach offers multiple perspectives within a standardized evaluation scheme. Its disadvantages are extra time consumed to train the team and conduct interviews and the intimidating effect it may have on candidates. Its advantage is that it incorporates more individuals into the process of analyzing a candidate's qualifications.[2] Team interviews foster the ideal of teamwork, and the involved employees share responsibility for the success or failure of the person hired. They also provide an opportunity to observe the candidate's ability to interact with groups, which may be important if the position will require that type of activity.

The composition of the interview team will depend on the position being filled. The team should include people with a common interest in the outcome of the selection process and people who have been in the organization long enough to share with the applicant some history of the organization and the department.[2]

Characteristics of an effective interview process include the following:

- Prior to the interview, the manager should provide the following to the candidate: information about the health-system institution, department, city, and state (if the applicant is not from the area); an agenda for the interview; the position description; travel directions to the facility; and clarification of expenses that will be incurred or reimbursed.
- The interview should be carefully planned. Consider the availability of those who need to participate in the process and allow adequate time for each event, including a tour of the facility (if needed).
- Interviewers should be well prepared. Preinterview information submitted by the candidate should be distributed to and reviewed by participants in advance of an interview.
- Carefully planned, open-ended questions should be developed in advance. Literature can be consulted to obtain sample questions and questions that are inadvisable or prohibited by law.[2–5] Human resources departments can usually assist in developing questions. (Refer to the appendix for sample questions.)
- To the extent possible, a core group of questions should be asked of all candidates as a means of comparing them. This does not negate the need to investigate different areas for each candidate or to pursue specific questions that surface during the interview.
- Questions should focus on predetermined criteria for the position and the qualifications of the candidates. The goal is to match the best candidate with the vacant position. Questions should focus on past performance, which is often a good indicator of future performance. In addition to questions regarding professional competency, the interview should contain questions that will help determine whether the applicant's attitudes and behaviors will be suitable for the job. Behavior-based selection criteria should be used when possible.
- The interviewer should give the candidate a realistic view of the position, including both favorable and unfavorable information. If the candidate is "oversold" on the position, dissatisfaction may set in when the truth becomes apparent.
- Performance standards and methods used for evaluation should be fully explained, and opportunities for professional growth should be presented.
- A description of employee benefits (e.g., medical insurance, vacation, sick leave, retirement benefits, and holidays) should be provided, either by the manager or by the human resources department.
- The initial salary and salary range for the position should be discussed with the candidate.
- The employee work schedule should be reviewed with the candidate.
- Any additional services or covered expenses the department offers should be outlined. Examples of these services or covered expenses include serving as a provider of continuing-education programs, travel ex-

penses and time off for continuing-education programs, payment of professional membership fees, and any other benefits that would attract the candidate to the position.

- A tour of the department should be provided.
- If the candidate is not from the area, a tour of the region should be given. Employees of the department or a real estate agency may show a candidate the area and describe the housing market and local schools.
- A follow-up letter is sent to the candidate after the interview to express thanks for interest in the position and the organization and to advise the candidate of the next steps. Timely and well-organized communication between recruiters and candidates is essential to a successful recruitment effort.

Each interview should be documented to keep track of each candidate's responses and to avoid confusion later. Documentation could include interview questions and the candidate's responses or simply a rating of the candidate's responses to specific questions. One person may be designated to collect and collate comments from a group interview. Documentation should occur immediately after the interview.[2] When considering a potential employee, the interviewer should examine punctuality, completeness and accuracy of the resumé or curriculum vitae, communication skills, compensation expectations, skills and knowledge pertinent to the position, and optimal fit with coworkers. The recruitment team should agree in advance on a systematic method for selecting the successful candidate.

Background Verification. The accuracy of information provided by the candidate should be verified by the human resources department. Information may be obtained from the following sources:

- Personal reference letters provided by the applicant,
- Letters of reference provided by previous employers or preceptors (with the applicant's permission),
- State board of pharmacy records,
- Academic records, and
- Legal background searches (when permitted by law and/or by the applicant).

Job Offer. The job offer should be made as quickly as possible after the interview process is completed. Offers should be made to candidates with enthusiasm and should include a deadline for response. Information about candidate selection should be kept confidential until the offer has been accepted. The organization may have specific policies and procedures regarding job offers.[2]

The salary offered to a candidate will usually be competitive with salaries for similar jobs in other organizations in the same market and compatible with the organization's existing salary structure. The market may vary, depending on the position. For example, the market for a pharmacy technician may be local, whereas the market for a pharmacist or pharmacy manager may be regional or national. To preserve equity within the organization, the salary offered to a candidate generally should be consistent with salaries of staff currently in that position. When exceptions are considered, it may become necessary to reassess the compensation of existing staff.

In addition to salary, other commitments made to a candidate should be expressed in writing as part of the formal job offer. These may include the following:

- Date on which employment will begin,
- Supervisor's name and position,
- Position description,
- Performance standards and evaluation system,
- Next performance review date,
- Next compensation increase date,
- Expected work schedule and whether it is subject to change depending on future needs of the department,
- Employee benefits (e.g., insurance, vacation, tuition assistance, sick leave, holidays, and retirement and pension benefits),
- Miscellaneous commitments (e.g., employment bonus, relocation expenses, licensure reimbursement, payment for professional association memberships, and payment for attendance at professional education programs), and
- Potential drug screening (as applicable and in keeping with the law) or employee physical examination and the dates of these activities.

Retention

Staff turnover is costly. The time required to recruit and train new employees has been shown to cause a temporary loss of productivity in the workplace.[6] Staff turnover also has a negative impact on staff morale, which may further reduce productivity and increase turnover. Because individuals have varied needs and wants that may change over time, there is no consistent formula for managers to apply to ensure employee retention.[7–9] Each organization's experience will depend on such factors as the age of employees, the employees' stages in life and career, the organizational structure, the work environment, and the work itself.

Retention may compete with recruitment. For example, creating staff positions with exclusively morning shifts may help retention but hurt recruitment, because fewer candidates are interested in evening shifts. When competing issues arise, pharmacy managers must balance them with the short- and long-term departmental goals and the current demand for employment.

Each organization should identify and assess retention factors by examining the unique aspects of the respective department and organization. For example, a committee broadly representing the organization could be established to determine major retention factors. On the basis of this assessment, a retention plan should be developed. The plan should be reviewed periodically as the needs of employees change; employee surveys may help determine these. The following factors may be considered in analyzing staff retention:

- *Training period.* The department should devote sufficient time and attention to training. Prepare for the new employee's first day by providing him or her with key material in advance and by developing an organized training schedule. Introduce the new employee to key people on the first day and have everyone in the department introduce themselves during the orientation period. Communicate with the new employee regularly during the training period and throughout the first three months.[10] Sufficient training time ensures that the new employee is comfortable in the new work environment and decreases the likelihood that he or she will become frustrated in the new position. Some organizations have developed a structured mentoring program in which a new employee is paired with a senior employee during the training period.

- *Intent to stay.* In several studies, this factor was the best predictor of staff retention.[11] Employees can simply be asked whether they intend to stay. Replies will reflect employee perceptions and should be considered in light of behavior (i.e., the actual turnover rate). Replies also may be influenced by the employees' fear of reprisal.

- *Job satisfaction.* Job satisfaction is a measure of the degree to which individuals like their jobs, their work environment, and relationships with their coworkers. Job satisfaction is important to retention, although the relationship may be direct or indirect. Employees can be asked how satisfied they are with their jobs; there are many survey instruments to assist pharmacy managers and directors in performing this task.[12] Job dissatisfaction does not necessarily lead to staff turnover if other factors are more important to the individual.[13,14]

- *Pay and benefits.* These refer to the remuneration for work performed and the organization's overall benefit plan. Pay may be hourly (a wage) or salaried and may include overtime premiums or bonuses and incentive plans. A benefit plan may include life, medical, dental, disability, and liability insurance; tuition payments; retirement packages; paid organizational membership dues; sick leave; paid vacation; child care; and prescription benefits. The value of specific benefits to an employee will likely change over time. Many organizations offer a benefits plan that gives the employee the option of choosing benefits individually suited to stages in his or her life and career.

- *Performance management.* Performance appraisal is a periodic assessment of an employee's performance throughout the year. Performance appraisal is only one step in a performance management process that includes appraisal, ongoing feedback, goal setting, and development. This process is important to the success of the manager, the employee, and the organization. The goal of performance management is to share information that will help the employee grow, both personally and professionally, and improve the organization. Periodic discussions with the employee are necessary to provide and receive feedback and to avoid surprises at the time of the scheduled performance appraisal.[15] Direct observation and evaluation by supervisors and coworkers can contribute to a meaningful appraisal.

- *Recognition and awards.* Employees often feel that recognition is lacking in the workplace.[7–10] New supervisors or managers should receive training in employee recognition, which includes both formal and informal feedback mechanisms, from structured employee of the month (or year) programs to a simple thank-you given in private or at a department meeting. Managers should identify how employees want to be recognized, through employee surveys or informal discussions.[10] Methods of employee recognition include

  - Thank-you notes,
  - Commendations,
  - Acknowledgment at department meetings,
  - Organization-wide events during National Pharmacy Week,
  - Employee of the month, quarter, or year,
  - Support for attendance at a professional meeting, and
  - Small awards such as movie tickets or gift certificates for coffee.[16]

- *Promotion opportunities.* These may be in the form of formal promotions, career advancement programs, training opportunities, or special project or committee appointments. Flat organizational structures provide fewer formal opportunities for staff promotion. Employees who have made personal investments in the organization—through expanded responsibilities associated with promotion—may have stronger feelings of loyalty that translate into increased retention. Succession planning is a key organizational strategy that ensures the availability of future leaders.

- *Job design.* This refers to the general tasks that an employee performs—the content of the work. Job design includes autonomy, the complexity of tasks, and the support and tools provided to the employee. Studies have found that job content is more highly correlated with retention as the level of an employee's education increases.[11] Motivational theories suggest that the job itself can motivate intrinsically and that success in the job can lead to increased employee satisfaction.

- *Peer relations.* This refers to working relationships with peers, nurses, physicians, and technical support staff. Peer relations are often rated highly as a reason for staying with an organization. It is difficult to predict during the interview process how a candidate's peer relations will develop, but past behaviors and discussion of hypothetical scenarios can provide some insight.

- *Kinship responsibilities.* This refers to family considerations, such as child care needs, spouse-employment transfers, and care for elderly relatives. Child and elder care needs are important for working parents. These considerations are also difficult to screen for during the interview process, and they will change over time. Legal restrictions prevent recruiters from asking some questions; the organization's human resources department should be able to offer advice on this issue.

- *Opportunity.* This refers to other options in the job market. Obviously, tight job markets (a relative lack of alternative positions) increase retention, whereas open job markets (those with many other open positions) may increase turnover. Managers should always be attentive to retaining good employees, but in open job markets they need to be especially attentive.

- *Staff-development opportunities.* This refers to job training, educational opportunities, and tuition reimbursement or other educational and personal growth opportunities for staff. Training and educational opportunities can affect recognition and awards, promotion opportunities, job design, and peer relations, so they can have a big impact on employee retention.

- *Management style.* This refers to the organizational structure and prevalent management style in the organization (e.g., on the spectrum from autocratic to participatory). The accessibility of management staff may be a factor as well as the extent to which staff input is encouraged. Each employee will prefer a particular management style; no one style will work equally well for all employees. Managers must be sensitive to the management styles that are effective for their staff.

- *Employee coaching.* This refers to the manager's mentorship role. Managers should provide feedback to employees regarding performance, teach specific job-related skills, hold formal and informal career discussions with employees, help employees achieve greater self-awareness, advise employees on how best to prepare for career options, and assist employees in preparing a yearly career-development plan.[10] In addition, it is important that managers recognize and acknowledge the employee's contributions to the health system.

- *Management survey.* This refers to the organization's commitment to identifying opportunities for improving management. Such opportunities can be identified by surveying employees about their manager's performance. The survey should be conducted by each manager's supervisor. Managers should also complete the survey to see how their rating compares with that of their staff. Action plans should be established on the basis of the survey results.[10] Such "360-degree" surveys should be managed with caution, however; they may create animosity and foster unhealthy relationships between management and staff.

- *Physical working conditions.* This refers to the physical characteristics and safety of the workplace, such as space, equipment, noise levels, parking accommodations, and cleanliness.

- *Scheduling.* This refers to opportunities for varied scheduling, vacation time, shift rotation, job sharing, flexible hours, and part-time work.

- *Motivation.* Extrinsic motivators for change (such as salary, promotion, and recognition) can affect behavior, but they cannot change values and attitudes.[17] In the workplace, change occurs most readily when people are motivated by the desire to bring their professional activities in line with their personal and professional values and beliefs. Living vision and value statements offer employees an opportunity to shape an inspiring organizational culture. Although each employee's motivations will be different, some theories of motivation can help managers understand what contributes to job satisfaction. Maslow's[14] hierarchy of needs, for example, states that employees will be happiest when they are working toward self-actualization, which requires that their more basic needs for security, esteem, belonging, and knowledge be satisfied first. Herzberg et al.'s[18] motivation/hygiene theory explains that employees cannot be motivated by the "hygiene" aspects of their work (organization policies, supervision, salary, peer relations, and working conditions), but that dissatisfaction with those aspects can interfere with motivating factors (the work itself, responsibility, achievement, recognition, and advancement).

- *Exit interview.* An interview should be scheduled with a director of the department, the human resources department, and the exiting employee. The director should ask in-depth questions to identify why the employee is leaving. The exit interview should explore the employee's opinion of the company, department, his or her direct manager as well as any other issues the employee may have for leaving. Pharmacy managers should validate and share this information with the appropriate management staff to decrease the likelihood that another employee may leave for a similar reason.[14]

References

1. Poremba AC. Determining the department's staffing: writing job descriptions. In: Pharmacy management toolkit: tools of the trade for pharmacy managers and directors [CD-ROM]. Bethesda, MD: American Society of Health-System Pharmacists; 2001.

2. Nimmo CM, ed. Human resources management. ACCRUE level II. Bethesda, MD: American Society of Hospital Pharmacists; 1991.

3. Yate M. Hiring the best. 3rd ed. Holbrook, MA: Adams; 1990.

4. Wilson R. Conducting better job interviews. Hauppauge, NY: Barrons; 1991.

5. Smart B. The smart interviewer. New York: Wiley; 1989.

6. Donovan L. The shortage. *RN.* 1980; 8:21–7.

7. Smith SN, Stewart JE, Grussing PG. Factors influencing the rate of job turnover among hospital pharmacists. *Am J Hosp Pharm.* 1986; 43:1936–41.

8. Porter LW, Stears RM. Organizational work and personal factors in employee turnover and absenteeism. *Psychol Bull.* 1973; 80:151–76.

9. Loveridge CE. Contingency theory: explaining staff nurse retention. *J Nurs Adm.* 1988; 18:22–5.

10. Branham FL. Keeping the people who keep you in business. 1st ed. New York: Amacon; 2001.

11. Cavanagh SJ. Predictions of nursing staff turnover. *J Adv Nurs.* 1990; 15:373–80.

12. Section 7.5: employee satisfaction. In: Pharmacy management toolkit: tools of the trade for pharmacy managers and directors [CD-ROM]. Bethesda, MD: American Society of Health-System Pharmacists; 2001.

13. Johns G. Organizational behavior: understanding life at work. Glenview, IL: Scott, Foresman; 1983.

14. Maslow AH. Motivation and personality. 2nd ed. New York: Harper & Rowe; 1970.

15. Chrymko MM. How to do a performance appraisal. *Am J Hosp Pharm.* 1991; 48:2600–1.

16. Nelson B. 1001 ways to reward employees. New York: Workman Publishing; 1994.

17. Nimmo CM, Holland RW. The practice change model: an innovative pharmacy-specific approach to motivating staff change. In: Pharmacy management toolkit: tools of the trade for pharmacy managers and directors [CD-ROM]. Bethesda, MD: American Society of Health-System Pharmacists; 2001.

18. Herzberg F, Mausner B, Snyderman BB. The motivation to work. 2nd ed. New York: Wiley; 1959.

Appendix—Sample Questions to Ask of Job Candidates[2]

Questions for Experienced Pharmacists and Technicians

- How did you become interested in pharmacy?
- What skills or traits do you think a pharmacist needs to be successful?
- What is the single greatest contribution you have made in your present (or most recent) position?
- What is something you have recommended or tried in your present (or most recent) position that did not work? Why didn't it?
- How are you evaluated in your present (most recent) job?
- What would your present (most recent) employer say are your strong points? Your weak points?
- Why did you (do you want to) leave your last (present) job?
- Do you prefer working on a team or alone? Why?
- What part of the job did you like the best and least?

Questions for Recent Pharmacy School Graduates

- What was your most rewarding college experience?
- Why did you want to study pharmacy?
- What would you change about your college experience if you could?
- Do you think your grades accurately reflect your academic achievements?
- What subjects did you like most and least? Why?

General Questions

- What qualities are you looking for in your next supervisor?
- What supervisory style do you think you have?
- What are your long-term career goals?
- How does this position fit in with your long-term career goals?
- What are you looking for in your next position that has been lacking in previous positions?

Subjects About Which You May Not Ask

- Race,
- National origin,
- Religion,

- Age,
- Marital or family status,
- Child care arrangements or childbearing plans,
- Arrest records (although convictions related to drug use would be appropriate),
- Credit rating and other financial information (unless the position involves financial responsibilities),
- Military discharge status, unless resulting from a military conviction, and
- General information that would point out handicaps or health problems unrelated to job performance.

Approved by the ASHP Board of Directors, September 27, 2002. Revised by the ASHP Council on Administrative Affairs. Supersedes the ASHP Technical Assistance Bulletin on the Recruitment, Selection, and Retention of Pharmacy Personnel dated April 27, 1994.

The bibliographic citation for this document is as follows: American Society of Health-System Pharmacists. ASHP guidelines on the recruitment, selection, and retention of pharmacy personnel. *Am J Health-Syst Pharm*. 2003; 60:587–93.

White Paper on Pharmacy Technicians 2002: Needed Changes Can No Longer Wait

Introduction

The counting and pouring now often alleged to be the pharmacist's chief occupation will in time be done by technicians and eventually by automation. The pharmacist of tomorrow will function by reason of what he knows, increasing the efficiency and safety of drug therapy and working as a specialist in his own right. It is in this direction that pharmaceutical education must evolve without delay.

—Linwood F. Tice, D.Sc.,
Dean, Philadelphia College of
Pharmacy and Science (1966)[1]

Health care and the profession of pharmacy have changed enormously since Dr. Tice articulated this vision more than 35 years ago. The role of the pharmacy technician has likewise undergone substantial change. Technicians have increased in number. They may access a wide array of training opportunities, some of which are formal academic programs that have earned national accreditation. Technicians may now seek voluntary national certification as a means to demonstrate their knowledge and skills. State boards of pharmacy are increasingly recognizing technicians in their pharmacy practice acts.

Nonetheless, Dr. Tice's vision remains unrealized. Although pharmacy technicians are employed in all pharmacy practice settings, their qualifications, knowledge, and responsibilities are markedly diverse. Their scope of practice has not been sufficiently examined. Basic competencies have not been articulated. Standards for technician training programs are not widely adopted. Board regulations governing technicians vary substantially from state to state.

Is there a way to bring greater uniformity in technician competencies, education, training, and regulation while ensuring that the technician work force remains sufficiently diverse to meet the needs and expectations of a broad range of practice settings? This is the question that continues to face the profession of pharmacy today as it seeks to fulfill its mission to help people make the best use of medications.

The purpose of this paper is to set forth the issues that must be resolved to promote the development of a strong and competent pharmacy technician work force. Helping pharmacists to fulfill their potential as providers of pharmaceutical care would be one of many positive outcomes of such a development. The paper begins with a description of the evolution of the role of pharmacy technicians and of their status in the work force today. The next section sets forth a rationale for building a strong pharmacy technician work force. The paper then turns to three issues that are key to realizing the pharmacy technician's potential: (1) education and training, (2) accreditation of training institutions and programs, and (3) certification. Issues relating to state regulation of pharmacy technicians are then discussed. The paper concludes with a call to action and a summary of major issues to be resolved.

Many of the issues discussed in this report were originally detailed in a white paper developed by the American Pharmaceutical Association (APhA) and the American Society of Health-System Pharmacists (ASHP), which was published in 1996.[2] For this reason, this paper focuses primarily on events that have occurred since that time. Other sources used in the preparation of this paper include Institute of Medicine (IOM) reports,[3,4] a report to the U.S. Congress on the pharmacy work force,[5] and input from professional associations representing pharmacists and technicians as well as from educators, regulators, and consumers.

The Pharmacy Technician: Past to Present

A pharmacy technician is "an individual working in a pharmacy [setting] who, under the supervision of a licensed pharmacist, assists in pharmacy activities that do not require the professional judgment of a pharmacist."[6] The technician is part of a larger category of "supportive personnel," a term used to describe all non-pharmacist pharmacy personnel.[7]

There have been a number of positive developments affecting pharmacy technicians in the past decade, including national certification, the development of a model curriculum for pharmacy technician training, and greater recognition of pharmacy technicians in state pharmacy practice acts. The role of the pharmacy technician has become increasingly well defined in both hospital and community settings. Technicians have gained greater acceptance from pharmacists, and their numbers and responsibilities are expanding.[8–11] They are starting to play a role in the governance of state pharmacy associations and state boards of pharmacy. Yet more needs to be done. There is still marked diversity in the requirements for entry into the pharmacy technician work force, in the way in which technicians are educated and trained, in the knowledge and skills they bring to the workplace, and in the titles they hold and the functions they perform.[12,13] The absence of uniform national training standards further complicates the picture. Because of factors such as these, pharmacists and other health professionals, as well as the public at large, have varying degrees of understanding and acceptance of pharmacy technicians and their role in health care delivery.

An awareness of developments relevant to pharmacy technical personnel over the last several decades is essential to any discussion of issues related to current and future pharmacy technicians.[14,15] Policy statements of a number of national pharmacy associations are listed in the appendix. A summary of key events of the past half century follows.

1950s–1990s. Beginning in the late 1950s, hospital pharmacy and ASHP took the lead in advocating the use of pharmacy technicians (although the term "pharmacy technician" had not yet come into use), in developing technician training programs, and in calling for changes needed to ensure that the role of technicians was appropriately articulated in state laws and regulations.[16] Among the initial objectives was to make a distinction between tasks to be performed by professional and nonprofessional staff in hospital and community settings. This was largely accomplished by 1969.[14,17]

In the community pharmacy sector, chain pharmacies supported the use of pharmacy technicians and favored on-the-job training. By contrast, the National Association of Retail Druggists (NARD, now the National Community Pharmacist Association [NCPA]), in 1974, stated its opposition to the use of technicians and other "subprofessionals of limited training" out of concern for public safety.[14]

Largely because of its origins, technician practice was initially better defined and standardized in hospitals than in community pharmacies. As the need for technicians in both settings became increasingly apparent, however, many pharmacists and pharmacy educators began to call for collaborative discussions and greater standardization on a number of issues related to pharmacy technicians, and in recent years, progress has been made toward this goal.

The Pharmacy Technician Work Force Today. Based on Pharmacy Technician Certification Board (PTCB) and Bureau of Labor Statistics (BLS) estimates, there are as many as 250,000 pharmacy technicians in the United States.[8,18] This is a significant increase over the 1996 estimate of 150,000.[2] BLS predicts that pharmacy technician employment will grow by 36% or more between 2000 and 2010.[8] This percentage of growth is "much faster than the average for all occupations," but in line with a majority of other supportive personnel in the health care sector.

Pharmacy technicians work in a wide variety of settings, including community pharmacies (approximately 70% of the total work force), hospitals and health systems (approximately 20%), long-term-care facilities, home health care agencies, clinic pharmacies, mail-order pharmacies, pharmaceutical wholesalers, managed care organizations, health insurance companies, and medical computer software companies.[8] The 2001 Schering Report found that 9 out of 10 community pharmacies employ pharmacy technicians.[10] Recent studies conducted in acute care settings indicate that this figure is nearly 100% for the hospital sector.[19]

What functions do technicians perform? Their primary function today, as in decades past, is to assist with the dispensing of prescriptions. A 1999 National Association of Chain Drug Stores (NACDS)/Arthur Andersen study revealed that, in a chain-pharmacy setting, pharmacy technicians' time was spent on dispensing (76%), pharmacy administration (3%), inventory management (11%), disease management (<1%), and miscellaneous activities, including insurance-related inquiries (10%).[21] Surveys conducted by PTCB have yielded similar results.[18,21] The nature of dispensing activities may be different in a hospital than in a community pharmacy. In hospitals, technicians may perform additional specialized tasks, such as preparing total parenteral nutrition solutions, intravenous admixtures, and medications used in clinical investigations and participating in nursing-unit inspections.[22]

In the past, pharmacists have traditionally been reluctant to delegate even their more routine work to technicians.[14] The 2001 Schering Report concluded that, in the past five years, pharmacists have become more receptive to pharmacy technicians. Indeed, much has changed in the scope of potential practice activities for pharmacy technicians and pharmacy's perception of the significant role technicians might play.[10,22] New roles for pharmacy technicians continue to emerge as a result of practice innovation and new technologies.[9,11] Despite their expanded responsibilities, many technicians believe that they can do more. For example, one study reported that 85% of technicians employed in chain pharmacies, compared with 58% of those working in independent

pharmacies, felt that their knowledge and skills were being used to the maximum extent.[10]

Pharmacy Technicians: The Rationale

Several developments in health care as a whole, and in pharmacy in particular, have combined to create an increasing demand for pharmacy technicians. Three of significant importance are the pharmacist work force shortage, the momentum for pharmaceutical care, and increased concern about safe medication use.

Pharmacist Work Force Shortage. In 1995, a report by the Pew Health Professions Commission predicted that automation and centralization of services would reduce the need for pharmacists and that the supply of these professionals would soon exceed demand.[23] The predicted oversupply has failed to materialize; in fact, there is now a national shortage of pharmacists. A 2000 report of the federal Health Resources and Services Administration (HRSA) stated, "While the overall supply of pharmacists has increased in the past decade, there has been an unprecedented demand for pharmacists and pharmaceutical care services, which has not been met by the currently available supply."[5] The work force shortage is affecting all pharmacy sectors. Ongoing studies (by the Pharmacy Manpower Project and others) indicate that the pharmacy personnel shortages will not be solved in the short term.[24]

For pharmacy practitioners, the results of the work force shortage are clear: more work must be done with fewer pharmacist staff. Between 1990 and 1999, the number of prescriptions dispensed in ambulatory care settings increased by 44%, while the number of active pharmacists per 100,000 people increased by only about 5%.[5] Chain pharmacists now fill an average of 86 prescriptions during a normal shift—a 54% increase since 1993.[25] NACDS and IMS HEALTH estimate that, between 1999 and 2004, the number of prescriptions will increase by 36% while the number of pharmacists will increase by only 4.5% (Figure 1).[26]

Faced with greater numbers of prescriptions to dispense, pharmacists have less time to counsel patients. Working conditions and schedules have deteriorated, and job-related stress has risen.[10] Professional satisfaction has diminished. Perhaps most ominous, fatigue and overwork increase the potential for medication errors.[5,27]

Increased use of technicians is one obvious way of reducing workload pressures and freeing pharmacists to spend more time with patients. A white paper issued in 1999 by APhA, NACDS, and NCPA emphasized the need for augmenting the pharmacist's resources through the appropriate use of pharmacy technicians and the enhanced use of technology.[28]

The situation in pharmacy is not unique. A report from the IOM concluded that the health care system, as currently structured, does not make the best use of its resources.[4] Broader use of pharmacy technicians, in itself, will not solve the pharmacist work force crisis. It would ensure, however, that the profession makes better use of existing resources.

Momentum for Pharmaceutical Care. More than a decade ago, Hepler and Strand[29] expressed the societal need for pharmaceutical care. Since that time, the concept has been refined, and its impact on the health care system and patient care has been documented. Studies have shown that pharmaceutical care can improve patient outcomes, reduce the

Figure 1. Community prescriptions and pharmacists, 1992–2005. Rx = prescriptions, RPh (FTE) = registered pharmacist (full-time equivalent). Reprinted, with permission, from reference 26.

incidence of negative therapeutic outcomes, and avoid the economic costs resulting from such negative outcomes.[30–33] Nonetheless, other studies indicate that pharmacists continue to spend much of their time performing routine product-handling functions.[19,20] Widespread implementation of pharmaceutical care, a goal for the entire profession, has been difficult to achieve thus far.

Technicians are instrumental to the advancement of pharmaceutical care. As Strand[34,35] suggested, prerequisites to successful implementation of pharmaceutical care include enthusiastic pharmacists, pharmacy supportive personnel willing to work in a pharmacy where dispensing is done by technicians rather than pharmacists, and a different mindset i.e., the pharmacist will no longer be expected to "count and pour" but to care for patients.

In other words, implementation of pharmaceutical care requires a fundamental change in the way pharmacies operate. Pharmacists must relinquish routine product-handling functions to competent technicians and technology. This is a difficult shift for many pharmacists to make, and pharmacists may need guidance on how to do it. For example, they may need training in how to work effectively with technicians. Recognizing this need, some practice sites have developed successful practice models of pharmacy technicians working with pharmacists to improve patient care. Several of these sites have been recognized through PTCB's "Innovations in Pharmaceutical Care Award."[36]

Safe Medication Use. Used inappropriately, medications may cause unnecessary suffering, increased health care expenditures, patient harm, or even death.[33] Ernst and Grizzle[37] estimated that the total cost of drug-related morbidity and mortality in the ambulatory care setting in 2000 was more than $177 billion—more than the cost of the medications themselves. They stressed the urgent need for strategies to prevent drug-related morbidity and mortality.

The problems associated with inappropriate medication use have received broad publicity in recent years. For example, *To Err Is Human: Building a Safer Health System* drew attention to medical errors.[3] It criticized the silence that

too often surrounds the issue. Many members of the public were shocked to realize that the system in which they place so much trust was far from perfect.

Sometimes pharmacists have been implicated in medication errors. Technicians, too, have not escaped culpability.[38–43] Several studies, most of which were performed in hospitals, have, however, demonstrated that appropriately trained and supervised pharmacy technicians can have a positive effect on equalizing the distributive workload, reducing medication errors, allowing more time for clinical pharmacy practice, and checking the work of other technical personnel.[44,45] One study found that pharmacy technicians, when specially trained for the purpose, were as accurate as pharmacists in checking for dispensing errors.[46] The United States Pharmacopeia Medication Errors Reporting Program (USPMERP) has noted the contributions that pharmacy technicians can make to medication error prevention through their involvement in inventory management (e.g., identifying problems relating to "look-alike" labeling and packaging).[47] USPMERP also affirms that a "team approach" and "proactive attitudes" of pharmacists and technicians are important elements in reducing medication errors. The National Coordinating Council for Medication Error Reporting and Prevention advocates that a series of checks be established to assess the accuracy of the dispensing process and that, whenever possible, an independent check by a second individual (not necessarily a pharmacist) should be made.[48]

Reports such as these call for an expanded role for pharmacy technicians in a much-needed, systematic approach to medication error prevention.

Preparing Pharmacy Technicians for Practice

Historical Overview. Originally, all pharmacy technicians received informal, on-the-job training. The majority of pharmacy technicians are probably still trained this way.[8,18,49,50] Nevertheless, formal training programs, some of which are provided at the work site, are becoming more widespread. As state regulations, medications, record-keeping, and insurance requirements have become more complex, there has been a move toward more formal programs.[51] Some employers have found that formal training improves staff retention and job satisfaction.[18,52] Another advantage of a formal training program is that it can confer a sense of vocational identity.[49]

Formal training programs for pharmacy technicians are not new; they were introduced in the armed forces in the early 1940s, and more structured programs were developed by the military in 1958. In the late 1960s, the Department of Health, Education, and Welfare recommended the development of "pharmacist aide" curricula in junior colleges and other educational institutions.[14] The first formal hospital-based technician training program was initiated around this time. Training programs proliferated in the 1970s as the profession sought to meet the need for a differentiated pharmacy work force.[53] Many of these programs were established in response to requests from hospital pharmacy administrators; at that time there was little interest in formally trained technicians in community pharmacies who continued to train technicians on the job.[54]

In the 1980s, ASHP issued training guidelines intended to help hospital pharmacists develop their own training programs.[7] ASHP recommended minimum entry requirements for trainees and a competency evaluation that included written, oral, and practical components. The guidelines were used not only by hospitals but by vocational schools and community colleges that wanted to develop certificate and associate degree programs.[49]

Acknowledging the importance of a common body of core knowledge and skills for all pharmacy technicians that would complement site-specific training, NACDS and NCPA developed a training manual, arranged into nine instructional sections and a reference section.[55] Each section has learning objectives, self-assessment questions, and competency assessment for the supervising pharmacist to complete. The manual focuses on the practical, legal, and procedural aspects of dispensing prescriptions, sterile-product compounding, patient interaction, and reimbursement systems. APhA and ASHP also produce technician training manuals and resource materials for pharmacy technicians.[56–60]

To date, most programs have referred to the "training" rather than the "education" of pharmacy technicians. Further discussion of the need for clarification of the education and training needs of pharmacy technicians is provided below.

Academic Training Programs. In 2002, approximately 247 schools and training institutions in 42 states offered a range of credentials, including associate degrees, diplomas, and certificates, to pharmacy technicians. The military also continues to provide formal training programs for pharmacy technicians.

Formal technician training programs differ in many respects, one of which is length. The *Accrediting Commission of Career Schools and Colleges of Technology School Directory* lists 36 "pharmacy" programs.[12] These programs vary in length from 540 to 2145 contact hours (24–87 weeks), with a median of 970 hours. ASHP, which accredits technician training programs, requires that programs have a minimum of 600 contact hours and a minimum duration of 15 weeks.[61] The Pharmacy Technicians Educators Council (PTEC), an association representing pharmacy technician educators, supports the ASHP minimum requirements.[62]

The minimum acceptable length of the program is a matter of debate. Some pharmacy technician educators de-

plore a move within the education system to get people into the work force quickly. They believe that the pharmacy profession should make it clear that, while work force shortages and the needs of the marketplace are important considerations, rapid-training strategies do not seem appropriate for health care personnel whose activities directly affect the safe and effective use of medications.[51] There should be a clear relationship between the nature and intensity of education, training, and the scope of practice.

Entrance requirements for training programs also vary. Some have expressed concern that a substantial number of trainees may lack the necessary basic skills and aptitude to perform the functions expected of technicians.[51] The fact that about 30% of a certified pharmacy technician's time is spent performing tasks that require mathematical calculations reinforces the importance of suitably qualified training applicants.[21] ASHP acknowledged the need for minimum qualifications for training program applicants more than 20 years ago, but the issue continues to be a matter of debate.[7]

Progress Toward Standardization: The Model Curriculum. The absence of national training standards and the resultant variations in program content, length, and quality are barriers to the development of a strong technician work force. The problem is not unique to pharmacy technician training; other occupations in the health care sector also lack national standards. Nonetheless, it is ironic that persons in certain other occupations whose services have far less impact on public safety than do those of pharmacy technicians (e.g., barbers and cosmetologists) have training programs that, on average, are longer and less diverse than are pharmacy technician programs.[63] Reflecting a common sentiment on this issue, a 1999 PTEC survey concluded that "Expansion of the role of pharmacy technicians must be in tandem with standardizing training and establishment of competencies. Increased responsibilities should be commensurate with increased education."[64] Likewise, there was a consensus at the Third PTCB Stakeholders' Forum, held in June 2001, that national standards for pharmacy technician training are needed.[65]

Progress toward standardization has been facilitated by the *Model Curriculum for Pharmacy Technician Training*.[66] Having taken the initiative and the leadership role, ASHP collaborated with several other pharmacy associations (APhA, the American Association of Pharmacy Technicians, PTEC, the American Association of Colleges of Pharmacy [first edition only], and NACDS [second edition only]) to develop the *Model Curriculum*. The first edition, released in 1996, was based on the findings of the 1992–94 *Scope of Pharmacy Practice Project*.[67] Many of the revisions in the second edition, released in 2001, were based on a 1999 PTCB task analysis and accounted for changes in the scope of activities of today's pharmacy technicians as well as changes expected to occur over the next five years.[21,22] Significant changes were made, for example, in sections dealing with the technician's role in enhancing safe medication use, assisting with immunizations, and using "tech–check–tech" (a system in which pharmacy technicians are responsible for checking the work of other technicians with minimal pharmacist oversight).

The organizations that developed the model curriculum do not expect that every training program will cover every goal and objective of the curriculum; rather, the curriculum should be seen as a "menu" of possible learning outcomes. The model curriculum provides a starting point for identifying core competencies for pharmacy technicians.[22] It acknowledges the need for a level of understanding of basic therapeutics, anatomy, physiology, and pharmacology. The curriculum does not include recommendations regarding the relative amount of time that should be allotted to each module, but such guidelines are under consideration.[68]

The Future Preparation of Pharmacy Technicians: Education Versus Training. Virtually all the consensus-development meetings and studies that have investigated training requirements for pharmacy technicians have called for the development of standardized training in some form.[51,69] APhA and ASHP concur with this position.[2,70,71]

Such a recommendation would best be accompanied by two important caveats. The first is that any national standards for education and training of pharmacy technicians will not eliminate the need for additional, site-specific training that focuses on local policies and procedures.[52,65] Second, standards-based education or training can conceivably be delivered successfully in a variety of different settings.

However, what exactly is meant when the terms education and training are applied to pharmacy technicians? They have tended in the past to be used somewhat interchangeably. However, a distinction needs to be made and a balance between the two needs to be reached to ensure that pharmacy technicians are adequately and appropriately prepared to perform, in a safe and efficient manner, the functions and responsibilities that are assigned to them—both now and in the future. As has already been noted in this paper, the roles and responsibilities of pharmacy technicians have evolved and expanded in recent years. While, in the main, pharmacy technicians perform routine tasks that do not require the professional judgment of a pharmacist, state pharmacy practice acts now recognize that pharmacy technicians are being assigned new and different functions in the practice setting, some of which may require a higher level of judgment or extensive product knowledge and understanding.

Training involves learning through specialized instruction, repetition and practice of a task or series of tasks until proficiency is achieved. Education, on the other hand, involves a deeper understanding of a subject, based on explanation and reasoning, through systematic instruction and teaching. People may be proficient in performing a task without knowing why they are doing it, why it is important, or the logic behind the steps being performed. While education (as described above) may involve a training component, both are vital to the learning (or preparation) of the technician. Barrow and Milburn[72] give a useful treatise on this subject. The education and training of pharmacy technicians and other supportive personnel must be commensurate with the roles they are performing. To ensure quality, both the education and training components should be standards based.

Accreditation of Pharmacy Technician Education and Training

The Council on Credentialing in Pharmacy (CCP) defines accreditation as "the process by which a private association, organization, or government agency, after initial and periodic evaluations, grants recognition to an organization that has met certain established criteria."[73] Accreditation is an integral aspect of ensuring a quality educational experience.

For pharmacy technician education and training, there are two types of accreditation: programmatic (also referred to as specialized) and institutional. Programmatic accreditation focuses specifically on an individual program, whereas institutional accreditation evaluates the educational institution as a whole, with less specific attention paid to the standards of individual programs offered by the institution. Institutional accreditors operate either on a regional or national basis; the latter usually has a more focused area of interest. A system of dual accreditation, in which institutional accreditation is conducted by regional accrediting bodies and programmatic accreditation is conducted by the American Council on Pharmaceutical Education (ACPE), has worked well for schools and colleges of pharmacy since the 1930s.

Based on information obtained from published directories, it is estimated that only 43% of the 247 schools and training institutions referred to earlier are accredited by bodies specializing in technical, allied health, and paraprofessional education; 36% have their programs accredited by ASHP; and 12% are accredited by both ASHP and one or more of the institutional accrediting bodies specializing in technical, allied health, and paraprofessional education.

Institutional Accreditation. For institutions offering pharmacy technician training, national institutional accreditation is carried out by at least four agencies: the Accrediting Commission of Career Schools and Colleges of Technology (ACCSCT), the Accrediting Bureau of Health Education Schools (ABHES), the Council on Occupational Education (COE), and the Accrediting Council for Independent Colleges and Schools (ACICS). All of these agencies are recognized by the U.S. Department of Education. None has a formal national affiliation with the profession of pharmacy.

Because there are no nationally adopted standards for pharmacy technician training, it is difficult for institutional accrediting bodies to set detailed program requirements. ACCSCT standards require programs to have an advisory committee, the majority of whose members represent employers in the field of training.[74] ABHES has a suggested curriculum outline for pharmacy technician programs. In an effort to improve the quality of their programs, COE and ABHES plan to switch from institutional to program accreditation.[75] Of some concern is the fact that such accreditation systems (for pharmacy technician training programs) would be outside the pharmacy profession and would not be based on national standards recognized by the profession.

Program Accreditation. Program accreditation for technician training is offered by ASHP. ASHP accreditation of technician training programs began in 1982 at the request of hospital pharmacists. Many hospital-based technician training programs were already using ASHP's guidelines and standards, but they expressed a need for a more formal method of oversight to ensure the quality of training. ASHP had already accredited pharmacy residency programs and moving into technician accreditation seemed a logical step.

Initially, nearly all ASHP-accredited programs were hospital based. This is no longer the case; of the 90 technician training programs currently accredited by ASHP, only 3 are hospital based. Over 90% of programs are located at vocational, technical, or community colleges.[76]

The objectives, standards, and regulations of the accreditation program, as well as a directory of accredited programs, are available on the ASHP Web site.[61,76–78] The accreditation standards are geared toward preparing technicians for all practice settings and require that pharmacy technicians be trained in a wide variety of practice environments and complete laboratory exercises before beginning their experiential training.

While accreditation is voluntary for both pharmacy degree programs and technician training programs, an important distinction exists. State boards of pharmacy and the National Association of Boards of Pharmacy (NABP) have recognized ACPE accreditation as an eligibility requirement for the North American Pharmacy Licensure Examination (NAPLEX).[79] Completion of an accredited program is not usually a prerequisite for employment, registration, or certification as a pharmacy technician. However, accreditation does bring a number of benefits. For the program, the benefits include enhanced recruitment potential for trainees, improved marketing, and the opportunity for peer review and quality improvement. For employers, completion of an accredited program may be an indication of the level of competence of a technician. Most importantly, accreditation provides all stakeholders with an objective, external, and independent evaluation of the quality of the education or training experience. Employers have a strong interest in the quality of training of their employees, not least of which is in terms of potential liability issues if the employer provides the training. Therefore, it would appear to be in the best interest of employers for the onus of quality assurance to rest with an independent party.

A New Role for ACPE? ASHP recognizes that the education, training, and utilization of pharmacy technicians now have broader professional implications than when it introduced its accreditation program began in 1982. For this reason, ASHP has asked ACPE to explore assuming responsibility for this function. Many people now believe that accreditation is best left to an independent agency that has no direct or indirect interest in the provision of training or in the activities of the graduates of the training program.[80]

Involving ACPE might have an additional advantage, should a decision be made to develop national training standards. ACPE, which has broad experience spearheading collaborative efforts to develop educational standards for pharmaceutical education, could be an appropriate organization to lead the process of developing uniform national standards for technician education and training. Responses to a 2000 ACPE survey indicate that more than 80% of respondents support further exploration of an ACPE role in this area.

Certification of Pharmacy Technicians

Certification is the process by which a nongovernmental agency or association grants recognition to an individual who has met certain predetermined qualifications specified by that agency or association.[2] For pharmacy, the PTCB, created in 1995, has been one of the most positive developments of the past decade.

"Certified pharmacy technician" (CPhT) is the only national credential available to pharmacy technicians. A credential is documented evidence of an individual's or program's qualifications or characteristics. Credentials may include diplomas, licenses, certificates, and certifications.[73] CCP was established in 1999. The development and application of credentialing standards for the pharmacy profession are integral components of CCP's vision and mission statements. PTCB was one of CCP's founding organizations. For a pharmacy technician, certification is an indication of the mastery of a specific core of knowledge.[2] Certification is mainly voluntary, although some state boards of pharmacy now require certification of technicians.

The PTCB examination is based on a task analysis that defined the work of pharmacy technicians nationwide: 64% of the exam is based on knowledge required to assist the pharmacist in serving patients, 25% on medication distribution and inventory control systems, and 11% on the administration and management of pharmacy practice.[21] By the end of 2001, more than 100,000 technicians had been certified with this program.[37] CPhTs must renew their certification every two years and complete at least 20 hours of pharmacy-related continuing education (including 1 hour of pharmacy law) during that period of time.

For many technicians, achieving PTCB certification is an important part of their professional development.[18] Many pharmacy chains have recognized the value of certification and provide assistance and incentives to staff to achieve certification, including reimbursement of costs, advancement to a higher grade, and a salary increase.[18] Studies have revealed that certified technicians remain in practice longer than do noncertified technicians.[81,82] Staff turnover, including both pharmacists and technicians, has decreased in pharmacies that employ certified technicians. Improved staff morale, higher productivity, reduced errors, and higher levels of customer satisfaction have also been noted. Additional benefits for employers include improved risk management, reduced technician training times, and lower training costs.[84] Some pharmacists feel more confident delegating dispensing activities to certified technicians than to technicians who are not certified.[10,21]

PTCB recognizes the need to reassess and modify its policies and procedures, as well as the examination, in response to the changing needs of pharmacy practice, the profession, and trends in the marketplace. To make such assessments, PTCB conducts research and seeks input from its stakeholders. PTCB also reviews its eligibility criteria for candidates who wish to sit for the certification examination. Under consideration are specialty certification assessments in areas such as preparation of intravenous admixtures and third-party-payment systems.

Regulation of Pharmacy Technicians

For many years, most state boards of pharmacy, often reflecting the attitudes of pharmacists, opposed recognizing technicians and expanding the scope of their activities.[52,14] As pharmacists' roles changed and use of supportive personnel expanded, these attitudes began to shift. Over the past five years, a majority of states have revised their pharmacy practice acts in areas related to technicians. Today, Ohio is the only state that does not formally address pharmacy technicians in state statutes or regulations.

NABP regularly surveys state pharmacy practice acts. The results of these surveys are bellwethers of change at the state level; collectively, they reveal trends. The most recent survey was conducted in 2001.[13] To highlight changes that have taken place since the publication of the 1996 "White Paper on Pharmacy Technicians,"[2] the results of NABP's 1996–1997[84] and 2001–2002[13] surveys were compared. NABP also appoints task forces to study and make recommendations on major issues. The deliberations of these task forces have resulted in, among other things, a call for formal recognition of pharmacy technicians, simplified state registration procedures, site-specific training, a national technician competency examination, and a disciplinary clearinghouse. Key developments in regulation, as evidenced in the

NABP surveys and in recent NABP task force recommendations and actions, are summarized below.

Changes in State Regulations: 1996–2001. *Terminology.* In the 1996–1997 NABP survey, at least 11 terms were used to describe pharmacy supportive personnel. At that time, 24 states used the term "pharmacy technician." By 2001, 38 states had adopted this designation.

Technician Registration. In its "model act," designed to provide boards of pharmacy with model language that can be used when developing state laws or board rules, NABP advocates that pharmacists be licensed and that pharmacy technicians be registered.[85] "Registration" is defined as the process of making a list or being included on a list. It carries no indication or guarantee of the registrant's knowledge or skills. "Licensure" is the process by which an agency of government grants permission to an individual to engage in a given occupation upon finding that the applicant has attained the minimal degree of competency necessary to ensure that the public health, safety, and welfare will be reasonably well protected.[2] Like NABP, ASHP and APhA support registration and oppose licensure of pharmacy technicians. APhA and ASHP believe that licensed pharmacists must retain responsibility and accountability for the quality of service in a pharmacy.[72,73,86]

By 2001, 24 states required registration and 5 required licensure of pharmacy technicians, in accordance with NABP's recommendations. Although the term "license" is used in these regulations, in some cases the process would appear to more closely resemble "registration" in terms of the definitions used in this paper. The increase in the number of states (up from 14 in 1996) that now require either registration or licensure of pharmacy technicians is noteworthy.

Pharmacist-to-Technician Ratios. Since 1996, at least 25 states have liberalized their pharmacist-to-technician ratios (from a norm of 1:1 or 1:2 to 1:2 or 1:3). Some states further relaxed ratios in sites where certified pharmacy technicians are employed. In their 1996 white paper, APhA and ASHP called for a reassessment of mandated arbitrary pharmacist-to-technician ratios.[2] This stance reflects the organizations' conviction that pharmacists should be responsible and accountable for pharmacy technicians under their charge.[70,71] NACDS believes that each practice setting should be allowed to determine its own optimal ratio.[87] Following the recommendation of a 1999 Task Force on Standardization of Technicians' Roles and Competencies,[88] NABP encouraged states to modify or eliminate ratios in pharmacy settings with quality assurance programs in place.

Standard Training Requirements. Between 1996 and 2001, the number of states that had incorporated training requirements into their regulations rose by 34% (from 19 to 26). Training requirements had been recommended in 1996 by an NABP task force.

The training requirements that state boards have put in place are, in some cases, minimal. Many states require nothing more than a training manual; there are no detailed minimum requirements. California, Kansas, Indiana, and Washington, on the other hand, have enacted competency-based regulations or well-defined standards for training program assessment. Some states require continuing education for renewal of registration or licensure; others are considering such a requirement.

Technician Certification. Louisiana, New Mexico, Texas, Utah, Virginia, and Wyoming have made certification a requirement for registration or licensure. Texas was the first

to introduce the requirement in 1996. The law was implemented in January 2001; a provision exists, however, for certain technicians to be exempted.[89] In Utah, the licensing authority has defined compliance with minimum training standards, as well as certification and the passing of a law examination, as requirements for licensure.[90] Alaska, Arizona, Kentucky, Massachusetts, Minnesota, North Carolina, Oregon, Tennessee, and Texas have altered pharmacist-to-technician ratios, responsibilities, supervision, or other requirements on the basis of a technician's certification status.

Levels of Personnel and Scope of Practice. Based on findings of its 1999 task force, NABP has recognized two levels of supportive personnel: pharmacy technician and certified pharmacy technician, and specified the scope of practice that would be allowed for technicians working under the supervision of a pharmacist.[91] Activities that cannot be performed by a pharmacy technician include drug-utilization review, clinical conflict resolution, prescriber contact concerning prescription drug order clarification or therapy modification, patient counseling, dispensing-process validation, prescription transfer, and compounding. The following activities cannot be performed by a certified pharmacy technician: drug-utilization review, clinical conflict resolution, prescriber contact concerning prescription drug order clarification or therapy modification, patient counseling, dispensing-process validation, and receipt of new prescription drug order when communicating by telephone or electronically unless the original information is recorded so the pharmacist can review the order as transmitted. The task force had recommended a third, and higher, level of supportive personnel—the pharmacist assistant—but NABP did not adopt this recommendation. APhA and ASHP likewise oppose the creation of this category of supportive personnel.[70,71]

Many of the changes in state regulations are reflected in the functions that technicians perform. For example, the number of states allowing a pharmacy technician to call a physician for refill authorization increased by 41% (from 25 to 36) in hospital and institutional settings and by 47% (from 24 to 36) in a community setting between 1996 and 2001. Few states have traditionally allowed pharmacy technicians in any work setting to accept called-in (new) prescriptions from a physician's office, and there was little change in this area over the past five years. There was also little change in the dispensing-related activities that pharmacy technicians perform; however, the percentage of states allowing these activities was already high (>85% in 1996). The only dispensing-related activity to show a more than 15% increase (in the number of states that allow it) in the past five years is the reconstitution of oral liquids, which increased by 22% (from 41 to 51) in hospitals and by 23% (from 40 to 50) in community settings. In hospital and institutional settings, the number of states allowing technicians to compound medications for dispensing increased by 33% (from 34 to 46); the number increased by 24% (from 34 to 43) in the community setting.

Competency Assessment. In May 2000, NABP resolved that it would (1) develop a national program to assess the competencies necessary for technicians to safely assist in the practice of pharmacy, (2) review existing technician certification programs to determine whether the development of its competence assessment program should be a cooperative effort with other groups, and (3) urge state boards to use this program as one criterion in determining the eligibility of technicians to assist in the practice of pharmacy.[92] NABP has now joined PTCB on the national certification program for pharmacy technicians and will work with state boards of pharmacy to encourage acceptance of the PTCB certification program as a recognized assessment tool for pharmacy technicians.[93] The use of the PTCB certification program will also be incorporated into NABP's *Model State Pharmacy Act and Model Rules*.

The Need for Regulation. The difficulties stemming from lack of regulatory oversight over pharmacy technicians go further than one might initially foresee. For example, if state regulations do not recognize a class of personnel (through registration or licensure), it is difficult to discipline such personnel in the event of misconduct. Several state boards have reported that the absence of such regulation is creating problems (Rouse MJ, personal communication, 2001 Oct and Nov). For example, in the absence of adequate controls, pharmacy technicians who have committed an act of misconduct, such as drug diversion, can move from site to site, or state to state, without being traced or being held accountable. NABP and many state executives and pharmacists have called for better systems of control and measures to track disciplinary actions. By 2000, at least 25 states had incorporated disciplinary procedures for technicians in their regulations.[92]

Among the regulatory issues that remain in flux, none is more important than defining the roles and responsibilities of supportive personnel and the titles they are assigned. Pharmacy supportive personnel perform a wide array of services. Some state regulations recognize this and have differentiated levels of supportive personnel; some states have specific requirements for technicians-in-training. Multiple levels of pharmacy supportive personnel may continue to be required in the future, and the levels may vary among and within practice settings. The profession needs to determine what these levels should be and to define the role and function, competencies, education, training, and level of supervision appropriate for each.

Time for Action

Pharmacy faces a serious work force shortage at a time when the public and health care providers alike are looking to pharmacists to assume expanded responsibility for better medication use. Better use of human resources is essential. When pharmacists limit their direct involvement in the technical aspects of dispensing, delegate this responsibility to pharmacy technicians working under their supervision, and increase the use of automated dispensing technology, they can fully concentrate on the services for which they are uniquely educated and trained. Only then will Dr. Tice's vision of the future become reality.

The utilization, education, training, and regulation of pharmacy technicians have changed dramatically in the past five years. National certification has played a particularly important role in these changes. Nonetheless, many challenges remain. Because these challenges are interrelated, resolving them requires a coordinated approach. The profession needs a shared vision for pharmacy technicians and other supportive personnel. This vision will provide the framework within which further necessary change can take place. Beginning with that much-needed vision, the major issues to be discussed and resolved might be expressed as follows:

1. *Vision*
    a. Define a vision for pharmacy technicians as an integral part of the vision and mission of the profession of pharmacy.
    b. Develop goals, objectives, and strategies to realize this vision, including determining who will lead the process and the specific roles, present and future, of all parties.
    c. Communicate the vision and goals to all stakeholders, including policymakers and the public.
2. *Roles, responsibilities, and competencies*
    a. Define the different levels of pharmacy supportive personnel and the responsibilities or functions appropriate for individuals at each level.
    b. Determine the competencies required for high-level performance at each level.
3. *Education and training*
    a. Establish standards (including eligibility criteria) for the education and training of each level of pharmacy supportive personnel.
    b. Establish requirements for maintenance of competence, where applicable, and create the systems to achieve this.
    c. Consider the cost implications of any new training model, and devise appropriate strategies to address cost concerns.
4. *Credentialing and accreditation*
    a. Develop or enhance appropriate credentials, in collaboration with PTCB and CCP, to reflect what is happening and required in practice.
    b. Determine what the most appropriate systems of accreditation for education and training programs for pharmacy technicians are and who should lead this process on behalf of the profession.
5. *Regulation*
    a. Determine the appropriate regulatory framework under which pharmacy technicians can optimally contribute to the achievement of pharmacy's mission.
    b. Work to bring about further changes in state pharmacy practice acts and regulations in order to achieve the desired regulatory framework.
    c. Work to bring about the development and adoption of standardized definitions and terminology for pharmacy supportive personnel.

Conclusion

Change does not come easily, and it is seldom embraced by everyone. As Kenneth Shine put it, when discussing the need for change in the health system: "The issue . . . will be whether these needed changes occur only begrudgingly as a reaction to external forces, or whether they occur proactively as a result of professional leadership."[94] The profession of pharmacy is changing in response to internal as well as external influences. Both pharmacists and pharmacy technicians are, therefore, part of an evolving partnership. Pharmacy must respond to the changes that are already taking place and be sufficiently creative and flexible to anticipate and accommodate future developments. The need to address the issues surrounding pharmacy technicians in a timely manner cannot be overemphasized. Proper preparation of pharmacy technicians to work with pharmacists is important in the promotion of public health and better use of medication. CCP, on behalf of its member organizations, offers this paper to provide a stimulus for professionwide action that can no longer wait.

References

1. Sonnedecker G, Kremers E. Kremers and Urdang's history of pharmacy. 4th ed. Madison, WI: American Institute of the History of Pharmacy; 1976:241.

2. American Society of Health-System Pharmacists. White paper on pharmacy technicians. *Am J Health-Syst Pharm.* 1996; 53:1793–6.

3. Kohn LT, Corrigan JM, Donaldson MS, eds. To err is human: building a safer health system. Washington, DC: National Academy Press; 1999.

4. Committee on Quality of Health Care in America. Crossing the quality chasm: a new health system for the 21st century. Washington, DC: National Academy Press; 2001.

5. Bureau of Health Professions. Report to Congress. The pharmacist workforce: a study of the supply and demand for pharmacists. Washington, DC: U.S. Department of Health and Human Services; 2000.

6. 1995 candidate handbook—national pharmacy technician certification examination. Washington, DC: Pharmacy Technician Certification Board; 1995:15.

7. American Society of Hospital Pharmacists. ASHP outcome competencies for institutional pharmacy technician training programs (with training guidelines). *Am J Hosp Pharm.* 1982; 39:317–20.

8. Bureau of Labor Statistics. Occupational outlook handbook. www.bls.gov/oco/ocos252.htm (accessed 2002 Apr 3).

9. Ervin KC, Skledar S, Hess MM, et al. Data analyst technician: an innovative role for the pharmacy technician. *Am J Health-Syst Pharm.* 2001; 58:1815–8.

10. Pharmacists, technicians, and technology: serving the patient. *Schering Report XXIII.* Kenilworth, NJ: Schering Laboratories; 2001.

11. Traynor K. Technician careers continue to evolve. *Newsl MD Society Health-Syst Pharm.* 2001; 24(4):1,4.

12. Accrediting Commission of Career Schools and Colleges of Technology directory. www.accsct.org/resource/resource_mainframe.html (accessed 2002 Apr 3).

13. 2001–2002 survey of pharmacy law. Park Ridge, IL: National Association of Boards of Pharmacy; 2001:34–44.

14. American Society of Hospital Pharmacists. Final report of the ASHP Task Force on Technical Personnel in Pharmacy. *Am J Hosp Pharm.* 1989; 46:1420–9.

15. American Society of Health-System Pharmacists. Chronology of ASHP activities for pharmacy technicians. www.ashp.org/technicians/chronology.html (accessed 2002 Mar 27).

16. Zellmer WA. Priorities for hospital pharmacy in the 1980s. *Am J Hosp Pharm.* 1980; 37:481. Editorial.

17. American Pharmaceutical Association. Report of the task force practitioner's and subprofessional's roles in pharmacy. *J Am Pharm Assoc.* 1969; 9:415–7.

18. Pharmacy Technician Certification Board: published and unpublished research, surveys, and employer consultations.

19. Ringold DJ, Santell JP, Schneider PJ. ASHP national survey of pharmacy practice in acute care settings: dispensing and administration. *Am J Health-Syst Pharm.* 2000; 57:1759–75.

20. Arthur Andersen LLP. Pharmacy activity cost and productivity study. www.nacds.org/user-assets/PDF_files/arthur_andersen.PDF (accessed 2002 Mar 27).

21. Muenzen PM, Greenberg S, Murer MM. PTCB task analysis identifies role of certified pharmacy technicians in pharmaceutical care. *J Am Pharm Assoc.* 1999; 39:857–64.

22. Model curriculum for pharmacy technician training. 2nd ed. Bethesda, MD: American Society of Health-System Pharmacists; 2001:iv,1.

23. Pew Health Professions Commission. Critical challenges: revitalizing the health professions for the twenty-first century. San Francisco: Center for Health Professions; 1995.

24. Gershon SK, Cultice JM, Knapp KK. How many pharmacists are in our future? The Bureau of Health Professions projects supply to 2020. *J Am Pharm Assoc.* 2000; 40:757–64.

25. National Association of Chain Drug Stores. Pharmacy: playing a growing role in America's health care. www.nacds.org/wmspage.cfm?parm1=378 (accessed 2001 Nov 29).

26. IMS HEALTH and NACDS Economics Department. Used with permission.

27. Kelly WN. Pharmacy contributions to adverse medication events. Conference report: understanding and preventing drug misadventures. www.ashp.com/public/proad/mederror/pkel.html (accessed 2002 Mar 27).

28. National Association of Chain Drug Stores, American Pharmaceutical Association, National Community Pharmacists Association. White paper. Implementing effective change in meeting the demands of community pharmacy practice in the United States; 1999.

29. Hepler CD, Strand LM. Opportunities and responsibilities in pharmaceutical care. *Am J Hosp Pharm.* 1990; 47:533–43.

30. American Pharmaceutical Association Foundation. Project ImPACT.www.aphafoundation.org/Project_Impact/Impact.htm (accessed 2002 Mar 28).

31. Johnson JA, Bootman JL. Drug-related morbidity and mortality: a cost-of-illness model. *Arch Intern Med.* 1995; 155:1949–56.

32. Johnson JA, Bootman JL. Drug-related morbidity and mortality and the economic impact of pharmaceutical care. *Am J Health-Syst Pharm.* 1997; 54:554–8.

33. Bootman JL, Harrison DL, Cox E. The health care cost of drug-related morbidity and mortality in nursing facilities. *Arch Intern Med.* 1997; 157:2089–96.

34. Strand LM. Building a practice in pharmaceutical care: Hoechst Marion Roussell lecture. *Pharm J.* 1998; 260:874–6.

35. Strand LM. Pharmaceutical care: Liverpool John Moores University seminar. *Pharm J.* 1998; 260:877–8.

36. Pharmacy Technician Certification Board Web site. www.ptcb.org/ (accessed 2002 Mar 28).

37. Ernst FR, Grizzle AJ. Drug-related morbidity and mortality: updating the cost-of-illness model. *J Am Pharm Assoc.* 2001; 41:192–9.

38. Lease D. Can you trust your pharmacist? http://speakout.com/activism/opinions/2850-1.html (accessed 2002 Mar 28).

39. Schuman D. When pharmacies make mistakes. www.news-sentinel.com (accessed 2002 Mar 28).

40. Levine J. Assistants' role in the spotlight: study finds mistakes by pharmacy technicians. http://my.webmd.com/content/article/1728.55198 (accessed 2002 Mar 28).

41. Stolberg SG. Death by prescription: the boom in medications brings rise in fatal risks. www.nytimes.com/library/national/science/060399sci-prescriptions.html (accessed 2002 Mar 28).

42. Hendren J. Pharmacy technicians dispense drugs: prescriptions often filled by lower paid technicians. www.capecodonline.com/cctimes/archives/2000/mar/7/prescriptionsoften7.htm (accessed 2002 Mar 28).

43. Dooley K. 'Support personnel' handle pills: few standards regulate important job. *Lexington Herald-Leader.* 2001; Oct 22:11.

44. Kalman MK, Witkowski DE, Ogawa GS. Increasing pharmacy productivity by expanding the role of pharmacy technicians. *Am J Hosp Pharm.* 1992; 49:84–9.

45. Woller TW, Stuart J, Vrabel R, et al. Checking of unit dose cassettes by pharmacy technicians at three Minnesota hospitals: pilot study. *Am J Hosp Pharm.* 1991; 48:1952–6.

46. Ness JE, Sullivan SD, Stergachis A. Accuracy of technicians and pharmacists in identifying dispensing errors. *Am J Hosp Pharm.* 1994; 51:354–7.

47. Cowley E, Baker KR. Liability for errors in expanded pharmacy practice: issues for technicians and pharmacists. *J Am Pharm Assoc.* 2000; 40(suppl 1):S56–7.

48. National Coordinating Council for Medication Error Reporting and Prevention. Recommendations for avoiding error-prone aspects of dispensing medications. www.nccmerp.org/rec_990319.htm (accessed 2002 Apr 1).

49. Ray MD. Training hospital pharmacy technicians. *Am J Hosp Pharm.* 1984; 41:2595. Editorial.

50. Reeder CE, Dickson M, Kozma CM, et al. ASHP national survey of pharmacy practice in acute care settings—1996. *Am J Health-Syst Pharm.* 1997; 54:653–69.

51. Keresztes J, Palmer M, Lang SM, et al., eds. National pharmacy technician conference: looking toward the future. *J Pharm Technol.* 2001; 17 (suppl):S1–26.

52. Sanford ME, Faccinetti NJ, Broadhead RS. Observational study of job satisfaction in hospital pharmacy technicians. *Am J Hosp Pharm.* 1984; 41:2599–606.

53. American Society of Hospital Pharmacists. ASHP long-range position statement on pharmacy manpower needs and residency training. *Am J Hosp Pharm.* 1980; 37:1220.

54. Eichelberger BM. College-based technician training programs: producing without planning? *Am J Hosp Pharm.* 1979; 36:992–3.

55. Schafermeyer KW, Hobson EH, eds. The community retail pharmacy technician training manual. 3rd ed. Alexandria, VA: National Association of Chain Drug Stores and National Community Pharmacists Association; 1999.

56. Marks SM, Hopkins WA Jr. Pharmacy technician certification: quick-study guide. 2nd ed. Washington, DC: American Pharmaceutical Association; 2000.

57. Posey LM. Complete review for the pharmacy technician. Washington, DC: American Pharmaceutical Association; 2001.

58. Hopkins WA Jr. Complete MATH review for the pharmacy technician. Washington, DC: American Pharmaceutical Association; 2001.

59. Manual for pharmacy technicians. 2nd ed. Bethesda, MD: American Society of Health-System Pharmacists; 1998.

60. Pharmacy technician certification review and practice exam. Bethesda, MD: American Society of Health-System Pharmacists; 1998.

61. American Society of Health-System Pharmacists Commission on Credentialing. Accreditation standard for pharmacy technician training programs. www.ashp.org/technicians/techstnd.pdf (accessed 2002 Apr 1).

62. The Pharmacy Technician Educators Council. PTEC recommended pharmacy technology program content. www.rxptec.org/rptpc.html (accessed 2002 Apr 1).

63. Rouse MJ. Analysis of 36 pharmacy technician programs, 36 barbering and styling programs, and 34 cosmetology and styling programs listed in the ACCSCT Directory; 2001 Nov.

64. Moscou K. Pharmacy technician educators' attitudes toward education and training requirements for pharmacy technicians. *J Pharm Technol.* 2000; 16:133–7.

65. Pharmacy Technician Certification Board. Third Annual Stakeholder Forum; Leesburg, VA: 2001 Jun 13–14. *(Proceedings not yet published.)*

66. American Society of Health-System Pharmacists. Model curriculum for pharmacy technician training. www.ashp.org/technicians/model_curriculum/ (accessed 2002 Apr 1).

67. Summary of the final report of the Scope of Pharmacy Practice Project. *Am J Hosp Pharm.* 1994; 51:2179–82.

68. Rouse MJ. Personal communication with Nimmo CM, model curriculum committee leader. 2001 Oct.

69. Technical personnel in pharmacy: directions for the profession in society. Proceedings of an invitational conference conducted by the University of Maryland Center on Drugs and Public Policy and sponsored by the ASHP Research and Education Foundation. *Am J Hosp Pharm.* 1989; 46:491–557.

70. American Pharmaceutical Association Policy statements.

71. Professional policies adopted at the 54th annual session of the ASHP House of Delegates. *Am J Health-Syst Pharm.* 2002; 59:1563–7.

72. Barrow W, Milburn G, eds. A critical dictionary of educational concepts. 2nd ed. New York, NY: Teachers College Press; 1970.

73. Council on Credentialing in Pharmacy. Guiding principles or pharmacy credentialing activities. www.pharmacycredentialing.org/ (accessed 2002 Apr 1).

74. Accrediting Commission of Career Schools and Colleges of Technology. Getting accredited. www.accsct.org/getting/get_mainframe.html (accessed 2002 Apr 1).

75. Rouse MJ. (Letters to Eaton CJ, Associate Executive Director, Accrediting Bureau of Health Education Schools, and Puckett G, Associate Executive Director, Council on Occupational Education.) 2001 Nov.

76. American Society of Health-System Pharmacists. ASHP-accredited pharmacy technician training program directory. www.ashp.org/directories/technician/index.cfm (accessed 2002 Apr 1).

77. American Society of Health-System Pharmacists Commission on Credentialing. ASHP regulations on accreditation of pharmacy technician training programs. www.ashp.org/technicians/techregs.pdf (accessed 2002 Apr 1).

78. American Society of Health-System Pharmacists. Pharmacy technicians. www.ashp.org/technicians/index.html (accessed 2002 Apr 1).

79. Pharmacist.com. Getting your license. www. pharmacist.com/articles/l_t_0001.cfm (accessed 2002 Apr 1).

80. Association of Specialized and Professional Accreditors. Member code of good practice. www.aspa-usa.org/ (accessed 2002 Apr 1).

81. Burkhart A. Pharmacy's challenging environment: technicians as part of the solution. Paper presented at APhA Annual Meeting. San Francisco, CA; 2001 Mar 19.

82. Nouri L. The utilization of certified pharmacy technicians with automation and technology. Paper presented at APhA Annual Meeting. Washington, DC; 2000 Mar 12.

83. Murer MM. Innovations for enhancing patient safety and new roles for certified pharmacy technicians. Paper presented at ASHP Midyear Clinical Meeting. New Orleans, LA; 2001 Dec 4.

84. 1996–1997 Survey of pharmacy law. Park Ridge, IL: National Association of Boards of Pharmacy; 1997:32–40.

85. The Model state pharmacy act and model rules. Park Ridge, IL: National Association of Boards of Pharmacy; 2001.

86. Gans JA, Manasse HR. Memorandum to executive directors of state boards of pharmacy, state pharmacists associations, and state health-system pharmacists societies. Bethesda, MD: 1997 Oct 20.

87. National Association of Chain Drug Stores. Issue brief. 2002 Apr.

88. National Association of Boards of Pharmacy. Report of the Task Force on Standardization of Technicians' Roles and Competencies. 2000 May 8.

89. Texas State Board of Pharmacy. Rule §291.29: exemption from pharmacy technician certification requirements. www.tsbp.state.tx.us/Pharmacytechs.htm (accessed 2002 Apr 2).

90. Utah Division of Occupational and Professional Licensing. Pharmacy Practice Act. www.dopl.utah.gov/ licensing/statutes_and_rules/58-17a.pdf (accessed 2002 Apr).

91. National Association of Boards of Pharmacy. Report of the NABP Committee on Law Enforcement/Legislation. 2000 Jan.

92. Madigan M. Regulatory evolution of pharmacy technicians. Paper presented at PTEC Annual Meeting. Toronto, Canada; 2001 Jul 10.

93. Pharmacy Technician Certification Board. News release 02-001. www.ptcb.org (accessed 2002 Apr 2).

94. Shine KI. President's report to the members. www. iom.edu/iom/iomhome.nsf/pages/2000+iom+ president+report (accessed 2002 Apr 2).

Appendix—Policy Statements of National Associations

The following statements are published with the permission of the respective organizations and were accurate as of March 2002, with the exception of (d), which was accurate as of June 2002.

(a) The American Association of Colleges of Pharmacy
(b) The American Association of Pharmacy Technicians
(c) The American Pharmaceutical Association
(d) The American Society of Health-System Pharmacists
(e) The National Association of Chain Drug Stores
(f) The National Community Pharmacists Association
(g) The National Pharmacy Technician Association
(h) The Pharmacy Technicians Educators Council

The American Association of Colleges of Pharmacy

www.aacp.org/Docs/AACPFuntions/AboutAACP/ 4308_CumulativePolicies,1980-2001.pdf

Policies On Supportive Personnel

- AACP supports inclusion in the professional pharmacy curriculum of didactic and experiential material related to the supervision and management of supportive personnel in pharmacy practices. *(Source: Professional Affairs Committee, 1990)*
- Training for technicians in pharmacy must be based on competencies derived from tasks that are deemed appropriate by the profession and currently performed by technical personnel. *(Source: Professional Affairs Committee, 1989)*
- Pharmacy schools should offer their assistance to supportive personnel training programs to assure that programs meet appropriate educational objectives. *(Source: Professional Affairs Committee, 1987)*
- Training for supportive personnel in pharmacy must be based on sound educational principles with clearly established competency objectives. *(Source: Professional Affairs Committee, 1987)*

The American Association of Pharmacy Technicians

www.pharmacytechnician.com/

Code of Ethics for Pharmacy Technicians

Preamble
Pharmacy Technicians are healthcare professionals who assist pharmacists in providing the best possible care for patients. The principles of this code, which apply to pharmacy technicians working in any and all settings, are based on the application and support of the moral obligations that guide the pharmacy profession in relationships with patients, healthcare professionals and society.

Principles
- A pharmacy technician's first consideration is to ensure the health and safety of the patient, and to use knowledge and skills to the best of his/her ability in serving patients.
- A pharmacy technician supports and promotes honesty and integrity in the profession, which includes a duty to observe the law, maintain the highest moral and ethical conduct at all times and uphold the ethical principles of the profession.
- A pharmacy technician assists and supports the pharmacists in the safe and efficacious and cost effective distribution of health services and healthcare resources.
- A pharmacy technician respects and values the abilities of pharmacists, colleagues and other healthcare professionals.
- A pharmacy technician maintains competency in his/ her practice and continually enhances his/her professional knowledge and expertise.

- A pharmacy technician respects and supports the patient's individuality, dignity, and confidentiality.
- A pharmacy technician respects the confidentiality of a patient's records and discloses pertinent information only with proper authorization.
- A pharmacy technician never assists in dispensing, promoting or distribution of medication or medical devices that are not of good quality or do not meet the standards required by law.
- A pharmacy technician does not engage in any activity that will discredit the profession, and will expose, without fear or favor, illegal or unethical conduct of the profession.
- A pharmacy technician associates with and engages in the support of organizations, which promote the profession of pharmacy through the utilization and enhancement of pharmacy technicians.

The American Pharmaceutical Association

www.aphanet.org

2001 Automation and Technical Assistance

APhA supports the use of automation for prescription preparation and supports technical and personnel assistance for performing administrative duties and facilitating pharmacist's provision of pharmaceutical care.

1996 Control of Distribution System (Revised 2001)

The American Pharmaceutical Association supports the pharmacists' authority to control the distribution process and personnel involved and the responsibility for all completed medication orders regardless of practice setting.
(*J Am Pharm Assoc.* NS36:396. June 1996)

1996 Technician Licensure and Registration

1. APhA recognizes, for the purpose of these policies, the following definitions:
   (a) Licensure: The process by which an agency of government grants permission to an individual to engage in a given occupation upon finding that the applicant has attained the minimal degree of competency necessary to ensure that the public health, safety, and welfare will be reasonably well protected. Within pharmacy, a pharmacist is licensed by a State Board of Pharmacy.
   (b) Registration: The process of making a list or being enrolled in an existing list.
2. APhA supports the role of the State Boards of Pharmacy in protecting the public in its interaction with the profession, including the Boards' oversight of pharmacy technicians, through their control of pharmacy and pharmacy licenses.
3. In States where the Board of Pharmacy chooses to exercise some direct oversight of technicians, APhA recommends a registration system.
4. APhA reaffirms its opposition to licensure of pharmacy technicians by statute or regulation.
(*J Am Pharm Assoc.* NS36:396. June 1996)

1971 Sub-professionals: Functions, Standards and Supervision

The committee recommends that APhA endorse the use of properly supervised supportive personnel in pharmacy practice as a positive step toward improving the quality and quantity of pharmaceutical services provided by the profession.
(*J Am Pharm Assoc.* NS11:277. May 1971)

1966 Sub-professionals

The committee would be opposed to any assumption of the pharmacist's professional functions by sub-professionals or technicians. There is a need to determine exactly what these functions are and the relative position of the pharmacy intern. Under no circumstance should a sub-professional program in pharmacy create an individual such as the former "qualified assistant" still practicing in some states.
(*J Am Pharm Assoc.* NS6:332. June 1966)

The American Society of Health-System Pharmacists

www.ashp.org
See also www.ashp.org/public/hq/ (accessed 2002 Apr 4).
See also www.ashp.org/public/hq/policy/2001Policy Positions.pdf (accessed 2002 Apr 4).

[Editor's note: ASHP policy position 0224 (below) has been superseded by ASHP policy position 0322, printed elsewhere in this book. ASHP policy positions are updated annually and can be accessed at ASHP's Web site at www.ashp.org/aboutashp/.]

0224

Credentialing of Pharmacy Technicians
Source: Council on Legal and Public Affairs
To advocate and support registration of pharmacy technicians by state boards of pharmacy (registration is the process of making a list or being enrolled in an existing list; registration should be used to help safeguard the public by interstate and intrastate tracking of the technician work force and preventing individuals with documented problems from serving as pharmacy technicians); further,

To advocate and support mandatory certification of all current pharmacy technicians and new hires within one year of date of employment (certification is the process by which a nongovernmental agency or association grants recognition to an individual who has met certain predetermined qualifications specified by that agency or association); further,

To advocate the adoption of uniform standards for the education and training of all pharmacy technicians to ensure competency; further,

To oppose state licensure of pharmacy technicians (licensure is the process by which an agency of government grants permission to an individual to engage in a given occupation upon a finding that the applicant has attained the minimal degree of competency necessary to ensure that the public health, safety, and welfare will be reasonably well protected); further,

To advocate that licensed pharmacists should be held accountable for the quality of pharmacy services provided and the actions of pharmacy technicians under their charge.

0212

Pharmacy Technician Training
Source: Council on Educational Affairs
To support the goal that technicians entering the pharmacy work force have completed an accredited program of training; further,

To encourage expansion of accredited pharmacy technician training programs.

0211

Image of and Career Opportunities for Pharmacy Technicians

Source: Council on Educational Affairs

To promote the image of pharmacy technicians as valuable contributors to health care delivery; further,

To develop and disseminate information about career opportunities that enhance the recruitment and retention of qualified pharmacy technicians.

0209

Substance Abuse and Chemical Dependency

Source: Council on Educational Affairs

To collaborate with appropriate professional and academic organizations in fostering adequate education on substance abuse and chemical dependency at all levels of pharmacy education (i.e., schools of pharmacy, residency programs, and continuing-education providers); further,

To support federal, state, and local initiatives that promote pharmacy education on substance abuse and chemical dependency; further,

To advocate the incorporation of education on substance abuse and chemical dependency into the accreditation standards for Doctor of Pharmacy degree programs and pharmacy technician training programs.

0025

Opposition to Creation of "Pharmacist Assistant" Category of Licensed Pharmacy Personnel

Source: House of Delegates

To reaffirm the following statement in the "White Paper on Pharmacy Technicians" (April 1996) endorsed by ASHP and the American Pharmaceutical Association:

"Although there is a compelling need for pharmacists to expand the purview of their professional practice, there is also a need for pharmacists to maintain control over all aspects of drug product handling in the patient care arena, including dispensing and compounding. No other discipline is as well qualified to ensure public safety in this important aspect of health care."

Further,

To note that some interest groups in pharmacy have advocated for the creation of a new category of licensed personnel called "Pharmacist Assistant" that would have (a) less education and training than pharmacists and (b) independent legal authority to perform many of the functions that are currently restricted to licensed pharmacists; further,

To support the optimal use of well trained, certified pharmacy technicians under the supervision of licensed pharmacists; further,

To oppose the creation of a category of licensed personnel in pharmacy such as "Pharmacist Assistant" that would have legal authority to perform independently those professional pharmacy functions that are currently restricted to licensed pharmacists.

8610

Pharmacy Technicians

Source: Council on Legal and Public Affairs

To work toward the removal of legislative and regulatory barriers preventing pharmacists from delegating certain technical activities to other trained personnel.

This policy was reviewed in 1997 by the Council on Legal and Public Affairs and by the Board of Directors and was found to still be appropriate.

The National Association of Chain Drug Stores

www.nacds.org

Issue Brief—Pharmacy Technicians (Issued October 2001; updated April 2002)

The Issue

Registration, training and certification of pharmacy support personnel (pharmacy technicians) and maximizing the duties that such pharmacy technicians can perform.

Background

Allowing pharmacy technicians to be utilized to the fullest extent possible without any ratio will:

- Enhance pharmacists availability to counsel patients and to confer with other health professionals;
- improve overall service to patients;
- ease workload and improve professional satisfaction for pharmacists; and,
- enhance efficiency and improve resources available for meeting the increased prescription volume and addressing the pharmacist shortages.

Certification of Pharmacy Technicians

- Certification should be voluntary and not mandatory.
- "Certification" exams should be effective tools for evaluating pharmacy technicians at the various pharmacy practice sites, such as community retail pharmacies, hospital pharmacies, and other practice settings.
- If pharmacy technicians decide to be certified they should be permitted to perform expanded duties and responsibilities.
- Pharmacy technicians, even if not certified, should be permitted to do routine nonjudgmental dispensing functions including, but not limited to, handling nonjudgmental third party and other payment issues, offering the patient the availability of the pharmacist for counseling, placing telephone calls to prescribers for refill requests, taking phone calls from prescribers' offices authorizing refill prescriptions, and preparing prescriptions for pharmacist's final review.

Pharmacy Technician Training and Examinations

- Boards of Pharmacy should allow for employer-based pharmacy technician training programs and examination pursuant to a Pharmacy Technician Training Manual.
- Boards of Pharmacy should recognize that employer-based technician training programs prepare technicians to work in their own particular practice setting, and that technician training programs should be designed to teach competencies relevant to the particular practice setting.

- Chain pharmacy technician training programs and examinations should receive Board approval.

NACDS Position

- Continue to permit an unlimited number of technicians and allow each practice setting to determine their optimal ratio.
- Allow technicians to perform non-judgmental tasks . . . those duties that do not require the expertise of a pharmacist.
- Allow technician training tailored to the pharmacy and to the company operations and standards.
- Allow certification to remain voluntary.
- Allow certified pharmacy technicians to perform additional duties and responsibilities commensurate with their competencies.
- Approve employer based training and examination pharmacy technician programs and recognize the importance of practice site specific training and examination programs such as community pharmacy based programs.
- Recognize the NACDS pharmacy technician training and examination program for certification of pharmacy technicians.

The National Community Pharmacists Association

www.ncpanet.org

NCPA supports the use of pharmacy technicians in community pharmacies to enhance the pharmacist's role in the provision of quality pharmacist care. NCPA believes the proper training and supervision of technicians by the pharmacist is critical to the health and safety of patients.

Technician Support and Technology:
Recognizing the current environment of regional shortages of pharmacists and the projected increase in prescription volume due to potential Medicare prescription drug benefit coverage and an aging population, NCPA recommends enhancing patient care and addressing manpower issues through the more efficient utilization of technician support and technology. NCPA strongly opposes the creation of any category of supportive personnel, which is not under the direct supervision of a licensed pharmacist.

The National Pharmacy Technician Association

www.pharmacytechnician.org/

Key Professional Issues
Medication Errors:
NPTA feels that the use of highly trained, educated and certified pharmacy technicians in the pharmacy profession will assist in efficiently and effectively reducing the occurrence of medication errors.

Technician Liability:
NPTA feels that with the emergence of national technician certification, producing increased roles and responsibilities, the issue of technician liability will become an evermore-present factor. Currently, NPTA does not have a position statement on technician liability.

Technician Education and Training:
NPTA fully supports formalized education and training programs at institutions of higher education. NPTA feels strongly that at some point, pharmacy technicians should be required to obtain a degree/certificate to be allowed to practice as a pharmacy technician. At this point, NPTA does not have a position statement on whether this degree should be a one or two year degree, when this policy should be implemented, or an appropriate approach for those already practicing. The requirement of formal education for pharmacy technicians, which is not present in most states, will be an integral part of the advancement of pharmacy practice, patient safety and a more efficient/effective healthcare system.

Technician Certification, Regulation and Credentialing
National Certification:
NPTA fully supports legislated requirements of certification by pharmacy technicians across the United States. National Certification is an appropriate and effective first step towards the educational and training goals for pharmacy technicians of the future.

Continuing Education:
NPTA strongly believes that an independent organization should be setup to accredit and monitor providers of pharmacy technician level continuing education programs. NPTA feels that while certified pharmacy technicians should be allowed to utilize ACPE CE Programs, that no organization (local, state or national) should make ACPE programs a requirement, since currently all ACPE programs are designed at the pharmacist's level.

The Pharmacy Technicians Educators Council

www.rxptec.org/

PTEC Recommendations and Goals
PTEC strongly recommends that all pharmacy education and programs seek ASHP accreditation.

PTEC strongly recommends that all pharmacy technician-training programs have a minimum of 600 contact hours, in accordance with ASHP accreditation standards.

In the short term, PTEC will:

- Work with AACP to design and implement programs which would provide step-wise technician training curriculum credits which could be used towards pharmacist training and education.
- Advocate a PTEC representative attend AACP board meetings, and invite AACP officers to attend PTEC board meetings.

PTEC advocates that:

- Within 5 years, all technician-training programs have a *minimum* of 600 contact hours; and
- Within 10 years, all technician-training programs evolve into 2-year associate degree programs.

PTEC recognizes the need for, and supports the development and introduction of, appropriate credentials for pharmacy technicians, including at the specialty level.

PTEC will work with AACP to design and implement programs which would provide step-wise technician-training curriculum credits that could be used towards pharmacist training and education.

The PTEC recommended pharmacy technology program content is published on its website: www.rxptec.org/rptpc.html

---

The following organizations have endorsed this document: Academy of Managed Care Pharmacy, American Association of Colleges of Pharmacy, American College of Apothecaries, American College of Clinical Pharmacy, American Council on Pharmaceutical Education, American Pharmaceutical Association, American Society of Consultant Pharmacists, American Society of Health-System Pharmacists, Board of Pharmaceutical Specialties, Commission for Certification in Geriatric Pharmacy, Pharmacy Technician Certification Board, and Pharmacy Technician Educators Council.

Development of this white paper was supported by an educational grant from PTCB.

Copyright © 2003, American Society of Health-System Pharmacists, Inc. All rights reserved.

The bibliographic citation for this document is as follows: American Society of Health-System Pharmacists. White paper on pharmacy technicians 2002: Needed changes can no longer wait. *Am J Health-Syst Pharm.* 2003; 60:37–51.

This document was also published in the *Journal of the American Pharmaceutical Association.*

Practice Settings

Practice Settings

Home Intravenous Therapy Benefit (0414)
Source: Council on Legal and Public Affairs
To support the continuation of a home intravenous therapy benefit under federal and private health insurance plans, and expand the home infusion benefit under Medicare Part B at an appropriate level of reimbursement for pharmacists' patient care services provided, medications, supplies, and equipment.
This policy supersedes ASHP policy 9004.

Pharmacists in Managed Care Settings (0205)
Source: Council on Administrative Affairs
To assume a leadership role as a membership organization in meeting the unique needs of pharmacists practicing in managed care settings (e.g., health maintenance organizations, preferred-provider organizations, pharmacy benefit management companies, and independent practice associations).
This policy supersedes ASHP policy 8801.

ASHP Guidelines: Minimum Standard for Home Care Pharmacies

Purpose

Home care pharmacies provide pharmaceutical products and clinical monitoring services to patients of all ages in their homes, including home infusion therapy, oral medications, home hospice pharmaceutical services, and parenteral and enteral nutrition. Pharmacists practicing in home care pharmacies provide a specialized form of pharmaceutical care to the patients they serve. Home care pharmacies, whether they are hospital-based, long-term-care pharmacies, community pharmacies, independent organizations, or multisite organizations, should be viewed as an integral component of the overall health care system.

Home care patients require systemwide continuity of care. Mechanisms should exist for appropriate and confidential sharing of patient information among responsible providers and caregivers across the continuum of care and in various components of health systems. Systemwide communication, through interfacing patient information systems, oral and written communication, and consistent product labeling, is important to optimize care and minimize the risk of health care misadventures.

The purpose of these guidelines is to outline the minimum requirements for the operation and management of pharmaceutical services to be provided by home care pharmacies. However, as noted, the provision of pharmaceutical care in the home care setting should be coordinated among other settings. Therefore, as applicable, these guidelines should be used in conjunction with minimum standards for other practice settings. Many of the topics outlined are the subject of other ASHP practice standards, which should be referred to for additional information and guidance. Because of differences in settings and in organizational arrangements and complexities, aspects of these guidelines may be more applicable to some settings than others. Managers of home care pharmacies should use their professional judgment in assessing and adapting these guidelines to meet their own needs and circumstances.

To ensure the safe, appropriate, and effective use of medications in the home, home care pharmacies should develop comprehensive services to address factors unique to home care. Caregivers such as family members, who often have no health care experience, should be trained to properly administer medications, operate medication administration devices, and monitor patients as necessary. Medications must be aseptically compounded, often in quantities sufficient for several days' use, and delivered under conditions that will ensure that product potency and purity are maintained. Vascular access should be maintained for the intended duration of therapy, which may range from days to years. Medication administration devices should be selected and maintained to accurately and safely administer a variety of therapeutic regimens. Potential complications should be anticipated, and a proactive plan of care should be established for monitoring, detecting, and managing complications. Economic considerations should be taken into account so that care is provided in the most cost-effective manner. Finally, home care pharmacies should have an effective organizational structure with the flexibility to meet the changing needs of patients, as well as to keep pace with the rapid growth of the industry and changes in health systems. As providers of pharmaceutical care in the home setting, pharmacists should be concerned with the outcomes of their services and not just the provision of these services. Effective management is necessary to ensure that quality outcomes of therapy are achieved.

The criteria for home care pharmacy that are covered in these guidelines are distributed among the following categories: (1) leadership and practice management, (2) drug information, education, and counseling, (3) care planning, monitoring, and continuity, (4) drug distribution and control, and (5) facilities, equipment, and information systems. Collectively, these criteria represent a minimum level of quality that all home care pharmacies should strive to provide consistently. While the scope of pharmaceutical services is likely to vary from site to site depending upon the needs of the patients served, these criteria are strongly linked to patient outcomes, and neglect of any one area may compromise quality.

Standard 1: Leadership and Practice Management

Effective leadership and practice management are necessary for the delivery of pharmaceutical services in a manner consistent with the needs of the home care patient, the needs of the home care organization and pharmacy, and the requirements for continuous improvement in patient care outcomes. The pharmacy manager should focus on the pharmacist's responsibility for providing pharmaceutical care and on the development of an infrastructure for supporting pharmaceutical care.

Managerial responsibilities include (1) setting the short-term and long-term goals of the pharmacy according to the needs of the patients served, (2) developing plans and schedules for achieving these goals, (3) directing implementation of the plans and the day-to-day activities associated with them, (4) determining whether the goals and schedules are being met, and (5) instituting corrective actions when necessary. The pharmacy manager, in carrying out these responsibilities, should supervise an adequate number of competent, qualified personnel. A part-time or contract manager has the same basic obligations and responsibilities as a full-time manager.

Managing the Pharmacy

Education and Training of the Home Care Pharmacy Manager. The home care pharmacy should be managed by a professionally competent, legally qualified pharmacist. The manager should be thoroughly knowledgeable about home care pharmacy practice and management. Completion of a pharmacy residency program and home care experience are desirable.

Pharmacy Mission. The pharmacy or its affiliated organization should have a written mission statement that, at a minimum, reflects both patient care and operational responsibilities. The statement should be consistent with the mission of the home care organization and parent health system, if applicable. The mission should be understood by employees, contract staff, and other participants (e.g., students and residents) in the pharmacy's activities. The development and prioritization of goals, objectives, and work plans should be consistent with the mission statement.

Laws and Regulations. Compliance with local, state, and federal laws and regulations applicable to the home care pharmacy is required. The pharmacy should maintain written or computerized documentation of compliance concerning requirements for procurement and distribution of drug products, patient information, and related safety from the state board of pharmacy, Food and Drug Administration, Drug Enforcement Administration, Health Care Financing Administration, and Occupational Safety and Health Administration, among others. Home care pharmacies dispensing drugs across state boundaries shall comply with out-of-state licensure requirements, as well as other state and federal interstate laws and regulations.

Policy and Procedure Manual. A policy and procedure manual governing the scope of the home care pharmaceutical services (e.g., administrative, operational, and clinical) should be available and properly maintained. The manual should be reviewed and revised annually or whenever necessary to reflect changes in procedures specific to the sites where the pharmacy's products and services are provided. All personnel should be familiar with the contents of the manual. Appropriate mechanisms should be established to ensure compliance with the policies and procedures.

Practice Standards and Guidelines. The practice standards and guidelines of accrediting and professional organizations, such as the American Society of Health-System Pharmacists (ASHP) and the Joint Commission on Accreditation of Healthcare Organizations (JCAHO), should be assessed and adapted when applicable to the home care organization, the scope of pharmaceutical services, and the patient population served.

Managing Financial Resources

Financial Management. Oversight of workload and financial performance should be managed in accordance with the home care organization's requirements. Management should provide for (1) determination and analysis of pharmacy service costs, (2) analysis of budgetary variances, (3) capital equipment acquisition, (4) patient revenue projections, and (5) justification of personnel commensurate with workload productivity. The pharmacy manager should be an integral participant in the home care organization's financial management process.

Drug Expenditures. Specific policies and procedures for managing drug expenditures should address such methods as competitive bidding, group purchasing, utilization- review programs, inventory management, and cost-effective patient services.

Manufacturers and Suppliers. Criteria for selecting drug product manufacturers and suppliers should be established by the pharmacy to ensure the quality of drug products and the best prices.

Reimbursement. The manager of the pharmaceutical services or home care organization should be knowledgeable about reimbursements for home care pharmaceutical services, medications, supplies, durable medical equipment, and, if applicable, nursing services support. Processes should exist for routine verification of patient reimbursement benefits and for counseling patients about their anticipated financial responsibility for planned therapies. A process should also exist for responding to service requests from medically indigent patients.

Managing Pharmaceutical Care

Committee Involvement. A pharmacist should be a member of and actively participate on committees responsible for establishing policies and procedures for medication use, patient care, and performance improvement, among other things. Also, pharmacists should participate in the activities of similar committees of a parent home care organization or health system, as applicable.

Medication Therapy Decisions. The pharmacist's prerogatives to initiate, monitor, and modify medication therapy for individual patients, consistent with laws, regulations, home care organization policy, and clinical protocols, should be clearly delineated and approved by the home care organization's authorized leadership.

Selection of Medications. Policies and procedures addressing the selection of medications should be available. These policies should be based on clinical appropriateness.

Home Care Medical Record Systems. Clinical actions and recommendations by pharmacists that are intended to ensure safe and effective use of medications and that have a potential effect on patient outcomes should be documented in patients' home care medical records. In addition, a patient medication profile should be maintained by all home care pharmacies regardless of where the dispensing of medications takes place. The home care medical record should include progress notes, laboratory test results, and other patient information related to determining the appropriateness of medications and monitoring their effects. The system should provide safeguards against the improper manipulation or alteration of records and provide an audit trail. An automated information system is preferred, but the system may be either manual or automated. If an automated information system is used, an auxiliary record-keeping procedure should be available for documenting medication information in case the automated system is inoperative.

Medication Histories. Pharmacists should prepare or have access to comprehensive medication histories for each patient's home care medical record and other databases (e.g., prescription and nonprescription medication profile), or both. A pharmacist-conducted medication history for each patient is desirable; however, a home care nurse may obtain and maintain current medication histories, provided this information is accessible to the pharmacist and other health care providers.

Patient Confidentiality. Patient confidentiality should be protected by safeguarding access to all sources of patient information, including financial (billing), medication profiles, and home care medical records. Patient information should be shared only with health care providers within the home care pharmacy, home care organization, or health system authorized to care for the patient. Written policies and procedures for access to and dissemination of confidential patient information should be available. All employees should respect patient privacy and maintain confidentiality during home visits and deliveries.

Clinical Protocols. The pharmacist should be involved in the home care organization's initiatives to develop model clinical protocols, care plans, pathways, or disease management guidelines to ensure that pharmaceutical care elements are included. Clinical protocols should be used whenever appropriate to maximize the safety of medication use in the home.

Preventive and Postexposure Immunization Programs. The pharmacy should participate in the development of policies and procedures concerning preventive and postexposure programs for infectious diseases (including, but not limited to, HIV infection, tuberculosis, and hepatitis) for patients and employees.

Substance-Abuse Programs. The pharmacy should assist in the development of, and participate in, substance-abuse prevention, education, and employee and patient assistance programs.

Twenty-Four-Hour Pharmaceutical Services. Home care pharmaceutical services should be available 24 hours a day, seven days a week. A pharmacist should be available for consultation or dispensing after hours. Home care pharmacy staff may be supplemented by knowledgeable and experienced part-time or on-call personnel to extend pharmaceutical services coverage.

Pharmacy Security and Access After Hours. Only authorized pharmacy personnel should have access to the pharmacy area. Other home care organization personnel may be in the pharmacy area only when an authorized pharmacist is present, in accordance with the home care organization's policies or as required by laws and regulations. In an emergency situation in which a pharmacist is not present, such as a fire or security alarm, policies and procedures should guide safe access to the pharmacy area and provide for notification of the pharmacist in charge or a designee.

Disaster Situations. Policies and procedures should be available for providing pharmaceutical services in case of an areawide disaster affecting the home care pharmacy or patients' home care settings. Patients should be informed about what to do to safely continue needed home therapies in the event of a disaster.

Institutional Review Board. The manager of the pharmacy, or a designee, should be a member of the home care organization's or health system's institutional review board.

Managing Human Resources

Work Schedules and Assignments. The pharmacy manager should ensure that work schedules, procedures, and assignments make the best use of pharmacy personnel and other resources. Resources should be sufficient to ensure patient safety.

Position Descriptions. The responsibilities and related competencies for home care pharmacy employees should be clearly defined in written position descriptions for all job categories.

Performance Evaluation. Policies and procedures should define the ongoing performance evaluations of home care pharmacy personnel. All home care pharmacy personnel should receive regular and timely evaluations. Performance should be evaluated on the basis of position description requirements and expected competencies.

Support Personnel. Sufficient support personnel (pharmacy technicians and customer service, procurement, delivery, clerical, and administrative personnel) should be available to facilitate the delivery of pharmaceutical care and services. Pharmacy technician certification by the Pharmacy Technician Certification Board is desirable; alternatively, technicians should complete an equivalent state-approved pharmacy technician training program, if available. Appropriate supervisory controls should be maintained and documented consistent with federal and state laws and regulations.

Education and Training. All personnel should possess the education and training needed to fulfill their responsibilities, including specific knowledge related to home care. All personnel should participate in continuing-education programs and activities relevant to home care practice as necessary to maintain or enhance their competence.

Recruitment and Selection of Personnel. Personnel should be recruited and selected on the basis of the requirements in the established job descriptions and candidates' job-related qualifications and prior performance. The pharmacy manager should assist in identifying the relevant professional and technical qualifications and should participate in candidate interviews and selections.

Orientation of Personnel. There should be an established procedure for orienting new and current personnel to the pharmacy, the home care organization, the health systems that the home care pharmacy serves, respective positions, relevant home care services, community resources, and the parent organization.

Managing Performance Improvement

Performance Improvement. There should be an ongoing, systematic program for assessing the delivery of pharmaceutical care and services. Performance improvement activities based on assessments should be integrated with the home care organization's or health system's overall performance improvement activities. Operational and outcomes data should be benchmarked with those of other home care pharmacies of similar size and scope. Outcomes, including follow-up actions, of performance improvement efforts should be documented and provided to the home care organization's managers and others, as appropriate.

Medication-Use Evaluation. An ongoing medication-use-evaluation program should be in place to ensure that medications are used appropriately, safely, and effectively.

Adverse Drug Reactions. An ongoing program should be in place for monitoring, reporting, and preventing adverse drug reactions. The pharmacist should submit reports of adverse drug reactions to FDA's MedWatch program and the drug's manufacturer, as appropriate.

Medication Errors. The home care organization should have an ongoing program to prevent medication errors. Pharmacists, physicians, nurses, and other appropriate home care personnel should monitor for and document medication errors. The home care organization should analyze the causes of medication errors and implement corrective actions. Medication errors should be reported to voluntary national reporting systems and, as required, to accrediting organizations.

Drug Product Recalls. Procedures should be in place for responding to drug and device product recalls, for identifying patients who received or used a recalled product, and for removing the drug or device product from the pharmacy or home when the recall is at the user level.

Standard 2: Drug Information, Education, and Counseling

The home care pharmacist should provide accurate, comprehensive general and patient-specific drug information to patients, caregivers, other pharmacists, physicians, nurses, and other health care providers, as appropriate, in response to requests, in the delivery of pharmaceutical care, or through educational programs. Physicians and nurses should receive adequate information about a medication's therapeutic use, dosage, potential adverse effects, and safe administration in the home—in particular, stability requirements—before the medication is administered.

Information about the stability of drugs for home infusion should include administration via a variety of alternative delivery devices. These may include portable infusion pumps, syringe pumps, implantable infusion devices, and common peripheral and central-line administration.

Up-to-date drug information resources should be available in the home care pharmacy, including current periodicals, the latest editions of drug compendiums and textbooks in appropriate pharmaceutical and biomedical subject areas, and any references required by state boards of pharmacy. Availability of drug information on electronic media is desirable. Information may be accessed and provided in conjunction with medical libraries and other resources.

Drug Information Requests. Responses to general and patient-specific drug information requests should be accurate and prompt. Drug information requests and responses should be documented and monitored for accuracy and timeliness as part of performance improvement activities.

Patient Education and Counseling. Home care pharmacists should be available for and actively participate in patient education and counseling. The pharmacist is responsible for ensuring that the patient and, as appropriate, the caregiver receive information, are counseled, and understand the patient's medication therapy. Patient education and counseling should be coordinated with the patient's other health care providers. The content and form of the education and counseling should be specific to the patient's assessed needs, abilities, and readiness, consistent with care plans and services provided. Patient and caregiver compliance, understanding, knowledge, and skills should be periodically reas-

sessed. A home care pharmacist should be readily accessible to patients and caregivers if questions arise. Patient education and counseling should be performed in accordance with applicable federal and state laws and regulations and documented in the patient's home care record.

Medication Teaching Materials. Educational material tailored to the patient and the medication therapy should be provided to the patient and the caregiver for use at home. Specifically, medication teaching materials for drugs most often used in home care practice should be available for dissemination to patients, caregivers, and other health care providers. These materials should be based on information most appropriate for safe medication use in the home. Educational materials should contain, but not be limited to, the following: name and description of the medication; usual dose; dosage interval; duration of therapy; goals of drug therapy; importance of compliance; proper aseptic technique in preparation for use (if applicable); proper administration of medication; inspection of medication, containers, and related supplies before use; common severe adverse effects, drug–drug interactions, drug–nutrient interactions, and their management; proper use of medication-related equipment and supplies; emergency-response instructions; instructions for storing, handling, and disposing of the drug; and procedures to follow if a dose is missed.

Dissemination of Drug Information. Pharmacists should keep the home care organization's staff informed about the use of medications on an ongoing basis through appropriate consultations, publications, and presentations. Pharmacists should ensure the timely dissemination of drug product recall notices, safety alerts, market withdrawals, and labeling changes.

Pharmacist Consultations. Pharmacists should provide oral or written consultations to other health professionals regarding medication therapy selection and management. Consultations should be documented in the patient's home care medical record.

Investigational Drug Information. The home care pharmacist should have access to information on all investigational studies and similar research projects involving medications and medication-related devices used in the home care, hospital, or alternate-site setting. The pharmacist should provide pertinent written information (to the extent such information exists) about the safe and proper use of investigational drugs, including possible adverse effects and adverse drug reactions, to nurses, pharmacists, physicians, and other health care providers participating in clinical drug research.

Standard 3: Care Planning, Monitoring, and Continuity

An important aspect of pharmaceutical care is optimizing medication use for individual patients. This should include processes designed to ensure the safe and effective use of medications and to increase the probability of desired patient outcomes. The pharmacist, in collaboration with the patient, caregiver, physician, nurse, and other health care providers, should be responsible for developing an individualized care plan for each patient.

Care Plan. The care plan should be based on information obtained from the initial pharmacy assessment and other relevant information obtained from the patient, caregiver, physician, nurse, and other health care providers. At a minimum, the plan should include actual or potential medication therapy problems and proposed solutions, desired outcomes or goals of the medication therapy, and the objective and subjective parameters for monitoring outcomes or goals and medication therapy-related problems. The plan should be developed at the initiation of medication therapy, reviewed, and updated, if necessary, on a regular basis according to the home care organization's policies. The degree of detail of the plan should be based on the complexity of the patient's health problems and drug therapy. The pharmacist is responsible for ensuring that the medication therapy (pharmaceutical care) elements of the plan are communicated to appropriate parties involved in the patient's care. All the patient's health care providers should routinely share care plan information and actions. The plans and updates should be a part of the patient's home care medical record.

Initial Patient Assessment. The pharmacist should ensure that each patient referral for home care is assessed for appropriateness on the basis of formal, predetermined admission criteria, as outlined in the ASHP Guidelines on the Pharmacist's Role in Home Care.[1] Before the start of home care services, patients should be informed of their rights and responsibilities. These should be explained in detail and given in writing to the patient and a family member or other caregiver. Once a patient is accepted for home care services, but before the initiation of therapy, the organization should ensure that the patient's current clinical status, home environment, and support systems are assessed. A thorough patient database should be prepared to identify pharmaceutical care needs and to provide the basis for ongoing medication therapy monitoring and for measuring patient outcomes. The patient database should be documented in the patient's home care medical record. Information that minimally should be included in the database is outlined in the ASHP Guidelines on the Pharmacist's Role in Home Care.[1] Information for the database can be gathered from the past and current medical record; laboratory test results; direct communication with the patient, caregiver, physician, nurse, and other health care providers; and the home care pharmacist's direct observations.

Medication Orders. Medication orders should be assessed by a pharmacist before the first dose is dispensed. A pharmacist should receive the physician's order. If not received by a pharmacist, the order should be verified by a pharmacist. The pharmacist should assess the order for the following:

1. Therapeutic appropriateness of the patient's medication regimen,
2. Therapeutic duplication in the patient's medication regimen,
3. Appropriateness of the route and method of administration of the medication,
4. Drug–drug, drug–nutrient, drug–laboratory test, and drug–disease interactions, and
5. Clinical and pharmacokinetic laboratory data for evaluating the efficacy of medication therapy and anticipating toxicity and adverse effects.

Any questions about the order should be resolved with the prescriber, and a written notation should be made in the patient's home care medical record or pharmacy copy of the prescriber's order. Information concerning changes should be communicated to the patient's other health care providers.

First-Dose Precautions. The pharmacist, in collaboration with other health care providers, should assess whether a first dose of a medication can be safely administered in the home or whether the patient should be referred to an alternative treatment site for the initiation of therapy. Policies and procedures should outline the situations and therapies for which medications for treating anaphylaxis should be dispensed so that the pharmacist can ensure that the appropriate medications are available when a first dose is to be administered.

Patient Education and Counseling. The home care pharmacist, or the nurse as the agent, should ensure that the patient, the caregiver, and other health care providers understand the proper use and administration of medications, including the intravenous access device and infusion device, as required. The home care pharmacist, or the nurse as the agent, should explain to the patient or the patient's agent the directions for use and any additional information. Also, prescriptions delivered outside the confines of the pharmacy should be discussed.

Medication Therapy Monitoring. After the initiation of medication therapy, the pharmacist collects and reviews data from physical and nutritional assessments, laboratory tests, and oral communication with the patient, caregiver, nurse, and physician (1) to evaluate the clinical status of the patient and the response to medication therapy, (2) to determine whether the patient's pharmaceutical care needs are being met, and (3) to ascertain whether the care plan designed for the patient is effective. The monitoring plan, which should be detailed in the care plan, guides medication therapy-monitoring activities and facilitates evaluation of the patient's progress by the pharmacist. Additionally, the pharmacist should, in collaboration with other professional staff members, monitor the following:

1. Functional status of the drug delivery system,
2. Patient utilization of medications, supplies, and equipment,
3. Patient compliance with the prescribed regimen,
4. Patient adaptation to delivery of care in the home, and
5. Patient satisfaction with the care and service delivered.

If the patient is responding and has no new identified pharmaceutical care needs or medication-related problems, but has not completed the course of therapy, pharmaceutical services should be continued as planned. If it is determined that the patient is not responding, or if new medication-related problems are identified, the plan should be revised and implemented.

Medical Emergencies. The home care pharmacist should participate in decisions about the emergency care of patients at home, including the development of protocols for using emergency drugs in the home.

Documentation of Pharmaceutical Care and Outcomes. The pharmacy should have an ongoing process for consistent documentation (and reporting to physicians, administrators, and others) of pharmaceutical care and patient outcomes resulting from medication therapy and other pharmacy actions. Patient privacy and confidentiality must be protected at all times.

Continuity of Care. The pharmacist should routinely contribute to processes ensuring that each patient receives pharmaceutical care regardless of transitions that occur across different health care settings (for example, among different components of a health system and different types of home care services). When home care patients are admitted to a hospital, the home care pharmacy should inform the hospital about (1) the medications the patient is currently receiving from the home care pharmacy and (2) known allergies. The home care pharmacy should recognize hospital policy when considering whether properly stored medications and medical equipment from the home can be used during the home care patient's hospitalization.

Standard 4: Medication Distribution and Control

The home care pharmacy should be responsible for the procurement, storage, distribution, and control of all drug products it dispenses (including medication-related devices and pharmaceutical diagnostics). Policies and procedures governing these functions should be developed by the pharmacy manager in collaboration with other appropriate home care organization staff members.

Processing the Medication Order

Medication Orders. All patient medication orders should be documented in the patient's home care medical record. The home care pharmacist should obtain a signed original of the prescriber's order, a direct copy of the prescriber's order, an oral order from the prescriber or his authorized agent, or an electronically transmitted, prescriber-entered order consistent with applicable laws and regulations. Safeguards should be in place to ensure the security of electronically transmitted prescriber orders. All medication orders should be reviewed by a pharmacist and assessed in relation to the medication profile and, as appropriate, an established procedure for using an approved list of medications for specific treatment circumstances and emergencies. A system should exist to ensure that medication orders are not inappropriately continued.

Prescribing. Policies and procedures should be available to ensure that heath care providers meet applicable state licensure and home care organization authorization, if required, for prescribing medications. The pharmacy should advocate and foster conformance with standardized, approved terminology and abbreviations when medications are being prescribed.

Therapeutic Purpose. Prescribers should be encouraged to routinely communicate the condition being treated or the therapeutic purpose of medications with all prescription and medication orders.

Preparing, Packaging, and Labeling Medications

Sterile Products. Home care pharmacists are responsible for ensuring the quality of sterile products intended for use in the home. Guidance is available for developing an adequately designed and equipped facility, training and validating em-

ployees, validating and documenting compounding procedures, practicing aseptic technique, monitoring the work environment, maintaining the facility and equipment, ensuring the quality of prepared products, and developing policies and procedures.[2,3]

Beyond-Use Dating. Home care pharmacies are often required to assign extended beyond-use dates to sterile products so that a multiple-day supply of medications can be dispensed and delivered. However, pharmacists should take into account circumstances that may affect the medication's potency and stability, including (1) delivery of sterile products to the home, either by the pharmacy's own vehicles or by a common carrier, (2) storage of sterile products in the home before use, (3) manipulation of sterile products in the home environment to add ingredients (such as vitamins) and to set up tubing and filters for administration, and (4) administration of products at temperatures that are warmer than controlled room temperature because of administration in outdoor or non-air-conditioned environments or the use of ambulatory infusion pumps worn close to the body.

Beyond-use dates should be based on the manufacturer's approved product labeling; however, information about the long-term stability of products for home use may not be included in the labeling. In addition, information may not accurately reflect the product's intended conditions of use in home care, including the concentration, diluent, container, and infusion conditions. The home care pharmacist should either consult the manufacturer for an appropriate beyond-use date or determine the date by reviewing the literature. Applying published stability data can introduce inaccuracies if the intended conditions of use differ greatly from the reported conditions. Pharmacists should maintain a record of the resources used for establishing beyond-use dates. A table or chart of accepted beyond-use dates, formulations, and conditions of use for commonly prepared products may be helpful in ensuring that assigned dates are consistent and appropriate. Patients should be trained to check products for current beyond-use dates prior to their use.

Packaging for Home Delivery. Products should be delivered in appropriate packaging to ensure that labeled storage requirements are met during transit under the expected environmental conditions. The pharmacy should develop and follow written procedures for packaging; these procedures should include privacy-protection considerations. Product confirmation after delivery should be used to ensure that the packaging procedures and materials used were effective in maintaining product integrity and temperature control during transit.

The stability of refrigerated products at room temperature should be taken into account when in the development of packaging procedures. A few refrigerated products have extended stability at room temperature and may be safely delivered without refrigerated packaging. Products that are stable for 24 hours or less at room temperature should always be delivered in temperature-controlled packaging (coolers, ice packs, etc.).

Labeling. Medications for home use should be labeled so that patients and caregivers can easily understand instructions for drug storage, preparation, and administration. Auxiliary labels should be used as necessary. When manipulation of medications is required before administration, labeling should clearly state current contents and the steps for measuring, reconstituting, or adding other ingredients. Labels for compounded medications should state the total content of the medication or nutrient per container so that it can be clearly known in case the patient is transferred to another treatment setting.[4] If medications are to be administered with an infusion device, pump settings should be included on the label.

Delivery and Handling of Medications in the Patient's Home

Delivery. Policies and procedures should be available to ensure product integrity and temperature control during home delivery or patient pickup of supplies and drugs. Delivery to the patient should include inventory management to avoid excessive accumulation of supplies and drugs. Excesses may indicate poor compliance, inadequate patient training, failure to assess patient needs, or ineffective inventory management by the patient.

When common carriers are used, the pharmacy is responsible for ensuring that the carrier can provide timely delivery, proper handling, and external temperature control. Delivery personnel should know the shipping requirements for each package. If refrigerated products are packaged so that product labels containing storage instructions are concealed, an exterior "Refrigerate" label should be used. To protect patient confidentiality, prescription labels with medication names and directions should not be used to label boxes. Box labels should include only the patient's name and address, the storage requirements, and delivery instructions.

Additional precautions (such as double bagging [including at least one leakproof container] and cushioning) should be used to safeguard hazardous products from breaking and leaking. The delivery person, patient, and caregiver must be trained to recognize and manage accidental spills. Packages containing hazardous products should have appropriate precautionary labels.

Universal Precautions in Patients' Homes. Home care pharmacy personnel delivering medications or supplies to patients' homes should use universal precautions. Patients and caregivers should be instructed on the application of universal precautions in the home. The provision of instructions on universal precautions, as well as the provision of other information and counseling, should be documented. Personnel should always wash their hands before assisting patients with the handling of supplies in the home.

Storage in the Home. The pharmacy should take precautions to ensure that medications are properly stored with respect to temperature, light, and other labeled storage conditions. If sterile or other products require refrigeration, appropriate methods should be used to segregate them from food to avoid contaminating the outside of the container. Patients, caregivers, or delivery personnel should be trained to check the refrigerator on a regular basis to determine whether temperatures are within an acceptable range to ensure product integrity. If the patient does not have an appropriate environment for storage of medications, the pharmacy should make alternative arrangements so that medications are properly stored. Drugs and supplies that do not require refrigeration should be stored in a separate, restricted location not accessible to children and pets.

Waste Disposal. Patients receiving hazardous drugs in the home should be instructed in proper waste-disposal methods that comply with federal and state laws and regulations. Needles and other sharps should be placed in appropriate disposal containers, and a process should be established for the safe removal and disposal of the waste. Local codes may have specific disposal requirements.

Medication Administration. Policies and procedures on the administration of medications should be available. Only personnel who are authorized by the home care organization and are appropriately trained should be permitted to administer medications to a patient. Pharmacists, where legally permitted, may be authorized to administer medications after receiving appropriate training.

The Patient's Own Medications. Drug products and related devices not dispensed by the home care pharmacy that are to be used during the patient's course of therapy should be documented in the patient's home care medical record. When home care patients are admitted to a hospital, the home care pharmacy should inform the hospital about the medications the patient is currently receiving from the home care pharmacy and about any known allergies. The home care pharmacy should recognize hospital policy when considering whether properly stored medications and medical equipment from the home can be used during the home care patient's hospitalization.

Drug Samples. The use of drug samples should be eliminated to the fullest extent possible. However, if samples are permitted, the pharmacy should control these products to ensure proper storage, records, labeling, and product integrity.

Controlling Certain Categories of Medications

Cytotoxic and Hazardous Drug Products. Policies and procedures for storing, handling, and disposing of cytotoxic and other hazardous drug products should be available to ensure patient and employee safety in compliance with applicable local, state, and federal laws and regulations. Employees should be specially trained, and their handling and disposal of these products should be monitored. Spill kits should be available.[5]

Controlled Substances. Policies and procedures for the storage, distribution, use, and accountability of controlled substances should be available to ensure appropriate use and to prevent diversion in compliance with applicable local, state, and federal laws and regulations.

Investigational Drugs. Policies and procedures for the safe and proper use of investigational drugs should be established and followed. The pharmacy should be responsible for overseeing the distribution and control of all investigational drugs. Investigational drugs should be dispensed and administered to consenting patients in accordance with an approved protocol. Home care pharmacists should initiate, participate in, and support medical and pharmaceutical research appropriate to the goals, objectives, and resources of the home care organization.

Standard 5: Facilities, Equipment, and Information Resources

To ensure optimal operational performance and quality patient care, adequate space, equipment, and supplies should be available for all professional and administrative functions related to medication use. These resources should be located in areas that facilitate the provision of services to patients, nurses, prescribers, and other health care providers and should be integrated with the home care organization's communication and delivery or transportation systems. Facilities should be constructed, arranged, and equipped to promote safe and efficient work and to avoid damage to or deterioration of drug products.

Medication Storage and Preparation. Facilities should be available for storing and preparing medications in the home care pharmacy under proper conditions of sanitation, temperature, light, moisture, ventilation, segregation, and security to ensure medication integrity and personnel safety and to prevent drug diversion. Adequate refrigeration and freezer capacity should be provided within the secure pharmacy area.

Medication Storage Area Inspections. All stocks of medications stored in the home care pharmacy or in the organization's facilities should be inspected routinely to ensure the absence of recalled, outdated, unusable, or mislabeled products. Inspections should include storage conditions that would compromise medication integrity, storage arrangements that might contribute to medication errors, and storage locations that might be vulnerable to drug diversion efforts.

Compounding and Packaging. Designated space and equipment for compounding and packaging sterile and nonsterile drug products should be available.[2,5] The compounding environment should be monitored and maintained on an ongoing basis.

Cytotoxic and Hazardous Drug Products. Appropriate facility space, equipment, and supplies for compounding cytotoxic and hazardous drug products should be available (to include a biological safety cabinet, spill kits, eye-washing station, and protective garb).[6]

Drug Information. Adequate space, resources, and information handling and communication technology should be available to facilitate the provision of drug and related information to patients, caregivers, health care providers, multidisciplinary team members, and referring physicians.

Pharmacist–Patient Consultation. Home care pharmacists will primarily consult patients or caregivers over the telephone. Home visits should be considered for enhancing compliance or simplifying complex drug-related patient issues.

Office and Meeting Space. Office and meeting areas should be available for administrative, clinical, technical, and reimbursement staff. Ideally, interdisciplinary team members from pharmacy, nursing, and reimbursement are located within a proximate space. Sufficient educational and training activities should be established. Adequate facilities and equipment should be established for decontaminating, cleaning, and maintaining infusion devices, including durable medical equipment.

Drug Delivery Systems, Administration Devices, and Automated Dispensing Devices. Home care pharmacists should provide leadership and advice in organizational and clinical decisions about the selection of drug delivery systems, administration devices, and automated compounding and dispensing devices and should participate in the evaluation, use, and monitoring of these systems and devices. The potential for medication errors associated with such systems and devices must be thoroughly evaluated. Policies and procedures should be available for the certification (calibration) and maintenance of equipment and devices. Equipment should be adequately maintained and certified in compliance with applicable standards, laws, and regulations. Equipment maintenance and certification should be documented.

Record Maintenance. Adequate space should be available for maintaining and storing records, including medication profiles and other patient information, management information, equipment maintenance sheets, controlled-substances inventory sheets, and material safety data sheets, among others, to ensure compliance with laws, regulations, accreditation requirements, and sound management practices. Appropriate licenses, permits, and tax stamps should be available.

Information Technology. Computer resources should be used to maintain patient medication profiles, perform necessary patient billing procedures, manage drug product inventories, and interface with other available computerized systems to obtain patient-specific clinical information for drug therapy monitoring and other clinical functions and to facilitate the continuity of care after patients transfer to and from other care settings.

References

1. American Society of Hospital Pharmacists. ASHP guidelines on the pharmacist's role in home care. *Am J Hosp Pharm.* 1993; 50:1940–4.
2. American Society of Hospital Pharmacists. ASHP technical assistance bulletin on quality assurance for pharmacy-prepared sterile products. *Am J Hosp Pharm.* 1993; 50:2386–98.
3. The United States pharmacopeia, 23rd rev., and The national formulary, 18th ed. Rockville, MD: United States Pharmacopeial Convention; 1994:1963–75.
4. Mirtallo J, Driscoll D, Helms R, et al. Safe practices for parenteral nutrition feeding formulations. *JPEN J Parenter Enteral Nutr.* 1998; 22:49–66.
5. American Society of Hospital Pharmacists. ASHP technical assistance bulletin on compounding nonsterile products in pharmacies. *Am J Hosp Pharm.* 1994; 51:1441–8.
6. American Society of Hospital Pharmacists. ASHP guidelines on handling cytotoxic and hazardous drugs. *Am J Hosp Pharm.* 1990; 47:1033–49.

Suggested Reading

1. Monk-Tutor MR. The U.S. home infusion market. *Am J Health-Syst Pharm.* 1998; 55:2019–25.

2. Monk-Tutor MR. Home care practice as a model for providing pharmaceutical care. *Am J Health-Syst Pharm.* 1998; 55:486–90.

3. Andrusko-Furphy KT. Oryx and performance measurement in home care. *Am J Health-Syst Pharm.* 1998; 55:2299–301.

4. Scheckelhoff K. Understanding the dynamics of the integrated health system. *Infusion.* 1997; 3(Apr):18–22.

5. Haidar TA, Grillo JA. An interdisciplinary critical pathway for home intravenous antibiotic therapies. *Infusion.* 1997; 3(Apr): 38–50.

6. Bemus AM, Lindley CM, Sawyer WT, et al. Task analysis of home care pharmacy. *Am J Health-Syst Pharm.* 1996; 53:2831–9.

7. Andrusko-Furphy K. Why does home care require so much documentation? *Consult Pharm.* 1994; 9:581–2.

8. McPherson ML, Ferris R. Establishing a home health care consulting practice. *Am Pharm.* 1994; NS34 (Feb):42–9.

Approved by the ASHP Board of Directors, November 14, 1998. Developed by the ASHP Council on Professional Affairs.

Barbara McKinnon, Pharm.D., Karen E. Bertch, Pharm.D., Lawrence P. Carey, Pharm. D., Terry D. Leach, Larry D. Pelham, M.S., FASHP, Brian G. Swift, Pharm.D., and J. Scott Reid, Pharm.D., are gratefully acknowledged for drafting this document.

The bibliographic citation for this document is as follows: American Society of Health-System Pharmacists. ASHP Guidelines on Minimum Standards for Home Care Pharmacists. *Am J Health-Syst Pharm.* 1999; 56:629–38.

ASHP Guidelines: Minimum Standard for Pharmaceutical Services in Ambulatory Care

In recent years there has been an increasing emphasis in health care on the provision of ambulatory care services. This shift away from acute hospital care is due to several factors. Managed care has created incentives to decrease hospitalization rates and length of stay. The number of elderly patients with multiple chronic medical conditions that require longitudinal management is growing. There is more focus in medicine on preventive health and patient education. Appropriate medication therapy in the ambulatory care setting is often the most common and most cost effective form of treatment, yet the clinical, humanistic, and economic consequences of adverse drug events and the inappropriate use of medications in this setting could be catastrophic.[1] As providers of pharmaceutical care to patients in the ambulatory care setting, pharmacists should be concerned with and take responsibility for the outcomes of their services in addition to the provision of these services.

The provision of pharmaceutical services for ambulatory patients occurs in a variety of settings including freestanding pharmacies, ambulatory clinics, hospital outpatient departments, assisted living centers, and others. Pharmacists in ambulatory care settings could also provide some aspects of pharmaceutical services to patients through a mail-order prescription service, patients receiving home care, and patients residing in long-term care and other extended-care settings. Organizational arrangements may vary with the pharmaceutical services operating independently, or as components in local health care organizations that may be independent or affiliated with larger local and regional health systems.[2,3] Furthermore, in some settings the delivery of pharmaceutical care may be independent and separated from distributive services. For brevity, these guidelines will use the terms pharmaceutical services and organizations to imply any arrangement.

The primary purpose of these guidelines is to outline the minimum requirements for the operation and management of pharmaceutical services for patients in the ambulatory care setting. Pharmaceutical services, especially the provision of pharmaceutical care, in the ambulatory care setting should be coordinated among other settings, therefore, these guidelines should be used, as applicable, in conjunction with minimum standards for other practice settings. Rather than including detailed advice in this document, readers should refer to other ASHP documents that address many of the topics outlined for additional information and guidance. Because of differences in settings and organizational arrangements and complexity, aspects of these guidelines may not be applicable in some settings. Ambulatory care pharmacists should use their professional judgement in assessing and adapting these guidelines to meet the needs of their own practice settings.

In circumstances where a pharmacy or network of pharmacies are contracted to provide pharmaceutical services to the organization's patients, the following minimal standards should be incorporated into contract language.

The criteria for pharmaceutical services in the ambulatory care setting that are covered in these guidelines are distributed among the following categories: (1) leadership and practice management, (2) medication therapy and pharmaceutical care, (3) drug distribution and control, and (4) facilities, equipment, and other resources. Collectively, the criteria represent a minimum level of quality that pharmaceutical services for ambulatory patients should strive to provide on a consistent basis. While the scope of pharmaceutical services will likely vary from site to site, depending upon the needs of the patients served, the criteria are strongly linked to patient outcomes and neglect in any one may compromise quality.

Standard I: Leadership and Practice Management

Effective leadership and practice management skills are necessary for the delivery of pharmaceutical services in a manner consistent with the organization's and patients' needs and for the continuous improvement in patient care outcomes. Pharmaceutical service management should focus on the pharmacist's responsibility to provide pharmaceutical care and the development of the personnel, facilities, and other resources to support that responsibility. The guidelines use the term, director of ambulatory care pharmaceutical services or, director, to indicate the person responsible for managing services. Depending on the health care organization's structure and other factors, designations such as manager, pharmacist-in-charge, or responsible pharmacists are used.

The director of ambulatory care pharmaceutical services should be responsible for (1) setting the short- and long-term goals of the pharmacy based on the needs of the patients served, the specific needs of the pharmacy (and any organizational arrangement of which the pharmaceutical services may be a component), and developments and trends in health care and ambulatory care pharmacy practice, (2) developing plans and schedules for achieving these goals, (3) directing the implementation of the plans and the day-to-day activities associated with them, (4) determining whether the goals and schedule are being met, and (5) instituting corrective actions where necessary.[4,5] The director, in carrying out the aforementioned responsibilities, should employ an adequate number of competent, qualified personnel.

Managing Pharmaceutical Services

Education and Training, Director. Pharmaceutical services should be managed by a professionally competent, legally qualified pharmacist. The director of the ambulatory care pharmaceutical service should be thoroughly knowledgeable about and have experience in ambulatory care pharmacy practice and management. The director should have completed an applicable accredited pharmacy residency program or have equivalent training and experience. Completion of an advanced management degree (e.g., M.B.A., M.H.A., M.S.) and/or practice management residency is desirable.

Mission. The pharmaceutical service should have a written

mission statement that, at a minimum, reflects patient care and customer service responsibilities and, if applicable, is consistent with the mission of the organization of which the pharmacy may be a component. The mission should be understood by every employee and other participants (e.g., students and residents) involved with the pharmacy's activities. The development and prioritization of goals, objectives, and work tasks should be consistent with the mission statement.

Laws and Regulations. Compliance with local, state, and federal laws and regulations applicable to pharmaceutical services in the ambulatory care setting is required. The pharmacy shall maintain written or computerized documentation of compliance with requirements concerning procurement and distribution of drug products, patient information, and related safety from the board of pharmacy, Food and Drug Administration, Drug Enforcement Administration, Health Care Financing Administration, Occupational Health and Safety Administration, among others. Ambulatory care pharmacies dispensing medications across state boundaries shall comply with out-of-state licensure requirements, as well as other state and federal interstate laws and regulations.

Policies and Procedures Manual. A policies and procedures manual governing the scope of ambulatory care pharmaceutical services (e.g., administrative, operational, and clinical) should be available and properly maintained. The manual should be reviewed and revised annually or whenever necessary to reflect changes in policies and procedures, scope of services, organizational arrangements, and other factors. All personnel should be familiar with the contents of the manual. Appropriate mechanisms should be established to ensure compliance with the policies and procedures.

Practice Standards and Guidelines. The practice standards and guidelines of the American Society of Health-System Pharmacists, the National Committee on Quality Assurance (NCQA), the Health Plan Employer Data and Information Set (HEDIS), and the Joint Commission on Accreditation of Healthcare Organizations (JCAHO) or other appropriate accrediting body should be assessed and adapted, as applicable. The pharmacy should strive to meet these standards regardless of the particular financial and organizational arrangements by which pharmaceutical services are provided to the organization and its patients.

Managing the Medication-Use Process

Medication-Use Policy Development. Medication-use policy decisions should be based on clinical, quality-of-life, and pharmacoeconomic factors that result in optimal patient care. Committees within the organization (e.g., pharmacy and therapeutics, infection control) that make decisions concerning medication use should include the active and direct involvement of physicians, pharmacists, and other appropriate health care professionals. The pharmacy should prepare and present to these committees drug product evaluation reports that consider all aspects of safety, effectiveness, and cost.

Clinical Care Plans and Disease State Management. Pharmacists should be involved as part of an interdisciplinary team in the development and implementation of clinical care plans (clinical practice guidelines, critical pathways) and disease state management programs involving medication therapy, collaborative care agreements, and treatment protocols. Emphasis should be placed on clinical care plans, primary care, and medication treatment protocols that cover dosage calculations and limits, and use of medications frequently associated with adverse events, including medication errors.[6,7] Primary care protocols should consider whole patient needs for health promotion and disease prevention measures as well as appropriate patient assessments, management of medication-related care problems, and referrals for acute medical care. The targeting of diseases should consider the prevalence of the disease in the population served by the organization and the potential for impact on clinical and economic outcomes.[8]

Drug Information. Pharmacists should provide accurate, comprehensive, general and patient-specific drug information to patients, caregivers, other pharmacists, physicians, nurses, and other health care providers, as appropriate, in response to requests, in the delivery of pharmaceutical care, or through educational programs and publications.

Drug information sources should include current professional and scientific periodicals and the latest editions of textbooks in appropriate pharmaceutical and biomedical subject areas. Available information sources should support research on patient care issues and facilitate provision of pharmaceutical care and safety in the medication-use process. This information may be accessed in conjunction with medical libraries and other available resources. Appropriate drug information sources should be readily accessible to professional staff.

If applicable, pharmacists should have access to information on all investigational studies and similar research projects involving medications and medication-related devices used by the organization. Pharmacists should provide pertinent written information (to the extent known) about the safe and proper use of investigational drugs, including possible adverse effects, to nurses, pharmacists, physicians, and other health care providers involved in the care of patients admitted to the investigational drug protocols.

Development of Patient Care Services. Pharmacists should be involved in the development, implementation, and evaluation of new or changing patient care services within the organization, such as the development of new clinic or office sites. These efforts should promote the continuity of pharmaceutical care across the continuum of care, practice settings, and geographically dispersed facilities.

Preventive and Postexposure Immunization Programs. The pharmacy should participate in the development of policies and procedures concerning preventive and postexposure programs for infectious diseases (including, but not limited to, HIV, tuberculosis, and hepatitis) for patients and employees. As appropriate, pharmacists should promote the use of and may administer immunizations, when legally allowed.

Substance-Abuse Programs. The pharmacy should assist in the development of and participate in the organization's substance-abuse prevention, education, and employee and patient assistance programs.

Medical Emergencies. The pharmacy should participate in the development of policies and procedures to ensure the availability, access, and security of emergency medications, including antidotes. Appropriately trained pharmacists should have an authorized role in responding to medical emergencies.

Institutional Review Board. Pharmacist's membership on the organization's institutional review board is preferred depending on the prevalence of clinical drug research.

Committee Involvement. A pharmacist should be a member of and actively participate in those committees responsible for establishing policies and procedures for medication-use, other aspects of patient care, and performance improvement and others, as appropriate. Also, pharmacists should participate in the activities of similar committees of a parent health system, as applicable.

Formulary Management and Integration. The pharmacy should maintain an up-to-date formulary of drug products approved by the medical staff. Drug products should be selected for the formulary through a medication-use policy development process (pharmacy and therapeutics committee or equivalent) that ensures the availability of the most appropriate drug products for the population served. The formulary should limit choices based on clinical evidence of efficacy and safety as well as cost to essential drug products with few duplicates. Drug products of marginal benefit should be eliminated or restricted, to the extent possible.

When applicable, the pharmacy should integrate the formularies (or approved drug lists) of third party payers into a patient care process that ensures optimal and cost-effective patient outcomes. Organizations with multiple practice settings such as acute inpatient and ambulatory care should coordinate formularies to promote continuity of care. A process should exist to obtain non-formulary drug products when medically necessary for the care of specific patients.

Disaster Services. Policies and procedures should exist for providing pharmaceutical services during facility, local, or area-wide disasters affecting the organization's patients. Appropriately trained pharmacists should be members of emergency preparedness teams and participate in drills. Patients should be informed about what to do in the event of a disaster to safely continue medication therapy.

Managing Performance Improvement

Performance Improvement. There should be an ongoing, systematic program for assessing the delivery of pharmaceutical care and services and of the utilization of medications in patient care.[9] Performance improvement activities based on assessments should be integrated with the organization's or health system's overall performance improvement activities, as applicable. Corrective actions should be planned and implemented for identified deficiencies and reassessed at appropriate time intervals. Operational and outcomes data should be bench-marked with those of other ambulatory care pharmaceutical services of similar size and scope. The results, including follow-up actions, of improvement efforts should be documented and provided to the organization's managers and others, as appropriate.

Medication-Use Evaluation. An ongoing program of monitoring drug utilization and costs should be in place to ensure that medications are used appropriately, safely, and effectively, and to increase the probability of desired patient

outcomes within defined populations of patients. The medication-use policy committee should define specific parameters for evaluation (disease state, pharmacological category, high-use/high cost drug products) as appropriate for the organization. Through the ongoing evaluation of medication-use, areas in need of improvement in medication prescribing and management can be identified and targeted for intervention.

Documentation and Measurement of Pharmaceutical Care, Interventions, and Outcomes. Pharmaceutical services should have an ongoing process for consistent documentation and measurement (and reporting to medical staff, administrators, and others) of pharmaceutical care, interventions, and patient outcomes from medication therapy (including patient satisfaction and quality of life) and pharmacists' contributions to patient care.[10]

Adverse Drug Reactions. An ongoing program should be in place for preventing, monitoring, and reporting adverse drug reactions. The program should include timely communications about the occurrences of adverse drug reactions to affected patients, their caregivers, and other providers. The pharmacy should submit adverse drug reaction reports to the FDA MedWatch program and drug products' manufacturers, as appropriate.

Medication Errors. The ambulatory care organization should have an ongoing program to prevent medication errors, including nonpunitive reporting and analysis. Pharmacists, physicians, nurses, and other health care personnel involved in the medication-use process should monitor for, document, and report medication errors. The organization, with the participation of pharmacists, should analyze the causes of medication errors and implement corrective actions. The occurrence of medication errors should be reported to voluntary national reporting systems (e.g., USP Medication Error Reporting Program and FDA MedWatch) and, as required, to accrediting organizations.

Integration of Population-Based and Patient-Specific Activities. A mechanism to ensure that the clinical and economic findings of population-based activities are appropriately incorporated into daily patient-specific practice should exist. Population-based activities provide insight and guidance in the treatment of the "average" patient, however, all variables identified in the patient-specific encounter should be considered in the therapeutic decision making for an individual patient.[11]

Managing Human Resources

Work Schedules and Assignments. The director should ensure that work schedules, procedures, and assignments optimize the use of personnel and other resources. Sufficient personnel should be available to ensure the safe and timely delivery of pharmaceutical services and patient care.

Position Descriptions. The responsibilities and related competencies of professional and supportive personnel should be clearly defined in written position descriptions. Pharmacists should be responsible for the provision of pharmaceutical care and for the supervision and management of support staff. Sufficient support staff (pharmacy technicians, clerical, secretarial) should be employed to facilitate the provision of pharmaceutical care. Technicians should be responsible for most aspects of drug distribution, including the processing of medication orders. This should be supervised and checked by a pharmacist. Roles of technicians and pharmacists should be clearly delineated to maximize the use of technicians in activities they can legally and safely perform.

Recruitment and Selection of Personnel. Personnel should be recruited and selected on the bases of requirements in established position descriptions. The personnel selection process should include an assessment of prior performance in job-related functions and the candidate's ability and willingness to contribute to achieving the pharmacy's mission. The director should assist in identifying the relevant professional and technical qualifications and should participate in candidate interviews and selections.

Performance Evaluation. Scheduled, periodic evaluations of performance should occur for all pharmacy personnel. Performance should be evaluated on the bases of position description requirements and expected competencies. Evaluations should include comments from professional and technical staff as well as other members of the health care team. Customer service should also be included in the evaluation process.

Education and Training. All personnel should possess the education and training needed to fulfill their responsibilities. All personnel should participate in relevant continuing education programs, staff development programs, and other activities as necessary to maintain or enhance their competence.

Pharmacist Licensure and Certification. All pharmacists shall possess a current state license to practice pharmacy. Board of Pharmaceutical Specialties' certification of pharmacists to provide specialty services to patients and selected patient care is encouraged, as applicable.

Technician Certification. Certification of pharmacy technicians by the Pharmacy Technician Certification Board should be strongly encouraged or required, as feasible. In addition, completion of an accredited training program is preferred.

Orientation of Personnel. All new personnel should be oriented to their positions' responsibilities and continued competencies, and applicable pharmacy and organization policies and procedures.

Managing Financial Resources

Budget Management. The pharmacy should have a budget consistent with the organization's financial management process that supports the scope of and demand for pharmaceutical services. Oversight of workload and financial performance should be managed in accordance with the organization's requirements. Management should provide for (1) determination and analysis of pharmaceutical service costs, (2) analysis of budgetary variances, (3) capital equipment acquisition, (4) patient revenue projections, and (5) justification of personnel commensurate with workload productivity.

Processes should enable the analysis of pharmaceutical services by unit-of-service and other parameters appropriate to the organization (e.g., organization-wide costs by medication therapy, clinical service, specific disease management categories, and patient health plan enrollment). The director should have an integral part in the organization's financial management process.

Drug Expenditures. Specific policies and procedures for managing drug expenditures should address such methods as competitive bidding, group purchasing, utilization review programs, inventory management, and cost-effective patient services.

Revenue, Reimbursement, and Compensation. The director should be knowledgeable about revenues for pharmaceutical services including reimbursement for the provision of drug products and related supplies and compensation for pharmacists' cognitive services. Processes should exist for routine verification of patient benefits and for counseling patients about their anticipated financial responsibility for planned medication therapies. A process should also exist for responding to services requests from medically indigent patients. (For additional information, see: Coding and Reimbursement Guide for Pharmacists, St. Anthony Publishing; Directory of Prescription Drug Patient Assistance Programs, Pharmaceutical Research and Manufacturers Association.)

Standard II: Medication Therapy and Pharmaceutical Care

At a minimum, pharmacists are responsible for assessing the legal and clinical appropriateness of medication orders (or prescriptions), educating and counseling patients on the use of their medications, monitoring the effects of medication therapy, and maintaining patient profiles and other records. In the ambulatory care setting these responsibilities are best accomplished through the provision of pharmaceutical care whether in the context of collaborative agreements with physicians or independent of such agreements. The pharmaceutical care activities may vary, however, depending on whether agreements are in place, pharmacists have delegated authorities in patient care, and these are supported by provisions in the organization's policies and procedures. Individual state laws and regulations may establish specific requirements and limits.

Providing Pharmaceutical Care

Pharmaceutical care involves establishing a relationship with the patient; obtaining patient and medication history information; assessing the appropriateness of medication orders; preventing, identifying and resolving medication or other problems; educating and counseling patients; and monitoring the patient and medication effects.[12] When authorized for collaborative medication therapy or primary care, pharmacists may also participate in medication therapy decision-making and administering medications.

Pharmaceutical Care Plan. Pharmacists should maintain a comprehensive, on-going pharmaceutical care plan, either separately or as a component of a multidisciplinary care plan, for each patient based on level of responsibilities. The pharmaceutical care plan, if separate, should be accessible to prescribers, pharmacists, and other health care providers involved in patient care. The pharmacist should be responsible for communicating the contents to the patient and other health care providers. The pharmaceutical care plan should, at a minimum, document the patient's medical and medication history, medication therapy assessment, and the medication therapy regimen, including drug name, strength, route of administration, indication of therapy, goal of therapy, monitoring parameters, and proposed length of therapy.

Depending on applicable laws and regulations and the organization's policies and procedures, the pharmaceutical care plan, or elements, may be a part of the patient's medical record or maintained in a separate pharmacy record or patient profile, preferably electronic.

Relationships with Patients. Patient-based medication therapy and pharmaceutical care begins with the relationship between the patient and the pharmacist. The ambulatory care pharmacist in the role of providing direct patient care should develop and maintain a level of rapport and trust with the patient and caregiver to effectively provide pharmaceutical care. The pharmacist should coordinate all aspects of the individual patient's pharmaceutical care and serve as a patient advocate. The pharmacist should be flexible and adapt to patient-specific variables such as the patient's perception of how their illness and/or symptoms impact his or her life and the patient's readiness for change.

Medication-Therapy Decisions. Pharmacists should actively participate in medication therapy decision-making and management through collaboration with the physician, patient, and other health care providers. By participating in collaborative drug therapy management, the pharmacist takes an active role in the initiation, management, and monitoring of medication therapy and takes responsibility for achieving desired therapeutic outcomes. The development of a collaborative care agreement between the pharmacist, prescriber, and the patient should occur in compliance with applicable laws and regulations and the organization's policies and procedures, as applicable.

Pharmacist Prescribing. When permitted by applicable state laws and regulations, pharmacist may be delegated prescriptive authority in accordance with established collaborative drug therapy management agreements.

Therapeutic Goals. The pharmacist and patient should work together and with other health care providers to set goals, timetables, and therapeutic milestones for all pharmacotherapy.

Patient and Medication History. Upon patient admission for ambulatory care services, a pharmacist should obtain, or conduct as necessary, a patient and medication history (or profile). The history should include, but not be limited to, known health problems and diseases, applicable measurements and laboratory values, known drug allergies and adverse drug experiences, and a comprehensive list of prescription and nonprescription medications and related medical devices currently being used. The history should be maintained and updated during subsequent patient encounters.

Medication Therapy Assessment. The pharmacist should assess medication orders, new and refill, prior to dispensing, to ensure safe and effective medication therapy. The assessment should include the appropriateness of the prescribed medication(s) for the patient's diagnosis and history, the identification of medication-related problems, and interventions for resolving the problems, if any. Problems should be resolved with the prescriber before further processing of the medication order. In addition, the assessment should produce a plan for monitoring patient adherence, therapeutic and adverse effects, and patient outcomes.

Patient Education and Counseling

Patient education and counseling are essential components of pharmaceutical care in the ambulatory care setting and pharmacists' provision should exceed the minimal legal requirements.[13] A simple offer to counsel is inconsistent with pharmacists' responsibilities. The pharmacist should ensure that the patient understands all information required for the safe and proper use of the medication and devices, as applicable. Directions for use should be clearly expressed. Supplementary written information should be provided as necessary to reinforce oral communications. Contingencies should be available to provide education, counseling, and written materials to non-English speaking patients, where applicable. Depending on need, this might require access to interpreters or bilingual pharmacists.

At a minimum, the pharmacist should verify that patients and caregivers, understand what medications (prescription, nonprescription, and alternative substances) they are using, why they are using them, how to use them, what therapeutic effects to expect, what potential adverse effects to watch for, and what actions to take if adverse effects occur. Counseling should also include the patients responsibility for adherence to and reporting on their experience with the medication therapy plan.

Medication Therapy Monitoring. The pharmacist should monitor patient understanding and adherence to their medication therapy plan and its effects and outcomes. During subsequent encounters with patients for medication order refills or follow up visits, pharmacists should obtain information, as appropriate, from patients, assess patient progress, identify any problems, and resolve problems either with the prescriber or in accord with a collaborative agreement.

Medication Administration. Only personnel who are permitted by law and regulation, authorized by the organization, and appropriately trained should administer medications to patients. Pharmacists should participate in establishing policies and procedures for medication administration in the ambulatory care setting. When legally permitted, medication administration by appropriately trained pharmacists may be within their scope of practice, depending on the ambulatory care setting's workload distribution among members of the health care team. As appropriate, pharmacists may witness now or one-time doses of medications self-administered by patients.

Supporting Pharmaceutical Care

Continuity of Care. Pharmacists should routinely contribute to processes that ensure each patient's pharmaceutical care is maintained regardless of transitions across the continuum of care and practice settings (e.g., between inpatient and community pharmacies or home care services).

Emergency Access to Pharmaceutical Care. Policies and procedures should exist within the organization to provide patients access to appropriate levels of pharmaceutical care during emergent situations 24 hours a day, including access to the pharmacist responsible for their care, if appropriate.

Medical Record Documentation. Clinical actions and recommendations by pharmacists that are designed to ensure safe and cost effective use of medications and that have a potential effect on patient outcomes should be documented in patients' medical records. Pharmacists' documentation in the patients' medical records may require organization-specific training and authorization.

Patient Confidentiality. Policies and procedures for access to and dissemination of confidential patient information should be available. Patient privacy and confidentiality should be protected by safeguarding access to all sources of patient information, including financial (billing), medication profiles, medical records, and organization reports, whether in computer databases or hard copy. Patient information should be shared only with authorized health care providers and others within the pharmacy or the organization as needed for the care of patients. Patient information should only be shared with family members and caregiver(s) upon the request of the patient. Privacy shall be maintained during all communication with a patient.

Standard III: Drug Distribution and Control

The pharmacy and/or contracted network pharmacies should be responsible for the procurement, distribution, and control of all drug products used in the treatment of the organization's patients. Policies and procedures governing medication distribution and control should be developed by the pharmacy in collaboration with other appropriate organization staff and committees.

Purchasing and Maintaining the Availability of Drug Products

Drug Product Availability. Drug products approved for routine use should be purchased, stored, and available in sufficient quantities to meet the needs of ambulatory care patients. Drug products not approved for routine use, but necessary to meet the needs of specific patients or categories of patients should be obtained in response to orders according to established policies and procedures.

Pharmaceutical Manufacturers and Suppliers. Criteria for selecting pharmaceutical manufacturers and suppliers or contracting with group purchasing organizations should be established by the pharmacy to ensure the quality and best price of drug products. Preference should be considered for manufacturers and suppliers that provide packaging and labeling designed to reduce vulnerability to medication errors (e.g., bar-coding).

Pharmaceutical Manufacturers' Representatives. Policies and procedures governing the activities of representatives (including related supplies and devices) within the pharmacy, ambulatory care setting, and organization should exist. Representatives should be provided written guidance

on their activities. All promotional materials and activities should be reviewed and approved by the pharmacy. Representatives should not have access to patient care areas.

Samples. The use of drug product samples should be prohibited to the extent possible. However, if samples are permitted under certain circumstances, policies and procedures for their use should exist. The pharmacy should control samples to ensure proper storage, record keeping, and product integrity, if allowed by state law and regulation. Samples dispensed to patients should meet all applicable packaging and labeling laws and regulations and standards.

Drug Product Storage Area Inspections. All stocks of drug products whether located within or outside the pharmacy area should be inspected routinely and managed by pharmacy and location staff to ensure the absence of outdated, unusable, recalled, or mislabeled products. Storage conditions should be monitored to ensure compliance with environmental requirements and to assess, document, and correct any conditions that might foster medication deterioration and storage arrangements that might contribute to medication errors. Appropriate security must prevent the access of unauthorized staff and others (technical, health care provider, housekeeping, patients and caregivers) to stock medications and medication order forms (prescription blanks).

Patient Care Area Stock. Stocks of drug products held in nonpharmacy areas (e.g., nursing station, clinic, or physicians' offices) for direct administration to ambulatory patients should be minimal. To the extent possible, stocks should be limited to medications for emergency, diagnostic, and routine treatments, including certain injectables (e.g., local anesthetics and vaccines). The potential for medication errors and adverse effects should be considered for any drug product stocked outside of the pharmacy. Drug products shall be under control at all times to prevent unauthorized access and diversion.

Emergency Medications. The pharmacy should ensure the availability, access, and security of emergency medications, including antidotes. Pharmacists should have an authorized role in responding to medical emergencies.

Drug Recall and New Prescribing Information. An ongoing program should exist for timely intervention and dissemination of information regarding drug recalls and release of new prescribing or adverse drug reaction information on specific drug products. For situations in which the potential for an adverse event is possible, the pharmacy should have procedures in place to identify all patients of the organization using the product, to identify the prescribers of the product, and to intervene with specific alternatives to reduce the risk of adverse events.

Policies and procedures should exist for removing recalled drug products from all storage and patient care areas, and when the recall is to the user level, for notifying patients who have received recalled products and for replacing patients' supplies.

Processing the Medication Order

Prescribing. Policies and procedures should be available to ensure that health care providers meet applicable state licensure and, if required, organizational authorization for prescribing medications. Medications should be administered and dispensed to ambulatory patients only upon the oral or written order of authorized prescribers. Oral new orders should be limited to non-routine and emergent situations and strongly discouraged for drug products and regimens prone to adverse events, including medication errors. A pharmacist should verify and reduce oral orders to writing as soon as possible.

The pharmacy should advocate and foster prescriber's conformance with the formulary, clinical care plans, and disease state management programs, and with standardized, approved terminology and abbreviations when prescribing medications. The pharmacy should advocate for the development and use of electronic prescribing systems (prescriber direct order entry).

Therapeutic Purpose. Prior to dispensing any medication, the pharmacist should substantiate the indication for which the medication was prescribed. Prescribers should be encouraged to routinely communicate the condition being treated or the therapeutic purpose of medications with all medication orders.

Medication Orders. Medication orders (or prescriptions) shall contain at a minimum the following information: patient name (and address), medication name, dose, frequency, route, quantity (duration), prescriber identification (and prescriber DEA number for controlled substances) and signature, and date. All medication orders shall be reviewed for legality and clinical appropriateness by a pharmacist before being dispensed. Any questions should be resolved with the prescriber, and a written notation made in the patient's pharmacy record or profile. Information concerning changes should be appropriately communicated to the patient, caregiver, and other involved health care providers.

Preparing, Packaging, and Labeling Medications

Preparation. The pharmacist should prepare or supervise the preparation, in a timely and accurate manner, those drug formulations, strengths, dosage forms, and packages prescribed, including those that are not commercially available but are needed in the care of patients.

Extemporaneous Compounding. Drug formulations, dosage forms, strengths, and packaging that are not available commercially but are deemed necessary for patient care should be prepared by appropriately trained personnel in accordance with applicable standards and regulations (e.g., FDA, U.S.P., state board of pharmacy). Adequate quality control and quality assurance procedures should exist for these operations. Commercially available products should be used to the maximum extent possible.

Sterile Products. All sterile medications for use in the ambulatory care facility or for use by patients in the home should be prepared in a suitable environment by appropriately trained personnel and labeled appropriately for the user. Quality control and quality assurance procedures for the preparation of sterile products should exist, including periodic assessment of personnel on aseptic technique.

Cytotoxic and Hazardous Drug Products. All cytotoxic and hazardous drug products for use in the ambulatory care facility or for use by patients in the home should be prepared in a suitable environment by appropriately trained personnel and labeled appropriately for the user. Special precautions, equipment, supplies (spill kits), and training for storage, handling, and disposal of cytotoxic and hazardous drug products should exist to ensure the safety of personnel, patients, and visitors. Quality control and quality assurance procedures for the preparation of cytotoxic and hazardous products should exist. Personnel handling cytotoxic and hazardous drug products should be monitored periodically for adverse effects.

Controlled Substances. Pharmacists are responsible for a lead role in the control of drug products that are subject to diversion and misuse. Pharmacists have primary responsibility for receipt, storage, security, distribution within the facility and to patients for home use, and disposal of controlled substances and for related records. Policies and procedures shall exist to ensure compliance with the Comprehensive Drug Abuse Prevention and Control Act of 1970 and with state laws and regulations that may be more stringent. Storage within the pharmacy and nonpharmacy (e.g., emergency room) areas are secure and have controlled access to only authorized personnel. Procedures are in place to detect and investigate inventory shrinkage.

Investigational Drugs. The pharmacy should be responsible for overseeing the distribution and control of all investigational drugs. Investigational drugs shall be approved for use by an institutional review board, and shall be dispensed and administered to consenting patients according to an approved protocol.

Non-FDA Approved Drugs. The pharmacy should seek and obtain documented authorization from appropriate organization committees for the pharmacologic use of any chemical substance that has not received FDA approval for any drug use. Documentation should exist to ensure that appropriate risk management measures (e.g., obtaining informed consent) have been taken.

Packaging. Medications dispensed to ambulatory care patients should be packaged and labeled in compliance with applicable federal and state laws and regulations and with USP and other standards. When feasible, dispensing in unopened manufacturers' and in tamper-evident packages is desirable. Packaging materials should be selected that preserve the integrity, cleanliness, and potency of compounded and commercially available drug products. Containers, including unit dose packages, for patient home use shall comply with the Poison Prevention Packaging Act.

Labeling. At a minimum, labels for patient home use of medications shall comply with applicable federal and state laws and regulations. Generally, labels contain: name, address, and telephone number of the pharmacy; date of dispensing; serial number of the prescription; patient's full name; name, strength, and dosage form of the medication; directions to the patient for use of the medication; name of the prescriber; precautionary information; authorized refills; and initials (or name) of the responsible pharmacist. Other information may be required by individual state law and regulation.

Drug Delivery Systems and Administration Devices. Pharmacists should provide leadership and advice in organizational and clinical decisions regarding drug delivery systems and administration devices, and should participate in the evaluation, use, and monitoring of these systems and devices. The potential for medication errors associated with such systems and devices should be thoroughly evaluated.

Mail Distribution. The pharmacy may mail medications to patients, preferably when part of a comprehensive pharmaceutical care program, which provides patients access to a pharmacist. Mailed medications shall conform to all federal and state laws and regulations. Outer mailing packages and medication containers should protect the medication from heat, humidity, and other environmental conditions that would affect stability.[14] A toll-free telephone service should be provided that is answered during normal business hours to enable communication between a patient or a physician of a patient and a pharmacist with access to the patient's records. The pharmacy should have procedures for investigating, replacing, and reporting, as required, medications lost during delivery. Special requirements for mailing controlled substances vary by state law and regulation.

Standard IV: Facilities, Equipment, and Other Resources

To ensure optimal performance and quality patient care, adequate space, equipment, and other resources should be available for all professional and administrative functions relating to medication use. Pharmaceutical services operations should be located in areas that facilitate provision of services to patients, nurses, prescribers, and other health care providers. Facilities should be constructed, arranged, and equipped to promote safe and efficient work flow for staff and patients and to avoid damage to or deterioration of drug products.

Information Technology. Computer-based (electronic) information systems are preferred to maintain patient pharmaceutical care plans and medication profiles; perform necessary patient billing procedures; manage drug product inventories; and interface with other available computerized systems to obtain patient specific clinical information. Information is essential for medication therapy monitoring and other clinical functions, to facilitate the continuity of care to and from other care settings, and to produce drug utilization, cost, and related reports.

Medication Storage and Preparation Areas. Facilities should exist to store and prepare drug products and medications under proper conditions of sanitation, temperature, light, moisture, ventilation, segregation, and security throughout the pharmacy and other patient care areas. Monitored, adequate refrigeration and freezer capacity should be available within the secure pharmacy area and, as necessary, in nonpharmacy areas.

Compounding and Packaging. Designated space and equipment for compounding and packaging of sterile and nonsterile drug products, including hazardous drug products, should exist. The compounding and packaging areas should be clean and orderly and routinely monitored and maintained to minimize the risk of errors and contamination of drug products.

Patient Assessment and Counseling Area. A designated area for private patient assessment and counseling by pharmacists should be available to enhance patients' knowledge, understanding, and adherence to prescribed medication therapy regimens and monitoring plans. Space should accommodate the pharmacist and patient and, as appropriate, parents, caregivers, or chaperons.

Automation. There should be policies and procedures on the evaluation, selection, use, calibration and monitoring, and maintenance of all automated pharmacy systems.[15] Automated dispensing systems and software may be useful in promoting accurate and efficient medication ordering and preparation, dispensing, and distribution. The potential for medication errors associated with automated systems should be thoroughly evaluated and eliminated to the extent possible. Automated dispensing systems should support the pharmacist's assessment of medication orders (and opportunity to intervene) and checking of filled orders before dispensing.

Automated dispensing systems and automated storage and distribution devices should be controlled by the pharmacy's computer-based information system. An interface with the organization's information system is strongly encouraged. A pharmacist should supervise the stocking of medications in automated dispensing systems and in automated storage and distribution devices. The maintenance, calibration, and certification, as required by applicable standards, laws, and regulations, should be ongoing and documented.

Record and Equipment Maintenance. Adequate space should exist for maintaining and storing records (e.g., equipment maintenance, controlled substances inventory, material safety data sheets) to ensure compliance with laws, regulations, accreditation requirements, and sound management practices. Appropriate licenses, permits, and tax stamps and other documents should be on display or on file as required. All nonautomated equipment should be adequately maintained and certified in accordance with applicable standards, laws, and regulations. Equipment maintenance and certification should be documented.

Office and Meeting Area. Adequate office and meeting areas should be available for administrative, educational, and training activities.

References

1. Johnson JA, Bootman JL. Drug-related morbidity and mortality, a cost-of-illness model. *Arch Intern Med.* 1995; 155:1949–56.
2. Lewis RK, Carter BL, Glover DG, Hutchinson RA. Comprehensive services in an ambulatory care pharmacy. *Am J Health-Syst Pharm.* 1995; 52:1793–7.
3. Segarra-Newnham M, Soisson KT. Provision of pharmaceutical care through comprehensive pharmacotherapy clinics. *Hosp Pharm.* 1997; 32(Jun):845–50.
4. Crane VS, Hatwig CA, Hayman JN, Hoffman R. Developing a management planning and control system for ambulatory pharmacy resources. *Pharm Pract Manage Q.* 1998; 18(1):52–71.
5. Rosum RW. Planning for an ambulatory care service. *Am J Health-Syst Pharm.* 1997; 54:1584, 1587.
6. Kernodle SJ. Improving health care with clinical practice guidelines and critical pathways: implications for

pharmacists in ambulatory practice. *Pharm Pract Manage Q.* 1997; 17(3):76–89.

7. LaCalamita S. Role of the pharmacist in developing critical pathways with warfarin therapy. *J Pharm Pract.* 1997; 10:398–410.

8. Curtiss FR. Lessons learned from projects in disease management in ambulatory care. *Am J Health-Syst Pharm.* 1997; 54:2217–29.

9. MacKinnon N. Performance measures in ambulatory pharmacy. *Pharm Pract Manage Q.* 1997; 17(1): 52–62.

10. Borgsdorf LR, Mian JS, and Knapp KK. Pharmacist-managed medication review in a managed care system. *Am J Hosp Pharm.* 1994; 51:772–7.

11. Mutnick AH, Sterba KJ, Szymusiak-Mutnick BA. Integration of quality assessment and a patient-specific intervention/outcomes program. *Pharm Pract Manage Q.* 1998: 17(4):25–36.

12. Hepler CD, Strand LM. Opportunities and responsibilities in pharmaceutical care. *Am J Hosp Pharm.* 1990; 47:533–43.

13. Lewis RK, Lasack NL, Lambert BL, Connor SE. Patient counseling—a focus on maintenance therapy. *Am J Health-Syst Pharm.* 1997; 54:2084–98.

14. United States Pharmacopeia. General Notices and Requirements—Preservation, Packaging, Storage, and Labeling. *Pharmacopeial Forum.* Nov-Dec 1998; 24 (6):7205–12.

15. Glover DG. Automated medication dispensing devices. *J Am Pharm Assn.* 1997; NS37(May-Jun):353–60.

Approved by the ASHP Board of Directors, April 21, 1999. Revised by the Council on Professional Affairs. Supersedes an earlier version, ASHP Guidelines on Pharmaceutical Services for Ambulatory Patients, dated November 14, 1990.

Richard K. Lewis, Pharm.D., MBA, Bryan F. Yeager, Pharm.D., Darryl G. Glover, Pharm.D., Jennifer White, Pharm.D., Aimee Gelhot, Pharm.D., and Christopher A. Hatwig, M.S., are gratefully acknowledged for drafting this revision.

The bibliographic citation for this document is as follows: American Society of Health-System Pharmacists. ASHP guidelines: minimum standard for pharmaceutical services in ambulatory care. *Am J Health-Syst Pharm.* 1999; 56:1744–53.

ASHP Guidelines: Minimum Standard for Pharmacies in Hospitals

Pharmacists work closely with other health practitioners to meet the needs of the public. The various societal needs for pharmaceutical care require that pharmacies provide a wide array of organized services. The primary purpose of this document is to serve as a guide for the provision of pharmaceutical services in hospitals; however, certain elements may be applicable to other health care settings. These Guidelines should also be useful in evaluating the scope and quality of these services.

As providers of pharmaceutical care, pharmacists are concerned with the outcomes of their services and not just the provision of these services. The elements of a pharmacy program that are critical to overall successful performance in a hospital include (1) leadership and practice management, (2) drug information and education, (3) activities to ensure rational medication therapy, (4) drug distribution and control, (5) facilities, and (6) participation in drug therapy research. Collectively, these elements represent a minimum level of practice that all hospital pharmacy departments must strive to provide on a consistent basis. While the scope of pharmaceutical services will likely vary from site to site, depending upon the needs of the patients served, these elements are inextricably linked to outcomes. Hence, failure to provide any of these services may compromise the overall quality of pharmaceutical care.

These Guidelines outline the minimum requirements for pharmaceutical services in hospitals. The reader is encouraged to review the ASHP practice standards referenced throughout this document for a more detailed description of the components of these services.

Standard I:
Leadership and Practice Management

Effective leadership and practice management skills are necessary for the delivery of pharmaceutical services in a manner consistent with the hospital's and patients' needs as well as continuous improvement in patient care outcomes. Pharmaceutical service management must focus on the pharmacist's responsibility to provide pharmaceutical care and to develop an organizational structure to support that mission.

The director of the pharmacy shall be responsible for (1) setting the short- and long-term goals of the pharmacy based on the needs of the patients served, the specific needs of the hospital (and any health system of which the hospital may be a component), and developments and trends in health care and hospital pharmacy practice, (2) developing plans and schedules for achieving these goals, (3) directing the implementation of the plans and the day-to-day activities associated with them, (4) determining whether the goals and schedule are being met, and (5) instituting corrective actions where necessary. The director of the pharmacy, in carrying out the aforementioned tasks, shall employ an adequate number of competent, qualified personnel. A part-time director of the pharmacy has the same basic obligations and responsibilities as a full-time director.

- *Education and training, director.* The pharmacy shall be managed by a professionally competent, legally

qualified pharmacist. The director of the pharmacy service must be thoroughly knowledgeable about hospital pharmacy practice and management. He or she should have completed a pharmacy residency program accredited by the American Society of Health-System Pharmacists.[1] An advanced management degree (e.g., M.B.A., M.H.A., M.S.) is desirable.

- *Pharmacy mission.* The pharmacy shall have a written mission statement that, at a minimum, reflects both patient care and operational responsibilities. Other aspects of the mission may be appropriate as well, for example, educational and research responsibilities in the case of teaching and research hospitals. The statement shall be consistent with the mission of the hospital (and health system of which the hospital may be a component). The mission should be understood by every employee and other participant (e.g., students and residents) in the pharmacy's activities.

- *Support personnel.* Sufficient support personnel (pharmacy technicians, clerical, secretarial) shall be employed to facilitate the implementation of pharmaceutical care. Pharmacy technicians should be certified by the Pharmacy Technician Certification Board and should have completed an accredited training program. Appropriate supervisory controls must be maintained and documented.

- *Work schedules and assignments.* The director of the pharmacy shall ensure that work schedules, procedures, and assignments optimize the use of personnel and resources.

- *Education and training.* All personnel must possess the education and training needed to fulfill their responsibilities. All personnel must participate in relevant continuing-education programs and activities as necessary to maintain or enhance their competence.[2]

- *Recruitment and selection of personnel.* Personnel must be recruited and selected on the basis of job-related qualifications and prior performance.

- *Orientation of personnel.* There must be an established procedure for orienting new personnel to the pharmacy, the hospital, and their respective positions.[3]

- *Performance evaluation.* Procedures for the routine evaluation of the performance of pharmacy personnel shall exist.

- *Position descriptions.* Areas of responsibility within the pharmacy shall be clearly defined. Written position descriptions for all categories of pharmacy personnel must exist and must be revised as necessary.

- *Operations manual.* An operations manual governing pharmacy functions (e.g., administrative, operational, and clinical) shall exist. It should include long-term goals for the pharmacy. The manual must be revised when necessary to reflect changes in procedures, organization, and objectives. All personnel should be familiar with the contents of the manual. Appropriate mechanisms to ensure compliance with the policies and procedures should be established.

- *Drug expenditures.* Policies and procedures for managing drug expenditures shall exist. They should address such methods as competitive bidding, group purchasing, utilization-review programs, and cost-effective patient services.[4]

- *Workload and financial performance.* A process shall exist to routinely monitor workload and financial performance. This process should provide for the determination and analysis of hospital and systemwide costs of medication therapy. A pharmacist should be an integral part of the hospital's financial management team.
- *Committee involvement.* A pharmacist should be a member of and actively participate in those committees responsible for establishing medication-related policies and procedures as well as those committees responsible for the provision of patient care.
- *Quality assessment and improvement.* There shall be an ongoing, systematic program for quality assessment and improvement of the pharmacy and medication-use process. This program should be integrated with the hospital's or health system's quality assessment and quality improvement activities. Quality improvement activities related to the distribution, administration, and use of medications shall be routinely performed. Feedback to appropriate individuals about the quality achieved shall be provided.
- *24-hour pharmaceutical services.* Adequate hours of operation for the provision of needed pharmaceutical services must be maintained; 24-hour pharmaceutical services should be provided if possible. Twenty-four-hour pharmaceutical services should exist in *all* hospitals with clinical programs that require intensive medication therapy (e.g., transplant programs, open-heart surgery programs, and neonatal intensive care units). When 24-hour pharmacy service is not feasible, a pharmacist must be available on an on-call basis.
- *After-hours pharmacy access.* In the absence of 24-hour pharmaceutical services, access to a limited supply of medications should be available to authorized nonpharmacists for use in carrying out urgent medication orders. The list of medications to be accessible and the policies and procedures to be used (including subsequent review of all activity by a pharmacist) shall be developed by the pharmacy and therapeutics (P&T) committee (or its equivalent). Items for such access should be chosen with safety in mind, limiting wherever possible medications, quantities, dosage forms, and container sizes that might endanger patients. Routine after-hours access to the pharmacy by nonpharmacists (e.g., nurses) for access to medications is strongly discouraged; this practice should be minimized and eliminated to the fullest extent possible. The use of well-designed night cabinets, after-hours medication carts, and other methods precludes the need for nonpharmacists to enter the pharmacy.[5] For emergency situations in which nonpharmacist access is necessary, policies and procedures should exist for safe access to medications by persons who receive telephone authorization from an on-call pharmacist.
- *Practice standards and guidelines.* The practice standards and guidelines of the American Society of Health-System Pharmacists and the Joint Commission on Accreditation of Healthcare Organizations (JCAHO) or other appropriate accrediting body should be viewed as applicable, and the hospital should strive to meet these standards regardless of the particular financial and organizational arrangements by which pharmaceutical services are provided to the facility and its patients.
- *Laws and regulations.* Applicable laws and regulations must be met and relevant documentation of compliance must be maintained (e.g., records, material safety data sheets, copies of state board regulations).
- *Patient confidentiality.* The pharmacist shall respect and protect patient confidentiality by safeguarding access to computer databases and reports containing patient information. Patient information should be shared only with authorized health professionals and others authorized within the hospital or health system as needed for the care of patients.

Standard II:
Drug Information and Education

The pharmacist shall provide patient-specific drug information and accurate and comprehensive information about drugs to other pharmacists, other health professionals, and patients as appropriate.

Up-to-date drug information shall be available, including current periodicals and recent editions of textbooks in appropriate pharmaceutical and biomedical subject areas. Electronic information is desirable. This information may be provided in conjunction with medical libraries and other available resources. Appropriate drug information resources shall be readily accessible to pharmacists located in patient care areas. No medication should be administered to a patient unless medical and nursing personnel have received adequate information about, and are familiar with, its therapeutic use, potential adverse effects, and dosage.

- *Drug information requests.* Responses to general and patient-specific drug information requests shall be provided in an accurate and timely manner. A process shall exist to assess and ensure the quality of responses to requests.
- *Medication-therapy monographs.* Medication-therapy monographs for medications under consideration for formulary addition or deletion shall be available. These monographs should be based on an analytical review of pertinent literature. Each monograph shall include a comparative therapeutic and economic assessment of each medication proposed for addition.
- *Patient education.* Pharmacists should be available for and actively participate in patient education. Pharmacists must help to ensure that all patients are given adequate information (including information on ethical issues, if any) about the medications they receive. Patient education activities shall be coordinated with the nursing, medical, and other clinical staff as needed.[6]
- *Dissemination of drug information.* Pharmacists should keep the hospital's staff informed about the use of medications on an ongoing basis through appropriate publications, presentations, and programs. Pharmacists should ensure timely dissemination of drug product information (e.g., recall notices, labeling changes).

Standard III:
Optimizing Medication Therapy

An important aspect of pharmaceutical care is optimizing medication use. This must include processes designed to ensure the safe and effective use of medications and increase the probability of desired patient outcomes. The pharmacist, in concert with the medical and nursing staff, must develop policies and procedures for ensuring the quality of medication therapy.

- *Medical record documentation.* Clinical actions and recommendations by pharmacists that are designed to ensure safe and effective use of medications and that have a potential effect on patient outcomes should be documented in patients' medical records.[7]
- *Medication histories.* Pharmacists should prepare or have immediate access to comprehensive medication histories for each patient's medical record or other databases (e.g., medication profile), or both. A pharmacist-conducted medication history for each patient is desirable.
- *Medication orders.* All prescribers' medication orders (except in emergency situations) must be reviewed for appropriateness by a pharmacist before the first dose is dispensed. Any questions regarding the order must be resolved with the prescriber at this time, and a written notation of these discussions must be made in the patient's medical record or pharmacy copy of the prescriber's order. Information concerning changes must be communicated to the appropriate health professional.
- *Medication-therapy monitoring.* Medication-therapy monitoring shall be conducted for appropriate patients and medication use. Medication-therapy monitoring includes an assessment of
  - a. The therapeutic appropriateness of the patient's medication regimen.
  - b. Therapeutic duplication in the patient's medication regimen.
  - c. The appropriateness of the route and method of administration of the medication.
  - d. The degree of patient compliance with the prescribed medication regimen.
  - e. Medication–medication, medication–food, medication–laboratory test, and medication–disease interactions.
  - f. Clinical and pharmacokinetic laboratory data to evaluate the efficacy of medication therapy and to anticipate toxicity and adverse effects.
  - g. Physical signs and clinical symptoms relevant to the patient's medication therapy.
- *Therapeutic purpose.* Prescribers should be encouraged to routinely communicate the condition being treated or the therapeutic purpose of medications with all prescription and medication orders.
- *Pharmacist consultations.* Pharmacists should provide oral and written consultations to other health professionals regarding medication-therapy selection and management.
- *Medication-use evaluation.* An ongoing medication-use evaluation program shall exist to ensure that medications are used appropriately, safely, and effectively.[8]
- *Medication-use policy development.* The pharmacist shall be a member of the P&T committee, the institu-

tional review board, and the infection control, patient care, medication-use evaluation, and other committees that make decisions concerning medication use.
- *Documentation of pharmaceutical care and outcomes.* The pharmacy shall have an ongoing process for consistent documentation (and reporting to medical staff, administrators, and others) of pharmaceutical care and patient outcomes from medication therapy and other pharmacy actions.
- *Continuity of care.* The pharmacist shall routinely contribute to processes ensuring that each patient's pharmaceutical care is maintained regardless of transitions that occur across different care settings (for example, among different components of a health system or between inpatient and community pharmacies or home care services).
- *Work redesign initiatives.* The pharmacist must be involved in work redesign initiatives such as patient-focused care, where they exist. These efforts should be such that pharmaceutical care is enhanced and supported.
- *Clinical care plans.* Pharmacists must be involved in the development of clinical care plans involving medication therapy.
- *Microbial resistance.* Policies and procedures addressing microbial resistance to anti-infectives shall exist. Pharmacists should review laboratory reports of microbial sensitivities and advise prescribers if microbial resistance is noted.
- *Medication-therapy decisions.* The pharmacist's prerogatives to initiate, monitor, and modify medication therapy for individual patients, consistent with laws, regulations, and hospital policy, shall be clearly delineated and approved by the P&T committee (or comparable body).
- *Immunization programs.* The pharmacy shall participate in the development of hospital policies and procedures concerning preventive and postexposure immunization programs for patients and hospital employees.[9]
- *Substance-abuse programs.* The pharmacy shall assist in the development of and participate in hospital substance-abuse prevention and employee assistance programs, where they exist.

Standard IV:
Medication Distribution and Control

The pharmacy shall be responsible for the procurement, distribution, and control of *all* drug products used in the hospital (including medication-related devices and pharmaceutical diagnostics) for inpatient and ambulatory patients.[10] Policies and procedures governing these functions shall be developed by the pharmacy with input from other appropriate hospital staff and committees.

- *Medication orders.* All patient medication orders shall be contained in the patient's medical record. A direct copy of the prescriber's order, either hard copy or prescriber-entered electronic transmission (preferred method), shall be received by the pharmacist. Order-transmittal safeguards should be used to ensure the security of the prescriber's order. All medication orders shall be reviewed by a pharmacist and assessed in relation to a medication profile before administration, unless an established procedure exists for the use of an approved list of medications for specific treatment circumstances and emergencies. A system shall exist to ensure that medication orders are not inappropriately continued.

- *Formulary.* A formulary of approved medications shall be maintained by the pharmacy.[11]

- *Prescribing.* Medications shall be prescribed by individuals who have been granted appropriate clinical privileges in the hospital and are legally permitted to order medications. The pharmacy shall advocate and foster practitioners' conformance with standardized, approved terminology and abbreviations to be used throughout the hospital when prescribing medications.

- *Medication administration.* Only personnel who are authorized by the hospital and appropriately trained shall be permitted to administer medications to a patient. This may include pharmacists and other pharmacy personnel.

- *Extemporaneous compounding.* Drug formulations, dosage forms, strengths, and packaging that are not available commercially but are needed for patient care shall be prepared by appropriately trained personnel in accordance with applicable practice standards and regulations (e.g., FDA, state board of pharmacy). Adequate quality assurance procedures shall exist for these operations.[12]

- *Sterile products.* All sterile medications shall be prepared and labeled in a suitable environment by appropriately trained personnel. Quality assurance procedures for the preparation of sterile products shall exist.[13]

- *Unit dose packaging.* Whenever possible, medications shall be available for inpatient use in single-unit packages and in a ready-to-administer form. Manipulation of medications before administration (e.g., withdrawal of doses from multidose containers, labeling containers) by final users should be minimized.[14]

- *Medication storage.* Medications shall be stored and prepared under proper conditions of sanitation, temperature, light, moisture, ventilation, segregation, and security to ensure medication integrity and personnel safety.

- *Adverse drug reactions.* An ongoing program for monitoring, reporting, and preventing adverse drug reactions shall be developed.[15]

- *Medication errors.* Pharmacists, with physicians and other appropriate hospital personnel, shall establish policies and procedures with respect to medication-error prevention and reporting.[5] Ongoing monitoring and review of medication errors with corresponding appropriate action should be maintained.

- *Drug product recalls.* A written procedure shall exist for the handling of a drug product recall. There should be an established process for removing from use any drugs or devices subjected to a recall.

- *Patient's own medications.* Drug products and related devices brought into the hospital by patients shall be identified by pharmacy and documented in the patient's medical record if the medications are to be used during hospitalization. They shall be administered only pursuant to a prescriber's order and according to hospital policies and procedures.

- *Vendors' representatives.* Written policies governing the activities of representatives of vendors of drug products (including related supplies and devices) within the hospital shall exist.[16]

- *Samples.* The use of medication samples shall be eliminated to the extent possible. However, if samples are permitted, the pharmacy must control these products to ensure proper storage, maintenance of records, and product integrity.

- *Manufacturers and suppliers.* Criteria for selecting drug product manufacturers and suppliers shall be established by the pharmacy to ensure high quality of drug products.[17]

- *Cytotoxic and hazardous drug products.* Policies and procedures for storage, handling, and disposal of cytotoxic and other hazardous drug products shall exist.[18]

- *Controlled substances.* Accountability procedures shall exist to ensure control of the distribution and use of controlled substances and other medications with a potential for abuse.[19]

- *Nondrug substances.* The pharmacy shall seek and obtain documented authorization from appropriate medical staff and hospital committees for the pharmacologic use of any chemical substance that has never received FDA approval for any drug use. Documentation must exist to ensure that appropriate risk management measures (e.g., obtaining informed consent) have been taken.

- *Medication storage area inspections.* All stocks of medications shall be inspected routinely to ensure the absence of outdated, unusable, or mislabeled products. Storage conditions that would foster medication deterioration and storage arrangements that might contribute to medication errors also must be assessed, documented, and corrected.

- *Floor stock.* Floor stocks of medications generally shall be limited to medications for emergency use and routinely used safe items (e.g., mouthwash, antiseptic solutions). The potential for medication errors and adverse effects must be considered for every medication allowed as floor stock.

- *Disaster services.* A procedure shall exist for providing pharmaceutical services in case of disaster.

- *Medical emergencies.* The pharmacy shall participate in hospital decisions about emergency medication kits and the role of pharmacists in medical emergencies.

- *Drug delivery systems, administration devices, and automated dispensing machines.* Pharmacists shall provide leadership and advice in organizational and clinical decisions regarding drug delivery systems, administration devices, and automated dispensing machines and should participate in the evaluation, use, and monitoring of these systems and devices.[20] The potential for medication errors associated with such systems and devices must be thoroughly evaluated.

Standard V: Facilities, Equipment, and Information Resources

To ensure optimal operational performance and quality patient care, adequate space, equipment, and supplies shall be available for all professional and administrative functions relating to medication use. These resources must be located in areas that facilitate the provision of services to patients, nurses, prescribers, and other health care providers and must be integrated with the hospital's communication and delivery or transportation systems. Facilities shall be constructed, arranged, and equipped to promote safe and efficient work and to avoid damage to or deterioration of drug products.

- *Medication storage.* Facilities shall exist to enable the storage and preparation of medications under proper conditions of sanitation, temperature, light, moisture, ventilation, segregation, and security to ensure medication integrity and personnel safety throughout the hospital.
- *Packaging and compounding.* Designated space and equipment for packaging and compounding drug products and preparing sterile products shall exist. There shall be a suitable work environment that promotes orderliness and efficiency and minimizes potential for contamination of products.[13,14]
- *Cytotoxic and hazardous drug products.* Special precautions, equipment, and training for storage, handling, and disposal of cytotoxic and other hazardous drug products shall exist to ensure the safety of personnel, patients, and visitors.[18]
- *Drug information.* Adequate space, resources, and information-handling and communication technology shall be available to facilitate the provision of drug information.
- *Consultation space.* In outpatient dispensing areas, a private area for pharmacist–patient consultations shall be available to enhance patients' knowledge of and compliance with prescribed medication regimens.
- *Office and meeting space.* Office and meeting areas shall be available for administrative, educational, and training activities.
- *Automation.* Automated mechanical systems and software may be useful in promoting accurate and efficient medication ordering and preparation, drug distribution, and clinical monitoring, provided they are safely used and do not hinder the pharmacist's review of (and opportunity to intervene in) medication orders before the administration of first doses. An interface with a comprehensive pharmacy computer system is encouraged. Pharmacy personnel must supervise the stocking of medications in dispensing machines.
- *Record maintenance.* Adequate space shall exist for maintaining and storing records (e.g., equipment maintenance, controlled substances inventory, material safety data sheets) to ensure compliance with laws, regulations, accreditation requirements, and sound management techniques. Appropriate licenses, permits, and tax stamps shall be present. Equipment shall be adequately maintained and certified in accordance with applicable practice standards, laws, and regulations. There shall be documentation of equipment maintenance and certification.
- *Computerized systems.* Computer resources should be used to support secretarial functions, maintain patient medication profile records, perform necessary patient billing procedures, manage drug product inventories, and interface with other available computerized systems to obtain patient-specific clinical information for medication therapy monitoring and other clinical functions and to facilitate the continuity of care to and from other care settings.

Standard VI: Research

The pharmacist should initiate, participate in, and support medical and pharmaceutical research appropriate to the goals, objectives, and resources of the specific hospital.[21]

- *Policies and procedures.* The pharmacist shall ensure that policies and procedures for the safe and proper use of investigational drugs are established and followed.[22]
- *Distribution and control.* The pharmacy shall be responsible for overseeing the distribution and control of all investigational drugs. Investigational drugs shall be approved for use by an institutional review board and shall be dispensed and administered to consenting patients according to an approved protocol.[22]
- *Institutional review board.* A pharmacist shall be included on the hospital's institutional review board.
- *Drug information.* The pharmacist shall have access to information on all investigational studies and similar research projects involving medications and medication-related devices used in the hospital. The pharmacist shall provide pertinent written information (to the extent known) about the safe and proper use of investigational drugs, including possible adverse effects and adverse drug reactions to nurses, pharmacists, physicians, and other health care professionals called upon to administer, dispense, and prescribe these medications.

References

1. American Society of Hospital Pharmacists. ASHP residency accreditation regulations and standards on definitions of pharmacy residencies and fellowships. *Am J Hosp Pharm.* 1987; 44:1142–4.
2. American Society of Hospital Pharmacists. ASHP statement on continuing education. *Am J Hosp Pharm.* 1990; 47:1855.
3. American Society of Hospital Pharmacists. ASHP technical assistance bulletin on the recruitment, selection, and retention of pharmacy personnel. *Am J Hosp Pharm.* 1994; 51:1811–5.
4. American Society of Hospital Pharmacists. ASHP technical assistance bulletin on assessing cost-containment strategies for pharmacies in organized health-care settings. *Am J Hosp Pharm.* 1992; 49:155–60.
5. American Society of Hospital Pharmacists. ASHP guidelines on preventing medication errors in hospitals. *Am J Hosp Pharm.* 1993; 50:305–14.
6. American Society of Hospital Pharmacists. ASHP statement on the pharmacist's role in patient education programs. *Am J Hosp Pharm.* 1991; 48:1780.
7. American Society of Hospital Pharmacists. ASHP guidelines for obtaining authorization for documenting pharmaceutical care in patient medical records. *Am J Hosp Pharm.* 1989; 46:338–9.
8. American Society of Hospital Pharmacists. ASHP guidelines on the pharmacist's role in drug-use evaluation. *Am J Hosp Pharm.* 1988; 45:385–6.
9. American Society of Hospital Pharmacists. ASHP technical assistance bulletin on the pharmacist's role in immunization. *Am J Hosp Pharm.* 1993; 50:501–5.
10. American Society of Hospital Pharmacists. ASHP statement on the pharmacist's responsibility for distribution and control of drug products. *Am J Hosp Pharm.* 1995; 52:747.
11. American Society of Hospital Pharmacists. ASHP statement on the formulary system. *Am J Hosp Pharm.* 1983; 40:1384–5.
12. American Society of Hospital Pharmacists. ASHP technical assistance bulletin on compounding nonsterile

products in pharmacies. *Am J Hosp Pharm.* 1994; 51:1441–8.

13. American Society of Hospital Pharmacists. ASHP technical assistance bulletin on quality assurance for pharmacy-prepared sterile products. *Am J Hosp Pharm.* 1993; 50:2386–98.

14. American Society of Hospital Pharmacists. ASHP technical assistance bulletin on single unit and unit dose packages of drugs. *Am J Hosp Pharm.* 1985; 42:378–9.

15. American Society of Hospital Pharmacists. ASHP guidelines on adverse drug reaction monitoring and reporting. *Am J Health-Syst Pharm.* 1995; 52:417–9.

16. American Society of Hospital Pharmacists. ASHP guidelines for pharmacists on the activities of vendors' representatives in organized health care systems. *Am J Hosp Pharm.* 1994; 51:520–1.

17. American Society of Hospital Pharmacists. ASHP guidelines for selecting pharmaceutical manufacturers and suppliers. *Am J Hosp Pharm.* 1991; 48:523–4.

18. American Society of Hospital Pharmacists. ASHP technical assistance bulletin on handling cytotoxic and hazardous drugs. *Am J Hosp Pharm.* 1990; 47: 1033–49.

19. American Society of Hospital Pharmacists. ASHP technical assistance bulletin on use of controlled sub-stances in organized health-care settings. *Am J Hosp Pharm.* 1993; 50:489–501.

20. American Society of Hospital Pharmacists. ASHP statement on the pharmacist's role with respect to drug delivery systems and administration devices. *Am J Hosp Pharm.* 1993; 50:1724–5.

21. American Society of Hospital Pharmacists. ASHP guidelines for the use of investigational drugs in organized health-care settings. *Am J Hosp Pharm.* 1991; 48:315–9.

22. American Society of Hospital Pharmacists. ASHP statement on pharmaceutical research in organized health-care settings. *Am J Hosp Pharm.* 1991; 48:1781.

Approved by the ASHP Board of Directors, September 22, 1995. Revised by the ASHP Council on Professional Affairs. Supersedes an earlier version dated November 14–15, 1984.

The bibliographic citation for this document is as follows: American Society of Health-System Pharmacists. ASHP guidelines: minimum standard for pharmacies in hospitals. *Am J Health-Syst Pharm.* 1995; 52:2711–7.

ASHP Guidelines on the Pharmacist's Role in Home Care

Purpose

The purpose of these guidelines is to define the role of the pharmacist in providing pharmaceutical care to patients in the home[1] or alternate-site setting. In broad terms, home care is the provision of specialized, complex pharmaceutical products and clinical assessment and monitoring to patients in their homes. This generally includes home infusion therapy and other injectable drug therapy and parenteral and enteral nutrition therapy. These therapies require resources and support beyond those of the traditional orally and topically administered therapies. Specific pharmacist education and training, drug product admixtures and administration techniques, equipment operation and maintenance, and patient monitoring are required to ensure successful outcomes. These guidelines outline the pharmacist's role in providing these services and products. They are not intended to apply to home health services that do not involve the provision of pharmaceutical services.

Many of the activities included in these guidelines are the subjects of other ASHP policy and guidance documents, which should be referred to for additional information. Pharmacists practicing in home care should use professional judgment in assessing ASHP's policy and guidance documents and in adapting them to meet their health care organizations' and patients' needs and circumstances.

Background

Home care services are provided by a variety of organizations, including hospitals, community pharmacies, home health agencies, hospices, and specialized infusion companies. Patients receive care in noninpatient settings, such as their homes and ambulatory infusion centers, or in alternate-site settings, such as skilled-nursing facilities. These guidelines apply to the provision of home care services by pharmacists practicing in all health care settings. It should be noted that different aspects of home care can be provided by different organizations. When services are shared among providers, pharmacists have a professional responsibility to ensure that all patient care responsibilities are defined, understood, agreed upon, and documented in advance by all providers.

Pharmacists' Responsibilities

Preadmission Assessment. The pharmacist should ensure that each patient referred for home care is assessed for appropriateness on the basis of admission criteria, including the following:

- The patient, family, and caregiver agree with provision of care services in the home.
- The patient or caregiver is willing to be educated about the correct administration of medications.
- The home environment is conducive to the provision of home care services (e.g., electricity and running water are present, and the home is clean).
- The home care provider has reasonable geographic access to the patient.

- There is psychosocial and family support (e.g., caregiver requirements and financial concerns are manageable, and the family environment is suitable).
- There is ongoing prescriber involvement in the assessment and treatment of the patient.
- The medical condition and prescribed medication therapy are suitable for home care services, and there is a prognosis with clearly defined outcome goals.
- The indication, dosage, and route and method of administration of medications are appropriate.
- Appropriate laboratory tests are ordered for monitoring the patient's response to medications.

Using the information collected during the preadmission assessment, the pharmacist, in conjunction with the other health care providers involved in the patient's care and the patient or caregiver, will determine the patient's appropriateness for home infusion services. The conclusions of the assessment should be communicated to all parties and appropriately documented.

Before the start of home care services, patients should be informed of their rights and responsibilities, including financial obligations. These should be explained in detail; given to the patient, family member, or other caregiver in writing; and documented in the patient's record.

In cases in which the first dose of a medication is to be given at home, the pharmacist should use clinical judgment in determining, in conjunction with the prescriber, home care nurse, and patient or caregiver, if home administration of the first dose is appropriate. Policies and procedures should define factors to be used in making this decision and precautions necessary when first doses are administered at home (e.g., emergency medications, monitoring and observation, and presence of a health care provider).[2]

Once a patient is accepted for home care, the pharmacist should assess the patient's current status and develop a patient database for ongoing drug therapy monitoring and as an evaluation tool for measuring patient outcomes. In most home care practice sites, the pharmacist is responsible for obtaining the medication order from the prescriber. In addition, the pharmacist should assess the legality and appropriateness of the medication order.

Initial Patient Database and Assessment. The complete patient database should be documented in the patient's home care record. This database should include, at a minimum, the following:

- The patient's name, address, telephone number, and date of birth,
- The person to contact in the event of an emergency, including the legal guardian or representative, if applicable,
- Information on the existence, content, and intent of an advance directive, if applicable,
- The patient's height, weight, and sex,
- All diagnoses,
- The location and type of intravenous access and when it was placed, if applicable,
- Pertinent laboratory test results,

- Pertinent medical history and physical findings,
- Nutrition screening test results,
- An accurate history of allergies,
- Initial and ongoing pharmaceutical assessments,
- A detailed medication profile, including all medications (prescription and nonprescription), immunizations, home remedies, and investigational and nontraditional therapies,
- The prescriber's name, address, and telephone number and any other pertinent information (e.g., Drug Enforcement Administration number),
- Other agencies and individuals involved in the patient's care and directions for contacting them,
- A history of medication use,
- A care plan and a list of drug-related problems, if any,
- Treatment goals and the expected duration of therapy,
- Indicators of desired outcomes,
- Patient education previously provided,
- Any functional limitations of the patient, and
- Any pertinent social history (e.g., alcohol consumption and tobacco use).

To obtain this information, the pharmacist could use the medical record; laboratory test results; direct communication with the patient, caregiver, nurse, and prescriber; and direct observation. When the pharmacist cannot directly observe the patient, the patient's home care nurse or other appropriate health care provider could provide the results of direct observation and physical assessment. If a shared-service agreement exists among multiple providers, the pharmacist should ensure that this agreement specifies the responsibilities of each provider for obtaining and sharing pertinent patient information.

Selection of Products, Devices, and Ancillary Supplies.
The pharmacist, in collaboration with other health care providers and the patient, is responsible for selecting infusion devices, ancillary drugs (e.g., heparin lock flush solution and 0.9% sodium chloride injection), and ancillary supplies (e.g., dressing kits, syringes, and administration sets).[3,4] Pharmacists should be thoroughly trained and knowledgeable in the selection, proper use, and maintenance of these devices, drugs, and supplies. Factors involved in the selection of devices and ancillary supplies may include the following:

- The stability and compatibility of prescribed medications in infusion device reservoirs,
- The ability of an infusion device to accommodate the appropriate volume of medication and diluent and to deliver the prescribed dose at the appropriate rate,
- The ability of the patient or caregiver to learn to operate an infusion device,
- The potential for patient complications and noncompliance,
- Patient convenience,
- Nursing or caregiver experience with therapies and selected devices,
- Prescriber preferences,
- Cost considerations, and
- The safety features of infusion devices.

The home care pharmacist, in consultation with the prescriber, should determine when emergency medications and supplies (e.g., anaphylaxis "kits") should be dispensed to home care patients. When standing orders for ancillary drugs or supplies or standardized treatment protocols are used, the pharmacist should review each protocol to determine its appropriateness for the patient.

Development of Care Plans. The pharmacist, in collaboration with the patient or caregiver and other health care providers, is responsible for developing an appropriate and individualized care plan for each patient. The pharmacist's contribution to the care plan should be based on information obtained from the initial pharmacy assessment and other relevant information obtained from the nurse, the prescriber, the patient, and the caregiver. At a minimum, the pharmacist's contribution to the care plan should include the following[5]:

- A description of actual or potential drug therapy problems and their proposed solutions,
- A description of desired outcomes of drug therapy provided,
- A proposal for patient education and counseling, and
- A plan specifying proactive objective and subjective monitoring (e.g., vital signs, laboratory tests, physical findings, patient response, toxicity, adverse reactions, and noncompliance) and the frequency with which monitoring is to occur.

The care plan should be developed at the start of therapy and regularly reviewed and updated. The degree of detail of the plan should be based on the complexity of drug therapy and the patient's condition.

The pharmacist is responsible for communicating care plan contributions to other health care providers involved in the patient's care, to the patient, and to the caregiver. Updates, as they occur, should be communicated to the appropriate persons. The care plan and updates should be a part of the patient's record.

Patient Education and Counseling. The pharmacist is responsible for ensuring that the patient or caregiver receives appropriate education and counseling about the patient's medication therapy. The pharmacist should verify that the patient or caregiver understands the therapy. Other health care providers may be involved. A home care pharmacist should be readily accessible if questions or problems arise. Supplementary written information should be provided to reinforce oral communications. Contingencies should be available to provide education, counseling, and written materials to patients who do not speak English. Depending on the need, this might require access to interpreters or bilingual pharmacists.

Professional judgment is required to determine what information should be included in patient education and counseling. The following should be considered:

- A description of medication therapy, including drug, dose, route of administration, dosage interval, and duration of therapy,
- The goals of medication therapy and indicators of progress toward those goals,
- Self-assessment techniques for monitoring the effectiveness of therapy,
- The importance of following the therapeutic plan,
- Proper aseptic technique,
- Proper care of the vascular-access device and site, if applicable,

- Precautions and directions for administering medications,
- Inspection of medications, containers, and supplies prior to use,
- Equipment use, maintenance, and troubleshooting,
- Home inventory management and procedures for securing additional supplies and medications when needed,
- Potential adverse effects, drug–drug interactions, drug–nutrient interactions, contraindications, and adverse reactions, and their management,
- Special precautions and directions for the preparation, storage, handling, and disposal of drugs, supplies, and biomedical waste,
- Information on contacting health care providers involved in the patient's care,
- Examples of situations that should be brought to the attention of the pharmacist or other health care providers involved in the patient's care (e.g., missed doses, doses not given at the proper time, and low supplies), and
- Emergency procedures.

Patient counseling and education should be performed in accordance with applicable state regulations and documented in the patient's home care record.

Clinical Monitoring. The pharmacist is responsible for ongoing clinical monitoring of the patient's drug therapy according to the care plan and for appropriately documenting and communicating the results of all pertinent monitoring activities to other health care providers involved in the patient's care. The pharmacist is also responsible for ensuring that relevant information is obtained from the patient, the caregiver, and other health care providers and for documenting this information in the patient's home care record.

Pharmacists may, in collaboration with prescribers and others, wish to develop clinical monitoring protocols for various therapies that could be individualized in specific care plans. Pharmacists may receive laboratory test results before other health care providers. In such cases, the pharmacist is responsible for communicating the test results to the prescriber and other health care providers. The pharmacist should provide an interpretive analysis of the information and recommendations for dosage adjustments and for continuation or discontinuation of drug therapy. The pharmacist should ensure that sufficient laboratory test results are readily available for monitoring the patient's therapy. In shared-service arrangements, clinical monitoring responsibilities should be delineated.

Effective communication with prescribers, nurses, and other health care providers. Effective communication among pharmacists, prescribers, nurses, and other health care providers is essential to ensuring continuous, coordinated care. The pharmacist should ensure that effective channels of communication about care are in place, including shared-service arrangements (e.g., regarding pain assessments and laboratory test data). Both oral and written communication methods can be used for communicating patient information. All relevant clinical communication should be documented in the patient's home care record. The pharmacist is responsible for protecting the patient's privacy and confidentiality while communicating this information to other health care providers. It is recommended that personnel involved in the care of the patient (e.g., nurses, pharmacists, dietitians, delivery representatives, and reimbursement coordinators) meet regularly to discuss the clinical status of the patient and any operational issues related to the patient's care.

The patient, the family, the caregiver, and all health care providers involved in the patient's care should have access to a pharmacist 24 hours a day. The pharmacist is responsible for providing a summary of all relevant clinical information to another pharmacist providing coverage for that patient (e.g., an on-call pharmacist) before transferring patient care responsibilities.

Communication with the Patient and the Caregiver. The pharmacist providing home care services should establish free and open channels of communication with the patient or the caregiver. The pharmacist should contact the patient or the caregiver, as appropriate, to

- Obtain information needed for the initial pharmacy assessment,
- Provide supplemental patient education and counseling as needed,
- Assess compliance with drug therapy,
- Assess progress toward the goal of therapy,
- Inform the patient how to contact the pharmacist when needed, and
- Assess drug therapy problems (e.g., failure to respond to therapy and adverse drug events).

All contacts with the patient should be documented in the patient's home care record.

Coordination of Drug Preparation, Delivery, Storage, and Administration. The pharmacist is responsible for ensuring the proper acquisition, compounding, dispensing, storage, delivery, and administration of all medications and related equipment and supplies. Compounding of sterile products should comply with applicable practice standards, accreditation standards, and pertinent state and federal laws and regulations. If these services are being provided by another pharmacy, the pharmacist should have reasonable assurance that these standards are being met by the pharmacy providing the service. Pharmacists may administer medications to patients in the home setting unless prohibited by applicable laws and regulations.

The pharmacist should ensure that the delivery of medications and supplies to the patient occurs in a timely manner to avoid interruptions in drug therapy. Furthermore, the pharmacist should ensure that storage conditions during delivery and while in the patient's home are consistent with the recommendations for storing the product and beyond-use dating. The temperature of home refrigerators or freezers in which medications are stored should be within acceptable limits and should be monitored by the patient or caregiver. The pharmacist should ensure that an adequate inventory of medications and ancillary supplies is available in the patient's home. It may be appropriate to provide additional inventory for unforeseen circumstances in which extra doses or supplies may be required (e.g., waste, breakage, and emergencies).

Standard Precautions for Employee and Patient Safety. A home care organization is responsible for helping teach employees, patients, family members, and caregivers about standard safety precautions. The pharmacist should ensure that the home care organization provides appropriate education for its employees and patients, including education about appropriate disposal and handling of medical waste, procedures for preventing and managing needle and sharps stick injuries, handling of cytotoxic and hazardous medications,[6] and material safety data sheets. The pharmacist should be a key resource in the development of such educational programs. The pharmacist should assume an active role in the home care organization's infection-control activities.

Documentation in the Home Care Record. A home care record should be developed and used for documenting the home care services provided to each patient. Written organizational policies and procedures should address the security of home care records and specify personnel authorized to review patient records and to make entries. The need to maintain confidentiality of patient information should be stressed to all personnel.

The pharmacist is responsible for documenting all pharmacy clinical activities in the patient's record in a timely manner. General clinician-oriented forms are preferred over specific nursing, pharmacy, and other health care professional forms to minimize duplication of information.

It may be advisable for organizations that provide multiple home care services (e.g., pharmacy, nursing, and respiratory therapy) to use a single home care record for documenting all clinical information regarding each patient. The patient's record should be accessible at all times to authorized personnel involved in the care of the patient, but confidentiality should be maintained.

Adverse Drug Event Reporting and Performance Improvement. The home care pharmacist should take a leadership role in the development of a program for reporting and monitoring all adverse drug events and device-related events, including adverse drug reactions and medication errors. The pharmacist should ensure that the prescriber is notified promptly of any suspected adverse drug events. Adverse drug events should serve as outcome indicators of quality, and the monitoring of adverse drug events should be a part of the organization's ongoing performance improvement program. Relevant trends should be integrated into staff development and inservice education programs for pharmacists and nurses to improve the quality of care and patient outcomes. Serious adverse drug reactions and device-related problems should be reported promptly to the manufacturer and to the Food and Drug Administration's MedWatch program. Medication errors should be reported to the USP Practitioner Reporting Program. Sentinel events should be reported to the Joint Commission on Accreditation of Healthcare Organizations.

Participation in Clinical Drug Research in the Home. The pharmacist should play a key role in the development of policies and procedures for handling investigational drugs and their protocols in the home care setting. When patient participation in clinical drug research is initiated in the institutional setting or another setting before the patient's transfer to the home care setting, it is important that the home care pharmacist obtain and keep on file sufficient information about the investigational drug protocol and drugs. If an investigational drug is dispensed or administered by the home care organization, a copy of the completed and signed informed consent should be placed in the patient's home care record. The home care pharmacist should review the proto-

col before the patient is admitted to the home care service to determine whether it would be appropriate to treat the patient at home. When investigational drug inventories are maintained in the home care pharmacy, the pharmacist is responsible for accurate record keeping. The pharmacist should be an active participant in coordinating and monitoring clinical drug research in home care.

Participation in Performance Improvement Activities. Pharmacists should be active participants in performance improvement activities in their organizations. A performance improvement program for home care should monitor patient satisfaction and outcomes. Aspects of care that may be monitored include, but are not limited to, the following:

* Unscheduled inpatient admissions,
* Unexpected discontinuation of infusion therapy,
* Interruption of infusion therapy,
* Development of infections or complications,
* Reported adverse drug reactions and adverse device-related reactions,
* Medication errors, and
* Medication-related problems.

The performance improvement program should include appropriate quality control measures for compounding sterile products and other activities.

Policies and Procedures. The home care pharmacist should be an active participant in the development of organizational policies and procedures. The organization should maintain current policies and procedures for all aspects of patient care and quality assurance. Activities that should be addressed in policies and procedures include criteria for accepting patients into home care services, patient education and counseling, drug preparation and dispensing, equipment maintenance, quality assurance in sterile product compounding, infection control, and documentation.

Licensure. Pharmacists who provide home care services must have an active license to practice pharmacy issued by the applicable state board of pharmacy and other credentials as required by local, state, or federal laws and regulations. Some states require special licensure or training for preparing sterile products. Pharmacists dispensing medications to patients who reside in other states may also be subject to laws and regulations in those states; additional licensure may be required. The pharmacist should know about all applicable federal and state laws and regulations.

Training, Continuing Education, and Competence. Pharmacists should receive training as necessary to ensure that they possess the knowledge and skills required for the provision of home care services. They should participate in ongoing continuing-education activities to update and enhance their knowledge and skills related to home care. Pharmacists should participate in an ongoing competence assessment program as part of an overall staff development program. A valid assessment of competence should consider the pharmacist's responsibilities and the types and ages of patients. The assessment should be conducted and documented on an ongoing basis for all pharmacists. When appropriate, pharmacists should assist in training and in continuing-education programs for other home care providers. Pharmacists should provide, to the extent possible in their organizations, student clerkship, externship, and internship training, as well as postgraduate residency training.

References

1. Pelham LD, Norwood MR. Home health care services. In: Brown TR, ed. Handbook of institutional pharmacy practice. 3rd ed. Bethesda, MD: American Society of Hospital Pharmacists; 1992:357–66.
2. McNulty TJ. Initiation of antimicrobial therapy in the home. *Am J Hosp Pharm.* 1993; 50:773–4.
3. Kwan J. High-technology i.v. infusion devices. *Am J Hosp Pharm.* 1991; 48:536–51.
4. Bowles C, McKinnon BT. Selecting infusion devices. *Am J Hosp Pharm.* 1993; 50:1228–30.
5. Hepler CD, Strand LM. Opportunities and responsibilities in pharmaceutical care. *Am J Hosp Pharm.* 1990; 47:533–43.
6. Schaffner A. Safety precautions in home chemotherapy. *Am J Nurs.* 1984; 84:346–7.

Developed through the ASHP Council on Professional Affairs with the assistance of the Executive Committee and Professional Practice Committee of the ASHP Section of Home Care Practitioners and approved by the ASHP Board of Directors on April 27, 2000.

The bibliographic citation for this document is as follows: American Society of Health System Pharmacists. ASHP guidelines on the pharmacist's role in home care. *Am J Health-Syst Pharm.* 2000; 57:1252–7.

ASHP Guidelines on Pharmaceutical Services in Correctional Facilities

Introduction

Pharmaceutical services in correctional facilities encompass many aspects of community, hospital, and consultant pharmacy practice. These guidelines are intended to address some of the unique aspects of pharmacy practice and services in correctional facilities. Some correctional facilities may not require, or be able to obtain, the services of a pharmacist. However, the concepts, principles, and recommendations contained in this standard are applicable to all correctional facilities, regardless of size or type. Thus, the part-time pharmacy director or consultant pharmacist has the same basic obligations and responsibilities as his or her full-time counterpart in larger settings. This document should serve as a guide for the provision of pharmaceutical services in correctional institutions.

Administration

Pharmaceutical services are an integral part of health care provided in correctional institutions. The pharmacist is usually responsible for multiple tasks ranging from the management of the pharmacy to the direct provision of services to inmate-patients. Two primary management responsibilities pertain to human and fiscal resources.

Personnel[1]

- Sufficient support personnel should be available to maximize the use of pharmacists in tasks requiring professional judgment. Appropriate supervisory controls for support personnel should be maintained. The use of pharmacy technicians graduated from ASHP-accredited pharmacy technician training programs is recommended. Pharmacy technicians should be certified by the Pharmacy Technician Certification Board.
- All personnel should possess the education and training needed to carry out their responsibilities. The competence of all staff may be enhanced through relevant continuing education. Credentialing of eligible staff as Certified Correctional Health Professionals through the National Commission on Correctional Health Care is recommended.
- A pharmacist should be available, at a minimum, on a consulting basis; the pharmacist should visit each facility no less than monthly. If the only pharmaceutical services provided are those of a consultant pharmacist, the consultant pharmacist should assume the role of pharmacy director.
- If the pharmacist is an employee of a contract vendor, he or she should be designated as the pharmacy director and assume the associated obligations and responsibilities.
- Health care services should be available to inmate-patients 24 hours a day. Pharmacist services should also be available, at least on an "on call" basis.
- Other pertinent guidelines of the American Society of Health-System Pharmacists, the National Commission on Correctional Health Care, and the American Correctional Association should be followed, and requirements set by federal, state, and local laws and regulations with respect to personnel should be met.

Fiscal Resources

Pharmacists serving correctional institutions should strive to manage expenses while providing optimal care to the inmate-patients. The pharmacist should

- Work with the administrators of the correctional institution to establish a budget for the operation of the pharmacy.
- Consider factors unique to each institution for the development of the budget (e.g., total inmate capacity, average daily inmate population, demographics of the inmate population).
- Make allowances for the disproportionate amount of chronic communicable disease in the prison population and the regional variability of diseases.
- Apply the ASHP Technical Assistance Bulletin on Assessing Cost-Containment Strategies for Pharmacies in Organized Health-Care Settings, as appropriate.[2]

Policies and Procedures

A policies and procedures manual specifically written to address aspects of pharmacy practice in the correctional facility should exist.

- All policies and procedures should conform to federal, state, and local laws and regulations.
- The pharmacy director should be familiar with the Standards for Health Services promulgated by the National Commission on Correctional Health Care and the standards of the American Correctional Association.
- The pharmacy director should be familiar with the constitutional rights of inmate-patients, current literature about inmates' rights, and court rulings affecting the practice of correctional health care in general and correctional pharmacy in particular. Attention to these concepts should be reflected in the manual.
- The pharmacy director should be familiar with current literature, laws, and regulations governing confidentiality, consent, and other areas of correctional health care that diverge from more traditional standards of pharmacy practice. Attention to these should be reflected in the manual.
- Transportation of inmate-patients' medications within and among facilities should be addressed.
- Security of drug products, entry into the pharmacy during the absence of a pharmacist, use of night cabinets, emergency supplies of medications, and disaster services should be addressed.
- Policies and procedures on the pharmacy's role in preparing lethal injections for capital punishment should exist.

Administrative Reports

Administrative reports generated by the pharmacy department will vary from facility to facility depending on the level of pharmaceutical services provided. Reports should include

- The amounts and cost of drugs and services furnished
- Destruction of unusable or outdated medications
- Inventory value and quantities
- Records of formal meetings with administrators, physicians, nurses, and other staff and any changes implemented as a result of those meetings
- Minutes of pharmacy and therapeutics committee meetings
- Medication administration records
- Reports of quality-control and quality-improvement activities
- Reports generated as required by applicable state laws regulating the practice of pharmacy. (While often not specifically written for the practice of correctional pharmacy, these laws are nonetheless usually pertinent to pharmacy practice within the correctional setting.)

Facilities

The pharmacy should be located within or in an area contiguous to the space provided for other health care services. Facilities should be adequate to accommodate appropriate security of all drug products, especially controlled substances.[3]

Purchasing, Distribution, and Control of Medications

Purchasing, distribution, and control of medications are essential elements of any pharmacy operation. Adequate methods to ensure that these responsibilities are met should exist.[4]

Purchasing

- The pharmacy director should be responsible for choosing the sources from which to obtain drug products.
- The pharmacy director should ensure that all medications meet applicable legal requirements. Guidance on the obligations of drug product suppliers and purchasers appears in the ASHP Guidelines for Selecting Pharmaceutical Manufacturers and Suppliers.[5]
- The pharmacy director should ensure that medications purchased from sources other than manufacturers or wholesalers (e.g., other pharmacies, contract providers) meet all applicable legal requirements. All suppliers should be able, at the request of the pharmacy director, to provide data on the quality of products.
- To the extent possible, all drug products should be contained in single-unit or unit dose packages.

Distribution

The pharmacist is responsible for the distribution and control of all drug products (including diagnostics and drug-related devices).

- A unit dose drug distribution and control system is recommended.

- The system employed should focus on patient safety and result in a minimal incidence of medication errors and adverse drug reactions. Ongoing processes for the monitoring and reporting of adverse drug reactions and the detection and prevention of medication errors should exist.
- The system employed should be cost-effective.
- The system employed should foster drug-control and drug-use monitoring.
- The system employed should foster patient compliance, recovery of drugs because of expired orders, and ultimate destruction of all unusable and outdated medications.
- Inmates should not be used in the distribution process.
- Patient confidentiality should be ensured in the distribution process (e.g., patients receiving medications for the treatment of AIDS).

Drug Storage

- The pharmacy director should ensure the proper security of medications stored in each location.
- The pharmacy director should ensure that drug products are stored in accordance with manufacturer or USP requirements.
- The pharmacy director should ensure that stored drug products are not expired.

Control

- A process for the recovery of medications dispensed to inmate-patients after the discontinuance of orders or in compliance with automatic stop orders should exist.
- A process for minimizing and eliminating unauthorized use of medications by anyone other than the intended patient (e.g., exchange of medications between inmates) should exist.
- A process for minimizing and eliminating pilferage should exist.
- A process for monitoring and preventing the dispensing of unusually large quantities of medications should exist.
- A process for preventing the dispensing of sufficient doses of any medication to enable potential suicide should exist. Individuals who are evaluated as high risks for suicide should be identified.
- A process for the security and dispensing of controlled substances should exist.
- The pharmacy director, in conjunction with the facility's medical staff and other responsible health authorities, should maintain policies and procedures for the routine review and renewal of medication orders and for any automatic discontinuance of orders.
- Access to patients' medication records should be limited to authorized personnel only. Complete access by the pharmacist should be ensured.
- A process for pharmacist review of medication orders to ensure patient safety and appropriateness of medication should exist. Medication orders (except in emergency situations) should be reviewed by the pharmacist before the first dose is dispensed.

Medication Administration

While medication administration is traditionally the responsibility of nurses, in the correctional setting some or all of this responsibility may be assigned to other personnel.

- The pharmacy director should be familiar with standards of the National Commission on Correctional Health Care with respect to medication administration by non-health-care personnel, and policies and procedures specifically addressing such administration should exist.
- The pharmacy director should participate in development of medication administration forms and ensure that all relevant information is incorporated into the forms.
- The pharmacy director should regularly educate all personnel involved in medication administration. These educational programs should include information on proper administration, indications, monitoring for adverse effects and allergic reactions, documentation, accountability, confidentiality, and the importance of compliance. Inmates who repeatedly refuse to take medications should be counseled by a pharmacist.
- Policies should be developed regarding the administration of medication to inmate-patients assigned to jobs or on work-release programs.
- Policies and procedures should be developed to ensure continuity of therapy upon release. Released inmates should have access to a limited supply of medications; either the drugs should be provided upon release or released inmates should have a prescription order transmitted to the pharmacy of their choice.

Documentation

- Medication administration records should be reviewed by the pharmacist at least monthly for proper documentation of medication administration.
- Review of the medication administration record should include assessments of documentation of medications administered, doses, frequency of administration, compliance, start and stop dates, and medication allergies.
- Pharmacist interventions should be documented in patients' medical records.
- The pharmacist should document refills in accordance with state laws and regulations.
- Policies and procedures should exist for documenting the transportation of medication among separate sites in correctional facilities, including accountability from pickup to drop off.
- A consistent pattern of refusal by an inmate-patient to take medication should be documented in the patient's medical record.
- Policies and procedures should exist for the proper documentation of the receipt, placement in inventory, dispensing, administration, and destruction of controlled substances.

Emergency Services

- A pharmacist should educate medical and correctional personnel on the proper use of medications stocked for emergency use.
- A pharmacist should be available on an on-call basis in case of emergencies.
- Policies and procedures for the use of emergency kits of medications in life-threatening situations should exist. These kits should be maintained by a pharmacist.

- The pharmacy director should maintain policies and procedures for accessibility of medications in case of riots or other emergency situations.
- The pharmacy director, in conjunction with the medical director or other responsible health authority and the correctional institution's administrator, should develop policies and the procedures that complement the standards of the National Commission on Correctional Health Care regarding emergency services.

Therapeutic Policies

- The pharmacy director should be a member of the pharmacy and therapeutics committee or its equivalent.
- A formulary should exist in accordance with the ASHP Statement on the Formulary System, the ASHP Guidelines on Formulary System Management, the ASHP Technical Assistance Bulletin on Drug Formularies, and the ASHP Technical Assistance Bulletin on the Evaluation of Drugs for Formularies.[6-9]
- Drug products selected for formulary inclusion should serve the needs of the inmate-patient population and at the same time be as cost-effective as possible. The pharmacy director should ensure that cost is not the only determinant for drug product selection.
- Procedures should exist for the provision of nonformulary medications when necessary.
- The pharmacy director should, in conjunction with the facility's medical staff, maintain policies and procedures for the use of investigational medications that ensure adherence to the rights of inmate-patients.
- The pharmacy director should, in conjunction with the facility's psychiatrist or medical director, maintain policies and procedures for the use of psychotropic medications.
- The pharmacy director should be familiar with laws and regulations governing the treatment of patients with AIDS and make appropriate procedural allowances for the treatment of these patients.
- The pharmacist should have input into decisions about infection control policies and procedures pertinent to medication use.

Quality Improvement

- The pharmacy director should encourage the development of and participate in an ongoing quality improvement process that includes drug-use evaluation and drug-regimen review.

Drug Information

- A program should exist for regular education of health care and pertinent non-health-care personnel with respect to medication use.
- An up-to-date resource library that includes current publications and those required by law and regulation should be maintained by the pharmacy.
- The pharmacist should provide drug consultations as required to nurses, physician assistants, physicians, and any others involved in initiating, executing, and monitoring medication therapy.
- The pharmacist should educate and counsel inmate-patients on the proper use of medications.

Research

- Policies and procedures for the use of investigational drugs within the correctional facility should exist. (Additional guidance on pertinent policies and procedures can be found in the ASHP Guidelines for the Use of Investigational Drugs in Organized Health-Care Settings.[10])
- The pharmacy director should adhere to the Federal Regulations on Medical Research in Correctional Facilities (45 C.F.R. 46, revised March 6, 1983) when devising policies and procedures for use of investigational drugs.
- Information on issues that affect pharmacy practice within the correctional environment (e.g., criminology, medical–legal issues, endemic patient population) should be maintained.

References

1. American Society of Hospital Pharmacists. ASHP guidelines: minimum standard for pharmacies in institutions. *Am J Hosp Pharm.* 1985; 42:372–5.
2. American Society of Hospital Pharmacists. ASHP technical assistance bulletin on assessing cost-containment strategies for pharmacies in organized health-care settings. *Am J Hosp Pharm.* 1992; 49:155–60.
3. American Society of Hospital Pharmacists. ASHP technical assistance bulletin on use of controlled substances in organized health-care settings. *Am J Hosp Pharm.* 1993; 50:489–501.
4. American Society of Hospital Pharmacists. ASHP technical assistance bulletin on drug distribution and control. *Am J Hosp Pharm.* 1980; 37:1097–103.
5. American Society of Hospital Pharmacists. ASHP guidelines for selecting pharmaceutical manufacturers and suppliers. *Am J Hosp Pharm.* 1991; 48:523–4.
6. American Society of Hospital Pharmacists. ASHP guidelines on formulary system management. *Am J Hosp Pharm.* 1992; 49:648–52.
7. American Society of Hospital Pharmacists. ASHP technical assistance bulletin on drug formularies. *Am J Hosp Pharm.* 1991; 48:791–3.
8. American Society of Hospital Pharmacists. ASHP technical assistance bulletin on the evaluation of drugs for formularies. *Am J Hosp Pharm.* 1988; 45:386–7.
9. American Society of Hospital Pharmacists. ASHP statement on the formulary system. *Am J Hosp Pharm.* 1983; 1384–5.
10. American Society of Hospital Pharmacists. ASHP guidelines for the use of investigational drugs in organized health-care settings. *Am J Hosp Pharm.* 1991; 48:315–9.

These guidelines were reviewed in 2003 by the Council on Professional Affairs and by the Board of Directors and were found to still be appropriate.

Approved by the ASHP Board of Directors, April 26, 1995. Developed by the Council on Professional Affairs. Drafted for council review by Ronald L. Rideman.

The bibliographic citation for this document is as follows: American Society of Health-System Pharmacists. ASHP guidelines on pharmaceutical services in correctional facilities. *Am J Health-Syst Pharm.* 1995; 52:1810–3.

Research

Research

Clinical Investigations of Drugs Used in Elderly and Pediatric Patients (0229)

Source: Council on Professional Affairs

To advocate increased enrollment of pediatric and geriatric patients in clinical trials of new medications; further,

To encourage pharmacodynamic and pharmacokinetic research in geriatric and pediatric patients to facilitate the safe and effective use of medications in these patient populations.

This policy supersedes ASHP policy 8711.

Institutional Review Boards and Investigational Use of Drugs (0230)

Source: Council on Professional Affairs

To support mandatory education and training on human subject protections and research bioethics for members of institutional review boards (IRBs), principal investigators, and all others involved in clinical research; further,

To advocate that IRBs include pharmacists as voting members; further,

To advocate that IRBs inform pharmacy of all approved clinical research involving drugs within the hospital or health system; further,

To advocate that pharmacists should act as liaisons between IRBs and pharmacy and therapeutics committees in the management and conduct of clinical drug research studies; further,

To strongly support pharmacists' management of drug products used in clinical research.

This policy supersedes ASHP policies 0119 and 0022.

Studies on Costs and Benefits of Clinical Pharmacy Services (8205)

Source: Council on Clinical Affairs

To request that the ASHP Research and Education Foundation encourage studies to assess costs and patient benefits of various clinical pharmacy services in different types and sizes of institutions.

This policy was reviewed in 1996 by the Council on Educational Affairs and by the Board of Directors and was found to still be appropriate.

ASHP Statement on Pharmaceutical Research in Organized Health-Care Settings

Pharmacy practice is grounded in the physicochemical, biological, and socioeconomic sciences. Hence, the continued and future success and self-esteem of the profession are dependent on the expanded knowledge base that can be produced through dynamic and rigorous scientific research and development. This research, to be meaningful and productive in terms of pharmacy's needs and goals in organized health-care settings, must include the participation of pharmacists practicing in those settings.

Pharmacists in organized health-care settings function in cooperation with other health-care professionals. They contribute a unique expertise to the drug-related aspects of patient care and take personal professional responsibility for the outcomes from the pharmaceutical care they provide to patients. Improvements in drug therapy depend on new knowledge generated by scientific research. Thus, pharmacists in organized health-care settings have a professional obligation to participate actively in and increase pharmacy-related and drug-related research efforts.[1,2]

Reflecting the collaborative nature of contemporary health care, this research should be multidisciplinary to be most beneficial. Thus, ASHP encourages pharmacists with a researchable idea or problem to seek the advice and active participation of people and organizations with scientific expertise such as

- College faculty (especially college of pharmacy faculty).
- Other staff and departments within the setting.
- Staff and departments in other health-care organizations.
- Industrial research personnel and laboratories.

It also is appropriate for pharmacists to function as principal investigators in research projects.

ASHP encourages pharmacists to increase their involvement in the following kinds of scientific research and development:

- Pharmaceutical research, including the development and testing of new drug dosage forms and drug prepa-

ration and administration methods and systems.
- Clinical research, such as the therapeutic characterization, evaluation, comparison, and outcomes of drug therapy and drug treatment regimens.
- Health services research and development, including behavioral and socioeconomic research such as research on cost–benefit issues in pharmaceutical care.
- Operations research, such as time and motion studies and evaluation of new and existing pharmacy programs and services.

This research will be a critical contribution of pharmacy to health care and must be fostered by all facets of the profession.

References

1. American Society of Hospital Pharmacists. ASHP guidelines for pharmaceutical research in organized health-care settings. *Am J Hosp Pharm.* 1989; 46:129–30.
2. American Society of Hospital Pharmacists. ASHP guidelines for the use of investigational drugs in organized health-care settings. *Am J Hosp Pharm.* 1991; 48:315–9.

Approved by the ASHP Board of Directors, November 14, 1990, and the ASHP House of Delegates, June 3, 1991. Revised by the ASHP Council on Professional Affairs. Supersedes a previous statement, "ASHP Statement on Institutional Pharmacy Research," approved by the ASHP House of Delegates on June 3, 1985, and the ASHP Board of Directors on November 14–15, 1984.

The bibliographic citation for this document is as follows: American Society of Hospital Pharmacists. ASHP statement on pharmaceutical research in organized health-care settings. *Am J Hosp Pharm.* 1991; 48:1781.

ASHP Guidelines for Pharmaceutical Research in Organized Health-Care Settings

The promotion of research in the health and pharmaceutical sciences and in pharmaceutical services is a purpose of the American Society of Hospital Pharmacists, as stated in its Charter.[1] In keeping with this purpose, pharmacists in organized health-care settings should understand the (1) basic need for research and systematic problem solving in pharmacy practice; (2) fundamental scientific approach; (3) basic components of a research plan; (4) process of documenting and reporting findings; and (5) responsibilities of investigators with respect to patients, employers, grantors, and science in general.

In its purest form, scientific research is the systematic, controlled, empirical, and critical investigation of hypothetical propositions (theories) about presumed relationships among natural phenomena.[2] Aspects of the research process (e.g., problem definition, systematic data gathering, interpretation, and reporting), however, are also applicable to resolving specific practice problems. Independent, intraprofessional, and interdisciplinary collaborative research and problem solving are encouraged.

Need

Since pharmacy is based on the theories of the pharmaceutical, medical, and social sciences, pharmacy's advancement is linked to advancement in those sciences. Scientific inquiry, through formal research and systematic problem solving, leads to an expansion of knowledge and thus to advancement. Both research and systematic problem solving in organized health-care settings are needed for developing knowledge in pharmaceutics and drug therapy and for evaluation, modification, and justification of specific practices. Therefore, an understanding of the research process is important to pharmacists in such settings.

Primary areas for research by pharmacists in organized health-care settings are those in which pharmacists possess special expertise or unique knowledge. These areas include drug therapy, pharmaceutics, bioavailability, pharmacy practice administration, sociobehavioral aspects of pharmaceutical service systems, and application of information handling and computer technology to pharmacy practice.

The Scientific Approach

Aspects of the scientific approach may be applied to formal research and systematic problem solving. The scientific approach consists of four basic steps:

1. *Problem—Obstacle—Idea.*[3] The scientist experiences an obstacle to understanding or curiosity as to why something is as it is. The scientist's first step is to express the idea in some reasonably manageable form, even if it is ill defined and tentative.
2. *Hypothesis.* The scientist looks back on experience for possible solutions—personal experience, the literature, and contacts with other scientists. A tentative proposition (hypothesis) is formulated about the relationship between two or more variables in the problem; for example, "If such and such occurs, then so and so results."

3. *Reasoning—Deduction.* The scientist deduces the consequences of the formulated hypothesis. The scientist may find that the deductions reveal a new problem that is quite different from the original one. On the other hand, deductions may lead to the conclusion that the problem cannot be solved with existing technical tools. Such reasoning can help lead to wider, more basic, and more significant problems as well as to more narrow (testable) implications of the original hypothesis.
4. *Observation—Test—Experiment.* If the problem has been well stated, the hypotheses have been adequately formulated, and the implications of the hypotheses have been carefully deduced, the next step is to test the relationships expressed by the hypotheses, that is, the relationships among the variables. All testing is for one purpose: putting the relationships among the variables to an empirical test. It is not the hypotheses that are tested but the deduced implications of the hypotheses. On the basis of the research evidence, each hypothesis is either accepted or rejected.

Components of a Research Plan

Formal research frequently requires the development of a written plan (protocol or proposal). In funded research, the plan may take the form of a grant application. A typical plan might include

1. A problem statement.
2. A review of available literature on the subject.
3. The objectives for the project, including the hypotheses and the to-be-tested relationships among variables.
4. A description of the methodology to be used.
5. A description of statistical analyses to be applied to the data collected.
6. A budget and time frame for the project (where applicable).
7. The expected applicability of the research findings.

Documentation and Reporting

The structure of a research report is similar to the structure of a research plan. A typical outline is as follows:

1. Problem.
    a. Theories, hypotheses, and definitions.
    b. Previous research: the literature.
2. Methodology.
    a. Sample and sampling method.
    b. Experimental procedures and instrumentation.
    c. Measurement of variables.
    d. Statistical methods of analysis.
    e. Pretesting and pilot studies.
3. Results, interpretation, and conclusions.

The statement of the problem sets the general stage for the reader and may be in question form. A common practice is to state the broader, general problem and then to state the hypotheses, both general and specific. All important variables should be defined, both in general and in operational terms, giving a justification for the definitions used, if needed.

The general and research literature related to the problem is discussed to explain the theoretical rationale of the problem, to tell the reader what research has and has not been carried out on the problem, and to show that this particular investigation has not been conducted before (except in the case of validating research).

The methodology section should meticulously describe what was done so as to enable another investigator to reproduce the research, reanalyze the data, and arrive at unambiguous conclusions about the adequacy of the methods. This section should tell what samples were used, how they were selected, and why they were selected. The means of measurement of the variables should be described. The data analysis methods should be outlined and justified. Where pilot studies and pretesting were used, they should be described.

Results and data should be condensed and expressed in concise form. Limitations and weaknesses of the study should be discussed. The question of whether the data support the hypotheses must be foremost in the mind of the report writer. Everything written should relate the results and data to the problem and the hypotheses.

Investigators' Responsibilities

Investigators bear a general responsibility to be scientifically objective in their research inquiries, conclusions, and reports. They bear a responsibility for being methodical and meticulous in the gathering of research data. They also bear both a fiduciary and a reporting responsibility to employers and grantors. In general, employee investigators are at least partially responsible to their employer organizations in the choice of research topics. Research funded from sources outside an investigator's organization may impose additional contractual obligations on the investigator and the organization.

In research involving patients, investigators are responsible for protecting patients from harm while the patients are participating in the research. All research involving patients should be reviewed and approved, before initiation, by an institutional review board. Written, informed consent should be obtained from every patient participating in each research project.[4] Meticulous recordkeeping is required regarding the clinical experience of patients participating in research projects.

Employee investigators bear responsibility for helping their organizations differentiate true, objective research from product marketing trials and promotions that may purport to be research projects. Grants for bona fide research typically bear a direct cost-recovery relationship to projects and typically involve the direct transfer of grant funds from grantors to the employee investigator's employer organization. Specific institutional policies vary widely, but employee investigators can generally better fulfill their fiduciary responsibilities when funds are not distributed directly from grantors to investigators. In keeping with their fiduciary responsibilities and their responsibility to be scientifically objective, investigators should be wary of arrangements in which prospective grantors offer inducements of value (gifts, trips, experiences, publicity, publications, etc.) to investigators, institutions, or patients before, during, or after the completion of proposed projects.

Investigators should make legitimate efforts to document publicly the findings of research in scientific, objectively refereed publications.

References

1.   American Society of Hospital Pharmacists. Governing documents of the American Society of Hospital Pharmacists. Bethesda, MD: American Society of Hospital Pharmacists; 1984.
2.   Kerlinger F. Foundations of behavioral research. New York: Holt, Rinehart and Winston; 1964:13.
3.   Dewey J. How we think. Boston: Heath; 1933:106–18, as adapted to the scientific framework by Kerlinger, op cit., p 13–5.
4.   American Society of Hospital Pharmacists. ASHP guidelines for the use of investigational drugs in institutions. *Am J Hosp Pharm*. 1983; 40:449–51.

Approved by the ASHP Board of Directors, September 30, 1988. Developed by the Council on Professional Affairs. Supersedes the "ASHP Guidelines for Scientific Research in Institutional Pharmacy" approved on November 15, 1977.

The bibliographic citation for this document is as follows: American Society of Hospital Pharmacists. ASHP guidelines for pharmaceutical research in organized health-care settings. *Am J Hosp Pharm*. 1989; 46:129–30.

ASHP Guidelines on Clinical Drug Research

Purpose

The use of drug products to manage diseases and improve patients' quality of life is increasing as more effective and safer agents become available. Research to develop these agents is occurring in health system practice settings throughout the world. The credibility of this research and the protection of human subjects is a major responsibility of all health professionals involved.

ASHP believes pharmacists should play a pivotal role in the management of drugs used in the conduct of clinical research.[1–3] Pharmacists have become essential components of health system infrastructures supporting clinical research with both approved drugs and investigational drugs.[a,b] Pharmacists' roles in clinical research generally fall into one of two categories: (1) drug storage, preparation, and record keeping, frequently through an investigational drug service, and (2) serving as a principal investigator or a subinvestigator, manager, or coordinator within a research team that may include other health care professionals, research sponsors, monitors, contract research organizations, institutional review boards (IRBs), and institutional administrators.

The purposes of this document are to (1) outline the principles of clinical research, (2) describe the roles of participants in clinical research, (3) define pharmacists' roles in the use of drugs in clinical research, and (4) provide guidance to pharmacists and others responsible for the medication management component of clinical research. ASHP believes these guidelines are applicable to clinical research conducted in any health-system practice setting. These guidelines are an interpretation of federal laws, regulations, and standards for pharmacy practice in health systems. They should be used in conjunction with the applicable federal and state laws and regulations, not as a substitute for them. This document uses the term *shall* when the content is based on law or regulation and the term *should* for advice based on other guidelines, professional judgment, or expert opinion.

Background

The United States has benefited from a system for researching and marketing drug products that is codified in federal and state laws and regulations. The federal Food, Drug, and Cosmetic Act and its amendments[4] regulate drug product quality, safety, and effectiveness. The Food and Drug Administration (FDA) is the federal agency charged with enforcing the act and promulgating regulations for its implementation. FDA regulations concerning the conduct of clinical research with drug products of particular relevance for health-system pharmacists include Title 21 Code of Federal Regulations (CFR) Part 50, Protection of Human Subjects; Title 21 CFR Part 56, Institutional Review Boards; and Title 21 CFR Part 312, Investigational New Drug Application. Also applicable are the Department of Health and Human Services regulations in Title 45 CFR Part 46, Protection of Human Subjects. Requirements for and guidance on compliance with regulations are provided in FDA Information Sheets.

FDA has also published the Good Clinical Practice Consolidated Guideline[5] that was prepared under the auspices of the International Conference on Harmonisation of Technical Requirements for Registration of Pharmaceuticals for Human Use. The guideline offers a unified standard for designing, conducting, recording, and reporting trials that involve the participation of human subjects in the United States, Japan, and the European Union. In particular, the guideline provides a clearer understanding of behavioral and compliance standards for regulated drug research.

Basic Principles

The institutional components and practice settings of health systems participating in clinical drug research shall develop mechanisms, generally in the form of policies and procedures, for the approval, planning, and implementation of protocols. Good clinical practices, consistent with national and international standards, are the cornerstone of drug research in humans. Principles consistent with good clinical practices include the following:

1. An organization participating in human drug research studies shall ensure that such studies contain adequate safeguards for human subjects, its staff, and the scientific integrity of the study. There shall be written policies and procedures for the approval, management, and control of research involving investigational (not FDA-approved) drugs and post-marketing studies of FDA-approved drugs used in a research protocol. All research team members shall be fully informed about and comply with these policies and procedures.

2. The clinical trial shall have adequate prior information to justify use of human subjects, have a clearly defined protocol, and have received IRB approval before implementation.

3. All drug studies shall meet accepted ethical, legal, and scientific standards and be conducted by appropriately qualified investigators. Investigator qualifications, such as prior training and experience in research and with certain disease states, are required to be reviewed by IRBs, study sponsors, and FDA if the research will be submitted under an investigational new drug application (IND).

4. Every member of the research team shall be qualified by experience or training to perform his or her respective role.

5. All subjects must freely provide informed consent (documented in writing) before treatment with study drugs is begun. Accurate and complete information about the study's objectives, risks, and benefits must be provided before consent is obtained from the subject or his or her legally authorized representative. No unreasonable inducements (i.e., coercion or undue influence) shall be offered to subjects to encourage their participation in the study.

6. All clinical trial data shall be recorded and the records stored in such a way that the subject's rights of privacy and confidentiality are protected. All records shall be managed in a way that permits accurate reporting, verification, and retrieval after archiving.

7. Qualified pharmacists and other nonphysicians may serve as principal investigators as long as medical decisions made for the subjects are always the responsibility of a qualified physician or dentist.

Health-System Organization and Oversight

The health system should have processes for the administration of research that ensure that the aforementioned principles are upheld and the following responsibilities are met.

1. The health system shall be able to review and approve a protocol in the context of federal, state, and local laws and regulations. The health system should consider whether its own sponsored research or intellectual property development of drugs requires an IND for drugs not commercially available and approved drugs for unlabeled uses. An IND may be required if proposed research on the use of a marketed drug is intended to support the sponsor's change in drug labeling, advertising, or indications for use; a significant increase in risk; or a change in dosage level or route of administration. The health system should consult FDA for guidance.

2. The health system should have a mechanism for review and approval of the financial aspects of drug research, whether the study is sponsored by government agencies, foundations, or the pharmaceutical industry or is not sponsored.[6] Financial aspects may include contractual agreements stipulating cost recovery for resources, intellectual property agreements, insurance provisions, indemnification terms, and conflict-of-interest statements. Cost identification, allocation, and recovery mechanisms are imperative items for review and approval.

3. As required by federal regulation, clinical research shall be reviewed and approved by an IRB or equivalent committee (21 CFR 56.109). This committee shall evaluate each proposed clinical research study in terms of human subject protections and compliance with recognized ethical, legal, and scientific standards. No clinical study may be initiated unless approved in writing by the committee. Spoken IRB approval may be granted in emergency situations for a single subject's access to an investigational drug, but emergency use shall be reported to the IRB within five days; subsequent use requires full IRB review. Studies on the use of drugs in emergency or critical care settings do not in themselves qualify for single-subject approval and emergency exemption. Specific regulations govern research in the emergency setting and should be consulted in preparing protocols, IRB submissions, and consent procedures.[c,7]

   Treatment IND protocols are also subject to IRB review and approval. These protocols permit patient access to investigational drugs through a special program established by a sponsor. The physician and patient must agree that use of the agent may be in the patient's best interest and must document this agreement on a consent form.

   The IRB shall monitor approved studies to ensure that they are carried out appropriately and that the protocols are reassessed at least annually. Health system policies and procedures shall provide guidance on the conversion of human subjects to other therapies in the event that approval of an existing protocol is withdrawn by the IRB. The investigational-drug pharmacist, pharmacy director, or pharmacy director's designee should be a member of the IRB and should be consulted by the committee whenever drug studies are reviewed.

4. Investigational drugs shall be used only under the supervision of the principal investigator or authorized subinvestigators, all of whom shall be members of the professional staff. The determination of qualifications for investigators is the responsibility of the sponsor, IRB, and FDA when appropriate. Properly qualified pharmacists with experience and training in research may serve as principal investigators or subinvestigators.

5. The principal investigator or designee is responsible for obtaining informed consent from each subject who is eligible for participation in the study (i.e., meets inclusion and exclusion criteria).[c] The informed consent process shall conform to current federal and state regulations. IRB approval of the consent form (and assent form for minors) is required. Review by legal counsel may be desirable. The following points shall be included in the consent document and in an accompanying oral explanation by the investigator:

   a. That the trial involves research.

   b. The nature and purpose of the study and its expected benefits and foreseeable risks or discomforts. The name and telephone number of the principal investigator and persons to contact for questions about the study or drug.

   c. A balanced description of the alternative treatments available, including their respective risks and benefits.

   d. A general description of the study procedures, identification of any procedures that are experimental, expected length of therapy with the drug, and the subject's responsibilities. The name(s) of the investigational drug(s), including brand and generic names of commercial products.

   e. A statement that (1) participation is voluntary, (2) the subject may withdraw from the study at any time, (3) refusal to participate in or withdrawal from the study will involve no penalty or loss of benefits to which the subject is otherwise entitled, and (4) the principal investigator may remove the subject from the study if circumstances warrant. The investigator shall supply any new information that may affect a subject's desire to continue in a study.

   f. The name and signature of the subject (or his or her legally authorized representative), the name and signature of the principal investigator or subinvestigator, and the name and signature of the person presenting the consent form, with lines for each to personally date the signature.

   g. A statement of who will have access to any study records that contain subject identifiers, including monitoring personnel from the study sponsor or FDA who may inspect the records to assess compliance with the study protocol and all regulations, or institutional personnel auditing the quality of clinical research or financial transactions.

   h. Compensation or treatment available for a research-related injury.

   i. Anticipated payments to subjects, pro rata terms, or expenses subjects may incur. Any costs for which the subject will be responsible.

   The consent form shall be as detailed as is practical, with the goal of minimizing the amount of information that must be presented orally yet enabling comprehension by most persons reading the form. For non-English-speaking subjects the consent form shall be in the subject's own language when feasible, or adequate interpretation shall be provided. For children able to read, an assent form shall be used to document their participation in the research process. The subject (or his or her representative) must have adequate time to read the consent form before signing it and shall receive a copy of the signed and dated form, along with any amendments to it. The subject shall retain a copy of the consent form. Additional copies of the consent form shall be kept on file as required by the sponsor, the IRB, the individual health system, and the medical records department.

Under certain protocols, patient drug or medical information may be collected from existing medical or pharmacy records. Pharmacists and investigators should consult the IRB to determine protocol-review and informed-consent requirements for any proposed studies.

6. The principal investigator is responsible for the proper maintenance of case report forms and all other study records required by the health system, the sponsor, and FDA.

7. The health system's medication-use system shall contain the following elements concerning drugs used in clinical research:

   a. Drugs shall be properly packaged in accordance with all applicable federal and state laws, regulations, and standards (e.g., FDA, *The United States Pharmacopeia and The National Formulary* [*USP–NF*], and the Poison Prevention Packaging Act).

   b. Drugs shall be labeled properly to ensure their safe use by the research and institutional staff and the subject.

   c. There shall be a mechanism to ensure that sufficient supplies of the drugs will be always available for the duration of the study.

   d. A mechanism shall be in place to allow the pharmacist or other designated health care provider, in a medical emergency during a randomized and blinded trial, to break the blinding code and reveal the identity of the study drug to other health care professionals. A reason to break the blind might be the need for a treatment decision that can be made only with knowledge of drug assignment.

   e. Nurses, pharmacists, physicians, and other health care practitioners (e.g., respiratory therapists, physician assistants) called on to administer or dispense investigational drugs should have adequate written information about (1) pharmacology (particularly adverse effects), (2) storage requirements, (3) method of dose preparation and administration, (4) disposal of unused drug, (5) precautions to be taken, including handling recommendations, (6) authorized prescribers, (7) human subject safety monitoring guidelines, and (8) any other material pertinent to safe and proper use of investigational drugs. These health care providers should be informed about the overall study objectives and procedures and shall have available a complete copy of the protocol for reference. Under all circumstances, investigational drugs shall be safely controlled, administered, and destroyed.

   f. Bulk supplies of the investigational drug shall be properly stored and adequately secured. When practical, all bulk supplies shall be stored in the pharmacy to ensure that storage, dispensing, accountability, and security are in compliance with federal and state laws and regulations and with standards used by the pharmacy department.

   g. There shall be a method for ensuring that only an authorized practitioner or designee prescribes the investigational drug.

   h. Records of the amount of investigational drug received from the sponsor and of its disposition (e.g., amounts dispensed to subjects or returned to sponsor) shall be maintained. These records shall be retained as required by regulation. Generally, records shall be maintained for at least two years after the date of an approved new-drug application (NDA) for the indication that is being investigated or, if the application is not approved or no application is filed, for at least two years after the investigation is discontinued and FDA is notified. Institutions should consider retaining records indefinitely. For studies involving international sites, records shall be maintained for 15 years after study closure. The sponsor may also request that records be stored longer than the minimum required time.

   i. If the subject is to receive the investigational drug at another facility, suitable arrangements shall be made for transfer of the drug. Sufficient information for safe use of the investigational drug, including copies of the subject's signed consent form, the study protocol, and the IRB approval letter, shall accompany the drug. The responsibilities of the facility to which the drug is transferred are based on whether that facility is providing care incidental to or as a participant in the research protocol.[8]

   j. The institution's records on investigational-drug studies should be designed so that various descriptive reports (e.g., names of all drugs under study, names of subjects who have received a given drug) can be generated conveniently and expeditiously. Once a study is closed, a copy of all pharmacy-related records should be provided to the principal investigator for storage. For its own records, the pharmacy should have a mechanism for long-term storage. The drug control responsibilities previously described shall be assigned to a pharmacist. If a pharmacist is not available, the investigator shall make arrangements to comply with these standards.

Pharmaceutical Services

A pharmacist should be responsible for ensuring that procedures for the control of drugs used in clinical research are developed and implemented. Each health system should develop a structure and procedures specific to its own needs and organization.

1. A copy of the IRB-approved research protocol and investigator's brochure or drug data sheet (see item 2 below), or both, and all amendments should be kept by a pharmacist.

2. Using the protocol and additional information (if needed) supplied by the principal investigator and sponsor, the pharmacist should prepare an investiga-

tional-drug data sheet that concisely summarizes for the medical, nursing, and pharmacy staffs information pertinent to use of the drug. This communication should contain, at a minimum

   a. Drug designation and common synonyms.

   b. Dosage forms and strengths.

   c. Usual dosage range, including dosage schedule and route of administration.

   d. Indications pursued in this study.

   e. Expected therapeutic effect to be studied.

   f. Expected and potential adverse effects, including symptoms of toxicity and their treatment.

   g. Drug–drug and drug–food interactions.

   h. Contraindications.

   i. Storage requirements.

   j. Instructions for dosage preparation and administration, including stability and handling guidelines.

   k. Instructions for disposition of unused doses.

   l. Names and telephone numbers of principal and authorized subinvestigators and study coordinators.

     Confidential copies should be distributed to the appropriate pharmacy staff and all areas within the health system where the investigational drug will be administered and the subjects monitored. Through the pharmacy or health-system computer system, this information can be made available to all staff members who need it. It is staff members' responsibility to become familiar with the information in these data sheets and to not share the information with persons who do not need it.

3. When it is practical, investigational-drug supplies should be stored in a pharmacy. When the drug is stored outside a pharmacy (e.g., small quantities in the investigator's office or in clinics where the drug is administered), methods used by the investigator responsible for the drug shall be audited by a pharmacist to ensure that storage, dispensing, accountability, and security comply with federal and state laws and regulations and with institutional policy.

4. The pharmacist shall maintain a perpetual inventory record for investigational drugs stored in the pharmacy. This record shall contain the drug's name, dosage form and strength, lot number, and expiration date; the name, address, and telephone number of the sponsor; the protocol number; and any other information needed for ordering the drug. Space shall be provided for recording data on the disposition of the drug (amounts received, transferred, wasted, or dispensed, with dates; the names of or codes for persons receiving the drug; and the names of prescribers), the amount currently on hand, the minimum reorder level, and the recorder's initials. The inventory record shall reflect drug doses that were dispensed but not administered and were returned to the pharmacist. These records are commonly audited by the sponsor, the sponsor's representatives, or FDA.[9,10]

5. The dispensing of investigational drugs should be integrated with the rest of the medication-use system, including, but not limited to, order review, profile maintenance, packaging, labeling, delivery, and quality-assurance procedures. However, prescription labels for investigational drugs shall be marked "investigational drug" or otherwise distinguished from other labels. The label should also include an alert to any possible hazards. There shall be a method for verifying that a valid, signed consent has been obtained. The investigational drug shall be dispensed only on the order of an authorized investigator or designee.

6. Educating patients and monitoring therapy (including adverse drug reaction monitoring) are two clinical functions that are particularly important and applicable to investigational drugs. The protocol should specify the provision of these functions by the pharmacists, the authorized investigator(s), and other members of the research team.

7. At the conclusion of the study, the pharmacist shall return, transfer, or dispose of all unused investigational drugs according to the specific instructions provided by the sponsor and in accordance with applicable regulations.

8. The pharmacist should prepare an annual or semiannual descriptive summary of investigational-drug use for the pharmacy director and pharmacy and therapeutics committee. This summary should include the number of studies in progress, a list of all drugs studied during the previous period, and a financial statement.

9. Drug costs and other expenses associated with drug studies (e.g., costs of record keeping and drug administration) should be properly allocated and reimbursed. Policies and procedures should address the role pharmacists play in billing sponsors, subjects, and third-party payers for services and goods related to research. In general, sponsors and health systems cannot charge subjects for an investigational drug. Sponsors may petition FDA for an exception. Health systems may charge subjects for drug preparation and other services necessary to deliver a final product, as is customary for delivery of services within the practice setting and when sponsors do not reimburse for this service. The anticipated costs of research should be described in the consent form. Subjects must be advised that they or their third-party payers are responsible for these charges and that a third-party payer may refuse to pay for charges related to research.

10. The investigational drugs shall be stored under appropriate environmental control in a limited-access area separate from routine drug stocks and shall be inventoried on a regular basis.

11. Pharmacists may be confronted with circumstances related to a patient who is receiving an investigational drug provided by an investigator at a nonaffiliated practice setting and is admitted to their own practice setting for care incidental to the research protocol. Pharmacists should have a policy for managing investigational drugs under those circumstances that meets FDA guidelines.[8]

12. Pharmacists must ensure the scientific integrity of drug studies by managing access to treatment-assignment records in blinded studies and by ensuring that the correct drug was dispensed. The pharmacist, investigator, and sponsor must agree on a procedure for unblinding treatment assignment in emergencies.

13. Pharmacists who are assigned to manage investigational drugs may at times have to delegate certain dispensing activities to other pharmacists within the health system. To ensure continuity of quality dispensing services, the responsible pharmacist should design and implement procedures for educating other members

of the pharmacy staff about the protocol and dispensing requirements. Often this can be accomplished by personal instruction and by preparing written directives and references for use by other pharmacists when they are called upon to dispense an investigational drug.

14. Pharmacists managing investigational drugs are in a unique position to monitor patient adherence to medication regimens. Because of the requirement that medication dispensed and returned be accounted for, pharmacists can readily surmise whether study patients are consuming the medication in the prescribed manner. At a minimum, pharmacists should counsel the investigator's research staff with regard to patient adherence. Pharmacists' skills in patient counseling should be used to support the investigators' efforts to encourage patients to adhere to their protocols.

Pharmaceutical Research Sponsors, Monitors, and Contract Research Organizations

The pharmaceutical company, or any study sponsor, that supports the use of investigational drugs in health systems should receive reliable and valid data. The following recommendations will serve as a guide to the pharmaceutical industry or other study sponsors to ensure that investigational drug use is managed appropriately and that studies are conducted effectively, efficiently, and safely.

1. Drugs shall be properly packaged in accordance with all applicable federal and state laws, regulations, and standards (e.g., FDA, *USP–NF*, and the Poison Prevention Packaging Act).

2. Drugs shall be properly labeled in accordance with applicable laws, regulations, and standards. If possible, ample space shall be left on the drug product container for further labeling by the pharmacist. Expiration dates and lot numbers should also be noted on the label.

3. A 24-hour telephone number should be available to study personnel, including the principal investigator and the pharmacy department. In the event of an emergency, information should be available pertaining to (1) adverse effects and their treatment, (2) emergency protocol management and dosing and administration guidelines, (3) the ability to break a "blinded code" to determine the treatment regimen, and (4) the mechanism for procuring a supply of medication under an emergency-use protocol.

4. Company representatives should be designated to handle routine requests, such as those for additional forms and resupply of investigational drugs. If possible, direct telephone or fax access should be available to expedite requests.

5. Investigational drugs should be shipped to the principal investigator in care of a pharmacist. The following information about procurement should also be supplied to the pharmacist:
   a. Name and telephone number of the sponsor's study monitor or field representative responsible for drug ordering.
   b. Estimated time for fulfillment of orders.
   c. Limits on quantities that can be ordered.
   d. Special ordering instructions.
   e. How the order is to be shipped (e.g., specific package-shipping firms).
   f. Disposition of invoice or drug receipt form once the drug is received.

6. The following information should be supplied by a sponsor or investigator to the pharmacist, preferably in an investigator's brochure, as applicable:
   a. Storage conditions required before and after preparation.
   b. Amounts and types of diluents for reconstitution and administration and the resulting final concentration of active drug.
   c. Stability of the prepared (i.e., ready-to-administer, reconstituted, or diluted) product and compatibility with drug delivery systems, diluents or i.v. fluids, containers, i.v. tubing, and filters.
   d. Known compatibility or incompatibility with other products.
   e. Light sensitivity.
   f. Filtration needs.
   g. Expiration dates or retest dates.
   h. Special instructions for preparation and administration.
   i. Acceptable and recommended routes and methods of administration, including rates of infusion for injectable products.
   j. Known adverse effects during or after administration (e.g., pain, phlebitis, and nausea) and how to avoid and treat them.
   k. Usual dosage regimens and highest dose tested for specific disease states, including dosage expressions for prescribing and labeling that could minimize misreading and misinterpretation.
   l. Contraindications.
   m. Drug interactions.
   n. Special precautions for storage, handling, and disposal of the drugs, including cytotoxic and hazardous drugs. For all hazardous drugs, the pharmacy department must be supplied with material safety data sheets.
   o. Pharmacology, including mechanism of action.
   p. Pharmacokinetic characteristics.

7. If all unused drugs are to be returned to the sponsor, information regarding storage and return procedures should be provided to the pharmacist. Drugs that are contaminated, outdated, or otherwise unsuitable should be returned to the sponsor or destroyed according to the institution's policies and procedures and applicable laws and regulations. These options should be agreed on beforehand by the sponsor and the pharmacist.

8. A complete current copy of the research protocol and investigator's brochure should be supplied to the pharmacist. Additional educational materials for use in informing pharmacists, physicians, and nurses about the investigational drug and research protocol should also be provided.

9. An appropriate allotment of research funds should be designated as reimbursement for
   a. Personnel.
   b. Storage facilities.
   c. Equipment.
   d. Ancillary products, such as diluents, syringes, and needles.
   e. Forms and miscellaneous clerical materials.

f. Computer and other data-processing costs.

g. Other expenses attributable to the pharmacist's involvement in the study.

h. Apportioned pharmacy overhead costs.

10. Sponsors should respond to requests for information from pharmacists involved in treating patients without formal research approval at that institution. This may occur, for example, when a patient is hospitalized (e.g., in an emergency) at a facility other than his or her usual care site.

11. When seeking marketing approval for an investigational drug, sponsors should consult pharmacists, physicians, and others involved in their investigational-drug studies for information. Because of their experience with the drug, these practitioners can supply valuable suggestions for labeling, packaging, palatability, routes of administration, and other dosage form characteristics, as well as information regarding patient monitoring and education.

12. The sponsor of an investigational drug study should provide final closure details within six months of trial completion. This includes prompt notification of closure, directions for drug disposition, and final audits of all study records.

13. These recommendations should also apply to the postmarketing approval of drugs under study for new indications or diseases.

References

1. Stolar MH, ed. Pharmacy-coordinated investigational drug services. Revised ed. Bethesda, MD: American Society of Hospital Pharmacists; 1986.

2. American Society of Health-System Pharmacists. ASHP guidelines: minimum standard for pharmacies in hospitals. *Am J Health-Syst Pharm.* 1995; 52:2711–7.

3. American Society of Hospital Pharmacists. ASHP statement on the use of medications for unlabeled uses. *Am J Hosp Pharm.* 1992; 49:2006–8.

4. Federal Food, Drug, and Cosmetic Act (21 U.S.C. 301 et seq.) 1938, as amended.

5. Food and Drug Administration, Department of Health and Human Services. International conference on harmonisation; good clinical practice consolidated guideline. *Fed Regist.* 1997; 62:25692–709.

6. Wermeling DP, Piecoro LT, Foster TS. Financial impact of clinical research on a health system. *Am J Health-Syst Pharm.* 1997; 54:1742–51.

7. Bailey EM, Habowski SR. How to apply for emergency use of an investigational agent. *Am J Health-Syst Pharm.* 1996; 53:208–10.

8. Food and Drug Administration. Use of investigational products when subjects enter a second institution. IRB operations and clinical investigation information sheet. http://www.fda.gov/oc/oha/useofinv.html (accessed August 25, 1997).

9. Food and Drug Administration. Institutional review board inspections. IRB operations and clinical investigation information sheet. http://ww.fda.gov/oc/oha/institut.html (accessed August 25, 1997).

10. Food and Drug Administration. Inspections of clinical investigators. IRB operations and clinical investigation information sheet. http://www.fda.gov/oc/oha/inspect.html (accessed August 25, 1997).

Suggested Internet Source

Food and Drug Administration information for clinical investigators. http://www.fda.gov/cder/about/smallbiz/clinical_investigator.htm.

Glossary[d]

Adverse Drug Reaction (ADR): In preapproval clinical experience with a new medicinal product or its new usages, particularly since the therapeutic dose(s) may not be established, all noxious and unintended responses to a medicinal product related to any dose should be considered adverse drug reactions. "Responses to a medicinal product" means that a causal relationship between a medicinal product and an adverse event is at least a reasonable possibility (i.e., that the relationship cannot be ruled out).

An ADR to a marketed medicinal product is a response to a drug that is noxious and unintended and that occurs at doses normally used in humans for prophylaxis, diagnosis, or therapy of diseases or for modification of physiological function.

Adverse Event (AE): An AE is any untoward medical event that occurs in a patient or clinical investigation subject administered a pharmaceutical product and that does not necessarily have a causal relationship to this treatment. An AE can therefore be any unfavorable and unintended sign (including an abnormal laboratory finding), symptom, or disease temporally associated with the use of a medicinal (investigational) product, whether or not related to the medicinal (investigational) product.

Audit: A systematic and independent examination of trial-related activities and documents to determine whether the evaluated trial-related activities were conducted and the data were recorded, analyzed, and accurately reported according to the protocol, sponsor's standard operating procedures, good clinical practice, and the applicable regulatory requirements.

Audit Report: A written evaluation by the sponsor's auditor of the results of the audit.

Case Report Form: A printed, optical, or electronic document designed to record all of the protocol-required information to be reported to the sponsor on each trial subject.

Clinical Trial or Study: Any investigation in human subjects that is intended to discover or verify the clinical, pharmacologic, or other pharmacodynamic effects of an investigational product, to identify any adverse reactions to an investigational product, or to study absorption, distribution, metabolism, and excretion of an investigational product with the object of ascertaining its safety, efficacy, or both. (The terms clinical trial and clinical study are synonymous.)

Clinical Trial/Study Report: A written description of a trial or study of any therapeutic, prophylactic, or diagnostic agent conducted in humans, in which the clinical and statistical description, presentations, and analyses are fully integrated into a single report.

Contract Research Organization: A person or organization (commercial, academic, or other) contracted by the sponsor to perform one or more of a sponsor's trial-related duties and functions.

Direct Access: Permission to examine, analyze, verify, and reproduce any records and reports that are important in the evaluation of a clinical trial. Any party (e.g., domestic and foreign regulatory authorities, sponsors, monitors, and auditors) with direct access should take all reasonable precautions within the constraints of the applicable regulatory requirements to maintain the confidentiality of subjects' identities and sponsors' proprietary information.

Documentation: All records, in any form (including but not limited to written, electronic, magnetic, and optical records and scans, roentgenograms, and electrocardiograms) that describe or record the methods, conduct, or results of a trial, the factors affecting a trial, and the actions taken.

Essential Documents: Documents that individually and collectively permit evaluation of the conduct of a study and the quality of the data produced.

Good Clinical Practice: A standard for the design, conduct, performance, monitoring, auditing, recording, analysis, and reporting of clinical trials that provides assurance that the data and reported results are credible and accurate and that the rights, integrity, and confidentiality of trial subjects are protected.

Independent Ethics Committee: An independent body (institutional, regional, national, or supranational review board or committee), constituted of medical or scientific professionals and nonmedical or nonscientific members, whose responsibility it is to ensure the protection of the rights, safety, and well-being of human subjects involved in a trial and to provide public assurance of that protection by, among other things, reviewing and approving or providing favorable opinion on the trial protocol and the suitability of the investigators, the facilities, and the methods and material to be used in obtaining and documenting informed consent of the trial subjects.

Informed Consent: A process by which a subject voluntarily confirms his or her willingness to participate in a particular trial, after having been informed of all aspects of the trial that are relevant to the decision to participate. Informed consent is documented by means of a written, signed, and dated form.

Investigator's Brochure: A compilation of clinical and nonclinical data on an investigational product that are relevant to the study of the product in human subjects.

Monitoring: Overseeing the progress of a clinical trial and ensuring that it is conducted, recorded, and reported in accordance with the protocol, standard operating procedures, good clinical practice, and the applicable regulatory requirements.

Monitoring Report: A written report from the monitor to the sponsor after each site visit or other trial-related communication, according to the sponsor's standard operating procedures.

Protocol: A document that describes the objectives, design, methods, statistical considerations, and organization of a trial. The protocol usually also gives the background and rationale for the trial, but these could be provided in other protocol-referenced documents. (Throughout the ICH GCP Guideline, the term protocol refers to protocol and protocol amendments.)

Serious Adverse Event or Serious Adverse Drug Reaction: Any untoward medical event that occurs in a patient or subject receiving a drug at any dose and results in death, is life-threatening, requires inpatient hospitalization or prolongation of existing hospitalization, results in persistent or significant disability or incapacity, or is a congenital anomaly or birth defect.

Source Data: All information in original records and certified copies of original records of clinical findings, observations, or other activities in a clinical trial that is necessary for the reconstruction and evaluation of the trial. Source data are contained in source documents (original records or certified copies).

Source Documents: Original documents, data, and records (e.g., hospital records, clinical and office charts, laboratory notes, memoranda, subjects' diaries or evaluation checklists, pharmacy dispensing records, recorded data from automated instruments, copies or transcriptions certified after verification as being accurate and complete, microfiches, photographic negatives, microfilm or magnetic media, roentgenograms, and subject files and records kept at the pharmacy, the laboratories, and the medicotechnical departments involved in the clinical trial).

Sponsor: An individual, a company, an institution, or an organization that takes responsibility for the initiation, management, or financing of a clinical trial.

Sponsor–Investigator: An individual who both initiates and conducts, alone or with others, a clinical trial, and under whose immediate direction the investigational product is administered to, dispensed to, or used by a subject. The term does not include any person other than an individual (e.g., it does not include a corporation or an agency). The obligations of a sponsor–investigator include both those of a sponsor and those of an investigator.

---

[a]In this document investigational drugs are defined as those that are being considered for but have not yet received marketing approval by FDA for human use and those that have FDA approval for at least one indication but are being studied for new indications, new routes of administration, or new dosage forms.
[b]The principles and procedures described here are applicable to all clinical drug studies, not just those involving investigational drugs.
[c]In certain emergency situations, prior consent may be waived (21 CFR 50.24).
[d]Definitions selected from reference 5.

These guidelines were reviewed in 2003 by the Council on Professional Affairs and by the Board of Directors and were found to still be appropriate.

Approved by the ASHP Board of Directors, November 15, 1997. Developed by the ASHP Council on Professional Affairs. Supersedes the ASHP Guidelines for the Use of Investigational Drugs in Organized Health-Care Settings, dated November 14, 1990.

The bibliographic citation for this document is as follows: American Society of Health-System Pharmacists. ASHP Guidelines on Clinical Drug Research. *Am J Health-Syst Pharm.* 1998; 55:369–76.

ASHP
Therapeutic Position Statements

ASHP Therapeutic Position Statement on the Use of the International Normalized Ratio System to Monitor Oral Anticoagulant Therapy

Statement of Position

ASHP supports the use of the International Normalized Ratio (INR) as a standardized method for reporting prothrombin time in patients receiving oral anticoagulant therapy. ASHP encourages the use of the INR system in all organized health care settings and clinical laboratories that measure prothrombin times, because the INR system reduces the differences in prothrombin time test results that are caused by using thromboplastins with varying sensitivities. ASHP encourages the education of all health care providers on the importance and appropriate use of the INR system.

Background

Oral anticoagulant therapy (primarily warfarin) must be closely monitored, because the anticoagulant response to fixed dosages varies among individuals and the safety and efficacy of the drugs are dependent on maintaining the anticoagulant effect within a defined therapeutic range.[1-3] Prothrombin time (PT) or "pro time" has been used for laboratory monitoring since its introduction by Quick et al. in 1935.[4] The PT is used because it measures the depression of three of the clotting factors of the extrinsic coagulation pathway (II, VII, and X). Warfarin inhibits the production of these vitamin K-dependent clotting factors. The PT test is performed by adding calcium and tissue thromboplastin to citrated plasma to activate the coagulation cascade. The time required for clotting to occur is expressed in seconds. To monitor warfarin therapy, the PT ratio had been traditionally calculated as the patient's PT divided by a mean normal PT.

The source of thromboplastin reagents used in North America has changed from human brain (1950) to rabbit brain (1970s and 1980s).[5] The change occurred primarily because rabbit brain thromboplastins, which are less responsive to the anticoagulant effects of warfarin than human brain thromboplastins are, were more readily available from commercial sources and less expensive than human brain thromboplastins. Although this was thought to be an inconsequential substitution, the change to less responsive rabbit brain thromboplastins resulted in a substantial decrease in the sensitivity of the PT test and, hence, lower measurements of PT values. Because this substitution was largely unrecognized by many clinicians, the average dose of warfarin used to treat thromboembolic disorders unnecessarily *increased* during the 1970s and 1980s in an attempt to maintain PT ratios at therapeutic goals.[5]

In response to this problem, the World Health Organization (WHO) developed an international reference standard, the International Sensitivity Index (ISI), to determine the responsiveness of the PT to the reduction in coagulation factors, as measured with a given thromboplastin.[6-11] Each lot of thromboplastin can be characterized by an ISI that calibrates the reagent with the first WHO reference human brain thromboplastin, which was assigned an ISI of 1.0.[11] In 1985, the International Committee on Thrombosis and He-mostasis/International Committee for Standardization in Haematology recommended adoption of a uniform calibration system in which the PT ratio is expressed in terms of the International Normalized Ratio (INR).[12] The INR is the PT ratio that would have been obtained if the WHO standard for thromboplastin reagent had been used.

Calculation Method

Any PT system (i.e., a combination of the thromboplastin reagent and the clotting instrument) can be related to the INR scale by calibration. The calibration is performed by measuring, with both the local thromboplastin and the WHO standard reagent, the PT of 20 healthy individuals and a number of patients receiving oral anticoagulants (60 patients are recommended). The PTs are plotted on double logarithmic scales, and the ISI is calculated by orthogonal regression analysis.[12] The commercial manufacturer of the thromboplastin reagent calculates the ISI and includes it in the product package insert. The ISI is specific for each lot. The lower the ISI, the more "sensitive" the reagent, and the closer the derived INR will be to the observed PT ratio. The INR, an exponential function, is calculated as follows:

$$INR = (PT/\bar{\chi})^{ISI} \text{ or } INR = (PT \text{ ratio})^{ISI}$$

where PT = patient prothrombin time expressed in seconds and $\bar{\chi}$ = mean of the range of the normal prothrombin time expressed in seconds.[a] Current literature indicates that thromboplastin reagents available in the United States have an ISI between 1.0 and 2.88.[13]

Calculation of the INR is relatively simple and can be performed with a hand-held calculator. For example, if the PT ratio is 1.7 and the ISI of thromboplastin is 2.6, the calculated INR = $1.7^{2.6}$ = 3.97. The relationship between the INR and PT ratio over a range of ISI values is shown in Figure 1.[14] Calculation should not be necessary for the practicing clinician if clinical laboratories routinely report INRs instead of PT ratios.

Failure to rely on the INR system may have resulted in significant errors in anticoagulant therapy due to the variability in thromboplastin reagent sensitivity.[15] Because of the large range of sensitivities of available commercial thromboplastins, it is no longer possible to establish standardized therapeutic ranges of anticoagulation by using the PT ratio or the uncorrected PT in seconds.[15] This variability in thromboplastin sensitivity is of particular concern if a patient's PT is measured at a variety of laboratories with different thromboplastin reagents. Although the INR system has not eliminated interlaboratory differences in PT, it does reduce the differences.[16,17] The INR system provides the best method of standardizing PT monitoring for the variable sensitivities of different thromboplastin reagents. Recommended therapeutic ranges of INRs are beyond the scope of this document, but readers are encouraged to review the October 1992 supplement to *Chest* for this information.

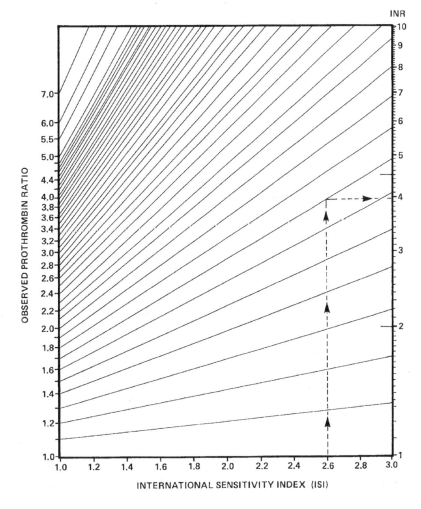

Figure 1. Nomogram showing relationship between INR and PT ratio over a range of ISI values. In the example shown, the INR is 3.97 when the observed PT ratio is 1.7 and the thromboplastin ISI is 2.6. Reprinted from reference 14, with permission.

Limitations of the INR System

As the use of the INR system to monitor warfarin therapy has increased, concerns have been raised about the reliability of this system. The specific problems, as identified by Hirsh and Poller,[18] include (1) lack of reliability of the INR system when used at the onset of warfarin therapy, (2) loss of INR system accuracy and precision when thromboplastins with high ISI values are used, (3) loss of accuracy of the INR with automated clot detectors, (4) lack of reliability of the ISI result provided by the manufacturer, (5) incorrect calculation of the INR resulting from the use of inappropriate control plasma, and (6) high INR values in overanticoagulated patients, producing unnecessary alarm. Hirsh and Poller offer potential solutions to these problems: (1) using INRs during the induction phase of warfarin treatment, on the basis of evidence that the PT ratio is less reliable than the INR and lack of evidence that the INR is not as reliable; (2) using sensitive thromboplastins with ISI values close to 1.0; (3) calibrating each new batch of thromboplastin with lyophilized plasmas with certified INR values; (4) calibrating with certified lyophilized plasma samples with known INR values to determine instrument-specific ISI; (5) educating laboratory personnel about the differences between mean normal PT and control PT; and (6) following a standard approach to treating patients with high INR values.

Summary

The INR system of standardizing PT measurements can minimize variability between laboratories, PT reagents, and instruments. The INR system can also facilitate international agreement on therapeutic ranges and allow direct comparison of clinical trials. This should provide greater uniformity in the management of oral anticoagulant therapy and ultimately may improve patient outcomes.[11] ASHP supports the use of the INR system on the basis of studies demonstrating that this system permits warfarin dosing that is less dependent on the variability of thromboplastin reagent sensitivity.

References

1. Hirsh J, Dalen JE, Deykin D, et al. Oral anticoagulants: mechanism of action, clinical effectiveness, and optimal therapeutic range. *Chest.* 1992; 102(Suppl): 312S–326S.

2. Hull R, Hirsh J, Carter C, et al. Different intensities of oral anticoagulant therapy in the treatment of proximal vein thrombosis. *N Engl J Med.* 1982; 307:1676–81.

3. Turpie AGG, Gunstensen J, Hirsh J, et al. Randomized comparison of two intensities of oral anticoagulant therapy after tissue valve replacement. *Lancet.*

1988; 1:1242–5.

4.   Quick AJ, Stanley-Brown M, Bancroft FW. A study of the coagulation defect in hemophilia and in jaundice. *Am J Med Sci.* 1935; 190:501–11.

5.   Hirsh J, Poller L, Deykin D, et al. Optimal therapeutic range for oral anticoagulants. *Chest.* 1989; 95(suppl 25):5S–11S.

6.   Bailey EL, Harper TA, Pinkerton PG. The "therapeutic range" of one-stage prothrombin time in control of anticoagulant therapy: the effect of different thromboplastin preparations. *Can Med Assoc J.* 1971; 105:1041–3.

7.   Zucker S, Cathey MG, Sox PJ, et al. Standardization of laboratory tests for controlling anticoagulant therapy. *Am J Clin Pathol.* 1970; 53:348–54.

8.   Latatto ZA, Thomson JM, Poller L. An evaluation of chromogenic substrates in the control of oral anticoagulant therapy. *Br J Haematol.* 1981; 47:301–18.

9.   Poller L. Laboratory control of anticoagulant therapy. *Semin Thromb Haemost.* 1986; 12:13–9.

10. Poller L. Progress in standardisation in anticoagulant control. *Hematol Rev.* 1987; 1:225–41.

11. Eckman MH, Levine HJ, Pauker SG. Effect of laboratory variation in the prothrombin time ratio results of oral anticoagulant therapy. *N Engl J Med.* 1993; 329:696–702.

12. Loelinger EA. ICSH/ICTH recommendations for reporting prothrombin time in oral anticoagulant control. *J Clin Pathol.* 1985; 38:133–4.

13. DuPont Pharma. ADOPT-INR. Accurate determination of prothrombin times; International Normalized Ratio. Wilmington, DE; 1993.

14. Poller L. A simple nomogram for the derivation of international normalised ratios for the standardisation of prothrombin times. *Thromb Haemost.* 1988; 60:18–20.

15. Bussey HI, Force RW, Bianco TM, et al. Reliance on prothrombin time ratio causes significant errors in anticoagulant therapy. *Arch Intern Med.* 1992; 152:278–82.

16. Ng VL, Levin J, Corash L, et al. Failure of the international normalized ratio to generate consistent results within a local medical community. *Am J Clin Pathol.* 1993; 99:689–94.

17. Le DT, Weibert RT, Sevilla BK, et al. The International Normalized Ratio (INR) for monitoring warfarin therapy: reliability and relation to other monitoring methods. *Ann Intern Med.* 1994; 120:552–8.

18. Hirsh J, Poller L. The international normalized ratio: a guide to understanding and correcting its problems. *Arch Intern Med.* 1994; 154:282–9.

---

[a]A well-defined mean normal PT must be used. The mean normal PT is determined by measuring the PT for fresh plasma samples obtained from at least 20 healthy individuals from both sexes over a range of age groups. The mean normal PT should be determined with the same thromboplastin reagent and on the same instrument as the patient's PT. The mean normal PT is reestablished for each new lot of reagent.

This therapeutic position statement was reviewed in 2002 by the Commission on Therapeutics and by the Board of Directors and was found to still be appropriate.

Approved by the ASHP Board of Directors November 16, 1994. Developed by the ASHP Commission on Therapeutics.

The bibliographic citation for this document is as follows: American Society of Health-System Pharmacists. ASHP therapeutic position statement on the use of the International Normalized Ratio system to monitor oral anticoagulant therapy. *Am J Health-Syst Pharm.* 1995; 52:529–31.

ASHP Therapeutic Position Statement on the Institutional Use of 0.9% Sodium Chloride Injection to Maintain Patency of Peripheral Indwelling Intermittent Infusion Devices

Statement of Position

0.9% Sodium chloride injection is a safe and effective means for maintaining catheter patency of peripheral indwelling intermittent infusion devices (PIIIDs) in adults. ASHP supports the use of 0.9% sodium chloride injection in preference to heparin-containing flush solutions (heparin flush) in the institutional setting, on the basis of clinical evidence indicating that 0.9% sodium chloride injection (1) is as effective as heparin flush in maintaining the patency of PIIIDs when blood is not aspirated into the device, (2) is safer to use than heparin flush because of less potential for adverse effects, (3) avoids drug incompatibilities associated with heparin flush, and (4) is a cost-effective alternative to heparin flush. Because of limited available scientific evidence to date, this recommendation is not applicable to children under the age of 12 years, patients in the home or other outpatient settings, catheters used for central venous or arterial access (including peripherally inserted central catheters and midline catheters), or the maintenance of patency in indwelling venipuncture devices used to obtain blood samples. Further research on PIIID patency in the aforementioned patient populations and settings is warranted.

Background

PIIIDs, commonly referred to as "heparin locks," are used to provide convenient intravenous (i.v.) access in patients who require intermittent i.v. administration of medications without a continuous infusion of i.v. fluids. The advantages of PIIIDs include patient mobility and comfort and reduced fluid load.[1-4] PIIIDs most commonly consist of an intravenously inserted catheter attached to a short external cannula with a resealable injection port that is designed to facilitate multiple needle entries; thus, these devices eliminate the unnecessary trauma of multiple venipunctures.[4]

A problem frequently encountered with a PIIID is the loss of patency because of clot formation within the catheter. To prevent clot formation, catheters are commonly flushed after each administration of i.v. medication and every 8 to 12 hours when the device is not in use.[5] Because of heparin's anticoagulant effects, dilute solutions of heparin in 0.9% sodium chloride injection (e.g., 10–100 units/mL) have traditionally been used to periodically flush and fill these devices and hence to prevent the formation of clots. Dilute heparin solutions are used to maintain patency while avoiding the systemic effects associated with therapeutic doses of heparin.[6] The optimum concentration of heparin and whether the drug is needed at all have not been established.[4,7-11]

Efficacy. Studies indicate that 0.9% sodium chloride injection alone is as effective as heparin-containing solutions in maintaining PIIID patency.[5,9,10,12-19] In several randomized, double-blind studies in which PIIIDs composed principally

of fluoroethylene propylene (FEP-Teflon®) were used, 0.9% sodium chloride injection for flushing was associated with patency rates similar to those achieved with flush solutions containing 10 or 100 units of heparin sodium per milliliter.[13-15] The frequency of phlebitis associated with the use of these solutions was also similar.[7-11,13-15] The type of solution used to maintain PIIID patency may not be as important as the positive pressure maintained in the i.v. line by the capped (sealed) injection device, which appears to prevent blood reflux and clot formation in the device.[10,11] Several studies provide a scientific basis for using heparin,[6,20,21] but most published research supports 0.9% sodium chloride injection as an effective alternative to heparin flush in maintaining the patency of PIIIDs. Limited data from children four weeks to 18 years of age suggest no difference between 0.9% sodium chloride injection alone and 0.9% sodium chloride injection with heparin 10 units/mL in maintaining device patency.[22] Until further controlled studies are conducted in this patient population, heparin, if it is used, should be administered in the smallest amount necessary to maintain patency of the device. One survey showed that it is common practice to flush catheter devices in neonates with heparin 1–2 units/mL.[23]

Adverse Effects of Heparin Flush Therapy. Heparin, even when used in small doses, may elicit adverse reactions in some patients. The potential for bleeding complications increases when patients receive multiple, unmonitored heparin flushes.[24] Repeated injections of heparin even in small doses can alter activated partial thromboplastin time results.[25] Allergic reactions are an inherent risk of using heparin. Although rare, heparin flush-associated thrombocytopenia and hemorrhage have been reported.[24,26-28] The risks of these adverse effects may be avoided by using 0.9% sodium chloride injection instead of heparin flush.

Drug Incompatibility. Heparin has been shown to be incompatible with many commonly used i.v. drugs.[29] If heparin flush has been used to maintain the patency of a PIIID and a drug must be administered that is incompatible with heparin, it is necessary to flush the catheter with 0.9% sodium chloride injection before and after administering the incompatible drug and then to refill the PIIID with heparin. This procedure is commonly referred to as "SASH" (sodium chloride—administration [of drug]—sodium chloride— heparin).[30] The use of 0.9% sodium chloride injection as a flushing agent avoids the numerous drug incompatibilities associated with heparin and obviates the need for SASH.

Cost Implications. Enhanced quality of patient care should be the primary reason for deciding to use 0.9% sodium chloride injection for flushing. Secondarily, the choice of 0.9% sodium chloride injection may avoid substantial costs associated with drugs, related supplies, and staff time.[11]

Summary

Because of current therapeutic evidence supporting the efficacy of 0.9% sodium chloride and the inherent risks associated with heparin, ASHP believes the use of 0.9% sodium chloride injection is appropriate for maintaining the patency of PIIIDs in adults in institutional settings.

References

1. Millam DA. Intermittent devices. *NITA.* 1981; 4(Mar–Apr):142–5.

2. Larkin M. Heparin locks. *NITA.* 1979; 2(May–Jun):18–9.

3. Thomas RB, Salter FJ. Heparin locks: their advantages and disadvantages. *Hosp Formul.* 1975; 10:536–8.

4. Deeb EN, Di Mattia PE. How much heparin in the lock? *Am J IV Ther.* 1976; 3(Dec–Jan):22–6.

5. Tuten SH, Gueldner SH. Efficacy of sodium chloride versus dilute heparin for maintenance of peripheral intermittent intravenous devices. *Appl Nurs Res.* 1991; 2:63–71.

6. Hanson RL, Grant AM, Majors KR. Heparin-lock maintenance with ten units of sodium heparin in one milliliter of normal saline solution. *Surg Gynecol Obstet.* 1976; 142:373–6.

7. Garrelts JC. White clot syndrome and thrombo-cytopenia: reasons to abandon heparin i.v. lockflush solution. *Clin Pharm.* 1992; 11:797–9.

8. Weber DR. Is heparin really necessary in the lock and, if so, how much? *DICP Ann Pharmacother.* 1991; 25:399–407.

9. Barrett PJ, Lester RL. Heparin versus saline flushing solutions in a small community hospital. *Hosp Pharm.* 1990; 25:115–8.

10. Dunn DL, Lenihan SF. The case for the saline flush. *Am J Nurs.* 1987; 87:798–9.

11. Goode CJ, Titler M, Rakel B, et al. *Nurs Res.* 1991; 40:324–30.

12. Fry B. Intermittent heparin flushing protocols. A standardization issue. *J Intraven Nurs.* 1992; 15 (May–Jun):160–3.

13. Epperson EL. Efficacy of 0.9% sodium chloride injection with and without heparin for maintaining indwelling intermittent injection sites. *Clin Pharm.* 1984; 3:626–9.

14. Garrelts JC, LaRocca J, Ast D, et al. Comparison of heparin and 0.9% sodium chloride injection in the maintenance of indwelling intermittent IV devices. *Clin Pharm.* 1989; 8:34–9.

15. Hamilton RA, Plis JM, Clay C, et al. Heparin sodium versus 0.9% sodium chloride injection for maintaining patency of indwelling intermittent infusion devices. *Clin Pharm.* 1988; 7:439–43.

16. Shearer J. Normal saline versus dilute heparin flush: a study of peripheral intermittent IV devices. *NITA.* 1987; 10:425–7.

17. Miracle V, Fangman B, Kayrouz P, et al. Normal saline vs. heparin lock flush solution: one institution's findings. *Ky Nurse.* 1989; 37(Jul–Aug):1, 6–7.

18. Ashton J, Gibson V, Summers S. Effects of heparin versus saline solution on intermittent infusion device irrigation. *Heart Lung.* 1990; 19:608–12.

19. Hook ML, Ose P. Heparin vs. normal saline. *J Intraven Nurs.* 1990; 13:150.

20. Cyganski JM, Donahue JM, Heaton JS. The case for the heparin flush. *Am J Nurs.* 1987; 87:796–7.

21. Holford NH, Vozeh S, Coates P, et al. More on heparin lock. *N Engl J Med.* 1977; 296:1300–1. Letter.

22. Lombardi TP, Gundersen B, Zammett LO, et al. Efficacy of 0.9% sodium chloride injection with or without heparin sodium for maintaining patency of intravenous catheters in children. *Clin Pharm.* 1988; 7:8332–6.

23. Romanowski GL, Zenk KE. Intravenous flush solutions for neonates. Paper presented at 26th Annual ASHP Midyear Clinical Meeting. New Orleans, LA: 1991 Dec 10.

24. Passannante A, Macik BG. Case report: the heparin flush syndrome: a cause of iatrogenic hemorrhage. *Am J Med Sci.* 1988; 296(Jul):71–3.

25. AHFS Drug Information 93. McEvoy GK, ed. Heparin sodium. Bethesda, MD: American Society of Hospital Pharmacists; 1993: 833.

26. Heeger PS, Backstrom JT. Heparin flushes and thrombocytopenia. *Ann Intern Med.* 1986; 105:143.

27. Doty JR, Alving BM, McDonnell DE, et al. Heparin-associated thrombocytopenia in the neurosurgical patient. *Neurosurgery.* 1986; 19:69–72.

28. Cines DB, Tomaski A, Tannenbaum S. Immune endothelial-cell injury in heparin-associated thrombocytopenia. *N Engl J Med.* 1987; 316:581–9.

29. Trissel LA. Handbook on injectable drugs. 7th ed. Bethesda, MD: American Society of Hospital Pharmacists; 1992.

30. Intravenous Nurses Society. Intravenous Nursing Standards of Practice. *J Intraven Nurs.* 1990; 13:S77–8.

This therapeutic position statement was reviewed in 1997 by the Commission on Therapeutics and by the Board of Directors and was found to still be appropriate.

Approved by the ASHP Board of Directors April 27, 1994. Developed by the Commission on Therapeutics.

The bibliographic citation for this document is as follows: American Society of Hospital Pharmacists. ASHP therapeutic position statement on the institutional use of 0.9% sodium chloride injection to maintain patency of peripheral indwelling intermittent infusion devices. *Am J Hosp Pharm.* 1994; 51:1572–4.

ASHP Therapeutic Position Statement on Strict Glycemic Control in Patients with Diabetes

Statement of Position

The American Society of Health-System Pharmacists (ASHP) supports strict glycemic control in all appropriate patients with diabetes mellitus. Strict glycemic control in patients with type 1 and type 2 diabetes mellitus has been shown to reduce the progression of some of the disease's chronic complications, including nephropathy, retinopathy, and neuropathy, and there are strong indications that such control may reduce the risks associated with macrovascular disease.

ASHP recognizes the need to improve glycemic control in patients with type 1 and 2 diabetes mellitus. The goal for most patients is to achieve a mean glycosylated hemoglobin (HbA$_{1c}$) concentration of <7%, as recommended by the American Diabetes Association (ADA),[1] although some patients may be able to achieve the <6.5% target recommended by the American College of Endocrinology (ACE).[2] The ability of a specific patient to achieve a glycemic goal depends on a variety of factors, including age, predisposition to hypoglycemia, comorbidities, and ability to follow treatment regimens. The medications used for glycemic control in patients with diabetes include insulin or insulin analogues and oral antidiabetic agents, given either alone or in combination.

Hypertension and dyslipidemias are prevalent conditions in patients with diabetes and contribute substantially to morbidity and mortality. In addition to strict glycemic control, aggressive treatment of hypertension and dyslipidemias is imperative to prevent adverse outcomes.

Background

Prevalence. The number of patients diagnosed with diabetes in the United States has increased threefold since 1960 and eightfold since 1935.[3,4] Several factors probably account for this increase, including the aging of the U.S. population, the reduction in mortality among people with diabetes, the increase in the ethnic-minority population, the improved sensitivity of biochemical measures, the change in diagnostic criteria (i.e., serum glucose concentration of ≥126 mg/dL), and the increased prevalence of obesity and physical inactivity.[3]

Pathophysiological Effects of Hyperglycemia. Several compelling mechanisms for glucose toxicity have been proposed: increased production of advanced glycosylation end products, alterations in the sorbitol pathway, and increased production of protein kinase C.

Nonenzymatically mediated glycosylation of proteins occurs at a rate proportional to glucose concentration and leads to the formation of advanced glycosylation end products.[5] Accumulation of these very stable end products causes thickened basement membranes and an inactivation of endothelium-derived relaxing factor, which results in microvascular constriction and leakage and oxidation of low-density lipoproteins.[6]

Alterations in the sorbitol pathway are caused by intracellular hyperglycemia. Peripheral hyperglycemia leads to intracellular hyperglycemia in non-insulin-dependent cell lines. Intracellular hyperglycemia increases flux through the polyol pathway. The increased production of sorbitol via this pathway results in a decrease in the uptake of myoinositol, which decreases Na$^+$-K$^+$-ATPase activity, leading to microvascular leakage and oxidation of low-density lipoproteins.

Hyperglycemia also induces the production of protein kinase C. Protein kinase C liberates vascular endothelial growth factor, which promotes the formation of fragile new blood vessels and causes endothelial damage.[7] Inhibition of protein kinase C may therefore reverse or reduce the rate of progression of microvascular disease.[8]

Effect of Glycemic Control on Complications

Three large prospective randomized trials and one large epidemiologic trial found a correlation between glycemic control and reduction in the progression of chronic complications associated with diabetes. Subsequent studies have confirmed these findings. The Diabetes Control and Complications Trial (DCCT) and the Kumamoto study examined the effects of strict glycemic control on the development and progression of diabetes-related complications in patients with type 1 and type 2 diabetes mellitus, respectively.[9,10] The United Kingdom Prospective Diabetes Study (UKPDS) compared intensive glycemic control with conventional treatments to determine whether intensive glycemic control could reduce the frequency of diabetes-related microvascular and macrovascular complications,[11] and the Wisconsin Epidemiologic Study of Diabetes Retinopathy (WESDR) studied the relationship between hyperglycemia and the frequency and progression of diabetes-related microvascular and macrovascular complications.[12]

The DCCT. In 1993, the DCCT Research Group published the results of a long-term prospective study that evaluated 1441 patients with type 1 diabetes mellitus.[9] Investigated was whether strict glycemic control prevents chronic complications (the primary prevention cohort, *n* = 726 patients) and reduces the progression of chronic complications present at the initiation of intensive treatment (the secondary intervention cohort, *n* = 715 patients). Patients from both cohorts were randomly assigned to intensive therapy or conventional therapy. The intensive therapy group received a basal dose of insulin plus additional doses with meals. Some patients used a subcutaneous insulin-infusion pump to deliver the basal infusion and bolus doses prior to meals; others injected a long-acting insulin as a basal dose and had three injections of regular insulin with meals. The conventional therapy group received one or two daily injections each of rapid-acting insulin and intermediate-acting insulin. The patients were studied for a mean of 6.5 years. Researchers halted the study early, after an independent monitoring committee determined that the data overwhelmingly supported the conclusion that glycemic control reduced the development and progression of diabetes-related microvascular complications (Table 1). Furthermore, the study showed that the reduction in the risk of microvascular complications increased as

Table 1.
Relative Reduction in Risk of Clinical Complications in Diabetes Patients Given Intensive Therapy[9]

Clinical Complication	Relative Risk Reduction (%)
Albuminuria	
Microalbuminuria	35
Macroalbuminuria	56
Clinical neuropathy	60
Retinopathy	
Initial appearance	27
Clinically significant	34–76
Severe	45

HbA_{1c} levels approached normal (e.g., patients with an HbA_{1c} concentration of 6% had a lower rate of progression of retinopathy than patients with an HbA_{1c} concentration of 7%). A key finding was that for every 1% reduction in HbA_{1c} there was a 30% reduction in microvascular complications.[13]

Although the DCCT was not designed to evaluate the effects of glycemic control on macrovascular disease, some of its indicators were evaluated. Intensive insulin therapy was associated with a significant relative reduction (34%) ($p < 0.02$) in the development of hypercholesterolemia (serum low-density-lipoprotein [LDL] cholesterol concentrations of >160 mg/dL). Targeted LDL cholesterol levels have been revised for all populations, including patients with diabetes. The National Cholesterol Education Program recommends that patients with diabetes achieve LDL cholesterol concentrations of <100 mg/dL.[14] Intensive insulin therapy also reduced the relative risk of macrovascular disease (peripheral and cardiovascular disease) by 41%, but the difference was not significant, probably because of the small number of patients who developed macrovascular disease.

There was a threefold increase in the development of severe hypoglycemia (i.e., hypoglycemia requiring the assistance of another person) in the intensive therapy group ($p < 0.001$). There were 62 severe hypoglycemic episodes per 100 patient-years in the intensive therapy group and 19 per 100 patient-years in the conventional therapy group.

The Kumamoto Study. Although the DCCT showed that strict glycemic control reduced complications in patients with type 1 diabetes mellitus, the question of applicability to patients with type 2 disease remained. Two years after the DCCT was published, the Kumamoto study demonstrated a relationship between glycemic control and a reduction in microvascular complications and neuropathic problems in patients with type 2 diabetes mellitus.[10] This study was a prospective randomized six-year trial in 110 nonobese Japanese patients who received either intensive or conventional insulin regimens similar to those used in the DCCT. One hundred two of the patients remained in the study for the entire six years. Intensive therapy consisted of three or more injections of insulin per day, and conventional therapy consisted of one or two injections per day. The goal of the intensive therapy was to maintain blood glucose levels close to normal, with HbA_{1c} concentrations of <7%. HbA_{1c} concentrations were 7% and 9% with intensive and conventional therapy, respectively ($p < 0.001$). The mean HbA_{1c} concentration of 7.1% in the intensive therapy group represented a reduction of 2.3% for patients in the secondary intervention cohort and 2.1% for those in the primary prevention cohort.

The Kumamoto study found that, after six years, 7.7%

of patients in the intensive therapy group had developed retinopathy, compared with 32% of the patients receiving conventional therapy. In the secondary intervention cohort, the cumulative percentages of patients with progressive retinopathy were 19.2% and 44% in the intensive and conventional therapy groups, respectively. Intensive therapy patients had a 70% relative reduction in the risk of development or progression of nephropathy. After six years of treatment, 9.6% of the patients in the intensive therapy group developed microalbuminuria or albuminuria, versus 30% in the conventional therapy group ($p = 0.005$). Significant differences in nerve conduction velocities and vibratory sensation thresholds were observed between the groups after six years ($p < 0.05$).

The study found no worsening of retinopathy or nephropathy in patients with HbA_{1c} concentrations of <6.5%, fasting blood glucose concentrations of <110 mg/dL, and two-hour postmeal glucose concentrations of <80 mg/dL. No episodes of severe hypoglycemia were observed.

The UKPDS. The UKPDS was a randomized, multicenter, prospective trial in 5102 patients with newly diagnosed type 2 diabetes mellitus.[11] The mean duration of this trial was 11 years. The primary goal was to determine whether intensive blood glucose control was better than conventional therapies in reducing the risk of microvascular and macrovascular complications. A secondary goal was to determine the advantages and disadvantages of particular glycemic control therapies. Of the 5102 patients in the trial, 4209 were randomly assigned: 342 to a metformin therapy group intended for obese patients and 3867 to therapy with insulin or sulfonylureas. Patients in both groups were further randomly assigned to intensive or conventional therapy. The goals for the patients in the conventional therapy group were a fasting plasma glucose concentration of <270 mg/dL and no symptoms of hyperglycemia. The goals for the patients in the intensive therapy group were a fasting plasma glucose concentration of <108 mg/dL and no symptoms of hyperglycemia. The average difference in HbA_{1c} values between the conventional and intensive therapy groups was only 0.9%, but this small reduction reduced by 12% ($p = 0.029$) the risk of any diabetes-related endpoint, including myocardial infarction, heart failure, angina, sudden death, stroke, amputation, retinal photocoagulation, renal failure, and vitreous hemorrhage. The authors reported a 16% reduction in the risk of both fatal and nonfatal myocardial infarction ($p = 0.052$) and a 25% reduction in microvascular disease ($p = 0.0099$). No increase in macrovascular problems was seen in patients being treated with sulfonylureas or insulin. Patients in the intensive therapy group gained more weight than patients in the conventional therapy group, but they had fewer diabetes-related complications.

There were no significant differences between patients who received intensive metformin treatment and those given intensive sulfonylurea or insulin treatment.[15] The UKPDS authors nevertheless concluded, "Since intensive glucose control with metformin appears to decrease the risk of diabetes-related endpoints in overweight diabetic patients and is associated with less weight gain and fewer hypoglycemic attacks than are insulin and sulfonylureas, it may be the first-line pharmacologic therapy of choice in these patients" (Table 2).

The WESDR. The WESDR was a large epidemiologic study of patients in an 11-county area of Wisconsin.[12] The goal was to study the relationship between hyperglycemia and chronic complications. The initial trial focused on diabetic retinopathy, but a follow-up trial examined the frequency and progression of microvascular and macrovascular complications over a 10-year period.[16] A strong correlation was reported between higher HbA$_{1c}$ values and loss of vision, retinopathy, renal failure, lower-extremity amputation, myocardial infarction, and overall mortality.

Management of Diabetes Mellitus

All health care providers can be involved in the treatment and management of patients with diabetes through education, pharmacotherapy management, patient monitoring, and encouragement.[17] Health care providers need to take responsibility for educating themselves, other providers, and patients about the risks and benefits of strict glycemic control, including the drug therapy and lifestyle changes used to achieve it. Providers can contribute by becoming a member of the diabetes care team and taking responsibility for designing therapeutic regimens that incorporate individualized treatment approaches to achieving glucose goals based on the patient's age, body weight, type of diabetes, renal function, and cognitive function. Diabetes is a chronic disease that requires continuous treatment and monitoring. Web sites offering health care providers relevant information are listed in the appendix.

Factors that must be considered when designing therapy regimens include the patient's age, understanding of the disease, motivation, and predisposition to hypoglycemia, as well as the age of onset and duration of the disease. ADA and ACE have established guidelines for practitioners (Table 3).[1,2] Patients with diabetes should try to maintain their glucose levels as close to normal as the constraints of hypoglycemic episodes and other patient-specific characteristics allow.

Table 2.
Relative Reduction in Risk of Diabetes-Related Endpoints between Intensive Treatment Regimens[15]

	Relative Risk Reduction[a] (%)	
Endpoint	Intensive Metformin Therapy	Intensive Sulfonylurea or Insulin Therapy
Any diabetes-related endpoint	32	7
Death	42	20
Myocardial infarction	39	21
Microvascular disease	29	16

[a]Differences in risk reduction between therapies were not significant.

Education. Several studies have concluded that educational interventions have a positive effect on patients with diabetes. Pharmacist counseling of older patients with diabetes has been shown to improve outcomes.[18] Another trial compared standard care of type 2 diabetes mellitus with pharmacist-directed primary care over a four-month period; pharmacist interventions resulted in significant reductions in fasting plasma glucose and HbA$_{1c}$ levels.[19]

Lifestyle and Pharmacotherapy Management. Strict glycemic control in patients with type 1 diabetes mellitus is best achieved by the intensive insulin treatment methods described in the DCCT: multiple daily injections or use of a subcutaneous insulin infusion pump. Methods for achieving strict glycemic control in patients with type 2 diabetes mellitus are more varied. Lifestyle changes (diet and exercise) are the foundation of prevention and management of type 2 disease; lifestyle changes and treatment with metformin have been shown to reduce the frequency of diabetes in high-risk individuals.[20] Diabetes is a progressive disease, and therefore patients who are unable to maintain glycemic control with a meal plan and exercise will need drug therapy. Sulfonylureas, biguanides, meglitinides, thiazolidinediones, α-glucosidase inhibitors, D-phenylalanine derivatives, insulin, or a combination of these medications may be needed. The use of combination therapy has burgeoned in the past few years; a detailed discussion of the various combination therapies is available elsewhere.[21]

Although strict glycemic control will benefit a majority of patients, it may be difficult to achieve in all patients because of the risks associated with severe hypoglycemia. Intensive therapy may not be appropriate for patients with a history of repeated severe hypoglycemic episodes or for those who display a lack of hypoglycemic awareness. Diabetes care for patients younger than 18 years requires consideration of complicated physical and emotional growth needs. The risk–benefit ratio of intensive therapy may be unfavorable for young patients (those less than 6 years old) because they may have a form of "hypoglycemic unawareness."[1] Intensive therapy is also inappropriate for patients without the cognitive ability or the motivation required to adhere to the regimen. The preconception care of women with preexisting diabetes or gestational diabetes represents special cases. ADA has clinical practice recommendations that outline standards of care for these patients.[22,23]

Unique problems may be encountered when a patient with diabetes is hospitalized. For example, glycemic needs may change dramatically, depending on oral intake, the amount of dextrose supplied in intravenous infusions, medication effects on blood glucose, infections, surgery, and the response to physiological stress. Glycemic regimens may

Table 3.
Recommendations for Glycemic Control by American Diabetes Association (ADA) and American College of Endocrinology (ACE)[1,2,a]

Biochemical Index	Normal Value	Goal Value		Additional Intervention Suggested by ADA
		ADA	ACE	
Preprandial blood glucose conc. (mg/dL)	<100	90–130	≤110	<80 or >140 (whole blood)
Postprandial blood glucose conc. (mg/dL)	<140	180	≤140	[b]
Bedtime blood glucose conc. (mg/dL)	<110	100–140 (whole blood)		<100 or >160
HbA$_{1c}$ conc. (%)	<6	<7	<6.5	>8

[a]Plasma values unless otherwise indicated.
[b]ADA was unable to reach consensus on a recommendation.

need to be significantly altered and continually adjusted while the patient receives acute care. Patients with type 2 diabetes mellitus who were not being treated with insulin prior to hospitalization may need insulin while hospitalized. Although the use of simple sliding-scale insulin regimens has been promoted, their efficacy has been brought into question, particularly when they are not used in combination with intermediate- or long-acting insulin.[24] A review of the inpatient management of diabetes has been published elsewhere and offers comprehensive guidelines.[25]

Monitoring. Patients with diabetes should be monitored for appropriate glycemic control and for comorbid conditions (e.g., hyperlipidemia and hypertension). ADA has established a set of guidelines for self-monitoring of blood glucose in patients with diabetes.[26] An expert panel concluded that self-monitoring should be used for (1) achieving and maintaining a specific level of glycemic control, (2) preventing and detecting hypoglycemia, (3) avoiding severe hypoglycemia, (4) adjusting care in response to changes in lifestyle in individuals requiring pharmacologic therapy, and (5) determining the need for initiating insulin therapy in patients with gestational diabetes mellitus.

The ADA position statement on bedside blood glucose monitoring in hospitals states that capillary blood glucose determination at the bedside is analogous to an additional vital sign for people with diabetes.[27] Capillary blood glucose determination at the bedside could shorten hospital stays and replace venipuncture measurement of blood glucose levels. Use of blood glucose monitoring requires (1) a clear administrative responsibility for the procedure, (2) well-defined policies and procedures, (3) a training program for personnel doing the testing, (4) quality-control procedures, and (5) regularly scheduled equipment maintenance.[25]

Summary

The deleterious effects of hyperglycemia have been documented from the biochemical to the pathophysiologic level. Given the research findings and the guidelines for glycemic control established by ADA and ACE, ASHP supports and encourages strict glycemic control in all appropriate patients with diabetes mellitus to reduce the progression of chronic complications.

References

1. American Diabetes Association. Standards of medical care for patients with diabetes mellitus. *Diabetes Care.* 2003; 26(suppl 1):S32–50.
2. American College of Endocrinology. Consensus Statement on Guidelines for Glycemic Control. *Endocr Pract.* 2002; 8 (Suppl 1):5–11.
3. Diabetes 2001 vital statistics. Alexandria, VA: American Diabetes Association; 2001.
4. Benjamin SM, Valdez R, Geiss LS et al. Estimated number of adults with prediabetes in the U.S. in 2000: opportunities for prevention. *Diabetes Care.* 2003; 26: 645–9.
5. Brownlee M, Cerami A, Vlassara H. Advanced glycosylation end products in tissue and the biochemical basis of diabetic complications. *N Engl J Med.* 1988; 318:1315–21.
6. Libby P. Atherosclerosis: the new view. *Sci Am.* 2002; 286(May):46–55.
7. Frank RN. Potential new medical therapies for diabetic retinopathy: protein kinase C inhibitors. *Am J Ophthalmol.* 2002; 133:693–8.
8. Setter SM, Campbell RK, Cahoon CJ. The emerging role of protein kinase C b (PKC b) in diabetes complications. *Adv Pharm.* 2003; 1:149–58.
9. Diabetes Control and Complications Trial Research Group. The effect of intensive treatment of diabetes on the development and progression of long-term complications in insulin-dependent diabetes mellitus. *N Engl J Med.* 1993; 329:977–86.
10. Ohkubo Y, Kishikawa H, Araki E et al. Intensive insulin therapy prevents the progression of diabetic microvascular complications in Japanese patients with noninsulin diabetes mellitus: a randomized, prospective 6-year study. *Diabetes Res Clin Pract.* 1995; 28:103–17.
11. UK Prospective Diabetes Study (UKPDS) Group. Intensive blood-glucose control with sulphonylureas or insulin compared with conventional treatment and risk of complications in patients with type 2 diabetes (UKPDS 33). *Lancet.* 1998; 352:837–53.
12. Klein R, Klein BE, Moss SE et al. Relationship of hyperglycemia to the long-term incidence and progression of diabetic retinopathy. *Arch Intern Med.* 1994; 154:2169–78.
13. Reduce HbA1c by just 1% and see what happens. www.diabetesincontrol.com/issue59/#item#1 (accessed 2003 Jul 25).
14. Executive summary of the third report of the National Cholesterol Education Program (NCEP) Expert Panel on Detection, Evaluation, and Treatment of High Blood Cholesterol in Adults (Adult Treatment Panel III). *JAMA.* 2001; 285:2486–97.
15. UK Prospective Diabetes Study (UKPDS) Group. Effect of intensive blood-glucose control with metformin on complications in overweight patients with type 2 diabetes (UKPDS 34). *Lancet.* 1998; 352:854–65.
16. Klein R. Hyperglycemia and microvascular and macrovascular disease in diabetes. *Diabetes Care.* 1995; 18:258–68.
17. McPherson ML. ASHP Ambulatory Care Clinical Skills Program: type 2 diabetes mellitus management module. Bethesda, MD: American Society of Health-System Pharmacists; 2000:4.
18. Baran RW, Crumlish K, Patterson H et al. Improving outcomes of community-dwelling older patients with diabetes through pharmacist counseling. *Am J Health-Syst Pharm.* 1999; 56:1535–9.
19. Coast-Senior EA, Kroner BA, Kelley CL et al. Management of patients with type 2 diabetes by pharmacists in primary care clinics. *Ann Pharmacother.* 1998; 32:636–41.
20. Diabetes Prevention Program Research Group. Reduction in the incidence of type 2 diabetes with lifestyle intervention or metformin. *N Engl J Med.* 2002; 346: 393–403.
21. Medications for the treatment of diabetes. Alexandria, VA: American Diabetes Association; 2000.
22. American Diabetes Association. Preconception care of women with diabetes. *Diabetes Care.* 2003; 26(suppl 1):S91–3.
23. American Diabetes Association. Gestational diabetes mellitus. *Diabetes Care.* 2003; 26(suppl 1):S103–5.
24. Queale WS, Seidler AJ, Brancati FL. Glycemic control and sliding scale insulin use in medical inpatients with

diabetes mellitus. *Arch Intern Med.* 1997; 157:545–52.

25. Hirsch IB, Brunzell J, Paauw DS. Inpatient management of adults with diabetes. *Diabetes Care.* 1995; 18:870–7.

26. American Diabetes Association. Self-monitoring of blood glucose. *Diabetes Care.* 1994; 17:81–6.

27. American Diabetes Association. Bedside blood glucose monitoring in hospitals. *Diabetes Care.* 2003; 26(suppl 1):S119.

Developed through the ASHP Commission on Therapeutics and approved by the ASHP Board of Directors on July 28, 2003

The bibliographic citation for this document is as follows: American Society of Health-System Pharmacists. ASHP Therapeutic Position Statement on Strict Glycemic Control in Patients with Diabetes. *Am J Health-Syst Pharm.* 2003; 60:2357–62

Appendix—Web Sites with Diabetes Information for Providers

Organization	URL
American Diabetes Association	www.diabetes.org
American Association of Clinical Endocrinologists	www.aace.com/clin
American Association of Diabetes Educators	www.aadenet.org
Juvenile Diabetes Research Foundation International	www.jdrf.org/index.php
American Dietetic Association	www.eatright.org
National Diabetes Education Program	www.ndep.nih.gov
National Institute of Diabetes and Digestive and Kidney Diseases	www.niddk.nih.gov/index.htm

ASHP Therapeutic Position Statement on the Safe Use of Niacin in the Management of Dyslipidemias

Statement of Position

ASHP supports the use of niacin products under the supervision of a qualified health care provider for the treatment of dyslipidemias in adults. Niacin is proven safe and effective in the management of most lipid disorders but requires ongoing monitoring by a health care provider to detect potential toxicities. Health care providers should teach patients how to minimize niacin's bothersome adverse effects and encourage long-term adherence. Because a variety of nonprescription niacin products with various potentials for toxicity are available, pharmacists should actively monitor patient selection of niacin products and discourage patient self-treatment with niacin. In addition, pharmacists should work in conjunction with patients and their primary care providers to ensure adequate monitoring for toxicity and effectiveness of therapy.

Background

Niacin (nicotinic acid) is effective for managing most primary and secondary dyslipidemias in adults and is classified, along with bile acid sequestrants (BAS) and 3-hydroxy-3-methylglutaryl coenzyme A (HMG-CoA) reductase inhibitors ("statins"), as a major drug for managing hypercholesterolemia by National Cholesterol Education Program (NCEP) Adult Treatment Panel II (ATP II).[1] Niacin is not recommended for routine use in children and adolescents with significant dyslipidemias because of limited information about its safety and efficacy in these populations.[2] Niacin effectively lowers serum total cholesterol (TC); low-density-lipoprotein cholesterol (LDL-C), the lipid component that is most directly related to the development of coronary heart disease (CHD); and triglycerides (TG). Niacin elevates high-density-lipoprotein cholesterol (HDL-C), the lipid component conferring cardioprotection. It was proved effective in the secondary prevention of coronary artery events in the Coronary Drug Project,[3] and it reduced overall mortality by 11% in the 15-year follow-up of that same study.[4] Niacin has been used successfully in combination with BAS and statins for reducing the rate of progression and increasing the likelihood of regression of atherosclerotic plaques in patients with established CHD.[5] Niacin also effectively lowers TG in patients at risk for pancreatitis and in patients with a history of pancreatitis secondary to elevated TG. For those patients able to tolerate the drug, niacin may be the least expensive agent per percent reduction in LDL-C.

Available Products

Niacin (nicotinic acid, vitamin B$_3$) products and products containing its metabolite nicotinamide (niacinamide) should not be confused. Both are equally effective as nutrients and cofactors, but only nicotinic acid has clinically important lipid-altering properties. Numerous immediate-release (IR) and extended-release (ER) niacin products are currently marketed. Most of these products are marketed as nutritional supplements rather than as prescription or nonprescription drugs. This is an important distinction, since regulatory requirements for the marketing of nutritional supplements differ substantially from those for prescription drugs. Nutritional supplements are not labeled according to USP standards and do not carry FDA-approved labeling for use as lipid-modifying agents. However, niacin products sold as nutritional supplements are available in strengths far exceeding the recommended dietary allowance for niacin and are often promoted directly to the public for use as lipid-modifying agents. Some products, such as Niacor (Upsher-Smith) and Nicolar (Rhône Poulenc-Rorer), have received FDA approval as lipid-modifying agents and are available by prescription only. From the limited information available, it appears that niacin dosage forms vary in their pharmaceutical, pharmacologic, and clinical properties and are not interchangeable.[6–8]

Significant differences in adverse-effect profiles and, possibly, effectiveness exist between IR and ER products. ER products were developed in an effort to reduce the adverse effects of niacin, notably flushing. While flushing may be less common with ER products, some may be more likely to cause gastrointestinal upset, elevated liver enzymes, and hepatitis.[6–8] At similar doses, ER products appear to lower LDL-C more effectively than IR products. Even though available data do not allow for precise identification of an equivalence ratio for the difference in LDL-C-lowering effects between ER and IR products, it is likely that 1500 mg of an ER product has roughly the same LDL-C-lowering effect as 3000 mg of an IR product.[6] Further hampering the establishment of an exact equivalence ratio are literature reports suggesting that ER products appear to be less effective than IR products in reducing TG and raising HDL-C.[6–8]

Adverse Effects

Dermatologic Reactions. Niacin has been reported to cause many dermatologic reactions, including flushing, pruritus, dry skin, and reversible acanthosis nigricans. The most common adverse effect associated with niacin is flushing. Flushing results from prostaglandin D$_2$-mediated vasodilation. However, tolerance to these effects may develop and is associated with decreased mediator release. Vasodilation can be of sufficient magnitude to lower blood pressure and can, rarely, precipitate angina in patients with existing coronary artery disease.

Acanthosis nigricans is manifested as hyperpigmented, velvety, verrucous plaques on the neck and axillae, under the breasts, and in the antecubital space and groin areas. It is also associated with numerous conditions and drugs other than niacin, such as obesity, diabetes, adenocarcinoma, and corticosteroid and estrogen use. It occurs more commonly with IR products, and its development in association with niacin requires drug discontinuation.[9] If the lesions do not resolve, other causes should be explored.

Gastrointestinal Effects. Gastrointestinal distress, including nausea, vomiting, abdominal pain, indigestion, heartburn, anorexia, and diarrhea, is commonly associated with niacin use. The frequency of gastrointestinal complaints is higher in users of ER niacin.[10] Active peptic ulceration during niacin therapy has been reported, although a direct causal relationship has not been established.[11] However, it seems prudent to avoid prescribing niacin to patients who have active peptic ulcer disease. Gastrointestinal distress can be minimized by dividing the total daily dose into a twice-daily or three-times-daily dosage regimen and by instructing patients to take niacin on a full stomach.

Hepatotoxicity. Hepatotoxicity is probably the most serious adverse effect of niacin, but because this possible toxicity has not been fully studied, the true frequency is not known. Rises in serum hepatic transaminases appear to be dose related with both IR and ER niacin products.[6,12] Patients with asymptomatic enzyme elevations three times the upper limit of normal should have their niacin therapy discontinued. These enzymatic changes are usually reversible upon discontinuation of drug therapy; however, there are a few case reports of fulminant hepatitis with ER products.[13] Elevations of hepatic transaminases less than three times the upper limit of normal may occur early in therapy but usually resolve with continued therapy or dosage reductions.

The frequency of hepatotoxicity appears to be greater with certain ER products[6] and may be more common when patients have replaced an IR niacin product with an ER product at the same dosage. Therefore, patients should be advised not to change niacin products without the advice of a qualified health care provider. Some investigators, however, have found a low frequency of hepatotoxicity with ER niacin products, suggesting that all ER niacin products may not be the same.[14–16] Clearly, additional research is needed. Because of this increased risk of hepatotoxicity with ER products, the maximum dosage recommended by NCEP for this dosage form is 2 g/day.[17]

NCEP further recommends that patients be started on IR niacin products and that ER products be considered only when IR products are not tolerated and alternative products are ineffective or not tolerated. If a switch from an IR to an ER product is to be accomplished, the ER product should be begun at a lower dosage (no more than 50% of the IR dosage) and the dosage gradually adjusted upward, since there is evidence that ER products may be more than twice as potent in lowering cholesterol as IR products.[12] Patients should be encouraged to report any signs or symptoms of hepatotoxicity (e.g., nausea, vomiting, malaise, loss of appetite, right-upper-quadrant pain, jaundice, and dark urine).

Glucose Intolerance. Niacin can reduce glucose tolerance, possibly by causing or aggravating insulin resistance.[18] Elevations in fasting glucose levels appear to be dose related for all niacin preparations. When niacin is used in diabetic patients, deterioration of glycemic control may result, possibly making its use as a first-line agent undesirable.

Uric Acid Effects. Niacin decreases urinary secretion of uric acid, which may result in increased plasma uric acid concentrations. The risk of uric acid elevations increases as the niacin dosage increases. Niacin should be avoided in patients who have a recent history of acute gout and who are not taking a uric acid-lowering medication, as well as in patients who have frequent gout attacks despite treatment. Niacin therapy may be considered in patients who have a history of gout but who are taking a uric acid-lowering medication and have not had an attack in the past year.

Use of Niacin in Combination with Other Lipid-Modifying Agents

Patients who maintain an elevated LDL-C concentration despite single-drug therapy may be responsive to combination therapy with niacin and either a BAS or a statin. Combination therapy may actually be more efficacious, safer, and more cost-effective than increasing the dose of the single agent. When LDL-C remains elevated and TG concentrations are <200 mg/dL, the addition of a BAS or a statin to niacin therapy may effectively lower LDL-C about 50%, compared with the 15–25% average reduction in LDL-C achieved by niacin alone.[19] Patients with severe hypercholesterolemia (such as familial hypercholesterolemia) may require LDL-C reductions of 40% or more and will generally need combination therapy to achieve a reduction of this magnitude. In patients with elevated LDL-C and elevated TG (200–400 mg/dL), the NCEP ATP II considers the combination of niacin with either a BAS or a statin to be effective and capable of reducing LDL-C by 60%; however, the niacin–statin combination does carry the possibility of increased risk of myopathy and hepatitis. The risk of myopathy with this combination may potentially be lessened when water-soluble statins are used. Although it is not necessary to avoid this combination, patients must be selected carefully and monitored closely for symptoms of muscle pain. It should be noted that the American Heart Association does not advocate the use of a BAS with niacin or statins when TG exceed 200 mg/dL because of the potential for further elevation of TG by the BAS.[20]

Dosage Guidelines

To enhance patient adherence and tolerability, all patients should be advised to take niacin with meals and to avoid concurrent use of alcohol or hot drinks. Also, unless it is contraindicated, patients should be advised to take 325 mg of aspirin 30 minutes before each IR niacin dose or 325 mg of enteric-coated aspirin 45–60 minutes before each IR niacin dose. Use of aspirin before a dose of ER niacin is optional, since flushing may be less. Patients should also be instructed to try using their niacin without aspirin periodically to determine whether the aspirin is providing any benefit. The following dosage regimens can be recommended:

Initiating Therapy with IR Niacin:

1. Initiate IR niacin at a low dosage (e.g., 50–100 mg orally twice daily during the first week).
2. Slowly increase the dosage of niacin over one month to reach a daily dose of 1–1.5 g (dividing the total daily dose into a twice-daily or three-times-daily regimen). Doubling the daily dose each week will result in this amount. Assess effects after four and eight weeks and, if necessary, continue to increase the dosage slowly until 3 g of IR niacin per day or a desired cholesterol level is reached.
3. A slower dosage-adjustment schedule may be required for some sensitive patients.

Initiating Therapy with ER Niacin:

1. Start with 250 mg orally twice daily during the first week.
2. Increase the dosage to 500 mg twice daily for the next three weeks.
3. Thereafter, increase the dosage weekly to no more than 2 g/day. (Although a maximum dosage of ER niacin of 2 g/day has been recommended by NCEP, the lowest dosage should be used whenever possible because of the potential for toxicity.)

Monitoring Therapy

Before a patient is started on niacin therapy there should be a baseline determination of serum hepatic transaminases, fasting glucose, and uric acid and a minimum of two fasting lipid profiles. These laboratory tests should be repeated four to six weeks after the dosage of niacin is stabilized. The NCEP ATP II recommends that a minimum of two fasting lipid profiles be used in evaluating the response to therapy; however, for compliant patients more than 50% from their LDL-C goal, only one determination may be sufficient. Once the LDL-C goal has been reached, fasting lipid profiles and toxicity monitoring should be repeated every 2–3 months for the first year and then every 6–12 months, provided that there is no sign of toxicity and the dosage is stable. Continued laboratory monitoring is very important, since there is a potential for late toxicity.

Role of the Pharmacist

Niacin cannot be safely or effectively administered without the active support and supervision of trained health care professionals. Given that many niacin products (either non-prescription drugs or nutritional supplements) are available without a prescription, pharmacists have a potentially large and important role in ensuring the appropriate use of this therapy. Needed services that pharmacists can provide by working with other health care professionals include:

1. Cautioning patients about the need for ongoing consultation with their physician or other health care provider when using niacin for its lipid-lowering effects, especially when any of the following conditions are present: chronic liver disease, active peptic ulcer disease, poorly controlled acid reflux disease, diabetes, hyperuricemia, and poorly controlled gout.
2. Informing patients about the benefits of therapy with niacin (as a reason to take it), including its effect on the lipid profile and on CHD and mortality outcomes.
3. Providing guidance in the selection of IR rather than ER dosage forms, including making IR dosage forms available for selection, cautioning about switching from IR to ER dosage forms, and encouraging the continued administration of the same dosage form to promote consistent effects on lipids.
4. Giving instructions on how to initiate niacin therapy, recommending a specific dosage-adjustment schedule, and empowering patients to interrupt therapy or reduce daily doses to accommodate transient adverse effects.
5. Instructing patients on how to avoid or manage symptoms associated with niacin's vasodilatory and gastrointestinal effects by administering doses with food,

slowing adjusting doses upward, administering prophylactic aspirin, avoiding alcohol and hot drinks if these beverages accentuate flushing, and using antihistamines and emollients for pruritus and dry skin, respectively.
6. Monitoring lipid profiles to determine whether the goal of therapy has been attained.
7. Monitoring for adverse effects, including vasodilation (e.g., flushing, itching, headache), hepatotoxicity (e.g., malaise, fatigue, anorexia, lethargy), hyperglycemia (e.g., increased thirst, appetite, and urination), gout, gastrointestinal upset, and acanthosis nigricans.
8. Monitoring and facilitating patients' adherence to therapy.
9. Encouraging patients to maintain regular contact with a health care professional to ensure the efficacy and safety of therapy.
10. Advising other health care professionals of the place of niacin therapy in the management of dyslipidemias.

Summary

ASHP supports the use of niacin as an effective therapy for the management of dyslipidemias in adults. Successful and safe therapy requires ongoing supervision and instruction by qualified health care providers to monitor the efficacy of therapy and minimize niacin's potential for adverse effects. Because many niacin products are available without a prescription, pharmacists are in a unique position to help ensure that patients make the best use of this medication.

References

1. Summary of the second report of the National Cholesterol Education Program (NCEP) Expert Panel on Detection, Evaluation, and Treatment of High Blood Cholesterol in Adults (Adult Treatment Panel II). *JAMA.* 1993; 269:3015–23.
2. Report of the Expert Panel on Blood Cholesterol Levels in Children and Adolescents. Bethesda, MD: National Heart, Lung, and Blood Institute, 1991; NIH publication no. 91-2732:70.
3. Coronary Drug Project Research Group. Clofibrate and niacin in coronary heart disease. *JAMA.* 1975; 231:360–81.
4. Canner PL, Berge KG, Wenger NK, et al., for the Coronary Drug Project Research Group. Fifteen year mortality in coronary drug project patients: long-term benefit with niacin. *J Am Coll Cardiol.* 1986; 8:1245–55.
5. Superko RH, Krauss RM. Coronary artery disease regression: convincing evidence for the benefit of aggressive lipoprotein management. *Circulation.* 1994; 90:1056–69.
6. McKenney JM, Proctor JD, Harris S, et al. A comparison of the efficacy and toxic effects of sustained vs. immediate-release niacin in hypercholesterolemic patients. *JAMA.* 1994; 271:672–7.
7. Christensen NA, Achor RWP, Berge KG, et al. Nicotinic acid treatment of hypercholesterolemia: comparison of plain and sustained-action preparations and report of two cases of jaundice. *JAMA.* 1961; 177:76–80.
8. Knopp RH, Ginsberg J, Albers JJ, et al. Contrasting effects of unmodified and time-release forms of niacin

on lipoproteins in hyperlipidemic subjects: clues to mechanism of action of niacin. *Metabolism.* 1985; 34:642–50.

9. Brown J, Winkelmann RK. Acanthosis nigricans: a study of 90 cases. *Medicine.* 1968; 47:33–51.

10. Gibbons LW, Gonzalez V, Gordon N, et al. The prevalence of side effects with regular and sustained-release nicotinic acid. *Am J Med.* 1995; 99:378–85.

11. Parsons WB. Activation of peptic ulcer by nicotinic acid: report of five cases. *JAMA.* 1960; 173:92–6.

12. Gray DR, Morgan T, Chretien SD, et al. Efficacy and safety of controlled-release niacin in dyslipoproteinemic veterans. *Ann Intern Med.* 1994; 121:252–8.

13. Mullin GE, Greenson JK, Mitchell MC. Fulminant hepatic failure after ingestion of sustained-release nicotinic acid. *Ann Intern Med.* 1989; 111:253–5.

14. Keenan JM, Fontaine PL, Wenz JB, et al. Niacin revisited: a randomized, controlled trial of wax-matrix sustained-release niacin in hypercholesterolemia. *Arch Intern Med.* 1991; 151:1424–32.

15. Knopp RH, Ginsberg J, Albers JJ, et al. Contrasting effects of unmodified and time-release forms of niacin on lipoproteins in hyperlipidemia subjects: clues to mechanism of action of niacin. *Metabolism.* 1985; 34:642–50.

16. Alderman JD, Pasternak RC, Sacks FM, et al. Effect of a modified, well-tolerated niacin regimen on serum total cholesterol, high density lipoprotein cholesterol and the cholesterol to high density lipoprotein ratio. *Am J Cardiol.* 1989; 64:725–9.

17. Second report of the Expert Panel on Detection, Evaluation, and Treatment of High Blood Cholesterol in Adults (Adult Treatment Panel II). Bethesda, MD: National Heart, Lung, and Blood Institute, 1993; NIH publication no. 933095:111–7.

18. Kahn SE, Beard JC, Schwartz MW, et al. Increased beta-cell secretory capacity as a mechanism for islet adaptation to nicotinic acid-induced insulin resistance. *Diabetes.* 1989; 38:562–8.

19. Tobert JA. Efficacy and long-term adverse effect pattern of lovastatin. *Am J Cardiol.* 1988; 62:28J–34J.

20. American Heart Association Consensus Panel. Preventing heart attack and death. *Circulation.* 1995; 92:1–5.

Approved by the ASHP Board of Directors, September 26, 1997. Developed by the ASHP Commission on Therapeutics.

The bibliographic citation for this document is as follows: American Society of Health-System Pharmacists. ASHP therapeutic position statement on the safe use of niacin in the management of dyslipidemias. *Am J Health-Syst Pharm.* 1997; 54:2815–9.

ASHP Therapeutic Position Statement on Antithrombotic Therapy in Chronic Atrial Fibrillation

Statement of Position

ASHP supports the routine use of antithrombotic therapy (warfarin or aspirin) for stroke prevention in patients with chronic atrial fibrillation (AF). Antithrombotic therapy given to patients with AF for primary prevention (before the first stroke or episode of systemic embolism) or as a secondary intervention (after stroke or systemic embolism has occurred) unequivocally reduces the risk of stroke. Warfarin is more effective than aspirin but carries a higher risk of bleeding and requires regular medical monitoring.

ASHP encourages the use of warfarin, if it can be administered safely, in all patients with chronic AF who are younger than 65 years and have clinical risk factors for stroke (Table 1) or who are older than 65. However, ASHP recognizes that, for patients who are ages 65 to 75 years and without clinical risk factors, either warfarin or aspirin may be an option, depending on individual patient circumstances. Aspirin may be an appropriate choice for AF patients younger than 65 with no risk factors and for any patient with AF who is not a candidate for warfarin therapy. There is no evidence that the combination of warfarin and aspirin is superior to warfarin alone for AF.

Many patients who are eligible for antithrombotic therapy remain unprotected, possibly because of prescriber concerns about the potential for hemorrhagic complications and the difficulty of managing oral anticoagulation. ASHP believes that the safe and effective use of warfarin is dependent on adequate patient education and monitoring—services that can be efficiently provided by pharmacists. ASHP encourages pharmacists to work actively with other health care providers to optimize anticoagulant therapy through the provision of these services.

Background

Atrial fibrillation is present in 2.3% of people over 40 years of age and in 5.9% of those over 65 years.[2] Most patients with AF are elderly (mean age, 75 years). Men are more likely to have AF than women during their lifetimes, but because more women than men live to age 75, equal numbers of men and women have AF.[2] The presence of valvular heart disease alone, especially rheumatic mitral valve disease, is associated with a significant increase in the risk of stroke and systemic embolism. Although never evaluated in a randomized trial, there is little doubt that long-term anticoagulant therapy is effective in reducing the frequency of systemic embolism in patients with rheumatic mitral valve disease and AF. It is strongly recommended, therefore, that warfarin therapy be used in patients with AF and rheumatic mitral valve disease.[3,4]

Nonrheumatic AF, usually defined as AF without evidence or a clinical history of mitral valve stenosis, afflicts about 2.2 million Americans, and the prevalence is higher in older age groups.[5–8] Nonrheumatic AF occurs most commonly in patients with hypertension or ischemic heart disease (coronary artery disease), hyperthyroidism, cardiomyopathy, and congestive heart failure. Consequently, this ASHP Therapeutic Position Statement focuses on nonrheumatic AF. Hereafter, the term "atrial fibrillation" ("AF") refers to nonrheumatic AF.

The risk of stroke in patients with AF is 5% per year, or five to six times higher than in an age-matched population without AF. Approximately 75,000 strokes occur each year in the United States in patients with AF.[1,9] The risk of stroke varies greatly depending on age and the presence of coexisting cardiovascular disease (appendix). In patients with AF, the major clinical risk factors for stroke are a history of hypertension, prior stroke or transient ischemic attack, recent heart failure, and thyrotoxicosis. Age and diabetes have also been identified in some studies as major risk factors. The annual event rate varies considerably depending on patient age and the presence of risk factors that were identified in an Atrial Fibrillation Investigators analysis.[11] Patients under the age of 65 years with no risk factors have an annual event rate of 0.3–3.1%. One or more risk factors increase the rate to 3.0–8.1% per year.[11] Among persons in the age range 65–75 years, the rates are 2.7–7.1% with no risk factors and 3.9–8.3% with one or more risk factors. Among persons older than 75 years, the annual risk ranges from 1.7% to 7.7% with no risk factors and from 4.7% to 13.9% with one or more risk factors. Analysis of placebo-treated patients in a large randomized clinical trial indicates that the annual rate of thromboembolism increases from 2.5% per year with no risk factors to 7.2% with one risk factor to 17.6% with two or more risk factors.[13] Therefore, stratification of patients on the basis of risk is useful for determining the best type of antithrombotic therapy.[13]

Thrombi that form in high-flow arteries are rich in platelets, and antiplatelet agents such as aspirin are thought to be optimal therapy. Because patients with AF frequently have vascular disease, thrombi may arise in high-flow areas such as the carotid circulation in addition to the cardiac chambers, and antiplatelet therapy may protect some patients in whom thrombi develop in this manner.[9,14] However, patients with AF may also develop thrombi in the atria, especially the atrial appendages, because of stasis or turbu-

Table 1.
Recommendations on Antithrombotic Therapy in Chronic Atrial Fibrillation[a]

Age (yr)	Risk Factors[b]	Recommendation
<65	Yes	Warfarin to achieve INR[c] of 2–3
<65	No	Aspirin or nothing
65–75	Yes	Warfarin to achieve INR of 2–3
65–75	No	Warfarin to achieve INR of 2–3 or aspirin
>75	Yes or no	Warfarin to achieve INR of 2–3

[a]Adapted from reference 1, with permission.
[b]Risk factors for stroke include previous transient ischemic attack or stroke, hypertension, heart failure, diabetes, clinical coronary artery disease, mitral stenosis, prosthetic heart valves, and thyrotoxicosis.
[c]INR = International Normalized Ratio.

lent blood flow. These cardiogenic emboli contain fewer platelets, are less responsive to antiplatelet therapy, and are best prevented by warfarin.

Patients with cardioembolic stroke typically have an abrupt onset of symptoms and die suddenly or are left with major neurologic sequelae. While the benefits of antithrombotic therapy in preventing stroke are well established, only about one quarter of patients with AF are receiving warfarin,[8] perhaps because of physician concerns about the small but important risk of serious hemorrhagic complications. It is therefore prudent that practitioners have a thorough understanding of the risks versus the benefits of this therapy.

The benefit of antithrombotic therapy can be expressed as the absolute risk reduction (difference in risk between the control group [x] and the treated group [y]; $x - y$) or the relative risk reduction (percent reduction in risk in the treated group [y] compared with the controls [x]; $[(x-y)/x] \times 100\%$). Comparing treatments by reporting only the relative risk ratio or the percent change in the event rate can be misleading. This is particularly true for antithrombotic therapy in AF, since the absolute risk of stroke varies widely, from about 1% with no risk factors to more than 15% with multiple risk factors (appendix).[13] A useful estimate of benefit can be calculated from the absolute risk reduction and expressed as the "number needed to treat" (NNT).[15] NNT is defined as the number of persons who need to be treated to prevent one event per year and is equal to 1/(treatment event rate – control event rate).

Evidence for Efficacy of Antithrombotic Therapy

Warfarin. There have been five randomized controlled trials of antithrombotic therapy for mostly primary prevention of stroke and systemic embolism in AF and one trial for secondary intervention (Table 2). Compared with placebo, warfarin reduces the relative risk of stroke by nearly 70% when the International Normalized Ratio (INR) target range is 1.5–4.5. If an on-therapy, or efficacy, analysis is used rather than an intention-to-treat analysis, the relative risk reduction is over 80%.[14] The absolute reduction in stroke risk by warfarin ranged from 2.5% per year to 4.7% per year in primary prevention studies and was 8.4% per year in the secondary intervention study (Table 2). This implies that 22–40 patients would need to be treated with warfarin to prevent one first-time stroke or systemic embolism per year. Prevention of one secondary event per year would require warfarin therapy in only 12 patients.

In a primary and secondary prevention trial, the efficacy of low-intensity, fixed-dose warfarin (INR, 1.2–1.5) plus aspirin (325 mg/day) was compared with that of conventional adjusted-dose warfarin therapy in high-risk AF patients.[22] Patients given adjusted-dose warfarin had a significantly lower rate of stroke and systemic embolism than patients given aspirin in combination with low-intensity warfarin therapy (1.9% per year versus 7.9% per year, or an absolute reduction in risk of 6.0% per year). Thus, 17 high-risk AF patients would need to be treated with adjusted-dose warfarin therapy to prevent one stroke not prevented by aspirin plus low-intensity warfarin therapy.[22] Reduction in disabling stroke by warfarin averaged only 1.5% per year in unselected AF patients.[11]

Intracranial hemorrhage during warfarin therapy in carefully monitored clinical trials occurs at a rate of 0.4–1.5% per year.[11,23] Thus, according to NNT analysis, one intracranial hemorrhage will occur per year for every 67–250 patients treated with warfarin. While the intracranial bleeding rate with warfarin is fairly low in low-risk patients, the absolute risk of intracranial hemorrhage may approach the absolute reduction in the risk of stroke. Knowledge of local trends in bleeding complications will help in balancing the risk with the benefit of anticoagulation. These principles should help clinicians more clearly discern the risk–benefit ratio of anticoagulants in a given patient and dispel their reluctance to prescribe this therapy in patients who would clearly benefit.

The risk–benefit ratios of warfarin treatment for chronic AF established in large clinical trials may not be generalizable to routine clinical practice because patients generally are more carefully selected and more intensively monitored in clinical trials.[11,24] Elderly persons over 75 years of age constitute the group of most concern. Several studies have shown that older patients may require smaller dosages of warfarin than younger patients to maintain a given level of anticoagulation and that they may be at greater risk for major hemorrhage.[25-27] Fihn, et al.[26] found that life-threatening and fatal complications were more common in patients 80 years of age or older (relative risk, 4.5; absolute event rate, 3.3% per year).

The optimal intensity of anticoagulation to adequately prevent stroke and minimize bleeding risk probably depends on the inherent stroke risk. In the Boston Area Anticoagulation Trial for Atrial Fibrillation (BAATAF) and Stroke Prevention in Nonrheumatic Atrial Fibrillation (SPINAF) primary prevention trials, low-intensity anticoagulation (estimated INR target range, 1.5–2.5) was highly effective for relatively low-risk patients.[17,19] In contrast, time-dependent analysis of warfarin efficacy in AF patients with prior stroke or transient ischemic attack suggested that more intensive anticoagulation (INR, 2.5–4.2) may be optimal.[22,28]

In a recent case–control study, Hylek, et al.[29] found that an INR of <2.0 was associated with an increased risk of ischemic stroke in patients with AF. This finding is useful for establishing the lower end of an INR range that should provide protection from stroke. The highest risk was for patients with an INR of <1.5. If patients are less than 75 years of age, an INR range of 2.0–3.0 is effective and safe; for some patients older than 75 years, the lower end of this range may be a reasonable target.

Recently, Palareti, et al.[27] found in a large cohort study that age was strongly correlated with the risk of major hemorrhage. The rate of major hemorrhage in patients over 70 years of age was four times that in patients ages 50–69 years. A higher target INR (2.5–4.0) may be considered for secondary intervention based largely on one large randomized trial.[28]

In summary, the current recommended range of intensity of anticoagulation in most patients with AF is an INR of 2.0–3.0.[1,11] Patients over the age of 75 who are at a higher risk of bleeding may require more intensive monitoring, and the need to lower the target INR to the lower half of the range of 2.0–3.0 should be considered in these patients.[22,26]

Aspirin. Aspirin is much less effective than warfarin in preventing stroke (primarily noncardioembolic stroke), and only the Stroke Prevention in Atrial Fibrillation (SPAF) study demonstrated a significant benefit from aspirin (Table 2).[10,30] However, in high-risk AF patients, the combination of aspirin and low-intensity fixed-dose warfarin (INR, 1.2–1.5)

Table 2.
Efficacy of Antithrombotic Therapy for Reducing Risk of Ischemic Stroke in Patients with Atrial Fibrillation[a]

Study	Type[b]	n	Target INR or Aspirin Dosage	Relative Risk Reduction, % (p)[c]	Absolute Risk Reduction (%/yr)	NNT
Warfarin versus Placebo						
AFASAK[16]	1°	671	2.8–4.2	58 (<0.05)	2.6	39
SPAF I[10]	1°	421	2.0–4.5[d]	65 (0.01)	4.7	22
BAATAF[17]	1°	420	1.5–3.0[d]	86 (0.002)	2.6	39
CAFA[18]	1°	378	2.0–3.0	33 (>0.05)	2.5	40
SPINAF[19]	1°	571	1.5–3.0[d]	79 (0.001)	3.4	30
EAFT[20]	2°	439	2.5–4.0	66 (0.001)	8.4	12
Aggregate[e]				68 (<0.001)		
Aspirin versus Placebo						
AFASAK[16]	1°	672	75 mg/day	18 (>0.05)	0.7	143
SPAF I[10]	1°	1120	325 mg/day	44 (0.01)	2.5	40
EAFT[20]	2°	782	300 mg/day	15 (>0.05)	1.3	77
Aggregate				21 (<0.05)		
Warfarin versus Aspirin						
SPAF II[21]	1°	1100	325 mg/day	31 (>0.05)	0.8	125
AFASAK[16]	1°	671	2.8–4.2, 75 mg/day	50 (0.05)	1.9	53
SPAF III[22]	1°	1044	2–3, 325 mg/day[f]	76 (0.001)	6.0	17
EAFT[20]	2°	455	2.5–4.0, 300 mg/day	62 (0.001)	6.4	16
Aggregate				55 (<0.01)		

[a]INR = International Normalized Ratio, NNT = number needed to treat to prevent one ischemic stroke per year, AFASAK = Atrial Fibrillation Aspirin Study of Anticoagulation from Kopenhaven, SPAF = Stroke Prevention in Atrial Fibrillation, BAATAF = Boston Area Anticoagulation Trial for Atrial Fibrillation, CAFA = Canadian Atrial Fibrillation Anticoagulation, SPINAF = Stroke Prevention in Nonrheumatic Atrial Fibrillation, EAFT = European Atrial Fibrillation Trial.
[b]1° = primary prevention (in several studies, 5–10% of patients had remote thromboembolism), 2° = secondary intervention (previous transient ischemic attack or stroke).
[c]Reduction compared with control (active treatment or placebo) by intention-to-treat analysis.
[d]INR estimated for BAATAF, SPAF I, and SPINAF, which used prothrombin time ratios.
[e]Average of all studies cited.
[f]Aspirin 325 mg/day plus warfarin given to achieve an INR in the range of 1.2–1.5.

did not confer sufficient efficacy in stroke prevention, while conventional adjusted-dose warfarin therapy (INR, 2.0–3.0) demonstrated a significant reduction (absolute risk reduction of 6.0% per year) compared with low-intensity warfarin plus aspirin.[22]

The key in selecting antithrombotic prophylaxis is stroke risk stratification. While there is consensus in identifying high-risk patients,[11,22] risk stratification for low-risk patients remains controversial. Subgroups of low-risk AF patients have been proposed whose inherent stroke rate would be low (<2% per year) (appendix), but none of the stratification schemes has been satisfactorily validated in a randomized clinical trial. Patients with AF who are younger than 65 years and have no identifiable risk factors receive little benefit from warfarin (appendix), and if any therapy is provided, aspirin at a dosage of 325 mg/day is considered adequate (Table 1).[11] While aspirin has not been proved to be of value, specifically for other low-risk AF patients, it is reasonable because of its low toxicity and its potential benefit for associated, sometimes occult, coronary artery disease.

Cost-Effectiveness of Therapy

Antithrombotic prophylaxis for AF is considered to be cost-effective if the rate of thromboembolism is high relative to the rate of major bleeding events.[31] Using direct costs, Gage, et al.[32] found that for patients with AF and one additional risk factor, warfarin therapy cost $8000 per quality-adjusted life-year (QALY) saved. Patients with low risk of stroke (appendix) or lone AF were more costly to treat; the estimated cost of warfarin therapy was about $370,000 per QALY saved. For patients who were not prescribed warfarin, aspirin was preferred to no therapy on the basis of both quality-adjusted

survival and cost in all cases, regardless of the number of risk factors present. Other investigators have also concluded that warfarin is cost-effective in high-risk patients with AF.[33,34] The Agency for Health Care Policy and Research has estimated that appropriate anticoagulant therapy in AF would save approximately $600 million annually in the prevention and treatment of stroke.[a]

Role of the Pharmacist

To optimize the safety and effectiveness of long-term oral anticoagulant therapy, the pharmacist should take an active role in educating and monitoring the patient. Patients should be adequately counseled on the full range of issues pertaining to anticoagulation, such as the indication for therapy, the laboratory test used to monitor anticoagulation, the need for close medical supervision, signs and symptoms of bleeding or thromboembolic complications, dietary interactions, drug interactions, alcohol consumption, and possible alterations in the response to warfarin in the presence of various underlying medical conditions. The pharmacist should also take an active role in closely monitoring and reporting newly observed adverse drug reactions and interactions. Long-term oral anticoagulant therapy should be regularly monitored by prothrombin time (PT) test, with conversion of the PT into the INR.[35,36] ASHP has previously endorsed the routine use of the INR for monitoring warfarin therapy.[36]

Safe and effective monitoring has been achieved through the establishment of specialty practice anticoagulation clinics, and there are numerous reports and trials that document the role of pharmacists in these clinics.[37–41] Clinics with personnel focused on anticoagulation therapy are capable of reducing hemorrhagic complication rates and thromboembolism rates compared with routine medical care (RMC).

Ansell and Hughes[38] recently summarized the literature relating to the outcome in patients undergoing anticoagulation therapy who were seen during RMC and in anticoagulation clinics (ACC) staffed by pharmacists and other health professionals. Their review showed that the rate of thromboembolism is reduced from 16.2% per patient-year in RMC to 2.4% per patient-year in ACC and that major hemorrhage is reduced from 10.9% to 2.8% per patient-year. Cost savings of $800 to $1600 per patient-year were also noted with ACC. Other studies conducted in pharmacist-run clinics support these findings.[39-41]

Pharmacists may also contribute to positive patient outcomes by helping to identify candidates for antithrombotic prophylaxis who are not receiving any form of therapy. Inpatients can be identified case by case or through screening of electrocardiograms. Inpatients and outpatients could be identified through diagnosis-related-group or International Classification of Diseases codes. Once patients are identified, pharmacists should encourage the appropriate use of warfarin and aspirin through one-on-one interactions and educational programs based on guidelines of the American College of Chest Physicians[1] and this ASHP Therapeutic Position Statement.

Summary

Stroke is a catastrophic, but largely preventable, consequence of AF. ASHP supports recommendations established by the American College of Chest Physicians (Table 1) for the use of antithrombotic therapy in appropriate patients to reduce the morbidity and mortality associated with stroke. The selection of warfarin versus aspirin should be based on the presence of clinical risk factors for stroke and the patient's ability to safely undergo anticoagulation therapy. Adequate patient education and monitoring are keys to the successful use of antithrombotic therapy, and ASHP believes that pharmacists can play an important role in providing these services.

References

1. Laupacis A, Albers G, Dalen J, et al. Antithrombotic therapy in atrial fibrillation. *Chest.* 1995; 108(suppl): 352S–9S.
2. Feinberg WM, Blackshear JL, Laupacis A, et al. Prevalence, age distribution, and gender of patients with atrial fibrillation. *Arch Intern Med.* 1995; 155:469–73.
3. Levine HJ, Pauker SG, Eckman MH. Antithrombotic therapy in valvular heart disease. *Chest.* 1995; 108(suppl):360S–70S.
4. Stein PD, Alpert JS, Copeland J, et al. Antithrombotic therapy in patients with mechanical and biological prosthetic heart valves. *Chest.* 1995; 108(suppl): 371S–9S.
5. Wolf PA, Abbot RD, Kannel WB. Atrial fibrillation as an independent risk factor for stroke: the Framingham Study. *Stroke.* 1991; 22:983–8.
6. Lake RR, Cullen KJ, deKlerk NH, et al. Atrial fibrillation in an elderly population. *Aust N Z J Med.* 1989; 19:321–6.
7. Philips SJ, Whisnant J, O'Fallon WM, et al. Prevalence of cardiovascular disease and diabetes in residents of Rochester, Minnesota. *Mayo Clin Proc.* 1990; 65:344–59.
8. Furberg CD, Psaty BM, Manolio TA, et al. Prevalence of atrial fibrillation in elderly subjects: the Cardiovascular Health Study. *Am J Cardiol.* 1994; 74:238–41.
9. Nelson KM, Talbert RL. Preventing stroke in patients with nonrheumatic atrial fibrillation. *Am J Hosp Pharm.* 1994; 51:1175–83.
10. Stroke Prevention in Atrial Fibrillation Investigators. The Stroke Prevention in Atrial Fibrillation study: final results. *Circulation.* 1991; 84:527–39.
11. Atrial Fibrillation Investigators. Risk factors for stroke and efficacy of antithrombotic therapy in atrial fibrillation: analysis of pooled data from five randomized controlled trials. *Arch Intern Med.* 1994; 154:1449–57.
12. Stroke Prevention in Atrial Fibrillation Investigators. Risk factors for thromboembolism during aspirin therapy in patients with atrial fibrillation: the Stroke Prevention in Atrial Fibrillation study. *J Stroke Cerebrovasc Dis.* 1995; 5:147–57.
13. Stroke Prevention in Atrial Fibrillation Investigators. Predictors of thromboembolism in atrial fibrillation: II. Echocardiographic features of patients at risk. *Ann Intern Med.* 1992; 116:6–12.
14. Hart RG, Talbert RL, Kadri K, et al. Warfarin for stroke prevention: a clinical review. *Neurologist.* 1996; 2:319–41.
15. Laupacis A, Sackett DL, Robert RS. An assessment of clinically useful measurements of the consequences of treatment. *N Engl J Med.* 1988; 318:1728–33.
16. Petersen P, Boysen G, Godtfredsen J, et al. Placebo-controlled, randomised trial of warfarin and aspirin for prevention of thromboembolic complications in chronic atrial fibrillation (AFASAK). *Lancet.* 1989; 1:175–8.
17. Boston Area Anticoagulation Trial for Atrial Fibrillation Investigators. The effect of low-dose warfarin on the risk of stroke in nonrheumatic atrial fibrillation. *N Engl J Med.* 1990; 323:1505–11.
18. Connolly SJ, Laupacis A, Gent M, et al. for the CAFA Study Co-investigators. Canadian Atrial Fibrillation Anticoagulation (CAFA) study. *J Am Coll Cardiol.* 1991; 18:349–55.
19. Veterans Affairs Stroke Prevention in Nonrheumatic Atrial Fibrillation Investigators. Warfarin in the prevention of stroke associated with nonrheumatic atrial fibrillation. *N Engl J Med.* 1992; 327:1406–12.
20. European Atrial Fibrillation Trial Study Group. Secondary prevention in nonrheumatic atrial fibrillation after transient ischemic attack or minor stroke. *Lancet.* 1993; 342:1255–62.
21. Stroke Prevention in Atrial Fibrillation Investigators. Warfarin versus aspirin for prevention of thromboembolism in atrial fibrillation: stroke prevention in atrial fibrillation. II Study. *Lancet.* 1994; 343:687–91.
22. Stroke Prevention in Atrial Fibrillation Investigators. Adjusted-dose warfarin versus low-intensity, fixed-dose warfarin plus aspirin for high-risk patients with atrial fibrillation: Stroke Prevention in Atrial Fibrillation III randomised clinical trial. *Lancet.* 1996; 348:633–8.
23. Hart RG, Boop BS, Anderson DC. Oral anticoagulants and intracranial hemorrhage. Facts and hypotheses. *Stroke.* 1995; 26:1471–7.
24. Bussey HI, Force RW, Bianco TM, et al. Reliance on prothrombin time ratios causes significant errors in anticoagulation therapy. *Arch Intern Med.* 1992; 152: 278–82.
25. Gottlieb LK, Salem-Schatz S. Anticoagulation in atrial fibrillation. Does efficacy in clinical trials translate

into effectiveness in practice? *Arch Intern Med.* 1994; 154:1945–53.

26. Fihn SD, Callahan CM, Martin DC, et al. The risk for and severity of bleeding complications in elderly patients treated with warfarin. *Ann Intern Med.* 1996; 124:970–9.

27. Palareti G, Leali N, Coccheri S, et al. Bleeding complications of oral anticoagulant treatment: an inception-cohort, prospective collaborative study. *Lancet.* 1996; 348:423–8.

28. European Atrial Fibrillation Trial Study Group. Optimal oral anticoagulant therapy in patients with nonrheumatic atrial fibrillation and recent cerebral ischemia. *N Engl J Med.* 1995; 333:5–10.

29. Hylek EM, Skates SJ, Sheehan MA, et al. An analysis of the lowest effective intensity of prophylactic anticoagulation for patients with nonrheumatic atrial fibrillation. *N Engl J Med.* 1996; 335:540–6.

30. Miller VT, Rothrock JF, Pearce LA, et al. Ischemic stroke in patients with atrial fibrillation: effect of aspirin according to stroke mechanism. *Neurology.* 1993; 43:32–6.

31. Eckman MH, Levine HJ, Pauker SG. Making decisions about antithrombotic therapy in heart disease. Decision analytic and cost-effectiveness issues. *Chest.* 1995; 108(suppl):457S–70S.

32. Gage BF, Cardinalli AB, Albers GW, et al. Cost-effectiveness of warfarin and aspirin for prophylaxis of stroke in patients with nonvalvular atrial fibrillation. *JAMA.* 1995; 274:1839–45.

33. Kan BD. Cost effectiveness of stroke prophylaxis for nonvalvular atrial fibrillation. *JAMA.* 1996; 275:909.

34. Gustafsson C, Asplund K, Britton M, et al. Cost effectiveness of primary stroke prevention in atrial fibrillation: Swedish national perspective. *BMJ.* 1992; 305:1457–60.

35. Hirsh J, Dalen JE, Deykin D, et al. Oral anticoagulants: mechanism of action, clinical effectiveness, and optimal therapeutic range. *Chest.* 1995; 108(suppl):231S–46S.

36. American Society of Health-System Pharmacists. ASHP therapeutic position statement on the use of the International Normalized Ratio system to monitor oral anticoagulant therapy. *Am J Health-Syst Pharm.* 1995; 52:529–31.

37. Conte RR, Kehoe WA, Nielson N, et al. Nine-year experience with a pharmacist-managed anticoagulation clinic. *Am J Hosp Pharm.* 1986; 43:2460–4.

38. Ansell JE, Hughes R. Evolving models of warfarin management: anticoagulation clinics, patient self-monitoring, and patient self-management. *Am Heart J.* 1996; 132:1095–100.

39. Radley AS, Hall J, Farrow M, et al. Evaluation of anticoagulant control in a pharmacist operated anticoagulant clinic. *J Clin Pathol.* 1995; 48:545–7.

40. Wilt VM, Gums JG, Ahmed OI, et al. Outcome analysis of a pharmacist-managed anticoagulation service. *Pharmacotherapy.* 1995; 15:732–9.

41. Chiquette E, Amato MG, Bussey HI. Comparison of an anticoagulation clinic with routine medical care. *Circulation.* 1995; 92(suppl 8):I–686.

Appendix—Risk of Stroke in Atrial Fibrillation

Stroke Prevention in Atrial Fibrillation Study,[10] Placebo Group. High-risk variables were history of hypertension, prior stroke or transient ischemic attack (TIA), diabetes, and recent heart failure. With high-risk variables absent, the thromboembolic risk rate was 1.4% per year (95% confidence interval [CI], 0.05–3.7% per year). With high-risk variables present, the rate was >7% per year. The fraction of AF patients at low risk was 38%.

Pooled Data from Atrial Fibrillation Investigators.[11] High-risk variables were history of hypertension, prior stroke or TIA, diabetes, and age >65 years. With high-risk variables absent, the thromboembolic risk rate was 1.0% per year (95% CI, 0.3–3.1%). With high-risk variables present, the rate was >5% per year. The fraction of AF patients at low risk was 15%.

Stroke Prevention in Atrial Fibrillation Study, Aspirin Group.[12] High-risk variables were history of hypertension, prior stroke or TIA, women older than 75 years, and impaired left ventricular function (including recent congestive heart failure or fractional shortening of ≤25% on M-mode echocardiography). With high-risk variables absent, the thromboembolic risk rate was 1% per year (95% CI, 0.5–2.3%). With high-risk variables present, the rate was >6% per year. The fraction of AF patients at low risk was 30%.

[a]Life-saving treatments to prevent stroke underused. Agency for Health Care Policy and Research news release. Washington, DC; 1995 Sep 7.

Approved by the ASHP Board of Directors, September 26, 1997. Developed by the ASHP Commission on Therapeutics.

The bibliographic citation for this document is as follows: American Society of Health-System Pharmacists. ASHP therapeutic position statement on antithrombotic therapy in chronic atrial fibrillation. *Am J Health-Syst Pharm.* 1998; 55:376–81.

ASHP Therapeutic Position Statement on the Preferential Use of Metronidazole for the Treatment of *Clostridium difficile*-Associated Disease

Statement of Position

ASHP supports the use of oral metronidazole as the preferred antimicrobial agent for treating *Clostridium difficile*-associated disease (CDAD). Oral metronidazole and oral vancomycin appear to be equally efficacious for the treatment of CDAD in most situations. However, routine use of oral vancomycin may contribute to the emergence of vancomycin-resistant *Enterococcus* species, and oral vancomycin is more costly than oral metronidazole. Oral vancomycin should be reserved for the most severe, potentially life-threatening forms of the disorder, for cases that fail to respond to oral metronidazole, and for patients who are unable to tolerate oral metronidazole or to whom metronidazole should not be given. Mild cases of CDAD may respond to discontinuation of the inciting agent, making antimicrobial treatment unnecessary and reducing the possibility of CDAD relapse. Asymptomatic carriers of *C. difficile* should not be treated for CDAD.

Background

CDAD is an infectious disorder that can develop when toxin-producing *C. difficile* is acquired as a component of the colonic microflora. If an individual harboring the organism is subsequently exposed to certain antimicrobial agents, *C. difficile* is able to evade eradication by spore formation, while many of the bacteria that help maintain normal microbial ecology in the colon are destroyed. This selective advantage for replication can result in the uncontrolled overgrowth of *C. difficile* and production of bacterial exotoxins that cause inflammation and cellular damage.[1,2] When symptomatic disease ensues, its severity ranges from self-limiting diarrhea to life-threatening enterocolitis with toxic megacolon.[2,3]

CDAD is predominantly, but not exclusively, a nosocomial disease.[1] Epidemic outbreaks of CDAD may occur within institutions, with patterns of antimicrobial use contributing to the initiation of an outbreak as well as compromising the efficacy of infection control measures intended to limit it.[4] The frequency of community-acquired CDAD is less than one case per 10,000 antimicrobial prescriptions,[5] compared with as many as one case per 100 hospitalized adult patients treated with an antimicrobial agent.[2] However, CDAD will likely become more common in the community setting as outpatient antimicrobial treatment of serious infections increases.

Minimum criteria for diagnosis of CDAD consist of mild to moderate diarrhea accompanied either by a positive *C. difficile* cytotoxin (or toxin b) test result or by endoscopically observed pseudomembranes.[1] Concurrent or recent antimicrobial use is usually present but is not a criterion for definitive diagnosis.[1] However, a recent study indicated that hospitalized patients without antimicrobial exposure during the previous month and either significant diarrhea or abdominal pain are unlikely to have a positive *C. difficile* cytotoxin test result.[6]

Virtually all antimicrobial agents and certain antineoplastic agents with antimicrobial activity have been implicated in precipitating CDAD,[3] but data suggest that second- and third-generation cephalosporins play an increasingly important role.[7-9] Amoxicillin and amoxicillin–clavulanate are among the most frequently implicated antimicrobial agents in community-acquired CDAD.[10] Although the time of onset of CDAD ranges from within one to two days after the initiation of therapy to as long as 10 weeks after drug discontinuation, most cases occur after several days of treatment or within the first few weeks after discontinuation of therapy.[2,3]

Asymptomatic colonization by *C. difficile* can occur, especially in healthy neonates and infants. Long-term carriage of the organism has been documented.[1,2] A well-designed study showed that treatment of asymptomatic carriers of *C. difficile* with either metronidazole or vancomycin is of no clinical value[11]; more recent data substantiate this.[12]

The initial steps in the management of all cases of CDAD are discontinuation of the precipitating agent, if feasible, and restoration of fluids and electrolytes, if needed.[2,3] Antimicrobial treatment should be reserved for cases that fail to respond promptly to this initial therapy and for cases in which discontinuation of the precipitating agent is not a therapeutic option.[2,3] In mild cases of CDAD (diarrhea accompanied by minimal or no constitutional symptoms), particularly those in individuals who are not elderly or debilitated, the patient should be monitored for symptomatic improvement for 48 hours before oral antimicrobial treatment is instituted. If symptomatic deterioration occurs, appropriate antimicrobial therapy should be started promptly.

Relative Efficacy of Oral Metronidazole and Oral Vancomycin in the Treatment of CDAD

Oral vancomycin was first reported to be effective in the treatment of CDAD in 1978.[13] In 1983, a small but well-designed clinical trial showed oral metronidazole to be equivalent to oral vancomycin for the treatment of CDAD.[14] By then oral vancomycin was already established as the drug of choice for CDAD.

Prospective, randomized comparisons have shown no significant difference in initial response rates or relapse rates between oral metronidazole and oral vancomycin in the treatment of CDAD.[1,2,14-17] Therefore, oral metronidazole is now the preferred therapy for most patients with CDAD.[1,3,18,19] Oral vancomycin is considered appropriate only in cases of severe, potentially life-threatening CDAD, when oral metronidazole fails, or when oral metronidazole is not tolerated or cannot be used.[3,18]

Severe CDAD is not clearly defined in the literature. It has been generally characterized in terms of pseudomembrane formation, fever exceeding 40 °C (104 °F), marked abdominal tenderness, and pronounced leukocytosis.[2,3,14] The detection of fecal leukocytes by microscopy also suggests more severe disease.[9] Even in these clinical circumstances, there is little objective evidence that oral vancomycin is superior to oral metronidazole.[14–16] In rare instances, ileus and toxic megacolon develop. These constitute potentially life-threatening conditions in which oral therapy is not feasible, but optimal drug therapy remains undefined.[2,7]

Role of Vancomycin in the Emergence of Vancomycin-Resistant Enterococci

Many studies have identified prior exposure to vancomycin as a risk factor for colonization and infection by vancomycin-resistant enterococci (VRE).[20] Although intravenous rather than oral vancomycin appears to be the most significant risk factor, oral vancomycin use has also been implicated.[20–23] An apparent association between CDAD and the acquisition of VRE has also been described.[20,24,25] In two European studies it was found that glycopeptide-resistant enterococci could be isolated readily from stool samples after oral administration of vancomycin to healthy adults.[26,27]

Concern over the probable role of indiscriminate use of vancomycin in the emergence of VRE culminated in the publication, by the Hospital Infection Control Practices Advisory Committee of the Centers for Disease Control and Prevention, of consensus guidelines for prudent vancomycin use.[18] The guidelines deem oral vancomycin "appropriate or acceptable . . . when antibiotic-associated colitis (AAC) fails to respond to metronidazole therapy or if AAC is severe and potentially life threatening" and state that its use for the "primary treatment of AAC" should be discouraged.

Vancomycin and Metronidazole Dosage Regimens

Since *C. difficile* usually does not escape the gastrointestinal tract, only antimicrobial levels within the intestinal lumen are of consequence. When vancomycin is administered orally, high fecal concentrations are obtained because of poor absorption. A regimen of vancomycin 125 mg (as the hydrochloride salt) four times daily provides the same clinical outcome as 500 mg four times daily because it yields a mean fecal vancomycin concentration well above the highest reported minimum inhibitory concentration for *C. difficile*.[28]

In contrast to oral vancomycin, oral metronidazole attains very low fecal concentrations because of nearly complete absorption. Although this has resulted in lingering concern about the efficacy of oral metronidazole in the treatment of serious cases of CDAD,[1] such concern seems unwarranted. Some unmetabolized metronidazole is eliminated in the feces via biliary excretion, and the drug appears to cross the intestinal wall into the lumen of the inflamed colon. Furthermore, successful treatment of CDAD with metronidazole is well documented.[1,14–16] Total daily dosages of oral metronidazole in the treatment of CDAD have ranged from 1000 to 2250 mg administered in three or four divided doses.[2] Of three major studies that found oral metronidazole and oral vancomycin to be therapeutically equivalent for CDAD, two used a daily metronidazole dosage of 1000 mg (250 mg four times daily),[7,14] and one used a daily dosage of 1500 mg (500 mg three times daily).[16] No direct comparisons of metronidazole dosages have been published.[2]

Ten days has been the usual duration of therapy when either oral agent is used for CDAD.[2] Symptomatic improvement may be apparent within 48 hours, but treatment is most likely to be successful if carried out for the full 10 days.[1] A slow or delayed response to therapy with either metronidazole or vancomycin may occur in patients with a pre-existing intestinal disorder and associated diarrhea.[17] However, therapeutic failure of metronidazole should not be assumed until a minimum of six days of treatment have been completed without symptomatic improvement.[7,14,16] Therapeutic failure rates of 2–5% can be anticipated with either oral metronidazole or oral vancomycin.[7,17]

Oral therapy is always preferable for the treatment of CDAD, but the oral route is not always feasible because of gastrointestinal obstruction or other reasons (e.g., toxic megacolon).[3] Treatment approaches in patients unable to tolerate oral medications have included i.v. vancomycin, i.v. metronidazole, and rectal vancomycin alone and in various combinations, but no comparative studies have been performed.[29] Because treatment failures have been reported with either i.v. metronidazole or i.v. vancomycin given alone,[30,31] consideration should be given to the concurrent use of i.v. metronidazole and either i.v. or rectal vancomycin.[3] Several regimens for the rectal administration of vancomycin have been described.[3,29] Because the available efficacy data are exclusively anecdotal, no definitive recommendations can be made regarding the treatment of CDAD in the patient who cannot take oral medications.

Treatment of Relapse

Approximately 15–35% of patients treated for CDAD with either oral metronidazole or oral vancomycin relapse within two months after completing initial therapy.[3] Relapse is defined as a return of symptoms and positive diagnostic test results after discontinuation of successful antimicrobial therapy for CDAD.[3] Most patients relapse only once, although multiple relapses occur in a small subset of patients.[2,17] Relapse frequency is unrelated to the antimicrobial selected for initial treatment of CDAD,[3,17] but additional exposure to antimicrobials given to treat other types of infection appears to be a significant risk factor for recurrence of CDAD, and the frequency of recurrence increases with the number of antimicrobials administered.[17]

A multitude of protocols for treating CDAD relapse are described in the literature, but no comparative studies have been conducted.[2,3,17] More than 90% of patients with CDAD who relapse respond to a single repeated course of oral medication, either metronidazole or vancomycin.[7] Since relapse is usually unrelated to antimicrobial resistance, the same agent used to treat CDAD initially can be used to treat the relapse.[2,3] Thus, patients with a first relapse of CDAD who were treated with oral metronidazole initially should receive a second 10-day course of metronidazole.[1] No definitive therapeutic recommendation can be made for a patient with multiple relapses. Therapeutic options are discussed in detail elsewhere.[2,3,17]

Special Populations

Asymptomatic carriage of toxin-producing *C. difficile* is common in newborn infants and in children less than two years of age, but CDAD is rare. It is also rare in older children. However, certain subpopulations, such as children with gastrointestinal motility disorders like Hirschsprung's disease (congenital megacolon) and severely neutropenic children with leukemia, are at increased risk.[32] Comparative studies of oral metronidazole and oral vancomycin for the treatment of CDAD have not been conducted in the pediatric population. Since the pharmacokinetic profile of oral metronidazole in children is similar to that in adults, there is no reason to consider oral metronidazole inferior to oral vancomycin for CDAD in pediatric patients. However, commercial oral vancomycin solution may prove more palatable than an extemporaneously prepared metronidazole suspension for children who are unable to swallow metronidazole tablets or for whom the available tablet formulation is not appropriate.[33]

Recommended dosages for the treatment of CDAD in children are oral metronidazole 30 mg/kg/day given in divided doses every six hours or oral vancomycin 40 mg/kg/day given in divided doses every six to eight hours.[19] The maximum dosage in pediatric patients should not exceed the adult dosage.

The risk of metronidazole therapy during the first trimester of pregnancy is uncertain, and metronidazole use during that trimester is controversial.[34] Metronidazole is excreted into breast milk. Oral vancomycin may therefore be the preferred agent for the treatment of CDAD during the first trimester and in nursing mothers.[3]

Therapeutic Alternatives

The use of an anion-exchange resin such as cholestyramine, with or without metronidazole or vancomycin therapy, offers no demonstrable benefit and should be discouraged.[2,3] Concomitant use of cholestyramine and oral vancomycin is particularly undesirable because of binding of vancomycin by cholestyramine. Antiperistaltic agents can cause retention of *C. difficile* toxins in the colon and should be avoided.[2,3] Oral bacitracin, which is expensive and less efficacious than metronidazole or vancomycin,[2] should generally not be used. Biotherapy, such as supplementation of the normal colonic microflora with *Saccharomyces boulardii*, may be a future approach to the prevention and treatment of CDAD.[35]

The Pharmacist's Role

Pharmacists should strive to optimize the treatment of CDAD by encouraging the preferential use of metronidazole when antimicrobial therapy is warranted. Currently, excessive use of oral vancomycin for CDAD is largely an institutional problem because CDAD is primarily a nosocomial disease. However, as CDAD becomes more common in the community setting, ambulatory care pharmacists too will have a responsibility for ensuring optimal treatment of this disease.

The availability of guidelines for vancomycin use alone may not result in major changes in prescribing behavior.[33,36–39] Additional strategies for influencing vancomycin prescribing may include tailored educational efforts and interventions that encourage physicians to prescribe oral metronidazole preferentially for the treatment of CDAD when antimicrobial therapy is indicated. In addition, pharmacists should become involved in implementing comprehensive antimicrobial management programs that can both help to prevent the development of bacterial resistance and reduce overall expenditures.[38]

Pharmacists should collaborate on studies designed to clarify the relationship between oral vancomycin use and the acquisition of vancomycin-resistant bacteria, participate in surveillance for vancomycin-resistant organisms, and contribute to infection-control measures directed against vancomycin-resistant pathogens.[40]

Finally, pharmacists can play a key role in communicating to patients the risks of resistance associated with the indiscriminate use of antimicrobial agents and the potential adverse effects of therapy. Improved patient understanding of these risks should result in better adherence to therapy.

Summary

ASHP supports preferential use of oral metronidazole for treating CDAD when antimicrobial therapy is indicated. Oral vancomycin should be reserved for severe, potentially life-threatening cases or when oral metronidazole cannot be used. Oral metronidazole is as safe and effective as oral vancomycin and is considerably less costly. In addition, preliminary data suggest that routine use of oral vancomycin for CDAD may contribute to the spread of VRE—emerging nosocomial pathogens that can be extraordinarily difficult to treat. Pharmacists should work to foster preferential prescribing of oral metronidazole for the treatment of CDAD. Pharmacists should also actively seek opportunities to educate health care providers and counsel patients about the risks associated with the indiscriminate use of vancomycin and other antimicrobial agents.

References

1. Gerding DDN, Johnson S, Peterson LR, et al. *Clostridium difficile*-associated diarrhea and colitis. *Infect Control Hosp Epidemiol.* 1995; 16:459–77.
2. Reinke CM, Messick CR. Update on *Clostridium difficile*-induced colitis, parts 1 and 2. *Am J Hosp Pharm.* 1994; 51:1771–81, 1892–901.
3. Fekety R. Guidelines for the diagnosis and management of *Clostridium difficile*-associated diarrhea and colitis. *Am J Gastroenterol.* 1997; 92:739–50.
4. Lai KK, Melvin ZS, Menard MJ, et al. *Clostridium difficile*-associated diarrhea: epidemiology, risk factors, and infection control. *Infect Control Hosp Epidemiol.* 1997; 18:628–32.
5. Hirschhorn LR, Trnka Y, Onderdonk A, et al. Epidemiology of community-acquired *Clostridium difficile*-associated diarrhea. *J Infect Dis.* 1994; 169:127–33.
6. Katz DA, Lynch ME, Littenberg B. Clinical prediction rates to optimize cytotoxin testing for *Clostridium difficile* in hospitalized patients with diarrhea. *Am J Med.* 1996; 100:487–95.
7. Olson MM, Shanholtzer CJ, Lee JT Jr, et al. Ten years of prospective *Clostridium difficile*-associated disease surveillance and treatment at the Minneapolis VA medical center, 1982–1991. *Infect Control Hosp Epidemiol.* 1994; 15:371–81.
8. Nelson DE, Auerbach SB, Baltch AL, et al. Epidemic *Clostridium difficile*-associated diarrhea: role of second- and third-generation cephalosporins. *Infect Control Hosp Epidemiol.* 1994; 15:88–94.
9. Manabe YC, Vinetz JM, Moore RD, et al. *Clostridium difficile* colitis: an efficient clinical approach to diagnosis. *Ann Intern Med.* 1995; 123:835–40.
10. Riley TV, Cooper M, Bell B, et al. Community-acquired *Clostridium difficile*-associated diarrhea. *Clin Infect Dis.* 1995; 20(suppl 2):S263–5.
11. Johnson S, Homann SR, Bettin KM, et al. Treatment of asymptomatic *Clostridium difficile* carriers (fecal excretors) with vancomycin or metronidazole: a randomized, placebo-controlled trial. *Ann Intern Med.*

1992; 117:297–302.

12. Samore MH, DeGirolami PC, Tlucko A, et al. *Clostridium difficile* colonization and diarrhea at a tertiary care hospital. *Clin Infect Dis.* 1994; 18:181–7.

13. Tedesco F, Markham R, Gurwith M, et al. Oral vancomycin for antibiotic-associated pseudomembranous colitis. *Lancet.* 1978; 2:226–8.

14. Teasley DG, Olson MG, Gebhard RI, et al. Prospective randomized trial of metronidazole versus vancomycin for *Clostridium difficile*-associated diarrhea and colitis. *Lancet.* 1983; 2:1043–6.

15. Anand A, Bahey B, Mir T, et al. Epidemiology, clinical manifestations, and outcome of *Clostridium difficile*-associated diarrhea. *Am J Gastroenterol.* 1994; 89:519– 23.

16. Wenisch C, Parschalk B, Hasenhundl M, et al. Comparison of vancomycin, teicoplanin, metronidazole, and fusidic acid for the treatment of *Clostridium difficile*-associated diarrhea. *Clin Infect Dis.* 1996; 22:813–8.

17. Fekety R, McFarland LV, Surawicz CM, et al. Recurrent *Clostridium difficile* diarrhea: characteristics of and risk factors for patients enrolled in a prospective, randomized, double-blinded trial. *Clin Infect Dis.* 1997; 24:324–33.

18. Centers for Disease Control and Prevention Hospital Infection Control Practices Advisory Committee. Recommendations for preventing the spread of vancomycin resistance. *Infect Control Hosp Epidemiol.* 1995; 16:105–13.

19. *Clostridium difficile.* In: Peter G, ed. American Academy of Pediatrics 1997 red book: report of the Committee on Infectious Diseases. 24th ed. Elk Grove Village, IL: American Academy of Pediatrics; 1997:177–8.

20. Gerding DN. Is there a relationship between vancomycin-resistant enterococcal infection and *Clostridium difficile* infection? *Clin Infect Dis.* 1997; 25(suppl 2):S206–10.

21. Fraise AP. The treatment and control of vancomycin-resistant enterococci. *J Antimicrob Chemother.* 1996; 38:753–6.

22. Carr JR, Fitzpatrick PE, Cumbo TJ, et al. A reduction in oral vancomycin use and a concomitant reduction in vancomycin-resistant *Enterococcus. Infect Control Hosp Epidemiol.* 1996; 17(suppl):25. Abstract.

23. Rao GG, Ojo F, Kolokithas D. Vancomycin-resistant gram-positive cocci: risk factors for fecal carriage. *J Hosp Infect.* 1997; 35:63–9.

24. Rafferty ME, McCormick MI, Bopp LH, et al. Vancomycin-resistant enterococci in stool specimens submitted for *Clostridium difficile* cytotoxin assay. *Infect Control Hosp Epidemiol.* 1997; 18:342–4.

25. Lam S, Singer C, Tucci V, et al. The challenge of vancomycin-resistant enterococci: a clinical and epidemiologic study. *Am J Infect Control.* 1995; 23:170–80.

26. Van der Auwera P, Pensart N, Korten V, et al. Influence of oral glycopeptides on the fecal flora of human volunteers: selection of highly glycopeptide-resistant enterococci. *J Infect Dis.* 1996; 173:1129–36.

27. Edlund C, Barkholt L, Olsson-Liljequist B, et al. Effect of vancomycin on intestinal flora of patients who previously received antimicrobial therapy. *Clin Infect Dis.* 1997; 25:729–32.

28. Fekety R, Silva J, Kaufman C, et al. Treatment of antibiotic-associated *Clostridium difficile* colitis with oral vancomycin: comparison of two dosage regimens. *Am J Med.* 1989; 86:15–9.

29. Bublin JG, Barton TL. Rectal use of vancomycin. *Ann Pharmacother.* 1994; 28:1357–8.

30. Oliva SL, Guglielmo BJ, Jacobs R, et al. Failure of intravenous vancomycin and intravenous metronidazole to prevent or treat antibiotic-associated pseudomembranous colitis. *J Infect Dis.* 1989; 159:1154–5. Letter.

31. Kleinfeld D, Donta ST. Reply. (Failure of intravenous vancomycin and intravenous metronidazole to prevent or treat antibiotic-associated pseudomembranous colitis.) *J Infect Dis.* 1989; 159:1155. Letter.

32. Zwiener BJ, Belknap WM, Quan R. Severe pseudomembranous enterocolitis in a child: case report and literature review. *Pediatr Infect Dis J.* 1989; 8:876–82.

33. Evans ME, Kortas KJ. Vancomycin use in a university medical center: comparison with Hospital Infection Control Practices Advisory Committee guidelines. *Infect Control Hosp Epidemiol.* 1996; 17:356–9.

34. Metronidazole. In: Briggs GG, Freeman RK, Yaffe SJ, eds. Drugs in pregnancy and lactation: a guide to fetal and neonatal risk. 4th ed. Baltimore: Williams & Wilkins; 1994:585–9.

35. Eddy JT, Stamatakis MK, Makela EH. *Saccharomyces boulardii* for the treatment of *Clostridium difficile*-associated colitis. *Ann Pharmacother.* 1997; 31:919–21.

36. Johnson SV, Hoey LL, Vance-Bryan K. Inappropriate vancomycin prescribing based on criteria from the Centers for Disease Control and Prevention. *Pharmacotherapy.* 1995; 15:579–85.

37. Watanakunakorn C. Prescribing pattern of vancomycin in a community teaching hospital with low prevalence of vancomycin-resistant enterococci. *Infect Control Hosp Epidemiol.* 1997; 18:767–9.

38. Carr JR, Fitzpatrick P, Izzo JL, et al. Changing the infection control paradigm from off-line to real time: the experience at Millard Fillmore Health System. *Infect Control Hosp Epidemiol.* 1997; 18:255–9.

39. Beidas S, Khamesian M. Vancomycin use in a university medical center: comparison with Hospital Infection Control Practices Advisory Committee guidelines. *Infect Control Hosp Epidemiol.* 1996; 17:773–4. Letter.

40. Schlaes DM, Gerding DN, John JF Jr, et al. Society for Healthcare Epidemiology of America and Infectious Diseases Society of America Joint Committee on the Prevention of Antimicrobial Resistance: guidelines for the prevention of antimicrobial resistance in hospitals. *Infect Control Hosp Epidemiol.* 1997; 18:275–91.

This therapeutic position statement was reviewed in 2002 by the Commission on Therapeutics and by the Board of Directors and was found to still be appropriate.

Approved by the ASHP Board of Directors April 22, 1998. Developed by the ASHP Commission on Therapeutics.

The bibliographic citation for this document is as follows: American Society of Health-System Pharmacists. ASHP therapeutic position statement on the preferential use of metronidazole for the treatment of *Clostridium difficile*-associated disease. *Am J Health-Syst Pharm.* 1998; 55:1407–11.

ASHP Therapeutic Position Statement on the Safe Use of Oral Nonprescription Analgesics

Statement of Position

Nonprescription oral analgesics are extensively used for the management of headache, fever, and mild to moderate aches and pains. When taken as directed for short-term use, these agents are generally safe and effective. However, there are a number of considerations regarding the optimal choice for a given patient and condition. Recent media coverage has highlighted controversies about the relative efficacy and safety of the various available agents, increasing the potential for public confusion about the appropriate choice of a nonprescription analgesic.

ASHP encourages the appropriate selection and use of nonprescription analgesics. Selection should include an assessment of the patient's condition; concurrent diseases and medications; patient characteristics and preferences; the safety, efficacy, and cost of nonprescription analgesics; and the patient's response to therapy. ASHP encourages health care providers, especially pharmacists, to take an active role in helping to ensure that patients make the best use of these medications. ASHP recognizes the role of patients in taking responsibility for their own care and encourages consumers to follow the instructions on the label and consult with a health care provider, particularly if they have a chronic condition or are taking other medications, so that potentially harmful drug effects or interactions can be avoided.

Background

Approximately 2% of the U.S. population consumes an analgesic, antipyretic, or nonsteroidal anti-inflammatory drug (NSAID) each day.[1] Between 1991 and 1995, sales of nonprescription analgesics increased by $370 million to $2.62 billion, indicating widespread use of these agents.[2] More than 150 nonprescription products containing aspirin, nonacetylated salicylates, ibuprofen, naproxen sodium, ketoprofen, or acetaminophen, either alone or in combination with other medications, are currently available for purchase by the U.S. public.

A number of epidemiologic studies have characterized the association between the consumption of the ingredients contained in nonprescription analgesics and toxicity to the kidney, liver, and gastrointestinal (GI) tract.[3-10] Annual U.S. costs associated with the toxicities of prescription and nonprescription use of acetaminophen, aspirin, and nonaspirin NSAIDs are estimated to be about $51.5 million, $458.6 million, and $1.35 billion, respectively.[7] Excessive consumption of analgesic ingredients on an ongoing basis without medical supervision is clearly not in keeping with the labeled use of nonprescription analgesic products. The availability of analgesics as single-agent products and as combination products not primarily marketed for pain relief underscores the need to guard against inadvertent or intentional excessive use.

Several types of nonprescription analgesics are available, each with different pharmacologic properties and toxicities. The introduction of several agents in the NSAID class to the nonprescription market has contributed to public confusion about the relative safety and efficacy of nonprescription analgesics. Recent media coverage has focused on the nephrotoxic effects of nonsalicylate NSAIDs and the hepatotoxic effect of acetaminophen in combination with ethanol. Warnings for people who consume three or more alcoholic drinks per day are now required by the Food and Drug Administration for all nonprescription drugs containing internal analgesics, including cough and cold remedies.[11] The potential for unintentional overdose is enhanced by the increasing number of combination products with brand names that the public would not recognize as products containing an analgesic. These issues heighten the importance of consumers seeking the assistance of a health care provider, such as their pharmacist, when selecting a nonprescription product.

Pain Responsive to Nonprescription Analgesics

Pain occurs when an organ or musculoskeletal or skin structure is injured by trauma, disease, muscle spasms, or inflammation. Pain-evoking stimuli have in common the ability to cause cells to release proteolytic enzymes and polypeptides that stimulate nerve endings and initiate the pain impulse. Prostaglandins sensitize nerve endings to polypeptide-induced stimulation.[12]

Pain is categorized, according to its origin, as somatic, visceral, or neuropathic. Somatic pain arises from the musculoskeletal system or the skin. Visceral pain originates in the organs of the thorax and the abdomen. Neuropathic pain occurs from injury to the somatic sensory pathways.

Conditions producing visceral pain include ischemia of organ or tissue (e.g., angina), spasm of visceral smooth muscle, and physical distention of an organ or stretching of its associated mesentery.[13] Unlike somatic pain, visceral pain may not be localized by the brain as coming from a specific organ and is often interpreted as coming from various skin or muscle segments (referred pain).

Nonprescription analgesics are very effective for mild to moderate somatic pain from skeletal muscle (myalgia), joints (arthralgia), osteoarthritis, and soft tissue and for dysmenorrhea and headache. They are less effective against visceral pain.[12] Nonprescription analgesics are commonly used for acute pain and are frequently used as adjunctive therapy in the management of chronic malignant or nonmalignant pain. It is unclear whether neuropathic pain is relieved by nonprescription analgesics.

Nonprescription Analgesics

Three classes of nonprescription analgesics are currently available: the para-aminophenols, which currently include only acetaminophen; the salicylates, which include aspirin (acetylsalicylic acid) and the nonacetylated salicylates (sodium salicylate, choline salicylate, and magnesium salicylate); and the propionic acid derivatives (ibuprofen, naproxen sodium, and ketoprofen). Because they have similar pharmacologic properties, the salicylates and propionic acid derivatives are collectively recognized as NSAIDs. These agents are available as brand-name and generic products and are often found in combination with one another as well as with analgesic adjuvants such as caffeine. Nonprescription analgesics are also frequently found in remedies promoted for the relief of cough, cold, and flu symptoms.

Pharmacologic Properties. NSAIDs have pharmacologic properties that include analgesic, antipyretic, and anti-inflammatory effects.[12] With the exception of choline salicylate and magnesium salicylate, NSAIDs also have antiplatelet effects. Analgesic effects of NSAIDs occur at lower dosages than those required for anti-inflammatory effects. At nonprescription dosages, most NSAIDs do not have significant anti-inflammatory effects.[14] Acetaminophen has analgesic and antipyretic activity; it has no clinically significant anti-inflammatory or antiplatelet activity.

The primary mechanism of action of NSAIDs is peripheral inhibition of cyclooxygenase, the enzyme responsible for synthesis of prostaglandins from arachidonic acid. Aspirin irreversibly inhibits cyclooxygenase, whereas other NSAIDs act reversibly on this enzyme.[15] The resulting decrease in prostaglandin synthesis reduces the sensitivity of peripheral pain receptors to pain impulses at the site of inflammation and trauma. Acetaminophen may inhibit prostaglandin synthesis centrally, which could account for the difference in adverse effects seen between acetaminophen and NSAIDs.

Prostaglandins have a variety of functions in the kidney, including vasodilation, diuresis, and natriuresis; thromboxane A_2 is a vasoconstrictor.[15,16] Blood pressure, blood volume, and electrolyte balance are some of the functions regulated by prostaglandins. Prostaglandins are also involved in maintaining the integrity of the stomach lining and the functional activity of platelets. Inhibition of prostaglandin synthesis by NSAIDs can therefore result in decreased renal perfusion, electrolyte imbalance, and gastric irritation. With the exception of choline salicylate and magnesium salicylate, platelet dysfunction with resultant bleeding can also occur.

Comparative Efficacy. Numerous clinical trials have compared the relative efficacy of nonprescription analgesics. A majority of these trials have been conducted for headache, dysmenorrhea, or pain associated with dental procedures, osteoarthritis, episiotomy, or athletic injury. Most of these studies did not demonstrate a significant difference in the analgesic efficacy of these agents at standard analgesic dosages. Clinical studies have shown superior pain control with one agent versus another, but many of those studies were single-dose studies, which often provide different outcomes than multiple-dose studies.

Nonsalicylate NSAIDs are superior to acetaminophen and salicylates for dysmenorrhea and pain from metastatic bone disease. They also may be more effective than salicylates or acetaminophen for pain associated with inflammation (e.g., dental pain, sunburn, gout, rheumatic disorders) when used at anti-inflammatory dosages.[12] However, pain relief is a subjective endpoint that is influenced by a host of factors, including prior experience and a belief that the pain will be relieved. Thus, individuals may perceive that a particular nonprescription analgesic is more effective than another for a specific type of pain.

Safety Considerations in Nonprescription Analgesic Selection

Renal Disease. Because of the previously described functions of prostaglandins in the kidney and the vascular system, patients taking nonprescription analgesics may be at risk for fluid and electrolyte disturbances, acute renal failure, acute interstitual nephritis, chronic renal failure, and analgesic-associated nephropathy (AAN).[4,5,17] While a majority of these effects are more commonly associated with use of nonsalicylate NSAIDs, AAN has been attributed to the long-term use of all nonprescription analgesics.[18] Combination analgesic products (those containing two or more nonnarcotic analgesics with or without caffeine, codeine, or another narcotic analgesic), particularly products containing phenacetin before its removal from the U.S. market in 1983, have been most commonly implicated in AAN.[18] However, the actual risk of non-phenacetin combinations continues to be debated.[19] Certain patient risk factors increase the potential for adverse renal effects, such as preexisting renal insufficiency, congestive heart failure, hypertension, liver disease, diabetes, atherosclerotic cardiovascular disease, and diuretic theapy.[17] Dehydration also increases the risk of drug-induced renal effects.[17]

Cardiovascular Disease. In addition to the increased risk of adverse renal effects, there are other reasons for patients with cardiovascular disease to be cautious of using NSAIDs. Regular use of NSAIDs may impair blood pressure control.[1] Further, patients with significant cardiovascular disease may have impaired ability to tolerate serious GI complications resulting from regular use of NSAIDs.[20] Although low-dose aspirin (50–325 mg per day) is now recommended for treatment of some cardiovascular diseases (e.g., ischemic stroke, acute myocardial infarction) and for use in conjunction with specific revascularization procedures, these indications require the advice and supervision of a health care provider to ensure safe, appropriate use.[21]

Diabetes Mellitus. It has been suggested that patients with diabetes mellitus may constitute a population at high risk for adverse effects after the ingestion of NSAIDs. Diabetic patients have lower pain tolerance than control subjects and thus may be more likely to require nonprescription analgesics.[22] Diabetes can alter the normal mechanisms for regulating vascular pressure, and these alterations may be further exacerbated by NSAIDs. Patients with diabetes have a high rate of end-stage renal disease[23] and are at increased risk of NSAID-induced nephropathy.[17] Although some uses of NSAIDs may be appropriate in the diabetic patient (e.g., the medically supervised use of low-dose aspirin for prevention of cardiovascular events[24]), the aforementioned concerns are arguments against indiscriminate use of nonprescription dosages of NSAIDs in this population.

Gastrointestinal Disease. Nonprescription NSAIDs can cause GI complications—dyspepsia, gastritis, ulcer formation, GI bleeding, and perforation—by the mechanisms of direct mucosal damage and systemic prostaglandin inhibition.[12,25-29] These complications are generally dose related. Gastritis is a local effect that can occur at low dosages and without the risk of ulcer formation.[12] Ulceration generally results from systemic prostaglandin inhibition and is most often initially asymptomatic. However, symptoms may not correlate with the presence or absence of ulceration.

Patients at highest risk for development of serious NSAID-associated ulcer complications (ulcer, bleeding, or complications from bleeding) include those with a history of GI disease, those older than 60 years of age, and those concomitantly using corticosteroids, anticoagulants, or nicotine.[7,30] Additional risk factors include cardiovascular disease, use of aspirin and other NSAIDs in combination, and concomitant use of aspirin or other NSAIDs with alcohol.[20,28,31] Patients with any of these risk factors should use NSAIDs cautiously and only after consulting a qualified health care provider. Acetaminophen has not been associated with GI toxicity and may be preferred for patients with GI risk factors.

Hepatic Disease. Although relatively uncommon, adverse hepatic effects ranging from mild to fatal have been associated with nonprescription analgesics taken for therapeutic purposes. Salicylates may cause acute, intrinsic hepatotoxicity when blood levels are high, especially in patients with preexisting hepatic impairment, juvenile arthritis, or rheumatic fever.[32] There have also been occasional reports of hepatic injury associated with ibuprofen and naproxen, but the relative risk for nonsalicylate NSAID-induced hepatotoxicity is considered to be low.[8,9]

Chronic alcohol abuse may increase the risk of liver toxicity from excessive acetaminophen use (i.e., the use of dosages exceeding the recommended daily dosage).[10,33] The proposed mechanism is that chronic alcohol ingestion concomitantly induces cytochrome P-450 enzymes and depletes glutathione, through both the effects of the alcohol and the malnutrition associated with alcoholism, leading to accumulation of acetaminophen's toxic metabolite. FDA recently issued a final rule that all nonprescription analgesics carry the warning that people who generally consume three or more alcoholic drinks per day should consult their physicians for advice on taking pain relievers and not exceed the recommended dosage of analgesic.[11]

Asthma. Approximately 20% of patients with asthma have potentially life-threatening hypersensitivity reactions after aspirin ingestion.[34] Many aspirin-intolerant patients are sensitive to other NSAIDs and to chemicals such as preservatives and food dyes (e.g., tartrazine yellow). Although the exact mechanism of aspirin or NSAID intolerance is unknown, it is postulated that aspirin-mediated inhibition of cyclooxygenase causes arachidonic acid to be metabolized through the lipoxygenase pathway rather than the cyclooxygenase pathway.[35] The end result is accumulation of leukotrienes, which can cause bronchospasm and anaphylaxis. Patients with a history of nasal polyps or aspirin-induced disorders such as severe rhinitis, sinusitis, urticaria, angioedema, bronchospasm, and anaphylaxis should avoid most NSAIDs. Choline salicylate, sodium salicylate, and acetaminophen are generally considered acceptable alternatives for most patients.

Coagulation Defects. Patients with coagulation defects such as von Willebrand's disease, hemophilia, thrombocytopenia, uremia, and cirrhosis should avoid NSAID-containing products.[36] Older adults and those who consume alcohol regularly or take anticoagulants may have prolonged bleeding time and should use nonprescription NSAIDs with care. Although all NSAIDs have the potential to prolong bleeding time, nonacetylated salicylates do not have as great an effect on platelet function and may be used with appropriate medical supervision. Although a possible interaction with warfarin has been noted, acetaminophen is generally considered the preferred agent for most patients with underlying conditions that affect coagulation.[37]

Hyperuricemia. Many patients with gout self-medicate with nonprescription analgesics in an attempt to relieve the pain associated with this condition. Salicylates at daily dosages of 1–2 g inhibit tubular secretion of uric acid and elevate plasma urate concentrations, which may worsen hyperuricemia.[12] In addition, salicylates antagonize the uricosuric effects of sulfinpyrazone and probenecid.[12] Therefore, salicylates should generally be avoided in patients with gout or hyperuricemia.

Not all patients with gout or hyperuricemia would be expected to have adverse effects with NSAIDs, particularly if they used the products infrequently at the recommended nonprescription dosages. However, patients with gout or hyperuricemia should seek the advice of a qualified health care provider when selecting nonprescription analgesics.

Special Populations. Safety issues associated with nonprescription analgesics are especially important in certain patient groups, including older adults, infants and children, and pregnant or lactating women. Older adults who suffer from arthritis, muscle aches and pain, headaches, and cold symptoms frequently self-medicate with nonprescription analgesics, using either single-agent or combination products. In a survey of patients 76 to 96 years of age, nonprescription analgesics and anti-inflammatory agents represented 35% of nonprescription drugs used.[38] Because geriatric patients commonly take prescription cardiovascular agents, diuretics, and anti-inflammatory medications, concomitant use of nonprescription analgesics should be closely monitored to prevent drug interactions.[38] In addition, older patients tend to be more sensitive to the effects of medications, may have decreased renal clearance, and often require dosage adjustment to minimize adverse effects.

In the pediatric population, the safe and effective use of nonprescription analgesics depends on proper dosing. Dosage should ideally be based on weight, and the medication should be administered with an appropriate measuring device. Age may be an alternative dosage guide for pediatric patients who are an appropriate weight for their age. Dosage adjustments will be required throughout the infant and toddler years because weight changes significantly during this developmental period. Appropriate attention to the concentrations of various liquid products is important to ensure safe dosing. Salicylates are not recommended as analgesics or antipyretics for children with symptoms of influenza or chickenpox because of the risk of Reye's syndrome.[39] Because the early symptoms of influenza and chickenpox may be difficult to distinguish from those of other illnesses, it may be prudent to avoid salicylates in children unless these are specifically prescribed by a physician. Both acetaminophen and ibuprofen[40] have been shown to be safe and effective for short-term use in children.

Maternal ingestion of nonprescription analgesics may affect the fetus, neonate, or breast-fed infant. In pregnant women, aspirin may affect maternal or fetal hemostasis, and high doses may cause birth defects, intrauterine growth retardation, or stillbirth. Administration of NSAIDs during the third trimester has been associated with premature closure of the patent ductus arteriosus.[41] In most circumstances, acetaminophen is considered the analgesic of choice for pregnant women. The American Academy of Pediatrics has determined that both acetaminophen and ibuprofen are compatible with breast-feeding.[42]

Patients scheduled for elective surgery constitute a special population in whom the bleeding risks associated with aspirin and NSAIDs must be considered. The decision to avoid use of NSAID-containing products before elective surgery depends on the bleeding risks associated with the surgery, the indication for NSAID therapy, patient risk factors, the specific agent and dosage employed, and the availability and appropriateness of alternative analgesics.

Drug Interactions. Drug interactions with aspirin, other salicylates, and NSAIDs number more than 100 and can be found in reviews and standard textbooks on drug interactions. Most reported interactions between salicylates or NSAIDs and other drugs are pharmacokinetic. However, pharmacodynamic interactions appear to be more important clinically in that it is largely the effect of these agents on arachidonic acid metabolism that renders patients more susceptible to adverse effects from concomitantly administered medications.[43] Interactions with salicylates and NSAIDs range from those of minor clinical importance to those with potentially life-threatening implications (e.g., increased risk of bleeding with oral anticoagulants).[43] Although some drug interactions have been noted only with specific agents, in many instances the pharmacologic and pharmacokinetic properties of salicylates and NSAIDs make it likely that nearly all the agents in these classes will interact similarly with another drug or class of drugs. Patients and their health care providers should be aware of any medication (prescription or nonprescription) that the patient is taking on a regular basis, because this may influence selection of a nonprescription analgesic. Few clinically important drug interactions with acetaminophen have been reported but include alcohol in excessive amounts, isoniazid, and rifampin.[10,44]

Other Considerations

Additional factors should be considered in the selection of nonprescription analgesics. The patient's pain should be assessed for its responsiveness to nonprescription analgesics and the need for physician referral. Nonprescription analgesics are indicated for self-treatment of mild to moderate pain and should be taken for no longer than 7–10 days. More severe pain or pain of longer duration requires evaluation by a physician. When these products are used as antipyretics, use should generally be limited to three days. Febrile infants younger than three months and older patients with a high fever or constitutional symptoms suggestive of a serious underlying infectious disease should be referred to a physician.[12]

When nonprescription analgesics are appropriate, drug selection should take into account not only the comparative safety and efficacy of available drug products but also available dosage forms and costs of therapy. These factors should be considered along with the patient's prior response to therapy, certain patient characteristics (e.g., allergies or physical impairment that may limit the ability to take medications), and patient preference.[12]

Appropriate use of nonprescription analgesics requires adherence to the instructions on the label. Patients should understand the limits of nonprescription therapy and the

importance of seeking medical attention should symptoms persist. Because pharmacists are often accessible at the point of purchase of nonprescription products, they are in a unique position to assist patients in the selection and optimal use of nonprescription analgesics.

Summary

Nonprescription analgesics are generally safe and effective when used correctly for mild to moderate pain or fever. However, these agents do have risks, and selection of the best agent for a given patient requires consideration of a number of medication and patient factors. Consumers are encouraged to read and follow label instructions and to consult with a qualified health care provider, such as their pharmacist, for help in sorting out these factors and ensuring the best possible outcomes from nonprescription analgesic therapy.

References

1. Matzke GR. Nonrenal toxicities of acetaminophen, aspirin, and nonsteroidal anti-inflammatory agents. *Am J Kidney Dis.* 1996; 28(suppl 1):S63–70.

2. 1995 report on consumer sales of analgesics. Northbrook, IL: Nielsen; 1996.

3. Whelton A. Renal effects of the over-the-counter analgesics. *J Clin Pharmacol.* 1995; 35:454–63.

4. Sandler DP, Burr FR, Weinberg CR. Nonsteroidal anti-inflammatory drugs and the risk for chronic renal disease. *Ann Intern Med.* 1991; 115:165–72.

5. Perneger TV, Whelton PK, Klag MJ. Risk of kidney failure associated with the use of acetaminophen, aspirin, and nonsteroidal anti-inflammatory drugs. *N Engl J Med.* 1994; 331:1675–9.

6. Wilcox CM, Shalek KA, Cotsonis G. Striking prevalence of over-the-counter nonsteroidal anti-inflammatory drug use in patients with upper gastrointestinal hemorrhage. *Arch Intern Med.* 1994; 154:42–6.

7. McGoldrick MD, Bailie GR. Nonnarcotic analgesics: prevalence and estimated economic impact of toxicities. *Ann Pharmacother.* 1997; 31:221–7.

8. Carson JL, Strom BL, Duff A, et al. Safety of nonsteroidal anti-inflammatory drugs with respect to acute liver disease. *Arch Intern Med.* 1993; 153:1331–6.

9. Garcia-Rodriquez LA, Williams R, Derby LE, et al. Acute liver injury associated with nonsteroidal anti-inflammatory drugs and the role of risk factors. *Arch Intern Med.* 1994; 154:311–6.

10. Whitcomb DC, Block GD. Association of acetaminophen hepatotoxicity with fasting and ethanol use. *JAMA.* 1994; 272:1845–50.

11. Food and Drug Administration. Over-the-counter drug products containing analgesic/antipyretic active ingredients for internal use: required alcohol warning. 21 CFR 201.322. *Fed Regist.* 1998; 63(205):56789–802.

12. Lipman AG. Internal analgesic and antipyretic products. In: American Pharmaceutical Association. Handbook of nonprescription drugs. 11th ed. Washington, DC: American Pharmaceutical Association; 1996.

13. Guyton AC. Textbook of medical physiology. 9th ed. Philadelphia, PA: W.B. Saunders; 1996:609–20.

14. Simon LS, Mills JA. Nonsteroidal antiinflammatory drugs. Part 2. *N Engl J Med.* 1980; 302:1237.

15. Oates JA, Fitzgerald GA, Branch RA, et al. Clinical implications of prostaglandin and thromboxane A$_2$ formation. Part 1. *N Engl J Med.* 1988; 319:689–98.

16. Oates JA, Fitzgerald GA, Branch RA, et al. Clinical implications of prostaglandin and thromboxane A$_2$ formation. Part 2. *N Engl J Med.* 1988; 319:761–7.

17. Whelton A, Hamilton CW. Nonsteroidal anti-inflammatory drugs: effects on kidney function. *J Clin Pharmacol.* 1991; 31:588–98.

18. Henrich WL, Agondoa LE, Barrett B, et al. Analgesics and the kidney: summary and recommendations to the Scientific Advisory Board of the National Kidney Foundation and the Ad Hoc Committee of the National Kidney Foundation. *Am J Kidney Dis.* 1996; 27:162–5.

19. Delzell E, Shapiro S. Commentary on the National Kidney Foundation position paper on analgesics and the kidney. *Am J Kidney Dis.* 1996; 28:783–5.

20. Silverstein FE, Graham DY, Senior JR, et al. Misoprostol reduces serious gastrointestinal complications in patients with rheumatoid arthritis receiving nonsteroidal anti-inflammatory drugs. *Ann Intern Med.* 1995; 123:241–9.

21. Food and Drug Administration. Internal analgesic, antipyretic, and antirheumatic drug products for over-the-counter human use: final rule for professional labeling of aspirin, buffered aspirin, and aspirin in combination with antacid drug products. 21 CFR part 343. *Fed Regist.* 1998; 63:56802–19.

22. Morley GK, Mooradian AB, Levine AS, et al. Mechanism of pain in diabetic peripheral neuropathy—effect of glucose on pain perception in humans. *Am J Med.* 1984; 77:79–82.

23. American Diabetes Association. Diabetic nephropathy. *Diabetes Care.* 1998; 21(suppl 1):S50–3.

24. American Diabetes Association. Aspirin therapy in diabetes. *Diabetes Care.* 1998; 21(suppl 1):S45–6.

25. Soll AH, Weinstein WM, Kurata J, et al. Nonsteroidal anti-inflammatory drugs and peptic ulcer disease. *Ann Intern Med.* 1991; 114:307–19.

26. Allison MC, Howatson AG, Torrance CJ, et al. Gastrointestinal damage associated with the use of nonsteroidal anti-inflammatory drugs. *N Engl J Med.* 1992; 327:749–54.

27. Griffin MR, Pieper JM, Daugherty JR, et al. Nonsteroidal anti-inflammatory drug use and increased risk for peptic ulcer disease in elderly persons. *Ann Intern Med.* 1991; 114:257–63.

28. Henry D, Dobson A, Turner C. Variability in the risk of major gastrointestinal complications from non-aspirin nonsteroidal anti-inflammatory drugs. *Gastroenterology.* 1993; 105:1078–88.

29. Peura DA, Lanza FL, Fostout CJ, et al. The American College of Gastroenterology Bleeding Registry: preliminary findings. *Am J Gastroenterol.* 1997; 92:924–8.

30. Gabriel SE, Jaakkimainen L, Bombardier C. Risk for serious gastrointestinal complications related to use of nonsteroidal anti-inflammatory drugs. *Ann Intern Med.* 1991; 115:787–96.

31. Deykin D, Jarson P, McMahon L. Ethanol potentiation of aspirin-induced prolongation of the bleeding time. *N Engl J Med.* 1982; 306:852–4.

32. Zimmerman HJ. Update of hepatotoxicity due to classes of drugs in common clinical use: nonsteroidal drugs, anti-inflammatory drugs, antibiotics, antihypertensives, and cardiac and psychotropic agents. *Semin Liver Dis.* 1990; 10:322–38.

33. Schiodt FV, Rochling FA, Casey DL, et al. Acetaminophen toxicity in an urban county hospital. *N Engl J Med.* 1997; 337:1112–7.

34. Settipane GA. Aspirin and allergic diseases: a review. *Am J Med.* 1983; 74:102–9.

35. Szczeklik A, Gryglewski RJ. Asthma and anti-inflammatory drugs: mechanisms and clinical patterns. *Drugs.* 1983; 25:533–43.

36. Schafer AL. Effects of nonsteroidal anti-inflammatory drugs on platelet function and systemic hemostasis. *J Clin Pharmacol.* 1995; 35:209–19.

37. Hylek EM, Heiman H, Skates SJ, et al. Acetaminophen and other risk factors for excessive warfarin anticoagulation. *JAMA.* 1998; 279:657–62.

38. Delafuente JC, Meuleman JR, Conlin M, et al. Drug use among functionally active, aged, ambulatory people. *Ann Pharmacother.* 1992; 26:179–83.

39. Arrowsmith JB, Kennedy DL, Kuritsky JN, et al. National patterns of aspirin use and Reyes syndrome reporting in the United States, 1980 to 1985. *Pediatrics.* 1987; 79:858–63.

40. Lesko SM, Mitchell AA. An assessment of the safety of pediatric ibuprofen. *JAMA.* 1995; 273:929–33.

41. Briggs GG, Freeman RK, Yaffe SJ. Drugs in pregnancy and lactation: a guide to fetal and neonatal risk. 5th ed. Baltimore: Williams & Wilkins; 1998.

42. American Academy of Pediatrics policy statement. The transfer of drugs and other chemicals into human milk. *Pediatrics.* 1994; 93:137–50.

43. Johnson AG, Seidemann P, Day RO. NSAID-related adverse drug interactions with clinical relevance. *Int J Clin Pharmacol Ther.* 1994; 32:509–32.

44. Nolan CM, Sandblom RE, Thummel KE, et al. Hepatotoxicity associated acetaminophen usage in patients receiving multiple drug therapy for tuberculosis. *Chest.* 1994; 105:408–11.

Approved by the ASHP Board of Directors, November 14, 1998. Developed by the ASHP Commission on Therapeutics.

Celeste M. Lindley, Pharm.D., M.S., FCCP, FASHP, is acknowledged for drafting this document.

The bibliographic citation for this document is as follows: American Society of Health-System Pharmacists. ASHP therapeutic position statement on the safe use of oral nonprescription analgesics. *Am J Health-Syst Pharm.* 1999; 56:1126–31.

ASHP Therapeutic Position Statement
on Smoking Cessation

Statement of Position

The negative effects of smoking on public health are well established, yet high rates of smoking persist for several reasons, especially the difficulty of overcoming nicotine addiction. Smoking is the single most important preventable cause of morbidity and mortality in the United States, accounting for more than one in every five deaths.[1] Nicotine addiction is also associated with other types of tobacco products, such as smokeless tobacco. The successful treatment of nicotine addiction often requires that complex social, psychological, behavioral, and pharmacologic factors be addressed and thus often necessitates the support and guidance of health care providers. ASHP encourages all health care providers, including pharmacists, to actively promote nicotine abstinence and smoking cessation and participate in the provision of smoking-cessation interventions. ASHP discourages the distribution of all tobacco products by pharmacists and pharmacies.

Prevalence of Smoking in the United States

There are approximately 47 million adult smokers in the United States; the highest prevalence is in the 25- to 44-year age group.[2] The prevalence of current smoking in adults is higher among Native Americans (36%), non-Hispanic blacks (26%), and non-Hispanic whites (26%) than among Hispanics (18%) and Asians or Pacific Islanders (17%).[2] Tobacco use is increasing among adolescents.[3] Of students in grades 9–12, approximately 35% smoke cigarettes and 11% use smokeless tobacco.[3] This is disturbing given that approximately 90% of all persons who become addicted to nicotine start using tobacco products before the age of 18 years. Peer influence can be very significant in the early stages of tobacco use in young people; the peer group provides expectations, cues for experimentation, and reinforcement.[4] Additional factors that can foster the use of tobacco products in young people include an overestimation of the prevalence of smoking in peers and adults, behavioral factors (e.g., associating tobacco use with bonding with peers, with being independent and mature, and with having a positive self-image), easy access to tobacco products, and cigarette advertisements.[4] Thus, efforts to decrease overall tobacco use must include preventing the onset of tobacco use in young people.[5] The recent Food and Drug Administration ruling prohibiting the sale and distribution of tobacco to children and adolescents represents the beginning of a more comprehensive approach in this direction.[6]

Health Consequences of Smoking

More than 400,000 Americans die of smoking-related illnesses each year, and the number of deaths is increasing.[1] Cigarette smoking increases the risk of coronary heart disease (CHD), cancer-related death, chronic obstructive pulmonary disease, peripheral vascular disease, stroke, and peptic ulcer disease. Smoking can also complicate a number of existing disorders, such as hypertension, diabetes mellitus, and asthma. Various substances in cigarettes can interact with several commonly prescribed drugs (e.g., benzodiazepines, heparin, oral contraceptives, theophylline, propoxyphene, tricyclic antidepressants), thus altering the actions or effectiveness of these drugs.[7] Cigarette smoking accounts for 30% of all deaths related to cancer and more than 80% of all lung cancers.[8,9] The risk of lung cancer and chronic obstructive pulmonary disease is higher among pipe and cigar smokers as well, although it is lower than for cigarette smokers.[10-12] The use of smokeless tobacco increases the risk of oropharyngeal cancer fourfold[13] and has been linked to cancers of the nasal cavity, the larynx, the esophagus, the stomach, and the urinary tract.[14] Smokeless-tobacco use is also associated with a variety of dental problems, including periodontal disease and tooth staining.[15]

Exposure to environmental tobacco smoke (ETS, also called secondhand smoke) increases the risk for death from heart disease or lung cancer.[16] Children exposed to ETS have an increased risk of middle ear effusions, asthma, and lower-respiratory-tract infections.[16] One study found that infants born to women who have been exposed to ETS also have an increased risk for asthma.[17] Smoking during pregnancy increases the risk of spontaneous abortion or miscarriage and of having a baby with low birth weight, congenital abnormalities, sudden infant death syndrome, or a respiratory disorder.[16,18] The relative risk for CHD is increased for both nonsmoking men and nonsmoking women exposed to spousal ETS.[19,20]

The annual medical cost associated with smoking-related illnesses in the United States is about $50 billion[8]; this does not include the estimated $47 billion in productivity and earnings lost annually as a consequence of smoking-related illness.[21,22]

Health Benefits of Smoking Cessation

The benefits of smoking cessation include an improved sense of taste and smell, a better feeling of physical well-being, monetary savings, better-smelling breath, the birth of healthier babies, and a reduced risk of CHD, of all types of smoking-related cancers, and of respiratory complications (e.g., chronic obstructive pulmonary disease, influenza, pneumonia, asthma). The risk of smoking-related disease continues to decrease as the duration of abstinence increases. People who quit smoking before age 50 have half the risk of dying over the next 15 years compared with people who continue to smoke.[8,23] After one year of abstinence, the excess risk of CHD-associated mortality is reduced by half and continues to decline with time.[23] The risk of lung cancer declines steadily and after 10 years is 30% to 50% the risk of people who continue smoking.[8] After smoking cessation, the risk of stroke returns to the level of persons who have never smoked. This risk reduction can occur within 5 years, but, in some cases, as many as 15 years of abstinence may be required.[12,24]

Nicotine Addiction

Addiction to nicotine involves the interplay of psychological, physical, behavioral, and social factors.[25,26] To be successful and to minimize the risk of relapse after the smoker quits, smoking-cessation strategies must address these factors. As for other addictive substances, the psychoactive (mood-altering) effects of nicotine are one of the most important contributing factors to the development of physical dependence on tobacco.[23,25,26] Nicotine is a potent central nervous system stimulant and may cause nausea and vomiting upon initial exposure, but tolerance to these effects develops rapidly. With continued use, nicotine improves cognitive performance, wakefulness, and mood and may reduce anxiety and irritability. The chronic use of nicotine requires increasingly higher nicotine doses to produce these effects.[25] Abrupt cessation after daily use of nicotine for several weeks or more may result in withdrawal symptoms such as irritability, anxiety, increased appetite, weight gain, dysphoria (depressed mood), decreased heart rate, impaired concentration, restlessness, insomnia, and a craving for nicotine.[27] Withdrawal symptoms usually begin within 24 hours of smoking cessation, typically peak in one to four days, and last for three to four weeks.[27] Nicotine withdrawal symptoms in smokeless-tobacco users are the same as in cigarette smokers.[15] Nicotine dependence and withdrawal are also likely to occur in pipe and cigar smokers.[12]

The inability to tolerate withdrawal symptoms is a major reason for relapse after smoking cessation. Other risk factors for relapse include concomitant psychiatric illness, alcohol use, drug use among peers, lack of social or family support, severe nicotine dependence, and a lack of involvement in work and leisure activities.[12] In addition, strong urges to smoke can occur when patients trying to quit encounter familiar situations (e.g., participating in social activities, relaxing after meals, having coffee or alcoholic beverages) in which smoking previously increased the pleasure of the activity. The risk of relapse is greatest in the first three months after the person stops smoking. During this time, approximately 65% of those who quit will relapse.[28] Relapse should not be considered a sign of failure but an opportunity for the health care provider to detect its cause and advise on subsequent treatment strategies. Many smokers are not willing to make a commitment to quit because they are uninformed, concerned about the effects of quitting, or discouraged by previous relapses. Some of these patients may respond to motivational interventions.[26,27] These smokers should also be informed that most smokers make repeated cessation attempts before achieving long-term abstinence. The risk of relapse can be minimized by reinforcing and supporting a person's decision to quit.[25,26,29] This can be done by expressing concern, encouraging the person to remain abstinent, reviewing the benefits of quitting, and extending the use of nicotine replacement therapy to alleviate withdrawal symptoms or prolonged craving.

Smoking-cessation interventions should be tailored to the needs of the individual patient. Smoking cessation is a dynamic process that occurs before, during, and after the person quits. Nicotine cravings, which can occur years after the patient quits, may trigger relapse at any time. Different smoking-cessation strategies are needed depending on what stage of quitting a smoker is at. The transtheoretical model of smoking cessation describes six stages (precontemplation, contemplation, preparation, action, maintenance, and re-

lapse) of the quitting process that can be readily identified by health care providers asking questions about a patient's behavior.[29,30] Because patients can fluctuate between stages, it is important to consider the stage a patient is at during each encounter so that appropriate strategies are implemented. It is also likely that many smokers decide to quit when they hear messages from many different sources, so comments from pharmacists and other health care providers are very important in moving someone closer to quitting.

Methods of Smoking Cessation

Smoking-cessation methods include both nonpharmacologic and pharmacologic interventions. Their effectiveness has primarily been evaluated in cigarette smokers; there is limited information about effectiveness in cigar or pipe smokers. However, pipe and cigar smokers who are nicotine dependent are likely to benefit from the treatments that work for cigarette smokers. Smoking-cessation techniques have been applied to users of smokeless tobacco in a few studies with small samples.[26,31,32]

Nonpharmacologic interventions include behavioral therapy (e.g., skills training and problem solving, relaxation techniques, nicotine weaning [fading]), educational and support groups, and self-help approaches (e.g., self-help manuals). No single intervention has been shown to be more effective than the others. Compared with no intervention, all these techniques can double the cessation rates.[26] In addition, the more intensive the intervention, the more effective it is.[33] Interventions that significantly increase cessation rates relative to no patient contact include skills training and problem solving, intratreatment social support (i.e., direct contact with a clinician during treatment), and aversion techniques.[26] Data on the effectiveness of hypnosis and acupuncture are lacking.[26,27] Most nonpharmacologic interventions are also considered highly cost-effective.[25,34] Readers are referred elsewhere for a detailed discussion of nonpharmacologic interventions.[26,27]

Pharmacologic interventions include nonprescription products, such as the nicotine patch and nicotine gum, and prescription medications, such as clonidine, buspirone or other anxiolytics, extended-release bupropion (and other antidepressants), and the nicotine inhaler and spray. Nicotine replacement therapy effectively alleviates the symptoms of nicotine withdrawal.[26,27,35,36] Abstinence rates with nicotine replacement therapy (involving the patch and gum) are highest when concurrent nonpharmacologic interventions are used, but they are also effective when used alone.[25,26,35] Nicotine replacement therapy generally doubles cessation rates compared with placebo, regardless of the intensity or level of concomitant psychosocial support provided.[26,27] A meta-analysis by Silagy et al.[35] found rates of continuous abstinence for 6 to 12 months to be 19% for patients receiving nicotine replacement therapy and 11% for control patients, representing a 71% increase in the rate of abstinence with the use of nicotine replacement therapy.[35]

Nicotine replacement therapy is safe for patients with cardiovascular disease. Studies have found either no evidence that it increases the risk of adverse cardiovascular events in patients with concomitant cardiac disease or[37-40] that the risk of cardiovascular events is small, even with concurrent smoking.[37] Common adverse effects with nicotine gum include mouth and throat soreness, nausea, vomiting, and jaw muscle ache.[41] The most common adverse effects with the nicotine patch are local dermatologic reactions (e.g., pruritus, rash, erythema).[41] The major adverse effects of nicotine nasal inhaler include nasal and throat irritation and coughing.[27,36]

An extended-release form of bupropion is the first non-nicotine agent to carry FDA-approved labeling as an aid to smoking cessation. Abstinence rates with bupropion have been shown to be significantly better than with placebo. Hurt et al.[42] reported the rate of continuous abstinence over a six-week period in nondepressed patients to be 10.5% in the placebo group, compared with 24.4% in the group receiving 300 mg of bupropion hydrochloride daily.[42] Insomnia and dry mouth were the most frequent adverse effects.[42] More studies are under way to further document bupropion's efficacy. Data are insufficient to support the effectiveness of buspirone, other anxiolytics, antidepressants (other than bupropion), psychostimulants (methylphenidate, amphetamines), or clonidine for smoking cessation.[26,27]

The more nicotine dependent the smoker, the more intensive the treatment required to provide effective therapy.[26,43] Recent data clearly show that all patients, even those with low nicotine dependence, will have a significantly better treatment result if provided with nicotine replacement therapy.[43] The Agency for Health Care Policy and Research (AHCPR), in its clinical practice guidelines for smoking cessation, recommends that every smoker, regardless of degree of nicotine dependence, be offered nicotine replacement therapy.[26]

Factors to consider in the selection and monitoring of a pharmacologic agent for smoking cessation include the agent's adverse-effect profile and the appropriateness of the drug delivery system or dosage form.[44-46] It is also important to recognize that smoking cessation (with or without pharmacologic interventions for smoking cessation) may alter the pharmacokinetics of certain drugs and thus necessitate change in their dosage.[7] The dosage and total duration of treatment with these pharmacologic agents for smoking cessation must be tailored to the needs of the individual patient.

AHCPR supports the combined use of nonpharmacologic and pharmacologic approaches in smoking-cessation programs.[26] Its guidelines address multiple strategies to help patients quit, including individual or group counseling, or brief advice to quit; aversion methods; nicotine replacement therapy (patch, gum, inhaler, spray); follow-up contact; and relapse-prevention strategies. AHCPR guidelines were published before bupropion's labeling for smoking cessation was approved by FDA. Readers are referred to the AHCPR guidelines for more details about these strategies.[26]

There is limited evidence of the effectiveness of nonpharmacologic interventions or the safety and efficacy of pharmacologic interventions in children and adolescents. More research is needed to determine effective smoking-cessation or tobacco treatment strategies in children and adolescents.

Pharmacists' Role

Pharmacists' expertise in drug therapy, their accessibility to the public, and their presence at the point of purchase of nicotine replacement products make them particularly suitable advocates for smoking cessation. Involvement of pharmacists in smoking-cessation activities is consistent with the proposed Healthy People 2010 initiative to increase to at least 75% the percentage of health care providers who routinely advise cessation and provide assistance and follow-up for all their tobacco-using patients.[47] Pharmacists should actively discourage smoking in all age groups and participate in public campaigns (community and self-directed programs) that educate the public on the health risks of smoking. To achieve the greatest impact on the prevalence of tobacco use, educational efforts should specifically target children and adolescents and their parents, other caregivers, siblings, and peers who smoke. Pharmacists should encourage adults with children to avoid smoking when they are in their children's presence to protect them from the harmful effects of ETS and to serve as appropriate nonsmoking role models.

Pharmacists in virtually any practice setting have opportunities to advise patients on the hazards of tobacco use, encourage behavioral change, and enhance the efforts of other providers. Pharmacists can identify patients who smoke, provide counseling to quit, refer interested patients to more intensive interventions, and counsel about pharmacotherapy for smoking cessation. Culturally appropriate smoking-cessation interventions should be used when necessary.

Pharmacists have a unique opportunity to assist patients in smoking cessation with prescription and nonprescription products. The patient encounter is an opportunity for pharmacists to provide information about the health risks of smoking and the correct use of pharmacotherapy for smoking cessation, to evaluate and monitor the use of pharmacotherapy for smoking cessation, to inform patients about possible drug interactions that may occur as a result of smoking cessation and suggest that the patients discuss these with their other providers, and to provide support and reinforcement during the quitting process. A mixed or inconsistent message will be created by pharmacists who encourage smoking cessation but continue to sell tobacco products. Pharmacists should demand that tobacco products not be sold at their practice sites.

Appropriately trained pharmacists are also qualified to direct smoking-cessation clinics. Pharmacists are well suited to educating patients about drug dosing, adverse effects, drug interactions, the effects of smoking on drugs, and the selection and correct use of a drug delivery system and to be actively involved in the management of drug therapy. Organized clinics also facilitate the provision of more intensive nonpharmacologic interventions.[48] Additional specialized training would be required for pharmacists to actively be involved in the provision of behavioral therapy. The effectiveness of pharmacist-directed smoking-cessation programs has been documented.[49]

Summary

Smoking continues to be the single most important preventable cause of morbidity and mortality in the United States. Pharmacists, in collaboration with other health care providers, have the opportunity to make a significant contribution to addressing this major public health problem. ASHP supports AHCPR's guidelines for smoking cessation. ASHP encourages all health care providers to actively promote smoking cessation and become participants in the provision of smoking-cessation programs or tobacco treatment interventions. Because a majority of smokers start smoking when they are less than 18 years old, emphasis must also be given to the prevention of smoking by children and adolescents.

References

1. Centers for Disease Control and Prevention. Smoking—attributable mortality and years of potential life lost—United States, 1984. *MMWR*. 1997; 46:444–51.

2. Centers for Disease Control and Prevention. Cigarette smoking among adults—United States, 1995. *MMWR*. 1997; 46:1217–20.

3. Centers for Disease Control and Prevention. Tobacco use and usual source of cigarettes among high school students—United States, 1995. *MMWR*. 1996; 45:413–8.

4. Centers for Disease Control and Prevention. Preventing tobacco use among young people. *MMWR*. 1994; 43(RR4):1–10.

5. Kessler DA. Nicotine addiction in young people. *N Engl J Med*. 1995; 333:186–9.

6. Food and Drug Administration. The regulations restricting the sale and distribution of cigarettes and smokeless tobacco to protect children and adolescents. Executive summary. Rockville, MD: U.S. Department of Health and Human Services. 1996 Aug 23.

7. Hansten P, Horn J. Drug interactions and quarterly updates. Vancouver, WA: Applied Therapeutics; 1995.

8. The health benefits of smoking cessation. A report of the Surgeon General, 1990. Washington, DC: U.S. Department of Health and Human Services, 1990; publication no. CDC 90–8416.

9. Cancer facts and figures 1997. Atlanta: American Cancer Society; 1997.

10. Henningfield JE, Harihan M, Kozlowski LT. Nicotine content and health risks of cigars. *JAMA*. 1996; 276:1857–9. Letter.

11. Nelson DE, Davis RM, Chrismon JH, et al. Pipe smoking in the United States, 1965-1991. *Prev Med*. 1996; 25(2):91–9.

12. The health consequences of smoking: nicotine addiction. A report of the Surgeon General, 1988. Washington, DC: U.S. Department of Health and Human Services, 1988; publication no. CDC 88-8406.

13. Winn DM, Blot WJ, Shy CM, et al. Snuff dipping and oral cancer among women in the southern United States. *N Engl J Med*. 1981; 304:745–9.

14. Gottlieb A, Pope SK, Rickert VI, et al. Patterns of smokeless tobacco use by young adolescents. *Pediatrics*. 1993; 91:75–8.

15. Goolsby MJ. Smokeless tobacco: the health consequences of snuff and chewing tobacco. *Nurs Pract*. 1992; 17:24–38.

16. American Heart Association. Active and passive tobacco exposure. *Circulation*. 1994; 90:2581–90.

17. Barber K, Mussin E, Taylor DK. Fetal exposure to involuntary maternal smoking and child respiratory disease. *Ann Allergy Asthma Immunol*. 1996; 76:427–30.

18. Charlton A. Children and passive smoking. *J Fam Pract*. 1994; 38:267–77.

19. Glantz SA, Parmley WW. Passive smoking and heart disease: epidemiology, physiology, and biochemistry. *Circulation*. 1991; 83:1.

20. Glantz SA, Parmley W. Passive smoking and heart disease: mechanisms and risk. *JAMA*. 1995; 273:1047–53.

21. Centers for Disease Control and Prevention. Medical care expenditures attributable to cigarette smoking—United States, 1993. *MMWR*. 1994; 43:469–72.

22. Centers for Disease Control and Prevention. Cigarette smoking among adults—United States, 1995. *MMWR*. 1996; 43: 925–9.

23. American Thoracic Society. Cigarette smoking and health. *Am J Respir Crit Care Med*. 1996; 153:861–5.

24. Kawachi I, Colditz GA, Stampfer MJ, et al. Smoking cessation and decreased risk of stroke in women. *JAMA*. 1993; 269:232–6.

25. Haxby DG. Treatment of nicotine dependence. *Am J Health-Syst Pharm*. 1995; 52:265–81.

26. Smoking cessation. Clinical practice guideline no. 18. Rockville, MD: Agency for Health Care Policy and Research, 1996 Apr; AHCPR publication no. 96–0692.

27. Diagnostic and statistical manual of mental disorders. 4th ed. Washington, DC: American Psychiatric Association; 1994: 243–7.

28. Hatziandieu EJ, Pierce JP, Lefkopoulou M, et al. Quitting smoking in the United States in 1986. *J Natl Cancer Inst*. 1990; 82:1402–6.

29. Hudmon KS, Berger BA. Pharmacy applications of the transtheoretical model in smoking cessation. *Am J Health-Syst Pharm*. 1995; 52:282–93.

30. Frank SH, Jaen CR. Office evaluation and treatment of the dependent smoker. *Prim Care*. 1993; 20:251–68.

31. Hatsukami D, Jensen J, Allen A, et al. Effects of behavioral and pharmacological treatment of smokeless tobacco users. *J Consult Clin Psychol*. 1996; 64(1):153–61.

32. Severson HH. Enough snuff. In: Smokeless tobacco or health. Smoking and tobacco control monograph. Washington, DC: U.S. Department of Health and Human Services, 1992; 2:279–90.

33. Cromwell J, Bartosch WJ, Fiore MC, et al. Cost-effectiveness of the clinical practice recommendations in the AHCPR guideline for smoking cessation. *JAMA*. 1997; 278:1759–66.

34. Law M, Tank JL. An analysis of the effectiveness of intervention intended to help people stop smoking. *Arch Intern Med*. 1995; 155:1933–41.

35. Silagy C, Mant D, Fowler G, et al. Meta-analysis of efficacy of nicotine replacement therapies in smoking cessation. *Lancet*. 1994; 343:139–42.

36. Schneider NG, Olmstead R, Nilsson F, et al. Efficacy of a nicotine inhaler in smoking cessation. *Addiction*. 1996; 91: 1293–306.

37. Benowitz NC, Gourlay SG. Cardiovascular toxicity of nicotine. *J Am Coll Cardiol*. 1997; 29:1422–31.

38. Benowitz NL, Fitzgerald GA, Wilson M, et al. Nicotine effects on eicosanoid formation and hemostatic function. *J Am Coll Cardiol*. 1993; 22:1159–67.

39. Working group for the study of transdermal nicotine in patients with coronary artery disease. Nicotine replacement therapy for patients with coronary artery disease. *Arch Intern Med*. 1994; 154:989–95.

40. Joseph AM, Norman SM, Ferry LH, et al. The safety of transdermal nicotine as an aid to smoking cessa-

tion in patients with cardiac disease. *N Engl J Med.* 1996; 335:1792–8.

41.   Risk/benefit of nicotine replacement in smoking cessation. *Drug Saf.* 1993; 8:49–56.

42.   Hurt RD, Sachs DPl, Glover ED, et al. A comparison of sustained-release bupropion and placebo for smoking cessation. *N Engl J Med.* 1997; 337:1195–202.

43.   Sachs DPL, Sawe U, Leischow SJ. Effectiveness of a 16-hour transdermal nicotine patch in a medical practice setting, without intensive group counseling. *Arch Intern Med.* 1993; 153:1881–90.

44.   Sachs DP. Effectiveness of the 4-mg dose of nicotine pola–crilex for the initial treatment of high-dependent smokers. *Arch Intern Med.* 1995; 155:1973–80.

45.   Dale LC, Hurt RD, Offord KP, et al. High-dose nicotine patch therapy. *JAMA.* 1995; 274:1353–8.

46.   Sachs DP, Benowitz NL. Individualizing medical treatment of tobacco dependence. *Eur Respir J.* 1996; 9:629–31.

47.   U.S. Department of Health and Human Services. Healthy People 2010 objectives: draft for public comment. Washington, DC: U.S. Government Printing Office; 1998 Sep 15.

48.   Sanders D, Gibson JS. Navy pharmacists energize smoking-cessation program. *Hosp Pharm.* 1997; 32:1493–7.

49.   Smith M, McGhan W, Lauger G. Pharmacist counseling and outcomes of smoking cessation. *Am Pharm.* 1995; NS35(8):20–32.

Approved by the ASHP Board of Directors, November 14, 1998. Developed by the ASHP Commission on Therapeutics.

Jutta C. Joseph, Pharm.D., is gratefully acknowledged for drafting this document.

The bibliographic citation for this document is as follows: American Society of Health-System Pharmacists. ASHP therapeutic position statement on smoking cessation. *Am J Health-Syst Pharm.* 1999; 56:460–4.

ASHP Therapeutic Position Statement on the Identification and Treatment of *Helicobacter pylori*-Associated Peptic Ulcer Disease in Adults

Statement of Position

In February 1994 a National Institutes of Health (NIH) consensus panel concluded that patients with peptic ulcer disease and *Helicobacter pylori* infection require treatment with antimicrobial agents in combination with antisecretory drugs (i.e., histamine H_2-receptor antagonists, proton-pump inhibitors), whether on first presentation with the illness or on recurrence.[1] Although professional organizations and societies have publicly supported the NIH panel,[2,3] many patients with peptic ulcer disease continue to receive inadequate treatment.

Effective treatment regimens for eradicating *H. pylori* infection include a variety of combinations of prescription and nonprescription agents. The complexity of these treatment regimens heightens the importance of patient education and monitoring to ensure compliance with and optimal response to therapy. ASHP encourages and supports pharmacists' involvement in the identification and treatment of patients with *H. pylori*-associated disease with the objective of decreasing peptic ulcer recurrence rates and associated morbidity and mortality. In addition, ASHP encourages pharmacists to work with other health care professionals in providing these services.

An association of *H. pylori* with peptic ulcer disease in children has been more difficult to prove. This is because *H. pylori* infection and peptic ulcer disease are both infrequent in children.[4] This Therapeutic Position Statement was developed for adult patients.

Background

Approximately 25 million people in the United States have had peptic ulcer disease during their lifetimes.[5] Each year, 500,000–850,000 patients are diagnosed with peptic ulcer disease. Complications of peptic ulcer disease are reportedly fatal in approximately 6,500 persons in the United States annually.[6,7] The economic burden of the disease is staggering; the direct cost of patient care and the indirect cost of productivity losses total an estimated $5.65 billion each year.[8]

Except for ulcers in patients taking nonsteroidal anti-inflammatory drugs (NSAIDs) or in those with gastrinoma (Zollinger-Ellison syndrome), 95% of duodenal ulcers and 80% of gastric ulcers are associated with infection with *H. pylori*.[9,10] Recent data suggest that only 80% of duodenal ulcers in the United States are associated with *H. pylori* infection.[11] The potential for NSAIDs to induce gastric ulcers has been known for several decades.[6] However, the role of *H. pylori* as an independent risk factor for peptic ulcer disease has been established only relatively recently.[12] Patients with peptic ulcer disease are not always tested and treated for *H. pylori* infection. Hood et al.[13] estimated that only 56% of inpatient Medicare beneficiaries with a principal diagnosis of peptic ulcer disease were screened for *H. pylori*. Of those, only 70% who tested positive for *H. pylori* were treated with antimicrobial therapy.

Public awareness of the cause of peptic ulcer disease is lacking. A population-based survey in 1997 found that only 27% of Americans were aware of the association between *H. pylori* and peptic ulcer disease.[14] Sixty percent of respondents believed that feeling overly stressed was the cause, while 17% thought the cause was eating spicy foods.

Over 50% of the world's population may be infected with *H. pylori*, and this organism is believed to be responsible for chronic gastritis, duodenal ulcers, and gastric ulcers.[12] However, although epidemiologic studies have shown an association between *H. pylori* and gastric cancer, clinical trials have not proved that eradicating *H. pylori* prevents this cancer.[15] Many investigations are being performed that may clarify *H. pylori*'s role, if any, in gastric cancer. Gastric cancer is the second leading cause of cancer-related deaths worldwide and the 10th leading cause in the United States.

Although the regimens can be complex, a limited array of medications are used in the treatment of *H. pylori*-induced peptic ulcer disease, including amoxicillin, clarithromycin, metronidazole, and tetracycline. Histamine H_2-receptor antagonists (e.g., cimetidine, famotidine, and ranitidine) and proton-pump inhibitors (e.g., lansoprazole and omeprazole) are frequently used in combination with antimicrobial regimens to suppress ulcer symptoms. Bismuth subsalicylate is also often used.

The association between *H. pylori* and peptic ulcer disease may be best demonstrated by ulcer recurrence rates. Patients with a duodenal ulcer who are treated with a single course of H_2-receptor antagonist therapy alone exhibit recurrence rates of 85–95% per year. Those receiving long-term maintenance on H_2-receptor antagonist therapy have recurrence rates of nearly 30% per year. Multiple studies have shown a large and significant decrease in ulcer recurrence if *H. pylori* is eradicated in patients with *H. pylori*-associated ulcers. The rate of duodenal ulcer recurrence is reported to be 6% or less in the 12 months after therapy. However, a meta-analysis of double-blind, randomized, North American trials in patients with duodenal ulcers documented by endoscopy and with *H. pylori* infection and eradication documented by biopsy revealed an ulcer recurrence rate of 20% within six months despite eradication of *H. pylori* infection.[16] Researchers hypothesize that this disparity in recurrence rates may be due to a variety of factors, such as differences in U.S. and non-U.S. populations (e.g., in NSAID use, smoking, and genetic factors), missed diagnoses of *H. pylori* infection after treatment, and increases in non-*H. pylori*-associated ulcers. Even though the rate of ulcer recurrence after *H. pylori* eradication may be somewhat higher in the United States than originally estimated, ulcer recurrence is five times less likely if *H. pylori* has been eradicated than if the infection persists.[16] Whether the rate of recurrence of *H. pylori*-associated ulcers is 6% or 20%, the primary cause of recurrence after antimicrobial therapy is failure to achieve eradication.

Eradication of *H. pylori*-associated peptic ulcer disease has not only a health benefit but an economic benefit. Using a Markov model, Sonnenberg and Townsend[17] compared the economic benefit of H_2-receptor antagonists (intermittent and maintenance therapy) with antimicrobial therapy for duodenal ulcers. The expected total cost per patient for 15 years was $995 for antimicrobial therapy, $10,350 for intermittent H_2-receptor antagonist therapy, and $11,186 for maintenance H_2-receptor antagonist therapy. Other pharmacoeconomic studies found similar economic benefits for antimicrobial therapy compared with conventional antisecretory therapy.[18–20]

Testing for *H. pylori* Infection

All patients with a documented acute gastric or duodenal ulcer—even if induced by NSAIDs—should be tested for *H. pylori* infection. Patients with a confirmed history of an ulcer and current symptoms should also be tested, whether they are taking antisecretory medications or not. Diagnostic testing must be performed before any patient is treated to confirm the presence of *H. pylori* infection.[1,21] In addition, treatment should be offered to any patient who tests positive for *H. pylori*, even in the absence of an ulcer.[21] A survey of primary care physicians and gastroenterologists found that 95% knew of the association between *H. pylori* and peptic ulcer disease; however, 50% of primary care physicians and 29% of gastroenterologists simply started patients on antisecretory therapy without testing for *H. pylori*.[22]

Peptic ulcer disease is diagnosed with 100% certainty by visualization on endoscopy. Examination of a biopsy specimen of the gastric mucosa allows for the identification of *H. pylori* infection. This diagnostic procedure is very expensive and can be uncomfortable for the patient. An alternative strategy for the patient who has symptoms of dyspepsia and has no documented history of an ulcer is the "test-and-treat" strategy. This entails testing the symptomatic patient for *H. pylori* and, if the result is positive, treating the *H. pylori* infection with an eradication regimen. Approximately 15–25% of dyspeptic patients actually have an ulcer, and another 20% have symptoms of non-ulcer-related dyspepsia that will disappear with eradication of *H. pylori*.[23-25] Therefore, some 35–45% of symptomatic patients with no history of ulcers or proven ulcers may benefit from testing for *H. pylori* and treatment. Decision analysis has shown this to be a cost-effective strategy.[26,27] However, some researchers disagree with this approach because of inconclusive findings of studies of whether *H. pylori* infection causes symptoms of dyspepsia and whether eradication of *H. pylori* infection provides symptomatic relief in patients with dyspepsia. Therefore, it seems that dyspeptic patients should be evaluated for testing and treatment on a case-by-case basis. Since antimicrobial resistance may occur, treating symptomatic patients without testing for *H. pylori* is discouraged. Also, routine screening of the general population for *H. pylori* is not recommended.

The diagnosis of *H. pylori* infection can be made by invasive and noninvasive tests. For symptomatic patients, it must be decided whether endoscopy, an invasive procedure, is needed. A formal diagnostic evaluation, including endoscopy, should be performed if a patient is older than 45 years with new-onset symptoms, is unresponsive to initial therapy, or has "alarm" symptoms like weight loss, bleeding, anemia, and dysphagia.[28] If endoscopy is performed, mucosal samples should be sent for histological testing, rapid urease testing, or both to identify *H. pylori* infection or cancer. Currently, culture of *H. pylori* is not required for initial diagnosis. When endoscopy is indicated, the test of first choice is a urease test

of an antral specimen. This test may be used only in patients not taking bismuth-containing medications, proton-pump inhibitors, or antimicrobials within the past four weeks because these medications decrease the test's sensitivity. Since blood in the gastric lumen may also compromise a urease test of an antral specimen, alternative testing may include histological examination of a specimen taken a distance from the ulcer crater and serologic testing.[15]

When endoscopy is not clinically indicated, antibody detection tests and urea breath tests (UBTs) are also available to detect *H. pylori* infection.[29,30] Antibody detection by serologic or whole-blood testing is safe, easy to perform in the outpatient setting, and inexpensive; however, there may be reduced performance with whole-blood testing in office-based practices. Serologic testing should be considered for patients with no alarm symptoms who have a history of documented ulcers but have not received treatment for *H. pylori*.[31] The nonradioactive (^{13}C) and radioactive (^{14}C) UBTs are more sensitive, specific, and expensive than serologic and whole-blood antibody detection tests and are better suited for follow-up testing to verify eradication.[28] False-negative results with UBTs are infrequent (rate, 1–3%) but can occur for patients currently or recently taking an antisecretory drug, bismuth subsalicylate, or an antimicrobial agent. Although guidelines recommend waiting four weeks after drug discontinuation before testing, recent studies suggest that a true-positive test result occurs one week after discontinuation.[21,32,33] Another noninvasive test was recently developed that detects antigen in the stool of patients with active *H. pylori* infection. Although only a few studies have been performed thus far, stool antigen testing has sensitivity and specificity similar to those of serologic testing and seems to be as effective as the UBT in screening for *H. pylori*.[34,35] Since this simple sampling method does not require trained personnel at the testing site or expensive equipment, the overall cost may be lower than that of other noninvasive tests.

Because testing is expensive, confirmation of *H. pylori* eradication is not necessary in all treated patients. Patients with documented peptic ulcers or with complicated or refractory ulcers should have eradication verified after therapy. This can be done by repeat endoscopy or UBT. Antibody detection by serologic or whole-blood testing is not reliable for confirming eradication and therefore should not be used.[1,21,28] The results of studies examining the role of the stool antigen test for determining posttreatment eradication have been inconsistent; therefore, this test is not currently recommended. Eradication cannot be verified until at least four weeks after the last dose of an antimicrobial and at least seven days after the last dose of a proton-pump inhibitor. Although no organism may appear to be present during these drug clearance intervals, this does not necessarily indicate that the organism has been eradicated from the body. All patients should be followed up clinically to assess symptom response and recurrence. Absence of symptoms upon the completion of antimicrobial therapy in patients who were previously symptomatic has been shown to be a sensitive and specific indicator of eradication of *H. pylori*.[36]

Treatment Regimens

H. pylori eradication, defined as absence of the bacterium four weeks after the completion of drug therapy, has been a challenge to investigators and health care professionals. All currently available treatment regimens have some limitations, and no single regimen is routinely recommended as the treatment of choice. Six regimens have been approved by the Food and Drug Administration (FDA) for treating *H. pylori* infection in patients with duodenal ulcers, and other regimens are endorsed by the Ad Hoc Committee on Practice Parameters of the American College of Gastroenterology (ACG) and the American Digestive Health Foundation (ADHF), an international consensus group. Treatment regimens recommended by ASHP for *H. pylori*-associated peptic ulcer disease are found in Table 1.[37–41]

Selection of an antimicrobial regimen should be based on efficacy (i.e., eradication rate), safety, drug interaction potential, antimicrobial resistance, tolerability, patient compliance with therapy, convenience, and cost. There are no drug regimens for *H. pylori* that are 100% effective; however, clinicians use regimens with eradication rates of 80% and higher with good clinical success. Compliance with the selected regimen directly predicts success, since poor compliance has been shown to decrease eradication rates and promote resistance.[42]

The use of a single drug—either an antisecretory agent or an antimicrobial—has very little efficacy in eradicating *H. pylori* (rates of 20–40%). Although successful treatment may be achieved with the concurrent use of only two drugs (i.e., an antimicrobial plus an antisecretory drug), eradication rates with these regimens are suboptimal, and the risk of antimicrobial resistance with two-drug regimens containing only one antimicrobial is increased. Three- and four-drug regimens containing two antimicrobials are preferred because of their ability to achieve higher eradication rates. In addition, antisecretory therapy as a component of these regimens helps increase eradication rates and reduce ulcer pain more rapidly.

Triple-drug therapy with bismuth subsalicylate, metronidazole, and tetracycline (BMT) has proven to be consistently effective.[43] This regimen received FDA approval on the basis of eradication rates of 77–82% in the submitted data. Other trials found an eradication rate of up to 90%.[44] All patients with an active ulcer being treated with BMT should receive an antisecretory agent. The addition of an H_2-receptor antagonist to BMT has increased eradication rates (89%), but the addition of a proton-pump inhibitor achieved an even higher rate (97%).[40] While many experts still believe 10–14 days of therapy is necessary to achieve high eradication rates, some studies have found a 7-day BMT regimen that includes a proton-pump inhibitor to be successful.[21]

Because of the complexity and approximately 30% adverse-effect rate of BMT, FDA has approved a simpler two-drug regimen that consists of clarithromycin plus omeprazole. This regimen, however, is consistently less effective than triple-drug regimens, may lead to increased resistance problems, and is categorically not recommended.

The addition of a second antimicrobial to two-drug therapy (consisting of clarithromycin plus a proton-pump inhibitor) has been shown to increase efficacy and decrease rates of resistance. FDA approved the combination of clarithromycin, amoxicillin, and lansoprazole for 10–14 days and the combination of clarithromycin, amoxicillin, and omeprazole for 10 days (Table 1). ACG and ADHF endorse the use of clarithromycin plus amoxicillin or metronidazole plus a proton-pump inhibitor. ADHF does not recommend fewer than 14 days of treatment, despite some evidence that shorter regimens can be effective. Some U.S. trials suggest that eradication rates are acceptable with 10 days of triple-drug therapy based on proton-pump inhibitors, but further studies are needed.[21] As investigators and clinicians become more familiar with shorter treatment regimens, recommendations regarding the optimal duration of therapy will need to be reexamined.[21,28]

While two FDA-approved regimens suggest continuing antisecretory therapy beyond the duration of antimicrobial therapy, limited data suggest that this is not necessary to achieve ulcer healing in patients with active, uncomplicated duodenal ulcer disease.[45] However, patients with large, refractory, or bleeding ulcers should continue antisecretory therapy until bacterial eradication has been documented.[28] These high-risk patients should be evaluated for continued long-term antisecretory maintenance therapy on the basis of co-morbidities, severity of illness, and NSAID use.

Triple-drug therapies containing a proton-pump inhibitor are at least as effective as FDA-approved two-drug therapy with omeprazole and clarithromycin and BMT and are associated with better compliance and tolerability than FDA-approved two-drug therapy with omeprazole and clarithromycin or BMT.[46,47] These triple-drug therapies have also been shown to be the most cost-effective. In decision-analytic models of duodenal ulcer disease, metronidazole and clarithromycin or BMT plus a proton-pump inhibitor had consistently lower direct costs and better outcomes than other regimens, including two-drug therapy with omeprazole and clarithromycin.[48,49]

The therapies listed in Table 1 should serve as a guide when choosing an antimicrobial regimen for *H. pylori*-associated peptic ulcer disease. Selection should be based on drug compliance history, allergies, local patterns of antimicrobial resistance, costs, and concomitant disease states. All regimens listed have shown eradication rates that indicate the potential for clinical cure.

The choice of an antimicrobial regimen after a treatment has failed is based on the original regimen. If treatment failure occurs in a patient receiving a clarithromycin-based

Table 1.
ASHP Treatment Recommendations for *Helicobacter pylori*-Associated Peptic Ulcer Disease

Regimen	Eradication Rate(s) (%)
Bismuth subsalicylate 525 mg q.i.d. + metronidazole 250 mg q.i.d. + tetracycline 500 mg q.i.d. each for 14 days + H_2-receptor antagonist in ulcer treatment doses for 28 days[a,b]	77, 82[37]
Clarithromycin 500 mg b.i.d. + amoxicillin 1 g b.i.d. + lansoprazole 30 mg b.i.d. each for 10–14 days[b]	84, 86, 92[38]
Clarithromycin 500 mg b.i.d. + amoxicillin 1 g b.i.d. + omeprazole 20 mg b.i.d. each for 10 days[b]	78, 90[39]
Bismuth subsalicylate 525 mg q.i.d. + metronidazole 500 mg t.i.d. or 250 mg q.i.d. + tetracycline 500 mg q.i.d. + proton-pump inhibitor (omeprazole 20 mg or lansoprazole 30 mg) b.i.d. each for 14 days	97.6[40]
Clarithromycin 500 mg b.i.d. + amoxicillin 1 g b.i.d. + omeprazole 20 mg b.i.d. each for 14 days	92[41]
Clarithromycin 500 mg b.i.d. + metronidazole 500 mg b.i.d. + proton-pump inhibitor (omeprazole 20 mg or lansoprazole 30 mg) b.i.d. each for 14 days	89–91[38]

[a]Ranitidine 150 mg b.i.d. used in trials evaluated for FDA approval.
[b]FDA approved this regimen for duodenal ulcers, but it also appears to be effective for gastric ulcers.

regimen, a triple-drug regimen not containing clarithromycin should be initiated; the same is true for metronidazole-based triple-drug therapies. If a patient does not respond to metronidazole, omeprazole, and clarithromycin, then the combination of BMT and a proton-pump inhibitor should be utilized. If a patient does not respond to two courses of eradication therapy, culture and susceptibility testing is necessary and a gastroenterologist should be consulted.

Antimicrobial Resistance

Worldwide antimicrobial resistance is a major determinant of the efficacy of eradication therapy for *H. pylori* infection, especially in the cases of metronidazole and clarithromycin. In geographic regions with a high prevalence of resistance to metronidazole, eradication rates with BMT may be 40–50% lower than in other areas. In the United States, resistance is lower than in European countries, and overall eradication rates with BMT remain close to 90%. However, U.S. data from 1993–99 suggest that primary resistance to metronidazole and clarithromycin is increasing.[50] Metronidazole resistance (defined as a minimum inhibitory concentration [MIC] of ≥32 µg/mL) was highly variable but increased from 8.7% in 1993 to 24.6% in 1999. Clarithromycin resistance (MIC, ≥1 µg/mL) increased significantly from 4.3% in 1993 to 10.5% in 1998 before dropping slightly in 1999 to 8.6%. Evaluating the relationship between clinical outcome and in vitro susceptibility of *H. pylori* to metronidazole is complicated by the lack of a standard method for determining MICs for *H. pylori*.[51] This increasing resistance may begin to have an impact on eradication rates and clinical outcomes in the United States.

The use of triple-drug therapy based on a proton-pump inhibitor (e.g., omeprazole, metronidazole, and clarithromycin) or of BMT plus a proton-pump inhibitor has been shown to be minimally affected by resistance to metronidazole in the United States. Resistance to clarithromycin is less common but may prove a larger obstacle to eradication than metronidazole resistance. The use of a clarithromycin-containing regimen when a resistant isolate is present has achieved eradication in less than 25% of patients.[52]

Role of the Pharmacist

Pharmacists should play a frontline role in the identification and treatment of patients with *H. pylori*-associated peptic ulcer disease. Pharmacists can identify candidates for *H. pylori* testing from prescription-refill lists for patients receiving maintenance antisecretory therapy to prevent ulcer recurrence. Preventing unnecessary testing and promoting appropriate testing for *H. pylori* are important aspects of pharmacy involvement in peptic ulcer management. Pharmacists in all practice settings should work to ensure that appropriate combination therapy is initiated and that monitoring for drug interactions and adverse effects is adequate.[53] Pharmacists can also assist in identifying patients who no longer require long-term antisecretory therapy once *H. pylori* has been successfully eradicated. Patients who request nonprescription H$_2$-receptor antagonists or antacids should be counseled on whether their symptoms warrant seeing a physician for further diagnostic evaluation.

Pharmacists are currently providing many of these services, sometimes from a specialty clinic. Pharmacist-managed clinics focusing on *H. pylori*-associated peptic ulcer disease have shown real benefit in improving patient care and decreasing the use of antisecretory therapy.[54–57] Published reports of pharmacist-managed *H. pylori* clinics indicate that patients are identified either by having received long-term maintenance acid suppression therapy or by referral from their primary care provider or team. In these clinics, not only do pharmacists identify patients, they also use serologic testing to identify *H. pylori;* choose treatment strategies based on patients' individual characteristics; counsel patients about the disease, treatment expectations, drug regimens, and adverse effects; and initiate follow-up at predetermined times. A cost avoidance of approximately $20,000 per year has been documented in two independent studies of pharmacist-managed *H. pylori* clinics treating 50–150 patients per year.[56,58] By discontinuing unneeded maintenance therapy, curing patients with antimicrobial regimens, and counseling patients about their drug therapy and disease, pharmacists can optimize patient care and contribute to an institution's cost-savings initiatives.

Since most of the regimens for treating *H. pylori*-associated peptic ulcer disease are complex, counseling patients about the importance of drug compliance is one of the most important activities a pharmacist can perform to improve eradication rates. Plans for increasing compliance may be suggested, such as taking medications with normal daily activities to help fit a routine and using compliance aids and calendars.

Patients and prescribers should understand that the usual precaution of separating tetracycline administration from the ingestion of food and bismuth subsalicylate is not necessary when tetracycline is used to treat *H. pylori* infection because its effect is local, not systemic. However, patients should still be cautioned about tetracycline–drug interactions that result from chelation (e.g., with calcium or iron), since this interaction inhibits tetracycline's ability to act locally. Pharmacists need to inform patients with gastroesophageal reflux disease (GERD) that GERD symptoms sometimes worsen after treatment. Worsened symptoms of GERD may be due to a loss of *H. pylori*-secreted ammonia buffering the gastric juice, an increase in acid secretion after healing of gastritis, or the possibility that proton-pump inhibitors may be less effective in an *H. pylori*-negative stomach.[57,59] Patients taking metronidazole should be warned about potential drug interactions (e.g., involving alcohol or warfarin). Patients should also be counseled about alarm symptoms (e.g., weight loss, bleeding, anemia, and dysphagia). Pharmacists are ideally suited to informing patients about peptic ulcer disease and answering questions about the disease or the treatment regimens. Patients who are knowledgeable about their disease are more likely to understand the importance of compliance with medication regimens. Pharmacists should explain the association between *H. pylori* infection and peptic ulcer disease, the tests that may be performed to detect *H. pylori*, treatment regimens, and adverse effects that may occur with specific treatment regimens.

Summary

ASHP supports the identification and treatment of *H. pylori* infection in appropriate patients as an effective method of reducing the morbidity and mortality associated with peptic ulcer disease. Successful and safe therapy requires extensive patient education and monitoring by qualified health care professionals to maximize patient understanding of and compliance with medication regimens and to minimize adverse events. Pharmacists are key to ensuring that patients use prescribed regimens appropriately so that *H. pylori* is eradicated and that clinical outcomes of associated peptic ulcer disease are optimal.

References

1. National Institutes of Health Consensus Panel on *Helicobacter pylori* in Peptic Ulcer Disease. *Helicobacter pylori* in peptic ulcer disease. *JAMA.* 1994; 272:65–9.

2. Puera DA. The report of the Digestive Health Initiative International Update Conference on *Helicobacter pylori. Gastroenterology.* 1997; 113:S4–8.

3. Soll AH, for the Practice Parameters Committee of the American College of Gastroenterology. Medical treatment of peptic ulcer disease. Practice guidelines. *JAMA.* 1996; 275:622–9.

4. Robinson DM, Abdel-Rahman SM, Nahata MC. Guidelines for the treatment of *Helicobacter pylori* in the pediatric population. *Ann Pharmacother.* 1997; 31:1247–9.

5. *Helicobacter pylori* and peptic ulcer disease. www.cdc.gov./ulcer/md.htm (accessed. 2000 Oct 2).

6. Wolfe MM, Lichtenstein DR, Singh G. Medical progress: gastrointestinal toxicity of nonsteroidal anti-inflammatory drugs. *N Engl J Med.* 1999; 340:1888–99.

7. National Digestive Disease Information Clearinghouse. Digestive diseases in the United States: epidemiology and impact. Washington, DC: Public Health Service, 1994; NIH publication no. 94-1447.

8. Sonnenberg A, Everhart J. Health impact of peptic ulcer in the United States. *Am J Gastroenterol.* 1997; 92:614–20.

9. Walsh JH, Peterson WL. The treatment of *Helicobacter pylori* infection in the management of peptic ulcer disease. *N Engl J Med.* 1995; 333:984–91.

10. Roll J, Weng A, Newman J. Diagnosis and treatment of *Helicobacter pylori* infection among California Medicare patients. *Arch Intern Med.* 1997; 157:994–8.

11. Peterson WL, Ciociola AA, Sykes DL and the RBC *H. pylori* Study Group. Ranitidine bismuth citrate plus clarithromycin is effective for healing duodenal ulcers, eradicating *H. pylori* and reducing ulcer recurrence. *Aliment Pharmacol Ther.* 1996; 10:251–61.

12. Goodwin CS, Mendall MM, Northfield TC. *Helicobacter pylori* infection. *Lancet.* 1997; 349:265–9.

13. Hood HM, Wark C, Burgess PA, et al. Screening for *Helicobacter pylori* and nonsteroidal anti-inflammatory drug use in Medicare patients hospitalized with peptic ulcer disease. *Arch Intern Med.* 1999; 159:149–54.

14. Centers for Disease Control and Prevention. Knowledge about causes of peptic ulcer disease in the United States: March-April 1997. *MMWR.* 1997; 46:985–7.

15. Pounder RE, Williams MP. The treatment of *Helicobacter pylori* infection. *Aliment Pharmacol Ther.* 1997; 11(suppl 1):35–41.

16. Laine L, Hopkins R, Girardi L. Has the impact of *Helicobacter pylori* therapy on ulcer recurrence in the United States been overstated? A meta-analysis of rigorously designed trials. *Am J Gastroenterol.* 1998; 93:1409–15.

17. Sonnenberg A, Townsend WF. Costs of duodenal ulcer therapy with antibiotics. *Arch Intern Med.* 1995; 155:922–8.

18. Taylor JL, Zagari M, Murphy K, et al. Pharmacoeconomic comparison of treatments for the eradication of *Helicobacter pylori. Arch Intern Med.* 1997; 157:87–97.

19. Vakil N, Fennerty MB. Cost-effectiveness of treatment regimens for the eradication of *Helicobacter pylori* in duodenal ulcer. *Am J Gastroenterol.* 1996; 91:239–45.

20. Fendrick AM, McCort JT, Chernew ME, et al. Immediate eradication of *Helicobacter pylori* in patients with previously documented peptic ulcer disease: clinical and economic effects. *Am J Gastroenterol.* 1997; 92:2017–24.

21. Howden CW, Hunt RH. Guidelines for the management of *Helicobacter pylori* infection. *Am J Gastroenterol.* 1998; 93:2330–8.

22. Breuer T, Goodman KJ, Malaty HM, et al. How do clinicians practicing in the U.S. manage *Helicobacter pylori*-related gastrointestinal diseases? A comparison of primary care and specialist physicians. *Am J Gastroenterol.* 1998; 98:553–61.

23. Blum AL, Talley NJ, O'Morain C, et al. Lack of effect of treating *Helicobacter pylori* infection in patients with nonulcer dyspepsia. *N Engl J Med.* 1998; 339:1875–81.

24. McColl K, Murray L, El-Omar E, et al. Symptomatic benefit from eradicating *Helicobacter pylori* infection in patients with nonulcer dyspepsia. *N Engl J Med.* 1998; 339:1869–74.

25. Friedman LS. *Helicobacter pylori* and nonulcer dyspepsia. *N Engl J Med.* 1998; 339:1928–30. Editorial.

26. Fendrick AM, Chernew ME, Hirth RA, et al. Alternative management strategies for patients with suspected peptic ulcer disease. *Ann Intern Med.* 1995; 123:260–8.

27. Ofman JJ, Etchason J, Fullerton S, et al. Management strategies for *Helicobacter pylori*-seropositive patients with dyspepsia: clinical and economic consequences. *Ann Intern Med.* 1997; 126:280–91.

28. American Digestive Health Foundation. The report of the Digestive Health Initiative International Update Conference on *Helicobacter pylori. Gastroenterology.* 1998; 113:S4–8.

29. Atherton JC. Non-endoscopic tests in the diagnosis of *Helicobacter pylori* infection. *Aliment Pharmacol Ther.* 1997; 11(suppl 1):11–20.

30. Savarino V, Vigneri S, Celle G. The 13C urea breath test in the diagnosis of *Helicobacter pylori* infection. *Gut.* 1999; 45(suppl 1):118–22.

31. Cutler AF, Havstad S, Ma CK, et al. Accuracy of invasive and noninvasive tests to diagnose *Helicobacter pylori* infection. *Gastroenterology.* 1995; 109:136–41.

32. Savarino V, Bisso G, Pivari M, et al. Effect of gastric acid suppression on 13C urea breath test: comparison of ranitidine with omeprazole. *Aliment Pharmacol Ther.* 2000; 14:291–7.

33. Connor SJ, Seow F, Ngu MC, et al. The effect of dosing with omeprazole on the accuracy of the 13C urea breath test in *Helicobacter pylori* infected subjects. *Aliment Pharmacol Ther.* 1999; 13:1287–93.

34. Vaira D, Malfertheiner P, Megraud F, et al. Diagnosis of *Helicobacter pylori* infection with a new non-invasive antigen-based assay. *Lancet.* 1999; 354:30–3.

35. Braden B, Teuber G, Dietrich CF, et al. Comparison of new faecal antigen test with (13)C-urea breath test for detecting *Helicobacter pylori* infection and monitoring eradication treatment: prospective clinical evaluation. *BMJ*. 2000; 320:148.

36. Phull PS, Halliday D, Price AB, et al. Absence of dyspeptic symptoms as a test for *Helicobacter pylori* eradication. *BMJ*. 1996; 312:349–50.

37. Peura D. *Helicobacter pylori:* rational management options. *Am J Med*. 1998; 105:424–30.

38. Prevpac package insert. Deerfield, IL: Tap Pharmaceuticals; 1999 Jan.

39. Biaxin package insert. North Chicago, IL: Abbott Laboratories; 2000 Apr.

40. Borody TJ, Andrews P, Fracchia G, et al. Omeprazole enhances efficacy of triple therapy in eradicating *Helicobacter pylori*. *Gut*. 1995; 37:477–81.

41. Laine L, Estrada R, Trujillo M, et al. Randomized comparison of differing periods of twice-a-day triple therapy for the eradication of *Helicobacter pylori*. *Aliment Pharmacol Ther*. 1996; 10:1029–33.

42. Graham DY, Lew GM, Malaty HM, et al. Factors influencing the eradication of *Helicobacter pylori* with triple therapy. *Gastroenterology*. 1992; 102:493–6.

43. Salcedo JA, Al-Kawas F. Treatment of *Helicobacter pylori* infection. *Arch Intern Med*. 1998; 158:842–51.

44. Graham D, Lew G, Klein P, et al. Effect of treatment of *Helicobacter pylori* infection on the long-term recurrence of gastric or duodenal ulcer. *Ann Intern Med*. 1992; 116:705–8.

45. Goh KL, Navaratnam P, Peh SC, et al. *Helicobacter pylori* eradication with short-term therapy leads to duodenal ulcer healing without the need for continued acid suppression therapy. *Eur J Gastroenterol Hepatol*. 1996; 8:421–3.

46. De Boer WA, Tytgat GN. Treatment of *Helicobacter pylori* infection. *BMJ*. 2000; 320:31–4.

47. Peterson WL, Fendrick M, Cave DR, et al. *Helicobacter pylori*-related disease. *Arch Intern Med*. 2000; 160:1285–91.

48. Taylor JL, Zagari M, Murphy K, et al. Pharmacoeconomic comparison of treatments for the eradication of *Helicobacter pylori*. *Arch Intern Med*. 1997; 157:87–97.

49. Vakil N, Fennerty B. Cost-effectiveness of treatment regimens for *H. pylori* infection based on a community practice effectiveness study. *Gastroenterology*. 1997; 112:A47. Abstract.

50. Meyer JM, Higgins KM, Wang W, et al. Evaluation of risk factors in The Surveillance of *Helicobacter pylori* Antimicrobial Resistance Partnership (SHARP) in the United States from 1993–1999. *Gastroenterology*. 2000; 118(suppl):A677.

51. Solnick JV. Antibiotic resistance in *Helicobacter pylori*. *Clin Infect Dis*. 1998; 27:90–2. Editorial.

52. Graham DY, de Boer WA, Tytgat GNJ. Choosing the best anti-*Helicobacter pylori* therapy: effect of antimicrobial resistance. *Am J Gastroenterol*. 1996; 91:1072–6.

53. Berardi RR. Peptic ulcer disease. In: DiPiro JT, Talbert RL, Yee GC, et al., eds. Pharmacotherapy: a pathophysiologic approach. 4th ed. Stamford, CT: Appleton & Lange; 1999:548–70.

54. Segarra-Newnham M, Siebert WF. Development and outcomes of an ambulatory clinic for *Helicobacter pylori* treatment. *Hosp Pharm*. 1998; 33:205–9.

55. Morreale AP. Pharmacist-managed *Helicobacter pylori* clinic. *Am J Health-Syst Pharm*. 1995; 52:183–5.

56. Forster K, Koo J, Heyworth MF. A pharmacist-managed *Helicobacter pylori* VAMC clinic. *P&T*. 1999; 24:184–7.

57. Labenz J, Blum AL, Bayerdorffer E, et al. Curing *Helicobacter pylori* infection in patients with duodenal ulcer may provoke reflux esophagitis. *Gastroenterology*. 1997; 112:1442–7.

58. Patchin GM, Wieland KA, Carmichael JM. Six months' experience with a pharmacist-run *Helicobacter pylori* treatment clinic. *Am J Health-Syst Pharm*. 1996; 53:2081–2.

59. O'Connor HJ. *Helicobacter pylori* and gastro-oesophageal reflux disease—clinical implications and management. *Aliment Pharmacol Ther*. 1999; 13:117–27.

Approved by the ASHP Board of Directors on November 11, 2000.

The bibliographic citation for this document is as follows: American Society of Health-System Pharmacists. ASHP therapeutic position statement on the identification and treatment of *Helicobacter pylori*-associated peptic ulcer disease in adults. *Am J Health-Syst Pharm*. 2001; 58:331–7.

ASHP Therapeutic Position Statement on the Safe Use of Pharmacotherapy for Obesity Management in Adults

Statement of Position

ASHP supports the safe and appropriate use of pharmacotherapy for weight loss in carefully selected adult patients at risk for obesity-related comorbidities. When indicated, weight-loss agents should be used only as an adjunct to dietary therapy, increased physical activity, and behavioral therapy by patients who have not successfully responded to these modalities. Pharmacotherapy should not be used solely for cosmetic weight loss or weight loss in patients with a low level of health risks. ASHP encourages pharmacists to work with patients and other health care providers to promote lifestyle changes as the primary treatment modality and to monitor the effectiveness and safety of weight-loss agents, when prescribed. The availability of nonprescription weight-loss products gives pharmacists a unique opportunity to educate patients about the effectiveness, potential adverse effects, and drug interactions of these medications.

Background

Obesity is a major public health concern because of its increasing prevalence and associated health risks. In this document, obesity and overweight are defined by body mass index (BMI), which is correlated with total body fat and estimates the relative risk of disease. BMI is calculated by weight in kilograms divided by height in meters squared (kg/m^2). Overweight is defined as a BMI of 25–29.9 kg/m^2, and obesity is defined as a BMI of $\geq$30 kg/m^2.[1]

It is estimated that 54% of U.S. adults over age 20 years are overweight, and the prevalence of obesity increased from 12.8% in 1960 to 22.5% in 1994.[1,2] These estimates are of concern because of the excessive health risks associated with obesity, including coronary heart disease, hypertension, type 2 diabetes mellitus, dyslipidemia, sleep apnea, osteoarthritis, and certain forms of cancer (e.g., endometrial, breast, prostate, and colon).[3] The negative health consequences of obesity make it the second leading cause of preventable death in the United States and impart a significant economic and psychosocial effect on society.[4] In 1990, obesity and its associated comorbidities contributed to $46 billion in direct costs and $23 billion in indirect costs in the United States.[5] In addition, obese persons report a decreased quality of life and frequently suffer from discrimination.[6] Reducing the health, financial, and psychosocial burdens of obesity has become a public health initiative. "Healthy People 2010," a project that defined national health goals, included several objectives, such as increasing the proportion of people at a healthy weight (BMI of 18.5–24.9 kg/m^2), decreasing the proportion of obese adults, and increasing regular physical activity.[7]

Management of Obesity

Obesity is the result of energy intake exceeding energy expenditure. Although the etiology of obesity is not completely understood, it is linked to several metabolic, genetic, and environmental factors.[8] Medications, such as glucocorticoids, insulin, sulfonylureas, antidepressants, progestins, and antipsychotics, can contribute to weight gain.[9]

Obesity is now recognized as a chronic disease that requires treatment to reduce its associated health risks. Although weight loss is an important treatment outcome, the main goal of obesity management should be to improve cardiovascular and metabolic values to reduce obesity-related morbidity and mortality. A 5–10% loss of body weight can substantially improve metabolic values, such as blood glucose, blood pressure, and lipid concentrations.[1] In addition, a 5–10% intentional reduction in body weight may reduce morbidity and mortality.[10] Therefore, one goal of obesity management should be an initial 10% weight loss to reduce health risks and improve patients' quality of life.[1] To retain the benefits of weight loss, obesity management should also include methods to maintain a lower body weight. Primary treatment modalities include dietary therapy, exercise, and behavior modification. Select patients may benefit from pharmacotherapy or surgical intervention. A discussion of treatment modalities other than pharmacotherapy is outside the scope of this statement, but resources and additional guidelines for the diagnosis and nonpharmacologic management of obesity can be found in the appendix.

Pharmacotherapy

Currently available prescription drugs for managing obesity reduce weight by inducing satiety or decreasing dietary fat absorption. Satiety is achieved by increasing synaptic levels of norepinephrine, serotonin, or both. Stimulation of serotonin receptor subtypes 1B, 1D, and 2C and α_1- and β_2-adrenergic receptors decreases food intake by regulating satiety.[11] Adrenergic agents (e.g., diethylpropion, benzphetamine, phendimetrazine, mazindol, and phentermine) act by modulating central norepinephrine and dopamine receptors through the promotion of catecholamine release. Aside from phentermine, other adrenergic agents are infrequently used, perhaps because of the lack of long-term, well-controlled data or the fear of their potential abuse.[12] Older adrenergic weight-loss drugs (e.g., amphetamine, methamphetamine, and phenmetrazine), which strongly engage in dopamine pathways, are no longer recommended because of the risk of their abuse.

Fenfluramine and dexfenfluramine, both serotonergic agents used to regulate appetite, are no longer available for use. Selective serotonin-reuptake inhibitor (SSRI) antidepressants have been studied for their effect on weight control, but results have shown limited effectiveness. Therefore, their use for this indication cannot be recommended at this time, either alone or in combination with phentermine.[13] New treatment options include sibutramine and orlistat. Sibutramine acts as a reuptake inhibitor of both norepinephrine and serotonin to regulate satiety.[14] Orlistat inhibits pancreatic lipase to reduce the absorption of dietary fat.[15]

Multiple discoveries, including the adipose-tissue protein leptin, neuropeptide-Y antagonism, β_3 stimulation, α_2 antagonism, and other hormonal or metabolic pathways, will lead to further research into compounds that may be effective for weight control. The roles of these chemicals and pathways are currently under investigation.[8,16] Drugs that do not currently have FDA-approved labeling for managing obesity, such as thyroid hormone, bupropion, and topiramate, are supported by limited data for this indication and cannot be recommended at this time.[12,17–19]

Efficacy

When used in conjunction with dietary therapy and exercise, pharmacotherapy typically results in modest weight reductions of 2–10 kg during the first six months.[13] This can be compared with a weight loss of about 8% by using a low-calorie diet for at least 6 months and an additional 1.5–3-kg loss if the diet is combined with physical activity for 9–24 months.[1] After six months of pharmacotherapy, minimal weight loss occurs, and weight is usually maintained if the drug is continued. In some patients, weight regain may occur despite continuous drug treatment. After drug discontinuation, weight is frequently regained to pretreatment levels or higher.

Because of the chronic nature of obesity and the need for long-term therapy in some patients, evaluation of drug efficacy studies should focus on those that provide placebo-controlled data for at least one year of therapy and posttherapy follow-up. Phentermine has not been studied as a monotherapy for longer than 36 weeks or approved for administration longer than a few weeks.[20] The combination of phentermine and fenfluramine has been evaluated for long-term use, and results have revealed improved efficacy and reduced adverse effects when compared with either agent alone.[21] Although fenfluramine and dexfenfluramine are no longer available, clinical studies of fenfluramine–phentermine therapy or dexfenfluramine alone revealed sustained weight loss over at least one year of treatment and serve as a benchmark for future drug evaluations.[21,22] Combined use of phentermine and fluoxetine has been reported, but no controlled data are available to recommend the use of this combination. A 24-week study of sibutramine showed dose-related weight loss with a mean 5.5-kg weight loss compared with placebo for study completers.[23] The results of a second study revealed a 3.0-kg mean difference for sibutramine 10 mg compared with placebo and a 4.3-kg mean difference for sibutramine 15 mg versus placebo for study completers at one year.[24] Another one-year study showed a 5.7-kg mean difference for sibutramine 10 mg versus placebo at study completion; subjects in this study entered a very-low-calorie diet phase for four weeks before drug or placebo administration.[25] Orlistat has been shown to provide sustained weight loss for up to two years of therapy[26,27] (Tables 1 and 2). Combinations of available agents have not been evaluated for safety or efficacy and cannot be recommended at this time. Pharmacists should ensure that patients are not currently taking other prescription, nonprescription, or herbal preparations for weight loss before recommending or dispensing prescription weight-loss medications.

Safety and Adverse Effects

The safety of prescription weight-loss agents is a source of debate among health care professionals. Adverse effects can be divided into two categories: those that occur shortly after initiating therapy that are dose-related minor effects, and the rare but serious effects that can occur long after therapy has begun. Initial adverse effects are directly related to the drug's mechanism of action and are often mild and transient. They can frequently be avoided by dosage and schedule adjustments, careful drug selection for patients at high risk for these effects, and appropriate patient education and monitoring after initiating therapy or following dosage adjustments.

Adverse effects related to adrenergic drugs, such as phentermine, include headache, insomnia, nervousness, irritability, tachycardia, hypertension, and palpitations. Sedative effects of serotonergic drugs include lethargy, somnolence, and asthenia. Other adverse effects of these agents include dry mouth, nausea, diarrhea, constipation, dreams or nightmares, and dizziness. The most common adverse effects of sibutramine are headache (30.3% versus 18.6% for placebo), dry mouth (17.2% versus 4.2% for placebo), constipation (11.5% versus 6.0% for placebo), and insomnia (10.7% versus 4.5% for placebo).[28] When compared with placebo, sibutramine has been associated with a mean increase in systolic or diastolic blood pressure (1–3 mm Hg) and heart rate (4–5 beats/min) in normotensive patients or patients with controlled hypertension. These effects can be serious, especially in patients with preexisting hypertension. The incidence of increased blood pressure is 2.1% for sibutramine compared with 0.9% for placebo.[28] Pharmacists should recommend or provide blood pressure monitoring for patients on sibutramine therapy. Sibutramine is contraindicated in patients with uncontrolled or poorly controlled hypertension.[28]

Orlistat is minimally absorbed, causing gastrointestinal effects, such as oily spotting (26.6% versus 1.3% for placebo), flatulence (23.9% versus 1.4% for placebo), fecal urgency (22.1% versus 6.7% for placebo), oily stool (20.0% versus 2.9% for placebo), oily evacuation (11.9% versus 0.8% for placebo), increased defecation (10.8% versus 4.1% for placebo), and fecal incontinence (7.7% versus 0.9% for placebo) (incidences are those reported for the first year of treatment with orlistat).[29] Despite these effects, completion rates and main reasons for withdrawal from clinical trials did not differ between orlistat and placebo users.[27] To minimize or avoid these fat-intake-related effects, patients should comply with a low-fat diet (less than 30% of calories derived from fat). Consulting a registered dietitian about dietary modifications to reduce fat intake would also benefit patients. Pharmacists should assess patients for and counsel them about potential adverse effects. Pharmacists should also explain to patients that orlistat is useful only if taken with a meal containing some fat; a dose should be skipped when a meal is fat free, since orlistat has no value in this situation.

Before prescribing any weight-loss agents, clinicians should determine if patients are at high risk for adverse effects from therapy or if any drug-specific contraindications are applicable (Table 2). None of the weight-loss drugs is approved for use in pregnant or lactating women or in pediatric patients as safety in these populations has not been established.

Sibutramine and orlistat are approved for one year and two years of therapy, respectively. The efficacy and safety of using these medications longer than two years are currently unknown. The possible long-term effects identified with older weight-loss agents raise concerns about the safety of prolonged use of weight-loss drugs in general. Cardiac valve abnormalities, potentially attributable to the serotonergic agents fenfluramine and dexfenfluramine, were reported in July 1997 and led to the voluntary withdrawal of these drugs from the market in September 1997.[30] At that time, data submitted to FDA from the echocardiograms of 291 asymptomatic patients exposed to fenfluramine or dexfenfluramine showed that approximately 30% had valvular abnormalities. More recent data suggest a lower prevalence (9–14%) of aortic regurgitation in anorectic-treated patients, which was significantly higher than in the untreated, and no increase of other valvular abnormalities was demonstrated.[31] A strong relationship between the occurrence of aortic regurgitation and the duration of drug therapy was also described, with the incidence climbing to 21.2% in patients receiving these drugs for longer than 18 months. The Centers for Disease Control and Prevention issued public health recommendations for patients exposed to fenfluramine and dexfenfluramine.[32] Echocardiographic evaluations of small numbers of patients receiving sibu-tramine treatment did not reveal cardiac abnormalities.[33] Sibutramine's action as a serotonin-reuptake inhibitor, rather than a serotonin-releasing agent, may reduce this drug's risk of causing valvular abnormalities. Until more data are available, patients should be made aware of this potential risk and carefully monitored. No cardiac abnormalities have been reported with orlistat use.

Primary pulmonary hypertension has been associated with the use of many weight-loss drugs, especially if prescribed longer than three months.[34,35] The mechanism for drug-induced primary pulmonary hypertension is unknown, but is postulated to be related to elevated serotonin levels, which cause pulmonary vasoconstriction. Although the risk of this adverse effect is extremely low (approximately 1 in 500,000),[34] patients receiving long-term anorectic therapy should be carefully questioned about dyspnea, chest pain, syncope, and edema and instructed to report any symptoms during therapy and within the first year following cessation of weight-loss drugs. The medication should be discontinued if these symptoms are considered possibly related to drug therapy.

Data from animal studies have provided some evidence of brain serotonin neurotoxicity caused by fenfluramine and dexfenfluramine use.[35] Serotonin plays a role in cognition, memory, mood, anxiety, aggression, sleep, and other neurologic functions. No clinical data exist showing drug induced neurotoxicity in humans. However, the potential for human clinical consequences of serotonin neurotoxicity are unknown, and further investigation of newer agents may be required.

Orlistat has been shown to reduce serum concentrations of fat-soluble vitamins (vitamins A, D, E, and K). Although most patients' plasma levels remained within normal ranges during clinical trials, a daily multivitamin supplement containing fat-soluble vitamins at bedtime is recommended. During Phase III and IV clinical trials of orlistat, 11 cases of breast cancer were reported. This is not believed to be related to orlistat use because the drug is minimally absorbed and the cancer preceded patients' study enrollment in the majority of cases. More recent studies were conducted by the manufacturer and have not reproduced these findings.[36]

Drug Interactions

The potential for drug–drug interactions should be assessed before initiating weight-loss agents. The combination of phentermine or sibutramine with monoamine oxidase inhibitors (MAOIs) is contraindicated, and at least 14 days should elapse between the administration of these agents.[28,37] Recent information indicates that phentermine has monoamine oxidase-inhibiting properties, suggesting that it should not be combined with other weight-loss medications.[38] Sibutramine

is not currently approved for use with other weight-loss drugs.[28] The risk of serotonin syndrome from the combination of serotonergic agents and sibutramine is not completely clear. Because sibutramine inhibits serotonin reuptake, combinations of sibutramine and other serotonergic drugs should be avoided, if possible.[28] If such a combination is prescribed, patients should be instructed about the signs and symptoms of this syndrome, including excitement, hypomania, restlessness, loss of consciousness, confusion, disorientation, anxiety, agitation, motor weakness, myoclonus, tremor, hyperreflexia, ataxia, incoordination, hyperthermia, shivering pupillary dilation, diaphoresis, emesis, and tachycardia, and how to reach medical help if they experience any of these symptoms.[39] Because of the serotonergic and adrennergic effects of many herbal weight-loss preparations (e.g., St. John's wort, ephedra), patients should be cautioned not to take these with sibutramine or phentermine. In addition, sibutramine is metabolized by the cytochrome P-450 isoenzyme 3A4, and inhibition or induction of this system may affect sibutramine plasma concentrations. In single-dose studies, orlistat decreased the absorption of fat-soluble vitamin supplements. Orlistat and cyclosporine should not be coadministered because of orlistat's potential to reduce cyclosporine levels, and doses of these drugs should be administered at least two hours apart. Patients should have their cyclosporine levels monitored more frequently if they are receiving concomitant therapy with orlistat.[29] In addition, patients taking other medications with a narrow therapeutic index (e.g., warfarin), which may be affected by fat malabsorption, should be closely monitored.

Other Therapeutic Options

There are many weight-loss products available to patients without a prescription. Products may include single components or combinations of ingredients, such as ephedrine, caffeine, benzocaine, chromium, psyllium, chitosan, and herbal preparations. Herbal ingredients frequently include ma huang (*Ephedra sinica*), St. John's wort (*Hypericum perforatum*), guarana (*Paulinia cupana*), kola nut (*Cola nitida, Cola acuminata,* and *Garcinia cola*), hydroxycitric acid (*Garcinia cambogia*), and others. These agents reportedly induce weight loss through various mechanisms. For example, ephedrine, ma huang, caffeine, guarana, and kola nut cause stimulatory effects, St. John's wort promotes the serotonergic regulation of satiety, ephedrine and ma huang induce thermogenesis, while psyllium and chitosan rely on their bulk formation to decrease hunger and fat absorption, respectively. Although these products are widely promoted to the public, there are few data to support their efficacy or safety as agents for weight reduction and long-term maintenance of weight loss. Controlled studies using chitosan or *G. cambogia* for weight reduction have revealed that their use was of no benefit.[40,41] No long-term data (longer than one year) are available for any of these agents.

Clinicians and patients should be cautious when using these products as there is a lack of available data to support the benefits of their use and their potential adverse effects. The results of the Hemorrhagic Stroke Project suggest that phenylpropanolamine found in appetite suppressants is an independent risk factor for hemorrhagic stroke in women.[42] The significant implications of this study prompted FDA to take steps in October 2000 to remove phenylpropanolamine from the market by requesting that all drug companies discontinue selling products that contain phenylpropanola-

Table 1.
Major Efficacy Studies of Prescription Weight-Loss Agents

Reference	No. Patients[a]	Treatment	Behavorial Modification	Duration of Active Treatment and Follow-up	Results[b]
Phentermine Resin (PHEN)					
20	108 (64)	PHEN 30 mg q.d. continuous vs. PHEN 30 mg q.d. 4 wk alternating with placebo for 4 wk vs. placebo	Calorie-restricted diet	36-wk active treatment, no follow-up after discontinuation	Weight loss at 36 wk: 12.2 kg for PHEN continuous, 13.0 kg for alternating regimen (as effective as continuous PHEN therapy). 4.8 kg for placebo
57	30 (22)	PHEN 30 mg q.d. vs. placebo	Calorie-restricted diet	3-mo active treatment, follow-up 3 mo after discontinuation	Weight loss at 3 mo: 5.8 kg for PHEN, 2.6 kg for placebo; weight loss at 6 mo: 6.3 kg for PHEN, 4.5 kg for placebo (not significantly different)
Fenfluramine (F) [c] + Phentermine Resin (PHEN)					
21[d]					
Phase I	121 (112)	F 60 mg extended release + PHEN 15 mg vs. placebo	Behavior modification sessions, diet, exercise	Wk 0–34: randomized, placebo controlled	Weight loss at 34 wk: 14.3 kg for treatment group, 4.6 kg for placebo group
Phase II	112 (83)	F + PHEN continuous vs. F + PHEN intermittent		Wk 34–104: open label	Weight loss at 104 wk: 12.6 kg for continuous treatment, 11.6 kg for intermittent treatment
Phase III	77 (59)	F + PHEN		Wk 104–156: open-label dosage adjustment	Weight loss at 156 wk: 9.4 kg below baseline
Phase IV	52 (51)	F 60 mg extended release + PHEN 15 mg vs. placebo		Wk 156–190: double blind, randomized	
Phase V	51 (48)	No medication		Wk 190–210: follow-up	Gained 2.7 kg after drug discontinuation; weight loss maintained in select patients, suggesting highly individualized success rate
Dexfenfluramine (D) [c]					
22	822 (483)	D 15 mg b.i.d. vs. placebo	Calorie-restricted diet	1-yr active treatment, no follow-up after discontinuation	Weight loss at 1 yr: 9.8 kg for treatment group, 7.2 kg for placebo; more than twice as many pts. lost >10% of initial weight in the D group
Sibutramine (S)					
23	1047 (683)	S 1, 5, 10, 15, 20, or 30 mg vs. placebo	Not stated	24-wk active treatment, no follow-up after discontinuation	Dose-related weight loss did not plateau at 24 wk, ranged from 8.3 kg with S 30 mg to 0.9 kg with placebo

Reference	No. of patients enrolling (completing)[a]	Drug regimen[c]	Diet	Duration[d]	Results[b]
25	205 (159)	S 10 mg q.d. vs. placebo	Very-low-calorie diet for initial 4 wk prior to drug/placebo therapy	12-mo active treatment, 3-mo follow-up after discontinuation	Predrug diet phase weight loss: 7.7 kg for S group, 7.4 kg for placebo group, weight change at 1-yr active treatment +0.5 kg for placebo group and −5.2 kg for S group, weight loss primarily in first 6 mo of S therapy
Orlistat (ORL)					
24	485 (256)	S 10 or 15 mg q.d. vs. placebo	Not stated	1-yr active treatment, no follow-up after discontinuation	Weight loss at 1 yr: 4.8 kg for S 10-mg group, 6.1 kg for S 15-mg group, 1.8 kg for placebo; 39% of pts. on S 15 mg lost at least 10% of body weight
26	688 (435)	ORL120 mg t.i.d. vs. placebo; Year 2: rerandomization of patients into treatment or placebo group	Mildly hypocaloric diet for 1st yr, eucaloric maintenance diet for 2nd yr	2-yr active treatment	Weight loss at 1 yr: 10.3 kg in ORL group, 6.1 kg in placebo group. Patients losing >10% body weight at 1 yr: 39% with ORL vs. 18% with placebo at 1 yr, ORL more effective at preventing weight gain in second year. Patients receiving placebo after 1 yr of ORL regained most of lost weight at 2-yr endpoint.
58	322 (254) Obese patients with type 2 diabetes mellitus taking oral sulfonyl-ureas	ORL 120 mg t.i.d. vs. placebo	Mildly hypocaloric diet	1-yr active treatment, no follow-up after discontinuation	Weight loss at 1 yr: 6.2 kg for treatment group, 4.3 kg for placebo group; modest but significant improvement in fasting glucose and glycohemoglobin levels with ORL
27	892 (403)	Year 1: ORL 120 mg t.i.d. vs. placebo; Year 2: rerandomization of patients into three groups: ORL 120 mg t.i.d., ORL 60 mg t.i.d., or placebo	Controlled-energy diet for year 1, weight maintenance diet for year 2	Year 2: active treatment group rerandomized, placebo subjects from year 1 continued with placebo in year 2	Weight loss at 1 yr: 8.8 kg for ORL group, 5.8 kg for placebo group; weight regained in year 2: 35.2% for ORL 120-mg group, 51.3% for ORL 60-mg group, and 63.4% for placebo

[a] Number of patients enrolling followed by the number of patients completing the study in parentheses.
[b] Expressed as mean weight loss.
[c] PHEN = phentermine resin, F = fenfluramine, D = dexfenfluramine, S = sibutramine, ORL = orlistat. Fenfluramine and dexfenfluramine were withdrawn from the U.S. market in September 1997.
[d] The patients remaining at the end of one phase were enrolled in the next phase of the study.

Table 2.
Dosing, Contraindications/High-Risk Patients, and Monitoring[a] of Select Prescription Weight-Control Agents

Treatment	Initial Dose	Recommended Adjustment	Contraindications and High-Risk Patients	Monitoring
Phentermine (Ionamin and others)	15-mg resin formulation p.o. before breakfast	Increase to 30-mg resin formulation p.o. before breakfast	Concurrent MAOI[b] therapy, agitated states, history of drug abuse, advanced arteriosclerosis, cardiovascular disease, moderate-to-severe HTN, hyperthyroidism, glaucoma	Blood pressure and pulse: baseline measurement and at regular intervals during therapy; symptoms of PPH
Sibutramine (Meridia)	10 mg p.o. q.d.	Increase to 15 mg if needed; decrease to 5 mg if initial dose not well tolerated	Concurrent MAOI or other weight-loss agent therapy, anorexia nervosa, uncontrolled or poorly controlled HTN, history of CAD, CHF, or arrhythmias, stroke, narrow angle glaucoma	Blood pressure and pulse: baseline measurement and at regular intervals during therapy; symptoms of PPH
Orlistat (Xenical)	120 mg p.o. t.i.d. before meals (do not take dose if meal is missed or contains no fat)	None described; higher doses provide no additional benefit	Chronic malabsorption syndrome, cholestasis	Symptoms of fat-soluble vitamin deficiency and need for multivitamin supplementation (taken >2 hr after dose)

[a]Not including weight-loss monitoring.
[b]MAOI = monoamine oxidase inhibitor, HTN = hypertension, CAD = coronary artery disease, CHF = congestive heart failure, PPH = primary pulmonary hypertension.

mine. Ma huang (an herbal form of ephedrine), guarana, and kola nut possess stimulant properties and can elevate blood pressure and heart rate. They should be avoided by patients with cardiovascular disease, hypertension, thyroid disease, and diabetes. Ephedrine-containing products have been associated with serious effects, such as severely high blood pressure, heart attacks, strokes, and death.[43] St. John's wort may produce photosensitivity in susceptible patients, and its long-term effects are not known. Combinations of ma huang or ephedrine with St. John's wort, which are known as "herbal fen-phen," are available to the public. FDA has warned consumers that these products may cause injury and has attempted to remove them from the market.[44] The safety of these herbal preparations is unknown, and case reports suggest their potential toxicity. Several products containing guar gum, a product that swells when wet, have been removed from the market because of reports of esophageal and intestinal obstruction. Adverse events caused by herbal weight-loss agents could be severe and include nephrotoxicity (linked to *Stephania tetrandra, Magnolia officinalis,* and ma huang)[45,46] and hepatotoxicity (linked to ma huang and germander).[47,48]

Patients prescribed MAOI therapy should not use phenylpropanolamine, ephedrine-like products, or St. John's wort because of the risk of hypertensive crisis. In addition, St. John's wort should not be used with other serotonergic agents to avoid the risk of serotonin syndrome. Potential drug interactions could occur in patients taking warfarin, digoxin, or oral contraceptives with St. John's wort.[49–51] Patients with preexisting cardiac disease (e.g., hypertension

and angina) should be counseled against using nonprescription and herbal preparations that could compromise their cardiovascular status, such as phenylpropanolamine, ephedrine, ma huang, guarana, and kola nut products.

Despite the growing popularity of herbal therapies, there are no adequate data to support their use for weight loss, and the short- and long-term adverse effects of these agents are largely unknown. Many products are not standardized, and the content can vary substantially from the label and between lots of the same product.[52] Furthermore, pharmacists should not recommend these products at this time. Patients using nonprescription or herbal preparations should be cautioned about adverse effects, drug interactions, and the potential impurities of herbal products.[53,54] Pharmacists should encourage patients to communicate their use of these products to their health care providers and monitor the use of weight-loss drugs for safety and efficacy.

Barriers to Pharmacotherapy

There are several barriers inhibiting the use of pharmacotherapy for obesity management. Previously, obesity was not recognized as a chronic disease, and attitudes toward treatment may have averted clinicians from considering drug therapy as an adjunct to long-term management. The fear of abuse and addiction often hinders their use, although newer weight-loss agents are less likely to cause physical dependence. The recent withdrawal of certain agents from the market because of their suspected long-term adverse effects has made patients and prescribers reluctant to use weight-loss drugs. Lastly, the high cost of the newer prescription agents frequently limits their use since their costs may not be covered by third-party payers.

Determining Suitable Candidates

The primary goal of the patient–clinician team should be to improve health by reducing comorbid risk factors rather than to achieve dramatic weight loss. Clinicians should provide patients with realistic expectations for weight loss and educate patients that modest weight loss (a reduction of 5%) may provide many health benefits. Patients should demonstrate high motivation for lifestyle modifications and should participate in a program that incorporates diet, exercise, and behavior modification. These modifications are essential to maintain lifelong weight control. The initial weight-loss goal should be a reduction of 10% from baseline weight over six months. Therefore, a loss of one to two pounds per week with lifestyle modifications over the first six months is recommended.[1]

Pharmacotherapy is not indicated when weight loss can be achieved through diet, exercise, and behavior modification. Patients may be considered for pharmacotherapy if they are at high risk for obesity-related comorbidities and if a six-month program of diet, behavioral therapy, and increased physical activity did not result in the loss of one pound per week.[1] The level of risk from obesity-related comorbidities can be estimated from the patient's BMI, waist circumference, and concomitant disease states (Table 3). Waist circumference correlates with abdominal fat mass, which is an independent predictor of health risk and morbidity. The level of risk aids in determining appropriate candidates for pharmacotherapy. An obese patient (BMI of $\geq$30 kg/m^2) with no concomitant risk factors or a patient with a BMI of $\geq$27 kg/m^2 with concomitant risk factors or diseases (e.g., hypertension, dyslipidemia, coronary heart disease, type 2 diabetes mellitus, and sleep apnea) is considered at high risk and may be considered a candidate for pharmacotherapy if lifestyle modifications are unsuccessful. Providers should carefully consider other conditions for treatment in patients with a BMI of $\geq$27 kg/m^2, such as concomitant disease states (e.g., osteoarthritis), familial risk factors, and patient quality of life.

The risks of not managing obesity should be compared with the potential risks of pharmacotherapy. When considering treatment options, the patient's lifestyle, concomitant disease states, and medications should be taken into consideration. The correlation between BMI and mortality may weaken with increasing age, and it is unknown if weight loss in patients over 65 years will prolong life.[1] Therefore, the

benefits should be weighed carefully against the potential adverse effects of pharmacotherapy that can occur in this population. Patients should demonstrate a full understanding of the potential risks and adverse effects of the agent chosen and understand that the safety and effectiveness of long-term pharmacotherapy are unknown.

Patient Monitoring

Patient monitoring is important once weight-loss medications have been initiated. The monitoring of safety and effectiveness should include monthly visits (if the patient is ambulatory) to measure weight, waist circumference, blood pressure, and heart rate and to assess any adverse effects of therapy for at least the first six months. Therapy is considered successful if, after six months of therapy, substantial weight loss (10% of body weight or more) is achieved and the patient has no serious adverse effects from the medication. At this point, the rate of weight loss generally reaches a plateau and weight maintenance should take priority. (If further weight loss is desired, lifestyle modifications can be made to further decrease caloric intake and increase energy expenditure.) Successful weight maintenance is defined as a weight regain of less than 3 kg (6.6 lb) in two years and a sustained reduction in waist circumference of at least 4 cm.[1] Because obesity is a chronic disease, weight is frequently regained after drug discontinuation.[13] Therefore, clinicians may choose long-term pharmacotherapy for patients who show adequate weight loss and tolerability during the first six months of therapy. However, the duration of treatment is currently under debate, and data about the long-term safety and efficacy of available agents are scarce. If treatment is continued beyond what is recommended on the package labeling, patients should be made aware of the unlabeled use of these medications, the potential adverse effects, and the lack of long-term efficacy and safety data. Patients should always be encouraged to continue life-style modifications, and their participation in these modifications should be continually assessed. Patients unable to lose at least 2 kg in the first four weeks of pharmacotherapy are unlikely to achieve a long-term response, and discontinuation of medications should be considered.[1]

Role of the Pharmacist

In all practice settings, pharmacists can play an important role in the management of overweight and obesity.[55,56] Pharmacists can collaborate with other health care professionals to identify overweight and obese patients and encourage lifestyle modifications. When pharmacotherapy is indicated, pharma-

Table 3.
Classification of Overweight and Obesity and Level of Associated Risk for Type 2 Diabetes Mellitus, Hypertension, and Cardiovascular Disease[1]

Item	BMI[a] (kg/m^2)	Obesity Class	Disease Risk Relative to Normal Weight and Waist Circumference	
			Men $\leq$102 cm ($\leq$40 in), Women $\leq$88 cm ($\leq$35 in)	Men >102 cm (>40 in), Women >88 cm (>35 in)
Underweight	<18.5	...	...	...
Normal	18.5–24.9	...	...	...
Overweight	25.0–29.9	...	Increased	High
Obesity	30.0–34.9	I	High	Very high
	35.0–39.9	II	Very high	Very high
Extreme obesity	$\geq$40	III	Extremely high	Extremely high

[a]BMI = body mass index.

cists can aid the health care team in selecting an appropriate agent considering patient-specific factors, such as concomitant disease states and medications. Pharmacists should be sympathetic to patients suffering from this chronic disease. Reinforcement of lifestyle modifications and provision of encouragement to patients on a monthly basis are important duties for every member of the treatment team. Increased frequency of patient contact may improve the success of weight loss and maintenance efforts. Identifying and monitoring patients using nonprescription or herbal weight-loss preparations are also important aspects of ensuring patient safety.

Summary

Obesity is a chronic disease that may require pharmacologic treatment in select patients at high risk in whom lifestyle modifications alone were unsuccessful. Although long-term therapy may be indicated in these patients, long-term safety and efficacy data for the current agents are not available. Patients should be informed of all known risks of therapy and, together with their health care providers, carefully consider the risks and benefits of treatment. Patients should be informed that pharmacotherapy has been proven to produce modest weight loss (10% weight loss) when used in conjunction with lifestyle modifications. The health benefits of modest weight loss should be stressed, and lifestyle changes should be continuously encouraged. Pharmacists can take an active role in the management of obesity by assisting in the selection of weight-loss agents and providing appropriate counseling and monitoring to ensure safe and effective drug therapy outcomes for patients using prescription and nonprescription products. Further evaluation of current and future therapies will be necessary to determine the role of long-term pharmacotherapy for the management of obesity.

References

1. National Heart, Lung, and Blood Institute. Clinical guidelines on the identification, evaluation, and treatment of overweight and obesity in adults. The evidence report. Washington, DC: U.S. Department of Health and Human Services, 1998; NIH publication no. 98-4083.

2. Flegal KM, Carroll MD, Kuczmarski RJ, et al. Overweight and obesity in the United States: prevalence and trends, 1960–1994. *Int J Obes.* 1998; 22:39–47.

3. Pi-Sunyer FX. Medical hazards of obesity. *Ann Intern Med.* 1993; 119(7, pt. 2):655–60.

4. McGinnis M, Foege WH. Actual causes of death in the United States. *JAMA.* 1993; 270:2207–12.

5. Wolf AM, Colditz GA. Social and economic effects of body weight in the United States. *Am J Clin Nutr.* 1996; 63(suppl):466s–9s.

6. Fontaine KR, Cheskin LJ, Barosky I. Health-related quality of life in obese persons seeking treatment. *J Fam Pract.* 1996; 43:265–70.

7. Healthy people 2010. Conference edition. Vols. 1 and 2. Washington, DC: U.S. Department of Health and Human Services; 2000.

8. Rosenbaum M, Leibel RL, Hirsch J. Obesity. *N Engl J Med.* 1997; 337:396–407.

9. Atkinson RL. A 33-year-old woman with morbid obesity. *JAMA.* 2000; 283:3236–43.

10. Williamson DF, Pamuk E, Thun M, et al. Prospective study of intentional weight loss and mortality in never-smoking overweight US white women aged 40–64 years. *Am J Epidemiol.* 1995; 141:1128–41.

11. Bray GA. The new era of drug treatment. Pharmacologic treatment of obesity: symposium overview. *Obes Res.* 1995; 3(suppl 4):415s–7s.

12. Bray GA. Use and abuse of appetite-suppressant drugs in the treatment of obesity. *Ann Intern Med.* 1993; 119(7, pt. 2):707–13.

13. National Task Force on the Prevention and Treatment of Obesity. Long-term pharmacotherapy in the management of obesity. *JAMA.* 1996; 276:1907–15.

14. McNeely W, Goa KL. Sibutramine. A review of its contribution to the management of obesity. *Drugs.* 1998; 56:1093–124.

15. McNeely W, Benfield P. Orlistat. *Drugs.* 1998; 56:241–9.

16. Mertens IL, Van Gaal LF. Promising new approaches to the management of obesity. *Drugs.* 2000; 60:1–9.

17. Peter CJ, Early JJ, Gibbs CM. Treatment of affective disorder and obesity with topiramate. *Ann Pharmacother.* 2000; 43:1262–5.

18. Dursun SM. Clozapine weight gain, plus topiramate weight loss. *Can J Psychiatry.* 2000; 45:198. Letter.

19. Voelker R. New weight loss tool. *JAMA.* 1999; 281:2277.

20. Munro JF, MacCuish AC, Wilson EM, et al. Comparison of continuous and intermittent anorectic therapy in obesity. *BMJ.* 1968; 1:352–4.

21. Weintraub M, Sundaresan PR, Madan M, et al. Long-term weight control studies I–VII. *Clin Pharmacol Ther.* 1992; 51:586–641.

22. Guy-Grand B, Apfelbaum M, Crepaldi G, et al. International trial of long-term dexfenfluramine in obesity. *Lancet.* 1989; 2:1142–5.

23. Bray GA, Blackburn GL, Ferguson JM, et al. Sibutramine produces dose-related weight loss. *Obes Res.* 1999; 7:189–98.

24. Jones SP, Smith IG, Kelly F, et al. Long term weight loss with sibutramine. *Int J Obes.* 1995; 19(suppl 2):41. Abstract.

25. Apfelbaum M, Vague P, Ziegler O, et al. Long-term maintenance of weight loss after a very-low-calorie diet: a randomized blinded trial of the efficacy and tolerability of sibutramine. *Am J Med.* 1999; 106:179–84.

26. Sjostrom L, Rissanen A, Andersen T, et al. Randomised placebo-controlled trial of orlistat for weight loss and prevention of weight regain in obese patients. *Lancet.* 1998; 352:167–73.

27. Davidson MH, Hauptman J, DiGirolamo M, et al. Weight control and risk factor reduction in obese subjects treated for 2 years with orlistat. *JAMA.* 1999; 281:235–42.

28. Meridia product monograph. Mount Olive, NJ: Knoll Pharmaceutical; 1998 Nov.

29. Xenical package insert. Nutley, NJ: Hoffmann–La Roche; 1999 May.

30. Connolly HM, Crary JL, McGoon MD, et al. Valvular heart disease associated with fenfluramine–phentermine. *N Engl J Med.* 1997; 337:581–8.

31. Gardin JM, Schumacher D, Constantine G, et al. Valvular abnormalities and cardiovascular status following exposure to dexfenfluramine or phentermine/

fenfluramine. *JAMA*. 2000; 283:1703–9.

32. Centers for Disease Control and Prevention. Cardiac valvulopathy associated with exposure to fenfluramine or dexfenfluramine: US Department of Health and Human Services interim public health recommendations. *MMWR Morb Mortal Wkly Rep*. Nov 1997; 46:1061–6.

33. Bach DS, Rissanen AM, Mendel CM, et al. Absence of cardiac valve dysfunction in obese patients treated with sibutramine. *Obes Res*. 1999; 7:363–9.

34. Abenhaim L, Moride Y, Brenot F, et al. Appetite-suppressant drugs and the risk of primary pulmonary hypertension. *N Engl J Med*. 1996; 335:609–16.

35. McCann UD, Seiden LS, Rubin LJ, et al. Brain serotonin neurotoxicity and primary pulmonary hypertension from fenfluramine and dexfenfluramine. *JAMA*. 1997; 278:666 72.

36. Xenical capsules Hoffmann–La Roche applicant no. 20-766. Approval date Apr 23, 1999. www.fda.gov/cder/foi/nda/99/020766a.htm (accessed 2001 Apr 3).

37. Ionamin package insert. Rochester, NY: Medeva Pharmaceuticals; 1996 Aug.

38. Ulus IH, Maher TJ, Wurtman RJ. Characterization of phentermine and related compounds as monoamine oxidase (MAO) inhibitors. *Biochem Pharmacol*. 2000; 59:1611–21.

39. Sporer KA. The serotonin syndrome: implicated drugs, pathophysiology, and management. *Drug Saf*. 1995:13:94–104.

40. Pittler MH, Abbot NC, Harkness EF, et al. Randomized, double-blind trial of chitosan for body weight reduction. *Eur J Clin Nutr*. 1999; 53:379–81.

41. Heymsfield SB, Allison DB, Vasselli JR, et al. *Garcinia cambogia* (hydroxycitric acid) as a potential antiobesity agent. *JAMA*. 1998; 280:1596–600.

42. Kernan WN, Viscoli CM, Brass LM, et al. Phenylpropanolamine and the risk of hemorrhagic stroke. *N Engl J Med*. 2000; 343:1826–32.

43. Centers for Disease Control and Prevention. Adverse events associated with ephedrine-containing products—Texas, December 1993–September 1995. *MMWR Morb Mortal Wkly Rep*. 1996; 45:689–92.

44. Food and Drug Administration. FDA warns against drug promotion of "herbal fen-phen." Rockville, MD: U.S. Department of Health and Human Services; 1997 Nov 6. (Talk Paper T97-56.)

45. Vanherweghem JL, Depierreux M, Tielemans C, et al. Rapidly progressive interstitial renal fibrosis in young women: association with slimming regimen including Chinese herbs. *Lancet*. 1993; 341:387–91.

46. Powell T, Hsu FF, Turk J, et al. Ma-huang strikes again: ephedrine nephrolithiasis. *Am J Kidney Dis*. 1998; 32:153–9.

47. Nadir A, Agrawal S, King PD, et al. Acute hepatitis associated with the use of a Chinese herbal product, ma-huang. *Am J Gastroenterol*. 1996; 91:1436–8.

48. Larrey D, Vial T, Pauwels A, et al. Hepatitis after germander (*Teucrium chamaedrys*) administration: another instance of herbal medicine hepatotoxicity. *Ann Intern Med*. 1992; 117:129–32.

49. Ernst E. Second thought about safety of St. John's wort. *Lancet*. 1999; 354:2014–6.

50. Fugh-Berman A. Herb–drug interactions. *Lancet*. 2000; 355:134–8.

51. Yue QY, Berquist C, Gerden B. Safety of St. John's wort (*Hypericum perforatum*). *Lancet*. 2000; 355:576–7. Letter.

52. Gurley BJ, Gardner SF, Hubbard MA. Content versus label claims in ephedra-containing dietary supplements. *Am J Health-Syst Pharm*. 2000; 57:963–9.

53. Miller LG. Herbal medicinals. *Arch Intern Med*. 1998; 158:2200–11.

54. Winslow LC, Kroll DJ. Herbs as medicines. *Arch Intern Med*. 1998; 158:2192–9.

55. Dombrowski SR. Pharmacist counseling on nutrition and physical activity—part 1 of 2: understanding current guidelines. *J Am Pharm Assoc*. 1999; 39:479–91.

56. Dombrowski SR, Ferro LA. Pharmacist counseling on nutrition and physical activity—part 2 of 2: helping patients make changes. *J Am Pharm Assoc*. 1999; 39:613–27.

57. Williams RA, Foulsham BM. Weight reduction in osteoarthritis using phentermine. *Practitioner*. 1981; 225:231–2.

58. Hollander PA, Elbein SC, Hirsch IB, et al. Role of orlistat in the treatment of obese patients with type 2 diabetes: a 1-year randomized double-blind study. *Diabetes Care*. 1998; 21:1288–94.

Appendix—Information Resources

Healthy People 2010: Healthy people 2010. Washington, DC: U.S. Department of Health and Human Services; 2000 (web.health.gov/healthypeople).

National Institutes of Health: National Heart, Lung, and Blood Institute. Clinical guidelines on the identification, evaluation, and treatment of overweight and obesity in adults. The evidence report. Washington, DC: U.S. Department of Health and Human Services; 1998. NIH publication no. 98-4083 (www.nhlbi.nih. gov).

The American Association of Clinical Endocrinologists/ American College of Endocrinology (AACE/ACE): AACE/ACE position statement on the prevention, diagnosis and treatment of obesity (1998 rev). *Endocr Prac*. 1998; 4:297–330 (www.aace.org).

U.S. Department of Agriculture: Center for Nutrition Policy and Promotion. Food guide pyramid. Washington, DC: U.S. Department of Health and Human Serv-ices; Home and Garden Bulletin No. 252(www.nal. usda. gov/fnic).

Center for Nutrition Policy and Promotion, U.S. Department of Agriculture, U.S. Department of Health and Human Services. Nutrition and your health: dietary guidelines for Americans. Washington, DC: U.S. Department of Health and Human Services, 2000; Home and Garden Bulletin No. 232. 5th ed. (www.usda.gov).

The LEARN Education Center: Brownell KD. The LEARN program for weight control. Dallas: American Health Publishing; 1997 (www.learneducation. com).

Pharmacy Weight Management Programs: Dombrowski SR. Pharmacist counseling on nutrition and physical activity—part 1 of 2: understanding current guidelines. *J Am Pharm Assoc*. 1999; 39:479–91.

Dombrowski SR, Ferro LA. Pharmacist counseling on nutrition and physical activity—part 2 of 2: helping patients make changes. *J Am Pharm Assoc*. 1999; 39:613–27.

Developed by the ASHP Commission on Therapeutics and Approved by the ASHP Board of Directors on April 23, 2001.

The bibliographic citation for this document is as follows: American Society of Health-System Pharmacists. ASHP therapeutic position statement on the safe use of pharmacotherapy for obesity management in adults. *Am J Health-Syst Pharm.* 2001; 58:1645–55.

ASHP Therapeutic Position Statement on the Use of β-Blockers in Survivors of Acute Myocardial Infarction

Statement of Position

The American Society of Health-System Pharmacists (ASHP) supports the use of β-adrenergic blocking agents (β-blockers) in patients surviving an initial acute myocardial infarction (MI). Strong and consistent evidence from randomized controlled trials has demonstrated that treatment with β-blockers can reduce morbidity and mortality in this patient population. Despite these findings, β-blockers are underused in clinical practice.

An analysis of prescribing patterns in the United States has identified several high-risk populations that receive suboptimal treatment with β-blockers. These populations include the elderly, patients with diabetes, and patients with diminished left ventricular systolic function. ASHP supports pharmacists' efforts to improve the use of β-blocker therapy in survivors of acute MI, particularly those in high-risk groups. ASHP recognizes that, for patients with underlying conditions such as bradycardia, atrioventricular conduction defects, and bronchospastic disease, β-blocker therapy may be contraindicated, depending on individual patient circumstances.

All health systems should adopt methods for identifying and resolving barriers to treatment with β-blockers in survivors of MI. ASHP recognizes that there is a strong need for health professionals to collaborate to improve β-blocker use in such patients, which will in turn improve clinical outcomes and the quality of care.[1-4]

Background

Cardiovascular disease is the leading cause of death in the United States. Nearly 650,000 people have a first MI each year, while another 450,000 have a recurrent MI.[5] Approximately 45% of patients with an MI in a given year die as a consequence; 50% of these patients will die before hospitalization.[1] The mortality rate is between 7% and 15% for hospitalized patients experiencing their first MI and increases significantly with subsequent MIs.[6,7] In addition, the risk of cardiovascular morbidity and mortality remains elevated after MI, with roughly 85% of deaths being cardiovascular in origin. The economic consequences of coronary artery disease in the United States are profound. Projected costs, direct and indirect, for coronary artery disease in the U.S. health care system in 2002 are about $112 billion.[5]

It is essential to implement therapeutic interventions after a coronary event that will improve survival and reduce health care costs. The administration of β-blockers is one such intervention. The pharmacologic benefits associated with β-blockers after MI are multifactorial and may involve antiischemic and antiarrhythmic mechanisms.

Beta-Blockers for Secondary Prevention of Coronary Artery Disease

The beneficial effects of β-blocker therapy after MI have been demonstrated in many trials. In a landmark trial, the Norwegian Multicenter Study, overall mortality declined 6.2% and recurrent MI declined 5.7% in patients treated with timolol for a mean of 17 months ($p = 0.0001$ and 0.006, respectively).[8] Persistent benefits were observed for up to six years after MI in patients who continued to receive timolol after the trial ended.[9] Similar results were observed in the Beta-Blocker Heart Attack Trial (BHAT), which found a 2.6% absolute reduction in mortality after two years of β-blocker therapy (a 7.2% mortality rate in the β-blocker group and a 9.8% rate in the placebo group) ($p < 0.005$).[10] In both trials, patients were started on β-blockers within 21 days of having an MI. Reductions in mortality occurred as a result of reductions in the risk of sudden death and other cardiovascular events. Data pooled from randomized trials of oral β-blockers used after MI indicated a 21% reduction in mortality from all causes and a 30% reduction in sudden death. In addition, the use of β-blockers for secondary prevention was associated with a 22% reduction in the risk of a second MI.[11]

A majority of these clinical trials enrolled patients without strong contraindications to β-blocker therapy. Patients recruited for the trials were often less than 70 years of age and typically had no clinical evidence of heart failure.[2] Thus, initial randomized trials often assessed the beneficial effects of β-blockers in low-risk post-MI patients. However, data indicate that patients at high risk, such as the elderly and those with evidence of left ventricular dysfunction, derive greater benefit from β-blocker therapy.[3]

Guidelines for Management of Acute MI

The American College of Cardiology (ACC) and the American Heart Association (AHA) have developed national guidelines for the management of patients with acute MI.[3] These recommendations are based on scientific evidence and expert opinion and are categorized according to the strength of the evidence or opinion (Table 1). According to the current ACC and AHA guidelines, β-blocker therapy should be initiated early (within 12 hours of onset of infarction) in patients without contraindications to therapy (a class I recommendation). However, treatment with β-blockers is a class IIb recommendation for patients with evidence of moderate left ventricular dysfunction and other contraindications. Lastly, β-blockers should be withheld in patients with evidence of severe left ventricular dysfunction during the period of acute infarction (a class III recommendation). Once initiated, β-blocker therapy should be continued indefinitely in all high-risk patients, including those with anterior MI, patients with evidence of complex ectopy or left ventricular dysfunction, and the elderly (a class I recommendation).

Low-risk patients and patients with non-ST-segment-elevation MI should also be considered for β-blocker therapy (a class IIa recommendation). Patients with relative contraindications to β-blockers, including those with moderate to severe heart failure, should not be absolutely excluded from receiving the therapy (Table 2). Such treatment should be considered in these patients if close monitoring can be

Table 1.
American College of Cardiology and American Heart Association Recommendations for Managing Acute Myocardial Infarction[3]

Class of Recommendations	Description
I	There is evidence or a general consensus that a treatment is effective and provides a therapeutic benefit.
IIa	Evidence or expert opinion regarding potential benefits is conflicting; however, the weight of evidence or opinion is in favor of the usefulness or efficacy of the therapy.
IIb	Evidence or expert opinion regarding potential benefits is conflicting; usefulness or efficacy is less well established by evidence or opinion.
III	Therapy has no demonstrable benefit and may be harmful.

Table 2.
Relative Contraindications to β–Blocker Therapy[3]

Heart rate, < 60 beats/min
Systolic arterial blood pressure, <100 mm Hg
Moderate or severe heart failure
Signs of peripheral hypoperfusion
PR interval >0.24 sec
Second- or third-degree atrioventricular block
Severe chronic obstructive pulmonary disease
History of asthma
Severe peripheral vascular disease
Insulin-dependent diabetes mellitus

ensured (a class IIb recommendation). According to the guidelines, while evidence of moderate to severe heart failure may preclude the use of intravenous β-blockers early in the MI period, such evidence is a strong indication for the use of oral β-blockers upon discharge.

Undertreatment with β-Blockers

Despite the clear benefits of β-blockers in survivors of acute MI, these agents continue to be underprescribed in these patients after discharge from the hospital. Failure to prescribe β-blockers after MI is common and in many cases is not due to a contraindication. Recent studies have found that fewer than 60% of eligible survivors of MI actually receive a β-blocker upon hospital discharge.[3,11–13] Utilization of β-blockers for secondary prevention remains low, even by cardiologists. In an analysis of insurance claims to 17 health plans submitted by 150 cardiologists, β-blockers were prescribed after discharge for only 48% of eligible patients.[14] The prescribing rates actually pertain to low-risk patients, since patients with diabetes or left ventricular systolic dysfunction were excluded.[15] In many studies of the prescribing of β-blockers after MI, patients with diabetes or evidence of heart failure during hospitalization have been categorized as ineligible for β-blocker therapy.[11,12] Data have established that β-blockers reduce morbidity and mortality in these high-risk populations.[16–30]

Special Populations

The Elderly. Approximately 84.9% of deaths from acute MI in the United States occur in people over the age of 65.[1] Several trials have documented the benefits of β-blockers in older post-MI patients. The Norwegian Multicenter Study demonstrated a 6.7% absolute reduction in mortality among patients 65–75 years of age treated with timolol compared with placebo ($p < 0.05$).[16] Similarly, in the BHAT, patients 60–69 years of age given propranolol had a 33% relative reduction in mortality compared with patients given placebo, whereas the relative reduction in mortality among patients ages 30–59 receiving propranolol was only 19%.[17] Elderly patients who have an MI are often not treated as aggressively as younger patients; undertreatment with β-blockers is one example. Several studies have analyzed the use of β-blockers among elderly patients after MI, and all have documented detrimental consequences, including reinfarction and death, of underutilization in this patient population.[11,16]

Soumerai et al.[18] evaluated the use of β-blockers among 5332 New Jersey Medicare recipients hospitalized with an acute MI between 1987 and 1992. Among the 3737 patients deemed eligible for therapy, only 21% received a β-blocker. Prescribing rates declined with advancing patient age. Patients 65–74 years of age were significantly more likely to receive β-blocker therapy than those ages 75–84 or patients who were 85 and older. Krumholz et al.[19] evaluated a similar sample of patients as part of the National Cooperative Cardiovascular Project (NCCP), which looked at the medical records of over 200,000 Medicare beneficiaries and assessed the use of β-blockers upon hospital discharge in 1994 and 1995. Overall, β-blockers were prescribed for 50% of patients deemed "ideal" candidates for therapy. Patients prescribed a calcium-channel blocker upon discharge were less likely to receive a β-blocker, despite evidence supporting such therapy in this patient population.[18,19]

Patients not treated with β-blockers after MI were at increased risk for subsequent cardiovascular morbidity and mortality in the NCCP. Among ideal candidates for β-blocker therapy, the absolute mortality rate after one year was 4.9% lower for those prescribed β-blockers than for those who were not (7.7% versus 12.6%) ($p < 0.001$).[19] In the analysis by Soumerai et al.,[18] mortality following two years of therapy was reduced by 43% (relative risk [RR] = 0.57, 95% confidence interval [CI] = 0.47–0.69) and rehospitalization was decreased by 22% (RR = 0.78, 95% CI = 0.67–0.90) among patients who were treated with a β-blocker compared with patients who were not. The reduction in mortality was consistent across all three age ranges (65–74, 75–84, and ≥85 years). Beta-blockers should be considered for every post-MI patient, regardless of age, unless contraindications exist.

Patients with Diabetes Mellitus. Despite their higher risk of subsequent morbidity and mortality, patients with diabetes mellitus are underprescribed β-blockers after MI. Chowdhury et al.[20] compared the use of β-blockers after MI among patients with and without diabetes. In general, β-blocker use was low in the entire population analyzed. However, use at one year was higher among patients without diabetes than patients with diabetes (34% versus 27%). Further analysis revealed that 42% of the patients without diabetes and 30%

of those with diabetes who were not prescribed a β-blocker lacked clear contraindications to therapy. Undertreatment with β-blockers in elderly patients with diabetes was also documented in a retrospective analysis of data from the NCCP.[21] Prescribing rates upon hospital discharge for patients without clear contraindications to β-blockers were 45% for patients with type 1 diabetes mellitus and 48% for patients with type 2 diabetes mellitus. After adjustments for additional contributing factors, patients with diabetes were less likely to receive a β-blocker upon hospital discharge than patients without diabetes.

Diabetic patients may have potential complications as a result of β-blocker therapy, which may be why these agents are underprescribed in this patient population after acute MI.[22] For instance, β-blockers mask the symptoms of hypoglycemia and inhibit glycogenolysis, thereby delaying recovery from hypoglycemic events. In addition, β-receptor blockade may reduce glycemic control in patients with diabetes. Consequently, β-blocker therapy has been considered relatively contraindicated in patients with diabetes.

Data on the safety of β-blockers in diabetic patients are emerging. For instance, in the UK Prospective Diabetes Study, treatment with a β-blocker was associated with reductions in macrovascular and microvascular complications that were similar to reductions produced by angiotensin-converting-enzyme (ACE) inhibitors.[23] However, patients receiving β-blockers were taking additional therapy to lower their glucose levels more frequently than were patients receiving an ACE inhibitor (66% versus 53%) ($p = 0.0015$). In the trials analyzing β-blocker use after MI, a β-blocker did not significantly increase the rate of diabetic complications requiring hospitalization.[20,21]

Excluding patients with diabetes from β-blocker therapy can have profound implications for the subsequent risk of mortality. In the analysis of data from the NCCP, receipt of a β-blocker after MI was associated with improved survival rates for patients with diabetes mellitus types 1 and 2.[21] The Diabetes and Insulin–Glucose Infusion in Acute Myocardial Infarction (DIGAMI) study indicated that the administration of β-blockers upon hospital discharge was associated with an approximate 50% reduction in mortality at one year ($p = 0.001$).[24] Every effort should be made to ensure that post-MI patients are not denied at least a therapeutic trial of a β-blocker on the basis of diabetes alone.

Patients with Left Ventricular Systolic Dysfunction. Clinical evidence of left ventricular systolic dysfunction after an acute MI has long been considered a contraindication to β-blocker therapy. Indeed, most clinical trials excluded patients with signs or symptoms of left ventricular systolic dysfunction because of concerns over precipitating clinical heart failure.[2] Patients with evidence of heart failure during hospitalization are often not considered candidates for β-blocker therapy; this leads to lower prescribing rates in this patient population. Reduced prescribing of β-blockers in the presence of clinical heart failure and the associated consequences have been documented in several analyses of post-MI patients.[25–28]

A retrospective analysis of data from the placebo group of the Multicenter Diltiazem Post-Infarction Trial found that administration of a β-blocker was less frequent among patients with diminished left ventricular systolic function and clinical evidence of heart failure.[25] However, within the population of patients with reduced left ventricular function (ejection fraction, <30%), the risk of congestive heart failure

was lower for patients who were given β-blockers than for those who were not (46% versus 61%, RR = 0.75, 95% CI = 0.48–1.19). The risk of death was also lower among patients receiving β-blockers compared with those not treated with these agents (24% versus 45%, RR = 0.53, 95% CI = 0.26–1.05).

Data from the Acute MI Ramipril Efficacy (AIRE) trial were analyzed to determine the rate at which β-blockers were prescribed after MI in patients with clinical evidence of heart failure.[26] Beta-blocker use was less frequent in patients with pronounced left ventricular dysfunction and heart failure and those who required treatment with diuretics. In addition, open-label therapy with an ACE inhibitor occurred less frequently among patients receiving β-blocker therapy. Univariate analysis demonstrated that β-blocker therapy was associated with significant reductions in all-cause mortality and clinical heart failure ($p < 0.001$).

Post hoc analysis of data from the BHAT revealed higher mortality rates for patients with evidence of left ventricular failure at randomization than for patients with preserved ventricular function (17% versus 7%).[27] However, among patients with diminished left ventricular function, mortality was lower among those randomized to treatment with a β-blocker than the placebo group (10% versus 17%). Administration of β-blockers to patients with diminished left ventricular systolic function contributed to the prolongation of life in 6 of every 100 patients treated.

Although these analyses were retrospective, it is evident that patients with diminished left ventricular function are at higher risk for subsequent morbidity and mortality and are likely to benefit from β-blocker therapy. Furthermore, recent clinical trials have confirmed the role of β-blockers in the management of patients with documented left ventricular systolic dysfunction.[28,29] In addition, the Carvedilol Post-Infarct Survival Control in Left Ventricular Dysfunction (CAPRICORN) study, a multicenter randomized controlled trial in 1959 post-MI patients with reduced left ventricular function (ejection fraction, <40%), documented an absolute reduction in all-cause mortality of 3% compared with placebo (12% versus 15%) ($p = 0.03$) after the administration of carvedilol 25 mg twice daily.[30] Reductions in nonfatal MI were also observed.

Given these trials, the presence of left ventricular systolic dysfunction should no longer be considered an absolute contraindication to β-blocker therapy. The ACC and AHA guidelines recommend that β-blockers be considered for patients with moderate to severe heart failure.[3] Such therapy should be implemented cautiously and with careful monitoring, as precipitation of an acute exacerbation of heart failure can occur. Only by increasing the utilization of β-blockers in such high-risk patients will the reductions in morbidity and mortality be achieved.

Cost-Effectiveness

Phillips et al.[31] used a computerized model of patients with coronary heart disease to examine the economic benefits associated with improvements in the use of β-blockers among all post-MI patients ages 35–84 who lacked clear contraindications to therapy. In the analysis, which assumed a societal perspective, the increased use of β-blockers was associated with a gain of 447,000 life-years and a projected saving of $18 million over a 20-year period. A cost of $4500 per quality-adjusted life-year gained was determined for post-MI patients.

Mechanisms for Improving β-Blocker Use

Although publishing therapeutic guidelines is the easiest and most universal method for educating prescribers, electronic publications and journal articles are relatively ineffective in changing prescribing. In a retrospective analysis, Holmboe et al.[32] found that the administration of β-blockers upon hospital discharge was not significantly more frequent among institutions with critical pathways than those without them. However, Sarasin et al.[33] reported that multiple interventions, including the distribution of preprinted therapeutic guidelines, inservice education, and bimonthly reminders, were effective at improving prescribing rates for β-blockers from 38% to 63% among post-MI patients. The use of multiple interventions makes it hard to identify the intervention with the greatest effect on physician prescribing, however. In addition, duplicating the interventions undertaken in the Sarasin et al. study may be ineffective at other institutions, since altering clinical decisions requires an understanding of the underlying clinical behavior. Each health care institution is different, and implementation of a single model is not likely to be universally effective. Instead, each institution must determine the types of interventions required to best improve prescribing within that organization. The Cooperative Cardiovascular Project found that providing feedback about prescribing rates to practitioners increased the frequency of administration of β-blockers to post-MI patients from 47% to 68%.[34]

Several national organizations interested in improving the quality of health care in the United States have identified the importance of tracking the use of β-blockers after MI. In 1997, the Health Care Financing Administration, now known as the Centers for Medicare and Medicaid Services, began a national program to track the quality of care provided to fee-for-service Medicare beneficiaries.[35] Data collected over a six-month period spanning 1998 and 1999 indicated that β-blockers were prescribed upon discharge to 72% of MI patients in the median state. Administration rates ranged from 47% in Mississippi to 93% in Massachusetts and the District of Columbia. The National Committee for Quality Assurance (NCQA) provides clinical performance information submitted by managed care organizations. The frequency of administration of β-blockers increased from an average of 62% of patients in 1996, when tracking by NCQA began, to an average of 85% of patients in 1999.[36] The Joint Commission on Accreditation of Healthcare Organizations plans to increase the use of performance data as part of its accreditation program for health systems.[37] Tracking β-blocker administration upon hospital discharge is one of the first five core measures.

Role of the Pharmacist

Interdisciplinary involvement in the assessment and improvement of β-blocker use after MI is warranted. All members of the health care team should strive to maximize prescribing of β-blockers after MI. Pharmacists have a responsibility for ensuring that the care provided achieves identifiable outcomes and improves the patient's quality of life. Consequently, pharmacists have a responsibility for identifying agents for which the weight of evidence indicates a therapeutic benefit but that have been erroneously omitted from a patient's medical regimen. Pharmacists' next responsibilities are ensuring that mechanisms for avoiding such oversights are implemented and that appropriate therapy is initiated and monitored.

Pharmacists can increase the use of β-blockers by participating in the development of national or institutional therapeutic guidelines and helping to identify potential candidates for β-blocker therapy after MI. For example, Cano and Lemoine[38] documented an increase in the rate of prescribing of post-MI β-blockers from 60% in 1996 to 90% in 1998 after a therapeutic pathway involving pharmacists was implemented. Hilleman[39] documented an increase in the frequency of administration of post-MI β-blockers from 74% in 1996–97 to 92% in 1999 after a pharmacist-directed concurrent drug-use evaluation was put in place.

Additional mechanisms for improving the use of β-blockers should be actively sought by pharmacists in all health care environments. The identification of potential candidates after discharge from the hospital may be more challenging; however, given the substantial benefits of β-blocker therapy, measures to identify such candidates in the community should be pursued. Finally, pharmacists are encouraged to document and report their efforts, which in turn will increase the use of β-blockers in these patients.

Recommendations for Therapy

After an acute MI, patients should be assessed for eligibility for β-blockers; therapy should ideally be implemented within the first few days after the event (if it has not already been initiated) and be continued indefinitely in patients lacking contraindications.[3] Contraindications vary, depending on the source consulted. The AHA and ACC guidelines include several relative contraindications to β-blocker therapy (Table 2).[3] Patients with underlying bronchospastic disease may have bronchospasm after the therapy is begun. Consequently, the guidelines include severe chronic obstructive pulmonary disease and a history of asthma as relative contraindications. However, β-blockers are not contraindicated in all patients with lung disease. Therefore, every effort should be made to determine the severity of the patient's pulmonary condition before therapy is begun. If the potential benefit appears to outweigh the potential risk, β_1-selective agents should be used preferentially. It should be noted, however, that β_1-receptor selectivity is dose related and that such selectivity is lost with the administration of higher dosages. The AHA and ACC guidelines also include the presence of severe peripheral vascular disease and type 1 diabetes mellitus as relative contraindications. In these patients, any β-blocker therapy should proceed cautiously and with appropriate monitoring.

Atenolol, propranolol, metoprolol, and timolol have FDA-approved labeling for use in patients who survive an MI; however, some clinicians believe that any β-blocker may be used, except agents with intrinsic sympathomimetic activity.[40] After implementation of therapy, the dosage should be carefully adjusted while the patient is monitored for symptomatic bradycardia and hypotension and signs and symptoms consistent with congestive heart failure. The β-blocker dosage should be increased to the maximum recommended when possible, including atenolol 100 mg/day, propranolol 180–240 mg/day, timolol 20 mg/day, and metoprolol 200 mg/day.[12] Recently, however, the dosages used in elderly patients have been questioned. Rochon et al.[41] observed that low-dose treatment (defined as dosages less than those achieved with standard tablet sizes) was associated with a 2.1% absolute reduction in hospitalization rates (RR = 1.53, 95% CI = 1.01–2.31) and similar one-year survival benefits among patients greater than 66 years of age. Similar results were reported by Barron et al.,[15] who observed a greater reduction in cardiovascular mortality for patients receiving low-dose β-blocker therapy (defined as dosages less than 50% of those found to be effective in clinical trials) (hazard ratio [HR] = 0.33) (p = 0.009) than for patients receiving high-dose therapy (HR = 0.82) (p = 0.51). Additional randomized clinical trials will be needed to determine the optimal dosage of β-blockers for elderly patients after MI.

Conclusion

Beta-blocker therapy reduces morbidity and mortality after acute MI. However, clinical practice falls short of achieving the full benefits of post-MI β-blocker therapy, particularly in the elderly, patients with left ventricular systolic dysfunction, and patients with diabetes. Health care professionals need to more actively promote rational use of β-blockers for all post-MI patients who lack clear contraindications to therapy. ASHP urges pharmacists to assume responsibility for providing care that achieves definite outcomes in these patients and improves their quality of life.

References

1. Yusuf S, Peto R, Lewis J et al. Beta-blockade during and after myocardial infarction: an overview of randomized trials. *Prog Cardiovasc Dis.* 1985; 27:335–71.
2. Beta-Blocker Pooling Project Research Group. The Beta-Blocker Pooling Project (BBPP): subgroup findings from randomized trials in post-MI patients. *Eur Heart J.* 1988; 9:8–16.
3. Ryan TJ, Antman EM, Brooks NH et al. 1999 Update: ACC/AHA guidelines for the management of patients with acute myocardial infarction. A report of the American College of Cardiology/American Heart Association Task Force on Practice Guidelines (Committee on Management of Acute Myocardial Infarction). *J Am Coll Cardiol.* 1999; 34:890–911.
4. McCormick D, Gurwitz JH, Lessard D et al. Use of aspirin, beta-blockers, and lipid-lowering medications before recurrent acute myocardial infarction: missed opportunities for prevention? *Arch Intern Med.* 1999; 159:561–7.
5. 2002 Heart and stroke statistical update. Dallas, TX: American Heart Association; 2001.
6. Moss AJ, Benhorn J. Prognosis and management after a first myocardial infarction. *N Engl J Med.* 1990; 322:743–53.
7. May GS, Eberlein KA, Furberg CD et al. Secondary prevention after myocardial infarction: a review of long-term trials. *Prog Cardiovasc Dis.* 1982; 24:331–52.
8. Norwegian Multicenter Study Group. Timolol-induced reduction in mortality and re-infarction in patients surviving acute myocardial infarction. *N Engl J Med.* 1981; 304:801–7.
9. Pedersen TR. Six year follow-up of the Norwegian Multicenter Study on timolol after acute myocardial infarction. *N Engl J Med.* 1985; 313:1055–8.
10. Beta-Blocker Heart Attack Trial Research group. A randomized trial of propranolol in patients with acute myocardial infarction; mortality results. *JAMA.* 1982; 247:1707–14.
11. Phillips BG, Yim JM, Brown EJ et al. Pharmacologic profile of survivors of acute myocardial infarction at United States academic hospitals. *Am Heart J.* 1996; 131:872–8.
12. Viskin S, Kitzis I, Lev E et al. Treatment with beta-adrenergic blocking agents after myocardial infarction: from randomized trials to clinical practice. *J Am Coll Cardiol.* 1995; 25:1327–32.
13. Meehan TP, Hennen J, Radford MJ et al. Process and outcome of care for acute myocardial infarction among Medicare beneficiaries in Connecticut: a quality improvement demonstration project. *Ann Intern Med.* 1995; 122:928–36.
14. Brand DA, Newcomer LN, Freiburger A et al. Cardiologist's practices compared with practice guidelines: use of beta-blockade after acute myocardial infarction. *J Am Coll Cardiol.* 1995; 26:1432–6.
15. Barron HV, Viskin S, Lundstrom RJ et al. Beta-blocker dosages and mortality after myocardial infarction. Data from a large health maintenance organization. *Arch Intern Med.* 1998; 158:449–53.
16. Gunderson T, Abrahmsen AM, Kjekshus J et al. Timolol-related reduction in mortality and reinfarction in patients ages 65–75 years surviving acute myocardial infarction. *Circulation.* 1982; 66:1179–84.
17. Hawkins CM, Richardson DW, Vokonas PS. Effect of propranolol in reducing mortality in older myocardial infarction patients. The Beta-Blocker Heart Attack Trial experience. *Circulation.* 1983; 67(6, pt. 2):I94–7.
18. Soumerai SB, McLaughlin TJ, Spiegelman D et al. Adverse outcomes of underuse of beta-blockers in elderly survivors of acute myocardial infarction. *JAMA.* 1997; 277:115–21.
19. Krumholz HM, Radford MJ, Wang Y et al. National use and effectiveness of beta-blockers for the treatment of elderly patients after acute myocardial infarction: National Cooperative Cardiovascular Project. *JAMA.* 1998; 280:623–9.
20. Chowdhury TA, Ladker SS, Dyer PH. Comparison of secondary prevention measures after myocardial infarction in subjects with and without diabetes mellitus. *J Intern Med.* 1999; 245:565–70.
21. Chen J, Marciniak TA, Radford MJ et al. Beta-blocker therapy for secondary prevention of myocardial infarction in elderly diabetic patients. Results from the National Cooperative Cardiovascular Project. *J Am Coll Cardiol.* 1999; 34:1388–94.
22. Lowel H, Koenig W, Engel S et al. The impact of diabetes mellitus on survival after myocardial infarction: can it be modified by drug treatment? Results of a population-based myocardial infarction register follow-up. *Diabetologia.* 2000; 43:218–26.
23. UK Prospective Diabetes Study Group. Efficacy of atenolol and captopril in reducing risk of macrovascular and microvascular complications in type 2 diabetes: UKPDS 39. *BMJ.* 1998; 317:713–20.
24. Malmberg K, Ryden L, Hamsten A et al. Mortality prediction in diabetic patients with myocardial infarction: experience from the DIGAMI study. *Cardiovasc Res.* 1997; 34:248–53.
25. Lichstein E, Hager WD, Gregory JJ et al. Relation between beta-adrenergic blocker use, various correlates of left ventricular function and the chance of developing congestive heart failure. The Multicenter Diltiazem Post-Infarction Research Group. *J Am Coll Cardiol.* 1990; 16:1327–32.

26. Spargias KS, Hall AS, Greenwood DC et al. Beta-blocker treatment and other prognostic variables in patients with clinical evidence of heart failure after acute myocardial infarction: evidence from the AIRE study. *Heart.* 1999; 81:25–32.

27. Furberg CD, Hawkins CM, Lichstein E et al., for the Beta-Blocker Heart Attack Trial Study Group. Effect of propranolol in postinfarction patients with mechanical or electrical complications. *Circulation.* 1984; 69:761–5.

28. Packer M, Bristow MR, Cohn JN et al., for the US Carvedilol Heart Failure Group. The effect of carvedilol on morbidity and mortality in patients with chronic heart failure. *N Engl J Med.* 1996; 334:1349–55.

29. MERIT-HF Study Group. Effect of metoprolol CR/XL in chronic heart failure: Metoprolol CR/XL Randomized Intervention Trial in Congestive Heart Failure (MERIT-HF). *Lancet.* 1999; 353:2001–7.

30. CAPRICORN Investigators. Effect of carvedilol on outcome after myocardial infarction in patients with left-ventricular dysfunction: the CAPRICORN randomized trial. *Lancet.* 2001; 357:1385–90.

31. Phillips KA, Shlipak MG, Coxson P et al. Health and economic benefits of increased beta-blocker use following myocardial infarction. *JAMA.* 2000; 284: 2748–54.

32. Holmboe ES, Meehan TP, Radford MJ et al. Use of critical pathways to improve the care of patients with acute myocardial infarction. *Am J Med.* 1999; 107:324–31.

33. Sarasin FP, Maschiangelo ML, Schaller MD et al. Successful implementation of guidelines for encouraging the use of beta-blockers in patients after acute myocardial infarction. *Am J Med.* 1999; 106:499–505.

34. Marciniak TA, Ellerbeck EF, Radford MJ et al. Improving the quality of care for Medicare patients with acute myocardial infarction: results from the Cooperative Cardiovascular Project. *JAMA.* 1998; 279:1351–7.

35. Jencks SF, Cuerdon T, Burwen DR et al. Quality of medical care delivered to Medicare beneficiaries: a profile at state and national levels. *JAMA.* 2000; 284: 1670–6.

36. National Committee for Quality Assurance. The state of managed care quality 2000. Washington, DC: National Committee for Quality Assurance; 2000.

37. Joint Commission on Accreditation for Healthcare Organizations. Plan for introducing Joint Commission hospital core measures requirements. www.jcaho.org/oryx_frm.html (accessed 2001 Jan 22).

38. Cano SB, Lemoine K. Promoting optimal use of beta-blockers after myocardial infarction. *Am J Health-Syst Pharm.* 1999; 56:858–9.

39. Hilleman DE. Acute myocardial infarction. Paper presented at ASHP Midyear Clinical Meeting. Las Vegas, NV; 2000 Dec.

40. Mehta RH, Eagle KA. Secondary prevention in acute myocardial infarction. *BMJ.* 1998; 316:838–42.

41. Rochon PA, Tu JV, Anderson GM et al. Rate of heart failure and 1-year survival for older people receiving low-dose beta-blocker therapy after myocardial infarction. *Lancet.* 2000; 356:639–44.

Approved by the ASHP Board of Directors on June 1, 2002. Developed by the ASHP Commission on Therapeutics.

The bibliographic citation for this document is as follows: American Society of Health-System Pharmacists. ASHP therapeutic position statement on the use of β-blockers in survivors of acute myocardial infarction. *Am J Health-Syst Pharm.* 2002; 59:2226–32.

ASHP Therapeutic Position Statement on the Use of Statins in the Prevention of Atherosclerotic Vascular Disease in Adults

Statement of Position

Atherosclerotic vascular disease (ASVD) is responsible for nearly 75% of all deaths from cardiovascular disease, and cardiovascular disease is the leading cause of death for both men and women in the United States.[1] Elevated cholesterol, specifically cholesterol contained in low-density-lipoprotein (LDL) particles, is an important risk factor for the development of ASVD. Diet and exercise therapy should be a fundamental part of all cholesterol-lowering treatment regimens. However, diet and exercise alone are often ineffective at significantly reducing blood cholesterol, and drug therapy is frequently needed to reach targeted goals. Therapy with 3-hydroxy-3-methylglutaryl coenzyme A (HMG-CoA) reductase inhibitors, or statins, has been shown to reduce the risk of fatal and nonfatal myocardial infarction (MI), unstable angina, and the need for revascularization procedures in hypercholesterolemic patients without known ASVD (primary prevention). In addition, statins have reduced all-cause mortality and stroke for patients with ASVD (secondary prevention). The American Society of Health-System Pharmacists (ASHP) supports the use of statins to lower blood cholesterol and reduce morbidity and mortality in patients at risk for atherosclerotic events.

Background

Pathophysiology of Atherosclerosis and Lipid Metabolism. Atherosclerosis is a multifactorial vascular process consisting of proliferation of intimal smooth muscle cells with accumulation of macrophages and T lymphocytes, an increase in the connective tissue matrix, and increases of cholesterol esters and free cholesterol in smooth muscle and endothelial cells.[2] Atherosclerotic lesions form when cholesterol-rich lipoproteins are deposited in macrophages, leading to foam-cell formation and eventually an atherosclerotic plaque. This plaque can rupture and form a nonocclusive or occlusive thrombus resulting in angina, MI, or sudden death.[3]

Cholesterol, triglycerides, and phospholipids are the major lipids in the body and are transported through the bloodstream as complex, water-soluble molecules called lipoproteins. Cholesterol is classified by the lipoprotein in which it is carried, such as very-low-density lipoprotein cholesterol, LDL cholesterol, intermediate-density-lipoprotein cholesterol, or high-density-lipoprotein (HDL) cholesterol. Total cholesterol is a sum of these components.

Prevalence of Hyperlipidemia in the United States. Nearly 102 million Americans have total blood cholesterol values of ≥200 mg/dL. These patients are candidates for dietary or cholesterol-lowering drug therapy.[1] Despite epidemiologic and interventional studies showing a direct relationship between elevated cholesterol and ASVD, hyperlipidemia continues to be undertreated.[4]

Pharmacology of Statins

Five statins are approved for use in the United States: atorvastatin, fluvastatin, lovastatin, pravastatin, and simvastatin. Several others are currently being developed. These agents work by inhibiting HMG-CoA reductase, the enzyme essential for the conversion of HMG-CoA to mevalonate. Competitive inhibition of this enzyme causes upregulation of LDL receptors on the surface of the liver and increased removal of LDL cholesterol from the blood. In addition, these agents lower triglycerides and have nonlipid effects that modify endothelial function, inflammatory responses, plaque stability, and thrombus formation.[5,6] The clinical significance of these effects is unknown. Although these drugs share the same mechanism of action in lowering cholesterol, they differ in chemical structure, pharmacokinetics, and pharmacologic potency. The chemical differences between statins produce variations in the effect that food has on the absorption, elimination half-lives, extent of protein binding, and cytochrome P-450 isoenzyme metabolism.[7] Current evidence does not support a definitive advantage of one product over another. In general, these drugs are well tolerated, and adverse effects on both liver and muscle are rare. The risk of myopathy with statin therapy is low. The risk of developing myopathy increases when a statin is used concomitantly with cyclosporine, erythromycin, a fibric-acid derivative, or niacin therapy. Data from 8000 patients taking lovastatin in the Expanded Clinical Evaluation of Lovastatin study revealed an increase of liver transaminases (three times the upper limit of normal) versus placebo of 1.5% and 0.1%, respectively.[8] Generally, monitoring of liver-function tests should occur before the initiation of statin therapy, 6–12 weeks after initiation of therapy, if the dosage is increased, and periodically thereafter.[9]

Patients with high LDL cholesterol and triglyceride levels can be difficult to treat and may benefit from the combination of a statin and a fibrate (gemfibrozil, fenofibrate, or clofibrate). While the reported frequency of myopathy associated with combination therapy is low (0.12%), caution should be exercised when statins and fibrates are used concomitantly because of the risk of severe myopathy, rhabdomyolysis, and renal failure.[10] The benefits should clearly balance the risks of combination statin–fibrate therapy, and the patient must be educated about the risks and warning signs of myopathy.

Current Guidelines for the Evaluation and Management of Lipid Disorders

In 2001, the National Cholesterol Education Program (NCEP) revised its guidelines for the evaluation and treatment of hyperlipidemia.[11] The NCEP guidelines identified an LDL cholesterol concentration of <100 mg/dL as the optimal level for all adults (Table 1). A complete lipid profile (total, LDL, and HDL cholesterol and triglyceride levels) and risk assessment are used to determine the risk classification of an adult.

Table 1.
Classification of Serum LDL Cholesterol Levels[11,a]

Category	Level (mg/dL)
Optimal	<100
Above optimal	100–129
Borderline high	130–159
High	160–189
Very high	≥190

[a]LDL = low-density lipoprotein.

Table 2.
Risk Factors for the Development of ASVD[11,a]

Positive Risk Factors	Negative Risk Factor
Patient age (men ≥45 yr; women ≥55 yr)	High HDL cholesterol level (≥60 mg/dL)
Family history of premature CHD[b]	
Cigarette smoking	
Hypertension (≥140/90 mm Hg or patient taking antihypertensive medication)	
Low HDL cholesterol level (<40 mg/dL)	

[a]ASVD = atherosclerotic vascular disease, CHD = coronary heart disease, HDL = high-density lipoprotein.
[b]CHD in male first-degree relative age <55 years or female first-degree relative age <65 years.

Table 3.
Treatment Based on LDL and Non-HDL Cholesterol Levels[11,a]

Treatment	mg/dL	
	Initiation Level	LDL Cholesterol Goal
Therapeutic lifestyle modification		
Without CHD and 0 or 1 risk factor	≥160	<160
Without CHD and 2+ risk factors	≥130	<130
With CHD or CHD risk equivalents	≥100	<100
Drug treatment		
Without CHD and 0 or 1 risk factor	≥190	<160
Without CHD and 2+ risk factors		<130
10-yr risk <10%	≥160	
10-yr risk 10–20%	≥130	
With CHD or CHD risk equivalents	≥130	<100

[a]LDL = low-density lipoprotein, HDL = high-density lipoprotein, CHD = coronary heart disease.

An individual's goal LDL cholesterol is determined by the presence of coronary heart disease (CHD) or CHD equivalents (diabetes mellitus or multiple risk factors that confer a 10-year risk for CHD that is greater than 20%) or the presence of major risk factors (Table 2). A patient's 10-year risk of having a CHD event is estimated from the Framingham risk score.[11] Treatment decisions should be based on both the LDL cholesterol level and risk of CHD (Table 3). For patients with triglyceride concentrations of >200 mg/dL who have achieved their goal LDL cholesterol level, non-HDL cholesterol may be utilized as a secondary treatment goal and can be estimated by subtracting HDL cholesterol from a patient's total cholesterol level. The American Heart Association and the American College of Cardiology published guidelines for the management of patients after MI that support recommendations in the NCEP guidelines.[12,13]

Evidence of Effectiveness

Statins effectively reduce LDL cholesterol by 20–55%. The degree of lipid-lowering response is dependent on agent selection, treatment dose, and individual patient response. LDL cholesterol reduction is a surrogate endpoint for reduction of ASVD, and effectiveness is best evaluated by reduc-

tion of events such as all-cause death, CHD death, need for revascularization procedures, and hospital admissions. Several large well-controlled trials have been conducted to assess the effect of statins on these endpoints in various patient groups.[14-18]

Primary Prevention Studies

The West of Scotland Coronary Prevention Study (WOSCOPS) and the Air Force/Texas Coronary Atherosclerosis Prevention Study (AFCAPS/TexCAPS) were prospective, randomized, double-blind comparisons of pravastatin and lovastatin, respectively, versus placebo. Individuals enrolled in AFCAPS/TexCAPS did not have clinically evident cardiovascular disease, while WOSCOPS participants had no history of MI.[14,15] A small percentage of WOSCOPS patients had other evidence of atherosclerosis, including angina (5%) and changes in the ST segment of their electrocardiograms (8%). Both pravastatin and lovastatin reduced the occurrence of acute major coronary events, the primary endpoint of these studies. All-cause mortality was 4.1% in the placebo group and 3.2% in the treatment group, demonstrating a reduction of 22% in WOSCOPS (95% confidence interval [CI] 0–40%) (p = 0.051). All-cause mortality was not assessed in AFCAPS/TexCAPS. In WOSCOPS, the time-to-event curves between the treatment and placebo groups became divergent after approximately six months. WOSCOPS also found a 31% reduction in the need for coronary angioplasty and a 37% reduction in revascularization procedures in patients who received pravastatin. Both studies provide compelling evidence that statin therapy significantly reduces atherosclerotic events for patients without evidence of CHD.

Genetic variations in the metabolism of cholesteryl ester transfer protein influence the progression of coronary atherosclerosis. Statin therapy has demonstrated the ability to slow this progression by lowering blood cholesterol and affecting nonlipid vascular function.[19] Genetic variability accounts for differences in the development of atherosclerosis and may explain differences in response to statin therapy. Further studies are needed to clarify this relationship.

Secondary Prevention Studies

Several large trials assessed the effect of statin therapy in patients with stable CHD. The Scandinavian Simvastatin Survival Study (4S), the Cholesterol And Recurrent Events (CARE) trial, and the Long-term Intervention with Pravastatin in Ischemic Disease (LIPID) study were randomized, double-blind, placebo-controlled trials of statins versus placebo in patients with a history of MI or angina pectoris.[16–18] The primary endpoints of all-cause mortality (4S), fatal and nonfatal MI (CARE), and mortality from CHD (LIPID) were significantly reduced in each trial (Table 4). These studies demonstrated that cholesterol reduction for stable patients with known coronary artery disease can reduce the rate of MI and CHD and ultimately improve overall survival rates. The Myocardial Ischemia Reduction with Aggressive Cholesterol Lowering (MIRACL) study found that statins also benefit patients with unstable CHD.[20]

The Effect of Statin Therapy on Stroke

A meta-analysis by Bucher et al.,[21] which involved 49,427 patients, found a reduction in fatal and non-fatal stroke associated with statin therapy compared with other lipid-lowering therapies (risk ratio 0.76 [95% CI, 0.62–0.92]). After analysis of studies of CHD endpoints, pravastatin and simvastatin were approved by the Food and Drug Administration for the prevention of stroke.

Long-Term Safety of Statin Therapy

Most patients will require long-term therapy to maintain serum cholesterol within a desired range. However, few studies have evaluated the long-term effects of statins on noncardiovascular mortality. The Prospective Pravastatin Pooling (PPP) project analyzed data from the cumulative experience of WOSCOPS, CARE, and LIPID.[22] Approximately 89% of the patients were male, and 25% of participants were older than 65 years. The mean exposure time to the study drug was 4.5 years. PPP did not identify a difference in noncardiovascular death or serious noncardiovascular adverse events between placebo and pravastatin. There were no confirmed cases of rhabdomyolysis. Studies evaluating long-term exposure are greatly needed to fully assess safety on a continuum.[23] It is important to remember that statins are category-X drugs and contraindicated in pregnant women and nursing mothers.

Heeschen et al.[24] reported that withdrawal of statin therapy from hospitalized cardiac patients was associated with increased rates of cardiac events. This report was generated from a subgroup analysis of the Platelet Receptor Inhibition in Ischemic Syndrome Management trial and supports the initiation and continuation of statin therapy for patients admitted to the hospital for acute coronary syndromes.

Effectiveness in Specific Patient Subgroups

Rates of CHD are highest in elderly patients. Although the relative risk of CHD is lower in the elderly than in the young or middle-aged, high cholesterol values lead to more CHD events in the elderly. Patients age 65–75 years who were treated with pravastatin in CARE (n = 1283) had clinically and statistically significant reductions in major coronary events, coronary death, coronary revascularization, and stroke, compared with patients receiving placebo.[25] Similar results were reported for elderly patients (n = 1121) in 4S.[26] A subgroup of patients 65–76 years who were treated with simvastatin had a statistically significant relative reduction of 34% for all-cause mortality, attributable to a 43% relative risk reduction for CHD mortality. Furthermore, the absolute risk reduction for patients 65 years or older was more than twice that of those less than 65 years for both total and CHD mortality. The Heart Protection Study (HPS) was the largest prospective intervention trial to date and compared simvastatin 40 mg daily to placebo in over 20,000 patients.[27] It was specifically designed to evaluate subpopulations of patients (e.g., differences in age, baseline LDL cholesterol values, sex, history of diabetes) and included 5806 patients 70 years of age or older. Vascular events were significantly reduced from 28.7% to 23.6% in the group that received simvastatin.

Patients with type 2 diabetes mellitus have a twofold to fourfold increased risk of CHD than do patients without diabetes.[28] The American Diabetes Association recommends statins as first-line therapy for diabetics with high LDL cholesterol levels.[29] LDL and HDL cholesterol levels of <100 and >40 mg/dL, respectively, are optimal for adult patients with diabetes; likewise, their triglyceride levels should be <150 mg/dL. HPS was the only intervention trial that specifically studied patients with concurrent diabetes and dyslipidemia and found significant vascular-event reduction with statin therapy. Subanalysis of other trials has also suggested the benefits of statins.[27] Analysis of CARE

Table 4.
Statin Therapy Trials for Reducing Risk of Coronary Events and Death in Patients with ASVD[a]

Trial	Treatment	Mean Duration (yr)	Treatment Effect on Primary Endpoint	p	NNT
Primary Prevention					
WOSCOPS[14] (n = 6595)	Pravastatin 40 mg daily	4.9	Coronary event; RRR, 31% (95% CI, 17–43%)	<0.001	42
AFCAPS/TexCAPS[15] (n = 6605)	Lovastatin 20–40 mg daily	5.2	Coronary event; RR, 0.63 (95% CI, 0.50–0.79)	<0.001	24
Secondary Prevention					
4S[16] (n = 4444)	Simvastatin 10–40 mg daily	5.4	Death; RR, 0.70 (95% CI, 0.58–0.85)	0.0003	25
CARE[17] (n = 4159)	Pravastatin 40 mg daily	5.0	Coronary event and MI; RRR, 24% (95% CI, 9–36%)	0.003	33
LIPID[18] (n = 9014)	Pravastatin 40 mg daily	6.1	CHD, death; RRR, 24% (95% CI, 12–35%)	<0.001	53

[a]ASVD = atherosclerotic vascular disease, NNT = number of patients needed to treat to prevent one primary endpoint event per trial duration, WOSCOPS = West of Scotland Coronary Prevention Study, RRR = relative risk reduction, CI = confidence interval, AFCAPS/TexCAPS = Air Force/Texas Coronary Atherosclerosis Prevention Study, RR = relative risk, 4S = Scandinavian Simvastatin Survival Study, CARE = Cholesterol and Recurrent Events trial, MI = myocardial infarction, LIPID = Long-term Intervention with Pravastatin in Ischemic Disease study.

and 4S found significant reductions in CHD occurrence in patients with diabetes who were treated with a statin.[28] The use of high-dose statin therapy (e.g., simvastatin 80 mg or atorvastatin 40 or 80 mg) to treat hypertriglyceridemia should be restricted to patients with high LDL cholesterol and triglyceride levels. Triglyceride reduction, achievable by strict glycemic control, should be attempted before the addition of lipid-lowering drug therapy.[29]

Therapeutic Alternatives

Other modalities exist for the treatment of dyslipidemia and should be considered if a statin cannot be used. Both niacin and bile-acid resins lower LDL cholesterol levels and reduce the number of CHD events. The Lipid Research Clinics Coronary Primary Prevention Trial found that patients treated with cholestyramine for seven years had a 19% reduction in nonfatal MI and a 24% decrease in CHD-related death.[30]

The Coronary Drug Project found a significant reduction in nonfatal MI with niacin therapy (27%) compared with placebo.[31] There was no significant effect on all-cause or cause-specific mortality. However, at 15 years, patients treated with niacin had an 11% decrease in mortality when compared with those taking placebo.[32] The mortality reduction was evident even though approximately 30% of the niacin-treated patients had poor compliance (i.e., took less than 60% of the prescribed amount of drug).

Adverse effects from niacin and bile-acid resins are often intolerable and result in poor medication compliance. A report of lipid-lowering therapy compliance from two health maintenance organizations found one-year discontinuation rates of 15% for lovastatin, 41% for bile-acid resins, and 46% for niacin.[33] Because hyperlipidemia generally requires lifelong therapy, high discontinuation rates reflect a failure to realize known treatment benefits. When compliance, adverse effects, and effectiveness are considered, statins should be first-line monotherapy in patients with known ASVD or multiple risk factors for ASVD. Patients may benefit from niacin or bile-acid resins if they cannot tolerate statins or if combination therapy is essential to managing mixed hyperlipidemias.

Cost of Prevention

The cost associated with treating lipid disorders must be assessed when considering a patient's risk of ASVD. When risk increases, treatment with a statin becomes more cost-effective. Analysis of statin trials indicates that they are cost-effective for patients with an annual coronary artery disease risk exceeding 1%.[34] This includes high- and moderate-risk primary prevention and secondary prevention. Analysis of WOSCOPS data (high-risk primary prevention) revealed a cost savings per quality-adjusted life year of $17,585, well below the $50,000 per life year saved, which is the figure frequently used as the upper limit of cost-effective therapy.[35]

Role of The Pharmacist

Pharmacists should participate in evaluating, monitoring, and treating hyperlipidemia and are encouraged to do so by NCEP. Pharmacists can play an active role in providing education about diet and drug therapy, treatment goals, benefits of therapy, the importance of compliance, and the monitoring of adverse effects.[36,37] Reviewing medication

profiles for drugs used to treat symptoms of CHD, such as sublingual or transdermal nitroglycerin, may identify potential candidates for statin therapy.[38] Cholesterol screening in community pharmacies can now be conducted with point-of-care testing machines, and patients can then be referred to their primary care provider for assessment and consideration for drug therapy.[39] Direct patient care can also be provided through pharmacist-managed lipid clinics in ambulatory care settings and in specialized pharmacies.[40] Opportunities for pharmacists to become involved include developing, implementing, and tailoring drug therapy and improving compliance, all of which can assist patients in reaching their therapeutic goal. Hyperlipidemia requires lifelong therapy, and educating patients about diet and drug therapy is essential for reducing the risk of cardiovascular events.

Summary

Elevated blood cholesterol levels contribute significantly to ASVD and are often undertreated or not treated at all. Evaluation and management of lipid disorders should be guided by current NCEP guidelines. For patients with elevated cholesterol levels after appropriate therapeutic lifestyle changes, statins are a safe and effective means of reducing cardiovascular events. Because of their proven safety and effectiveness, ASHP supports the use of statins as first-line therapy for the primary and secondary prevention of atherosclerotic events.

References

1. American Heart Association. 2002 heart and stroke statistical update. www.americanheart.org/presenter (accessed 2002 May 14).
2. Libby P. The vascular biology of atherosclerosis. In: Braunwald E, ed. Heart disease: a textbook of cardiovascular medicine. Philadelphia: Saunders; 2001: 995–1009.
3. Kullo IJ, Edwards WD, Schwartz RS. Vulnerable plaque: pathobiology and clinical implications. *Ann Intern Med.* 1998; 129:1050–60.
4. Kwiterovich PO Jr. State-of-the-art update and review: clinical trials of lipid-lowering agents. *Am J Cardiol.* 1998; 82(12A):3U–17U.
5. Rosenson RS, Tangney CC. Antiatherothrombotic properties of statins. Implications for cardiovascular event reduction. *JAMA.* 1998; 279:1643–50.
6. Grundy SM. Consensus statement: role of therapy with "statins" in patients with hypertriglyceridemia. *Am J Cardiol.* 1998; 81(4A):1B–6B.
7. Illingworth DR, Tobert JA. A review of clinical trials comparing HMG-CoA reductase inhibitors. *Clin Ther.* 1994; 16:366–85.
8. Bradford RH, Shear CL, Chremos AN, et al. Expanded Clinical Evaluation of Lovastatin (EXCEL) study results. *Arch Intern Med.* 1991; 151:43–9.
9. McEvoy GK, ed. AHFS drug information 2002. Bethesda, MD: American Society of Health-System Pharmacists; 2002.
10. Shek A, Ferrill MJ. Statin–fibrate combination therapy. *Ann Pharmacother.* 2001; 35:908–17.
11. Executive summary of the third report of the National Cholesterol Education Program (NCEP) Expert Panel on Detection, Evaluation, and Treatment of High Blood

Cholesterol in Adults (Adult Treatment Panel III). *JAMA.* 2001; 285:2486–97.

12. Smith SC, Blair SN, Criqui MH, et al. AHA consensus panel statement. Preventing heart attack and death in patients with coronary heart disease. *J Am Coll Cardiol.* 1995; 26:292–4.

13. Ryan TJ, Anderson JL, Antman EM, et al. ACC/AHA guidelines for the management of patients with acute myocardial infarction: a report of the American College of Cardiology/American Heart Association Task Force on Practice Guidelines (Committee on Management of Acute Myocardial Infarction). *J Am Coll Cardiol.* 1996; 28:1328–428.

14. Shepherd J, Cobbe SM, Ford I, et al. Prevention of coronary heart disease with pravastatin in men with hypercholesterolemia. *N Engl J Med.* 1995; 333:1301–7.

15. Downs JR, Clearfield M, Weis S, et al. Primary prevention of acute coronary events with lovastatin in men and women with average cholesterol levels: results of AFCAPS/TexCAPS. *JAMA.* 1998; 279:1615–22.

16. Pederson TR, Kjekshus J, Berg K, et al. Randomised trial of cholesterol lowering in 4444 patients with coronary heart disease: the Scandinavian Simvastatin Survival Study (4S). *Lancet.* 1994; 344:1383–9.

17. Sacks FM, Pfeffer MA, Moye LA, et al. The effect of pravastatin on coronary events after myocardial infarction in patients with average cholesterol levels. *N Engl J Med.* 1996; 335:1001–9.

18. Prevention of cardiovascular events and death with pravastatin in patients with coronary heart disease and a broad range of initial cholesterol levels. *N Engl J Med.* 1998; 339:1349–57.

19. Kuivenhoven JA, Jukema JW, Zwinderman AH, et al. The role of a common variant of the cholesteryl ester transfer protein gene in the progression of coronary artheroslerosis. *N Engl J Med.* 1998; 338:86–93.

20. Effects of atorvastatin on early recurrent ischemic events in acute coronary syndromes. *JAMA.* 2001; 285:1711–8.

21. Bucher HC, Griffith LE, Guyatt GH. Effect of HMGcoA reductase inhibitors on stroke. A meta-analysis of randomized, controlled trials. *Ann Intern Med.* 1998; 128:89–95.

22. Pfeffer MAS, Keech A, Sacks FM, et al. Safety and tolerability of pravastatin in long-term clinical trials: Prospective Pravastatin Pooling (PPP) project. *Circulation.* 2002; 105:2341–6.

23. Gaziano JM, Hebert PR, Hennekens CH. Cholesterol reduction: weighing the benefits and risks. *Ann Intern Med.* 1996; 124:914–8.

24. Heeschen C, Hamm CW, Laufs U, et al. Withdrawal of statins increases event rates in patients with acute coronary syndromes. *Circulation.* 2002; 105:1446–52.

25. Lewis SJ, Moyé LA, Sacks FM, et al. Effect of pravastatin on cardiovascular events in older patients with myocardial infarction and cholesterol levels in the average range. Results of the Cholesterol And Recurrent Events (CARE) trial. *Ann Intern Med.* 1998; 129:681–9.

26. Meittinen TA, Pyörälä K, Olsson AG, et al. Cholesterol-lowering therapy in women and elderly patients with myocardial infarction or angina pectoris. Findings from the Scandinavian Simvastatin Survival Study (4S). *Circulation.* 1997; 96:4211–8.

27. MRC/BHF Heart Protection Study of cholesterol lowering with simvastatin in 20,536 high-risk individuals: a randomised placebo-controlled trial. *Lancet.* 2002; 360:7–22.

28. Haffner SM. Management of dyslipidemia in adults with diabetes. *Diabetes Care.* 1998; 21:160–78.

29. American Diabetes Association. Management of dyslipidemia in adults with diabetes. *Diabetes Care.* 2003; 26(suppl 1):S83–6.

30. The Lipid Research Clinics Coronary Primary Prevention Trial results. I. Reduction in incidence of coronary heart disease. *JAMA.* 1984; 251:351–64.

31. Clofibrate and niacin in coronary heart disease. *JAMA.* 1975; 231:360–81.

32. Canner PL, Berge KG, Wenger NK, et al. Fifteen year mortality in Coronary Drug Project patients: long-term benefit with niacin. *J Am Coll Cardiol.* 1986; 8:1245–55.

33. Andrade SE, Walker AM, Gottlieb LK, et al. Discontinuation of antihyperlipidemic drugs—do rates reported in clinical trials reflect rates in primary care settings? *N Engl J Med.* 1995; 332:1125–31.

34. Hay JW, Yu WM, Ashraf T. Pharmacoeconomics of lipid-lowering agents for primary and secondary prevention of coronary artery disease. *Pharmacoeconomics.* 1999; 15:47–74.

35. Hay JW. Economic modeling and sensitivity analysis. *Value Health.* 1998; 1:187–93.

36. Shibley MC, Pugh CB. Implementation of pharmaceutical care services for patients with hyperlipidemias by independent community pharmacy practitioners. *Ann Pharmacother.* 1997; 31:713–9.

37. Bluml BM, McKenney JM, Cziraky MJ. Pharmaceutical care services and results in Project ImPACT: hyperlipidemia. *J Am Pharm Assoc.* 2000; 40:157–65.

38. Tullio CJ, Goode DL. Identifying ambulatory care patients with coronary heart disease who need cholesterol management. *Am J Health-Syst Pharm.* 1998; 55:1769–71.

39. Interim Report from Project ImPact: Hyperlipidemia. Collaborative practice model shows promise for improving patient care. *J Am Pharm Assoc.* 1998; 38:529–34.

40. Furmaga EM. Pharmacist management of a hyperlipidemia clinic. *Am J Hosp Pharm.* 1993; 50:91–5.

Approved by the ASHP Board of Directors on September 27, 2002. Developed by the ASHP Commission on Therapeutics.

The bibliographic citation for this document is as follows: American Society of Health-System Pharmacists. ASHP therapeutic position statement on the use of statins in the prevention of atherosclerotic vascular disease in adults. *Am J Health-Syst Pharm.* 2003; 60:593–8.

ASHP Therapeutic Position Statement on the Use of Low-Molecular-Weight Heparins for Adult Outpatient Treatment of Acute Deep-Vein Thrombosis

Statement of Position

The American Society of Health-System Pharmacists believes that the use of low-molecular-weight-heparin (LMWH) therapy for the treatment of acute deep-vein thrombosis (DVT) in appropriate adult outpatients is as safe and effective as traditional inpatient therapy with unfractionated heparin (UFH). Outpatient treatment of acute DVT with LMWHs is often more cost-effective than traditional inpatient therapy and is associated with greater patient satisfaction. When opportunities exist, health care professionals are encouraged to actively participate in developing, implementing, and monitoring outpatient DVT treatment programs.

Background

Traditionally, patients who are diagnosed with acute DVT are hospitalized for administration and monitoring of intravenous UFH therapy. Warfarin sodium is overlapped with UFH for a minimum of five days until the patient's International Normalized Ratio (INR) is therapeutic for two consecutive days, at which time UFH can be discontinued.[1] LMWHs have several unique properties that may offer advantages over UFH in the initial treatment of DVT, including a more predictable anticoagulant response, a longer plasma half-life, and reduced frequencies of thrombocytopenia and osteopenia.[1] Three LMWHs are currently available in the United States (Table 1).[2-5] Pharmacokinetic and pharmacodynamic properties vary among LMWHs, and data are insufficient to determine whether these agents are clinically interchangeable.[6,7]

The goals of outpatient treatment of DVT are the same as those of traditional inpatient treatment: arrest thrombus growth, prevent recurrence, limit limb swelling, and prevent embolization and the postphlebitic syndrome. Outpatient therapy has the added benefits of decreasing overall DVT treatment costs and improving quality of life.[8]

Evidence of Efficacy and Safety

Randomized controlled clinical trials comparing LMWHs with UFH for the treatment of acute DVT in hospitalized patients suggest that LMWH therapy is at least as safe and effective as conventional UFH therapy (Table 2).[9-17] LMWHs are administered in weight-based, individualized doses and do not require routine frequent monitoring of activated partial thromboplastin time (aPPT). Although thrombocytopenia occurs infrequently with LMWHs, a platelet count measured between days 5 and 7 of therapy is helpful in monitoring for the occurrence of heparin-induced thrombocytopenia in heparin-naive patients.[1]

Clinical trials comparing LMWHs administered in the outpatient setting with conventional inpatient UFH therapy have demonstrated that both were equally safe and effective for acute DVT in appropriately selected patients.[9,11,18,19] Levine et al.[9] reported that patients with proximal DVT randomized

to treatment with traditional UFH in the hospital and those randomized to outpatient treatment with enoxaparin 1 mg/kg subcutaneously every 12 hours did not have significant differences in rates of recurrent thromboembolism or major bleeding. The rate of recurrent thromboembolism was 6.7% in the UFH group and 5.3% in the enoxaparin group.

Evidence that outpatient LMWH therapy is as safe and effective as inpatient UFH therapy was also provided by an international, multicenter, randomized, controlled trial involving nadroparin.[18] The LMWH was as effective as UFH therapy, cost less, and had few or no measurable adverse effects on physical or mental well-being. A systematic review also suggested that outpatient treatment of DVT with LMWHs is efficacious and safe.[20]

The success of outpatient DVT treatment programs in many health care systems demonstrates that acute DVT may be safely and effectively managed in everyday clinical practice outside the hospital setting.[12,13,19] In fact, the strength of available literature supporting the use of LMWHs in the treatment of acute DVT has led to a reevaluation of the use of UFH for this indication. Guidelines from the American College of Chest Physicians (ACCP) state that "LMWH offers the major benefits of convenience of dosing and facilitation of outpatient treatment."[1] ACCP recommends that LMWHs be preferred over UFH for the treatment of acute DVT or pulmonary embolism (PE). Evidence supporting outpatient treatment of PE with LMWHs exists but is less robust than that for outpatient treatment of DVT.[12,21,22]

Cost-Effectiveness

Hospitalization adds appreciably to the cost of treating acute DVT. Even though LMWH drug costs are much higher than those of UFH, avoiding hospitalization or decreasing its length substantially lowers the overall cost of DVT treatment.

An economic evaluation of an existing outpatient DVT treatment program in a large group-model health maintenance organization (HMO) revealed an average cost saving of $2828 (in 1998 dollars) for each patient treated at home with LMWHs.[13] Another retrospective pharmacoeconomic evaluation of outpatient DVT treatment with LMWHs in a large HMO documented a mean cost difference of $2583 per patient in favor of the LMWH group.[23] These savings are consistent with previously published data from a non-managed care environment that estimated the saving associated with outpatient treatment of DVT at $2750 per patient (in 1998 dollars).[8] A trial of the inpatient administration of LMWHs versus UFH for DVT found that the average cost saving per patient treated with LMWHs was $509 (in 1998 dollars).[24] The authors estimated that if 37% of the patients receiving LMWHs had been treated as outpatients, the average cost saving per patient would have increased to $1159. By a similar analysis, if 92% of the LMWH-treated patients had received the therapy as outpatients, the cost saving would have been $2165 per patient.

During a two-year evaluation period, the previously mentioned group-model HMO realized a total cost saving of

Table 1.
Heparin Profiles[a]

Variable	Unfractionated Heparin[2]	Dalteparin[3,b]	Enoxaparin[4,c]	Tinzaparin[5,d]
Mean molecular weight	15,000	5,000	4,500	5,500–7,500
Bioavailability	30–60	81–93	92	86.7
Plasma half-life (min)[e]	45–60	119–139	129–180	204–210
Dosage recommendations for DVT[f]	Various	200 international units/kg subcutaneous once daily or 100 international units/kg subcutaneous q 12 hr for 5–7 days in conjunction with warfarin	1 mg/kg subcutaneous q 12 hr or 1.5 mg/kg once daily[g] for 5–7 days in conjunction with warfarin	175 international units/kg subcutaneous once daily for 5–7 days in conjunction with warfarin

[a]DVT = deep-vein thrombosis.
[b]Lacks FDA-approved labeling for use in the treatment of DVT or pulmonary embolism (PE).
[c]FDA has approved labeling for use in inpatient treatment of acute DVT with or without PE or for outpatient treatment of acute DVT without PE.
[d]FDA has approved labeling for use in the inpatient treatment of acute DVT with or without PE.
[e]Inpatients with normal renal function.
[f]Based on actual body weight; dosing for patients weighing >120 or <40 kg is controversial (anti-Xa activity monitoring has been suggested for these patients).
[g]Once-daily administration may be less effective in very obese patients and patients with cancer.

Table 2.
Adverse Outcomes of Treatment of Deep-Vein Thrombosis with Low-Molecular-Weight Heparins and Unfractionated Heparin (UFH)

Outcome	Frequency (%)			
	UFH[9,10]	Dalteparin[11,12]	Enoxaparin[9,13]	Tinzaparin[10]
Death	6.7–9.6	1.2–7	4.3–4.6	4.7
Major bleeding	1.2–5	0.9–2	0.8–2.0	0.5
Pulmonary embolism	0.8–2.7	0.9	0.8–1.5	1.4
Recurrence of thrombus extension	4.1–5.9	1.6–3.6	2.6–4.5	1.4

over $1 million (in 1998 dollars)—enough to offset the entire operating budget for a centralized clinical pharmacy anticoagulation service.[13] Sensitivity analysis demonstrated that the savings realized by this organization were robust. For example, tripling the acquisition cost of LMWHs would reduce the average cost saving to only $1953 per DVT episode managed at home. Break-even analysis demonstrated that, for the cost of traditional inpatient treatment to equal outpatient treatment, either LMWH acquisition costs would have to increase by 750% or costs for inpatient therapy would have to decrease by 77%. Health systems should, therefore, explore outpatient treatment of DVT. The associated financial savings can offset the cost of developing, implementing, and maintaining the service.

Access to care, support by ancillary care providers, insurance coverage, patient satisfaction, and quality of life need to be considered to ensure that therapy can be obtained and be safe and effective. LMWH therapy can be a financial burden for patients who lack an outpatient prescription drug benefit; many insurance plans do not cover the cost of self-administered outpatient LMWH therapy. It is important to consider all aspects of care and to be aware that, in special situations, inpatient treatment of DVT may be preferable.

Patient Satisfaction

Anecdotal experience and the results of formal evaluations indicate a high degree of patient satisfaction and comfort with outpatient DVT treatment. Using the Medical Outcomes Study Short-Form 36[25] to compare changes in health-related quality of life, O'Brien et al.[8] observed a greater improvement in social functioning for patients treated with

LMWHs as outpatients than for those treated with UFH as inpatients. These results are consistent with the findings of a separate study that used a 5-point Likert scale to determine that 91% of patients completing the survey were "very pleased" to have their DVT treated at home.[19]

Successful Outpatient DVT Treatment Programs

The medical literature contains numerous reports of successful outpatient DVT treatment programs.[12,13,19,23] These programs have been implemented in a variety of health care systems and tailored to the needs and strengths of each system. Successful implementation of these programs relies on detailed care plans that begin at the point of entry into the system and on collaborative efforts by a variety of practitioners, departments, laboratory personnel, home care services, social workers, case managers, risk management personnel, and financial planners.

Before starting outpatient DVT therapy, practitioners should ensure that patients understand the implications of their disease and the rationale behind treatment. The correct use and potential adverse effects of LMWHs and warfarin should be thoroughly reviewed with patients. Patients should be taught to identify signs and symptoms of complications and to seek medical attention immediately should they occur. During initial therapy, frequent patient contact is essential for early detection of potential problems and to ensure that patients have their questions and concerns addressed promptly. Follow-up contact should be scheduled to ask patients about signs and symptoms that may suggest bleeding, thrombus extension, and PE. Once LMWH therapy is completed (in approximately five to seven days), patient contact can be less frequent. Practitioners should document their patient care activities in the medical record. Occasionally, some patients are unwilling or unable to comply with the demands of outpatient DVT treatment. Outpatient treatment may still be accomplished by using home health nursing services, having patients come to the medical office for daily LMWH injections, or admitting patients to a skilled-nursing facility. The added costs incurred by these services still make outpatient treatment of DVT attractive compared with the cost of hospitalization.[13]

Special Patient Populations

Outpatient DVT treatment requires careful patient selection. There is no consensus yet about which patients are the best candidates for home therapy; a comparison of exclusion criteria used in outpatient DVT treatment programs is provided in Table 3.[26] In the opinion of the advocates of strict exclusion criteria, careful patient selection and risk stratification reduce the rate of thromboembolic complications.[27] Proponents of a less restrictive approach argue that strict exclusion criteria may unnecessarily withhold outpatient treatment with LMWHs from many patients. Further investigation is necessary to determine whether the lower rate of thromboembolic complications observed in programs with strict exclusion criteria represents a true reduction in the complication rate or a selection bias. For example, cancer patients with DVT are denied the option of outpatient therapy in some programs. However, preliminary evidence suggests that the mortality rate among cancer patients treated with LMWHs is lower than the rate among patients treated with

UFH.[28] Recent evidence has also demonstrated that patients with cancer and DVT or PE had fewer recurrences of DVT when they were treated with an LMWH alone (dalteparin 200 International Units/kg subcutaneously once daily for one month, followed by 150 International Units/kg once daily for five months) than when they received usual therapy with an LMWH followed by oral anticoagulation therapy.[29] Outpatient DVT therapy with LMWHs also offers terminally ill cancer patients the opportunity to spend more time at home.

According to strict exclusion criteria, approximately 60% of patients with acute DVT are eligible for some form of outpatient LMWH therapy (Table 3). A less restrictive approach increases the fraction of eligible patients to 75–95% while maintaining the same efficacy and safety found in clinical trials.[12,13,19]

Patients with concomitant diseases that could affect LMWH pharmacokinetics may be less suitable candidates for outpatient DVT therapy. Altered pharmacokinetics (as in patients with renal dysfunction and pregnant patients) may result in insufficient or excessive anticoagulation, increasing the risk of therapeutic failure or bleeding. In these circumstances, outpatient therapy should be undertaken with caution, and vigilant monitoring for complications is indicated.

Plasma concentrations of LMWHs are not routinely monitored; however, anti-factor Xa activity can be measured and used to approximate the LMWH concentration in the blood. The College of American Pathologists reports that this assay is routinely performed in approximately 18% of all laboratories.[30] The minimal anti-Xa level needed for a therapeutic effect has not been established, but an inverse relationship between thrombus propagation and anti-Xa level

Table 3.
Outcomes of and Exclusion Criteria for Outpatient Deep-Vein Thrombosis (DVT) Treatment Programs

Variable	Ref. 26 ($n = 102$)	Ref. 19 ($n = 89$)	Ref. 12 ($n = 194$)	Ref. 13 ($n = 391$)
Exclusion criteria	Platelet count, <100 × 10³/mm³ Active bleeding History of gastrointestinal bleeding within 6 mo Underlying liver disorder History of familial bleeding disorder Hypertensive urgency or emergency Hypercoagulable state Catheter-associated DVT History of heparin sensitivity Pregnant or lactating Pulmonary embolism Iliofemoral thrombosis >30% of ideal body weight Renal insufficiency Recent surgery Other comorbid medical conditions Other factors increasing risk of home treatment	High risk of bleeding Additional medical condition requiring hospital admission Incapable of self-treatment at home	Concurrent illness requiring hospital admission for >48 hr Active bleeding Inpatient status without discharge in the next 48 hr Pulmonary embolism DVT with pain requiring i.v. narcotics Age, <18 yr Likelihood of poor compliance	Hospital admission required for concurrent symptomatic disease Pulmonary embolism Active bleeding Pregnant
Major bleeding complication rate (%)	0	1.1	2.1	0.8
Thromboembolic complication rate (%)	1.9	6.7	3.6	4.1
Outpatient treatment (%)	42 (61 with abbreviated hospital admission)	>75 (including <24-hr hospital admission)	95	78

has been observed.[31,32] Furthermore, high anti-Xa levels have been associated with bleeding.[33] The exact role of anti-Xa activity monitoring is currently not well defined. Monitoring anti-Xa activity has been suggested for patients who are small, obese, pregnant, or renally impaired, as well as for children.[34] Blood samples for measuring anti-Xa activity should be collected three to four hours after LMWH administration.[30] Therapeutic ranges of 0.6–1.0 and 1.0–2.0 International Units/mL have been suggested for twice-daily and once-daily LMWH therapy, respectively.[34] Inhibition of factor Xa is not the sole contributor to LMWH's anticoagulant effect. Adjusting LMWH dosages on the basis of anti-factor Xa activity is therefore difficult to justify.[35] In addition, dosage-adjustment algorithms similar to those used with UFH and aPTT measurements are not currently available for LMWH and anti-factor Xa measurements.

Barriers to Outpatient Treatment with LMWHs

Some patients are unable or unwilling to self-inject LMWHs or cannot adhere to the rigorous schedule of blood drawings or finger sticks necessary for monitoring outpatient transition to oral warfarin therapy. Options for these patients include visiting-nurse services, admission to a skilled-nursing facility, and admission to the hospital. Point-of-care INR-monitoring devices for warfarin therapy may provide a means for patients who do not live close to a clinical laboratory or who have limited mobility.

LMWH therapy may be a financial burden for patients who do not have prescription drug insurance. As more successful programs are developed and the cost savings are appreciated, more broad-based coverage for outpatient DVT treatment may become available. Health care professionals should continue to document the clinical and financial outcomes associated with outpatient DVT treatment programs. Presenting favorable outcomes data to health plans may facilitate approval of coverage on a more widespread basis.

Commercially available doses do not always meet patient-specific needs, and some institutions have therefore elected to repackage weight-based LMWH doses. Repackaging LMWHs may be attractive from an economic perspective and for ease of administration; however, not all pharmacies are equipped with cleanrooms with laminar-airflow hoods or barrier isolators, which are necessary to ensure the sterility of repackaged LMWH syringes. Well-publicized reports of patients being harmed by compounded injectables substantiate that effective compounding practices must be followed to ensure the quality and safety of the product.[36,37] In addition, repackaged enoxaparin syringes must be refrigerated,[38] which may be problematic for patients who do not have ready access to a refrigerator. Repackaged dalteparin syringes have been shown to retain 90% of anti-Xa activity for 15 days at room temperature.[39]

Outpatient DVT therapy with LMWHs requires a well-coordinated system of communication and follow-up. Patients should have access to a provider 24 hours a day, seven days a week to address questions and concerns in a timely manner. This may present problems to health care systems that are inaccessible after hours or on weekends and holidays. The availability of an anticoagulation management service has been shown to be beneficial in the outpatient management of DVT.[12,13,19]

Elements of an outpatient LMWH therapy program can be considered without a dedicated anticoagulation management service providing 24-hour support. For example, a health system with limited resources can develop an outpatient LMWH treatment protocol through the combined efforts of primary care providers, affiliated urgent care centers, emergency department physicians, and health-system pharmacists and nurses. The protocol would clearly specify criteria for identifying appropriate candidates for the therapy and outline procedures for initial treatment and education, all of which could be the responsibility of the urgent care and emergency room physicians. Follow-up care during standard outpatient hours of operation can be provided by primary care providers or pharmacists and nurses trained and dedicated to monitoring outpatients who are receiving LMWHs for acute DVT. After-hours care can be managed by the provider's on-call service or emergency department. The overall coordination of care should be the responsibility of a designated health care professional, who should be notified as soon as possible following the decision to initiate treatment. The success of outpatient LMWH treatment will depend on close communication among all involved health care professionals with the help of a coordinator, along with adequate training of providers and patients receiving LMWH therapy.

Summary

Outpatient treatment of DVT with LMWHs offers the opportunity to dramatically reduce the cost of treating DVT and improve the quality of life without compromising clinical outcomes. Given the choice, most patients are willing to be treated at home and are comfortable with or willing to accept the idea of giving themselves injections of LMWHs. Establishing comprehensive outpatient treatment guidelines is important to ensure that adequate support is provided by the anticoagulation provider. Pharmacists have assumed lead roles in developing and maintaining successful outpatient DVT treatment programs. Because of the safety, effectiveness, and potential savings associated with treating patients with acute DVT in the outpatient setting, ASHP encourages health care professionals to become or remain actively involved in the development and documentation of innovative outpatient DVT treatment programs. These programs will also facilitate the use of newer antithrombotic agents as they become available and receive approval for outpatient DVT treatment.[10,26]

References

1. Hyers TM, Giancarlo A, Hull RD et al. Antithrombotic therapy for venous thromboembolic disease. *Chest.* 2001; 119:176S–93S.

2. Heparin sodium package insert. Kalamazoo, MI: Pharmacia & Upjohn; 2000 Jan.

3. Fragmin (dalteparin) package insert. Kalamazoo, MI: Pharmacia & Upjohn; 2003 May.

4. Lovenox (enoxaparin) package insert. Bridgewater, NJ: Aventis; 2003 Jan.

5. Innhep (tinzaparin) package insert. Boulder, CO: Pharmion; 2003 Jan.

6. Prandoni P. Low-molecular-weight heparins: are they interchangeable? Yes. *J Thromb Haemost.* 2003; 1:10–1.

7. Nenci GG. Low-molecular-weight heparins: are they interchangeable? No. *J Thromb Haemost.* 2003; 1:12–3.

8. O'Brien B, Levine M, Willan A et al. Economic evalu-

ation of outpatient treatment with low-molecular-weight heparin for proximal vein thrombosis. *Arch Intern Med.* 1999; 159:2298–304.

9. Levine M, Jent M, Hirsh J et al. A comparison of low-molecular-weight heparin administered primarily at home with unfractionated heparin administered in the hospital for proximal deep-vein thrombosis. *N Engl J Med.* 1996; 334:677–81.

10. Hull RD, Raskob GE, Pineo GF et al. Subcutaneous low-molecular-weight heparin compared with continuous intravenous heparin in the treatment of proximal-vein thrombosis. *N Engl J Med.* 1992; 337:663–9.

11. Lindmarker P, Holmstrom M. Use of low molecular weight heparin (dalteparin), once daily, for the treatment of deep vein thrombosis. A feasibility and health economic study in an outpatient setting. *J Intern Med.* 1996; 240:395–401.

12. Wells PS, Kovacs MJ, Bormanis J et al. Expanding eligibility for outpatient treatment of deep venous thrombosis and pulmonary embolism with low-molecular-weight heparin. *Arch Intern Med.* 1998; 158:1809–12.

13. Tillman DJ, Charland SL, Witt DM. Effectiveness and economic impact associated with a program for outpatient management of acute deep vein thrombosis in a group model health maintenance organization. *Arch Intern Med.* 2000; 160:2926–32.

14. Hull RD, Raskob GE, Pineo GF et al. Subcutaneous low-molecular-weight heparin compared with continuous intravenous heparin in the treatment of proximal deep-vein thrombosis. *N Engl J Med.* 1992; 326:975–82.

15. Lensing AW, Prins MH, Davidson BL et al. Treatment of deep venous thrombosis with low-molecular-weight heparin: a meta-analysis. *Arch Intern Med.* 1995; 155:601–7.

16. Leizorovicz A. Comparison of the efficacy and safety of low-molecular-weight heparins and unfractionated heparin in the initial treatment of deep vein thrombosis. *Drugs.* 1996; 52(suppl 7):30–7.

17. Merli G, Spiro TE, Olsson CG et al. Subcutaneous enoxaparin once or twice daily compared with intravenous unfractionated heparin for treatment of venous thromboembolic disease. *Ann Intern Med.* 2001; 134:191–202.

18. Koopman MM, Prandoni P, Piovella F et al. Treatment of venous thrombosis with intravenous unfractionated heparin administered in the hospital as compared with subcutaneous low-molecular-weight heparin administered at home. *N Engl J Med.* 1996; 334:682–7.

19. Harrison L, McGinnis J, Crowther M et al. Assessment of outpatient treatment of deep-vein thrombosis with low-molecular-weight heparin. *Arch Intern Med.* 1998; 158:2001–3.

20. Diagnosis and treatment of deep venous thrombosis and pulmonary embolism. Rockville, MD: Agency for Healthcare Research and Quality, AHRQ Evidence Report/Technology Assessment no. 68; 2003.

21. Columbus Investigators. Low-molecular-weight heparin in the treatment of patients with venous thromboembolism. *N Engl J Med.* 1997; 337:657–62.

22. Kovacs MJ, Anderson D, Morrow B et al. Outpatient treatment of pulmonary embolism with dalteparin. *Thromb Haemost.* 2000; 83:209–11.

23. Spyropoulos AC, Hurley JS, Ciesla GN et al. Management of acute proximal deep vein thrombosis. Pharmacoeconomic evaluation of outpatient treatment with enoxaparin vs inpatient treatment with unfractionated heparin. *Chest.* 2002; 122:108–14.

24. Hull RD, Raskob GE, Rosenbloom D et al. Treatment of proximal vein thrombosis with subcutaneous low-molecular-weight heparin vs. intravenous heparin. An economic perspective. *Arch Intern Med.* 1997; 157:289–94.

25. Ware JE, Snow KK, Kosinski M et al. SF-36 Health Survey: manual and interpretation guide. Boston: Nimrod; 1993.

26. Spyropoulos AC, Kardos J, Wigal P. Outcomes analysis of the outpatient treatment of venous thromboembolic disease using the low-molecular-weight heparin enoxaparin in a managed care organization. *J Manag Care Pharm.* 2000; 6:298–304

27. Spyropoulos AC. Outpatient protocols for treatment of venous thromboembolism using low-molecular-weight heparin: to treat or not to treat at home. *Arch Intern Med.* 1999; 159:1139–40.

28. Gould MK, Dembitzer AD, Doyle RL et al. Low-molecular-weight heparins compared with unfractionated heparin for treatment of acute deep vein thrombosis. A meta-analysis of randomized, controlled trials. *Ann Intern Med.* 1999; 130:800–9.

29. Lee AY, Levine MN, Baker RI et al. Low-molecular-weight heparin versus a coumarin for the prevention of recurrent venous thromboembolism in patients with cancer. *N Engl J Med.* 2003; 349:146–53.

30. Laposata M, Green D, Van Cott EM et al. College of American Pathologists Conference XXXI on Laboratory Monitoring of Anticoagulant Therapy. The clinical use and laboratory monitoring of low-molecular-weight heparin, danaparoid, hirudin and related compounds, and argatroban. *Arch Pathol Lab Med.* 1998; 122:799–807.

31. Alhenc-Gelas M, Jestin-Le Guernic C, Vitoux JF et al. Adjusted versus fixed doses of the low-molecular-weight heparin fragmin in the treatment of deep vein thrombosis. *Thromb Haemost.* 1994; 71:698–702.

32. Levine MN, Planes A, Hirsh J et al. The relationship between antifactor Xa level and clinical outcome in patients receiving enoxaparin low molecular weight heparin to prevent deep vein thrombosis after hip replacement. *Thromb Haemost.* 1989; 62:940–4.

33. Nieuwenhuis HK, Albada J, Banga JD et al. Identification of risk factors for bleeding during treatment of acute venous thromboembolism with heparin or low molecular weight heparin. *Blood.* 1991; 78:2337–43.

34. Hirsh J, Warkentin TE, Shaughnessy SG et al. Heparin and low-molecular-weight heparin: mechanisms of action, pharmacokinetics, dosing, monitoring, efficacy and safety. *Chest.* 2001; 119:64S–94S.

35. Rosenbloom D, Ginsberg JS. Arguments against monitoring levels of anti-factor Xa in conjunction with low-molecular-weight heparin therapy. *Can J Hosp Pharm.* 2002; 55:15–9.

36. American Society of Health-System Pharmacists. ASHP guidelines on quality assurance for pharmacy-prepared sterile products. *Am J Health-Syst Pharm.* 2000; 57:1150–69.

37. Pharmaceutical compounding—sterile preparations. The United States pharmacopeia, 27th rev., and The national formulary, 22nd ed. Rockville, MD: United

States Pharmacopeial Convention; 2004.

38. Charland SL, Davis DD, Tillman DJ. Activity of enoxaparin sodium in tuberculin syringes for 10 days. *Am J Health-Syst Pharm.* 1998; 55:1296–8.

39. Louie S, Chin A, Gill MA. Activity of dalteparin sodium in polypropylene syringes. *Am J Health-Syst Pharm.* 2000; 57:760–2.

Developed through the ASHP Commission on Therapeutics and approved by the ASHP Board of Directors on April 15, 2004.

The bibliographic citation for this document is as follows: American Society of Health-System Pharmacists. ASHP Therapeutic Position Statement on the Use of Low-Molecular-Weight Heparins for Adult Outpatient Treatment of Acute Deep-Vein Thrombosis. *Am J Health-Syst Pharm.* 2004; 61: 1950–5.

ASHP Therapeutic Position Statement on Strategies for Identifying and Preventing Pneumococcal Resistance

Statement of Position

The American Society of Health-System Pharmacists (ASHP) supports the establishment of state and national surveillance systems to track the prevalence of drug-resistant *Streptococcus pneumoniae* so that appropriate antimicrobial regimens can be used to treat infections caused by this common community-acquired pathogen.

ASHP supports continued educational efforts to promote the rational use of antimicrobials as a strategy for preventing the development of drug-resistant bacteria.

ASHP supports the vaccination of all persons at risk for acquiring pneumococcal disease. Use of pneumococcal vaccines is a reliable strategy to decrease the morbidity and mortality associated with invasive infections due to *S. pneumoniae*.

Background

S. pneumoniae, also known as pneumococcus, is the most common cause of community-acquired bacterial respiratory-tract infections. It is a frequent cause of meningitis, bacteremia, otitis media, and community-acquired pneumonia. Infections caused by *S. pneumoniae* have been associated with increased morbidity and mortality, especially in children under two years of age and elderly adults. Infections caused by *S. pneumoniae* have typically been successfully treated with a variety of antimicrobials, including penicillin, cephalosporins, and erythromycin. In the early 1990s the first reports of penicillin nonsusceptible *S. pneumoniae* (PNSP) began to appear in the United States; penicillin nonsusceptible strains include both intermediately resistant and resistant strains of *S. pneumoniae*. During the past decade the reports of increasing resistance of *S. pneumoniae* to penicillin and cephalosporins continued, and in the late 1990s reports of increasing resistance to trimethoprim–sulfamethoxazole, macrolides, and fluoroquinolones began to appear. Many isolates developed resistance to multiple classes of drugs and became known as multi-drug resistant *S. pneumoniae* (MDRSP). The increasing prevalence of MDRSP is creating a challenge for health care providers in treating this common community-acquired pathogen.

The clinical significance of drug-resistant *S. pneumoniae* on treatment outcomes is unclear. Most of the available data on clinical outcomes are from retrospective reviews, case–control studies, and case reports. There is evidence that meningitis due to PNSP does not respond to treatment with either penicillin or standard doses of cephalosporins, leading to poor clinical outcomes.[1] In contrast, there does not appear to be a significant difference in clinical outcome, primarily mortality, when pneumonia or other nonmeningeal infections due to PNSP are treated with penicillin or cephalosporins. On the contrary, macrolides and fluoroquinolones with poor in vitro activity against *S. pneumoniae* have been associated with poor clinical outcomes and even treatment failures. It is likely that clinical outcomes be depend on the mechanism and degree of resistance, the site of infection, and the pharmacokinetic and pharmacodynamic characteristics of the antimicrobial agents used in treatment.

Definitions. NCCLS, previously known as the National Committee for Clinical Laboratory Standards, revised the definitions of *S. pneumoniae* susceptibility to several antimicrobials in its 2002 standards. *S. pneumoniae* resistant to penicillin is defined in terms of the minimum inhibitory concentration (MIC) of penicillin. Strains may be distinguished as susceptible (MIC < 0.06 μg/mL), intermediately resistant (MIC 0.12–1.0 μg/mL), or highly resistant (MIC ≥ 2 μg/mL).[2] The most notable change in 2002 was the increase in breakpoint values for susceptibility of nonmeningitis isolates of *S. pneumoniae*. NCCLS took into account the pharmacokinetic and pharmacodynamic factors of a drug in redefining susceptibility breakpoints. The definition of multidrug-resistant *S. pneumoniae* is a strain resistant to three or more classes of antimicrobials.

Epidemiology. Numerous national and international surveillance studies have been conducted to determine the prevalence of *S. pneumoniae* resistance.[3–7] These networks used similar methodologies and specimens: clinical isolates of *S. pneumoniae* from sterile body sites or the respiratory tract, with susceptibility testing in accordance with NCCLS standards. Although these studies showed differing resistance rates to the antimicrobials tested, some common trends emerged (Table 1). The incidence of strains highly resistant to penicillin has surpassed that of intermediately resistant

Table 1.
Susceptibility of *Streptococcus pneumoniae* Isolates to Commonly Used Antimicrobials

Ref.	n	% Resistant Isolates					
		IR Penicillin	Resistant Penicillin	Ceftriaxone[a]	Erythromycin	Trimethoprim–Sulfamethoxazole	Levofloxacin
3	3,447	9.6	15.5	NA[b]	19.2	24.0	0.7
4[c]	2,432	12.0	25.0	4.3	28.8	37.5	NA
5	10,012	14.2	21.2	NA	27.9	NA	1.0
6	1,531	12.7	21.5	NA	25.7	30.3	0.3
7	7,671	15.5	18.4	1.7	NA	26.0	0.9

[a]NCCLS nonmeningitis breakpoints.
[b]NA = not applicable.
[c]U.S. data only.

strains. The rates of resistance to non-β-lactams have also increased: the prevalence of macrolide resistance is 20–30%, and trimethoprim–sulfamethoxazole resistance ranges between 24% and 38%. *S. pneumoniae* resistance to levofloxacin is hovering around 1%. However, there have been reports from Canada[8] and the Centers for Disease Control and Prevention (CDC)[9] of increasing resistance of *S. pneumoniae* to fluoroquinolones. Most fluoroquinolone-resistant isolates are resistant to other antimicrobials. Fluoroquinolone-resistant organisms are more likely to be found in persons over 65 years of age, the population with the highest use of fluoroquinolones.

Persons at risk. The greatest risk factor for becoming infected with a drug-resistant strain of *S. pneumoniae* is prior antimicrobial use. Other risk factors include carriage of *S. pneumoniae*, daycare attendance, exposure to children who attend daycare, severe medical comorbidities, immunosuppression, and high alcohol intake.[1] Smoking has been identified as a risk factor for developing invasive *S. pneumoniae* infections.[10] The risk of invasive *S. pneumoniae* infections is 4-fold if the patient is a smoker and 2.5-fold if the patient is exposed to secondhand smoke. The risk of invasive disease declines over time for persons who have stopped smoking.

Mechanisms of resistance. Resistance of *S. pneumoniae* to β-lactams is due to genetic mutations leading to alterations in three or four of the five high-molecular-weight penicillin-binding proteins (PBPs).[11] The degree of *S. pneumoniae* resistance is dependent on which PBPs are involved and the affinity of the β-lactam agent to the PBP. The differences in expression of these PBPs explain the differences in susceptibility to a variety of β-lactams.

S. pneumoniae resistance to macrolides occurs primarily through two mechanisms: active drug efflux (M phenotype) or ribosomal modification (MLS$_\beta$ phenotype).[12] Active drug efflux confers resistance to all agents within the class, whereas ribosomal modification confers resistance not only to the macrolides but also to clindamycin and streptogramins. Approximately 75% of macrolide-resistant *S. pneumoniae* found in the United States is attributable to active drug efflux.

Resistance of *S. pneumoniae* to fluoroquinolones is primarily a result of mutations of the *parC* and *gyrA* genes, although efflux pumps may also play a role.[13] Alterations in the parC subunit of topoisomerase IV result in the reduced susceptibility of *S. pneumoniae* to gatifloxacin, levofloxacin, and moxifloxacin. This single-step mutation is difficult to detect clinically because isolates with a *parC* mutation are reported as susceptible using standard laboratory testing. This is concerning because isolates with single-step mutations are the progenitors for fully drug-resistant strains of *S. pneumoniae*, which have additional mutations in the gyrA subunit of DNA gyrase.

Establishment of Surveillance Systems

Surveillance systems are an integral component of combating bacterial resistance. The data gathered from surveillance systems can be used for many purposes, such as identifying and tracking global outbreaks, setting public health policy, determining appropriate treatments for different infections, and heightening awareness of health care providers to local resistance trends that may affect the routine care of patients.

Health systems should develop a mechanism for the surveillance of bacterial resistance. Ideally, the surveillance system should identify trends in bacterial susceptibility patterns and correlate this with antimicrobial use in both health systems and communities.[14] The clinical microbiology laboratory, pharmacy, information systems, and infection control departments play important roles in maintaining an active surveillance system. Surveillance systems for tracking the prevalence of *S. pneumoniae* include two approaches, each providing differing types of information. The more common system uses culture data from clinical isolates causing invasive disease, which give an indication of the resistance patterns of strains actually causing clinical infection. The other approach determines the community *S. pneumoniae* carriage rate by testing nasopharyngeal swabs from individuals without clinical illness, demonstrating which strains could cause clinical infection. However, one study found that nasopharyngeal swabs overestimate the rate of *S. pneumoniae* colonization because of misidentification of oral streptococci as *S. pneumoniae*.[15] The importance of accurately identifying *S. pneumoniae* and determining susceptibility cannot be overstated.

Guidelines for the treatment of common community-acquired infections developed by various national organizations can be found in the appendix. These guidelines incorporate data from large surveillance studies of microbial resistance to make recommendations for initial treatment regimens. Local surveillance data can be used to tailor national guidelines when developing local recommendations for empirical treatments.

Participation in an active surveillance system should not be limited to individual institutions. Health systems should actively participate in state and national surveillance initiatives. Sentinel surveillance, which incorporates data from a small number of laboratories to determine trends for a much larger area, can accurately detect large changes in the susceptibility of *S. pneumoniae*, but it infrequently detects emerging resistance profiles, such as the fluoroquinolone resistance of *S. pneumoniae*.[16] Sentinel surveillance is also useful in showing trends in susceptibility over time. CDC, the Food and Drug Administration, and the National Institutes of Health have launched an action plan to combat antimicrobial resistance.[17] One of the four major components of this plan is the enhancement of surveillance systems. CDC will coordinate efforts with state and local health departments to develop national, regional, state, and local surveillance networks. The data gained from this initiative can be used to target areas with a high prevalence of PNSP for pneumococcal vaccination programs and efforts to promote the judicious use of antimicrobials.

Rational Use of Antimicrobials

There is an abundance of literature showing the relationship between antimicrobial-use patterns and the development of resistance. However, the bulk of this literature has been generated from hospital or institutional studies and has little bearing on PNSP. Since *S. pneumoniae* is primarily a community-acquired pathogen, antimicrobial use in the outpatient setting has the greatest influence on the susceptibility profile of *S. pneumoniae*. Few studies have shown a relationship between outpatient prescription use and *S. pneumoniae* susceptibility patterns. In the United States, Diekema and colleagues[18] found a positive correlation between high usage rates of outpatient β-lactam agents and the decreased penicillin susceptibility of *S. pneumoniae*. No correlation was found between the use of other antimicrobial classes (e.g., macrolides, tetracyclines, and fluoroquinolones) and the decreased penicillin susceptibility of *S. pneumoniae*. Bronzwaer et al.[19] found a relationship between high outpatient use of β-lactam agents and macrolides and the decreased penicillin susceptibility of *S. pneumoniae* in Europe. A major limitation of both of these studies was the failure to track patient adherence to prescribed regimens; however, these studies demonstrated that the community burden of high antimicrobial use is substantial and plays a role in the development of microbial resistance.

Several national organizations,[14] CDC, and the World Health Organization have advocated judicious antimicrobial-use stewardship as a mechanism to limit the development of bacterial resistance. One of the cornerstones of antimicrobial-use stewardship is the appropriate use of antimicrobials. Approximately 50% of adults'[20] and over 20% of children's[21] prescriptions for antibacterials are unnecessary. These agents were usually prescribed for treatment of the common cold, upper-respiratory-tract infections, and bronchitis, ailments often caused by viruses that do not respond to antibacterials.

Hennessy et al.[22] attempted to demonstrate that decreased outpatient antimicrobial use could reduce the carriage of PNSP. In a controlled intervention trial in rural Alaska, investigators provided extensive education to the health care providers and the public on the management of respiratory-tract infections and the appropriate use of antimicrobials. They tracked the nasal carriage of penicillin-susceptible *S. pneumoniae* and PNSP, as well as antimicrobial use in the region for a three-year period. During the first year they found a significant decrease in the nasal carriage of PNSP and antimicrobial use. However, the carriage of PNSP increased to almost preintervention levels in the following two years of the study, despite the continued low rate of antimicrobial use. This suggests that changing antimicrobial-use patterns is only one part of solving a complex problem. Such changes will likely need to be coupled with other programs, including aggressive vaccination, to show a significant effect on decreasing the carriage of *S. pneumoniae*.

Education of health care providers and the public is essential for ensuring the rational use of antimicrobials. Pharmacists can play a significant role in educating both groups,[23] assuming roles as educators to assist in disseminating vital information that encourages the rational use of antimicrobials.

Educating the public about antimicrobial use and misuse is essential because consumers play a key role in drug utilization. In focus groups, patients have indicated that if physicians explain why an antimicrobial was not needed, they would be satisfied with not receiving a prescription for one.[24] For many reasons, most health care providers cannot or do not spend the time necessary to adequately educate their patients or patients' caregivers on the potential dangers of the inappropriate use of antimicrobials. Pharmacists are encouraged to assume responsibility for educating patients about these dangers. A mass media campaign geared to the public on the dangers of emerging infectious diseases has been underway for several years.[25] This campaign should be tailored for the needs of individual communities.

Vaccination

Infections caused by *S. pneumoniae* continue to cause significant morbidity and mortality despite the availability of effective vaccines. Both the 23-valent pneumococcal polysaccharide vaccine (PPV) and the 7-valent pneumococcal conjugate vaccine (PCV7) have been shown to be highly effective in providing protection against the most commonly isolated pneumococcal serotypes that cause human disease, including those serotypes known to be antimicrobial resistant. While the use of these vaccines will not prevent the development of drug-resistant *S. pneumoniae*, they will likely prevent invasive infection caused by a drug-resistant organism. PPV is recommended for all adults aged 65 years or older.[26] It may also be given to select groups of high-risk patients over 2 years of age. This vaccine does not produce an adequate immunological response in children under 2 years old and should not be used in that population. PCV7 was added to the standard recommended pediatric vaccines in October 2000.[27] The PCV7 series should be given to all children beginning at age 2 months. The CDC National Immunization Program has established current recommendations for pneumococcal vaccine administration.[28]

PPV was licensed in the early 1980s and has demonstrated good immunogenicity in both young and older adults; however, an individual will not develop an immune response to all 23 pneumococcal serotypes.[29] The reason for this is unclear. Despite the vaccine's long-standing availability and documented effectiveness, less than 60% of eligible persons actually receive it.[30] One of the Healthy People 2010 goals is for 90% of eligible adults to receive pneumococcal vaccine.[30] This is an excellent opportunity for pharmacists to improve the vaccination rate of older adult patients and help promote national health care goals.

Revaccination with PPV is recommended for adults over age 65 years if the first dose was administered when he or she was under 65 years old at the time of vaccination and at least five years have elapsed since the first dose.[26] In addition, persons younger than 65 years with immunocompromising conditions may receive a one-time revaccination if five years have elapsed since the first dose of PPV. Revaccination with PPV results in a somewhat blunted immune response and is associated with increased injection-site reactions.[29]

PCV7 for children has been available since February 2000. Use of this vaccine has been shown to decrease the carriage rate of *S. pneumoniae* and the incidence of invasive pneumococcal disease, acute otitis media, and pneumonia in vaccinated populations.[31,32] The rate of vaccine-specific serotype *S. pneumoniae* carriage in vaccinated children remains below the rate for nonvaccinated children over prolonged periods of time. Widespread vaccination of children with PCV7 has shown a "herd effect" in decreasing the carriage rate of *S. pneumoniae* in children, who are an important vector for the transmission of *S. pneumoniae* to other children and adults.[31] This indirect effect was recently documented by the CDC Active Bacterial Core Surveillance Network, which found a decrease of 32% in invasive disease in adults age 20–39 years, 8% for those 40–64 years of age, and 18% for those 65 years or older.[32] This is similar to what was seen with widespread use of the *Haemophilus influenzae* type B vaccine and the marked decrease in *H. influenzae*-related infections.

Most people who succumb to preventable infections had visited a health care provider in the preceding year but were not vaccinated.[33-37] Clinicians need to ensure that people receive proper immunizations[38,39] and pharmacists can promote vaccination efforts by serving as educators, facilitators, and vaccinators. Although vaccinations are typically administered in the ambulatory care setting, clinicians seize opportunities to vaccinate hospitalized patients as well. Pharmacists have demonstrated that they can increase the number of persons receiving needed vaccines in both inpatient and ambulatory care settings.[40]

Summary

The incidence of drug-resistant *S. pneumoniae* continues to increase, causing significant morbidity and mortality. Health care providers should seize the opportunity to promote the judicious use of antimicrobials and aggressive vaccination with the pneumococcal vaccines as a means to lessen this significant health problem.

References

1. Pallares R, Fenoll A, Linares J et al. The epidemiology of antibiotic resistance in *Streptococcus pneumoniae* and the clinical relevance of resistance to cephalosporins, macrolides and quinolones. *Int J Antimicrob Agents.* 2003; 22(suppl 1):S15–24.

2. Performance standards for antimicrobial susceptibility testing; 12th informational supplement. Wayne, PA: NCCLS; 2002. NCCLS document M100–S12.

3. Centers for Disease Control and Prevention. Active bacterial core surveillance report, emerging infections program network, *Streptococcus pneumoniae,* 2001. www.cdc.gov/ncidod/dbmd/survreports/spneu01.pdf (accessed 2004 Jul 30).

4. Jacobs MR, Felmingham D, Appelbaum PC et al. The Alexander Project 1998–2000: susceptibility of pathogens isolated from community-acquired respiratory tract infection to commonly used antimicrobial agents. *J Antimicrob Chemother.* 2003; 52:229–46.

5. Doern G, Rybak MJ. Activity of telithromycin against *Streptococcus pneumoniae* resistant to penicillin, macrolides and fluoroquinolones isolated from respiratory tract infections: PROTEK US year 2 (2001–2002). Paper presented at the 43rd Annual Interscience Conference on Antimicrobial Agents and Chemotherapy. Chicago, IL; 2003 Sept 16.

6. Doern GV, Heilmann KP, Huynh HK et al. Antimicrobial resistance among clinical isolates of *Streptococcus pneumoniae* in the United States during 1999–2000, including a comparison of resistance rates since 1994–1995. *Antimicrob Agents Chemother.* 2001; 45:1721–9.

7. Karlowsky JA, Thornsberry C, Jones ME et al. Factors associated with relative rates of antimicrobial resistance among *Streptococcus pneumoniae* in the United States: results from the TRUST surveillance program (1998–2002). *Clin Infect Dis.* 2003; 36:963–70.

8. Chen DK, McGeer A, de Azavedo JC et al. Decreased susceptibility of *Streptococcus pneumoniae* to fluoroquinolones in Canada. *N Engl J Med.* 1999; 341:233–9.

9. Centers for Disease Control and Prevention. Resistance of *Streptococcus pneumoniae* to fluoroquinolones—United States, 1995–1999. *MMWR.* 2001; 50:800–4.

10. Nuorti JP, Butler JC, Farley MM et al. Cigarette smoking and invasive pneumococcal disease. *N Engl J Med.* 2000; 342:681–9.

11. Appelbaum PC. Resistance among *Streptococcus pneumoniae*: implications for drug selection. *Clin Infect Dis.* 2002; 34:1613–20.

12. Lynch JP, Martinez FJ. Clinical relevance of macrolide-resistant *Streptococcus pneumoniae* for community-acquired pneumonia. *Clin Infect Dis.* 2002; 34 (suppl 1):S27–46.

13. Hooper DC. Fluoroquinolone resistance among gram-positive cocci. *Lancet Infect Dis.* 2002; 2:530–8.

14. Shlaes DM, Gerding DN, John JF Jr et al. Society for Healthcare Epidemiology of American and Infectious Diseases Society of America Joint Committee on Prevention of Antimicrobial Resistance: guidelines for the prevention of antimicrobial resistance in hospitals. *Clin Infect Dis.* 1997; 25:584–99.

15. Wester CW, Ariga D, Nathan C et al. Possible overestimation of penicillin resistant *Streptococcus pneumoniae* colonization rates due to misidentification of oropharyngeal streptococci. *Diagn Microbiol Infect Dis.* 2002; 42:263–8.

16. Schrag SJ, Zell ER, Schuchat A et al. Sentinel surveillance: a reliable way to track antibiotic resistance in communities? *Emerg Infect Dis.* 2002; 8:496–502.

17. Centers for Disease Control and Prevention. National Center for Infectious Diseases: antimicrobial resistance. www.cdc.gov/drugresistance/ (accessed 2004 Aug 1).

18. Diekema DJ, Brueggemann AB, Doern GV. Antimicrobial-drug use and changes in resistance in *Streptococcus pneumoniae*. *Emerg Infect Dis.* 2000; 6:552–6.

19. Bronzwaer SL, Cars O, Buchholz U et al. A European study on the relationship between antimicrobial use and antimicrobial resistance. *Emerg Infect Dis.* 2002; 8:278–82.

20. Gonzales R, Steiner JF, Sande MA. Antibiotic prescribing for adults with colds, upper respiratory tract infections, and bronchitis by ambulatory care physicians. *JAMA.* 1997; 278:901–4.

21. Nyquist AC, Gonzales R, Steiner JF et al. Antibiotic prescribing for children with colds, upper respiratory tract infections, and bronchitis. *JAMA.* 1998; 279:875–7. [Erratum, *JAMA.* 1998; 279:1702.]

22. Hennessy TW, Petersen KM, Bruden D et al. Changes in antibiotic-prescribing practices and carriage of penicillin-resistant *Streptococcus pneumoniae*: a controlled intervention trial in rural Alaska. *Clin Infect Dis.* 2002; 34:1543–50.

23. Dickerson LM, Mainous AG III, Carek PJ. The pharmacist's role in promoting optimal antimicrobial use. *Pharmacotherapy.* 2000; 20:711–23.

24. Avorn J, Solomon DH. Cultural and economic factors that (mis)shape antibiotic use: the nonpharmacologic basis of therapeutics. *Ann Intern Med.* 2000; 133:128–35.

25. Freimuth V, Linnan HW, Potter P. Communicating the threat of emerging infections to the public. *Emerg Infect Dis.* 2000; 6:337–47.

26. Centers for Disease Control and Prevention. Prevention of pneumococcal diseases: recommendations of the Advisory Committee on Immunization Practices. *MMWR.* 1997; 46(RR-8):1–24.

27. Centers for Disease Control and Prevention. Preventing pneumococcal disease among infants and young children: recommendations of the Advisory Committee on Immunization Practices. *MMWR.* 2000; 49(RR-9):1–35.

28. Centers for Disease Control and Prevention. National Immunization Program. www.cdc.gov/nip/ (accessed 2004 Aug 1).

29. Artz AS, Ershler WB, Longo DL. Pneumococcal vaccination and revaccination of older adults. *Clin Microbiol Rev.* 2003; 16:308–18.

30. Office of Disease Prevention and Health Promotion, Department of Health and Human Services. Healthy people 2010. www.healthypeople.gov (accessed 2004 Aug 1).

31. Dagan R, Fraser D. Conjugate pneumococcal vaccine and antibiotic-resistant *Streptococcus pneumoniae*: herd immunity and reduction of otitis morbidity. *Pediatr Infect Dis J.* 2000; 19:S79–88.

32. Whitney CG, Farley MM, Hadler J et al. Decline in invasive pneumococcal disease after the introduction of protein-polysaccharide conjugate vaccine. *N Engl J Med.* 2003; 348:1737–46.

33. Williams WW, Hickson MA, Kane MA et al. Immunization policies and vaccine coverage among adults. The risk for missed opportunities. *Ann Intern Med.* 1988; 108:616–25. [Erratum, *Ann Intern Med.* 1988; 109:348.]

34. Fedson DS, Harward MP, Reid RA et al. Hospital-based pneumococcal immunization. Epidemiologic rationale from the Shenandoah study. *JAMA.* 1990; 264:1117–22.

35. Fedson DS. Influenza and pneumococcal immunization strategies for physicians. *Chest.* 1987; 91:436–43.

36. Magnussen CR, Valenti WM, Mushlin AI. Pneumococcal vaccine strategy. Feasibility of a vaccination program directed at hospitalized and ambulatory patients. *Arch Intern Med.* 1984; 144:1755–7.

37. Vondracek TG, Pham TP, Huycke MM. A hospital-based pharmacy intervention program for pneumococcal vaccination. *Arch Intern Med.* 1998; 158:1543–7.

38. American Society of Health-System Pharmacists. ASHP guidelines on the pharmacist's role in immunization. *Am J Health-Syst Pharm.* 2003; 60:1371–7.

39. Grabenstein JD, Bonasso J. Health-system pharmacists' role in immunizing adults against pneumococcal disease and influenza. *Am J Health-Syst Pharm.* 1999; 56(suppl 2):S2–25.

40. Noped JC, Schomberg R. Implementing an inpatient pharmacy-based pneumococcal vaccination program. *Am J Health-Syst Pharm.* 2001; 58:1852–5.

Developed through the ASHP Commission on Therapeutics and approved by the ASHP Board of Directors on April 15, 2004.

The bibliographic citation for this document is as follows: American Society of Health-System Pharmacists. ASHP Therapeutic Position Statement on Strategies for Identifying and Preventing Pneumococcal Resistance. *Am J Health-Syst Pharm.* 2004; 61: in press.

Appendix—Selected Guidelines for the Treatment of Common Community-Acquired Respiratory-Tract Infections

Bronchitis

Snow V, Mottur-Pilson C, Hickner JM et al. for the American College of Physicians–American Society of Internal Medicine. Principles of appropriate antibiotic use for treatment of acute bronchitis in adults. *Ann Intern Med.* 2001; 134:518–20.

Community-Acquired Pneumonia

Mandell LA, Bartlett JG, Dowell SF et al. Update of practice guidelines for the management of community-acquired pneumonia in immunocompetent adults. *Clin Infect Dis.* 2003; 37:1405–33.

Otitis Media

American Academy of Pediatrics Subcommittee on Diagnosis and Management of Acute Otitis Media. Diagnosis and management of acute otitis media. *Pediatrics.* 2004; 113:1451–65.

American Academy of Family Physicians, American Academy of Otolaryngology-Head and Neck Surgery, American Academy of Pediatrics. Subcommittee on Diagnosis and Management of Otitis Media with Effusion. Otitis media with effusion. *Pediatrics.* 2004; 113:1412–29.

Sinusitis

American Academy of Pediatrics. Subcommittee on Management of Sinusitis and Committee on Quality Improvement. Clinical practice guideline: management of sinusitis. *Pediatrics.* 2001; 108:798–808.

Snow V, Mottur-Pilson C, Hickner JM, for the American College of Physicians–American Society of Internal Medicine. Principles of appropriate antibiotic use for acute sinusitis in adults. *Ann Intern Med.* 2001; 134:495–7.

ASHP
Therapeutic Guidelines

ASHP Therapeutic Guidelines on Antimicrobial Prophylaxis in Surgery

The ASHP Therapeutic Guidelines on Antimicrobial Prophylaxis in Surgery,[1] which have provided practitioners with standardized effective regimens for the rational use of prophylactic antimicrobials, have been revised as described in this document on the basis of new clinical evidence and additional concerns. Recommendations are provided for adult and pediatric patients (1 to 21 years of age), including infants (one month to 2 years of age). Geriatric patients, newborns (premature and full-term), and patients with renal or hepatic dysfunction are not specifically addressed. Therefore, the guidelines may not be applicable to these patients, or certain adjustments to the recommendations may be necessary. The higher occurrence of resistant organisms and the importance of controlling health care costs are also considered.

Prophylaxis refers to the prevention of an infection and can be characterized as primary prophylaxis, secondary prophylaxis (suppression), or eradication. Primary prophylaxis refers to the prevention of an initial infection. Secondary prophylaxis refers to the prevention of recurrence or reactivation of a preexisting infection (e.g., prevention of the recurrence of a latent herpes simplex virus infection). Eradication refers to the elimination of a colonized organism to prevent the development of an infection (e.g., eliminating methicillin-resistant *Staphylococcus aureus* [MRSA] from the nares of health care workers). These guidelines focus on primary prophylaxis. Secondary prophylaxis and eradication are not addressed.

Guideline Development and Use

These guidelines were prepared by the Rocky Mountain Poison and Drug Center under contract to ASHP. The project was coordinated by a drug information pharmacist who worked with a multidisciplinary consortium of writers and consulted with six physicians on staff at the University of Colorado Health Sciences Center. The project coordinator worked in conjunction with an independent panel of eight clinical pharmacy specialists with expertise in either adult or pediatric infectious disease. The panel was appointed by ASHP. Panel members and contractors were required to disclose any possible conflicts of interest before their appointment. The guidelines underwent multidisciplinary field review to evaluate their validity, reliability, and utility in clinical practice. The final document was approved by the ASHP Commission on Therapeutics and the ASHP Board of Directors.

The recommendations in this document may not be appropriate for use in all clinical situations. Decisions to follow these recommendations must be based on the professional judgment of the clinician and consideration of individual patient circumstances and available resources.

These guidelines reflect current knowledge (at the time of publication) on antimicrobial prophylaxis in surgery. Given the dynamic nature of scientific information and technology, periodic review, updating, and revision are to be expected.

Strength of evidence for recommendations. The primary literature from the previous ASHP Therapeutic Guidelines on Antimicrobial Prophylaxis in Surgery[1] was reviewed together with the primary literature between the date of the previous guidelines and August 1997, identified by a MEDLINE search. Particular attention was paid to study design, with greatest credence given to randomized, controlled, double-blind studies. Established recommendations by experts in the area (i.e., Centers for Disease Control and Prevention [CDC], American College of Obstetricians and Gynecologists [ACOG]) were also considered.

Guideline development included consideration of the following characteristics: validity, reliability, clinical applicability, flexibility, clarity, and a multidisciplinary nature as consistent with ASHP's philosophy on therapeutic guidelines.[2] Recommendations on the use of an antimicrobial are substantiated by the strength of evidence that supports the recommendation. The strength of evidence represents only support for or against prophylaxis and does not apply to the antimicrobial choice, dose, or dosage regimen. Studies supporting the recommendations for the use of an antimicrobial were classified as follows:

Level I: (evidence from large, well-conducted randomized, controlled clinical trials or a meta-analysis)

Level II: (evidence from small, well-conducted randomized, controlled clinical trials)

Level III: (evidence from well-conducted cohort studies)

Level IV: (evidence from well-conducted case–control studies)

Level V: (evidence from uncontrolled studies that were not well conducted)

Level VI: (conflicting evidence that tends to favor the recommendation)

Level VII: (expert opinion)

This system has been used by the Agency for Health Care Policy and Research, and ASHP supports it as an acceptable method for organizing strength of evidence for a variety of therapeutic or diagnostic recommendations.[2] Each recommendation was assigned a category corresponding to the strength of evidence that supports the use or nonuse of antimicrobial prophylaxis:

Category A: (levels I–III)
Category B: (levels IV–VI)
Category C: (level VII)

A category C recommendation represents a consensus of the expert panel based on the clinical experience of individual panel members and a paucity of quality supporting literature. In cases for which opinions were markedly divided, the recommendations indicate that a substantial number of panel members supported an alternative approach.

Pediatrics. Pediatric patients are subject to many prophylaxis opportunities that are similar to those for adults. Although pediatric-specific prophylaxis data are sparse, available data have been evaluated and are presented in this document. However, in most cases, the pediatric recommendations, including recommendations for infants, have been extrapolated from adult data.

Clinical studies to determine the optimal dosages of antimicrobials used for pediatric prophylaxis are essentially nonexistent. In contrast, there are sufficient pharmacokinetic studies for most agents used that appropriate pediatric dosages can be estimated that provide systemic exposure, and presumably efficacy, similar to that demonstrated in the adult efficacy trials. It is also common clinical practice to use antimicrobial prophylaxis in pediatric patients in a manner that is similar, if not identical, to that used in adults. Therefore, the pediatric dosages provided in these guidelines are based largely on pharmacokinetic equivalence and the generalization of the adult efficacy data to pediatric patients.[3,4] Because pediatric trials have generally not been conducted, a strength of evidence has not been applied to these recommendations. With few exceptions (e.g., aminoglycoside dosages), pediatric dosages should not exceed the maximum adult recommended dosages. If dosages are calculated on a milligram-per-kilogram basis for children weighing more than 40–50 kg, the calculated dosage will exceed the maximum recommended dosage for adults; thus adult dosages should be used.

Resistance. The basis for guideline development was to recommend an effective antimicrobial with the narrowest spectrum of activity. Alternative antimicrobials were included on the basis of documented efficacy. Individual health systems must consider specific resistance patterns at their practice site when adopting these recommendations.

When considering the use of antimicrobials for prophylaxis, one must also take into account the risks of contributing to the development of antimicrobial resistance. In numerous studies of prophylaxis, both surgical[5,6] and nonsurgical,[7–16] attempts have been made to evaluate the impact of antimicrobial prophylaxis on the development of resistance. Numerous studies[5,7–13] demonstrated an increase in resistance, yet other studies[6,14–16] failed to demonstrate the emergence of resistance. Most of the studies demonstrating the development of resistance involved the use of broad-spectrum antimicrobials.[5,7–13] Thus, currently recommended practice is to use narrow-spectrum antimicrobials for the shortest duration to reduce the likelihood of the development of antimicrobial resistance.

The frequency with which MRSA has been recovered from various infection sites has increased steadily throughout the United States.[17–19] The frequency of methicillin resistance among staphylococcal strains rose from 2.4% in 1975 to 29% in 1991.[19] CDC's National Nosocomial Infections Surveillance identified a rapid increase in vancomycin-resistant enterococci (VRE) from 0.3% in 1989 to 7.9% in 1993. The rate of high-level enterococcal resistance to penicillin and aminoglycosides increased simultaneously. The use of vancomycin has been reported consistently as a risk factor for infection and colonization with VRE and may increase the possibility of the emergence of vancomycin-resistant *S. aureus* or vancomycin-resistant *Staphylococcus epidermidis*.[20] In response, the Hospital Infection Control Practices Advisory Committee (HICPAC), with the support of other major organizations, developed measures for preventing and controlling vancomycin resistance.[21] The ASHP guidelines are consistent with the HICPAC recommendations. The following situations are appropriate or acceptable for use of vancomycin: prophylaxis of endocarditis (as recommended by the American Heart Association [AHA]) before certain procedures and for major surgical procedures involving implantation of prosthetic materials or devices (e.g., cardiac and vascular procedures, total hip replacement) at institutions with a high rate of infections due to MRSA or methicillin-resistant *S. epidermidis* (MRSE). Use of vancomycin for routine surgical prophylaxis should be discouraged (other than in a patient with a life-threatening allergy to β-lactam antimicrobials).

Cost. Pharmacoeconomic studies have been lacking or inadequate with regard to the prophylactic use of antimicrobials; therefore, a cost-minimization approach was employed in developing these guidelines. When antimicrobials have been shown to be equally efficacious and safe, the recommendation is based on the least expensive agent (on the basis of average wholesale price). The other antimicrobials are considered to be alternative agents. The recommendation of an antimicrobial is determined primarily by efficacy and secondarily by cost. Because of variations in cost from one health system to another, health systems must tailor the choice of antimicrobials to their individual acquisition costs.

Goals of Surgical Prophylaxis

Ideally, an anti-infective drug for surgical prophylaxis should achieve the following goals: (1) prevent postoperative infection of the surgical site, (2) prevent postoperative infectious morbidity and mortality, (3) reduce the duration and cost of health care (when the costs associated with the management of postoperative infection are considered, the cost-effectiveness of prophylaxis becomes evident),[22,23] (4) produce no adverse effects, and (5) have no adverse consequences for the microbial flora of the patient or the hospital.[24] To achieve these goals, an anti-infective drug should be (1) active against the pathogens most likely to contaminate the wound, (2) given in an appropriate dosage and at a time that ensures adequate concentrations at the incision site during the period of potential contamination, (3) safe, and (4) administered for the shortest effective period to minimize adverse effects, development of resistance, and cost.[24] The benefits of preventing postoperative infection pertain to both outpatient and inpatient surgeries. Other guidelines on antimicrobial prophylaxis in surgery have been published.[25]

Although prophylactic antimicrobials play an important part in reducing the rate of postoperative wound infection, other factors, such as the surgeon's experience, the length of the procedure, hospital and operating-room environments, and the underlying medical condition of the patient, have a strong impact on wound infection rates. Medical conditions associated with an increased risk of postoperative infection include extremes of age, undernutrition, obesity, diabetes, hypoxemia, remote infection, corticosteroid therapy, recent operation, chronic inflammation, and prior site irradiation.[26] Antimicrobial prophylaxis may be justified for any procedure if the patient has an underlying medical condition associated with a risk of wound infection or if the patient is immunocompromised (e.g., malnourished, neutropenic, receiving immunosuppressive agents). These variables should be considered in evaluations of infection-control problems.

Antimicrobial prophylaxis is beneficial in surgical

procedures associated with a high rate of infection (clean-contaminated or contaminated operations), for implantation of prosthetic materials, and in any procedure in which postoperative infection, however unlikely, may have severe consequences. Other clean procedures that may warrant prophylaxis are breast procedures[27,28] and hernia procedures,[27] although more data are needed.

The modified National Research Council wound classification criteria are as follow[26,29]:

- Clean surgical procedures (primarily closed, elective procedures involving no acute inflammation, no break in technique, and no transection of gastrointestinal [GI], oropharyngeal, genitourinary [GU], biliary, or tracheobronchial tracts)

- Clean-contaminated procedures (procedures involving transection of GI, oropharyngeal, GU, biliary, or tracheobronchial tracts with minimal spillage or with minor breaks in technique; clean procedures performed emergently or with major breaks in technique; reoperation of clean surgery within seven days; or procedures following blunt trauma)

- Contaminated procedures (clean-contaminated procedures during which acute, nonpurulent inflammation is encountered or major spillage or technique break occurs; procedures performed within four hours of penetrating trauma or involving a chronic open wound)

- Dirty procedures (procedures performed when there is obvious preexisting infection [abscess, pus, necrotic tissue present]; preoperative perforation of GI, oropharyngeal, biliary, or tracheobronchial tracts; or penetrating trauma greater than four hours old)

Typically, prophylactic antimicrobials are not indicated for clean surgical procedures. However, prophylaxis is justified for procedures involving prosthetic placement because of the potential for severe complications if postoperative infections involve the prosthesis. Antimicrobial prophylaxis is justified for the following types of surgical procedures: cardiothoracic, GI tract (e.g., colorectal and biliary tract operations), head and neck (except clean procedures), neurosurgical, obstetric or gynecologic, orthopedic (except clean procedures), urologic, and vascular. The use of antimicrobials for dirty and contaminated procedures is not classified as prophylaxis but as treatment for a presumed infection; therefore, dirty and contaminated procedures are not discussed in these guidelines.[30]

It is difficult to establish significant differences in efficacy between prophylactic antimicrobials and placebo when infection rates are low. A small sample size increases the likelihood of Type II error; therefore, there may be no apparent difference between the antimicrobial and placebo when in fact the antimicrobial has a beneficial effect.[31] A valid study would be placebo controlled and randomized with a large enough sample in each group to avoid Type II error. A large sample is rarely achieved in well-controlled studies of surgical prophylaxis. Thus, some of the surgical prophylaxis efficacy data are at risk for Type II error. Because of this obstacle, prophylaxis is recommended in some cases because the complications of postoperative infection (e.g., removal of an infected device) necessitate precautionary measures despite the lack of statistical support.

Selection of Antimicrobial Agents

The selection of an appropriate antimicrobial agent for specific patients should take into account not only comparative efficacy but also adverse-effect profiles and patient drug allergies. A discussion of adverse-effect profiles of the antimicrobials is beyond the scope of these guidelines. There is little evidence to suggest that the newer antimicrobials, with broader antibacterial activity in vitro, result in lower rates of postoperative wound infection than older drugs whose spectrum of activity is narrower. Because most comparative studies have a small number of patients, a significant difference between antimicrobials cannot be detected; therefore, antimicrobial selection is based on cost, adverse-effect profile, ease of administration, pharmacokinetic profile, and antibacterial activity. The agent chosen should have activity against the most common surgical wound pathogens. For clean-contaminated operations, the agent of choice should be effective against common pathogens found in the GI and GU tracts. In clean operations, the gram-positive cocci—S. aureus and S. epidermidis—predominate. For most procedures, cefazolin should be the agent of choice because of its relatively long duration of action, its effectiveness against the organisms most commonly encountered in surgery, and its relatively low cost.

Specific recommendations for the selection of prophylactic antimicrobials for various surgical procedures are provided in Table 1. Equivalent pediatric dosages have been included in Table 2; however, these recommendations are based on data derived primarily from adult patients and from tertiary references.[3,4,35] Neonatal (full-term and preterm) dosages are not provided. The reader is referred to Neofax for neonatal dosages.[36] There are few data on the use of surgical antimicrobial prophylaxis in the pediatric population. Available pediatric clinical data were evaluated and are presented in the efficacy section after the adult data.

Development of Colonization or Resistance. One factor that may influence the selection of cefazolin is the occurrence of surgical wound infections despite prophylaxis with cefazolin. An infection-control surveillance study of surgical wound infections implicated β-lactamase production as a possible cause of cefazolin and cefamandole failure.[39] β-lactamase-producing S. aureus isolates associated with the wound infections rapidly hydrolyzed cefamandole and cefazolin. Isolates of S. aureus taken from patients who had received cefazolin were more resistant than isolates taken from patients who had received cefamandole, and the cefazolin-associated isolates were capable of hydrolyzing cefazolin more rapidly. These findings may have important implications for the use of first-generation cephalosporins, particularly cefazolin, for surgical prophylaxis. However, the overall frequency of cefazolin failure as a result of resistance is low, and cefazolin continues to be the drug of choice. New studies comparing cefazolin with agents that are more resistant to β-lactamase, such as cefamandole and cefuroxime, may be needed.

A second factor that may discourage the selection of cefazolin is the recognition that MRSA and methicillin-resistant, coagulase-negative staphylococci are resistant to all cephalosporins. These organisms have been associated with infection after cardiothoracic, orthopedic, vascular, and cerebrospinal shunting procedures. This resistance pattern may influence drug selection in hospitals with a high frequency of such isolates. However, vancomycin use should be restricted because of the increase in vancomycin-resistant enterococci. The only situations in which vancomycin is appropriate for surgical prophylaxis are major surgical pro-

Table 1.
Recommendations for Surgical Antimicrobial Prophylaxis in Adults

Type of Surgery	Recommended Regimen[a]	Alternative Regimens[a]	Strength of Evidence[b]
Cardiothoracic	Cefazolin 1 g i.v. at induction of anesthesia and q 8 hr for up to 72 hr[c,d]	Cefuroxime 1.5 g i.v. at induction of anesthesia and q 12 hr for up to 72 hr, cefamandole 1 g i.v. at induction of anesthesia and q 6 hr for up to 72 hr, vancomycin 1 g i.v. with or without gentamicin 2 mg/kg i.v.[e]	A
Gastrointestinal			
Gastroduodenal			
Procedures involving entry into the lumen of the gastrointestinal tract	Cefazolin 1 g i.v. at induction of anesthesia		A
Highly selective vagotomy, Nissen's fundoplication, and Whipple's procedure	Cefazolin 1 g i.v. at induction of anesthesia		C
Biliary tract			
Open procedure	Cefazolin 1 g i.v. at induction of anesthesia		A
Laparoscopic procedure	None		B
Appendectomy for uncomplicated appendicitis	Cefoxitin, cefotetan, or cefmetazole 1–2 g i.v. at induction of anesthesia	Piperacillin 2 g i.v. at induction of anesthesia; if patient is allergic to penicillin, metronidazole 500 mg i.v. plus gentamicin 2 mg/kg i.v. at induction of anesthesia	A
Colorectal	Neomycin sulfate 1 g plus erythromycin base 1 g p.o. (after mechanical bowel preparation is completed[f]) at 19, 18, and 9 hr before surgery; if oral route is contraindicated, cefoxitin, cefotetan, or cefmetazole 2 g i.v. at induction of anesthesia; for patients undergoing high-risk surgery (e.g., rectal resection), oral neomycin and erythromycin plus an i.v. cephalosporin		A
Head and neck			
Clean	None		B
With placement of prosthesis	Cefazolin 1 g i.v. at induction of anesthesia		C
Clean-contaminated	Cefazolin 2 g i.v. at induction of anesthesia and q 8 hr for 24 hr or clindamycin 600 mg i.v. at induction of anesthesia and q 8 hr for 24 hr	Addition of gentamicin 1.7 mg/kg i.v. to clindamycin regimen or of metronidazole 500 mg i.v. q 8 hr to cefazolin regimen is controversial; single-dose regimens might be preferable, but this approach is controversial	A
Elective craniotomy or cerebrospinal fluid shunting	Cefazolin 1 g i.v. at induction of anesthesia	Oxacillin 1 g or nafcillin 1 g i.v. at induction of anesthesia; vancomycin 1 g i.v.[g]	A
Obstetric or gynecologic			
Cesarean delivery[h]	Cefazolin 2 g i.v. immediately after clamping of umbilical cord		B (low risk), A (high risk)
Hysterectomy (vaginal, abdominal, or radical)[i]	Cefazolin 1 g i.v. or cefotetan 1 g i.v. at induction of anesthesia	Cefoxitin 1 g i.v. at induction of anesthesia	A
Ophthalmic	Topical neomycin–polymyxin B–gramicidin 1–2 drops or tobramycin 0.3% or gentamicin 0.3% 2 drops instilled before procedure[j]	Addition of tobramycin 20 mg by subconjunctival injection is optional	C
Orthopedic			
Clean, not involving implantation of foreign materials[k]	None		C
Hip fracture repair[l]	Cefazolin 1 g i.v. at induction of anesthesia and q 8 hr for 24 hr	Vancomycin 1 g i.v.[g]	A
Implantation of internal fixation devices[l]	Cefazolin 1 g i.v. at induction of anesthesia and q 8 hr for 24 hr	Vancomycin 1 g i.v.[g]	C
Total joint replacement	Cefazolin 1 g i.v. at induction of anesthesia and q 8 hr for 24 hr	Vancomycin 1 g i.v.[g]	A

Continued on next page

Table 1 (*continued*)
Recommendations for Surgical Antimicrobial Prophylaxis in Adults

Type of Surgery	Recommended Regimen[a]	Alternative Regimens[a]	Strength of Evidence[b]
Urologic (high-risk patients only[m])	Trimethoprim 160 mg with sulfamethoxazole 800 mg p.o. or lomefloxacin 400 mg p.o. 2 hr before surgery (if oral agents used) or cefazolin 1 g i.v. at induction of anesthesia (if injection preferred)		A
Vascular[n]	Cefazolin 1 g i.v. at induction of anesthesia and q 8 hr for 24 hr	Vancomycin 1 g i.v with or without gentamicin 2 mg/kg i.v.[g]	A
Transplantation			
Heart	Cefazolin 1 g i.v. at induction of anesthesia and q 8 hr for 48–72 hr[d]	Cefuroxime 1.5 g i.v. at induction of anesthesia and q 12 hr for 48–72 hr, cefamandole 1 g i.v. at induction of anesthesia and q 6 hr for 48–72 hr, or vancomycin 1 g i.v. with or without gentamicin 2 mg/kg i.v.[e]	A
Lung and heart–lung[o,p]	Cefazolin 1 g i.v. at induction of anesthesia and q 8 hr for 48–72 hr	Cefuroxime 1.5 g i.v. at induction of anesthesia and q 12 hr for 48–72 hr, cefamandole 1 g i.v. at induction of anesthesia and q 6 hr for 48–72 hr, or vancomycin 1 g i.v.[g]	B
Liver	Cefotaxime 1 g i.v. plus ampicillin 1 g i.v. at induction of anesthesia and q 6 hr during procedure and for 48 hr beyond final surgical closure	Antimicrobials that provide adequate coverage against gram-negative aerobic bacilli, staphylococci, and enterococci may be appropriate	B
Pancreas and pancreas–kidney	Cefazolin 1 g i.v. at induction of anesthesia		B
Kidney	Cefazolin 1 g i.v. at induction of anesthesia		A

[a]If a short-acting agent is used, it should be readministered if the operation takes more than three hours. If an operation is expected to last more than six to eight hours, it would be reasonable to administer an agent with a longer half-life and duration of action or to administer a short-acting agent at three-hour intervals during the procedure. Readministration may also be warranted if prolonged or excessive bleeding occurs or there are factors that may shorten the half-life (e.g., extensive burns). Readministration may not be warranted in patients in whom the half-life is prolonged (e.g., patients with renal insufficiency or failure).

[b]Strength of evidence that supports the use or nonuse of prophylaxis is classified as A (levels I–III), B (levels IV–VI), or C (level VII). Level I evidence is from large, well-conducted randomized, controlled clinical trials. Level II evidence is from small, well-conducted randomized, controlled clinical trials. Level III evidence is from well-conducted cohort studies. Level IV evidence is from well-conducted case–control studies. Level V evidence is from uncontrolled studies that were not well conducted. Level VI evidence is conflicting evidence that tends to favor the recommendation. Level VII evidence is expert opinion.

[c]Duration is based on expert panel consensus. Prophylaxis for 24 hours or less may be appropriate.

[d]There is currently no evidence to support continuing antimicrobial prophylaxis until chest and mediastinal drainage tubes are removed.

[e]According to Hospital Infection Control Practices Advisory Committee guidelines[21] or American Heart Association recommendations for penicillin-allergic patients at high risk for endocarditis.[32]

[f]Mechanical bowel preparation is required for nonobstructed patients undergoing elective operations.

[g]According to Hospital Infection Control Practices Advisory Committee guidelines.[21]

[h]The American College of Obstetricians and Gynecologists (ACOG) considers the use of prophylaxis controversial in low-risk patients.[33] ACOG does not routinely recommend prophylaxis in low-risk patients because of concerns about adverse effects, development of resistant organisms, and relaxation of standard infection-control measures and proper operative technique.

[i]According to ACOG guidelines, first-, second-, and third-generation cephalosporins can be used for vaginal, abdominal, and radical hysterectomies.[34]

[j]The necessity of continuing topical antimicrobials postoperatively has not been established by data.

[k]Laminectomy and knee, hand, and foot surgeries. The evaluated studies did not include arthroscopy and did not identify specific procedures, like carpal tunnel release; however, arthroscopy and other procedures not involving implantation are similar enough to be included with clean orthopedic procedures not involving implantation.

[l]Procedures involving internal fixation devices (e.g., nails, screws, plates, wires).

[m]High risk is defined as prolonged postoperative catheterization, positive urine cultures, or hospital infection rate of greater than 20%.

[n]Prophylaxis is not indicated for brachiocephalic procedures. Although there are no data, patients undergoing brachiocephalic procedures involving vascular prostheses or patch implantation (e.g., carotid endarterectomy) may benefit from prophylaxis.

[o]Patients undergoing lung transplantation with negative pretransplant cultures should receive antimicrobial prophylaxis as appropriate for other types of cardiothoracic surgeries.

[p]Patients undergoing lung transplantation for cystic fibrosis should receive 7–14 days of prophylaxis with antimicrobials selected according to pretransplant culture and susceptibility results. This may include additional antibacterial agents or antifungal agents.

Table 2.
Antimicrobial Regimens for Surgical Prophylaxis in Pediatric Patients[a]

Type of Surgery	Preferred Regimen[b]	Alternative Regimens[b]
Cardiothoracic	Cefazolin 20–30 mg/kg i.v. at induction of anesthesia and q 8 hr for up to 72 hr[c,d]	Cefuroxime 50 mg/kg i.v. at induction of anesthesia and q 8 hr for up to 72 hr,[c,d] vancomycin 15 mg/kg i.v. with or without gentamicin 2 mg/kg i.v.[e]
Gastrointestinal		
Gastroduodenal (procedures involving entry into the lumen of the gastrointestinal tract, highly selective vagotomy, Nissen's fundoplication, and Whipple's procedure)	Cefazolin 20–30 mg/kg i.v. at induction of anesthesia	
Biliary tract		
Open procedures	Cefazolin 20–30 mg/kg i.v. at induction of anesthesia	
Laparoscopic procedures	None	
Appendectomy for uncomplicated appendicitis	Cefoxitin 20–40 mg/kg i.v., cefotetan 20 40 mg/kg i.v., cefotaxime 25–50 mg/kg i.v., or ceftizoxime 25–50 mg/kg i.v. at induction of anesthesia	Piperacillin 50 mg/kg i.v. at induction of anesthesia; if patient is allergic to penicillin, metronidazole 10 mg/kg i.v. plus gentamicin 2 mg/kg i.v. at induction of anesthesia
Colorectal	Neomycin sulfate 20 mg/kg plus erythromycin base 10 mg/kg p.o. (after mechanical bowel preparation is completed) at 19, 18, and 9 before surgery; if oral route is contraindicated, cefoxitin or cefotetan 30–40 mg/kg i.v. at induction of anesthesia; for patients undergoing high-risk surgery (e.g., rectal resection), oral neomycin and erythromycin plus an i.v. cephalosporin	
Head and neck		
Clean	None	
With placement of prosthesis	Cefazolin 20–30 mg/kg i.v at induction of anesthesia	
Clean-contaminated	Cefazolin 30–40 mg/kg i.v. at induction of anesthesia and q 8 hr for 24 hr or clindamycin 15 mg/kg i.v. at induction of anesthesia and q 8 hr for 24 hr	Addition of gentamicin 2.5 mg/kg i.v. to clindamycin regimen or of metronidazole 10 mg/kg i.v. q 8 hr to cefazolin regimen is controversial; single-dose regimens might be preferable, but this approach is controversial
Elective craniotomy or cerebrospinal-fluid shunting	Cefazolin 20–30 mg/kg i.v. at induction of anesthesia	Vancomycin 15 mg/kg i.v.[f]
Obstetric or gynecologic		
Cesarean delivery[g]	Cefazolin 2 g i.v. immediately after clamping of umbilical cord	
Hysterectomy (vaginal, abdominal, or radical)[h]	Cefazolin 1 g i.v. or cefotetan 1 g i.v. at induction of anesthesia	Cefoxitin 1 g i.v. at induction of anesthesia
Ophthalmic	Topical neomycin–polymyxin B–gramicidin 1–2 drops or tobramycin 0.3% or gentamicin 0.3% 2 drops instilled before procedure[i]	
Orthopedic		
Clean, not involving implantation of foreign materials[j]	None	
Hip fracture repair,[k] implantation of internal fixation devices,[k] total joint replacement	Cefazolin 20–30 mg/kg i.v. at induction of anesthesia and q 8 hr for 24 hr	Vancomycin 15 mg/kg i.v.[f]
Urologic procedures (high-risk patients only[l])	Trimethoprim 6–10 mg/kg plus sulfamethoxazole 30–50 mg/kg p.o. 2 hr before surgery (if oral agents used) or cefazolin 20–30 mg/kg i.v. at induction of anesthesia (if injection preferred)	
Vascular procedures[m]	Cefazolin 20–30 mg/kg i.v. at induction of anesthesia and q 8 hr for 24 hr	Vancomycin 15 mg/kg i.v. with or without gentamicin 2 mg/kg i.v.[f]
Transplantation		
Heart	Cefazolin 20–30 mg/kg i.v. at induction of anesthesia and q 8 hr for 48–72 hr[d]	Cefuroxime 50 mg/kg i.v. at induction of anesthesia and q 8 hr for 48–72 hr,[c,d] vancomycin 15 mg/kg with or without gentamicin 2 mg/kg i.v.[e]

Continued on next page

Table 2. (*continued*)
Antimicrobial Regimens for Surgical Prophylaxis in Pediatric Patients[a]

Type of Surgery	Preferred Regimen[b]	Alternative Regimens[b]
Transplantation		
Lung and heart–lung[n,o]	Cefazolin 20–30 mg/kg i.v. at induction of anesthesia and q 8 hr for 48–72 hr[d]	Cefuroxime 50 mg/kg i.v. at induction of anesthesia and q 8 hr for 48–72 hr,[d] vancomycin 15 mg/kg i.v.[f]
Liver	Cefotaxime 50 mg/kg i.v. plus ampicillin 50 mg/kg i.v. at induction of anesthesia and q 6 hr for 48 hr beyond final surgical closure	Antimicrobials that provide adequate coverage against gram-negative aerobic bacilli, staphylococci, and enterococci may be appropriate
Pancreas and pancreas–kidney	Cefazolin 20 mg/kg i.v. at induction of anesthesia	
Kidney	Cefazolin 20 mg/kg i.v. at induction of anesthesia	

[a]The recommendations included in this table have been extrapolated from adult data. The pediatric dosages are approximately equivalent to the adult dosages listed in Table 1. With few exceptions (aminoglycosides), pediatric dosages should not exceed the maximum dosage recommended for adults. Adult dosages should be used for children weighing more than 40–50 kg because a dosage calculated on a milligram-per-kilogram basis will exceed the maximum recommended dosage for adults.[34,35] Dosages for neonates (full-term and preterm) are not provided. The reader is referred to Neofax for neonatal dosing.[36]

[b]If a short-acting agent is used, it should be readministered if the operation takes more than three hours. If an operation is expected to last more than six to eight hours, it would be reasonable to administer an agent with a longer half-life and duration of action or to administer a short-acting agent at three-hour intervals during the procedure. Readministration may also be warranted if prolonged or excessive bleeding occurs or there are factors that may shorten the half-life (e.g., extensive burns). Readministration may not be warranted in patients in whom the half-life is prolonged (e.g., patients with renal insufficiency or failure).

[c]Duration is based on expert panel consensus. Prophylaxis for 24 hours or less may be appropriate.

[d]There is currently no evidence to support continuing antimicrobial prophylaxis until chest and mediastinal drainage tubes are removed.

[e]According to Hospital Infection Control Practices Advisory Committee guidelines[21] or American Heart Association recommendations for penicillin-allergic patients at high risk for endocarditis.[32] Pediatric cancer patients may require dosages greater than the standard dosage.[37,38]

[f]According to Hospital Infection Control Practices Advisory Committee guidelines.[21]

[g]The American College of Obstetricians and Gynecologists (ACOG) considers the use of prophylaxis controversial in low-risk patients.[33] ACOG does not routinely recommend prophylaxis in low-risk patients because of concerns about adverse effects, development of resistant organisms, and relaxation of standard infection-control measures and proper operative technique.

[h]According to ACOG guidelines, first-, second-, and third-generation cephalosporins can be used for vaginal, abdominal, and radical hysterectomies.[34]

[i]The necessity of continuing topical antimicrobials postoperatively has not been established by data.

[j]Laminectomy and knee, hand, and foot surgeries. The evaluated studies did not include arthroscopy procedures and did not identify specific procedures, like carpal tunnel release; however, arthroscopy and other procedures not involving implantation are similar enough to be included with clean orthopedic procedures not involving implantation.

[k]Procedures involving internal fixation devices (e.g., nails, screws, plates, wires).

[l]High risk is defined as prolonged postoperative catheterization, positive urine cultures, or hospital infection rate of greater than 20%.

[m]Prophylaxis is not indicated for brachiocephalic procedures. Although there are no data, patients undergoing brachiocephalic procedures involving vascular prosthesis or patch implantation (e.g., carotid endarterectomy) may benefit from prophylaxis.

[n]Patients undergoing lung transplantation with negative pretransplant cultures should receive antimicrobial prophylaxis as appropriate for other types of cardiothoracic surgeries.

[o]Patients undergoing lung transplantation for cystic fibrosis should receive 7–14 days of prophylaxis with antimicrobials selected according to pretransplant isolates and susceptibilities. This may include additional antibacterial or antifungal agents.

cedures involving the implantation of prosthetic materials or devices at institutions that have a high rate of infections caused by MRSA or MRSE or in patients who have a life-threatening allergy to β-lactam antimicrobials.[21] A high rate of infection caused by MRSA is defined as >20% by our expert panel consensus. However, some institutions consider >10% to be a high MRSA infection rate and 20% to be a low infection rate for MRSE. Each institution is encouraged to develop guidelines for the proper use of vancomycin, as applicable to the institution. Consistent with the HICPAC recommendations, a single dose of vancomycin administered immediately before surgery is sufficient unless the procedure lasts more than six hours or major blood loss occurs, in which case the dose should be repeated.[21] Prophylaxis should be discontinued after a maximum of two doses.

The use of antimicrobials for prophylaxis in surgery contributes to changes in individuals' and institutions' bacterial flora. Studies have demonstrated that the use of antimicrobials prophylactically can alter bacterial flora, leading to colonization or resistance,[5,40–45] although another study, which involved patients undergoing colorectal surgery, showed no effect on the emergence of resistant bacteria.[6] The bacterial flora affected include, but are not limited to, *Clostridium difficile*, enterococci, *Pseudomonas* species, and *Serratia* species.

Colonization with *C. difficile* has been demonstrated with prophylaxis of more than 24 hours' duration[40] and single-dose prophylaxis.[41] Colonization with *C. difficile* may lead to complications such as colitis. A retrospective review demonstrated that 55% of the *C. difficile*-associated colitis cases were associated with surgical patients receiving preoperative cephalosporins.[42]

Surgical prophylaxis may be a contributing factor to the development of VRE. An increase in VRE infection has been demonstrated in solid-organ transplant patients.[43,44] Although transplant patients receive multiple courses of antimicrobials, including vancomycin, throughout their hospital course, the use of prophylactic antimicrobials may contribute to the development of resistance. A descriptive report demonstrated higher VRE infection rates among patients on the organ transplantation service (13.2 infections per 1000 admissions) and the surgical intensive care unit (5.6 infections per 1000 admissions) compared with the medical intensive care unit (4.8 infections per 1000 admissions) and the internal medicine service (1.8 infections per 1000 admissions).[43] In a hospital surveillance study, 32 (10.4%) of the 307 patients in whom VRE were cultured were transplant recipients[44]; 24 (75%) of 32 patients developed VRE within 30 days (mean time) of transplantation. In an infant–toddler surgical ward, colorectal prophylaxis was an independent risk factor for colonization with a β-lactamase-producing, gentamicin-resistant strain of *Enterococcus faecalis*.[45]

The development of resistance to *Pseudomonas* species and *Serratia* species from the use of surgical prophylaxis has also been demonstrated.[5] An increased rate of *Pseudomonas* and *Serratia* resistance to gentamicin was detected, with a subsequent decrease in resistance after gentamicin was removed from the prophylactic regimen for open-heart surgery.

Timing. Prophylaxis implies delivery of the drug to the operative site before contamination occurs. Thus, the anti-infective drug should be given before the initial incision to ensure its presence in an adequate concentration in the targeted tissues. A landmark study demonstrated that, in a guinea pig model, antimicrobials administered before or around the time of *S. aureus* inoculation reduced the rate of infection, whereas administration after *S. aureus* exposure was less effective.[46] The effect of administering an antimicrobial in the fourth postoperative hour was no different from that seen in a control group. This was confirmed in a prospective clinical study that demonstrated that giving antimicrobials more than two hours before surgery was no more effective than giving no antimicrobials or postoperative antimicrobials alone.[47] By consensus, the ideal time of administration is within 30 minutes to one hour before the incision. For most procedures, scheduling administration at the time of induction of anesthesia ensures adequate concentrations during the period of potential contamination.[30] The exceptions are cesarean procedures, in which the antimicrobial should be administered after cross-clamping of the umbilical cord,[48,49] and colonic procedures, in which oral antimicrobials should be administered starting 19 hours before the scheduled time of surgery.[50–56]

Duration. The shortest effective duration of antimicrobial administration for preventing postoperative infection is not known; however, postoperative antimicrobial administration is not necessary for most procedures.[57] For most procedures, the duration of antimicrobial prophylaxis should be 24 hours or less, with the exception of cardiothoracic procedures (up to 72 hours' duration) and ophthalmic procedures (duration not clearly established). The duration of cardiothoracic prophylaxis is based on expert panel consensus because the data do not delineate the optimal duration of prophylaxis. Prophylaxis for 24 hours or less may be appropriate for cardiothoracic procedures. At a minimum, antimicrobial coverage must be provided from the time of incision to closure of the incision. If a short-acting agent is used, it should be readministered if the operation extends beyond three hours in duration.[58] Readministration may also be warranted if prolonged or excessive bleeding occurs or there are factors that may shorten the half-life of the antimicrobial (e.g., extensive burns). Readministration may not be warranted in patients for whom the half-life is prolonged (e.g., patients with renal insufficiency or failure). If an operation is expected to last more than six to eight hours, it would be reasonable to administer an agent with a longer half-life and duration of action or to consider administering a short-acting agent at three-hour intervals during the procedure.

Route of Administration

Antimicrobials used for prophylaxis in surgery may be administered intravenously, orally, or topically. The preferred route of administration varies with the type of surgery, but, for a majority of procedures, intravenous administration is ideal because it produces reliable and predictable serum and tissue concentrations. Oral antimicrobials are often used for gut decontamination in elective colorectal operations and are an option in urologic procedures.

The use of topical antimicrobial agents, paste, and irrigations is beyond the scope of these guidelines. Intravenous and oral administration are the main focus of the guidelines, with the exception of ophthalmic procedures, for which topical administration is the primary route of administration.

Cardiothoracic Surgery

Background. Approximately 4 million cardiothoracic surgeries are performed annually in the United States.[59] Of these, approximately 500,000 are coronary-artery bypass graft (CABG) procedures and approximately 600,000 are open-heart procedures. A relatively small number involve heart or heart–lung transplants and repair of congenital heart defects in children.

Patients who have cardiac conditions such as prosthetic cardiac valves, previous bacterial endocarditis, acquired valvular dysfunction, hypertrophic cardiomyopathy, and mitral valve prolapse with valvular regurgitation are at risk for developing bacterial endocarditis when undergoing open-heart surgery. Few controlled trials have demonstrated a benefit of prophylaxis. However, because of the morbidity and mortality associated with bacterial endocarditis, the AHA recommends antimicrobial prophylaxis.[32]

Mediastinitis and sternal wound infection are rare but serious complications of cardiothoracic surgery. The frequency of these infections with or without associated sternal dehiscence is 0.7% to 1.5%; however, the associated mortality rate is 13% to 33%.[60] Risk factors for these complications include chronic obstructive pulmonary disease, prolonged stay in the intensive care unit, respiratory failure, connective tissue disease, and male sex. Advanced age, lengthy surgery, and diabetes mellitus have also been identified as risk factors.[61]

Organisms. The primary intent of early antimicrobial prophylaxis in open-heart surgery was to reduce the frequency of postoperative endocarditis after valve repair. Early studies showed that coagulase-positive and coagulase-negative staphylococci were the primary pathogens infecting prosthetic valves.[62–64] As a result, most early prophylactic regimens were directed against staphylococci, with semisynthetic penicillins and first-generation cephalosporins emerging as the drugs of choice. With the advent of the CABG procedure and an expansion in the number of cardiothoracic procedures performed in the United States, prophylaxis must cover a broader spectrum of aerobic gram-negative pathogens that cause wound infections postoperatively at the sternal incision and the saphenous vein harvest sites.[64–67]

Efficacy. The postoperative infection rate in clean cardiothoracic surgeries is intrinsically low, and the extent of superiority of one regimen over another is relatively small. Antimicrobial prophylaxis in cardiothoracic surgery is associated with a fivefold lower rate of postoperative wound infection compared with placebo (approximately 5% versus 20% to 25%).[68] Early placebo-controlled studies using a semisynthetic penicillin[69] or cephradine[70] were terminated early because of high infection rates in the placebo groups. Postoperative wound infection rates ranged from 9.1% to 54% in the placebo groups, compared with 0% to 6.7% in groups receiving antimicrobials. Since the routine administration of prophylactic antimicrobials for cardiothoracic surgeries, postoperative wound infection rates have ranged from 0.8% to 25%.

Choice. Cephalosporins were compared with antistaphylococcal penicillins as prophylactic agents for cardiothoracic surgery in five studies. The antistaphylococcal penicillins were used in combination with another penicillin, an aminoglycoside, or both in four of these studies.[71–75] In four of the five studies, there were fewer total wound infections in the cephalosporin-treated patients; however, none of the differences were significant.

Published trials comparing cefazolin, cefamandole, and cefuroxime as prophylactic antimicrobials for cardiothoracic surgery have revealed fewer total infections in the second-generation cephalosporin-treated patients; however, none of the differences were significant.[76–82] Both sternal and total wound infection rates (sternal plus leg wound infection) ranged from 2.5% to 18.8% in cefazolin-treated patients and from 0% to 13.5% in cefamandole- or cefuroxime-treated patients. Total wound infection rates were lower in patients receiving the second-generation cephalosporin in seven of the eight comparison groups. Leg wound infection rates were lower in five of the eight second-generation cephalosporin treatment groups. Meta-analysis of these results did not yield significant differences between agents when sternal and leg wounds were analyzed separately.[68] In another study, in which cefazolin and cefamandole, both with the addition of gentamicin, were compared, there was a significantly lower rate of sternal and total wound infection in the cefamandole–gentamicin group.[77] Three randomized, prospective, double-blind studies did not favor the second-generation cephalosporins: One study demonstrated no clinically or statistically significant difference between cefazolin and cefuroxime prophylaxis in 702 patients undergoing heart surgery,[83] a second study showed that cefuroxime-treated patients developed more sternal wound infections than cefazolin-treated patients,[84] and a third study showed no difference in rates of postsurgical site wound infection among cefamandole, cefazolin, and cefuroxime.[82]

In a study that compared second-generation cephalosporins, cefamandole was found to be superior to cefonicid in preventing perioperative infections.[85] No differences in total wound infection rates were found in another study in which cefuroxime was compared with ceftriaxone in 512 patients.[78] Vancomycin was superior to penicillin G in preventing total wound infections.[86]

In summary, cefamandole and cefuroxime were each associated with a lower frequency of wound infection than cefazolin, although significant differences were not consistently demonstrated. There were no differences in wound infection rates in a study that compared cefazolin with ceftriaxone. In addition, no differences in outcome were seen in studies in which cefamandole was compared with cefuroxime. No differences were found between antistaphylococcal penicillin regimens (often used in combination with aminoglycosides or other penicillins) and single-agent first- or second-generation cephalosporin regimens. These results are further supported by the results of a 30-year meta-analysis.[68]

Cephalosporins, as single agents, are at least as effective as combination regimens of antistaphylococcal penicillins and aminoglycosides and are much easier to administer. Cefazolin has been the traditional cephalosporin of choice. Further trials in a large number of patients would be required in order to demonstrate the superiority of cefamandole or cefuroxime.

There are limited data regarding the choice of an antimicrobial for penicillin-allergic patients undergoing cardiovascular procedures. Although vancomycin offers coverage against potential gram-positive pathogens, the addition of an aminoglycoside may be prudent when colonization and infection with gram-negative organisms are expected (such as a saphenous vein site).

Duration. The optimal duration of antimicrobial prophylaxis for cardiothoracic surgery was addressed by five studies, all using cephalothin as the prophylactic antimicrobial.[66,87–90] Dosages and durations in the short-duration groups ranged from a single 1-g dose of cephalothin (as the sodium) to 2 g every six hours for two days. Long treatment regimens ranged from 2 g of cephalothin preoperatively followed by 1 g every six hours for three days to 2 g every six hours for six days. Total wound infection rates were lower in the short-duration treatment groups in two of four studies, although the differences were not significant. In another randomized study, there was no significant difference between single-dose ceftriaxone and cefuroxime three times daily until the end of the second postoperative day.[90] The researchers concluded that a single dose of ceftriaxone was a viable alternative to cefuroxime for 48 hours as prophylaxis in cardiothoracic surgical procedures. A European randomized, prospective study in 844 evaluable patients demonstrated that a single dose of cefuroxime 20 mg/kg (as the sodium) at induction of anesthesia was as effective as the same dose at induction of anesthesia followed by 750 mg three times daily for three consecutive days.[91]

Pediatric Efficacy. No well-controlled studies have evaluated the efficacy of antimicrobial prophylaxis in pediatric patients undergoing cardiovascular procedures. A survey indicated that the predominant practice in pediatric cardiovascular surgery is to use cefazolin for two days or less or until transthoracic medical devices are removed.[92]

Recommendations. For patients undergoing cardiothoracic procedures, the recommended regimen is cefazolin 1 g (as the sodium) intravenously at induction of anesthesia and every 8 hours for up to 72 hours. This duration is based on consensus of the expert panel because the data do not delineate the optimal duration of prophylaxis. Prophylaxis for 24 hours or less may be appropriate for cardiothoracic procedures. Currently there is no evidence to support continuing prophylaxis until chest and mediastinal drainage tubes are removed. Cefuroxime 1.5 g (as the sodium) intravenously at induction of anesthesia and every 12 hours for up to 72 hours or cefamandole 1 g (as the nafate) at induction of anesthesia and every six hours for up to 72 hours are suitable alternatives. Further studies are needed to demonstrate the efficacy of single-dose prophylaxis. Vancomycin 1 g (as the hydrochloride) intravenously over one hour, with or without gentamicin 2 mg/kg (as the sulfate) intravenously, should be reserved as an alternative on the basis of guidelines from HICPAC and AHA.[21,32] (Strength of evidence for prophylaxis = A.)

Pediatric Dosage. The recommended regimen for pediatric patients undergoing cardiothoracic procedures is cefazolin 20–30 mg/kg (as the sodium) intravenously at induction of anesthesia and every 8 hours for up to 72 hours. Cefuroxime 50 mg/kg (as the sodium) intravenously at induction of anesthesia and every 8 hours for up to 72 hours is an acceptable alternative. Vancomycin 15 mg/kg (as the hydrochloride) intravenously over one hour, with or without gentamicin 2 mg/kg (as the sulfate) intravenously, should be reserved as an alternative on the basis of guidelines from HICPAC and AHA.[21,32]

Gastroduodenal Surgery

Background. The gastroduodenal procedures considered in this document include resection with or without vagotomy for gastric or duodenal ulcers, resection for gastric carcinoma, revision required in order to repair strictures of the gastric outlet, and gastric bypass. Studies addressing antimicrobial prophylaxis for gastroesophageal reflux disease procedures (Nissen's fundoplication), pancreatoduodenectomy (Whipple's procedure), or highly selective vagotomy for ulcers could not be identified.

The stomach is an effective barrier to bacterial colonization; this is at least partially related to its acidity. The stomach and the duodenum typically contain small numbers of organisms ($<10^4$ CFU/mL), the most common of which are streptococci, lactobacilli, diphtheroids, and fungi.[93,94] Treatment with agents that increase gastric pH significantly increases the concentration of gastric organisms.[95–97] Alterations in gastric and duodenal bacterial flora as a result of increases in gastric pH have the potential to increase the postoperative infection rate.[98,99]

The risk of postoperative infection in gastroduodenal surgery depends on a number of factors. Patients who are at highest risk include those with achlorhydria, decreased gastric motility, gastric outlet obstruction, morbid obesity, gastric bleeding, or cancer.[100]

Organisms. The most common organisms cultured from wound infections after gastroduodenal surgery are coliforms (*Escherichia coli, Proteus* species, *Klebsiella* species), staphylococci, streptococci, enterococci, and, occasionally, *Bacteroides* species.[101–108]

Efficacy. In one large study, wound infection rates in patients not receiving antimicrobial prophylaxis were 6% after vagotomy and drainage, 13% after gastric ulcer surgery, 17% after surgery for gastric cancer, and 25% in patients with gastroduodenal bleeding.[109] Results of randomized, controlled trials clearly indicate that prophylactic antimicrobials are effective in decreasing postoperative infection rates in gastroduodenal surgery. Relative to other types of GI tract surgery, the number of clinical trials evaluating antimicrobial prophylaxis for gastroduodenal surgery is limited. The most common definition of wound infection used in those studies was the presence of purulent discharge. In placebo-controlled trials, infection rates ranged from 0% to 7% for patients receiving cephalosporins and from 21% to 44% for patients receiving placebo.[102,103,105–107,110–112] The difference was significant in most studies.

No efficacy data are available on highly selective vagotomy, Nissen's fundoplication, or Whipple's procedure. Despite the lack of data, the expert panel supports the use of a single dose of cefazolin 1 g (as the sodium) intravenously for prophylaxis of these procedures.

Choice. No differences between first- and second-generation cephalosporins were found. The most frequently used agents were first-generation[103,105,108,110–113] and second-generation[101,102,104,106,107,113] cephalosporins. Ticarcillin,[108] amoxicillin–clavulanate,[114] mezlocillin,[104] and ciprofloxacin[101,115] were also evaluated. Relatively few studies have compared the efficacy of different agents in reducing postoperative infection rates. In comparative studies, ticarcillin (intravenous) and cephalothin (intravenous) were similarly effective,[108] as were ciprofloxacin (intravenous and oral) and cefuroxime (intravenous).[101]

Duration. Available data indicate that single-dose and multidose regimens are similarly effective. Two studies compared single- and multidose regimens of either cefamandole[113] or amoxicillin–clavulanate.[114] There was no significant difference in wound infection rates. No studies have evaluated the use of a single dose of a first-generation cephalosporin.

Pediatric Efficacy. No well-controlled studies have evaluated the efficacy of antimicrobial prophylaxis in pediatric patients undergoing gastroduodenal surgery.

Recommendation. Antimicrobial prophylaxis in gastroduodenal surgery should be considered for patients at highest risk for postoperative infections, such as patients with increased gastric pH (e.g., patients receiving histamine H$_2$-receptor antagonists), decreased gastric motility, gastric outlet obstruction, gastric bleeding, or cancer. Antimicrobials are not needed when the lumen of the intestinal tract is not entered.

A single dose of cefazolin 1 g (as the sodium) given intravenously at induction of anesthesia is recommended in procedures during which the lumen of the intestinal tract is entered. A single dose of cefazolin 1 g given intravenously at induction of anesthesia is recommended for highly selective vagotomy, Nissen's fundoplication, and Whipple's procedure. (Strength of evidence for prophylaxis = A when the lumen of the intestinal tract is entered.) (Strength of evidence for prophylaxis = C for highly selective vagotomy, Nissen's fundoplication, and Whipple's procedure.)

Pediatric Dosage. The recommended regimen for pediatric patients undergoing gastroduodenal surgery during which the lumen of the intestinal tract is entered, highly selective vagotomy, Nissen's fundoplication, and Whipple's procedure is a single dose of cefazolin 20–30 mg/kg (as the sodium) intravenously at induction of anesthesia.

Biliary Tract Surgery

Background. Biliary tract surgeries include cholecystectomy, exploration of the common bile duct, and choledochoenterostomy. The overall risk of postoperative infection in biliary tract surgery is approximately 5% to 20%.[116] The biliary tract is usually sterile; therefore, the risk of infection is low. However, it is generally accepted that patients with bacteria in the bile at the time of surgery are at higher risk of postoperative infection.[117,118] Factors that place patients at a higher risk of infection include obesity, age greater than 70 years, an acute episode of cholecystitis or cholelithiasis within the previous six months, diabetes mellitus, or a history of obstructive jaundice or bile duct obstruction.[116,119]

Organisms. The organisms most commonly associated with infection after biliary tract surgery include *E. coli, Klebsiella* species, and enterococci; less frequently, other gramnegative organisms, streptococci, or staphylococci are isolated. Anaerobes are occasionally reported, most commonly *Clostridium* species.[117,119–128]

Efficacy. Data from randomized, controlled trials support the use of prophylactic antimicrobials in all patients undergoing biliary tract surgery. Significantly lower rates of postoperative wound infection have been demonstrated, even in patients at low risk.

Numerous studies have evaluated the use of prophylactic antimicrobials during biliary tract surgery. Although the definition of wound infection varied between studies, the presence of purulent discharge was the most common definition. First-generation,[121,127,129–138] second-generation,[118–120,122,123,126,133,135,136,138–143] and third-generation[123,124,132,141] cephalosporins have been studied more extensively than other antimicrobials. Limited data are available for ampicillin–

gentamicin,[144] mezlocillin,[142] piperacillin,[137] amoxicillin–clavulanate,[143] and ciprofloxacin.[124,145]

Although many studies had an insufficient sample size to demonstrate a significant benefit of antimicrobial prophylaxis, a meta-analysis of 42 clinical trials that compared prophylactic antimicrobials with placebo demonstrated that active treatment significantly reduced the risk of wound infection.[116] In that analysis, the overall wound infection rate was 15% in the control group. Wound infection rates were 9% lower in the antimicrobial treatment group than the control group. When patients were stratified by low or high risk and by early or late wound inspection (early in hospital or late at follow-up), antimicrobial prophylaxis was still effective in preventing wound infections in all groups, although the largest benefit was in high-risk patients with a later wound inspection.

Laparoscopic cholecystectomy has replaced open cholecystectomy as the standard of practice because of a reduction in recovery time and a shorter hospital stay. There have been few studies of antimicrobial prophylaxis for laparoscopic cholecystectomy. The studies that have addressed this procedure were not randomized, controlled studies. In one study at the Mayo Clinic, 95% of 195 patients received a preoperative dose of an antimicrobial, usually a first-generation cephalosporin. Erythema at the trocar site was noted in 6% of patients, and wound separation was noted in 5% of patients; however, no treatment was necessary.[146] A nonrandomized study showed 14 infections in 228 patients who received antimicrobial prophylaxis and no infections in 188 patients who received only a chlorhexidine scrub before surgery.[147] The patients in this study were assigned to treatment groups according to the attending physician's treatment preference. In a study in the United Kingdom, cefuroxime 1.5 g (as the sodium) was administered at induction of anesthesia to 253 consecutive patients. At two weeks, 0.8% of patients had wound infections, 0.8% had chest infections, and 0.4% had an intra-abdominal abscess. No complications were noted at 12 months.[148] Current data do not support antimicrobial prophylaxis for laparoscopic cholecystectomies.

Choice. The data do not indicate a significant difference among first-, second-, and third-generation cephalosporins. Several studies have compared first-generation cephalosporins with second- or third-generation agents.[127,132–136,138] With one exception,[136] there was no significant difference among agents. This was confirmed by a meta-analysis that found no significant difference among first-, second-, and third-generation cephalosporins.[116] Other studies found no significant differences between ampicillin and cefamandole,[126] ciprofloxacin and ceftriaxone,[124] cefonicid and mezlocillin,[142] cefuroxime with or without metronidazole and mezlocillin,[149] amoxicillin–clavulanate and mezlocillin,[150] amoxicillin–clavulanate and cefamandole,[143] and oral and intravenous ciprofloxacin and intravenous cefuroxime.[145]

Duration. The effect of treatment duration on outcome has been evaluated. A single dose of a cephalosporin was compared with multiple doses in several studies; no significant differences were found.[118,120,121,132,139–141,151] The largest study compared one dose of cefuroxime with three doses in 1004 patients with risk factors for infection who were undergoing biliary tract surgery.[118] There was no significant difference in the rates of minor or major wound infection between the single- and multiple-dose groups.

Pediatric Efficacy. No well-controlled studies have evaluated the efficacy of antimicrobial prophylaxis in pediatric patients undergoing biliary tract surgery.

Recommendation. A single dose of cefazolin 1 g (as the sodium) administered intravenously at induction of anesthesia is recommended for open procedures in the biliary tract. (Strength of evidence for prophylaxis = A.) Antimicrobial prophylaxis is not recommended in laparoscopic cholecystectomies. (Strength of evidence against prophylaxis = B.)

Pediatric Dosage. The recommended regimen for pediatric patients undergoing open procedures in the biliary tract is a single dose of cefazolin 20–30 mg/kg (as the sodium) intravenously at induction of anesthesia.

Appendectomy

Background. Cases of appendicitis can be described as complicated or uncomplicated on the basis of the pathology. Patients with uncomplicated appendicitis have an acutely inflamed appendix. Complicated appendicitis usually includes perforated or gangrenous appendicitis, including peritonitis or abscess formation. However, in some studies patients with gangrenous appendicitis are considered to have uncomplicated disease because these patients generally have a lower infectious complication rate than patients with perforation. Because complicated appendicitis is treated as a presumed infection, it has not been addressed in these guidelines.

Approximately 80% of patients with appendicitis have uncomplicated disease.[24] Postoperative infection has been reported in 9–30% of patients with uncomplicated appendicitis who do not receive prophylactic antimicrobials.[152-156] Postoperative infection was usually defined as purulent wound discharge with or without positive cultures. Laparoscopic appendectomy has been reported to produce similar or lower rates of infection as open appendectomy when antimicrobials are used; however, there have been no randomized, controlled studies.[157]

Organisms. The most common microorganisms isolated from wound infections after appendectomy are anaerobic and aerobic gram-negative enteric organisms. *Bacteroides fragilis* is the most commonly cultured anaerobe, and *E. coli* is the most frequent aerobe, indicating that the bowel flora constitute a major source for pathogens.[24,158,159] Aerobic and anaerobic streptococci, *Staphylococcus* species, and *Enterococcus* species also have been reported. *Pseudomonas aeruginosa* has been reported infrequently.

Efficacy. As a single agent, metronidazole was no more effective in appendectomy than placebo.[152,155] Cefazolin was generally less effective than placebo, with postoperative infection rates above 10%.[153] This is likely due to its limited activity against anaerobes. Clindamycin was more effective than placebo, although the postoperative infection rate tended to be relatively high (17%).[153]

Choice. Randomized, controlled trials have failed to identify an agent that is clearly superior to other agents in the prophylaxis of postappendectomy infectious complications. The second- and third-generation cephalosporins appear to have similar efficacy and are the recommended agents on the basis of cost and tolerability. Given the relatively equivalent efficacy between agents, a cost-minimization approach is reasonable; the choice of agents should be based on local drug acquisition costs.

A wide range of antimicrobials have been evaluated for prophylaxis in uncomplicated appendicitis. The most commonly used agents were cephalosporins. In general, second-generation cephalosporins (cefoxitin, cefotetan) and third-generation cephalosporins (cefoperazone, cefotaxime) were effective, with postoperative infection rates of <5% in most studies.[156,160-166] However, one study[165] showed that single-dose cefotetan was significantly more effective than single-dose cefoxitin, perhaps because of the longer half-life of cefotetan.

Piperacillin 2 g (as the sodium) was comparable to cefoxitin 2 g (as the sodium) in a well-controlled study.[166] Metronidazole was less effective than cefotaxime, with infection rates above 10%.[160] However, when metronidazole was combined with ampicillin[167] or gentamicin,[162,168] the postoperative infection rates were 3% to 6%. Clindamycin was more effective than cefazolin, although the postoperative infection rate tended to be relatively high (17%).[153]

Duration. In most of the studies of second- or third-generation cephalosporins or metronidazole combinations, a single dose[160-162,165,166,168] or two or three doses[156,163,167] were given. Although direct comparisons were not done, there was no discernible difference in postoperative infection rates between single-dose and multidose administration in most studies.

Pediatric Efficacy. Two pediatric studies demonstrated no difference in infection rates between placebo and antimicrobials: metronidazole, penicillin plus tobramycin, and piperacillin[169] and single-dose metronidazole and single-dose metronidazole plus cefuroxime.[170] As a single agent, metronidazole was no more effective than placebo in two double-blind studies that included children 10 years of age and older[152] and 15 years of age and older.[155] In a randomized study that included pediatric patients, ceftizoxime and cefamandole demonstrated significantly lower infection rates and duration of hospitalization than placebo.[171] Both cefoxitin and a combination of gentamicin and metronidazole were associated with a lower rate of postoperative infection in a randomized study that included pediatric patients less than 16 years of age.[162] Second-generation cephalosporins (cefoxitin) and third-generation cephalosporins (cefoperazone, cefotaxime) were effective, with postoperative infection rates of <5% in two studies that included pediatric patients less than 12 years of age.[156,162,163]

Recommendation. For uncomplicated appendicitis, the recommended regimen is a cephalosporin with anaerobic and aerobic activity (cefoxitin, cefotetan, cefmetazole) 1–2 g intravenously at induction of anesthesia. An alternative is piperacillin 2 g (as the sodium) intravenously. For penicillin-allergic patients, an alternative is metronidazole 500 mg plus gentamicin 2 mg/kg (as the sulfate) intravenously at the induction of anesthesia. (Strength of evidence for prophylaxis = A.)

Pediatric Dosage. The recommended regimen for pediatric patients undergoing procedures for uncomplicated appendicitis is a single intravenous dose of cefoxitin 20–40 mg/kg (as the sodium), cefotetan 20–40 mg/kg (as the disodium), or cefotaxime or ceftizoxime 25–50 mg/kg (as the sodium) at induction of anesthesia. An alternative is piperacillin 50 mg/kg (as the sodium) intravenously at induction of anesthesia. For penicillin-allergic patients, an alternative is metronidazole 10 mg/kg plus gentamicin 2 mg/kg (as the sulfate) intravenously at induction of anesthesia.

Colorectal Surgery

Background. Wound infections are a frequent complication of surgery of the colon or rectum. Other septic complications, such as fecal fistula, intra-abdominal abscesses, peritonitis, and septicemia, are serious concerns but much less common.[172] Infectious complication rates range from 30% to 60% when antimicrobial prophylaxis is not used.[24,173] Patients receiving appropriate antimicrobial prophylaxis have infection rates of <10%. A pooled analysis of clinical trials of antimicrobial prophylaxis in colon surgery also demonstrated that the use of antimicrobials significantly reduces mortality (11.2% for control versus 4.5% for treatment).[174] The type and duration of surgery can affect the risk of infection. Rectal resection is associated with a higher risk of infection than intraperitoneal colon resection.[175,176] Surgeries lasting 3.5 hours or more are associated with a higher risk of infection than shorter procedures.[24] Other risk factors include impaired host defenses, age of >60 years, hypoalbuminemia, poor preoperative bowel preparation, bacterial contamination of the surgical wound,[177] corticosteroid therapy, and malignancy.[178]

The removal of feces and intestinal fluid by mechanical preparation is considered a prerequisite for colorectal surgery. Mechanical preparation also reduces the high concentrations of bacteria in the bowel. Traditional three- to four-day regimens of clear liquids, cathartics, and enemas have been replaced by single-day lavage techniques.[179–186]

The choice of antimicrobials for prophylaxis in colorectal surgery should be guided by the spectrum of activity of the agent. Agents should have activity against the anaerobic and aerobic flora of the bowel. There have been three main approaches to the prophylaxis of infections after colorectal surgery: oral agents, intravenous agents (usually cephalosporins), and combinations of oral and intravenous agents. Although numerous clinical trials have been conducted, the central issues of determining the most appropriate regimen (oral versus intravenous versus an oral–intravenous combination) and the optimal choice of antimicrobial have yet to be fully resolved.

Organisms. The infecting organisms in colorectal surgery are derived from the bowel lumen, where there are high concentrations of organisms. *B. fragilis* and other obligate anaerobes are the most frequently isolated organisms from the bowel, with concentrations 1,000 to 10,000 times higher than those of aerobes.[187] *E. coli* is the most common aerobe. *B. fragilis* and *E. coli* make up approximately 20% to 30% of the fecal mass. They are the most frequently isolated pathogens from infected wounds after colon surgery.[187]

Efficacy. Results from randomized, controlled trials unequivocally support the use of prophylactic antimicrobials in all patients undergoing colorectal surgery. Postoperative infection rates tend to be lower when oral antimicrobials are used for prophylaxis than after the use of intravenous agents; therefore, oral antimicrobials are preferred.

Oral regimens. A variety of oral agents administered after mechanical bowel preparation have been evaluated for prophylaxis for colorectal surgery. The most common combinations have been an aminoglycoside (neomycin and, less often, kanamycin) plus an agent that will provide sufficient anaerobic activity, usually erythromycin[50–56,188] or metronidazole.[56,182,188–192] In placebo-controlled studies,[6,50,188,192,193] the oral combination was significantly more effective than placebo in reducing wound infections. Postoperative wound infection rates ranged from 0% to 11% with neomycin plus erythromycin[50–56] and from 2% to 13% with neomycin and metronidazole.[189–191] Combinations of neomycin and tetracycline[6,193] and neomycin and clindamycin[189] have also been used successfully, with postoperative wound infection rates of <10%. The use of metronidazole as a single agent appears to be less effective, with reported wound infection rates of 12% to 15%.[194,195]

Oral antimicrobials have been compared with intravenous agents in a few studies. Oral neomycin plus oral erythromycin was significantly more effective than intravenous gentamicin and intravenous metronidazole[54] but was similarly effective as intravenous cefoxitin,[52] intravenous cefamandole,[53] and intravenous ceftriaxone plus intravenous metronidazole.[55]

Intravenous regimens. A wide range of intravenous antimicrobials have been evaluated for prophylaxis in colorectal surgery. Cephalosporins are the most common agents, usually administered as a single agent. First-generation cephalosporins produced inconsistent results.[196–200] With one exception,[199] single-agent first-generation cephalosporins were generally ineffective, with postoperative wound infection rates ranging from 12% to 39%.[196,197] This is not surprising given the lack of *B. fragilis* activity of these agents. Second-generation cephalosporins have been widely evaluated. In single-agent therapy, wound infection rates ranged from 0% to 17%[176,198,201–209]; however, more than half of the studies found rates of >10%. Third-generation agents have been evaluated in a few trials; postoperative wound infection rates were 8% to 19% with single-agent use.[205,210,211] In some studies, second- or third-generation cephalosporins were combined with other intravenous agents, most commonly metronidazole.[201,209–212] However, in three of four studies, a combination of a second- or third-generation cephalosporin plus metronidazole was no more effective than the cephalosporin alone.[201,209–211] Other intravenous agents that have been evaluated either alone or in combination include aminoglycosides,[54,101,213–217] clindamycin,[213] ampicillin,[214,218,219] ampicillin plus a β-lactamase inhibitor,[216,220] doxycycline,[218,221–223] ticarcillin plus a β-lactamase inhibitor,[215,224] piperacillin,[206,225] piperacillin plus a β-lactamase inhibitor,[225] imipenem,[212] and ciprofloxacin.[115]

Combination oral and intravenous regimens. Combinations of oral and intravenous antimicrobials have been used in an attempt to further reduce postoperative infection rates. Regimens include oral neomycin and erythromycin plus intravenous administration of a cephalosporin,[52,175,176,197,198,226,227] metronidazole,[228,229] or gentamicin plus clindamycin.[213] Postoperative wound infection rates in these studies ranged from 0% to 7%. With one exception,[175] there was no significant difference between oral neomycin–erythromycin plus an intravenous antimicrobial and oral neomycin–erythromycin alone.[52,197,213,226] When combination oral and intravenous agents were compared with intravenous agents alone, combination therapy tended to be superior in four of five studies[52,176,197,198,228]; the difference was significant in two of the studies.[176,197] In one study,[176] the difference was even greater among patients undergoing rectal resection, a procedure associated with a high risk of infection. The postoperative wound infection rates after rectal resection were 23% and 11%, respectively, for patients receiving intravenous cefoxitin and cefoxitin plus oral neomycin and erythromycin.

Duration. Single and multiple doses were compared in several studies.[203–205,211,219,222] However, only two of these studies[219,222] compared single doses with multiple doses of the same antimicrobial. There was no significant difference in infection rates between single-dose and multidose administration, with only one exception. A single dose of cefotaxime plus metronidazole was significantly more effective than three doses of cefotaxime alone.[211]

Pediatric Efficacy. No well-controlled studies have evaluated the efficacy of antimicrobial prophylaxis in pediatric patients undergoing colorectal surgery. The safety, efficacy, tolerability, and cost-effectiveness of intestinal lavage have been demonstrated in pediatric patients.[230,231]

Recommendation. Patients undergoing colorectal surgery should receive mechanical bowel preparation. Numerous bowel preparations are available. Lavage solutions are contraindicated in patients with obstruction.

Oral neomycin sulfate 1 g and erythromycin base 1 g should be given after the bowel preparation is complete at 19, 18, and 9 hours before surgery. If the oral route is contraindicated, a single 2-g dose of an intravenous cephalosporin with both aerobic and anaerobic activity (e.g., cefoxitin, cefotetan, cefmetazole) should be given at induction of anesthesia. Because there is no demonstrable difference in efficacy among these cephalosporins, the choice should be based on local drug acquisition costs. In patients undergoing high-risk surgery, such as rectal resection, a combination of oral neomycin–erythromycin plus a cephalosporin administered intravenously is recommended. (Strength of evidence for prophylaxis = A.)

Pediatric Dosage. Pediatric patients undergoing colorectal surgery should undergo mechanical bowel preparation. Numerous bowel preparations are available. Lavage solutions are contraindicated in patients with obstruction. One regimen for pediatric patients is polyethylene glycol–electrolyte lavage solution given orally or by nasogastric tube at a rate of 25–40 mL/kg/hr until rectal effluent is clear.[230,231]

Oral neomycin sulfate 20 mg/kg and erythromycin base 10 mg/kg should be given after the bowel preparation is complete at 19, 18, and 9 hours before surgery. If the oral route is contraindicated, a single 30–40 mg/kg intravenous dose of cefoxitin or cefotetan should be given at induction of anesthesia. In patients undergoing high-risk surgery, such as rectal resection, a combination of oral neomycin and erythromycin plus a cephalosporin administered intravenously is recommended.

Head and Neck Surgery

Background. Elective surgical procedures of the head and neck can be categorized as clean or clean-contaminated. Clean procedures include parotidectomy, thyroidectomy, and submandibular-gland excision. Clean-contaminated procedures include all procedures involving an incision through the oral or pharyngeal mucosa.[232] These vary considerably from tonsillectomy, adenoidectomy, and rhinoplasty to complicated tumor-debulking procedures requiring massive reconstruction.

In prospective, randomized, double-blind trials comparing placebo with antimicrobials in clean-contaminated surgeries, patients receiving placebo had postoperative wound infection rates of 36% to 78%.[233-235] Antimicrobials are associated with dramatically lower rates of postoperative wound infection. Infection rates below 10% may be expected when appropriate antimicrobial prophylaxis is given.[233,234,236-241]

Postoperative wound infection rates are affected by age, nutritional status, and the presence of concomitant medical conditions such as diabetes mellitus. The hospital course, including length of hospitalization before surgery, duration of antimicrobial use before surgery, length of surgery, and presence of implants, can also affect postoperative wound infection rates. If the patient has cancer, the stage of the malignancy before operation and preoperative radiation therapy must also be assessed.[242-244]

Organisms. The normal flora of the mouth and the oropharynx are responsible for most infections that follow clean-contaminated head and neck procedures. The predominant oropharyngeal organisms include various streptococci (aerobic and anaerobic species), *S. epidermidis*, *Peptococcus*, *Peptostreptococcus*, and numerous anaerobic gram-negative bacteria, including *Bacteroides* species (but almost never *B. fragilis*) and *Veillonella*. Nasal flora include *Staphylococcus* species and *Streptococcus* species. Anaerobic bacteria are approximately 10 times more common than aerobic bacteria in the oropharynx. As a result, postoperative wound infections are primarily polymicrobial. Both aerobic and anaerobic bacteria are cultured from infected wounds in more than 90% of cases.[245-248] It has been suggested that aerobic gram-negative bacteria are colonizers rather than pathogens in most patients.[237,246]

Efficacy for Clean Procedures. Systemic administration of prophylactic antimicrobials has not proven effective in reducing wound infection rates in patients undergoing clean procedures of the head and neck; however, randomized, blinded studies have not been performed for clean procedures. A retrospective review of 438 patients undergoing clean procedures (parotidectomy, thyroidectomy, or submandibular gland excision) demonstrated that 80% of the patients had not received prophylactic antimicrobials; the associated wound infection rate was 0.7%. Patients receiving antimicrobials had a similar wound infection rate.[249] Another retrospective cohort study of 192 patients who underwent surgery between 1976 and 1989 did not demonstrate any difference in infection rates between patients who did and patients who did not receive perioperative antimicrobials.[250] However, the authors calculated that the excess cost due to patients who developed a postoperative wound infection was in excess of $36,000 and that the cost of administering prophylaxis to 100 patients is less than this amount. These retrospective data alone do not justify prophylaxis. Other factors besides cost need to be considered, including the potential for resistance, adverse events, and prosthetic placement.

Pediatric Efficacy for Clean Procedures. No well-controlled studies have evaluated the effect of antimicrobial prophylaxis in the pediatric population undergoing clean surgical procedures of the head and neck.

Efficacy for Clean-Contaminated Procedures. Three double-blind, placebo-controlled trials established superiority of antimicrobials over placebo in clean-contaminated procedures.[233,234,238] In one trial, 101 patients were randomly assigned to receive placebo every eight hours for four doses, cefazolin 500 mg (as the sodium) every eight hours for four doses, cefotaxime 2 g (as the sodium) every eight hours for four doses, or cefoperazone 2 g (as the sodium) every eight hours for four doses.[234] Infection rates were 78% in the placebo group, 33% in the cefazolin group, 10% in the cefotaxime group, and 9% in the cefoperazone group. The difference between each antimicrobial group and the placebo group was significant. The length of hospital stay for infected patients was twice that of noninfected patients. The second study demonstrated a wound infection rate of 12% with ampicillin plus cloxacillin, compared with 28% with placebo.[238] Although the wound infection rate (27%) for cefamandole 2 g (as the nafate) followed by 1 g every eight hours for a total of three doses was relatively high compared with the previous studies, cefamandole did demonstrate superiority over placebo (wound infection rate of 55%).[233] Another study involving cefoperazone, cefotaxime, and placebo demonstrated similar results.[235]

Choice. Various studies of prophylaxis for clean-contaminated procedures have demonstrated wound infection rates of less than 10% with clindamycin plus gentamicin,[236,251] clindamycin plus amikacin,[252] cefazolin plus metronidazole,[241] cefuroxime alone,[253] and cefuroxime plus metronidazole.[253] A prospective, randomized, double-blind study compared clindamycin 600 mg (as the hydrochloride) intravenously for a total of four doses with clindamycin 600 mg plus gentamicin 1.7 mg/kg (as the sulfate) intravenously for a total of four doses in 104 patients undergoing clean-contaminated oncological head and neck surgery.[237] The combination of gentamicin plus clindamycin demonstrated no significant advantage over clindamycin alone. The postoperative infection rate was 3.8% in both groups. The authors concluded that clindamycin alone appears effective as a prophylactic agent and that broad-spectrum antimicrobials such as cefoxitin may be unnecessary. Because clindamycin is not active against aerobic gram-negative bacteria, the authors concluded that these bacteria are probably colonizers rather than pathogens. This study suggests that aerobic gram-negative coverage (as provided by gentamicin) may be unnecessary. However, the study lacked sufficient power to show a difference among groups.

Cefazolin offers coverage against potential aerobic and anaerobic organisms, except *B. fragilis*, in clean-contaminated procedures of the head and neck. Although the need for coverage against *B. fragilis* has not been substantiated by the literature, some people consider the addition of metronidazole to cefazolin acceptable when colonization with *B. fragilis* is expected.

Dosage. Cefazolin 500 mg (as the sodium) three times daily for a total of one and five days demonstrated high infection rates (35% and 18%, respectively).[251] Another study showed similar results with cefazolin.[236] Two major flaws with these studies were the dose (500 mg) and the administration time (three hours preoperatively).

In a randomized trial, cefazolin 2 g (as the sodium) was compared with moxalactam 2 g (as the disodium), each given one hour before surgery and three more times, for a total of four doses.[254] Infection rates were not significantly different: 8.5% in the cefazolin group and 3.4% in the moxalactam group. A prospective, randomized multicenter trial compared the effectiveness of clindamycin 900 mg (as the hydrochloride) with that of cefazolin 2 g (as the sodium) before surgery and continued every 8 hours for a total of 24 hours in patients undergoing major procedures (pectoralis major myocutaneous flap reconstruction).[255] Wound infections developed in 19.6% of patients in the clindamycin group and 21.6% of patients in the cefazolin group. This difference was not significant. These two trials demonstrated that, when administered at the appropriate time, cefazolin 2 g is effective.

In a prospective, double-blind trial, 159 patients were randomly assigned to receive amoxicillin 1750 mg (as the trihydrate) with clavulanic acid 250 mg (as clavulanate potassium), clindamycin 600 mg (as the hydrochloride) plus gentamicin 80 mg (as the sulfate), or cefazolin 2 g (as the sodium).[256] All groups received a total of three intravenous doses (the cefazolin group received one 2-g dose followed by two doses of 1 g each). There was no significant difference in wound infection rates among these regimens.

Duration. There was no difference in efficacy between one day and five days of clindamycin plus gentamicin prophylaxis in a randomized, unblinded study.[236] Other studies involving prophylaxis for a total duration of one day or less also demonstrated wound infection rates of 10% or less.[235,237,239,240,251,253,254] Single-dose prophylaxis has not been studied.

Pediatric Efficacy for Clean-Contaminated Procedures. No well-controlled studies have evaluated the efficacy of antimicrobial prophylaxis in pediatric patients undergoing clean-contaminated surgery of the head and neck.

Recommendation. *Clean procedures.* Infection rates in clean head and neck surgical procedures are generally less than 2%. Antimicrobial prophylaxis is not justified in patients undergoing clean surgical procedures of the head and neck. If there is prosthetic placement, cefazolin 1 g (as the sodium) intravenously at induction of anesthesia is appropriate. (Strength of evidence against prophylaxis = B.) (Strength of evidence for prophylaxis with prosthesis placement = C.)

Clean-contaminated procedures. The preferred regimens for patients undergoing clean-contaminated head and neck procedures are cefazolin 2 g (as the sodium) intravenously at induction of anesthesia and every 8 hours for 24 hours or clindamycin 600 mg (as the hydrochloride) intravenously at induction of anesthesia and every 8 hours for 24 hours. The necessity of giving gentamicin with clindamycin or metronidazole with cefazolin remains controversial; if these combinations are selected, the dosages are gentamicin 1.7 mg/kg (as the sulfate) intravenously and metronidazole 500 mg intravenously every eight hours. Agents should be administered at induction of anesthesia. Prophylaxis should not exceed 24 hours. Single-dose regimens may be preferable, particularly when cost and the possibility of resistance are considered; however, this approach remains controversial. (Strength of evidence for prophylaxis = A.)

Pediatric Dosage. *Clean procedures.* Antimicrobial prophylaxis is not recommended in pediatric patients undergoing clean head and neck procedures unless there is prosthetic placement. In these cases, cefazolin 20–30 mg/kg (as the sodium) administered intravenously at induction of anesthesia is appropriate.

Clean-contaminated procedures. The recommended regimen for pediatric patients undergoing clean-contaminated head and neck procedures is cefazolin 30–40 mg/kg (as the sodium) intravenously at induction of anesthesia and every 8 hours for 24 hours or clindamycin 15 mg/kg (as the hydrochloride) intravenously, at induction of anesthesia and every 8 hours for 24 hours. The addition of gentamicin 2.5 mg/kg (as the sulfate) intravenously to clindamycin remains controversial, as does the addition of metronidazole 10 mg/kg intravenously every eight hours to cefazolin. Agents should be administered at induction of anesthesia. Single-dose regimens may be preferable, particularly when cost and the possibility of resistance are considered; however, this approach remains controversial.

Neurosurgery

Background. Clean neurosurgical procedures are those during which there is no break in surgical technique and no entry into the respiratory or GI tract. Clean procedures usually carry a risk of postoperative wound infection of less than 5%. In many hospitals the risk is 1% to 2%.[257] It is therefore understandable that the use of injectable antimicrobials for such procedures is controversial. In addition, it is difficult to design clinical trials that could enable a distinction between infection rates of 2% and 5%. Clean-contaminated neurosurgical procedures (e.g., surgical approach through the nasopharynx or transphenoid sinus) are not addressed in these guidelines because there is a lack of data and there are no sufficiently similar procedures from which to extrapolate data.

Examples of clean neurosurgical procedures include elective craniotomy for the repair of aneurysms, correction of arteriovenous malformations, and removal of various types of brain tumors. There can be major differences (e.g., immune status, nutrition) between a person who undergoes elective surgery for a nonmalignant condition and a patient with cancer. These variables make clinical trial results difficult to interpret. Some craniotomies for ruptured aneurysms must be done on an emergency basis, and meticulous preparation of the skin cannot be ensured. Neurosurgical procedures after trauma occurring outside the hospital should never be included in comparative trials and would be considered contaminated surgery. Laminectomies (with or without the use of the operating microscope) are performed by orthopedic surgeons and neurosurgeons. Many studies include laminectomies and elective craniotomies in trials of clean neurosurgical procedures. The microscope introduces an additional source of potential contamination that should be considered. Laminectomies are addressed in this section and the orthopedic section.

Ventricular fluid-shunting procedures (ventriculo–peritoneal shunts), performed to control increased intracranial pressure in patients with hydrocephalus, have also been included in some clinical trials of clean neurosurgical procedures. Because this procedure involves the placement of a foreign body (pressure-release valve and tubing) in the cranium, another variable is introduced. Most infectious disease consultants believe that such shunting operations should be studied as a separate entity.[258] Ventricular fluid-shunting procedures are also performed after serious head trauma and in some elective craniotomy procedures to drain cerebrospinal fluid (CSF) and lower intracranial pressure. The drains are left in place for varying lengths of time, ranging from 48 hours to seven days.

Postoperative central nervous system (CNS) shunt infections are associated with serious morbidity and mortality. The rate of infection is generally reported as 5% to 20%.[259–261] Infections after surgery include meningitis, ventriculitis (most common infection), and, less frequently, wound infection.[258] In most cases, antimicrobial therapy without shunt removal is not effective in eradicating the infecting organism.[262–267] Therefore, shunt removal or replacement, in addition to intravenous antimicrobial therapy, is common practice.

Organisms. Data from most published clinical trials indicate that wound infections are primarily associated with gram-

positive bacteria. *S. aureus* and coagulase-negative staphylococci are responsible for more than 85% of such infections and are isolated in mixed cultures with other gram-positive bacteria in an additional 5% to 10% of cases. Gram-negative bacteria are isolated as the sole cause of postoperative neurosurgical wound infections in only 5% to 8% of cases.[268–273] Therefore, most clinical trials of antimicrobial prophylaxis use a drug with primary activity against staphylococci: clindamycin, erythromycin, penicillinase-stable penicillins (oxacillin, nafcillin, and methicillin), first-generation cephalosporins, and vancomycin.

Staphylococci account for 75% to 80% of CNS and wound infections after shunting procedures. Gram-negative bacteria are responsible for only 10% to 20% of such infections.[261,274–281]

Efficacy for Clean Neurosurgical Procedures. Although the efficacy of antimicrobials in lowering postoperative wound infection rates after elective craniotomy and laminectomy has not been demonstrated in a pivotal clinical trial, a single dose of an antimicrobial effective against *S. aureus* can be recommended. The strongest evidence supporting prophylaxis is a meta-analysis of eight prospective, randomized, placebo-controlled trials in craniotomy patients.[282] The following data also support prophylaxis.

Studies, mostly published before 1980, of prophylactic antimicrobials in clean neurosurgery cases were uncontrolled, nonrandomized, and retrospective.[268,269,283–287] These studies seemed to favor some type of prophylactic regimen. In 1980, an excellent review of most of these studies concluded that a final recommendation regarding antimicrobial prophylaxis in clean neurosurgical procedures must await the results of controlled clinical trials.[288] A randomized, nonblinded, clinical trial involving 402 cases (including craniotomy and spinal operations) demonstrated the superiority of antimicrobial prophylaxis (vancomycin and gentamicin with a streptomycin irrigation during the surgical procedure) in preventing infections compared with controls.[271]

Prospective studies involving large numbers of patients have also demonstrated lower neurosurgical postoperative infection rates when antimicrobial prophylaxis is used.[270,289–291] One such study in craniotomy, spinal surgery, and shunting procedures was stopped early because of an excessive number of wound infections in the placebo group.[273]

Choice. In a blinded study, 826 patients undergoing clean neurological procedures were randomly assigned to receive either a single dose of ceftizoxime 2 g (as the sodium) or a combination of a single dose of vancomycin 1 g (as the hydrochloride) and gentamicin 80 mg (as the sulfate).[292] Patients undergoing cranial, spinal, or transphenoidal neurosurgical procedures who were not undergoing placement of a shunt or another foreign body were included. The rate of primary and secondary wound infections was not different between the treatment groups. Ceftizoxime was better tolerated than the vancomycin–gentamicin combination. CSF and blood samples were obtained from 19 craniotomy patients. Ceftizoxime and gentamicin were detectable in all samples. Vancomycin was detectable in the serum in all cases but was undetectable in some CSF samples. The researchers concluded that ceftizoxime is as effective as the combination of gentamicin and vancomycin but is less toxic and has better CSF penetration.

A meta-analysis also did not demonstrate a significant difference between antimicrobial regimens.[282]

Duration. A meta-analysis did not demonstrate a significant difference between single-dose and multi-dose regimens for clean neurosurgical procedures.[282]

Pediatric Efficacy for Clean Neurosurgical Procedures. A randomized, placebo-controlled, double-blind trial that included pediatric patients undergoing clean neurosurgical procedures was stopped prematurely because of an excessive number of wound infections in the placebo group.[273] The overall rate of infection was 2.8% in the antimicrobial group and 11.7% in the placebo group.

Efficacy for CSF-Shunting Procedures. Because CNS infections after shunting procedures are responsible for substantial mortality and morbidity, especially in children, the possible role of prophylactic antimicrobials in such procedures has been the subject of numerous small, but well-conducted, randomized, controlled trials.[293–300] Meticulous surgical and aseptic technique and short operation time were determined to be important factors in lowering infection rates after shunt placement. Although the number of patients studied in each trial was small, two meta-analyses of the data demonstrated that the use of antimicrobial prophylaxis in CSF-shunting procedures reduces the risk of infection by approximately 50%.[301,302]

    Choice. Because no antimicrobial has been demonstrated to have greater efficacy over the others for CSF-shunting procedures, a single dose of cefazolin appears to be the best choice.

    Duration. In most studies, prophylaxis was continued for 24 to 48 hours postoperatively, but regimens of different durations were not compared for efficacy. There is a lack of data evaluating the continuation of extraventricular drains with and without antimicrobial prophylaxis.

Pediatric Efficacy for CSF-Shunting Procedures. A retrospective pediatric study of 1201 CSF-shunting procedures failed to demonstrate a significant difference in infection rates between patients who received antimicrobials (2.1%) and those who did not receive antimicrobials (5.6%). Two randomized, prospective studies that included pediatric patients did not demonstrate a significant difference in infection rates between the control group and the groups that received cefotiam[300] or methicillin.[297] A randomized, double-blind, placebo-controlled study that included pediatric patients undergoing ventriculoperitoneal shunt surgeries failed to demonstrate that the use of perioperative sulfamethoxazole–trimethoprim reduced the frequency of shunt infection.[293]

    Other studies have demonstrated efficacy for prophylactic antimicrobials.[295,303] A single-center, randomized, double blind, placebo-controlled trial of perioperative rifampin plus trimethoprim was performed in pediatric patients.[303] Among patients receiving rifampin plus trimethoprim, the infection rate was 12%, compared with 19% in patients receiving placebo. The study was ended (because of the high infection rates) before significance could be achieved. Infection rates at the study institution had been 7.5% in the years before the study. An open randomized study institution that included pediatric patients demonstrated a lower infection rate in a group receiving oxacillin (3.3%) than in a control group (20%).[295]

Recommendation. A single dose of cefazolin 1 g (as the sodium) intravenously at induction of anesthesia is recommended for patients undergoing clean neurosurgical procedures or CSF-shunting procedures. Alternatively, a single

intravenous dose of one of the β-lactamase-stable penicillins might be used (oxacillin 1 g [as the sodium] or nafcillin 1 g [as the sodium]). Vancomycin 1 g (as the hydrochloride) intravenously over one hour should be reserved as an alternative on the basis of previously outlined guidelines from HICPAC.[21] (Strength of evidence for prophylaxis for clean neurosurgical procedures = A.) (Strength of evidence for prophylaxis for CSF-shunting procedures = A.)

Pediatric Dosage. The recommended regimen for pediatric patients undergoing clean neurosurgical procedures or CSF-shunting procedures is a single dose of cefazolin 20–30 mg/kg (as the sodium) intravenously at induction of anesthesia. Vancomycin 15 mg/kg (as the hydrochloride) intravenously should be reserved as an alternative on the basis of previously outlined guidelines from HICPAC.[21,32]

Cesarean Delivery

Background. Approximately 1 million infants are born by cesarean delivery in the United States annually.[304] The rate of cesarean delivery has risen from 5% to 25% over the past two decades.[305] Postpartum infectious complications are common after cesarean delivery. Endometritis (infection of the uterine lining) is usually identified by uterine tenderness and sometimes abnormal or foul-smelling lochia. Wound infection is usually defined as the presence of pus at the incision site. Although febrile morbidity, or temperature elevation in an asymptomatic patient, is often considered in evaluations of antimicrobial prophylaxis, it appears that this temperature elevation is often not associated with an identifiable infectious source or with symptoms specific for infection. It may occur in women with normal physical examination results and sometimes disappears without treatment. In controlled trials, increased temperature occurred with equal frequency in placebo and treatment groups.[306,307] Moreover, women with febrile morbidity appear not to be those who later develop clinical infection. The presence or absence of febrile morbidity is not an appropriate indication of the efficacy of antimicrobial prophylaxis and therefore will not be considered in these guidelines.

    Endometritis has been reported to occur in up to 85% of patients in high-risk populations.[308] High-risk patients are defined as women who have not received prenatal care; who are poorly nourished; who have prolonged labor, especially in the presence of ruptured membranes; or who have undergone multiple vaginal examinations or frequent invasive monitoring. A majority of these women are of lower socioeconomic status. In contrast, women in upper or middle socioeconomic populations, who tend to be better nourished and to have received appropriate prenatal care, are at lower risk; the postpartum rate of endometritis in these patients ranges from 5% to 15%.

    The factor most frequently associated with infectious morbidity in postcesarean delivery is prolonged labor in the presence of ruptured membranes. Intact chorioamniotic membranes serve as a protective barrier against bacterial infection. Rupture of the membrane exposes the uterine surface to bacteria from the birth canal. The vaginal fluid with its bacterial flora is drawn up into the uterus when it relaxes between contractions during labor. Women undergoing labor for six to eight hours or longer in the presence of ruptured membranes should be considered at high risk for developing endometritis.[306] Other risk factors include systemic illness, poor hygiene, obesity, and anemia.

Organisms. The natural microflora of the vaginal tract are often involved in endometritis and include various aerobic and anaerobic streptococci, enterococci, staphylococci, enteric gram-negative bacilli, and anaerobic gram-negative bacteria such as *Bacteroides bivius, B. fragilis,* and *Fusobacterium* species.[306] In contrast, the organisms causing wound infections after delivery most often are *S. aureus* and other staphylococci, streptococci, and Enterobacteriaceae. Anaerobes are also present but less commonly than with endometritis.[309]

Efficacy. Most investigations of the efficacy of prophylactic antimicrobials in cesarean delivery have been conducted in high-risk patients. There has been considerable controversy about the necessity for prophylaxis in low-risk women undergoing cesarean delivery.

Despite multiple clinical trials assessing the efficacy of broad-spectrum antimicrobials or multiple doses of antimicrobials for prophylaxis in cesarean delivery, the data support the use of narrow-spectrum agents, such as first-generation cephalosporins, administered as a single dose intravenously immediately after clamping of the umbilical cord.[310,311]

Low-risk patients. Two early investigations showed significantly lower rates of postcesarean endometritis in low-risk patients with the use of prophylactic antimicrobials.[312,313] Some authorities have dismissed these benefits, arguing that limited morbidity, theoretical risks, and excessive costs do not justify prophylaxis in these patients.[314]

A randomized, prospective study compared the use of a 1-g dose of cefazolin (as the sodium) with no prophylaxis in 307 low-risk patients undergoing cesarean delivery.[315] The outcomes investigated were endometritis, wound infection, febrile morbidity, and use of antimicrobials for presumed or confirmed infection. The study showed significantly lower febrile morbidity and therapeutic antimicrobial use in the treatment group, although the sample was not large enough to enable a significant reduction in endometritis and wound infection to be detected.

A large-scale prospective study in more than 1800 low-risk women who underwent cesarean delivery was conducted from 1980 to 1982.[316] Although prophylaxis was uncontrolled for, endometritis and wound infection rates were significantly lower (0.7% and 0.2%, respectively in the group receiving prophylaxis than the group not receiving prophylaxis (2.1% and 2%, respectively). A case–control study, including the prospective data and women at high risk, determined that patients undergoing a first-time cesarean delivery were five times more likely to develop endometritis than those who had had a cesarean delivery in the past. On the basis of certain assumptions, the investigators calculated that more than $9 million could be saved annually by administering prophylaxis to low-risk patients. The cost of adverse effects was considered negligible. Thus, antimicrobial prophylaxis may be appropriate for low-risk cesarean deliveries.

However, ACOG considers the use of prophylaxis to be controversial in low-risk patients.[33] ACOG does not routinely recommend prophylaxis in low-risk patients because of concerns about adverse effects, development of resistant organisms, and relaxation of standard infection-control measures and proper operative technique.

High-risk patients. There have been more than 40 placebo-controlled, prospective trials evaluating the efficacy of prophylactic antimicrobials in cesarean delivery, most of which have been carried out in high-risk populations. A meta-analysis of these data, which combined high- and low-risk patients undergoing both emergency and elective cesarean deliveries, suggests that the rate of serious infections and endometritis is 75% lower and the rate of wound infections 65% lower among antimicrobial-treated patients than control patients.[317]

Choice. Although more than 20 different drugs have been used alone or in combination for antimicrobial prophylaxis during cesarean delivery, most obstetricians currently use either a penicillin or a cephalosporin.[318] ACOG recommends a first-generation cephalosporin, with extended-spectrum agents reserved for treatment rather than prophylaxis.[33]

In a large-scale study involving more than 1600 high-risk patients, several single-dose regimens, including cefazolin 2 g (as the sodium) or piperacillin 4 g (as the sodium), were comparably effective.[319] This provides two disparate choices, with drugs that offer differing spectra of activity with roughly equivalent efficacy. Two large-scale, randomized, double-blind trials offer a potential solution to this dilemma.[320,321] Both studies involved hundreds of high-risk patients and compared cefazolin, which has poor *Bacteroides* coverage, with cefoxitin or moxalactam, which has excellent *Bacteroides* coverage. In both studies, cefoxitin and moxalactam were slightly less effective than cefazolin in preventing endometritis, although the differences did not reach significance.

In another study of nearly 350 high-risk women undergoing cesarean delivery, a two-dose regimen of cefoxitin or piperacillin was given starting immediately after the cord was clamped.[322] Despite its superior in vitro activity against enterococci, *P. aeruginosa*, and several enteric gram-negative bacillary species, piperacillin was found to be no more effective than cefoxitin.

Timing. Unlike other surgical procedures for which antimicrobials are ideally administered just before incision, administration of antimicrobials in cesarean delivery is usually delayed until after cord clamping. This is done principally to avoid suppression of the infant's normal bacterial flora. Although toxicity in the infant is of potential concern, a majority of drugs used for this procedure (primarily β-lactams) have a documented record of safety in the treatment of infections during pregnancy, and many are used in the treatment of neonatal sepsis. ACOG and the American Academy of Pediatrics recommend administration of prophylactic antimicrobials after cord clamping.[33,34]

The issue of timing was addressed in three controlled trials. A large, randomized trial in 642 women undergoing cesarean delivery[49] and a smaller randomized, placebo-controlled study[48] demonstrated no difference in infectious complications, regardless of whether the antimicrobials were given preoperatively or after the cord was clamped. In the larger study, infants who were not exposed to antimicrobial agents in utero required significantly fewer evaluations for neonatal sepsis. A third case–control study demonstrated that a second- or third-generation cephalosporin given before incision was superior to cefazolin given as three 1-g doses starting immediately after cord clamping.[323] Thus, antimicrobials provide effective prophylaxis, even when given after clamping of the umbilical cord.[49]

Duration. Most recent trials of antimicrobial prophylaxis for cesarean delivery have assessed the efficacy of a single dose versus multiple doses (usually up to 24 hours). Early studies used regimens that lasted as long as five or six days. Two prospective, randomized studies found that a five-day course of a cephalosporin was no more efficacious than a 24-hour course.[324,325] A third study, by contrast, found that a three-day course of ampicillin was significantly more effective than three doses of ampicillin.[326] The explanation for this difference is unclear. The efficacy of several types of β-lactam antimicrobials given in various regimens to nearly 1600 patients was assessed in an open, randomized, comparative study.[319] One group of patients was given three doses of cefazolin, and the two other groups received a single dose of cefazolin, either 1 or 2 g (as the sodium). One dose of cefazolin 2 g was superior to three doses of cefazolin 1 g. One dose of cefazolin 1 g was no different than three doses of cefazolin 1 g. It does not seem necessary to extend prophylaxis beyond a single dose. These data also suggest that cefazolin 2 g is more efficacious than cefazolin 1 g.

Pediatric Efficacy. No well-controlled studies have evaluated the effect of antimicrobial prophylaxis for low- or high-risk adolescents undergoing cesarean delivery.

Recommendation. The recommended regimen for all women (low and high risk) undergoing cesarean delivery is a single dose of cefazolin 2 g (as the sodium) intravenously immediately after clamping of the umbilical cord. (Strength of evidence for prophylaxis for low-risk women = B.) (Strength of evidence for prophylaxis for high-risk women = A.)

Pediatric Dosage. The recommended regimen for low- and high-risk adolescents undergoing cesarean delivery is a single dose of cefazolin 2 g (as the sodium) intravenously immediately after clamping of the umbilical cord.

Hysterectomy

Background. Hysterectomy is second only to cesarean delivery as the most frequently performed major gynecologic operation in the United States, with approximately 590,000 hysterectomies being performed annually. Although there appears to be a downward trend in the rate since the mid-1980s, it is not yet known whether a true decline has occurred because of recent changes in the National Hospital Discharge Survey sampling method.[327]

Uterine fibroid tumors account for 30% of all presurgical diagnoses leading to hysterectomy; other common diagnoses are dysfunctional uterine bleeding, genital prolapse, endometriosis, chronic pelvic pain, pelvic inflammatory disease, endometrial hyperplasia, and cancer.[327] The proportion of patients undergoing concurrent unilateral or bilateral oophorectomy increases with age; this procedure is performed in approximately two thirds of women over the age of 60 years who undergo hysterectomy.[309]

Hysterectomy may be performed by a transvaginal or transabdominal approach. During a vaginal hysterectomy, the uterus and, occasionally, one or two fallopian tubes, the ovaries, or a combination of ovaries and fallopian tubes are removed through the vagina. No abdominal incision is made. Because the procedure is performed in an organ that is normally colonized with bacteria, it is associated with a high risk of postoperative infection. Abdominal hysterectomy involves removal of the uterus and, in some cases, one or both fallopian tubes, the ovaries, or a combination of ovaries and fallopian tubes. Because bacterial contamination associated with this procedure is minimal, postoperative infection rates in women receiving no antimicrobial prophylaxis have often been lower than those in women undergoing vaginal hysterectomy.[328–333] Radical hysterectomy, which entails removal

of the uterus, fallopian tubes, and ovaries and extensive stripping of the pelvic lymph nodes, is performed in patients with extension of cervical cancer. Many factors increase the risk of postoperative infection. Nonetheless, because of the low rate of contamination associated with this procedure, the need for prophylaxis has not been established.

Infections after hysterectomy include operative site infections: vaginal cuff infection, pelvic cellulitis, and pelvic abscess. Wound infections are usually diagnosed by the presence of pus or a purulent discharge.[307]

Risk factors for infection after vaginal or abdominal hysterectomy include longer duration of surgery, young age, diabetes, obesity, peripheral vascular disease, collagen disease, anemia, poor nutritional status, and previous history of postsurgical infection.[309,328,334,335] The depth of subcutaneous tissue is also a significant risk factor for transabdominal hysterectomy.[336] Factors that increase the risk of postoperative infection in women undergoing radical hysterectomy for cervical cancer include extended length of surgery, blood loss and replacement, presence of malignancy, prior radiation therapy, obesity, and presence of indwelling drainage catheters.[337,338]

Organisms. The vagina is normally colonized with a wide variety of bacteria, including gram-positive and gram-negative aerobes and anaerobes. The normal flora of the vagina include staphylococci, streptococci, enterococci, lactobacilli, diphtheroids, *E. coli*, anaerobic streptococci, *Bacteroides* species, and *Fusobacterium* species.[307,339] Postoperative vaginal flora differ from preoperative flora; enterococci, gram-negative bacilli, and *Bacteroides* species increase postoperatively. Postoperative changes in flora may occur independently of prophylactic antimicrobial administration and are not by themselves predictive of postoperative infection.[307,340,341] Postoperative infections associated with vaginal hysterectomy are frequently polymicrobial; enterococci, aerobic gram-negative bacilli, and *Bacteroides* species are isolated most frequently. Postoperative wound infections after abdominal and radical hysterectomy are also polymicrobial; gram-positive cocci and enteric gram-negative bacilli predominate, and anaerobes are also frequently isolated.[341,342]

Efficacy for Vaginal Hysterectomy. The rate of postoperative infection (wound and pelvic sites) in women administered placebo or no prophylactic antimicrobials ranges from 14% to 57%.[328–333,335,340,343–354] A number of antimicrobial agents, including clindamycin,[355] metronidazole,[331,354,356,357] penicillins,[307,345,353,355,357–360] ampicillin,[345,361,362] tetracycline derivatives,[333,352,363] streptomycin,[345] and first-generation,[328–330,344,347,351,353,356,358,360,361,364–367] second-generation,[307,349,350,357–359,363] and third-generation[355,367] cephalosporins have been studied as perioperative prophylaxis for vaginal hysterectomy. Overall, the use of antimicrobials markedly reduces the frequency of postoperative infection after vaginal hysterectomy to a generally acceptable rate of less than 10%.

Choice. Cephalosporins are the most frequently used antimicrobials for prophylaxis in vaginal hysterectomy. Cefazolin is the drug of choice. Cefazolin has been associated with postoperative infection rates ranging from 0% to 12%.[346,347,351,368–370] Postoperative infection rates with various second- and third-generation cephalosporins have ranged between 0% and 16%.[349,350,355,357–359,363,371] Studies directly comparing different cephalosporins have shown no significant differences in rates of infection.[372–381] Studies directly comparing the first-generation cephalosporins with second-

or third-generation cephalosporins indicate that first-generation cephalosporins (primarily cefazolin) are equivalent to second- and third-generation agents.[367–370,382]

In light of the organisms encountered in the vaginal canal and comparative studies conducted among different classes of cephalosporins, the expert panel considers cefazolin and cefotetan appropriate first-line choices for prophylaxis during vaginal hysterectomy and cefoxitin a suitable alternative. The ACOG guidelines support the use of a first-, second-, or third-generation cephalosporin for prophylaxis.[383]

Duration. The trend in recent years has been toward use of single-dose regimens of antimicrobials, administered immediately before surgery. Studies comparing single doses of one antimicrobial with multidose regimens of a different antimicrobial have shown the two regimens to be equally effective.[346,356,363,368–371,373–379,384–392] Although there have been few comparative trials involving single-dose cefazolin,[346,370] clinical experience indicates that this regimen is effective for most women. In addition, the drug's relatively long serum half-life (1.8 hours) suggests that a single dose would be sufficient. The exception is when the procedure lasts three hours or longer or if blood loss exceeds 1500 mL, in which case a second dose is warranted.

Efficacy for Abdominal Hysterectomy. At least 25 placebo-controlled or nonantimicrobial-controlled studies involving abdominal hysterectomy have been performed.[328–333,342,347,348,351–354,360,393–403] First- and second-generation cephalosporins and metronidazole have been studied more widely than any other agents. A meta-analysis of 25 controlled, randomized trials demonstrated the efficacy of antimicrobial prophylaxis with any of these agents in the prevention of postoperative infections.[404] The infection rate was 21.1% with placebo or no prophylaxis and 9.0% with any antimicrobial. Cefazolin was significantly more effective than placebo or no prophylaxis, with an infection rate of 11.4%.

Choice. Studies comparing second-generation cephalosporins and comparing second- and third-generation cephalosporin regimens have not shown significant differences in rates of serious infections.[376,387–392,405–407] Few comparisons have been made between second-generation cephalosporins and cefazolin. Cefazolin has been at least as effective in preventing infectious complications as third-generation cephalosporins.[369,384,399,408] However, in one double-blind, controlled study, the risk of major operative site infection requiring antimicrobial therapy was significantly higher with cefazolin (11.6%; relative risk, 1.84; 95% confidence interval, 1.03–3.29) than with cefotetan (6.3%).[334] A total of 511 women undergoing abdominal hysterectomy participated in this study and received a single dose of cefazolin 1 g (as the sodium) or cefotetan 1 g (as the disodium).

In light of the organisms involved in infectious complications from abdominal hysterectomy and the lack of superior efficacy demonstrated in comparative trials, the expert panel considers cefazolin or cefotetan an appropriate choice for prophylaxis and cefoxitin a suitable alternative. The ACOG guidelines state that first-, second-, and third-generation cephalosporins can be used for prophylaxis.[383]

Duration. A 24-hour antimicrobial regimen has been shown to be as effective as longer courses of prophylaxis for abdominal hysterectomy,[400,409] and many single-dose prophylaxis regimens have proved as effective as multidose regimens.[369,371,376,385,387–392,410] Single doses of cefotetan, ceftizoxime, or cefotaxime appear to be as effective as multiple doses of cefoxitin.[380,387,388,390–392,406]

Efficacy for Radical Hysterectomy. Six small prospective, placebo-controlled trials evaluated the impact of antimicrobial prophylaxis on wound infection rates after radical hysterectomy.[337,411–414] Rates of infection in the placebo groups ranged from 17% to 87%. In all six trials, the frequency of postoperative infection was lower with antimicrobial prophylaxis. Infection rates in antimicrobial-treated patients ranged from 0% to 64% (but generally from 0% to 15%). The antimicrobial agents used were cefoxitin, cefamandole, mezlocillin, and doxycycline. In one study in which cefamandole was given by injection and by intraperitoneal irrigation, postoperative infection rates were less than 4%.[411]

Choice. There is a lack of data comparing first- and second-generation cephalosporins. The optimal choice for prophylaxis has not been determined, but second-generation cephalosporins have demonstrated efficacy.[337,411,413] Because similar approaches are used in abdominal and radical hysterectomy and in light of the results of a recent study (described in Efficacy for abdominal hysterectomy),[334] a single dose of cefotetan may be applicable to radical hysterectomy procedures.

Appropriate cephalosporins identified by the expert panel members are cefazolin and cefotetan; an alternative is cefoxitin. The ACOG guidelines state that first-, second-, and third-generation cephalosporins can be used for prophylaxis.[383]

Duration. The optimal duration of antimicrobial prophylaxis for radical hysterectomy has not been established. The duration of prophylaxis ranged from one dose[414] to four days.[337,413] A 24-hour regimen of mezlocillin appears to be as effective as other antimicrobial regimens of longer duration.[412] A prospective, randomized study demonstrated no difference between a single dose of piperacillin plus tinidazole and a multidose (three-dose) regimen of the two drugs.[415]

Pediatric Efficacy. No well-controlled studies have evaluated the efficacy of antimicrobial prophylaxis in adolescents undergoing vaginal, abdominal, or radical hysterectomy.

Recommendation. The recommended regimen for women undergoing vaginal hysterectomy, abdominal hysterectomy, or radical hysterectomy is a single intravenous dose of cefazolin 1 g (as the sodium) or cefotetan 1 g (as the disodium) at induction of anesthesia. An alternative is cefoxitin 1 g (as the sodium) intravenously at induction of anesthesia. (Strength of evidence for prophylaxis for vaginal hysterectomy = A.) (Strength of evidence for prophylaxis for abdominal hysterectomy = A.) (Strength of evidence for prophylaxis for radical hysterectomy = A.)

Pediatric Dosage. The recommended regimen for adolescent women undergoing vaginal hysterectomy, abdominal hysterectomy, or radical hysterectomy is a single dose of cefazolin 1 g (as the sodium) or cefotetan 1 g (as the disodium) intravenously at induction of anesthesia. An alternative is cefoxitin 1 g (as the sodium) intravenously at induction of anesthesia.

Ophthalmic Surgeries

Background. Ophthalmic procedures include cataract extractions, vitrectomies, keratoplasties, implants, glaucoma operations, strabotomies, and retinal detachment repair. Most of the available studies involve cataract procedures.[416–427]

There is a low rate of postoperative ophthalmic infection (bacterial endophthalmitis),[417,418,424,428] but this is a devastating complication that may lead to an early loss of light sense and eventual loss of the eye if the infection is not eradicated.[420,424,425] Possible risk factors for developing postoperative ophthalmic infections include poor surgical technique, "weak ocular tissue" (not defined by the author), and multiple ophthalmic operations.[420] The duration of follow-up in studies that determined the postoperative endophthalmitis rate ranged from less than one week to 12 days[416,421,424,429]; 97% of cases of postoperative endophthalmitis occurred within the first 7 days of the 12-day follow-up period.[416] However, the appropriate duration of follow-up is not established.

Organisms. Approximately 90% of postoperative ophthalmic infections are caused by *S. aureus* or *S. epidermidis.*[420,425,430] The other organisms identified are *Streptococcus pneumoniae*, *Acinetobacter* species, and *P. aeruginosa.*[430] Virulent pathogens such as *P. aeruginosa*, *Bacillus cereus*, and *S. aureus* can cause eye destruction within 24 hours.[431]

Efficacy. Numerous studies have evaluated the effectiveness of prophylactic regimens in eradicating bacteria and reducing bacterial count on the conjunctivas, lower eyelid, eyelashes, and inner canthus (corner of the eye) preoperatively and postoperatively. There is a lack of controlled trials in the literature. The following studies had many flaws, including retrospective or uncontrolled design, inadequate follow-up, lack of confirmation of infection with cultures, difficulties in distinguishing between bacterial endophthalmitis and aseptic postoperative inflammation, inadequate aseptic surgical techniques, and inadequate preoperative and postoperative care.

Studies have shown that topical antimicrobials reduce ocular flora.[419,421,422,425,427] The studies evaluating bacteria eradication do not provide definitive antimicrobial choices, dosages, or duration of treatment because elimination of ophthalmic flora does not equate with a lower rate of infections. Although up to 95% of eye cultures are positive, few develop into infections.[420–422,425] Ciprofloxacin, norfloxacin, and ofloxacin have demonstrated antibacterial activity against organisms (staphylococcal and gram-negative organisms, in particular *Pseudomonas* species) that cause postoperative endophthalmitis,[432–435] but they cannot be recommended because of a lack of trials using fluoroquinolones prophylactically.

Choice. There have been no controlled efficacy studies supporting a particular choice of antimicrobial prophylaxis for ophthalmic surgeries. Because of the very low rate of infections (0.05% to 0.82%),[416–418,424,428,436] an enormous patient population would be required to allow determination of the most effective antimicrobial. The most efficacious antimicrobial cannot be determined from the available data because of study flaws.

A series of 16,000 cataract-extraction procedures demonstrated an infection rate of 0.6% (6 infections per 1,000 cases) with the use of an ointment containing neomycin 0.5% (as the sulfate), polymyxin B 0.1% (as the sulfate), and erythromycin 0.5% compared with 0.02% (3 infections per 15,000 cases) with the use of an ointment containing chloramphenicol 0.4%, polymyxin B 0.1% (as the sulfate), and erythromycin 0.5%.[417] Although these infection rates appear to favor chloramphenicol over neomycin, the superiority of chloramphenicol cannot be concluded because of limitations in the study design.

An open-label, nonrandomized, parallel trial demonstrated a lower rate of culture-proven endophthalmitis (0.06%) in a suite of operating rooms that used povidone-iodine preparation than in a similar suite that used topical silver protein solution (0.24%).[436] The intraocular procedures included vitrectomy, extracapsular cataract extraction, phacoemulsifications, secondary intraocular lens procedure, trabeculectomy, and penetrating keratoplasty. Recommendations cannot be made for the use of povidone-iodine as a single agent because of limitations of the study design (open-label, nonrandomized, without placebo control) and the surgeon's continued use of "customary" prophylactic antimicrobials (not identified) before, during, and after the procedure.

Prophylactic antimicrobials were administered during alternating cases in a series of 974 patients undergoing cataract extraction, glaucoma operations, corneal transplant, and pupillary membrane needling.[424] The prophylactic antimicrobial regimen was a subconjunctival combination of penicillin G 100,000 units and 3.3% streptomycin. There were seven postoperative infections (1.4%) among patients who had not received antimicrobials, compared with one infection (0.2%) among patients who received subconjunctival antimicrobials. In a follow-up series in which antimicrobials were used routinely in 1480 consecutive cases, the rate of infection was 0.14%. Organisms causing the postoperative infections in patients who received prophylactic antimicrobials were penicillin- and streptomycin-resistant *Proteus vulgaris* and *P. aeruginosa* and penicillin-sensitive *S. aureus* in a penicillin-allergic patient who received subconjunctival streptomycin only.

Route. The most often studied routes of administration are preoperative topical application and perioperative subconjunctival injection. Human data directly comparing administration routes have not been reported. Animal data demonstrated that topical application was highly effective in eliminating *Staphylococcus* and *Pseudomonas* species from the cornea but that antimicrobials administered periocularly or by intravenous injection did not significantly reduce the number of *Staphylococcus* or *Pseudomonas* organisms in the cornea.[437] Local reactions during the early postoperative period have been reported more frequently in eyes receiving subconjunctival antimicrobials than those in which no antimicrobials were used. These reactions, consisting of conjunctival hyperemia and chemosis (chemical action transmitted through a membrane) at the site of injection, usually subsided within two to four days. No systemic or serious local effects from the injections were reported.[424] Subconjunctival injections have been administered perioperatively or postoperatively because of the practicality of administering ophthalmic injections in a sedated and anesthetized patient. The ideal circumstance would be subconjunctival administration preoperatively once anesthesia is induced.

A concurrent series of 6618 patients undergoing cataract extraction were randomly assigned to receive periocular penicillin G 500,000 units or no periocular injection.[429] All patients were administered topical antimicrobials: chloramphenicol 0.5% and sulfamethazine 10% 15 to 20 hours before surgery, an unidentified ophthalmic antimicrobial ointment the day before surgery, polymyxin B 5000 units/mL (as the sulfate) and neomycin 2.5 mg/mL (as the sulfate) at the end of the procedure, an unidentified ophthalmic antimicrobial ointment the first day postoperatively, and sulfamethazine 5% solution for approximately another six days postoperatively starting the second postoperative day. The infection rate was 0.15% with the combination of topical antimicrobials and periocular penicillin, compared with 0.45% with only topical antimicrobials. Other routes, including intraocular antimicrobials and antimicrobial-soaked collagen shields,[438] are not widely accepted at this time because of the lack of safety and efficacy data. Topical only is the most common route of administration because of ease of administration, lack of complications, high efficacy in eliminating bacterial flora, and low cost.

Duration and timing. The available data do not specifically address duration and timing of antimicrobial administration. In studies to determine infection rates, the duration of preoperative antimicrobials ranged from one to five days. Postoperative topical antimicrobial regimens ranged from no postoperative antimicrobials to administration of antimicrobials until the time of patient discharge (approximately seven days).[416,424,429] The following data may provide some guidance. A series of 2508 cataract extraction procedures demonstrated that penicillin ophthalmic ointment had to be applied every two to three hours for three to eight days to eliminate pathogenic staphylococci from the conjunctiva and the eyelids.[425] Two consecutive patient groups undergoing open lacrimal surgery were retrospectively reviewed.[439] Both groups received topical antimicrobial drops (not further defined). The infection rate was 1.6% (2 of 128 patients) in the group that received postoperative antimicrobials and 7.9% (12 of 152 patients) in the group that did not receive postoperative antimicrobials. The study was not designed to determine the best postoperative antimicrobial, but, in a majority of cases, cephalexin 250 mg orally four times daily for five days was used. Although this study demonstrated a fivefold lower rate of infection with postoperative antimicrobials, recommendations for postoperative antimicrobial prophylaxis cannot be made until controlled studies are performed. Duration and timing cannot be extrapolated from general surgery (nonophthalmic) data because of the lack of data on antimicrobial pharmacokinetics in the eye (e.g., duration, distribution, and elimination from the aqueous humor). Recommendations on timing and duration are based solely on expert opinion.

Despite the lack of well-controlled trials, the consequences of bacterial endophthalmitis support the use of prophylactic antimicrobials. No definitive studies have delineated superiority of antimicrobial route, timing, or duration. The suggested antimicrobials are relatively similar in cost.

Pediatric Efficacy. No well-controlled studies have evaluated the efficacy of antimicrobial prophylaxis in pediatric patients undergoing ophthalmic surgery.

Recommendation. The prophylactic antimicrobials used in ophthalmic procedures should provide coverage against *Staphylococcus* species and gram-negative organisms, in particular *Pseudomonas* species. The necessity of continuing topical antimicrobials postoperatively has not been established. The frequency of administration is based on usual treatment regimens.

Antimicrobials that are appropriate include commercially available neomycin–polymyxin B–gramicidin solution one or two drops topically and tobramycin 0.3% or gentamicin 0.3% solution two drops topically before the procedure. Continuation of antimicrobials postoperatively is not supported by data. Addition of a subconjunctival antimicrobial, tobramycin 20 mg (as the sulfate), is optional. (Strength of evidence for prophylaxis = C.)

Pediatric Dosage. The recommendations for the use of topical antimicrobials in pediatric patients undergoing ophthalmic procedures are the same as for adults. Subconjunctival tobramycin cannot be recommended because there is a lack of pediatric data and dosages cannot be extrapolated from the insufficient adult data.

Orthopedics

Background. Antimicrobial prophylaxis will be discussed for total joint-replacement surgery, repair of hip fractures, implantation of internal fixation devices (screws, nails, plates, and pins), and clean orthopedic procedures (not involving replacement or implantations). Open (compound) fractures are often associated with extensive wound contamination and are virtually always managed with empirical antimicrobial therapy and surgical debridement. This practice is viewed as treatment rather than prophylaxis.[440] Although antimicrobials are given to patients with prosthetic joints who undergo dental procedures to reduce the likelihood of prosthesis infection,[441] this practice has not been sufficiently studied and is beyond the scope of these guidelines.

Postoperative wound infection is one of the more frequent complications of orthopedic surgery, and it often has devastating results,[442] frequently requiring removal of the implanted hardware and a prolonged course of antimicrobials for cure. Although early studies did not support the routine use of prophylactic antimicrobials,[443,444] these studies were flawed by an improper choice of agent(s), inappropriate dosage or route of administration, or failure to institute therapy until well beyond the time of the initial surgical incision. Later work has established that antimicrobial prophylaxis is indicated in some types of orthopedic procedures.[442,445–452]

Organisms. Organisms that make up the skin flora are the most frequent causes of postoperative infections in orthopedic surgery. The pathogens involved in total joint replacement are *S. epidermidis* (40% of infected patients), *S. aureus* (35%), gram-negative bacilli (15%), anaerobes (5%), and others (5%).[24]

Clean Orthopedic Procedures Not Involving Implantation of Foreign Materials

Background. The need for antimicrobial prophylaxis in clean orthopedic procedures is not well established.[452,453] Included in this category are knee, hand, and foot surgeries and laminectomy with and without fusion. These procedures do not normally involve the implantation of foreign materials. The evaluated data do not include arthroscopy procedures and do not identify specific procedures, like carpal tunnel release; however, arthroscopy and other procedures not involving implantation are similar enough to be included with clean orthopedic procedures not involving implantation. The risks of wound infection and long-term sequelae are quite low for procedures not involving implantation. The duration of procedures may be a risk factor, with longer procedures having higher infection rates; the difference was significant in one study[453] but not in another.[452] Neither study formally evaluated procedures performed on the feet of patients with diabetes. Diabetic patients are at a higher risk for infection, and their infections are typically polymicrobial; therefore, recommendations for procedures performed on the feet of patients with diabetes cannot be extrapolated from the following efficacy data.

Efficacy. The most extensive investigation of the efficacy of antimicrobial prophylaxis in clean orthopedic procedures was performed in the early 1970s.[452] In a randomized, double-blind, prospective study, the efficacy of cephaloridine was compared with that of placebo in reducing postoperative wound infection in more than 1500 patients undergoing clean orthopedic procedures (internal fixation device involvement was not identified). Infection rates for the two groups differed significantly: 5% with placebo and 2.8% with perioperative cephaloridine. Drug fever (loosely defined as fever occurring on the day the study drug was administered) was noted in 34 antimicrobial-treated patients and 14 placebo recipients.

Given the small difference in infection rates between groups and the lack of serious long-term sequelae from postoperative infections associated with these procedures, many authorities have questioned the need for antimicrobial prophylaxis. Attempts to correlate infection rate with the type of clean orthopedic procedure or with certain patient characteristics (e.g., age, disease) have been unsuccessful. Although one study demonstrated that prophylaxis with cefamandole was more effective than placebo when procedures were longer than two hours, prophylaxis was not more effective than placebo in procedures shorter than two hours.[453] These results were not consistent with those of the previously discussed study,[452] whose series was much larger and failed to demonstrate a difference in infection rates with procedures lasting longer than two hours.

The low rate of infection, coupled with the absence of serious morbidity as a consequence of postoperative infection, does not justify the expense or potential for toxicity and resistance associated with routine use of antimicrobial prophylaxis in this setting.

Pediatric Efficacy. No well-controlled studies have evaluated the efficacy of antimicrobial prophylaxis in pediatric patients undergoing clean orthopedic procedures.

Recommendation. Antimicrobial prophylaxis is not recommended for patients undergoing clean orthopedic procedures not involving implantation of foreign materials. (Strength of evidence against prophylaxis = C.)

Pediatric Dosage. Antimicrobial prophylaxis is not recommended for pediatric patients undergoing clean orthopedic procedures not involving implantation of foreign materials.

Hip Fracture Repair and Other Orthopedic Procedures Involving the Implantation of Internal Fixation Devices

Background. Data support the use of antimicrobial prophylaxis for hip fracture repairs. In contrast, there is a lack of data to support the use of prophylaxis for procedures other than hip fracture repairs that involve the implantation of internal fixation devices (e.g., high tibial osteotomy and ligament reconstruction). When internal fixation procedures involve the implantation of foreign bodies such as nails, screws, plates, and wires, postoperative infection can produce extensive morbidity—prolonged and repeated hospitalization, sepsis, persistent pain, and device replacement[442,454]—and possible death. No cost analysis is available to support the

use of prophylaxis for any orthopedic procedure; however, the assumed costs for the associated morbidity may be adequate to justify prophylaxis. Consequently, antimicrobial prophylaxis is frequently used, even though the infection rate is low. For example, the frequency of infection after hip fracture repair with or without prophylaxis is generally less than 5%.[442,450]

Efficacy. *Hip fracture repair.* The efficacy of antimicrobial prophylaxis in hip fracture repair was studied in three double-blind, randomized, placebo-controlled trials.[442,450,455] One study demonstrated a significant difference in postoperative wound infections after hip fracture repair in patients receiving placebo (4.8%, or 7 of 145 patients) and patients given nafcillin 0.5 g (as the sodium) intramuscularly every six hours for two days (0.8%, or 1 of 135 patients).[442] Some prostheses were used, but a majority of patients had pin or plate implantation. The duration of follow-up was one year. There was no difference in the frequency of infected wound hematomas between the two groups.

In another study involving 307 patients with hip fractures, a significant difference was demonstrated for major postoperative wound infection rates: 4.7% in the placebo group compared with 0.7% in patients given preoperative cephalothin 1 g (as the sodium) intravenously and every 4 hours thereafter for 72 hours.[450] The duration of follow-up was not identified. Patients who received cephalothin for prophylaxis tended to be colonized with cephalothin-resistant organisms (in urine, sputum, and blood).

Despite having a small sample size (127 patients) and an unusually high rate of wound infection in the control group, one study showed prophylaxis to be beneficial in preventing postoperative wound infection compared with no prophylaxis.[451] In contrast to the previously described studies, a randomized, double-blind, single-hospital study involving 352 patients undergoing hip fracture fixation failed to show a significant difference between four doses of cefazolin, one dose of cefazolin, and placebo.[455] These regimens did not differ in efficacy even when both treatment groups were combined and compared with the placebo group. Although hip fracture repairs are associated with low infection rates, results from these three studies[442,450,451] and the morbidity and costs associated with infectious complications in hip fracture repair support the use of short-term prophylactic antimicrobials. The long-term benefits of prophylaxis have not been determined.

Procedures other than hip surgery involving implantation of internal fixation devices. The evidence supporting antimicrobial prophylaxis for the implantation of internal fixation devices is not as strong for nonhip surgeries as for hip replacement or repair. In a randomized, double-blind study of 122 patients undergoing open reduction and internal fixation of closed ankle fractures, no difference was demonstrated between cephalothin 1 g (as the sodium) intravenously every six hours for a total of four doses and placebo.[456] However, the sample was too small. Despite the lack of studies evaluating prophylaxis for procedures involving the implantation of internal fixation devices, consideration of antimicrobial use is warranted, especially in complicated procedures, because of the associated morbidity and assumed costs of infections involving implanted devices.

Choice. Studies comparing antimicrobials are lacking. The antimicrobials that have been studied most often for prophylaxis in orthopedic surgery are first-generation cephalosporins. First-generation cephalosporins (particularly cefazolin) are the most suitable agents for orthopedic prophylaxis because their spectrum of activity includes *Staphylococcus* species and gram-negative bacilli (such as *E. coli*), they have desirable pharmacokinetic characteristics (adequate bone penetration),[457] and they are easy to administer, low in cost, and safe. Second- and third-generation cephalosporins offer no major advantages over first-generation agents. Second- and third-generation cephalosporins are more expensive; furthermore, indiscriminate use is likely to promote resistance, particularly among nosocomial gram-negative bacilli. Therefore, the use of a second- or third-generation cephalosporin as orthopedic surgical prophylaxis should be avoided. The increasing prevalence of MRSA warrants discriminate use of alternative antimicrobials. No studies have evaluated vancomycin as a prophylactic agent in orthopedic procedures. However, vancomycin has adequate activity against the most common pathogens involved and would be an acceptable alternative under certain circumstances.[21] Only patients with a serious β-lactam allergy or patients in institutions with a high rate of infection due to MRSA or MRSE should be administered vancomycin.

Duration. One study evaluated the duration of therapy in patients undergoing orthopedic surgery. A double-blind, randomized study compared one day of cefuroxime alone with one day of cefuroxime followed by oral cephalexin for a total of six days in 121 evaluable patients undergoing implantation surgery for intertrochanteric hip fracture repair.[458] This study, combined with the total joint-replacement studies, supports a duration of 24 hours or less.

Pediatric Efficacy. No well-controlled studies have evaluated the efficacy of antimicrobial prophylaxis in pediatric patients undergoing hip fracture repair or implantation of internal fixation devices.

Recommendation. Despite the lack of substantial data, the use of antimicrobial prophylaxis in hip fracture repair and in other orthopedic procedures involving the implantation of internal fixation devices may be substantiated by the morbidity (possible removal of an infected internal fixation device) and costs associated with infectious events. The recommended regimen is cefazolin 1 g (as the sodium) intravenously at induction of anesthesia and continued every 8 hours for 24 hours. Vancomycin 1 g (as the hydrochloride) intravenously over one hour should be reserved as an alternative agent on the basis of previously outlined guidelines from HICPAC.[21] (Strength of evidence for prophylaxis for hip fracture repair = A.) (Strength of evidence for prophylaxis for implantation procedures = C.)

Pediatric Dosage. Despite the lack of substantial data, the use of antimicrobial prophylaxis in hip fracture repair and in other orthopedic procedures involving the implantation of internal fixation devices may be substantiated by the morbidity (possible removal of an infected internal fixation device) and costs associated with infectious events. The recommended regimen for pediatric patients is cefazolin 20–30 mg/kg (as the sodium) intravenously at the induction of anesthesia and every 8 hours for 24 hours. Vancomycin 15 mg/kg (as the hydrochloride) intravenously should be reserved as an alternative on the basis of previously outlined guidelines from HICPAC.[21,32]

Total Joint Replacement

Background. It is estimated that more than 200,000 hip or knee replacements are performed each year in North America.[459] The frequency of infections complicating hip, knee, elbow, or shoulder replacement is low, ranging from 0.6% to 11%.[454] With the introduction of antimicrobial prophylaxis and the use of "ultraclean" operating rooms, the infection rate has declined substantially, generally to less than 1%.[447,448,454] The two main types of infectious complications of total joint arthroplasty are superficial and deep infections of the prosthesis. Infections of the joint prosthesis may occur early (less than one year after the procedure) or late (occurring after the first year). Infection after joint arthroplasty can be disastrous, frequently requiring removal of the prosthesis and a prolonged course of antimicrobials for cure. An analysis of the costs associated with operations in Europe demonstrated that 90% of the total expense was associated with keeping the patient in a hospital bed.[460] The stay for joint revision was much longer than the stay for primary joint replacement.

A 1992 survey documented low use of antimicrobial-impregnated bone cement and cement beads in the United States (for fewer than one procedure per month); a majority of the antimicrobial-impregnated cement was used in community hospitals.[461] Total hip arthroplasty, total knee arthroplasty, and chronic osteomyelitis were the most common indications for use. A wide variety of antimicrobials are used in these products, a majority of which have not been adequately studied in the clinical setting. Inadequate quality control during mixing and use has been identified. Prophylaxis with antimicrobial-impregnated bone cement and cement beads is not recommended. Readers are referred to a review of this topic for additional information about tissue penetration, clinical application, and safety.[462]

Efficacy. A majority of studies that have evaluated prophylactic antimicrobials in joint-replacement surgery have been conducted in patients undergoing total hip arthroplasty. There is a lack of data involving elbow and shoulder arthroplasty; however, these procedures are similar enough to justify inclusion with total hip arthroplasty.

A double-blind, randomized, placebo-controlled trial involving 2137 hip replacements in 2097 patients evaluated the efficacy of prophylactic cefazolin.[447] Cefazolin 1 g (as the sodium) was given before surgery and continued every six hours for a total of five days. After a two-year follow-up period, a significant difference in the rate of "hip infection" was found between the placebo group and the cefazolin group (3.3% and 0.9%, respectively). When these results were further analyzed for the type of operating-room environment, a significant difference was observed only when surgery was carried out in a conventional operating room. Antimicrobial prophylaxis did not significantly reduce infection when hip replacement surgery was performed in a "hypersterile" (laminar airflow) operating room (1.3% with placebo versus 0.8% with cefazolin). This study was well designed in that sufficient numbers of patients were enrolled to reduce the probability of Type I and Type II errors in terms of the efficacy of prophylaxis.

Choice. (Readers are also referred to Procedures other than hip surgery involving implantation of internal fixation devices.) Cefazolin has been compared with cefuroxime[463] and cefonicid.[464] A double-blind multicenter study of 1354 patients undergoing total joint (hip or knee) arthroplasty compared intravenous cefuroxime 1.5 g (as the sodium) preoperatively followed by 750 mg every eight hours for a total of three doses with intravenous cefazolin 1 g (as the sodium) preoperatively followed by 1 g every eight hours for a total of nine doses.[463] The preoperative doses were administered 50 to 60 minutes before incision. Follow-up assessments were performed at two to three months and one year after the procedure. An intention-to-treat analysis demonstrated no significant difference in the wound infection rate between cefuroxime (3%) and cefazolin (3%). All three late wound infections (identified at one-year follow-up) developed in the cefazolin group. The second trial was a double-blind, randomized, controlled trial that compared three doses of cefazolin with three doses of cefonicid in 102 patients undergoing joint replacement or insertion of a metallic device for fixation.[464] The median duration of follow-up was 106 to 109 days. There were six postoperative infections among 52 patients in the cefazolin group and no infections among the 50 patients in the cefonicid group. This difference was significant. However, three of the six infections in the cefazolin group were urinary tract infections.

Antimicrobials incorporated in bone cement is a viable method for prophylaxis. However, there are limited clinical data on the use of this method. One prospective, randomized clinical trial performed in two centers involved 401 patients undergoing total joint arthroplasty. Intravenous cefuroxime was compared with cefuroxime in bone cement.[465] All patients were followed for two years. The overall rate of deep infection (infection extending to the deep fascia, with persistent wound discharge or joint pain, positive or negative cultures from deep tissues, and delay in wound healing) was 1%. No significant difference was demonstrated between the two groups. There were no late deep infections (deep infection present for at least three months and occurring up to two years after the operation). Another prospective, randomized, controlled study that compared gentamicin-impregnated bone cement with systemic antimicrobials (cloxacillin, dicloxacillin, cephalexin, or penicillin) had similar results.[466] Antimicrobial bone cement has not been shown to be superior to intravenous antimicrobials.

The impact of ultraclean operating rooms on deep infection after joint-replacement surgery was evaluated in more than 8000 hip or knee operations.[448] A significantly lower rate of deep infection was observed with the use of ultraclean operating rooms than with conventional rooms (0.6% versus 1.5%, respectively). Although not strictly controlled in this study, the use of prophylactic antimicrobials (primarily flucloxacillin) was associated with an even lower rate of deep infection of the prosthesis.

Taken together, studies reported in the medical literature suggest that a short course of antimicrobial prophylaxis can significantly reduce the rate of postoperative infection, particularly late, deep-seated infection, in joint-replacement surgery. Although infectious complications are infrequent, the consequences of an infected joint prosthesis can be devastating. The use of ultraclean operating rooms significantly reduces the rate of deep infection after joint-replacement surgery, regardless of whether antimicrobials are given.[447,448] Because such operating environments are not widely available, antimicrobial prophylaxis using agents with activity primarily against *S. aureus* is indicated in patients undergoing joint-replacement surgery.

Duration. Two studies demonstrate that prophylactic antimicrobials are essential in total joint replacement, but the studies are not particularly helpful in guiding duration of use.[446,447] Studies involving total hip replacement have used antimicrobials for 12 hours to 14 days postoperatively.[442,445–451,467] A duration of 24 hours was supported in a randomized

trial of 358 patients undergoing total hip arthroplasty, total knee arthroplasty, or hip fracture repair that compared one day with seven days of either nafcillin or cefazolin.[467] The difference in infection rates between groups was not significant. The timing and duration of prophylaxis for total joint replacement have not been established, although there is general agreement that the first dose should be given about 30 minutes before the initial incision and the second dose given intraoperatively if the procedure takes more than three hours. The duration of prophylaxis remains controversial,[24] although the available data do not support prophylaxis beyond 24 hours.

A discussion of whether prophylaxis should be continued until postoperative surgical drainage tubes are removed is outside the scope of these guidelines; however, drainage tubes carry the risk of infection and thus are a variable in postoperative infections. There is a lack of data evaluating the risk of infection with and without continued antimicrobial prophylaxis in patients with surgical drainage tubes still in place. Continuation of antimicrobials may be warranted until the tubes are removed; however, there are no available data to support continuing prophylaxis.

Pediatric Efficacy. No well-controlled studies have evaluated the efficacy of antimicrobial prophylaxis in pediatric patients undergoing total joint replacement.

Recommendation. The recommended regimen for patients undergoing total hip, elbow, knee, or shoulder replacement is cefazolin 1 g (as the sodium) intravenously at induction of anesthesia and every 8 hours for 24 hours. Although continuing prophylaxis until drainage tubes are removed may be warranted, there is currently no evidence to support this practice. Vancomycin 1 g (as the hydrochloride) intravenously over one hour should be reserved as an alternative agent on the basis of previously outlined guidelines from HICPAC.[21] (Strength of evidence for prophylaxis = A.)

Pediatric Dosage. The recommended regimen for pediatric patients undergoing total hip, elbow, knee, or shoulder replacement is cefazolin 20–30 mg/kg (as the sodium) intravenously at induction of anesthesia and every 8 hours for 24 hours. Vancomycin 15 mg/kg (as the hydrochloride) intravenously should be reserved as an alternative on the basis of previously outlined guidelines from HICPAC.[21,32]

Urologic Surgery

Background. The efficacy of antimicrobial prophylaxis in urologic surgery has been investigated in many clinical trials, particularly in patients undergoing prostatectomy through the urethra, more commonly known as transurethral resection of the prostate (TURP).[385,468–488] Many patients undergoing resection of bladder tumors have also been studied.[470,489] Non-TURP transurethral procedures, like urethral dilatation and stone extraction, involve the same organisms and risk factors as TURP. Therefore, any transurethral procedure is similar enough to be included with TURP. Prostatectomy can also be performed through the perineum (perineal) and into the bladder (suprapubic). However, perineal procedures may involve different organisms on the basis of the proximity to the anus. There is a lack of studies addressing perineal prostatectomy; therefore, the following recommendations do not include perineal prostatectomy. *S. aureus* may be the only organism causing infection after suprapubic procedures. However, there is a lack of studies, so the following recommendations do not include suprapubic procedures.

The most common infectious complication after urologic surgery is bacteriuria, the frequency of which has varied from 0% to 54% in reported studies. More serious infections, including bacteremia, are rare after TURP. Risk factors for infection after urologic surgery include age over 60 years, prolonged preoperative hospital stay, and wound contamination.[490] Bacteriuria before open prostatectomy has also been identified as a risk factor for postoperative wound infection in patients with or without an indwelling catheter.[491] Other factors that contribute to postoperative complications are the length of postoperative catheterization and the mode of irrigation (closed versus open). No significant correlation between infection rate and diagnosis of benign prostate hyperplasia or prostate carcinoma has been identified.[480] Therefore, neither of these diagnoses is considered a risk factor. The major objective of prophylaxis is the prevention of bacteremia and surgical wound infection and secondarily the prevention of postoperative bacteriuria.[24] The benefits of preventing postoperative bacteriuria are unknown; however, a majority of studies have regarded postoperative bacteriuria, regardless of the presence or absence of infectious signs and symptoms, as a postoperative complication. Therapeutic antimicrobials directed at the appropriate pathogens and for the appropriate duration should be used in patients with preoperative urinary tract infection.

Organisms. *E. coli* is the most common isolate in patients with postoperative bacteriuria; however, other gram-negative bacilli and enterococci also cause infection.

Efficacy. A wide range of antimicrobial regimens, including cephalosporins,[385,469,471,473,475,477,479,480,483,484,486–489] aminoglycosides,[468,474,481,482] carbenicillin,[470,472] piperacillin–tazobactam,[487] trimethoprim–sulfamethoxazole,[473,476,486] nitrofurantoin,[478] and fluoroquinolones,[485,488,492–494] have been evaluated.

Four studies did not demonstrate a difference in the frequency of postoperative bacteriuria when prophylactic antimicrobials were compared with controls.[469–472] The postoperative bacteriuria rate was 10% or less for the control groups and 6% or less for the prophylactic antimicrobial groups. In eight studies, the rate of postoperative bacteriuria was 25% in the control groups and 5% or less in the antimicrobial groups.[474–476,478–482] These studies included only patients with sterile urine preoperatively. Postoperative bacteriuria was defined as greater than 10^5 CFU/mL. In most of the studies, patients who received antimicrobial prophylaxis did not have fewer febrile episodes or shorter hospital stays than control patients.

Choice. No single antimicrobial regimen appears superior. Broad-spectrum antimicrobials, such as aminoglycosides or second- and third-generation cephalosporins, are no more effective than first-generation cephalosporins or oral agents (trimethoprim–sulfamethoxazole or nitrofurantoin). One prospective, randomized study demonstrated that norfloxacin is effective in preventing stricture formation after TURP.[485] This study is relevant in that bacterial infection is believed to be the partial cause of stricture formation. Other trials have demonstrated the efficacy of lomefloxacin, another fluoroquinolone, for antimicrobial prophylaxis in urologic surgical procedures. One open-label, randomized trial showed that oral lomefloxacin is effective in preventing postsurgical bacteriuria after visual laser ablation of the prostate.[494] Additional studies indicated that oral lomefloxacin is as effective as intravenous cefotaxime or cefuroxime in the prevention of infections after transurethral surgical procedures.[488,492,493] Other fluoroquinolones may provide the same benefit as lomefloxacin; however, there are no efficacy data at this time to support recommendation of these agents.

Duration. In a large number of the trials, prophylaxis was continued for up to three weeks postoperatively.[468,470,472, 474–476,478,480] The most recent studies suggest that continuation of prophylaxis after the preoperative dose is unnecessary.[385,479,481–486,495] However, one study suggests that giving one dose of cefotaxime one hour before catheter removal instead of at the induction of anesthesia may be beneficial.[496]

Pediatric Efficacy. Most urologic studies evaluated prophylaxis for TURP or resection of bladder tumors, and pediatric patients therefore would be unlikely to have been included.

Recommendation. Considering the low risk of serious infection after urologic surgery, antimicrobial prophylaxis should be considered only in patients at high risk of postoperative bacteriuria (patients likely to require prolonged postoperative catheterization and patients with a positive urine culture) or in hospitals with infection rates of greater than 20%. Low-risk patients do not appear to benefit from the use of perioperative antimicrobials. If oral antimicrobials are used, a single dose of trimethoprim 160 mg with sulfamethoxazole 800 mg or lomefloxacin 400 mg (as the hydrochloride) should be administered two hours before surgery. If an injectable agent is preferred, cefazolin 1 g (as the sodium) intravenously at induction of anesthesia is recommended. Continuation of antimicrobial prophylaxis postoperatively is not recommended. (Strength of evidence for prophylaxis = A.)

Pediatric Dosage. Prophylaxis for urologic surgery in pediatric patients should be considered only in patients at high risk of postoperative bacteriuria (e.g., patients likely to require prolonged postoperative catheterization and patients with a positive urine culture) or in hospitals with infection rates of greater than 20%. If oral antimicrobials are used, a single dose of trimethoprim 6–10 mg/kg with sulfamethoxazole 30–50 mg/kg two hours before surgery is recommended. If an injectable agent is preferred, a single dose of cefazolin 20–30 mg/kg (as the sodium) intravenously at induction of anesthesia is recommended. Fluoroquinolones are not recommended in pediatric patients.

Vascular Surgery

Background. Infection after vascular surgery often is associated with extensive morbidity and mortality. Postoperative infection is particularly devastating if it involves the vascular graft material. As a result, antimicrobial prophylaxis is widely used with surgical revascularization.[497] Patients undergoing brachiocephalic procedures do not appear to benefit from antimicrobial prophylaxis. Although there are no data, patients undergoing brachiocephalic procedures (e.g., carotid endarterectomy) involving vascular prosthesis or patch implantation may benefit from prophylaxis. Risk factors for postoperative surgical wound infection in patients undergoing vascular surgery include lower-extremity surgery, delayed surgery after hospitalization, diabetes mellitus, and a history of vascular surgery.[498] Another risk factor is short duration of antimicrobial prophylaxis, which was defined as a 1.5-g dose of intravenous cefamandole (as the nafate) at induction of anesthesia and 750 mg of cefamandole four and eight hours after the first dose.[498]

Organisms. The predominant organisms involved include *S. aureus, S. epidermidis,* and enteric gram-negative bacilli. At some institutions, MRSA could be an organism of concern.

Efficacy. Prophylactic antimicrobials decrease the rate of infection after procedures involving the lower abdominal vasculature and procedures required for dialysis access. The duration of follow-up for late wound complications was at least once after hospital discharge (not further defined) for most studies,[499–501] one month,[498,502,503] six months,[504] and up to three years.[505]

In the first randomized, prospective, double-blind placebo-controlled study in patients undergoing peripheral vascular surgery (*n* = 462), the infection rate was significantly lower with cefazolin than placebo (0.9% and 6.8%, respectively).[499] Four deep graft infections were observed in the placebo group; none occurred in the patients who received cefazolin. No infections were observed in patients who underwent brachiocephalic (*n* = 103), femoral artery (*n* = 56), or popliteal (*n* = 14) procedures. Cefazolin-susceptible *S. aureus* was the predominant pathogen; however, gram-negative aerobic bacilli, coagulase-negative staphylococci, and enterococci were also isolated.

In a subsequent controlled trial, intravenous cephradine, topical cephradine, or both were evaluated in patients undergoing peripheral vascular surgery.[505] The infection rate was significantly different between the cephradine groups (less than 6%) and the control group (25%). There were no significant differences in the infection rate among the groups that received cephradine, regardless of route. Ten of 16 infected patients grew *S. aureus; E. coli* and other gram-negative bacilli were infrequently associated with infection.

Patients undergoing vascular-access surgery for hemodialysis also benefit from the administration of antistaphylococcal antimicrobials.[504] Two of 19 cefamandole-treated patients and 8 of 19 placebo recipients developed an infection after undergoing polytetra-fluoroethylene vascular-access grafts.

Choice. More recent studies have demonstrated that cefazolin remains the preferred cephalosporin for use in vascular surgery.[500,501] There was no significant difference in infection rates between cefazolin and cefuroxime in patients undergoing abdominal aortic and lower-extremity peripheral vascular surgery[500] or between cefazolin and cefamandole in patients undergoing aortic or infrainguinal arterial surgery.[501]

There are limited data regarding the choice of an antimicrobial for penicillin-allergic patients undergoing vascular procedures. Although vancomycin offers coverage against potential gram-positive pathogens, the addition of an aminoglycoside may be prudent when colonization and infection with gram-negative organisms are expected. Given the lack of data regarding vancomycin as a single agent, definitive conclusions are not possible.

Duration. A prospective, randomized, double-blind study compared infection rates of a one-day and a three-day course of cefuroxime with placebo in patients undergoing peripheral vascular surgery.[502] The infection rates were 16.7%, 3.8%, and 4.3% in the placebo, one-day, and three-day groups, respectively. The difference in the infection rates between the one-day and three-day groups was not significant. A prospective study that analyzed risk factors for surgical wound infection after vascular surgery found that patients randomly assigned to receive a short course of antimicrobial prophylaxis, defined as 1.5 g of cefamandole (as the nafate) at induction of anesthesia followed by 750 mg of cefamandole four and eight hours after the first dose, were more likely to develop surgical wound infection than patients randomly assigned to receive a longer course of antimicrobial prophylaxis, defined as 1.5 g of cefamandole (as the nafate) at induction of anesthesia and 750 mg every 6 hours for 48 hours after surgery.[498]

Route. The question of oral versus intravenous treatment was addressed in a multicenter, randomized, double-blind, prospective trial in 580 patients undergoing arterial surgery involving the groin.[503] Patients received two doses of ciprofloxacin 750 mg orally or three doses of cefuroxime 1.5 g intravenously on the day of surgery. The wound infection rate within 30 days of surgery was 9.2% (27 patients) in the ciprofloxacin group and 9.1% (26 patients) in the cefuroxime group. Although oral ciprofloxacin was shown to be as effective as intravenous cefuroxime in one study, this study did not address the well-founded concern about resistance developing with routine use of fluoroquinolones[506]; therefore, intravenous cefazolin remains the first-line agent for this indication. The study did, however, demonstrate the need for more studies regarding efficacy of oral agents for postoperative prophylaxis.

Pediatric Efficacy. No well-controlled studies have evaluated the efficacy of surgical prophylaxis in pediatric patients undergoing vascular surgery.

Recommendation. The recommendation for patients undergoing vascular surgery is cefazolin 1 g (as the sulfate) intravenously at induction of anesthesia and every 8 hours for 24 hours. Vancomycin 1 g (as the hydrochloride) intravenously over one hour, with or without gentamicin 2 mg/kg (as the sulfate) intravenously, should be reserved as an alternative on the basis of previously outlined guidelines from HICPAC.[21] Although there are no data, patients undergoing brachiocephalic procedures involving vascular prosthesis or patch implantation (e.g., carotid endarterectomy) may benefit from prophylaxis. (Strength of evidence for prophylaxis = A.)

Pediatric Dosage. The recommended regimen for pediatric patients undergoing vascular surgery is cefazolin 20–30 mg/kg (as the sodium) intravenously at induction of anesthesia and every 8 hours for 24 hours. Vancomycin 15 mg/kg (as the hydrochloride) intravenously over one hour, with or without gentamicin 2 mg/kg (as the sulfate) intravenously, should be reserved as an alternative on the basis of previously outlined guidelines from HICPAC.[21] Although there are no data, patients undergoing brachiocephalic procedures involving vascular prosthesis or patch implantation (e.g., carotid endarterectomy) may benefit from prophylaxis.

Solid Organ Transplantation

Few well-designed, prospective, comparative studies of antimicrobial prophylaxis have been conducted in patients undergoing solid organ transplantation, and no formal recommendations are available from professional organizations or expert consensus panels. As a result, multiple regimens are in use at different transplant centers. A recent survey of four major U.S. centers performing combined pancreas–kidney transplantation identified four different prophylactic regimens using from one to four different drugs for two to seven days postoperatively.[507]

The recommendations given for each of the solid organ transplant procedures represent an attempt to provide guidelines for safe and effective surgical prophylaxis based on the best available literature. These recommendations will undoubtedly vary considerably from protocols in use at various transplantation centers around the United States.

Heart Transplantation

Background. Heart transplantation has emerged as a standard therapeutic option for selected patients with end-stage cardiac disease. Approximately 4000 heart transplants are performed worldwide each year, including approximately 100 in children less than 16 years of age.[508] Survival rates after heart transplantation are approximately 79% at one year and 65% at five years, illustrating the tremendous progress that has been made over the past two decades. Infection continues to be an important cause of morbidity and mortality after heart transplantation and is the major cause of death in approximately 15%, 40%, and 10% of patients at <1 month, 1–12 months, and >12 months posttransplant, respectively.

Despite the large number of heart transplantation surgeries performed, few studies have specifically examined postoperative infection rates in this population. General cardiothoracic surgery has been associated with surgical wound infection rates of 9% to 55% in the absence of antimicrobial prophylaxis.[69,70,88] Because heart transplantation is similar to other cardiothoracic surgeries, similar considerations regarding the need for antimicrobial prophylaxis apply (see Cardiothoracic surgery).[509]

Organisms. Similar to other types of cardiothoracic surgery, coagulase-positive and coagulase-negative staphylococci are the primary pathogens that cause surgical wound infection after heart transplantation. *S. aureus* was the cause of all wound infections in one study involving heart transplantation.[510]

Efficacy. In an open-label, noncomparative study, the wound infection rate was 4.5% among 96 patients administered cefotaxime plus flucloxacillin preoperatively and for 72 hours after surgery.[510] This rate of infection was similar to that seen in other cardiothoracic, non-heart-transplantation procedures in which antimicrobial prophylaxis was used. Although antimicrobial prophylaxis appears to be effective in significantly reducing infection rates, no randomized, controlled trials have specifically addressed the use of antimicrobial prophylaxis in heart transplantation.

Choice. Antimicrobial prophylaxis for heart transplantation is similar to that used for other types of cardiothoracic procedures.[509] First- and second-generation cephalosporins are considered to be equally efficacious and are the preferred agents. There appear to be no significant differences in efficacy among prophylactic regimens using agents such as cefazolin, cephalothin, cefuroxime, and cefamandole.[511] The use of antistaphylococcal penicillins, either alone or in combination with aminoglycosides or cephalosporins, has not been demonstrated to provide efficacy superior to that of cephalosporin monotherapy (see Cardiothoracic surgery).

Duration. On the basis of data concerning other cardiothoracic procedures, prophylactic regimens of 48 to 72 hours' duration appear similar in efficacy to longer regimens.

Pediatric Efficacy. There are no data specifically addressing antimicrobial prophylaxis for heart transplantation in pediatric patients. Pediatric patients should be treated according to recommendations for other types of cardiothoracic procedures.

Recommendation. On the basis of data for other types of cardiothoracic surgery, antimicrobial prophylaxis is indicated for all patients undergoing heart transplantation. The recommended regimen is cefazolin 1 g (as the sodium) intravenously at induction of anesthesia and every 8 hours for 48 to 72 hours. Currently there is no evidence to support continuing prophylaxis until chest and mediastinal drainage tubes are removed. Cefuroxime 1.5 g (as the sodium) intravenously at induction of anesthesia and every 12 hours for 48 to 72 hours and cefamandole 1 g (as the nafate) intravenously at induction of anesthesia and every 6 hours for 48 to 72 hours are acceptable alternatives. Further studies are needed to demonstrate the efficacy of single-dose prophylaxis. Vancomycin 1 g (as the hydrochloride) intravenously with or without gentamicin 2 mg/kg (as the sulfate) should be reserved as an alternative agent on the basis of previously outlined guidelines from HICPAC and AHA.[21,32] (Strength of evidence for prophylaxis = A.)

Pediatric Dosage. The recommended regimen for pediatric patients undergoing heart transplantation is cefazolin 20–30 mg/kg (as the sodium) intravenously at induction of anesthesia and every 8 hours for 48 to 72 hours. Cefuroxime 50 mg/kg (as the sodium) at induction of anesthesia and every 8 hours for 48 to 72 hours is an acceptable alternative. Vancomycin 15 mg/kg (as the hydrochloride) intravenously with or without gentamicin 2 mg/kg (as the sulfate) should be reserved as an alternative on the basis of previously outlined guidelines from HICPAC and AHA.[21,32]

Lung and Heart–Lung Transplantation

Background. Lung transplantation has become an accepted mode of therapy for a variety of end-stage, irreversible lung diseases. The most common diseases for which lung transplantation is performed are chronic obstructive pulmonary disease, emphysema associated with α_1-antitrypsin deficiency, cystic fibrosis, idiopathic pulmonary fibrosis, and primary pulmonary hypertension.[512] Approximately 1000 single-lung, bilateral-lung, and heart–lung transplants are performed in the United States every year.[508,512] National survival rates after lung transplantation are approximately 70% at one year and 50% at five years; differences in rates between single-lung and double-lung transplants are not significant.[508] Survival rates after heart–lung transplants are somewhat lower: approximately 60% at one year and 40% at five years.

Bacterial, fungal, and viral infections are the most common complications and causes of death within the first 90 days after lung or heart–lung transplantation.[512–514] Bacterial infections, particularly surgical wound infections and pneumonia, are common in the immediate postoperative period. The frequent occurrence of bacterial pneumonias is directly related to the procedure being performed. Thus antimicrobial prophylaxis is routinely administered to patients undergoing lung or heart–lung transplantation with the aim of preventing bacterial pneumonia as well as wound infection.

Although much has been published about general infectious complications associated with lung transplantation, there are no data specifically addressing the optimal prophylactic antimicrobial regimens. Fungal and viral infections are late complications not directly associated with the surgical procedure. Prophylaxis of these infections is beyond the scope of this document.

Organisms. Similar to other cardiothoracic surgeries, coagulase-positive and coagulase-negative staphylococci are the primary pathogens that cause wound infection after lung transplantation. Patients undergoing lung transplantation are also at risk for bacterial pneumonia due to colonization or infection of the lower and upper airways of the donor, the recipient, or both.[512] The donor lung appears to be a major route of transmission of pathogens; 75% to 90% of bronchial washings from donor organs are positive for at least one bacterial organism.[515,516]

Organ recipients may also be the source of infection of the transplanted organ. This is particularly true in patients with cystic fibrosis because of the frequent presence of *P. aeruginosa* in the upper airways and sinuses before transplantation.[514] These pathogens are often highly resistant to antimicrobials because of the frequent administration of broad-spectrum agents during the previous course of the disease. Multiresistant strains of *Burkholderia (Pseudomonas) cepacia* and *Stenotrophomonas maltophilia* may be a problem in cystic fibrosis patients in some transplant centers.[514,517]

Infections with *Candida* and *Aspergillus* species are also common after lung transplantation. The occurrence of early *Candida* infections has been associated with colonization of the donor lung before transplantation.[516,518]

Efficacy. No randomized, controlled trials regarding antimicrobial prophylaxis for lung transplantation have been conducted. The rate of bacterial pneumonia within the first two weeks after surgery has reportedly been decreased from 35% to approximately 10% by routine antimicrobial prophylaxis.[519–521] Improvements in surgical technique and postoperative patient care may also be important factors in the apparently lower rates of pneumonia after lung transplantation.

Choice. No formal studies have addressed optimal prophylaxis for patients undergoing lung transplantation. Antimicrobial prophylaxis for lung and heart–lung transplantation should generally be similar to that for other cardiothoracic procedures (see Cardiothoracic surgery). First- and second-generation cephalosporins are considered to be equally efficacious and are the preferred agents for these procedures. However, prophylactic regimens should be modified to include coverage for any potential bacterial pathogens that have been isolated from the recipient's airways or the donor lung.[512] Patients with end-stage cystic fibrosis should receive antimicrobials on the basis of the known susceptibilities of pretransplant isolates, particularly *P. aeruginosa.*

It has been suggested that antifungal prophylaxis should be considered when pretransplant cultures reveal fungi in the donor lung.[512] Because of the serious nature of fungal infections in the early posttransplant period and the availability of relatively nontoxic antifungal agents, prophylaxis with fluconazole should be considered when *Candida* is isolated from the donor lung and itraconazole should be considered when *Aspergillus* is isolated.[512] Amphotericin B may also be considered.[522] No antifungal prophylaxis is necessary in the absence of positive fungal cultures from the donor lung.

Duration. No well-conducted studies have addressed the optimal duration of antimicrobial prophylaxis for lung transplantation. In the absence of positive cultures from the donor or the recipient, prophylactic regimens of 48 to 72 hours' duration are probably similar in efficacy to longer regimens.[522] In patients with positive pretransplant cultures from donor or recipient organs or patients with positive cultures posttransplant, prophylaxis should be continued for longer. Antimicrobial prophylaxis should be appropriately modified according to the specific organisms isolated and antimicrobial susceptibilities. It has been recommended that prophylactic regimens be continued for 7 to 14 days postoperatively in transplant recipients with positive cultures, particularly patients with cystic fibrosis and previous *P. aeruginosa* infection.[512,514,522]

Pediatric Efficacy. There are few data specifically concerning antimicrobial prophylaxis for lung transplantation in pediatric patients. Pediatric patients should be treated according to recommendations for other types of cardiothoracic procedures and as previously discussed for adult lung transplantation.[522]

Recommendation. On the basis of data from other types of cardiothoracic surgery, all patients undergoing lung transplantation should receive antimicrobial prophylaxis because of the high risk of infection. Patients with negative pretransplant cultures should receive antimicrobial prophylaxis as appropriate for other types of cardiothoracic surgeries. The recommended regimen is cefazolin 1 g (as the sodium) intravenously at induction of anesthesia and every 8 hours for 48 to 72 hours. There is no evidence to support continuing prophylaxis until chest and mediastinal drainage tubes are removed. Cefuroxime 1.5 g (as the sodium) intravenously at induction of anesthesia and every 12 hours for 48 to 72 hours and cefamandole 1 g (as the nafate) intravenously at induction of anesthesia and every 6 hours for 48 to 72 hours are acceptable alternatives. Further studies are needed to demonstrate the efficacy of single-dose prophylaxis. Vancomycin 1 g (as the hydrochloride) intravenously should be reserved as an alternative on the basis of previously outlined guidelines from HICPAC.[21]

The prophylactic regimen should be modified to provide coverage against any potential pathogens (e.g., *P. aeruginosa*) isolated from the donor lung or the recipient. Prophylactic regimens directed against *P. aeruginosa* may include one or two drugs with activity against this pathogen, although two-drug therapy is recommended for prophylaxis and is mandatory should prophylaxis fail and an actual infection develop. The regimen may also include antifungal agents such as fluconazole if donor lung cultures are positive for *Candida* and itraconazole if cultures are positive for *Aspergillus.* The following doses would be appropriate: fluconazole 200–400 mg intravenously or orally, or itraconazole 200 mg orally as tablet or suspension. If the use of amphotericin B is desired, doses of 0.1–0.25 mg/kg intravenously may be used. Patients undergoing lung transplantation for cystic fibrosis should receive 7 to 14 days of prophylaxis with antimicrobials selected according to pretransplant culture and susceptibility results. (Strength of evidence for prophylaxis = B.)

Pediatric Dosage. As used for other cardiothoracic procedures, the recommended regimen for pediatric patients undergoing lung or heart–lung transplantation is cefazolin 20–30 mg/kg (as the sodium) intravenously at induction of anesthesia and every 8 hours for 48 to 72 hours. Cefuroxime 50 mg/kg (as the sodium) intravenously at induction of anesthesia and every 8 hours for 48 to 72 hours is an acceptable alternative. Vancomycin 15 mg/kg (as the hydrochloride) intravenously should be reserved as an alternative on the basis of previously outlined guidelines from HICPAC.[21] If these regimens require modification for potential pathogens isolated from the donor or the recipient, the dosages are as appropriate for the specific agent(s) chosen. Patients undergoing lung transplantation for cystic fibrosis should receive 7 to 14 days of prophylaxis with antimicrobials selected according to pretransplant isolates and susceptibilities. These antimicrobials may be antibacterial or antifungal agents.

Liver Transplantation

Background. Liver transplantation is a life-saving procedure for many patients with end-stage hepatic disease for whom there are no other medical or surgical options. Approximately 6000 liver transplants are performed worldwide each year, with one- and five-year survival rates of 76% and 65%, respectively.[523,524] Infection remains a major cause of morbidity and mortality in liver transplant recipients. Infections may occur in 42% to 83% of patients within three months of transplantation and are the cause of death in 4% to 23% of patients; these rates are highly variable and do not seem to have substantially changed in spite of advances in surgical technique and medical management.[523–529]

Liver transplantation is often considered to be the most technically difficult of the solid organ transplant procedures. Surgical procedures longer than 8 to 12 hours have been consistently identified as one of the most important risk factors for early infectious complications, including wound infections, intra-abdominal infections, and biliary tract infections.[523,527,529] Other important risk factors for infectious complications include previous hepatobiliary surgery, high pretransplantation serum bilirubin concentration, and surgical complications such as anastomotic leakage. In spite of the high rate of infections directly related to the transplantation procedure, there are few well-controlled studies concerning optimal antimicrobial prophylaxis in this setting.

Organisms. The pathogens most commonly associated with early wound and intra-abdominal infections are those derived from the normal flora of the intestinal lumen and the skin. Aerobic gram-negative bacilli, including *E. coli*, *Klebsiella* species, *Enterobacter* species, and *Citrobacter* species, are common causes of wound and intra-abdominal infections and account for up to 65% of all bacterial pathogens.[523,524,527,529–531] Infections due to *P. aeruginosa* may also occur but are much less frequent in the early postoperative period. *P. aeruginosa* is most commonly associated with late pneumonias, vascular infections, and secondary bacteremias.[523,524,527,529]

Enterococci are particularly common pathogens and may be responsible for 20% to 46% of wound and intra-abdominal infections. *S. aureus* and coagulase-negative staphylococci are also common causes of postoperative wound infections.[524,525,527–529] Although *Candida* species commonly cause late infections, they are less frequent causes of early postoperative infections.

Efficacy. In evaluating the efficacy of prophylactic regimens, it is important to differentiate between early infections (variously defined as those occurring within 14 to 30 days after surgery) and late infections (those occurring >30 days after surgery). Infections occurring in the early postoperative period are most commonly associated with biliary, vascular, and abdominal surgeries involved in the transplantation procedure itself and are thus most preventable with prophylactic antimicrobial regimens.[523–525,527] The frequency of these infections varies from 10% to 55% despite antimicrobial prophylaxis.[523–525,527,532] It is difficult to assess the efficacy of prophylactic regimens in reducing the rate of infection because prophylaxis has been routinely used in light of the complexity of the surgical procedure; therefore, reliable rates of infection in the absence of prophylaxis are not available. No controlled studies have compared prophylaxis with no prophylaxis.

Choice. Antimicrobial prophylaxis should be directed against the pathogens most commonly isolated from early infections (i.e., gram-negative aerobic bacilli, staphylococci, enterococci). Traditional prophylactic regimens have thus consisted of a third-generation cephalosporin (usually cefotaxime because of relatively greater staphylococcal activity) plus ampicillin.[525,526,528–530,532] The use of cefoxitin and of ampicillin–sulbactam has also been reported; the efficacy of these regimens compared with that of cefotaxime plus ampicillin cannot be assessed because of different definitions of infection used in the various studies. No randomized, controlled studies have been conducted to compare the efficacy of other antimicrobial prophylactic regimens in the prevention of early postoperative infections.

At least one study used mechanical bowel preparation in conjunction with oral erythromycin base and neomycin sulfate, followed by systemic administration of cefotaxime plus ampicillin.[526] Infection rates in that study did not appear to be different from those in studies that did not use preoperative gut sterilization.

Several studies have examined the use of selective bowel decontamination in order to eliminate aerobic gram-negative bacilli and yeast from the bowel before surgery.[525,530–534] These studies used combinations of nonabsorbable antibacterials (aminoglycosides, polymyxin E) and antifungals (nystatin or amphotericin B) administered orally and applied to the oropharyngeal cavity, in combination with systemically administered antimicrobials. The results of these studies are conflicting and do not currently support the routine use of selective bowel decontamination in patients undergoing liver transplantation.[523]

Duration. No studies have assessed the optimal duration of antimicrobial prophylaxis in liver transplantation. Although antimicrobials were administered for five days in older studies,[526,529] more recent studies have limited the duration of prophylaxis to 48 hours, with no apparent difference in early infection rates.[525,527,530,532]

Pediatric Efficacy. There are few data specifically concerning antimicrobial prophylaxis in liver transplantation in pediatric patients. The combination of cefotaxime plus ampicillin has been reportedly used in children undergoing living-related-donor liver transplantation; the efficacy of this regimen appeared to be favorable.[528]

Recommendation. All patients undergoing liver transplantation should receive antimicrobial prophylaxis because of the high risk of infectious morbidity and mortality associated with these procedures. Cefotaxime 1 g (as the sodium) plus ampicillin 1 g (as the sodium) should be administered intravenously at induction of anesthesia, repeated every 6 hours during the procedure, and given every 6 hours for 48 hours beyond final surgical closure. Other antimicrobial regimens that provide adequate coverage against gram-negative aerobic bacilli, staphylococci, and enterococci may be appropriate, but no randomized, comparative clinical trials have been conducted. (Strength of evidence for prophylaxis = B.)

Pediatric Dosage. The recommended regimen for pediatric patients undergoing liver transplantation is cefotaxime 50 mg/kg (as the sodium) plus ampicillin 50 mg/kg (as the sodium) intravenously at induction of anesthesia and repeated every 6 hours for 48 hours beyond final surgical closure. Other antimicrobial regimens that provide adequate coverage against gram-negative aerobic bacilli, staphylococci, and enterococci may be appropriate, but no randomized, comparative clinical trials have been conducted.

Pancreas and Pancreas–Kidney Transplantation

Background. Pancreas transplantation is an accepted therapeutic intervention for type 1 diabetes mellitus; it is the only therapy that consistently achieves euglycemia without dependence on exogenous insulin. Simultaneous pancreas–kidney transplantation is an accepted procedure for patients with type 1 diabetes and severe diabetic nephropathy. Infectious complications are a major source of morbidity and mortality in patients undergoing pancreas or pancreas–kidney transplantation; the frequency of wound infection is reportedly 7% to 50%.[535–539] These patients may be at increased risk of wound and other infections because of the combined immunosuppressive effects of diabetes and the immunosuppressive drugs used to prevent graft rejection.[537] Other factors associated with increased wound infection rates include prolonged (more than four hours) operating time, organ donor of >55 years of age, and enteric rather than bladder drainage of pancreatic duct secretions.[537]

Organisms. A majority of superficial wound infections after pancreas or pancreas–kidney transplantation are caused by staphylococci (both coagulase-positive and coagulase-negative) and gram-negative aerobic bacilli (particularly *E. coli* and *Klebsiella* species). Deep wound infections also are frequently associated with gram-positive and gram-negative aerobes, as well as *Candida* species.[535–541]

Efficacy. Although no placebo-controlled studies have been conducted, several open-label, noncomparative studies have suggested that antimicrobial prophylaxis substantially decreases the rate of superficial and deep wound infections after pancreas or pancreas–kidney transplantation. Wound infection rates were 2.4% to 5% with various prophylactic regimens, compared with 7% to 50% for historical controls in the absence of prophylaxis.[507,540] However, even with antimicrobial prophylaxis, wound infection rates as high as 33% have been reported[537]; the reason for the wide disparity in infection rates observed with prophylaxis is not readily apparent.

Choice. Because of the broad range of potential pathogens, several studies have used multidrug prophylactic regimens, including imipenem–cilastatin plus vancomycin[537]; tobramycin, vancomycin, and fluconazole[540]; and cefotaxime,

metronidazole, and vancomycin.[542] These three regimens resulted in overall wound infection rates of 33%, 2.4%, and 30%, respectively. A recent study evaluated wound infection rates in pancreas–kidney transplantation after single-agent, single-dose prophylaxis with cefazolin.[507] Only two patients (5%) developed superficial wound infections, defined as the presence of erythema and purulent drainage. Although four additional patients (11%) developed deep wound infections, all infections were associated with bladder anastomotic leaks or transplant pancreatitis. On the basis of limited studies, it appears that multidrug regimens offer no distinct advantage over cefazolin.

Duration. Recent studies have evaluated the use of prophylactic regimens ranging from a single preoperative dose of cefazolin to multidrug regimens of two to five days' duration.[507,537,540,542] Although longer durations of antimicrobial prophylaxis have been recommended,[543] these appear to offer no clear advantages over the single-dose regimen.

Pediatric Efficacy. There are no data concerning antimicrobial prophylaxis for pancreas or pancreas–kidney transplantation in pediatric patients.

Recommendation. The recommended regimen for patients undergoing pancreas or pancreas–kidney transplantation is cefazolin 1 g (as the sodium) intravenously at induction of anesthesia. (Strength of evidence for prophylaxis = B.)

Pediatric Dosage. The recommended regimen for pediatric patients undergoing pancreas or pancreas–kidney transplantation is cefazolin 20 mg/kg (as the sodium) intravenously administered at induction of anesthesia.

Kidney Transplantation

Background. Approximately 10,000 kidney transplants are performed in the United States each year.[544] The rate of postoperative infection after this procedure has been reported to range from 10% to 56%.[545–552] Graft loss due to infection occurs in up to 33% of cases.[548] Mortality associated with postoperative infections is substantial and ranges from approximately 5% to 30%.[546,548,550,553,554]

Well-defined risk factors for wound infection after renal transplantation include contamination of organ perfusate; factors related to the procedure, such as ureteral leakage and hematoma formation; immunosuppressive therapy; and obesity.[554] In one study, the frequency of wound infection was 12% in patients receiving immunosuppression with azathioprine plus prednisone but only 1.7% in patients receiving cyclosporine plus prednisone.[555]

Organisms. Postoperative wound infections are typically caused by flora of the skin (particularly *S. aureus* and *S. epidermidis*) and of the urinary tract (most frequently *E. coli*). Enterococci and other gram-negative aerobic pathogens are less frequent causes of postoperative infections after kidney transplantation.[545–552,555,556]

Efficacy. A number of studies have clearly demonstrated that antimicrobial prophylaxis significantly decreases postoperative infection rates in patients undergoing kidney transplantation. These have included at least one randomized controlled trial[545] and many prospective and retrospective studies comparing infection rates with prophylaxis and historical infection rates at specific transplant centers.[546–549,552,555–557] A recent study evaluated wound infection rates in the absence of systemic prophylaxis and found only a 2% rate among 102 patients undergoing renal transplantation.[558] Possible explanations given for the very low infection rate included local wound irrigation with cefazolin, improved organ procurement techniques, and careful surgical technique employed by a single, very experienced surgical team. This study emphasizes the importance of good surgical technique during the transplant procedure as an effective means of reducing infectious complications. However, on the basis of available literature, the routine use of systemic antimicrobial prophylaxis is justified in patients undergoing renal transplantation.

Three studies using a triple-drug regimen consisting of an aminoglycoside, an antistaphylococcal penicillin, and ampicillin demonstrated infection rates of less than 2%, compared with 10% to 25% with no antimicrobial prophylaxis.[549,552] Piperacillin plus cefuroxime was also shown to be efficacious; infection rates were 3.7%, compared with 19% in patients not receiving prophylaxis.[545] Several studies have shown that single-agent prophylaxis with an antistaphylococcal penicillin,[556] a first-generation cephalosporin,[547,548] a second-generation cephalosporin,[557] or a third-generation cephalosporin such as cefoperazone or ceftriaxone[555,559] can reduce postoperative infection rates to between 0% and 8.4%. Antimicrobial prophylaxis with agents providing good coverage against gram-positive cocci and gram-negative enteric pathogens is very effective in reducing infection rates in patients undergoing kidney transplantation.

Choice. The data do not indicate a significant difference between single-agent regimens and regimens using two or more drugs.[545,549,552] Also, there appear to be no significant differences between single-agent regimens employing antistaphylococcal penicillins or first-, second-, or third-generation cephalosporins.[547,548,555–557,559] Studies have directly compared antimicrobial regimens in a prospective, controlled fashion. Single-agent prophylaxis with both cefazolin and ceftriaxone has been reported to result in infection rates of 0%.[547,559]

Duration. Studies have used various prophylactic regimens ranging from a single preoperative dose of cefazolin or ceftriaxone to multidrug regimens of two to five days' duration.[545–549,552,555–557] There appear to be no significant differences in wound infection rates between single-dose and multidose regimens.

Pediatric Efficacy. Although pediatric patients were included in studies demonstrating the efficacy of antimicrobial prophylaxis, there are few data specific to pediatric patients.

Recommendation. The recommended regimen for patients undergoing kidney transplantation is cefazolin 1 g (as the sodium) intravenously at induction of anesthesia. (Strength of evidence for prophylaxis = A.)

Pediatric Dosage. The recommended regimen for pediatric patients undergoing kidney transplantation is cefazolin 20 mg/kg (as the sodium) intravenously at induction of anesthesia.

References

1. ASHP Commission on Therapeutics. ASHP therapeutic guidelines on antimicrobial prophylaxis in surgery. *Clin Pharm.* 1992; 11:483–513.
2. Dotson LR, Witmer DR. Development of ASHP thera-peutic guidelines. *Am J Health-Syst Pharm.* 1995; 52:254–5.
3. Taketomo CK, Hodding JH, Kraus DM. Pediatric dosage handbook. Hudson, OH: Lexi-Comp; 1996.
4. Koren G, Prober CG, Gold R, eds. Antimicrobial therapy in infants and children. New York: Marcel Dekker; 1988.
5. Roberts NJ, Douglas RG. Gentamicin use and *Pseudomonas* and *Serratia* resistance: effect of a surgical prophylaxis regimen. *Antimicrob Agents Chemother.* 1978; 13:214–20.
6. Bartlett J, Condon R, Gorbach S et al. Veterans Administration Cooperative Study on bowel preparation for elective colorectal operations: impact of oral antibiotic regimen on colonic flora, wound irrigation cultures and bacteriology of septic complications. *Ann Surg.* 1978; 188:249–54.
7. Rozenberg-Arska M, Dekker AW, Verhoef J. Ciprofloxacin for selective decontamination of the alimentary tract in patients with acute leukemia during remission induction treatment: the effect on fecal flora. *J Infect Dis.* 1985; 152:104–7.
8. Harrison GA, Stross WP, Rubin MP et al. Resistance in oral streptococci after repeated three-dose erythromycin prophylaxis. *J Antimicrob Chemother.* 1985; 15:471–9.
9. Murray BE, Rensimer ER, DuPont HL. Emergence of high-level trimethoprim resistance in fecal *Escherichia coli* during oral administration of trimethoprim or trimethoprim-sulfamethoxazole. *N Engl J Med.* 1982; 306:130–5.
10. Kern WV, Andriof E, Oethinger M et al. Emergence of fluoroquinolone-resistant *Escherichia coli* at a cancer center. *Antimicrob Agents Chemother.* 1994; 38:681–7.
11. Dupeyron C, Mangeney N, Sedrati L et al. Rapid emergence of quinolone resistance in cirrhotic patients treated with norfloxacin to prevent spontaneous bacterial peritonitis. *Antimicrob Agents Chemother.* 1994; 38:340–4.
12. Tetteroo GWM, Wagenvoort JHT, Bruining HA. Bacteriology of selective decontamination: efficacy and rebound colonization. *J Antimicrob Chemother.* 1994; 34:139–48.
13. Kotilainen P, Nikoskelainen J, Huovinen P. Emergence of ciprofloxacin-resistant coagulase-negative staphylococcal skin flora in immunocompromised patients receiving ciprofloxacin. *J Infect Dis.* 1990; 161:41–4.
14. Kauffman CA, Liepman MK, Bergman AG et al. Trimethoprim/sulfamethoxazole prophylaxis in neutropenic patients. Reduction of infections and effect on bacterial and fungal flora. *Am J Med.* 1983; 74:599–607.
15. Weinstein JW, Roe M, Towns M et al. Resistant enterococci: a prospective study of prevalence, incidence, and factors associated with colonization in a university hospital. *Infect Control Hosp Epidemiol.* 1996; 17:36–41.
16. Kunova A, Trupl J, Kremery V Jr. Low incidence of quinolone resistance in gram-negative bacteria after five-years use of ofloxacin in prophylaxis during afebrile neutropenia. *J Hosp Infect.* 1996; 32:155–6. Letter.
17. Preheim L, Rimland D, Bittner M. Methicillin-resistant

Staphylococcus aureus in Veterans Administration Medical Centers. *Infect Control.* 1987; 8:191–4.

18. Thornsberry C. Methicillin-resistant staphylococci. *Clin Lab Med.* 1989; 9:255–67.

19. Panlilio AL, Culver DH, Gaynes RP et al. Methicillin-resistant *Staphylococcus aureus* in US hospitals, 1975–1991. *Infect Control Hosp Epidemiol.* 1992; 13:582–6.

20. Centers for Disease Control and Prevention. Nosocomial enterococci resistant to vancomycin—United States, 1989–1993. *MMWR.* 1993; 42:597–9.

21. Centers for Disease Control and Prevention. Recommendations for preventing the spread of vancomycin resistance: recommendations of the Hospital Infection Control Practices Advisory Committee (HICPAC). *MMWR.* 1994; 44:1–13.

22. Boyce J, Potter-Bynoe G, Dziobek L. Hospital reimbursement patterns among patients with surgical wound infections following open heart surgery. *Infect Control Hosp Epidemiol.* 1990; 11:89–93.

23. Roach A, Kernodle D, Kaiser A. Selecting cost-effective antimicrobial prophylaxis in surgery: are we getting what we pay for? *DICP Ann Pharmacother.* 1990; 24:183–5.

24. Gorbach SL, Condon RE, Conte JE Jr et al. Evaluation of new anti-infective drugs for surgical prophylaxis. Infectious Diseases Society of America and the Food and Drug Administration. *Clin Infect Dis.* 1992; 15(suppl 1):S313–38.

25. Antimicrobial prophylaxis in surgery. *Med Lett Drugs Ther.* 1997; 39:97–102.

26. Page CP, Bohnen JM, Fletcher R et al. Antimicrobial prophylaxis for surgical wounds. Guidelines for clinical care. *Arch Surg.* 1993; 128:79–88.

27. Platt R, Zaleznik DF, Hopkins CC et al. Perioperative antibiotic prophylaxis for herniorrhaphy and breast surgery. *N Engl J Med.* 1990; 322:153–60.

28. Platt R, Zucker JR, Zaleznik DF et al. Perioperative antibiotic prophylaxis and wound infection following breast surgery. *J Antimicrob Chemother.* 1993; 31:43–8.

29. National Academy of Sciences–National Research Council. Postoperative wound infections: the influence of ultraviolet irradiation of the operating room and of various other factors. *Ann Surg.* 1964; 160:1–195.

30. Kernodle DS, Kaiser AB. Surgical and trauma-related infections. In: Mandell GL, Bennett JE, Dolin R, eds. Principles and practice of infectious diseases. 4th ed. New York: Churchill Livingstone; 1995:2742–55.

31. Freiman JA, Chalmers TC, Smith H et al. The importance of beta, the type II error and sample size in the design and interpretation of the randomized control trial. *N Engl J Med.* 1978; 299:690–4.

32. Dajani AS, Taubert KA, Wilson W et al. Prevention of bacterial endocarditis. Recommendations by the American Heart Association. *JAMA.* 1997; 277:1794–801.

33. American College of Obstetricians and Gynecologists (ACOG). Antimicrobial therapy for obstetric patients. *ACOG Ed Bull.* 1998; 245:1–10.

34. Guidelines for perinatal care. 4th ed. Elk Grove Village, IL: American Academy of Pediatrics and American College of Obstetricians and Gynecologists; 1997.

35. Peter G, ed. 1997 Red book: report of the Committee on Infectious Diseases. 24th ed. Elk Grove Village, IL: American Academy of Pediatrics; 1997.

36. Young TE, Mangum OB. Neofax: a manual of drugs used in neonatal care. 10th ed. Columbus, NC: Ross Laboratories; 1997.

37. Chang D. Influence of malignancy on the pharmacokinetics of vancomycin in infants and children. *Pediatr Infect Dis J.* 1995; 14:667–73.

38. Chang D, Liem L, Malogolowkin M. A prospective study of vancomycin pharmacokinetics and dosage requirements in pediatric cancer patients. *Pediatr Infect Dis J.* 1994; 13:969–74.

39. Kernodle DS, Classen DC, Burke JP et al. Failure of cephalosporins to prevent *Staphylococcus aureus* surgical wound infection. *JAMA.* 1990; 263:961–6.

40. Kriesel D, Savel TG, Silver AL et al. Surgical antibiotic prophylaxis and *Clostridium difficile* toxin positivity. *Arch Surg.* 1995; 130:989–93.

41. Privitera G, Scarpellini P, Ortisi G et al. Prospective study of *Clostridium difficile* intestinal colonization and disease following single-dose antibiotic prophylaxis surgery. *Antimicrob Agents Chemother.* 1991; 35:208–10.

42. Jobe BA, Grasley A, Deveney KE et al. *Clostridium difficile* colitis: an increasing hospital-acquired illness. *Am J Surg.* 1995; 169:480–3.

43. Morris JG, Shay DK, Hebden JN. Enterococci resistant to multiple antimicrobial agents, including vancomycin: establishment of endemicity in a university medical center. *Ann Intern Med.* 1995; 123:250–9.

44. Sastry V, Brennan PJ, Levy MM. Vancomycin-resistant enterococci: an emerging problem in immunosuppressed transplant recipients. *Transplant Proc.* 1995; 27:954–5.

45. Rhinehart E, Smith NE, Wennersten C. Rapid dissemination of beta-lactamase producing aminoglycoside resistant *Enterococcus faecium* among patients and staff on an infant-toddler surgical ward. *N Engl J Med.* 1990; 323:1814–8.

46. Burke JF. The effective period of preventive antibiotic action in experimental incisions and dermal lesions. *Surgery.* 1961; 50:161–8.

47. Classen DC, Evans RS, Pestotnik SL et al. The timing of prophylactic administration of antibiotics and the risk of surgical-wound infection. *N Engl J Med.* 1992; 326:281–6.

48. Gordon HP, Phelps D, Blanchard K. Prophylactic cesarean section antibiotics: maternal and neonatal morbidity before and after cord clamping. *Obstet Gynecol.* 1979; 53:151–6.

49. Cunningham FG, Leveno KJ, DePalma RT et al. Perioperative antimicrobials for cesarean delivery: before or after cord clamping. *Obstet Gynecol.* 1983; 62:151–4.

50. Clarke J, Condon R, Bartlett J et al. Preoperative oral antibiotics reduce septic complications of colon operations: results of a prospective randomized, double-blind clinical study. *Ann Surg.* 1977; 186:251–9.

51. Nichols R, Broldo P, Condon P et al. Effect of preoperative neomycin-erythromycin intestinal preparation on the incidence of infectious complications following colon surgery. *Ann Surg.* 1973; 178:453–62.

52. Stellato T, Danziger L, Gordon N et al. Antibiotics in elective colon surgery: a randomized trial of oral, systemic, and oral/systemic antibiotics for prophylaxis. *Am Surg.* 1990; 56:251–4.

53. Petrelli N, Contre DC, Herrera L et al. A prospective

randomized trial of perioperative prophylactic cefamandole in elective colorectal surgery for malignancy. *Dis Colon Rectum.* 1988; 31:427–9.

54. Felip JF, Bonet EB, Eisman FI et al. Oral is superior to systemic antibiotic prophylaxis in operations upon the colon and rectum. *Surg Gynecol Obstet.* 1984; 158:359–62.

55. Kling PA, Dahlgren S. Oral prophylaxis with neomycin and erythromycin in colorectal surgery; more proof for efficacy than failure. *Arch Surg.* 1989; 124:705–7.

56. Lewis RT, Goodall RG, Marien B et al. Is neomycin necessary for bowel preparation in surgery of the colon? Oral neomycin plus erythromycin versus erythromycin-metronidazole. *Dis Colon Rectum.* 1989; 32:265–70.

57. DiPiro JT, Cheung RP, Bowden TA et al. Single-dose systemic antibiotic prophylaxis of surgical wound infections. *Am J Surg.* 1986; 152:552–9.

58. Scher KS. Studies on the duration of antibiotic administration for surgical prophylaxis. *Am Surg.* 1997; 63:59–62.

59. American Heart Association. 1996 statistical supplement. Dallas: Heart and stroke facts.

60. Demmy TL, Sang BP, Liebler GA et al. Recent experience with major sternal wound complications. *Ann Thorac Surg.* 1990; 49:458–62.

61. Kutsal A, Ibrisim E, Catav Z et al. Mediastinitis after open heart surgery. Analysis of risk factors and management. *J Cardiovasc Surg.* 1991; 32:38–41.

62. Kittle C, Reed W. Antibiotics and extracorporeal circulation. *J Thorac Cardiovasc Surg.* 1961; 41:34–48.

63. Slonim R, Litwak R, Gadboys H et al. Antibiotic prophylaxis of infection complicating open-heart operations. *Antimicrob Agents Chemother.* 1963; 3:731–5.

64. Goodman J, Schaffner W, Collins H et al. Infection after cardiovascular surgery. *N Engl J Med.* 1968; 278:117–23.

65. Fekety F, Cluff L, Sabiston D et al. A study of antibiotic prophylaxis in cardiac surgery. *J Thorac Cardiovasc Surg.* 1969; 57:757–63.

66. Conte J, Cohen S, Roe B et al. Antibiotic prophylaxis and cardiac surgery: a prospective double-blind comparison of single-dose versus multi-dose regimens. *Ann Intern Med.* 1972; 76:943–9.

67. Firor W. Infection following open-heart surgery, with special reference to the role of prophylactic antibiotics. *J Thorac Cardiovasc Surg.* 1967; 53:371–8.

68. Kreter B, Woods M. Antibiotic prophylaxis for cardiothoracic operations. Meta-analysis of thirty years of clinical trials. *J Thorac Cardiovasc Surg.* 1992; 104:590–9.

69. Fong I, Baker C, McKee D. The value of prophylactic antibiotics in aorta-coronary bypass operations. *J Thorac Cardiovasc Surg.* 1979; 78:908–13.

70. Penketh A, Wansbrough-Jones M, Wright E et al. Antibiotic prophylaxis for coronary artery bypass graft surgery. *Lancet.* 1985; 1:1500. Letter.

71. Hill D, Yates A. Prophylactic antibiotics in open heart surgery. *Aust N Z J Med.* 1975; 81:414–7.

72. Myerowitz P, Caswell K, Lindsay W et al. Antibiotic prophylaxis for open-heart surgery. *J Thorac Cardiovasc Surg.* 1977; 73:625–9.

73. Cooper D, Norton R, Mobin M et al. A comparison of two prophylactic antibiotic regimens for open-heart surgery. *J Cardiovasc Surg (Torino).* 1980; 21:279–86.

74. Bailey J, Perciva H. Cefamandole as a prophylactic in cardiac surgery. *Scand J Infect Dis.* 1980(suppl 25):112–7.

75. Ghoneim A, Tandon A, Ionescu M. Comparative study of cefamandole versus ampicillin plus cloxacillin: prophylactic antibiotics in cardiac surgery. *Ann Thorac Surg.* 1982; 33:152–8.

76. Slama T, Sklar S, Misinski J et al. Randomized comparison of cefamandole, cefazolin and cefuroxime prophylaxis in open-heart surgery. *Antimicrob Agents Chemother.* 1986; 29:744–7.

77. Kaiser A, Petracek M, Lea J et al. Efficacy of cefazolin, cefamandole, and gentamicin as prophylactic agents in cardiac surgery. *Ann Surg.* 1987; 206:791–7.

78. Geroulanos S, Oxelbark S, Donfried B et al. Antimicrobial prophylaxis in cardiovascular surgery. *Thorac Cardiovasc Surg.* 1987; 35:199–205.

79. Conklin C, Gray R, Neilson D et al. Determinants of wound infection incidence after isolated coronary artery bypass surgery in patients randomized to receive prophylactic cefuroxime or cefazolin. *Ann Thorac Surg.* 1988; 46:172–7.

80. Wellens F, Pirlet M, Larbuisson R et al. Prophylaxis in cardiac surgery: a controlled, randomized comparison between cefazolin and cefuroxime. *Eur J Cardiothorac Surg.* 1995; 9:325–9.

81. Galbraith U, Schilling J, von Segesser LK et al. Antibiotic prophylaxis in cardiovascular surgery: a prospective, randomized, comparative trial of one-day cefazolin vs single-dose cefuroxime. *Drugs Exp Clin Res.* 1993; 19:229–34.

82. Townsend TR, Reitz BA, Bilker WB et al. Clinical trial of cefamandole, cefazolin, and cefuroxime for antibiotic prophylaxis in cardiac operations. *J Thorac Cardiovasc Surg.* 1993; 106:664–70.

83. Curtis JJ, Boley TM, Walls JT et al. Randomized, prospective comparison of first- and second-generation cephalosporins as infection prophylaxis for cardiac surgery. *Am J Surg.* 1993; 166:734–7.

84. Doebbeling B, Pfaller M, Kuhns K et al. Cardiovascular surgery prophylaxis: a randomized, controlled comparison of cefazolin and cefuroxime. *J Thorac Cardiovasc Surg.* 1990; 99:981–9.

85. Gelfand MS, Simmons BP, Schoettle P et al. Cefamandole versus cefonicid prophylaxis in cardiovascular surgery: a prospective study. *Ann Thorac Surg.* 1990; 49:435–9.

86. Joyce F, Szczepanski K. A double-blind comparative study of prophylactic antibiotic therapy in open heart surgery: penicillin G versus vancomycin. *Thorac Cardiovasc Surg.* 1986; 34:100–3.

87. Goldman D, Hopkins C, Karchmer A et al. Cephalothin prophylaxis in cardiac valve surgery; a prospective, double-blind comparison of two-day and six-day regimens. *J Thorac Cardiovasc Surg.* 1977; 73:470–9.

88. Austin T, Coles J, McKenzie P et al. Cephalothin prophylaxis and valve replacement. *Ann Thorac Surg.* 1977; 23:333–6.

89. Hillis D, Rosenfeldt F, Spicer W et al. Antibiotic prophylaxis for coronary bypass grafting. *J Thorac Cardiovasc Surg.* 1983; 86:217–21.

90. Sisto T, Laurikka J, Tarkka MR. Ceftriaxone vs cefuroxime for infection prophylaxis in coronary bypass surgery. *Scand J Thorac Cardiovasc Surg.* 1994; 28:143–8.

91. Nooyen SMH, Overbeek BP, Brutel de la Riviere A et al. Prospective randomised comparison of single-dose versus multiple-dose cefuroxime for prophylaxis in coronary artery bypass grafting. *Eur J Clin Microbiol Infect Dis.* 1994; 13:1033–7.

92. Lee KR, Ring JC, Leggiadro RJ. Prophylactic antibiotic use in pediatric cardiovascular surgery: a surgery of current practice. *Pediatr Infect Dis J.* 1995; 14:267–9.

93. Gorbach SL, Plaut AG, Nahas L et al. Studies of intestinal microflora: II. Microorganisms of the small intestine and their relations to oral fecal flora. *Gastroenterology.* 1967; 53:856–67.

94. Gorbach SL. Intestinal microflora. *Gastroenterology.* 1971; 60:1110–29.

95. Ruddell WSJ, Axon ATR, Findlay JM et al. Effect of cimetidine on the gastric bacterial flora. *Lancet.* 1980; 1:672–4.

96. Driks MR, Craven DE, Bartolome RC et al. Nosocomial pneumonia in intubated patients given sucralfate as compared with antacids or histamine type 2 blockers. *N Engl J Med.* 1987; 317:1376–82.

97. Long J, Desantis S, State D et al. The effect of antisecretagogues on gastric microflora. *Arch Surg.* 1983; 118:1413–5.

98. Sjostedt S, Levin P, Malmborg AS et al. Septic complications in relation to factors influencing the gastric microflora in patients undergoing gastric surgery. *J Hosp Infect.* 1989; 12:191–7.

99. Feretis CB, Contou CT, Papoutsis GG et al. The effect of preoperative treatment with cimetidine on postoperative wound sepsis. *Am Surg.* 1984; 50:594–8.

100. LoCiero J, Nichols RL. Sepsis after gastroduodenal operations; relationship to gastric acid, motility, and endogenous microflora. *South Med J.* 1980; 73:878–80.

101. McArdle CS, Morran CG, Pettit L et al. Value of oral antibiotic prophylaxis in colorectal surgery. *Br J Surg.* 1995; 82:1046–8.

102. Nichols RL, Webb WR, Jones JW et al. Efficacy of antibiotic prophylaxis in high risk gastroduodenal operations. *Am J Surg.* 1982; 143:94–8.

103. Stone HH. Gastric surgery. *South Med J.* 1977; 70(suppl 1):35–7.

104. Morris DL, Yound D, Burdon DW et al. Prospective randomized trial of single-dose cefuroxime against mezlocillin elective gastric surgery. *J Hosp Infect.* 1984; 5:200–4.

105. Lewis RT, Allan CM, Goodall RG et al. Discriminate use of antibiotic prophylaxis in gastroduodenal surgery. *Am J Surg.* 1979; 138:640–3.

106. Lewis RT, Allan CM, Goodall RG et al. Cefamandole in gastroduodenal surgery: a controlled prospective, randomized, double-blind study. *Can J Surg.* 1982; 25:561–3.

107. Mitchell NJ, Evans DS, Pollock D. Pre-operative, single-dose cefuroxime antimicrobial prophylaxis with and without metronidazole in elective gastrointestinal surgery. *J Antimicrob Chemother.* 1980; 6:393–9.

108. Brown J, Mutton TP, Wasilauskas BL et al. Prospective, randomized, controlled trial of ticarcillin and cephalothin as prophylactic antibiotics for gastrointestinal operations. *Am J Surg.* 1982; 143:343–8.

109. Cruse PJ, Foord R. The epidemiology of wound infection: a ten-year prospective study of 62,939 wounds. *Surg Clin North Am.* 1980; 60:27–40.

110. Pories WJ, Van Rij AM, Burlingham BT et al. Prophylactic cefazolin in gastric bypass surgery. *Surgery.* 1981; 90:426–32.

111. Polk H, Lopez-Meyer J. Postoperative wound infection: a prospective study of determinant factors and prevention. *Surgery.* 1969; 66:97–103.

112. Evans C, Pollock AV. The reduction of surgical wound infections by prophylactic parenteral cephaloridine. *Br J Surg.* 1973; 60:434–7.

113. Stone HH, Haney BH, Kolb LD et al. Prophylactic and preventive antibiotic therapy. Timing, duration and economics. *Ann Surg.* 1979; 189:691–9.

114. Bates T, Roberts JV, Smith K et al. A randomized trial of one versus three doses of Augmentin as wound prophylaxis in at-risk abdominal surgery. *Postgrad Med J.* 1992; 68:811–6.

115. McArdle CS, Morran CG, Anderson JR et al. Oral ciprofloxacin as prophylaxis in gastroduodenal surgery. *J Hosp Infect.* 1995; 30:211–6.

116. Meijer WS, Schmitz PIM, Jeeke J. Meta-analysis of randomized, controlled clinical trials of antibiotic prophylaxis in biliary tract surgery. *Br J Surg.* 1990; 77:282–90.

117. Cainzos M, Potel J, Puente JL. Prospective, randomized, controlled study of prophylaxis with cefamandole in high-risk patients undergoing operations upon the biliary tract. *Surg Gynecol Obstet.* 1985; 160:27–32.

118. Meijer WS, Schmitz PI. Prophylactic use of cefuroxime in biliary tract surgery: randomized, controlled trial of single versus multiple dose in high-risk patients. Galant Trial Study Group. *Br J Surg.* 1993; 80:917–21.

119. Grant MD, Jones RC, Wilson SE et al. Single-dose cephalosporin prophylaxis in high-risk patients undergoing surgical treatment of the biliary tract. *Surg Gynecol Obstet.* 1992; 174:347–54.

120. Lapointe RW, Roy AF, Turgeon PL et al. Comparison of single-dose cefotetan and multidose cefoxitin as intravenous prophylaxis in elective, open biliary tract surgery: a multicentre, double-blind, randomized study. *Can J Surg.* 1994; 37:313–8.

121. Strachan CJL, Black J, Powis SJA et al. Prophylactic use of cephazolin against wound sepsis after cholecystectomy. *Br Med J.* 1977; 1:1254–6.

122. Berne TV, Yellin AE, Appleman MD et al. Controlled comparison of cefmetazole with cefoxitin for prophylaxis in elective cholecystectomy. *Surg Gynecol Obstet.* 1990; 170:137–40.

123. Wilson SE, Hopkins JA, Williams RA. A comparison of cefotaxime versus cefamandole in prophylaxis for surgical treatment of the biliary tract. *Surg Gynecol Obstet.* 1987; 164:207–12.

124. Kujath P. Brief report: antibiotic prophylaxis in biliary tract surgery. *Am J Med.* 1989; 87(suppl 5A):255–7.

125. Garibaldi RA, Skolnck D, Maglio S et al. Postcholecystectomy wound infection. *Ann Surg.* 1986; 204:650–4.

126. Levi JU, Martinez OV, Hutson DG et al. Ampicillin versus cefamandole in biliary tract surgery. *Am Surg.* 1984; 50:412–7.

127. Kellum JM, Duma RJ, Gorbach SL et al. Single-dose antibiotic prophylaxis for biliary surgery. *Arch Surg.* 1987; 122:918–22.

128. Muller EL, Pitt HA, Thompson JE et al. Antibiotics in infections of the biliary tract. *Surg Gynecol Obstet.*

1987; 165:285–92.

129. Stone HH, Hooper CA, Kolb LD et al. Antibiotic prophylaxis in gastric, biliary and colonic surgery. *Ann Surg.* 1976; 184:443–52.

130. Elliot DW. Biliary tract surgery. *South Med J.* 1977; 70(suppl 1):31–4.

131. Chetlin SH, Elliot DW. Preoperative antibiotics in biliary surgery. *Arch Surg.* 1973; 107:319–23.

132. Kellum JM, Gargano S, Gorbach SL et al. Antibiotic prophylaxis in high-risk biliary operations: multicenter trial of single preoperative ceftriaxone versus multidose cefazolin. *Am J Surg.* 1984; 148:15–21.

133. Drumm J, Donovan IA, Wise R. A comparison of cefotetan and cefazolin for prophylaxis against wound infection after elective cholecystectomy. *J Hosp Infect.* 1985; 6:227–80.

134. Plouffe JF, Perkins RL, Fass RJ et al. Comparison of the effectiveness of moxalactam and cefazolin in the prevention of infection in patients undergoing abdominal operations. *Diagn Microbiol Infect Dis.* 1985; 3:25–31.

135. Crenshaw CA, Glanges E, Webber CE et al. A prospective, randomized, double-blind study of preventive cefamandole therapy in patients at high risk for undergoing cholecystectomy. *Surg Gynecol Obstet.* 1981; 153:546–52.

136. Leaper DJ, Cooper MJ, Turner A. A comparison trial between cefotetan and cephazolin for wound sepsis prophylaxis during elective upper gastrointestinal surgery with an investigation of cefotetan penetration into the obstructed biliary tree. *J Hosp Infect.* 1986; 7:269–76.

137. Krajden S, Yaman M, Fuksa M et al. Piperacillin versus cefazolin given perioperatively to high-risk patients who undergo open cholecystectomy: a double-blind, randomized trial. *Can J Surg.* 1993; 36:245–50.

138. Sirinek KR, Schauer PR, Yellin AE et al. Single-dose cefuroxime versus multiple-dose cefazolin as prophylactic therapy for high-risk cholecystectomy. *J Am Coll Surg.* 1994; 178:321–5.

139. Maki DG, Lammers JL, Aughey DR. Comparative studies of multiple-dose cefoxitin vs. single-dose cefonicid for surgical prophylaxis in patients undergoing biliary tract operations or hysterectomy. *Rev Infect Dis.* 1984; 6(suppl 4):887–95.

140. Fabian TC, Zellner SR, Gazzaniga A et al. Multicenter open trial of cefotetan in elective biliary surgery. *Am J Surg.* 1988; 155:77–80.

141. Garcia-Rodriquez JA, Puig-LaCalle J, Arnau C et al. Antibiotic prophylaxis with cefotaxime in gastroduodenal and biliary surgery. *Am J Surg.* 1989; 158:428–32.

142. Targarona EM, Garau J, Munoz-Ramos C et al. Single-dose antibiotic prophylaxis in patients at high risk for infection in biliary surgery: a prospective and randomized study comparing cefonicid with mezlocillin. *Surgery.* 1990; 107:327–34.

143. Krige JE, Isaacs S, Stapleton GN et al. Prospective, randomized study comparing amoxicillin-clavulanic acid and cefamandole for the prevention of wound infection in high-risk patients undergoing elective biliary surgery. *J Hosp Infect.* 1992; 22(suppl A):33–41.

144. McLeish AR, Keighley MRB, Bishop HM. Selecting patients requiring antibiotics in biliary surgery by immediate gram stains of bile at surgery. *Surgery.* 1977; 81:473–7.

145. McArdle CS. Oral prophylaxis in biliary tract surgery. *J Antimicrob Chemother.* 1994; 33:200–2.

146. Donohue JH, Farnell MB, Grant CS et al. Laparoscopic cholecystectomy: early Mayo Clinic experience. *Mayo Clin Proc.* 1992; 67:449–55.

147. Frantzides CT, Sykes A. A reevaluation of antibiotic prophylaxis in laparoscopic cholecystectomy. *J Laparoendosc Surg.* 1994; 4:375–8.

148. Watkin DS, Wainwright AM, Thompson MH et al. Infection after laparoscopic cholecystectomy: are antibiotics really necessary? *Eur J Surg.* 1995; 161:509–11.

149. Cann KJ, Watkins RM, George C et al. A trial of mezlocillin versus cefuroxime with or without metronidazole for the prevention of wound sepsis after biliary and gastrointestinal surgery. *J Hosp Infect.* 1988; 12:207–14.

150. Menzies D, Gilbert JM, Shepherd MJ et al. A comparison between amoxycillin/clavulanate and mezlocillin in abdominal surgical prophylaxis. *J Antimicrob Chemother.* 1989; 24:203–8B.

151. Katz S, Glicksman A, Levy Y et al. Cefuroxime prophylaxis in biliary surgery: single versus triple dose. *Israel J Med Sci.* 1993; 29:673–6.

152. Ahmed ME, Ibrahim SZ, Arabi YE et al. Metronidazole prophylaxis in acute mural appendicitis: failure of a single intra-operative infusion to reduce wound infection. *J Hosp Infect.* 1987; 10:260–4.

153. Donovan IA, Ellis D, Gatehouse D et al. One-dose antibiotic prophylaxis against wound infection after appendectomy: a randomized trial of clindamycin, cefazolin sodium and a placebo. *Br J Surg.* 1979; 66:193–6.

154. Gilmore OJ, Martin TD. Aetiology and prevention of wound infection in appendectomy. *Br J Surg.* 1974; 62:567–72.

155. Keiser TA, Mackenzie RL, Feld LN. Prophylactic metronidazole in appendectomy: a double-blind controlled trial. *Surgery.* 1983; 93:201–3.

156. Winslow RE, Rem D, Harley JW. Acute nonperforating appendicitis: efficacy of brief antibiotic prophylaxis. *Arch Surg.* 1983; 118:651–5.

157. Wilson AP. Antibiotic prophylaxis and infection control measures in minimally invasive surgery. *J Antimicrob Chemother.* 1995; 36:1–5.

158. Stone HH. Bacterial flora of appendicitis in children. *J Pediatr Surg.* 1976; 11:37–42.

159. Keighley MR. Infection: prophylaxis. *Br Med Bull.* 1988; 44:374–402.

160. Lau WY, Fan ST, Yiu TF et al. Prophylaxis of post-appendectomy sepsis by metronidazole and cefotaxime: a randomized, prospective and double-blind trial. *Br J Surg.* 1983; 70:670–2.

161. Lau WY, Fan ST, Chu KW et al. Randomized, prospective, and double-blind trial of new beta-lactams in the treatment of appendicitis. *Antimicrob Agents Chemother.* 1985; 28:639–42.

162. Lau WY, Fan ST, Chu KW et al. Cefoxitin versus gentamicin and metronidazole in prevention of post-appendectomy sepsis: a randomized, prospective trial. *J Antimicrob Chemother.* 1986; 18:613–9.

163. O'Rourke MGE, Wynne MJ, Morahan RJ et al. Prophylactic antibiotics in appendectomy: a prospective, double-blind, randomized study. *Aust N Z J Surg.* 1984; 54:535–41.

164. Panichi G, Pantosi AL, Marsiglio F. Cephalothin or cefoxitin in appendectomy? *J Antimicrob Chemother.* 1980; 6:801–4. Letter.

165. Liberman MA, Greason KL, Frame S et al. Single-dose cefotetan or cefoxitin versus multiple-dose cefoxitin as prophylaxis in patients undergoing appendectomy for acute nonperforated appendicitis. *J Am Coll Surg.* 1995; 180:77–80.

166. Salam IM, Abu Galala KH, el Ashaal YI et al. A randomized prospective study of cefoxitin versus piperacillin in appendicectomy. *J Hosp Infect.* 1994; 26:133–6.

167. Lau WY, Fan ST, Yiu TF et al. Prophylaxis of postappendectomy sepsis by metronidazole and ampicillin; a randomized, prospective and double-blind trial. *Br J Surg.* 1983; 70:155–7.

168. Al-Dhohayan A, al-Sebayl M, Shibl A et al. Comparative study of augmentin versus metronidazole/gentamicin in the prevention of infections after appendectomy. *Eur Surg Res.* 1993; 25:60–4.

169. Kizilcan F, Tanyel FC, Buyukpamukcu N et al. The necessity of prophylactic antibiotics in uncomplicated appendicitis during childhood. *J Pediatr Surg.* 1992; 27:586–8.

170. Soderquist-Elinder C, Hirsch K, Bergdahl S et al. Prophylactic antibiotics in uncomplicated appendicitis during childhood—a prospective randomized study. *Eur J Pediatr Surg.* 1995; 5:282–5.

171. Browder W, Smith JW, Vivoda LM et al. Nonperforative appendicitis: a continuing surgical dilemma. *J Infect Dis.* 1989; 159:1088–94.

172. Bartlett S, Burton R. Effects of prophylactic antibiotics on wound infection after elective colon and rectal surgery. *Am J Surg.* 1983; 145:300–9.

173. Burton RC. Postoperative wound infection in colon and rectal surgery. *Br J Surg.* 1973; 60:363–8.

174. Baum M, Anish D, Chalmers T et al. A survey of clinical trials of antibiotic prophylaxis in colon surgery: evidence against further use of no treatment controls. *N Engl J Med.* 1981; 305:795–9.

175. Coppa G, Eng K, Gouge T et al. Parenteral and oral antibiotics in elective colorectal surgery: a prospective randomized trial. *Am J Surg.* 1983; 145:62–5.

176. Coppa G, Eng K. Factors involved in antibiotic selection in elective colon and rectal surgery. *Surgery.* 1988; 104:853–8.

177. Svensson LG. Prophylactic antibiotic administration. *S Afr J Surg.* 1985; 23:55–62.

178. Singh JJ, Wexner SD. Laparoscopy for colorectal cancer. In: Keighley MRB, Williams N, eds. Surgery of the anus, rectum and colon. 2nd ed. London: Saunders; 1999.

179. Davis G, Santa Ana C, Morawiski S et al. Development of a lavage solution associated with minimal water and electrolyte absorption or secretion. *Gastroenterology.* 1980; 78:991–5.

180. Beck D, Harford F, DiPalma JA. Comparison of cleansing methods in preparation for colon surgery. *Dis Colon Rectum.* 1985; 28:491–5.

181. Jagelman D, Fazio V, Lavery I et al. Single-dose piperacillin versus cefoxitin combined with 10 percent mannitol bowel preparation as prophylaxis in elective colorectal operations. *Am J Surg.* 1987; 154:478–81.

182. Wolff B, Beart R, Dozios R et al. A new bowel preparation for elective colon and rectal surgery: a prospective, randomized clinical trial. *Arch Surg.* 1988; 123:895–900.

183. Cohen SM, Wexner SD, Binderow SR et al. Prospective, randomized, endoscopic-blinded trial comparing precolonoscopy bowel cleansing methods. *Dis Colon Rectum.* 1994; 37:689–96.

184. Smith LE, Solla JA, Rothenberger DA. Current status. Preoperative bowel preparation. A survey of colon and rectal surgeons. *Dis Colon Rectum.* 1990; 33:154–9.

185. DiPalma JA, Marshall JB. Comparison of a new sulfate-free polyethylene glycol electrolyte lavage solution versus a standard solution for colonoscopy cleansing. *Gastrointest Endosc.* 1990; 36:285–9.

186. Oliveira L, Wexner SD, Daniel N et al. Mechanical bowel preparation for elective colorectal surgery. A prospective, randomized, surgeon-blinded trial comparing sodium phosphate and polyethylene glycol-based oral lavage solutions. *Dis Colon Rectum.* 1997; 40:585–91.

187. Nichols RL. Prophylaxis for intraabdominal surgery. *Rev Infect Dis.* 1984; 6(suppl 1):276–82.

188. Wapnick S, Gunito R, Leveen HH et al. Reduction of postoperative infection in elective colorectal surgery with preoperative administration of kanamycin and erythromycin. *Surgery.* 1979; 85:317–21.

189. Gahhos FN, Richards GK, Hinchey EJ et al. Elective colon surgery: clindamycin versus metronidazole prophylaxis. *Can J Surg.* 1982; 25:613–6.

190. Dion YM, Richards GK, Prentis JJ et al. The influence of oral metronidazole versus parenteral preoperative metronidazole on sepsis following colon surgery. *Ann Surg.* 1980; 192:221–6.

191. Beggs FD, Jobanputra RS, Holmes JT. A comparison of intravenous and oral metronidazole as prophylactic in colorectal surgery. *Br J Surg.* 1982; 69:226–7.

192. Goldring J, McNaught W, Scott A et al. Prophylactic oral antimicrobial agents in elective colonic surgery: a controlled trial. *Lancet.* 1975; 2:997–9.

193. Washington J, Dearing W, Judd E et al. Effect of preoperative antibiotic regimen on development of infection after intestinal surgery. *Ann Surg.* 1974; 180:567–72.

194. Willis A, Fergunson I, Jones P et al. Metronidazole in prevention and treatment of *Bacteroides* infections in elective colonic surgery. *Br Med J.* 1977; 1:607–10.

195. Hagen TB, Bergan T, Liavag I. Prophylactic metronidazole in elective colorectal surgery. *Acta Chir Scand.* 1980; 146:71–5.

196. Lewis RT, Allan CM, Goodall RG et al. Are first-generation cephalosporins effective for antibiotic prophylaxis in elective surgery of the colon? *Can J Surg.* 1983; 26:504–7.

197. Condon RE, Bartlett JG, Nichols RL et al. Preoperative prophylactic cephalothin fails to control septic complications of colorectal operations: results of a controlled clinical trial. *Am J Surg.* 1979; 137:68–74.

198. Kaiser A, Herrington J, Jacobs J et al. Cefoxitin vs erythromycin, neomycin and cefazolin in colorectal surgery: importance of the duration of the operative procedure. *Ann Surg.* 1983; 198:525–30.

199. McDermott F, Polyglase A, Johnson W et al. Prevention of wound infection in colorectal resections by preoperative cephazolin with and without metronidazole. *Aust N Z J Surg.* 1981; 51:351–3.

200. Jones RN, Wojeski W, Bakke J et al. Antibiotic pro-

phylaxis to 1,036 patients undergoing elective surgical procedures. A prospective randomized comparative trial of cefazolin, cefoxitin, and cefotaxime in a prepaid medical practice. *Am J Surg.* 1987; 153:341–6.

201. Morton A, Taylor E, Wells G. A multicenter study to compare cefotetan alone with cefotetan and metronidazole as prophylaxis against infection in elective colorectal operations. *Surg Gynecol Obstet.* 1989; 169:4–45.

202. Hoffman C, McDonald P, Watts J. Use of perioperative cefoxitin to prevent infection after colonic and rectal surgery. *Ann Surg.* 1981; 193:353–6.

203. Periti P, Mazzei T, Tonelli F. Single-dose cefotetan vs multiple dose cefoxitin—antimicrobial prophylaxis in colorectal surgery: results of a prospective, multicenter, randomized study. *Dis Colon Rectum.* 1989; 32:121–7.

204. Jagelman D, Fabian T, Nichols R et al. Single-dose cefotetan versus multiple dose cefoxitin as prophylaxis in colorectal surgery. *Am J Surg.* 1988; 155:71–6.

205. Shatney CH. Antibiotic prophylaxis in elective gastrointestinal tract surgery: a comparison of single-dose preoperative cefotaxime and multiple-dose cefoxitin. *J Antimicrob Chemother.* 1984; 14(suppl B):241–5.

206. Galandiuk S, Polk HC, Jagelman DG et al. Reemphasis of priorities in surgical antibiotic prophylaxis. *Surg Gynecol Obstet.* 1989; 169:219–22.

207. Arnaud JP, Bellissant E, Boissel P et al. Single-dose amoxycillin-clavulanic acid vs cefotetan for prophylaxis in elective colorectal surgery: a multicentre, prospective, randomized study. The PRODIGE Group. *J Hosp Infect.* 1992; 22(suppl A):23–32.

208. Periti P, Tonelli F, Mazzei T et al. Antimicrobial chemoimmunoprophylaxis in colorectal surgery with cefotetan and thymostimulin: prospective, controlled, multicenter study. Italian Study Group on Antimicrobial Prophylaxis in Abdominal Surgery. *J Chemother.* 1993; 5:37–42.

209. Skipper D, Karran SJ. A randomized, prospective study to compare cefotetan with cefuroxime plus metronidazole as prophylaxis in elective colorectal surgery. *J Hosp Infect.* 1992; 21:73–7.

210. Lumley JW, Siu SK, Pillay SP et al. Single-dose ceftriaxone as prophylaxis for sepsis in colorectal surgery. *Aust N Z J Surg.* 1992; 62:292–6.

211. Hakansson T, Raahave D, Hansen OH et al. Effectiveness of single-dose prophylaxis with cefotaxime and metronidazole compared with three doses of cefotaxime alone in elective colorectal surgery. *Eur J Surg.* 1993; 159:177–80.

212. Karran SJ, Sutton G, Gartell P et al. Imipenem prophylaxis in elective colorectal surgery. *Br J Surg.* 1993; 80:1196–8.

213. Barbar MS, Hirxberg BC, Rice C et al. Parenteral antibiotics in elective colon surgery? A prospective, controlled clinical study. *Surgery.* 1979; 86:23–9.

214. Madsen M, Toftgaard C, Gaversen H et al. Cefoxitin for one day vs ampicillin and metronidazole for three days in elective colorectal surgery: a prospective, randomized, multicenter study. *Dis Colon Rectum.* 1988; 31:774–7.

215. Blair J, McLeod R, Cohen Z et al. Ticarcillin/clavulanic acid (Timentin) compared to metronidazole/netilmicin in preventing postoperative infection after elective colorectal surgery. *Can J Surg.* 1987; 30:120–2.

216. AhChong K, Yip AW, Lee FC et al. Comparison of

prophylactic ampicillin/sulbactam with gentamicin and metronidazole in elective colorectal surgery: a randomized clinical study. *J Hosp Infect.* 1994; 27:149–54.

217. Mendes da Costa P, Kaufman L. Amikacin once daily plus metronidazole versus amikacin twice daily plus metronidazole in colorectal surgery. *Hepatogastroenterology.* 1992; 39:350–4.

218. Roland M. Prophylactic regimens in colorectal surgery: an open randomized consecutive trial of metronidazole used alone or in combination with ampicillin or doxycycline. *World J Surg.* 1986; 10:1003–8.

219. Juul PZ, Klaaborg KE, Kronborg O. Single or multiple doses of metronidazole and ampicillin in elective colorectal surgery: a randomized trial. *Dis Colon Rectum.* 1987; 30:526–8.

220. Kwok SP, Lau WY, Leung KL et al. Amoxicillin and clavulanic acid versus cefotaxime and metronidazole as antibiotic prophylaxis in elective colorectal resectional surgery. *Chemotherapy.* 1993; 39:135–9.

221. Bergman L, Solhaug JH. Single-dose chemoprophylaxis in elective colorectal surgery. *Ann Surg.* 1987; 205:77–81.

222. Goransson G, Nilsson-Ehle I, Olsson S et al. Single- versus multiple-dose doxycycline prophylaxis in elective colorectal surgery. *Acta Chir Scand.* 1984; 150:245–9.

223. Andaker L, Burman LG, Eklund A et al. Fosfomycin/metronidazole compared with doxycycline/metronidazole for the prophylaxis of infection after elective colorectal surgery: a randomized, double-blind, multicentre trial in 517 patients. *Eur J Surg.* 1992; 158:181–5.

224. University of Melbourne Colorectal Group. A comparison of single-dose Timentin with mezlocillin for prophylaxis of wound infection in elective colorectal surgery. *Dis Colon Rectum.* 1989; 32:940–3.

225. Stewart M, Taylor EW, Lindsay G. Infection after colorectal surgery: a randomized trial of prophylaxis with piperacillin versus sulbactam/piperacillin. West of Scotland Surgical Infection Study Group. *J Hosp Infect.* 1995; 29:135–42.

226. Condon RE, Bartlett J, Greenlee H et al. Efficacy of oral and systemic antibiotic prophylaxis in colorectal operations. *Arch Surg.* 1983; 118:496–502.

227. Condon RE. Preoperative antibiotic bowel preparation. *Drug Ther.* 1983; Jan:29–37.

228. Hinchey E, Richards G, Lewis R et al. Moxalactam as single agent prophylaxis in the prevention of wound infection following colon surgery. *Surgery.* 1987; 101:15–9.

229. Jagelman DG, Fazio VW, Lavery IC et al. A prospective, randomized, double-blind study of 10% mannitol mechanical bowel preparation combined with oral neomycin and short-term, perioperative, intravenous Flagyl as prophylaxis in elective colorectal resections. *Surgery.* 1985; 98:861–5.

230. Sondheimer JM, Sokol RJ, Taylor S et al. Safety, efficacy, and tolerance of intestinal lavage in pediatric patients undergoing diagnostic colonoscopy. *J Pediatr.* 1991; 119:148–52.

231. Tuggle DW, Hoelzer DJ, Tunell WP et al. The safety and cost-effectiveness of polyethylene glycol electrolyte solution bowel preparation in infants and children. *J Pediatr Surg.* 1987; 22:513–5.

232. Weber RS, Callender DL. Antibiotic prophylaxis in clean-comtaminated head and neck oncologic surgery.

Ann Otol Rhinol Laryngol. 1992; 101:16–20.

233. Saginur R, Odell PF, Poliquin JF. Antibiotic prophylaxis in head and neck cancer surgery. *J Otolaryngol.* 1988; 17:78–80.

234. Mandell-Brown M, Johnson JT, Wagner RL. Cost-effectiveness of prophylactic antibiotics in head and neck surgery. *Otolaryngol Head Neck Surg.* 1984; 92:520–3.

235. Johnson JT, Yu VL, Myers EN et al. Efficacy of two third-generation cephalosporins in prophylaxis for head and neck surgery. *Arch Otolaryngol.* 1984; 110:224–7.

236. Johnson JT, Myers EN, Thearle PB et al. Antimicrobial prophylaxis for contaminated head and neck surgery. *Laryngoscope.* 1984; 94:46–51.

237. Johnson JT, Yu VL, Myers EN et al. An assessment of the need for gram-negative bacterial coverage in antibiotic prophylaxis for oncological head and neck surgery. *J Infect Dis.* 1987; 155:331–3.

238. Dor P, Klastersky J. Prophylactic antibiotics in oral pharyngeal and laryngeal surgery for cancer: a double-blind study. *Laryngoscope.* 1973; 83:1992–8.

239. Mombelli G, Coppens L, Dor P et al. Antibiotic prophylaxis in surgery for head and neck cancer. Comparative study of short and prolonged administration of carbenicillin. *J Antimicrob Chemother.* 1981; 7:665–7.

240. Myers EN, Thearle PB, Sigler BA et al. Antimicrobial prophylaxis for contaminated head and neck surgery. *Laryngoscope.* 1984; 94:46–51.

241. Robbins KT, Byers RM, Fainstein V et al. Wound prophylaxis with metronidazole in head and neck surgical oncology. *Laryngoscope.* 1988; 98:803–6.

242. Robbins KT, Favrot S, Hanna D et al. Risk of wound infection in patients with head and neck cancer. *Head Neck.* 1990; 12(2):143–8.

243. Tabet JC, Johnson JT. Wound infection in head and neck surgery: prophylaxis, etiology and management. *J Otolaryngol.* 1990; 3:143–8.

244. Girod DA, McCulloch TM, Tsue TT et al. Risk factors for complications in clean-contaminated head and neck surgical procedures. *Head Neck.* 1995;17(1):7–13.

245. Becker GD, Welch WD. Quantitative bacteriology of closed-suction wound drainage in contaminated surgery. *Laryngoscope.* 1990; 100:403–6.

246. Johnson JT, Yu VL. Role of aerobic gram-negative rods, anaerobes, and fungi in wound infection after head and neck surgery: implications for antibiotic prophylaxis. *Head Neck.* 1989; 11(1):27–9.

247. Rubin J, Johnson JT, Wagner RL et al. Bacteriologic analysis of wound infection following major head and neck surgery. *Arch Otolaryngol Head Neck Surg.* 1988; 114:969–72.

248. Brown BM, Johnson JT, Wagner RL. Etiologic factors in head and neck wound infections. *Laryngoscope.* 1987; 97:587–90.

249. Johnson JT, Wagner RL. Infection following uncontaminated head and neck surgery. *Arch Otolaryngol Head Neck Surg.* 1987; 113:368–9.

250. Blair EA, Johnson JT, Wagner RL et al. Cost-analysis of antibiotic prophylaxis in clean head and neck surgery. *Arch Otolaryngol Head Neck Surg.* 1995; 121:269–71.

251. Brand B, Johnson JT, Myers EN et al. Prophylactic perioperative antibiotics in contaminated head and neck surgery. *Otolaryngol Head Neck Surg.* 1982; 990:315–8.

252. Gerard M, Meunier F, Dor P et al. Antimicrobial prophylaxis for major head and neck surgery in cancer patients. *Antimicrob Agents Chemother.* 1988; 32:1557–9.

253. Sharpe DAC, Renuich P, Mathews KHN et al. Antibiotic prophylaxis in oesophageal surgery. *Eur J Cardiothorac Surg.* 1992; 6:561–4.

254. Johnson JT, Yu VL, Myers EN et al. Cefazolin vs moxalactam? A double-blind, randomized trial of cephalosporins in head and neck surgery. *Arch Otolaryngol Head Neck Surg.* 1986; 112:151–3.

255. Johnson JT, Wagner RL, Schuller DE et al. Prophylactic antibiotics for head and neck surgery with flap reconstruction. *Arch Otolaryngol Head Neck Surg.* 1992; 118:488–90.

256. Rodrigo JP, Alvarez JC, Gomez JR et al. Comparison of three prophylactic antibiotic regimens in clean-contaminated head and neck surgery. *Head Neck.* 1997; 19:188–93.

257. Ehrenkranz NJ. Surgical wound infection occurrence in clean operations. Risk stratification for interhospital comparisons. *Am J Med.* 1981; 50:909–14.

258. Fan-Havard P, Nahata MC. Treatment and prevention of infections of cerebrospinal fluid shunts. *Clin Pharm.* 1987; 6:866–80.

259. Keucher TR, Mealey J. Long-term results after ventriculoatrial and ventriculoperitoneal shunting for infantile hydrocephalus. *J Neurosurg.* 1979; 50:179–86.

260. Yogev R, Davis T. Neurosurgical shunt infections—a review. *Childs Brain.* 1980; 6:74–80.

261. Renier D, Lacombe J, Pierre-Kahn A et al. Factors causing acute shunt infection—computer analysis of 1174 patients. *J Neurosurg.* 1984; 61:1072–8.

262. O'Brien M, Parent A, Davis B. Management of ventricular shunt infections. *Childs Brain.* 1979; 5:304–9.

263. Schoenbaum SC, Gardner P, Shillito J. Infection of cerebrospinal fluid shunts: epidemiology, clinical manifestations and therapy. *J Infect Dis.* 1975; 131:534–52.

264. Walters BC, Hoffman HJ, Hendrick EB et al. Cerebrospinal fluid shunt infection. Influences on initial management and subsequent outcome. *J Neurosurg.* 1984; 60:1014–21.

265. Wilson HD, Bean JR, James HE et al. Cerebrospinal fluid antibiotic concentrations in ventricular shunt infections. *Childs Brain.* 1978; 4:74–82.

266. James HE, Walsh JW, Wilson HD et al. The management of cerebrospinal fluid shunt infections. A clinical experience. *Acta Neurochir.* 1981; 59:157–66.

267. Mates S, Glaser J, Shapiro K. Treatment of cerebrospinal fluid shunt infections with medical therapy alone. *Neurosurgery.* 1982; 11:781–3.

268. Horwitz NH, Curtin JA. Prophylactic antibiotics and wound infections following laminectomy for lumbar disc disease. A retrospective study. *J Neurosurg.* 1975; 43:727–31.

269. Savitz MH, Malis LI. Prophylactic clindamycin for neurosurgical patients. *N Y State J Med.* 1976; 76:64–7.

270. Haines SJ, Goodman ML. Antibiotic prophylaxis of postoperative neurosurgical wound infection. *J Neurosurg.* 1982; 56:103–5.

271. Geraghty J, Feely M. Antibiotic prophylaxis in neurosurgery. A randomized, controlled trial. *J Neurosurg.* 1984; 60:724–6.

272. Mollman HD, Haines SJ. Risk factors for postoperative neurosurgical wound infection. A case-control study. *J Neurosurg.* 1986; 64:902–6.

273. Shapiro M, Wald U, Simchen E et al. Randomized clinical trial of intra-operative antimicrobial prophylaxis of infection after neurosurgical procedures. *J Hosp Infect.* 1986; 8:283–95.

274. George R, Leibrock L, Epstein M. Long-term analysis of cerebrospinal fluid shunt infections—a 25-year experience. *J Neurosurg.* 1979; 51:804–11.

275. Bayston R. Hydrocephalus shunt infections and their treatment. *J Antimicrob Chemother.* 1985; 15:259–61.

276. Forrest DM, Cooper DG. Complications of ventriculoatrial shunts. A review of 455 cases. *J Neurosurg.* 1968; 29:506–12.

277. Odio C, McCracken JC, Nelson JD. CSF shunt infections in pediatrics—a seven-year experience. *Am J Dis Child.* 1984; 138:1103–8.

278. Petrak RM, Pottage JC, Harris AA et al. *Haemophilus influenzae* meningitis in the presence of a cerebrospinal fluid shunt. *Neurosurgery.* 1986; 18:79–81.

279. Sells CJ, Shurtleff DB, Coeser JD. Gram-negative cerebrospinal fluid shunt-associated infections. *Pediatrics.* 1977; 59:614–8.

280. Shapiro S, Boaz J, Kleiman M et al. Origins of organisms infecting ventricular shunts. *Neurosurgery.* 1988; 22:868–72.

281. Gardner P, Leipzig TJ, Sadigh M. Infections of mechanical cerebrospinal fluid shunts. *Curr Clin Top Infect Dis.* 1988; 9:185–214.

282. Barker FG II. Efficacy of prophylactic antibiotics for craniotomy: a meta-analysis. *Neurosurgery.* 1994; 35:484–90.

283. Wright RL. Septic complication of neurosurgical spinal procedures. Springfield, IL: Thomas; 1970:26–39.

284. Wright RL. Postoperative craniotomy infections. Springfield, IL: Thomas; 1966:26–31.

285. Tenney JH, Vlahov D, Daleman M et al. Wide variation in risk of wound infection following clean neurosurgery. Implication for perioperative antibiotic prophylaxis. *J Meirpsirg.* 1986; 62:243–7.

286. Savitz MH, Malis LI, Meyers BR. Prophylactic antibiotics in neurosurgery. *Surg Neurol.* 1974; 2:95–100.

287. Malis LI. Prevention of neurosurgical infection by intraoperative antibiotics. *Neurosurgery.* 1979; 5:339–43.

288. Haines SJ. Systemic antibiotic prophylaxis in neurological surgery. *Neurosurgery.* 1980; 6:355–61.

289. Quartey GRC, Polyzoidis K. Intraoperative antibiotic prophylaxis in neurosurgery: a clinical study. *Neurosurgery.* 1981; 8:669–71.

290. Savitz MH, Katz SS. Prevention of primary wound infection in neurosurgical patients: a 10-year study. *Neurosurgery.* 1986; 18:685–8.

291. Blomstedt GC, Kytta J. Results of a randomized trial of vancomycin prophylaxis in craniotomy. *J Neurosurg.* 1988; 69:216–20.

292. Pons VG, Denlinger SL, Guglielmo BJ et al. Ceftizoxime versus vancomycin and gentamicin in neurosurgical prophylaxis: a randomized, prospective, blinded clinical study. *Neurosurgery.* 1993; 33:416–22.

293. Wang EL, Prober CG, Hendrick BE. Prophylactic sulfamethoxazole and trimethoprim in ventriculoperitoneal shunt surgery. A double-blind, randomized, placebo-controlled trial. *JAMA.* 1984; 251:1174–7.

294. Blomstedt GC. Results in trimethoprim-sulfamethoxazole prophylaxis in ventriculostomy and shunting procedures. *J Neurosurg.* 1985; 62:694–7.

295. Djindjian M, Fevrier MJ, Ottervbein G et al. Oxacillin prophylaxis in cerebrospinal fluid shunt procedures: results of a randomized, open study in 60 hydrocephalic patients. *Surg Neurol.* 1986; 24:178–80.

296. Blum J, Schwarz M, Voth D. Antibiotic single-dose prophylaxis of shunt infections. *Neurosurg Rev.* 1989; 12:239–44.

297. Schmidt K, Gjerris F, Osgaard O et al. Antibiotic prophylaxis in cerebrospinal fluid shunting: a prospective randomized trial in 152 hydrocephalic patients. *Neurosurgery.* 1985; 17:1–5.

298. Griebel R, Khan M, Tan L. CSF shunt complications: an analysis of contributory factors. *Childs Nerv Syst.* 1985; 1:77–80.

299. Lambert M, MacKinnon AE, Vaishnav A. Comparison of two methods of prophylaxis against CSF shunt infection. *Z Kinderchir.* 1984; 39(suppl):109–10.

300. Zentner J, Gilsbach J, Felder T. Antibiotic prophylaxis in cerebrospinal fluid shunting: a prospective randomized trial in 129 patients. *Neurosurg Rev.* 1995; 18:169–72.

301. Haines SJ, Walters BC. Antibiotic prophylaxis for cerebrospinal fluid shunts: a metanalysis. *Neurosurgery.* 1994; 34:87–92.

302. Langley JM, LeBlanc JC, Drake J et al. Efficacy of antimicrobial prophylaxis in placement of cerebrospinal fluid shunts: meta-analysis. *Clin Infect Dis.* 1993; 17:98–103.

303. Walters BC, Goumnerova L, Hoffman HJ et al. A randomized, controlled trial of perioperative rifampin/trimethoprim in cerebrospinal fluid shunt surgery. *Childs Nerv Syst.* 1992; 8:253–7.

304. Taffel SM, Placek PJ, Meien M. 1988 U.S. C-section rate at 24.7 per 100 births—a plateau? *New Engl J Med.* 1990; 323:199–200.

305. Lopez-Zeno JA, Peaceman AM, Adashek JA et al. A controlled trial of a program for the active management of labor. *New Engl J Med.* 1992; 326:450–4.

306. Faro S. Infectious disease relations to cesarean section. *Obstet Gynecol Clin North Am.* 1989; 16:363–71.

307. Hemsell DL. Infections after gynecologic surgery. *Obstet Gynecol Clin North Am.* 1989; 16:381–400.

308. Amstey MT, Sheldon GW, Blyth JF. Infectious morbidity after primary cesarean section in a private institution. *Am J Obstet Gynecol.* 1980; 136:205–10.

309. Faro S. Antibiotic prophylaxis. *Obstet Gynecol Clin North Am.* 1989; 16:279–89.

310. Crombleholme WR. Use of prophylactic antibiotics in obstetrics and gynecology. *Clin Obstet Gynecol.* 1988; 31:466–72.

311. Jakobi P, Weissmann A, Zimmer EZ et al. Single dose cefazolin prophylaxis for cesarean section. *Am J Obstet Gynecol.* 1988; 158:1049–52.

312. Duff P, Smith PN, Keiser JF. Antibiotic prophylaxis in low-risk cesarean section. *J Reprod Med.* 1982; 27:133–8.

313. Apuzzio JJ, Reyelt C, Pelosi MA et al. Prophylactic antibiotics for cesarean section: comparison of high- and low-risk patients for endometritis. *Obstet Gynecol.* 1982; 59:693–8.

314. Duff P. Prophylactic antibiotics for cesarean delivery: a simple cost-effective strategy for prevention of post-

operative morbidity. *Am J Obstet Gynecol.* 1987; 157:794–8.

315. Jakobi P, Weissman A, Sigler E et al. Post-Cesarean section febrile morbidity. Antibiotic prophylaxis in low-risk patients. *J Reprod Med.* 1994; 39:707–10.

316. Ehrenkranz NJ, Blackwelder WC, Pfaff SJ et al. Infections complicating low-risk cesarean sections in community hospitals: efficacy of antimicrobial prophylaxis. *Am J Obstet Gynecol.* 1990; 162:337–43.

317. Enkin M, Enkin E, Chalmers I et al. Prophylactic antibiotics in association with cesarean section. In: Chalmers I, Enkin M, Keiser MJNC, eds. Effective care in pregnancy and childbirth. Vol 1. London: Oxford University; 1989:1246–69.

318. Galask R. Changing concepts in obstetric antibiotic prophylaxis. *Am J Obstet Gynecol.* 1987; 157:491–5.

319. Faro S, Martens MG, Hammill HA et al. Antibiotic prophylaxis: is there a difference? *Am J Obstet Gynecol.* 1990; 162:900–9.

320. Stiver HG, Forward KR, Livingstone RA et al. Multicenter comparison of cefoxitin vs cefazolin for prevention of infectious morbidity after nonelective cesarean section. *Am J Obstet Gynecol.* 1985; 145:158–63.

321. Rayburn W, Varner M, Galask R et al. Comparison of moxalactam and cefazolin as prophylactic antibiotics during cesarean section. *Antimicrob Agents Chemother.* 1985; 27:337–9.

322. Benigno BB, Ford LC, Lawrence WD et al. A double-blind, controlled comparison of piperacillin and cefoxitin in the prevention of post-operative infection in patients undergoing cesarean section. *Surg Gynecol Obstet.* 1986; 162:1–7.

323. Fejgin MD, Markov S, Goshen S et al. Antibiotic for cesarean section: the case for 'true' prophylaxis. *Int J Gynecol Obstet.* 1993; 42:257–61.

324. D'Angelo LJ, Sokol RJ. Short- versus long-course prophylactic antibiotic treatment in cesarean section patients. *Obstet Gynecol.* 1980; 55:583–6.

325. Scarpignato C, Caltabiano M, Condemi V et al. Short-term vs long-term cefuroxime prophylaxis in patients undergoing emergency cesarean section. *Clin Ther.* 1982; 5:186–91.

326. Elliott JP, Freeman RK, Dorchester W. Short- versus long-course of prophylactic antibiotics in cesarean section. *Am J Obstet Gynecol.* 1982; 143:740–4.

327. Carlson KJ, Nichols DH, Schiff I. Indications for hysterectomy. *N Engl J Med.* 1993; 328:856–60.

328. Jennings RH. Prophylactic antibiotics in vaginal and abdominal hysterectomy. *South Med J.* 1978; 71:251–4.

329. Allen J, Rampone J, Wheeless C. Use of a prophylactic antibiotic in elective major gynecologic operations. *Obstet Gynecol.* 1972; 39:218–24.

330. Stage AH, Glover DD, Vaughan JE. Low-dose cephradine prophylaxis in obstetric and gynecologic surgery. *J Reprod Med.* 1982; 27:113–9.

331. Vincelette J, Finkelstein F, Aoki FY et al. Double-blind trial of perioperative intravenous metronidazole prophylaxis for abdominal and vaginal hysterectomy. *Surgery.* 1983; 93:185–9.

332. Mayer W, Gordon M, Rothbard MJ. Prophylactic antibiotics. Use in hysterectomy. *N Y State J Med.* 1976; 76:2144–7.

333. Wheeless CR Jr, Dorsey JH, Wharton LR Jr. An evaluation of prophylactic doxycycline in hysterectomy patients. *J Reprod Med.* 1978; 21:146–50.

334. Hemsell D, Johnson ER, Hemsell PG et al. Cefazolin is inferior to cefotetan as single-dose prophylaxis for women undergoing elective total abdominal hysterectomy. *Clin Infect Dis.* 1995; 20:677–84.

335. Goosenberg J, Emich JP Jr, Schwarz RH. Prophylactic antibiotics in vaginal hysterectomy. *Am J Obstet Gynecol.* 1969; 105:503–6.

336. Soper DE, Bump RC, Hurt GW. Wound infection after abdominal hysterectomy: effect of the depth of subcutaneous tissue. *Am J Obstet Gynecol.* 1995; 173:465–71.

337. Marsden DE, Cavanagh D, Wisniewski BJ et al. Factors affecting the incidence of infectious morbidity after radical hysterectomy. *Am J Obstet Gynecol.* 1985; 152:817–21.

338. Mann W, Orr J, Shingleton H et al. Perioperative influences on infectious morbidity in radical hysterectomy. *Gynecol Oncol.* 1981; 11:207–12.

339. Rein MF. Vulvovaginitis and cervicitis. Mandell GL, Bennett JE, Dolin R, eds. Principles and practice of infectious diseases. 4th ed. New York: Churchill Livingstone; 1995:1070–5.

340. Ohm MJ, Galask RP. The effect of antibiotic prophylaxis on patients undergoing vaginal operations. II. Alterations of microbial flora. *Am J Obstet Gynecol.* 1975; 123:597–604.

341. Ohm MJ, Galask RP. The effect of antibiotic prophylaxis on patients undergoing total abdominal hysterectomy. II. Alterations of microbial flora. *Am J Obstet Gynecol.* 1976; 125:448–54.

342. Appelbaum P, Moodley J, Chatterton S et al. Metronidazole in the prophylaxis and treatment of anaerobic infection. *S Afr Med J.* 1978; 1:703–6.

343. Ledger WJ, Sweet RL, Headington JT. Prophylactic cephaloridine in the prevention of postoperative pelvic infections in premenopausal women undergoing vaginal hysterectomy. *Am J Obstet Gynecol.* 1972; 115:766–74.

344. Breeden JT, Mayo JE. Low-dose prophylactic antibiotics in vaginal hysterectomy. *Obstet Gynecol.* 1974; 43:379–85.

345. Glover MW, Van Nagell JR Jr. The effect of prophylactic ampicillin on pelvic infection following vaginal hysterectomy. *Am J Obstet Gynecol.* 1976; 126:385–8.

346. Lett WJ, Ansbacher R, Davison BL et al. Prophylactic antibiotics for women undergoing vaginal hysterectomy. *J Reprod Med.* 1977; 19:51–4.

347. Holman J, McGowan J, Thompson J. Perioperative antibiotics in major elective gynecologic surgery. *South Med J.* 1978; 71:417–20.

348. Roberts JM, Homesley HD. Low-dose carbenicillin prophylaxis for vaginal and abdominal hysterectomy. *Obstet Gynecol.* 1978; 52:83–7.

349. Mickal A, Curole D, Lewis C. Cefoxitin sodium: double-blind vaginal hysterectomy prophylaxis in premenopausal patients. *Obstet Gynecol.* 1980; 56:222–5.

350. Hemsell DL, Cunningham FG, Kappus S et al. Cefoxitin for prophylaxis in premenopausal women undergoing vaginal hysterectomy. *Obstet Gynecol.* 1980; 56:629–34.

351. Polk B, Tager I, Shapiro M et al. Randomized clinical trial of perioperative cefazolin in preventing infection after hysterectomy. *Lancet.* 1980; 1:437–40.

352. Savage EW, Thadepalli H, Rambhatla K et al. Minocycline prophylaxis in elective hysterectomy. *J Reprod Med.* 1984; 29:81–7.

353. Davey PG, Duncan ID, Edward D et al. Cost-benefit analysis of cephradine and mezlocillin prophylaxis for abdominal and vaginal hysterectomy. *Br J Obstet Gynaecol.* 1988; 95:1170–7.

354. Willis A, Bullen C, Ferguson I et al. Metronidazole in the prevention and treatment of *Bacteroides* infection in gynaecological patients. *Lancet.* 1974; 2:1540–3.

355. Mozzillo N, Diongi R, Ventriglia L. Multicenter study of aztreonam in the prophylaxis of colorectal, gynecologic and urologic surgery. *Chemotherapy.* 1989; 35(suppl 1):58–71.

356. Hamod KA, Spence MR, Roshenshein NB et al. Single and multidose prophylaxis in vaginal hysterectomy: a comparison of sodium cephalothin and metronidazole. *Am J Obstet Gynecol.* 1980; 136:976–9.

357. Friese S, Willems FTC, Loriaux SM et al. Prophylaxis in gynaecological surgery: a prospective, randomized comparison between single-dose prophylaxis with amoxicillin/clavulanate and the combination of cefuroxime and metronidazole. *J Antimicrob Chemother.* 1989; 24(suppl B):213–6.

358. Benigno BB, Evard J, Faro S et al. A comparison of piperacillin, cephalothin, and cefoxitin in the prevention of postoperative infections in patients undergoing vaginal hysterectomy. *Surg Gynecol Obstet.* 1986; 163:421–7.

359. Faro S, Pastorek JG, Aldridge KE et al. Randomized, double-blind comparison of mezlocillin versus cefoxitin prophylaxis for vaginal hysterectomy. *Surg Gynecol Obstet.* 1988; 166:431–5.

360. Grossman J, Greco T, Minkin MJ et al. Prophylactic antibiotics in gynecologic surgery. *Obstet Gynecol.* 1979; 53:537–44.

361. Rapp RP, Van Nagell JR, Donaldson ES et al. A double-blind, randomized study of prophylactic antibiotics in vaginal hysterectomy. *Hosp Formul.* 1982; 1:524–9.

362. Benson WL, Brown RL, Schmidt PM. Comparison of short and long courses of ampicillin for vaginal hysterectomy. *J Reprod Med.* 1985; 30:874–6.

363. Hemsell DI, Hemsell PG, Nobles BJ. Doxycycline and cefamandole prophylaxis for premenopausal women undergoing vaginal hysterectomy. *Surg Gynecol Obstet.* 1985; 161:462–4.

364. Forney JP, Morrow CP, Townsend DE et al. Impact of cephalosporin prophylaxis on colonization: vaginal hysterectomy morbidity. *Am J Obstet Gynecol.* 1976; 125:100–5.

365. Ledger WJ, Child MA. The hospital care of patients undergoing hysterectomy: an analysis of 12,026 patients from the Professional Activity Study. *Am J Obstet Gynecol.* 1973; 117:423–30.

366. Ohm MJ, Galask RP. The effect of antibiotic prophylaxis on patients undergoing vaginal operations. I. The effect of morbidity. *Am J Obstet Gynecol.* 1975; 123:590–6.

367. Hemsell D, Hemsell PG, Nobles BJ et al. Moxalactam versus cefazolin prophylaxis for vaginal hysterectomy. *Am J Obstet Gynecol.* 1983; 147:379–85.

368. Hemsell D, Menon M, Friedman A. Ceftriaxone or cefazolin prophylaxis for the prevention of infection after vaginal hysterectomy. *Am J Surg.* 1984; 148:22–6.

369. Hemsell DL, Johnson ER, Bawdon RE et al. Ceftriaxone and cefazolin prophylaxis for hysterectomy. *Surg Gynecol Obstet.* 1985; 161:197–203.

370. Soper D, Yarwood R. Single-dose antibiotic prophylaxis in women undergoing vaginal hysterectomy. *Obstet Gynecol.* 1987; 53:879–82.

371. Hemsell DL, Johnson ER, Heard MC et al. Single dose piperacillin versus triple dose cefoxitin prophylaxis at vaginal and abdominal hysterectomy. *South Med J.* 1989; 82:438–42.

372. Blanco JD, Lipscomb KA. Single-dose prophylaxis in vaginal hysterectomy: a double-blind, randomized comparison of ceftazidime versus cefotaxime. *Curr Ther Res.* 1984; 36:389–93.

373. Rapp RP, Connors E, Hager WD et al. Comparison of single-dose moxalactam and a three-dose regimen of cefoxitin for prophylaxis in vaginal hysterectomy. *Clin Pharm.* 1986; 5:988–93.

374. Roy S, Wilkins J. Single-dose cefotaxime versus 3- to 5-dose cefoxitin for prophylaxis of vaginal or abdominal hysterectomy. *J Antimicrob Chemother.* 1984; 14(suppl B):217–21.

375. Roy S, Wilkins J, Hemsell DL et al. Efficacy and safety of single-dose ceftizoxime vs. multiple-dose cefoxitin in preventing infection after vaginal hysterectomy. *J Reprod Med.* 1988; 33(suppl 1):149–53.

376. Roy S, Wilkins J, Galaif E et al. Comparative efficacy and safety of cefmetazole or cefoxitin in the prevention of postoperative infection following vaginal and abdominal hysterectomy. *J Antimicrob Chemother.* 1989; 23(suppl D):109–17.

377. Mercer LJ, Murphy HJ, Ismail MA et al. A comparison of cefonicid and cefoxitin for preventing infections after vaginal hysterectomy. *J Reprod Med.* 1988; 33:223–6.

378. Hemsell DL, Heard ML, Nobles BJ et al. Single-dose cefoxitin prophylaxis for premenopausal women undergoing vaginal hysterectomy. *Obstet Gynecol.* 1984; 63:285–90.

379. Mendelson J, Portnoy J, De Saint Victor JR et al. Effect of single and multidose cephradine prophylaxis on infectious morbidity of vaginal hysterectomy. *Obstet Gynecol.* 1979; 53:31–5.

380. McGregor JA, Phillips LE, Dunne JT et al. Results of a double-blind, placebo-controlled clinical trial program of single-dose ceftizoxime versus multiple-dose cefoxitin as prophylaxis for patients undergoing vaginal and abdominal hysterectomy. *J Am Coll Surg.* 1994; 178:123–31.

381. Multicenter Study Group. Single-dose prophylaxis in patients undergoing vaginal hysterectomy: cefamandole versus cefotaxime. *Am J Obstet Gynecol.* 1989; 160:1198–201.

382. Jacobson JA, Hebertson R, Kasworm E. Comparison of ceforanide and cephalothin prophylaxis for vaginal hysterectomies. *Antimicrob Agents Chemother.* 1982; 22:643–6.

383. American College of Obstetricians and Gynecologists (ACOG). Antibiotics and gynecologic infections. *ACOG Educ Bull.* 1997; 237:1–8.

384. Campillo F, Rubio JM. Comparative study of single-dose cefotaxime and multiple doses of cefoxitin and cefazolin as prophylaxis in gynecologic surgery. *Am J Surg.* 1992; 164:12S–15S.

385. Turano A. New clinical data on the prophylaxis of

infections in abdominal, gynecologic, and urologic surgery. Multicenter Study Group. *Am J Surg.* 1992; 164(4A suppl):16S–20S.

386. D'Addato F, Canestrelli M, Repinto A et al. Perioperative prophylaxis in abdominal and vaginal hysterectomy. *Clin Exp Obstet Gynecol.* 1993; 20:95–101.

387. Orr JW Jr, Varner RE, Kilgore LC et al. Cefotetan versus cefoxitin as prophylaxis in hysterectomy. *Am J Obstet Gynecol.* 1986; 154:960–3.

388. Orr JW Jr, Sisson PF, Barrett JM et al. Single center study results of cefotetan and cefoxitin prophylaxis for abdominal or vaginal hysterectomy. *Am J Obstet Gynecol.* 1988; 158:714–6.

389. Eron LJ, Gordon SF, Harvey LK et al. A trial using early preoperative administration of cefonicid for antimicrobial prophylaxis with hysterectomies. *DICP Ann Pharmacother.* 1989; 23:655–8.

390. Berkeley AS, Orr JW, Cavanagh D et al. Comparative effectiveness and safety of cefotetan and cefoxitin as prophylactic agents in patients undergoing abdominal or vaginal hysterectomy. *Am J Surg.* 1988; 155:81–5.

391. Berkeley AS, Freedman KS, Ledger WJ et al. Comparison of cefotetan and cefoxitin prophylaxis for abdominal and vaginal hysterectomy. *Am J Obstet Gynecol.* 1988; 158:706–9.

392. Gordon SF. Results of a single center study of cefotetan prophylaxis in abdominal or vaginal hysterectomy. *Am J Obstet Gynecol.* 1988; 158:710–4. (Erratum published in *Am J Obstet Gynecol.* 1989; 160:1025.)

393. Mathews D, Ross H. Randomized, controlled trial of a short course of cephaloridine in the prevention of infection after abdominal hysterectomy. *Br J Obstet Gynecol.* 1978; 85:381–5.

394. Duff P. Antibiotic prophylaxis for abdominal hysterectomy. *Obstet Gynecol.* 1982; 60:25–9.

395. Walker EM, Gordon AJ, Warren RE et al. Prophylactic single-dose metronidazole before abdominal hysterectomy. *Br J Obstet Gynaecol.* 1982; 89:957–61.

396. Manthorpe T, Justesen T. Metronidazole prophylaxis in abdominal hysterectomy. A double-blind, controlled trial. *Acta Obstet Gynecol Scand.* 1982; 61:243–6.

397. Ohm MJ, Galask RP. The effect of antibiotic prophylaxis on patients undergoing total abdominal hysterectomy. I. Effect on morbidity. *Am J Obstet Gynecol.* 1976; 125:442–7.

398. Hemsell DL, Reisch J, Nobles B et al. Prevention of major infection after elective abdominal hysterectomy. Individual determination required. *Am J Obstet Gynecol.* 1983; 147:520–3.

399. Berkeley AS, Haywork SD, Hirsch JC et al. Controlled, comparative study of moxalactam and cefazolin for prophylaxis of abdominal hysterectomy. *Surg Gynecol Obstet.* 1985; 161:457–61.

400. Gonen R, Hakin M, Samberg I et al. Short-term prophylactic antibiotic for elective abdominal hysterectomy: how short? *Eur J Obstet Gynecol Reprod Biol.* 1985; 20:229–34.

401. Senior C, Steirad J. Are preoperative antibiotics helpful in abdominal hysterectomy? *Am J Obstet Gynecol.* 1986; 154:1004–8.

402. McDonald PJ, Sanders T, Higgins G et al. Antibiotic prophylaxis in hysterectomy: cefotaxime compared to ampicillin-tinidazole. *J Antimicrob Chemother.* 1985; 14(suppl B):223–30.

403. Mamsen A, Hansen V, Moller BR. A prospective randomized double-blind trial of ceftriaxone versus no treatment for abdominal hysterectomy. *Eur J Obstet Gynecol Reprod Biol.* 1992; 47:235–8.

404. Mittendorf R, Aronson MP, Berry RE et al. Avoiding serious infections associated with abdominal hysterectomy: a meta-analysis of antibiotic prophylaxis. *Am J Obstet Gynecol.* 1993; 169:1119–24.

405. Hemsell DL, Johnson ER, Bawdon RE et al. Cefoperazone and cefoxitin prophylaxis for abdominal hysterectomy. *Obstet Gynecol.* 1984; 63:467–72.

406. Tchabo JG, Cutting ME, Butler C. Prophylactic antibiotics in patients undergoing total vaginal or abdominal hysterectomy. *Int Surg.* 1985; 70:349–52.

407. Hemsell DL, Martin NJ Jr, Pastorek JG II et al. Single-dose antimicrobial prophylaxis at abdominal hysterectomy. Cefamandole vs cefotaxime. *J Reprod Med.* 1988; 33:939–44.

408. Tuomala RE, Fischer SG, Munoz A et al. A comparative trial of cefazolin and moxalactam as prophylaxis for preventing infection after abdominal hysterectomy. *Obstet Gynecol.* 1985; 66:372–6.

409. Scarpignato C, Labruna C, Condemi V et al. Comparative efficacy of two different regimens of antibiotic prophylaxis in total abdominal hysterectomy. *Pharmatherapeutica.* 1980; 2:450–5.

410. Hemsell DL, Hemsell PG, Heard ML et al. Preoperative cefoxitin prophylaxis for elective abdominal hysterectomy. *Am J Obstet Gynecol.* 1985; 153:225–6.

411. Miyazawa K, Hernandez E, Dillon MB. Prophylactic topical cefamandole in radical hysterectomy. *Int J Gynaecol Obstet.* 1987; 25:133–8.

412. Micha JP, Kucera PR, Birkett JP et al. Prophylactic mezlocillin in radical hysterectomy. *Obstet Gynecol.* 1987; 69:251–4.

413. Sevin B, Ramos R, Lichtinger M et al. Antibiotic prevention of infection complicating radical abdominal hysterectomy. *Obstet Gynecol.* 1984; 64:539–45.

414. Rosenshein NB, Ruth JC, Villar J et al. A prospective randomized study of doxycycline as a prophylactic antibiotic in patients undergoing radical hysterectomy. *Gynecol Oncol.* 1983; 15:201–6.

415. Mayer HO, Petru E, Haas J et al. Perioperative antibiotic prophylaxis in patients undergoing radical surgery for gynecologic cancer: single dose versus multiple dose administration. *Eur J Gynaecol Oncol.* 1993; 14:177–81.

416. Christy NE, Lall P. Postoperative endophthalmitis following cataract surgery. *Arch Ophthalmol.* 1973; 90:361–6.

417. Allen HF, Mangiaracine AB. Bacterial endophthalmitis after cataract extraction. *Arch Ophthalmol.* 1974; 91:3–7.

418. Allen HF, Mangiaracine AB. Bacterial endophthalmitis after cataract extraction: a study of 22 infections in 20,000 operations. *Arch Ophthalmol.* 1964; 57:454–62.

419. Fahmy JA. Bacterial flora in relation to cataract extraction: effects of topical antibiotics on the preoperative conjunctival flora. *Acta Ophthalmol.* 1980; 58:567–75.

420. Burns RP. Postoperative infections in an ophthalmologic hospital. *Am J Ophthalmol.* 1959; 48:519–26.

421. Burns RP, Hansen T, Fraunfelder FT et al. An experimental model for evaluation of human conjunctivitis

and topical antibiotic therapy: comparison of gentamicin and neomycin. *Can J Ophthalmol.* 1968; 3:132–7.

422. Burns RP, Oden M. Antibiotic prophylaxis in cataract surgery. *Trans Am Ophthalmol Soc.* 1972; 70:43–57.

423. Ormerod LD, Becker LE, Cruise RJ et al. Endophthalmitis caused by the coagulase-negative staphylococci factors influencing presentation after cataract surgery. *Ophthalmology.* 1993; 100:724–9.

424. Kolker AE, Freeman MI, Pettit TH. Prophylactic antibiotics and postoperative endophthalmitis. *Am J Ophthalmol.* 1967; 63:434–9.

425. Dunnington JH, Locatcher-Khorazo D. Value of cultures before operation for cataract. *Arch Ophthalmol.* 1945; 34:215–9.

426. Dallison IW, Simpson AJ, Keenan JI et al. Topical antibiotic prophylaxis for cataract surgery: a controlled trial of fusidic acid and chloramphenicol. *Aust N Z J Ophthalmol.* 1989; 17:289–93.

427. Apt L, Isenberg SJ, Yoshimori R et al. The effect of povidone-iodine solution applied at the conclusion of ophthalmic surgery. *Am J Ophthalmol.* 1995; 119:701–5.

428. Kattan HM, Flynn HW Jr, Pflugfelder SC et al. Nosocomial endophthalmitis survey: current incidence of infection after intraocular surgery. *Surv Ophthalmol.* 1991; 98:227–38.

429. Christy NE, Sommer A. Antibiotic prophylaxis of postoperative endophthalmitis. *Ann Ophthalmol.* 1979; 11:1261–5.

430. Mahajan VM. Acute bacterial infections of the eye: their aetiology and treatment. *Br J Ophthalmol.* 1983; 67:191–4.

431. O'Brien TP, Green RW. Endophthalmitis. Mandell GL, Bennett JE, Dolin R, eds. Principles and practice of infectious diseases. 4th ed. New York: Churchill Livingstone; 1995:1120–9.

432. Neu HC. Microbiologic aspects of fluoroquinolones. *Am J Ophthalmol.* 1991; 112:15S–24S.

433. Shungu DL, Tutlane VK, Weinberg E et al. In vitro antibacterial activity of norfloxacin and other agents against ocular pathogens. *Chemotherapy.* 1985; 31:112–8.

434. Osato MS, Jensen HG, Trousdale MD et al. The comparative in vitro activity of ofloxacin and selected ophthalmic antimicrobial agents against ocular bacterial isolates. *Am J Ophthalmol.* 1989; 108:380–6.

435. Miller IM, Vogel R, Cook TJ et al., and The Worldwide Norfloxacin Ophthalmic Study Group. Topically administered norfloxacin compared with topically administered gentamicin for the treatment of external ocular bacterial infections. *Am J Ophthalmol.* 1992; 113:638–44.

436. Speaker MG, Menikoff JA. Prophylaxis of endophthalmitis with topical povidone-iodine. *Ophthalmology.* 1991; 98:1769–75.

437. Leibowitz HM, Ryan WJ Jr, Kupferman A. Route of antibiotic administration in bacterial keratitis. *Arch Ophthalmol.* 1981; 99:1420.

438. Starr MB, Lally JM. Antimicrobial prophylaxis for ophthalmic surgery. *Surv Ophthalmol.* 1995; 36:485–501.

439. Walland MJ, Rose GE. Soft tissue infections after open lacrimal surgery. *Ophthalmology.* 1994; 101:608–11.

440. Eron LJ. Prevention of infection following orthopedic surgery. *Antibiot Chemother.* 1985; 33:140–64.

441. Nguyen TT, Garibaldi JA. Cephalosporin vs penicillin. *J Calif Dent Assoc.* 1994; 22:46–55.

442. Boyd RJ, Burke JF, Colton T. A double-blind clinical trial of prophylactic antibiotics in hip fractures. *J Bone Joint Surg.* 1973; 55A:1251–8.

443. Olix ML, Klug TJ, Coleman CR et al. Prophylactic penicillin and streptomycin in elective operations on bones, joints, and tendons. *Surg Forum.* 1960; 10:818–9.

444. Schonholtz GJ, Borgia CA, Blair JD. Wound sepsis in orthopedic surgery. *J Bone Joint Surg.* 1962; 44A:1548–52.

445. Ericson C, Lidgren L, Lindberg L. Cloxacillin in the prophylaxis of postoperative infections of the hip. *J Bone Joint Surg.* 1973; 55A:808–13.

446. Carlsson AS, Lidgren L, Lindberg L. Prophylactic antibiotics against early and late deep infections after total hip replacements. *Acta Orthop Scand.* 1977; 48:405–10.

447. Hill C, Mazas F, Flamant R et al. Prophylactic cefazolin versus placebo in total hip replacement. *Lancet.* 1981; 1:795–7.

448. Lidwell OM, Lowbury EJL, White W et al. Effect of ultraclean air in operating room on deep sepsis in the joint after total hip or knee replacement: a randomized study. *Br Med J.* 1982; 285:10–4.

449. Pollard JP, Hughes SPF, Scott JE et al. Antibiotic prophylaxis in total hip replacement. *Br Med J.* 1979; 1:707–9.

450. Burnett JW, Gustilo RB, Williams DN et al. Prophylactic antibiotics in hip fractures. *J Bone Joint Surg.* 1980; 62A:457–62.

451. Tengve B, Kjellander J. Antibiotic prophylaxis in operations on trochanteric femoral fractures. *J Bone Joint Surg.* 1978; 60A:97–9.

452. Pavel A, Smith RL, Ballard A et al. Prophylactic antibiotics in clean orthopedic surgery. *J Bone Joint Surg.* 1974; 56A:777–82.

453. Henley MB, Jones RE, Wyatt RWB et al. Prophylaxis with cefamandole nafate in elective orthopedic surgery. *Clin Orthop.* 1986; 209:249–54.

454. Fitzgerald RH. Infections of hip prosthesis and artificial joints. *Infect Dis Clin North Am.* 1989; 3:329–38.

455. Buckley R, Hughes G, Snodgrass T et al. Perioperative cefazolin prophylaxis in hip fracture surgery. *Can J Surg.* 1990; 33:122–7.

456. Paiement GD, Renaud E, Dagenais G et al. Double-blind, randomized prospective study of the efficacy of antibiotic prophylaxis for open reduction and internal fixation of closed ankle fractures. *J Orthop Trauma.* 1994; 8:64–6.

457. Cunha BA, Gossling HR, Pasternak HS et al. The penetration characteristics of cefazolin, cephalothin, and cephradine into bone in patients undergoing total hip replacement. *J Bone Joint Surg.* 1977; 59A:856–9.

458. Hedstrom SA, Lidgren L, Sernbo I et al. Cefuroxime prophylaxis in trochanteric hip fracture operations. *Acta Orthop Scand.* 1987; 58:361–4.

459. Harris WH, Sledge CV. Total hip and total knee replacement. *New Engl J Med.* 1990; 323:725.

460. Dreghorn CR, Roughneen P, Graham J et al. The real cost of joint replacement. *Br Med J.* 1986; 292:1636–7.

461. Fish DN, Hoffman HM, Danziger LH. Antibiotic-impregnated cement use in U.S. hospitals. *Am J Hosp Pharm.* 1992; 49:2469–74.

462. Wininger DA, Fass RJ. Antibiotic-impregnated cement and beads for orthopedic infections. *Antimicrob Chemother.* 1996; 40:2675–9.

463. Mauerhan DR, Nelson CL, Smith DL et al. Prophylaxis against infection in total joint arthroplasty. *J Bone Joint Surg.* 1994; 76A:39–45.

464. Liebergall M, Mosheiff R, Rand N et al. A double-blinded, randomized, controlled clinical trial to compare cefazolin and cefonicid for antimicrobial prophylaxis in clean orthopedic surgery. *Israel J Med Sci.* 1995; 31:62–4.

465. McQueen MM, Hughes SPF, May P et al. Cefuroxime in total joint arthroplasty. Intravenous or in bone cement. *J Arthroplasty.* 1990; 5:169–72.

466. Josefsson G, Kolmert L. Prophylaxis with systematic antibiotics versus gentamicin bone cement in total hip arthroplasty. A ten-year survey of 1,688 hips. *Clin Orthop.* 1993; 292:210–4.

467. Nelson CL, Green TG, Porter RA et al. One day versus seven days of preventive antibiotic therapy in orthopedic surgery. *Clin Orthop.* 1983; 176:258–63.

468. Gibbons RP, Stark RA, Gorrea RJ et al. The prophylactic use—or misuse—of antibiotics in transurethral prostatectomy. *J Urol.* 1978; 119:381–3.

469. Ferrie B, Scott R. Prophylactic cefuroxime in transurethral resection. *Urol Res.* 1984; 12:279–81.

470. Upton JD, Das S. Prophylactic antibiotics in transurethral resection of bladder tumors: are they necessary? *Urology.* 1986; 27:421–3.

471. Houle AM, Mokhless I, Sarto N et al. Perioperative antibiotic prophylaxis for transurethral resection of the prostate: is it justified? *J Urol.* 1989; 142:317–9.

472. Fair WR. Perioperative use of carbenicillin in transurethral resection of the prostate. *Urology.* 1986; 27(suppl 2):15–8.

473. Shah P, Williams G, Chaudary M et al. Short-term antibiotic prophylaxis and prostatectomy. *Br J Urol.* 1981; 53:339–43.

474. Morris MJ, Golovsky D, Guinness MDG et al. The value of prophylactic antibiotics in transurethral prostatic resection: a controlled trial, with observations on the origin of postoperative infection. *Br J Urol.* 1976; 48:479–84.

475. Gonzalez R, Wright R, Blackard CE. Prophylactic antibiotics in transurethral prostatectomy. *J Urol.* 1976; 116:203–5.

476. Hills NH, Bultitude MI, Eykyn S. Co-trimoxazole in prevention of bacteriuria after prostatectomy. *Br Med J.* 1976; 2:498–9.

477. Dorflinger T, Madsen PO. Antibiotics prophylaxis in transurethral surgery. *Urology.* 1984; 24:643–6.

478. Matthew AD, Gonzales R, Jeffords D et al. Prevention of bacteriuria after transurethral prostatectomy with nitrofurantoin macrocrystals. *J Urol.* 1978; 120:442–3.

479. Childs SJ, Wells WB, Mirelman S. Antibiotic prophylaxis for genitourinary surgery in community hospitals. *J Urol.* 1983; 130:305–8.

480. Nielsen OS, Maigaard S, Frimødt-Møller N et al. Prophylactic antibiotics in transurethral prostatectomy. *J Urol.* 1981; 126:60–2.

481. Charton M, Vallancien G, Veillon B et al. Antibiotic prophylaxis or urinary tract infection after transurethral resection of the prostate: a randomized study. *J Urol.* 1987; 138:87–9.

482. Ramsey E, Sheth NK. Antibiotic prophylaxis in patients undergoing prostatectomy. *Urology.* 1983; 21:376–8.

483. Slavis SA, Miller JB, Golji H et al. Comparison of single-dose antibiotic prophylaxis in uncomplicated transurethral resection of the prostate. *J Urol.* 1992; 147:1301–6.

484. Raz R, Almog D, Elhanan G et al. The use of ceftriaxone in the prevention of urinary tract infection in patients undergoing transurethral resection of the prostate (TURP). *Infection.* 1994; 22:347–9.

485. Hammarsten J, Lindqvist K. Norfloxacin as prophylaxis against urethral strictures following transurethral resection of the prostate: an open, prospective, randomized study. *J Urol.* 1993; 150:1722–4.

486. Viitanen J, Talja M, Jussila E et al. Randomized controlled study of chemoprophylaxis in transurethral prostatectomy. *J Urol.* 1993; 150:1715–7.

487. Brewster SF, MacGowan AP, Gingell JC. Antimicrobial prophylaxis for transrectal prostatic biopsy: a prospective, randomized trial of cefuroxime versus piperacillin/tazobactam. *Br J Urol.* 1995; 76:351–4.

488. Crawford ED, Berger NS, Davis MA et al. Prevention of urinary tract infection and bacteremia following transurethral surgery: oral lomefloxacin compared to parenteral cefotaxime. *J Urol.* 1992; 147:1053–5.

489. DeBessonet DA, Merlin AS. Antibiotic prophylaxis in elective genitourinary tract surgery: a comparison of single-dose preoperative cefotaxime and multiple-dose cefoxitin. *J Antimicrob Chemother.* 1984; 14(suppl B):271–5.

490. Taha SA, Sayed AAK, Grant C et al. Risk factors in wound infection following urologic operations: a prospective study. *Int Surg.* 1992; 77:128–30.

491. Richter S, Lang R, Zur F et al. Infected urine as a risk factor for postprostatectomy wound infection. *Infect Control Hosp Epidemiol.* 1991; 12:147–9.

492. Klimberg IW, Childs SJ, Madore RJ et al. A multicenter comparison of oral lomefloxacin versus parenteral cefotaxime as prophylactic agents in transurethral surgery. *Am J Med.* 1992; 92(suppl 4):121–5.

493. Charton M, Mombet A, Gattegno B. Urinary tract infection prophylaxis in transurethral surgery: oral lomefloxacin versus parenteral cefuroxime. *Am J Med.* 1992; 92(suppl 4A):4A–118S.

494. Costa FJ. Lomefloxacin prophylaxis in visual laser ablation of the prostate. *Urology.* 1994; 44:933–6.

495. Hall JC, Christiansen KJ, England P et al. Antibiotic prophylaxis for patients undergoing transurethral resection of the prostate. *Urology.* 1996; 47:852–6.

496. Duclos JM, Larrouturou P, Sarkis P. Timing of antibiotic prophylaxis with cefotaxime for prostatic resection: better in the operative period or at urethral catheter removal? *Am J Surg.* 1992; 164(4A suppl): 21S–23S.

497. Burnakis TG. Surgical antimicrobial prophylaxis: principles and guidelines. *Pharmacotherapy.* 1984; 4:248–71.

498. Richet S, Chidiac C, Prat A et al. Analysis of risk factors for surgical wound infections following vascular surgery. *Am J Med.* 1991; 91:171S–172S.

499. Kaiser A, Clayton KR, Mulherin JL et al. Antibiotic prophylaxis in vascular surgery. *Ann Surg.* 1978; 188:283–9.

500. Edwards WH, Kaiser AB, Kernodle DS et al. Cefur-

oxime versus cefazolin as prophylaxis in vascular surgery. *J Vasc Surg.* 1992; 15:35–42.

501. Edwards WH Jr, Kaiser AB, Tapper S et al. Cefamandole versus cefazolin in vascular surgical wound infection prophylaxis: cost-effectiveness and risk factors. *J Vasc Surg.* 1993; 18:470–5.

502. Hasselgren P-O, Ivarson L, Risberg B et al. Effects of prophylactic antibiotics in vascular surgery. A prospective, randomized, double-blind study. *Ann Surg.* 1984; 200:86–92.

503. Risberg B, Drott C, Dalman P et al. Oral ciprofloxacin versus intavenous cefuroxime as prophylaxis against postoperative infection in vascular surgery: a randomized double-blind, prospective multicentre study. *Eur J Endovasc Surg.* 1995; 10:346–51.

504. Bennion RS, Hiatt JR, Williams RA et al. A randomized, prospective study of perioperative antimicrobial prophylaxis for vascular access surgery. *J Cardiovasc Surg.* 1985; 26:270–4.

505. Pitt HA, Postier RG, Mcgowan WA et al. Prophylactic antibiotics in vascular surgery. Topical, systemic, or both. *Ann Surg.* 1980; 192:356–64.

506. Murray BE. Problems and dilemmas of antimicrobial resistance. *Pharmacotherapy.* 1992; 12:86–93.

507. Barone GW, Hudec WA, Sailors DM et al. Prophylactic wound antibiotics for combined kidney and pancreas transplants. *Clin Transplant.* 1996; 10:386–8.

508. Hosenpud JD, Novick RJ, Bennett LE et al. The registry of the International Society for Heart and Lung Transplantation: thirteenth official report—1996. *J Heart Lung Transplant.* 1996; 15:655–74.

509. Kaiser AB. Use of antibiotics in cardiac and thoracic surgery. In: Sabiston DC Jr, Spencer FC, eds. Surgery of the chest. 6th ed. Philadelphia: W. B. Saunders; 1995:98–116.

510. Khaghani A, Martin M, Fitzgerald M et al. Cefotaxime and flucloxacillin as antibiotic prophylaxis in cardiac transplantation. *Drugs.* 1988; 35(suppl 2):124–6.

511. Petri WA Jr. Infections in heart transplant recipients. *Clin Infect Dis.* 1994; 18:141–8.

512. Trulock EP. Lung transplantation. *Am J Respir Crit Care Med.* 1997; 155:789–818.

513. Davis RD Jr, Pasque MK. Pulmonary transplantation. *Ann Surg.* 1995; 221:14–28.

514. Kotloff RM, Zuckerman JB. Lung transplantation for cystic fibrosis. Special considerations. *Chest.* 1996; 109:787–98.

515. Dowling RD, Zenati M, Yousem S et al. Donor-transmitted pneumonia in experimental lung allografts. *J Thorac Cardiovasc Surg.* 1992; 103:767–72.

516. Low DE, Kaiser LR, Haydock DA et al. The donor lung: infectious and pathologic factors affecting outcome in lung transplantation. *J Thorac Cardiovasc Surg.* 1993; 106:614–21.

517. Steinbach S, Sun L, Jiang R-Z et al. Transmissibility of *Pseudomonas cepacia* infection in clinic patients and lung-transplant recipients with cystic fibrosis. *New Engl J Med.* 1994; 331:981–7.

518. Zenati M, Dowling RD, Dummer JS et al. Influence of the donor lung on development of early infections in lung transplant recipients. *J Heart Transplant.* 1990; 9:502–9.

519. Dauber JH, Paradis IL, Dummer JS. Infectious complications in pulmonary allograft recipients. *Clin Chest Med.* 1990; 11:291–308.

520. Deusch E, End A, Grimm M et al. Early bacterial infections in lung transplant recipients. *Chest.* 1993; 104:1412–6.

521. Paradis IL, Williams P. Infection after lung transplantation. *Semin Respir Infect.* 1993; 8:207–15.

522. Noyes BE, Kurland G, Orenstein DM. Lung and heart-lung transplantation in children. *Pediatr Pulmonol.* 1997; 23:39–48.

523. Kibbler CC. Infections in liver transplantation: risk factors and strategies for prevention. *J Hosp Infect.* 1995; 30(suppl):209–17.

524. Wade JJ, Rolando N, Hayllar K et al. Bacterial and fungal infections after liver transplantation: an analysis of 284 patients. *Hepatology.* 1995; 21:1328–36.

525. Arnow PM, Carandang GC, Zabner R et al. Randomized controlled trial of selective bowel decontamination for prevention of infections following liver transplantation. *Clin Infect Dis.* 1996; 22:997–1003.

526. Colonna JO II, Drew WJ, Brill JE et al. Infectious complications in liver transplantation. *Arch Surg.* 1988; 123:360–4.

527. George DL, Arnow PM, Fox AS et al. Bacterial infection as a complication of liver transplantation: epidemiology and risk factors. *Rev Infect Dis.* 1991; 13:387–96.

528. Uemoto S, Tanaka K, Fujita S et al. Infectious complications in living related liver transplantation. *J Pediatr Surg.* 1994; 29:514–7.

529. Kusne S, Dummer JS, Singh N et al. Infections after liver transplantation. An analysis of 101 consecutive cases. *Medicine.* 1988; 67:132–43.

530. Arnow PM, Furmaga K, Flaherty JP et al. Microbiological efficacy and pharmacokinetics of prophylactic antibiotics in liver transplant patients. *Antimicrob Agents Chemother.* 1992; 36:2125–30.

531. Gorensek MJ, Carey WD, Washington JA II et al. Selective bowel decontamination with quinolones and nystatin reduces gram-negative and fungal infections in orthotopic liver transplant recipients. *Cleve Clin J Med.* 1993; 60:139–44.

532. Bion JF, Badger I, Crosby HA et al. Selective decontamination of the digestive tract reduces gram-negative pulmonary colonization but not systemic endotoxemia in patients undergoing elective liver transplantation. *Crit Care Med.* 1994; 22:40–9.

533. Raakow R, Steffen R, Lefebre B et al. Selective bowel decontamination effectively prevents gram-negative bacterial infections after liver transplantations. *Transplant Proc.* 1990; 22:1556–7.

534. Weisner RH, Hermans PE, Rakela J et al. Selective bowel decontamination to decrease gram-negative aerobic bacterial and candidal colonization and prevent infection after orthotopic liver transplantation. *Transplantation.* 1988; 45:570–4.

535. Barker RJ, Mayes JT, Schulak JA. Wound abscesses following retroperitoneal pancreas transplantation. *Clin Transplant.* 1991; 5:403–7.

536. Douzdjian V, Abecassis MM, Cooper JL et al. Incidence, management, and significance of surgical complications after pancreas-kidney transplantation. *Surg Gynecol Obstet.* 1993; 177:451–6.

537. Everett JE, Wahoff DC, Statz C et al. Characterization and impact of wound infection after pancreas transplantation. *Arch Surg.* 1994; 129:1310–7.

538. Ozaki CF, Stratta RJ, Taylor RJ et al. Surgical compli-

cations in solitary pancreas and combined pancreas-kidney transplantations. *Am J Surg.* 1992; 164:546–51.

539. Sollinger HW, Ploeg RJ, Eckhoff DE et al. Two hundred consecutive simultaneous pancreas-kidney transplants with bladder drainage. *Surgery.* 1993; 114:736–44.

540. Freise CE, Stock PG, Roberts JP et al. Low postoperative wound infection rates are possible following simultaneous pancreas-kidney transplantation. *Transplant Proc.* 1995; 27:3069–70.

541. Smets YFC, van der Pijl JW, van Dissel JT et al. Major bacterial and fungal infections after 50 simultaneous pancreas-kidney transplantations. *Transplant Proc.* 1995; 27:3089–90.

542. Douzdjian V, Gugliuzza KK. Wound complications after simultaneous pancreas-kidney transplants: midline versus transverse incision. *Transplant Proc.* 1995; 27:3130–2.

543. Stratta RJ, Taylor RJ, Gill IS. Pancreas transplantation: a managed cure approach to diabetes. *Curr Probl Surg.* 1996; 33:709–816.

544. U.S. Renal Data System. 1995 annual report. *Am J Kidney Dis.* 1995; 26:S1–186.

545. Cohen J, Rees AJ, Williams G. A prospective randomized controlled trial of perioperative antibiotic prophylaxis in renal transplantation. *J Hosp Infect.* 1988; 11:357–63.

546. Hoy WE, May AG, Freeman RB. Primary renal transplant wound infections. *N Y State J Med.* 1981; 81:1469–73.

547. Kohlberg WI, Tellis VA, Bhat DJ et al. Wound infections after transplant nephrectomy. *Arch Surg.* 1980; 115:645–6.

548. Muakkassa WF, Goldman MH, Mendez-Picon G et al. Wound infections in renal transplant patients. *J Urol.* 1983; 130:17–9.

549. Novick AC. The value of intraoperative antibiotics in preventing renal transplant wound infections. *J Urol.* 1981; 125:151–2.

550. Ramos E, Karmi S, Alongi SV et al. Infectious complications in renal transplant recipients. *South Med J.* 1980; 73:752–4.

551. Rubin RH, Wolfson JS, Cosimi AB et al. Infection in the renal transplant recipient. *Am J Med.* 1981; 70:405–11.

552. Tilney NL, Strom TB, Vineyard GC et al. Factors contributing to the declining mortality rate in renal transplantation. *New Engl J Med.* 1978; 299:1321–5.

553. Lai M-K, Huang C-C, Chu S-H et al. Surgical complications in renal transplantation. *Transplant Proc.* 1994; 26:2165–6.

554. Schmaldienst S, Hoerl WH. Bacterial infections after renal transplantation. *Nephron.* 1997; 75:140–53.

555. Koyle MA, Glasscock RJ, Ward HJ et al. Declining incidence of wound infection in cadaveric renal transplant recipient. *Urology.* 1988; 31:103–6.

556. Judson RT. Wound infection following renal transplantation. *Aust N Z J Surg.* 1984; 54:223–4.

557. Del Rio G, Dalet F, Chechile G. Antimicrobial prophylaxis in urologic surgery: does it give some benefit? *Eur Urol.* 1993; 24:305–12.

558. Stephan RN, Munschauer CE, Kumar MSA. Surgical wound infection in renal transplantation. Outcome data in 102 consecutive patients without perioperative systemic antibiotic coverage. *Arch Surg.* 1997; 132:1315–9.

559. Capocasale E, Mazzoni MP, Tondo S et al. Antimicrobial prophylaxis with ceftriaxone in renal transplantation. Prospective study of 170 patients. *Chemotherapy.* 1994; 40:435–40.

Developed through the ASHP Commission on Therapeutics and approved by the ASHP Board of Directors on April 21, 1999. Supersedes an earlier version dated April 22, 1992.

Pharmacy, School of Pharmacy, University of California, San Francisco, CA.

[c]During the development of these guidelines, Dr. Dotson Jaggers was a Clinical Affairs Associate, ASHP.

The recommendations in this document do not indicate an exclusive course of treatment to be followed. Variations, taking into account individual circumstances, may be appropriate.

The bibliographic citation for this document is as follows: American Society of Health-System Pharmacists. ASHP therapeutic guidelines on antimicrobial prophylaxis in surgery. *Am J Health-Syst Pharm.* 1999; 56:1839–88.

Sedation, Analgesia, and Neuromuscular Blockade of the Critically Ill Adult: Revised Clinical Practice Guidelines for 2002

The critically ill and injured patient is invariably anxious, confused, uncomfortable, and in pain from immobility, wounds, and indwelling tubes and is generally distressed by the adverse environs of the intensive care unit. The restlessness associated with critical illness must nearly always, by necessity, be quelled with sedation and analgesia. Clinicians must sometimes use neuromuscular blockade as a last resort. The knowledge and practice of using sedatives, analgesics, and neuromuscular receptor blocking agents originated in and migrated out of the operating theater and postanesthesia recovery units. However, critical care clinicians have discovered that the sustained use of these agents in intentive care units has consequences that are different from those seen in the immediate perioperative period.

The Society of Critical Care Medicine (SCCM) and the American College of Critical Care Medicine (ACCM) systematically reviewed, developed, and, in 1995, published clinical practice guidelines (CPGs) for sedation, analgesia, and neuromuscular blockade in the critically ill patient.[1,2] These CPGs are the most popular and requested of the SCCM and ACCM documents because of the complexities involved in achieving appropriate levels of sedation and analgesia without inducing complications. Recommendations stemming from the 1995 CPGs, although evidence based, were limited because of the lack of prospective randomized trials comparing agents. Since that time, new evidence has emerged and ACCM believes that the CPGs require updating. ACCM and SCCM have joined forces with the American Society of Health-System Pharmacists (ASHP) to develop new CPGs on the sustained use of sedatives, analgesics, and neuromuscular blocking agents in the critically ill adult.[3,4] The quality of care can be improved by implementing the best known and tested standards, measuring the consequences of what we do, and reducing variability found in practice through the use of protocols. CPGs, in tandem with protocol development, can serve as educational tools, improve outcomes, and reduce costs.[5,6] Evidence suggests that, in real practice, recommendations such as these are often not followed.[7]

"Clinical practice guidelines" are defined by the Institute of Medicine as "systematically developed statements to assist the practitioner and patient in decisions about appropriate health care for specific clinical circumstances."[8] Clinicians need to differentiate CPGs from a summary or review article.[9–11] CPGs are vitally different from review articles and greatly valued for several reasons. Ideally, CPGs are created by a multidisciplinary task force of clinicians, including physicians, nurses, and pharmacists, as well as other health care professionals,

under the auspices of the recommendations developed by critical evaluation of the graded scientific literature. CPGs are typically more comprehensive and far-reaching in scope than review articles and serve as virtual guiding lights by providing a useful construct of available evidence and expert decision-making against which individual decisions by clinicians and programs can be evaluated.[12]

A comprehensive literature search was performed to develop the CPGs. Published studies identified through a MEDLINE search (Sedation and Analgesia 1994–2001; Neuromuscular blocking agents 1994–2001) were reviewed, as were the reference lists of the retrieved documents and abstracts from meetings of professional associations. The literature was critically evaluated for research design, patient selection, medication dose, administration route, combination treatment, test measures, statistics, and results.

The medical literature ranged in quality from prospective randomized trials and retrospective observations to expert opinions (Table 1). Pertinent references were assigned a score to account for variance in quality. The recommendations of SCCM, ACCM, and ASHP (Joint Task Force) were graded according to the strength and quality of the scientific evidence (Table 2). A substantial effort was made by the Joint Task Force to adhere to the methodology for developing scientifically sound CPGs as prescribed by the American Medical Association, the Institute of Medicine, and the Canadian Medical Association.[13–17] The 2002 clinical practice guidelines state the rationale, benefits, and harms of the recommendations, describe the expected health outcomes, and cite and rank the evidence. These CPGs will be reviewed and updated in three to five years.

There are major additions, besides the updating of the science, to the 2001 CPGs being issued by the Joint Task Force,[3,4] compared with the 1995 guidelines. These guide-

Table 1.
Categories of Literature Evaluation[a]

Level	Type of Evidence
1	Results from a single PRCT[b] or from a meta-analysis of PRCTs
2	Results from a single PRCT or from a meta-analysis of PRCTs, in which the confidence interval for the treatment effect overlaps the minimal clinically important benefit
3	Results from nonrandomized, concurrent, cohort studies
4	Results from nonrandomized, historical, cohort studies
5	Results from case series
6	Recommendation based on expert opinion

[a]After the authors have identified and classified their respective studies, they grade the articles on the basis of the results of the review.
[b]PRCT = prospective, randomized, controlled trial.

Table 2.
Grades of Recommendations

Grade	Type of Evidence
A	Methods strong, results consistent, PRCTs[a], no heterogeneity
B	Methods strong, results inconsistent, PRCTs, heterogeneity present
C	Methods weak, observational studies

[a]PRCT = prospective, randomized, controlled trial.

lines are the most comprehensive documents in the fields of sedation, analgesia, and neuromuscular blockade of the critically ill patient. Graded recommendations are provided and summarized in list form for efficient review at the end of each document. Clear one-page algorithms are also included in each document for sedation, analgesia, and neuromuscular blockade. There is a special focus on appropriate goals for treatment and an absolute insistence on monitoring the level of sedation, pain relief, and the degree of neuromuscular blockade or weakness to better titrate pharmacologic therapy. Moreover, tapering high-dose opioids or sedatives after prolonged treatment (more than a week) is now formally recommended to avoid withdrawal symptoms. Sleep deprivation, its contribution to states of agitation and delirium, and therapeutic approaches to relieve insomnia in critically ill patients are given new and special attention. *Use of neuromuscular blockade remains a last resort* and should always be preceded by adequate sedation. It should always be discontinued as soon as possible to avoid complications. Both documents address cost-effectiveness for their respective modalities.[3,4]

The CPGs issued for 2002 are comprehensive and based on available evidence. This field is still constrained by a dearth of high-quality, randomized, prospective trials comparing agents, monitoring techniques, and scoring scales. Critical care clinicians have a clarion mandate to understand these CPGs, to integrate this information in a manner that is appropriate for their practice setting, and to establish protocols to reduce practice variability and the complications that usually accompany variation. Once this information is applied at the bedside, there is a final obligation to measure the effects of its implementation and the ensuing consequences. The recommendations in these documents may not be appropriate for use in all clinical situations. Decisions to follow these recommendations must be based on professional judgment, level of care, individual patient circumstances, and available resources.

References

1. Shapiro BA, Warren J, Egol AB, et al. Practice parameters for intravenous analgesia and sedation for adult patients in the intensive care unit: an executive summary. *Crit Care Med.* 1995; 23:1596–600.
2. Shapiro BA, Warren J, Egol AB, et al. Practice parameters for sustained neuromuscular blockade in the adult critically ill patient: an executive summary. *Crit Care Med.* 1995; 23:1601–5.
3. Society of Critical Care Medicine and American Society of Health-System Pharmacists. Clinical practice guidelines for the sustained use of sedatives and analgesics in the critically ill adult. *Am J Health-Syst Pharm.* 2002; 59:150–78.
4. Society of Critical Care Medicine and American Society of Health-System Pharmacists. Clinical practice guidelines for sustained neuromuscular blockade in the adult critically ill patient. *Am J Health-Syst Pharm.*
2002; 59:179–95.
5. Price J, Ekleberry A, Grover A, et al. Evaluation of clinical practice guidelines on outcome of infection in patients in the surgical intensive care unit. *Crit Care Med.* 1999; 27:2118–24.
6. Luce J. Reducing the use of mechanical ventilation. *N Engl J Med.* 1996; 335:1916–7.
7. Rhoney DH, Murry KR. A national survey of the use of sedating and neuromuscular blocking agents in the intensive care unit. *Crit Care Med.* 1998; 26:A24. Abstract.
8. Institute of Medicine. Clinical practice guidelines: directions for a new program. Washington, DC: National Academy Press, 1990; 38.
9. Ostermann ME, Keenan SP, Seiferling RA, et al. Sedation in the intensive care unit: a systematic review. *JAMA.* 2000; 283:1451–9.
10. Lerch C, Park GR. Sedation and analgesia. *Br Med Bull.* 1999; 55:76–95.
11. Elliot JM, Bion JF. The use of neuromuscular blocking drugs in intensive care practice. *Acta Anaesthesiol Scand Suppl.* 1995; 106:70–82.
12. Wright J, Bibby J, Hughes J. Evidence-based practice. Guiding lights. *Health Serv J.* 1999; 109:30–1.
13. Institute of Medicine Committee to Advise the Public Health Service on Clinical Practice Guidelines. Clinical practice guidelines: directions of a new program. Washington, DC: National Academy Press; 1990.
14. Attributes to guide the development and evaluation of practice parameters. Chicago, IL: American Medical Association; 1990.
15. Quality of care program: the guidelines for Canadian clinical practice guidelines. Ottawa, Ontario: Canadian Medical Association; 1993.
16. Shaneyfelt TM, Mayo-Smith MF, Rothwangl J. Are guidelines following guidelines? The methodological quality of clinical practice guidelines in the peer-reviewed medical literature. *JAMA.* 1999; 281:1900–5.
17. Cook D, Giacomini M. The trials and tribulations of clinical practice guidelines. *JAMA.* 1999; 281:1950–1.

Developed through the Task Force of the American College of Critical Care Medicine (ACCM) of the Society of Critical Care Medicine (SCCM), in collaboration with the American Society of Health-System Pharmacists (ASHP), and in alliance with the American College of Chest Physicians. No external funding was provided.

The bibliographic citation for this document is as follows: Society of Critical Care Medicine and American Society of Health-System Pharmacists. Sedation, analgesia, and neuromuscular blockade of the critically ill adult: revised clinical practice guidelines for 2002. *Am J Health-Syst Pharm.* 2002; 59:147–9.

Clinical Practice Guidelines for Sustained Neuromuscular Blockade in the Adult Critically Ill Patient

The decision to treat a patient in the intensive care unit (ICU) with neuromuscular blocking agents (NMBAs) (for reasons other than the placement of an endotracheal tube) is a difficult one that is guided more commonly by individual practitioner preference than by standards based on evidence-based medicine. Commonly cited reasons for the use of NMBAs in the ICU are to facilitate mechanical ventilation or different modes of mechanical ventilation and to manage patients with head trauma or tetanus. Independent of the reasons for using NMBAs, we emphasize that all other modalities to improve the clinical situation must be tried, using NMBAs only as a last resort.

In 1995 the American College of Critical Care Medicine (ACCM) of the Society of Critical Care Medicine (SCCM) published guidelines for the use of NMBAs in the ICU. The present document is the result of an attempt to reevaluate the literature that has appeared since the last guidelines were published and, based on that review, to update the recommendations for the use of NMBAs in the ICU. Appendix A summarizes our recommendations. Using methods previously described to evaluate the literature and grade the evidence,[1] the task force reviewed the physiology of the neuromuscular receptor, the pharmacology of the NMBAs currently used in the ICU, the means to monitor the degree of blockade, the complications associated with NMBAs, and the economic factors to consider when choosing a drug.

Neuromuscular Junction in Health and Disease

The neuromuscular junction consists of a motor nerve terminus, the neurotransmitter acetylcholine, and the postsynaptic muscle endplate. (Figure 1.) The impulse of an action potential causes the release of acetylcholine from synaptic vesicles (each containing about 10,000 molecules of acetylcholine) diffusing across the 20-nm gap to the postsynaptic endplate. The motor endplate contains specialized ligand-gated, nicotinic acetylcholine receptors (nAChRs), which convert the chemical signal (i.e., binding of two acetylcholine molecules) into electrical signals (i.e., a transient permeability change and depolarization in the postsynaptic membrane of striated muscle).

There are depolarizing and nondepolarizing NMBAs. Depolarizing NMBAs physically resemble acetylcholine and, therefore, bind and activate acetylcholine receptors. Succinylcholine is currently the only available depolarizing NMBA and is not used for long-term use in ICUs.

Nondepolarizing NMBAs also bind acetylcholine receptors but do not activate them—they are competitive antagonists. The difference in the mechanism of action also accounts for different effects in certain diseases. If there is a long-term decrease in acetylcholine release, the number of acetylcholine receptors within the muscle increases. This upregulation causes an increased response to depolarizing NMBAs but a resistance to nondepolarizing NMBAs (i.e., more receptors must be blocked). Conditions in which there are fewer acetylcholine receptors (e.g., myasthenia gravis) lead to an increase in sensitivity to nondepolarizing NMBAs.

Adult skeletal muscle retains an ability to synthesize both the mature adult nAChR as well as an immature nAChR variant in which a gamma subunit is substituted for the normal epsilon subunit. Synthesis of immature (fetal) receptors may be triggered in the presence of certain diseases (e.g., Guillain-Barré syndrome, stroke) and other conditions producing loss of nerve function. These immature nAChRs are distinguished by three features. First, immature receptors are not localized to the muscle endplate but migrate across the entire membrane surface.[2] Second, the immature receptors are metabolically short-lived (<24 hours) and more ionically active, having a 2- to 10-fold longer channel "open time." Lastly, these immature receptors are more sensitive to the depolarizing effects of such drugs as succinylcholine and more resistant to the effects of competitive antagonists, such as pancuronium. This increase in the number of immature acetylcholine receptors may account for the tachyphylaxis seen with NMBAs and some of the complications associated with their use. For the remainder of this document, only nondepolarizing NMBAs will be discussed.

Pharmacology of Neuromuscular-Receptor Blockers

Aminosteroidal Compounds. The aminosteroidal compounds include pancuronium, pipecuronium, vecuronium, and rocuronium (Tables 1 and 2).[3–11]

Pancuronium. Pancuronium, one of the original NMBAs used in ICUs, is a long-acting, nondepolarizing compound that is effective after an intravenous bolus dose of 0.06–0.1 mg/kg for up to 90 minutes. Though it is commonly given as an i.v. bolus, it can be used as a continuous infusion[12] by adjusting the dose to the degree of neuromuscular blockade that is desired (Table 1). Pancuronium is vagolytic (more than 90% of ICU patients will have an increase in heart rate of ≥10 beats/min), which limits its use in patients who cannot tolerate an increase in heart rate.[12] In patients with renal failure or cirrhosis, pancuronium's neuromuscular blocking effects are prolonged because of its increased elimination half-life and the decreased clearance of its 3-hydroxypancuronium metabolite that has one-third to one-half the activity of pancuronium.

Pipecuronium. Pipecuronium is another long-acting NMBA with an elimination half-life of about two hours, similar to pancuronium's. Khuenl-Brady and colleagues[13] conducted an open-label evaluation of pipecuronium compared with pancuronium in 60 critically ill patients to determine the minimum doses required for ventilatory management. The administration of 8 mg of either drug followed by intermittent boluses of 4–6 mg when needed resulted in optimal paralysis. Patients were paralyzed for a mean duration of 62.6 hours (45–240 hours) and 61.5 hours (46–136 hours) with pancuronium and pipecuronium, respectively. No adverse effects were attributed to either drug. Perhaps because of this lack of difference and because there are no recent studies examining pipecuronium's use in the ICU, most clinicians continue to use the more familiar drug, pancuronium.

Figure 1. Neuromuscular Junction. Schematic model of the organization and structure of the neuromuscular junction, with focus and enlargement on the postsynaptic membrane. Agrin is the nerve-derived protein that triggers receptor clustering during synapse formation. Receptor aggregation appears to occur in distinct steps, however, initiated with acetylcholine receptors (AChR) localized together by rapsyn. Meanwhile, D-dystroglycan, the extracellular component of dystrophin-associated glycoprotein complex (DGC), is the agrin receptor which transduces final AChR clustering. This process utilizes the structural organization of additional proteins like utrophin, which stabilize the mature, immobile domains by interaction with the underlying cytoskeleton (actin). When completed, this process concentrates AChR density 1000-fold compared to typical muscle membrane. ACh = acetylcholine, MuSK = muscle-specific-receptor kirase, MASC = MuSK-accessory specificity component. (Reprinted with permission, from Wall MH, Prielipp RC. Monitoring the neuromuscular junction. In: Lake C, Blitt CD, Hines RL, eds. Clinical Monitoring: Practical Applications for Anesthesia and Critical Care. Philadelphia: W.B. Saunders, 2000, Figure 10-3.)

Vecuronium. Vecuronium is an intermediate-acting NMBA that is a structural analogue of pancuronium and is not vagolytic. An i.v. bolus dose of vecuronium 0.08–0.1 mg/kg, produces blockade within 60–90 seconds that typically lasts 25–30 minutes. After an i.v. bolus dose, vecuronium is given as a 0.8–1.2-µg/kg/min continuous infusion, adjusting the rate to the degree of blockade desired. Because up to 35% of a dose is renally excreted, patients with renal failure will have decreased drug requirements. Similarly, because up to 50% of an injected dose is excreted in bile, patients with hepatic insufficiency will also have decreased drug requirements to maintain adequate blockade. The 3-desacetylvecuronium metabolite has 50% of the pharmacologic activity of the parent compound, so patients with organ dysfunction may have increased plasma concentrations of both the parent compound and the active metabolite, which contributes to the prolongation of blockade if the dose is not adjusted. Vecuronium has been reported to be more commonly associated with prolonged blockade once discontinued, compared with other NMBAs.[a] Members of the task force believe that vecuronium is being used with decreased frequency in the ICU.

Vecuronium has been studied in open-label prospective trials.[14,15] In one of these studies, the mean infusion rate for vecuronium was 0.9 ± 0.1 µg/kg/min for a mean duration of 80 ± 7 hours. Recovery of a train-of-four (TOF) ratio of ≥0.7 was significantly longer than with cisatracurium.[15] Recovery time averaged 1–2 hours but ranged from ≤30 minutes to more than 48 hours.

Although Rudis et al.[14] observed no difference in the incidence of prolonged blockade between patients receiving vecuronium with and without concomitant administration of corticosteroids, the opinion of the task force was that patients receiving vecuronium and corticosteroids were at increased risk of prolonged weakness once the drug was discontinued.

Rocuronium. Rocuronium is a newer nondepolarizing NMBA with a monoquaternary steroidal chemistry that has an intermediate duration of action and a very rapid onset. When given as a bolus dose of 0.6–1 mg/kg, blockade is almost always achieved within two minutes, with maximum blockade occurring within three minutes. Continuous infusions are begun at 10 µg/kg/min.[8] Rocuronium's metabolite, 17-des-acetylrocuronium, has only 5–10% activity compared with the parent compound.

Sparr, Khuenl-Brady, and colleagues[8,9] studied the dose requirements, recovery times, and pharmacokinetics of rocuronium in 32 critically ill patients, 27 of whom were given intermittent bolus doses, and 5 received a continuous infusion. The median duration of drug administration was 29 hours and 63.4 hours in the bolus dose and infusion groups, respectively. The mean dose of rocuronium required to maintain 80% blockade was 0.34 mg/kg, and the median infusion rate required to maintain one twitch of the TOF was 0.54 mg/kg/hr. The median time from the last bolus dose to the appearance of TOF response was 100 minutes; in the infusion group, the TOF response returned 60 minutes after the infusion was stopped.

Rapacuronium. Rapacuronium, a propionate analogue of vecuronium, was marketed as a nondepolarizing NMBA as an alternative to succinylcholine. It was withdrawn from

Table 1.
Selected Neuromuscular Blocking Agents[a] for ICU Use

	Benzylisoquinolinium Drugs				
Variable	D-Turbocurarine (Curare)	Cisatracurium (Nimbex)	Atracurium (Tracrium)	Doxacurium (Nuromax)	Mivacurium (Mivacron)
Introduced (yr)	1942	1995	1983	1991	1992
ED$_{95}$[b] dose (mg/kg)	0.51	0.05	0.25	0.025–0.03	0.075
Initial dose (mg/kg)	0.1–0.2	0.1–0.2	0.4–0.5	0.025–0.05	0.15–0.25
Duration (min)	80	45–60	25–35	120–150	10–20
Infusion described	. . .	Yes	Yes	Yes	Yes
Infusion dose (μg/ kg/min)	. . .	2.5–3	4–12	0.3–0.5	9–10
Recovery (min)	80–180	90	40–60	120–180	10–20
% Renal excretion	40-45	Hofmann elimination	5–10 (uses Hofmann elimination)	70	Inactive metabolites
Renal failure	Increased duration	No change	No change	Increased duration	Increased duration
% Biliary excretion	10–40	Hofmann elimination	Minimal (uses Hofmann elimination)	Insufficient data	. . .
Hepatic failure	Minimal change to mild increased effect	Minimal to no change	Minimal to no change	. . .	Increased duration
Active metabolites	No	No	No, but can accumulate laudanosine	. . .	No
Histamine release hypotension	Marked	No	Minimal but dose dependent	No	Minimal but dose dependent
Vagal block tachycardia	Minimal	No	No	No	No
Ganglionic blockade hypotension	Marked	No	Minimal to none	No	No
Prolonged ICU block	. . .	Rare	Rare	Insufficient data	Insufficient data

	Aminosteroidal Drugs			
	Pancuronium (Pavulon)	Vecuronium (Norcuron)	Pipecuronium (Arduan)	Rocuronium (Zemuron)
Introduced (yr)	1972	1984	1991	1994
ED$_{95}$[b] dose (mg/kg)	0.05	0.05	0.05	0.3
Initial dose (mg/kg)	0.06–0.1	0.08–0.1	0.085–0.1	0.6–1
Duration (min)	90–100	35–45	90–100	30
Infusion described	Yes	Yes	No	Yes
Infusion dose (μg/ kg/min)	1–2	0.8–1.2	0.5–2	10–12
Recovery (min)	120–180	45–60	55–160	20–30
% Renal excretion	45–70	50	50+	33
Renal failure	Increased effect	Increased effect, especially metabolites	Increased duration	Minimal
% Biliary excretion	10–15	35–50	Minimal	<75
Hepatic failure	Mild increased effect	Variable, mild	Minimal	Moderate
Active metabolites	Yes, 3-OH and 17-OH-pancuronium	Yes, 3-desacetyl-vecuronium	Insufficient data	No
Histamine release hypotension	No	No	No	No
Vagal block tachycardia	Modest to marked	No	No	Some at higher doses
Ganglionic blockade hypotension	No	No	No	No
Prolonged ICU block	Yes	Yes	Insufficient data	Insufficient data

[a]Based on drugs for use in a 70-kg man. Modified with permission from Prielipp and Coursin. Reference 3.
[b]ED$_{95}$ = effective dose for 95% of patients studied.

the market on March 27, 2001, because of reports of morbidity (bronchospasm) and mortality associated with its use.

Benzylisoquinolinium Compounds. The benzylisoquinolinium compounds include D-tubocuranine, atracurium, cisa-

tracurium, doxacurium, and mivacurium (Tables 1 and 3).[12,15,16,31]

D-Tubocurarine. Tubocurarine was the first nondepolarizing NMBA to gain acceptance and usage in the ICU. This long-acting benzylisoquinolinium agent is rarely used

Table 2.
ICU Studies of Aminosteroidal Drugs[a]

Reference	Type of Study	Patients	Results	Level of Evidence
4	Prospective, observational, cohort	30	Median time to recovery with pancuronium was 3.5 hr in infusion group vs. 6.3 hr in the bolus dose group.	3
5	Prospective, open-label	25 PICU	Increased infusion requirements for pancuronium with anticonvulsants.	3
6	Prospective, open-label	6	Vecuronium clearance increased in 3 and decreased in 2 patients. V_D did not change.	3
7	Survey	. . .	Neuromuscular blockade monitored clinically with only 8.3% using TOF. All respondents indicated concomitant use of sedatives and/or opioids (75%).	5
8	Prospective, open-label	30 SICU	25 trauma patients received rocuronium 50-mg i.v. bolus dose followed by maintenance doses of 25 mg whenever TOF = 2, five patients were on continuous infusion at 25 mg/hr. Duration 1–5 days, recovery approximately 3 hr, and plasma clearance similar between groups.	3
9	Prospective, open-label	32	An initial dose of rocuronium 50 mg followed by maintenance doses of 25 mg with TOF = 2 (n = 27) or by continuous infusion to maintain TOF (n = 5). Pharmacokinetic data tabulated. Crossover with patients reported by Khuenl-Brady et al.[8]	3
10	Prospective, randomized, controlled	20 CABG	Pancuronium (n = 10) was compared to rocuronium (n = 10). Incidence of residual block higher with pancuronium than rocuronium. No effect on time to extubation.	2
11	Prospective, open-label	12 ICU	12 patients, 4 with MODS. Patients given 0.6-mg/kg bolus dose of rocuronium followed by repeated bolus (n = 2) or continuous infusion (n = 10) started at 10–12 µg/kg/min and adjusted to TOF = 1–4. No evidence of prolonged blockade.	3

[a]PICU = pediatric intensive care unit, SICU = surgical intensive care unit, CABG = coronary artery bypass grafting, ICU = intensive care unit, TOF = train-of-four, V_D = volume of distribution, MODS = multiple organ dysfunction syndrome.

Table 3.
ICU Studies of Benzylisoquinolinium Drugs[a]

Reference	Type of Study	Patients	Dose	Results	Level of Evidence
16	Review	. . .	. . .	Review of pharmacokinetics	5
17	Prospective, open-label, controlled	14 with hepatic failure vs. 11 controls	Cisatracurium 0.1-mg/kg i.v. bolus dose	V_D greater in liver patients but no differences in elimination $t_{1/2}$ or in duration of action	5
18	Prospective, randomized, single-blind	20 ICU	Cisatracurium (n = 12) 0.25 mg/kg/hr Atracurium (n = 8) 0.62 mg/kg/hr	Similar mean recovery time	2
19	Prospective, randomized	12 ICU	Cisatracurium 0.1-mg/kg bolus dose + 0.18-mg/kg/ hr infusion Atracurium: 0.5 mg/kg + 0.6-mg/kg/hr infusion	Measured V_D, Cl, $T_{1/2}$. Laudanosine concentration was lower in patients on cisatracurium	2
20	Randomized, open-label	61 ICU	Cisatracurium (n = 26) 0.1-mg/kg bolus, followed by an infusion of 3 µg/kg/min; 14 pts infusion only Atracurium (n = 18) 0.5 mg/kg bolus followed by an infusion of 10 µg/kg/min; 3 pts infusion only Infusion adjusted to one twitch.	118 ± 19 min recovery no change in HR, BP, and ICP with bolus	3

(Continued on next page)

Table 3 (*continued*)

Reference	Type of Study	Patients	Dose	Results	Level of Evidence
15	Prospective, randomized, double-blind, multicenter	58 ICU	Cisatracurium 2.5-µg/kg/min Vecuronium 1-µg/kg/min	Recovery profiles were significantly different with more prolonged recovery noted for vecuronium. TOF monitoring could not eliminate prolonged recovery and myopathy	1
21	Prospective, blinded, cross-over	14 with brain injury	Cisatracurium 0.15 mg/kg bolus Atracurium 0.75 mg/kg bolus	No change in ICP, CPP, CBF, MAP, $ETCO_2$, and HR and no histamine-related symptoms, with $3xED_{95}$ cisatracurium With $3xED_{95}$ atracurium, ICP, CPP, CBF, and MAP decreased within 2–4 min. Five patients had typical histamine reaction; excluding these five patients, there was no difference in any variable compared with cisatracurium	2
22	Observational, prospective, open-label	24 with brain injury	0.1 or 0.2-mg/kg cisatracurium bolus dose	No change from baseline in ICP, CPP, MAP, $ETCO_2$, HR, and CBF velocity in both groups	5
23	Case	. . .	. . .	. . .	4
24	Case	. . .	. . .	. . .	4
25	Review	. . .	. . .	. . .	4
26	Editorial	. . .	. . .	. . .	4
27	Review	. . .	. . .	. . .	5
28	Review	. . .	. . .	. . .	5
12	Multicenter, prospective, double-blind, randomized	40 critically ill	Doxacurium 0.04-mg/kg bolus dose, 0.025-mg/kg maintenance; pancuronium: 0.07 mg/kg bolus dose, 0.05-mg/kg mainte-nance	No difference in adverse reactions or onset of blockade; pancuronium had a more prolonged and variable recovery time	1
29	Prospective, open-label	8 mechanical ventilated ICU with HD monitoring and pHi <7.35	Doxacurium: 0.03-mg/kg load; 0.03-mg/kg/hr infusion	DO_2 + VO_2 decreased, pHi increased; VO_2 is decreased and pHi increased. NMBA causes redistribution of blood flow to splanchnic beds	5
30	Prospective, open-label study	8 ICU with traumatic head injury	Doxacurium 0.05 mg/kg then 0.25 µg/kg/min	No significant effect in HR, BP, ICP. No adverse effects	5
31	Case report	4 with atracurium tachyphy-laxis	Doxacurium 0.25–0.75 µg/kg/min	No tachyphylaxis noted	5

[a]ICU = intensive care unit, TOF = train-of-four, V_D = volume of distribution, HR = heart rate, BP = blood pressure, ICP = intracranial pressure, CPP = cerebral perfusion pressure, CBF = cerebral blood flow, MAP = mean arterial pressure, NMBA = neuromuscular blocking agent, $ETCO_2$ = end tidal carbon dioxide, ED_{95} = effective dose for 95% of patients studied, HD = hemodynamic flow, pHi = gastric mucosal pH, DO_2 = oxygen delivery, VO_2 = oxygen consumption, CBF = cerebral blood flow.

in ICUs because it induces histamine release and autonomic ganglionic blockade. Hypotension is rare, however, when the agent is administered slowly in appropriate dosages (e.g., 0.1–0.2 mg/kg). Metabolism and elimination are affected by both renal and hepatic dysfunction.

Atracurium. Atracurium is an intermediate-acting NMBA with minimal cardiovascular adverse effects and is associated with histamine release at higher doses. It is inactivated in plasma by ester hydrolysis and Hofmann elimination so that renal or hepatic dysfunction does not affect the duration of blockade.

Laudanosine is a breakdown product of Hofmann elimination of atracurium and has been associated with central nervous system excitation. This has led to concern about the possibility of precipitating seizures in patients who have received extremely high doses of atracurium or who are in hepatic failure (laudanosine is metabolized by the liver). There has been only one report of a surgical patient who had a seizure while receiving atracurium.[32]

Atracurium has been administered to various critically ill patient populations, including those with liver failure,[17] brain injury,[21] or multiple organ dysfunction syndrome (MODS), to facilitate mechanical ventilation. In these reports, atracurium infusion rates varied widely, but they typically ranged from 10 to 20 µg/kg/min with doses adjusted to clinical endpoints or by TOF monitoring. Infusion durations ranged from ≤24 hours to >200 hours. Recovery of normal neuromuscular activity usually occurred within one to two hours after stopping the infusions and was independent of organ function. Long-term infusions have been associated with the development of tolerance, necessitating significant dose increases or conversion to other NMBAs.[31,33] Atracurium has been associated with persistent neuromuscular weakness as have other NMBAs.[34–38]

Cisatracurium. Cisatracurium, an isomer of atracurium, is an intermediate-acting benzylisoquinolinium NMBA that is increasingly used in lieu of atracurium. It produces few, if any, cardiovascular effects and has a lesser tendency to produce mast cell degranulation than atracurium. Bolus doses of 0.1–0.2 mg/kg result in paralysis in an average of 2.5 minutes, and recovery begins at approximately 25 minutes; maintenance infusions should be started at 2.5–3 µg/kg/min. Cisatracurium is also metabolized by ester hydrolysis and

Hofmann elimination, so the duration of blockade should not be affected by renal or hepatic dysfunction. Prolonged weakness has been reported following the use of cisatracurium.[38]

Cisatracurium has been compared with atracurium and vecuronium for facilitating mechanical ventilation in several open-label prospective trials.[15,18–21] Cisatracurium infusion rates ranged from 2 to 8 μg/kg/min and were adjusted to clinical endpoints or to TOF count. Infusion durations varied from 4 to 145 hours. Recovery of a TOF ratio >0.7 occurred within 34–85 minutes after drug discontinuation and was independent of organ function. These recovery times are similar to those seen with atracurium[18,21] and less than those observed with vecuronium.[15]

Doxacurium. Doxacurium, a long-acting benzylisoquinolinium agent, is the most potent NMBA currently available. Doxacurium is essentially free of hemodynamic adverse effects. Initial doses of doxacurium 0.05–0.1 mg/kg may be given with maintenance infusions of 0.3–0.5 μg/kg/min and adjusted to the degree of blockade desired. An initial bolus dose lasts an average of 60–80 minutes. Doxacurium is primarily eliminated by renal excretion. In elderly patients and patients with renal dysfunction, a significant prolongation of effect may occur.

Murray and colleagues[12] conducted a prospective, randomized, controlled, multicenter comparison of intermittent doses of doxacurium and pancuronium in 40 critically ill patients requiring neuromuscular blockade to optimize mechanical ventilation or to lower intracranial pressure (ICP). Patients were given another bolus dose based on TOF monitoring and were paralyzed for a mean duration of 2.6 days with doxacurium or 2.2 days with pancuronium. There was a clinically significant increase in heart rate after the initial bolus dose of pancuronium compared with baseline (120 ± 23 versus 109 ± 22 beats/min, respectively) without any differences after the initial dose of doxacurium (107 ± 21 versus 109 ± 21 beats/min, respectively). Once the drugs were discontinued, the pancuronium group had a more prolonged and variable recovery time (279 ± 229 min) than the doxacurium group (135 ± 46 min).

Mivacurium. Mivacurium is one of the shortest-acting NMBAs currently available. It consists of multiple stereoisomers and has a half-life of approximately two minutes, allowing for rapid reversal of the blockade. There are little data to support its use as a continuous infusion in the ICU.

Indications

NMBAs are indicated in a variety of situations (Table 4).[8,9,12–15,17–21,30,39,42] There have been no studies randomizing patients who are considered candidates for NMBAs to a placebo versus an NMBA. We therefore reviewed many studies comparing one NMBA to another to assess the clinical indications for enrolling patients in these studies. The most common indications for long-term administration of NMBAs included facilitation of mechanical ventilation, control of ICP, ablation of muscle spasms associated with tetanus, and decreasing oxygen consumption (Figure 2). NMBAs are often used to facilitate ventilation and ablate muscular activity in patients with elevated ICP or seizures but have no direct effect on either condition. Patients who are being treated for seizures who also take NMBAs should have electroencephalographic monitoring to ensure that they are not actively seizing while paralyzed.

With the exception of atracurium and cisatracurium, which need to be given continuously because of their short half-lives, bolus administration of NMBAs offers potential advantages for controlling tachyphylaxis; monitoring for accumulation, analgesia, and amnesia; and limiting complications related to prolonged or excessive blockade; and improving economics. However, in many ICUs, NMBAs are administered continuously, achieving adequate paralysis and faster recovery with TOF monitoring.

Facilitate Mechanical Ventilation. Numerous reports have described the use of NMBAs to facilitate mechanical ventilation. Most of the reports are limited to case studies, small prospective open-label trials, and small randomized open-label and double-blind trials enrolling a wide variety of critically ill patients to whom NMBAs were given to prevent respiratory dyssynchrony, stop spontaneous respiratory efforts and muscle movement, improve gas exchange, and facilitate inverse ratio ventilation. However, none of these reports compared NMBAs to placebos.

Manage Increased ICP. The data supporting the use of NMBAs to control ICP are limited to a case report and an open-label trial. Prielipp[30] evaluated doxacurium use in eight patients with severe head injury in an open-label prospective study. NMBAs were given to facilitate ventilation or to manage brain injuries. Patients received an initial bolus injection of doxacurium 0.05 mg/kg followed by a continuous infusion of 0.25 μg/kg/min adjusted to maintain one twitch of the TOF. Doxacurium had no effect on ICP, heart rate, or blood pressure. Infusion rates were similar at the beginning (1 ± 0.1 mg/hr) and at the end (1.3 ± 0.2 mg/hr) of the study. TOF responses returned at 118 minutes; a TOF ratio of 0.7 was measured at 259 ± 24 minutes. No adverse events were reported.

McClelland et al.[40] treated three patients with atracurium for four to six days to manage increased ICP. Patients could undergo a neurologic examination within minutes after discontinuing atracurium. No adverse events were reported. There have been no controlled studies evaluating the role of NMBAs in the routine management of increased ICP.

Treat Muscle Spasms. Case studies describe the use of NMBAs in the treatment of muscle contractures associated with tetanus, drug overdoses, and seizures; many were published before 1994.

Anandaciva and Koay[41] administered a continuous rocuronium infusion to control muscle tone in patients with tetanus. Muscle spasms recurred at an infusion rate of 8 μg/kg/min, and neither administering a bolus dose of 0.9 mg/kg nor increasing the infusion rate to 10 μg/kg/min controlled the muscle contractures but did increase heart rate. Switching to a different NMBA could control the spasms.

Decrease Oxygen Consumption. Freebairn et al.[42] evaluated the effects of vecuronium on oxygen delivery, oxygen consumption, oxygen extraction ratios, and gastric intramucosal pH in a randomized, placebo-controlled crossover trial in 18 critically ill patients with severe sepsis. Although the infusion of vecuronium achieved an adequate level of paralysis and improved respiratory compliance, it did not alter intramucosal pH, oxygen consumption, oxygen delivery, or oxygen extraction ratios.

Recommended Indications

There are no prospective, randomized, controlled trials as-

Table 4.
Indications for the Long-Term Use of Neuromuscular Blocking Agents in Critically Ill Patients[a]

Indication	Agents (n)	Study Design	Underlying Diseases	Reference	Level of Evidence
Facilitate Mechanical Ventilation					
Facilitate management	Cisatracurium (40), atracurium (21)	Randomized, open-label	Hepatic failure, sepsis, cardiogenic shock, ARDS	20	2
Beneficial to management	Cisatracurium (12), atracurium (8)	Randomized, single-blind	Cardiac arrest, respiratory failure, postneuro-surgery, trauma, multiorgan failure, asthma, cardiogenic shock	18	2
Facilitate management	Cisatracurium (6), atracurium (6)	Randomized, open-label	Multiple	19	2
Facilitate management	Cisatracurium (28), vecuronium (30)	Randomized, double-blind	Head trauma, intracranial hemorrhage, trauma, ARDS, sepsis, hepatic or renal failure, tetanus	15	2
Optimize mechanical ventilation, increase ICP	Doxacurium (19), pancuronium (21)	Prospective, randomized, double-blind	Not reported	12	2
Facilitate mechanical ventilation	Pipecuronium (30), pancuronium (30)	Prospective, open-label	Head injury, multiple trauma, sepsis, multiorgan failure	13	3
Facilitate mechanical ventilation; dose-finding pharmacokinetic study	Rocuronium (32)	Prospective, open-label	Respiratory failure, multiple trauma, blunt brain trauma	9	3
Facilitate mechanical ventilation; dose-finding pharmacokinetic study	Rocuronium (30)	Prospective, open-label	Multiple trauma and/or blunt brain trauma	8	3
Deterioration in gas exchange	Vecuronium and atracurium (1)	Case report	Respiratory failure in a kidney/pancreas transplant patient	39	5
Control ICP					
Facilitate mechanical ventilation and/or management of traumatic brain injury	Doxacurium (8)	Prospective, open-label	Severe head injury	30	3
Control ICP	Atracurium (4)	Case report	Severe head injury	40	5
Control Muscle Spasms					
Control tetanospasms	Rocuronium (1)	Case report	Tetanus	41	5
Decrease Oxygen Consumption					
Determine effect on oxygen delivery, consumption, and gastric intramucosal pH	Vecuronium (18)	Prospective, randomized, controlled, cross-over	Severe sepsis and septic shock	42	2

[a]ARDS = acute respiratory distress syndrome, ICP = intracranial pressure.

Figure 2. Use of neuromuscular blocking agents (NMBAs) in the ICU.

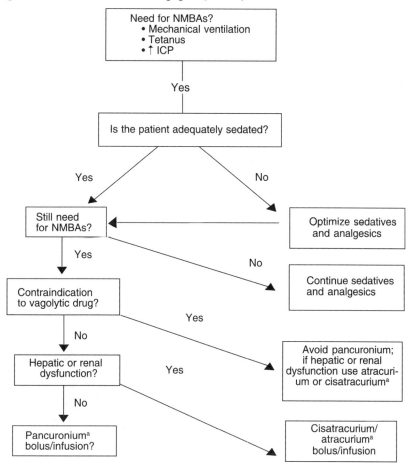

[a]Monitor train-of-four ratio, protect eyes, position patient to protect pressure points, and address deep venous thrombosis prophylaxis. Reassess every 12–24 hours for continued NMBA indication.

signing patients to an NMBA versus a placebo with a goal of documenting if such patients could be managed by means other than NMBA therapy.

Recommendation: NMBAs should be used for an adult patient in an ICU to manage ventilation, manage increased ICP, treat muscle spasms, and decrease oxygen consumption only when all other means have been tried without success. (Grade of recommendation = C)

Recommended Drugs

There has, in essence, been no study since the last guidelines were published that questions the use of pancuronium for the majority of patients in an ICU. Those prospective, randomized, controlled trials (PRCTs) that have been conducted do not clearly show the benefits of using newer agents or any other agents instead of pancuronium.

There are no well-designed studies with sufficient power to make this a level A recommendation, but there is evidence in the literature that patients on pancuronium fare as well as or better than patients receiving any other NMBA.

The two adverse effects of pancuronium that are commented on frequently are vagolysis and an increase in heart rate. Therefore, patients who would not tolerate an increase in heart rate, i.e., those with cardiovascular disease, should probably receive an NMBA other than pancuronium. The indications for the use of an NMBA must outweigh the risk

of tachycardia, and that is based on interpretation of the severity of the patient's underlying cardiovascular disease. For example, a patient with a history of atrial fibrillation now in sinus rhythm and otherwise hemodynamically stable might better tolerate pancuronium than a patient who is hospitalized with cardiogenic pulmonary edema and managed with mechanical ventilation. The clinician should choose an NMBA on the basis of other patient characteristics. Any benzylisoquinolinium compound or aminosteroidal compound could be substituted for pancuronium in these circumstances.

There are no ideal PRCTs that support this recommendation, but there are data suggesting that patients recover more quickly following administration of cisatracurium or atracurium compared with patients receiving other NMBAs if they have evidence of hepatic or renal disease.

Recommendations: The majority of patients in an ICU who are prescribed an NMBA can be managed effectively with pancuronium. (Grade of recommendation = B)

For patients for whom vagolysis is contraindicated (e.g., those with cardiovascular disease), NMBAs other than pancuronium may be used. (Grade of recommendation = C)

Because of their unique metabolism, cisatracurium or atracurium is recommended for patients with significant hepatic or renal disease. (Grade of recommendation = B)

Monitoring

Monitoring neuromuscular blockade is recommended (Table 5).[12,14,43–55] Monitoring the depth of neuromuscular blockade may allow use of the lowest NMBA dose and may minimize adverse events. No PRCT has reported that reducing the dose of an NMBA can prevent persistent weakness. Despite this lack of evidence and the lack of a standardized method of monitoring, assessment of the depth of neuromuscular blockade in ICU patients is recommended.[43]

Visual, tactile, or electronic assessment of the patient's muscle tone or some combination of these three is commonly used to monitor the depth of neuromuscular blockade. Observation of skeletal muscle movement and respiratory effort forms the foundation of clinical assessment; electronic methods include the use of ventilator software allowing plethysmographic recording of pulmonary function to detect spontaneous ventilatory efforts and "twitch monitoring," i.e., the assessment of the muscular response by visual, tactile, or electronic means to a transcutaneous delivery of electric current meant to induce peripheral nerve stimulation (PNS).

Table 5.
Monitoring the Degree of Neuromuscular Blockade[a]

Monitoring Method	Study Design	Reference	Level of Evidence
TOF vs. clinical assessment to guide dosing	Prospective, randomized, single-blind	14	2
TOF vs. clinical assessment to compare depth of neuromuscular blockade	Prospective, nonrandomized	43	4
Complications with various monitoring methods	Retrospective, nonrandomized cohort	44	4
Use of TOF in comparing NMBAs	Multicenter, double-blind, PRCT	12	2
Methods of monitoring NMBAs	Editorial	45	6
Methods of monitoring NMBAs	Review	46	6
Comparison of common NMBAs/pharmacology	Review	25	6
Frequency of NMBA monitoring methods	Nonrandomized, historic, descriptive	47	4
Comparison of NMBA monitoring methods	Editorial	48	6
Comparison of NMBA monitoring methods	Expert opinion	49	6
Comparison of NMBA monitoring methods	Expert opinion	50	6
Technical aspects and problems in NMBA monitoring	Review	51	6
Technical problems with NMBAs monitoring	Review	52	6
Technical problems with NMBA monitoring	Review	53	5
Methods of assessing depth of NMBA	Prospective, randomized, blinded	54	2
Patient assessment during NMBA use	Review	55	6

[a]TOF = train-of-four, NMBA = neuromuscular blocking agent, PRCT = prospective, randomized, controlled trial.

Since the last practice guidelines were published, only two studies have examined the best method of monitoring the depth of neuromuscular blockade, and none have compared the efficacy or accuracy of specific techniques. The first study was a prospective, randomized, single-blinded trial of 77 patients in a medical ICU who were administered vecuronium based on either clinical parameters (patient breathed above the preset ventilatory rate) or TOF monitoring, with a goal of one of four twitches.[44] PNS resulted in a significantly lower total dose and lower mean infusion rate of NMBA as well as a faster time to recovery of neuromuscular function and spontaneous ventilation.

A second study sought to compare the depth of blockade induced by atracurium either by "best clinical assessment" (i.e., maintenance of patient-ventilator synchrony and prevention of patient movement) or TOF monitoring (with a goal of three of four twitches). Analysis of the 36 medical ICU patients in this prospective, nonrandomized trial revealed no difference in the total dose, mean dose, or the mean time to clinical recovery.[43] This may have been due to sample size or study design.

An additional study examining the results of the implementation of a protocol using PNS to monitor the level of blockade in patients receiving a variety of NMBAs found a reduction in the incidence of persistent neuromuscular weakness.[49]

Other methods of electronic monitoring of the depth of blockade are fraught with difficulties; TOF monitoring of PNS remains the easiest and most reliable method available,[43,44,46–50] despite its shortcomings and technical pitfalls.[51–53] Currently, there is no universal standard for twitch monitoring. The choice of the number of twitches necessary for "optimal" blockade is influenced by the patient's overall condition and level of sedation. The choice of the "best" nerve for monitoring may be influenced by site accessibility, risk of false positives, considerations for the effect of stimulation on patient visitors, and whether faint twitches should be included in the assessment of blockade.[54–56] Despite these gaps in research-generated knowledge, evidence-based practice appears to be influencing the increasing frequency with which PNS is utilized.[47] The low correlation of blockade measured peripherally compared with that of the phrenic nerve and diaphragm underscores the importance of three issues: (1) more than one method of monitoring should be utilized, (2) poor technique in using any device will invariably produce inaccurate results, and (3) more clinical studies are necessary to determine the best techniques.

Recommendations for Monitoring Degree of Blockade

Even though the patient may appear quiet and "comfortable," experienced clinicians understand the indications and therapeutic limits of NMBAs. Despite multiple admonitions that NMBAs have no analgesic or amnestic effects, it is not uncommon to find a patient's degree of sedation or comfort significantly overestimated or even ignored. It is difficult to assess pain and sedation in the patient receiving NMBAs, but patients must be medicated for pain and anxiety, despite the lack of obvious symptoms or signs. In common practice, sedative and analgesic drugs are adjusted until the patient does not appear to be conscious and then NMBAs are administered. There have been no studies of the use of electrophysiologic monitoring in assessing adequacy of sedation or analgesia.

In a phenomenological study of 11 critically ill adult trauma patients who required therapeutic NMBA, patients compared their feelings of vagueness to dreaming.[56] Few patients recalled pain or painful procedures. Family members understood the rationale for the use of the drugs and remembered being encouraged to touch and talk with patients. The use of effective pain and sedation protocols and a liberalized visiting policy may have affected the findings.

Recommendations: Patients receiving NMBAs should be assessed both clinically and by TOF monitoring (Grade of recommendation = B), with a goal of adjusting the degree of neuromuscular blockade to achieve one or two twitches. (Grade of recommendation = C)

Before initiating neuromuscular blockade, patients should be medicated with sedative and analgesic drugs to provide adequate sedation and analgesia in accordance with the physician's clinical judgment to optimize therapy. (Grade of recommendation = C)

Complications

Skeletal muscle weakness in ICU patients is multifactorial, producing a confusing list of names and syndromes, including acute quadriplegic myopathy syndrome (AQMS), floppy man syndrome, critical illness polyneuropathy (CIP), acute myopathy of intensive care, rapidly evolving myopathy, acute myopathy with selective lysis of myosin filaments, acute steroid myopathy, and prolonged neurogenic weakness (Table 6).[57,58]

There are probably two adverse events related to prolonged paralysis following discontinuation of NMBAs. We define the first, "prolonged recovery from NMBAs," as an increase (after cessation of NMBA therapy) in the time to recovery of 50–100% longer than predicted by pharmacologic parameters. This is primarily due to the accumulation of NMBAs or metabolites. By comparison, the second, AQMS, presents with a clinical triad of acute paresis, myonecrosis with increased creatine phosphokinase (CPK) concentration, and abnormal electromyography (EMG). The latter is characterized by severely reduced compound motor action potential (CMAP) amplitudes and evidence of acute denervation. In the beginning, these syndromes are characterized by neuronal dysfunction; later (days or weeks), muscle atrophy and necrosis may develop.[59]

Prolonged Recovery from NMBAs. The steroid-based NMBAs are associated with reports of prolonged recovery and myopathy.[57,60] This association may reflect an increased risk inferred by these NMBAs or may reflect past practice patterns in which these drugs may have been more commonly used.[61] Steroid-based NMBAs undergo extensive hepatic metabolism, producing active drug metabolites. For instance, vecuronium produces three metabolites: 3-des-, 17-des-, and 3,17-desacetyl vecuronium.[62] The 3-desacetyl metabolite is estimated to be 80% as potent as the parent compound. The 3-desacetyl vecuronium metabolite is poorly

Table 6.
Weakness in ICU Patients: Etiologies and Syndromes[a]

1. Prolonged recovery from NMBAs (secondary to parent drug, drug metabolite, or drug–drug interaction)
2. Myasthenia gravis
3. Lambert-Eaton syndrome
4. Muscular dystrophy
5. Guillain-Barré syndrome
6. Central nervous system injury or lesion
7. Spinal cord injury
8. Steroid myopathy
9. Mitochondrial myopathy
10. HIV-related myopathy
11. Acute myopathy of intensive care
12. Disuse atrophy
13. Critical illness polyneuropathy
14. Severe electrolyte toxicity (e.g., hypermagnesemia)
15. Severe electrolyte deficiency (e.g., hypophosphatemia)

[a]ICU = intensive care unit, NMBAs = neuromuscular blocking agents, HIV = human immunodeficiency virus.

dialyzed, minimally ultrafiltrated, and accumulates in patients with renal failure because hepatic elimination is decreased in patients with uremia. Thus, the accumulation of both 3-desacetyl vecuronium and its parent compound, vecuronium, in patients with renal failure contributes to a prolonged recovery by this ICU subpopulation. Other explanations have been proposed. One suggests that the basement membrane of the neuromuscular junction acts as a reservoir of NMBAs, maintaining NMBAs at the nAChRs long after the drug has disappeared from the plasma.[63]

Drug–drug interactions that potentiate the depth of motor blockade (Table 7) may also prolong recovery. The specific interaction of NMBAs and exogenous corticosteroids is discussed later.[57,62–65]

Physiologic changes of the nAChRs are enhanced when patients are immobilized or denervated secondary to spinal cord injury, and perhaps during prolonged NMBA drug-induced paralysis. The nAChRs may be triggered to revert to a fetal–variant structure (Figure 3), characterized by an increase in total number, frequent extrajunctional proliferation, and resistance to nondepolarizing NMBAs. The proliferation and distribution of these altered receptors across the myomembrane may account for tachyphylaxis and the neuromuscular blocking effects of these drugs.

AQMS. AQMS, also referred to as postparalytic quadriparesis, is one of the most devastating complications of NMBA therapy and one of the reasons that indiscriminate use of NMBAs is discouraged (Table 8).[65,66] This entity must be differentiated from other neuromuscular pathologies (Table 6) seen in an ICU and requires extensive testing. Reports of AQMS in patients receiving NMBAs alone are quite limited; no experimental model has been able to produce the histopathology of this syndrome by administering NMBAs. Afflicted patients demonstrate diffuse weakness that persists long after the NMBA is discontinued and the drug and its active metabolites are eliminated. Neurologic examination reveals a global motor deficit affecting muscles in both the upper and lower extremities and decreased motor reflexes. However, extraocular muscle function is usually preserved. This myopathy is characterized by low-amplitude CMAPs, and muscle fibrillations but normal (or nearly normal) sensory nerve conduction studies.[63,67] Muscle biopsy shows prominent vacuolization of muscle fibers without inflammatory infiltrate, patchy type 2 muscle fiber atrophy, and sporadic myofiber necrosis.[64] Modest CPK increases (0 to 15-fold above normal range) are noted in approximately 50% of patients and are probably dependent on the timing of enzyme measurements and the initiation of the myopathic process. Thus, there may be some justification in screening patients with serial CPK determinations during infusion of NMBAs, particularly if the patients are concurrently treated with corticosteroids. Also, since AQMS develops after prolonged exposure to NMBAs, there may be some rationale to daily "drug holidays" (i.e., stopping the drugs for a few to several hours and restarting them only when necessary). However, no one has demonstrated that drug holidays decrease the frequency of AQMS. Other factors that may contribute to the development of the syndrome include nutritional deficiencies, concurrent drug administration with aminoglycosides or cyclosporine, hyperglycemia, renal and hepatic dysfunction, fever, and severe metabolic or electrolyte disorders.

Evidence supports, but occasionally refutes,[14] the association of concurrent administration of NMBAs and corti-

Table 7.
Drug–Drug Interactions of Neuromuscular Blocking Agents (NMBAs)

Drugs that potentiate the action of nondepolarizing NMBAs	Drugs that antagonize the actions of nondepolarizing NMBAs
Local anesthetics	Phenytoin
Lidocaine	Carbamazepine
Antimicrobials (aminoglycosides, polymyxin B, clindamycin, tetracycline)	Theophylline
Antiarrhythmics (procainamide, quinidine)	Ranitidine
Magnesium	
Calcium channel blockers	
β-Adrenergic blockers	
Immunosuppresive agents (cyclophosphamide, cyclosporine)	
Dantrolene	
Diuretics	
Lithium carbonate	

Figure 3. Acetylcholine Receptor. The mature nicotinic acetylcholine receptor (AChR) (left) with its glycoprotein subunits arranged around the central cation core. Two molecules of acetylcholine bind simultaneously to the two alpha subunits to convert the channel to an open state. The immature, or fetal-variant, receptor is shown on the right, with a single subunit substitution which follows major stress such as burns or denervation. These immature receptors are characterized by 10-fold greater ionic activity, rapid metabolic turnover, and extrajunctional proliferation. (Reprinted, with permission, from Martyn JAJ, White DA, Gronert GA et al. Up-and-down regulation of skeletal muscle acetylcholine receptors. *Anesthesiology.* 1992; 76:825.)

costeroids with AQMS.[59,63,68,69] The incidence of myopathy may be as high as 30% in patients who receive corticosteroids and NMBAs. While no period of paralysis is risk free, NMBA administration beyond one or two days increases the risk of myopathy in this setting.[63] Similarly, there is an inconsistent correlation with the dose of corticosteroids, but total doses in excess of 1 g of methylprednisolone (or equivalent) probably increase the risk. Afflicted patients manifest an acute, diffuse, flaccid weakness and an inability to wean from mechanical ventilation. Sensory function is generally preserved.[63] Muscle biopsy shows extensive type 2 fiber atrophy, myonecrosis, disarray of sarcomere architecture, and an extensive, selective loss of myosin. Experimental evidence in animals shows that denervation for ≥24 hours induces profound negative nitrogen balance and increases expression of steroid receptors in muscle. Such denervation sensitizes muscle to even normal corticosteroid concentrations, and evidence suggests that the combination of dener-

vation and high-dose corticosteroids precipitates myosinolysis.

Acute myopathy in ICU patients is also reported after administration of the benzylisoquinolinium NMBAs (i.e., atracurium, cisatracurium, doxacurium).[24,34,69] Common to all these reports is the coadministration of benzylisoquinolinium NMBAs and large doses of corticosteroids, aminoglycosides, or other drugs that affect neuromuscular transmission.

Recommendations: For patients receiving NMBAs and corticosteroids, every effort should be made to discontinue NMBAs as soon as possible. (Grade of recommendation = C)

Drug holidays (i.e., stopping NMBAs daily until forced to restart them based on the patient's condition) may decrease the incidence of AQMS. (Grade of recommendation = C)

Other nerve and muscle disorders have been recognized in the last decade in ICU patients (Table 6). For instance, CIP is a sensory and motor polyneuropathy identified in elderly, septic patients or those with MODS.[58,66,70] EMG testing reveals decreased CMAP, fibrillation potentials, and positive sharp waves.[60,63,64] CIP is primarily an axonopathy and may be related to microvascular ischemia of the nerve but is not directly related to the use of NMBAs. Recovery from ICU myopathy requires a protracted (weeks or months) hospitalization. One economic analysis of 10 patients who developed AQMS showed the median additional hospital charge to be $66,000 per patient.[65] As for any critically ill patient, particularly immobilized patients, deep venous thrombosis (DVT) prophylaxis and physical therapy to maintain joint mobility are important.

Patients receiving NMBAs are also at risk of developing keratitis and corneal abrasion. Prophylactic eye care is highly variable and recommendations may include methylcellulose drops, ophthalmic ointment, taping the eyelids shut to ensure complete closure, or eye patches. In a study of 69 paralyzed or heavily sedated patients by Lenart and Garrity,[71] there was strong evidence that the use of an artificial tear ointment prevented corneal exposure. In this randomized study, patients served as their own controls.

Myositis Ossificans (Heterotopic Ossification). Myositis ossificans can develop in patients who are paralyzed for long periods of time, but inflammation is not characteristic of the ailment. The name is misleading because the process in-

Table 8.
Potential Complications of Neuromuscular Blockade Use in the ICU[a]

Complications and contraindications of succinylcholine in the ICU	General complications associated with NMBAs in the ICU
Loss of airway	Awake, paralyzed patient–anxiety and panic
Hyperkalemia	Risk of ventilator disconnect or airway mishap
Plasma pseudocholinesterase deficiency	Autonomic and cardiovascular effects (i.e., vagolytic)
	Decreased lymphatic flow
	Risk of generalized deconditioning
	Skin breakdown
	Peripheral nerve injury
	Corneal abrasion, conjunctivitis
	Myositis ossificans
	Risk of prolonged muscle weakness, AQMS
	Potential central nervous system toxicity

[a]NMBA = neuromuscular blocking agent, AQMS = acute quadriplegic myopathy syndrome.

volves connective tissue (not muscle). The name originates from the ossification that occurs within the connective tissue of muscle but may also be seen in ligaments, tendons, fascia, aponeuroses, and joint capsules. The acquired form of the disease may occur at any age in either sex, especially around the elbows, thighs, and buttocks. The basic defect is the inappropriate differentiation of fibroblasts into osteoblasts and is usually triggered by trauma and muscle injury, paraplegia or quadriplegia, tetanus, and burns. Treatment consists of promoting an active range of motion around the affected joint and surgery when necessary.

Tachyphylaxis. For reasons mentioned earlier, tachyphylaxis to NMBAs can and does develop.

Coursin and colleagues[31] administered doxacurium to four patients who developed tolerance to atracurium infusions (range, 16 to 40 µg/kg/min). Patients were successfully blocked with infusion rates of doxacurium 0.25–0.75 µg/kg/min.

Tschida et al.[72] described a patient whose atracurium requirement escalated from 5 to 30 µg/kg/min over 10 days. The patient was successfully blocked with a pancuronium infusion of 10–50 µg/kg/min for a period of five days.

Fish and Singletary[33] describe a patient who was inadequately blocked with a 60-µg/kg/min infusion of atracurium but adequately paralyzed for seven days with 2.3-mg/kg/hr infusion of vecuronium. Tachyphylaxis then developed to vecuronium which prompted discontinuation of NMBAs. Two days later, 50-µg/kg/min atracurium infusions were required with high-dose midazolam and fentanyl infusions to achieve adequate oxygenation and acceptable airway pressures.

Recommendations: Patients receiving NMBAs should have prophylactic eye care (Grade of recommendation = B), physical therapy (Grade of recommendation = C), and DVT prophylaxis. (Grade of recommendation = C)

Patients who develop tachyphylaxis to one NMBA should try another drug if neuromuscular blockade is still required. (Grade of recommendation = C)

Economics

There have been few formal pharmacoeconomic evaluations of NMBAs. In one of these economic evaluations, medication-related cost savings were found when voluntary

prescribing guidelines for NMBAs were initiated in the operating room of a university hospital.[73] In another study that involved randomization to one of three NMBAs, there were no significant cost differences between atracurium, vecuronium, and rocuronium for surgeries lasting two hours or less, but vecuronium and rocuronium were economically advantageous if the duration of surgery was two to four hours.[74] In a third retrospective study, long-acting NMBAs (e.g., D-tubocurarine and pancuronium) were associated with prolonged postoperative recovery compared with shorter-acting agents (e.g., atracurium, mivacurium, and vecuronium). The authors noted in the discussion section of the paper that based on intrainstitutional recovery room costs, delays in recovery times seen with the longer-acting agents offset the expected savings in drug costs.[75] For patients transferred to the ICU, this may not be a major problem.

Two pharmacoeconomic investigations involving NMBAs in the ICU evaluated the costs associated with prolonged recovery following discontinuation of nondepolarizing NMBAs. In one study, overall costs were lower when TOF monitoring was employed.[76] In another study, patients who had prolonged motor weakness after discontinuing NMBAs were compared with a control group[77]; ICU and hospital costs were substantially higher in the patients with prolonged weakness.

A study involving 40 academic medical centers with patients undergoing coronary artery bypass graft surgery found no significant differences in duration of intubation or duration of ICU or hospital stay among patients who received pancuronium ($n = 732$), vecuronium ($n = 130$), or both ($n = 242$) agents.[78] It is unknown if these results pertain to subgroups of patients, such as those with renal or hepatic dysfunction. If the results of this study are confirmed, the choice of agent could be based solely on cost minimization using medication purchase cost information and equipotent dosage regimens.

A prospective, randomized trial comparing TOF to standard clinical assessment showed decreased NMBA usage and faster return of spontaneous ventilation with TOF monitoring.[14] TOF has the potential to decrease costs associated with NMBA use in ICUs.

Appendix B describes the basic steps involved in conducting a cost-effectiveness analysis of the NMBAs. Consequently, intrainstitutional data and assumptions can be used to perform the analysis along with local value judgments involved in selecting the appropriate agent(s).

Recommendation: Institutions should perform an economic analysis using their own data when choosing NMBAs for use in an ICU. (Grade of recommendation = C)

---

[a] Food and Drug Administration. Report of Anesthetic and Life Support Drugs Advisory Committee Meeting. Rockville, MD: U.S. Department of Health and Human Services; 1992 Nov 23.

References

1. Society of Critical Care Medicine and American Society of Health-System Pharmacists. Sedation, analgesia, and neuromuscular blockade of the critically ill adult: revised clinical practice guidelines for 2002. *Am J Health-Syst Pharm.* 2002; 59:147–9.

2. Coakley JH, Nagendran K, Yarwood GD, et al. Patterns of neurophysiological abnormality in prolonged critical illness. *Intensive Care Med.* 1998; 24:801–7.

3. Prielipp RC, Coursin DB. Applied pharmacology of common neuromuscular blocking agents in critical care. *New Horizons.* 1994; 2:34–47.

4. De Lemos JM, Carr RR, Shalansky KF, et al. Paralysis in the critically ill: intermittent bolus pancuronium compared with continuous infusion. *Crit Care Med.* 1999; 27:2648–55.

5. Tobias JD, Lynch A, McDuffee A, et al. Pancuronium infusion for neuromuscular block in children in the pediatric intensive care unit. *Anesth Analg.* 1995; 81:13–6.

6. Segredo V, Caldwell JE, Wright PM, et al. Do the pharmacokinetics of vecuronium change during prolonged administration in critically ill patients? *Br J Anaesth.* 1998; 80:715–9.

7. Appadu BL, Greiff JM, Thompson JP. Postal survey on the long-term use of neuromuscular block in the intensive care unit. *Intensive Care Med.* 1996; 22:862–6.

8. Khuenl-Brady KS, Sparr H, Pühringer F, et al. Rocuronium bromide in the ICU: dose finding and pharmacokinetics. *Eur J Anaesthesiol Suppl.* 1995; 11:79–80.

9. Sparr HJ, Wierda JMKH, Proost JH, et al. Pharmacodynamics and pharmacokinetics of rocuronium in intensive care patients. *Br J Anaesth.* 1997; 78:267–73.

10. McEwin L, Merrick PM, Bevan DR. Residual neuromuscular blockade after cardiac surgery: pancuronium vs rocuronium. *Can J Anaesth.* 1997; 44:891–5.

11. Stene J, Murray M, de Ruyter M, et al. Selective rocuronium pharmacodynamics and kinetics during ICU infusion. *Anesthesiology.* 1998; 89:A477. Abstract.

12. Murray MJ, Coursin DB, Scuderi PE, et al. Double-blind, randomized, multicenter study of doxacurium vs. pancuronium in intensive care unit patients who require neuromuscular-blocking agents. *Crit Care Med.* 1995; 23:450–8.

13. Khuenl-Brady KS, Reitstatter B, Schlager A, et al. Long-term administration of pancuronium and pipecuronium in the intensive care unit. *Anesth Analg.* 1994; 78:1082–6.

14. Rudis MI, Sikora CP, Angus E, et al. A prospective, randomized, controlled evaluation of peripheral nerve stimulation versus standard clinical dosing of neuromuscular blocking agents in critically ill patients. *Crit Care Med.* 1997; 25:575–83.

15. Prielipp RC, Coursin DB, Scuderi PB, et al. Comparison of the infusion requirements and recovery profiles of vecuronium and cisatracurium 51W89 in intensive care unit patients. *Anesth Analg.* 1995; 81:3–12.

16. Hull CJ. Pharmacokinetics and pharmacodynamics of the benzylisoquinolinium muscle relaxants. *Acta Anaesthesiol Scand Suppl.* 1995; 106:13–7.

17. De Wolf AM, Freeman JA, Scott VL, et al. Pharmacokinetics and pharmacodynamics of cisatracurium in patients with end-stage liver disease undergoing liver transplantation. *Br J Anaesth.* 1996; 76:624–8.

18. Pearson AJ, Harper NJ, Pollard BJ. The infusion requirements and recovery characteristics of cisatracurium or atracurium in intensive care patients. *Intensive Care Med.* 1996; 22:694–8.

19. Boyd AH, Eastwood NB, Parker CJ, et al. Comparison of the pharmacodynamics and pharmacokinetics of an infusion of cisatracurium (51W89) or atracurium in critically ill patients undergoing mechanical ventilation in an intensive therapy unit. *Br J Anaesth.* 1996; 76:382–8.

20. Newman PJ, Quinn AC, Grounds RM, et al. A comparison of cisatracurium (51W89) and atracurium by infusion in critically ill patients. *Crit Care Med.* 1997; 25:1139–42.

21. Schramm WM, Papousek A, Michalek-Sauberer A, et al. The cerebral and cardiovascular effects of cisatracurium and atracurium in neurosurgical patients. *Anesth Analg.* 1998; 86:123–7.

22. Schramm WM, Jesenko R, Bartuneka A, et al. Effects of cisatracurium on cerebral and cardiovascular hemodynamics in patients with severe brain injury. *Acta Anaesthesiol Scand.* 1997; 41:1319–23.

23. Grigore AM, Brusco L Jr, Kuroda M, et al. Laudanosine and atracurium concentrations in a patient receiving long-term atracurium infusion. *Crit Care Med.* 1998; 26:180–3.

24. Davis NA, Rodgers JE, Gonzalez ER, et al. Prolonged weakness after cisatracurium infusion: a case report. *Crit Care Med.* 1998; 26:1290–2.

25. Reeves ST, Turcasso NM. Nondepolarizing neuromuscular blocking drugs in the intensive care unit: a clinical review. *South Med J.* 1997; 90:769–74.

26. Miller RD. Use of neuromuscular blocking drugs in intensive care unit patients. *Anesth Analg.* 1995; 81:1–2.

27. Bion J, Prielipp RC, Bihari D, et al. Cisatracurium in intensive care. *Curr Opin Anesthesiol.* 1996; 9:S47–51.

28. Werba A, Schultz AM, Hetz H, et al. Benzylisochinoline muscle relaxants in clinical practice. *Acta Anaesthesiol Scan Suppl.* 1997; 111:109–10.

29. Marik PE, Kaufman D. The effects of neuromuscular paralysis on systemic and splanchnic oxygen utilization in mechanically ventilated patients. *Chest.* 1996; 109:1038–42.

30. Prielipp RC, Robinson JC, Wilson JA, et al. Dose response, recovery, and cost of doxacurium as a continuous infusion in neurosurgical intensive care unit patients. *Crit Care Med.* 1997; 25:1236–41.

31. Coursin DB, Meyer DA, Prielipp RC. Doxacurium infusion in critically ill patients with atracurium tachyphylaxis. *Am J Health Syst-Pharm.* 1995; 52:635–9.

32. Manthous CA, Chatila W. Atracurium and status epilepticus. *Crit Care Med.* 1995; 23:1440–2.

33. Fish DN, Singletary TJ. Cross-resistance to both atracurium- and vecuronium-induced neuromuscular blockade in a critically ill patient. *Pharmacotherapy.* 1997; 17:1322–7.

34. Meyer KC, Prielipp RC, Grossman JE, et al. Prolonged weakness after infusion of atracurium in two intensive care unit patients. *Anesth Analg.* 1994; 78:772–4.

35. Manthous CA, Chatila W. Prolonged weakness after the withdrawal of atracurium. *Am J Resp Crit Care Med.* 1994; 150:1441–3.

36. Branney SW, Haenal JB, Moore FA, et al. Prolonged

paralysis with atracurium infusion: a case report. *Crit Care Med.* 1994; 22:1699–701.

37.   Rubjo ER, Seelig CB. Persistent paralysis after prolonged use of atracurium in the absence of corticosteroids. *South Med J.* 1996; 89:624–6.

38.   Hoey LL, Joslin SM, Nahum A, et al. Prolonged neuromuscular blockade in two critically ill patients treated with atracurium. *Pharmacotherapy.* 1995; 15:254–9.

39.   Prielipp RC, Jackson MJ, Coursin DB. Comparison of neuromuscular recovery after paralysis with atracurium versus vecuronium in an ICU patient with renal insufficiency. *Anesth Analg.* 1994; 78:775–8.

40.   McClelland M, Woster P, Sweasey T, et al. Continuous midazolam/atracurium infusions for the management of increased intracranial pressure. *J Neurosci Nurs.* 1995; 27:96–101.

41.   Anandaciva S, Koay CW. Tetanus and rocuronium in the intensive care unit. *Anaesthesia.* 1996; 51:505–6.

42.   Freebairn RC, Derrick J, Gomersall CD, et al. Oxygen delivery, oxygen consumption, and gastric intramucosal pH are not improved by a computer-controlled, closed-loop, vecuronium infusion in severe sepsis. *Crit Care Med.* 1997; 25:72–7.

43.   Strange C, Vaughan L, Franklin C, et al. Comparison of train-of-four and best clinical assessment during continuous paralysis. *Am J Resp Crit Care Med.* 1997; 156:1556–61.

44.   Frankel H, Jeng J, Tilly E, et al. The impact of implementation of neuromuscular blockade monitoring standards in a surgical intensive care unit. *Am Surg.* 1996; 62:503–6.

45.   Sladen RN. Neuromuscular blocking agents in the intensive care unit: a two-edged sword. *Crit Care Med.* 1995; 23:423–8.

46.   Ford EV. Monitoring neuromuscular blockade in the adult ICU. *Am J Crit Care.* 1995; 4:122–30.

47.   Kleinpell R, Bedrosian C, McCormick L. Use of peripheral nerve stimulators to monitor patients with neuromuscular blockade in the ICU. *Am J Crit Care.* 1996; 5:449–54.

48.   Murray MJ. Monitoring of peripheral nerve stimulation versus standard clinical assessment for dosing of neuromuscular blocking agents. *Crit Care Med.* 1997; 25:561–2.

49.   Tavernier B, Rannou JJ, Vallet B. Peripheral nerve stimulation and clinical assessment for dosing of neuromuscular blocking agents in critically ill patients. *Crit Care Med.* 1998; 26:804–5.

50.   Barnette RE, Fish DJ. Monitoring neuromuscular blockade in the critically ill. *Crit Care Med.* 1995; 23:1790–1.

51.   Rudis M, Guslits B, Zarowitz B. Technical and interpretative problems of peripheral nerve stimulation in monitoring neuromuscular blockade in the intensive care unit. *Ann Pharmacother.* 1996; 30:165–72.

52.   Tschida SJ, Loey LL, Bryan KV. Inconsistency with train-of-four monitoring in a critically ill paralyzed patient. *Pharmacotherapy.* 1995; 15:540–5.

53.   Tschida SJ, Loey LL, Mather D. Train-of-four: to use or not to use. *Pharmacotherapy.* 1995; 15:546–50.

54.   Martin R, Bourdua I, Theriault S, et al. Neuromuscular monitoring: does it make a difference? *Can J Anesth.* 1996; 43:585–8.

55.   Luer JM. Sedation and chemical relaxation in critical pulmonary illness: suggestions for patient assessment

and drug monitoring. *AACN Clin Issues.* 1995; 6:333–43.

56.   Johnson KL, Cheung RB, Johnson SB, et al. Therapeutic paralysis of critically ill trauma patients: perceptions of patients and their family members. *Am J Crit Care.* 1999; 8:490–8.

57.   Watling SM, Dasta JF. Prolonged paralysis in intensive care unit patients after the use of neuromuscular blocking agents: a review of the literature. *Crit Care Med.* 1994; 22:884–93.

58.   Nates J, Cooper D, Day B, et al. Acute weakness syndromes in critically ill patients—a reappraisal. *Anaesth Intensive Care.* 1997; 25:502–13.

59.   Road J, Mackie G, Jiang T, et al. Reversible paralysis with status asthmaticus, steroids, and pancuronium: clinical electrophysiological correlates. *Muscle Nerve.* 1997; 20:1587–90.

60.   Lacomis D, Giuliani MJ, Van Cott A, et al. Acute myopathy of intensive care: clinical, electromyographic, and pathological aspects. *Ann Neurol.* 1996; 40:645–54.

61.   Elliot J, Bion J. The use of neuromuscular blocking drugs in intensive care practice. *Acta Anaesthesiol Scand Suppl.* 1995; 106:70–82.

62.   Leatherman J, Fluegel W, David W, et al. Muscle weakness in mechanically ventilated patients with severe asthma. *Am J Resp Crit Care Med.* 1996; 153:1686–90.

63.   David W, Roehr C, Leatherman J. EMG findings in acute myopathy with status asthmaticus, steroids and paralytics: clinical and electrophysiologic correlation. *Electromyogr Clin Neurophysiol.* 1998; 38:371–6.

64.   Faragher MW, Day BJ, Dennett X. Critical care myopathy: an electrophysiological and histological study. *Muscle Nerve.* 1996; 19:516–8.

65.   Latronico N, Fenzi F, Recupero D, et al. Critical illness myopathy and neuropathy. *Lancet.* 1996; 347:1579–82.

66.   Bolton CF. Muscle weakness and difficulty in weaning from the ventilator in the critical care unit. *Chest.* 1994; 106:1–2.

67.   Barohn RJ, Jackson CE, Rogers SJ, et al. Prolonged paralysis due to nondepolarizing neuromuscular blocking agents and corticosteroids. *Muscle Nerve.* 1994; 17:647–54.

68.   Zochodne DW, Ramsay DA, Shelley S. Acute necrotizing myopathy of intensive care: electrophysiologic studies. *Muscle Nerve.* 1994; 17:285–92.

69.   Marik PE. Doxacurium-corticosteroid acute myopathy: another piece to the puzzle. *Crit Care Med.* 1996; 24:1266–7.

70.   Hund E, Fogel W, Krieger D, et al. Critical illness polyneuropathy: clinical findings and outcomes of a frequent cause of neuromuscular weaning failure. *Crit Care Med.* 1996; 24:1328–33.

71.   Lenart SG, Garrity J. Eye care for the mechanically ventilated patient receiving neuromuscular blockade or propofol. *Mayo Clin Proc.* In press.

72.   Tschida SJ, Hoey LL, Nahum A, et al. Atracurium resistance in a critically ill patient. *Pharmacotherapy.* 1995; 15:533–9.

73.   Gora-Harper ML, Hessel E, Shadick D. Effect of prescribing guidelines on the use of neuromuscular blocking agents. *Am J Health-Syst Pharm.* 1995; 52:1900–4.

74. Loughlin KA, Weingarten CM, Nagelhout J, et al. A pharmacoeconomic analysis of neuromuscular blocking agents in the operating room. *Pharmacotherapy.* 1996; 16:942–50.

75. Ballantyne JC, Chang Y. The impact of choice of muscle relaxant on postoperative recovery time: a retrospective study. *Anesth Analg.* 1997; 85:476–82.

76. Zarowitz BJ, Rudis MI, Lai K, et al. Retrospective pharmacoeconomic evaluation of dosing vecuronium by peripheral nerve stimulation versus standard clinical assessment in critically ill patients. *Pharmacotherapy.* 1997; 17:327–32.

77. Rudis MI, Guslits BJ, Peterson EL, et al. Economic impact of prolonged motor weakness complicating neuromuscular blockade in the intensive care unit. *Crit Care Med.* 1996; 24:1749–56.

78. Butterworth J, James R, Prielipp RC, et al. Do shorter-acting neuromuscular blocking drugs or opioids associate with reduced intensive care unit or hospital length of stay after coronary artery bypass grafting? *Anesthesiology.* 1998; 88:1437–46.

Appendix A—Summary of Recommendations

1. NMBAs should be used for an adult patient in an ICU to manage ventilation, manage increased ICP, treat muscle spasms, and decrease oxygen consumption only when all other means have been tried without success.[1] (Grade of recommendation = C)

2. The majority of patients in an ICU who are prescribed an NMBA can be managed effectively with pancuronium. (Grade of recommendation = B)

3. For patients for whom vagolysis is contraindicated (e.g., those with cardiovascular disease), NMBAs other than pancuronium may be used. (Grade of recommendation = C)

4. Because of their unique metabolism, cisatracurium or atracurium is recommended for patients with significant hepatic or renal disease. (Grade of recommendation = B)

5. Patients receiving NMBAs should be assessed both clinically and by TOF monitoring (Grade of recommendation = B), with a goal of adjusting the degree of neuromuscular blockade to achieve one or two twitches. (Grade of recommendation = C)

6. Before initiating neuromuscular blockade, patients should be medicated with sedative and analgesic drugs to provide adequate sedation and analgesia in accordance with the physician's clinical judgment to optimize therapy. (Grade of recommendation = C)

7. For patients receiving NMBAs and corticosteroids, every effort should be made to discontinue NMBAs as soon as possible. (Grade of recommendation = C)

8. Drug holidays (i.e., stopping NMBAs daily until forced to restart them based on the patient's condition) may decrease the incidence of AQMS. (Grade of recommendation = C)

9. Patients receiving NMBAs should have prophylactic eye care (Grade of recommendation = B), physical therapy (Grade of recommendation = C), and DVT prophylaxis. (Grade of recommendation = C)

10. Patients who develop tachyphylaxis to one NMBA should try another drug if neuromuscular blockade is still required. (Grade of recommendation = C)

11. Institutions should perform an economic analysis using their own data when choosing NMBAs for use in an ICU. (Grade of recommendation = C)

Appendix B—Determination of Cost Effectiveness Using Intrainstitutional Data[a]

1. For each adverse effect (e.g., prolonged recovery) of any given neuromuscular blocking agent (NMBA), add all associated costs together and multiply this figure by the probability of the occurrence of the adverse effect.
   If adverse effects A, B, and C are associated with an NMBA, then

   (Drug cost + cost A1) (probability of occurrence expressed as a decimal) = $U
   (Drug cost + cost B1) (probability of occurrence expressed as a decimal) = $V
   (Drug cost + cost C1) (probability of occurrence expressed as a decimal) = $W

2. Calculate the product of the drug cost multiplied by the probability of occurrence of no adverse effects expressed as a decimal; add this product to the cost multiplied by the probability factor for each adverse effect calculated in step 1.

   (Drug cost) (probability of occurrence of no adverse effects) + $U + $V + $W = average cost of all pathways for agent
   Note: The probabilities of all adverse effects plus the probability of no adverse effects associated with the NMBA must add up to 1.

3. Determine the cost effectiveness of the agent by dividing the total costs associated with the agent by the probability of occurrence of no adverse effects expressed as a decimal.
   Example using pancuronium:

   a. [$224 (drug cost for 4 days of therapy) + $1000 (estimated cost of 1 extra day of ICU stay due to prolonged paralysis
      resulting from renal dysfunction)] [0.07 (estimated probability of renal dysfunction)] = $85.68
      [$224 (drug cost for 4 days of therapy) + $1000 (estimated cost of 1 extra day of ICU (intensive care unit) stay due to prolonged paralysis
      resulting from hepatic dysfunction)] [0.04 (estimated probability of hepatic dysfunction)] = $48.96
   b. [$224 (drug cost for 4 days of therapy, assuming no adverse effects) × 0.89 (estimated probability of no adverse effects)]
      + $85.68 + $48.96 = $334.00
   c. Cost effectiveness of pancuronium = 334.00/0.89 (probability of no adverse effects) = $375.28

Note that the term "adverse effects" includes problems such as prolonged paralysis resulting from decreased medication elimination due to impaired organ function. If a neuromuscular blocking agent is eliminated by more than one organ (e.g., kidney and liver), prolonged paralysis may result from impaired elimination due to a combination of organ problems. For example, one adverse effect may be prolonged paralysis associated with renal dysfunction, while another adverse effect may be prolonged paralysis associated with hepatic dysfunction, while a third adverse effect may be prolonged paralysis associated with combined renal and hepatic dysfunction.

Developed through the Task Force of the American College of Critical Care Medicine (ACCM) of the Society of Critical Care Medicine (SCCM), in collaboration with the American Society of Health-System Pharmacists (ASHP), and in alliance with the American College of Chest Physicians; and approved by the Board of Regents of ACCM and the Council of SCCM on November 15, 2001 and the ASHP Board of Directors on November 17, 2001.

Members of the 2001–2002 Commission on Therapeutics are William L. Greene, Pharm.D., BCPS, FASHP, *Chair*; Mary Lea Gora-Harper, Pharm.D., BCPS, *Vice Chair*; Kate Farthing, Pharm.D.; Charles W. Ham, Pharm.D., M.B.A.; Rita K. Jew, Pharm.D.; Rex S. Lott, Pharm.D.; Keith M. Olsen, Pharm.D., FCCP; Joseph J. Saseen, Pharm.D., BCPS; Beth A. Vanderheyden, Pharm.D., BCPS; Amy M. Blachere, R.Ph., *Student Member*; Jill E. Martin, Pharm.D., FASHP, *Board Liaison*; Dennis Williams, Pharm.D., FASHP, FCCP, FAPHA, BCPS, *Liaison Section of Clinical Specialist*; and Cynthia L. LaCivita, Pharm.D., *Secretary*.

Members of the Neuromuscular Blockade Task Force are Michael J. Murray, M.D., Ph.D., FCCM, *Chair*, Professor and Chair of Anesthesiology, and Dean, Mayo School of Health Sciences, Mayo Clinic Jacksonville, FL; Stanley Nasraway, Jr., M.D., FCCM, *Executive Director of Task Force*, Associate Professor, Surgery, Medicine, and Anesthesia, Tufts-New England Medical Center, Boston, MA; Jay Cowen, M.D., Director, Medical Intensive Care Unit, LeHigh Valley Hospital, Allentown, PA; Heidi F. DeBlock, M.D., Department of Surgery, Albany Medical Center, Albany, NY; Brian L. Erstad, Pharm.D., FCCM, Department of Pharmacy Practice & Science, College of Pharmacy, University of Arizona, Tucson, AZ; Anthony W. Gray, Jr., M.D., FCCM, Section of Pulmonary and Critical Care, Medicine and Surgical Critical Care, Lahey Clinic Medical Center, Burlington, MA; Judith Jacobi, Pharm.D., FCCM, BCPS, Critical Care Pharmacy Specialist, Methodist Hospital–Clarian Health Partners, Indianapolis, IN; Philip D. Lumb, M.B., B.S., FCCM, Professor and Chairman, Department of Anesthesiology, Keck School of Medicine of USC, Los Angeles, CA; William T. McGee, M.D., M.H.A., Critical Care Division, Departments of Medicine & Surgery, Baystate Medical Center, Springfield, MA; William T. Peruzzi, M.D., FCCM, Associate Professor of Anesthesiology, Northwestern University School of Medicine, Chief, Section of Critical Care Medicine, Northwestern Memorial Hospital, Chicago, IL; Richard C. Prielipp, M.D., FCCM, Section Head, Critical Care and Department of Anesthesiology, Wake Forest University School of Medicine, Medical Center Boulevard, Winston-Salem, NC; Greg Susla, Pharm.D., FCCM, Clinical Center Pharmacy Department, National Institutes of Health, Bethesda, MD; Ann N. Tescher, R.N., Clinical Nurse Specialist, Mayo Clinic, Rochester, MN; Cynthia L. LaCivita, Pharm.D., Clinical Affairs Associate, *ASHP Staff Liaison*; Deborah L. McBride, Director of Publications, *SCCM Staff Liaison*.

Reviewers: American College of Chest Physicians; American Academy of Neurology; American Association of Critical Care Nurses; American Nurses Association; American Pharmaceutical Association; American College of Clinical Pharmacy; Joe Dasta, Pharm.D.; Doug Fish, Pharm.D.; Erkan Hassan, Pharm.D.; H. Mathilda Horst, M.D.; Carlayne E. Jackson, M.D.; Karen Kaiser, R.N.; Kathleen M. Kelly, M.D.; Carl Schoenberger, M.D.; Lori Schoonover, R.N.; and Gayle Takaniski, Pharm.D.

The recommendations in this document do not indicate an exclusive course of treatment to be followed. Variations, taking into account individual circumstances, may be appropriate.

The bibliographic citation is as follows: Society of Critical Care Medicine and American Society of Health-System Pharmacists. Clinical practice guidelines for sustained neuromuscular blockade in the adult critically ill patient. *Am J Health Syst Pharm.* 2002; 59:179–95.

Clinical Practice Guidelines for the Sustained Use of Sedatives and Analgesics in the Critically Ill Adult

Maintaining an optimal level of comfort and safety for critically ill patients is a universal goal for critical care practitioners. The American College of Critical Care Medicine (ACCM) of the Society of Critical Care Medicine's (SCCM's) practice parameters for the optimal use of sedatives and analgesics was published in 1995 and recommended a tiered approach to the use of sedatives and analgesics, largely on the basis of expert opinion.[1] These clinical practice guidelines replace the previously published parameters and include an evaluation of the literature published since 1994 comparing the use of these agents. The reader should refer to the accompanying introduction for a description of the methodology used to develop these guidelines.[2]

This document is limited to a discussion of prolonged sedation and analgesia. Consistent with the previous practice guidelines, this document pertains to patients older than 12 years. The majority of the discussion focuses on the care of patients during mechanical ventilation. A discussion of regional techniques is not included. Appendix A summarizes the recommendations made herein.

Analgesia

In these guidelines, "analgesia" is defined as the blunting or absence of sensation of pain or noxious stimuli. Intensive care unit (ICU) patients commonly have pain and physical discomfort from obvious factors, such as preexisting diseases, invasive procedures, or trauma. Patient pain and discomfort can also be caused by monitoring and therapeutic devices (such as catheters, drains, noninvasive ventilating devices, and endotracheal tubes), routine nursing care (such as airway suctioning, physical therapy, dressing changes, and patient mobilization), and prolonged immobility.[3,4] Unrelieved pain may contribute to inadequate sleep, possibly causing exhaustion and disorientation. Agitation in an ICU patient may result from inadequate pain relief. Unrelieved pain evokes a stress response characterized by tachycardia, increased myocardial oxygen consumption, hypercoagulability, immunosuppression, and persistent catabolism.[5,6] The combined use of analgesics and sedatives may ameliorate the stress response in critically ill patients.[7,8] Pain may also contribute to pulmonary dysfunction through localized guarding of muscles around the area of pain and a generalized muscle rigidity or spasm that restricts movement of the chest wall and diaphragm.[9] Effective analgesia may diminish pulmonary complications in postoperative patients.[10]

Some patients recall unrelieved pain when interviewed about their ICU stays.[3,11,12] The perception of pain can be influenced by several factors, such as the expectation of pain, prior pain experiences, a patient's emotional state, and the cognitive processes of the patient.[11] Patients should be educated about the potential for pain and instructed to communicate their needs in an appropriate manner (such as using an assessment tool or other communication techniques). The goals of therapy should also be communicated to the patient and family. In many cases, pain will be managed but not completely eliminated. Fear of potent analgesics and misconceptions about pain and analgesics

should be addressed. Similarly, practitioner bias against the adequate use of opioids or misplaced fears of adverse effects or addiction may produce inadequate prescribing or administration.[13,14] Educating practitioners and assessing the quality of a pain management program may improve analgesia therapy, but such programs have not been universally successful.[4,15] The importance of appropriate pain management programs has been reinforced by the Joint Commission on Accreditation of Healthcare Organizations's (JCAHO's) establishment of standards on pain assessment and management.

> *Recommendation: All critically ill patients have the right to adequate analgesia and management of their pain. (Grade of recommendation = C)*

Pain Assessment. There is a limited amount of literature that directly addresses pain assessment in the critical care unit. The articles reviewed in this report include descriptions of pain assessment tools used for critically ill patients, even if these tools were not validated in this population. Studies of pain in the critically ill indicate the importance of systematic and consistent assessment and documentation.[16] The most reliable and valid indicator of pain is the patient's self-report.[17] The location, characteristics, aggravating and alleviating factors, and intensity of pain should be evaluated. Assessment of pain intensity may be performed with unidimensional tools, such as a verbal rating scale (VRS), visual analogue scale (VAS), and numeric rating scale (NRS). VAS comprises a 10-cm horizontal line with descriptive phrases at either end, from "no pain" to "severe pain" or "worst pain ever." Variations include vertical divisions or numeric markings. VAS is reliable and valid for many patient populations.[18] Though not specifically tested in the ICU, VAS is frequently used there.[19-22] Elderly patients may have difficulty with VAS.[20] NRS is a zero to ten point scale and patients choose a number that describes the pain, with ten representing the worst pain. NRS is also valid, correlates with VAS, and has been used to assess pain in cardiac surgical patients.[21] Because patients can complete the NRS by writing or speaking, and because it is applicable to patients in many age groups, NRS may be preferable to VAS in critically ill patients.

Multidimensional tools, such as the McGill Pain Questionnaire (MPQ) and the Wisconsin Brief Pain Questionnaire (BPQ), measure pain intensity and the sensory, affective, and behavioral components of that pain but take longer to administer and may not be practical for the ICU environment.[18,22] The MPQ and BPQ are reliable and valid tools but have not been tested or used in the ICU.

Although the most reliable indicator of pain intensity is what the patient reports, critically ill patients are often unable to communicate their level of pain if sedated, anesthetized, or receiving neuromuscular blockade. Neither the VAS nor the NRS will resolve this problem as they rely on the patient's ability to communicate with the care provider. Behavioral–physiological scales may be useful in assessing pain in these patients. Moderate agreement was found between the VAS and the observer-reported Faces scale for all observations, but less agreement was noted as the pain intensity increased.[19] The verbal descriptive scale (VDS) used in another trial showed moderate correlation (r> 0.60) with a behavioral pain scale in assessing pain in postanesthesia patients.[23] A behavioral–physiological scale was compared with an NRS and a moderate-to-strong correlation was observed between the scales.[24] The behavioral–physiological scale also assessed pain-related behaviors (movement, facial expression, and posturing) and physiological indicators (heart rate, blood pressure, and respiratory rate). However, such nonspecific parameters might be misinterpreted or affected by observer bias, leading to an underestimation of the degree of pain experienced by the patient.[12,24–27]

Family members or other surrogates have been evaluated for their ability to assess the amount of pain experienced by noncommunicative ICU patients. While surrogates could estimate the presence or absence of pain in 73.5% of patients, they less accurately described the degree of pain (53%).[28]

The most appropriate pain assessment tool will depend on the patient involved, his/her ability to communicate, and the caregiver's skill in interpreting pain behaviors or physiological indicators.

Recommendations: Pain assessment and response to therapy should be performed regularly by using a scale appropriate to the patient population and systematically documented. (Grade of recommendation = C)

The level of pain reported by the patient must be considered the current standard for assessment of pain and response to analgesia whenever possible. Use of the NRS is recommended to assess pain. (Grade of recommendation = B)

Patients who cannot communicate should be assessed through subjective observation of pain-related behaviors (movement, facial expression, and posturing) and physiological indicators (heart rate, blood pressure, and respiratory rate) and the change in these parameters following analgesic therapy. (Grade of recommendation = B)

Analgesia Therapy. Nonpharmacologic interventions including attention to proper positioning of patients, stabilization of fractures, and elimination of irritating physical stimulation (e.g., proper positioning of ventilator tubing to avoid traction on the endotracheal tube) are important to maintain patient comfort. Application of heat or cold therapy may be useful. Other nonpharmacologic techniques to promote patient comfort are discussed later in this document.

Pharmacologic therapies include opioids, nonsteroidal anti-inflammatory drugs (NSAIDs), and acetaminophen. Opioids mediate analgesia by interacting with a variety of central and peripheral opioid receptors. The opioids currently available have activity at a variety of these receptors, although the μ- and κ-receptors are most important for analgesia. Interaction at other receptors may contribute to adverse effects. The analgesic agents most commonly used in ICU patients (fentanyl, morphine, and hydromorphone) are addressed later.[29] Although alfentanil has previously been reported as an analgesic with sedative effects, it will not be extensively discussed because it is not commonly used in North America.[29]

Comparative trials of opioids have not been performed in critically ill patients. The selection of an agent depends on its pharmacology and potential for adverse effects. The characteristics of commonly used opioids and nonopioids are reviewed in Table 1.[30–32] Desirable attributes of an opioid include rapid onset, ease of titration, lack of accumulation of the parent drug or its metabolites, and low cost. Fentanyl has the most rapid onset and shortest duration, but repeated dosing may cause accumulation and prolonged effects. Morphine has a longer duration of action, so intermittent doses may be given. However, hypotension may result from vasodilation and an active metabolite may cause prolonged sedation in the presence of renal insufficiency. Hydromorphone's duration of action is similar to morphine's, but hydromorphone lacks a clinically significant active metabolite or histamine release. Meperidine has an active metabolite that causes neuroexcitation (apprehension, tremors, delirium, and seizures) and may interact with antidepressants (contraindicated with monoamine oxidase inhibitors and best avoided with selective serotonin-reuptake inhibitors), so it is not recommended for repetitive use.[17,33,34] Because codeine lacks analgesic potency, it is not useful for most patients. Remifentanil has not been widely studied in ICU patients and requires the use of a continuous infusion because of its very short duration of action.[35] The short duration of action could be beneficial in selected patients requiring interruptions for neurologic examination.[35]

Disease states, such as renal or hepatic insufficiency may alter opioid and metabolite elimination. Titration to the desired response and assessment of the drug's prolonged effect are necessary in all patients. The elderly may have reduced opioid requirements.[30,31,36–39]

Adverse effects of opioid analgesics are common and occur frequently in ICU patients. Of greatest concern are respiratory, hemodynamic, central nervous system, and gastrointestinal effects. Respiratory depression is a concern in spontaneously breathing patients or those receiving partial ventilatory support. Hypotension can occur in hemodynamically unstable patients, hypovolemic patients, or those with elevated sympathetic tone.[40] Opioid-mediated hypotension in euvolemic patients is a result of the combination of sympatholysis, vagally mediated bradycardia, and histamine release (when using codeine, morphine, or meperidine).[41,42] Opioid-induced depression of the level of consciousness may cloud the clinical assessment of critically ill patients, and hallucinations may increase agitation in some patients. Gastric retention and ileus are common in critically ill patients, and intestinal hypomotility is enhanced by opioids.[43,44] Routine prophylactic use of a stimulant laxative may minimize constipation. Small-bowel intubation may be needed for enteral nutrition because of gastric hypomotility.[45] Opioids may increase intra-cranial pressure with traumatic brain injury, although the data are inconsistent and the clinical significance is unknown.[46–48]

Opioid administration techniques. Preventing pain is more effective than treating established pain. When patients are administered drugs on an "as needed" basis, they may receive less than the prescribed dose and encounter significant delays in treatment, although the impact on patient outcome has not been well documented.[49] Analgesics should be administered on a continuous or scheduled intermittent basis, with supplemental bolus doses as required.[17] Intravenous administration usually requires lower and more frequent doses than intramuscular administration to titrate to patient comfort. Intramuscular administration is not recom-

Table 1.
Pharmacology of Selected Analgesics[1,17,30-32]

Agent	Equianalgesic Dose (i.v.)	Half-life	Metabolic Pathway	Active Metabolites (Effect)	Adverse Effects	Intermittent Dose[a]	Infusion Dose Range (Usual)	Infusion Cost per day 70 kg[b]
Fentanyl	200 µg	1.5–6 hr	Oxidation	No metabolite, parent accumulates	Rigidity with high doses	0.35–1.5 µg/kg i.v. q 0.5–1 hr	0.7–10 µg/kg/hr	100 µg/h: $26.00
Hydromorphone	1.5 mg	2–3 hr	Glucuronidation	None	...	10–30 µg/kg i.v. q 1–2 hr	7–15 µg/kg/hr	0.75 mg/hr: $5.00–11.00
Morphine	10 mg	3–7 hr	Glucuronidation	Yes (sedation, especially in renal insufficiency)	Histamine release	0.01–0.15 mg/kg i.v. q 1–2 hr	0.07–0.5 mg/kg/hr	5 mg/hr: $3.50–12.00
Meperidine	75–100 mg	3–4 hr	Demethylation and hydroxylation	Yes (neuroexcitation, especially in renal insufficiency or high doses)	Avoid with MAOIs[c] and SSRIs[d]	Not recommended	Not recommended	...
Codeine	120 mg	3 hr	Demethylation and glucuronidation	Yes (analgesia, sedation)	Lacks potency, histamine release	Not recommended	Not recommended	...
Remifentanil	...	3–10 min	Plasma esterase	None	...	...	0.6–15 µg/kg/hr	10 µg/kg/hr: $170.00
Ketorolac	...	2.4–8.6 hr	Renal	None	Risk of bleeding, GI and renal adverse effects	15–30 mg i.v. q 6h, decrease if age > 65 yr or wt < 50 kg or renal impairment, avoid > 5 days use.	...	...
Ibuprofen	...	1.8–2.5 hr	Oxidation	None	Risk of bleeding, GI and renal adverse effects	400 mg p.o. q 4–6 hr	...	...
Acetaminophen	...	2 hr	Conjugation	...	...	325–650 mg p.o. q 4–6 hr, avoid > 4 g/day	...	...

[a]More frequent doses may be needed for acute pain management in mechanically ventilated patients.
[b]Cost based on 2001 average wholesale price.
[c]MAOIs = monoamine oxidase inhibitors.
[d]SSRIs = selective serotonin-reuptake inhibitors.

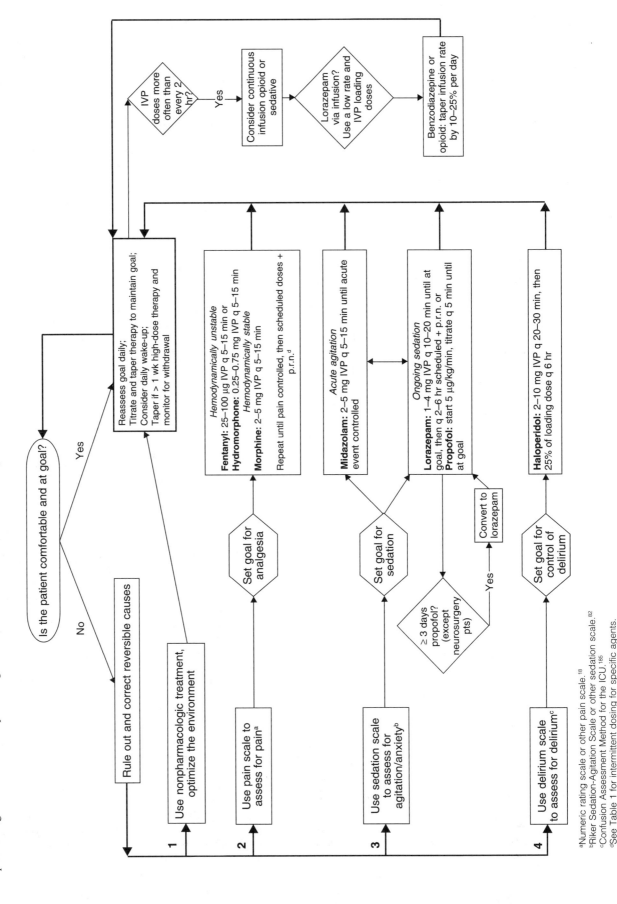

Figure 1. Algorithm for the sedation and analgesia of mechanically ventilated patients. This algorithm is a general guideline for the use of analgesics and sedatives. Refer to the text for clinical and pharmacologic issues that dictate optimal drug selection, recommended assessment scales, and precautions for patient monitoring. Doses are approximate for a 70-kg adult. IVP = intravenous push.

[a]Numeric rating scale or other pain scale.[18]
[b]Riker Sedation-Agitation Scale or other sedation scale.[82]
[c]Confusion Assessment Method for the ICU.[185]
[d]See Table 1 for intermittent dosing for specific agents.

mended in hemodynamically unstable patients because of altered perfusion and variable absorption. When a continuous infusion was used, a protocol incorporating daily awakening from analgesia and sedation allowed more effective analgesic titration and a lower total dose of morphine.[50] Daily awakening was associated with a shorter duration of ventilation and ICU stay.[50] A pain management plan and therapy goal should be established for each patient and reevaluated as the clinical condition changes. An algorithm that illustrates the potential use of opioid analgesics for mechanically ventilated patients is shown in Figure 1. Analgesic orders should be written to allow titration to achieve the analgesic goal and to balance the potential impact of adverse effects.

In noncritically ill patients, patient-controlled analgesia (PCA) has been reported to result in stable drug concentrations, a good quality of analgesia, less sedation, less opioid consumption, and potentially fewer adverse effects, including respiratory complications.[10,51] In addition, a basal rate or continuous infusion mode can be used for consistent analgesia during sleep. Patient selection is important when PCA is used, and particular attention should be paid to the patient's cognition, hemodynamic reserve, and previous opioid exposure. PCA devices can also be used for nurse-controlled analgesia. The elimination of paperwork can improve the timeliness of analgesic administration.

Fentanyl may also be administered via a transdermal patch in hemodynamically stable patients with more chronic analgesic needs. The patch provides consistent drug delivery, but the extent of absorption varies depending on the permeability, temperature, perfusion, and thickness of the skin. There is a large interpatient variability in peak plasma concentrations. Fentanyl patches are not a recommended modality for acute analgesia because of their 12–24-hour delay to peak effect and similar lag time to complete offset once the patch is removed. Breakthrough pain should be treated with rapid-acting agents.

The use of a reversal agent, such as naloxone, is not recommended after prolonged analgesia, because it can induce withdrawal and may cause nausea, cardiac stress, and arrhythmias. Analgesics with agonist–antagonist action, such as nalbuphine, butorphanol, and buprenorphine, can also elicit withdrawal symptoms and should be avoided during prolonged opioid use.

Recommendations: A therapeutic plan and goal of analgesia should be established for each patient and communicated to all caregivers to ensure consistent analgesic therapy. (Grade of recommendation = C)

If intravenous doses of an opioid analgesic are required, fentanyl, hydromorphone, and morphine are the recommended agents. (Grade of recommendation = C)

Scheduled opioid doses or a continuous infusion is preferred over an "as needed" regimen to ensure consistent analgesia. A PCA device may be utilized to deliver opioids if the patient is able to understand and operate the device. (Grade of recommendation = B)

Fentanyl is preferred for a rapid onset of analgesia in acutely distressed patients. (Grade of recommendation = C)

Fentanyl or hydromorphone are preferred for patients with hemodynamic instability or renal insufficiency. (Grade of recommendation = C)

Morphine and hydromorphone are preferred for intermittent therapy because of their longer duration of effect. (Grade of recommendation = C)

Nonopioid analgesics. NSAIDs provide analgesia via the nonselective, competitive inhibition of cyclooxygenase (COX), a critical enzyme in the inflammatory cascade. NSAIDs have the potential to cause significant adverse effects, including gastrointestinal bleeding, bleeding secondary to platelet inhibition, and the development of renal insufficiency. Patients with hypovolemia or hypoperfusion, the elderly, and those with preexisting renal impairment may be more susceptible to NSAID-induced renal injury.[52,53] Prolonged use (more than five days) of ketorolac has been associated with a twofold increase in the risk of renal failure and an increased risk of gastrointestinal and operative-site bleeding.[54,55] NSAIDs should not be administered to patients with asthma and aspirin sensitivity.

Administration of NSAIDs may reduce opioid requirements, although the analgesic benefit of NSAIDs has not been systematically studied in critically ill patients. Many oral agents are available, and ibuprofen and naproxen are available in liquid form. Ketorolac is currently the only parenteral NSAID. The safety of ketorolac administration in patients with severe renal insufficiency or those undergoing dialysis has not been determined.

The role, if any, of the more selective COX-2 inhibitors in the critically ill remains unknown. Selective COX-2 inhibiting agents cause less gastrointestinal irritation with long-term use than traditional NSAIDs.[56] The slow onset of action of some agents may decrease their utility for acute pain management.

Acetaminophen is an analgesic used to treat mild to moderate pain. In combination with an opioid, acetaminophen produces a greater analgesic effect than higher doses of the opioid alone.[57] The role of acetaminophen in critical care is limited to relieving mild pain or discomfort, such as that associated with prolonged bed rest or use as an antipyretic. Care must be taken to avoid excessive and potentially hepatotoxic doses, especially in patients with depleted glutathione stores resulting from hepatic dysfunction or malnutrition. Acetaminophen should be maintained at less than 2 g per day for patients with a significant history of alcohol intake or poor nutritional status and less than 4 g per day for others (Table 1).[58]

Recommendations: NSAIDs or acetaminophen may be used as adjuncts to opioids in selected patients. (Grade of recommendation = B)

Ketorolac therapy should be limited to a maximum of five days, with close monitoring for the development of renal insufficiency or gastrointestinal bleeding. Other NSAIDs may be used via the enteral route in appropriate patients. (Grade of recommendation = B)

Sedation

The indications for sedative agents are not well defined. Sedatives are common adjuncts for the treatment of anxiety and agitation. The causes of anxiety in critically ill patients are multifactorial and are likely secondary to an inability to communicate amid continuous noise (alarms, personnel, and equipment), continuous ambient lighting, and excessive stimulation (inadequate analgesia, frequent vital signs, repositioning, lack of mobility, and room temperature). Sleep deprivation and the circumstances that led to an ICU admission may increase patient anxiety, affecting up to 50% of ICU patients.[38,59] Efforts to reduce anxiety, including frequent reorientation, maintenance of patient comfort, provision of adequate analgesia, and optimization of the environment, may be supplemented with sedatives. Some patients with respiratory failure require sedation to facilitate mechanical ventilation, although sedation should not be used in lieu of appropriate ventilation strategies.

Agitation is common in ICU patients of all ages, occurring at least once in 71% of patients in a medical–surgical ICU.[38] Agitation can be caused by multiple factors, such as extreme anxiety, delirium, adverse drug effects, and pain.[38] However, not all patients with anxiety will exhibit agitation; some patients may be fearful, anxious, and withdrawn. When patients exhibit signs of anxiety or agitation, the first priority is to identify and treat any underlying physiological disturbances, such as hypoxemia, hypoglycemia, hypotension, pain, and withdrawal from alcohol and other drugs. The prevalence of drug and alcohol abuse in the general population is high, and these substances are commonly associated with traumatic injury.[60–62] Patients in the ICU should be assessed for symptoms of intoxication or withdrawal upon admission and for several weeks thereafter.[60–62] When possible, patients should be questioned about the use of herbal medicines because these products may contribute to significant drug interactions and adverse effects.[63]

Recent studies have confirmed that agitation may have a deleterious effect on patients by contributing to ventilator dysynchrony, an increase in oxygen consumption, and inadvertent removal of devices and catheters.[38,64–67] Sedatives reduce the stress response and improve the tolerance of routine ICU procedures.[68] The use of sedatives to maintain patient safety and comfort is often essential to the ICU therapeutic care plan. The sedation of mechanically ventilated patients is often medically necessary and should be based on an individualized assessment and the patient's needs. Sedatives should be administered intermittently or on an "as needed" basis to determine the dose that will achieve the sedation goal. Sedatives, as outlined in this guideline, are not intended to be used as a method of restraint and are not to be "used as a means of coercion, discipline, convenience, or retaliation by staff" (Federal regulation 42 CFR 482.13). It is important to consider this principle in order to follow the intent of the Centers for Medicare and Medicaid Services regulation regarding restraints.

An analgesic may be the appropriate initial therapy when pain is the suspected cause of acute agitation. Although opioids may produce sedating effects, they do not diminish awareness or provide amnesia for stressful events. Sedative–amnestic therapy is required to reliably attain amnesia.[69–72] Without amnesia, many patients who recall their ICU stay report unpleasant or frightening memories, which may contribute to post-traumatic stress disorder (PTSD) symptoms.[21,73] However, some patients have vivid hypnogogic hallucinations (dreams just before loss of consciousness) with sedative–amnestic therapy.[74] As sedation blunts explicit memory, these hallucinations may be patients' only memory of the ICU experience.[75] Recalling

delusions, without memory of real events, may also contribute to acute PTSD-related symptoms.[75] Other data suggest that PTSD may be experienced by 4–15% of ICU survivors.[76,77] Amnestic sedatives may paradoxically contribute to agitation and disorientation because patients may not remember where they are or why they are in the ICU.

Recommendation: Sedation of agitated critically ill patients should be started only after providing adequate analgesia and treating reversible physiological causes. (Grade of recommendation = C)

Sedation Assessment. *Subjective assessment of sedation and agitation.* Frequent assessment of the degree of sedation or agitation may facilitate the titration of sedatives to predetermined endpoints.[78–80] An ideal sedation scale should provide data that are simple to compute and record, accurately describe the degree of sedation or agitation within well-defined categories, guide the titration of therapy, and have validity and reliability in ICU patients. Many scales are available, but a true gold-standard scale has not been established.[79] Several scales have construct validity with good correlation between the scales' measures and other measures of sedation. None of the scales have been tested for their ability to detect a patient's response to changes in sedative therapy, dosage, or withdrawal. However, a defined sedation goal, using the Ramsay scale and a protocol-driven sedation plan, was shown to reduce the duration of mechanical ventilation and length of stay.[80] The authors did not report other patient outcome measures relative to the adequacy of analgesia or sedation.

The Riker Sedation–Agitation Scale (SAS) was the first scale proven to be reliable and valid in critically ill adults.[81,82] SAS scores a patient's level of consciousness and agitation from a seven-item list describing patient behavior (Table 2). Excellent inter-rater reliability has been demonstrated and validity has been shown with two other scales. The Motor Activity Assessment Scale (MAAS), adapted from the SAS, has also been validated and shown reliable for use in critically ill patients.[83] The MAAS has seven categories to describe patient behaviors in response to stimulation (Table 2). The Ramsay scale measures three levels of awake states and three levels of asleep states (Table 2).[84] It has been shown to have an acceptable interrater reliability compared with the SAS, but has been criticized for its lack of clear discrimination and specific descriptors to differentiate between the various levels.[82,85] Nevertheless, the Ramsay scale has been used in many comparative sedation trials and is widely used clinically. The Vancouver Interaction and Calmness Scale (VICS) has also been validated for the assessment of sedation in adult critically ill patients.[86] With the VICS scoring system, patients are assessed independently for the ability to interact and communicate and for their level of activity or restlessness. The VICS has not been tested to identify optimal sedation endpoints. Another scale, the Observer's Assessment of Alertness/Sedation Scale, is often used in the operating room but lacks the ability to assess agitation and has never been tested in the ICU.[87] The COMFORT scale has been extensively tested and applied in the ICU environment, but only in children.[88]

The appropriate target level of sedation will primarily depend on a patient's acute disease process and any therapeutic and supportive interventions required. A common target level of sedation in the ICU is a calm patient that can be easily aroused with maintenance of the normal sleep–

Table 2.
Scales Used to Measure Sedation and Agitation

Score	Description	Definition
Riker Sedation–Agitation Scale (SAS)[82]		
7	Dangerous agitation	Pulling at endotracheal tube (ETT), trying to remove catheters, climbing over bedrail, striking at staff, thrashing side-to-side
6	Very agitated	Does not calm despite frequent verbal reminding of limits, requires physical restraints, biting ETT
5	Agitated	Anxious or mildly agitated, attempting to sit up, calms down to verbal instructions
4	Calm and Cooperative	Calm, awakens easily, follows commands
3	Sedated	Difficult to arouse, awakens to verbal stimuli or gentle shaking but drifts off again, follows simple commands
2	Very sedated	Arouses to physical stimuli but does not communicate or follow commands, may move spontaneously
1	Unarousable	Minimal or no response to noxious stimuli, does not communicate or follow commands
Motor Activity Assessment Scale (MAAS)[83]		
6	Dangerously agitated	No external stimulus is required to elicit movement and patient is uncooperative pulling at tubes or catheters or thrashing side to side or striking at staff or trying to climb out of bed and does not calm down when asked
5	Agitated	No external stimulus is required to elicit movement and attempting to sit up or moves limbs out of bed and does not consistently follow commands (e.g., will lie down when asked but soon reverts back to attempts to sit up or move limbs out of bed)
4	Restless and cooperative	No external stimulus is required to elicit movement and patient is picking at sheets or tubes or uncovering self and follows commands
3	Calm and cooperative	No external stimulus is required to elicit movement and patient is adjusting sheets or clothes purposefully and follows commands
2	Responsive to touch or name	Opens eyes or raises eyebrows or turns head toward stimulus or moves limbs when touched or name is loudly spoken
1	Responsive only to noxious stimulus[a]	Opens eyes or raises eyebrows or turns head toward stimulus or moves limbs with noxious stimulus
0	Unresponsive	Does not move with noxious stimulus
Ramsay Scale[84]		
1	Awake	Patient anxious and agitated or restless or both
2		Patient cooperative, oriented and tranquil
3		Patient responds to commands only
4	Asleep	A brisk response to a light glabellar tap or loud auditory stimulus
5		A sluggish response to a light glabellar tap or loud auditory stimulus
6		No response to a light glabellar tap or loud auditory stimulus

[a]Noxious stimulus = suctioning or 5 seconds of vigorous orbital, sternal, or nail bed pressure.

wake cycle, but some may require deep levels of sedation to facilitate mechanical ventilation. The desired level of sedation should be defined at the start of therapy and re-evaluated on a regular basis as the clinical condition of the patient changes. Regimens should be written with the appropriate flexibility to allow titration to the desired endpoint, anticipating fluctuations in sedation requirements throughout the day.

Objective assessment of sedation. Objective testing of a patient's level of sedation may be helpful during very deep sedation or when therapeutic neuromuscular blockade masks observable behavior. Vital signs, such as blood pressure and heart rate, are not specific or sensitive markers of the level of sedation among critically ill patients. Tools utilized in objective assessment include heart rate variability and lower-esophageal contractility, but most are based on a patient's electroencephalogram (EEG). The raw EEG signal has been manipulated in several devices to simplify bedside interpretation and improve reliability. For example, the bispectral index (BIS) uses a digital scale from 100 (completely awake) to 0 (isoelectric EEG).[89] Most of the literature about the use of BIS in the operating room supports strong agreement between BIS and patient recall or level of hypnosis.[90] Elective surgery patients receiving sedatives have shown a strong inverse correlation between hypnotic drug effect and BIS.[91,92]

Although the BIS may be a promising tool for the objective assessment of sedation or hypnotic drug effect, it has limitations in the ICU environment.[93–95] BIS scores may vary between patients at the same subjective level of sedation, and subjective scales may be more reproducible during light sedation.[93,94] Muscle-based electrical activity may artificially elevate BIS scores if the patient has not received neuromuscular blockade.[94] A new version of BIS software is being tested for improved applicability in measuring ICU sedation. BIS has not been tested in patients with metabolic impairments or structural abnormalities of the brain. Studies have not compared the patient outcomes of using BIS versus subjective scales. Although BIS is likely to be useful when patients are deeply comatose or under neuromuscular blockade, routine use of this device cannot be recommended until the value and validity are confirmed.

Recommendations: A sedation goal or endpoint should be established and regularly redefined for each patient. Regular assessment and response to therapy should be systematically documented. (Grade of recommendation = C)

The use of a validated sedation assessment scale (SAS,

MAAS, or VICS) is recommended. (Grade of recommendation = B)

Objective measures of sedation, such as BIS, have not been completely evaluated and are not yet proven useful in the ICU. (Grade of recommendation = C)

Sedation Therapy. *Benzodiazepines.* Benzodiazepines are sedatives and hypnotics that block the acquisition and encoding of new information and potentially unpleasant experiences (anterograde amnesia) but do not induce retrograde amnesia. Although they lack any analgesic properties, they have an opioid-sparing effect by moderating the anticipatory pain response.[96,97] Benzodiazepines vary in their potency, onset and duration of action, uptake, distribution, metabolism, and presence or absence of active metabolites (Table 3). Patient-specific factors, such as age, concurrent pathology, prior alcohol abuse, and concurrent drug therapy, affect the intensity and duration of activity of benzodiazepines, requiring individualized titration. Elderly patients exhibit slower clearance of benzodiazepines or their active metabolites and have a larger volume of drug distribution, contributing to a marked prolongation of elimination.[111] Compromised hepatic or renal function may slow the clearance of benzodiazepines or their active metabolites. Induction or inhibition of hepatic or intestinal enzyme activity can alter the oxidative metabolism of most benzodiazepines.[112]

Benzodiazepine therapy should be titrated to a predefined endpoint, often requiring a series of loading doses. Hemodynamically unstable patients may experience hypotension with the initiation of sedation. Maintenance of sedation with intermittent or "as needed" doses of diazepam, lorazepam, or midazolam may be adequate to accomplish the goal of sedation.[78] However, patients requiring frequent doses to maintain the desired effect may benefit from a continuous infusion by using the lowest effective infusion dose. Continuous infusions must be used cautiously, as accumulation of the parent drug or its active metabolites may produce inadvertent oversedation. Frequent reassessment of a patient's sedation requirements and active tapering of the infusion rate can prevent prolonged sedative effects.[80] However, awakening times after several days of sedation may be quite unpredictable in clinical use. In contrast, tolerance to benzodiazepines may occur within hours to several days of therapy, and escalating doses of midazolam have been reported.[113,114] While not well described in the literature, paradoxical agitation has also been observed during light sedation and may be the result of drug-induced amnesia or disorientation.

Diazepam has been shown to provide rapid onset and awakening after single doses (Table 3).[78,115] Because of its long-acting metabolites, a prolonged duration of sedative effect may occur with repeated doses, but this may be acceptable for long-term sedation.[78] Lorazepam has a slower onset but fewer potential drug interactions because of its metabolism via glucuronidation (Table 3).[98,112] The slow onset makes lorazepam less useful for the treatment of acute agitation. Maintenance of sedation can be accomplished with intermittent or continuous intravenous administration. Lorazepam has an elimination half-life of 12–15 hours, so an infusion is not readily titratable. Loading doses given by i.v. push should be used initially with relatively fixed infusion rates. Lorazepam infusions should be prepared using the 2 mg/mL injection and diluted to a concentration of 1 mg/mL or less and mixed in a glass bottle.[116,117] Despite these

Table 3.
Pharmacology of Selected Sedatives[1,30–32,98–110]

Agent	Onset After i.v. Dose	Half-life of Parent Compound	Metabolic Pathway	Active Metabolite	Unique Adverse Effects	Intermittent i.v. Dose[a]	Infusion Dose Range (Usual)	Cost per day 70 kg patient[b]
Diazepam	2–5 min	20–120 hr	Desmethylation and hydroxylation	Yes (prolonged sedation)	Phlebitis	0.03–0.1 mg/kg q 0.5–6 hr	...	20 mg q 4 hr: $5.00–20.50
Lorazepam	5–20 min	8–15 hr	Glucuronidation	None	Solvent-related acidosis/renal failure in high doses	0.02–0.06 mg/kg q 2–6 hr	0.01–0.1 mg/kg/hr	48 mg/day: $55.00
Midazolam	2–5 min	3–11 hr	Oxidation	Yes (prolonged sedation, especially with renal failure)	...	0.02–0.08 mg/kg q 0.5–2 hr	0.04–0.2 mg/kg/hr	6 mg/hr: $65.00–309.00
Propofol	1–2 min	26–32 hr	Oxidation	None	Elevated triglycerides, pain on injection	...	5–80 µg/kg/min	50 µg/kg/min: $235.00–375.00
Haloperidol	3–20 min	18–54 hr	Oxidation	Yes (EPS)[c]	QT interval prolongation	0.03–0.15 mg/kg q 0.5–6 hr	0.04–0.15 mg/kg/hr	10 mg q 6 h: $62.00–65.00

[a]More frequent doses may be needed for management of acute agitation in mechanically ventilated patients.
[b]Cost based on 2001 average wholesale price.
[c]EPS = extrapyramidal symptoms.

precautions, precipitation may develop.[118] An alternative is to administer undiluted lorazepam as an infusion using a PCA device.[78] The lorazepam solvents polyethylene glycol (PEG) and propylene glycol (PG) have been implicated as the cause of reversible acute tubular necrosis, lactic acidosis, and hyperosmolar states after prolonged high-dose infusions. The dosing threshold for this effect has not been prospectively defined, but these case reports described doses that exceeded 18 mg/hr and continued for longer than four weeks and higher doses (>25 mg/hr) continuing for hours to days.[119–121] It seems prudent to avoid doses of this magnitude. Alternatively, lorazepam and diazepam may be administered via the enteral route in tablet or liquid form.[122] Large doses of liquid lorazepam (i.e., 60 mg of 2 mg/mL every six hours) may lead to diarrhea because of the high PEG and PG content.[123]

Midazolam has a rapid onset and short duration with single doses, similar to diazepam (Table 3).[115] The rapid onset of midazolam makes it preferable for treating acutely agitated patients. Accumulation and prolonged sedative effects have been reported in critically ill patients using midazolam who are obese or have a low albumin level or renal failure.[99–103] Prolonged sedative effects may also be caused by the accumulation of an active metabolite, alpha-hydroxymidazolam, or its conjugated salt, especially in patients with renal insufficiency.[101–105] Significant inhibition of midazolam metabolism has been reported with propofol, diltiazem, macrolide antibiotics, and other inhibitors of cytochrome P450 isoenzyme 3A4, which could influence the duration of effect.[107,108,112] Daily discontinuation of midazolam infusions (wake up) with retitration to a Ramsay scale endpoint reduced midazolam requirements and was associated with a reduction in the duration of mechanical ventilation and length of ICU stay.[50] However, the patients in this trial were off of midazolam for an average of 5.3 hours per day, so this research technique may be difficult to implement. Patients should be closely monitored for self-extubation or the removal of other monitoring devices during the daily awakening sessions.

The routine use of a benzodiazepine antagonist, such as flumazenil, is not recommended after prolonged benzodiazepine therapy because of the risks of inducing withdrawal symptoms and increasing myocardial oxygen consumption with as little as 0.5 mg of flumazenil.[124] An i.v. dose of flumazenil 0.15 mg is associated with few withdrawal symptoms when administered to patients receiving midazolam infusions.[125] If flumazenil is used to test for prolonged sedation after several days of benzodiazepine therapy, a single low dose is recommended.

Propofol. Propofol is an intravenous, general anesthetic agent. However, sedative and hypnotic properties can be demonstrated at lower doses. Compared with benzodiazepines, propofol produces a similar degree of amnesia at equisedative doses in volunteers.[69] In a clinical trial of ICU patients, propofol did not produce amnesia as often as midazolam.[70] Like the benzodiazepines, propofol has no analgesic properties.

Propofol has a rapid onset and short duration of sedation once discontinued (Table 3). While most of the early literature documents the comparatively rapid resolution of sedation after propofol infusions, a slightly longer recovery has been reported after more than 12 hours of infusion.[110,126] No changes in kinetic parameters have been reported in patients with renal or hepatic dysfunction.

Propofol is available as an emulsion in a phospholipid vehicle, which provides 1.1 kcal/mL from fat and should be counted as a caloric source. Long-term or high-dose infusions may result in hypertriglyceridemia.[127–129] Other adverse effects most commonly seen with propofol include hypotension, bradycardia, and pain upon peripheral venous injection. The hypotension is dose related and more frequent after bolus dose administration. Elevation of pancreatic enzymes has been reported during prolonged infusions of propofol.[130,131] Pancreatitis has been reported following anesthesia with propofol, although a causal relationship has not been established.[132] Prolonged use (>48 hours) of high doses of propofol (>66 µg/kg/min infusion) has been associated with lactic acidosis, bradycardia, and lipidemia in pediatric patients and doses >83 µg/kg/min have been associated with an increased risk of cardiac arrest in adults.[133,134] The adults at highest risk for cardiac complications received > 100 µg/kg/min infusion of a 2% propofol solution to achieve deep sedation after neurologic injury.[134] FDA has specifically recommended against the use of propofol for the prolonged sedation of pediatric patients. Patients receiving propofol should be monitored for unexplained metabolic acidosis or arrhythmias.

Alternative sedative agents should be considered for patients with escalating vasopressor or inotrope requirements or cardiac failure during high-dose propofol infusions.

Propofol requires a dedicated i.v. catheter when administered as a continuous infusion because of the potential for drug incompatibility and infection. Improper aseptic technique with propofol in the operating room has led to nosocomial postoperative infection.[135] However, a clinically relevant incidence of infectious complications has not been reported with ICU use.[136] The manufacturers suggest that propofol infusion bottles and tubing should hang no more than 12 hours and solutions transferred from the original container should be discarded every 6 hours. A preservative has been added to propofol to decrease the potential for bacterial overgrowth in case the vial would become contaminated. One of the propofol formulations contains edetic acid (Diprivan, AstraZeneca) and the manufacturer recommends a drug holiday after more than seven days of infusion to minimize the risk of trace element abnormalities. Another product (propofol, Gensia Sicor) contains sodium metabisulfite, which may produce allergic reactions in susceptible patients. Sulfite sensitivity occurs more frequently in patients with asthma.

While propofol appears to possess anticonvulsant activity, excitatory phenomena, such as myoclonus, have been observed. There are several case reports and small, uncontrolled studies describing the efficacy of propofol in refractory status epilepticus (after traditional treatment regimens have failed or are not tolerated) and electroconvulsive shock therapy.[137,138] Case reports have also described roles for propofol in delirium tremens refractory to high-dose benzodiazepine therapy.[139]

Propofol has been used to sedate neurosurgical patients to reduce elevated intracranial pressure (ICP).[140,141] The rapid awakening from propofol allows interruption of the infusion for neurologic assessment. Propofol may also decrease cerebral blood flow and metabolism. Propofol and morphine produced improved control of ICP compared with morphine alone in the treatment of severe traumatic brain injury (TBI).[141] Propofol reduced elevated ICP more effectively than fentanyl following severe TBI.[142] High doses of propofol should be used cautiously in this setting.[134] Propofol infusions used to reduce elevated ICP may need to be continued longer than usually recommended for routine sedation.[141]

Central α-agonists. Clonidine has been used to augment the effects of general anesthetics and narcotics and to treat drug withdrawal syndromes in the ICU.[143,144] The more selective α-2 agonist, dexmedetomidine, was recently approved for use as a sedative with analgesic-sparing activity for short-term use (<24 hours) in patients who are initially receiving mechanical ventilation. Patients remain sedated when undisturbed, but arouse readily with gentle stimulation. Dexmedetomidine reduces concurrent analgesic and sedative requirements and produces anxiolytic effects comparable to benzodiazepines.[145–148] Rapid administration of dexmedetomidine may produce transient elevations in blood pressure. Patients maintained on dexmedetomidine may develop bradycardia and hypotension, especially in the presence of intravascular volume depletion or high sympathetic tone. The role of this new agent in the sedation of ICU patients remains to be determined.

Sedative Selection. Acute agitation arises from a variety of etiologies, including pain. A short-acting opioid analgesic, such as fentanyl, may provide immediate sedation and patient comfort; however, fentanyl has not been compared with other sedatives in a controlled trial. Midazolam and diazepam also have a rapid onset of sedation.[115] Propofol has a rapid onset, but hypotension and infusion-site pain can result from bolus dose administration. Cautious use of sedatives is recommended for patients not yet intubated because of the risk of respiratory depression.

Comparative trials of prolonged sedation have been performed in a variety of critical care settings. Many were supported by pharmaceutical industry research grants; as a result, newer products have been evaluated more frequently. Outcome is usually described in terms of the speed of onset, ability to maintain the target level of sedation, adverse effects, time required for awakening, and ability to wean from mechanical ventilation. Most of the prospective, randomized trials are experimentally flawed because they are unblinded, use uncontrolled amounts of opioids, and exclude patients with obesity or renal or hepatic insufficiency. This limits their general applicability. There is a need for more large, high-quality, randomized trials of the effectiveness of different sedative agents.[149] Most of the trials used a Ramsay scale for assessment, so the depth of sedation can generally be compared among the trials. The trials are summarized in Tables 4–6.

Duration of therapy. Short-term (<24 hours), randomized, open-label trials of sedation have compared propofol and midazolam most often (eight of nine trials) (Table 4). An opioid was available to all patients. Awakening times for patients taking propofol ranged from 1 to 105 minutes versus 1 to 405 minutes for patients receiving midazolam.[128,150–157] Time to extubation has also been compared, but other variables may influence this outcome measure. Clinically, these agents produced similar outcomes following <24 hours of infusion (Table 4).

An intermediate duration of sedation (one to three days) was reported in three randomized open-label trials (Table 5). Propofol and midazolam were compared for sedation of medical ICU patients and a mixed medical–surgical ICU population with respiratory failure.[157,158] Patients receiving propofol had statistically more predictable awakening times than patients receiving midazolam in both trials. Clinically, this time difference was not as significant

and did not produce more rapid discharge from the ICU.[157] In a three-way comparison of midazolam, lorazepam, and propofol infusions for sedation of surgical ICU patients, the authors concluded that lorazepam was the preferred agent in this population.[118] Overall, these agents were similar in the levels of sedation provided, the time required to achieve adequate sedation, and the number of dose adjustments per day. However, midazolam produced adequate sedation during a greater percentage of time while propofol was associated with more undersedation and lorazepam with more oversedation. Morphine was provided on an as needed basis and the average dose was similar in all three groups. Awakening times were not reported. Precipitation of lorazepam infusions was reported.[118]

Nine open-label, randomized trials comparing long-term sedation (more than three days) were reviewed in these guidelines (Table 6).[70,127–129,157,159–163] Most of the trials compared propofol with midazolam. All trials included opioid therapy, although administration was not controlled. Most studies used a Ramsay scale for patient assessment. In these trials, propofol consistently produced more rapid awakening than midazolam with a statistical and, probably, a clinical difference.[70,127–129,160,161] Propofol patients awakened and were extubated in 0.25–4 hours while midazolam patients required 2.8–10 hours to awaken and up to 49 hours for extubation (Table 6).[157] The greatest difference in time to awakening was seen when a deep level of sedation was the goal of therapy (Ramsay level 4–5). Patients receiving propofol awakened from deep sedation significantly faster than those receiving midazolam.[127–129] Lorazepam and midazolam were also compared for long-term sedation.[159,162] One of these studies used a double-blind study design.[162] There was no statistically significant difference in awakening time between these agents when titrated to similar levels of sedation, although the awakening times associated with lorazepam appeared to be more predictable.

Sedative comparison. Four trials compared lorazepam with midazolam.[118,154,159,162] Intermittent lorazepam doses produced sedation comparable to a midazolam infusion during an eight-hour observation period.[154] Both lorazepam and midazolam have the potential to cause accumulation and prolonged drug effects or oversedation if administered excessively via continuous infusion, especially when deep levels of sedation are attempted.[118,159] However, a rigorous protocol of assessment and titration of lorazepam infusions to moderate levels of sedation produced a less variable awakening time with lorazepam than with midazolam, although the absolute difference in awakening time was not statistically significant.[159] A nurse-managed sedation protocol, which included the active titration of lorazepam infusions to a defined endpoint, avoided a prolonged sedative effect compared with physician management of infusion rates.[80] A blinded trial of lorazepam versus midazolam found that the lorazepam infusions were easier to manage than midazolam infusions because fewer dose adjustments were required to maintain the desired level of sedation.[162] In this trial, wide inter- and intrapatient variability was noted between sedative plasma concentrations and the Ramsay score. No difference was noted in patient recovery when patients were evaluated for 24 hours after the end of the infusion. Awakening times were not reported in two of the other trials.[118,154]

When titrated to a standard endpoint, midazolam and propofol provide comparable levels of sedation with a similar onset of effect.[128,150–153,155–157] As shown in Table 4, there

Table 4.
Clinical Trials with Less Than 24 hours of Sedation[a]

Level of Evidence (Reference)	Population Type (No. Patients)	Exclusion Criteria	Trial Design	Drugs	Mean Dosage	Actual Duration	Sedation Endpoint or Goal	Outcome Measure	Significance or Conclusion
1 (150)	MICU/SICU (100)	Obese, head injury, NMBA use	Multicenter, open-label	Propofol Midazolam Morphine: to all patients	Propofol: 1.77 mg/kg/hr Midazolam: 0.1 mg/kg/hr	Propofol: 20.2 hr Midazolam: 21.3 hr	Ramsay level 2–4	Awakening time: most awake at end of infusion, longest: Propofol: 105 min, Midazolam: 405 min	No statistical analysis reported
2 (128)	MICU/SICU (88 total, 40 short-term sedation)	Neurologic injury, ongoing NMBA use	Open-label	Propofol Midazolam Morphine: to all patients	Propofol: 2.3 mg/kg/hr Midazolam: 0.17 mg/kg/hr	Propofol: 11.9 hr Midazolam: 11.9 hr	Ramsay level 2–5 and modified GCS	Time to extubation: Propofol: 0.3 hr Midazolam: 2.5 ± 0.9 hr	$p < 0.05$, Propofol more rapid extubation
2 (151)	CABG (30)	Obese, renal or hepatic insufficiency	Open-label	Propofol Midazolam Sufentanil: to all patients	Propofol: 2.71 ± 1.13 mg/kg/hr Midazolam: 0.09 ± 0.03 mg/kg/hr	Propofol: 9.5 hr Midazolam: 9.8 hr	Ramsay level 5	Time to extubation: Propofol: 250 ± 135 min Midazolam: 391 ± 128 min	$p < 0.01$, Propofol more rapid extubation
1 (152)	CABG (84)	Renal or hepatic insufficiency	Open-label	Propofol Midazolam Morphine: p.r.n.	Propofol: 0.7 ± 0.09 mg/kg/hr Midazolam: 0.018 ± 0.001 mg/kg/hr	Propofol: 9.2 hr Midazolam: 9.4 hr	Ramsay level 3	Time to extubation: Propofol: 4.3 hr Midazolam: 3.5 hr	Not statistically significant
1 (153)	SICU (60)	None	Open-label, consecutive patients	Propofol Midazolam Morphine: p.r.n.	Propofol: 114.8 mg/hr (80.1 ± 21.1 kg) Midazolam: 2.1 ± 1.3 mg/hr (74.2 ± 24 kg)	16 hr observation, total sedation duration not defined	Ramsay level 3 and response to stimulation	Postsedation score at 5, 30, 60, and 90 min: Propofol scores lower at 5 and 30 min	$p < 0.05$, Midazolam more heavily sedated
1 (154)	MICU/SICU (61% trauma)	Cardiac insufficiency, neurosurgical or unstable	Multicenter, open-label	Lorazepam Midazolam Morphine: p.r.n.	Lorazepam: 1.6 ± 0.1 mg i.v. push, Midazolam: 14.4 ± 1.2 mg infusion over 8 hr	8 hr	Multiple scales: anxiety, amnesia, pain, GCS, Ramsay level 3	Adequacy of sedation	Comparable sedation scores

(Continued on next page)

Table 4 *(Continued)*

Level of Evidence (Reference)	Population Type (No. Patients)	Trial Design	Exclusion Criteria	Drugs	Mean Dosage	Actual Duration	Sedation Endpoint or Goal	Outcome Measure	Significance or Conclusion
1 (155)	Cardiac surgery (41)	Double-blind	Renal, hepatic, or cardiac failure	Propofol Midazolam Morphine: p.r.n.	Propofol: 0.64 ± .17 mg/kg/hr Midazolam: 0.015 ± 0.001 mg/kg/hr	Propofol: 4 hr Midazolam: 4 hr	Ramsay level 2–4	Awakening time: Propofol: 88.6 ± 51 min Midazolam: 93.8 ± 59.4 min	Not statistically significant
1 (156)	CABG (75)	Double-blind	Renal failure, neurologic history, hepatic failure, cardiovascular dysfunction	Propofol Midazolam Both Propofol and Midazolam Morphine: to all patients	Propofol: 1.2 ± 0.03 mg/kg/hr Midazolam: 0.08 ± 0.01 mg/kg/hr Propofol and Midazolam: Propofol: 0.22 ± 0.03 mg/kg/hr, Midazolam: 0.02 mg/kg/hr	Propofol: 14.4 hr Midazolam: 14.1 hr Propofol and Midazolam: 14.7 hr	Modified GCS	Time to extubation: Propofol: 0.9 ± 0.3 hr Midazolam: 2.3 ± 0.8 hr Propofol and Midazolam: 1.2 ± 0.6 hr	$p = 0.01$, Midazolam vs. Propofol or Propofol and Midazolam
2 (157)	MICU/SICU (99)	Multicenter, open-label, intention-to-treat analysis	Neurosurgery, coma, seizures	Propofol Midazolam Opiates: p.r.n.	Actual doses not specified	≤24 hr - post hoc stratum Propofol: $n = 21$ Midazolam: $n = 26$	Ramsay scale, level was specified daily	Time to extubation: Propofol: 5.6 hr Midazolam: 11.9 hr	$p = 0.029$ Overall: Propofol: 60.2% of time at target Ramsay score Midazolam: 44% of time at target Ramsay score, $p < 0.05$

aMICU = medical intensive care unit, SICU = surgical intensive care unit, NMBA = neuromuscular blocking agent, GCS = Glasgow Coma Score, CABG = coronary artery bypass graft.

is generally no statistical or clinical difference in awakening times between propofol and midazolam when used for short-term sedation. Data from longer trials of sedation (more than 72 hours) suggest that propofol is associated with more reliable and rapid awakening, both statistically and clinically, than midazolam.[106,127,128,156,158,160] Following long-term sedation, propofol awakening times ranged from 0.25 to 2.5 hours and midazolam awakening times ranged from 2.8 to 30 hours (Table 6). One center's comparison of two concentrations of propofol (1% and 2%) versus midazolam used in trauma patients has shown that midazolam provides deep levels of sedation more reliably than propofol, but the awakening times were much longer with midazolam.[127,163] More patients receiving 1% propofol experienced failure because of elevated triglycerides, but the 2% propofol group experienced failure because of inadequate sedation. Failure of propofol to provide adequate sedation of trauma patients was reported elsewhere, although an explanation was not apparent.[118]

Economic comparison. Several of these studies presented limited pharmacoeconomic data. In most reports, the sedative costs were the only costs considered (cost minimization).[118,154–156,162] Some studies included a portion of the costs for ICU patient care.[128,161] A sedative with a low acquisition cost may be cited as the least expensive agent for prolonged sedation (e.g., lorazepam).[1,32,118] A complete economic analysis should consider costs associated with the evaluation and treatment of sedation-induced adverse effects (e.g., prolonged sedation, infection, and hypertriglyceridemia), therapy failures (additional agents or high doses required), and drug preparation and administration costs (precipitation and tubing changes) to determine the total cost of therapy. The cost of sedation-induced prolongation of ventilation or length of ICU stay is likely to reduce the potential difference in acquisition costs between benzodiazepines and propofol.[164] Institutional vari-

Table 5.
Clinical Trials with One to Three Days of Sedation[a]

Level of Evidence (Reference)	Population (No. Patients)	Exclusion Criteria	Design	Drugs	Mean Dosage	Actual Duration	Sedation Endpoint/Goal	Outcome Measure	Significance/Conclusion
1 (158)	MICU with respiratory failure (73)	. . .	Open-label	Propofol Midazolam Morphine: p.r.n.	Propofol: 1.25 ± 0.87 mg/kg/hr Midazolam: 3.1 ± 3.2 mg/hr	Up to 3 days	Behavior scale	Awakening: defined by eye opening ability to follow with eyes, hand grasp, and tongue protrusion	Many awake during infusion, Propofol: smaller range of awakening times. Used daily wake-up to reassess patients
2 (118)	Surgical or Trauma ICU (31)	Alcohol abuse, head injury, dialysis	Open-label	Propofol Midazolam Lorazepam Morphine: p.r.n.	Propofol: 2 ± 1.5 mg/kg/hr Midazolam: 0.04 ± 0.03 mg/kg/hr Lorazepam: 0.02 ± 0.01 mg/kg/hr	Propofol: 86.4 ± 72 hr Midazolam: 60 ± 72 hr Lorazepam: 72 ± 52.8 hr	Ramsay level 2–4	Time with adequate sedation: Midazolam: 79% Propofol: 62% Lorazepam: 68%	Lorazepam vs. midazolam $p = 0.03$ Midazolam vs. Propofol $p = 0.01$ Propofol: more undersedation 31% Lorazepam: more oversedation 14% and precipitation 18%
2 (157)	MICU or SICU (99)	Neurosurgery, coma, seizures	Multicenter, Open-label, intention-to-treat analysis	Propofol Midazolam Opioids: p.r.n.	Actual doses not specified	24–72 hr = post hoc stratum Propofol: $n = 21$ Midazolam: $n = 17$	Ramsay scale, level was specified daily	Time to extubation Propofol: 7.4 hr Midazolam: 31.3 hr	$p = 0.068$, Enrollment ended early, insufficient power Overall: Propofol: 60.2% of time at target Ramsay score Midazolam: 44% of time at target Ramsay score, $p < 0.05$

[a]MICU = medical intensive care unit, ICU = intensive care unit, SICU = surgical intensive care unit.

Table 6.
Clinical Trials of More Than Three Days of Sedation

Level of Evidence (Reference)	Population (No. Patients)	Exclusion Criteria	Design	Drugs	Mean Dosage	Actual Duration	Sedation Endpoint/Goal	Outcome Measure	Significance/ Conclusion
2 (128)	MICU/SICU[a] (88 total, 28 medium-term, 20 long-term sedation)	Neurologic injury, ongoing NMBA use	Open-label	Propofol Midazolam Morphine: to all patients	Propofol 2.3 mg/kg/hr Midazolam 0.17 mg/kg/hr	Medium: Propofol: 116 hr Midazolam: 113 hr Long Propofol: 312 hr Midazolam: 342 hr	Ramsay level 2–5 and modified GCS	Time to extubation: Medium: Propofol: 0.4 ± 0.1 hr Midazolam: 13.5 ± 4 hr Long Propofol: 0.8 ± 0.3 hr Midazolam: 36.6 ± 6.8 hr	Medium: $p < 0.05$ Long: $p < 0.05$
1 (159)	MICU (20)	CNS abnormal	Open-label	Lorazepam Midazolam Morphine: to all patients	Lorazepam: 0.06 ± 0.04 mg/kg/hr Midazolam: 0.24 ± 0.16 mg/kg/hr	Lorazepam: 77 hr Midazolam: 108 hr	Ramsay level 2–3	Return to baseline mental status: Lorazepam: 261 ± 189 min, Midazolam: 1815 ± 2322 min	Not statistically significant
1 (160)	MICU/SICU (98)	Renal, hepatic, or cardiac failure, ongoing NMBA use	Open-label, multicenter	Propofol Midazolam Morphine: p.r.n.	Propofol: 2.8 ± 1.1 mg/kg/hr Midazolam: 0.14 ± 0.1 mg/kg/hr	Propofol: 81 hr Midazolam: 88 hr	Own sedation scale	Awakening lightly sedated: Propofol: 14 ± 0.8 min Midazolam: 64 ± 20 min Deep sedation: Propofol: 27 ± 16 min Midazolam: 237 ± 222 min	Light: $p < 0.05$ Heavy: $p < 0.01$
1 (129)	MICU/SICU (108 consecutive)	Chronic liver disease, head injury, ongoing NMBA use	Open-label	Propofol Midazolam Morphine: to all patients	Propofol: 3.07–5.7 mg/kg/hr Midazolam: 14 ± 0.1 mg/kg/hr	Propofol: 139 hr Midazolam: 141 hr	Ramsay level 4–5	Time to t-tube Propofol: 4 ± 3.9 hr Midazolam: 48.9 ± 47.2 hr	$p = 0.0001$ Propofol: high triglycerides 12% men, 50% women

(Continued on next page)

2 (70)	MICU/SICU (68 consecutive)	None	Open-label	Propofol; Midazolam; Morphine: p.r.n.	Propofol: 1.8 ± 0.08 mg/kg/hr; Midazolam: 0.07 ± 0.003 mg/kg/hr	Propofol: 99 hr; Midazolam: 141 hr	Ramsay level 2–3 also rated amnesia	Awakening: Propofol: 1.8 ± 0.4 hr; Midazolam: 2.8 ± 0.4 hr; Amnesia: Propofol: 29%; Midazolam: 100%	$p < 0.02$ More propofol patients with agitation upon awakening
2 (161)	MICU/SICU (26)	Hepatic or renal insufficiency, head injury, ongoing NMBA use	Open-label	Propofol + alfentanil; Midazolam + morphine	Alfentanil: 0.5–2 μg/kg/hr; Propofol: 1–4 mg/kg/hr; Morphine: 17–70 μg/kg/hr; Midazolam: 0.03–0.2 mg/kg/hr	...	Own scale, goal: moderate-heavy sedation	Time to extubation: Propofol: 3 hr (1–13 hr); Midazolam: 50 hr (1–121 hr)	$p = 0.006$
1 (127)	Trauma ICU (100 consecutive)	Renal or hepatic failure	Open-label	Propofol; Midazolam; Propofol + midazolam; Morphine: p.r.n.	Propofol: 2.12 ± 1.2 mg/kg/hr; Midazolam: 0.19 ± 0.09 mg/kg/hr; Propofol and Midazolam: Propofol: 1.6 ± 0.05 mg/kg/hr, Midazolam: 0.14 ± 0.08 mg/kg/hr	Propofol: 5.2 days; Midazolam: 6.6 days; Propofol and Midazolam: 7.2 days	Own scale, goal: moderate to heavy sedation	Awakening (excluding head trauma): Propofol: 110 ± 50 min; Midazolam: 660 ± 400 min; Propofol and Midazolam: 190 ± 200 min	Midazolam vs Propofol or Propofol and Midazolam: $p < 0.01$; Propofol: high triglyceride levels
1 (162)	MICU (64)	Head injury, ongoing NMBA use	Blinded	Lorazepam; Midazolam; Fentanyl p.r.n.	Lorazepam: 23.1 ± 14.4 mg/day; Midazolam: 372 ± 256 mg/day	Lorazepam: 141 hr; Midazolam: 141 hr	Addenbrooke sedation scale, initial moderate to heavy sedation, tapering to	Awakening similar, times not reported	Satisfactory sedation: Lorazepam: 87 ± 10.5%, Midazolam: 66.2 ± 23.1%p

(Continued on next page)

ables (bed availability) or patient-specific factors (other injuries and the need for observation) may impact a patient's length of stay more than the sedation regimen. More rapid extubation with propofol was not associated with a shorter length of stay in a multicenter Canadian trial.[157] Research that considers all of these cost factors is needed to estimate the overall cost of sedative regimens. Since the frequency of sedation-induced adverse effects has not been well described, there are insufficient data to create pharmacoeconomic models comparing the potential costs of sedative regimens. The acquisition costs of sedatives vary widely among institutions, and costs may decline with the availability of generic products (Table 3).

Multidisciplinary development and implementation of sedation guidelines have been shown to reduce direct drug costs (from $81.54 to $18.12 per patient per day), ventilator time (317 to 167 hours), and the lengths of ICU stay (19.1 to 9.9 days) and total stay without a change in mortality.[165] Although an economic analysis was not performed, a nursing-implemented sedation protocol using lorazepam reduced the duration of sedation and mechanical ventilation and the tracheostomy rate.[80] A systematic multi-disciplinary team approach to sedation and analgesia will produce clinical and economic benefits.

An algorithm was developed to incorporate many of the assessment issues with the therapy options in this document (Figure 1). When using this algorithm, the pharmacology, potential adverse effects, and therapeutic issues discussed in this document should be considered.

Recommendations: Midazolam or diazepam should be used for rapid sedation of acutely agitated patients. (Grade of recommendation = C)

Propofol is the preferred sedative when rapid awakening (e.g., for neurologic assessment or extubation) is important. (Grade of recommendation = B)

Midazolam is recommended for short-term use only, as it produces unpredictable awakening and time to extubation when infusions continue longer than 48–72 hours. (Grade of recommendation = A)

Lorazepam is recommended for the sedation of most patients via intermittent i.v. administration or continuous infusion. (Grade of recommendation = B)

Table 6 (continued)

Level of Evidence (Reference)	Population (No. Patients)	Exclusion Criteria	Design	Drugs	Mean Dosage	Actual Duration	Sedation Endpoint/Goal	Outcome Measure	Significance/ Conclusion
2 (163)	Trauma ICU (63 consecutive)	Renal or hepatic failure	Open-label	Propofol 2% Midazolam Morphine: to all patients	Propofol: 6400 ± 1797 mg/day Midazolam: 297.8 ± 103.8 mg/day	Propofol: 6.5 hr Midazolam 11.1 hr	Own scale, goal: moderate to heavy sedation	Awakening (no head trauma) Propofol: 145 ± 50 min Midazolam: 372 ± 491 min	Awakening: not statistically significant Less triglyceride elevation than historical control (reference 117)
2 (157)	MICU/SICU (99)	Neurosurgery, coma, seizures	Multicenter, open-label, intention-to-treat analysis	Propofol Midazolam Opioids: p.r.n.	Actual doses not specified	24–72 hr - post hoc stratum Propofol: $n = 4$ Midazolam: $n = 10$	Ramsay scale, level was specified daily	Time to extubation: Propofol: 8.4 hr Midazolam: 46.8 hr	$p = 0.03$, enrollment ended early, insufficient power limits conclusion Overall: Propofol: 60.2% of time at target Ramsay score Midazolam: 44% of time at target Ramsay score, $p < 0.05$

[a]MICU = medical intensive care unit, ICU = intensive care unit, NMBA = neuromuscular blocking agent, GCS = Glasgow Coma Score, SICU = surgical intensive care unit.

The titration of the sedative dose to a defined endpoint is recommended with systematic tapering of the dose or daily interruption with retitration to minimize prolonged sedative effects. (Grade of recommendation = A)

Triglyceride concentrations should be monitored after two days of propofol infusion, and total caloric intake from lipids should be included in the nutrition support prescription. (Grade of recommendation = B)

The use of sedation guidelines, an algorithm, or a protocol is recommended. (Grade of recommendation = B)

Sedative and Analgesic Withdrawal

Patients exposed to more than one week of high-dose opioid or sedative therapy may develop neuroadaptation or physiological dependence. Rapid discontinuation of these agents could lead to withdrawal symptoms. Opioid withdrawal signs and symptoms include dilation of the pupils, sweating, lacrimation, rhinorrhea, piloerection, tachycardia, vomiting, diarrhea, hypertension, yawning, fever, tachypnea, restlessness, irritability, increased sensitivity to pain, cramps, muscle aches, and anxiety. Benzodiazepine withdrawal signs and symptoms include dysphoria, tremor, headache, nausea, sweating, fatigue, anxiety, agitation, increased sensitivity to light and sound, paresthesias, muscle cramps, myoclonus, sleep disturbances, delirium, and seizures. Propofol withdrawal has not been well described but appears to resemble benzodiazepine withdrawal.

The occurrence of sedative and analgesic withdrawal has been described in both adult and pediatric ICU populations.[166-168] In adults, withdrawal is associated with the length of stay, mechanical ventilation, and the dose and duration of analgesic and sedative therapy. Patients at highest risk include those who stay greater than seven days in the ICU, receive greater than 35 mg/day of lorazepam, or greater than 5 mg/day of fentanyl.[166]

Studies of pediatric patients have found that the rate of medication weaning may be very important in the development of withdrawal syndromes.[167,169] Although not tested prospectively, it has been recommended that daily dose decrements of opioids not exceed 5–10% in high-risk patients.[170] If the drug is administered intermittently, changing the therapy to longer-acting agents may also attenuate withdrawal symptoms.[171] Another recommendation for opioid weaning is to decrease a continuous infusion rate by 20–40% initially and make additional reductions of 10% every 12–24 hours, depending on the patient's response.[172] Conversion to a continuous subcutaneous infusion has also been used for gradual fentanyl and midazolam weaning in children.[173] Patient care costs may be increased unnecessarily if sedatives and analgesics are withdrawn too slowly.

Recommendation: The potential for opioid, benzodiazepine, and propofol withdrawal should be considered after high doses or more than approximately seven days of continuous therapy. Doses should be tapered systematically to prevent withdrawal symptoms. (Grade of recommendation = B)

Delirium

As many as 80% of ICU patients have delirium, characterized by an acutely changing or fluctuating mental status, inattention, disorganized thinking, and an altered level of consciousness that may or may not be accompanied by agitation. Placing severely ill patients in a stressful environment for prolonged periods exacerbates the clinical symptoms of delirium.[174-177] Delirium is usually characterized by fluctuating levels of arousal throughout the day, associated with sleep–wake cycle disruption, and hastened by reversed day–night cycles.[178] Delirium may be associated with confusion and different motoric subtypes: hypoactive, hyperactive, or mixed.[179,180] Hypoactive delirium, which is associated with the worst prognosis, is characterized by psychomotor retardation manifested by a calm appearance, inattention, decreased mobility, and obtundation in extreme cases. Hyperactive delirium is easily recognized by agitation, combative behaviors, lack of orientation, and progressive confusion following sedative therapy.

Assessment of Delirium. The gold standard criteria used to diagnose delirium is the clinical history and examination as guided by the *Diagnostic and Statistical Manual of Mental Disorders, 4th edition (DSM-IV).*[177] Although many scales and diagnostic instruments have been developed to facilitate the recognition and diagnosis of delirium, these scales routinely exclude ICU patients because it is often difficult to communicate with them.[178,181] Several groups of delirium investigators have recently collaborated to develop and validate a rapid bedside instrument to accurately diagnose delirium in ICU patients, who are often nonverbal because they are on mechanical ventilation. This instrument is called the Confusion Assessment Method for the ICU (CAM-ICU).[181,182] The work was begun by Hart and colleagues with their publication of the Cognitive Test for Delirium and a later version called the Abbreviated Cognitive Test for Delirium.[183,184] These two investigations were limited because they included approximately 20 patients each and ex-cluded some of the most severely ill patients who are often cared for in the ICU. These factors led the authors to recommend that additional research with delirium assessment tools be conducted before routine application in mechanically ventilated patients.[184]

Collaboration among specialists in pulmonary and critical care, neurology, psychiatry, neuropsychology, and geriatrics has led to the development of a useful assessment tool.[182,185] It is based on the Confusion Assessment Method (CAM), which was designed specifically for use by health care professionals without formal psychiatric training, and incorporates *DSM-IV* criteria for the diagnosis of delirium.[186] CAM, which is the most widely used delirium assessment instrument for non-psychiatrists, is easy to use and has demonstrated utility in important clinical investigations.[187,188]

Critical care nurses can complete delirium assessments with the CAMICU in an average of 2 minutes with an accuracy of 98%, compared with a full *DSM-IV* assessment by a geriatric psychiatric expert, which usually requires at least 30 minutes to complete. The CAM-ICU assessments have a likelihood ratio of over 50 for diagnosing delirium and high inter-rater reliability (kappa = 0.96).[185] In the two subgroups expected to present the greatest challenge to the CAM-ICU (i.e., those over 65 years and those with suspected dementia), the instrument retained excellent inter-rater reliability, sensitivity, and specificity. To complete the CAM-ICU, patients are observed for the presence of an acute onset of mental status change or a fluctuating mental status, inattention, disorganized thinking, or an altered level of consciousness (Table 7). With the CAM-ICU, delirium was

Table 7.
The Confusion Assessment Method for the Diagnosis of Delirium in the ICU (CAM-ICU)[182,185]

Feature	Assessment Variables
1. Acute Onset of mental status changes or Fluctuating Course	Is there evidence of an acute change in mental status from the baseline?
	Did the (abnormal) behavior fluctuate during the past 24 hours, i.e., tend to come and go or increase and decrease in severity?
	Did the sedation scale (e.g., SAS or MAAS) or coma scale (GCS) fluctuate in the past 24 hours?[a]
	Did the patient have difficulty focusing attention?
2. Inattention	Is there a reduced ability to maintain and shift attention?
	How does the patient score on the Attention Screening Examination (ASE)? (i.e., Visual Component ASE tests the patient's ability to pay attention via recall of 10 pictures; auditory component ASE tests attention via having patient squeeze hands or nod whenever the letter "A" is called in a random letter sequence)
3. Disorganized thinking	If the patient is already extubated from the ventilator, determine whether or not the patient's thinking is disorganized or incoherent, such as rambling or irrelevant conversation, unclear or illogical flow of ideas, or unpredictable switching from subject to subject.
	For those still on the ventilator, can the patient answer the following 4 questions correctly?
	1. Will a stone float on water?
	2. Are there fish in the sea?
	3. Does one pound weigh more than two pounds?
	4. Can you use a hammer to pound a nail?
	Was the patient able to follow questions and commands throughout the assessment?
	1. "Are you having any unclear thinking?"
	2. "Hold up this many fingers." (examiner holds two fingers in front of patient)?
	3. "Now do the same thing with the other hand." (not repeating the number of fingers)
4. Altered level of consciousness (any level of consciousness other than alert (e.g., vigilant, lethargic, stupor, or coma))	Alert: normal, spontaneously fully aware of environment, interacts appropriately
	Vigilant: hyperalert
	Lethargic: drowsy but easily aroused, unaware of some elements in the environment, or not spontaneously interacting appropriately with the interviewer; becomes fully aware and appropriately interactive when prodded minimally
	Stupor: difficult to arouse, unaware of some or all elements in the environment, or not spontaneously interacting with the interviewer; becomes incompletely aware and inappropriately interactive when prodded strongly; can be aroused only by vigorous and repeated stimuli and as soon as the stimulus ceases, stuporous subjects lapse back into the unresponsive state.
	Coma: unarousable, unaware of all elements in the environment, with no spontaneous interaction or awareness of the interviewer, so that the interview is impossible even with maximal prodding

PATIENTS ARE DIAGNOSED WITH DELIRIUM IF THEY HAVE BOTH FEATURES 1 AND 2 AND EITHER FEATURE 3 OR 4.

[a]SAS = Sedation–Analgesia Scale, MAAS = Motor Activity Assessment Scale, GCS = Glasgow Coma Scale.

diagnosed in 87% of the ICU patients with an average onset on the second day and a mean duration of 4.2 ± 1.7 days.[185] Ongoing research will assist in understanding the etiology of delirium and the effects of therapeutic interventions.

Another instrument for delirium screening was validated in ICU patients by comparison with a psychiatric evaluation.[189] The use of these tools in prospective trials will delineate the long-term ramifications of delirium on the clinical outcomes of ICU patients. The study of delirium and other forms of cognitive impairment in mechanically ventilated patients and other risk factors for neuropsychological sequelae after ICU care may be an important advancement in the monitoring and treatment of critically ill patients.

Recommendation: Routine assessment for the presence of delirium is recommended. (The CAM-ICU is a promising tool for the assessment of delirium in ICU patients.) (Grade of recommendation = B)

Treatment of Delirium. Inappropriate drug regimens for sedation or analgesia may exacerbate delirium symptoms. Psychotic or delirious patients may become more obtunded and confused when treated with sedatives, causing a paradoxical increase in agitation.[190]

Neuroleptic agents (chlorpromazine and haloperidol) are the most common drugs used to treat patients with delirium. They are thought to exert a stabilizing effect on cerebral function by antagonizing dopamine-mediated neurotransmission at the cerebral synapses and basal ganglia. This effect can also enhance extrapyramidal symptoms (EPS). Abnormal symptomatology, such as hallucinations, delusions, and unstructured thought patterns, is inhibited, but the patient's interest in the environment is diminished, producing a characteristic flat cerebral affect. These agents also exert a sedative effect.

Chlorpromazine is not routinely used in critically ill patients because of its strong anticholinergic, sedative, and α-adrenergic antagonist effects. Haloperidol has a lesser sedative effect and a lower risk of inducing hypotension than chlorpromazine. Droperidol, a chemical congener of haloperidol, is reported to be more potent than haloperidol but has been associated with frightening dreams and may have a higher risk of inducing hypotension because of its direct vasodilating and antiadrenergic effects.[191,192] Droperidol has not been studied in ICU patients as extensively as haloperidol.

Haloperidol is commonly given via intermittent i.v. injection.[193] The optimal dose and regimen of haloperidol have not been well defined. Haloperidol has a long half-life (18–54 hours) and loading regimens are used to achieve a rapid response in acutely delirious patients. A loading regimen starting with a 2-mg dose, followed by repeated doses (double the previous dose) every 15–20 minutes while agitation persists, has been described.[193,194] High doses of haloperidol (>400 mg per day) have been reported, but QT prolongation may result. However, the safety of this regimen has been questioned.[192,195–200] Once the delirium is controlled, regularly scheduled doses (every four to six hours) may be continued for a few days; then therapy should be tapered over several days. A continuous infusion of haloperidol (3–25 mg/hr) has been used to achieve more consistent serum concentrations.[81,201] The pharmacokinetics of haloperidol may be affected by other drugs.[202]

Neuroleptic agents can cause a dose-dependent QT-interval prolongation of the electrocardiogram, leading to an increased risk of ventricular dysrhythmias, including torsades de pointes.[195–200] Significant QT prolongation has been reported with cumulative haloperidol doses as low as 35 mg, and dysrhythmias have been reported within minutes of administering i.v. doses of 20 mg or more.[199] A history of cardiac disease appears to predispose patients to this adverse event.[200] The actual incidence of torsades de pointes associated with halperidol use is unknown, although a historical case-controlled study suggests it may be 3.6%.[199]

EPS can occur with these agents. A slowly eliminated active metabolite of haloperidol appears to cause EPS.[203–208] EPS has been reported less frequently after i.v. versus oral haloperidol administration, but concurrent benzodiazepine use may mask EPS appearance. Self-limited movement disorders can be seen several days after tapering or discontinuing haloperidol and may last for up to two weeks.[209] Treatment of EPS includes discontinuing the neuroleptic agent and a clinical trial of diphenhydramine or benztropine mesylate.

Other adverse effects have also been described. Haloperidol therapy for the control of agitation after a traumatic brain injury may prolong the duration of posttraumatic amnesia, but the effect on functional recovery has not been well demonstrated in humans.[210] Although haloperidol is the most common antipsychotic agent associated with neuroleptic malignant syndrome and has been implicated in approximately 50% of reported episodes (only three cases were reported in critically ill patients receiving intravenous haloperidol), its adverse effects may be underreported.[211–214]

Haloperidol therapy for acutely agitated or delirious patients has not been studied prospectively in agitated ICU patients, but its utility has been suggested in case series.[81,193,201]

Recommendations: Haloperidol is the preferred agent for the treatment of delirium in critically ill patients. (Grade of recommendation = C)

Patients should be monitored for electrocardiographic changes (QT interval prolongation and arrhythmias) when receiving haloperidol. (Grade of recommendation = B)

Sleep

Sleep is believed to be important to recover from an illness. Sleep deprivation may impair tissue repair and overall cellular immune function.[215] Sleeplessness induces additional stress in critical care patients.[3,216] Allowing a patient to obtain an adequate amount of sleep may be difficult in a critical care unit. Sleep in the ICU has been characterized by few complete sleep cycles, numerous awakenings, and infrequent rapid-eye-movement (REM) sleep.[217] Atypical sleep patterns were demonstrated in critically ill patients receiving high doses of sedatives.[218]

Sleep Assessment. Similar to pain assessment, the patient's own report is the best measure of sleep adequacy, since polysomnography is not a clinically feasible tool in the critical care setting. If self-report is not possible, systematic observation of a patient's sleep time by nurses has been shown to be a valid measure.[219] A VAS or questionnaire can be used to assess sleep for specific patients.[220]

Nonpharmacologic Strategies. *Titrating environmental stimulation.* Nonpharmacologic interventions to promote sleep and increase overall patient comfort may include environment modification, relaxation, back massage, and music therapy. Noise in critical care settings is an environmental hazard that disrupts sleep.[221–223] Sources of noise include equipment, alarms, telephones, ventilators, and staff conversations. Noise levels above 80 decibels cause arousal from sleep. Sleep occurs best below 35 decibels.[222] Earplugs effectively decreased noise and increased REM sleep in healthy volunteers in a study that simulated noise heard in an ICU.[224] A creative unit design with single rooms may ameliorate noise and provide lighting that better reflects a day–night orientation.[225] Lighting mimicking the 24-hour day helps patients achieve normal sleep patterns, so bright lights should be avoided at night. In addition, care should be coordinated to minimize frequent interruptions during the night.

Relaxation. Head-to-toe relaxation may benefit anxious critically ill patients who can follow directions. Relaxation will lead to a parasympathetic response and a decrease in respiratory rate, heart rate, jaw tension, and blood pressure. Relaxation techniques include deep breathing followed by the sequential relaxation of each muscle group.[226] Relaxation, in combination with music therapy, is effective in patients with myocardial infarction.[227]

Music therapy. Music therapy relaxes patients and decreases their pain. Music intervention with cardiac surgery patients, during the first postoperative day, decreased noise annoyance, heart rate, and systolic blood pressure.[228] In mechanically ventilated patients, music therapy decreased anxiety and promoted relaxation.[229] Music therapy is a proven intervention for anxious patients in other critical care settings.[229–231] Music can decrease heart rate, respiratory rate, myocardial oxygen demand, and anxiety scores and improve sleep.[232,233] When selecting music, a patient's personal preference should be considered.

Massage. Back massage is an alternative or adjunct to pharmacologic therapy in critically ill patients. Approximately 5–10 minutes of massage initiates the relaxation response and increases a patient's amount of sleep.[234,235]

Pharmacologic Therapy to Promote Sleep. Patients may remain sleep-deprived despite nonpharmacologic interventions. Most patients need a combination of analgesics, sedatives, and relaxation techniques to decrease pain and anxiety and promote sleep. Sedative-hypnotics can induce sleep in healthy individuals, but little is known of their use in the critically ill. There was no difference in sleep quality between two groups of nonintubated ICU patients receiving midazolam or propofol.[59] Oral hypnotics, such as benzodiazepines or zolpidem, are used in nonintubated patients to decrease sleep latency while increasing total sleep time without affecting sleep architecture in stages three and four and REM sleep.[215]

Recommendation: Sleep promotion should include optimization of the environment and nonpharmacologic methods to promote relaxation with adjunctive use of hypnotics. (Grade of recommendation = B)

References

1. Shapiro BA, Warren J, Egol AB, et al. Practice parameters for intravenous analgesia and sedation for adult patients in the intensive care unit: an executive summary. *Crit Care Med.* 1995; 23:1596–600.

2. Society of Critical Care Medicine and American Society of Health-System Pharmacists. Sedation, analgesia, and neuromuscular blockade of the critically ill adult: revised clinical practice guidelines for 2002. *Am J Health-Syst Pharm.* 2002; 59:147–9.

3. Novaes MA, Knobel E, Bork AM, et al. Stressors in ICU: perception of the patient, relatives and healthcare team. *Intensive Care Med.* 1999; 25:1421–6.

4. Desbiens NA, Wu AW, Broste SK, et al. Pain and satisfaction with pain control in seriously ill hospitalized adults: findings from the SUPPORT research investigators. *Crit Care Med.* 1996; 24:1953–61.

5. Epstein J, Breslow MJ. The stress response of critical illness. *Crit Care Clin.* 1999; 15:17–33.

6. Lewis KS, Whipple JK, Michael KA, et al. Effect of analgesic treatment on the physiological consequences of acute pain. *Am J Hosp Pharm.* 1994; 51:1539–54.

7. Mangano DT, Silician D, Hollenberg M, et al. Postoperative myocardial ischemia; therapeutic trials using intensive analgesia following surgery. *Anesthesiology.* 1992; 76:342–53.

8. Parker SD, Breslow MJ, Frank SM, et al. Catecholamine and cortisol responses to lower extremity revascularization: correlation with outcome variables. *Crit Care Med.* 1995; 23:1954–61.

9. Desai PM. Pain management and pulmonary dysfunction. *Crit Care Clin.* 1999; 15:151–66.

10. Gust R, Pecher S, Gust A, et al. Effect of patient-controlled analgesia on pulmonary complications after coronary artery-bypass grafting. *Crit Care Med.* 1999; 27:2218–23.

11. Carroll KC, Atkins PJ, Herold GR, et al. Pain assessment and management in critically ill postoperative and trauma patients: a multisite study. *Am J Crit Care.* 1999; 8:105–17.

12. Ferguson J, Gilroy D, Puntillo K. Dimensions of pain and analgesic administration associated with coronary artery bypass in an Australian intensive care unit. *J Adv Nurs.* 1997; 26:1065–72.

13. Whipple JK, Lewis KS, Quebbeman EJ, et al. Analysis of pain management in critically ill patients. *Pharmacotherapy.* 1995; 15:592–9.

14. Sun X, Weissman C. The use of analgesics and sedatives in critically ill patients: Physicians' orders versus medications administered. *Heart Lung.* 1994; 23:169–76.

15. Caswell DR, Williams JP, Vallejo M, et al. Improving pain management in critical care. *Jt Comm J Qual Improvement.* 1996; 22:702–12.

16. Hamill-Ruth RJ, Marohn ML. Evaluation of pain in the critically ill patient. *Crit Care Clin.* 1999; 15:35–54.

17. Acute Pain Management Guideline Panel. Acute pain management: operative or medical procedures and trauma. Clinical practice guideline. Rockville, MD: Agency for Health Care Policy and Research, 1992; AHCPR publication no. 92–0032.

18. Ho K, Spence J, Murphy MF. Review of pain management tools. *Ann Emerg Med.* 1996; 27:427–32.

19. Terai T, Yukioka H, Asada A. Pain evaluation in the intensive care unit: observer-reported faces scale compared with self-reported visual analog scale. *Reg Anesth Pain Med.* 1998; 23:147–51.

20. Puntillo KA. Dimensions of procedural pain and its analgesic management in critically ill surgical patients. *Am J Crit Care.* 1994; 3:116–28.

21. Meehan DA, McRae ME, Rourke DA, et al. Analgesia administration, pain intensity, and patient satisfaction in cardiac surgical patients. *Am J Crit Care.* 1995; 4:435–42.

22. Melzack R, Katz J. Pain measurement in persons in pain. In: Wall PD, Melzack R, eds. Textbook of pain. Edinburgh, Scotland: Churchill Livingstone; 1994:337–51.

23. Mateo OM, Krenzischek DA. A pilot study to assess the relationship between behavioral manifestations of pain and self-report of pain in post anesthesia care unit patients. *J Post Anesth Nurs.* 1992; 7:15–21.

24. Puntillo KA, Miaskowski C, Kehrle K, et al. Relationship between behavioral and physiological indicators of pain, critical care patients' self-reports of pain, and opioid administration. *Crit Care Med.* 1997; 25:1159–66.

25. Sjostrom B, Haljamae H, Dahlgren LO, et al. Assessment of postoperative pain: impact of clinical experience and professional role. *Acta Anaesthesiol Scand.* 1997; 41:339–44.

26. Hall-Lord ML, Larsson G, Steen B. Pain and distress among elderly intensive care unit patients: comparison of patients' experiences and nurses' assessments. *Heart Lung.* 1998; 27:123–32.

27. Stannard D, Puntillo K, Miaskowski C, et al. Clinical judgement and management of postoperative pain in critical care patients. *Am J Crit Care.* 1996; 5:433–41.

28. Desbiens NA, Mueller-Rizner N. How well do surrogates assess the pain of seriously ill patients? *Crit Care Med.* 2000; 28:1347–52.

29. Watling SM, Dasta JF, Seidl EC. Sedatives, analgesics, and paralytics in the ICU. *Ann Pharmacother.* 1997; 31:148–53.

30. Wagner BKJ, O'Hara DA. Pharmacokinetics and pharmacodynamics of sedatives and analgesics in the treatment of agitated critically ill patients. *Clin Pharmacokinet.* 1997; 33:426–53.

31. Barr JB, Donner A. Optimal intravenous dosing strategies for sedatives and analgesics in the ICU. *Crit Care Clin.* 1995 11:827–47.

32. AmeriSource Corporation, ECHO software, version 3.1Q, release 00112. Accessed 2001 Feb 6.

33. Danziger LH, Martin SJ, Blum RA. Central nervous system toxicity associated with meperidine use in hepatic disease. *Pharmacotherapy.* 1994; 14:235–8.

34. Hangmeyer KO, Mauro LS, Mauro VF. Meperidine-related seizures associated with patient-controlled analgesia pumps. *Ann Pharmacother.* 1993; 27:29–32.

35. Tipps LB, Coplin WM, Murry KR, et al. Safety and feasibility of continuous infusion of remifentanil in the neurosurgical intensive care unit. *Neurosurgery.* 2000; 46:596–602.

36. Lay TD, Puntillo KA, Miaskowski MI. Analgesics prescribed and administered to intensive care cardiac surgery patients: does patient age make a difference? *Prog Cardiovasc Nurs.* 1996; 11:17–24.

37. Macintyre PE, Jarvis DA. Age is the best predictor of postoperative morphine requirements. *Pain.* 1995; 64:357–64.

38. Fraser GL, Prato S, Berthiaume D, et al. Evaluation of agitation in ICU patients: incidence, severity, and treatment in the young versus the elderly. *Pharmacotherapy.* 2000; 20:75–82.

39. Hofbauer R, Tesinsky P, Hammerschmidt V, et al. No reduction in the sufentanil requirement of elderly patients undergoing ventilatory support in the medical intensive care unit. *Eur J Anaesthesiol.* 1999; 16:702–7.

40. McArdle P. Intravenous analgesia. *Crit Care Clin.* 1999; 15:89–105.

41. Grossman M, Abiose A, Tangphao O, et al. Morphine-induced venodilation in humans. *Clin Pharmacol Ther.* 1996; 60:554–60.

42. Flacke JW, Flacke WE, Bloor BC, et al. Histamine release by four narcotics: a double-blind study in humans. *Anesth Analg.* 1987; 66:723–30.

43. Yuan C, Foss JF, O'Connor MF, et al. Effects of low-dose morphine on gastric emptying in healthy volunteers. *J Clin Pharmacol.* 1998; 38:1017–20.

44. Heyland DK, Tougas G, King D, et al. Impaired gastric emptying in mechanically ventilated, critically ill patients. *Intensive Care Med.* 1996; 22:1339–44.

45. Bosscha K, Nieuwenhuijs VB, Vos A, et al. Gastrointestinal motility and gastric tube feeding in mechanically ventilated patients. *Crit Care Med.* 1998; 26:1510–7.

46. Albanese J, Viviand X, Potie F, et al. Sufentanil, fentanyl, and alfentanil in head trauma patients: a study on cerebral hemodynamics. *Crit Care Med.* 1999; 27:407–11.

47. Sperry RJ, Bailey PL, Reichman MV, et al. Fentanyl and sufentanil increase intracranial pressure in head trauma patients. *Anesthesiology.* 1992; 77:416–20.

48. DeNaal M, Munar F, Poca MA, et al. Cerebral hemodynamic effects of morphine and fentanyl in patients with severe head injury. *Anesthesiology.* 2000; 92:11–9.

49. Dasta JF, Fuhrman TM, McCandles C. Patterns of prescribing and administering drugs for agitation and pain in patients in a surgical intensive care unit. *Crit Care Med.* 1994; 22:974–80.

50 Kress JP, Pohlman AS, O'Connor MF, et al. Daily interruption of sedative infusions in critically ill patients undergoing mechanical ventilation. *N Engl J Med.* 2000; 342:1471–7.

51. Boldt J, Thaler E, Lehmann A, et al. Pain management in cardiac surgery patients: comparison between standard therapy and patient-controlled analgesia regimen. *J Cardiothorac Vasc Anesth.* 1998; 12:654–8.

52. Pearce CJ, Gonzalez FM, Wallin JD. Renal failure and hyperkalemia associated with ketorolac tromethamine. *Arch Intern Med.* 1993; 153:1000–2.

53. Schlondorff D. Renal complications of nonsteroidal anti-inflammatory drugs. *Kidney Int.* 1993; 44:643–53.

54. Feldman HI, Kinman JL, Berlin JA, et al. Parenteral ketorolac: the risk for acute renal failure. *Ann Intern Med.* 1997; 126:193–9.

55. Strom BL, Berlin JA, Kinman JL, et al. Parenteral ketorolac and risk of gastrointestinal and operative site bleeding. *JAMA.* 1996; 275:376–82.

56. Bombardier C, Laine L, Reicin A, et al. Comparison of upper gastrointestinal toxicity of rofecoxib and naproxen in patients with rheumatoid arthritis. *N Engl J Med.* 2000; 343:1520–8.

57. Peduta VA, Ballabio M, Stefanini S. Efficacy of propacetamol in the treatment of postoperative pain. Morphine sparing effect in orthopedic surgery. Italian Collaborative Group on Propacetamol. *Acta Anaesthesiol Scand.* 1998; 42:293–8.

58. Zimmerman HJ, Maddrey W. Acetaminophen hepatotoxicity with regular intake of alcohol. Analysis of instances of therapeutic misadventure. *Hepatology.* 1995; 22:767–73.

59. Treggiari-Venzi M, Borgeat A, Fuchs-Buder T, et al. Overnight sedation with midazolam or propofol in the ICU: effects on sleep quality, anxiety and depression. *Intensive Care Med.* 1996; 22:1186–90.

60. Jenkins DH. Substance abuse and withdrawal in the intensive care unit: contemporary issues. *Surg Clin North Am.* 2000; 80:1033–53.

61. Cornwell EE, Belzberg H, Velmahos G, et al. The prevalence and effect of alcohol and drug abuse on cohort-matched critically injured patients. *Am Surg.* 1998; 64:461–5.

62. Spies CD, Rommelspacher H. Alcohol withdrawal in the surgical patient: prevention and treatment. *Anesth Analg.* 1999; 88:946–54.

63. Kaye AD, Clarke RC, Sabar R, et al. Herbal medicines: current trends in anesthesiology practice—a hospital survey. *J Clin Anesth.* 2000; 12:468–71.

64. Atkins PM, Mion LC, Mendelson W, et al. Characteristics and outcomes of patients who self-extubate from ventilatory support: a case-control study. *Chest.* 1997; 112:1317–23.

65. Vassal T, Anh NGD, Gabillet JM, et al. Prospective evaluation of self-extubations in a medical intensive care unit. *Intensive Care Med.* 1993; 19:340–2.

66. Fraser GL, Riker RR, Prato BS, et al. The frequency and cost of patient-initiated device removal in the ICU. *Pharmacotherapy.* 2001; 21:1–6.

67. Conti J, Smith D. Haemodynamic responses to extubation after cardiac surgery with and without continued sedation. *Br J Anaesth.* 1998; 80:834–6.

68. Cohen D, Horiuchi K, Kemper M, et al. Modulating effects of propofol on metabolic and cardiopulmonary responses to stressful intensive care unit procedures. *Crit Care Med.* 1996; 24:612–7.

69. Veselis RA, Reinsel RA, Feshchenko VA, et al. The comparative amnestic effects of midazolam, propofol, thiopental, and fentanyl at equi-sedative concentrations. *Anesthesiology.* 1997; 87:749–64.

70. Weinbroum AA, Halpern P, Rudick V, et al. Midazolam versus propofol for long-term sedation in the ICU: a randomized prospective comparison. *Intensive Care Med.* 1997; 23:1258–63.

71. Wagner BK, O'Hara DA, Hammond JS. Drugs for amnesia in the ICU. *Am J Crit Care.* 1997; 6:192–201.

72. Wagner BK, Zavotsky KE, Sweeney JB, et al. Patient recall of therapeutic paralysis in a surgical critical care unit. *Pharmacotherapy.* 1998; 18:358–63.

73. Schelling G, Stoll C, Meier M, et al. Health-related

quality of life and posttraumatic stress disorder in survivors of adult respiratory distress syndrome. *Crit Care Med.* 1998; 26:651–9.

74. Jones C, Griffiths RD. Disturbed memory and amnesia related to intensive care. *Memory.* 2000; 8:79–94.

75. Jones C, Griffiths RD, Humphris G, et al. Memory, delusions, and the development of acute post-traumatic stress disorder-related symptoms after intensive care. *Crit Care Med.* 2001; 29:573–80.

76. Schnyder U, Morgeli H, Nigg C, et al. Early psychological reactions to life-threatening injuries. *Crit Care Med.* 2000; 28:86–92.

77. Scragg P, Jones A, Fauvel N. Psychological problems following ICU treatment. *Anaesthesia.* 2001; 56:914.

78. Watling SM, Johnson M, Yanos J. A method to produce sedation in critically ill patients. *Ann Pharmacother.* 1996; 30:1227–31.

79. DeJonghe B, Cook D, Appere-De-Vecchi C, et al. Using and understanding sedation scoring systems: a systematic review. *Intensive Care Med.* 2000; 26: 275–85.

80. Brook AD, Ahrens TS, Schaiff R, et al. Effect of a nursing-implemented sedation protocol on the duration of mechanical ventilation. *Crit Care Med.* 1999; 27:2609–15.

81. Riker RR, Fraser GL, Cox PM. Continuous infusion of haloperidol controls agitation in critically ill patients. *Crit Care Med.* 1994; 22:89–97.

82. Riker RR, Picard JT, Fraser GL. Prospective evaluation of the Sedation-Agitation Scale for adult critically ill patients. *Crit Care Med.* 1999; 27:1325–9.

83. Devlin JW, Boleski G, Mlynarek M, et al. Motor Activity Assessment Scale: a valid and reliable sedation scale for use with mechanically ventilated patients in an adult surgical intensive care unit. *Crit Care Med.* 1999; 27:1271–5.

84. Ramsay MA, Savege TM, Simpson BR, et al. Controlled sedation with alphaxalone-alphadolone. *Br Med J.* 1974; 2:656–9.

85. Hansen-Flaschen J, Cowen J, Polomano RC. Beyond the Ramsay scale: need for a validated measure of sedating drug efficacy in the intensive care unit. *Crit Care Med.* 1994; 22:732–3.

86. DeLemos J, Tweeddale M, Chittock DR. Measuring quality of sedation in adult mechanically ventilated critically ill patients: the Vancouver Interaction and Calmness Scale. *J Clin Epidemiol.* 2000; 53:908–19.

87. Chernik DA, Gillings D, Laine H, et al. Validity and reliability of the Observer's Assessment of Alertness/ Sedation Scale: study with intravenous midazolam. *J Clin Psychopharmacol.* 1990; 10:244–51.

88. Ambuel B, Hamlett KW, Marx CM, et al. Assessing distress in pediatric intensive care environments: the COMFORT scale. *J Pediatr Psychol.* 1992; 17:95109.

89. Rosow C, Manberg PJ. Bispectral index monitoring. *Anesthesiol Clin North Am.* 1998; 2:89–107.

90. Liu J, Singh H, White PF. Electroencephalographic bispectral index correlates with intraoperative recall and depth of propofol-induced sedation. *Anesth Analg.* 1997; 84:185–9.

91. Doi M, Gajraj RJ, Mantzaridis H, et al. Relationship between calculated blood concentration of propofol and electrophysiological variables during emergence from anesthesia: comparison of bispectral index, spectral edge frequency, median frequency, and auditory

evoked potential index. *Br J Anaesth.* 1997; 78:180–4.

92. Liu J, Singh H, White PF. Electroencephalogram bispectral analysis predicts the depth of midazolam-induced sedation. *Anesthesiology.* 1996; 84:64–9.

93. Simmons LE, Riker RR, Prato BS, et al. Assessing sedation levels in mechanically ventilated ICU patients with the bispectral index and the sedation–agitation scale. *Crit Care Med.* 1999; 27:1499–504.

94. Riker RR, Simmons LE, Fraser GL, et al. Validating the sedation-agitation scale with the bispectral index and visual analog scale in adult ICU patients after cardiac surgery. *Intensive Care Med.* 2001; 27:853–8.

95. De Deyne C, Struys M, Decruyenaere J, et al. Use of continuous bispectral EEG monitoring to assess depth of sedation in ICU patients. *Intensive Care Med.* 1998; 24:1294–8.

96. Ghoneim MM, Mewaldt SP. Benzodiazepines and human memory: a review. *Anesthesiology.* 1990; 72: 926–38.

97. Gilliland HE, Prasad BK, Mirakhur RK, et al. An investigation of the potential morphine sparing effect of midazolam. *Anaesthesia.* 1996; 51:808–11.

98. Greenblatt DJ, Ehrenberg BL, Gunderman J, et al. Kinetic and dynamic study of intravenous lorazepam: comparison with intravenous diazepam. *J Pharmacol Exp Ther.* 1989; 250:134–9.

99. Vree TB, Shimoda M, Driessen JJ, et al. Decreased plasma albumin concentration results in increased volume of distribution and decreased elimination of midazolam in intensive care patients. *Clin Pharmacol Ther.* 1989; 46:537–44.

100. Driessen JJ, Vree TB, Guelen PJ. The effects of acute changes in renal function on the pharmacokinetics of midazolam during long-term infusion in ICU patients. *Acta Anaesthesiol Belg.* 1991; 42:149–55.

101. Greenblatt DJ, Abernethy DR, Locniskar A, et al. Effect of age, gender, and obesity on midazolam kinetics. *Anesthesiology.* 1984; 61:27–35.

102. Patel IH, Soni PP, Fukuda EK, et al. The pharmacokinetics of midazolam in patients with congestive heart failure. *Br J Clin Pharmacol.* 1990; 29:565–9.

103. Macgilchrist AJ, Birnie GG, Cook A, et al. Pharmacokinetics and pharmacodynamics of intravenous midazolam in patients with severe alcoholic cirrhosis. *Gut.* 1986; 27:190–5.

104. Boulieu R, Lehmann B, Salord F, et al. Pharmacokinetics of midazolam and its main metabolite 1-hydroxymidazolam in intensive care patients. *Eur J Drug Metab Pharmacokinet.* 1998; 23:255–8.

105. Malacrida R, Fritz ME, Suter P, et al. Pharmacokinetics of midazolam administered by continuous infusion to intensive care patients. *Crit Care Med.* 1992; 20:1123.

106. Bauer TM, Ritz R, Haberthur C, et al. Prolonged sedation due to accumulation of conjugated metabolites of midazolam. *Lancet.* 1995; 346:145–7.

107. Hamaoka N, Oda Y, Hase I, et al. Propofol decreases the clearance of midazolam by inhibiting CYP3A4: an in vivo and in vitro study. *Clin Pharmacol Ther.* 1999; 66:110–7.

108. Gorski JC, Jones DR, Haehner-Daniels BD, et al. The contribution of intestinal and hepatic CYP3A to the interaction between midazolam and clarithromycin. *Clin Pharmacol Ther.* 1998; 64:133–43.

109. Ahonen J, Olkkola KT, Salmenpera M, et al. Effect of diltiazem on midazolam and alfentanil disposition in

patients undergoing coronary artery bypass grafting. *Anesthesiology.* 1996; 85:1246–52.

110. Bailie GR, Cockshott ID, Douglas EJ, et al. Pharmacokinetics of propofol during and after long-term continuous infusion for maintenance of sedation in ICU patients. *Br J Anaesth.* 1992; 68:486–91.

111. Hammerlein A, Derendorf H, Lowenthal DT. Pharmacokinetic and pharmacodynamic changes in the elderly. *Clin Pharmacokinet.* 1998; 35:49–64.

112. Michalets EL. Update: clinically significant cytochrome P-450 drug interactions. *Pharmacotherapy.* 1999; 18:84–112.

113. Shelly MP, Sultan MA, Bodenham A, et al. Midazolam infusions in critically ill patients. *Eur J Anaesthesiol.* 1991; 8:21–7.

114. Nishiyama T. Sedation during artificial ventilation by continuous intravenous infusion of midazolam: effects of hepatocellular or renal damage. *J Intensive Care Med.* 1997; 12:40–4.

115. Ariano RE, Kassum DA, Aronson KJ. Comparison of sedative recovery time after midazolam versus diazepam administration. *Crit Care Med.* 1994; 22:1492–6.

116. Newton DW, Narducci WA, Leet WA, et al. Lorazepam stability in and sorption from intravenous admixture solutions. *Am J Hosp Pharm.* 1983; 40:424–7.

117. Hoey LL, Vance-Bryan K, Clarens DM, et al. Lorazepam stability in parenteral solutions for continuous intravenous administration. *Ann Pharmacother.* 1996; 30:343–6.

118. McCollam JS, O'Neil MG, Norcross ED, et al. Continuous infusions of lorazepam, midazolam and propofol for sedation of the critically-ill surgery trauma patient: a prospective, randomized comparison. *Crit Care Med.* 1999; 27:2454–8.

119. Laine GA, Hamid Hossain SM, Solis RT, et al. Polyethylene glycol nephrotoxicity secondary to prolonged high-dose intravenous lorazepam. *Ann Pharmacother.* 1995; 29:1110–4.

120. Seay RE, Graves PJ, Wilkin MK. Comment: possible toxicity from propylene glycol in lorazepam infusion. *Ann Pharmacother.* 1997; 31:647–8.

121. Arbour RB. Propylene glycol toxicity related to high-dose lorazepam infusion: case report and discussion. *Am J Crit Care.* 1999; 8:499–506.

122. Lugo RA, Chester EA, Cash J, et al. A cost analysis of enterally administered lorazepam in the pediatric intensive care unit. *Crit Care Med.* 1999; 27:417–21.

123. Shepherd MF, Felt-Gunderson PA. Diarrhea associated with lorazepam solution in a tube-fed patient. *Nutr Clin Pract.* 1996; 11:117–20.

124. Kamijo Y, Masuda T, Nishikawa T, et al. Cardiovascular response and stress reaction to flumazenil injection in patients under infusion with midazolam. *Crit Care Med.* 2000; 28:318–23.

125. Breheny FX. Reversal of midazolam sedation with flumazenil. *Crit Care Med.* 1992; 20:736–9.

126. Kowalski SD, Rayfield CA. A post hoc descriptive study of patients receiving propofol. *Am J Crit Care.* 1999; 8:507–13.

127. Sanchez-Izquierdo-Riera JA, Caballero-Cubedo RE, Perez-Vela JL, et al. Propofol versus midazolam: safety and efficacy for sedating the severe trauma patient. *Anesth Analg.* 1998; 86:1219–24.

128. Carrasco G, Molina R, Costa J, et al. Propofol versus midazolam in short-, medium-, and long-term sedation of critically ill patients. *Chest.* 1993; 103:557–64.

129. Barrientos-Vega R, Sanchez-Soria MM, Morales-Garcia C, et al. Prolonged sedation of critically ill patients with midazolam or propofol: impact on weaning and costs. *Crit Care Med.* 1997; 25:33–40.

130. Kumar AN, Achwartz DE, Lim KG. Propofol-induced pancreatitis: recurrence of pancreatitis after rechallenge. *Chest.* 1999; 115:1198–9.

131. Possidente CJ, Rogers FB, Osler TM, et al. Elevated pancreatic enzymes after extended propofol therapy. *Pharmacotherapy.* 1998; 18:653–5.

132. Leisure GS, O'Flaherty J, Green L, et al. Propofol and postoperative pancreatitis. *Anesthesiology.* 1996; 84:224–7.

133. Bray RJ. Propofol infusion syndrome in children. *Paediatr Anaesth.* 1998; 8:491–9.

134. Cremer OL, Moons KGM, Bouman EAC, et al. Long-term propofol infusion and cardiac failure in adult head-injured patients. *Lancet.* 2001; 357:117–8.

135. Bennett SN, McNeil MM, Bland LA, et al. Postoperative infections traced to contamination of an intravenous anesthetic, propofol. *N Engl J Med.* 1995; 333:147–54.

136. Webb SA, Roberts B, Breheny FX, et al. Contamination of propofol infusions in the intensive care unit: incidence and clinical significance. *Anaesth Intensive Care.* 1998; 26:162–4.

137. Avramov MN, Husain MM, White PF. The comparative effects of methohexital, propofol, and etomidate for electroconvulsive therapy. *Anesth Analg.* 1995; 81:596–602.

138. Stecker MM, Kramer TH, Raps EC, et al. Treatment of refractory status epilepticus with propofol: clinical and pharmacokinetic findings. *Epilepsia.* 1998; 39:18–26.

139. McCowan C, Marik P. Refractory delirium tremens treated with propofol: a case series. *Crit Care Med.* 2000; 28:1781–4.

140. Herregods L, Verbeke J, Rolly G, et al. Effect of propofol on elevated intracranial pressure. Preliminary results. *Anaesthesia.* 1988; 43(suppl):107–9.

141. Kelly DF, Goodale DB, Williams J, et al. Propofol in the treatment of moderate and severe head injury: a randomized, prospective double-blinded pilot trial. *J Neurosurg.* 1999; 90:1042–52.

142. Herregods L, Mergaert C, Rolly G, et al. Comparison of the effects of 24-hour propofol or fentanyl infusions on intracranial pressure. *J Drug Dev.* 1989; 2(suppl 2):99–100.

143. Spies CD, Dubisz N, Neumann T, et al. Therapy of alcohol withdrawal syndrome in intensive care unit patients following trauma: results of a prospective, randomized trial. *Crit Care Med.* 1996; 24:414–22.

144. Ip Yam PC, Forbes A, Kox WJ. Clonidine in the treatment of alcohol withdrawal in the intensive care unit. *Br J Anaesth.* 1992; 69:328.

145. Aantaa RE, Kanto JH, Scheinin M. Dexmedetomidine pre-medication for minor gynecologic surgery. *Anesth Analg.* 1990; 4:407–13.

146. Venn RM, Bradshaw CJ, Spencer R, et al. Preliminary UK experience of dexmedetomidine, a novel agent for postoperative sedation in the intensive care unit. *Anaesthesia.* 1999; 54:1136–42.

147. Hall JE, Uhrich TD, Barnet JA, et al. Sedative, amnestic, and analgesic properties of small-dose dexmedetomidine infusions. *Anesth Analg.* 2000;

90:699–705.

148. Belleville JP, Ward DS, Bloor BC, et al. Effects of intravenous dexmedetomidine in humans. *Anesthesiology.* 1992; 77:1125–33.

149. Osterman ME, Keenan SP, Seiferling RA, et al. Sedation in the intensive care unit, a systematic review. *JAMA.* 2000; 283:1451–9.

150. Aitkenhead AR, Willatts SM, Park GR, et al. Comparison of propofol and midazolam for sedation in critically ill patients. *Lancet.* 1989; 2(8665):704–9.

151. Roekaerts PM, Huygen FJ, deLange S. Infusion of propofol versus midazolam for sedation in the intensive care unit following coronary artery surgery. *J Cardiothorac Vasc Anesth.* 1993; 7:142–7.

152. Higgins TL, Yared JP, Estafanous FG, et al. Propofol versus midazolam for intensive care unit sedation after coronary artery bypass grafting. *Crit Care Med.* 1994; 22:1415–23.

153. Ronan KP, Gallagher TJ, George B, et al. Comparison of propofol and midazolam for sedation in intensive care unit patients. *Crit Care Med.* 1995; 23:286–93.

154. Cernaianu AC, DelRossi AJ, Flum DR, et al. Lorazepam and midazolam in the intensive care unit: a randomized, prospective, multicenter study of hemodynamics, oxygen transport, efficacy, and cost. *Crit Care Med.* 1996; 24:222–8.

155. Searle NR, Taillefer J, Gagnon L, et al. Propofol or midazolam for sedation and early extubation following cardiac surgery. *Can J Anaesth.* 1997; 44:629–35.

156. Carrasco G, Cabre L, Sobrepere G, et al. Synergistic sedation with propofol and midazolam in intensive care patients after coronary artery bypass grafting. *Crit Care Med.* 1998; 26:844–51.

157. Hall RI, Sandham D, Cardinal P, et al. Propofol vs midazolam for ICU sedation. A Canadian multicenter randomized trial. *Chest.* 2001; 119:1151–9.

158. Kress JP, O'Connor MF, Pohlman AS, et al. Sedation of critically ill patients during mechanical ventilation. *Am J Resp Crit Care Med.* 1996; 153:1012–8.

159. Pohlman AS, Simpson KP, Hall JB. Continuous intravenous infusions of lorazepam versus midazolam for sedation during mechanical ventilatory support: a prospective, randomized study. *Crit Care Med.* 1994; 22:1241–7.

160. Chamorro C, DeLatorre FJ, Montero A, et al. Comparative study of propofol versus midazolam in the sedation of critically ill patients: results of a prospective, randomized, multicenter trial. *Crit Care Med.* 1996; 24:932–9.

161. Manley NM, Fitzpatrick RW, Long T, et al. A cost analysis of alfentanil + propofol vs. morphine + midazolam for the sedation of critically ill patients. *Pharmacoeconomics.* 1997; 12:247–55.

162. Swart E, van Schijndel RJM, van Loenen AC, et al. Continuous infusion of lorazepam versus midazolam in patients in the intensive care unit: sedation with lorazepam is easier to manage and is more cost effective. *Crit Care Med.* 1999; 27:1461–5.

163. Sandiumenge Camps A, Sanchez-Izquierdo Riera JA, Toral Vazquez D, et al. Midazolam and 2% propofol in long-term sedation of traumatized critically ill patients: efficacy and safety comparison. *Crit Care Med.* 2000; 28:3612–9.

164. Kollef MH, Levy NT, Ahrens TS, et al. The use of continuous i.v. sedation is associated with prolongation of mechanical ventilation. *Chest.* 1998; 114:541–8.

165. Mascia MF, Koch M, Medicis JJ. Pharmacoeconomic impact of rational use guidelines on the provision of analgesia, sedation, and neuromuscular blockade in critical care. *Crit Care Med.* 2000; 28:2300–6.

166. Cammarano WB, Pittet JF, Weitz S, et al. Acute withdrawal syndrome related to the administration of analgesic and sedative medications in adult intensive care unit patients. *Crit Care Med.* 1998; 26:676–84.

167. Katz R, Kelly HW, His A. Prospective study on the occurrence of withdrawal in critically ill children who received fentanyl by continuous infusion. *Crit Care Med.* 1994; 22:763–77.

168. Fonsmark L, Rasmussen YH, Carl P. Occurrence of withdrawal in critically ill children. *Crit Care Med.* 1999; 27:196–9.

169. Carr DB, Todres ID. Fentanyl infusion and weaning in the pediatric intensive care unit: toward science-based practice. *Crit Care Med.* 1994; 22:725–7.

170. Buck M, Blumer J. Opioids and other analgesics: adverse effects in the intensive care unit. *Crit Care Clin.* 1991; 7:615–37.

171. American Pain Society. Principles of analgesic use in the treatment of acute pain and cancer pain. 3rd ed. Skokie, IL: 1992.

172. Anand KJS, Ingraham J. Tolerance, dependence, and strategies for compassionate withdrawal of analgesics and anxiolytics in the pediatric ICU. *Crit Care Nurse.* 1996; 16:87–93.

173. Tobias JD. Subcutaneous administration of fentanyl and midazolam to prevent withdrawal after prolonged sedation in children. *Crit Care Med.* 1999; 27:2262–5.

174. Koolhoven I, Tjon-A-Tsien MRS, van der Mast RC. Early diagnosis of delirium after cardiac surgery. *Gen Hosp Psychiatry.* 1996; 18:448–51.

175. Sanders KM, Stern TA, O'Gara PT, et al. Delirium during intra-aortic balloon pump therapy. *Psychosomatics.* 1992; 33:35–44.

176. Dyer CB, Ashton CM, Teasdale TA. Postoperative delirium. A review of 80 primary data collection studies. *Arch Intern Med.* 1995; 155:461–5.

177. American Psychiatric Association. DSM-IV: diagnostic and statistical manual of mental disorders. Washington, DC: American Psychiatric Press; 1994.

178. Trzepacz PT. Delirium—advances in diagnosis, pathophysiology, and treatment. *Psychiatr Clin North Am.* 1996; 19:429–49.

179. Lipowski ZJ. Delirium in the elderly patient. *N Engl J Med.* 1989; 320:578–82.

180. Meagher DJ, Trzepacz PT. Motoric subtypes of delirium. *Semin Clin Neuropsychiatry.* 2000; 5:75–85.

181. Ely EW, Siegel MD, Inouye S. Delirium in the intensive care unit: an underrecognized syndrome of organ dysfunction. *Semin Resp Crit Care Med.* 2001; 22:115–26.

182. Ely EW, Margolin R, Francis J, et al. Evaluation of delirium in critically ill patients: Validation of the confusion assessment method for the intensive care unit (CAM-ICU). *Crit Care Med.* 2001; 29:1370–9.

183. Hart RP, Levenson JL, Sessler CN, et al. Validation of a cognitive test for delirium in medical ICU patients. *Psychosomatics.* 1996; 37:533–46.

184. Hart RP, Best ALN, Sessler CN, et al. Abbreviated cognitive test for delirium. *J Psychosom Res.* 1997; 43:417–23.

185. Ely EW, Inouye SK, Bernard GR, et al. Delirium in mechanically ventilated patients: validity and reliability of the confusion assessment method for the intensive care unit (CAM-ICU). *JAMA.* 2001; 286:2703–10.

186. Inouye SK, van Dyck CH, Alessi CA, et al. Clarifying confusion: the confusion assessment method. *Ann Intern Med.* 1990; 113:941–8.

187. Smith MJ, Breitbart WS, Meredith MP. A critique of instruments and methods to detect, diagnose, and rate delirium. *J Pain Symptom Manage.* 1995; 10:35–77.

188. Inouye SK, Bogardus ST, Charpentier PA, et al. A multicomponent intervention to prevent delirium in hospitalized older patients. *N Engl J Med.* 1999; 340:669–76.

189. Bergeron N, Dubois MJ, Dumont M, et al. Intensive care delirium screening checklist: evaluation of a new screening tool. *Intensive Care Med.* 2001; 27:859–64.

190. Breitbart W, Marotta R, Platt MM, et al. A double-blind trial of haloperidol, chlorpromazine, and lorazepam in the treatment of delirium in hospitalized AIDS patients. *Am J Psychiatry.* 1996; 153:231–7.

191. Frye MA, Coudreaut MF, Hakeman SM, et al. Continuous droperidol infusion for management of agitated delirium in an intensive care unit. *Psychosomatics.* 1995; 36:301–5.

192. Faigel DO, Metz DC, Kochman ML. Torsade de pointes complicating the treatment of bleeding esophageal varices: association with neuroleptics, vasopressin, and electrolyte imbalance. *Am J Gastroenterol.* 1995; 90:822–4.

193. Tesar GE, Murray GB, Cassem NH. Use of haloperidol for acute delirium in intensive care setting. *J Clin Psychopharmacol.* 1985; 5:344–7.

194. Tesar GE, Stern TA. Rapid tranquilization of the agitated intensive care unit patient. *J Intensive Care Med.* 1988; 3:195–201.

195. DiSalvo TG, O'Gara PT. Torsade de pointes caused by high-dose intravenous haloperidol in cardiac patients. *Clin Cardiol.* 1995; 28:285–90.

196. Metzger E, Friedman R. Prolongation of the corrected QT and torsades de pointes cardiac arrhythmia associated with intravenous haloperidol in the medically ill. *J Clin Psychopharmacol.* 1993; 13:128–32.

197. Wilt JL, Minnema AM, Johnson RF, et al. Torsade de pointes associated with the use of intravenous haloperidol. *Ann Intern Med.* 1993; 119:391–4.

198. Hunt N, Stern TA. The association between intravenous haloperidol and torsades de pointes. *Psychosomatics.* 1995; 36:541–9.

199. Sharma ND, Rosman HS, Padhi D, et al. Torsades de pointes associated with intravenous haloperidol in critically ill patients. *Am J Cardiol.* 1998; 81:238–40.

200. Lawrence KR, Nasraway SA. Conduction disturbances associated with administration of butyrophenone antipsychotics in the critically ill: a review of the literature. *Pharmacotherapy.* 1997; 17:531–7.

201. Seneff MG, Mathews RA. Use of haloperidol infusions to control delirium in critically ill adults. *Ann Pharmacother.* 1995; 29:690–3.

202. Kudo S, Ishizaki T. Pharmacokinetics of haloperidol. *Clin Pharmacokinet.* 1999; 37:435–56.

203. Fang J, Baker GB, Silverstone PH, et al. Involvement of CYP3A4 and CYP2D6 in the metabolism of haloperidol. *Cell Mol Neurobiol.* 1997; 17:227–33.

204. Tsang MW, Shader RI, Greenblatt DJ. Metabolism of

haloperidol: clinical implications and unanswered questions. *J Clin Psychopharmacol.* 1994; 14:159–62.

205. Avent KM, Riker RR, Fraser GL, et al. Metabolism of haloperidol to pyridinium species in patients receiving high doses intravenously: is HPTP an intermediate? *Life Sci.* 1997; 61:2383–90.

206. Eyles DW, McLennan HR, Jones A, et al. Quantitative analysis of two pyridinium metabolites of haloperidol in patients with schizophrenia. *Clin Pharmacol Ther.* 1994; 56:512–20.

207. Usuki E, Pearce R, Parkinson A, et al. Studies on the conversion of haloperidol and its tetrahydropyridine dehydration product to potentially neurotoxic pyridinium metabolites by human liver microsomes. *Chem Res Toxicol.* 1996; 9:800–6.

208. Eyles DW, McGrath JJ, Pond SM. Formation of pyridinium species of haloperidol in human liver and brain. *Psychopharmacology.* 1996; 125:214–9.

209. Riker RR, Fraser GL, Richen P. Movement disorders associated with withdrawal from high-dose intravenous haloperidol therapy in delirious ICU patients. *Chest.* 1997; 111:1778–81.

210. Rao N, Jellinek HM, Woolston DC. Agitation in closed head injury: haloperidol effects on rehabilitation outcome. *Arch Phys Med Rehabil.* 1985; 66:30–4.

211. Shalev A, Hermesh H, Munitz H. Mortality from neuroleptic malignant syndrome. *J Clin Psychiatry.* 1989; 50:18–25.

212. Still J, Friedman B, Law E, et al. Neuroleptic malignant syndrome in a burn patient. *Burns.* 1998; 24:573–5.

213. Levitt AJ, Midha R, Craven JL. Neuroleptic malignant syndrome with intravenous haloperidol. *Can J Psychiatry.* 1990; 35:789. Letter.

214. Burke C, Fulda GJ, Casellano J. Neuroleptic malignant syndrome in a trauma patient. *J Trauma.* 1995; 39:796–8.

215. Krachman SL, D'Alonzo GE, Criner GJ. Sleep in the intensive care unit. *Chest.* 1995; 107:1713–20.

216. Stein-Parbury J, McKinley S. Patients' experiences of being in an intensive care unit: a select literature review. *Am J Crit Care.* 2000; 9:20–7.

217. Redeker NS. Sleep in acute care settings: an integrative review. *J Nurs Scholarsh.* 2000; 32:31–8.

218. Cooper AB, Thornley KS, Young GB, et al. Sleep in critically ill patients requiring mechanical ventilation. *Chest.* 2000; 117:809–18.

219. Edwards GB, Schuring LM. Pilot study: validating staff nurses' observations of sleep and wake states among critically ill patients using polysomnography. *Am J Crit Care.* 1993; 2:125–31.

220. Richardson SJ. A comparison of tools for the assessment of sleep pattern disturbance in critically ill adults. *Dimens Crit Care Nurs.* 1997; 16:226–39.

221. Meyers TJ, Eveloff SE, Bauer MS, et al. Adverse environmental conditions in the respiratory and medical ICU settings. *Chest.* 1994; 105:1211–6.

222. Aaron JN, Carlisle CC, Carskadon MA, et al. Environmental noise as a cause of sleep disruption in an intermediate respiratory care unit. *Sleep.* 1996; 19:707–10.

223. Freedman NS, Kotzer N, Schwab RJ. Patient perception of sleep quality and etiology of sleep disruption in the intensive care unit. *Am J Resp Crit Care Med.* 1999; 159:1155–62.

224. Wallace CJ, Robins J, Alvord LS, et al. The effect of earplugs on sleep measures during exposure to simu-

lated intensive care unit noise. *Am J Crit Care.* 1999; 8:210–9.

225. Horsburgh CR. Healing by design. *N Engl J Med.* 1995; 333:735–40.

226. Griffin JP, Myers S, Kopelke C, et al. The effects of progressive muscular relaxation on subjectively reported disturbance due to hospital noise. *Behav Med.* 1988; 14:37–42.

227. Guzzetta CE. Effects of relaxation and music therapy on patients in a coronary care unit with presumptive myocardial infarction. *Heart Lung.* 1989; 18:609–16.

228. Byers JF, Smyth KA. Effect of a music intervention on noise annoyance, heart rate, and blood pressure in cardiac surgery patients. *Am J Crit Care.* 1997; 6:183–91.

229. Chlan L. Effectiveness of a music therapy intervention on relaxation and anxiety for patients receiving ventilatory assistance. *Heart Lung.* 1998; 27:169–76.

230. Updike P. Music therapy results for ICU patients. *Dimens Crit Care Nurs.* 1990; 9:39–45.

231. Bolwerk CA. Effects of relaxing music on state anxiety in myocardial infarction patients. *Crit Care Nurs Q.* 1990; 13:63–72.

232. White JM. Effects of relaxing music on cardiac autonomic balance and anxiety after acute myocardial infarction. *Am J Crit Care.* 1999; 8:220–30.

233. Zimmerman L, Nieveen J, Barnason S, et al. The effects of music interventions on postoperative pain and sleep in coronary artery bypass graft (CABG) patients. *Sch Inq Nurs Pract.* 1996; 10:153–70.

234. Labyak SE, Metzger BL. The effects of effleurage backrub on the physiological components of relaxation: a meta-analysis. *Nurs Res.* 1997; 46:59–62.

235. Richards KC. Effect of a back massage and relaxation intervention on sleep in critically ill patients. *Am J Crit Care.* 1998; 7:288–99.

Appendix A—Summary of Recommendations

1. All critically ill patients have the right to adequate analgesia and management of their pain. (Grade of recommendation = C)

2. Pain assessment and response to therapy should be performed regularly by using a scale appropriate to the patient population and systematically documented. (Grade of recommendation = C)

3. The level of pain reported by the patient must be considered the current standard for assessment of pain and response to analgesia whenever possible. Use of the NRS is recommended to assess pain. (Grade of recommendation = B)

4. Patients who cannot communicate should be assessed through subjective observation of pain-related behaviors (movement, facial expression, and posturing) and physiological indicators (heart rate, blood pressure, and respiratory rate) and the change in these parameters following analgesic therapy. (Grade of recommendation = B)

5. A therapeutic plan and goal of analgesia should be established for each patient and communicated to all caregivers to ensure consistent analgesic therapy. (Grade of recommendation = C)

6. If intravenous doses of an opioid analgesic are required, fentanyl, hydromorphone, and morphine are the recommended agents. (Grade of recommendation = C)

7. Scheduled opioid doses or a continuous infusion is preferred over an "as needed" regimen to ensure consistent analgesia. A PCA device may be utilized to deliver opioids if the patient is able to understand and operate the device. (Grade of recommendation = B)

8. Fentanyl is preferred for a rapid onset of analgesia in acutely distressed patients. (Grade of recommendation = C)

9. Fentanyl or hydromorphone are preferred for patients with hemodynamic instability or renal insufficiency. (Grade of recommendation = C)

10. Morphine and hydromorphone are preferred for intermittent therapy because of their longer duration of effect. (Grade of recommendation = C)

11. NSAIDs or acetaminophen may be used as adjuncts to opioids in selected patients. (Grade of recommendation = B)

12. Ketorolac therapy should be limited to a maximum of five days, with close monitoring for the development of renal insufficiency or gastrointestinal bleeding. Other NSAIDs may be used via the enteral route in appropriate patients. (Grade of recommendation = B)

13. Sedation of agitated critically ill patients should be started only after providing adequate analgesia and treating reversible physiological causes. (Grade of recommendation = C)

14. A sedation goal or endpoint should be established and regularly redefined for each patient. Regular assessment and response to therapy should be systematically documented. (Grade of recommendation = C)

15. The use of a validated sedation assessment scale (SAS, MAAS, or VICS) is recommended. (Grade of recommendation = B)

16. Objective measures of sedation, such as BIS, have not been completely evaluated and are not yet proven useful in the ICU. (Grade of recommendation = C)

17. Midazolam or diazepam should be used for rapid sedation of acutely agitated patients. (Grade of recommendation = C)

18. Propofol is the preferred sedative when rapid awakening (e.g., for neurologic assessment or extubation) is important. (Grade of recommendation = B)

19. Midazolam is recommended for short-term use only, as it produces unpredictable awakening and time to extubation when infusions continue longer than 48–72 hours. (Grade of recommendation = A)

20. Lorazepam is recommended for the sedation of most patients via intermittent i.v. administration or continuous infusion. (Grade of recommendation = B)

21. The titration of the sedative dose to a defined endpoint is recommended with systematic tapering of the dose or daily interruption with retitration to minimize prolonged sedative effects. (Grade of recommendation = A)

22. Triglyceride concentrations should be monitored after two days of propofol infusion, and total caloric intake from lipids should be included in the nutrition support prescription. (Grade of recommendation = B)

23. The use of sedation guidelines, an algorithm, or a protocol is recommended. (Grade of recommendation = B)

24. The potential for opioid, benzodiazepine, and propofol withdrawal should be considered after high doses or more than approximately seven days of continuous therapy. Doses should be tapered systematically to prevent withdrawal symptoms. (Grade of recommen-

dation = B)

25. Routine assessment for the presence of delirium is recommended. (The CAM-ICU is a promising tool for the assessment of delirium in ICU patients.) (Grade of recommendation = B)

26. Haloperidol is the preferred agent for the treatment of delirium in critically ill patients. (Grade of recommendation = C)

27. Patients should be monitored for electrocardiographic changes (QT interval prolongation and arrhythmias) when receiving haloperidol. (Grade of recommendation = B)

28. Sleep promotion should include optimization of the environment and nonpharmacologic methods to promote relaxation with adjunctive use of hypnotics. (Grade of recommendation = B)

Developed through the Task Force of the American College of Critical Care Medicine (ACCM) of the Society of Critical Care Medicine (SCCM), in collaboration with the American Society of Health-System Pharmacists (ASHP), and in alliance with the American College of Chest Physicians; and approved by the Board of Regents of ACCM and the Council of SCCM on November 15, 2001, and the ASHP Board of Directors on November 17, 2001.

Members of the 2001–2002 Commission on Therapeutics are William L. Greene, Pharm.D., BCPS, FASHP, *Chair*; Mary Lea Gora-Harper, Pharm.D., BCPS, *Vice Chair*; Kate Farthing, Pharm.D.; Charles W. Ham, Pharm.D., M.B.A.; Rita K. Jew, Pharm.D.; Rex S. Lott, Pharm.D.; Keith M. Olsen, Pharm.D., FCCP; Joseph J. Saseen, Pharm.D., BCPS; Beth A. Vanderheyden, Pharm.D., BCPS; Amy M. Blachere, R.Ph., *Student Member*; Jill E. Martin, Pharm.D., FASHP, *Board Liaison*; Dennis Williams, Pharm.D., FASHP, FCCP, FAPHA, BCPS, *Liaison Section of Clinical Specialist*; and Cynthia L. LaCivita, Pharm.D., *Secretary*.

Members of the Sedation and Analgesia Task Force are Judith Jacobi, Pharm.D., FCCM, BCPS, *Chair*, Critical Care Pharmacy Specialist, Methodist Hospital-Clarian Health Partners, Indianapolis, IN; Stanley A. Nasraway, Jr., M.D., FCCM, *Executive Director of Task Force*, Associate Professor, Surgery, Medicine, and Anesthesia, Tufts-New England Medical Center, Boston, MA; H. Scott Bherke, M.D., Medical Director of Trauma, Methodist Hospital, Indianapolis, IN; Donald B. Chalfin, M.D., M.S., FCCM, Director, Division of Research and Attending Intensivist, Department of Emergency Medicine, Maimonides Medical Center, and Associate Professor of Clinical Epidemiology and Social Medicine, Albert Einstein College of Medicine, New York, NY; William M. Coplin, M.D., Associate Professor, Departments of Neurology & Neurological Surgery, Wayne State University, and Chief, Neurology, Medical Director, Neurotrauma and Critical Care, Detroit Receiving Hospital, Detroit, MI; Douglas B. Coursin, M.D., Associate

Director, Departments of Emergency and Critical Care Medicine, Trauma Life Support Center, University of Wisconsin, Madison, WI; David W. Crippen, M.D., FCCM, Director, SICU, St. Francis Medical Center, Pittsburgh, PA; Dorrie Fontaine, R.N., D.N.Sc., FAAN, Associate Professor, and Associate Dean for Undergraduate Studies, Georgetown University, School of Nursing, Washington, DC; Gilles L. Fraser, Pharm.D., FCCM, Department of Critical Care Medicine, Maine Medical Center, Portland, ME; Barry D. Fuchs, M.D., Medical Director, MICU, Hospital of the University of Pennsylvania, Philadelphia, PA; Ruth M. Kelleher, R.N., Department of Nursing, New England Medical Center, Boston, MA; Philip D. Lumb, M.D., B.S., FCCM, Professor and Chairman, Department of Anesthesiology, Keck School of Medicine of USC, Los Angeles, CA; Paul E. Marik, M.D.B.Ch., FCCM, Department of Critical Care Medicine, University of Pittsburgh Medical School, Pittsburgh, PA; Michael F. Mascia, M.D., M.P.H., Medical Director, Outpatient Surgical Services, Tulane University School of Medicine, New Orleans, LA; Michael J. Murray, M.D., Ph.D., FCCM, Department of Anesthesiology and Critical Care Service, Mayo Medical Center, Rochester, MN; William T. Peruzzi, M.D., FCCM, Associate Professor of Anesthesiology, Northwestern University School of Medicine, Chief, Section of Critical Care Medicine, Northwestern Memorial Hospital, Chicago, IL; Richard R. Riker, M.D., Assistant Chief, Department of Critical Care Medicine, Maine Medical Center, Portland, ME; Eric T. Wittbrodt, Pharm.D., Assistant Professor of Clinical Pharmacy, Philadelphia College of Pharmacy, University of the Sciences in Philadelphia, Philadelphia, PA; Cynthia L. LaCivita, Pharm.D., Clinical Affairs Associate, *ASHP Staff Liaison*; Deborah L. McBride, Director of Publications, *SCCM Staff Liaison*.

Reviewers: American College of Chest Physicians; American Academy of Neurology; American Association of Critical Care Nurses; American Nurses Association; American Pharmaceutical Association; American College of Clinical Pharmacy; Stephanie E. Cooke, Pharm.D.; Joe Dasta, Pharm.D.; Doug Fish, Pharm.D.; Erkan Hassan, Pharm.D.; H. Mathilda Horst, M.D.; Carlayne E. Jackson, M.D.; Karen Kaiser, R.N.; Kathleen Kelly, M.D.; Maria Rudis, Pharm.D.; Carl Schoenberger, M.D.; Lori Schoonover, R.N.; Gayle Takaniski, Pharm.D.; Dan Teres, M.D.; and Karen Thompson, M.D.

The recommendations in this document do not indicate an exclusive course of treatment to be followed. Variations, taking into account individual circumstances, may be appropriate.

The bibliographic citation is as follows: Society of Critical Care Medicine and American Society of Health-System Pharmacists. Clinical practice guidelines for the sustained use of sedatives and analgesics in the critically ill adult. *Am J Health-Syst Pharm.* 2002; 59:150–78.

ASHP Therapeutic Guidelines for Nonsurgical Antimicrobial Prophylaxis

The ASHP Therapeutic Guidelines for Nonsurgical Antimicrobial Prophylaxis,[1] which have provided practitioners with standardized effective regimens for the rational use of prophylactic antimicrobials, have been revised as described in this document on the basis of new clinical evidence and additional concerns. Recommendations are provided for adult and pediatric patients (1 to 21 years of age), including infants (one month to 2 years of age). Geriatric patients, newborns (premature and full-term), and patients with renal or hepatic dysfunction are not specifically addressed (with the exception of neonatal prevention of human immunodeficiency virus [HIV] infection). Therefore, the guidelines may not be applicable to these patients, or certain adjustments to the recommendations may be necessary. The higher occurrence of resistant organisms and the importance of controlling health care costs are also considered.

Prophylaxis refers to the prevention of an infection and can be characterized as primary prophylaxis, secondary prophylaxis (suppression), or eradication. Primary prophylaxis is the prevention of an initial infection. Secondary prophylaxis is the prevention of recurrence or reactivation of a preexisting infection (e.g., a latent herpes simplex virus [HSV] infection). Eradication is the elimination of a colonized organism to prevent the development of an infection (e.g., eliminating methicillin-resistant *Staphylococcus aureus* [MRSA] from the nares of health care workers). These guidelines focus on primary prophylaxis. Secondary prophylaxis and eradication are not addressed (with the exception of secondary prophylaxis with antiviral agents in granulocytopenic patients).

Antimicrobial prophylaxis is indicated in selected patients to prevent certain infections that are not a direct result of a surgical procedure. The following guidelines address (1) prevention of infection in specialized settings, including endocarditis in patients at risk who are undergoing dental, respiratory, gastrointestinal (GI), or genitourinary (GU) procedures; nosocomial pneumonia in mechanically ventilated patients; and meningitis after nonpenetrating head trauma associated with a basilar skull fracture, (2) prevention of infection in anticipation of or after defined exposures, including influenza A in patients at risk; malaria and traveler's diarrhea in persons traveling abroad; tuberculosis (TB); and HIV infection in occupational exposure, (3) prevention of perinatally acquired infection, including HIV, HSV-2, and group B streptococcal disease, and (4) prevention of opportunistic infections in the immunocompromised host, including afebrile granulocytopenic cancer patients, afebrile bone marrow transplant recipients, and HIV-infected persons.

The following guidelines review the persons at risk for infection, the efficacy of prophylaxis, and the current recommendations regarding patient eligibility and drug selection. The duration of prophylaxis is addressed only in cases for which data are available. Antimicrobial selection for specific patients should consider not only efficacy but also the agents' adverse-effect profiles, comparative costs, and the patient's drug allergies. Discussion of the adverse-effect profile of the antimicrobials is beyond the scope of these guidelines. Patient preference may also play an important

role in the use of prophylaxis. Examples are perinatal prophylaxis to prevent HIV infection, perinatal prophylaxis to prevent group B streptococcus, prophylaxis for occupational exposure to HIV, and prevention of influenza A.

Guideline Development and Use

These guidelines were prepared by the Rocky Mountain Poison and Drug Center under contract to ASHP. The project was coordinated by a drug information pharmacist who worked with a multidisciplinary consortium of writers and consulted with six physicians on staff at the University of Colorado Health Sciences Center. The project coordinator worked in conjunction with an independent panel of eight clinical pharmacy specialists with expertise in either adult or pediatric infectious disease. The panel was appointed by ASHP. Panel members and contractors were required to disclose any possible conflicts of interest before their appointment. The guidelines underwent multidisciplinary field review to evaluate their validity, reliability, and utility in clinical practice. The final document was approved by the ASHP Commission on Therapeutics and the ASHP Board of Directors.

The recommendations in this document may not be appropriate for use in all clinical situations. Decisions to follow these recommendations must be based on the professional judgment of the clinician and consideration of individual patient circumstances and available resources.

These guidelines reflect current knowledge (at the time of publication) on nonsurgical antimicrobial prophylaxis. Given the dynamic nature of scientific information and technology, periodic review, updating, and revision are to be expected.

Strength of Evidence for Recommendations. The primary literature from the previous ASHP Therapeutic Guidelines on Nonsurgical Antimicrobial Prophylaxis[1] was reviewed together with the primary literature published between the date of the previous guidelines and August 1997, identified by a MEDLINE search. Particular attention was paid to study design, with greatest credence given to randomized, controlled, double-blind studies. Established recommendations by experts in the area (i.e., the American Heart Association's [AHA's] recommendations on bacterial endocarditis, recommendations of the Centers for Disease Control and Prevention [CDC], and the U.S. Public Health Service [USPHS] and Infectious Diseases Society of America [IDSA] Prevention of Opportunistic Infections Working Group recommendations for the HIV population) were also considered.

Guideline development included consideration of the following characteristics: validity, reliability, clinical applicability, flexibility, clarity, and a multidisciplinary nature as consistent with ASHP's philosophy on therapeutic guidelines.[2] Recommendations for the use of an antimicrobial are substantiated by the strength of evidence that supports the recommendation. The strength of evidence represents only support for or against prophylaxis and does not apply to the antimicrobial choice, dose, or dosage regimen. The strength of evidence supporting the recommendations for the use of an antimicrobial was classified as follows:

Level I: (evidence from large, well-conducted randomized, controlled clinical trials or a meta-analysis

Level II: (evidence from small, well-conducted randomized, controlled clinical trials)

Level III: (evidence from well-conducted cohort studies)

Level IV: (evidence from well-conducted case–control studies)

Level V: (evidence from uncontrolled studies that were not well conducted)

Level VI: (conflicting evidence that tends to favor the recommendation)

Level VII: (expert opinion)

This system has been used by the Agency for Health Care Policy and Research (AHCPR), and ASHP supports it as an acceptable method for organizing strength of evidence for a variety of therapeutic or diagnostic recommendations.[2] Each recommendation was assigned a category corresponding to the strength of evidence that supports the use or nonuse of antimicrobial prophylaxis:

Category A: (levels I–III)
Category B: (levels IV–VI)
Category C: (level VII)

A category C recommendation represents a consensus of the expert panel based on the clinical experience of individual panel members and a paucity of quality supporting literature. In cases for which opinions were markedly divided, the recommendations indicate that a substantial number of panel members supported an alternative approach.

Pediatrics. Pediatric patients are subject to many prophylaxis opportunities that are similar to those for adults. Although pediatric-specific prophylaxis data are sparse, available data have been evaluated and are presented in this document. However, in most cases, the pediatric recommendations have been extrapolated from adult data.

Clinical studies to determine the optimal dosages of antimicrobials used for pediatric prophylaxis are essentially nonexistent. In contrast, there are sufficient pharmacokinetic studies for most agents used such that appropriate pediatric dosages can be estimated that provide similar systemic exposure, and presumably efficacy, as that demonstrated by the adult efficacy trials. It is also common clinical practice to use antimicrobial prophylaxis in pediatric patients in a similar, if not identical, manner as in adults. Therefore, the pediatric dosages provided in these guidelines are based largely on pharmacokinetic equivalence and the generalization of the adult efficacy data to pediatric patients.[3,4] Because pediatric trials have generally not been conducted, a strength of evidence has not been applied to these recommendations. With few exceptions (e.g., aminoglycoside dosages), pediatric dosages should not exceed the maximum adult recommended dosages. If dosages are calculated on a milligram-per-kilogram basis for children weighing more than 40–50 kg, the calculated dosage will exceed the maximum recommended dosage for adults; thus adult dosages should be used.

Resistance. The basis for guideline development was to recommend an effective antimicrobial with the most narrow spectrum of activity. Alternative antimicrobials were included on the basis of documented efficacy. Individual health systems must take into consideration specific resistance patterns at their practice site when adopting these recommendations.

When considering the use of antimicrobials for prophylaxis, one must also consider the risks of contributing to the development of antimicrobial resistance. In numerous studies of prophylaxis, both surgical[5,6] and nonsurgical,[7–16] attempts have been made to evaluate the impact of antimicrobial prophylaxis on the development of resistance. Numerous studies[5,7–13] demonstrated an increase in resistance, yet other studies[6,14–16] failed to demonstrate the emergence of resistance. Most of the studies demonstrating the development of resistance involved the use of broad-spectrum antimicrobials.[5,7–13] Thus, current recommended practice is to use narrow-spectrum antimicrobials for the shortest duration to reduce the development of antimicrobial resistance.

The frequency with which methicillin-resistant staphylococci have been recovered from various infection sites has increased steadily throughout the United States.[17–19] The frequency of methicillin resistance among staphylococcal strains rose from 2.4% in 1975 to 29% in 1991.[19] CDC's National Nosocomial Infections Surveillance identified a rapid increase in vancomycin-resistant enterococci (VRE) from 0.3% in 1989 to 7.9% in 1993. The rate of high-level enterococcal resistance to penicillin and aminoglycosides increased simultaneously. The use of vancomycin has been reported consistently as a risk factor for infection and colonization with VRE and may increase the possibility of the emergence of vancomycin-resistant *S. aureus* or vancomycin-resistant *Staphylococcus epidermidis*.[20] In response, the Hospital Infection Control Practices Advisory Committee (HICPAC), with the support of other major organizations, developed control measures for preventing and controlling vancomycin resistance.[21] The ASHP guidelines are consistent with the HICPAC recommendations. The following situations are appropriate or acceptable for use of vancomycin: prophylaxis of endocarditis (as recommended by AHA) before certain procedures and for major surgical procedures involving implantation of prosthetic materials or devices (e.g., cardiac and vascular procedures, total hip replacement) at institutions with a high rate of infections due to MRSA or methicillin-resistant *S. epidermidis*. Use of vancomycin for routine surgical prophylaxis should be discouraged (other than in a patient with life-threatening allergy to β-lactam antimicrobials).

Cost. Pharmacoeconomic studies have been lacking or inadequate with regard to the prophylactic use of antimicrobials; therefore, a cost-minimization approach was employed in developing these guidelines. When antimicrobials have been shown to be equally efficacious and safe, the recommendation is based on the least expensive agent (on the basis of average wholesale price). The other antimicrobials are considered to be alternative agents. The recommendation of an antimicrobial is determined primarily by efficacy and secondarily by cost. Because of variations in cost from one health system to another, health systems must tailor the choice of antimicrobials to their individual acquisition costs.

Endocarditis

Background. The incidence of infective endocarditis is difficult to estimate because of the difficulty of accurate diagnosis and the variability in reporting criteria. However, estimates have ranged from one to six cases per 100,000 people annually.[22,23] Infective endocarditis continues to cause serious morbidity and mortality despite treatment advances.[24-27] A study of 300 episodes of endocarditis occurring in 287 patients demonstrated that complications are common.[26] Complications included cardiac, neurologic, septic, and renal complications; extracranial systemic arterial embolism; septic pulmonary embolism; and complications related to surgical treatment. A cohort study with a 15-year follow-up involving 112 patients addicted to nonintravenous drugs demonstrated survival rates of 90% at 2 years, 88% at 5 years, 81% at 10 years, and 61% at 15 years.[27]

Several guidelines for prophylaxis before medical and dental procedures are available.[23,28-33] The rationale for prophylactic therapy is that, if the appropriate antimicrobial is present at the time of bacteremia, organisms are unable to colonize to the tissue in sufficient numbers to cause endocarditis. The various guidelines attempt to identify patient groups and procedures associated with a higher risk of infective endocarditis. AHA's most recent recommendations contain the following changes: a single dose of oral amoxicillin with no follow-up dose, a lower amoxicillin dose, and cephalexin, cefodroxil, azithromycin, and clarithromycin as alternatives to erythromycin for penicillin-allergic patients.[29] Although erythromycin remains an appropriate choice for prophylaxis, the committee did not specifically recommend it because of the GI adverse effects and the complicated pharmacokinetics of the various formulations compared with the newer agents in this class.

The most common causative organisms identified in patients with endocarditis are viridans streptococci and are known to cause bacteremia after dental or respiratory tract procedures.[24,26,29,34,35] Viridans streptococci that have been isolated in endocarditis include *S. gordonii, S. sanguis, S. mitis, S. oralis, S. adjacens, S. defectivus, S. mutans,* and *S. sobrinus.*[36] Other organisms identified include *S. aureus,*[24,29,34,37] *S. epidermidis,*[32,37] enterococci,[24,29,34] and, less commonly, gram-negative bacteria and fungi.[24,34] Reports of staphylococcal endocarditis are notably higher among patients undergoing valvular surgery.[34,37] Enterococci are most commonly implicated after high-risk GU and GI procedures.[29]

The costs and benefits of prophylaxis have been analyzed for at-risk patients undergoing procedures that produce bacteremia as well as for some subgroups of patients, notably those with mitral valve prolapse.[38] The cost of treating a patient with endocarditis has been estimated to be $46,000. For oral erythromycin and amoxicillin prophylaxis regimens, the estimated net cost was about $0.75 and $1.50, respectively, per dental procedure, compared with approximately $12,000 and $19,000 to treat each case of infective endocarditis prevented.[38] The cost–benefit analysis clearly favors prophylaxis.

Persons at Risk. Animal data and the results of in vitro studies support the concept that the development of infective endocarditis involves deposition of platelets and fibrin on an altered endocardial surface followed by bacterial colonization of these sites.[34] Persons at highest risk are those who have prosthetic cardiac valves, including bioprosthetic and homograft valves; previous bacterial endocarditis; complex cyanotic congenital heart disease (e.g., single ventricle states, transposition of the great arteries, tetralogy of Fallot); and surgically constructed systemic pulmonary shunts or conduits. Persons at moderate risk are those who have congenital cardiac malformations, including patent ductus arteriosus, ventricular septal defect, primum atrial septal defect, coarctation of the aorta, and bicuspid aortic valve; acquired valvar dysfunction (e.g., rheumatic heart disease); hypertrophic cardiomyopathy; and mitral valve prolapse with valvar regurgitation or thickened leaflets, including myxomatous mitral valve degeneration with regurgitation.[29]

Special considerations are involved in prescribing prophylaxis for bacterial endocarditis in patients with a history of rheumatic fever. These patients often receive secondary antimicrobial prophylaxis to prevent colonization or infection of the upper respiratory tract by group A streptococci and subsequent recurrent attacks of rheumatic fever. The secondary prophylactic therapy often continues into adulthood and may have to be continued for life in patients with a history of rheumatic carditis.[29]

Efficacy. There have been no randomized or placebo-controlled prospective clinical trials in humans to evaluate the efficacy of endocarditis prophylaxis before dental or medical procedures. Available data are from retrospective case–control studies. One study demonstrated that antimicrobial prophylaxis given before dental procedures was protective in 91% of patients with cardiac lesions.[39] In contrast, a case–control study of 438 patients who developed endocarditis after a medical or dental procedure demonstrated that only about 6% of endocarditis cases were preventable.[40] A retrospective analysis of a national registry identified cases of apparent failure of endocarditis prophylaxis.[41] Although the results call into question the effectiveness of antimicrobial regimens for endocarditis prophylaxis, care must be taken in interpreting case registry data, and it should be noted that only 12% of patients had received a regimen that followed the AHA guidelines at the time. Given the rarity of endocarditis, it would take an estimated 6000 patients with preexisting valvular heart disease who were undergoing dental procedures to show a significant benefit of prophylactic antimicrobials.[23] Because endocarditis prophylaxis is currently commonplace, it is unlikely that such a trial will be done.

The evidence supporting the use of prophylactic antimicrobials for high-risk patients with cardiac lesions before medical or dental procedures that produce bacteremia is incomplete but suggests that the benefits of prophylaxis against endocarditis outweigh the risks and costs for these patients. The choice of antimicrobials recommended by the AHA guidelines for endocarditis prophylaxis is based on the organisms that most frequently produce infective endocarditis and on the types of bacteremia produced by specific procedures.[29] AHA also used relevant literature on procedure-related endocarditis, including the results of animal experiments of endocarditis and retrospective analyses of human endocarditis cases.

Although there are no supporting data, ciprofloxacin has been recommended for antimicrobial prophylaxis in patients undergoing endoscopic retrograde cholangiopancreatography (ERCP) by a working party for the British Society of Gastroenterology Endoscopy Committee.[33] For this procedure, the choice of antimicrobial is directed at the pathogens most likely to cause gram-negative sepsis after ERCP rather than at enterococci, the organisms most commonly associated with endocarditis resulting from GI procedures. Most panel members considered ciprofloxacin or any fluoroquinolone to be an acceptable alternative agent for patients undergoing ERCP. However, a minority of panel members believed that fluoroquinolones, in general, should be avoided because of classwide resistance.

The development of resistant organisms is a concern associated with the use of antimicrobial prophylaxis against bacterial endocarditis. A prospective, uncontrolled study demonstrated resistant streptococci in the mouths of 8 out of 20 healthy adult volunteers administered oral penicillin V.[42] The relevance of these findings with respect to endocarditis prophylaxis is unclear because the number of resistant strains was low relative to the number of total oral streptococci.

Pediatric Efficacy. No well-controlled studies have evaluated the effect of prophylaxis against bacterial endocarditis in pediatric patients. The AHA guidelines provide pediatric dosage recommendations.[29]

Recommendation. The choice of antimicrobials for bacterial endocarditis prophylaxis is based on the procedure and the patient's level of risk for endocarditis (Table 1). Dental procedures for which prophylaxis is recommended include dental extractions, periodontal procedures (including surgery, scaling and root planing, probing, and recall maintenance), dental implant placement and reimplantation of avulsed teeth, endodontic (root canal) instrumentation or surgery only beyond the apex, subgingival placement of antimicrobial fibers or strips, initial placement of orthodontic bands but not brackets, intraligamentary local anesthetic injections, and prophylactic cleaning of teeth or implants when bleeding is anticipated. Prophylaxis is optional when there may be substantial bleeding, such as with operative and prosthodontic restorative dentistry, including restoration of decayed teeth (filling cavities) and replacement of missing teeth. Respiratory tract procedures for which prophylaxis is warranted include tonsillectomy and adenoidectomy, surgical operations that involve respiratory mucosa, and bronchoscopy with a rigid bronchoscope. Prophylaxis is optional for high-risk patients undergoing bronchoscopy with a flexible bronchoscope, with or without biopsy. Esophageal procedures include sclerotherapy for esophageal varices and esophageal stricture dilation. GI procedures include endoscopic retrograde cholangiography with biliary obstruction, biliary tract surgery, and surgical operations that involve intestinal mucosa. Prophylaxis is optional for high-risk patients undergoing transesophageal echocardiography and endoscopy with or without GI biopsy. GU tract procedures include prostatic surgery, cystoscopy, and urethral dilation. Prophylaxis is optional for high-risk patients undergoing vaginal hysterectomy and vaginal delivery. A list of related procedures, such as endotracheal intubation, for which endocarditis prophylaxis is not recommended because of the lesser risk of associated bacteremia can be found in the AHA guidelines. Patients who take an oral penicillin for secondary prophylaxis are often colonized by penicillin-, amoxicillin-, or ampicillin-resistant viridans streptococci. These patients should receive clindamycin, azithromycin, or clarithromycin instead of penicillin, amoxicillin, or ampicillin.[29]

Dental, respiratory tract, and esophageal procedures in patients at moderate or high risk. The recommended regimen for moderate- or high-risk patients undergoing dental, respiratory tract, or esophageal procedures is amoxicillin 2 g orally one hour before the procedure. For patients unable to take oral medications, the alternative is ampicillin 2 g (as the sodium) i.v. or i.m. within 30 minutes of the procedure. For patients allergic to penicillin, the alternative is clindamycin 600 mg (as the hydrochloride) orally one hour before the procedure, cephalexin or cefadroxil 2 g orally one hour before the procedure, or azithromycin or clarithromycin 500 mg orally one hour before the procedure. An acceptable alternative is erythromycin 800 mg (as the ethylsuccinate) or 1 g (as the stearate) orally two hours before the procedure and then half the dose six hours after the initial dose. For penicillin-allergic patients and patients unable to take oral medications, the alternative is clindamycin 600 mg (as the phosphate) i.v. within 30 minutes before the procedure or cefazolin 1 g (as the sodium) i.v. or i.m. within 30 minutes of the procedure.

GI and GU procedures for patients at moderate risk. For moderate-risk patients undergoing GI or GU procedures, the recommended regimen is amoxicillin 2 g orally one hour before the procedure or ampicillin 2 g (as the sodium) i.v. or i.m. within 30 minutes of the start of the procedure. For patients allergic to ampicillin or amoxicillin, the alternative is vancomycin 1 g (as the hydrochloride) i.v. over one to two hours (complete infusion within 30 minutes of the start of the procedure). For ERCP procedures, a fluoroquinolone such as ciprofloxacin given at a dose of 750 mg (as the base or hydrochloride) orally 60 to 90 minutes before the procedure is considered by some to be an acceptable alternative regimen.

GI and GU procedures for patients at high risk. The recommended regimen for high-risk patients undergoing GI or GU procedures is ampicillin 2 g (as the sodium) i.v. or i.m. plus gentamicin 1.5 mg/kg (as the sulfate; not to exceed 120 mg) i.v. or i.m. within 30 minutes of the start of the procedure followed by ampicillin 1 g i.v. or i.m. or amoxicillin 1 g orally six hours later. For patients allergic to ampicillin or amoxicillin, the alternative is vancomycin 1 g (as the hydrochloride) i.v. over one to two hours (complete infusion within 30 minutes of the start of the procedure) plus gentamicin 1.5 mg/kg (not to exceed 120 mg) i.v. or i.m. (complete injection within 30 minutes of the start of the procedure). For patients undergoing an ERCP procedure, ciprofloxacin 750 mg (as the base or hydrochloride) orally (any fluoroquinolone may be appropriate) given 60 to 90 minutes before the procedure may be considered an acceptable alternative regimen. (Strength of evidence for prophylaxis = B)

Pediatric Dosage. The choice of antimicrobials for endocarditis prophylaxis in pediatric patients is based on the procedure and the patient's level of risk for endocarditis. Readers are referred to the adult recommendations for the choice of antimicrobials. The equivalent pediatric initial doses are oral amoxicillin 50 mg/kg, oral clindamycin 20 mg/kg (as the hydrochloride), ampicillin 50 mg/kg (as the sodium) i.v. or i.m., clindamycin 20 mg/kg (as the phosphate) i.v., gentamicin 1.5 mg/kg (as the sulfate) i.v., and vancomycin 20 mg/kg (as the hydrochloride) i.v. The total pediatric dose should not exceed the total adult dose.

Meningitis After Nonpenetrating Head Trauma Associated with Basilar Skull Fracture

Background. The reported frequency of acute intracranial infection after basilar skull fractures is highly variable and ranges from 0% to 50%.[43–45] No prospective study involving patients with basilar skull fractures has compared the development of meningitis in patients with documented cerebrospinal fluid (CSF) leakage with development in patients without clinically detectable CSF leakage. No prospective study has investigated the time course for the development of meningitis after a basilar skull fracture. Although most central nervous system (CNS) infections are reported to develop within days to weeks after nonpenetrating head trauma, meningitis has been reported to occur months to years later.[46]

Several organisms have been isolated from the CSF of patients developing meningitis after basilar skull fractures. These include both gram-positive organisms (*Streptococcus* and *Staphylococcus*) and gram-negative organisms (*Escherichia coli, Serratia, Haemophilus, Klebsiella,* and *Acinetobacter*).[43,46–48] The most common organisms are *Streptococcus pneumoniae,* group A β-hemolytic streptococci, and *H. influenzae.*[49]

Persons at Risk. Basilar skull fractures after nonpenetrating head trauma are often, but not necessarily, associated with an interruption of the meninges. Meningeal tears, occurring in proximity to the nasopharynx, nasal or mastoid sinuses, or the external auditory canal, predispose patients with basilar skull fractures to meningitis. The direct spread of pathogenic organisms colonizing these contiguous-airspace areas is believed to be the cause of subsequent meningeal infection.

Efficacy. No prospective, randomized, double-blind, placebo-controlled trials have evaluated the potential benefits and risks of prophylactic antimicrobial administration after the diagnosis of basilar skull fracture. Only two reported studies have used prospective data collection in investigating this issue.[50,51] No recommendations could be made because these studies contained numerous flaws.

Most retrospective case series involving adults with basilar skull fractures have not supported the use of prophylactic antimicrobials.[47,48,52] Retrospective case series in which it was claimed that prophylactic antimicrobials were associated with a lower frequency of meningitis have been flawed by the nature of retrospective data collection, a small sample size, a lack of standardized antimicrobial regimens, and failure to account for confounding variables such as neurosurgical intervention and injury severity.[53] In contrast, a meta-analysis demonstrated a significantly lower frequency of meningitis (2.5% versus 10%) when prophylactic antimicrobials were administered to patients with CSF leakage.[54] Prophylactic antimicrobials may have a role in patients with CSF leakage. However, the meta-analysis, because of its limitations (including an inadequate amount of specific details on the choice, dosage, and duration of antimicrobial therapy; on the duration of CSF leakage; and on the latency of the meningitis), provides inadequate data for a specific recommendation.

Resistance. Retrospective case series in which it was claimed that prophylactic antimicrobials were responsible for the selection of more invasive, pathogenic, and antimicrobial-resistant organisms have been less numerous but equally as flawed as studies in which there was an alleged benefit from prophylactic antimicrobial administration.

Pediatric Efficacy. No well-controlled studies have evaluated the effect of prophylaxis for pediatric patients with a basilar skull fracture after nonpenetrating head trauma, either with or without CSF leakage. Retrospective case series involving children with basilar skull fractures have not supported the use of prophylactic antimicrobials.[47,48,55]

Recommendation. Prophylactic administration of antimicrobials to patients with a basilar skull fracture after nonpenetrating head trauma, either with or without CSF leakage, is not recommended (Table 1). (Strength of evidence against prophylaxis = C)

Pediatric Dosage. Prophylaxis for pediatric patients with a basilar skull fracture after nonpenetrating head trauma, either with or without CSF leakage, is not recommended.

Nosocomial Pneumonia in Patients Receiving Mechanical Ventilation

Background. The frequency of nosocomial pneumonia in the medical, surgical, and cardiothoracic intensive care unit (ICU) ranges from 10% to 65%, with case mortality rates of 13% to 55%.[56] CDC recently developed comprehensive guidelines for the prevention of nosocomial pneumonia.[57]

Selective decontamination of the GI tract has been widely used in Europe as a prophylactic regimen for ventilator-associated nosocomial pneumonia. These regimens are intended to reduce the rate of respiratory tract colonization, reduce the rate of nosocomial infections, and therefore reduce patient mortality. The most common regimens have included two components: (1) administration of a combination of oral nonabsorbable antimicrobials, such as aminoglycosides, colistin, and amphotericin B, to prevent GI microorganisms, and (2) application of a paste containing the same agents to the oral mucosa to prevent upper-respiratory-tract colonization. Vancomycin has been included in some regimens in an effort to prevent *S. aureus* infections. In addition, some investigators have included a brief course of an i.v. antimicrobial to treat an "incubating" pneumonia that may have been acquired at the time of admission.[58–64]

The most frequently isolated pathogens include gram-negative bacilli (most commonly *Pseudomonas aeruginosa* and Enterobacteriaceae), *S. aureus,* and coagulase-negative staphylococci. Although *Candida* is frequently isolated, it is a rare cause of pneumonia.[60,63,65]

Proper pharmacoeconomic evaluations of selective decontamination have not been conducted. A few studies have calculated the relative costs (primarily drug acquisition costs) of selective decontamination compared with placebo. In one study, selective decontamination was associated with lower overall antimicrobial and hospitalization costs.[66] In contrast, the cost of selective decontamination results in a higher total cost of ICU care (antimicrobials, microbiological surveillance, and nursing time) compared with the cost of placebo[63] and a higher cost of antimicrobials (both topical and systemic) compared with placebo.[67] A recent analysis showed that, to prevent one case of nosocomial pneumonia, 6 patients would have to be treated with selective decontamination and that, to prevent one death, 23 patients would have to be treated.[57]

Persons at Risk. Patients requiring prolonged mechanical ventilation are at greatest risk for nosocomial pneumonia. Oropharyngeal and gastric colonization by pathogenic organisms with subsequent aspiration is a major mechanism of ventilator-associated nosocomial pneumonia.[60] Other risk factors for nosocomial pneumonia include advanced age, organ system failure, prior administration of antimicrobials, supine head position during mechanical ventilation, longer ICU stay, and diagnosis of trauma.[56,65] Concomitant use of a histamine H_2-receptor antagonist (ranitidine or cimetidine) has been identified as a risk factor for nosocomial pneumonia in some,[68–70] but not all,[71–76] studies.

Efficacy. Selective decontamination has been the subject of investigation for more than 20 years and is practiced widely in Europe. However, most of the early studies were either not randomized[77,78] or not placebo controlled.[58,59,79–81] The use of selective decontamination has not been studied in the United States, primarily because of a widespread concern about the possibility of overgrowth of resistant organisms. Results of well-controlled trials indicate that, although selective decontamination is associated with a lower rate of bacterial colonization and nosocomial pneumonia, there is no significant benefit in terms of ICU stay, hospital stay, or mortality.

For the development of these guidelines, only randomized, double-blind, placebo-controlled trials with a clearly stated definition of pneumonia were evaluated.[60,63,64,66,67,82–84] In these studies, the use of selective decontamination was very effective in reducing respiratory tract colonization of bacteria, particularly gram-negative bacilli and *Candida* species. In three studies, there was a significantly lower frequency of pneumonia among patients receiving selective decontamination than among placebo recipients.[64,83,84] The frequency of pneumonia ranged from 15% to 28% among patients receiving selective decontamination and from 33% to 78% among patients receiving placebo. With one exception,[64] however, there was no difference in mortality between treated and placebo groups. In addition, selective decontamination had no effect on the duration of ICU or hospital stay.[60,63,64,67,82,83] A meta-analysis supported these conclusions.[85] It showed that nosocomial pneumonia was significantly lower among patients receiving selective decontamination than control patients; however, there was no significant difference between groups in mortality rate.

Resistance. The development of resistant organisms is the greatest concern associated with the use of selective decontamination and may explain why reducing the rate of pneumonia is not associated with lower mortality. Two long-term studies showed that, although the rate of colonization with gram-negative bacilli was lower, the rate of gram-positive bacilli colonization was higher.[61,86] A trend toward a higher rate of staphylococcal pneumonia among patients receiving selective decontamination has been demonstrated.[67] The addition of vancomycin to the antimicrobial regimen in order to decrease the rate of *S. aureus* colonization was not consistently associated with a reversal of this trend.[83] In addition, selective decontamination regimens do not cover *Enterococcus faecalis,* and five cases of *E. faecalis* colonization and endocarditis have been reported in patients receiving these regimens.[62] Selective decontamination was also associated with significantly higher resistance to cefotaxime and tobramycin.[64] However, the long-term use of selective decontamination has also been reported to have no effect on antimicrobial resistance or nosocomial pathogens.[87]

Pediatric Efficacy. No well-controlled studies have yet evaluated the effect of prophylaxis for mechanically ventilated pediatric patients.

CDC recently developed comprehensive guidelines for the prevention of nosocomial pneumonia.[57] CDC views selective decontamination for mechanically ventilated patients as an unresolved issue and therefore has no recommendations for or against the use of selective decontamination.

Recommendation. Because there is no significant benefit in terms of ICU stay, hospital stay, or mortality, the routine use of selective decontamination in mechanically ventilated patients cannot be recommended (Table 1). (Strength of evidence against prophylaxis = A)

Pediatric Dosage. Selective decontamination is not recommended in mechanically ventilated pediatric patients.

Influenza A

Background. Influenza A infection is associated with fever, myalgia, sore throat, nonproductive cough, and secondary bacterial pneumonia and may result in death. The illness increases health care use secondary to increases in hospital admissions and visits to physicians' offices, clinics, and emergency rooms. More than 20,000 influenza-associated deaths occurred during each of nine different U.S. epidemics from 1972–73 to 1990–92, and more than 40,000 influenza-associated deaths occurred during each of four of those epidemics.[88]

Persons at Risk. Groups at high risk for influenza-related complications include (1) persons 65 years of age and older, (2) residents of nursing homes and other chronic care facilities, (3) adults and children with chronic disorders of the pulmonary or cardiovascular system, including children with asthma, (4) adults and children who have required regular medical follow-up or hospitalization during the preceding year because of chronic metabolic diseases (including diabetes mellitus), renal dysfunction, hemoglobinopathy, or immunosuppression (including immunosuppression caused by medications or HIV infection) and who are expected to have inadequate antibody response to the vaccine, (5) children and teenagers (six months to 18 years of age) who are receiving long-term aspirin therapy and who therefore might be at risk for developing Reye syndrome after influenza, and (6) women who will be in the second or third trimester of pregnancy during the influenza season.[89]

Groups that can transmit influenza to persons at high risk include (1) physicians, nurses, and other personnel in hospital or outpatient health care settings, (2) employees of nursing homes or chronic care facilities who have contact with patients or residents, (3) providers of home care to persons at high risk (e.g., visiting nurses, volunteers), and (4) household members (including children) of persons in high-risk groups.[89]

Efficacy. Amantadine and rimantadine were both approved by FDA for prophylactic and therapeutic use against influenza A. Double-blind, placebo-controlled, clinical trials have demonstrated that the prophylactic effectiveness of amantadine and rimantadine is similar.[90–95] Amantadine and rimantadine were highly effective in preventing influenza-like illness; the rate of illness was 78% and 65% lower, respectively, compared with placebo.[94] The efficacy rates for

Table 1.
Prevention of Infection in Specialized Settings[a]

Infection and Setting[b]	Eligible Patients[c]	Recommended Regimen[d]	Alternative Regimens[d,e]	Strength of Evidence[f]
Bacterial endocarditis Dental, respiratory tract, or esophageal procedure	Adult; moderate or high risk[g]	Amoxicillin 2 g p.o. 1 hr before procedure or ampicillin 2 g i.v. or i.m. 30 min before procedure[h]	Clindamycin 600 mg, cephalexin 2 g, cefadroxil 2 g, azithromycin 500 mg, or clarithromycin 500 mg p.o. 1 hr before procedure; erythromycin ethylsuccinate 800 mg or erythromycin stearate 1 g p.o. 2 hr before procedure, then half initial dose p.o. 6 hr after initial dose; or clindamycin 600 mg i.v. or cefazolin 1 g i.v. or i.m. 30 min before procedure	B
	Pediatric; moderate or high risk[g]	Amoxicillin 50 mg/kg p.o. 1 hr before procedure or ampicillin 50 mg/kg i.v. or i.m. 30 min before procedure[h]	Clindamycin 20 mg/kg, cephalexin 50 mg/kg, cefadroxil 50 mg/kg, azithromycin 15 mg/kg, or clarithromycin 15 mg/kg 1 hr before procedure; erythromycin ethylsuccinate or stearate 20 mg/kg p.o. 2 hr before procedure, then 10 mg/kg p.o. 6 hr after initial dose; or clindamycin 20 mg/kg i.v. or cefazolin 25 mg/kg i.m. or i.v. 30 min before procedure	NA
Gastrointestinal or genitourinary procedure	Adult; moderate risk	Amoxicillin 2 g p.o. 1 hr before procedure or ampicillin 2 g i.v. or i.m. 30 min before procedure	Vancomycin 1 g i.v. over 1–2 hr, completing infusion within 30 min of starting procedure; for ERCP, ciprofloxacin 750 mg p.o. 60–90 min before procedure[i]	B
	Adult; high risk	Ampicillin 2 g i.v. or i.m. plus gentamicin 1.5 mg/kg (maximum 120 mg) i.v. or i.m. 30 min before procedure, then ampicillin 1 g i.v. or i.m. or amoxicillin 1 g p.o. 6 hr later[h]	Vancomycin 1 g i.v. over 1–2 hr plus gentamicin 1.5 mg/kg (maximum 120 mg) i.v. or i.m., completing both i.v. infusions within 30 min of starting procedure; for ERCP, ciprofloxacin 750 mg p.o. 60–90 min before procedure[i]	B
	Pediatric; moderate risk	Amoxicillin 50 mg/kg p.o. 1 hr before procedure or ampicillin 50 mg/kg i.v. or i.m. 30 min before procedure	Vancomycin 20 mg/kg i.v. over 1–2 hr, completing infusion within 30 min of starting procedure	NA
	Pediatric; high risk	Ampicillin 50 mg/kg i.v. or i.m. (maximum 2 g) plus gentamicin 1.5 mg/kg (maximum 120 mg) i.v. or i.m. 30 min before procedure, then ampicillin 25 mg/kg i.v. or i.m. or amoxicillin 25 mg/kg p.o. 6 hr later	Vancomycin 20 mg/kg i.v. over 1–2 hr plus gentamicin 1.5 mg/kg (maximum 120 mg) i.v. or i.m., completing both infusions within 30 min of starting procedure	NA

Continued on next page

prevention of laboratory-documented influenza were 91% for amantadine and 85% for rimantadine.[94]

Amantadine and rimantadine are not active against influenza B, which is responsible for approximately 20% of all influenza epidemics. In a given year, influenza B may be the only virus circulating.[96] Rimantadine has a lower frequency of CNS adverse effects, including nervousness, anxiety, difficulty concentrating, and lightheadedness.[89]

Resistance. In a 10-year study of one community, the investigators failed to detect naturally occurring drug-resistant strains of influenza A virus in untreated patients.[97] However, rimantadine-resistant influenza A virus isolates have been recovered from rimantadine-treated index patients, and the resistance can be transmitted and cause illness in other family members taking rimantadine for postexposure prophylaxis.[98] Amantadine-resistant influenza A was reported in a nursing facility where amantadine-resistant virus was shed by patients being treated for influenza with amantadine and caused illness in patients receiving the drug prophylactically.[99]

Pediatric Efficacy. Double-blind, placebo-controlled clinical trials in pediatric patients (ages 1–18 years) have demonstrated that prophylactic rimantadine is efficacious; the in-

Table 1 *(continued)*

Infection and Setting[b]	Eligible Patients[c]	Recommended Regimen[d]	Alternative Regimens[d,e]	Strength of Evidence[f]
Meningitis Nonpenetrating head trauma	Adult; basilar skull fracture	Not recommended	None	C
	Pediatric; basilar fracture	Not recommended	None	NA
Nosocomial pneumonia Intensive care unit	Adult; mechanical ventilation	Not recommended	None	A
	Pediatric; mechanical ventilation	Not recommended	None	NA

[a]Adult recommendations adapted from American Heart Association (AHA) recommendations (reference 29).

[b]Dental procedures include extractions, periodontal procedures (including surgery, scaling and root planing, probing, and recall maintenance), dental implant placement and reimplantation of avulsed teeth, endodontic (root canal) instrumentation or surgery only beyond the apex, subgingival placement of antimicrobial fibers or strips, initial placement of orthodontic bands but not brackets, intraligamentary local anesthetic injections, and prophylactic cleaning of teeth or implants when bleeding is anticipated. Prophylaxis is optional for procedures in which there may be significant bleeding, such as operative and prosthodontic restorative dentistry, including restoration of decayed teeth (filling cavities), and replacement of missing teeth. Respiratory tract procedures include tonsillectomy or adenoidectomy, surgical operations that involve respiratory mucosa, and bronchoscopy with a rigid bronchoscope. Prophylaxis is optional for high-risk patients undergoing bronchoscopy with a flexible bronchoscope, with or without biopsy. Esophageal procedures include sclerotherapy for esophageal varices and esophageal stricture dilation. Gastrointestinal tract procedures include endoscopic retrograde cholangiography with biliary obstruction, biliary tract surgery, and surgical operations that involve intestinal mucosa. Prophylaxis is optional for high-risk patients undergoing transesophageal echocardiography and endoscopy with or without gastrointestinal biopsy. Genitourinary tract procedures include prostatic surgery, cystoscopy, and urethral dilation. Prophylaxis is optional for high-risk patients undergoing vaginal hysterectomy or vaginal delivery.

[c]Moderate-risk patients include those with most congenital cardiac malformations, including the uncorrected conditions of patent ductus arteriosus, ventricular septal defect, primum atrial septal defect, coarctation of the aorta, and bicuspid aortic valve; acquired valvar dysfunction (e.g., rheumatic heart disease); hypertrophic cardiomyopathy; and mitral valve prolapse with valvar regurgitation or thickened leaflets (including myxomatous mitral valve degeneration with regurgitation). High-risk patients include those with prosthetic cardiac valves, including bioprosthetic and homograft valves; previous history of bacterial endocarditis; complex cyanotic congenital heart disease (e.g., single ventricle states, transposition of the great arteries, tetralogy of Fallot); and surgically constructed systemic–pulmonary shunts or conduits.

[d]When oral and parenteral regimens are indicated, the oral is preferred; the parenteral is to be used if the patient cannot take oral medication.

[e]For patients allergic to penicillin. Cephalosporins should not be used in patients with immediate-type hypersensitivity reaction (urticaria, angioedema, or anaphylaxis) to penicillins.

[f]Strength of evidence that supports the use or nonuse of prophylaxis is classified as A (levels I–III), B (levels IV–VI), or C (level VII). Level I evidence is from large, well-conducted randomized, controlled clinical trials. Level II evidence is from small, well-conducted randomized, controlled clinical trials. Level III evidence is from well-conducted cohort studies. Level IV evidence is from well-conducted case–control studies. Level V evidence is from uncontrolled studies that were not well conducted. Level VI evidence is conflicting evidence that tends to favor the recommendation. Level VII evidence is expert opinion. Strength-of-evidence classification not applied (NA) to pediatric recommendations.

[g]AHA recommends the same prophylactic regimen for dental, respiratory tract, and esophageal procedures in high- and moderate-risk patients.

[h]Patients who take an oral penicillin for secondary prophylaxis are often colonized by penicillin–amoxicillin- or ampicillin-resistant viridans streptococci. These patients should receive clindamycin, azithromycin, or clarithromycin instead of penicillin, amoxicillin, or ampicillin.

[i]Any fluoroquinolone may be appropriate for patients undergoing endoscopic retrograde cholangiopancreatography (ERCP).

fection rate was 30% in the placebo group and less than 10% in the rimantadine group.[100,101] Infection was defined by a positive viral throat culture or a fourfold increase in antibody titer. A double-blind, placebo-controlled trial in pediatric patients (average age of eight years) demonstrated that prophylactic amantadine is efficacious; the infection rate was 30% in the placebo group and 10% in the amantadine group.[102] Infection was defined by a temperature of 101 °F or more with a fourfold or more increase in titer of complement fixation plus hemagglutination inhibition.

Recommendation. Chemoprophylaxis is not a substitute for vaccination. Practitioners should refer to CDC annually for specific vaccine recommendations.

CDC recommends chemoprophylaxis with amantadine or rimantadine against influenza A in persons at risk (see above) for developing complications under certain circumstances: (1) persons at high risk who were vaccinated after influenza A activity began, because the development of antibodies can take as long as two weeks, (2) persons providing care to those at high risk who are not vaccinated; prophylaxis should be considered for all employees, regardless of their vaccination status, if the outbreak is caused by a variant strain of influenza A that might not be controlled by the vaccine, (3) persons who have immune deficiency and who are expected to have an inadequate antibody response to influenza vaccine, (4) persons for whom influenza vaccine is

contraindicated, including persons who have severe anaphylactic hypersensitivity to egg protein or other vaccine components, and (5) other persons who wish to avoid influenza A illness.

Factors that should be considered before initiation of chemoprophylaxis are cost, adherence, and potential adverse effects.[89] No well-controlled studies of pregnant women have been conducted, and the drug should be used during pregnancy only when the potential benefits outweigh the possible risk to the fetus.

On the basis of cost minimization, the regimen of choice is usually amantadine hydrochloride 100 mg orally twice daily (Table 2). An alternative regimen is rimantadine hydrochloride 100 mg orally twice daily for persons who cannot tolerate the CNS adverse effects of amantadine. Prophylaxis should be continued for 10 days after exposure. When an antiviral agent is used in conjunction with the vaccine, prophylaxis should be continued for two weeks after administration of the vaccine. If the vaccine is unavailable or contraindicated, prophylaxis should be continued for the duration of influenza A activity in the community. (Strength of evidence for prophylaxis = A)

Pediatric Dosage. Amantadine is the first drug of choice for influenza A prophylaxis; rimantadine is an alternative. Readers are referred to the adult recommendations for the indications to use chemoprophylaxis.

The dosage of amantadine hydrochloride in children of ages one to eight years and in older children who weigh less than 40 kg is 5–9 mg/kg/day orally in two divided doses (up to 200 mg daily).[3] For children 9 to 12 years of age who weigh more than 40 kg, the dosage of amantadine hydrochloride is 100 mg orally twice daily. The dosage of rimantadine hydrochloride in children less than 10 years of age is 5 mg/kg orally once daily (up to 150 mg daily). For children older than 10 years, the dosage of rimantadine hydrochloride is 100 mg orally twice daily. Prophylaxis should be continued for 10 days after exposure to influenza A. When an antiviral agent is used in conjunction with the vaccine, prophylaxis should be continued for two weeks after the last dose of vaccine (one dose is recommended for children older than nine years; two doses of vaccine are required for children up to nine years of age who have not been previously vaccinated). If the vaccine is unavailable or contraindicated, prophylaxis should be continued for the duration of influenza A activity in the community.

Malaria

Background. Malaria is caused by one or more of four parasites from the genus *Plasmodium: P. falciparum, P. vivax, P. ovale,* and *P. malariae. P. falciparum* infection is the most dangerous and may produce severe metabolic effects and microvascular disease. Microvascular disease can affect most organ systems, including the kidneys, the lungs, the GI system, and the CNS. *P. falciparum* infection can result in death. *P. vivax* and *P. ovale* do not cause microvascular complications and have less severe sequelae. *P. malariae* infection may produce an immune complex (parasite antigens, host antibodies, and complement) glomerulonephritis, which usually occurs three to six months after the malaria-transmission season.[103]

Persons at Risk. Malaria is so common that a person who has traveled in a malarious area for two months or longer should be considered to have malaria until proven otherwise.[104] The frequency of infection in high-risk areas varies from 20%[105] to almost 100%.[106] Persons who previously lived in an endemic area, moved away, and return to the area should also be considered at risk for developing malaria.

Efficacy. Various drug regimens and combinations have been used to prevent malaria infection. Chloroquine is the drug of choice for people traveling to regions where resistance has not developed. In chloroquine-resistant areas, mefloquine has been shown to be effective for malaria prophylaxis. In a large-scale study, five different treatment groups, including chloroquine and placebo, were compared. Malaria occurred less frequently in the groups taking mefloquine and a fixed combination of mefloquine plus sulfadoxine plus pyrimethamine, although the difference between these groups and the groups taking chloroquine or placebo was not significant.[107]

A study comparing mefloquine, chloroquine plus pyrimethamine plus sulfadoxine, and chloroquine alone in 334 patients showed that the *P. falciparum*-associated malaria infection rate was 79% lower in the mefloquine group than the chloroquine control group, which had a 69% infection rate.[108] Chloroquine plus pyrimethamine plus sulfadoxine was associated with an infection rate that was only 18% lower than that in the chloroquine control group. In a randomized, double-blind, placebo-controlled study of 567

men in Nigeria, the following regimens were compared: mefloquine, mefloquine plus sulfadoxine and pyrimethamine, pyrimethamine plus sulfadoxine, chloroquine, and placebo.[105] This study did not demonstrate a significant difference in prevention of new parasitemias between groups. However, during the treatment phase of the study, three patients developed symptomatic *P. falciparum* infection in the placebo group, compared with no patients in the treatment groups. In the posttherapy follow-up segment of the study, four more placebo patients and one patient in the group receiving mefloquine plus sulfadoxine and pyrimethamine (33 days after the last dose) developed symptomatic malaria. The infection rate was probably not high enough to enable a significant difference between groups to be detected. A study of 609 adult military personnel demonstrated that a 100-mg daily dose of doxycycline was 64% more efficacious in preventing malaria than a combination of pyrimethamine and dapsone.[106] Two studies, one comparing primaquine plus chloroquine with chloroquine alone[109] and the second comparing primaquine with chloroquine, demonstrated the efficacy of primaquine for malaria prophylaxis.[110]

Resistance. Malaria resistant to chloroquine is common. Malarious areas that do not have chloroquine-resistant *P. falciparum* are Central America and the Caribbean. Resistance is uncommon in the Middle East. Malarious areas where chloroquine-resistant malaria is common include Southeast Asia, sub-Saharan Africa, and northern South America.[111]

Pediatric Efficacy. A randomized study demonstrated that mefloquine hydrochloride 125 mg weekly was equally effective as primaquine and doxycycline in preventing symptomatic and asymptomatic malaria infections in children of ages 9–14 years.[112] Despite the fact that mefloquine's efficacy is comparable to that of primaquine and doxycycline, CDC recommends that mefloquine be reserved for chloroquine-resistant areas.

Recommendation. *Nonantimicrobial measures.* Implementing measures to reduce the risk of mosquito bites is the nonantimicrobial approach to preventing malaria. Travelers should remain in well-screened areas, use mosquito nets, and wear clothing that covers their entire body. Insect repellents should be used on exposed areas of skin. The most effective mosquito repellent is *N,N*-diethyl metatoluamide (DEET). DEET-containing repellents should be used according to directions and should be used sparingly on children. Adults should use 30–35% DEET on exposed skin; pediatric preparations containing 6–10% DEET are also available.[111] For current travel recommendations, contact the CDC travel hotline at (888) 232-3299 or (888) 232-3228 or see http://www.cdc.gov (select Travelers' Health).

Areas of chloroquine susceptibility. Chloroquine alone is recommended for malaria prophylaxis in areas of chloroquine susceptibility (Table 2). The adult dosage is chloroquine phosphate 500 mg (300 mg base) once a week initiated one week before entry into the malarious area and continuing for four weeks after departure from the area.[111]

Areas of chloroquine resistance. Mefloquine is recommended for malaria prophylaxis in areas of chloroquine resistance. The adult dosage is mefloquine hydrochloride 250 mg (228 mg base) once weekly beginning one week before travel and continued for four weeks after the person leaves the malarious area. Mefloquine should not be used by travelers with a history of epilepsy, psychiatric disorders, or a known hypersensitivity to mefloquine. An alternative is doxycycline 100 mg (as the calcium, hyclate, or monohydrate) daily beginning one day before travel and continued for four weeks after the person leaves the area. Doxycycline should not be used by pregnant women.[111] Another alternative is chloroquine phosphate (same dosage as previously described) with or without chloroguanide hydrochloride (proguanil) 200 mg/day during exposure and for four weeks after last exposure plus combination tablets of pyrimethamine (25 mg/tablet) and sulfadoxine (500 mg/tablet) as presumptive treatment—three tablets for febrile illness when medical care is not immediately available.[113] (Strength of evidence for prophylaxis = B)

Pediatric Dosage. *Areas of chloroquine susceptibility.* Chloroquine is recommended for malaria prophylaxis in children in areas of chloroquine susceptibility. The pediatric dosage is chloroquine phosphate 8.3 mg/kg (5 mg/kg base) orally once a week. The maximum weekly dose is 498 mg of chloroquine phosphate (300 mg base).

Areas of chloroquine resistance. Mefloquine hydrochloride is the drug of choice for malaria prophylaxis in children in areas of chloroquine resistance. The pediatric dosage is mefloquine hydrochloride 5 mg/kg (4.6 mg/kg base) weekly for children weighing less than 15 kg, one quarter of a 250-mg mefloquine hydrochloride tablet per week for children weighing 15–19 kg, half a tablet per week for children weighing 20–30 kg, three quarters of a tablet per week for children weighing 31–45 kg, and one tablet weekly for children weighing more than 45 kg.[111,112] An alternative is doxycycline 2 mg/kg/day (as the calcium, hyclate, or monohydrate) (maximum daily dose, 100 mg/day) for children older than eight years. Doxycycline should not be used in children less than eight years of age. Another suggested alternative is chloroquine phosphate (same dosage as previously described), with or without chloroguanide hydrochloride 50 mg/day for children younger than 2 years, 100 mg/day for ages 2–6 years, 150 mg/day for ages 7–10 years, or 200 mg/day for children older than 10 years plus combination pyrimethamine (25 mg/tablet) and sulfadoxine (500 mg/tablet) for presumptive treatment (one quarter of a tablet for children younger than 1 year, half a tablet for 1–3 years, one tablet for 4–8 years, two tablets for 9–14 years, and three tablets for children older than 14 years).[113]

Traveler's Diarrhea

Background. Traveler's diarrhea is a common affliction among people traveling from industrialized countries to developing countries. Traveler's diarrhea frequently starts during the first week of travel, and the risk of diarrhea persists with prolonged stays in endemic areas.[114] The syndrome is characterized by a twofold increase in the frequency of unformed bowel movements, often accompanied by such symptoms as abdominal cramping, nausea, fever, chills, urgency, and malaise. Symptoms are usually self-limiting and resolve within three to four days; 60% of persons affected recover within the first 48 hours. For some, the duration of symptoms may be as long as one week or even longer than three months (1% of travelers per year of stay).[115] Complications from traveler's diarrhea are rare.

The most common bacterial pathogens associated with traveler's diarrhea are *E. coli*, *Shigella*, *Salmonella*, *Campylobacter jejuni*, *Vibrio parahaemolyticus*, *Vibrio cholerae*, and *Vibrio fluvialis*. Although far less common, diarrhea may be due to protozoa (*Entamoeba histolytica*, *Giardia lamblia*, or *Cryptosporidium*). Viruses such as rotaviruses, Norwalk virus, and adenoviruses have also been implicated in traveler's diarrhea.[116]

Persons at Risk. Risk factors for traveler's diarrhea include young age, inexperience in traveling to an endemic area, high socioeconomic status, and prolonged stay. The illness is believed to result from the ingestion of fecally contaminated food or water. Foods associated with increased risk include salads, uncooked fruits and vegetables, unpasteurized dairy products, and raw meat and shellfish.[117]

Travel to some less-developed countries is associated with a high frequency of diarrhea. Travelers to such countries would appear to benefit most from antimicrobial prophylaxis. The frequency of traveler's diarrhea is highest among persons traveling to Latin America (mean, 53%; range, 21–100%), Africa (mean, 54%; range, 36–62%), the Middle East (percentage not available), and Asia (mean, 54%; range, 21–57%) and lowest among persons traveling to industrialized countries.[115]

Efficacy. Various antimicrobials, including trimethoprim–sulfamethoxazole,[118] doxycycline,[119] trimethoprim,[118,120] ciprofloxacin,[121–123] and norfloxacin,[124,125] have been shown to decrease the frequency of diarrhea in persons traveling for short periods (less than three weeks). Bismuth subsalicylate reduced the frequency and severity of traveler's diarrhea by up to 65% among college students traveling to Mexico.[126] The benefit of prophylaxis lasts only as long as the antimicrobial is taken.[120] In a contrasting study, doxycycline was not shown to be significantly more protective than placebo.[127] Despite the demonstrable efficacy of prophylaxis, CDC does not recommend prophylaxis for traveler's diarrhea because, even if untreated, the condition is most often mild and transient.[117] Furthermore, antimicrobial therapy places otherwise healthy people at unnecessary risk of toxicity and superinfection and encourages the emergence of resistant organisms.

Pediatric Efficacy. No well-controlled studies have yet evaluated the effect of prophylaxis of traveler's diarrhea in children.

Recommendation. Prophylaxis of traveler's diarrhea is not recommended. Traveler's diarrhea, even when untreated, is most often mild and transient. The antimicrobials used as prophylaxis against traveler's diarrhea place the otherwise healthy person at unnecessary risk of toxicity and superinfection and encourage the emergence of resistant organisms. A National Institutes of Health consensus panel recommended that travelers who are otherwise healthy not take antimicrobials for the prevention of traveler's diarrhea.[116] In addition, CDC does not recommend antimicrobial prophylaxis, focusing instead on prevention of traveler's diarrhea through dietary control (Table 2). Consumption of boiled, bottled, or chemically disinfected water and avoidance of uncooked fruits and vegetables, unpasteurized dairy products, and raw meat or shellfish are the safest methods for avoiding traveler's diarrhea.[117] Immunocompromised patients may be viable candidates for prophylaxis (trimethoprim–sulfamethoxazole, bismuth subsalicylate, and ciprofloxacin are all effective), but no studies in this population are available. (Strength of evidence against prophylaxis = C)

Pediatric Dosage. Prophylaxis of traveler's diarrhea is not recommended for children.

Tuberculosis

Background. Before the 1990s, the incidence of TB had been declining in the United States. In the early 1990s there was a 9% increase in the reported TB cases (25,000 cases reported in 1990).[128] Much of this increase is attributable to the spread of HIV infection and the increase in immigrants with TB.[129] Between 1993 and 1996 the number of cases reported decreased, with 21,000 reported in 1996.[128]

Most new cases of TB in the United States occur in patients in whom the primary infection with *Mycobacterium tuberculosis* occurred at an earlier date. Prevention of TB reactivation is the basis for selective periodic screening of patients at risk for exposure to *M. tuberculosis* and the use of antimicrobial preventive therapy in selected patients with positive skin-test results.

Persons at Risk. The Advisory Council for the Elimination of Tuberculosis (ACET) recommends that the following persons should be screened for TB[130]:

1. Close contacts (i.e., persons sharing the same household or other enclosed environments) of a person known or suspected to have TB.
2. Persons infected with HIV.
3. Persons who inject illicit drugs or other locally identified high-risk substance users (i.e., crack cocaine users).
4. Persons with one of the following medical conditions: diabetes mellitus, conditions requiring prolonged high-dose corticosteroid therapy and other immunosuppressive therapy, chronic renal failure, some hematologic disorders, other specific malignancies, ≥10% below ideal body weight, silicosis, gastrectomy, jejunoileal bypass, and abnormal chest radiograph showing fibrotic lesions consistent with old, healed TB.
5. Residents and employees of high-risk congregate settings.
6. Health care workers who serve high-risk clients.
7. Foreign-born persons, including children, recently arrived from countries that have a high incidence or prevalence of TB.
8. Some medically underserved, low-income populations.
9. High-risk racial or ethnic minority populations, as defined locally.
10. Infants, children, and adolescents exposed to adults in high-risk categories.

Efficacy. Isoniazid is the only drug with proven efficacy in the prophylaxis of TB. Prophylaxis can reduce the risk of TB by more than 90% in infected persons who adhere to therapy.[131] The efficacy of isoniazid preventive therapy in HIV-infected persons has been investigated only in small trials; however, the drug appears to confer protection.[129]

Resistance. Outbreaks of multidrug-resistant TB (defined as infection with a strain of *M. tuberculosis* resistant to both isoniazid and rifampin) have added to the concern about the re-emergence of TB.[129,132] TB caused by multidrug-resistant organisms may be associated with a very high mortality rate (72–89%).[129] The most important factors that contribute to the emergence of drug resistance are (1) the use of antituberculosis medications in uncontrolled nonprescription preparations available in many foreign countries, (2) poor adherence, and (3) improper therapy, usually the failure to employ adequate antituberculosis therapy at the beginning of treatment.[131] The level of patient adherence is inversely correlated with the duration of therapy. More than one year of therapy provides the maximum benefit, whereas six months confers a lesser benefit but is associated with higher adherence.[133] Because poor adherence contributes to resistance, the recommended duration of prophylaxis is six months.[130] Improving patient adherence is an important strategy for reducing the occurrence of multidrug-resistant TB and has been previously addressed by ASHP.[134]

Pediatric Efficacy. No well-controlled studies have yet evaluated the effect of prophylaxis for TB in children. Pediatric recommendations are provided by CDC.[113,130,135–137]

Recommendation. Official recommendations for the prevention of TB have been published by ACET.[130,135,138] The recommendation to start preventive therapy is based on risk factors and skin-test results (Table 2). Preventive therapy is indicated for the following skin-test results and risk factors:

1. In persons of any age with an induration of ≥5 mm who have had recent close contact with persons who have active TB, who have HIV infection or risk factors for HIV infection but unknown HIV status, or who have fibrotic chest radiographs consistent with healed TB.
2. In persons of any age with an induration of ≥10 mm who are intravenous drug users known to be HIV seronegative and who have other medical conditions (see risk factors).
3. In persons with an induration of ≥10 mm who are residents or employees of high-risk congregate settings (prisons and jails, nursing homes and other long-term-care facilities for the elderly, health care facilities, mental institutions, and homeless shelters), foreign-born persons recently arrived (i.e., within the past five years) from countries with a high prevalence or incidence of TB, some medically underserved, low-income populations (i.e., migrant farm workers, homeless persons), high-risk racial or ethnic minority populations (as defined locally), or infants, children, and adolescents exposed to adults in high-risk categories.
4. In persons less than 35 years of age with an induration of ≥10 mm or in persons 35 years of age or older with an induration of ≥15 mm who are recent converters (within the past two years).
5. In persons with an induration of ≥15 mm who do not meet any of the previous criteria.[130,135]

The recommended dosage of isoniazid is 300 mg orally daily for six months. An alternative dosage is 15 mg/kg (up to 900 mg) twice weekly for patients who must have therapy directly observed. In patients with immunosuppression or with radiographic abnormalities suggestive of "old" TB, the recommended duration of prophylaxis is 12 months. In patients who cannot take isoniazid because of adverse effects, oral rifampin 600 mg every day with or without ethambutol

Table 2.
Prevention of Infection in Anticipation of or after Defined Exposure[a]

Infection and Setting	Eligible Patients	Recommended Regimen	Alternative Regimens	Strength of Evidence[b]
Influenza A[c]	Adult high-risk patients[d] and groups that can transmit infection to high-risk patients[e]	Amantadine 100 mg p.o. b.i.d. before and throughout epidemic period[f]	Rimantadine 100 mg p.o. b.i.d. in patients unable to tolerate central nervous system effects of amantadine	A
	Pediatric high-risk patients[d] and groups that can transmit infection to high-risk patients[e]	Amantadine 5–9 mg/kg/day (maximum 200 mg/day) p.o. in 2 divided doses if 1–8 yr old and <40 kg; amantadine 100 mg p.o. b.i.d. if 9–12 yr old or >40 kg[f]; use before and throughout epidemic period	Rimantadine 5 mg/kg (maximum 150 mg/day) p.o. daily if <10 yr old; rimantadine 100 mg p.o. b.i.d. if >10 yr old	NA
Malaria				
Travel in areas of chloroquine susceptibility	Adult travelers to countries endemic for malaria	Chloroquine phosphate 500 mg (300 mg base) p.o. weekly starting 1 wk before travel, continue 4 wk after leaving area	None	B
	Pediatric travelers to countries endemic for malaria	Chloroquine phosphate 8.3 mg/kg (5 mg/kg base) p.o. weekly (maximum 498 mg/wk chloroquine phosphate) starting 1 wk before travel, continue 4 wk after leaving area	None	NA
Travel in areas of chloroquine resistance	Adult travelers to countries endemic for malaria	Mefloquine hydrochloride 250 mg p.o. weekly starting 1 wk before travel, continue 4 wk after leaving area	Doxycycline 100 mg p.o. daily starting 1 day before travel, continue 4 wk after leaving area; or chloroquine (same adult dosage and duration as above) with or without chloroguanide 200 mg/day p.o. during exposure and for 4 wk after last exposure plus pyrimethamine–sulfadoxine 3 tablets p.o. as presumptive treatment for febrile illness when medical care not immediately available (pyrimethamine 25 mg and sulfadoxine 500 mg per tablet)	B
	Pediatric travelers to countries endemic for malaria	Mefloquine hydrochloride 5 mg/kg p.o. weekly if <15 kg, 0.25 tablet weekly if 15–19 kg, 0.5 tablet weekly if 20–30 kg, 0.75 tablet weekly if 31–45 kg, 1 tablet weekly if >45 kg (1 tablet = 250 mg mefloquine hydrochloride)	Doxycycline 2 mg/kg/day (maximum 100 mg/day) p.o. if >8 yr old (not to be used in younger children); or chloroquine (same pediatric dosage and duration as above) with or without chloroguanide 50 mg/day p.o. if <2 yr old, 100 mg/day if 2–6 yr old, 150 mg/day if 7–10 yr old, 200 mg/day if >10 yr old plus pyrimethamine–sulfadoxine 0.25 tablet p.o. if <1 yr old, 0.5 tablet if 1–3 yr old, 1 tablet if 4–8 yr old, 2 tablets if 9–14 yr old, 3 tablets if >14 yr old as presumptive treatment for febrile illness when medical care not immediately available (pyrimethamine 25 mg and sulfadoxine 500 mg per tablet)	NA
Traveler's diarrhea				
Travel to underdeveloped countries	None (adult and pediatric)	Not recommended	None	C

Continued on next page

Table 2 *(continued)*

Infection and Setting	Eligible Patients	Recommended Regimen	Alternative Regimens	Strength of Evidence[b]
Tuberculosis[h]				
PPD induration ≥5 mm	Adults with recent close contact with person with active TB; HIV infected or with risk factors for HIV, fibrotic chest radiographs consistent with healed TB	Isoniazid 300 mg p.o. a daily for 6 mo; 12 mo if HIV infected or with radiographic evidence of old TB	Isoniazid 15 mg/kg (maximum 900 mg) p.o. twice weekly in directly observed therapy; if unable to take isoniazid, rifampin 600 mg p.o. daily with or without ethambutol 15 mg/kg/day p.o.; if exposed to multidrug-resistant TB and with high likelihood of infection, pyrazinamide 25 mg/kg/day p.o. with ethambutol 15 mg/kg/day p.o. or with a fluoro-quinolone (ofloxacin 400 mg or ciprofloxacin 750 mg p.o. b.i.d.). Pyridoxine 50 mg p.o. daily generally not necessary[j]	A
	Children with same eligibility as nonpediatric patients with induration ≥5 mm	Isoniazid 10 mg/kg/day (maximum 300 mg/day) p.o. for 6 mo	If unable to take isoniazid, rifampin 10–20 mg/kg/day (maximum 600 mg/day) p.o. as single daily dose; if exposed to multidrug-resistant TB and with high likelihood of infection, pyrazinamide 20–40 mg/kg/day (maximum 2 g/day) p.o. in divided doses (every 12–24 hr) plus ethambutol 15–25 mg/kg/day (maximum 2.5 g/day) p.o.[i] Pyridoxine prophylaxis 1–2 mg/kg/day p.o. generally not necessary[j]	NA
PPD induration ≥10 mm	Adult i.v. drug users known to be HIV seronegative; adults with certain conditions[k] Adult residents and employees of high-risk congregate settings;[l] foreign-born persons recently arrived from country with high prevalence or incidence of TB; some medically underserved, low-income populations; high-risk racial or ethnic minorities	Adult isoniazid as above	Adult isoniazid alternatives as above	A

Continued on next page

hydrochloride 15 mg/kg/day may be used. In patients infected with an isoniazid-resistant organism, rifampin with or without isoniazid or ethambutol has been recommended. Prophylaxis with pyridoxine hydrochloride 50 mg daily to prevent peripheral neuritis or convulsions due to isoniazid is generally not necessary, except for persons with conditions in which neuropathy is common (diabetes, uremia, alcoholism, malnutrition), pregnant women, and persons with a seizure disorder. For persons exposed to multidrug-resistant TB and with a high likelihood of being infected (with an induration of >5 mm, anergic, or with HIV infection), oral pyrazinamide 25 mg/kg/day and oral ethambutol hydrochloride 15 mg/kg/day or pyrazinamide and a fluoroquinolone (ciprofloxacin 750 mg twice a day or ofloxacin 400 mg twice a day) for 12 months are recommended. (Strength of evidence for prophylaxis = A)

Pediatric Dosage. The recommendation for TB prophylaxis in children is isoniazid 10 mg/kg/day (maximum daily dose, 300 mg) administered as a single daily dose for six months. For children unable to take isoniazid, rifampin 10–20 mg/kg/day (maximum daily dose, 600 mg) in a single daily dose is recommended. Prophylaxis with pyridoxine hydrochloride 1–2 mg/kg/day to prevent peripheral neuritis or convulsions due to isoniazid is generally not necessary, except for persons with conditions in which neuropathy is common (diabetes, uremia, malnutrition), children or adolescents on meat- or milk-deficient diets, breast-feeding infants, and children with a seizure disorder. For children exposed to multidrug-resistant TB and with a high likelihood of being infected, pyrazinamide 20–40 mg/kg/day with doses given every 12–24 hours (maximum daily dose, 2 g) and ethambutol hydrochloride 15–25 mg/kg/day (maximum daily dose, 2.5 g) should be used. Ethambutol is generally not recommended for children whose visual acuity cannot be monitored. However, ethambutol should be considered for all children with organisms resistant to other drugs when susceptibility to ethambutol has been demonstrated or is likely.

Occupational Exposure to HIV

Persons at Risk. The risk of HIV seroconversion through occupational exposure in health care workers is approxi-

Table 2 *(continued)*

Infection and Setting	Eligible Patients	Recommended Regimen	Alternative Regimens	Strength of Evidence[b]
PPD induration ≥10 mm and patient <35 yr old	Adult converter within last 2 yr	Adult isoniazid as above	Adult isoniazid alternatives as above	A
PPD induration ≥10 mm	Children with the same eligibility as adults with induration ≥10 mm; exposure to high-risk categories	Pediatric isoniazid as above	Pediatric isoniazid alternatives as above	NA
PPD induration ≥15 mm and patient ≥35 yr old	Adult converter within last 2 yr	Adult isoniazid as above	Adult isoniazid alternatives as above	A
PPD induration ≥15 mm	Adults with none of above adult eligibility criteria	Adult isoniazid as above	Adult isoniazid alternatives as above	A
PPD induration ≥15 mm	Children with none of above pediatric eligibility criteria	Pediatric isoniazid as above	Pediatric isoniazid alternatives as above	NA

[a]PPD = purified protein derivative (tuberculin skin test), TB = tuberculosis.

[b]Strength of evidence that supports the use or nonuse of prophylaxis is classified as A (levels I–III), B (levels IV–VI), or C (level VII). Level I evidence is from large, well-conducted randomized, controlled clinical trials. Level II evidence is from small, well-conducted randomized, controlled clinical trials. Level III evidence is from well-conducted cohort studies. Level IV evidence is from well-conducted case–control studies. Level V evidence is from uncontrolled studies that were not well conducted. Level VI evidence is conflicting evidence that tends to favor the recommendation. Level VII evidence is expert opinion. Strength-of-evidence classification not applied (NA) to pediatric recommendations.

[c]Prophylaxis is recommended for the following: (1) Persons at high risk vaccinated after influenza A activity has begun. The development of antibodies can take as long as two weeks. Children who receive influenza vaccine for the first time can require as long as six weeks of prophylaxis (i.e., prophylaxis for two weeks after the second dose of vaccine has been received). (2) Persons providing care to those at high risk who are not vaccinated. Prophylaxis should be considered for all employees, regardless of their vaccination status, if the outbreak is caused by a variant strain of influenza A that might not be controlled by the vaccine. (3) Persons who have immune deficiency who are expected to have an inadequate antibody response to influenza vaccine. (4) Persons for whom influenza vaccine is contraindicated, including persons who have severe anaphylactic hypersensitivity to egg protein or other vaccine components. (5) Other persons who wish to avoid influenza A illness.

[d]Groups at high risk for influenza-related complications include (1) persons at least 65 years old, (2) residents of nursing homes and other chronic care facilities, (3) adults and children with chronic disorders of the pulmonary or cardiovascular systems, including children with asthma, (4) adults and children who have required regular medical follow-up or hospitalization during the preceding year because of chronic metabolic diseases (including diabetes mellitus), renal dysfunction, hemoglobinopathies, or immunosuppression, (5) children and teenagers (six months–18 years old) who are receiving long-term aspirin therapy and therefore might be at risk for developing Reye's syndrome after influenza, and (6) women who will be in the second or third trimester of pregnancy during the influenza season. No well-controlled studies have been conducted in pregnant women, and chemoprophylaxis should be used during pregnancy only when the potential benefits outweigh the possible risk to the fetus.

[e]Groups that can transmit influenza to persons at high risk include (1) physicians, nurses, and other health care personnel, (2) employees of nursing homes and chronic care facilities who have contact with patients or residents, (3) providers of home care to persons at high risk (e.g., visiting nurses, volunteers), and (4) household members (including children) of persons in high-risk groups.

[f]Continue for 10 days after exposure. When used in conjunction with vaccine, continue for two weeks after vaccine (after the second of two vaccine doses required in children younger than nine years who have not previously been vaccinated). If vaccine is unavailable or contraindicated, continue for the duration of influenza activity in the community.

[g]Household members of persons in high-risk groups.

[h]Adapted from recommendations of the Centers for Disease Control and Prevention (reference 130).

[i]Ethambutol is generally not recommended for children whose visual acuity cannot be monitored. However, ethambutol should be considered for all children with organisms resistant to other drugs when susceptibility to ethambutol has been demonstrated or is likely.

[j]Pyridoxine prophylaxis to prevent isoniazid-associated peripheral neuritis or convulsions is generally not necessary, except in persons with conditions in which neuropathy is common (diabetes, uremia, alcoholism, malnutrition), pregnant women, children or adolescents on meat- or milk-deficient diets, breast-feeding infants, and persons with a seizure disorder.

[k]Certain conditions include HIV infection, diabetes mellitus, conditions requiring prolonged high-dose corticosteroid therapy and other immunosuppressive therapy (including bone marrow and organ transplantation), chronic renal failure, some hematologic disorders (e.g., leukemias, lymphomas), other specific malignancies (e.g., carcinoma of the head and neck), ≥10% below ideal weight, silicosis, gastrectomy, and jejonoileal bypass.

[l]Correctional institutions, nursing homes, mental institutions, other long-term residential facilities, and shelters for the homeless.

mately 0.3% from a percutaneous injury from a needle or other device.[139,140] The risk after mucous membrane or skin exposure to HIV-infected blood is approximately 0.1% or <0.1%, respectively.[141] Variables related to the risk of HIV transmission include volume of blood involved in the exposure, stage of HIV disease, and plasma HIV RNA level in the source patient as well as site and mechanism of exposure.[142,143] In a case–control study involving 33 case patients from France, Italy, the United Kingdom, and the United States, the risk of HIV seroconversion was higher when exposure was associated with a deep injury, visible blood on the device involved, a device previously placed in a source patient's vein or artery, or exposure to a terminally ill AIDS patient.[144] The risk of HIV seroconversion was lower with postexposure use of zidovudine.

Efficacy. Animal data on zidovudine have been inconclusive, and human experience has been limited.[144–150] Evaluation of zidovudine in humans is difficult because the low occurrence of HIV seroconversion after occupational exposure necessitates a very large sample to demonstrate a prophylactic effect.

In a case–control study involving national surveillance from the United States, France, Italy, and the United Kingdom, zidovudine prophylaxis was associated with an almost 80% lower risk of HIV seroconversion after percutaneous exposure to HIV-infected blood.[144] Caution should be used in interpreting these results because of retrospective data collection, use of cases and controls, differing sources of cases and controls, and reporting or ascertainment bias.

Because well-controlled trials of chemoprophylaxis after occupational exposure have not been conducted, recommendations must be extrapolated from trials in patients with HIV infection. Single- and combination-drug therapies have been studied for treatment in HIV-infected patients. Although there are no data showing that monotherapy is more efficacious than combination therapy in postexposure prophylaxis, combination therapy has demonstrated greater efficacy than monotherapy in HIV-infected patients[151–154] and is the standard of care for the treatment of these patients.[155] The combination of zidovudine and didanosine, zidovudine plus zalcitabine, or didanosine alone slows the progression of HIV disease and is superior to treatment with zidovudine alone.[151] The combination of indinavir, zidovudine, and lamivudine demonstrated undetectable viral RNA levels at week 24 in 22 of 24 patients. In contrast, only 9 of 24 patients treated with indinavir alone and 0 of 24 patients treated with zidovudine and lamivudine had undetectable levels.[153]

For HIV prophylaxis after occupational exposure, CDC recommends the combination of zidovudine, lamivudine, and indinavir or nelfinavir in persons at highest risk for seroconversion.[156,157] Zidovudine and lamivudine may be better tolerated and appear to have comparable antiretroviral potency, although there are no comparative markers and the potency is based on surrogate markers (HIV RNA levels and CD4+ lymphocyte counts).[158] Indinavir may be better tolerated than the other protease inhibitors. The addition of indinavir to the zidovudine and lamivudine combination enhances the antiretroviral potency.[153] However, there are no clinical data showing that three antiviral agents are more efficacious than two in postexposure prophylaxis.

Changes in drug protocols may be appropriate on the basis of factors such as antiretroviral drug resistance profile of HIV from the source patient as well as medical conditions, concurrent drug therapy, drug toxicity in the exposed worker, and patient adherence. A variable to consider when choosing antiretroviral agents is the antiretroviral therapy of the source patient. Some experts give the health care worker at least two antiretrovirals that the source patient is not taking because of the concern about resistance. Although not included in the CDC recommendations, alternative regimens have consisted of stavudine plus lamivudine and stavudine plus didanosine. Alternative regimens may be required in certain situations, such as the source person's virus being resistant to the standard regimen.[157] An alternative to indinavir is nelfinavir. Because most occupational exposures to HIV do not result in seropositivity, potential toxicity should be considered when postexposure prophylaxis is prescribed. One third of health care workers in two surveillance studies prematurely discontinued zidovudine because of adverse effects.[139,149] Another concern is adherence to the drug regimen. Despite a lack of efficacy data, some experts choose a combination product containing zidovudine and lamivudine for better adherence.

Resistance. There are no data available on the resistance rates with prophylactic antivirals in the setting of occupational exposure; however, development of resistance is common when antivirals are used to treat HIV-infected persons.[155]

Pediatric Efficacy. Not applicable.

Recommendation. The best means of preventing HIV seroconversion from occupational exposure is to reduce the likelihood of exposure through the use of standard precautions during procedures and in the handling of blood and other body fluids. In the case of occupational exposure, current guidelines have been proposed by USPHS[156,157] and supported by an international panel.[155,158] The recommendations are provisional because of limited data on efficacy and toxicity of postexposure prophylaxis and risk for HIV seroconversion after different types of exposure. The recommended dosages are zidovudine 300 mg orally twice daily or 200 mg three times a day, lamivudine 150 mg orally twice a day, and indinavir 800 mg (as the sulfate) orally three times a day or nelfinavir 750 mg (as the mesylate) orally three times a day (Table 3). Prophylaxis is continued for four weeks.

Alternative regimens with other nucleoside reverse-transcriptase inhibitors, protease inhibitors, or nonnucleoside reverse-transcriptase inhibitors may be required. Postexposure prophylaxis should be initiated promptly, preferably within one to two hours after HIV exposure. Although animal studies suggest that postexposure prophylaxis is not effective when started later than 24–36 hours after exposure,[141,159] the interval after which there is no benefit from postexposure prophylaxis for humans is undefined. CDC recommends prophylaxis for all high-risk exposures. CDC does not recommend prophylaxis for lower-risk exposures, with the provision that these exposed health care workers be offered the option of receiving prophylaxis. Specific considerations by route of exposure follow.

Percutaneous exposure to blood. When a large volume of blood (e.g., in the case of deep injury with a large-diameter hollow needle that was previously in the source patient's vein or artery, especially involving an injection of the source patient's blood) or blood containing a high HIV titer (e.g., if the source patient has acute retroviral illness or end-stage AIDS, in which case viral load measurement may be considered but has not been evaluated in relation to prophylaxis) or both are involved, zidovudine plus lamivudine plus indinavir should be recommended. (These situations are regarded as presenting the highest or increased risk.)

When neither a large volume of blood nor blood with a high titer of HIV (e.g., a solid suture-needle injury from a source patient with asymptomatic HIV infection) is involved, prophylaxis is not recommended. The exposed worker may be offered zidovudine plus lamivudine. (This scenario is regarded as presenting no increased risk.)

Percutaneous exposure to fluid containing visible blood or tissue. When fluid (including semen, vaginal secretions, and cerebrospinal, synovial, pleural, peritoneal, pericardial, and amniotic fluids) is involved, prophylaxis is not recommended. The exposed worker may be offered zidovudine plus lamivudine.

Percutaneous exposure to other fluid. When other fluid (e.g., urine) is involved, prophylaxis is not recommended and should not be offered.

Mucous membrane exposure and skin exposure. Regarding skin, risk is increased for exposures involving a high titer of HIV, prolonged contact, an extensive area, or an area in which skin integrity is visibly compromised. For skin exposures without increased risk, the risk of drug toxicity outweighs the benefit of postexposure prophylaxis. When blood or skin exposure is involved, prophylaxis is not recommended. The exposed worker may be offered zidovudine plus lamivudine. Addition of indinavir is optional (associated with an increased risk of toxicity).

When fluid containing visible blood, other fluid (including semen, vaginal secretions, and cerebrospinal, synovial, pleural, peritoneal, pericardial, and amniotic fluids), or tissue is involved, prophylaxis is not recommended. The exposed worker may be offered zidovudine plus lamivudine.

When other fluid (e.g., urine) is involved, prophylaxis is not recommended and should not be offered. (Strength of evidence for prophylaxis = C)

Pediatric Dosage. Not applicable.

Resources. The following resources may be useful in the event of occupational exposure to HIV: CDC's home page (http://www.cdc.gov), the Epidemiology and Prevention Center at the University of California, San Francisco (http://epi-center.ucsf.edu), and a 24-hour hotline on caring for occupational exposure (888-448-4911). Health care professionals are encourged to register pregnant women receiving antiretrovirals with the antiretroviral pregnancy registry (800-258-4263) and to register health care professionals receiving prophylaxis with the HIV postexposure prophylaxis registry (888-737-4448).

Perinatally Acquired HIV Infection

Background. Maternal–infant transmission of HIV is the primary means by which young children become infected. Approximately 7000 infants are born to HIV-infected women each year in the United States; 1000–2000 of these children will be infected with HIV.[160] It has been demonstrated that the maternal–infant transmission rate is 15–40%.[161–163]

Persons at Risk. All infants born to HIV-infected women are considered at high risk for HIV infection. Infection may occur in utero, during labor and delivery, or by breastfeeding.[164] The presence of ruptured maternal membranes for more than four hours before delivery has been shown to nearly double the risk of maternal–infant transmission.[165] Transmission risk may be increased in women with low CD4+ lymphocyte counts or AIDS,[165,166] but this has not been consistently reported. Two recent studies have demonstrated that the risk of transmission is significantly associated with maternal viral load at the time of study entry or delivery.[167,168] Although the two studies did not stratify plasma HIV RNA levels versus transmission rates in the same way, it is clear that the risk of transmission increases significantly as viral load increases. In one study the transmission rate was 0% among 63 women with <20,000 RNA copies per mL of plasma compared with 100% transmission among 13 women with >80,000 RNA copies per mL of plasma.[167] Maternal HIV RNA levels are thus highly predictive of perinatal transmission risk. However, even low-level maternal viremia may be associated with a significant risk of perinatal transmission, while high maternal viral loads do not result in perinatal transmission to all infants. It is currently unclear whether routine maternal HIV viral load measurements will be useful because of the poor predictive value of maternal viral load for perinatal transmission risk.[169]

Efficacy. CDC issued official recommendations for prophylaxis of maternal–infant transmission of HIV in 1994 based solely on the results of the AIDS Clinical Trials Group Protocol 076 (ACTG 076). ACTG 076 demonstrated that the relative risk of maternal–infant transmission was 67.5% lower with zidovudine than with placebo (8.3% and 25.5%,

respectively).[163] Subsequent studies have similarly demonstrated differences in transmission between no prophylaxis (19–29%) and zidovudine monotherapy (3–14%).[166,170–172]

Although ACTG 076 specifically studied women with CD4+ lymphocyte counts of >200 cells/μL, subsequent studies have found that benefits of prophylaxis can be demonstrated regardless of CD4+ lymphocyte count or plasma HIV RNA levels.[162,166–168,170] There is also no apparent association between efficacy of prophylaxis and clinical stage of disease.

Studies addressing the use of nonzidovudine monotherapy or combination therapy with agents from one or more antiretroviral drug classes have not yet been completed. However, CDC recommends an initial triple-drug regimen consisting of two nucleoside-analogue reverse-transcriptase inhibitors and a protease inhibitor for the treatment of HIV infection. The recommended triple-drug regimen has potential additional efficacy in the prevention of maternal–infant transmission of HIV.[155] Studies are currently being conducted to evaluate the safety and efficacy of multiple-drug regimens for prevention of vertical transmission.

The CDC recommendations call for prophylaxis of HIV-infected pregnant women to begin at 14–34 weeks of gestation. Because zidovudine has been shown to be mutagenic in a mammalian in vitro cell-transformation assay and because it was associated with embryotoxic effects and fetal resorptions in animal studies, antiretroviral drug use during the first trimester of pregnancy is not recommended. However, observational studies have demonstrated no apparent association of fetal abnormalities with zidovudine use throughout pregnancy.[170,173,174] The frequency of congenital malformations in ACTG 076 or subsequent studies was not increased.[163] Studies in rodents have raised hypothetical concerns about the possible transplacental carcinogenicity of zidovudine. However, a panel of experts convened by NIH recently concluded that the proven benefits of zidovudine in reducing the risk of perinatal transmission outweigh these hypothetical concerns. Thus zidovudine continues to be used as standard therapy according to recommended protocols during weeks 14–34 of pregnancy.[169] Prophylaxis regimens are also associated with minimal maternal toxicity and appear to be safe for the infant as well.[163]

Resistance. Because ACTG 076 specifically studied antiretroviral-therapy-naive women, the effects of previous antiretroviral therapy on prophylaxis efficacy are of interest. Prophylaxis appears to remain beneficial, even in women with an extensive previous history of antiretroviral drug use.[162,166] However, limited data suggest that maternal–infant transmission of virus resistant to antiretroviral drugs may occur in these women.[162] The frequency and significance of this occurrence are unclear. Whether short-term use of zidovudine during pregnancy is associated with induction of viral resistance to antiretroviral agents is also unclear at this time.

Pediatric Efficacy. No well-controlled studies have evaluated the effect of prophylaxis in HIV-infected adolescent girls to prevent maternal–infant HIV transmission, although adult data are applicable.

Recommendation. Antiretroviral prophylaxis of maternal–infant HIV transmission is indicated when the potential benefits of drug therapy are believed to outweigh the risks to the mother or the infant (Table 4). The CDC prophylaxis regimen consists of three separate components: antepartum, intrapartum, and neonatal. As many as possible of these components should be used in prophylaxis, depending on the time of identification of eligible patients and the availability of care. Although some form of antiretroviral prophylaxis is recommended or offered in all scenarios, therapy should be instituted only after consultation with the woman and careful discussion of the potential benefits and risks involved. Decisions about the use of antiretroviral drugs during pregnancy should be made only after careful assessment of many factors, including the degree of maternal immunodeficiency (based on CD4+ lymphocyte count), the risk for maternal disease progression (based on viral load measurements), history of prior or current antiretroviral drug therapy, gestational age, and supportive care needs. Decisions about the initiation or continuation of therapy should be based on the same factors used for similar decisions in nonpregnant women, with additional consideration of the risk to the fetus and the infant. Current recommendations stress that the antiviral regimens should be selected with consideration of the proven benefit of antiretroviral therapy for the health of the infected woman as well as the potential reduction in risk of HIV transmission to the child. Ultimately, the final decision to accept or reject zidovudine treatment recommended for the woman and her child is the right and responsibility of the woman.[169] Recommendations also generally address four scenarios:

1. Pregnant HIV-infected women (with any CD4+ lymphocyte count) who are at >14 weeks' gestation and without a history of extensive (more than six months) antiretroviral therapy: recommend or offer all components of prophylaxis.
2. Pregnant HIV-infected women who have a history of extensive previous antiretroviral therapy before pregnancy: recommend or offer all components of prophylaxis.
3. Pregnant HIV-infected women who have not received antepartum antiretroviral therapy and who are in labor: recommend or offer intrapartum and neonatal components of prophylaxis.
4. Infants born to HIV-infected women who have received no intrapartum antiretroviral therapy: recommend or offer neonatal component of prophylaxis. It is advised that therapy for the infant be initiated as soon as possible (preferably within hours) after delivery. No data support offering antiretroviral therapy to the infant if therapy cannot be initiated within 24 hours after delivery.

Although combination antiretroviral therapy is standard in the general treatment of HIV-infected adults, the additional benefits and risks of combination therapy for prevention of perinatal transmission are as yet undetermined. Although combination regimens are considered optimal for long-term maternal benefits, zidovudine monotherapy is acceptable if the woman wants to minimize exposure of the fetus to other drugs. Because zidovudine is the only drug that has been proven to reduce the risk of perinatal transmission, all combinations of antiretroviral agents should include zidovudine as part of the initial therapeutic regimen. For patients already receiving regimens that do not include zidovudine, the addition of zidovudine or substitution of zidovudine for another nucleoside reverse-transcriptase inhibitor is recommended.[169] Zidovudine should be administered as follows:

- For antepartum prevention, zidovudine 100 mg orally five times daily, initiated at 14–34 weeks' gestation and continued for the remainder of the pregnancy.
- For intrapartum prevention, during labor, zidovudine 2 mg/kg i.v. over one hour, followed by 1 mg/kg/hr i.v. by continuous infusion until delivery.
- Neonatal dosage: zidovudine syrup 2 mg/kg orally every six hours for six weeks, beginning 8–12 hours after birth. (Strength of evidence for prophylaxis = A)

Pediatric Dosage. In the case of adolescent pregnancy, the adult recommendations should be used. Additional guidelines for the prevention of perinatal transmission of HIV can be found at http://www.hivatis.org/pedguide.html, the Web site of the HIV/AIDS Treatment Information Service.

Perinatally Acquired Herpes Simplex Virus Type 2 Infection

Background. Approximately 1500 to 2000 cases of neonatal herpes are reported each year in the United States, an annual incidence of 1 in every 7500 births. HSV-2 accounts for nearly 70% of neonatal herpes and may be acquired congenitally, natally, or postnatally. The presence of primary HSV, but probably not recurrent HSV, during pregnancy increases the frequency of spontaneous abortion twofold to fourfold and increases the frequency of preterm labor twofold. Congenital anomalies may occur with primary, recurrent, or even asymptomatic disease.[175]

Persons at Risk. The risk of HSV infection in newborns of HSV-infected mothers is greatly increased. Cesarean birth is recommended for mothers if an HSV lesion will come into contact with the baby at the time of delivery.[176] The neonatal infection rates are greater in mothers with primary HSV infection than in mothers with recurrence of previously acquired HSV, 30–40% versus 3–5%, respectively.[175] However, distinguishing between primary and recurrent HSV infection in women on the basis of clinical findings is difficult. Most newborns infected with HSV are born to women who have asymptomatic or unrecognized infection.[176] HSV-1 and HSV-2 produce equal severity of disease. The use of fetal scalp monitors or other invasive instrumentation antenatally increases the risk of perinatal HSV transmission. Antiviral prophylaxis is based on the presumption that reduction in the frequency of active HSV lesions at delivery will reduce the rate of cesarean delivery, newborn HSV exposure, and subsequent neonatal HSV disease.[177] Nearly 1600 cesarean births must be performed to prevent one case of neonatal herpes infection (a cost per neonatal herpes case averted of $2.5 million and a cost per quality-adjusted life-year gained of $203,000).[178]

Efficacy. The efficacy of prophylaxis with acyclovir in the prevention of HSV disease in newborns is not known; however, use of this regimen has been associated with a lower rate of cesarean deliveries.[177,179] Data on prophylaxis to prevent HSV-2 are limited to a case series in mothers with recurrent genital HSV-2,[180] a placebo-controlled, double-blind study of mothers with first-episode herpes,[177] and a placebo-controlled study in mothers with frequent recurrent genital herpes.[179]

One series of five mothers with recurrent genital herpes (HSV-2) received different acyclovir dosages after 37 weeks' gestation, and acyclovir plasma concentrations and viral cultures from the genital area were followed until birth.[180] This small uncontrolled study suggests that mothers with recurrent genital HSV infection may still have asymptomatic viral shedding and transmission to the newborn despite treatment with acyclovir.

In a placebo-controlled, double-blind study, 46 pregnant women with first-episode genital herpes were randomly assigned to receive either oral acyclovir 400 mg three times daily or placebo from 36 weeks' gestation to delivery.[177] The frequency of symptomatic recurrent HSV lesions at the time of delivery was 8% for the acyclovir recipients and 34% for the placebo recipients, demonstrating a significant reduction in HSV disease at time of delivery. The rate of cesarean section was also lower in the treatment group than the placebo group (19% versus 40%, respectively). Apparently the obstetrician had a greater sense of security with the acyclovir group because of fewer lesions. However, no newborn in either group developed HSV disease, and there were no differences in neonatal outcomes between the groups. No benefit in reducing the risk for neonatal HSV was demonstrated, possibly because of the relatively low infection rate and the enormous number of patients needed to detect differences. Acyclovir was well tolerated by both the mother and the fetus. The results of this study suggest that acyclovir suppressive therapy decreases the rate of cesarean section in mothers with genital herpes, but no conclusive benefits for the prevention of disease in the newborn could be demonstrated.

Another study also demonstrated the benefit of oral acyclovir in reducing active HSV lesions at delivery and the cesarean delivery rate.[179] The study was placebo controlled but was not randomized or blinded in women with frequently recurring genital herpes (an average of three symptomatic recurrences over the last six months of pregnancy). Ninety-two women with recurrent genital herpes received either acyclovir 200 mg orally four times daily or placebo for one to two weeks before delivery. No cesarean sections were performed specifically because of the presence of herpes lesions in the acyclovir-treated group ($n = 46$), while 9 (20%) of 46 patients in the placebo group had cesarean sections because of active herpes lesions at the time of delivery. There were no cases of neonatal herpes in either group. A lower cesarean delivery rate in primary HSV-infected mothers is an important benefit to the mothers. There are no data available showing that famciclovir or valacyclovir reduces active HSV lesions at delivery or the cesarean delivery rate, although famciclovir and valacyclovir are efficacious against HSV. The CDC pregnancy outcome registry from 1984 to 1993 indicated no increased risk of birth defects among infants born to women exposed to acyclovir during pregnancy.[181]

Resistance. There are no data available on the development of resistance with perinatal prophylactic antivirals. Acyclovir-resistant HSV is most commonly reported in severely immunocompromised patients and infrequently in immunocompetent patients with extended treatment courses.[182]

Pediatric Efficacy. No well-controlled studies have evaluated the effect of prophylaxis in adolescent girls to prevent maternal–infant transmission of HSV, although adult data should be applicable.

Recommendation. The efficacy of prophylactic antivirals in pregnant women with genital HSV infection is not well established, although acyclovir administration has been associated with lower cesarean delivery rates. If prophylaxis is chosen, the recommended regimen is acyclovir 400 mg orally three times daily from 36 weeks' gestation to delivery in primary HSV-infected mothers (Table 4). An alternative is valacyclovir 1 g (as the hydrochloride) orally twice a day. For mothers with frequently recurring genital HSV (six episodes a year), the recommended regimen is acyclovir 200 mg four times daily for one to four weeks before delivery. Alternatives are famciclovir orally 125 mg twice a day or valacyclovir orally 500 mg (as the hydrochloride) twice a day. Prophylaxis is not recommended in pregnant women with a remote history of genital HSV (no recent recurrence or HSV seropositive). (Strength of evidence for prophylaxis = A for prevention of cesarean delivery in mothers with primary HSV infection and B for recurrent genital HSV. Strength of evidence against prophylaxis = C for mothers with a remote history of genital HSV)

Health care professionals are encouraged to register pregnant women receiving acyclovir with the acyclovir pregnancy registry at 888-825-5249, extension 39441.

Pediatric Dosage. According to adult efficacy data, acyclovir is associated with lower cesarean delivery rates in HSV-infected mothers and lower risks inherent in the surgical procedure. Adolescents should receive the adult dosage of acyclovir: acyclovir 400 mg orally three times daily from 36 weeks' gestation to delivery in primary HSV-infected adolescents. An alternative is valacyclovir 1 g (as the hydrochloride) orally twice a day. Acyclovir 200 mg orally four times daily for one to four weeks before delivery is recommended for mothers with frequently recurring genital HSV (six episodes a year). Alternatives are famciclovir orally 125 mg twice a day or valacyclovir orally 500 mg (as the hydrochloride) twice a day. Prophylaxis is not recommended in pregnant adolescents with a remote history of genital HSV (no recent recurrence or HSV seropositive).

Perinatally Acquired Group B Streptococcal Infection

Background. Group B streptococci are the pathogens most frequently implicated in neonatal sepsis in the United States and are directly implicated in 20% of all episodes of peripartum sepsis.[183] Two distinct disease types—early onset and late onset—have been described. Early-onset sepsis (less than seven days after birth) results from intrauterine infection and is more common than late-onset disease (seven days to three months).[184,185] Early-onset disease is associated with a higher mortality rate.[185] It is estimated that 0.2–0.5% of all neonates in the United States develop sepsis involving group B streptococci, with a fatality rate of 25%.[183,184] The annual morbidity and mortality rates associated with group B streptococci in the United States are approximately 12,000 infants and 50,000 pregnant women.[185]

A pharmacoeconomic analysis showed that intrapartum prophylactic antimicrobials administered to colonized women with labor complications (fever, rupture of membranes for more than 12 hours, or labor onset before 37 weeks of gestation) could save approximately $16 million in direct medical costs.[186]

Persons at Risk. Because group B streptococci are transmitted from mother to neonate during delivery, infants born to mothers with cervical or vaginal colonization are at greatest risk for sepsis. Approximately 10–34% of pregnant women have vaginal or rectal colonization.[187] Virtually 100% of group B streptococcal carriers can be detected when selective broth media for lower vagina and anorectum cultures are used.[185] Of infants born to colonized mothers, 40–73% become colonized themselves, but only 1–2% develop sepsis.[185,187]

Several maternal factors increase the risk of infection in infants of mothers who are colonized by group B streptococci. These include gestation of less than 37 weeks, rupture of membranes more than 18 hours before delivery, fever during labor, previous delivery of an infant infected with group B streptococcal disease, group B streptococcal bacteriuria during pregnancy, high inoculum of group B streptococci in genital cultures, age of mother of less than 20 years, low concentration of serotype-specific antibody to the group B streptococcal capsular polysaccharide in the serum, and African-American race. Multiple gestation may also be a factor.[187]

Efficacy. Several randomized trials have demonstrated that intrapartum administration of antimicrobials is effective in reducing the rate of vertical transmission of group B streptococci.[188–191] In one study, the frequency of early-onset group B streptococcal disease was significantly different in the infants whose mothers received prophylaxis (0%) compared with those who received no treatment (6.3%).[188] In a meta-analysis of controlled trials and cohort studies, the use of antimicrobial prophylaxis was associated with a 30-fold lower frequency of early-onset group B streptococcal infection.[192]

Resistance. The development of resistant Enterobacteriaceae after the use of ampicillin or amoxicillin prophylaxis for group B streptococcus in women with premature rupture of the membranes has been described[193] and should be considered in the risk–benefit assessment of the use of prophylactic antimicrobials.

Pediatric Efficacy. No well-controlled studies have evaluated the effect of prophylaxis in adolescent girls to prevent perinatal group B streptococcal infection, although adult data are likely to be applicable.

Table 3.
Prevention of Human Immunodeficiency Virus Infection after Occupational Exposure[a]

Setting	Eligible Patients	Recommended Regimen	Alternative Regimens	Strength of Evidence[b]
Percutaneous exposure to blood	Persons with highest- and increased-risk exposure[c]	Zidovudine 300 mg p.o. b.i.d. or 200 mg p.o. t.i.d. plus lamivudine 150 mg p.o. b.i.d. plus either indinavir 800 mg p.o. t.i.d. or nelfinavir 750 mg p.o. t.i.d. for 4 wk	[d]	C
	Persons with exposure of no increased risk[e]	Not recommended	Offer zidovudine 300 mg p.o. b.i.d. or 200 mg p.o. t.i.d. plus lamivudine 150 mg p.o. b.i.d.[d]	C
Other percutaneous exposure	Persons exposed to fluid containing blood, other fluid,[f] or tissue	Not recommended	Offer zidovudine 300 mg p.o. b.i.d. or 200 mg p.o. t.i.d. plus lamivudine 150 mg p.o. b.i.d.[d]	C
	Persons exposed to other fluid (e.g., urine)	Not recommended	Do not offer	C
Exposure of mucous membrane or skin[g]	Persons exposed to blood	Not recommended	Offer zidovudine 300 mg p.o. b.i.d. or 200 mg p.o. t.i.d. plus lamivudine 150 mg p.o. b.i.d.; addition of indinavir or nelfinavir is optional[d]	C
	Persons exposed to fluid containing blood, other fluid,[f] or tissue	Not recommended	Offer zidovudine 300 mg p.o. b.i.d. or 200 mg p.o. t.i.d. plus lamivudine 150 mg p.o. b.i.d.[d]	C
	Persons exposed to other fluid (e.g., urine)	Not recommended	Do not offer	C

[a]Adapted from recommendations of the Centers for Disease Control and Prevention (CDC, reference 157).

[b]Strength of evidence that supports the use or nonuse of prophylaxis is classified as A (levels I–III), B (levels IV–VI), or C (level VII). Level I evidence is from large, well-conducted randomized, controlled clinical trials. Level II evidence is from small, well-conducted randomized, controlled clinical trials. Level III evidence is from well-conducted cohort studies. Level IV evidence is from well-conducted case–control studies. Level V evidence is from uncontrolled studies that were not well conducted. Level VI evidence is conflicting evidence that tends to favor the recommendation. Level VII evidence is expert opinion. Strength-of-evidence classification not applied (NA) to pediatric recommendations.

[c]Highest and increased-risk exposures involve a larger volume of blood (e.g., deep injury with large diameter hollow needle previously in source patient's vein or artery, especially involving an injection of source patient's blood) or blood containing a high titer of HIV. A high titer of HIV is defined as blood from a person with acute retroviral illness or end-stage AIDS; viral load measurement may be considered, but its use in relation to prophylaxis has not been evaluated.

[d]Alternative regimens with other nucleoside reverse-transcriptase inhibitors, protease inhibitors, or nonnucleoside reverse-transcriptase inhibitors may be required. Alternative regimens may be required in certain situations (e.g., resistance of source's virus to standard regimen).[157] Other regimens have not been approved by CDC.

[e]There is no increased risk if exposure was to neither a large volume of blood nor blood with a high titer of HIV (e.g., solid suture-needle injury from a source patient with asymptomatic HIV infection).

[f]Other fluids include semen, vaginal secretions, and cerebrospinal, synovial, pleural, peritoneal, pericardial, and amniotic fluids.

[g]For skin exposures, the risk is increased if the fluid contains a high titer of HIV, there is prolonged contact, the exposed area is large, or the integrity of the exposed skin is visibly compromised. For skin exposures without increased risk, the risk of drug toxicity outweighs the benefit of postexposure prophylaxis.

Recommendation. Two acceptable strategies for the prevention of perinatal group B streptococcal infection have been proposed by CDC and the American Academy of Pediatrics (AAP)/American College of Obstetricians and Gynecologists (ACOG).[187,194] The two strategies include screening at 35–37 weeks and using only risk factors. Regardless of the strategy used, women should be given antimicrobial prophylaxis if they had a previous delivery of an infant with group B streptococcal disease or group B streptococcal bacteriuria during the pregnancy. The prenatal screening strategy includes screening all pregnant women at 35–37 weeks and offering antimicrobial prophylaxis to all pregnant women with positive group B streptococcal cultures. If the results of group B streptococcal cultures are not known at the time of labor, intrapartum prophylaxis should be administered if one of the following risk factors is present: delivery at <37 weeks' gestation (for ruptured membranes without labor at <37 weeks, group B streptococcal culture should be collected and either antimicrobials given until cultures are completed and negative or antimicrobials begun once positive culture results are available), duration of membrane rupture of ≥18 hours before delivery, or intrapartum fever (≥38 °C). The risk-factor strategy is based only on the presence of the preceding intrapartum risk factors; intrapartum antimicrobial prophylaxis is administered if one or more of these risk factors are present.

The recommendation for intrapartum therapy is penicillin G 5 million units i.v. load, then 2.5 million units i.v. every four hours until delivery (Table 4). An alternative regimen is ampicillin 2 g (as the sodium) i.v., then 1 g i.v. every four hours until delivery. Patients allergic to penicillin may receive clindamycin 900 mg (as the phosphate) i.v. every eight hours or erythromycin 500 mg (as the lactobionate) i.v. every six hours until delivery. (Strength of evidence for prophylaxis = A)

Pediatric Dosage. CDC and AAP have published official recommendations on antimicrobial prophylaxis of perinatal group B streptococcal infection and empirical management of neonates born to women receiving intrapartum chemoprophylaxis.[176,187] Readers are referred to the adult recommendations for at-risk patients who require prophylaxis.

Opportunistic Infections in Afebrile Granulocytopenic Patients

Persons at Risk. Patients with granulocytopenia (usually defined as <500 granulocytes/mm³ for at least seven days) are at an increased risk of serious infection and death. Patients with hematologic malignancies, especially patients with acute leukemia, who are receiving antineoplastic therapy are at particular risk for infection. Patients receiving antineoplastic conditioning for bone marrow transplantation (BMT) also experience severe granulocytopenia and have significant risk of infection. Many of the studies evaluated for this review included patients with leukemia as well as patients undergoing BMT. Therefore, recommendations for patients undergoing BMT are included in this section.

The degree and duration of granulocytopenia are the greatest risk factors for the development of infection. Patients with severe granulocytopenia (<100 granulocytes/mm³) are at greatest risk. Although patients with a duration of granulocytopenia of less than one week can become febrile and require antimicrobials, they generally respond quickly to therapy.[195] Other risk factors include mucosal and skin lesions, indwelling catheters, instrumentation, severe periodontal disease, dental procedures, postobstructive pneumonia, status of the malignancy or organ engraftment, and compromise of other immune responses.[196] Patients who have granulocytopenia related to antineoplastic therapy are at greater risk of infection than patients with granulocytopenia due to other causes (e.g., aplastic anemia, HIV infection). This is presumably due to alterations in the mucosal integrity induced by chemotherapy, which allows enhanced bacterial or fungal colonization.[195]

Another risk factor for fungal infections is the administration of broad-spectrum antimicrobials.[197,198] Fungal infections are particularly common in patients undergoing allogeneic BMT because these patients receive an intense conditioning regimen in addition to immunosuppressive agents to prevent or treat graft-versus-host disease.[197]

The use of colony-stimulating factors has a beneficial effect on granulocyte recovery and thus eliminates the need for extended duration of antimicrobial prophylaxis. The frequency and severity of infection are inversely related to absolute neutrophil count in patients with acute leukemia.[199] Colony-stimulating factors (granulocyte colony-stimulating factor, granulocyte/macrophage colony-stimulating factor, and macrophage colony-stimulating factor) have been associated with a lower severity and duration of neutropenia and infectious complications and a shorter duration of therapeutic antimicrobial administration. Colony-stimulating factors have also been associated with a shorter duration of therapeutic antimicrobials and hospitalization in BMT patients.[200] Although the use of colony-stimulating factors in the prevention of fungal infections is controversial, there is some evidence of a beneficial effect.[201] A concern with administering colony-stimulating factors is the regrowth of leukemic blasts in the bone marrow. Because the use of colony-stimulating factors eliminates the need for prolonged prophylaxis, there is potential for use to alter or influence the interpretation of study results.

Historically, antibacterial prophylaxis has been directed primarily toward gram-negative aerobic bacteria, especially *E. coli*, *Klebsiella pneumonia*, and *P. aeruginosa*. However, the prevalence of gram-positive bacteria (staphylococci and streptococci) is increasing, perhaps because of the increased use of indwelling catheters and the use of prophylactic regimens for selective intestinal decontamination. The most common fungal pathogens are *Candida* and *Aspergillus* species. Cytomegalovirus (CMV) infection is a major cause of morbidity in patients undergoing BMT. Before the use of antiviral prophylaxis regimens, the risk of reactivation of latent infection was 80% and the risk of a seronegative recipient acquiring CMV from either blood transfusion or seropositive marrow was 40%.[202]

The goal of antimicrobial prophylaxis in granulocytopenic patients is to prevent infection, the cause of death in 50–80% of these patients. Unless otherwise specified, only trials of a concurrent, randomized design were considered.

Bacterial Prophylaxis. *Efficacy.* Most studies of antibacterial prophylaxis were conducted in patients receiving chemotherapy for acute leukemia or undergoing BMT. Agents such as trimethoprim–sulfamethoxazole and, more recently, the fluoroquinolones (e.g., ciprofloxacin, norfloxacin, ofloxacin) have been used to achieve a selective antimicrobial effect by reducing the aerobic bacterial flora of the colon without suppressing the anaerobic flora. This practice theoretically preserves resistance to colonization by undesirable aerobic gram-negative bacilli. Data are lacking on the use of penicillin or cephalosporins plus aminoglycosides for prophylaxis, even though a plethora of data are available on these agents for empirical treatment in febrile neutropenic patients.[203] The available data demonstrate a lower number of infectious episodes.[204-236] However, the lack of improvement in mortality and the risk of drug-resistant bacteria may outweigh the benefit of reducing infectious episodes. IDSA recommends against the use of routine antibacterial prophylaxis, with the exception of using trimethoprim–sulfamethoxazole for patients at risk (e.g., patients with childhood leukemias, histiocytosis, or AIDS) for *Pneumocystis carinii* pneumonitis. The quinolones may be considered for short periods if the potential for resistant organisms is appreciated and outweighed by the benefits.[203]

Treatment with trimethoprim–sulfamethoxazole was superior to no drug and to placebo in reducing measures of acquired infection (e.g., duration of fever, duration of antimicrobial use, number of infections, number of gram-negative bacteremias) in most,[204-207] but not all,[237] studies. Norfloxacin prophylaxis was associated with a lower rates of gram-negative infections but not gram-positive infections compared with placebo.[208] Similarly, norfloxacin plus oral amphotericin B was associated with a lower frequency of gram-negative and overall infections compared with amphotericin B alone.[209] With one exception,[210] vancomycin[211-213] or teicoplanin[214] was effective as prophylaxis (lower rate of gram-positive infections, catheter-related infections, and use of empirical antimicrobials).

Use of prophylactic antimicrobials in patients with granulocytopenia has become so well established that most studies do not contain a control group. Studies have focused on comparisons among the various antimicrobial regimens. Comparisons have included trimethoprim–sulfamethoxazole versus fluoroquinolones,[215-226] fluoroquinolones versus fluoroquinolones,[215,227-229] fluoroquinolones with and without added coverage for gram-positive infections,[230-233] and fluoroquinolone versus vancomycin plus polymyxin B.[234,235]

Trimethoprim–sulfamethoxazole was generally superior to nalidixic acid in reducing either gram-negative or overall infection rates.[216,226] In contrast, newer fluoroquinolones (ciprofloxacin, norfloxacin, ofloxacin) were generally associated with a lower rate of gram-negative infections than trimethoprim–sulfamethoxazole.[218,221,223] Trimethoprim–sulfamethoxazole is generally less well tolerated than fluoroquinolones and is associated with delayed recovery from granulocytopenia.[220,223,226] There was no significant difference in the overall infection rates between fluoroquinolones and trimethoprim–sulfamethoxazole. Prophylaxis with fluoroquinolones was associated with a higher frequency of infections by gram-positive bacteria, especially viridans streptococci.[217,219]

Comparisons between fluoroquinolones have been the subject of several investigations.[215,227-229] Ciprofloxacin was more effective than norfloxacin in preventing fever and microbiologically documented infection in one large trial.[229] However, comparisons between ciprofloxacin and ofloxacin found no difference in efficacy.[215,228]

The addition of an antimicrobial with gram-positive coverage (e.g., a penicillin or macrolide) to fluoroquinolones is effective in decreasing the frequency of gram-positive infections associated with the use of quinolones alone.[230-233] The combination was effective in reducing the frequency of bacteremia, especially that due to streptococcal species. Despite supportive data for reducing gram-positive bacter-

emia, the combination of fluoroquinolones plus prophylaxis for gram-positive bacteremia (penicillin, vancomyicn, or macrolides) was not associated with a lower rate of fever-related morbidity or infection-related mortality in a meta-analyis.[236]

Resistance. The emergence of resistance has been a problem with the major prophylactic antibacterial agents. *E. coli* resistance to trimethoprim–sulfamethoxazole, including the isolation of a self-transferable plasmid, has been reported.[238,239] Fluoroquinolones have also been associated with the emergence of resistant organisms, primarily gram-positive bacteria[240,241] but also *E. coli*.[242]

Pediatric efficacy. Few controlled trials in pediatric patients have been reported. Among children of ages 2 to 16 years undergoing BMT, there was a lower frequency of septicemia in the group receiving i.v. ceftazidime plus teicoplanin than in the control group.[243] In 44 children with granulocytopenia, norfloxacin was associated with a lower number of febrile episodes than trimethoprim–sulfamethoxazole, although there was no difference in the mean number of febrile days or the use of systemic antimicrobials.[244] The mean ages were eight and six years, respectively. No arthropathies were noted in children receiving norfloxacin.

Fungal Prophylaxis. *Efficacy.* Numerous recent studies have evaluated the efficacy of antifungal prophylaxis in granulocytopenic patients with hematologic malignancies (primarily acute leukemia) or in patients receiving BMT. Both topical and systemic agents have been used. Topical agents include amphotericin B, nystatin, and clotrimazole administered orally or by inhalation.[245-248] Systemic agents include i.v. amphotericin B and oral or i.v. azoles (e.g., fluconazole, ketoconazole, itraconazole).[249-259] The Eastern Cooperative Oncology Group (ECOG) recommends continued clinical investigation of the use of fungal prophylaxis because of the toxicity and limited efficacy in the treatment of invasive fungal infections. ECOG recommends that fluconazole or low-dose amphotericin B be considered for patients undergoing BMT.[202] The risk of drug resistance and fungal colonization by less susceptible strains may outweigh the benefit of reducing infectious episodes. IDSA recommends against the routine use of antifungals, with the exception that fluconazole may be used if the frequency of systemic infection due to *C. albicans* is high and that due to other *Candida* species is low.[203]

Low-dose (0.1 mg/kg/day) i.v. amphotericin B was associated with a lower rate of systemic fungal infection, number of days with fever, and number of days of high-dose (1 mg/kg/day) amphotericin B treatment required in patients undergoing BMT compared with placebo.[249] Despite being associated with a lower number of yeast colonizing the oropharyngeal area, low-dose (0.1 mg/kg/day) i.v. amphotericin B was associated with a significantly greater frequency of infusion-related adverse effects (chills, fever, nausea, and vomiting) but not systemic toxicities (electrolytes, renal function, and hepatic enzymes) compared with placebo.[250]

Oral or i.v. fluconazole or ketoconazole was associated with a lower frequency of fungal colonization and superficial fungal infections compared with placebo in studies involving patients undergoing BMT only,[255] hematologic malignancies only,[253,256] and both.[251,252,254] However, fluconazole did not have a favorable effect on infection-

Table 4.
Prevention of Perinatally Acquired Infection[a]

Infection and Setting	Eligible Patients	Recommended Regimen	Alternative Regimens	Strength of Evidence[b]
HIV[c]				
Antepartum prevention of transmission	All pregnant HIV-infected women at >14 wk gestation	Zidovudine 100 mg p.o. 5 times daily, starting at 14–34 wk of gestation, continued for remainder of pregnancy	None	A
Intrapartum prevention of transmission	All pregnant HIV-infected women	During labor, zidovudine 2 mg/kg i.v. over 1 hr, then 1 mg/kg/hr i.v. continuous infusion until delivery	None	A
Prevention of neonatal infection	All neonates born to HIV-infected women	Zidovudine syrup 2 mg/kg p.o. q 6 hr for 6 wk, beginning 8–12 hr after birth	None	A
HSV-2				
Reduction of cesarean delivery rate	Women with primary genital HSV	Acyclovir 400 mg p.o. t.i.d. from 36 wk gestation to delivery[d]	Valacyclovir 1 g p.o. b.i.d.	A[e]
	Women with frequent recurrent genital HSV[f]	Acyclovir 200 mg p.o. q.i.d. for 1–4 wk before delivery[d]	Famciclovir 125 mg p.o. b.i.d. or valacyclovir 500 mg p.o. b.i.d.	B[e]
	Women with remote history of genital HSV[g]	Not recommended	None	C
Group B streptococcus[h] Intrapartum prevention of neonatal sepsis	Women with (1) previous delivery of infant with group B streptococcal disease or (2) group B streptococcal bacteriuria during current pregnancy	Intrapartum penicillin G 5 million units i.v. load, then 2.5 million units q 4 hr until delivery	Ampicillin 2 g i.v. load, then 1 g i.v. q 4 hr until delivery, clindamycin 900 mg i.v. q 8 hr, or erythromycin 500 mg i.v. q 6 hr until delivery	A

[a]HIV = human immunodeficiency virus, HSV = herpes simplex virus.
[b]Strength of evidence that supports the use or nonuse of prophylaxis is classified as A (levels I–III), B (levels IV–VI), or C (level VII). Level I evidence is from large, well-conducted randomized, controlled clinical trials. Level II evidence is from small, well-conducted randomized, controlled clinical trials. Level III evidence is from well-conducted cohort studies. Level IV evidence is from well-conducted case–control studies. Level V evidence is from uncontrolled studies that were not well conducted. Level VI evidence is conflicting evidence that tends to favor the recommendation. Level VII evidence is expert opinion. Strength-of-evidence classification not applied (NA) to pediatric recommendations.
[c]The mother has the right and responsibility to accept or reject the recommendation for zidovudine treatment for herself and her child.
[d]If acyclovir is used, register patient in the acyclovir pregnancy registry (telephone 888-825-5249, extension 39441).
[e]For prevention of cesarean section.
[f]Frequent means six or more herpes episodes a year.
[g]Remote means no recent recurrence or woman is HSV seropositive.
[h]Acceptable strategies for preventing infection include prenatal screening and considering risk factors. Regardless of strategy, antimicrobial prophylaxis should be used in all women who are eligible as indicated in the table. In prenatal screening, culture for group B streptococci is performed at 35–37 weeks of gestation, and antimicrobial prophylaxis is offered if the culture is positive. If culture results are not known at the time of labor, intrapartum prophylaxis should be administered if one of the following conditions is present: (1) delivery after 37 weeks of gestation (for ruptured membranes without labor at <37 weeks, perform group B streptococcal culture and give antimicrobials until cultures are completed and negative, or begin antimicrobials once positive culture results are available), (2) duration of membrane rupture is ≥18 hours before delivery, or (3) intrapartum fever (≥38 °C). In the risk-factor strategy, antimicrobial prophylaxis is administered if one of the numbered conditions in the previous sentence is present.

related health care costs and was associated with prolonged severe neutropenia.[254] Two of these studies also found a lower use of i.v. amphotericin B for empirical therapy.[251,255] However, with one exception,[255] there was no significant difference in the frequency of systemic fungal infections with fluconazole prophylaxis compared with placebo.[252–254,256] The efficacy of reducing systemic infections could not be assessed because of the small number of patients in the study.[251] Even though fluconazole was associated with a lower frequency of systemic fungal infections due to *C. albicans*, there was no difference in the frequency of non-*C. albicans* and *Torulopsis glabrata* infections between the fluconazole group and the placebo group.[255] Itraconazole was ineffective in preventing fungal infections for patients with hematologic malignancies who were not undergoing BMT.[260]

Fluconazole was associated with a lower frequency of systemic and superficial fungal infections in a double-blind, randomized, placebo-controlled, multicenter trial in patients undergoing BMT.[258] However, fluconazole did not prevent *C. krusei* infections. Fluconazole was associated with a lower frequency of superficial infections compared with a nystatin–miconazole combination in patients with hematologic malignancies and patients undergoing BMT.[245] Fluconazole was associated with a lower frequency of serious infections compared with nystatin–clotrimazole in patients with hematologic malignancies and BMT patients.[246] Ketoconazole was no more effective than oral nystatin in preventing fungal infections in patients undergoing BMT.[259] Compared with oral amphotericin B, systemic treatment with fluconazole has been associated with a lower frequency of superficial infections in some patients with hematologic malignancies and in patients undergoing BMT.[247,248] Other studies that involved only patients with hematologic malignancies did not demonstrate this effect.[261–263] There was no significant difference between these treatments in the frequency of systemic fungal infections.

One study compared i.v. amphotericin B with either i.v. or oral fluconazole.[257] Although there was no significant difference in infection rates between the treatments, fluconazole was associated with a significantly greater success rate, defined as lack of discontinuation of prophylaxis due to toxicity or the decreased occurrence of a possible fungal infection.

A disadvantage of the azole antifungals is a lack of effectiveness against *Aspergillus*. A single-center trial failed to demonstrate a difference in deep mycoses between placebo (8 infections out of 76 patients) and fluconazole 400 mg/day (8 infections out of 75 patients) because the predominant mycosis was aspergillosis.[254] The efficacy of fluconazole in preventing *Aspergillus* infections could not be determined in a multicenter trial involving 356 patients because of the low frequency of *Aspergillus*.[258] During selection of an agent for antifungal prophylaxis, the need for coverage of *Aspergillus* should be considered.[254,264,265]

The optimal fluconazole prophylaxis dosage has not been established. The most commonly used dosage is 400 mg/day, based on the results of a double-blind, multicenter trial in BMT patients in which the dosage was arbitrarily chosen.[258] However, the Working Party of the British Society for Antimicrobial Chemotherapy[265] recommends 50 mg/day on the basis of an open, randomized, multicenter trial.[247] Dosages lower than 400 mg/day may be effective but have not been well studied.

Resistance. Resistant non-*albicans* strains of *Candida*[258,266–269] and breakthrough infections caused by *T. glabrata*[258,261,270] after prophylaxis with fluconazole have also been reported.

Pediatric Efficacy. Fluconazole,[269,271] ketoconazole,[272,273] and itraconazole[273] have been used in children, although only one study was controlled.[272] In that study, ketoconazole was associated with a lower rate of fungal colonization but not of documented infections or fever of unknown origin requiring systemic treatment with amphotericin B.

Viral Prophylaxis. *Efficacy.* There are no data supporting antiviral prophylaxis for granulocytopenic patients with hematologic malignancies. There is a lack of data supporting primary antiviral prophylaxis (CMV-negative recipients, CMV-positive donors) in granulocytopenic BMT patients. Intravenous immunoglobulin (IVIG) has been associated with a lower frequency of CMV infection in CMV-seronegative recipients of allogeneic BMT.[274]

Data support the use of antivirals for secondary prophylaxis (suppressive therapy). In patients undergoing BMT who had positive cultures for CMV, prophylaxis with ganciclovir was associated with a lower rate of CMV infection and mortality compared with placebo.[275,276] The ganciclovir i.v. dosages were 5 mg/kg (as the sodium) twice daily for the first 7 days and then once daily for the first 100 days after transplantation[275] and 5 mg/kg daily for 5 days per week for 120 days. Intravenous acyclovir 500 mg/m^2 (as the sodium) three times a day for one month followed by oral acyclovir 800 mg four times daily for six months was superior to oral acyclovir 200–400 mg four times daily alone in preventing CMV infection and in improving survival.[277] Oral acyclovir 200 mg every six hours to 400 mg five times a day for 18 to 35 days is also effective in preventing the reactivation of HSV infections in seropositive patients undergoing BMT.[278–280]

Resistance. There are no data available on the development of resistance with primary prophylaxis against CMV in granulocytopenic patients. Only one of the several studies of secondary prophylaxis evaluated the sensitivity of the vi-

ruses. No acyclovir-resistant HSV was isolated in a study of secondary prophylaxis.[280] However, ganciclovir-resistant CMV strains during long-term ganciclovir therapy in AIDS patients have been reported.[281,282]

Pediatric Efficacy. No well-controlled studies have yet evaluated the effect of prophylaxis for viral infections in granulocytopenic pediatric patients.

Recommendation: Bacterial Prophylaxis. Prophylaxis is generally not recommended for patients with hematologic malignancies or BMT patients who are expected to experience prolonged (seven days or more) granulocytopenia because of the lack of demonstrated improvement in mortality and the risk of drug-resistant bacteria (Table 5). Exceptions are trimethoprim–sulfamethoxazole for patients at risk (e.g., patients with childhood leukemia, histiocytosis, or AIDS) for *P. carinii* pneumonitis. The quinolones may be considered for short periods if the potential for resistant organisms is appreciated and outweighed by the benefits. The dosage is trimethoprim 160 mg and sulfamethoxazole 800 mg orally twice daily. If quinolones are used, the dosage is ciprofloxacin 500 mg orally twice daily, ciprofloxacin 400 mg (as the lactate) i.v. twice daily, or ofloxacin 200 mg orally or i.v. twice daily. Prophylaxis should start when antineoplastic therapy begins for patients with hematologic malignancies and from the start of the conditioning regimen for BMT patients. Prophylaxis should continue until the granulocyte count exceeds 500/mm^3 or until fever occurs. If fever occurs, presumptive therapy with an appropriate antimicrobial should be initiated. (Strength of evidence against prophylaxis = C)

Pediatric Dosage in Bacterial Prophylaxis. Prophylaxis is not recommended for pediatric patients with hematologic malignancies or BMT patients who are expected to experience prolonged (seven days or more) granulocytopenia because of the lack of demonstrated improvement in mortality and the risk of drug-resistant bacteria. Exceptions are trimethoprim–sulfamethoxazole for pediatric patients at risk (e.g., patients with childhood leukemia, histiocytosis, or AIDS) for *P. carinii* pneumonitis. The regimen is trimethoprim 6–10 mg/kg/day and sulfamethoxazole 30–50 mg/kg/day divided twice daily. Prophylaxis should start when antineoplastic therapy begins for patients with hematologic malignancies and from the start of the conditioning regimen for BMT patients. Prophylaxis should continue until the granulocyte count exceeds 500/mm^3 or until fever occurs. Although children have been treated with ciprofloxacin without the occurrence of arthropathy, further safety data are needed before widespread use can be recommended in this patient population. Norfloxacin has also been used safely in children, but data are limited.

Recommendation: Fungal Prophylaxis. Fungal prophylaxis is generally not recommended for patients with hematologic malignancies or BMT patients who are expected to experience prolonged (seven days or more) granulocytopenia. However, if the risk of *C. albicans* infection is high and the risk of infection with other *Candida* species is low, fluconazole may be an option.[203] The significant risks (increasing the prevalence of non-*albicans Candida* species and other more resistant fungal infections) and the associated costs should be considered. The dosage is fluconazole 400 mg orally or i.v. once daily. An alternative is i.v. amphotericin B 0.1–0.25 mg/kg/day. Prophylaxis should start when antineoplastic therapy begins for patients with hematologic malignancies and from the start of the conditioning regimen for BMT patients. Prophylaxis should be continued until the granulocyte count exceeds 500/mm³ or until fever occurs. (Strength of evidence against prophylaxis = C)

Pediatric Dosage in Fungal Prophylaxis. Fungal prophylaxis is not recommended for pediatric patients with hematologic malignancies or BMT patients who are expected to experience prolonged (seven days or more) granulocytopenia. However, if the risk of *C. albicans* infection is high and the risk of infection with other *Candida* species is low, fluconazole may be an option.[203] The significant risks (increasing the prevalence of non-*albicans Candida* species and other more resistant fungal infections) and the associated costs should be considered. The dosage is fluconazole 3–5 mg/kg/day orally or i.v. for fungal prophylaxis. An alternative is i.v. amphotericin B 0.1–0.25 mg/kg/day. Prophylaxis should start when antineoplastic therapy begins for patients with hematologic malignancies and from the start of the conditioning regimen for BMT patients. Prophylaxis should be continued until the granulocyte count exceeds 500/mm³ or until fever occurs.

Recommendation: Viral Prophylaxis. Although antiviral therapy for secondary prophylaxis (suppressive therapy) is acceptable in BMT patients, antiviral therapy for primary prophylaxis is not recommended for granulocytopenic patients, including BMT patients. (Strength of evidence against primary prophylaxis = C)

Pediatric Dosage in Viral Prophylaxis. Primary prophylaxis is not recommended for granulocytopenic pediatric patients, including BMT patients.

Opportunistic Infections in HIV-Infected Persons

The prophylaxis and treatment of opportunistic infections in HIV-infected patients is a rapidly changing area of infectious diseases. Because of the intensive research being conducted and the frequent introduction of new drugs or drug regimens, this area is continually evolving. The recommendations presented in this section are based on available clinical information and the formal recommendations that were current at the time this document was prepared.[283–285] Because of the rapid progression of practice related to this area, readers should be mindful of the possibility that the CDC recommendations may have been revised since publication of these guidelines.

Recommendations concerning prophylaxis of opportunistic infections in HIV-infected patients were largely based on the official guidelines of CDC and IDSA.[284] However, there are several situations for which new information has become available since publication of the CDC guidelines and for which there are new unofficial guidelines or clinical practice standards. Formal CDC guidelines as well as newer information were used to develop the recommendations presented in this document.

Combination antiretroviral drug regimens, particularly those containing protease inhibitors, are capable of increasing CD4+ lymphocyte counts by as many as 100–250 cells/μL over baseline values at the initiation of therapy. Although studies are currently being conducted, it is not yet known whether these increases in CD4+ lymphocytes induced by antiretroviral therapy are sufficient to restore immune function to the degree that drug therapies providing prophylaxis against opportunistic infections may be discontinued. Current data are insufficient to indicate whether these patients are no longer at high risk even though their CD4+ lymphocytes were significantly depleted at an earlier time. Most experts recommend that, until such data become available, prophylactic therapies be initiated on the basis of the lowest documented CD4+ lymphocyte count and that prophylactic therapies be continued regardless of subsequent therapy-induced increases in the CD4+ lymphocyte counts.[286]

Candidiasis, histoplasmosis, and coccidioidomycosis in HIV-infected persons

Background. The frequency of mucocutaneous infections due to *C. albicans* and other *Candida* species is considerably higher in HIV-infected patients, both adults and children. These infections manifest primarily as oropharyngeal, esophageal, or vulvovaginal candidiasis. The occurrence of oropharyngeal candidiasis is related to the severity of HIV disease; this infection occurs in up to 62% of previously asymptomatic persons, 43–78% of persons with AIDS-related complex, and 54–93% of persons with AIDS.[287] Esophageal candidiasis is the AIDS-defining illness in approximately 15% of adult cases reported to CDC and 14.3% of cases in children.[288,289] New or increased severity of vulvovaginal candidiasis has been reported in up to 52% of HIV-infected women, and the cumulative frequency of recurrent infections is approximately 33% in women.[290] Disseminated candidiasis or other invasive infections as a complication of HIV disease are uncommon.

Disseminated histoplasmosis is the AIDS-defining illness in approximately 1% of adult cases reported to CDC and 0.4% of cases in children.[291,292] However, this infection occurs in approximately 5% of HIV-infected patients who live in histoplasmosis-endemic areas. Disseminated histoplasmosis in endemic areas may be due to primary infection, reactivation, or reinfection.

Coccidioidomycosis is a relatively uncommon infection among HIV-infected patients, responsible for only 0.25% of AIDS-defining illnesses overall. However, as with histoplasmosis, the frequency of infection is considerably higher among HIV-infected persons living in endemic areas. Coccidioidomycosis may occur in up to 25% of HIV-infected patients living in endemic areas.[293–295]

Persons at Risk. Esophageal candidiasis in adults is more common among women than men (21% versus 14%, respectively), higher among blacks than whites (17% versus 14%), and higher among intravenous drug users than homosexual males (17% versus 13%).[288] The reported median CD4+ lymphocyte counts at the time of occurrence of esophageal candidiasis were 24 cells/μL for women and 39 cells/μL for men.[288] Low CD4+ cell count (<50 cells/μL) is the only risk factor for *Candida* colonization of various mucocutaneous sites and esophageal disease yet identified.[288] It would appear, therefore, that the only potential indication for primary prophylaxis of mucocutaneous candidiasis is a documented CD4+ cell count of <50 cells/μL.

The risk of developing disseminated histoplasmosis also appears to be highest in AIDS patients with advanced immunosuppression (CD4+ lymphocyte count of <75 cells/μL).[291] In addition, residence in a histoplasmosis-endemic area is required in order to place patients at high risk of infection.[292,296] Risk factors for coccidioidomycosis are similar to those for histoplasmosis, with residence in an endemic area and CD4+ lymphocyte counts of <250 cells/μL being the most significant risk factors for development of active infection.[295,297]

Efficacy. Antifungal agents have not been shown to have clear benefit in the prophylaxis of systemic infections. One prospective, randomized trial compared oral fluconazole with clotrimazole troches for the primary prophylaxis of localized infections due to *Candida* species.[298] After a median follow-up period of 35 months, the frequency of both oropharyngeal and esophageal candidiasis was approximately six times lower among patients receiving fluconazole. These benefits of therapy were most pronounced in patients with CD4+ lymphocyte counts of <50 cells/μL, consistent with previous observations regarding high-risk groups. However, the frequency of oropharyngeal candidiasis in fluconazole-treated patients was still 10.6%, and prophylactic therapy was not associated with a lower overall mortality among study patients.

Limited data suggest that fluconazole prophylaxis has little benefit in the prevention of disseminated histoplasmosis in HIV-infected patients; infection rates among patients receiving fluconazole did not differ significantly from rates among untreated patients.[298–300] The role of ketoconazole and itraconazole in the prevention of histoplasmosis is currently unclear. It is also unclear whether chemoprophylaxis is of benefit in preventing coccidioidomycosis. Although active coccidioidomycosis has developed in HIV-infected persons during treatment with oral antifungal therapy for other indications, no formal prophylaxis studies have been conducted.[295,301]

Resistance. In addition to the questionable overall benefits of prophylaxis, there are also concerns about the emergence of *Candida* resistance to azole antifungal agents among patients receiving chronic suppressive therapy. Reports have documented the development of fluconazole-resistant *Candida* species among oncology, BMT, and HIV-infected patients receiving fluconazole prophylaxis.[302–304] The occurrence of infection due to non-*Candida* species that are resistant to fluconazole and amphotericin B has also been documented during long-term fluconazole prophylaxis.[305,306]

Pediatric Efficacy. No well-controlled studies have evaluated the effect of prophylaxis of *Candida* infection, histoplasmosis, or coccidioidomycosis in children. Recommendations are provided by CDC, USPHS, and IDSA.[283–285]

Recommendation. Candida. Routine primary prophylaxis of mucocutaneous *Candida* infections is not recommended for HIV-infected adults because of the effectiveness of therapy for acute disease, infrequent occurrence of serious invasive disease, questionable mortality benefits of prophylaxis, concerns about the development of azole-resistant *Candida* species, potential for multiple drug interactions involving the azole antifungals, and costs of routine prophylaxis.[288,307] Azole antifungal agents may be used in patients at high risk of infection (i.e., CD4+ lymphocyte count of <50 cells/mL), but these patients should be very carefully selected and therapy instituted on an individual basis and only in unusual circumstances.[284] If primary antifungal prophylaxis is to be initiated, oral fluconazole 100–200 mg every day is preferred (Table 6). Although itraconazole has been

shown to be effective in the treatment of acute candidiasis, this drug has not yet been clearly demonstrated to be effective as a prophylactic agent, and use of itraconazole is not recommended for this purpose.[284]

Disseminated histoplasmosis or coccidioidomycosis. Routine prophylaxis in HIV-infected adults is not recommended for disseminated histoplasmosis or coccidioidomycosis. In addition to the lack of substantive data on prophylaxis, the potential development of azole-resistant fungal strains and cost-effectiveness of prophylaxis are concerns that should discourage routine practice.[283,284,286,293] Prophylactic use of azole antifungal agents, specifically itraconazole 200 mg orally every day, may be considered for patients with advanced HIV infection (CD4+ lymphocyte count of <100 cells/μL) who live in endemic areas. Patients should be carefully selected on a case-by-case basis; prophylaxis should not be routinely instituted. The oral bioavailability of itraconazole capsules has been shown to be approximately 50% lower in persons with AIDS than in healthy volunteers. In contrast, the administration of itraconazole oral solution to persons with AIDS has been shown to achieve plasma levels approximately 50–70% higher than those achieved after administration of the oral capsule. Therefore, the oral solution may be the preferred dosage form if itraconazole is to be administered in this population.[308,309] (Strength of evidence against prophylaxis = B)

Pediatric Dosage. Candida. Routine primary prophylaxis of mucocutaneous *Candida* infections is not currently recommended for children. Antifungal agents may be used in patients at high risk of infection (i.e., CD4+ lymphocyte count of <750 cells/μL for children less than one year of age, <500 cells/μL for children one to five years of age, and <200 cells/μL for children six years of age or older), but these patients should be carefully selected and therapy instituted on an individual basis. Antifungal agents include nystatin (100,000 units/μL) 4–6 mL orally every six hours and topical clotrimazole 10 mg orally five times a day. The use of azole antifungal agents is not recommended in the pediatric population.

Disseminated histoplasmosis or coccidioidomycosis. Routine prophylaxis of disseminated histoplasmosis or coccidioidomycosis in HIV-infected children is not recommended. Prophylactic use of azole antifungal agents (fluconazole 3–6 mg/kg orally every day or itraconazole 2–5 mg/kg orally every 12–24 hours) may be considered for patients with advanced HIV infection (i.e., CD4+ lymphocyte count of <750 cells/μL for children less than one year of age, <500 cells/μL for children one to five years of age, and <200 cells/μL for children six years of age or older) who live in endemic areas (Table 6). Patients should be carefully selected on a case-by-case basis; prophylaxis should not be routinely instituted.

Cryptococcus Neoformans Infections in HIV-Infected Persons

Background. Infection with *Cryptococcus neoformans* is a major cause of morbidity and mortality among patients infected with HIV. The most frequent manifestation in HIV-infected patients is cryptococcal meningitis; this infection occurs as the AIDS-defining illness in approximately 6% of all patients with advanced HIV disease and is associated with mortality rates of 25–40%.[298,310,311] Children are less prone to development of cryptococcal meningitis, with infection reported in approximately 1% of pediatric AIDS cases.[310]

Persons at Risk. Cryptococcal disease is assumed to represent primary infection as a result of environmental exposure. Although the primary environmental source of cryptococcal exposure is unknown, exposure to areas heavily contaminated with pigeon droppings has been associated with high rates of infection (although not necessarily clinical disease).[310] Persons with HIV infection working or living in contaminated areas may be at increased risk of cryptococcal meningitis. African-American race appears to be an independent risk factor for cryptococcal disease.[310] The most consistently identified risk factor for cryptococcal disease in HIV-infected persons is the CD4+ lymphocyte count. The highest risk of cryptococcal meningitis is associated with CD4+ lymphocyte counts of <100 cells/µL.[300,312] In a study of fluconazole prophylaxis, 78% of AIDS patients who developed cryptococcal disease had CD4+ lymphocyte counts of <50 cells/µL.[298] Thus, the patients at highest risk of cryptococcal infections are those with HIV infection and a CD4+ lymphocyte count of <50 cells/µL.[284,285] Such patients may be considered for prophylaxis, although these risk factors do not constitute a true indication for therapy.

Efficacy. A retrospective study of patients receiving fluconazole for other indications found the rate of cryptococcal infections to be only 0.3%, compared with 4.8% in untreated control patients.[300] Two additional case–control studies also demonstrated a significantly lower rate of cryptococcal disease in patients receiving fluconazole for other reasons.[313,314] Only one prospective, randomized trial has specifically evaluated primary prophylaxis.[298] The frequency of cryptococcal infections was approximately 1% in patients receiving oral fluconazole, compared with 7% among patients receiving clotrimazole troches. This overall difference in infection rates was significant and was most pronounced for patients with CD4+ lymphocyte counts of <50 cells/µL. However, no difference in mortality was demonstrated between groups. It must again be emphasized that this finding is applicable only to primary prophylactic therapies and not to regimens for secondary prophylaxis.

Resistance. There are concerns about the emergence of azole-resistant *C. neoformans* strains during prolonged fluconazole prophylaxis. In addition, the cost-effectiveness of prophylaxis for this indication remains to be established.

Pediatric Efficacy. No well-controlled studies have evaluated the effect of prophylaxis of cryptococcal disease in pediatric patients. Recommendations are provided by CDC, USPHS, and IDSA.[283,284]

Recommendation. In the absence of demonstrated survival benefits for prophylaxis and given the concerns about development of azole-resistant strains and cost-effectiveness, prophylaxis of cryptococcal disease should not be routinely recommended for HIV-infected adults.[284] If prophylaxis is to be used, the recommended regimen is fluconazole 200 mg orally every day (Table 6). Although itraconazole 200 mg orally every day is recommended by CDC as an alternative to fluconazole, at least one clinical study has shown fluconazole to be superior to itraconazole in this setting.[315]

Patients should be carefully selected on an individual basis and should be evaluated for factors that may place them at high risk of infection (CD4+ lymphocyte count of <50 cells/µL and residence in an endemic geographic area). (Strength of evidence against prophylaxis = A)

Pediatric Dosage. Primary prophylaxis for cryptococcal disease in pediatric patients is not recommended. As is the case for adults, there are no data on the value of routine prophylaxis of HIV-infected children. Prophylactic use of azole antifungal agents (fluconazole 3–6 mg/kg orally every day or itraconazole 2–5 mg/kg orally every 12–24 hours) may be considered for patients with advanced HIV infection (i.e., CD4+ lymphocyte count of <750 cells/µL for children less than one year of age, <500 cells/µL for children one to five years of age, and <200 cells/µL for children six years of age or older) who live in endemic areas. However, patients should be carefully selected on a case-by-case basis; prophylaxis should not be routinely instituted.

Disseminated *Mycobacterium Avium* Complex Infection in HIV-Infected Persons

Background. Infection with *Mycobacterium avium* complex (MAC) occurs as a late-stage complication of HIV infection. Disseminated, nonpulmonary MAC infection is an AIDS-defining illness and may involve infection of the blood, bone marrow, liver, spleen, GI tract, and other body sites.[316] Disseminated MAC develops in 12–25% of adults with AIDS and is associated with a higher risk of death.[317] Disseminated MAC is also an important opportunistic infection in children and occurs in approximately 6% of children with AIDS; the frequency is somewhat higher (approximately 13%) in children with hemophilia- or transfusion-related HIV infection.[318] Because disseminated MAC commonly occurs in both adults and children with AIDS and is associated with a significant mortality risk, CDC issued formal recommendations for prophylaxis of MAC in 1993; these were updated in 1995 and again in 1997.[284,307,319]

Persons at Risk. Disseminated MAC infection is most common in HIV-infected persons with CD4+ lymphocyte counts of <100 cells/µL; more than 93% of all MAC infections occur in patients with very low CD4+ lymphocyte counts.[316,320] In one study, the median CD4+ lymphocyte count at time of MAC diagnosis was only 13 cells/µL.[320] Two randomized, controlled trials of rifabutin prophylaxis against disseminated MAC disease demonstrated a significantly lower frequency of infection in adult patients with CD4+ lymphocyte counts of <100 cells/µL.[321] The original recommendations, therefore, specified that prophylaxis against MAC infection should be instituted in all HIV-positive adults with CD4+ lymphocyte counts of <100 cells/µL.[319] However, subsequent analysis of the prophylaxis trials revealed that rifabutin prophylaxis was associated with a lower frequency of MAC bacteremia only in patients with CD4+ lymphocyte counts of <50–75 cells/µL; beneficial effects were not significant with CD4+ lymphocyte counts of 75–99 cells/µL.[316]

In children, as in adults, the risk of development of disseminated MAC infection is directly related to decreasing CD4+ lymphocyte counts.[318] However, the median CD4+ lymphocyte count is usually higher than in adults when disseminated MAC disease occurs.[318]

Efficacy. Two randomized, double-blind, placebo-controlled trials established the efficacy of rifabutin for the prophylaxis of disseminated MAC disease in patients with advanced HIV infection.[321] In the first trial, MAC bacteremia developed in 8% of patients receiving rifabutin prophylaxis, compared with 17% of patients receiving placebo. This twofold significant difference in the rate of disseminated MAC disease was also demonstrated in the second study; bacteremia developed in 9% and 18% of patients treated with rifabutin and placebo, respectively. Beneficial effects of rifabutin prophylaxis on symptoms, signs, and laboratory markers of advanced HIV disease were also observed in the treatment groups. However, the difference in survival rates between the rifabutin and placebo groups is unclear; this difference was not significant in the original analysis but was subsequently found to be significant (26% difference in mortality) when complete follow-up data were analyzed at a later date.[322] The overall observed failure rate of rifabutin prophylaxis (8%) and the frequent adverse effects necessitating rifabutin discontinuation (16%) in these studies have tempered enthusiasm for prophylaxis with this agent. In addition, rifabutin has clinically significant drug–drug interactions with the protease inhibitors, making it less than ideal for many persons with advanced HIV infection. Finally, there are concerns about the development of rifamycin resistance among other mycobacterial strains (e.g., *M. tuberculosis*) as a consequence of widespread rifabutin use.

In a randomized, double-blind, placebo-controlled trial of clarithromycin as prophylaxis against disseminated MAC disease in patients with AIDS and CD4+ lymphocyte counts of <100 cells/μL, the rate of MAC infection was 16% in the placebo group but only 6% among patients receiving clarithromycin.[323] Clarithromycin treatment was associated with significantly lower mortality than placebo (32% versus 41%, respectively). The observation that 58% of MAC organisms isolated from patients receiving clarithromycin were subsequently clarithromycin resistant has raised concerns about the long-term suitability of this agent.[316] Clarithromycin has also been shown to be more effective than rifabutin in the prevention of disseminated MAC disease, although a clear survival benefit was not shown.[324] Although associated with fewer drug interactions, clarithromycin is an inhibitor of the cytochrome P-450 system, particularly the 3A isoenzyme, and thus has the potential for causing drug interactions with the protease inhibitors and other agents metabolized by this pathway.[325] Patients should therefore be closely monitored during therapy that includes both clarithromycin and protease inhibitors.

Azithromycin has also been evaluated for the prophylaxis of disseminated MAC disease. A prospective, randomized, double-blind trial compared once-weekly azithromycin, rifabutin, or both agents in combination in high-risk AIDS patients with CD4+ lymphocyte counts of <100 cells/μL.[326] The risk of infection in the azithromycin group was significantly lower than in the rifabutin group (7.6% versus 15.3%, respectively). The risk of infection was even lower with combination therapy (2.8% infection rate); however, dose-limiting adverse effects were significantly more frequent in this group. No survival benefits were demonstrated in any treatment group. The results of this study indicate that azithromycin may also be considered an appropriate agent for the prevention of disseminated MAC disease in high-risk patients.

Resistance. Drug-resistant MAC disease occurred in 58% of persons taking clarithromycin,[323] 11% of persons taking

azithromycin,[326] and no persons taking rifabutin.[321,326] As stated previously, there are concerns about the development of rifamycin resistance among other mycobacterial strains, such as *M. tuberculosis,* because of widespread rifabutin use; as yet there are few data on the relevance of these concerns.

CDC originally recommended rifabutin as the preferred agent for routine MAC prophylaxis.[307] However, rifabutin has several disadvantages, including lack of demonstrated survival benefits in randomized, controlled studies; treatment failures; adverse effect rates; and potentially significant drug interactions. More recent data indicate that clarithromycin and azithromycin are the agents of choice for this indication. Clarithromycin has demonstrated survival benefits, is well tolerated, and is associated with fewer clinically significant drug interactions than rifabutin. Azithromycin also has demonstrated efficacy in reducing the frequency of disseminated MAC disease, has demonstrated efficacy in reducing other bacterial infections, has the potential advantage of once-weekly dosing, is well tolerated, and is not a significant inhibitor of cytochrome P-450. Because of proven and potential benefits of the macrolide antimicrobials, relative to rifabutin, clarithromycin and azithromycin are the preferred agents for primary prophylaxis of disseminated MAC disease. The combination of clarithromycin and rifabutin is no more effective than clarithromycin alone and should not be used. Although possibly more effective than azithromycin monotherapy, the combination of azithromycin and rifabutin is also associated with more adverse effects, higher cost, potential for drug interactions, and disadvantages that affect patient adherence; this combination is therefore not recommended.[284,285]

Pediatric Efficacy. No well-controlled studies have evaluated the effect of prophylaxis in the pediatric population. Recommendations are provided by CDC, USPHS, and IDSA.[283–285]

Recommendation. Prophylaxis against MAC in HIV-infected adults is recommended when the CD4+ lymphocyte count is <50–75 cells/μL (Table 7). The recommended regimen is oral azithromycin 1200 mg weekly or oral clarithromycin 500 mg twice daily. Rifabutin 300 mg every day orally, either alone or in combination with azithromycin, is recommended as an alternative agent. Selection of a specific agent should be based on individual patient characteristics and concurrent medications. (Strength of evidence for prophylaxis = A)

Pediatric Dosage. Although prophylaxis of MAC infection in children has not been rigorously evaluated, primary prophylaxis is presumed to be effective and is recommended in the following groups of children: six years of age or older with a CD4+ lymphocyte count of <50 cells/μL, two to six years of age with a CD4+ lymphocyte count of <75 cells/μL, one to two years of age with a CD4+ lymphocyte count of <500 cells/μL, and less than one year of age with a CD4+ lymphocyte count of <750 cells/μL. Oral azithromycin 20 mg/kg (up to a maximum of 1200 mg) once each week or clarithromycin 7.5 mg/kg (up to a maximum of 500 mg) every 12 hours is the preferred regimen for prophylaxis in these groups. Azithromycin 5 mg/kg (up to a maximum of 250 mg) every day may be used as an alternative. Rifabutin 300 mg every day orally for children 6–12 years old and 5 mg/kg every day orally for children less than 6 years old is recommended as an alternative agent when clarithromycin and azithromycin are poorly tolerated.

P. carinii Pneumonia in HIV-Infected Persons

Background. *P. carinii* pneumonia (PCP) is the most common serious opportunistic infection among HIV-infected persons in the United States. Approximately 51% of all adults and adolescents diagnosed with AIDS between 1982 and 1992 had one or more episodes of PCP. The total number of cases of PCP in the United States is estimated at approximately 60,000 per year.[327] Although the overall percentage of PCP infection among persons with AIDS decreased from 61% to 43% during that time, PCP remained the most common AIDS-defining condition. The annual incidence of PCP was 4.2% in 1985 and decreased to 2.5% in 1991, presumably as a result of widespread, effective efforts at prophylaxis.[328] The most recent CDC recommendations for primary prophylaxis of PCP in both adults and children were issued in 1995.[307,329]

PCP is also the most common AIDS-defining condition among children, being reported in 37% of pediatric AIDS cases reported to CDC through 1992.[318] The incidence of PCP during the first year of life is approximately 12–13%. This incidence has not decreased substantially in spite of the availability of effective prophylaxis, largely because of the failure to identify children born to HIV-infected mothers in time to promptly begin prophylaxis.[330]

PCP is an important cause of mortality among adults with AIDS; the mortality rate for first episodes is approximately 15–18%.[331] Each episode of PCP among adults is associated with a mean hospital stay of 14.4 days at a cost of $13,485.[331] Prophylaxis of PCP has important implications for medical resource use and prevention of morbidity and mortality for HIV-infected persons.

Persons at Risk. Among HIV-infected adults, the risk for developing PCP increases dramatically when the CD4+ lymphocyte count falls below 200 cells/μL. The yearly incidence of PCP is approximately 18% in patients with ≤200 cells/μL, compared with 7% in all HIV-infected persons with a CD4+ lymphocyte count of >200 cells/μL.[332,333] Most cases of PCP occur in persons with CD4+ lymphocyte counts of <50 cells/μL. Although CD4+ lymphocyte counts are the most important marker for risk of development of PCP, unexplained fever (>100 °F for two weeks or more) and oropharyngeal candidiasis have also been identified as independent risk factors for PCP.[332,334]

Among HIV-infected children, the risk of PCP is highest among infants less than one year of age. More than 50% of cases of PCP occur in children of three to six months of age in whom HIV infection was perinatally acquired.[335,336] The need for prophylaxis is difficult to correlate with CD4+ lymphocyte counts in children less than one year of age, and cell counts may fall very rapidly between measurements; children under one year of age are thus considered at high

Table 5.
Prevention of Opportunistic Infection in Nonpediatric and Pediatric Patients with Granulocytopenia or Receiving Bone Marrow Transplant

Infection	Eligible Patients	Recommended Regimen	Alternative Regimens	Strength of Evidence[a]
Bacterial	Patients expected to have granulocyte count of <500/mm³ for ≥7 days	Not recommended[b]	For adult patients, trimethoprim 160 mg with sulfamethoxazole 800 mg p.o. b.i.d., ciprofloxacin 500 mg p.o. b.i.d. or 400 mg i.v. b.i.d., or ofloxacin 200 mg i.v. or p.o. b.i.d.[c]	C
			For pediatric patients, trimethoprim 6–10 mg/kg/day with sulfamethoxazole 30–50 mg/kg/day p.o. (divided into two daily doses)[c]	NA
Fungal	Patients expected to have granulocyte count of <500/mm³ for ≥7 days	Not recommended[d]	For adult patients, fluconazole 400 mg i.v. or p.o. daily or amphotericin B 0.1–0.25 mg/kg/day i.v.[c]	C
			For pediatric patients, fluconazole 3–5 mg/kg/day i.v. or p.o. daily or amphotericin B 0.1–0.25 mg/kg/day i.v.[c]	NA
Viral	Patients with positive cytomegalovirus culture after transplantation	Primary prophylaxis is not recommended	For adult and pediatric patients with bone marrow transplant, secondary prophylaxis (suppressive therapy) includes ganciclovir i.v. for at least 3 mo or acyclovir i.v. for 1 mo followed by oral acyclovir	C[e]

[a]Strength of evidence that supports the use or nonuse of prophylaxis is classified as A (levels I–III), B (levels IV–VI), or C (level VII). Level I evidence is from large, well-conducted randomized, controlled clinical trials. Level II evidence is from small, well-conducted randomized, controlled clinical trials. Level III evidence is from well-conducted cohort studies. Level IV evidence is from well-conducted case–control studies. Level V evidence is from uncontrolled studies that were not conducted. Level VI evidence is conflicting evidence that tends to favor the recommendation. Level VII evidence is expert opinion. Strength-of-evidence classification not applied (NA) to pediatric recommendations.

[b]Exceptions are (1) trimethoprim–sulfamethoxazole for patients at risk (e.g., those with childhood leukemias, histiocytosis, or AIDS) for *Pneumocystis carinii* pneumonitis and (2) quinolones for short periods if the potential for resistant organisms is appreciated and outweighed.

[c]Prophylaxis should start when antineoplastic therapy begins (for patients with hematologic malignancies) or when the conditioning regimen begins (for patients receiving bone marrow transplants) and continue until the granulocyte count exceeds 500 cells/mm³ or until fever occurs. If fever occurs, presumptive therapy with appropriate antimicrobials should be initiated.

[d]If the risk of infection with *Candida albicans* is high but the risk of infection with other *Candida* species is low, then fluconazole may be an option. The significant risks (e.g., increasing the prevalence of non-*albicans Candida* species and other more resistant fungal infections) and the costs associated with those risks should be considered before prophylaxis is started.

[e]Applies to the recommendation against primary prophylaxis for nonpediatric patients.

risk for PCP, regardless of CD4+ lymphocyte counts.[330,336] Correlation of PCP infection with CD4+ lymphocyte counts is more reliable in older children; 84% of children one to five years of age had CD4+ lymphocyte counts of ≤500 cells/mL at the time of PCP diagnosis, and 100% of children six years of age or older had CD4+ lymphocyte counts of ≤200 cells/ mL. The risk of PCP and the need for primary prophylaxis are thus based on CD4+ lymphocyte counts in children one year of age or older.

Efficacy. Randomized, placebo-controlled studies have demonstrated that prophylaxis very effectively reduces the frequency of PCP among HIV-infected adults. Compared with patients receiving no prophylactic therapy in whom PCP infection rates were 29–53% per year, patients receiving PCP prophylaxis had infection rates of 0–5% per year.[337–342] Prophylactic efficacy has been demonstrated for a number of agents and regimens, and current recommendations include several regimens. Although adverse effects have been associated with PCP prophylaxis in 2–40% of patients, the risk of such adverse effects is acceptable compared with the potential benefits. Routine PCP prophylaxis is therefore justified for all patients who meet the indications for prophylaxis.

Recent CDC recommendations list several regimens for prophylaxis of PCP in adults.[284] Trimethoprim–sulfamethoxazole has repeatedly been shown to be extremely effective in patients who can tolerate potential adverse effects of therapy.[337,340,341,343,344] Trimethoprim–sulfamethoxazole is therefore the preferred therapy for PCP prophylaxis because of excellent efficacy, ability to prevent extrapulmonary *Pneumocystis* infection, prophylactic efficacy against both *Toxoplasma gondii* and systemic bacterial infections as well as PCP, and low cost. Other recommended regimens that have shown efficacy comparable to that of trimethoprim–sulfamethoxazole include dapsone, dapsone plus pyrimethamine, and aerosolized pentamidine.[327,338,340]

For persons unable to tolerate trimethoprim–sulfamethoxazole, dapsone is usually preferred over aerosolized pentamidine because of increased efficacy in persons with very low CD4+ lymphocyte counts (<100 cells/μL), ease of administration, lower expense, and efficacy in the prophylaxis of toxoplasmosis. It is worth noting that dapsone prophylaxis is considerably less effective at total daily doses of <100 mg[340]; therefore, persons who do not tolerate dapsone at this dosage should receive either dapsone in combination with pyrimethamine or aerosolized pentamidine. Although previously the preferred agent for PCP prophylaxis, aerosolized pentamidine is now considered an alternative to trimethoprim–sulfamethoxazole because of lesser efficacy in persons with a CD4+ lymphocyte count of <100 cells/μL, higher costs, failure to protect against extrapulmonary *Pneumocystis* infection, and lack of prophylactic efficacy against toxoplasmosis.[284]

Resistance. The inability to culture *P. carinii* has impeded identification of resistance. Although antimicrobial resistance is a potential mechanism for failure of PCP prophylaxis, clinical treatment failures related to the occurrence of drug resistance have not been demonstrated with trimethoprim–sulfamethoxazole[338,340] or aerosolized pentamidine.[338,339]

Pediatric Efficacy. Although no randomized, placebo-controlled trials of PCP prophylaxis have been conducted in children, a recent retrospective study showed that the risk for PCP among children receiving prophylaxis was more than four times lower than in those who were not (yearly infection rate of 4% versus 25%, respectively).[345] Observational studies have also demonstrated a lower frequency of PCP among children who received prophylaxis compared with those who did not.[330] Pediatric recommendations are provided by CDC, USPHS, and IDSA.[284,285]

Recommendation. Primary prophylaxis against PCP in adults is indicated for patients at high risk (HIV-infected adults with CD4+ lymphocyte counts of ≤200 cells/μL, unexplained fever of >100 °F for two or more weeks, or a history of oropharyngeal candidiasis) (Table 7). Trimethoprim 160 mg and sulfamethoxazole 800 mg orally every day is the recommended regimen. Alternatives are trimethoprim 80 mg and sulfamethoxazole 400 mg orally every day, trimethoprim 160 mg and sulfamethoxazole 800 mg orally three times a week, dapsone 50 mg orally twice daily or 100 mg orally every day, dapsone 50 mg orally every day plus pyrimethamine 50 mg orally every week plus leucovorin 25 mg (as the calcium) orally every week, dapsone 200 mg orally every week plus pyrimethamine 75 mg orally every week plus leucovorin 25 mg orally every week, and aerosolized pentamidine isethionate 300 mg/month by Respirgard II nebulizer (Marquest Medical Products). (Strength of evidence for prophylaxis = A)

Pediatric Dosage. Children born to HIV-infected mothers should be administered prophylaxis beginning at four to six weeks of age; prophylaxis should be discontinued if the child is subsequently determined to be HIV-negative. The need for prophylaxis after the age of 12 months is determined on the basis of age-specific CD4+ lymphocyte counts. PCP prophylaxis is indicated for children one to five years of age in whom the CD4+ lymphocyte count falls to ≤500 cells/μL or a CD4+ lymphocyte percentage of <15%. In children 6–12 years of age, PCP prophylaxis is indicated for CD4+ lymphocyte counts of ≤200 cells/μL or a CD4+ lymphocyte percentage of <15%.

Trimethoprim 150 mg/m²/day and sulfamethoxazole 750 mg/m²/day in two divided doses orally three times a week on consecutive days is the preferred regimen in all children between the ages of one month and five years. Alternative dosages are not proven to be effective in this age group and are not recommended. Children 6–12 years of age may receive the preferred regimen administered in a single daily dose; an alternative schedule in this age group is the same dose given daily in two divided doses, or two divided doses three times a week on alternate days. Children unable to tolerate trimethoprim–sulfamethoxazole should receive dapsone 2 mg/kg (not to exceed 100 mg) every day orally, aerosolized pentamidine isethionate 300 mg every month for children five years old or older, or pentamidine isethionate i.v. 4 mg/kg every two to four weeks.

Toxoplasmic Encephalitis in HIV-Infected Persons

Background. Toxoplasmic encephalitis (TE) is one of the most important neurologic complications of HIV infection in adults. Infections due to *T. gondii* are second only to cryptococcal meningitis as common AIDS-related infections of the CNS. Studies from the United States and Europe have shown TE to be the AIDS-defining illness in 5% to 23% of cases.[346,347] TE is associated with early mortality in approximately 16% of patients, and 40–50% of surviving patients will have residual neurologic deficits.[348] Although primary prophylaxis against PCP has been widely adopted for many years, prophylaxis for *T. gondii* infections has not previously been widespread. Improved understanding of the epidemiology of and risk factors for toxoplasmosis, as well as recent studies demonstrating that *Pneumocystis* prophylaxis regimens are also effective against toxoplasmosis, have led to official recommendations for the primary prophylaxis of TE in HIV-infected adults.[284]

Unlike with adults, TE as a complication of AIDS is relatively rare in children. The infection accounted for <1% of AIDS-defining illnesses in pediatric cases reported to CDC through 1992.[346] TE in children is more likely to be the result of maternal–fetal transmission of toxoplasmosis by HIV-infected mothers.[346] Because of the very low frequency, there are currently no formal recommendations for prophylaxis of toxoplasma infections in children.

Persons at Risk. It is believed that *T. gondii* infections in HIV-infected persons are due to reactivation of latent infection originally acquired much earlier in life. The risk of TE is therefore associated with the presence of immunoglobulin G antibodies to *Toxoplasma* that indicate previous infection. Approximately 5–40% of HIV-infected adults are seropositive for *Toxoplasma*[349,350]; the risk of developing TE in this population is approximately 27-fold higher than among HIV-infected persons who are seronegative.[347] HIV-infected persons who are both seropositive for immunoglobulin G to *Toxoplasma* and have CD4+ lymphocyte counts of <100 cells/μL have a 10–50% risk of developing TE.[347,349,351]

Efficacy. Both retrospective and prospective, comparative studies have demonstrated that trimethoprim–sulfamethoxazole effectively prevents the occurrence of TE in high-risk patients. Prophylaxis with trimethoprim 160 mg and sulfamethoxazole 800 mg daily is associated with the development of TE in 0–3% of patients, compared with 33–48% of persons receiving no prophylaxis.[340,348,352-354] Trimethoprim–sulfamethoxazole is preferred for prophylaxis of toxoplasmosis because of its demonstrated efficacy against PCP as well as TE, conferring the ability of a single prophylactic regimen to be effective against two important opportunistic infections.

Dapsone alone appears to be less effective. Although one comparative study showed dapsone to be as effective as trimethoprim–sulfamethoxazole or aerosolized pentamidine,[340] other animal and human studies have had conflicting results regarding dapsone's efficacy for this indication. The combination of dapsone and pyrimethamine appears to be more effective than dapsone alone. Three open, prospective trials demonstrated that dapsone plus pyrimethamine and leucovorin effectively prevents the occurrence of toxoplasmosis, has comparable efficacy to that of trimethoprim–sulfamethoxazole, and is superior to aerosolized pentamidine.[352,353,355,356] In these studies, the frequency of TE in the dapsone–pyrimethamine groups ranged from 0% to 14%, compared with infection rates of 2% in patients receiving trimethoprim–sulfamethoxazole and 25% in patients receiving aerosolized pentamidine. Combination therapy with dapsone plus pyrimethamine is thus appropriate alternative therapy for prophylaxis of TE and PCP in patients unable to tolerate recommended regimens of trimethoprim–sulfamethoxazole.[284]

Pyrimethamine alone is also unacceptable as prophylaxis against TE. Although two studies have shown pyrimethamine to be effective,[357,358] an additional study showed no difference in the frequency of TE between the pyrimethamine-treated group and the placebo group.[359] Additional studies are needed to determine the role of pyrimethamine monotherapy in patients unable to tolerate either trimethoprim–sulfamethoxazole or dapsone-containing regimens for prophylaxis of TE.

Pediatric Efficacy. No well-controlled studies have yet evaluated the efficacy of TE prophylaxis in the pediatric population. Pediatric recommendations are provided by USPHS and IDSA.[284]

Recommendation. Primary prophylaxis against TE in all HIV-infected adults is not routinely recommended. Rather, prophylaxis should be reserved for carefully selected high-risk patients with advanced disease. Avoiding exposure to *T. gondii* is an important aspect of disease prevention. Because the risk of acquiring new strains of *Toxoplasma* is unknown, seropositive and seronegative persons who are infected with HIV should be advised about preventive practices. These include eating red meats only if they have been well cooked; practicing hand washing after gardening, yard work, or other outdoor activities; and, if there is a cat in the household, changing the litter box daily to prevent maturation of infectious oocysts.[346]

Primary prophylaxis against TE is indicated only for HIV-infected patients with advanced disease (CD4+ lymphocyte counts of <100 cells/μL) who are also immunoglobulin G seropositive for *T. gondii* (Table 7). Trimethoprim 160 mg and sulfamethoxazole 800 mg orally every day is the preferred regimen for all patients who are able to tolerate the drug. Alternative dosages are trimethoprim 80 mg and sulfamethoxazole 400 mg orally every day and trimethoprim 160 mg and sulfamethoxazole 800 mg orally three times a week. Dapsone 50 mg orally every day plus pyrimethamine 50 mg every week is an acceptable alternative regimen in patients unable to tolerate trimethoprim–sulfamethoxazole. Leucovorin 25 mg (as the calcium) orally every week may also be administered with this regimen to prevent hematologic toxicity. Dapsone alone, pyrimethamine alone, and aerosolized pentamidine are not recommended as alternative regimens because of insufficient efficacy data or demonstrated inferior efficacy. (Strength of evidence against primary prophylaxis = A)

Pediatric Dosage. Primary prophylaxis against TE in HIV-infected pediatric patients is not recommended. In children with immunoglobulin G antibody seropositive to *T. gondii* and a CD4+ lymphocyte count indicating severe immunosuppression (<12 months of age with CD4+ lymphocyte counts of <750 cells/μL or a CD4+ lymphocyte percentage of <15%, 1–5 years of age with a CD4+ lymphocyte count of <500 cells/μL or a CD4+ lymphocyte percentage of <15%, or 6–12 years of age with a CD4+ lymphocyte count of <200 cells/μL or a CD4+ lymphocyte percentage of <15%), secondary prophylaxis may be an option and should be administered with trimethoprim 150 mg/m^2/day and sulfamethoxazole 750 mg/m^2/day orally every day. An alternative regimen for children one month old and older is dapsone 2 mg/kg or 15 mg/m^2 (not to exceed 25 mg) orally every day plus pyrimethamine 1 mg/kg orally every day plus leucovorin 5 mg (as the calcium) orally every three days.

Table 6.
Prevention of Fungal Infections in Patients Infected with Human Immunodeficiency Virus

Infection	Eligible Patients[a]	Recommended Regimen[b]	Alternative Regimens	Strength of Evidence[c]
Mucocutaneous candidiasis	Adults with CD4+ <50[d]	Not recommended	Fluconazole 100–200 mg p.o. daily	B
	Children 1–5 yr old with CD4+ <500 or ≥6 yr old with CD4+ <200[d]	Not recommended	Nystatin suspension (100,000 units/mL) 4–6 mL p.o. q 6 hr or clotrimazole troches 10 mg p.o. 5 times daily	NA
Disseminated histoplasmosis	Adult residents of endemic area with CD4+ <100[d]	Not recommended	Itraconazole[e] 200 mg p.o. daily	B
	Pediatric residents of endemic area 1–5 yr old with CD4+ <500 or ≥6 yr old with CD4+ <200[d]	Not recommended	Itraconazole[e] 2–5 mg/kg p.o. q 12–24 hr, fluconazole 3–6 mg/kg p.o. q 24 hr	NA
Coccidioidomy-cosis	Adult residents of endemic area with CD4+ <100[d]	Not recommended	Itraconazole[e] 200 mg p.o. daily	B
	Pediatric residents of endemic area 1–5 yr old with CD4+ <500 or ≥6 yr old with CD4+ <200	Not recommended	Itraconazole[e] 2–5 mg/kg p.o. q 12–24 hr, fluconazole 3–6 mg/kg p.o. q 24 hr	NA
Cryptococcal meningitis	Adult residents of endemic area with CD4+ <50[d]	Not recommended	Fluconazole 200 mg p.o. daily or itraconazole 200 mg p.o. daily	A
	Pediatric residents of endemic area 1–5 yr old with CD4+ <500 or ≥6 yr old with CD4+ <200	Not recommended	Fluconazole 3–6 mg/kg p.o. daily or itraconazole 2–5 mg/kg p.o. q 12–24 hr	NA

[a]Criteria are for patients infected with the human immunodeficiency virus. CD4+ = CD4+ lymphocyte count (cells/μL).

[b]Refer to recommendation of Centers for Disease Control and Prevention for detailed information and dosage for children younger than one year (reference 284).

[c]Strength of evidence that supports the use or nonuse of prophylaxis is classified as A (levels I–III), B (levels IV–VI), or C (level VII). Level I evidence is from large, well-conducted randomized, controlled clinical trials. Level II evidence is from small, well-conducted randomized, controlled clinical trials. Level III evidence is from well-conducted cohort studies. Level IV evidence is from well-conducted case–control studies. Level V evidence is from uncontrolled studies that were not well conducted. Level VI evidence is conflicting evidence that tends to favor the recommendation. Level VII evidence is expert opinion. Strength-of-evidence classification not applied (NA) to pediatric recommendations.

[d]Patients should be carefully selected and therapy instituted on an individual basis.

[e]Oral solution may be the preferred dosage form.

CMV Disease in HIV-Infected Persons

Background. CMV is the cause of significant morbidity and mortality among persons with advanced HIV disease. CMV disease, manifested either as retinitis or involvement of other organs, was the AIDS-defining illness in 9.4% of AIDS cases in adults and 9.3% of cases in children reported to CDC through 1992.[360] CMV retinitis occurs in approximately 25–40% of all adults with AIDS.[361,362] However, the true importance of CMV in HIV-infected patients is better illustrated by the fact that 75–90% of patients examined at autopsy have evidence of CMV infection of the retina, brain, GI tract, lungs, or adrenal glands.[363,364] Further, CMV is an immediate cause of death in 30% of patients dying of AIDS-related complications.[365] Prevention and effective management of CMV disease is clearly an important issue in the treatment of HIV-infected persons.

Persons at Risk. Although primary infection may occur in HIV-infected persons, CMV disease usually represents a reactivation of latent infection; 95–98% of homosexual men and injection drug users with HIV infection are seropositive for antibodies to CMV at the time of diagnosis.[366] Reactivation of CMV infection is closely related to the degree of HIV-associated immunosuppression. HIV-infected persons with CD4+ lymphocyte counts of <200 cells/μL are at increased risk of developing CMV disease, while those with CD4+ lymphocyte counts of <100 cells/μL are at even greater risk.[365,367] Retinitis due to CMV occurs primarily in patients with CD4+ lymphocyte counts of <50 cells/μL; the median time to development of retinitis in adults with this advanced degree of HIV disease is six months.[368] Viremia has also been demonstrated to be a significant predictor of

the development of CMV disease in HIV-infected patients. One study demonstrated the probability of patients with CMV viremia developing CMV disease to be nearly 80% within one year of the first positive blood culture; these patients had a 22-fold higher risk of CMV disease than HIV-infected patients without viremia.[369] Measurements of CMV viral load may also be of value in the identification of high-risk patients. Detection and quantitation of CMV DNA in plasma by polymerase chain reaction have been demonstrated to be more useful than either urine or blood cultures in identifying patients at high risk for later developing CMV disease.[370]

Routine prophylaxis of CMV disease is not yet recommended. However, prophylaxis for HIV-infected adults with CD4+ lymphocyte counts of <50 cells/μL and who are also seropositive for antibodies to CMV may be considered for selected patients.[284] Further information about the use of CMV viral load data to identify high-risk patients will be available in the future and may also eventually assist clinicians with decisions to institute CMV prophylaxis.

Efficacy. High-dose oral acyclovir is not effective in preventing CMV. A double-blind, placebo-controlled trial of oral acyclovir 800 mg orally four times a day demonstrated virtually no difference in the occurrence of CMV disease between treated and placebo groups.[371] However, a prospective, randomized, double-blind, placebo-controlled study evaluating the efficacy of ganciclovir for preventing CMV disease yielded some impressive results.[372] Patients enrolled in this study, nearly 90% of whom had CD4+ lymphocyte counts of <50 cells/μL, were randomly assigned to receive either ganciclovir 1000 mg orally three times a day or placebo. The study was stopped after a median follow-up

Table 7.
Prevention of Opportunistic Infection in Patients Infected with Human Immunodeficiency Virus[a]

Infection	Eligible Patients[b]	Recommended Regimen	Alternative Regimens	Strength of Evidence[c]
Disseminated *Mycobacterium avium* complex	Adults with CD4+ <50–75	Azithromycin 1200 mg p.o. weekly or clarithromycin 500 mg p.o. b.i.d.	Rifabutin 300 mg p.o. daily with or without azithromycin 1200 mg p.o. weekly	A
	Children 6–12 yr old with CD4+ <50	Azithromycin 20 mg/kg (maximum 1200 mg) p.o. weekly or clarithromycin 7.5 mg/kg (maximum 500 mg) p.o. q 12 hr	Rifabutin 300 mg p.o. daily or azithromycin 5 mg/kg (maximum 250 mg) p.o. daily	NA
	Children 2–6 yr old with CD4+ <75, 1–2 yr old with CD4+ <500, or <1 yr old with CD4+ <750	Azithromycin 20 mg/kg (maximum 1200 mg) p.o. weekly or clarithromycin 7.5 mg/kg (maximum 500 mg) p.o. q 12 hr	Rifabutin 5 mg/kg p.o. daily when suspension available or azithromycin 5 mg/kg (maximum 250 mg) p.o. daily	NA
PCP	Adult or adolescent >2 yr old with CD4+ ≤200, unexplained fever for ≥2 wk, or history of oropharyngeal candidiasis	TMP 160 mg and SMX 800 mg p.o. daily, TMP 80 mg and SMX 400 mg p.o. daily, or TMP 160 mg and SMX 800 mg p.o. thrice weekly	Dapsone 50 mg p.o. b.i.d. or 100 mg p.o. daily; dapsone 50 mg p.o. daily plus pyrimethamine 50 mg and leucovorin 25 mg p.o. weekly; dapsone 200 mg, pyrimethamine 75 mg, and leucovorin 25 mg p.o. weekly; or aerosolized pentamidine 300 mg monthly via Respirgard II nebulizer	A
	Children 6–12 yr old not previously receiving PCP prophylaxis with CD4+ ≤200 or <15%	TMP 150 mg/m^2/day and SMX 750 mg/m^2/day p.o. in 2 divided doses thrice weekly on consecutive days, in single daily dose thrice weekly on consecutive days, in 2 divided doses daily, or in 2 divided doses thrice weekly on alternate days	Dapsone 2 mg/kg (maximum 100 mg) p.o. daily, pentamidine 4 mg/kg i.v. q 2–4 wk, or aerosolized pentamidine 300 mg monthly via Respirgard II nebulizer	NA
	Children 1–5 yr old not previously receiving PCP prophylaxis with CD4+ ≤500 or <15%	TMP 150 mg/m^2/day and SMX 750 mg/m^2/day p.o. in 2 divided doses thrice weekly on consecutive days	Dapsone 2 mg/kg (maximum 100 mg) p.o. daily or pentamidine 4 mg/kg i.v. q 2–4 wk	NA
Toxoplasma gondii encephalitis	Adult with IgG antibody seropositive for *Toxoplasma* and CD4+ <100	Primary prophylaxis not recommended	TMP 160 mg and SMX 800 mg p.o. daily, TMP 80 mg and SMX 400 mg p.o. daily, TMP 160 mg and SMX 800 mg p.o. thrice weekly, or dapsone 50 mg p.o. daily, pyrimethamine 50 mg, leucovorin 25 mg p.o. weekly, and SMX 750 mg/m^3/day	A[d]
	Children ≥6 yr old with IgG antibody seropositive for *Toxoplasma* and CD4+ <200 or <15% or 1–5 yr old with IgG antibody seropositive for *Toxoplasma* and CD4+ <500 or <15%	Primary prophylaxis not recommended	TMP 150 mg/m^2/day p.o. in 2 divided daily doses, or dapsone 2 mg/kg or 15 mg/m^2 (maximum 25 mg) p.o. daily, pyrimethamine 1 mg/kg p.o. daily, and leucovorin 5 mg p.o. q 3 days	NA
CMV disease	Adult with CD4+ <50 and positive for CMV antibody	Primary prophylaxis not recommended	Ganciclovir 1000 mg p.o. t.i.d.	B[d]
	Children ≥6 yr old with CD4+ <200 or <15% and positive for CMV antibody or 1–5 yr old with CD4+ <500 or <15% and positive for CMV antibody	Primary prophylaxis not recommended	Oral ganciclovir under investigation but not yet recommended for use	NA
Primary HSV	Adult and pediatric patients susceptible to HSV as determined by seronegativity for antibody to HSV	Primary prophylaxis not recommended	None	C[e]

Continued on next page

Table 7 (continued)

Infection	Eligible Patients[b]	Recommended Regimen	Alternative Regimens	Strength of Evidence[c]
Primary VZV	Adult and pediatric patients suceptible to VZV as determined by having no prior VZV infection, by being seronegative for antibody to VZV, and having no history of significant exposure to persons with active varicella or herpes zoster	Primary prophylaxis not recommended	Immunoprophylaxis in susceptible patients[f]	C[e]

[a]CD4+ = CD4+ lymphocyte count (cells/µL), TMP = trimethoprim, SMX = sulfamethoxazole, PCP = *Pneumocystis carinii* pneumonia, IgG = immunoglobulin G, CMV = cytomegalovirus, HSV = herpes simplex virus, VZV = varicella zoster virus.
[b]Criteria are for patients infected with the human immunodeficiency virus.
[c]Strength of evidence that supports the use or nonuse of prophylaxis is classified as A (levels I–III), B (levels IV–VI), or C (level VII). Level I evidence is from large, well-conducted randomized, controlled clinical trials. Level II evidence is from small, well-conducted randomized, controlled clinical trials. Level III evidence is from well-conducted cohort studies. Level IV evidence is from well-conducted case–control studies. Level V evidence is from uncontrolled studies that were not well conducted. Level VI evidence is conflicting evidence that tends to favor the recommendation. Level VII evidence is expert opinion. Strength-of-evidence classification not applied (NA) to pediatric recommendations.
[d]For primary prophylaxis.
[e]Against primary prophylaxis in nonpediatric patients.
[f]Refer to recommendation of Centers for Disease Control and Prevention for detailed information (reference 284).

period of 367 days when interim analysis revealed that the rates of both overall CMV disease and CMV retinitis were 50% lower among patients receiving ganciclovir. Although not significant, there was also a trend toward a higher rate of survival among patients receiving ganciclovir.

Oral ganciclovir may prove to have an important role in the prevention of CMV disease. However, the routine use of ganciclovir is not yet recommended because of several concerns. An unpublished study showed that oral ganciclovir does not prevent CMV disease. However, there were methodological differences between the two studies. First, in the study by Spector, et al.,[372] patients underwent dilated ophthalmoscope examination at regular intervals, while Crumpacker[373] defined endpoints clinically. Second, as with prophylaxis of various fungal infections, there are additional concerns about the true mortality benefits of prophylaxis, the toxicity of oral ganciclovir, the development of ganciclovir-resistant CMV strains during long-term ganciclovir therapy, and the cost-effectiveness of routine prophylaxis. Although oral ganciclovir is promising, until these concerns have been adequately addressed, the routine use of ganciclovir prophylaxis in HIV-infected patients at risk of CMV disease cannot be advocated.

Resistance. There are no data on the development of resistance with prophylaxis against CMV. However, ganciclovir-resistant CMV strains during long-term ganciclovir therapy have been reported.[281,282]

Pediatric Efficacy. No well-controlled studies have yet evaluated the effect of prophylaxis for CMV in pediatric patients. Pediatric recommendations are not provided by CDC, USPHS, or IDSA.[284]

Recommendation. Primary prophylaxis of CMV disease is not routinely recommended because of insufficient data demonstrating clinical efficacy versus benefits and concerns about the development of drug-resistant CMV strains during long-term antiviral use. The use of oral ganciclovir 1000 mg three times a day has been recommended in carefully selected patients who are seropositive for antibodies to CMV and have advanced HIV infection (CD4+ lymphocyte count

of <50 cells/µL) (Table 7). (Strength of evidence against primary prophylaxis = B)

Pediatric Dosage. Primary prophylaxis against CMV is not recommended for pediatric patients. Primary prophylaxis with ganciclovir may eventually be an option for patients who are seropositive for antibodies to CMV and have severe immunosuppression. Although currently under study, the efficacy of oral ganciclovir for primary prophylaxis is not yet demonstrated to be beneficial in children and is not recommended at this time.

Herpes Simplex and Varicella-Zoster Virus Infections in HIV-Infected Persons

Background. HSV infections are common in all populations. In adults in the United States, seroprevalence rates are >80% for HSV-1 (oral mucosal lesions) and 20–30% for HSV-2 (genital lesions).[360] In HIV-infected persons, reactivation of HSV occurs frequently and can result in chronic mucocutaneous disease; however, disseminated HSV disease occurs rarely.[374] Varicella-zoster virus (VZV) is the cause of varicella or chickenpox, a childhood disease that occurs in more than 90% of persons. Although VZV infection in HIV-negative children is usually self-limiting and without complication, primary infections in HIV-infected children and adults may be associated with severe disease that may occasionally be fatal (usually because of pulmonary complications).[360] Adults with HIV infection are approximately nine times more likely than HIV-negative persons to develop recurrent VZV (herpes zoster or shingles).[375] Because seroprevalence of both HSV and VZV are so common in the general population, measures to prevent primary infection with these viruses are valid only for HIV-infected individuals who are still seronegative.

Persons at Risk. HSV reactivation is common in HIV-infected persons. Reactivation appears more common with HSV-2 than with HSV-1, and reactivation of both strains appears to be relatively independent of the stage of HIV disease.[360] Severe mucocutaneous HSV disease does not commonly appear until advanced HIV disease (CD4+ lymphocyte count of <100 cells/µL) is present. There are no known risk factors for more severe complications of reactivated HSV infection (meningitis, encephalitis).[360] Maternally transmitted primary HSV infections in children are not usually clinically serious, but features of reactivated HSV are similar to those seen in HIV-infected adults.

No other clear risk factors for herpes zoster in HIV-infected persons have yet been identified,[360] although there appears to be an association between a decreasing CD4+ lymphocyte count and the severity of VZV disease in HIV-infected children.[376]

Efficacy. Other than measures designed to prevent exposure to HSV, no other strategies have been proven effective in the prevention of primary HSV infections. The role of acyclovir or other antiviral agents in the prophylaxis of primary HSV infections is unknown; therefore chemoprophylaxis of HSV is not recommended. This is particularly true in light of the frequent occurrence (11–17% of patients) of acyclovir-resistant HSV in HIV-infected persons receiving long-term acyclovir therapy.[377]

Although data from controlled studies are lacking, CDC has issued recommendations that varicella-zoster immune globulin (VZIG) be administered to susceptible (no history of prior infection or VZV seronegative) HIV-infected adults after significant exposure to persons with active VZV infections.[284] The need for VZIG should be evaluated on an individual basis according to the HIV-infected patient's medical condition and the degree of exposure. Significant exposure is defined as more than one hour of household contact or exposure to a VZV-infected patient in the same room or an adjacent bed.[284] When indicated, VZIG should be administered within 96 hours after exposure. Other forms of antiviral chemoprophylaxis have not been adequately studied and are not recommended. In addition, use of the live-attenuated varicella vaccine for prevention of primary VZV infection is not recommended because of a lack of efficacy and safety studies in HIV-infected persons.[284]

Resistance. There are no data on the development of resistance as a result of primary prophylaxis against HSV or VZV. Acyclovir-resistant HSV is most commonly reported in severely immunocompromised patients and infrequently in immunocompetent patients with extended treatment courses.[182]

Pediatric Efficacy. Although data from controlled studies are lacking, CDC, USPHS, and IDSA have issued recommendations that VZIG be administered to susceptible (no history of prior infection or VZV seronegative) HIV-infected children after significant exposure to persons with active VZV infections.[284]

Recommendation. Primary chemoprophylaxis for HSV and VZV is not recommended. Because severe HSV disease in all age groups is a result of reactivation rather than primary infection, and because HSV-2 reactivation is much more problematic than HSV-1, prophylaxis efforts are directed toward prevention of primary infections in persons seronegative for antibodies to HSV-2.[307,360] This is most effectively accomplished through the use of latex condoms by sexually active HIV-infected adults rather than chemoprophy-

laxis.[283,307] HIV-infected persons with no reliable history of VZV infection or documented seronegativity for antibodies to VZV are possibly susceptible to primary infection and should avoid exposure to individuals with either varicella or herpes zoster.[360]

Because of the increased severity of primary VZV infection in HIV-infected adults, susceptible persons should be administered VZIG after significant exposure to persons with active varicella or herpes zoster.[283,307] For detailed information on immunoprophylaxis, readers are referred to the CDC guidelines.[284] No other forms of prophylaxis are indicated. (Strength of evidence against primary prophylaxis = C)

Pediatric Dosage. Primary chemoprophylaxis for HSV and VZV is not recommended for pediatric patients. Because of the higher severity of primary VZV infection in HIV-infected children, susceptible persons should be administered VZIG after significant exposure to persons with active varicella or herpes zoster.[284] For detailed information on immunoprophylaxis, readers are referred to the CDC guidelines.[284] No other forms of prophylaxis are indicated.

References

1. ASHP Commission on Therapeutics Task Force. ASHP therapeutic guidelines on nonsurgical antimicrobial prophylaxis. *Clin Pharm.* 1990; 9:423–45.
2. Dotson LR, Witmer DR. Development of ASHP therapeutic guidelines. *Am J Health-Syst Pharm.* 1995; 52:254–5.
3. Taketomo CK, Hodding JH, Kraus DM. Pediatric dosage handbook. Hudson, OH: Lexi-Comp; 1996.
4. Koren G, Prober CG, Gold R, eds. Antimicrobial therapy in infants and children. New York: Marcel Dekker; 1988.
5. Roberts NJ, Douglas RG. Gentamicin use and *Pseudomonas* and *Serratia* resistance: effect of a surgical prophylaxis regimen. *Antimicrob Agents Chemother.* 1978; 13:214–20.
6. Bartlett J, Condon R, Gorbach S, et al. Veterans Administration Cooperative Study on bowel preparation for elective colorectal operations: impact of oral antibiotic regimen on colonic flora, wound irrigation cultures and bacteriology of septic complications. *Ann Surg.* 1978; 188:249–54.
7. Rozenberg-Arska M, Dekker AW, Verhoef J. Ciprofloxacin for selective decontamination of the alimentary tract in patients with acute leukemia during remission induction treatment: the effect on fecal flora. *J Infect Dis.* 1985; 152:104–7.
8. Harrison GA, Stross WP, Rubin MP, et al. Resistance in oral streptococci after repeated three-dose erythromycin prophylaxis. *J Antimicrob Chemother.* 1985; 15:471–9.
9. Murray BE, Rensimer ER, DuPont HL. Emergence of high-level trimethoprim resistance in fecal *Escherichia coli* during oral administration of trimethoprim or trimethoprim-sulfamethoxazole. *N Engl J Med.* 1982; 306:130–5.
10. Kern WV, Andriof E, Oethinger M, et al. Emergence of fluoroquinolone-resistant *Escherichia coli* at a cancer center. *Antimicrob Agents Chemother.* 1994; 38:681–7.
11. Dupeyron C, Mangeney N, Sedrati L, et al. Rapid emergence of quinolone resistance in cirrhotic patients

treated with norfloxacin to prevent spontaneous bacterial peritonitis. *Antimicrob Agents Chemother.* 1994; 38:340–4.

12. Tetteroo GWM, Wagenvoort JHT, Bruining HA. Bacteriology of selective decontamination: efficacy and rebound colonization. *J Antimicrob Chemother.* 1994; 34:139–48.

13. Kotilainen P, Nikoskelainen J, Huovinen P. Emergence of ciprofloxacin-resistant coagulase-negative staphylococcal skin flora in immunocompromised patients receiving cipro-floxacin. *J Infect Dis.* 1990; 161:41–4.

14. Kauffman CA, Liepman MK, Bergman AG, et al. Trimethoprim/sulfamethoxazole prophylaxis in neutropenic patients. Reduction of infections and effect on bacterial and fungal flora. *Am J Med.* 1983; 74:599–607.

15. Weinstein JW, Roe M, Towns M, et al. Resistant enterococci: a prospective study of prevalence, incidence, and factors associated with colonization in a university hospital. *Infect Control Hosp Epidemiol.* 1996; 17:36–41.

16. Kunova A, Trupl J, Kremery V Jr. Low incidence of quinolone resistance in gram-negative bacteria after five-years use of ofloxacin in prophylaxis during afebrile neutropenia. *J Hosp Infect.* 1996; 32:155–60. Letter.

17. Preheim L, Rimland D, Bittner M. Methicillin-resistant *Staphylococcus aureus* in Veterans Administration Medical Centers. *Infect Control.* 1987; 8:191–4.

18. Thornsberry C. Methicillin-resistant staphylococci. *Clin Lab Med.* 1989; 9:255–67.

19. Panlilio AL, Culver DH, Gaynes RP, et al. Methicillin-resistant *Staphylococcus aureus* in US hospitals, 1975–1991. *Infect Control Hosp Epidemiol.* 1992; 13:582–6.

20. Centers for Disease Control and Prevention. Nosocomial enterococci resistant to vancomycin—United States, 1989–1993. *MMWR.* 1993; 42:597–9.

21. Centers for Disease Control and Prevention. Recommendations for preventing the spread of vancomycin resistance: recommendations of the Hospital Infection Control Practices Advisory Committee (HICPAC). *MMWR.* 1994; 44:1–13.

22. Scheld WM, Sande MA. Endocarditis and intravascular infections. In: Mandell GL, Bennett JE, Dolan R eds. Principles and practice of infectious diseases, 4th ed. New York: Churchill Livingstone; 1995:740–99.

23. Durack DT, Phil D. Prevention of infective endocarditis. *N Engl J Med.* 1995; 332:38–44.

24. Von Reyn CF, Levy BS, Arbeit RD, et al. Infective endocarditis: an analysis based on strict case definitions. *Ann Intern Med.* 1981; 94:505–18.

25. Durack DT, Phil D. Current issues in prevention of infective endocarditis. *Am J Med.* 1985; 78:149–56.

26. Mansur AJ, Grinberg M, da Luz PL, et al. The complications of infective endocarditis. A reappraisal in the 1980s. *Arch Intern Med.* 1992; 152:2428–32.

27. Tornos MP, Permanyer-Miralda G, Olona M, et al. Long-term complications of native valve infective endocarditis in non-addicts. A 15-year follow-up study. *Ann Intern Med.* 1992; 117:567–72.

28. Dajani AS, Bisno AL, Chung KJ, et al. Prevention of bacterial endocarditis. Recommendations by the American Heart Association. *JAMA.* 1990; 264:2919–22.

29. Dajani AS, Taubert KA, Wilson W, et al. Prevention of

bacterial endocarditis. Recommendations by the American Heart Association. *JAMA.* 1997; 277:1794–801.

30. Prevention of bacterial endocarditis. *Med Lett Drugs Ther.* 1989; 31:12.

31. Simmons NA. Recommendations for endocarditis prophylaxis. The Endocarditis Working Party for Antimicrobial Chemotherapy. *J Antimicrob Chemother.* 1993; 31:437–8.

32. Woods R. FDI Commission Working Group. Antibiotic prophylaxis for infective endocarditis. *Int Dent J.* 1994; 44(3):215–22.

33. Mani V, Cartwright K, Dooley J, et al. Antibiotic prophylaxis in gastrointestinal endoscopy: a report by a working party for the British Society of Gastroenterology Endoscopy Committee. *Endoscopy.* 1997; 29:114–9.

34. Rossiter SJ, Stinson EB, Oyer PE, et al. Prosthetic valve endocarditis. *J Thorac Cardiovasc Surg.* 1978; 76:795–803.

35. Kaye D. Prophylaxis for infective endocarditis: an update. *Ann Intern Med.* 1986; 104:419–23.

36. Mandell GL, Douglas RG Jr, Bennet JE, eds. Principles and practice of infectious diseases. New York: Wiley; 1995.

37. Antunes MJ, Sanches MF, Fernandes LE. Antibiotic prophylaxis and prosthetic valve endocarditis. *J Heart Valve Dis.* 1992; 1:201–5.

38. Devereux RB, Frary CJ, Kramer-Fox R, et al. Cost-effectiveness of infective endocarditis prophylaxis for mitral valve prolapse with or without a mitral regurgitant murmer. *Am J Cardiol.* 1994; 74:1024–9.

39. Imperiale TF, Horwitz R. Does prophylaxis prevent postdental infective endocarditis? A controlled evaluation of protective efficacy. *Am J Med.* 1990; 88:131–6.

40. Vander Meer JM, Van Wijk W, Thompson J, et al. Efficacy of antibiotic prophylaxis for prevention of native-valve endocarditis. *Lancet.* 1992; 339:135–9.

41. Durack DT, Phil D, Kaplan EL, et al. Apparent failures of endocarditis prophylaxis. Analysis of 52 cases submitted to a national registry. *JAMA.* 1983; 250:2318–22.

42. Fleming P, Feigal RJ, Kaplan EL, et al. The development of penicillin-resistant oral streptococci after repeated penicillin prophylaxis. *Oral Surg Oral Med Oral Pathol.* 1990; 70:440–4.

43. Baltas I, Tsoulfa S, Sakellariou P, et al. Posttraumatic meningitis: bacteriology, hydrocephalus and outcome. *Neurosurgery.* 1994; 35:422–7.

44. Calvert CA, Cairns H. Discussion on injuries of the frontal and ethmoidal sinuses. *Proc R Soc Med.* 1942; 35:805–10.

45. Chandra RK. Immunocompetence in undernutrition. *J Pediatr.* 1972; 81:1194.

46. Eljamel MS, Foy PM. Acute traumatic CSF fistulae: the risk of intracranial infection. *Br J Neurosurg.* 1990; 4:381–5.

47. Dagi TF, Meyer FB, Poletti CA. The incidence and prevention of meningitis after basilar skull fracture. *Am J Emerg Med.* 1983; 3:295–8.

48. MacGee EE, Cauthen JC, Brackett CE. Meningitis following acute traumatic cerebrospinal fluid fistula. *J Neurosurg.* 1976; 33:312–6.

49. Mandell GL, Douglas RG Jr, Bennett JE, eds. Principles and practice of infectious diseases. New York: Wiley; 1995.

50. Klatersky J, Sadeghi M, Brihaye J. Antimicrobial prophylaxis in patients with rhonorrhoea or otorrhea; a double blind study. *Surg Neurol.* 1976; 6:111–4.

51. Ignelzi RJ, VanderArk GD. Analysis of the treatment of basilar skull fractures with and without antibiotics. *J Neurosurg.* 1975; 43:721–6.

52. Ignelzi RJ, VanderArk GD. Cerebral mucormycosis following open head trauma. *J Neurosurg.* 1975; 42:593–6.

53. Leech PJ, Paterson A. Conservative and operative management for cerebrospinal-fluid leakage after closed head injury. *Lancet.* 1973; 1:1013–6.

54. Brodie HA. Prophylactic antibiotics for posttraumatic cerebrospinal fluid fistulae. A meta-analysis. *Arch Otolaryngol Head Neck Surg.* 1997; 123:749–52.

55. Einhorn A, Mizrahi EM. Basilar skull fractures in children. The incidence of CNS infection and the use of antibiotics. *Am J Dis Child.* 1978; 132:1121–4.

56. Kollef MH. Ventilator-associated pneumonia. A multivariate analysis. *JAMA.* 1993; 270:1965–70.

57. Centers for Disease Control and Prevention. Guidelines for prevention of nosocomial pneumonia. *MMWR.* 1997; 46:1–77.

58. Kerver AJH, Rommes JH, Mevissen-Verhage AE, et al. Prevention of colonization and infection in critically ill patients: a prospective study. *Crit Care Med.* 1988; 16:1087–93.

59. Ledingham IM, Alcock SR, Eastaway AT, et al. Triple regimen of selective decontamination of the digestive tract, systemic cefotaxime, and microbiological surveillance for prevention of acquired infection in intensive care. *Lancet.* 1988; 1:785–90.

60. Ferrer M, Torres A, Gonzalez J, et al. Utility of selective digestive decontamination in mechanically ventilated patients. *Ann Intern Med.* 1994; 120:389–95.

61. Saunders GL, Hammond JM, Potgieter PD, et al. Microbiological surveillance during selective decontamination of the digestive tract (SDD). *J Antimicrob Chemother.* 1994; 34:529–44.

62. Sijpkens YW, Buurke EJ, Ulrich C, et al. *Enterococcus faecalis* colonisation and endocarditis in five intensive care patients as late sequelae of selective decontamination. *Intensive Care Med.* 1995; 21:231–4.

63. Hammond JM, Potgieter PD, Saunders GL, et al. Double-blind study of selective decontamination of the digestive tract in intensive care. *Lancet.* 1992; 340:5–9.

64. Rocha LA, Martin MJ, Pita S, et al. Prevention of nosocomial infection in critically ill patients by selective decontamination of the digestive tract. A randomized, double-blind, placebo-controlled study. *Intensive Care Med.* 1992; 18:398–404.

65. Vincent JL, Bihari DJ, Suter PM, et al. The prevalence of nosocomial infection in intensive care units in Europe. Results of the European Prevalence of Infection in Intensive Care Study. EPIC International Advisory Committee. *JAMA.* 1995; 274:639–44.

66. Langlois-Karaga A, Bues-Charbita J, Davignon A, et al. Selective digestive decontamination in multiple trauma patients: cost and efficacy. *Pharm World Sci.* 1995; 17:12–6.

67. Gastinne H, Wolff M, Delatour F, et al. A controlled trial in intensive care units of selective decontamination of the digestive tract with nonabsorbable antibiotics. The French Study Group on Selective Decontami-nation of the Digestive Tract. *N Engl J Med.* 1992; 326:594–9.

68. Apte NM, Karnad DR, Medhedar TP, et al. Gastric colonization and pneumonia in intubated critically ill patients receiving stress ulcer prophylaxis: a randomized, controlled trial. *Crit Care Med.* 1992; 20:590–3.

69. Prod'hom G, Leuenberger P, Koerfer J, et al. Nosocomial pneumonia in mechanically ventilated patients receiving antacid, ranitidine, or sucralfate as prophylaxis for stress ulcer. A randomized controlled trial. *Ann Intern Med.* 1994; 120:653–62.

70. Mustafa NA, Akturk G, Ozen I, et al. Acute stress bleeding prophylaxis with sucralfate versus ranitidine and incidence of secondary pneumonia in intensive care unit patients. *Intensive Care Med.* 1995; 21:287.

71. Martin LF, Booth FV, Karlstadt RG, et al. Continuous intravenous cimetidine decreases stress-related upper gastrointestinal hemorrhage without promoting pneumonia. *Crit Care Med.* 1993; 21:19–30.

72. Ryan P, Dawson J, Teres D, et al. Nosocomial pneumonia during stress ulcer prophylaxis with cimetidine and sucralfate. *Arch Surg.* 1993; 128:1353–7.

73. Thomason MH, Payseur ES, Hakenewerth AM, et al. Nosocomial pneumonia in ventilated trauma patients during stress ulcer prophylaxis with sucralfate, antacid, and ranitidine. *J Trauma.* 1996; 41:503–8.

74. Mahul PH, Auboyer C, Jospe R, et al. Prevention of nosocomial pneumonia in intubated patients: respective role of mechanical subglottic secretions drainage and stress ulcer prophylaxis. *Intensive Care Med.* 1992; 18:20–5.

75. Pickworth KK, Falcone RE, Hoogeboom JE, et al. Occurrence of nosocomial pneumonia in mechanically ventilated trauma patients: a comparison of sucralfate and ranitidine. *Crit Care Med.* 1993; 21:1856–62.

76. Cook DJ, Reeve BK, Guyatt GH, et al. Stress ulcer prophylaxis in critically ill patients. Resolving discordant meta-analysis. *JAMA.* 1996; 275:308–14.

77. Stoutenbeek CP, Van Saene HK, Miranda DR, et al. The effect of selective decontamination of the digestive tract on colonisation and infection rate in multiple trauma patients. *Intensive Care Med.* 1984; 10:185–92.

78. Borthen L, Heimdahl A, Nord CE. Comparison between two non-absorbable antibiotic regimens for decontamination of the oropharynx. *Infection.* 1984; 12:349–54.

79. Stoutenbeek CP, Van Saene HKF, Miranda DR, et al. The effect of oropharyngeal decontamination using topical nonabsorbable antibiotics in the incidence of nosocomial respiratory tract infections in multiple trauma patients. *J Trauma.* 1987; 27:357–64.

80. Unertl K, Ruckdeschl G, Selman HK, et al. Prevention of colonization and respiratory infections in long-term ventilated patients by local antimicrobial prophylaxis. *Intensive Care Med.* 1987; 13:106–13.

81. Van Uffelen R, Rommes JH, Van Saene HKF. Preventing lower airway colonization and infection in mechanically ventilated patients. *Crit Care Med.* 1987; 15:99–102.

82. Hammond JM, Potgieter PD. Is there a role for selective decontamination of the digestive tract in primarily infected patients in the ICU? *Anaesth Intensive Care.*

1995; 23:168–74.

83. Korinek AM, Laisne MJ, Nicolas MH, et al. Selective decontamination of the digestive tract in neurosurgical intensive care unit patients: a double-blind, randomized, placebo-controlled study. *Crit Care Med.* 1993; 21:1466–73.

84. Pugin J, Auckenthaler R, Lew DP, et al. Oropharyngeal decontamination decreases incidence of ventilator-associated pneumonia. A randomized, placebo-controlled, double-blind clinical trial. *JAMA.* 1991; 265:2704–10.

85. Kollef MH. The role of selective digestive tract decontamination on mortality and respiratory tract infections. A meta-analysis. *Chest.* 1994; 105:1101–8.

86. Nardi G, Valentinis U, Proietti A, et al. Epidemiological impact of prolonged systematic use of topical SDD on bacterial colonization of the tracheobronchial tree and antibiotic resistance. A three-year study. *Intensive Care Med.* 1993; 19:273–8.

87. Hammond JM, Potgieter PD. Long-term effects of selective decontamination on antimicrobial resistance. *Crit Care Med.* 1995; 23:637–45.

88. Centers for Disease Control and Prevention. Update: influenza activity—worldwide, 1995. *JAMA.* 1995; 274:1005–7.

89. Centers for Disease Control and Prevention. Prevention and control of influenza: recommendations of the advisory committee on immunization practices (ACIP). *MMWR.* 1997; 46:1–25.

90. Togo Y, Hornick RB, Dawkins AT. Studies on induced influenza in man. Double-blind study designed to assess the prophylactic efficacy of an analogue of amantadine hydrochloride against A2/Rockville/1/65 strain. *JAMA.* 1968; 203:87–92.

91. Dawkins AT, Gallager LR, Togo Y, et al. Studies on induced influenza in man. Double-blind study designed to assess the prophylactic efficacy of an analogue of amantadine hydrochloride. *JAMA.* 1968; 203:93–7.

92. Monto AS, Gunn RA, Bandyk MG, et al. Prevention of Russian influenza by amantadine. *JAMA.* 1979; 241:1003–7.

93. Pettersson RF, Hellstrom PE, Penttinen K, et al. Evaluation of amantadine in the prophylaxis of influenza A (H1N1) virus infection: a controlled field trial among young adults and high-risk patients. *J Infect Dis.* 1980; 142:377–83.

94. Dolin R, Reichman RC, Madore HP, et al. A controlled trial of amantadine and rimantadine in the prophylaxis of influenza A infection. *N Engl J Med.* 1982; 307:580–4.

95. Reuman PD, Bernstein DI, Keefer MC, et al. Efficacy and safety of low dosage amantadine hydrochloride as prophylaxis for influenza A. *Antiviral Res.* 1989; 11:27–40.

96. Douglas RG. Prophylaxis and treatment of influenza. *N Engl J Med.* 1990; 322:443–50.

97. Belshe RB, Burk B, Newman F, et al. Resistance of influenza A virus to amantadine and rimantadine: results of one decade of surveillance. *J Infect Dis.* 1989; 159:430–5.

98. Hayden FG, Belshe RB, Clover RD, et al. Emergence and apparent transmission of rimantadine-resistant influenza A in families. *N Engl J Med.* 1989; 321:1696–702.

99. Degelau J, Somani SK, Cooper SL, et al. Amantadine-resistant influenza A in a nursing facility. *Arch Intern Med.* 1992; 152:390–2.

100. Clover RD, Crawford SA, Abell TD, et al. Effectiveness of rimantadine prophylaxis of children within families. *Am J Dis Child.* 1986; 140:706–9.

101. Crawford SA, Clover RD, Abell TD, et al. Rimantadine prophylaxis in children: a follow-up study. *Pediatr Infect Dis J.* 1988; 7:379–83.

102. Quilligan JJ, Hirayama M, Baernstein HD. The suppression of A2 influenza in children by the chemoprophylactic use of amantadine. *J Pediatr.* 1966; 69:572–5.

103. Krogstad DJ. Plasmodium species (malaria). In: Mandell GL, Douglas RG Jr, Bennett JE, eds. Principles and practice of infectious diseases. New York: Wiley; 1995:2414–27.

104. White NJ. The treatment of malaria. *N Engl J Med.* 1996; 335:800–6.

105. Salako LA, Adio RA, Walker O, et al. Mefloquine-sulphadoxine-pyrimethamine (Fansimef, Roche) in the prophylaxis of *Plasmodium falciparum* malaria: a double-blind, comparative, placebo-controlled study. *Ann Trop Med Parasitol.* 1992; 86:575–81.

106. Watanasook C, Singharaj P, Suriyamongkol V, et al. Malaria prophylaxis with doxycycline in soldiers deployed to the Thai-Kampuchean border. *Southeast Asian J Trop Med Public Health.* 1989; 20:61–4.

107. Bunnag D, Malikul S, Chittamas S, et al. Fansimef for prophylaxis of malaria: a double-blind randomized placebo controlled trial. *Southeast Asian J Trop Med Public Health.* 1992; 23:777–82.

108. Boudreau EF, Pang LW, Chaikummao S, et al. Comparison of mefloquine, chloroquine plus pyrimethamine-sulfadoxine (Fansidar), and chloroquine as malarial prophylaxis in eastern Thailand. *Southeast Asian J Trop Med Public Health.* 1991; 22:183–9.

109. Fryauff DJ, Baird JK, Basri H, et al. Randomized placebo-controlled trial of primaquine for prophylaxis of falciparum and vivax malaria. *Lancet.* 1995; 346:1190–3.

110. Baird JK, Fryauff DJ, Basri H, et al. Primaquine for prophylaxis against malaria among nonimmune transmigrants in Irian Jaya, Indonesia. *Am J Trop Med Hyg.* 1995; 52:479–84.

111. Centers for Disease Control and Prevention. Prescription drugs for malaria. CDC document 221012. 1995 Nov 28.

112. Weiss WR, Oloo AJ, Johnson A, et al. Daily primaquine is effective for prophylaxis against falciparum malaria in Kenya: comparison with mefloquine, doxycycline, and chloroquine plus proguanil. *J Infect Dis.* 1995; 171:159–75.

113. American Academy of Pediatrics. Red book: report of the Committee on Infectious Diseases. 24th ed. Elk Grove Village, IL: American Academy of Pediatrics; 1997.

114. Hoge CW, Shlim DR, Echeverria P, et al. Epidemiology of diarrhea among expatriate residents living in a highly endemic environment. *JAMA.* 1996; 275:533–8.

115. Castelli F, Carosi G. Epidemiology of traveler's diarrhea. *Chemotherapy.* 1995; 41(suppl 1):20–32.

116. Travelers' diarrhea. Consensus conference. *JAMA.* 1985; 253:2700–4.

117. Centers for Disease Control and Prevention. Food and

water and traveler's diarrhea. CDC document 220004. 1993 Mar 25.

118. DuPont HL, Galindo E, Evans DG, et al. Prevention of travelers' diarrhea with trimethoprim-sulfamethoxazole and trimethoprim alone. *Gastroenterology.* 1983; 84:75–80.

119. Sack RB. Antimicrobial prophylaxis of travelers' diarrhea: a summary of studies using doxycycline or trimethoprim and sulfamethoxazole. *Scand J Gastroenterol.* 1983; 84:111–7.

120. Sack RB. Antimicrobial prophylaxis of travelers' diarrhea: a selected summary. *Rev Infect Dis.* 1986; 8:S160–6.

121. Pichler H, Diridl G, Wolf D. Ciprofloxacin versus placebo in the treatment of acute bacterial diarrhea. Paper presented at 14th International Congress of Chemotherapy. Kyoto, Japan; 1985 Jun 23–28.

122. Rademaker CM, Hoepelman IM, Wolfhagen MJ, et al. Results of a double-blind, placebo-controlled study using ciprofloxacin for prevention of travelers' diarrhea. *Eur J Clin Microbiol Infect Dis.* 1989; 8:690–4.

123. Parry H, Howard AJ, Galpin OP, et al. The prophylaxis of travellers' diarrhoea; a double-blind, placebo-controlled trial of ciprofloxacin during a Himalayan expedition. *J Infect.* 1994; 28:337–8. Letter.

124. Johnson PC, Ericsson CD, Morgan DR, et al. Prophylactic norfloxacin for acute travelers' diarrhea. *Clin Res.* 1984; 32:870A. Abstract.

125. Scott DA, Haberberger RL, Thornton SA, et al. Norfloxacin for the prophylaxis of travelers' diarrhea in U.S. military personnel. *Am J Trop Med Hyg.* 1990; 42:160–4.

126. DuPont HL, Ericsson CD, Johnson PC, et al. Use of bismuth subsalicylate for the prevention of travelers' diarrhea. *Rev Infect Dis.* 1990; 12:S64–7.

127. Echeverria P, Sack RB, Blacklow NR, et al. Prophylactic doxycycline for travelers' diarrhea in Thailand. *Am J Epidemiol.* 1984; 120:912–21.

128. Centers for Disease Control and Prevention. Tuberculosis morbidity—United States, 1996. *MMWR.* 1997; 46:695–700.

129. Cohn DL. Treatment and prevention of tuberculosis in HIV-infected persons. *Infect Dis Clin North Am.* 1994; 8:399–412.

130. Centers for Disease Control and Prevention. Screening for tuberculosis and tuberculosis infection in high-risk populations. Recommendations of the Advisory Council for the Elimination of Tuberculosis. *MMWR.* 1995; 44:19–34.

131. American Academy of Pediatrics Committee on Infectious Diseases. Chemotherapy for tuberculosis in infants and children. *Pediatrics.* 1992; 89:161–5.

132. Wolinsky E. Statement of the Tuberculosis Committee of the Infectious Diseases Society of America. *Clin Infect Dis.* 1993; 16:627–8.

133. Essentials of tuberculosis control for the practising physician. Tuberculosis Committee, Canadian Thoracic Society. *Can Med Assoc J.* 1994; 150:1561–71.

134. American Society of Health-System Pharmacists. ASHP therapeutic position statement on strategies for preventing and treating multidrug-resistant tuberculosis. *Am J Health-Syst Pharm.* 1997; 54:428–31.

135. Centers for Disease Control and Prevention. The use of preventive therapy for tuberculous infection in the United States. Recommendations of the Advisory Committee for Elimination of Tuberculosis. *MMWR.* 1990; 39:9–12.

136. Starke JR, Correa AG. Management of mycobacterial infection and disease in children. *Pediatr Infect Dis J.* 1995; 14:455–70.

137. Ad Hoc Committee of the Scientific Assembly on Microbiology, Tuberculosis and Pulmonary Infections. Treatment of tuberculosis and tuberculosis infection in adults and children. *Clin Infect Dis.* 1995; 21:9–27.

138. Centers for Disease Control and Prevention. Management of persons exposed to multidrug-resistant tuberculosis. *MMWR.* 1992; 42:61–71.

139. Tokars JI, Marcus R, Culver DH, et al. Surveillance of HIV infection and zidovudine use among health care workers after occupational exposure to HIV-infected blood. *Ann Intern Med.* 1993; 118:913–9.

140. Henderson DK, Fahey BJ, Willy M, et al. Risk for occupational transmission of human immunodeficiency virus type 1 (HIV-1) associated with clinical exposures: a prospective evaluation. *Ann Intern Med.* 1990; 113:740–6.

141. Gerberding JL. Management of occupational exposures to blood-borne viruses. *N Engl J Med.* 1995; 332:444–51.

142. Petrosillo N, Puro V, Jagger J, et al. The Italian multicenter study on nosocomial and occupational risk of infections in dialysis. The risks of occupational exposure and infection by human immunodeficiency virus, hepatitis B virus, and hepatitis C virus in the dialysis setting. *Am J Infect Control.* 1995; 23:278–85.

143. Gerberding JL. Risks to health care workers from occupational exposure to hepatitis B virus, human immunodeficiency virus, and cytomegalovirus. *Infect Dis Clin North Am.* 1989; 3:735–45.

144. Cardo DM, Culver DH, Ciesielski CA, et al. CDC and Prevention Needlestick Surveillance Group. *N Engl J Med.* 1997; 337:1485–90.

145. Durand E, LeJeunne C, Hughes FC. Failure of prophylactic zidovudine after suicidal self-inoculation of HIV-infected blood. *N Engl J Med.* 1991; 324:1062.

146. Jones PD. HIV transmission by stabbing despite zidovudine prophylaxis. *Lancet.* 1991; 338:884.

147. Lange JMA, Boucher CAB, Hollak CEM, et al. Failure of zidovudine prophylaxis after accidental exposure to HIV-1. *N Engl J Med.* 1990; 332:1375–7.

148. Looke DFM, Grove DI. Failed prophylactic zidovudine after needlestick injury. *Lancet.* 1990; 335:1280.

149. Puro V, Ippolito G, Guzzanti E, et al. Zidovudine prophylaxis after accidental exposure to HIV: the Italian experience. *AIDS.* 1992; 6:963–9.

150. LaFon SW, Mooney BD, McMullen JP, et al. A double-blind, placebo-controlled study of the safety and efficacy of Retrovir (zidovudine, ZDV) as a chemoprophylactic agent in health care workers (HCW) exposed to HIV. 30th Interscience Conference on Antimicrobial Agents and Chemotherapy. Washington, DC: American Society for Microbiology; 1990:167. Abstract.

151. Hammer SM, Katzenstein DA, Hughes MD, et al., for the AIDS Clinical Trials Group Study 175 Study Team. A trial comparing nucleoside monotherapy with combination therapy in HIV-infected adults with CD4 cell counts from 200 to 500 per cubic millimeter. *N Engl J Med.* 1996; 335:1081–90.

152. Berry P, Kahn J, Cooper R, et al. Antiretroviral activity and safety of indinavir (IDV) alone and in combination

with zidovudine (ZDV) in ZDV-naive patients with CD4 cell counts of 50–500 cells/mm³. XI International Conference on AIDS. Vancouver, British Columbia, Canada; 1996 Jul 7–12. Abstract.

153. Gulick R, Mellors J, Havlir D, et al. Potent and sustained antiretroviral activity of indinavir in combination with zidovudine and lamivudine. Third Conference on Retroviruses and Opportunistic Infections. Washington, DC; 1996 Jan 28 to Feb 1. Abstract.

154. Gulick R, Mellors J, Havlir D, et al. Potent and sustained antiretroviral activity of indinavir (IDV), zidovudine (ZDV) and lamivudine (3TC). XI International Conference on AIDS. Vancouver, British Columbia, Canada; 1996 Jul 7–12. Abstract.

155. Carpenter CC, Fischl MA, Hammer SM, et al. Antiretroviral therapy for HIV infection in 1997. Updated recommendations of the International AIDS Society-USA Panel. *JAMA.* 1997; 277:1962–9.

156. Centers for Disease Control and Prevention. Update: provisional recommendations for chemoprophylaxis after occupational exposure to human immunodeficiency virus. *MMWR.* 1996; 45:468–72.

157. Centers for Disease Control and Prevention. Public Health Service guidelines for the management of health-care worker exposures to HIV and recommendations for postexposure prophylaxis. *MMWR.* 1998; 47:1–35.

158. Carpenter CCJ, Fischl MA, Hammer SM, et al. Antiretroviral therapy for HIV infection in 1996 [recommendations of an international panel]. *JAMA.* 1996; 276:146–54.

159. Niu MT, Stein DS, Schnittmann SM. Primary human immunodeficiency virus type 1 infection: review of pathogenesis and early treatment interventions in humans and animal retrovirus infections. *J Infect Dis.* 1993; 168:1490–501.

160. Centers for Disease Control and Prevention. Recommendations for the use of zidovudine to reduce perinatal transmission of human immunodeficiency virus. *MMWR.* 1994; 43:1–20.

161. Working Group on Mother-to-Child Transmission of HIV-1 in Africa, America, and Europe: results from 13 perinatal studies. *J Acquir Immune Defic Syndr.* 1995; 8:506–10.

162. Frenkel LM, Wagner LE II, Demeter LM, et al. Effects of zidovudine use during pregnancy on resistance and vertical transmission of human immunodeficiency virus type 1. *Clin Infect Dis.* 1995; 20:1321–6.

163. Connor EM, Sperling RS, Gelber R, et al. Reduction of maternal-infant transmission of human immunodeficiency virus type 1 with zidovudine treatment. *N Engl J Med.* 1994; 331:1173–80.

164. Mofenson L. Epidemiology and determinants of vertical HIV transmission. *Semin Pediatr Infect Dis.* 1994; 5:252–65.

165. Landesman SH, Kalish LA, Burns DN, et al. Obstetrical factors and the transmission of human immunodeficiency virus type I from mother to child. *N Engl J Med.* 1996; 334:1617–23.

166. Matheson PB, Abrams EJ, Thomas PA, et al. Efficacy of antenatal zidovudine in reducing perinatal transmission of human immunodeficiency virus type 1. *J Infect Dis.* 1995; 172:353–8.

167. Dickover RE, Garratty EM, Herman SA, et al. Identification of levels of maternal HIV-1 RNA associated with risk of perinatal transmission. Effect of maternal zidovudine treatment on viral load. *JAMA.* 1996; 275:599–605.

168. Sperling RS, Shapiro DE, Coombs RW, et al. Maternal viral load, zidovudine treatment, and the risk of transmission of human immunodeficiency virus type-1 from mother to infant. *N Engl J Med.* 1996; 335:1621–9.

169. Centers for Disease Control and Prevention. Public Health Service Task Force recommendations for the use of antiretroviral drugs in pregnant women infected with HIV-1 for maternal health and for reducing perinatal HIV-1 transmission in the United States. *MMWR.* 1998; 47(RR-2):1–30.

170. Boyer PJ, Dillon M, Navaie M, et al. Factors predictive of maternal-fetal transmission of HIV-1. Preliminary analysis of zidovudine given during pregnancy and/or delivery. *JAMA.* 1994; 271:1925–30.

171. Fiscus SA, Adimora AA, Schoenbach VJ, et al. Perinatal HIV infection and the effect of ZDV therapy on transmission in rural and urban counties. *JAMA.* 1996; 275:1483–8.

172. Simpson BJ, Shapiro ED, Andiman WA. Reduction in the risk of vertical transmission of HIV-1 associated with treatment of pregnant women with orally administered zidovudine alone. *J Acquir Immune Defic Syndr Hum Retrovirol.* 1997; 14:145–52.

173. Kumar RN, Hughes PF, Khurranna A. Zidovudine use during pregnancy: a report on 104 cases and the occurrence of birth defects. *J Acquir Immune Defic Syndr.* 1994; 7:1034–9.

174. Ferrazin A, De Maria A, Gotta C, et al. Zidovudine therapy of HIV-1 infection during pregnancy: assessment of the effect on the newborns. *J Acquir Immune Defic Syndr.* 1993; 6:376–9.

175. Overall JC. Herpes simplex virus infection of the fetus and newborn. *Pediatr Ann.* 1994; 23:131–6.

176. American Academy of Pediatrics and American College of Obstetricians and Gynecologists. Guidelines for perinatal care. 4th ed. 1997.

177. Scott LL, Sanchez PJ, Jackson GL, et al. Acyclovir supression to prevent cesarean delivery after first-episode genital her-pes. *Obstet Gynecol.* 1996; 87:69–73.

178. Randolph AG, Washington AE, Prober CG. Cesarean delivery for women presenting with genital herpes lesions. Efficacy, risks, and costs. *JAMA.* 1993; 270:77–82.

179. Stray-Pedersen B. Acyclovir in late pregnancy to prevent neonatal herpes simplex. *Lancet.* 1990; 336:756.

180. Haddad J, Langer B, Astruc D, et al. Oral acyclovir and recurrent genital herpes during late pregnancy. *Obstet Gynecol.* 1993; 82:102–4.

181. Centers for Disease Control and Prevention. Pregnancy outcomes following systemic prenatal acyclovir exposure—June 1, 1984–June 30, 1993. *MMWR.* 1993; 42:806–9.

182. Wagstaff AJ, Faulds D, Goa KL. Aciclovir. A reappraisal of its antiviral activity, pharmacokinetic properties and therapeutic efficacy. *Drugs.* 1994; 47:153–205.

183. Walsh JA, Hutchins S. Group B streptococcal disease: its importance in the developing world and prospect for prevention with vaccines. *Pediatr Infect Dis J.* 1989; 8:271–6.

184. Boyer KM, Gotoff SP. Antimicrobial prophylaxis of neonatal group B streptococcal sepsis. *Clin Perinatol.* 1988; 15:831–50.

185. American Academy of Pediatrics Committee on Infec-

tious Diseases and Committee on Fetus and Newborn: guidelines for prevention of group B streptococcal (GBS) infection by chemoprophylaxis. *Pediatrics.* 1992; 90:775–8.

186. Mohle-Boetani JC, Schuchat A, Plikaytis BD, et al. Comparison of prevention strategies for neonatal group B streptococcal infection. A population-based economic analysis. *JAMA.* 1993; 270:1442–8.

187. Prevention of perinatal group B streptococcal disease: a public health perspective. *MMWR.* 1996; 45:1–24.

188. Boyer KM, Gotoff SP. Prevention of early-onset neonatal group B streptococcal disease with selective intrapartum chemoprophylaxis. *N Engl J Med.* 1986; 314:1665–9.

189. Easmon CSF, Hastings MJG, Deeley J, et al. The effect of intrapartum chemoprophylaxis on the vertical transmission of group B streptococci. *Br J Obstet Gynaecol.* 1983; 90:633–5.

190. Morales WJ, Lim DV, Walsh AF. Prevention of neonatal group B streptococcal sepsis by the use of a rapid screening test and selective intrapartum chemoprophylaxis. *Am J Obstet Gynecol.* 1986; 155:979–83.

191. Teres FO, Matorras R, Perea AG, et al. Prevention of neonatal group B streptococcal sepsis. *Pediatr Infect Dis J.* 1987; 6:874.

192. Allen UD, Navas L, King SM. Effectiveness of intrapartum penicillin prophylaxis in preventing early onset group B streptococcal infection: results of a meta-analysis. *Can Med Assoc J.* 1993; 149:1659–65.

193. McDuffie RS Jr, McGregor JA, Gibbs RS. Adverse perinatal outcome and resistant Enterobacteriaceae after antibiotic usage for premature rupture of the membranes and group B streptococcus carriage. *Obstet Gynecol.* 1993; 82:487–9.

194. American College of Obstetricians and Gynecologists Committee on Obstetric Practice. Prevention of early-onset group B streptococcal disease in newborns. Committee opinion. Danvers, MA: Copyright Clearance Center; 1996 Jun. ISSN 1074–861X.

195. Pizzo PA. Management of fever in patients with cancer and treatment-induced neutropenia. *N Engl J Med.* 1993; 328:1323–32.

196. Infectious Diseases Society of America. Guidelines for use of antimicrobial agents in neutropenic patients with unexplained fever. *J Infect Dis.* 1990; 161:381–96.

197. Uzun O, Anaissie EJ. Antifungal prophylaxis in patients with hematologic malignancies: a reappraisal. *Blood.* 1995; 86:2063–72.

198. Guiot HF, Fibbe WE, van't Wout JW. Risk factors for fungal infection in patients with malignant hematologic disorders: implications for empirical therapy and prophylaxis. *Clin Infect Dis.* 1994; 18:525–32.

199. Body GP, Buckley M, Sathe YS, et al. Quantitative relationships between circulating leukocytes and infections in patients with acute leukemia. *Ann Intern Med.* 1966; 64:328–40.

200. Lieschke GJ, Burgess AW. Granulocyte colony-stimulating factor and granulocyte-macrophage colony-stimulating factor. *N Engl J Med.* 1992; 327:99–106.

201. Klastersky J. Prevention and therapy of fungal infections in cancer patients. A review of recently published information. *Support Care Cancer.* 1995; 3:393–401.

202. Rowe JM, Ciobanu N, Ascensao J, et al. Recommended guidelines for the management of autologous and allogeneic bone marrow transplantation. A report from the Eastern Cooperative Oncology Group (ECOG). *Ann Intern Med.* 1994; 120:143–58.

203. Hughes WT, Armstrong D, Bodey GP, et al. 1997 guidelines for the use of antimicrobial agents in neutropenic patients with unexplained fever. *Clin Infect Dis.* 1997; 25:551–73.

204. Dekker AW, Rozenberg-Arska M, Sixma JJ, et al. Prevention of infection with trimethoprim/sulfamethoxazole plus amphotericin B in patients with acute nonlymphocytic leukemia. *Ann Intern Med.* 1981; 95:555–9.

205. Gualtieri RJ, Donowitz GR, Kaiser DL, et al. Double-blind randomized study of prophylactic trimethoprim/sulfamethoxazole in granulocytopenic patients with hematologic malignancies. *Am J Med.* 1983; 74:934–40.

206. Gurwith MJ, Brunton JL, Lank BA, et al. A prospective controlled investigation of prophylactic trimethoprim-sulfamethoxazole in hospitalized granulocytopenic patients. *Am J Med.* 1979; 66:248–56.

207. Pizzo PA, Robichaud KH, Edwards BK, et al. Oral antibiotic prophylaxis in patients with cancer: a double-blind randomized placebo-controlled trial. *J Pediatr.* 1983; 102:125–33.

208. Karp JE, Merz WG, Hendricksen C, et al. Oral norfloxacin for prevention of gram-negative bacterial infections in patients with acute leukemia and granulocytopenia. *Ann Intern Med.* 1987; 106:1–7.

209. Yamada T, Dan K, Nomura T. Prevention of bacterial and fungal infection in acute leukemia patients: a new and potent combination of oral norfloxacin and amphotericin B. *Intern Med.* 1993; 32:710–5.

210. Teinturier C, Hartmann O, Lemerle J, et al. Prevention of gram-positive infections in patients treated with high-dose chemotherapy and bone marrow transplantation: a randomized, controlled trial of vancomycin. *Pediatr Hematol Oncol.* 1995; 12:73–7.

211. Lamy T, Michelet C, Dauriac C, et al. Benefit of prophylaxis by intravenous systemic vancomycin in granulocytopenic patients: a prospective, randomized trial among 59 patients. *Acta Haematologica.* 1993; 90:109–13.

212. Attal M, Schlaifer D, Rubie H, et al. Prevention of gram-positive infections after bone marrow transplantation by systemic vancomycin: a prospective, randomized trial. *J Clin Oncol.* 1991; 9:865–70.

213. Vassilomanolakis M, Plataniotis G, Koumakis G, et al. Central venous catheter-related infections after bone marrow transplantation in patients with malignancies: a prospective study with short-course vancomycin prophylaxis. *Bone Marrow Transplant.* 1995; 15:77–80.

214. Lim SH, Smith MP, Machin SJ, et al. A prospective randomized study of prophylactic teicoplanin to prevent early Hickman catheter-related sepsis in patients receiving intensive chemotherapy for haematological malignancies. *Eur J Haematol.* 1993; 54:10–3.

215. Arning M, Wolf HH, Aul C, et al. Infection prophylaxis in neutropenic patients with acute leukaemia—a randomized, comparative study with ofloxacin, ciprofloxacin and cotrimoxazole/colistin. *J Antimicrob Chemother.* 1990; 26:137–42.

216. Bow EJ, Rayner E, Scott BA, et al. Selective gut decontamination with nalidixic acid or trimethoprim/sulfamethoxazole for infection prophylaxis in neutropenic cancer patients: relationship of efficacy to anti-

microbial spectrum and timing of administration. *Antimicrob Agents Chemother.* 1987; 31:551–7.

217. Bow EJ, Rayner E, Louie TJ. Comparison of norfloxacin with cotrimoxazole for infection prophylaxis in acute leukemia. *Am J Med.* 1988; 84:847.

218. Dekker AW, Rozenberg-Arska M, Verhoef J. Infection prophylaxis in acute leukemia: a comparison of ciprofloxacin with trimethoprim/sulfamethoxazole and colistin. *Ann Intern Med.* 1987; 106:7–12.

219. Donnelly JP, Maschmeyer G, Daenen S. Selective oral antimicrobial prophylaxis for the prevention of infection in acute leukaemia—ciprofloxacin versus co-trimoxazole plus colistin. The EORTC-Gnotobiotic Project Group. *Eur J Cancer.* 1992; 28A:873–8.

220. Imrie KR, Prince HM, Couture F, et al. Effect of antimicrobial prophylaxis on hematopoietic recovery following autologous bone marrow transplantation: ciprofloxacin versus co-trimoxazole. *Bone Marrow Transplant.* 1995; 15:267–70.

221. Kern W, Kurrle E. Ofloxacin versus trimethoprim-sulfamethoxazole for prevention of infection in patients with acute leukemia and granulocytopenia. *Infection.* 1991; 19:73–80.

222. Lew MA, Kehoe K, Ritz J, et al. Prophylaxis of bacterial infections with ciprofloxacin in patients undergoing bone marrow transplantation. *Transplantation.* 1991; 51:630–6.

223. Lew MA, Kehoe K, Ritz J, et al. Ciprofloxacin versus trimethoprim/sulfamethoxazole for prophylaxis of bacterial infections in bone marrow transplant recipients: a randomized, controlled trial. *J Clin Oncol.* 1995; 13:239–50.

224. Liang RH, Yung RW, Chan TK, et al. Ofloxacin versus cotrimoxazole for prevention of infection in neutropenic patients following cytotoxic chemotherapy. *Antimicrob Agents Chemother.* 1990; 34:215–8.

225. Orlandi E, Navarra A, Cruciani M, et al. Norfloxacin versus cotrimoxazole for infection prophylaxis in granulocytopenic patients with acute leukemia. A prospective randomized study. *Haematologica.* 1990; 75:296–8.

226. Wade JC, DeJongh CA, Newman KA, et al. Selective antimicrobial modulation as prophylaxis against infection during granulocytopenia: trimethoprim/sulfamethoxazole vs. nalidixic acid. *J Infect Dis.* 1983; 147:624–34.

227. D'Antonio D, Iacone A, Fioritoni G, et al. Comparison of norfloxacin and pefloxacin in the prophylaxis of bacterial infection in neutropenic cancer patients. *Drugs Exp Clin Res.* 1992; 18:141–6.

228. D'Antonio D, Piccolomini R, Iacone A, et al. Comparison of ciprofloxacin, ofloxacin and pefloxacin for the prevention of the bacterial infection in neutropenic patients with haematological malignancies. *J Antimicrob Chemother.* 1994; 33:837–44.

229. Prevention of bacterial infection in neutropenic patients with hematologic malignancies. A randomized, multicenter trial comparing norfloxacin with ciprofloxacin. The GIMEMA Infection Program. Gruppo Italiano Malattie Ematologiche Maligne dell'Adulto. *Ann Intern Med.* 1991; 115:7–12.

230. Broun ER, Wheat JL, Kneebone PH, et al. Randomized trial of the addition of gram-positive prophylaxis to standard antimicrobial prophylaxis for patients undergoing autologous bone marrow transplantation.

Antimicrob Agents Chemother. 1994; 38:576–9.

231. Fanci R, Leoni F, Bosi A, et al. Chemoprophylaxis of bacterial infections in granulocytopenic patients with ciprofloxacin vs ciprofloxacin plus amoxicillin. *J Chemother.* 1993; 5:119–23.

232. Reduction of fever and streptococcal bacteremia in granulocytopenic patients with cancer. A trial of oral penicillin V or placebo combined with pefloxacin. International Antimicrobial Therapy Cooperative Group of the European Organization for Research and Treatment of Cancer. *JAMA.* 1994; 272:1183–9.

233. Kern WV, Hay B, Kern P, et al. A randomized trial of rox-ithromycin in patients with acute leukemia and bone marrow transplant recipients receiving fluoroquinolone prophylaxis. *Antimicrob Agents Chemother.* 1994; 38:465–72.

234. Winston DJ, Ho WG, Nakao SL, et al. Norfloxacin vs. vancomycin/polymixin for prevention of infections in granulocytopenic patients. *Am J Med.* 1986; 80:884–90.

235. Winston DJ, Ho WG, Bruckner DA, et al. Ofloxacin versus vancomycin/polymixin for prevention of infections in granulocytopenic patients. *Am J Med.* 1990; 88:36–42.

236. Cruciani M, Rampazzo R, Malena M, et al. Prophylaxis with fluoroquinolones for bacterial infections in neutropenic patients: a meta-analysis. *Clin Infect Dis.* 1996; 23:795–805.

237. Ward TT, Thomas RG, Fye CL, et al. Trimethoprim sulfamethoxazole prophylaxis in granulocytopenic patients with acute leukemia: evaluation of serum antibiotic levels in a randomized, double-blind, placebo-controlled Department of Veterans Affairs Cooperative Study. *Clin Infect Dis.* 1993; 17:323–32.

238. Wilson JM, Guiney DG. Failure of oral trimethoprim/sulfamethoxazole prophylaxis in acute leukemia. *N Engl J Med.* 1982; 306:16–20.

239. Murray BE, Rensimer ER, DuPont HL. Emergence of high-level trimethoprim resistance in fecal *Escherichia coli* during oral administration of trimethoprim or trimethoprim/sulfamethoxazole. *N Engl J Med.* 1982; 306:130–5.

240. Giuliano M, Pantosti A, Gentile G, et al. Effects of oral and intestinal microfloras of norfloxacin and pefloxacin for selective decontamination in bone marrow transplant patients. *Antimicrob Agents Chemother.* 1989; 33:1709–13.

241. Classen DC, Burke JP, Ford CD, et al. *Streptococcus mitis* sepsis in bone marrow transplant patients receiving oral antimicrobial prophylaxis. *Am J Med.* 1990; 89:441–6.

242. Carratala J, Fernandez-Sevilla A, Tubau F, et al. Emergence of quinolone-resistant *Escherichia coli* bacteremia in neutropenic patients with cancer who have received prophylactic norfloxacin. *Clin Infect Dis.* 1995; 20:557–60.

243. Avril M, Hartmann O, Valteau-Couanet D, et al. Antiinfective prophylaxis with ceftazidime and teicoplanin in children undergoing high-dose chemotherapy and bone marrow transplantation. *Pediatr Hematol Oncol.* 1994; 11:63–73.

244. Cruciani M, Concia E, Navarra A, et al. Prophylactic cotrimoxazole versus norfloxacin in neutropenic children—prospective randomized study. *Infection.* 1989; 17:65–9.

245. Egger T, Gratwohl A, Tichelli A, et al. Comparison of

fluconazole with oral polyenes in the prevention of fungal infections in neutropenic patients. A prospective, randomized, single-center study. *Support Care Cancer.* 1995; 3:139–46.

246. Ellis ME, Clink H, Ernst P, et al. Controlled study of fluconazole in the prevention of fungal infections in neutropenic patients with haematological malignancies and bone marrow transplant recipients. *Eur J Clin Microbiol Infect Dis.* 1994; 13:3–11.

247. Philpott-Howard NJ, Wade JJ, Mufti GJ, et al.Randomized comparison of oral fluconazole versus oral polyenes for the prevention of fungal infection in patients at risk of neutropenia. Multicentre Study Group. *J Antimicrob Chemother.* 1993; 31:973–84.

248. Quirk PC, Osborne PJ, Walsh LJ. Australian Dental Research Fund Trebitsch Scholarship. Efficacy of antifungal prophylaxis in bone marrow transplantation. *Aust Dent J.* 1995; 40:267–70.

249. Riley DK, Pavia AT, Beatty PG, et al.The prophylactic use of low-dose amphotericin B in bone marrow transplant patients. *Am J Med.* 1994; 97:509–14.

250. Perfect JR, Klotman ME, Gilbert CC, et al. Prophylactic intravenous amphotericin B in neutropenic autologous bone marrow transplant recipients. *J Infect Dis.* 1992; 165:891–7.

251. Chandrasekar PH, Gatney CM. Effect of fluconazole prophylaxis on fever and use of amphotericin in neutropenic cancer patients. Bone Marrow Transplantation Team. *Chemotherapy.* 1994; 40:136–43.

252. Hansen RM, Reinerio N, Sohnle PG, et al. Ketoconazole in the prevention of candidiasis in patients with cancer: a prospective, randomized, controlled, double-blind study. *Arch Intern Med.* 1987; 147:710–2.

253. Palmblad J, Lonnqvist B, Carlsson B, et al. Oral ketoconazole prophylaxis for *Candida* infections during induction therapy for acute leukaemia in adults: more bacteraemias. *J Intern Med.* 1992; 231:363–70.

254. Schaffner A, Schaffner M. Effect of prophylactic fluconazole on the frequency of fungal infections, amphotericin B use, and health care costs in patients undergoing intensive chemotherapy for hematologic neoplasias. *J Infect Dis.* 1995; 172:1035–41.

255. Slavin MA, Osborne B, Adams R, et al. Efficacy and safety of fluconazole prophylaxis for fungal infections after marrow transplantation—a prospective, randomized, double-blind study. *J Infect Dis.* 1995; 171:1545–52.

256. Winston DJ, Chandrasekar PH, Lazarus HM, et al. Fluconazole prophylaxis of fungal infections in patients with acute leukemia. Results of a randomized, placebo-controlled, double-blind, multicenter trial. *Ann Intern Med.* 1993; 118:495–503.

257. Bodey GP, Anaissie EJ, Elting LS, et al. Antifungal prophylaxis during remission induction therapy for acute leukemia: fluconazole versus intravenous amphotericin B. *Cancer.* 1994; 73:2099–106.

258. Goodman JL, Winston DJ, Greenfield RA, et al. A controlled trial of fluconazole to prevent fungal infections in patients undergoing bone marrow transplantation. *N Engl J Med.* 1992; 326:845–51.

259. Shepp DH, Kosterman A, Siegel MS, et al. Comparative trial of ketoconazole and nystatin for prevention of fungal infection in neutropenic patients treated in a protective environment. *J Infect Dis.* 1985; 152:1257–63.

260. Vreugdenhil G, Van Dijke BJ, Donnelly JP, et al. Efficacy of itraconazole in the prevention of fungal infections among neutropenic patients with hematologic malignancies and intensive chemotherapy. A double-blind, placebo-controlled study. *Leuk Lymphoma.* 1993; 11:353–8.

261. Akiyama H, Mori S, Tanikawa S, et al. Fluconazole versus oral amphotericin B in preventing fungal infection in chemotherapy-induced neutropenic patients with haematological malignancies. *Mycoses.* 1993; 36:373–8.

262. Menichetti F, Del Favero A, Martino P, et al. Preventing fungal infection in neutropenic patients with acute leukemia: fluconazole compared with oral amphotericin B. The GIMEMA Infection Program. *Ann Intern Med.* 1994; 120:913–8.

263. Rozenberg-Arska M, Dekker AQ, Branger J, et al. A randomized study to compare oral fluconazole to amphotericin B in the prevention of fungal infections in patients with acute leukaemia. *J Antimicrob Chemother.* 1991; 27:369–76.

264. Beyer J, Schwartz S, Heinemann V, et al. Strategies in prevention of invasive pulmonary aspergillosis in immunosuppressed or neutropenic patients. *Antimicrob Agents Chemother.* 1994; 38:911–7.

265. Working Party of the British Society for Antimicrobial Chemotherapy. Working Party Report. Chemoprophylaxis for candidosis and aspergillosis in neutropenia and transplantation: a review and recommendations. *J Antimicrob Chemother.* 1994; 32:5–21.

266. Chandrasekar PH, Gatny CM. The effect of fluconazole prophylaxis on fungal colonization in neutropenic cancer patients. Bone Marrow Transplantation Team. *J Antimicrob Chemother.* 1994; 33:309–18.

267. Ellis ME, Qadri SM, Spence D, et al. The effect of fluconazole as prophylaxis for neutropenic patients on the isolation of *Candida* spp. from surveillance cultures. *J Antimicrob Chemother.* 1994; 33:1223–8.

268. Wingard JR, Merz WG, Rinaldi MG, et al. Increase in *Candida krusei* infection among patients with bone marrow transplantation and neutropenia treated prophylactically with fluconazole. *N Engl J Med.* 1991; 325:1274–7.

269. Cesaro S, Rossetti F, Perilongo G, et al. Fluconazole prophylaxis and *Candida fungemia* in neutropenic children with malignancies. *Haematologica.* 1993; 78:249–51.

270. Wingard JR, Merz WG, Rinaldi MG, et al. Association of *Torulopsis glabrata* infections with fluconazole prophylaxis in neutropenic bone marrow transplant patients. *Antimicrob Agents Chemother.* 1993; 37:1847–9.

271. Cap J, Mojzesova A, Kayserova E, et al. Fluconazole in children: first experience with prophylaxis in chemotherapy-induced neutropenia in pediatric patients with cancer. *Chemotherapy.* 1993; 39:438–42.

272. Benhamou E, Hartmann O, Nogues C, et al. Does ketoconazole prevent fungal infection in children treated with high dose chemotherapy and bone marrow transplantation? Results of a randomized, placebo-controlled trial. *Bone Marrow Transplant.* 1991; 7:127–31.

273. Ninane J, Sluysman T, Vermylen C, et al. Itraconazole versus ketoconazole prophylaxis in immunodeficient children: results of 2 consecutive nonrandomized stud-

ies. *Pediatr Hematol Oncol.* 1988; 6:349–53.

274. Messori A, Rampazzo R, Scroccaro G, et al. Efficacy of hyperimmune anti-cytomegalovirus immunoglobulins for the prevention of cytomegalovirus infection in recipients of allogeneic bone marrow transplantation: a meta-analysis. *Bone Marrow Transplant.* 1994; 13:163–7.

275. Goodrich JM, Mori M, Gleaves CA, et al. Early treatment with ganciclovir to prevent cytomegalovirus disease after allogeneic bone marrow transplantation. *N Engl J Med.* 1991; 325:1601–7.

276. Schmidt GM, Horak DA, Niland JC, et al. A randomized, controlled trial of prophylactic ganciclovir for cytomegalovirus pulmonary infection in recipients of allogeneic bone marrow transplants; The City of Hope-Stanford-Syntex CMV Study Group. *N Engl J Med.* 1991; 324:1005–11.

277. Prentice HG, Gluckman E, Powles RL, et al., for the European Acyclovir for CMV Prophylaxis Study Group. Impact of long-term acyclovir on cytomegalovirus infection and survival after allogeneic bone marrow transplantation. *Lancet.* 1994; 343:749–53.

278. Gluckman E, Lotsberg J, Devergie A, et al. Prophylaxis of herpes infections after bone marrow transplantation by oral acyclovir. *Lancet.* 1983; 2:706–8.

279. Saral R, Burns WH, Laskin OL, et al. Acyclovir prophylaxis of *Herpes simplex* virus infections: a randomized, double-blind, controlled trial in bone marrow transplant recipients. *N Engl J Med.* 1981; 305:63–7.

280. Wade JC, Newton B, Flournoy N, et al. Oral acyclovir for prevention of *Herpes simplex* virus reactivation after marrow transplantation. *Ann Intern Med.* 1984; 100:823–8.

281. Sarasini A, Baldanti F, Furione M, et al. Double resistance to ganciclovir and foscarnet of four human cytomegalovirus strains recovered from AIDS patients. *J Med Virol.* 1995; 47:237–44.

282. Drew WL, Miner RC, Busch DF, et al. Prevalence of resistance in patients receiving ganciclovir for serious cytomegalovirus infection. *J Infect Dis.* 1991; 163:716–9.

283. Kaplan JE, Masur H, Holmes KK, et al. USPHS/IDSA guidelines for the prevention of opportunistic infections in persons infected with human immunodeficiency virus: an overview. *Clin Infect Dis.* 1995; 21(suppl 1):S12–31.

284. Centers for Disease Control and Prevention. USPHS/IDSA guidelines for the prevention of opportunistic infections in persons infected with human immunodeficiency virus. *MMWR.* 1997; 46(RR-12):1–46.

285. USPHS/IDSA Prevention of Opportunistic Infection Working Group. Preface to the 1997 USPHS/IDSA guidelines for the prevention of opportunistic infections in persons infected with human immunodeficiency virus. *Clin Infect Dis.* 1997; 25(suppl 3):S299–312.

286. USPHS/IDSA Prevention of Opportunistic Infection Working Group. 1997 USPHS/IDSA guidelines for the prevention of opportunistic infections in persons infected with human immunodeficiency virus: disease-specific recommendations. *Clin Infect Dis.* 1997; 25(suppl 3):S313–35.

287. Schmidt-Westhausen A, Schiller RA, Pohle HD, et al. Oral *Candida* and *Enterobacteriaceae* in HIV-1 infection: correlation with clinical candidiasis and antimy-cotic therapy. *J Oral Pathol Med.* 1991; 20:469–72.

288. Reef SE, Mayer KH. Opportunistic candidal infections in patients infected with human immunodeficiency virus: prevention issues and priorities. *Clin Infect Dis.* 1995; 21(suppl 1):S99–102.

289. Eyster ME, Rabkin CS, Hilgartner MW, et al. Human immunodeficiency virus-related conditions in children and adults with hemophilia: rates, relationship to CD4 counts, and predictive value. *Blood.* 1993; 81:828–34.

290. Imam N, Carpenter CCJ, Mayer KH, et al. Hierarchical pattern of mucosal *Candida* infections in HIV-seropositive women. *Am J Med.* 1990; 89:142–6.

291. Nightingale SD, Parks JM, Pounders SM, et al. Disseminated histoplasmosis in patients with AIDS. *South Med J.* 1990; 83:624–30.

292. Wheat LJ, Connolly-Stringfield PA, Baker RL, et al. Disseminated histoplasmosis in the acquired immunodeficiency syndrome: clinical findings, diagnosis and treatment, and review of the literature. *Medicine (Baltimore).* 1990; 69:361–74.

293. McNeil MM, Ampel NM. Opportunistic coccidioidomycosis in patients infected with human immunodeficiency virus: prevention issues and priorities. *Clin Infect Dis.* 1995; 21(suppl 1):S111–3.

294. Fish DG, Ampel NM, Galgiani JN, et al. Coccidioidomycosis during human immunodeficiency virus infection: a review of 77 patients. *Medicine (Baltimore).* 1990; 69:384–91.

295. DiTomasso JP, Ampel NM, Sobonya RE, et al. Bronchoscopic diagnosis of pulmonary coccidioidomycosis: comparison of cytology, culture, and transbronchial biopsy. *Diagn Microbiol Infect Dis.* 1994; 18:83–7.

296. Hajjeh RA. Disseminated histoplasmosis in persons infected with human immunodeficiency virus. *Clin Infect Dis.* 1995; 21(suppl 1):S108–10.

297. Ampel NM, Dols CL, Galgiani JN. Coccidioidomycosis during human immunodeficiency virus infection: results of a prospective study in a coccidioidal endemic area. *Am J Med.* 1993; 94:235–40.

298. Powderly WG, Finkelstein DM, Feinberg J, et al. A randomized trial comparing fluconazole with clotrimazole troches for the prevention of fungal infections in patients with advanced human immunodeficiency virus infection. *N Engl J Med.* 1995; 332:700–5.

299. Pottage JC Jr, Sha BE. Development of histoplasmosis in a human immunodeficiency virus-infected patient receiving fluconazole. *J Infect Dis.* 1991; 164:622–3. Letter.

300. Nightingale SD, Cal SX, Peterson DM, et al. Primary prophylaxis with fluconazole against systemic fungal infections in HIV-positive patients. *AIDS.* 1992; 6:191–4.

301. Arguinchona HL, Ampel NM, Dols CL. Persistent coccidioidal seropositivity without clinical evidence of active coccidioidomycosis in patients infected with human immunodeficiency virus. *Clin Infect Dis.* 1995; 20:1281–5.

302. Sanguineti A, Carmichael JK, Campbell K. Fluconazole-resistant *Candida albicans* after long-term suppressive therapy. *Arch Intern Med.* 1993; 153:1122–4.

303. Kitchen VS, Savage M, Harris JRW. *Candida albicans* resistance in AIDS. *J Infect.* 1991; 22:204–5.

304. Willocks L, Leen CLS, Brettle RP, et al. Fluconazole resistance in AIDS patients. *J Antimicrob Chemother.*

1991; 28:937–9.

305. Powderly WG. Mucosal candidiasis caused by non-*albicans* species of *Candida* in HIV-positive patients. *AIDS.* 1992; 6:604–5. Letter.

306. Berg J, Clancy JC, Nguyen MH. The hidden danger of primary fluconazole prophylaxis for patients with AIDS. *Clin Infect Dis.* 1998; 26:186–7.

307. Centers for Disease Control and Prevention. USPHS/IDSA guidelines for the prevention of opportunistic infections in persons infected with human immunodeficiency virus: a summary. *MMWR.* 1995; 44(RR-8):1–34.

308. Smith D, van de Velde V, Woestenborghs R, et al. The pharmacokinetics of oral itraconazole in AIDS patients. *J Pharm Pharmacol.* 1992; 44:618–9.

309. Reynes J, Bazin C, Ajana F, et al. Pharmacokinetics of itraconazole (oral solution) in two groups of human immunodeficiency virus-infected adults with oral candidiasis. *Antimicrob Agents Chemother.* 1997; 41:2554–8.

310. Pinner RW, Hajjeh RA, Powderly WG. Prospects for preventing cryptococcosis in persons infected with human immunodeficiency virus. *Clin Infect Dis.* 1995; 21(suppl 1):S103–7.

311. Saag MA, Powderly WG, Cloud GA, et al. Comparison of amphotericin B with fluconazole in the treatment of acute AIDS-associated cryptococcal meningitis. *N Engl J Med.* 1992; 326:83–9.

312. Crowe SM, Carlin JB, Stewart KI. Predictive value of CD4 numbers for the development of opportunistic infections and malignancies in HIV-infected persons. *J Acquir Immune Defic Syndr.* 1991; 4:770–6.

313. Ammassari A, Linzalone A, Murri R, et al. Fluconazole for primary prophylaxis of AIDS-associated cryptococcosis: a case-control study. *Scand J Infect Dis.* 1995; 27:235–7.

314. Quagliarello VJ, Viscoli C, Horwitz RI. Primary prevention of cryptococcal meningitis by fluconazole in HIV-infected patients. *Lancet.* 1995; 345:548–52.

315. Saag MS, Cloud GC, Graybill JR, et al. Comparison of fluconazole versus itraconazole as maintenance therapy of AIDS-associated cryptococcal meningitis. 35th Interscience Conference on Antimicrobial Agents and Chemotherapy, San Francisco. Washington, DC: American Society for Microbiology; 1995:I218. Abstract.

316. Ostroff SM, Spiegel RA, Feinberg J, et al. Preventing disseminated *Mycobacterium avium* complex disease in patients infected with human immunodeficiency virus. *Clin Infect Dis.* 1995; 21(suppl 1):S72–6.

317. Chaisson RE, Moore RD, Richman DD, et al. Incidence and natural history of *Mycobacterium avium*-complex infections in patients with advanced human immunodeficiency virus disease treated with zidovudine. *Am Rev Respir Dis.* 1992; 146:285–9.

318. Horsburgh CR, Caldwell MB, Simonds RJ. Epidemiology of disseminated nontuberculous mycobacterial disease in children with acquired immunodeficiency syndrome. *Pediatr Infect Dis J.* 1993; 12:219–22.

319. Centers for Disease Control and Prevention. Recommendations on prophylaxis and therapy for disseminated *Mycobacterium avium* complex for adults and adolescents infected with human immunodeficiency virus. *MMWR.* 1993; 42:14–21.

320. Nightingale SD, Byrd LT, Southern PM, et al. Incidence of *Mycobacterium avium-intracellulare* complex bacteremia in human immunodeficiency virus-positive patients. *J Infect Dis.* 1992; 165:1082–5.

321. Nightingale SD, Cameron DW, Gordin FM, et al. Two controlled trials of rifabutin prophylaxis against *Mycobacterium avium* complex infection in AIDS. *N Engl J Med.* 1993; 329:828–33.

322. Moore RD, Chaisson RE. Survival analysis of two controlled trials of rifabutin prophylaxis against *Mycobacterium avium* complex in AIDS. *AIDS.* 1995; 9:1337–42.

323. Pierce M, Crampton S, Henry D, et al. A randomized trial of clarithromycin as prophylaxis against disseminated *Mycobacterium avium* complex infection in patients with advanced acquired immunodeficiency syndrome. *N Engl J Med.* 1996; 335:384–91.

324. Benson CA, Cohn DL, Williams P, et al. A phase II prospective, randomized, double-blind study of the safety and efficacy of clarithromycin vs. rifabutin vs. clarithromycin plus rifabutin for prevention of *Mycobacterium avium* complex disease in HIV+ patients with CD4 counts less or equal to 100 cells/mL. 3rd Conference on Retroviruses and Opportunistic Infections. Alexandria, VA: Infectious Diseases Society of America; 1996. Abstract.

325. Piscitelli SC, Flexner C, Minor JR, et al. Drug interactions in patients infected with human immunodeficiency virus. *Clin Infect Dis.* 1996; 23:685–93.

326. Havlir DV, Dube MP, Sattler FR, et al., for the California Collaborative Treatment Group. Prophylaxis against disseminated *Mycobacterium avium* complex with weekly azithromycin, daily rifabutin, or both. *N Engl J Med.* 1996; 335:392–8.

327. Masur H. Prevention and treatment of *Pneumocystis* pneumonia. *N Engl J Med.* 1992; 327:1853–60.

328. Simonds RJ, Hughes WT, Feinberg J, et al. Preventing *Pneumocystis carinii* pneumonia in persons infected with human immunodeficiency virus. *Clin Infect Dis.* 1995; 21(suppl 1):S44–8.

329. Centers for Disease Control and Prevention. 1995 revised guidelines for prophylaxis against *Pneumocystis carinii* pneumonia for children infected with or perinatally exposed to human immunodeficiency virus. *MMWR.* 1995; 44(RR-4):1–11.

330. Simonds RJ, Lindegren ML, Thomas P, et al. Prophylaxis of *Pneumocystis carinii* pneumonia among children with perinatally acquired human immunodeficiency virus infection in the United States. *N Engl J Med.* 1995; 332:786–90.

331. Gallant JE, McAvinue SM, Moore RD, et al. The impact of prophylaxis on outcome and resource utilization in *Pneumocystis carinii* pneumonia. *Chest.* 1995; 107:1018–23.

332. Phair J, Munoz A, Saah A, et al. Response to letter to the editor. *N Engl J Med.* 1990; 322:1608.

333. Chu SY, Hanson DL, Ciesielski C, et al. Prophylaxis against *Pneumocystis carinii* pneumonia at higher CD4+ T-cell counts. *JAMA.* 1995; 273:848. Letter.

334. Phair J, Munoz A, Detels R, et al. The risk of *Pneumocystis carinii* pneumonia among men infected with human immunodeficiency virus type 1. *N Engl J Med.* 1990; 322:161–5.

335. Simonds RJ, Oxtoby MJ, Caldwell MB, et al. *Pneumocystis carinii* pneumonia among children with perinatally acquired human immunodeficiency virus infection in the United States, 1982–1992. *JAMA.*

1993; 270:470–3.

336. European Collaborative Study Group. CD4 T cell count as predictor of *Pneumocystis carinii* pneumonia in children born to mothers infected with HIV. *Br Med J.* 1994; 308:437–40.

337. Fischl MA, Dickinson GM, La Voie L. Safety and efficacy of trimethoprim and sulfamethoxazole chemoprophylaxis for *Pneumocystis carinii* pneumonia in AIDS. *JAMA.* 1988; 259:1185–9.

338. May TH, Beuscart C, Reynes J, et al. Trimethoprim-sulfamethoxazole versus aerosolized pentamidine for primary prophylaxis of *Pneumocystis carinii* pneumonia: a prospective, randomized, controlled clinical trial. *J Acquir Immune Defic Syndr.* 1994; 7:457–62.

339. Lidman C, Berglund O, Tynell E, et al. Aerosolized pentamidine as primary prophylaxis for *Pneumocystis carinii* pneumonia: efficacy, mortality and morbidity. *AIDS.* 1994; 8:935–9.

340. Bozzette SA, Finkelstein DM, Spector SA, et al. A randomized trial of three antipneumocystis agents in patients with advanced human immunodeficiency virus infection. *N Engl J Med.* 1995; 332:693–9.

341. Schneider MME, Nielsen TL, Nelsing S, et al. Efficacy and toxicity of two doses of trimethoprim-sulfamethoxazole as primary prophylaxis against *Pneumocystis carinii* pneumonia in patients with human immunodeficiency virus. *J Infect Dis.* 1995; 171:1632–6.

342. Ena J, Amador C, Pasqua F, et al. Once-a-month administration of intravenous pentamidine to patients infected with human immunodeficiency virus as prophylaxis for *Pneumocystis carinii* pneumonia. *Clin Infect Dis.* 1994; 18:901–4.

343. Mallolas J, Zamora L, Gatell JM, et al. Primary prophylaxis for *Pneumocystis carinii* pneumonia: a randomized trial comparing cotrimoxazole, aerosolized pentamidine and dapsone plus pyrimethamine. *AIDS.* 1993; 7:59–64.

344. Ioannidis JPA, Cappelleri JC, Skolnik PR, et al. A meta-analysis of the relative efficacy and toxicity of *Pneumocystis carinii* prophylactic regimens. *Arch Intern Med.* 1996; 156:177–88.

345. Thea DM, Lambert G, Weedon J, et al. Benefit of primary prophylaxis before 18 months of age in reducing the incidence of *Pneumocystis carinii* pneumonia and early death in a cohort of 112 human immunodeficiency virus-infected infants. *Pediatrics.* 1996; 79:59–64.

346. Richards FO Jr, Kovacs JA, Luft BJ. Preventing toxoplasmic encephalitis in persons infected with human immunodeficiency virus. *Clin Infect Dis.* 1995; 21(suppl 1):S49–56.

347. Oksenhendler E, Charreau I, Tournerie C, et al. *Toxoplasma gondii* infection in advanced HIV infection. *AIDS.* 1994; 8:483–7.

348. Carr A, Tindall B, Brew BJ, et al. Low-dose trimethoprim-sulfamethoxazole prophylaxis for toxoplasmic encephalitis in patients with AIDS. *Ann Intern Med.* 1992; 117:106–11.

349. Luft BJ, Remington JS. Toxoplasmic encephalitis in AIDS. *Clin Infect Dis.* 1992; 15:211–22.

350. Israelski DM, Chmiel JS, Poggensee L, et al. Prevalence of *Toxoplasma* infection in a cohort of homosexual men at risk of AIDS and *Toxoplasma* encephalitis. *J Acquir Immune Defic Syndr.* 1993; 6:414–8.

351. Beaman MH, Luft BJ, Remington JS. Prophylaxis for toxoplasmosis in AIDS. *Ann Intern Med.* 1992; 117:163–4.

352. Podzamczer D, Salazar A, Jimenez J, et al. Intermittent trimethoprim-sulfamethoxazole compared with dapsonepyrimethamine for the simultaneous primary prophylaxis of *Pneumocystis* pneumonia and toxoplasmosis in patients infected with HIV. *Ann Intern Med.* 1995; 122:755–61.

353. Podzamczer D, Satin M, Jimenez J, et al. Thrice weekly cotrimoxazole is better than weekly dapsone-pyrimethamine for primary prevention of *Pneumocystis carinii* pneumonia in HIV-infected patients. *AIDS.* 1993; 7:501–6.

354. Hardy WD, Feinber J, Finkelstein DM, et al. Trimethoprim-sulfamethoxazole versus aerosolized pentamidine for secondary prophylaxis of *Pneumocystis carinii* pneumonia in AIDS patients receiving zidovudine: AIDS Clinical Trial Group protocol 012. *N Engl J Med.* 1992; 327:1842–8.

355. Girard PM, Landman R, Gaudebout C, et al. Dapsone-pyrimethamine compared with aerosolized pentamidine as primary prophylaxis against *Pneumocystis carinii* pneumonia and toxoplasmosis in HIV infection. *N Engl J Med.* 1993; 328:1514–20.

356. Clotet B, Romeu J, Sirera G. Twice-weekly dapsone-pyrimethamine for preventing PCP and cerebral toxoplasmosis. *AIDS.* 1991; 5:601–2.

357. Bachmeyer C, Gorin I, Deleuze J, et al. Pyrimethamine as primary prophylaxis for toxoplasmic encephalitis in patients infected with human immunodeficiency virus: open study. *Clin Infect Dis.* 1994; 18:479–80. Letter.

358. Leport C, Chene G, Morlat P, et al. Pyrimethamine for primary prophylaxis of toxoplasmic encephalitis in patients with human immunodeficiency virus infection: a double-blind, randomized trial. *J Infect Dis.* 1996; 173:91–7.

359. Jacobson MA, Besch CL, Child C, et al. Primary prophylaxis with pyrimethamine for toxoplasmic encephalitis in patients with advanced human immunodeficiency virus disease: results of a randomized trial. *J Infect Dis.* 1994; 169:384–94.

360. Stewart JA, Reef SE, Pellett PE, et al. Herpesvirus infections in persons infected with human immunodeficiency virus. *Clin Infect Dis.* 1995; 21(suppl 1):S114–20.

361. Jacobson MA, Mills J. Serious cytomegalovirus disease in the acquired immunodeficiency syndrome (AIDS): clinical findings, diagnosis, and treatment. *Ann Intern Med.* 1988; 108:585–94.

362. Jabs DA, Enger C, Bartlett JG. Cytomegalovirus retinitis and acquired immunodeficiency virus syndrome. *Arch Ophthalmol.* 1989; 107:75–80.

363. McKenzie R, Travis WD, Dolan SA, et al. The causes of death in patients with human immunodeficiency virus infection: a clinical and pathologic study with emphasis on the role of pulmonary diseases. *Medicine (Baltimore).* 1991; 70:326–43.

364. Reichert CM, O'Leary TJ, Levens DL, et al. Autopsy pathology in the acquired immune deficiency syndrome. *Am J Pathol.* 1983; 112:357–82.

365. Masur H. Introduction. Symposium: clinical implications of herpesvirus infections in patients with AIDS. *Am J Med.* 1992; 92(suppl 2A):S1–2.

366. Drew WL. Cytomegalovirus infection in patients with

AIDS. *J Infect Dis.* 1988; 158:449–56.

367. Gallant JE, Moore RD, Richman DD, et al. Incidence and natural history of cytomegalovirus disease in patients with advanced human immunodeficiency virus disease treated with zidovudine. The Zidovudine Epidemiology Study Group. *J Infect Dis.* 1992; 166:1223–7.

368. Pertel P, Hirschtick R, Phair J, et al. Risk of developing cytomegalovirus retinitis in persons infected with the human immunodeficiency virus. *J Acquir Immune Defic Syndr.* 1992; 5:1069–74.

369. Gerard L, Leport C, Flandre P, et al. Cytomegalovirus (CMV) viremia and the CD4+ lymphocyte count as predictors of CMV disease in patients infected with human immunodeficiency virus. *Clin Infect Dis.* 1997; 24:836–40.

370. Shinkai M, Bozzette SA, Powderly W, et al. Utility of urine and blood cultures and plasma DNA polymerase chain reaction for identification of AIDS patients at risk for developing human cytomegalovirus disease. *J Infect Dis.* 1997; 175:302–8.

371. Youle MS, Gazzard BG, Johnson MA, et al. Effects of high-dose oral acyclovir on herpesvirus disease and survival in patients with advanced HIV disease: a double-blind, placebo-controlled study. *AIDS.* 1994; 8:641–9.

372. Spector SA, McKinley GF, Lalezari JP, et al. Oral ganciclovir for the prevention of cytomegalovirus disease in persons with AIDS. *N Engl J Med.* 1996; 334:1491–7.

373. Crumpacker CS. Ganciclovir. *N Engl J Med.* 1996; 335:721–9.

374. Safrin S, Ashley R, Houlihan C, et al. Clinical and serologic features of herpes simplex virus infection in patients with AIDS. *AIDS.* 1991; 5:1107–10.

375. Holmberg SD, Buchbinder SP, Conley LJ, et al. The spectrum of medical conditions and symptoms before AIDS in HIV-infected homosexual and bisexual men. *Am J Epidemiol.* 1995; 141:395–404.

376. Jura E, Chadwick EG, Joseph SH, et al. Varicella-zoster infections in children infected with human immunodeficiency virus. *Pediatr Infect Dis.* 1989; 8:586–90.

377. Whitley RJ, Gnann JW Jr. Acyclovir: a decade later. *N Engl J Med.* 1992; 327:782–9.

This official ASHP practice standard was developed through the ASHP Commission on Therapeutics and approved by the ASHP Board of Directors on November 14, 1998. Supersedes an earlier version dated May 1990.

Members of the 1998–1999 ASHP Commission on Therapeutics are Austin J. Lee, Pharm.D., BCPS, FASHP, Chair; C. Wayne Weart, Pharm.D., FASHP, Vice Chair; G. Dennis Clifton, Pharm.D.; Matthew A. Fuller, Pharm.D., BCPS, BCPP; Kent M. Nelson, Pharm.D., BCPS; William L. Green, Pharm.D., BCPS, FASHP; Mary Beth Gross, Pharm.D.; Michael D. Katz, Pharm.D.; Shirley J. Reitz, Pharm.D.; Jane E. DeWitt, Student Member; Donald T. Kishi, Pharm.D., Board Liaison; and Leslie Dotson Jaggers, Pharm.D., BCPS, Secretary.

Project Coordinator: Debbie Denzel, Pharm.D. Clinical Information Specialist Rocky Mountain Poison and Drug Center Denver, CO 80220

Expert Panel: John A. Bosso, Pharm.D., BCPS Professor of Pharmacy Practice and Administration, College of Pharmacy, Professor of Pediatrics, College of Medicine, Medical University of South Carolina 171 Ashley Avenue Charleston, SC 29425-0810; Steven C. Ebert, Pharm.D., FCCP Clinical Associate Professor of Pharmacy, University of Wisconsin, Clinical Specialist in Infectious Diseases, Department of Pharmacy, Meriter Hospital Madison, WI 53715; John F. Flaherty, Jr., Pharm.D., FCCP Clinical Sciences Liaison, Gilead Sciences Inc. Foster City, CA 94044; B. Joseph Guglielmo, Jr., Pharm.D. Professor and Vice Chairman, Department of Clinical Pharmacy, School of Pharmacy, University of California, San Francisco, San Francisco, CA 94143-0622; David P. Nicolau, Pharm.D. Coordinator for Research, Department of Medicine, Division of Infectious Diseases, Department of Pharmacy, Hartford Hospital, Hartford, CT 06102; Karen Plaisance, Pharm.D., BCPS Associate Professor, School of Pharmacy, University of Maryland, Baltimore, MD 21201; Joseph T. DiPiro, Pharm.D. Professor, College of Pharmacy, University of Georgia and Medical College of Georgia, Augusta, GA 30912-2390; Larry H. Danziger, Pharm.D. Professor of Pharmacy Practice, College of Pharmacy, University of Illinois at Chicago, Chicago, IL 60612-7230.

Major Contributor: Doug Fish, Pharm.D. Assistant Professor Department of Pharmacy Practice School of Pharmacy University of Colorado Health Sciences Center Denver, CO 80262.

Contributors: Richard Dart, M.D., Ph.D., Lada Kokan, M.D., Edwin Kuffner, M.D., Jodi Schonbok, Luke Yip, M.D., Rocky Mountain Poison and Drug Consultation Center, Denver, CO 80220: Bret Fulton, Louisville, CO 80027; Christopher Paap, Pharm.D., Assistant Professor, Department of Pharmacy Practice, School of Pharmacy, University of Colorado Health Sciences Center, Denver, CO 80262

The bibliographic citation for this document is as follows: American Society of Health-System Pharmacists. ASHP therapeutic guidelines for nonsurgical antimicrobial prophylaxis. *Am J Health-Syst Pharm.* 1999; 56:1201–50.

ASHP Therapeutic Guidelines on the Pharmacologic Management of Nausea and Vomiting in Adult and Pediatric Patients Receiving Chemotherapy or Radiation Therapy or Undergoing Surgery

These therapeutic guidelines are intended to assist health care professionals in the appropriate management of adult and pediatric patients with nausea and vomiting induced by chemotherapeutic agents, radiation therapy, or surgery. There has been a renewed interest in the treatment of nausea and vomiting based on an improved understanding of the physiologic mechanisms involved in emesis. This interest has led to a continued proliferation of clinical trials of antiemetic therapies. Mild cases of nausea or vomiting may be discomforting, but frequently symptoms are self-limiting and treatment can be simple and inexpensive. More severe nausea and vomiting can result in dehydration, malnutrition, and metabolic disturbances, which can have a substantial effect on quality of life, survival, and health care costs. Even mild nausea and vomiting may have late sequelae, such as anticipatory emesis in patients receiving chemotherapy. Therefore, primary prevention of nausea and vomiting is paramount.

The availability of new antiemetic agents and formulations has raised questions about the most cost-effective way to manage nausea and vomiting. Antiemetic therapy was selected for guideline development because (1) nausea and vomiting occur frequently, (2) there is a lack of consistency in selection of therapeutic agents in clinical practice, and (3) nausea and vomiting are preventable, which means there is potential for a significant impact on clinical, humanistic, and economic outcomes.

Nausea, vomiting, and retching are three separate entities that are assessed independently. Nausea is a subjectively unpleasant sensation associated with flushing, tachycardia, and an awareness of the urge to vomit. Vomiting, or emesis, is characterized by contraction of the abdominal muscles, descent of the diaphragm, and opening of the gastric cardia, resulting in expulsion of stomach contents from the mouth. Retching involves spasmodic contractions of the diaphragm, thoracic, and abdominal wall muscles without expulsion of gastric contents. Many medications, medical conditions, and procedures have been shown to induce nausea and vomiting (Table 1).

As a drug class, chemotherapeutic agents frequently induce nausea and vomiting; however, not all of these agents have the same propensity to induce symptoms. In the absence of antiemetic agents, vincristine is associated with nausea and vomiting in less than 10% of patients while cisplatin induces these symptoms in more than 90% of patients.[1] In one study, vomiting occurred in 47 (98%) of 48 patients receiving cisplatin without antiemetic therapy.[4] Patients had a median of six emetic episodes in the first 24 hours after administration of cisplatin. Vomiting continued after rescue therapy with antiemetics in 77% of patients during this 24-hour period.

The frequency of postoperative nausea and vomiting is influenced by the surgical procedure, the age and sex of the patient, and other medications administered, but the overall frequency, defined by large-scale clinical trials, has been estimated to be 20–30%.[5–7]

Radiation therapy, with or without concomitant chemotherapy, has also been shown to induce nausea and vomiting. Nausea and vomiting occur most commonly when the gastrointestinal (GI) tract is irradiated. It has been estimated that more than 80% of patients receiving mid- and upper-hemibody radiation experience nausea and vomiting.[8–12] Specific factors that increase the risk of nausea and vomiting with chemotherapy, radiation therapy, or surgery are addressed in a subsequent section of this document.

Hundreds of studies have assessed the effect of pharmacologic therapy on nausea and vomiting associated with precipitating factors; however, the quality of the literature varies significantly.[13–16] Methodological concerns with published antiemetic trials that make comparisons between treatment options difficult include the following[13,15,16]:

- Inclusion of heterogeneous patient populations (e.g., selection of patients receiving chemotherapeutic agents with differing levels of emetogenicity or patients undergoing differing types of surgery).
- Use of a variety of doses, routes of administration, schedules, and combinations of antiemetic agents.
- Lack of randomization.
- Inadequate blinding of investigators or patients to study medications.
- Rarity of placebo controls (primarily because of ethical considerations).
- Insufficient sample size to provide enough power to detect a difference between study groups if there was a true difference.
- Inadequate assessment of nausea, vomiting, and retching, including what was measured, who performed the assessment, and scales of measurement.
- Inconsistent definition of successful treatment.
- Rarity of outcomes data, including humanistic, economic, and other clinical outcomes (e.g., adverse effects of medications).

Several reviews discuss this topic more extensively.[13–16]

Nausea and vomiting can potentially affect large numbers of patients; however, current evidence suggests a lack of consistency in the management of these symptoms in clinical practice.[1–3,5–7,13,17–20] Pharmacologic management should be based on systematic evaluation of currently available scientific evidence and on medication-specific and patient-specific variables, including the type of emetic stimulus; the ability and willingness of patients to use oral, rectal, or injectable medications; prior alcohol use; age; concomitant diseases or medications; the frequency, duration, and severity of symptoms; sex; the success of previous treatment; suspected cause and precipitating factors; and patient preference.

Adverse effects of antiemetics also need to be considered when specific agents are selected. Table 2 lists common adverse effects of antiemetic agents.

Antiemetic agents are most useful when given prophylactically; it is much easier to prevent symptoms than to control them. When preventive measures are successful, adverse clinical, humanistic, and economic outcomes can be avoided.

Severe or protracted nausea and vomiting can result in dehydration, malnutrition, metabolic disturbances (e.g., metabolic alkalosis, hyponatremia, hypochloremia, and hypokalemia), and aspiration pneumonia.[3,21,22] These complications can be life threatening; infants and children are at particularly high risk. The pressure generated by vomiting can cause rupture of the esophagus (Boerhaave's syndrome) or linear mucosal tears (Mallory-Weiss syndrome) in the region of the cardioesophageal junction, with resulting hematemesis. Patients receiving chemotherapy may be unable to tolerate subsequent courses of chemotherapy, or the symptoms may be so severe that the patient refuses further cycles of chemotherapy.[19,21]

The effects of uncontrolled nausea and vomiting on quality of life are also an important consideration.[20,23–26] Much of the research assessing quality-of-life implications of nausea and vomiting relates to patients receiving cancer chemotherapy. Studies have shown that nausea and vomiting secondary to chemotherapy reduce the patient's ability to complete household tasks, enjoy meals, spend time with others, and maintain activities of daily living and recreation.[24,25] Nausea and vomiting can be so distressing that patients may be unable to work, care for themselves, or take their prescribed medications. Vomiting seems to have a greater impact on daily functioning than nausea.

The Functional Living Index—Cancer (FLIC) and the Functional Living Index—Emesis (FLIE) are two instruments used in research to evaluate the impact of chemotherapy-induced nausea and vomiting on quality of life. The FLIE contains nine items for assessing nausea and another nine for vomiting and addresses the effect of nausea and vomiting on physical activities, social and emotional function, and the ability to enjoy meals. The possible score ranges from 18 to 126, with lower scores indicating a more negative impact on the patient's functional living as a result of nausea and vomiting. Lindley and colleagues[24] demonstrated a significant and dramatic decline in the quality of life of outpatients receiving chemotherapy by using the FLIE. The mean FLIE score decreased from 115 immediately before chemotherapy to 85 three days after chemotherapy in patients with emesis. This study also showed cost-related consequences of chemotherapy-induced emesis: 23% of patients missed work, 22% were unable to prepare meals, 12% were unable to take care of themselves, and 12% were unable to take prescribed medications on at least one occasion. The economic significance was not assessed but warrants further study.[24]

More recently, Osoba and colleagues[26] used a health-related quality of life (HQL) questionnaire to assess symptoms in chemotherapy-naïve patients who received either moderately or highly emetogenic chemotherapy. This study showed significant worsening of scores in cognitive function, global quality of life, fatigue, anorexia, insomnia, and dyspnea in patients who vomited compared with those who did not vomit within seven days after chemotherapy. The study also indicated that global quality of life, physical function, role function, social function, fatigue, and anorexia were significantly worse before chemotherapy in patients who subsequently vomited than in those who did not vomit. This suggests that HQL scores may have value in

Table 1.
Classes of Drugs, Medical Conditions, and Procedures That May Induce Nausea and Vomiting[1-3]

Drug or Drug Class
  Anesthetic agents (e.g., thiopental, halothane)
  Antidepressants (e.g., fluoxetine, sertraline, paroxetine, fluvoxamine)
  Antimicrobials (e.g., imipenem–cilastatin, erythromycin, vancomycin, metronidazole, trimethoprim–sulfamethoxazole, nitrofurantoin)
  Antifungals (e.g., itraconazole)
  Contrast media
  Corticosteroids
  Cytotoxic agents (e.g., cisplatin, cyclophosphamide)
  Ergot alkaloids (e.g., dihydroergotamine, ergotamine, methysergide, pergolide)
  Estrogen-containing substances
  Iron formulations (e.g., iron dextran, ferrous gluconate, ferrous fumarate, ferrous sulfate, ferrous phosphate)
  Levodopa and carbidopa
  Nonsteroidal anti-inflammatory drugs
  Opioids (e.g., morphine, fentanyl)
  Potassium salts (e.g., acetate, phosphate, chloride [oral more than i.v.], gluconate)
  Tramadol
Medical Condition or Procedure
  Anxiety
  Cerebral metastases
  Gastrointestinal malignancies
  Hepatitis
  Hypercalcemia
  Hepatic metastases
  Intestinal obstruction
  Migraine headaches
  Morning sickness and hyperemesis gravidarum
  Motion sickness
  Menière's disease
  Motility disorders (e.g., gastroparesis, irritable bowel syndrome)
  Pain
  Pancreatitis
  Peritonitis
  Renal colic
  Radiation therapy
  Surgery

predicting which patients might experience chemotherapy-induced emesis and thus require additional antiemetic strategies for adequate emesis control.

The choice of antiemetic agent may affect resource use and costs. An inappropriate agent or dose may result in increases in cost associated with rescue therapy or wasted drug (e.g., 32 mg of ondansetron when 8 mg would have sufficed), nursing time, cleanup time, emergency room or clinic visits, hospital admission, or complicated and extended hospital stay. These types of issues, in addition to patient satisfaction, may ultimately affect managed care contracts.

Scope

These guidelines address the management of adult and pediatric patients with nausea and vomiting induced by chemotherapeutic agents, radiation therapy, or surgery. The guidelines were written to be applicable to both the inpatient and outpatient setting. Management of populations at risk of nausea and vomiting associated with other medications, procedures, or medical conditions are not within the scope of this document. Nonpharmacologic strategies such as music therapy, hypnosis, progressive muscle relaxation, diversion therapy, guided imagery, biofeedback, self-hypnosis, dietary modifications, and acupressure may be valuable adjuvants but are beyond the scope of this document.[27-32] Some standard regimens could not be incorporated into the guidelines because of a lack of randomized clinical trials. The guidelines should not be routinely applied to patients with a relative contraindication to any of the agents recommended.

Guideline Development and Use

The ASHP Therapeutic Guidelines on the Pharmacologic Management of Nausea and Vomiting in Adult and Pediatric Patients Receiving Chemotherapy or Radiation Therapy or Undergoing Surgery were prepared by the University of Kentucky Drug Information Center under contract to ASHP. The project was coordinated by the director of the center, who worked in conjunction with an independent panel of seven clinical specialists (a physician, a nurse, and five pharmacists) representing adult and pediatric hematology–oncology and surgery–anesthesia. The panel was appointed by ASHP. Panel members and contractors were required to disclose any possible conflicts of interest before appointment.

The scientific literature is the foundation for the recommendations. A comprehensive literature search was performed. Published studies identified through a MEDLINE search (1966 to April 1998) were reviewed, as were the reference lists of the retrieved documents and abstracts from meetings of professional associations, when appropriate. The literature was critically evaluated, including examination of research design, patient selection, medication dose, route, combination treatment, test measures, statistics, and results. Recommendations were graded A, B, C, or D according to the strength of scientific evidence:

A. Strong research-based evidence (multiple relevant and high-quality scientific studies),

B. Moderate research-based evidence (one relevant, high-quality scientific study or multiple adequate scientific studies),

C. Limited research-based evidence (at least one adequate scientific study in patients with nausea and vomiting, published in a reputable medical journal), and

D. Panel interpretation of information that did not meet inclusion criteria as research-based evidence.

The same system was previously used by an AHCPR panel of experts to develop guidelines.[33] The strength of evidence appears in parentheses after the recommendation and reflects both the overall quality of the studies and the strength of the study design.

The primary clinical endpoint that was considered as the definition of complete response in the studies was the number of patients with no vomiting episodes. Secondary endpoints included the number of patients with no nausea or retching and documentation of reduction in the number of emetic episodes or the severity of nausea. Clinical trials describing pharmacologic management that influenced humanistic or economic outcomes were strongly considered.

A panel of experts was created to ensure that applicable studies were included in the analysis, to provide expert judgment when the literature was of poor quality or lacking, and to provide insight into the clarity, practicality, and flexibility of the document in clinical practice. The guidelines were circulated in draft form, and all members of the panel had the opportunity to comment on the recommenda-

Table 2.
Adverse Effects of Antiemetic Agents

Medication	Adverse Effects[a]
Antihistamines Diphenhydramine, hydroxyzine	Most common: sedation, dry mouth, constipation; less common: confusion, blurred vision, urinary retention
Belladonna alkaloid Scopolamine	Most common: dry mouth, drowsiness, impaired eye accommodation; rare: disorientation, memory disturbances, dizziness, hallucinations
Benzamides Benzquinamide, metoclopramide, trimethobenzamide	Most common: sedation, restlessness, diarrhea (metoclopramide), agitation, central nervous system depression; less common: extrapyramidal effects (more frequent with higher doses), hypotension, neuroleptic syndrome, supraventricular tachycardia (with i.v. administration)
Benzodiazepines Lorazepam	Most common: sedation, amnesia; rare: respiratory depression, ataxia, blurred vision, hallucinations, paradoxical reactions (weeping, emotional reactions)
Butyrophenones Droperidol, haloperidol	Most common: sedation, hypotension, tachycardia; less common: extrapyramidal effects, dizziness, increase in blood pressure, chills, hallucinations
Cannabinoids Dronabinol	Most common: drowsiness, euphoria, somnolence, vasodilation, vision difficulties, abnormal thinking, dysphoria; less common: diarrhea, flushing, tremor, myalgia
Corticosteroids Dexamethasone, methylprednisolone	Most common: gastrointestinal upset, anxiety, insomnia; less common: hyperglycemia, facial flushing, euphoria, perineal itching or burning (with dexamethasone, probably secondary to vehicle and rate of injection)
Phenothiazines Prochlorperazine, promethazine, chlorpromazine, triethylperazine	Most common: sedation, lethary, skin sensitization; less common: cardiovascular effects, extrapyramidal effects, cholestatic jaundice, hyperprolactinemia; rare: neuroleptic malignant syndrome, hematologic abnormalities
Serotonin Antagonists Ondansetron, granisetron, dolasetron	Most common: headache, asymptomatic prolongation of electrocardiographic interval; less common: constipation, asthenia, somnolence, diarrhea, fever, tremor or twitching, ataxia, lightheadedness, dizziness, nervousness, thirst, muscle pain, warm or flushing sensation on i.v. administration; rare: transient elevations in serum transaminases

[a]Most common = >10%, less common = 1–10%, rare = <1%. Based on FDA-approved labeling and generalized to the drug class.

tions and strengths of evidence. The guidelines underwent multidisciplinary field review to evaluate their validity, reliability, and utility in clinical practice. The final document was approved by the ASHP Commission on Therapeutics and the ASHP Board of Directors. The guidelines are scheduled for review and update in two to four years.

The recommendations in this document may not be appropriate for use in all clinical situations. Decisions to follow these recommendations must be based on the professional judgment of the clinician, individual patient circumstances, and available resources.

Assessment of Nausea and Vomiting

The goal of prophylaxis and treatment is to either alleviate or minimize nausea and vomiting, depending on patient-specific and causative factors (e.g., operative procedure, cytotoxic agent). Nausea and vomiting should be considered as two separate entities and should be assessed as such. The severity and duration of nausea and the number of episodes and duration of vomiting and retching are important considerations. Systematically documenting nausea and vomiting provides the basis for adjusting the medication to suit the individual patient's needs—adjusting the antiemetic dose or dosage interval, providing scheduled doses of antiemetics, adding an as-needed antiemetic agent for breakthrough nausea and vomiting, or changing the route of administration. When nausea and vomiting are being assessed, it is important to select a clinically justified time frame for measuring changes.

Methods for assessing nausea and vomiting[14] are well established for chemotherapy-induced nausea and vomiting; however, they are described to a lesser extent for radiation therapy-induced and postoperative nausea and vomiting. Methods as simple as specifying present or absent or yes or no have been used, as have 3-point, 4-point, 5-point, 6-point, and 10-point scales. Visual-analogue scales are another alternative. Regardless of the method used, it is important for the patient to perform the assessment instead of relying on the perception of the caregiver.

The visual-analogue scale, which is used to quantify the intensity of nausea on a 100-mm line with two extremes, can be vertical (with 100 mm representing severe symptoms on the top and 0 mm representing the absence of symptoms on the bottom) or horizontal.[34] This instrument may be particularly beneficial for patients with sight impairment or a low level of literacy. The scale can be altered for children, with a smiling face at the top and a frowning face on the bottom. Patients are asked to mark the scale at a point that best indicates the sensation at the time. The measurement should be taken at the most likely time of nausea or at regular intervals. It is recommended that, if feasible, the patient be seated at the time of measurement rather than remaining supine, in order to more accurately assess the intensity.[35] The four-point scale has also been frequently used and is preferred by some because of its simplicity.[14] Nausea is graded by the patient as "none," "mild," "moderate," or "severe."

Vomiting and retching are assessed separately from nausea; this assessment should be done in an objective manner. Retching needs to be clearly differentiated from vomiting. The number and duration of episodes should be recorded over a 24-hour period. If chemotherapy is being administered, antiemetic efficacy should also be evaluated between courses. Patients should be interviewed about control of nausea and vomiting.

Patients should be monitored for the occurrence of adverse effects, adherence to treatment, hydration status, food intake, and wound dehiscence if applicable. Adverse effects of the antiemetics should also be monitored (Table 2), as should the ramifications of uncontrolled nausea and vomiting (e.g., electrolyte disturbances, dehydration). The overall period for which the patient needs to be assessed depends on patient-specific and causative factors.

Physiology of Chemotherapy-Induced Nausea and Vomiting

The mechanism of chemotherapy-induced nausea and vomiting is a complex interaction between neurotransmitters and receptors in the central and peripheral nervous systems (Figure 1). The process is initiated by the stimulation of dopamine, opiate, histamine, acetylcholine, neurokinin 1 (NK_1) or serotonin receptors. Dopamine type 2 and serotonin type 3 ($5\text{-}HT_3$) receptors seem to be the most important in chemotherapy-induced nausea and vomiting.

There has been a vast amount of research on the role of serotonin in this process. Both cancer chemotherapy and radiation therapy are known to induce emesis at least in part by causing enterochromaffin cells lining the GI tract to release serotonin.[36-38] The serotonin binds to vagal afferent $5\text{-}HT_3$ receptors in the GI tract, which send impulses to the vomiting center located in the lateral reticular formation of the medulla in the brain. The vomiting center is a physiological rather than an anatomic entity, consisting of intertwined neural networks in the nucleus tractus solitarii of the medulla oblongata. The vomiting center also receives impulses from the chemoreceptor trigger zone (CTZ), the brain cortex, and the vestibular apparatus.

The CTZ is considered to play an important role in chemotherapy-induced emesis. The CTZ is located in the area postrema, in the floor of the fourth ventricle. It lies outside the blood–brain barrier where it is accessible to

Figure 1. Pathways and neurotransmitter receptors in chemotherapy-induced nausea and vomiting. GI = gastrointestinal, CTZ = chemoreceptor trigger zone, NTS = nucleus tractus solitarius, D_2 = dopamine type 2 receptor, $5\text{-}HT_3$ = serotonin type 3 receptor, M = muscarinic receptor, H_1 = histamine type 1 receptor, NK_1 = tachykinin neurokinin type 1 receptor.

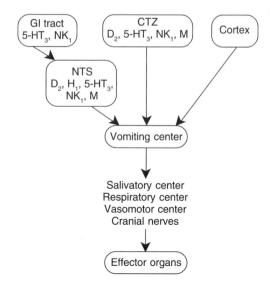

circulating emetogenic substances (e.g., chemotherapeutic agents) in both the blood and the cerebrospinal fluid. This location is important because most chemotherapeutic agents do not cross the blood–brain barrier. The CTZ sends impulses to the vomiting center, which in turn initiates the vomiting cascade by sending efferent impulses to the respiratory, vasomotor, and salivary centers and to cranial nerves VIII and X. Subsequently, impulses are sent to the abdominal muscles, the diaphragm, the stomach, and the esophagus, ultimately resulting in emesis.

The influence of the limbic system on the emetic response is less well understood. The limbic region of the brain, within the cerebral cortex, initiates emesis from chemotherapy indirectly. This region of the brain is responsible for anticipatory or learned responses, which is important if nausea and vomiting are not adequately controlled during a patient's initial course of chemotherapy. This process relates more to the psychological components of nausea and vomiting than to those causing direct stimulation.

Acute Versus Delayed Nausea and Vomiting. Chemotherapy-induced nausea and vomiting can be divided into three distinct types: acute, delayed, and anticipatory. Traditionally, acute nausea or vomiting is defined as that occurring within the first 24 hours after administration of cancer chemotherapy. Delayed nausea or vomiting is defined as that beginning at least 24 hours after administration of cancer chemotherapy; it may last for longer than 120 hours. In placebo-controlled trials reported by Gralla, et al.,[39] Homesley, et al.,[40] Cubeddu, et al.,[41] and Cupissol, et al.,[42] 98% of patients receiving cisplatin at doses of 50–120 mg/m² had emesis within 24 hours after the dose. Kris, et al.[43] described the frequency and severity of symptoms 24–144 hours after administration of cisplatin. Symptoms were greatest 48–72 hours after cisplatin therapy. Some 61% of patients had delayed emesis, with a median number of emetic episodes of two per patient; 78% of patients had delayed nausea. DeMulder and colleagues[44] studied a group of patients receiving cisplatin 50–100 mg/m² and observed delayed emesis in 62% of patients given oral metoclopramide and 65% of patients given oral ondansetron over a five-day period.

Delayed emesis has also been described in patients receiving less emetogenic doses of cisplatin and in patients receiving combinations containing an anthracycline plus cyclophosphamide. There are no placebo-controlled trials quantifying delayed emesis among patients receiving cyclophosphamide and doxorubicin combinations at various dosages. However, Schmoll[45] demonstrated that the frequency of delayed vomiting among patients given either metoclopramide or ondansetron was 34% and 17%, respectively, during the 24–48 hours after chemotherapy and 16% and 11%, respectively, during the 48–72 hours after chemotherapy. Jones, et al.[46] noted delayed emesis for up to 120 hours after administration of cyclophosphamide and anthracycline combinations despite treatment with either dexamethasone or ondansetron.

The time frame of 24 hours as the definition of delayed as opposed to acute was arbitrarily assigned. However, when the course of vomiting was examined over the 24 hours after administration of cisplatin 120 mg/m², two vomiting peaks were noted—one at approximately 4 hours and one at 18 hours—with virtually no vomiting between those times.[4,39,47] High-dose metoclopramide and ondansetron attenuated the first peak, but neither eliminated or attenuated the second peak. When serotonin metabolites (5-hydroxyindoleacetic acid, or 5-HIAA) are measured in the urine after high-dose cisplatin therapy, a peak is found at 6 hours but not at 48 hours.[48] This suggests that serotonin is not the primary mediator of symptoms for delayed emesis and is confirmed by the lower efficacy rate of ondansetron for preventing delayed emesis than for preventing acute emesis.[44,49,50] These observations of the pattern of emesis after high-dose cisplatin suggest that delayed emesis may begin as early as 16 hours after chemotherapy.

The pattern of emesis after administration of high-dose cyclophosphamide differs from the time course of emesis induced by cisplatin. Cyclophosphamide is associated with a more prolonged pattern of emesis, demonstrating a latency period of approximately 10 hours, after which nausea and vomiting begin and continue for up to three days.[44] Reasons for the latency period are unclear, but data suggest that conversion of cyclophosphamide to active metabolites may be required. There is little or no elevation of urinary 5-HIAA in patients given high doses of cyclophosphamide.[44] This may be because cyclophosphamide induces less serotonin release from enterochromaffin cells than cisplatin does, which may account for the less severe emesis produced by cyclophosphamide. Serotonin antagonists have not demonstrated superiority over dexamethasone with or without metoclopramide in treating delayed emesis after cyclophosphamide-based chemotherapy.[45,46] This lends further support to the hypothesis that delayed emesis may begin at less than 24 hours and that additional neurophysiological mechanisms may be involved.

Breakthrough Nausea and Vomiting. Breakthrough nausea and vomiting are nausea and vomiting that occur despite preventive therapy. Antiemetic treatment administered to patients who have not responded to prophylactic regimens prescribed for acute or delayed nausea and vomiting is often referred to as rescue therapy.

Anticipatory Vomiting. Anticipatory vomiting is defined as a learned or conditioned response typically occurring when nausea and vomiting have been controlled poorly with previous administration of chemotherapy.[6] It occurs before, during, or after the administration of chemotherapy but before acute chemotherapy-related symptoms would be expected to occur. Anticipatory nausea and vomiting are not controlled by antiemetic agents or other pharmacologic interventions but have been treatable through behavioral modification and other nonpharmacologic approaches. Behavioral interventions may be effective because they produce physiological relaxation, divert attention away from the conditional stimulus and toward neutral or relaxing images, and enhance feelings of control.[51–53] Although reports suggest that the amnestic and anxiolytic properties of lorazepam may help prevent anticipatory nausea and vomiting by blocking the memory of emesis associated with chemotherapy, this has not been substantiated by large, randomized trials.[54–56] Efforts should be directed at preventing nausea and vomiting by administering the most effective antiemetic with the initial course of emesis-producing chemotherapy.

Factors to Consider in the Selection of an Agent for Chemotherapy-Induced Nausea and Vomiting

Because no single agent is completely effective (i.e., resulting in the absence of nausea and vomiting) in all patients, individualization of therapy is important. Considerations in the selection of an agent for the prevention and treatment of nausea and vomiting include the type, dose, and schedule of chemotherapy; the type of symptoms (acute or delayed); the outcome of previous therapy; anticipated adverse effects (Table 2); the frequency and severity of nausea and vomiting; and patient preference.

The primary factor that influences the frequency and severity of chemotherapy-induced nausea and vomiting is the emetic potential of the cytotoxic agent (Table 3). For most chemotherapeutic agents (e.g., cisplatin), higher doses are more emetogenic than lower doses (Table 4).[6,13,21,58–62] Slowing the infusion rate by prolonging the infusion time may decrease the risk of emesis. For example, increasing the infusion time of cisplatin from one hour to eight hours resulted in a small but significant reduction in emesis.[58]

Patient-specific factors also affect the risk of nausea and vomiting (Table 4).[6,13,21,58–62] Patients younger than 50 years have more nausea and vomiting than older patients. Because they have greater physiological reserves, younger patients may receive more aggressive chemotherapy, leading to more nausea and vomiting. Women are more susceptible to nausea and vomiting than men.[6] Limited evidence suggests that people who have had motion sickness or pregnancy-related nausea and vomiting may be more apt to have problems with chemotherapy. Patients who use alcohol heavily or who have done so in the past have a reduced risk of emesis. Patients who have vomited repeatedly after prior doses of chemotherapy are more likely to have nausea and vomiting with subsequent doses.[13]

Knowledge of the patterns of emesis after administration of specific chemotherapeutic agents aids in the selection of antiemetic agents and dosage schedules that will allow for adequate protection at the expected time of onset and for the duration of both acute and delayed nausea and vomiting.[63] Table 5 shows the expected onset and duration of emesis for commonly used chemotherapeutic agents.[16,63–66]

Mechlorethamine induces emesis within 30 minutes after intravenous administration, whereas other agents with very high emetic potential (e.g., cisplatin, dacarbazine, streptozocin) usually do not induce emesis for at least one hour after administration. With moderately emetogenic agents (e.g., daunorubicin, doxorubicin, ifosfamide), emesis often develops within six hours.[63] A later onset of acute emesis occurs with certain agents, particularly cyclophosphamide. This variability in occurrence and onset suggests that individual drugs may cause emesis by different mechanisms and that some agents (e.g., cyclophosphamide) require metabolic activation to cause emesis, delaying the onset.[64]

The duration of emesis also is agent dependent. Most chemotherapeutic drugs can cause emesis for approximately 12–24 hours after administration. Two exceptions are cisplatin, with a duration of emesis of more than 24 hours, and cyclophosphamide, with a duration of 6–36 hours.

The rate of drug administration affects the onset, intensity, and duration of chemotherapy-induced emesis. The occurrence of emesis after a continuous infusion typically peaks within the first day of treatment and gradually

Table 3.
Emetogenicity of Chemotherapeutic Agents[57,a]

Level 1 (Less Than a 10% Frequency)	Level 3 (30–60% Frequency)
Androgens	Aldesleukin[c]
Bleomycin	Cyclophosphamide (i.v., ≤750 mg/m²)
Busulfan (oral, <4 mg/kg/day)	Dactinomycin (≤1.5 mg/m²)
Chlorambucil (oral)	Doxorubicin hydrochloride (20–60 mg/m²)
Cladribine	Epirubicin hydrochloride (≤90 mg/m²)
Corticosteroids	Idarubicin
Fludarabine	Ifosfamide
Hydroxyurea	Methenamine (oral)
Interferon	Methotrexate (250–1000 mg/m²)
Melphalan (oral)	Mitoxantrone (≤15 mg/m²)
Mercaptopurine	Level 4 (60–90% Frequency)
Methotrexate (≤50 mg/m²)[b]	Carboplatin
Thioguanine (oral)	Carmustine (<250 mg/m²)
Tretinoin	Cisplatin (<50 mg/m²)
Vinblastine	Cyclophosphamide (>750 mg/m² to ≤1500 mg/m²)
Vincristine	Cytarabine (≥1 g/m²)
Vinorelbine	Dactinomycin (>1.5 mg/m²)
Level 2 (10–30% Frequency)	Doxorubicin hydrochloride (>60 mg/m²)
Asparaginase	Irinotecan
Cytarabine (<1 g/m²)[b]	Melphalan (i.v.)
Docetaxel	Methotrexate (≥1000 mg/m²)
Doxorubicin hydrochloride (<20 mg/m²)	Mitoxantrone (>15 mg/m²)
Etoposide	Procarbazine (oral)
Fluorouracil (<1000 mg/m²)	Level 5 (More Than a 90% Frequency)
Gemcitabine	Carmustine (>250 mg/m²)
Methotrexate (>50 mg/m²; <250 mg/m²)	Cisplatin (≥50 mg/m²)
Mitomycin	Cyclophosphamide (>1500 mg/m²)
Paclitaxel	Dacarbazine (≥500 mg/m²)
Teniposide	Lomustine (>60 mg/m²)
Thiotepa	Mechlorethamine
Topotecan	Pentostatin
	Streptozocin

[a]The most highly emetogenic agent in the combination should be identified, and the contribution of other agents should be considered by using the following rules: (1) Level 1 agents do not contribute to the emetogenicity of a given regimen. (2) Adding one or more level 2 agents increases the emetogenicity of the combination by one level greater than the most emetogenic agent in the combination. (3) Adding level 3 and 4 agents increases the emetogenicity of the combination by one level per agent.
[b]When methotrexate and cytarabine are coadministered intrathecally to pediatric patients, the level of emetogenicity is increased to level 3.
[c]Corticosteroids should not be used as antiemetics.

Table 4.
Risk Factors for Chemotherapy-Induced Emesis[a]

Treatment-Specific Factors
Drug
Dose
Infusion rate
Patient-Specific Factors
Age
Sex
Alcohol use
History of motion sickness or nausea during pregnancy
Prior exposure to chemotherapeutic agents

[a]See text for details.

diminishes, leaving the patient almost symptom-free by the end of the regimen. Emesis occurs earlier and is more severe when cytarabine is administered rapidly than when it is infused more slowly.[64]

When more than one cycle of chemotherapy is given, emesis tends to be progressively less well controlled; however, with procarbazine, dacarbazine, bleomycin, and the androgens, nausea diminishes over repeated cycles as patients become more tolerant of the adverse effects. The degree of tolerance varies depending on the frequency of cycles, the interval between cycles, and the characteristics of the chemotherapy.

Likewise, in patients receiving chemotherapy over multiple days, including bone marrow transplant preparative regimens or leukemia induction regimens, emesis control declines after the first day and reaches a low by the third or fourth day. Emesis begins to resolve as the drugs are metabolized and excreted from the body. Patients receiving chemotherapy over multiple days experience both acute and delayed effects of the chemotherapeutic agents employed.[16,67] Strategies for preventing emesis over multiple-day cycles usually employ antiemetics aimed at preventing symptoms of acute emesis on the first day and symptoms of both acute and delayed emesis for up to six days after the period of acute emesis.

The administration of drugs at specific times during the circadian or biological cycle also may affect the frequency and severity of chemotherapy-induced emesis. Patients receiving cisplatin during the evening hours (at or after 1800) have less emesis than those who receive the same dose in the morning (at or after 0600).[68]

Other factors may also contribute to the overall risk of nausea and vomiting (Table 1) but not necessarily increase the frequency or severity of nausea and vomiting secondary to chemotherapy.

Prevention of Chemotherapy-Induced Nausea and Vomiting

Recommendation 1. The emetic potential of the chemotherapeutic agent (Table 3) is the primary factor to consider when deciding whether to administer pharmacologic prophylaxis and which antiemetic(s) to select. (Strength of evidence = A)

Table 3 shows a method for determining the emetic potential of combination therapy. The method has been adapted from an article published by Hesketh and colleagues.[57] In contrast to previously developed algorithms, this method includes newer chemotherapeutic agents and takes into account factors such as dose, route, and combination chemotherapy. The table was created on the basis of panel consensus after examination of clinical trials that used

Table 5.
Onset and Duration of Emesis[16,63-66]

Chemotherapeutic Agent	Onset of Emesis after Administration (hr)	Duration of Emesis (hr)
Aldesleukin	0–6	N.A.[a]
Androgens	48–100[b]	Variable
Asparaginase or pegaspargase	1–3	N.A.
Bleomycin	3–6	N.A.
Busulfan	N.A.	N.A.
Carboplatin (200–400 mg/m²)	2–6	1–48
Carmustine	2–6	4–24
Chlorambucil (oral)	48–72	N.A.
Cisplatin	1–6	>24
Cladribine	N.A.	N.A.
Corticosteroids	N.A.	N.A.
Cyclophosphamide[c]	6–12	6–36
Cytarabine (>1000 mg/m²)	6–12	3–5
Dacarbazine[d]	2–6	6–24
Dactinomycin	2–6	12–24
Daunorubicin	2–6	<24
Docetaxel	N.A.	N.A.
Doxorubicin	2–6	6–24
Etoposide	3–6	6–12
Fludarabine	N.A.	N.A.
Fluorouracil	3–6	3–6
Gemcitabine	N.A.	N.A.
Hydroxyurea	6–12	N.A.
Idarubicin	N.A.	N.A.
Ifosfamide	3–6	6–12
Interferon-beta	N.A.	N.A.
Irinotecan	2–6	6–12
Lomustine	3–6	6–12
Mechlorethamine	0.5–2	6–24
Melphalan (oral)	6–12	N.A.
Mercaptopurine	4–8	N.A.
Methotrexate	4–12	3–12
Mitomycin	2–6	18–24
Mitoxantrone (<15 mg/m²)	N.A.	N.A.
Paclitaxel	N.A.	N.A.
Pentostatin	N.A.	N.A.
Procarbazine (oral)[b]	24–27	Variable
Semustine	3–6	6–12
Streptozocin	2–6	12–24
Teniposide	3–6	6–12
Thioguanine	4–8	N.A.
Thiotepa	6–12	Variable
Vinblastine	4–8	N.A.
Vincristine	4–8	N.A.

[a]Not available.
[b]Development of tolerance possible.
[c]High dose.
[d]Characteristically, vomiting lessens with each subsequent dose when dacarbazine is given over five days.

chemotherapeutic agents, antiemetic review articles that addressed emetogenic classification, and antiemetic trials that contained a placebo control as well as the collective clinical experience of the panel. The recommendations for combined therapy need to be validated in several patient populations. The table provides the framework for recommendations on whether to provide antiemetic prophylaxis for patients and on the selection of agents. Newer agents that are not included in the guidelines established by Hesketh, et al. have been added to the table on the basis of the literature and panel consensus. This table was developed for adult patients and should be used cautiously in the pediatric population because of different degrees of emetogenicity, different dosages, and different combinations of chemotherapeutic agents used in this patient group. However, the table is considered to be generally applicable to children receiving chemotherapeutic agents.

Recommendation 2. Adult and pediatric patients receiving chemotherapeutic agent(s) with emetic potential classified as level 2 through 5 should receive pharmacologic prophylaxis against nausea and vomiting each day on which chemotherapy is given. (Strength of evidence = B) Antiemetic prophylaxis is not required when the level of emetogenicity is 1.

(a) Adult and pediatric patients receiving level-2 chemotherapeutic regimens can receive dexamethasone or methylprednisolone alone for prophylaxis of nausea and vomiting. (Strength of evidence = B) Prochlorperazine is also an option for adults. (Strength of evidence = D)

(b) Adult and pediatric patients receiving chemotherapeutic agent(s) with emetic potential of level 3 through 5 should receive a corticosteroid (dexamethasone or methylprednisolone) in combination with a 5-HT$_3$ receptor antagonist. (Strength of evidence = A for adults and C for pediatric patients)

(c) Orally and intravenously administered antiemetics are generally equivalent in efficacy and safety for both adult and pediatric patients. (Strength of evidence = B for adults and C for pediatric patients) The decision as to which formulation to use should be based on patient-specific factors and cost.

(d) The decision as to which 5-HT$_3$ receptor antagonist to use should be based on the acquisition cost of comparable doses. (Strength of evidence = A) (Tables 6 and 7) Dosage recommendations for adult and pediatric patients differ.

Efficacy of 5-HT$_3$ Receptor Antagonists. Ondansetron, granisetron, and dolasetron prevent the serotonin-stimulated emetic response by blocking the 5-HT$_3$ receptors of the vagal afferent nerves in the GI tract and the CTZ. Clinical trials have demonstrated the safety and efficacy of ondansetron, granisetron, and dolasetron for the prevention of acute nausea and vomiting in pediatric and adult patients, including patients receiving moderately emetogenic (cyclophosphamide) or highly emetogenic (cisplatin) chemotherapeutic agents.[41,42,46,47,69–108]

The safety of granisetron, ondansetron, and dolasetron has been demonstrated in clinical trials, with headache being the most common event (14%) and asthenia (5%), somnolence (4%), diarrhea (4%), constipation (3%), and fever (<1%) occurring infrequently. These effects are not dose or route dependent. A safety advantage of the 5-HT$_3$ receptor antagonists over metoclopramide has been demonstrated. In one study, the frequency of adverse effects was significantly less with granisetron than with metoclopramide (61% versus 77% respectively, $p = 0.003$).[109] Extrapyramidal effects and agitation were significantly less frequent ($p <0.0001$ and $p = 0.030$, respectively) with ondansetron than with metoclopramide.

In general, the 5-HT$_3$ receptor antagonists are well-tolerated agents. Few patients have withdrawn from clinical trials of these agents because of adverse effects. Significant differences among the 5-HT$_3$ receptor antagonists in the rate of adverse effects have generally not been seen.

The 5-HT$_3$ receptor antagonists as a class may cause electrocardiographic (ECG) interval changes (PR, Qt$_c$, and ST prolongation and QRS widening). With dolasetron, these changes are related in magnitude and frequency to blood levels of the active metabolite hydrodolasetron. These ECG changes are thought to occur secondary to the blockade of sodium channels.[110] The effects of dolasetron versus ondansetron on ECG recordings were studied in healthy volunteers.[111] The changes were acute, transient, and asymptomatic. Dolasetron was associated with significant dose-related increases in heart rate and PR and QRS intervals between zero and four hours. Ondansetron produced a significant increase in QT interval and decrease in heart rate. All values returned to baseline after eight hours.

5-HT$_3$ Receptor Antagonists versus Metoclopramide. Ondansetron, granisetron, and dolasetron have been compared with metoclopramide, with and without dexamethasone, in cisplatin-treated adult patients.[44,79,83,91,112–120] A large double-blind, randomized study examined the efficacy and safety of antiemetic prophylaxis with either ondansetron (0.15 mg/kg i.v. for three doses starting 30 minutes before chemotherapy and then every two hours for two doses) plus dexamethasone phosphate (20 mg i.v. daily) or metoclopramide (3 mg/kg i.v. given 30 minutes before chemotherapy and two hours after chemotherapy) plus dexamethasone phosphate (20 mg i.v. daily) and diphenhydramine hydrochloride (50 mg i.v. daily) in patients receiving cisplatin at a dose of at least 50 mg/m^2.[121] Complete protection from vomiting was found more frequently in the patients receiving ondansetron plus dexamethasone (79%) than in the patients receiving the metoclopramide combination (60%, $p <0.002$).[122] These results were maintained for up to three consecutive cycles of chemotherapy.

Similar results have been found in patients receiving granisetron or dolasetron. In a double-blind, randomized study comparing granisetron (1 mg orally twice daily) alone, granisetron (1 mg orally twice daily) plus dexamethasone phosphate (12 mg i.v. on day 1 only), and metoclopramide (3 mg/kg as a loading dose before cisplatin with a 4-mg/kg i.v. infusion over eight hours administered at the same time as cisplatin, and, on days 1–6, metoclopramide 10 mg orally three times daily) plus dexamethasone phosphate (12 mg i.v. on day 1) in patients receiving cisplatin at a dose of at least 50 mg/m^2, complete protection from emesis and nausea was found in 43.7%, 54.7%, and 37.2%, respectively, on the day cisplatin was administered.[115] The granisetron–dexamethasone combination was superior to both granisetron alone and the metoclopramide–dexamethasone combination ($p = 0.007$).

In a multicenter, double-blind, randomized trial, the efficacy and safety of dolasetron 1.2 or 1.8 mg/kg i.v. and metoclopramide 7 mg/kg i.v. were compared in 226 patients for the prevention of acute nausea and vomiting associated with high-dose cisplatin (>80 mg/m^2).[119] Complete response was obtained in 57% of patients receiving dolasetron 1.8 mg/kg, 48% of patients receiving dolasetron 1.2 mg/kg, and 35% of patients receiving metoclopramide. Both doses of dolasetron were more effective ($p = 0.0009$ for 1.8 mg/kg, $p = 0.0058$ for 1.2 mg/kg) than metoclopramide. Twelve percent of the patients receiving metoclopramide reported extrapyramidal symptoms, which is not unexpected with the large doses that were used.[119]

Studies have shown that, in patients receiving moderately emetogenic chemotherapy, ondansetron (8 mg orally three times daily, with the first dose sometimes administered intravenously) is at least as effective as metoclopramide (60 mg i.v. followed by 20 mg orally three times daily) and better tolerated.[123–125]

Table 6.
Standard Dosages and Costs of Antiemetics for Management of Chemotherapy-Induced Nausea and Vomiting in Adults

Agent	Dosage	Cost/Dose ($)[a]	Cost/Day($)[a]
Prophylaxis			
Ondansetron[b]	24 mg p.o. (tablet or suspension) 30 min before chemotherapy	38.46	. . .[c]
	8 mg i.v. 30 min before chemotherapy	48.90	. . .
Granisetron[b]	2 mg p.o. 30 min before chemotherapy	82.56	. . .
	10 µg/kg i.v. 30 min before chemotherapy	121.77[d]	. . .
Dolasetron[b]	100–200 mg p.o. 30 min before chemotherapy	66.00	. . .
	1.8 mg/kg or 100 mg i.v. 30 min before chemotherapy	149.88	. . .
Dexamethasone[f]	20 mg p.o. 30 min before chemotherapy	1.60	. . .
	20 mg i.v. 30 min before chemotherapy	3.08	. . .
Treatment			
Lorazepam	1–2 mg p.o. or sl q 6 hr	0.19–0.38	0.76–1.52
	1–2 mg i.m. or i.v. q 6 hr	5.19–10.30	20.76–41.52
Prochlorperazine	5–20 mg p.o. q 6 hr	2.54–2.16	2.16–8.64
	5–20 mg i.m. or i.v. q 6 hr	1.10–4.38	4.40–17.52
	25 mg rectally q 12 hr	3.39	6.78
	15–30 mg (extended-release capsule) p.o. q 12 hr	1.64–3.28	3.28–6.00
Metoclopramide	2 mg/kg i.v. q 2–4 hr for 2–5 doses; for delayed nausea and vomiting, 0.5 mg/kg or 30 mg i.v. q 4–6 hr for 3–5 days	3.94	7.88–19.70
	2 mg/kg p.o. q 2–4 hr for 2–5 doses; for delayed nausea and vomiting, 0.5 mg/kg or 30 mg p.o. q 4–6 hr for 3–5 days	0.51	1.02–2.55
Dexamethasone	10–20 mg p.o. q 4–6 hr	0.80–1.60	3.20–9.60
	10–20 mg i.v. q 4–6 hr	2.33–4.22	9.32–27.96
Haloperidol	1–4 mg p.o. q 6 hr	0.20–0.80	0.80–3.12
	1–4 mg i.m. or i.v. q 6 hr	0.75–3.00	3.00–12.00
Dronabinol	5–15 mg/m² (~5–20 mg) p.o. q 3–6 hr	5.87–22.49	23.48–179.92

[a]1998 *Red Book*.
[b]For use with chemotherapeutic agents having an emetogenic potential of level 3, 4, or 5.
[c]Not applicable.
[d]For a 70-kg patient.
[e]For use with chemotherapeutic agents having an emetogenic potential of level 2, 3, 4, or 5. Not recommended for use with aldesleukin.

Selecting a 5-HT₃ Receptor Antagonist. At equipotent doses, granisetron, ondansetron, and dolasetron do not appear to differ in efficacy or safety in patients treated with moderately or highly emetogenic chemotherapeutic regimens.[90,91,105,107,126–139] The comparative trials included a variety of combinations of chemotherapeutic agents as well as i.v. and oral antiemetic therapies at varying regimens. Two of the most recent trials were performed by Navari, et al.[105] and Roila.[136] The study by Navari, et al. was a large, double-blind study in which ondansetron (0.15 mg/kg i.v. for three doses) was compared with granisetron (10 or 40 µg/kg i.v.) in 987 chemotherapy-naïve patients receiving cisplatin (>70 mg/m²). The rate of complete protection from vomiting was similar among all three groups (51%, 47%, and 48%, respectively; *p* >0.05). Neither agent was used in combination with dexamethasone.

In the study by Roila,[136] ondansetron 8 mg plus dexamethasone phosphate 20 mg i.v. was compared with granisetron 3 mg and dexamethasone phosphate 20 mg i.v. in 973 chemotherapy-naïve patients receiving cisplatin at a dose of at least 50 mg/m². Neither group received the doses approved by FDA for the prevention of emesis in patients receiving highly emetogenic chemotherapy. The doses used were those approved by regulatory agencies in Europe (where the study was performed) for this indication. Complete protection from vomiting was similar between the two groups (79.3% and 79.9%, respectively).

A randomized, double-blind, parallel trial compared dolasetron 1.8 or 2.4 mg/kg i.v. with ondansetron 32 mg i.v. for the prevention of nausea and vomiting after highly

emetogenic chemotherapy.[138] All treatments were given over 15 minutes beginning 30 minutes before cisplatin administration. The complete response rates for dolasetron 1.8 and 2.4 mg/kg and ondansetron were 44.4%, 40%, and 42.7%, respectively. No significant differences were noted among treatment groups.

Granisetron and ondansetron were shown in a multicenter trial not to differ significantly in their effect on functional status (as defined by using the FLIE) before and 72 hours after cancer chemotherapy.[140]

The results of these trials and other data suggest that the choice of whether to use ondansetron, dolasetron, or granisetron should be based primarily on acquisition costs for comparable dosage regimens.

Intravenous versus Oral 5-HT₃ Receptor Antagonists. If adult or pediatric patients are able to take medication orally, therapy should generally be given via that route. There is strong evidence to support the use of oral dolasetron and granisetron in adult patients receiving highly emetogenic chemotherapy. There are as yet few published data to support the use of oral ondansetron in adult patients receiving highly emetogenic chemotherapy or the use of oral 5-HT₃ receptor antagonists in pediatric patients receiving highly emetogenic chemotherapy. Oral administration may obviate the need for i.v. access, is easier in outpatients, is usually less expensive, and is generally preferred over the i.v. route by the patient if he or she does not have i.v. access. Preclinical studies also suggest that oral therapy may have an advantage

Table 7.
Standard Dosages and Costs of Antiemetics for Management of Chemotherapy-Induced Nausea and Vomiting in Pediatric Patients

Drug	Dosage	Cost($)[a]		
		Per Regimen	Per Dose	Per Day
Prophylaxis				
Ondansetron	If 4–11 yr of age, 4 mg p.o. 30 min before and 4 and 8 hr after chemotherapy; may also be given as a single 12-mg dose 30 min before chemotherapy	34.65		
	If >11 yr of age, 8 mg p.o. 30 min before and 4 and 8 hr after chemotherapy; may also be given as single 24-mg dose 30 min before chemotherapy	55.02		
	If >3 yr of age, 0.15 mg/kg i.v. 30 min before and 4 and 8 hr after chemotherapy	146.70		
Granisetron	If ≥2 yr of age, 20–40 µg/kg i.v. 30 min before chemotherapy	34.79–69.58		
Dexamethasone	10–14 mg/m² p.o. in single or divided doses	1.44		
	10–14 mg/m² i.v. in single or divided doses	4.41		
Dolasetron	1.8 mg/kg p.o. 30 min before chemotherapy	49.80		
	1.8 mg/kg i.v. 30 min before chemotherapy	53.95		
Methylprednisolone	0.5–1 mg/kg p.o. 30 min before and 4 and 8 hr after chemotherapy (maximum total dose, 4 mg/kg); may also be given as single dose 30 min before chemotherapy	4.05–8.10		
	0.5–1 mg/kg i.v. 30 min before and 4 and 8 hr after chemotherapy (maximum total dose, 4 mg/kg); may also be given as single dose 30 min before chemotherapy	1.80–3.60		
Treatment				
Lorazepam	0.05 mg/kg (maximum, 3 mg) p.o. q 8–12 hr as needed		0.19	0.57–1.14
	0.05 mg/kg (maximum, 3 mg) i.v. q 8–12 hr as needed		5.19	15.57–31.14
Chlorpromazine	If >6 mo of age, 0.55 mg/kg p.o. q 4–6 hr as needed		0.07	0.28–0.42
	If >6 mo of age, 1.1 mg/kg rectally q 6–8 hr as needed (maximum of 40 mg per dose if age is <5 yr or weight is <22 kg)		3.25	9.75–13.00
	If >6 mo of age, 0.55 mg/kg i.v. q 6–8 hr as needed (maximum of 40 mg per dose if age is <5 yr or weight is <22 kg)		0.26	0.78–1.04
Methylprednisolone	0.5–1 mg/kg p.o. q 12 hr as needed		1.62–2.70	3.24–5.40
	0.5–1 mg/kg i.v. q 12 hr as needed		0.60–1.20	1.20–2.40
Dexamethasone	5–10 mg/m² p.o. q 12 hr as needed		0.48–1.44	0.96–2.88
	5–10 mg/m² i.v. q 12 hr as needed		1.19–2.33	2.34–4.66

[a]Based on 1998 *Red Book* prices. For 20-kg child or child with body surface area of 0.8 m².

over i.v. therapy because the oral formulation may act locally on the GI serotonin receptors.[36,141] There will be situations in which the i.v. route is preferred (e.g., patients unable to take oral medication because of vomiting at the time of or shortly after administration; pediatric patients receiving multiday, highly emetogenic drug combinations).

The efficacy and safety of an oral antiemetic regimen versus i.v. therapy was examined in patients receiving moderately and highly emetogenic chemotherapy in three recent studies.[135,142,143] In the trials by Perez, et al.[135] and Gralla, et al.,[142] 2 mg of oral granisetron was comparable in efficacy to 32 mg of i.v. ondansetron, with no significant difference in adverse events. In a study by Navari, et al.,[143] the oral combination of dolasetron and dexamethasone was associated with a clinically relevant longer time to first emetic episode than i.v. dolasetron and dexamethasone. Although there are some data showing that oral ondansetron may not be equivalent to the i.v. formulation, inadequate doses may have been used.[117]

Selecting a Dose of 5-HT₃ Receptor Antagonist. Several dose-finding studies have shown that ondansetron administered as a single i.v. dose of 8 or 32 mg is as effective as the formerly recommended multiple-dose regimen (0.15 mg/kg plus two additional doses administered at least four hours apart) or an infusion regimen (8 mg plus a continuous infusion of 1 mg/hr for 24 hours) in patients receiving high doses of cisplatin.[73,144,145] Seynaeve, et al.[144] evaluated 535 patients who received a single 32-mg i.v. dose of ondansetron, an 8-mg i.v. dose followed by a continuous infusion of 1 mg/hr for 24 hours, or a single 8-mg i.v. dose given before cisplatin chemotherapy. Control of emesis was similar among the three groups. Other studies support the efficacy of using an 8-mg dose.[127,146]

In a study by Hesketh and colleagues,[65] the efficacy and safety of i.v. ondansetron 32, 24, and 8 mg each combined with 20 mg of i.v. dexamethasone phosphate were examined in patients receiving chemotherapy of high, moderately high, or moderate emetic potential, respectively. This was not a randomized trial but a trial in which the different doses were based on chemotherapy treatments the patients received. Patients had good control of acute emesis across a wide spectrum of chemotherapy regimens, with a complete response obtained in 72%, 88%, and 77% of patients in the high, moderately high, and moderate categories, respectively. Roila, et al.[136] demonstrated the equivalence of ondansetron 8 mg i.v. with granisetron 3 mg i.v. when each was used with i.v. dexamethasone. In a large-scale, double-blind study involving 699 patients, the efficacy of ondansetron 32 mg i.v. was found to be superior to the 8-mg i.v. dose.[145]

On the basis of these studies, a single dose of 8 mg i.v. is recommended for most adult patients if ondansetron is used for the prevention of nausea and vomiting in patients receiving chemotherapy of emetogenic levels 3 to 5. Most of the data supporting i.v. ondansetron doses of 8 mg were based on cisplatin regimens administered in doses of 75 mg/m², on average. It is unclear whether patients receiving cisplatin doses exceeding 100 mg/m² would benefit from higher ondansetron doses. In pediatric patients, 0.15 mg/kg has been used, but lower doses may be effective. Tables 6 and 7 list the recommended dosages for adult and pediatric patients.

The efficacy and tolerability of ondansetron 24 mg orally plus dexamethasone 12 mg orally were compared with the efficacy and tolerability of ondansetron 8 mg i.v. plus dexamethasone phosphate 20 mg i.v. in patients receiving highly emetogenic chemotherapy.[147] A total of 562 patients were randomly assigned to receive oral (262 patients) or i.v. (266 patients) therapy. Complete or major control of emesis was achieved in 90% of the patients in the oral group and 89% in the i.v. group. There was no significant difference in efficacy or tolerability between 24 mg of oral ondanisetron plus dexamethasone and 8 mg of i.v. ondansetron plus dexamethasone in the prevention of acute nausea and vomiting with highly emetogenic chemotherapy.

Many of the available studies with i.v. granisetron have used 40 μg/kg instead of the 10-μg/kg dose approved by FDA. However, clinical studies have shown that both doses are comparable in most patients, and therefore it is recommended that 10 μg/kg or 1 mg be used in adults.[97,148,149] This was further confirmed in a recent large-scale clinical trial in which a 1-mg i.v. dose was similar in efficacy to a 3-mg i.v. dose.[105] In pediatric patients, doses higher than 10 μg/kg may be necessary.[80]

Dose-ranging studies have been performed to determine the optimal dose of dolasetron for the prevention of nausea and vomiting[102,104,150–158] in adult and pediatric patients.[105,107,153–161] An i.v. dose of 1.8 mg/kg has been shown to be safe and effective in adults and pediatric patients. Oral doses of 25, 50, 100, and 200 mg in adults were compared in a pooled analysis performed by Rubenstein, et al.[154] in patients receiving moderately emetogenic chemotherapy. Fewer patients who received the 25-mg dose had a complete response compared with those who received the 100- and 200-mg dose (p <0.001). The difference between the 100- and 200-mg dose was not significant (p = 0.052); therefore, the 100-mg oral dose is recommended for the prevention of nausea and vomiting in adult patients receiving moderately emetogenic chemotherapy, but a dose of 200 mg may be required in patients receiving highly emetogenic chemotherapy.

Combining 5-HT₃ Receptor Antagonists with Dexamethasone. When combination antiemetic therapy is being considered, agents with different mechanisms of action should

be selected if possible. The mechanism by which corticosteroids exert their antiemetic activity is unknown, but investigators have theorized that it may be inhibition of prostaglandin synthesis or modification of the blood–cerebrospinal fluid barrier for chemotherapeutic agents. Another theory is that corticosteroids inhibit cortical input into the vomiting center. Several double-blind, large-scale trials have shown that the combination of ondansetron or granisetron with dexamethasone is significantly more effective than either agent alone against high-dose cisplatin-induced emesis.[67,68,98,115,139,159–168]

In a study by Joss,[169] 215 patients were randomly assigned to receive ondansetron 8 mg i.v. plus placebo or the same dose of ondansetron with dexamethasone phosphate 8 mg i.v. 15 minutes before and four and eight hours after administration of highly emetogenic chemotherapy. In chemotherapy-naïve patients, the combination of ondansetron plus dexamethasone was significantly better than ondansetron and placebo in protecting the patients completely from emesis (81% versus 64%, respectively; p = 0.04).

The combination of granisetron with dexamethasone has been found to be superior to granisetron alone in patients receiving moderately emetogenic chemotherapeutic agents. One study evaluated 428 patients who were being treated with moderately emetogenic chemotherapy (cyclophosphamide 600–1000 mg/m², doxorubicin >50 mg/m², epirubicin >75 mg/m², or carboplatin >300 mg/m² alone or in combination) and randomly assigned to receive one of three antiemetic drug regimens.[162] One group of patients received dexamethasone phosphate 8 mg i.v. before chemotherapy and dexamethasone 4 mg orally immediately before the start of chemotherapy and every 6 hours for 24 hours (four doses). Another group received granisetron 3 mg i.v. 20 minutes before chemotherapy. A third group received the combination of granisetron and dexamethasone (granisetron 3 mg i.v. 20 minutes before chemotherapy, followed by dexamethasone phosphate 8 mg i.v., then dexamethasone 4 mg orally immediately before the start of chemotherapy; the dexamethasone dose was repeated every six hours for a total of four doses). Patients who received the combination regimen were found to have complete protection from vomiting, nausea, and both nausea and vomiting (93%, 72%, and 70%, respectively) more frequently compared with those who received dexamethasone (71%, 55%, and 49%) and granisetron alone (72%, 48%, and 43%). Combination therapy was significantly better than either agent alone in providing complete protection from either nausea or vomiting. This effect was maintained through several cycles of chemotherapy.[163] Dexamethasone alone was as effective as granisetron alone in preventing emesis induced by moderately emetogenic chemotherapy.

Similar to ondansetron and granisetron, the efficacy of dolasetron was enhanced by the addition of dexamethasone.[139]

Although there has been concern that corticosteroids may interfere with the antitumor effects of chemotherapy through immunosuppressive mechanisms, this has not been documented in clinical trials. The known benefits of corticosteroids as antiemetics outweigh these unproven theoretical concerns. However, this may not be the case with some biological agents, such as aldesleukin. The coadministration of glucocorticoids such as dexamethasone with aldesleukin should be avoided.[170] Interleukin-2 produced by T-helper cells stimulates the production of the immune system's T-killer cells to activate an immune response against the tumor.

Dexamethasone may decrease the antitumor effectiveness of aldesleukin by inhibiting the activity of the T-helper cells, thereby decreasing T-killer-cell activity.[171–173]

Corticosteroids are used for the treatment of many malignancies and are usually administered as a single dose before chemotherapy. It is extremely unlikely that using these agents as antiemetics in this way would lead to clinically significant adverse reactions. Corticosteroids should be used with caution in patients with unstable diabetes mellitus. Data supporting the use of additional agents (e.g., D_2 antagonists) in combination with 5-HT$_3$ receptor antagonists are emerging.[174]

Use of Dexamethasone Alone or Prochlorperazine with Mildly to Moderately Emetogenic Chemotherapy. High doses of corticosteroids, such as methylprednisolone 250 mg and dexamethasone 20 mg, given intravenously or orally, have demonstrated useful antiemetic activity when used alone for the prevention of acute nausea in patients receiving mildly to moderately emetogenic chemotherapy.[175–179] Dexamethasone has been shown to be at least as effective as prochlorperazine in these patients.[178,179] Markman, et al.[178] demonstrated that patients receiving moderately emetogenic chemotherapy have significantly less nausea and vomiting (p <0.02 and p <0.03, respectively), less somnolence (p <0.001), and less suppression of appetite (p <0.02) with dexamethasone than with prochlorperazine. Few associated effects are reported with dexamethasone and include mood changes, increased appetite, and a feeling of well-being.

Prochlorperazine is a reasonable alternative to dexamethasone in adults. Phenothiazines, such as prochlorperazine, were the first agents reported to provide significant antiemetic activity in patients receiving chemotherapy and have been used for more than 30 years.[179,180] They have been shown to be effective in the prevention of nausea and vomiting in patients receiving mildly to moderately emetogenic chemotherapy.

Pediatrics. Several reports support the safety and efficacy of ondansetron, granisetron, and dolasetron in pediatric patients.[75,80,89,92,96,100–104,106,171,181–184] Ondansetron is commercially available as an oral solution, whereas granisetron and dolasetron are not. Granisetron hydrochloride injection has been shown to be stable in apple juice, orange juice, cola, and electrolyte-replacement solution for at least one hour when stored at room temperature.[185,186] Dolasetron injection mixed in apple or apple–grape juice may be kept for up to two hours at room temperature before use.[110]

Ondansetron was compared with metoclopramide plus dexamethasone in a randomized, controlled study of 30 patients ages 1 to 15 years who received moderately emetogenic chemotherapeutic agents.[101] Patients received ondansetron 3–8 mg/m² i.v. over three to five minutes before chemotherapy followed by 3–8 mg/m² i.v. or orally and every 12 hours for three days. Intravenous metoclopramide was given at a dose of 10 mg/m² before chemotherapy and every six hours for at least three days. Dexamethasone was given at a dose of 2 or 4 mg/m² i.v. or orally three times daily. In the 24 hours after the start of chemotherapy, ondansetron was more effective than the metoclopramide–dexamethasone combination: 93% of patients receiving ondansetron and 33% of patients receiving metoclopramide in combination with dexamethasone had a complete (no emetic episodes) or major (1 to 2 emetic episodes) response. The dose of metoclopramide in this study (approximately 0.33 mg/kg) was low. Most studies that have demonstrated the efficacy of metoclopramide

for chemotherapy-induced nausea and vomiting have used doses greater than 1 mg/kg.

Similar results were found by Hahlen and colleagues[102] when granisetron was compared with a chlorpromazine–dexamethasone combination. Children were assigned on a single-blind basis to receive either granisetron or a combination of dexamethasone and chlorpromazine for the duration of ifosfamide treatment (two to three days). On each treatment day, granisetron 20 µg/kg was infused immediately before ifosfamide. Two subsequent doses (20 µg/kg) were permitted within each 24-hour period. In the other group, dexamethasone phosphate 2 mg/m² was infused 30 minutes before ifosfamide therapy each day, followed by 2 mg/m² 8 and 16 hours later. At the start of the study, the chlorpromazine dosage was 0.5 mg/kg i.v. 25 minutes before ifosfamide infusion and at four- to six-hour intervals. This dosage proved too sedating and was subsequently reduced to 0.3 mg/kg followed by 0.3–0.5 mg/kg at four- to six-hour intervals. During the first 24 hours, 50% of the patients in the granisetron group experienced either no vomiting or one vomiting episode, compared with 21% of the patients in the chlorpromazine and dexamethasone group (p = 0.005).

Dolasetron has been used in the pediatric population.[104,106] Doses of 0.6–2.4 mg/kg were evaluated in 46 children receiving moderately to highly emetogenic chemotherapy.[104] Complete response rates ranged from 10% to 67% and did not necessarily correlate with dose.

The value of adding dexamethasone to a 5-HT$_3$ receptor antagonist was evaluated in a study by Alvarez, et al.[98] involving 34 children 3 to 18 years of age. The children were given ondansetron 0.15 mg/kg i.v. 30 minutes before chemotherapy and at four and eight hours in combination with either placebo or dexamethasone 4–8 mg/m² i.v. every four to six hours. All the patients received highly emetogenic chemotherapy, including cisplatin, cyclophosphamide, and ifosfamide. Complete response (no episodes of emesis) occurred in 61% of the patients who received ondansetron plus dexamethasone and 23% of the patients who received ondansetron plus placebo. Significance was not determined. Although a total dose of 0.45 mg/kg was used, reduced doses of ondansetron have been shown to be effective.

Both dexamethasone and methylprednisolone are used in pediatric patients. Although most of the literature supporting the addition of corticosteroids relates to dexamethasone, the risk of perineal irritation is lower with methylprednisolone.[187] In adult patients, this adverse effect has been shown to be minimized by slowing the infusion rate. Although corticosteroids can be used, many children receiving moderately emetogenic chemotherapy regimens have leukemia or lymphoma and already receive a corticosteroid as part of their chemotherapy regimen.

Chlorpromazine has been shown to be effective in pediatric patients receiving moderately emetogenic chemotherapeutic agents.[188–192] One of the most frequent adverse effects of chlorpromazine is sedation.

Pharmacoeconomic Issues. Johnson and colleagues[193] evaluated the clinical and economic outcomes associated with the use of ondansetron in patients receiving chemotherapy. The objectives of the study were to (1) retrospectively compare lengths of hospital stay and overall hospital costs for patients receiving ondansetron or "standard" antiemetic therapy, (2) concurrently examine the hospital costs associated with managing an episode of severe nausea and vomiting in patients receiving chemotherapy, and (3) concurrently compare quality-of-life scores for patients admitted for chemotherapy who received ondansetron or standard therapy. The recommended indication for ondansetron at the study institution was for patients receiving moderately to highly emetogenic chemotherapy or patients intolerant to other antiemetic regimens. Ondansetron was not used routinely to prevent or treat delayed episodes of nausea and vomiting. The standard dosage regimen for ondansetron at the study institution was the manufacturer's recommended dose of 0.15 mg/kg i.v. over 15 minutes, 30 minutes before chemotherapy, and four and eight hours later for each cycle of chemotherapy. The study by Johnson, et al. supports a shorter hospital stay for patients who received ondansetron than for those who received standard therapy when severity of illness and disease are controlled for. The hospital costs per admission were lower, hospital revenue per admission was higher, and resource consumption was lower in the patients receiving ondansetron versus the standard therapy group. Of the 52 patients who were asked to participate in the quality-of-life analysis, 27 completed the FLIC portion of the questionnaire. Mean scores were lower after chemotherapy was administered in both the ondansetron and standard therapy groups; there was not a significant difference between the two groups. Major limitations of this study were that standard antiemetic therapy and antineoplastic doses were not defined. Other studies that have examined the economic impact of 5-HT$_3$ receptor antagonists[192,194–199] generally support their use with highly emetogenic chemotherapy. These studies differ in their methods and definitions of outcomes.

For the prevention of acute emesis, the 5-HT$_3$ receptor antagonists are more expensive than other antiemetics, but they are more effective. In an economic analysis conducted by Dranitsaris and colleagues,[200] patients with breast cancer who received FEC or FAC chemotherapy (fluorouracil–epirubicin–cyclophosphamide or fluorouracil–doxorubicin–cylophosphamide) and ondansetron for acute or delayed emesis were studied. Total costs (primary, rescue, and failure costs) were $56.73 and $51.31 for the ondansetron and comparitor groups, respectively. Patients in the comparitor group received metoclopramide i.v., diphenhydramine i.v., and lorazepam sublingually. Beyond the first 24 hours, 5-HT$_3$ receptor antagonists became an increasingly more expensive option (i.e., less value for money).

In contrast, Zbrozek and colleagues[201] suggested that ondansetron provides only a small benefit at a large overall cost compared with metoclopramide. There were, however, several limitations to their cost-utility analysis. The authors assumed that successful treatment of nausea and vomiting is analogous to the improvement of chronic mild to moderate angina. However, it is difficult to extrapolate the improvement in quality of life and satisfaction of patients with angina to cancer patients at high risk for chemotherapy-induced nausea and vomiting. In addition, the authors' definitions of successful treatment and associated costs were not inclusive or reflective of clinical practice. The time that patients were at risk for nausea and vomiting was arbitrarily set at one day. Because cost-utility analysis has an implied extrapolation to a full year (quality adjusted life year), this would make sense if chemotherapy were repeated every day. Because chemotherapy is usually repeated only once a month, the cost utility is reduced.

From pharmacoeconomic studies it appears that 5-HT$_3$ receptor antagonists are a cost-effective choice for adults and children receiving moderately to highly emetogenic agents.

Treatment of Breakthrough Chemotherapy-Induced Nausea and Vomiting

Recommendation 3. All patients receiving chemotherapy should have antiemetics available on an as-needed basis for rescue for breakthrough nausea and vomiting. (Strength of evidence = A) Patients should be educated on the appropriate administration of and expectations for therapy and should be reassured that every effort is being made to prevent symptoms. In adults, lorazepam, methylprednisolone, prochlorperazine, metoclopramide, dexamethasone, haloperidol, and dronabinol are effective. (Strength of evidence = C) In pediatric patients, chlorpromazine, lorazepam, or methylprednisolone (or dexamethasone) is recommended. (Strength of evidence = B) The choice of agent should be based on patient-specific factors (e.g., anticipated adverse effects, past success) and cost.

Agents available for the management of nausea and vomiting include chlorpromazine, prochlorperazine, methylprednisolone, lorazepam, metoclopramide, dexamethasone, haloperidol, and dronabinol. These agents differ in their mechanism of action, dosage, adverse effects, and cost.

Chlorpromazine, prochlorperazine, and haloperidol are thought to exert their antiemetic activity by inhibiting dopamine at the CTZ. The anticholinergic activity of these agents may also contribute to their antiemetic effects. Metoclopramide exerts its activity by inhibiting the dopa-mine receptors, and, at high doses, 5-HT$_3$ receptors in the GI tract and CTZ. Lorazepam is thought to inhibit the limbic system and cortical input into the vomiting center. The mechanism of action of dronabinol is unknown. The efficacy of these rescue medications, especially haloperidol, dronabinol, prochlorperazine, and promethazine, has not been well documented in the medical literature.

Tables 6 and 7 list recommended dosages and costs of lorazepam, chlorpromazine, prochlorperazine, metoclopramide, methylprednisolone, dexamethasone, haloperidol, and dronabinol for the treatment of chemotherapy-induced nausea and vomiting. At recommended dosages, these agents are generally associated with a low risk of adverse effects in most patients and are generally inexpensive. Metoclopramide has been associated with frequent adverse effects in children, including dystonic reactions.[202–208] Table 2 lists the most common adverse effects of the different classes of agents used.

Granisetron, dolasetron, and ondansetron have also been shown to be effective in the treatment of breakthrough nausea and vomiting, but their superiority over more traditional, less expensive agents has not been determined. Results from several noncomparative trials demonstrate that ondansetron and granisetron are effective in treating chemotherapy-induced emesis refractory to conventional therapy.[42,209–211]

The cannabinoids have complex central nervous system effects, including central sympathomimetic action. Evidence supports the selective use of pure tetrahydrocannabinol (THC) preparations to treat nausea associated with chemotherapy rather than the reclassification of crude marijuana as a prescribable medicine.[212] Because the oral form of THC can be abused, only the amount necessary for a single cycle should be prescribed.

The reader is referred to recommendation 10 for guidance in managing patients who do not respond to initial therapy with an antiemetic agent.

Prevention of Delayed Chemotherapy-Induced Emesis

Recommendation 4. For the prevention of delayed emesis after cisplatin therapy in adults, dexamethasone with metoclopramide or a 5-HT$_3$ receptor antagonist is recommended. (Strength of evidence = A) The choice of agent should be based on patient-specific factors and cost. For delayed emesis after cyclophosphamide, doxorubicin, or carboplatin therapy, a 5-HT$_3$ receptor antagonist with dexamethasone is recommended. (Strength of evidence = B) Prochlorperazine in combination with dexamethasone has also been used and is available in extended-release and rectal dosage forms, but the evidence to support this combination is limited. (Strength of evidence = D) In pediatric patients, chlorpromazine, lorazepam, or a 5-HT$_3$ receptor antagonist can be used in combination with a corticosteroid. (Strength of evidence = C)

Delayed emesis occurs most frequently with cisplatin and cyclophosphamide. Patients who have problems with delayed nausea and vomiting during their initial cycle of chemotherapy are more likely to have an occurrence during subsequent cycles.

The use of metoclopramide in combination with dexamethasone was shown to be effective in a double-blind, controlled trial comparing placebo, dexamethasone, and the combination of dexamethasone and metoclopramide in cisplatin-treated patients.[48] Delayed vomiting was prevented in 11% of placebo recipients, 35% of patients receiving dexamethasone, and 52% of patients treated with the combination of metoclopramide and dexamethasone, with the greatest benefits at two to three days after cisplatin therapy. Patients received dexamethasone 8 mg orally twice daily for two days then 4 mg orally twice daily for two days plus metoclopramide 0.5 mg/kg orally four times daily for four days.

Oral ondansetron was shown to be effective in a randomized placebo-controlled trial.[213] The patients who received ondansetron had significantly fewer emetic episodes on days 2 and 3 combined, day 4, and day 5 than the patients who received placebo (p <0.002). On days 2 and 3, the complete response rate was 36% for patients receiving ondansetron and 26% for placebo recipients.

The Italian Group for Antiemetic Research[214] compared the efficacy and safety of oral ondansetron 8 mg twice daily with that of oral metoclopramide 20 mg every six hours, both combined with intramuscular dexamethasone phosphate (8 mg twice daily on days two and three and 4 mg twice daily on day four), in 322 patients who had been given cisplatin 50 mg/m² or more. All patients received the same i.v. prophylactic regimen for acute emesis (ondansetron 8 mg and dexamethasone phosphate 20 mg). Complete protection from delayed emesis and nausea was achieved in 62% and 44% of patients with ondansetron and 60% and 54% of patients with metoclopramide, respectively. These differences were not significant (p ≥0.05). There was no difference in the occurrence of adverse effects between the two groups, with the exception of constipation and heartburn, which occurred more frequently in patients receiving ondansetron plus dexamethasone (18.4% versus 8.1%, p <0.008, and 8.9% versus 3.1%, p <0.035, respectively).

The advantage of prochlorperazine is that, in addition to an oral and i.v. formulation, commercially available rectal and extended-release oral products may be an option in some patients. Two preliminary studies assessed the efficacy of using the combination of metoclopramide, dexamethasone, and prochlorperazine for up to one week after cisplatin therapy. The treated groups had superior results to those of the control group.[215,216] The combination of prochlorperazine, diphenhydramine, and lorazepam has also been shown to be effective.[217]

Physiology of Radiation Therapy-Induced Nausea and Vomiting

Radiation therapy-induced emesis is a very complex process. The exact mechanism remains to be fully elucidated.[11,218] It has been suggested that the vomiting center and the vagal nuclei, stimulated either directly by radiation or indirectly through chemical mediators, may play a critical role in producing the emetogenic effects of radiation.[10] Possible chemical mediators include ß-endorphin, prostaglandins, histamine, methionine, encephalin, and catecholamines.[10,11] Recently, it has been postulated that serotonin, released from the enterochromaffin cells of the GI tract, may induce vomiting through interactions with visceral afferent fibers and the 5-HT$_3$ receptors.[218]

Factors to Consider in the Selection of an Agent for Radiation Therapy-Induced Nausea and Vomiting

Many patients receiving radiation therapy will require no medication for prevention or treatment of nausea and vomiting. In general, nausea and vomiting associated with radiation therapy is not as predictable or severe as chemotherapy-induced nausea and vomiting.

The site of radiation is a primary factor to consider in efforts to anticipate the risk, onset, peak, and duration of nausea and vomiting with radiation therapy. Essentially all patients who receive total body irradiation have nausea and vomiting, especially if radiation therapy is combined with highly emetogenic chemotherapeutic agents.[8–12] In contrast, the risk of emesis is low if only the extremities are irradiated.[9] About 83% of patients receiving mid- and upper-hemibody irradiation have nausea and vomiting; the frequencies are 50% for fractionated radiation of the upper abdomen and 39% for lower-hemibody irradiation.[9,219] With fractionated radiation of the upper abdomen, the onset is in two to three weeks. The onset is more rapid (40–90 minutes) with total body irradiation or mid-, upper-, or lower-hemibody irradiation.

Other radiation-related risk factors include the dose, dose rate, and field size (Table 8).[8–12] The risk of nausea and vomiting is greater if radiation is delivered as a single high dose than if it is given as fractionated smaller doses, if higher dose rates are used, and with larger field sizes (e.g., total body irradiation).[11,219]

Chemotherapy given immediately before or concurrent with radiation therapy increases the risk of nausea and vomiting. Other factors include the psychological state of the patient (e.g., the presence of anxiety) and other stimuli, including smell, taste, and vestibular stimulation. Females are more apt to have nausea and vomiting than males, as are patients over the age of 10 years. Readers are referred to other resources for an overview of radiation therapy.[9,11,220]

Studies of the management of nausea and vomiting in patients receiving radiation therapy are limited. Most of the studies are not well controlled. Determination of the most

Table 8.
Risk Factors for Radiation Therapy-Induced Emesis[a]

Treatment-Related Factors
   Site of irradiation
   Dose of radiation
   Dose rate
   Field size
Other Factors
   Recent or concurrent cytotoxic therapy
   Patient's psychological state
   Sensory stimuli
   Patient's sex
   Patient's age

[a]See text for details.

appropriate antiemetic regimen is difficult because of the variability in design, patient selection, dosage regimen, irradiation treatment (site, dosage, duration), use of concomitant chemotherapy, definition of successful therapy, and variability in time course during which nausea and vomiting were assessed.

Prevention of Radiation Therapy-Induced Nausea and Vomiting

Recommendation 5. Patients receiving total or hemibody irradiation (with or without concomitant chemotherapeutic agents) or single-exposure, high-dose radiation therapy to the upper abdomen should receive preventive therapy for nausea and vomiting with each day of therapy. (Strength of evidence = A) A 5-HT$_3$ receptor antagonist should be used both in adults and in pediatric patients. (Strength of evidence = B) Oral therapy should be encouraged; however, i.v. therapy is an acceptable option. (Strength of evidence = B) There is no evidence to support the use of 5-HT$_3$ receptor antagonists 24 hours beyond the last dose of radiation.

Animal studies have demonstrated that, after irradiation, serotonin is released from the enterochromaffin cells of the intestine.[38] Emesis produced by radiation appears to be mediated through activation of peripheral or central 5-HT$_3$ receptors by the release of serotonin. 5-HT$_3$ receptor antagonists have been shown to be effective in alleviating radiation-induced emesis in ferrets.[221] Published studies support the efficacy of ondansetron, granisetron, and dolasetron for the prevention of emesis caused by radiation therapy.[12,222–237] Frequently patients receive total body irradiation and chemotherapy concomitantly. Selection of an antiemetic agent should be based on both the level of emetogenicity of chemotherapy and risk factors associated with radiation-induced emesis. Readers are referred to Tables 6 and 7 for dosage regimens.

Ondansetron has been shown to be more effective than low-dose metoclopramide in patients undergoing radiation therapy. A multicenter, randomized, double-blind study compared oral ondansetron 8 mg with oral metoclopramide 10 mg in adult patients receiving 8 to 10 GY to the abdomen in a single exposure.[224] Both medications were given one to two hours before radiation and every eight hours for five days. On day 1 of radiation, ondansetron was associated with complete control of emesis in 97% of the patients, compared with 46% of the patients treated with metoclopramide (p <0.001). On days 2–5, the differences were no longer significant, with control in 68% and 65% of patients on days 2 and 3 with

ondansetron and metoclopramide, respectively, and 97% and 95% of patients on days 4 and 5 for ondansetron and metoclopramide, respectively. There are several limitations of the study. The dose of metoclopramide was low, the methods were not well described, and several other variables (e.g., concomitant medications or diseases, dose of radiation) could have influenced the results of the study.

Ondansetron was compared with prochlorperazine for the prevention of nausea and vomiting in 135 adults undergoing fractionated irradiation of the upper abdomen.[235] Antiemetic therapy was administered throughout radiation therapy at the following dosages: ondansetron 8 mg orally three times daily and prochlorperazine 10 mg orally three times daily. Some 61% of the patients who received ondansetron and 35% of those given prochlorperazine had a complete response, with no emetic episodes throughout their treatment course (p = 0.002). One of the limitations of the study is the low doses of prochlorperazine used.

Prentice and colleagues[237] compared i.v. granisetron with the combination of metoclopramide, dexamethasone, and lorazepam in 30 bone marrow transplant patients receiving total body irradiation. The patients in the granisetron group received a mean total radiation dose of 750 cGY and the combination-therapy group, 749 cGY; the doses were administered over a mean time of 1.2 hours in both groups. All patients had received chemotherapy, including high-dose cyclophosphamide, which was completed at least 66 hours before radiation therapy. After 24 hours, eight patients in the granisetron group and two in the combination-therapy group had a complete response.

In a double-blind, placebo-controlled trial, the efficacy of dolasetron 0.3, 0.6, and 1.2 mg i.v. for the prevention of nausea and vomiting after radiation therapy was examined.[238] Significantly fewer patients in the placebo group than in the groups receiving 0.3, 0.6, or 1.2 mg had complete control of vomiting (54%, 100%, 93%, and 83%; p = 0.002).

If patients are able to take medication orally, therapy should be given by that route. This recommendation is based on potential therapeutic benefits, ease of administration, patient preference, and cost.

Limited evidence supports the use of the 5-HT$_3$ receptor antagonists during radiation therapy in the pediatric population.[70,75,233,239,240] Most studies included children of various ages, and sometimes data in children were combined with data from adult patients. In an uncontrolled study by Jurgens and colleagues,[231] 15 children between the ages of two and seven years received undefined conditioning regimens of chemotherapy, total body irradiation, and ondansetron before bone marrow transplantation. Ondansetron was given intravenously at doses of 5 mg/m^2 or 8 mg immediately before the chemotherapy regimen, according to the body surface area. Intravenous or oral therapy at a dose of 2, 4, or 8 mg (according to body surface area) was continued three times daily during chemotherapy administration and total body irradiation and for a further two days if a noncisplatin conditioning regimen was used and five days if cisplatin was used. Complete or major control of emesis (zero to two emetic episodes) was achieved in 57% of the patients on their worst day of total body irradiation.

The 5-HT$_3$ receptor antagonist should be given with each day of radiation therapy. There is no evidence to support the use of 5-HT$_3$ receptor antagonists 24 hours beyond the last dose of radiation therapy.

Treatment of Radiation Therapy-Induced Nausea and Vomiting

Recommendation 6. If an agent is needed to treat established radiation therapy-induced emesis in adults, prochlorperazine, metoclopramide, or thiethylperazine is recommended. 5-HT$_3$ receptor antagonists are also an option. Chlorpromazine and lorazepam can be used in pediatric patients. (Strength of evidence = D)

Prochlorperazine, metoclopramide, and thiethylperazine have been used for the treatment of nausea and vomiting caused by radiation therapy.[6,224,241,242] They are generally effective, have few adverse effects, and are available in different formulations—oral, injectable, and rectal (prochlorperazine only). Metoclopramide, although not commercially available as a rectal formulation, has been given rectally.[243] The choice of agent should be based on anticipated adverse effects (Table 2), previous successes, and cost. If combination therapy is needed for severe nausea and vomiting, combination therapy should include medications with different mechanisms of action and adverse effect profiles. Patients should then receive prophylactic ondansetron or granisetron before each subsequent radiation treatment.

Treatments for nausea and vomiting secondary to radiation therapy in the pediatric population are not well substantiated. Recommendations to use chlorpromazine and lorazepam for treatment of radiation-induced nausea and vomiting are based on data from pediatric patients receiving the medications for treatment of nausea and vomiting secondary to other precipitating factors (e.g., chemotherapy).

Physiology of Postoperative Nausea and Vomiting

Many of the pathways in the control of postoperative nausea and vomiting are complex and have not been fully elucidated. With cancer chemotherapy-induced emesis, the agent is the stimulus. With postoperative nausea and vomiting, however, a wide range of stimuli contributes to the emetic response of patients.[2,5,7,244–248]

Factors to Consider in the Selection of an Agent for Postoperative Nausea and Vomiting

Antiemetic selection should be based on safety and efficacy, patient factors, risk factors for nausea and vomiting, and costs. Many factors influence the risk and severity of postoperative nausea and vomiting (Table 9). They can be classified as pertaining to the patient, the operative procedure, anesthesia, or the postoperative period.

Certain patient characteristics increase the risk of postoperative nausea and vomiting.[2,5,7,244–248] The risk is higher in adults than in children, in women (particularly premenopausal women) than in men, in obese patients, in patients who have a high level of preoperative anxiety, and in patients who have a low threshold for nausea (e.g., patients with a history of motion sickness or patients who have previously had postoperative nausea and vomiting).[5,244,246] The risk is also higher in patients with delayed gastric emptying secondary to disorders such as GI obstruction, gastroesophageal reflux disease, chronic cholecystitis, neuromuscular disorders, and intrinsic neuropathies.[5] Gastric hypomotility can compli-

Table 9.
Risk Factors for Postoperative Nausea and Vomiting[a]

> *Patient-Specific Factors*
>   Age
>   Sex
>   Weight
>   Threshold for nausea
>   Psychological stress
>   Delayed gastric emptying
> *Operative Procedure*
>   Indication for surgery
>   Type of surgery
>   Duration of procedure
>   Intubation procedure
> *Anesthetic-Related Factors*
>   Preanesthetic medication
>   Oral intake
>   Gastric distension
>   Anesthetic
>   Reversal of muscle relaxation
>   Duration of anesthesia
>   Use of opioids
> *Postoperative Factors*
>   Presence of pain
>   Patient movement
>   Oral intake

[a]See text for details.

cate conditions such as scleroderma, myotonic dystrophy, progressive muscular dystrophies, amyloidosis, and familial visceral myopathies.

The operative procedure also affects rates of postoperative nausea and vomiting.[2,5,7,244–248] If nausea and vomiting are components of the disorder being treated (e.g., increased intracranial pressure, upper GI obstruction), the rate of postoperative nausea and vomiting may be increased.[5] Certain types of procedures are associated with nausea and vomiting: intra-abdominal, major gynecological, orthopedic, ear–nose–throat, or laparoscopic surgery; adenotonsil-lectomy; and surgery for strabismus.[5,7,244] Intubation may evoke nausea and vomiting, and longer procedures are associated with more nausea and vomiting than shorter ones.[5,244]

Anesthesia-related factors must also be considered.[2,5,7,244–248] The preanesthetic medication can influence the risk of postoperative nausea and vomiting. Morphine and other opioids can increase the risk; atropine decreases the risk.[245,248] The risk of nausea and vomiting is generally less with regional nerve block procedures than with general anesthesia.[5] General anesthetics vary in their propensity to cause postoperative nausea and vomiting. Etomidate and ketamine may increase the risk. Nitrous oxide and inhalation agents may also cause nausea, with the risk ranked as follows: ether and cyclopropane > halothane > enflurane > isoflurane > sevoflurane and desflurane. Propofol decreases the risk. Other factors that increase the risk of postoperative nausea or vomiting include a longer duration of anesthesia, the administration of opioids, the reversal of muscle relaxation, and gastric distension caused by suctioning or vigorous positive pressure ventilation via face mask. The presence of food in the stomach during induction of anesthesia increases the risk of nausea and vomiting both during induction and during the postoperative period.

During the postoperative period, nausea may be increased by sudden motion or changes in position or by unrelieved visceral or pelvic pain. Another factor is the timing of oral intake after surgery.[5,247]

There is extensive literature addressing antiemetic selection for the prevention and treatment of postoperative nausea and vomiting. Although significant progress has been made over the years in the prevention of symptoms, patients continue to have difficulty with nausea and vomiting postoperatively. Vomiting can result in dehydration, electrolyte imbalance, prolongation of stay in the recovery room, hospital admissions, and loss of work. Although the data available to support agent selection is vast, the medications are difficult to compare because of the heterogeneity of the patient populations studied, small sample sizes, lack of consistency in definition of outcomes, and changes in anesthetic techniques over time.

Prevention of Postoperative Nausea and Vomiting

Recommendation 7. Patients who are at high risk of vomiting should receive antiemetic prophylaxis against postoperative nausea and vomiting. (Strength of evidence = C)

Not all surgical patients require medication for the prophylaxis of nausea and vomiting. Approximately 10% of patients will have symptoms in the recovery room and 30% will have symptoms for the first 24 hours after surgery.[249] For some of these patients, the nausea is only transient. Administration of antiemetic medications, although considered generally safe, does place a patient at risk for adverse effects (Table 2). With some medications (e.g., metoclopramide, ondansetron), the dose of the antiemetic may be lower for prophylaxis of postoperative nausea and vomiting than chemotherapy-induced nausea and vomiting, and therefore adverse effects may be less common. The decision to provide antiemetic therapy should be based on the presence of risk factors for nausea and vomiting and the potential for serious sequalae from vomiting (e.g., head and neck surgery). A patient who has several risk factors (see Factors to Consider in the Selection of an Agent for Postoperative Nausea and Vomiting and Table 9) would be considered at high risk. Important factors contributing to a high risk of nausea and vomiting include the type of surgical procedure, history of motion sickness or postoperative nausea and vomiting, the patient's sex, and the administration of anesthetics known to cause the symptoms.

Propofol has been shown to decrease the frequency of nausea and vomiting in adults and children undergoing surgical procedures.[250,251] A meta-analysis of 84 trials involving more than 6000 patients (of whom 3098 were treated with propofol) demonstrated that propofol does not have any clinically relevant antiemetic properties as an induction agent. When used for maintenance of anesthesia, propofol has relevant clinical effects (i.e., absence of nausea and vomiting) in the short term, when the potential for developing postoperative nausea and vomiting is greater than 20%.[252]

Recommendation 8. When prophylaxis is indicated, droperidol or a 5-HT$_3$ receptor antagonist is recommended for the prevention of postoperative nausea and vomiting in adult and pediatric patients. (Strength of evidence = A) Other medications that have been studied extensively and that are considered to be alternatives include chlorpromazine, prochlorperazine, metoclopramide, and promethazine. (Strength of evidence = B) Because droperidol and 5-HT$_3$ receptor antagonists are effective, the choice of agent should

be based on patient-specific factors and cost. Metoclopramide and prochlorperazine should generally not be used in pediatric patients. (Strength of evidence = C)

Efficacy of Droperidol. Droperidol is thought to exert its antiemetic properties by blocking dopamine receptors. Several trials have examined the efficacy of droperidol for the prophylaxis of postoperative nausea and vomiting in adults.[253–296] A majority of trials that compared droperidol with placebo showed that the medication was effective in preventing nausea and vomiting in a variety of surgeries (e.g., gynecological, orthopedic, ophthalmic, cesarean section). Although efficacy was established when the drug was given before induction and at the end of surgery, better results were demonstrated when the medication was given intraoperatively.

Tables 10 and 11 show medications, dosages, and costs for antiemetics used for prophylaxis and treatment of nausea and vomiting postoperatively. Lower doses of droperidol (5–20 µg/kg) have been used successfully in procedures associated with a moderately high frequency of emesis (e.g., laparoscopy) but have limited efficacy for the more emetogenic procedures (e.g., surgery for strabismus). Higher doses of droperidol (2.5–5 mg in adults and 50–75 µg/kg in children) may be more effective in higher risk patients, although the patients should be monitored for adverse effects (e.g., sedation, dysphoria). Droperidol may cause restlessness and akathisia, which are of particular concern in outpatient surgeries.[264,267,268,270,276]

Droperidol is generally well tolerated in the doses typically used for postoperative nausea and vomiting. Sedation is one of the most common adverse effects. Fortney, et al.,[296] in a large study of antiemetic prophylaxis in high-risk outpatients, found no significant differences among placebo, two dosages of droperidol, and ondansetron in terms of the occurrence of hypotension, sedation, or agitation and anxiety. In addition, patient satisfaction scores did not differ between the groups receiving one of the two dosages of droperidol and the ondansetron group. Dysphoria and akathisia reported by other investigators were not seen in this study. Mortensen[260] found that, after minor gynecological surgery, significantly more patients who received droperidol were rated as excessively drowsy in recovery compared with placebo recipients but that there was no difference between placebo and droperidol recipients in duration of stay in the recovery ward. Extrapyramidal reactions rarely occur with droperidol in adults but may occur more frequently in pediatric patients.

Droperidol versus Metoclopramide. High doses (2 mg/kg) of metoclopramide have been used for chemotherapy-induced nausea and vomiting, but lower doses (0.1–0.2 mg/kg for adults and children) have been studied for the management of postoperative nausea and vomiting. Many of the studies of the efficacy and safety of metoclopramide for postoperative nausea and vomiting[256,262,263,266,269,271,272,276,282–284,287,293,295,297–320] have yielded mixed results and involved diverse patient populations.[262,266,271,272,276,289,293,295,300–302,308,309,312] Although most studies support the efficacy of metoclopramide, several studies in which droperidol was compared with metoclopramide showed significantly better results with droperidol.[256,269,271,276,290,295]

In a randomized trial by DeSilva and colleagues,[293] the prophylactic antiemetic efficacy of i.v. ondansetron, droperidol, perphenazine, and metoclopramide was com-

Table 10.
Standard Dosages and Costs of Antiemetics for Management of Postoperative Nausea and Vomiting in Adults

Agent	Dosage	Cost/Dose ($)[a]
Prophylaxis		
Droperidol	0.625–1.25 mg i.v. 5 min before termination of anesthesia	0.43–0.86
Ondansetron	4 mg i.v. immediately before induction of anesthesia	24.45
	8 mg p.o. 1 hr before induction of anesthesia	38.46
Dolasetron	12.5 mg i.v. intraoperatively	18.60
	100 mg p.o. 1 hr before induction of anesthesia	66.00
Metoclopramide	10 mg i.v. given near end of procedure (20 mg may be used)	3.94–7.88
Promethazine	25 mg p.o. 1 hr before induction of anesthesia	0.04
	12.5–25 mg i.v. immediately before induction of anesthesia	0.28–0.55
Prochlorperazine	5–15 mg p.o. 1 hr before induction of anesthesia	0.54–1.62
	5–10 mg i.m. 1–2 hr before induction of anesthesia; may repeat once in 30 min if needed	1.10–2.20
	5–10 mg i.v. 15–30 min before induction of anesthesia; may repeat once as needed	1.10–2.20
Granisetron	20–40 µg/kg i.v.	243.54–487.08
Treatment		
Ondansetron	1–4 mg i.v. postoperatively	18.33–24.45
Metoclopramide	10 mg i.v. q 4–6 hr as needed postoperatively	3.94
Promethazine	10–25 mg p.o. q 4–6 hr as needed postoperatively	0.04
	12.5–25 mg i.m. or i.v. q 4 hr as needed postoperatively	0.28–0.55
Prochlorperazine	5–15 mg p.o. postoperatively	0.54–1.62
	5–10 mg i.m.; may repeat once in 30 min as needed	1.10–2.29
	5–10 mg i.v.; may repeat once as needed	1.10–2.20
Chlorpromazine	10-25 mg p.o. q 4–6 hr as needed	0.07–0.09
	12.5–25 mg i.m. if no hypotension; may repeat in 1 hr as needed	0.25–0.50
Droperidol	0.625–0.125 mg i.v. as needed	1.07–2.13
Dolasetron	12.5 mg i.v. postoperatively	18.73

[a]Costs do not take into account waste that occurs when precise dosage forms are not available and reflect the February 1998 average wholesale price taken from the 1998 *Red Book*.

pared with that of placebo in 360 patients undergoing total abdominal hysterectomy. The patients had no organic disease or only mild to moderate systemic disease without functional impairment (a physical status score of I or II on the American Society of Anesthesiologists assessment scale). A significantly larger percentage of patients who received i.v. ondansetron, droperidol, or perphenazine were free of severe emetic episodes (63%, 76%, and 70%, respectively) compared with patients who received placebo. There was no significant difference between metoclopramide (50%) and placebo (43%). Patients who received droperidol or perphenazine had nausea scores that were significantly lower than the scores for placebo recipients (p <0.02). Nausea scores of patients medicated with ondansetron or metoclopramide were not significantly different from those of placebo recipients.

Sedation, hypotension, and tachycardia are the most common adverse effects of droperidol (Table 2). The most common adverse effects of metoclopramide are sedation (up to 10%) and extrapyramidal effects. Intravenous administration has also resulted in hypotension, supraventricular tachycardia, and bradycardia.[300,321–325] Neuroleptic malignant syndrome has been rarely reported with metoclopramide and droperidol.[326]

Efficacy of 5-HT₃ Receptor Antagonists. Placebo-controlled trials support the efficacy of ondansetron for the prevention of postoperative nausea and vomiting in adults[293,327–355] and children.[289,291,292,356–363] On the basis of these studies, ondansetron can be given as a single i.v. dose of 4 mg for adults and 0.05 mg/kg (range, 0.05–0.15 mg/kg) for children by slow i.v. injection at induction of anesthesia. A quantitative review of the literature by Tramer, et al.[252] suggests that, for every 100 patients treated with ondansetron versus no prophylaxis for postoperative nausea and vomiting, 20 pa-

tients would not vomit. Ondansetron is the only 5-HT₃ receptor antagonist commercially available as an oral solution. Granisetron and dolasetron have been found to be stable over the short term in compounded suspensions.

Studies support the use of granisetron for the prevention of postoperative nausea and vomiting in adults and pediatric patients,[364–373] although this medication has not been studied as extensively for this indication as ondansetron. Granisetron administered as a single i.v. dose of 20–40 µg/kg has been shown to be effective; however, a large-scale study supports the use of lower doses. Wilson and colleagues[371] compared the efficacy of three i.v. doses of granisetron (0.1, 1, and 3 mg) with that of placebo in a double-blind manner in 527 adults undergoing elective open abdominal surgery or vaginal hysterectomy during general anesthesia. Antiemetic prophylaxis with a single 1- or 3-mg i.v. dose of granisetron resulted in a significantly higher percentage of patients without emetic episodes (63% with 1 mg and 62% with 3 mg) than with placebo (34%, p <0.001). A significantly greater percentage of patients achieved total control during the postoperative periods of 0–6 and 0–24 hours.

Randomized, double-blind, placebo-controlled, dose-ranging studies show the efficacy and safety of i.v. and oral dolasetron in preventing postoperative nausea and vomiting.[374–381] A pivotal randomized, double-blind study by Graczyk and colleagues[374] assessed the efficacy and safety of single i.v. doses of dolasetron 12.5, 25, and 50 mg compared with placebo in 635 patients undergoing outpatient gynecological surgery. Dolasetron or placebo was given 15 minutes before the end of anesthesia. Efficacy was determined by evaluating the percentage of patients who had a complete response (no episodes of vomiting and no doses of rescue antiemetics for 24 hours after recovery). All three i.v. doses of dolasetron were superior to placebo in preventing

Table 11.
Standard Dosages and Costs of Antiemetics for Management of Postoperative Nausea and Vomiting in Pediatric Patients

Agent	Dosage	Cost/Dose ($)[a]
Prophylaxis		
Dolasetron	>2 yr old: 1.8 mg/kg i.v. immediately before induction	53.95
Ondansetron	0.05 mg/kg i.v. (range, 0.05–0.15 mg/kg)	18.33
Droperidol	0.015–0.075 mg/kg/dose i.v.	1.38–6.88
Treatment		
Chlorpromazine	0.55 mg/kg p.o. or i.m.	10.22
Droperidol	0 1 mg/kg/dose i.v.	1.38
Ondansetron	0.05 mg/kg/dose i.v.	18.33

[a]For a 20-kg child and taken from the 1998 *Red Book*.

postoperative nausea and vomiting ($p < 0.0003$). The complete response rates were 50.3%, 51.6%, and 55.6%, respectively, for the 12.5-, 25-, and 50-mg dolasetron doses, compared with 30.6% for placebo. Of the doses tested, 12.5 mg was the lowest maximally effective dose.

The sole comparative trial of dolasetron for postoperative nausea and vomiting was a randomized double-blind, placebo-controlled comparison of dolasetron 25 or 50 mg i.v. and ondansetron 4 mg i.v. in 514 patients.[375] Patients received placebo or one of the three antiemetic regimens upon induction of anesthesia. Efficacy was measured by the rate of complete response to antiemetic therapy (no emesis or use of rescue medications) and total response (complete response plus no nausea). Complete and total response rates were higher for dolasetron 50 mg i.v. and ondansetron 4 mg i.v. than for dolasetron 25 mg i.v. or placebo. Complete response rates were 71% for dolasetron 50 mg, 64% for ondansetron 4 mg, 51% for dolasetron 25 mg, and 49% for placebo. The authors concluded that dolasetron 50 mg i.v. was equivalent to ondansetron 4 mg i.v., given at the induction of anesthesia, for prevention of postoperative nausea and vomiting. The dose of dolasetron used was four times the FDA-approved dose of 12.5 mg given intraoperatively.

Dolasetron has not been studied for the prevention of postoperative nausea and vomiting in pediatric patients. Therefore, the appropriate dose is unknown. For preventing nausea and vomiting secondary to chemotherapy in pediatric patients, doses of 1.8 mg/kg have been used.

The antiemetic efficacy of ondansetron 4 mg, tropisetron 5 mg, granisetron 3 mg, metoclopramide 10 mg, and placebo was examined in a prospective, randomized double-blind trial in 132 patients undergoing cholecystectomy.[370] For the 24-hour recovery period after surgery, the percentages of emesis-free patients were 65% for ondansetron, 52% for tropisetron, 48% for granisetron, 29% for metoclopramide, and 28% for placebo. The three 5-HT$_3$ receptor antagonists did not differ significantly in efficacy.

Prevention of nausea and vomiting with oral dolasetron has been studied in two randomized, double-blind, placebo-controlled trials.[380,381] Warriner, et al.[381] and Diemunsch, et al.[380] used nearly identical study designs. Both studied dolasetron in oral doses of 25, 50, 100, and 200 mg given before the induction of anesthesia. One study enrolled 373 patients[381] and the other, 789 patients.[380] Complete response was defined in both trials as no vomiting or use of

rescue medication for 24 hours postoperatively. Warriner, et al. reported that only the 100- and 200-mg oral doses of dolasetron were superior to placebo in terms of the percentage of complete responses (54.1% for 100 mg and 49.35% for 200 mg; $p < 0.003$ and $p < 0.01$, respectively, versus placebo [29.3%]). In the study by Diemunsch, et al., complete response rates were higher for dolasetron 50, 100, and 200 mg (>47%) than for placebo (35%) or dolasetron 25 mg (45%). No increase in efficacy was seen at doses greater than 50 mg. These two trials collectively support the use of oral dolasetron 100 mg to prevent postoperative nausea and vomiting.

The 5-HT$_3$ receptor antagonists are generally well tolerated, with headache being the most frequently occurring effect.

Droperidol versus the 5-HT$_3$ Receptor Antagonists. Fortney, et al.[296] randomly assigned more than 2000 patients at high risk for developing postoperative nausea and vomiting to receive placebo, droperidol 0.625 mg, droperidol 1.25 mg, or ondansetron 4 mg i.v. before the induction of anesthesia. The patients received a standard induction with a barbiturate and were allowed to receive midazolam, fentanyl, or alfentanil as premedication. All three of the treatments were superior to placebo in terms of complete responses at 0–2 hours postoperatively (droperidol 0.625 mg, 63%; droperidol 1.25 mg, 69%; ondansetron 4 mg, 62%; placebo, 46%) and 24 hours postoperatively (48%, 56%, 53%, and 35%, respectively). Ondansetron 4 mg was equivalent to droperidol 0.625 mg in terms of the number of complete responses at 0–2 hours (63% versus 62%), and droperidol 1.25 mg was superior to ondansetron 4 mg at 0–2 hours (69% versus 62%). All three treatment groups had similar efficacy in the 0–24 hours postoperatively. Headache was more frequent among the ondansetron-treated patients than the droperidol-treated patients. There were no significant differences among the treatment groups with regard to the frequency of hypotension, sedation, or agitation and anxiety. Patient satisfaction scores were similar for all treatment groups.

Results were mixed when droperidol was compared with ondansetron in adult surgical patients. Some studies showed no difference in the frequency of nausea and vomiting.[290,293,346,382] Alon and colleagues[282,383] did not find a difference in the frequency of vomiting but found that droperidol prevented nausea to a greater degree than ondansetron. In the study by Paxton and colleagues,[351] at one, two, and four hours after surgery, the scores for nausea were significantly lower in the ondansetron group than in the groups receiving metoclopramide, droperidol, or placebo; thereafter, there was no significant difference between the groups. All medications were given before induction of anesthesia. Two investigators reported that droperidol was superior to ondansetron.[294,383]

In a large-scale placebo-controlled study by Tang and colleagues,[384] ondansetron 4 mg i.v. was compared with droperidol 0.625 or 1.25 mg i.v. for the prevention of nausea and vomiting associated with outpatient gynecological surgery. The frequency of nausea and vomiting, times to achieve recovery, and patient-evaluated scores on visual-analogue scales for sedation, anxiety, pain, and nausea were recorded along with postdischarge emetic episodes, medications, quality of sleep, time to resumption of food intake and normal activity, and time to return to work. The frequency of nausea and vomiting in the hospital and after discharge, the need for rescue antiemetic therapy, and recovery and discharge times were similar for both droperidol groups and the ondansetron group, but these groups differed significantly from the placebo group. The cost-effectiveness ratios for both droperidol groups were significantly lower than those for the ondansetron and placebo groups. The authors concluded that droperidol 0.625 mg i.v. is comparable to ondansetron 4 mg i.v. for the prevention of emesis without increasing adverse effects or delaying discharge and is more cost-effective.

Watcha and Smith[385] compared the cost-effectiveness of ondansetron, droperidol, and metoclopramide in the prevention of postoperative nausea and vomiting. The total incremental costs associated with prophylactic ondansetron, metoclopramide, and droperidol were $37.74, $28.43, and $18.17 per patient, respectively. For ondansetron, prophylactic use was cost-effective only when the frequency of emesis exceeded 33%, whereas prophylactic droperidol was cost-effective even when the frequency was as low as 10%.

Droperidol has been compared with ondansetron for the prevention of postoperative nausea and vomiting in pediatric patients, with mixed results.[286,288,289,291,292,386] One of the studies found ondansetron to be significantly more effective than droperidol[289]; the other five studies found no significant difference between the two agents.[286,288,291,292,292,386] However, many of these studies did not have a sufficient sample size to allow a significant difference to be detected.[286,288,291] Lawhorn and colleagues[286] demonstrated that ondansetron provides antiemetic control for up to 24 hours; droperidol lasts for a significantly shorter period.

Fujii, et al.[372,387] compared the efficacy of droperidol with that of granisetron. In one study,[387] 80 patients scheduled for elective laparoscopic cholecystectomy were randomly assigned to receive placebo, droperidol 1.25 mg i.v., or granisetron 3 mg i.v. administered before induction of anesthesia. Nausea and vomiting occurred in 46% of placebo recipients, 41% of patients who received droperidol, and 15% of patients who received granisetron (p <0.05). Four patients in the placebo group, two in the droperidol group, and none in the granisetron group required rescue therapy. The dose of granisetron was four times higher than doses used to prevent nausea and vomiting in patients receiving chemotherapy. In another trial, Fujii, et al.[372] compared granisetron 40 μg/kg, droperidol 1.25 or 2.5 mg, and placebo in 100 patients undergoing gynecological surgery. The efficacy of granisetron in preventing nausea and vomiting was similar to that of droperidol 2.5 mg. In this study, a higher dose of droperidol and a lower dose of granisetron were used. Although granisetron is effective for the prevention of postoperative nausea and vomiting, the optimal dose is unknown.

Other Antiemetic Agents. Other agents have been tested for their efficacy in the prevention and treatment of postoperative nausea and vomiting, but studies are limited in number and quality. Representative agents include prochlorperazine,[257,388–390] cyclizine,[391–395] benzquinamide,[396–399] dronabinol,[400] trimethobenzamide,[401,402] dimenhydrinate,[403] thiethylperazine,[404,405] chlorpromazine,[403,406–410] promethazine,[281,388,408] haloperidol,[257,317,318,411] ephedrine,[283,412] clonidine,[373] hydroxyzine,[260,413] perphenazine,[293,319,320,395,401,403,414–417] dexamethasone,[372,417] and midazolam.[418]

In October 1997, FDA approved a scopolamine patch (Transderm Scop, Novartis) for the prevention of nausea and vomiting related to anesthesia and some pain relievers used during or after surgery. The most common adverse effects

associated with use of the patch are dry mouth and visual disturbances.[419] Large-scale clinical trials to compare scopolamine with droperidol or 5-HT$_3$ receptor antagonists in a variety of populations need to be completed so that the role of this medication in the management of postoperative nausea and vomiting can be better defined.

Treatment of Postoperative Nausea and Vomiting

Recommendation 9. Droperidol or 5-HT$_3$ receptor antagonists are recommended for adult and pediatric patients with established postoperative nausea and vomiting. (Strength of evidence = A) Other medications that have been studied extensively and that are considered to be alternatives include chlorpromazine, prochlorperazine, and promethazine. (Strength of evidence = B) The choice of agent should be based on patient-specific factors and cost. Prochlorperazine and metoclopramide should generally not be used in pediatric patients.

When ondansetron is used to treat postoperative nausea and vomiting, doses of 1–4 mg i.v. are effective.[344,345,420,421] In a study by Scuderi and colleagues,[344] 500 surgical patients undergoing endotracheal anesthesia received 1, 4, or 8 mg of ondansetron or placebo in a randomized, double-blind fashion in response to nausea or vomiting. Complete response to therapy (0–2 hours) was found in 57%, 61%, and 57% of the patients receiving 1, 4, and 8 mg, respectively, which was significantly better than the complete response rate in the placebo group (30%, p <0.001). For the 0- to 24-hour period, the complete response rate was 15% in the placebo group and 41%, 47%, and 47%, respectively, in the groups receiving ondansetron 1, 4, and 8 mg. A typical dose for pediatric patients is 50 μg/kg.

Dolasetron i.v. was evaluated for the treatment of established postoperative nausea and vomiting in several studies.[376,378,402,422,423] Diemunsch, et al.[376] and Kovac, et al.[378] used similar randomized, double-blind study designs and methods to assess the efficacy and safety of dolasetron 12.5, 25, 50, and 100 mg i.v. and placebo in more than 1000 predominantly female patients during the 24-hour period after surgery. In both studies, patients were enrolled after experiencing at least one episode of moderate to severe postoperative nausea or vomiting lasting more than five minutes in the 2-hour period after surgery.

Kovac, et al. reported that the percentage of patients with complete responses was significantly higher with dolasetron (all doses) than with placebo at 2 and 24 hours (p <0.05). The 12.5-mg dose was as effective as 25, 50, and 100 mg after 24 hours (complete response rate of 35%, versus 28%, 29%, and 29%, respectively). Nausea scores were significantly lower in patients treated with dolasetron 25 and 100 mg than in the placebo group (p <0.05).

Diemunsch and colleagues[376] reported that all four dolasetron groups had higher complete response rates after 24 hours than the placebo group (p <0.05). The group receiving 50 mg had the highest complete response rate (37.3%); response rates for the 12.5-, 25-, and 100-mg groups were 24.2%, 27.7%, and 25.0%, respectively.

Because of the inconsistency in findings between Kovac, et al.[378] and Diemunsch, et al.,[376,422] Watkins, et al.[379] combined the data from the two trials to attempt to make a more concrete recommendation for the safest and most effective dose to employ in the treatment of established postoperative nausea or vomiting. In the pooled analysis, all i.v. doses of dolasetron were more efficacious than placebo in terms of complete response (p <0.003) and antinausea effects (p <0.027). Patterns of adverse events were similar with placebo and all doses of dolasetron. The investigators concluded that the overall efficacy of dolasetron did not increase with higher doses, and the dose of 12.5 mg i.v. was recommended for use in treating established nausea or vomiting postoperatively.

Dolasetron has not been studied for the treatment of postoperative nausea and vomiting in pediatric patients.

Managing Patients Who Are Unresponsive to Prophylactic Antiemetic Therapy

Recommendation 10. When patients do not respond to initial therapy with an antiemetic agent, it is recommended that an agent from another pharmacologic class be added, that the dose of the antiemetic be increased to the maximum within an accepted range, or that a combination of both approaches be used. (Strength of evidence = D)

Evidence suggesting how to manage patients who do not respond to prophylactic antiemetics during the first cycle of chemotherapy, during radiation therapy, or after surgery is limited. In these circumstances, the patients undergoing chemotherapy or radiation therapy should receive rescue antiemetic agents as treatment. Postoperatively and for patients scheduled to receive their next cycle of chemotherapy or radiation therapy, an agent from another pharmacologic class can be added, the dose of the antiemetic may be increased to the maximum within the accepted range (increasing the dose of i.v. ondansetron from 8 to 16 mg for chemotherapy-induced nausea and vomiting or up to 4 mg for postoperative nausea and vomiting), or a combination of both approaches may be used. There is no documented benefit to further increasing the dose once the maximum dose has been reached in the accepted range (e.g., ondansetron 32 mg for chemotherapy-induced nausea and vomiting, 8 mg for postoperative nausea and vomiting). The maximum is generally the FDA-approved dose. An exception to this may be postoperative use of ondansetron 8 mg.

Conclusion

Appropriate management of nausea and vomiting in adult and pediatric patients receiving chemotherapeutic agents or radiation therapy or undergoing surgery has the potential to substantially improve clinical, humanistic, and economic outcomes.

References

1. Mitchelson F. Pharmacological agents affecting emesis: a review (part I). *Drugs.* 1992; 43:295–315.
2. Mitchelson F. Pharmacological agents affecting emesis: a review (part II). *Drugs.* 1992; 43:443–63.
3. Hanson JS, McCallum RW. The diagnosis and management of nausea and vomiting: a review. *Am J Gastroenterol.* 1985; 80:210–8.
4. Kris MG, Cubedden LX, Gralla RJ, et al. Are more antiemetic trials with placebo necessary? Report of patient data from randomized trials of placebo antiemetics with cisplatin. *Cancer.* 1996; 78:2193–8.
5. Watcha MF, White PF. Postoperative nausea and vomiting: its etiology, treatment, and prevention. *Anesthesiology.* 1992; 77:162–84.
6. Grunberg SM, Hesketh PJ. Control of chemotherapy-induced emesis. *N Engl J Med.* 1993; 329:1790–6.
7. Naylor RJ, Inall FC. The physiology and pharmacology of postoperative nausea and vomiting. *Anaesthesia.* 1994; 49:2–5.
8. Chaillet MP, Cosset JM, Socie G, et al. Prospective study of the clinical symptoms of therapeutic whole body irradiation. *Health Phys.* 1993; 64:370–4.
9. Danjoux CE, Rider WD, Fitzpatrick PJ. The acute radiation syndrome. *Clin Radiol.* 1979; 30:581–4.
10. DuBois A, Walker RI. Prospects for management of gastrointestinal injury associated with the acute radiation syndrome. *Gastroenterology.* 1988; 95:500–7.
11. Westbrook C, Glaholm J, Barrett A. Vomiting associated with whole body irradiation. *Clin Radiol.* 1987; 38:263–6.
12. Henriksson R, Lomberg H, Israelsson G, et al. The effect of ondansetron on radiation-induced emesis and diarrhoea. *Acta Oncologica.* 1992; 31:767–9.
13. Olver IN, Simon RM, Aisner J. Antiemetic studies: a methodological discussion. *Cancer Treat Rep.* 1986; 70:555–63.
14. Morrow GR. The assessment of nausea and vomiting: past problems, current issues, and suggestions for further research. *Cancer.* 1984; 53(suppl):2267–80.
15. Gralla RJ, Clark RA, Kris MG, et al. Methodology in anti-emetic trials. *Eur J Cancer.* 1991; 27(suppl 1):S5–8.
16. Aapro M. Methodological issues in antiemetic studies. *Invest New Drugs.* 1993; 11:243–53.
17. Newman V, Fullerton JT, Anderson PO. Clinical advances in the management of severe nausea and vomiting during pregnancy. *J Obstet Gynecol Neonatal Nurs.* 1993; 22:483–90.
18. Palazzo MGA, Strunin L. Anaesthesia and emesis: I. Etiology. *Can Anaesth Soc J.* 1984; 31:178–87.
19. Laszlo J. Emesis as limiting toxicity in cancer chemotherapy. In: Laslo J, ed. Antiemetics and cancer chemotherapy. Baltimore: Williams & Wilkins; 1982:1–5.
20. Coates A, Abraham S, Kaye SB, et al. On the receiving end—patient perception of the side effects of cancer chemotherapy. *Br J Cancer Clin Oncol.* 1983; 19:203–8.
21. Laszlo J, Gralla RJ, Einhorn LH, et al. Antiemetics: a round table discussion. *Drugs.* 1983; 25(suppl 1):74–80.
22. Graves T. Emesis as a complication of cancer chemotherapy: pathophysiology, importance, and treatment. *Pharmacotherapy.* 1992; 12:337–45.
23. Coates A, Gebaki V, Signorine D, et al. Prognostic value of quality-of-life scores during chemotherapy for advanced breast cancer. *J Clin Oncol.* 1992; 10:1833–8.
24. Lindley CM, Hirsch JD, O'Neill CV, et al. Quality of life consequences of chemotherapy-induced emesis. *Qual Life Res.* 1992; 1:331–40.
25. O'Brien BJ, Rusthoven J, Rocchi A, et al. Impact of chemotherapy-associated nausea and vomiting on patients' functional status and costs: survey of five Canadian centres. *Can Med Assoc J.* 1993; 149:296–302.
26. Osoba D, Zee B, Warr D, et al. Quality of life studies in chemotherapy-induced emesis. *Oncology.* 1996; 53(suppl 1):92–5.
27. Redd WH, Andrykowski MA. Behavioral interventions in cancer treatment: controlling aversion reactions to chemotherapy. *J Consult Clin Psychol.* 1982; 50:1018–29.

Recommendations

1. The emetic potential of the chemotherapeutic agent (Table 3) is the primary factor to consider when deciding whether to administer pharmacologic prophylaxis and which antiemetic(s) to select. (Strength of evidence = A)

2. Adult and pediatric patients receiving chemotherapeutic agent(s) with emetic potential classified as level 2 through 5 should receive pharmacologic prophylaxis against nausea and vomiting each day on which chemotherapy is given. (Strength of evidence = B) Antiemetic prophylaxis is not required when the level of emetogenicity is 1.

   (a) Adult and pediatric patients receiving level-2 chemotherapeutic regimens can receive dexamethasone or methylprednisolone alone for prophylaxis of nausea and vomiting. (Strength of evidence = B) Prochlorperazine is also an option for adults. (Strength of evidence = D)

   (b) Adult and pediatric patients receiving chemotherapeutic agent(s) with emetic potential of level 3 through 5 should receive a corticosteroid (dexamethasone or methylprednisolone) in combination with a 5-HT$_3$ receptor antagonist. (Strength of evidence = A for adults and C for pediatric patients)

   (c) Orally and intravenously administered antiemetics are generally equivalent in efficacy and safety for both adult and pediatric patients. (Strength of evidence = B for adults and C for pediatric patients) The decision as to which formulation to use should be based on patient-specific factors and cost.

   (d) The decision as to which 5-HT$_3$ receptor antagonist to use should be based on the acquisition cost of comparable doses. (Strength of evidence = A) (Tables 6 and 7) Dosage recommendations for adult and pediatric patients differ.

3. All patients receiving chemotherapy should have antiemetics available on an as-needed basis for rescue for breakthrough nausea and vomiting. (Strength of evidence = A) Patients should be educated on the appropriate administration of and expectations for therapy and should be reassured that every effort is being made to prevent symptoms. In adults, lorazepam, methylprednisolone, prochlorperazine, metoclopramide, dexamethasone, haloperidol, and dronabinol are effective. (Strength of evidence = C) In pediatric patients, chlorpromazine, lorazepam, or methylprednisolone (or dexamethasone) is recommended. (Strength of evidence = B) The choice of agent should be based on patient-specific factors (e.g., anticipated adverse effects, past success) and cost.

4. For the prevention of delayed emesis after cisplatin therapy in adults, dexamethasone with metoclopramide or a 5-HT$_3$ receptor antagonist is recommended. (Strength of evidence = A) The choice of agent should be based on patient-specific factors and cost. For delayed emesis after cyclophosphamide, doxorubicin, or carboplatin therapy, a 5-HT$_3$ receptor antagonist with dexamethasone is recommended. (Strength of evidence = B) Prochlorperazine in combination with dexamethasone has also been used and is available in extended-release and rectal dosage forms, but the evidence to support this combination is limited. (Strength of evidence = D) In pediatric patients, chlorpromazine, lorazepam, or a 5-HT$_3$ receptor antagonist can be used in combination with a corticosteroid. (Strength of evidence = C)

5. Patients receiving total or hemibody irradiation (with or without concomitant chemotherapeutic agents) or single-exposure, high-dose radiation therapy to the upper abdomen should receive preventive therapy for nausea and vomiting with each day of therapy. (Strength of evidence = A) A 5-HT$_3$ receptor antagonist should be used both in adults and in pediatric patients. (Strength of evidence = B) Oral therapy should be encouraged; however, i.v. therapy is an acceptable option. (Strength of evidence = B) There is no evidence to support the use of 5-HT$_3$ receptor antagonists 24 hours beyond the last dose of radiation.

6. If an agent is needed to treat established radiation therapy-induced emesis in adults, prochlorperazine, metoclopramide, or thiethylperazine is recommended. 5-HT$_3$ receptor antagonists are also an option. Chlorpromazine and lorazepam can be used in pediatric patients. (Strength of evidence = D)

7. Patients who are at high risk of vomiting should receive antiemetic prophylaxis against postoperative nausea and vomiting. (Strength of evidence = C)

8. When prophylaxis is indicated, droperidol or a 5-HT$_3$ receptor antagonist is recommended for the prevention of postoperative nausea and vomiting in adult and pediatric patients. (Strength of evidence = A) Other medications that have been studied extensively and that are considered to be alternatives include chlorpromazine, prochlorperazine, metoclopramide, and promethazine. (Strength of evidence = B) Because droperidol and 5-HT$_3$ receptor antagonists are effective, the choice of agent should be based on patient-specific factors and cost. Metoclopramide and prochlorperazine should generally not be used in pediatric patients. (Strength of evidence = C)

9. Droperidol or 5-HT$_3$ receptor antagonists are recommended for adult and pediatric patients with established postoperative nausea and vomiting. (Strength of evidence = A) Other medications that have been studied extensively and that are considered to be alternatives include chlorpromazine, prochlorperazine, and promethazine. (Strength of evidence = B) The choice of agent should be based on patient-specific factors and cost. Prochlorperazine and metoclopramide should generally not be used in pediatric patients.

10. When patients do not respond to initial therapy with an antiemetic agent, it is recommended that an agent from another pharmacologic class be added, that the dose of the antiemetic be increased to the maximum within an accepted range, or that a combination of both approaches be used. (Strength of evidence = D)

28. Cotanch PH. Relaxation training for control of nausea and vomiting in patients receiving chemotherapy. *Cancer Nurs.* 1983; 6:277–83.

29. Stoudemire A, Cotanch P, Laszlo J. Recent advances in the pharmacologic and behavioral management of chemotherapy-induced emesis. *Arch Intern Med.* 1984; 144:1029–33.

30. Wickham R. Managing chemotherapy-related nausea and vomiting: the state of the art. *Oncol Nurs Forum.* 1989; 16:563–74.

31. Burish TG, Jenkins RA. Effectiveness of biofeedback and relaxation training in reducing the side effects of cancer chemotherapy. *Cancer Nurs.* 1983; 6:277-83.

32. King CR. Nonpharmacologic management of chemotherapy-induced nausea and vomiting. *Oncol Nurs Forum.* 1997; 24:41–8.

33. Bigos S, Bowyer O, Braen G, et al. Acute low back problems in adults. Clinical practice guideline no.14. Rockville, MD: Agency for Health Care Policy and Research, Public Health Service, U.S. Department of Health and Human Services, December 1994; AHCPR publication no. 95–0642.

34. Gift AG. Visual analogue scales: measurement of subjective phenomena. *Nurs Res.* 1989; 38:286–8.

35. Rhodes VA, Johnson MH, McDaniel RW. Nausea, vomiting, and retching: the management of the symptom experience. *Semin Oncol Nurs.* 1995; 11:256–65.

36. Blower P. A pharmacologic profile of oral granisetron (Kytril tablets). *Semin Oncol.* 1995; 22(suppl 10):3–5.

37. Costall B, Domeney AM, Naylor J, et al. 5-hydroxy-tryptamine M-receptor antagonism to prevent cisplatin-induced emesis. *Neuropharmacology.* 1986; 25:959–61.

38. Matsuoka O, Tsuchiya T, Furukawa Y. The effect of x-irradiation on 5-hydroxytryptamine (serotonin) contents in the small intestines of experimental animals. *J Radiat Res.* 1962; 32:104–8.

39. Gralla RJ, Itri LM, Pisko CE, et al. Antiemetic efficacy of high-dose metoclopramide: randomized trials with placebo and prochlorperazine in patients with chemotherapy-induced nausea and vomiting. *N Engl J Med.* 1981; 305:905–9.

40. Homesley HD, Gainey JM, Jobson VW, et al. Cisplatin chemotherapy and emesis in patients given metoclopramide and controls. *N Engl J Med.* 1982; 307:250. Letter.

41. Cubeddu LX, Hoffmann IS, Fuenmayor NT, et al. Efficacy of ondansetron (GR 38032F) and the role of serotonin in cisplatin-induced nausea and vomiting. *N Engl J Med.* 1990; 322:810–6.

42. Cupissol DR, Serrou B, Caubel M. The efficacy of granisetron as a prophylactic anti-emetic and intervention agent in high-dose cisplatin-induced emesis. *Eur J Cancer.* 1990; 26(suppl 1):S23–7.

43. Kris MG, Gralla RJ, Clark RA, et al. Incidence, course, and severity of delayed nausea and vomiting following the administration of high-dose cisplatin. *J Clin Oncol.* 1985; 3:1379-84.

44. DeMulder PHM, Seynaeve C, Vermorken JB, et al. Ondansetron compared with high-dose metoclopramide in prophylaxis of acute and delayed cisplatin-induced nausea and vomiting: a multicenter, randomized, double-blind cross-over study. *Ann Intern Med.* 1990; 113:834–40.

45. Schmoll HJ. The role of ondansetron in the treatment of emesis induced by non-cisplatin-containing chemotherapy regimens. *Eur J Cancer Clin Oncol.* 1989; 25(suppl 1):535–9.

46. Jones AL, Hill AS, Soukop M, et al. Comparison of dexamethasone and ondansetron in the prophylaxis of emesis induced by moderately emetogenic chemotherapy. *Lancet.* 1991; 338:483–7.

47. Marty M, Pouillart P, Scholl S, et al. Comparison of the 5-hydroxytryptamine-3 (serotonin) antagonist ondansetron (GR 38032F) with high-dose metoclopramide in the control of cisplatin-induced emesis. *N Engl J Med.* 1990; 322:816–21.

48. Wilder-Smith OHG, Borgeat A, Chappuis P, et al. Urinary serotonin metabolite excretion during cisplatin chemotherapy. *Cancer.* 1993; 72:2239–41.

49. Kris MG, Gralla RJ, Tyson LB, et al. Controlling delayed vomiting: double-blind, randomized trial comparing placebo, dexamethasone alone, and metoclopramide plus dexamethasone in patients receiving cisplatin. *J Clin Oncol.* 1989; 7:108–14.

50. Gandara DR. Progress in control of acute and delayed emesis induced by cisplatin. *Eur J Cancer.* 1991; 27:9–11.

51. Morrow GR, Morrell C. Behavioral treatment for the anticipatory nausea and vomiting induced by cancer chemotherapy. *N Engl J Med.* 1982; 307:1476–80.

52. Morrow GR, Rosenthal SN. Models, mechanisms and management of anticipatory nausea and vomiting. *Oncology.* 1996; 53:4–7.

53. Tyc VL, Mulhern RK. Anticipatory nausea and vomiting in pediatric cancer patients: an analysis of conditioning and coping variables. *Dev Behav Pediatr.* 1997; 18:27–33.

54. Laszlo J, Clark RA, Hanson DC, et al. Lorazepam in cancer patients treated with cisplatin: a drug having antiemetic, amnestic, and anxiolytic effects. *J Clin Oncol.* 1985; 3:864–9.

55. Triozzi PL, Goldstein D, Laszlo J. Contributions of hemzodiazepines to cancer therapy. *Cancer Invest.* 1988; 6:103–11.

56. Malik IA, Khan WA, Qazilbash M, et al. Clinical efficacy of lorazepam in prophylaxis of anticipatory, acute, and delayed nausea, and vomiting induced by high doses of cisplatin. A prospective randomized trial. *Am J Clin Oncol.* 1995; 18(2):170–5. Abstract.

57. Hesketh PJ, Kris MG, Grunberg SM, et al. Proposal for classifying the acute emetogenicity of cancer chemotherapy. *J Clin Oncol.* 1997; 15:103–9.

58. Jordan NS, Schauer PK, Schauer A, et al. The effect of administration rate on cisplatin-induced emesis. *J Clin Oncol.* 1985; 3:559–61.

59. Laszlo J. Nausea and vomiting as major complications of cancer chemotherapy. *Drugs.* 1983; 25(suppl 1):1–7.

60. Morrow GR. Clinical characteristics associated with the development of anticipatory nausea and vomiting in cancer patients undergoing chemotherapy treatment. *J Clin Oncol.* 1984; 2:1170–6.

61. Nerenz DR, Leventhal H, Easterling DV, et al. Anxiety and drug taste as predictors of anticipatory nausea in cancer chemotherapy. *J Clin Oncol.* 1986; 4:224–33.

62. Triozzi PL, Laszlo J. Optimum management of nausea and vomiting in cancer chemotherapy. *Drugs.* 1987; 34:136–49.

63. Borison HL, McCarthy LE. Neuropharmacology of chemotherapy-induced emesis. *Drugs.* 1983; 25(suppl 1):8–17.

64. Tortorice PV, O'Connell MB. Management of chemotherapy-induced nausea and vomiting. *Pharmacotherapy.* 1990; 10:129–45.

65. Hesketh PJ, Beck T, Uhlenhopp M, et al. Adjusting the dose of intravenous ondansetron plus dexamethasone to the emetogenic potential of the chemotherapy regimen. *J Clin Oncol.* 1995; 13:2117–22.

66. Bilgrami S, Fallon BG. Chemotherapy-induced nausea and vomiting: easing patients' fear and discomfort with effective antiemetic regimens. *Postgrad Med.* 1993; 94:55–64.

67. Hesketh PJ. Treatment of chemotherapy-induced emesis in the 1990s: impact of the 5-HT₃ receptor antagonists. *Support Care Cancer* 1994; 2:286–92.

68. Hrushesky WJM. The clinical application of chronobiology to oncology. *Am J Anat.* 1983; 168:519–42.

69. Bremer K, for the Granisetron Study Group. A single blind study of the efficacy and safety of intravenous granisetron compared with alizapride plus dexamethasone in the prophylaxis and control of emesis in patients receiving 5 day cytostatic therapy. *Eur J Cancer.* 1992; 28A:1018–22.

70. Carden PA, Mitchell SL, Water KD, et al. Prevention of cyclophosphamide/cytarabine-induced emesis with ondansetron in children with leukemia. *J Clin Oncol.* 1990; 8:1531–5.

71. Chevallier B, on behalf of the Granisetron Study Group. Efficacy and safety of granisetron compared with high-dose metoclopramide plus dexamethasone in patients receiving high-dose cisplatin in a single-blind study. *Eur J Cancer.* 1990; 26:S33–6.

72. Marty M, on behalf of the Granisetron Study Group. A comparative study of the use of granisetron, a selective 5-HT₃ antagonist, versus a standard anti-emetic regimen of chlorpromazine plus dexamethasone in the treatment of cytostatic-induced emesis. *Eur J Cancer.* 1990; 26(suppl 1):S28–32.

73. Marty M, D'Allens H. Etude randomisee en double-insu comparant l'efficacite de l'ondansetron selon deux modes d'administration: injection unique et perfusion continue. *Cahiers Cancer.* 1990; 2:541–6.

74. Marty M, on behalf of the Granisetron Study Group. A comparison of granisetron as a single agent with conventional combination antiemetic therapies in the treatment of cytostatic-induced emesis. *Eur J Cancer.* 1992; 28A (suppl):S12–6.

75. Pinkerton CR, Williams D, Wootton C, et al. 5-HT₃ antagonist ondansetron—an effective outpatient antiemetic in cancer treatment. *Arch Dis Child.* 1990; 65:822–5.

76. Soukop M, on behalf of the Granisetron Study Group. A comparison of two dose levels of granisetron in patients receiving high-dose cisplatin. *Eur J Cancer.* 1990; 26:S15–29.

77. Dicato MA. Oral treatment with ondansetron in the outpatient setting. *Eur J Cancer.* 1991; 27(suppl 1):S18–9.

78. Fraschini G, Ciociola A, Esparza L, et al. Evaluation of three oral dosages of ondansetron in the prevention of nausea and emesis associated with cyclophosphamide-doxorubicin chemotherapy. *J Clin Oncol.* 1991; 9:1268–74.

79. Hainsworth J, Harvey W, Pendergrass K, et al. A single-blind comparison of intravenous ondansetron, a selective serotonin antagonist, with intravenous metoclopramide in the prevention of nausea and vomiting associated with high-dose cisplatin chemotherapy. *J Clin Oncol.* 1991; 9:721–8.

80. Lemerle J, Amaral D, Southall DP, et al. Efficacy and safety of granisetron in the prevention of chemotherapy-induced emesis in paediatric patients. *Eur J Cancer.* 1991; 27:1081–3.

81. Rosso R, Campora E, Cetto G, et al. Oral ondansetron (GR 38032F) for the control of acute and delayed cyclophosphamide-induced emesis. *Anticancer Res.* 1991; 11:937–40.

82. Blijham GH, on behalf of the Granisetron Study Group. Does granisetron remain effective over multiple cycles? *Eur J Cancer.* 1992; 28A:S17–21.

83. Diehl V, on behalf of the Granisetron Study Group. Fractionated chemotherapy—granisetron or conventional antiemetics? *Eur J Cancer.* 1992; 28A:S21–8.

84. Kamanabrou D, on behalf of the Granisetron Study Group. Intravenous granisetron—establishing the optimal dose. *Eur J Cancer.* 1992; 28A:S6–11.

85. Beck TM, Ciociola AA, Jones SE, et al. Efficacy of oral ondansetron in the prevention of emesis in outpatients receiving cyclophosphamide-based chemotherapy. *Ann Intern Med.* 1993; 118:407–13.

86. Buser KS, Joss RA, Piquet D, et al. Oral ondansetron in the prophylaxis of nausea and vomiting induced by cyclophosphamide, methotrexate, and 5-fluorouracil (CMF) in women with breast cancer. Results of a prospective, randomized, double-blind, placebo-controlled study. *Ann Oncol.* 1993; 4:475–9.

87. De Wet M, Falkson G, Rapoport BL. Repeated use of granisetron in patients receiving cytostatic agents. *Cancer.* 1993; 71:4043–9.

88. Ohmatsu H, Eguchi K, Shinkai T, et al. A randomized cross-over study of high-dose metoclopramide plus dexamethasone versus granisetron plus dexamethasone in patients receiving chemotherapy with high-dose cisplatin. *Jpn J Cancer Res.* 1994; 85:1151–8.

89. Hachimi-Idrissi S, De Schepper J, Maurus R, et al. Prevention of emesis by ICS 205-930 in children receiving cytotoxic chemotherapy. *Eur J Cancer.* 1993; 29A:854–6.

90. Jantunen IT, Muhonen TT, Kataja VV, et al. 5-HT₃ receptor antagonists in the prophylaxis of acute vomiting induced by moderately emetogenic chemotherapy—a randomized study. *Eur J Cancer.* 1993; 29A:1669–72.

91. Kirchner V, Aapro P, Alberto P, et al. Early clinical trial of MDL 73.147EF: a new 5-HT₃ receptor antagonist for the prevention of chemotherapy-induced nausea and vomiting. *Ann Oncol.* 1993; 4:481–4.

92. Matera MG, Di Tullio M, Lucarelli C, et al. Ondansetron, an antagonist of 5-HT₃ receptors, in the treatment of antineoplastic drug-induced nausea and vomiting in children. *J Med.* 1993; 24:161–70.

93. Warr D, Wilan A, Venner P, et al. A randomised, double-blind comparison of granisetron with high-dose metoclopramide, dexamethasone and diphenhydramine for cisplatin-induced emesis. *Eur J Cancer.* 1993; 29A:33–6.

94. Cubeddu LX, Pendergrass K, Ryan T, et al. Efficacy of oral ondansetron, a selective antagonist of 5-HT₃ receptors, in the treatment of nausea and vomiting associated with cyclophosphamide-based chemothera-

pies. Ondansetron Study Group. *Am J Clin Oncol.* 1994; 17:137–46.

95. Jacobson SJ, Shore RW, Greenberg M, et al. The efficacy and safety of granisetron in pediatric cancer patients who had failed standard antiemetic therapy during anticancer chemotherapy. *Am J Pediatr Hematol Oncol.* 1994; 16:231–5.

96. Miyajima Y, Numata S, Katayama I, et al. Prevention of chemotherapy-induced emesis with granisetron in children with malignant diseases. *Am J Pediatr Hematol Oncol.* 1994; 16:236–41.

97. Navari RM, Kaplan HG, Gralla RJ, et al. Efficacy and safety of granisetron, a selective 5 hydroxy-tryptamine-3 receptor antagonist, in the prevention of nausea and vomiting induced by high-dose cisplatin. *J Clin Oncol.* 1994; 12:2204–10.

98. Alvarez O, Freeman A, Bedros A, et al. Randomized double-blind crossover of ondansetron-dexamethasone versus ondansetron-placebo study for the treatment of chemotherapy-induced nausea and vomiting in pediatric patients with malignancies. *Am J Pediatr Hematol Oncol.* 1995; 17:145–50.

99. Clavel M, Bonneterre J, d'Allens H, et al. Oral ondansetron in the prevention of chemotherapy-induced emesis in breast cancer patients. *Eur J Cancer.* 1995; 31A:15–9.

100. Craft AW, Price L, Eden OB, et al. Granisetron as antiemetic therapy in children with cancer. *Med Pediatr Oncol.* 1995; 25:28–32.

101. Dick GS, Meller ST, Pinkerton CR. Randomised comparison of ondansetron and metoclopramide plus dexamethasone for chemotherapy induced emesis. *Arch Dis Child.* 1995; 73:243–5.

102. Hahlen K, Quintana E, Pinkerton CR, et al. A randomized comparison of intravenously administered granisetron versus chlorpromazine plus dexamethasone in the prevention of ifosfamide-induced emesis in children. *J Pediatr.* 1995; 126:309–13.

103. Holdsworth MT, Raisch DW, Duncan MH, et al. Assessment of chemotherapy-induced emesis and evaluation of a reduced-dose intravenous ondansetron regimen in pediatric outpatients with leukemia. *Ann Pharmacother.* 1995; 29:16–21.

104. Leclerc JM, Greenberg M, Lau R, et al. Open label IV dolasetron mesylate in pediatric patients receiving moderately to highly emetogenic chemotherapy: pharmacokinetics, efficacy and safety. *Support Care Cancer.* 1995; 3:343. Abstract.

105. Navari RM, Madajewicz S, Anderson N, et al. Oral ondansetron for the control of cisplatin-induced delayed emesis: a large, multicenter, double-blind, randomized comparative trial of ondansetron versus placebo. *J Clin Oncol.* 1995; 13:2408–16.

106. Yanofsky R, Pyesmany A, Pritchard S, et al. Open label oral dolasetron mesylate in pediatric patients receiving moderately to highly emetogenic chemotherapy: pharmacokinetics, efficacy and safety. *Support Care Cancer.* 1995; 3:344. Abstract.

107. Fauser A, Duclos B, Chemaissani A, et al. Therapeutic equivalence of single oral doses of dolasetron mesylate and multiple doses of ondansetron for the prevention of emesis after moderately emetogenic chemotherapy. *Eur J Cancer.* 1996; 32A:1523–9.

108. Kris MG, Pendergrass KB, Navari TH, et al. Prevention of acute emesis in cancer patients following high-

dose cisplatin with the combination of oral dolasetron and dexamethasone. *J Clin Oncol.* 1997; 15:2135–8.

109. Granisetron Study Group. The antiemetic efficacy and safety of granisetron compared with metoclopramide plus dexamethasone in patients receiving fractionated chemotherapy over 5 days. *J Cancer Res Clin Oncol.* 1993; 119:555–9.

110. Anzamet product information. Kansas City, MO: Hoechst Marion Roussel; 1997.

111. Benedict CR, Arbogast R, Martin L, et al. Single-blind study of the effects of intravenous dolasetron mesylate versus ondansetron on electrocardiographic parameters in normal volunteer. *J Cardiovasc Pharmacol.* 1996; 28:53–9.

112. Sledge GW, Einhorm L, Nagy C. Phase III double-blind comparison of intravenous ondansetron and metoclopramide as antiemetic therapy for patients receiving multiple-day cisplatin-based chemotherapy. *Cancer.* 1992; 70:2524–8.

113. Soukop M, McQuade B, Hunter E, et al. Ondansetron compared with metoclopramide in the control of emesis and quality of life during repeated chemotherapy for breast cancer. *Oncology.* 1992; 49:295–304.

114. Roila F. Ondansetron plus dexamethasone compared to the 'standard' metoclopramide combination. *Oncology.* 1993; 50:163–7.

115. Heron JF, Goedhals L, Jordaan JP, et al. Oral granisetron alone and in combination with dexamethasone: a double-blind randomized comparison against high-dose metoclopramide plus dexamethasone in prevention of cisplatin-induced emesis. *Ann Oncol.* 1994; 5:579–84.

116. Chiou TJ, Wei CH, Hsieh, et al. Comparison of intravenous granisetron with metoclopramide in the treatment of chemotherapy-induced emesis. *Chung Hua I Hsueh Tsa Chih.* 1995; 56:23–30.

117. Tsavaris N, Charalambidis G, Ganas N, et al. Ondansetron versus metoclopramide as antiemetic treatment during cisplatin-based chemotherapy. A prospective study with special regard to electrolyte imbalance. *Acta Oncol.* 1995; 34:243–6.

118. Soukop M. Management of cyclophosphamide-induced emesis over repeat courses. *Oncology.* 1996; 53:39–45.

119. Chevallier B, Cappelaere P, Splinter T, et al. A double-blind, multicentre comparison of intravenous dolasetron mesilate and metoclopramide in the prevention of nausea and vomiting in cancer patients receiving high-dose cisplatin chemotherapy. *Support Care Cancer.* 1997; 5:22–30.

120. Du Bois A, McKenna CJ, Andersson H, et al. A randomized, double-blind, parallel-group study to compare the efficacy and safety of ondansetron (GR38032F) plus dexamethasone with metoclopramide plus dexamethasone in the prophylaxis of nausea and emesis by carboplatin chemotherapy. *Oncology.* 1997; 54:7–14.

121. Italian Group for Antiemetic Research. Ondansetron plus dexamethasone versus metoclopramide plus dexamethasone plus diphenhydramine in prevention of cisplatin-induced emesis. *Lancet.* 1992; 340:96–9.

122. Italian Group for Antiemetic Research. Difference in persistence of efficacy of two antiemetic regimens on acute emesis during cisplatin chemotherapy. *J Clin Oncol.* 1993; 11:2396–404.

123. Bonneterre J, Chevallier B, Metz R, et al. A randomized double-blind comparison of ondansetron and

metoclopramide in the prophylaxis of emesis induced by cyclophosphamide, fluorouracil, and doxorubicin or epirubicin chemotherapy. *J Clin Oncol.* 1990; 8:1063–9.

124. Kaasa S, Kvaloy S, Dicato MA, et al. A comparison of ondansetron with metoclopramide in the prophylaxis of chemotherapy-induced nausea and vomiting: a randomized, double-blind study. *Eur J Cancer.* 1990; 26:311–4.

125. Marschner NW, Adler M, Nagel GA, et al. Double-blind, randomised trial of the antiemetic efficacy and safety of ondansetron and metoclopramide in advanced breast cancer patients treated with epirubicin and cyclophosphamide. *Eur J Cancer.* 1991; 27:1137–40.

126. Noble A, Bremer K, Goedhals L, et al. A double-blind, randomised crossover comparison of granisetron and ondansetron in 5-day fractionated chemotherapy: assessment of efficacy, safety, and patient preference. *Eur J Cancer.* 1994; 30A:1083–8.

127. Ruff P, Paska W, Goedhals L, et al. Ondansetron compared with granisetron in the prophylaxis of cisplatin-induced acute emesis; a multicenter double-blind, randomized, parallel-group study. *Oncology.* 1994; 51:113–8.

128. Bonneterre J, Hecquet B. Granisetron (IV) compared with ondansetron (IV plus oral) in the prevention of nausea and vomiting induced by moderately-emetogenic chemotherapy: a cross-over study. *Bull Cancer.* 1995; 82:1038–43.

129. Italian Group for Antiemetic Research. Ondansetron versus granisetron, both combined with dexamethasone, in the prevention of cisplatin-induced emesis. *Ann Oncol.* 1995; 6:805–10.

130. Stewart A, McQuade B, Cronje JDE, et al. Ondansetron compared with granisetron in the prophylaxis of cyclophosphamide induced emesis in out-patients: a multicentre double-blind, double-dummy, randomised, parallel group study. *Oncology.* 1995; 52:202–10.

131. Harris E, Hakimian D, Dempsey C, et al. Comparative outcomes of granisetron and ondansetron for prevention of chemotherapy induced nausea and vomiting. *Proc Am Soc Clin Oncol.* 1997; 15:540. Abstract.

132. Martoni A, Angelelli B, Guaraldi M, et al. An open randomised cross-over study on granisetron versus ondansetron in the prevention of acute emesis induced by moderate dose cisplatin-containing regimens. *Eur J Cancer.* 1996; 32:82–5.

133. Mantovani G, Maccio A, Curreli L, et al. Comparison of granisetron, ondansetron and tropisetron in the prophylaxis of acute nausea and vomiting induced by cisplatin for the treatment of head and neck cancer: a randomized controlled trial. *Cancer.* 1996; 77:941–8.

134. Pion JM, Fournier C, Darloy, et al. Oral granisetron vs ondansetron. A comparative double-blind cross-over multicenter study of preventive anti-emetic in moderately emetogenic chemotherapy by the French Northern Oncology group. *Proc Am Soc Clin Oncol.* 1997; 15:530. Abstract.

135. Perez EA, Hesketh P, Sanbach J, et al. Comparison of single-dose oral granisetron versus intravenous ondanseron in the prevention of nausea and vomiting induced by moderately emetogenic chemotherapy: a multicenter, double-blind, randomized parallel study. *J Clin Oncol.* 1998; 16:754–60.

136. Roila F for the Italian Group for Antiemetic Research.

Ondansetron versus granisetron, both combined with dexamethasone in the prevention of cisplatin-induced emesis. *Ann Oncol.* 1995; 6:805–10.

137. Audhuy B, Cappelaere P, Martin M, et al. A double-blind, randomized comparison of the anti-emetic efficacy of two intravenous doses of dolasetron mesilate and granisetron in patients receiving high dose cisplatin chemotherapy. *Eur J Cancer.* 1996; 32A:807–13

138. Hesketh P, Navari R, Grote T, et al. Double-blind, randomized comparison of the antiemetic efficacy of intravenous dolasetron mesylate and intravenous ondansetron in the prevention of acute cisplatin-induced emesis in patients with cancer. *J Clin Oncol.* 1996; 14:2242–9.

139. Lofters W, Pater J, Zee, et al. Phase III double-blind comparison of dolasetron mesylate and ondanseton: an evaluation of the additive role of dexamethasone in the prevention of acute and delayed nausea and vomiting due to moderately emetogenic chemotherapy. *J Clin Oncol.* 1997; 15:2966–73.

140. Farley PA, Dempsey CL, Shillington AA, et al. Patients' self-reported functional status after granisetron or ondansetron therapy to prevent chemotherapy-induced nausea and vomiting at six cancer centers. *Am J Health-Syst Pharm.* 1997; 54:2478–82.

141. Marr HE, Davey PT, Boyle EA, et al. Further studies of the antiemetic activity of granisetron against whole body X-irradiation or cisplatin-induced emesis in the ferret. *Pharmacology.* 1994; 48:283–92.

142. Gralla RJ, Navari RM, Hesketh PJ, et al. Single dose oral granisetron has equivalent antiemetic efficacy to intravenous ondansetron for highly emetogenic cisplatin-based chemotherapy. *J Clin Oncol.* 1998; 16:1568–73.

143. Navari RM, Pendergrass KB, Grote TH, et al. All oral regimens of dolasetron and dexamethasone to prevent emesis caused by high dose cisplatin. Proceedings of American Society of Clinical Oncology, Philadelphia, PA, May 20. 1996; 15:537.

144. Seynaeve C, Schuller J, Buser K, et al. Comparison of the anti-emetic efficacy of different doses of ondansetron, given as either a continuous infusion or a single intravenous dose, in acute cisplatin-induced emesis. A multicentre, double-blind, randomised, parallel group study. *Br J Cancer.* 1992; 66:192–7.

145. Beck TM, Hesketh PJ, Madajewicz S, et al. Stratified, randomized, double-blind comparison of intravenous ondansetron administered as a multiple-dose regimen versus two single-dose regimens in the prevention of cisplatin-induced nausea and vomiting. *J Clin Oncol.* 1992; 10:1969–75.

146. Pectasides D, Mylonakis A, Varthalitis J, et al. Comparison of two different doses of ondansetron plus dexamethasone in the prophylaxis of cisplatin-induced emesis. *Oncology.* 1997; 54:1–6.

147. Krzakowski M, Graham E, Goedhal L, et al. A multicenter, double-blind comparison of IV and oral administration of ondansetron plus dexamethasone for acute cisplatin-induced emesis. Ondansetron Acute Emesis Study Group. *Anticancer Drugs.* 1998; 9:593–8.

148. Riviere A. Dose finding study of granisetron in patients receiving high-dose cisplatin chemotherapy. The Granisetron Study Group. *Br J Cancer.* 1994; 69:967–71.

149. Perez EA, Navari RM, Kaplan HG, et al. Efficacy and safety of different doses of granisetron for the prophy-

laxis of cisplatin-induced emesis. *Support Care Cancer.* 1997; 5:31–7.

150. Conroy T, Fauser A, Spielmann M, et al. Acute antiemetic efficacy and safety of dolasetron mesylate, a 5-HT$_3$ antagonist, in cancer patients treated with cisplatin. *Am J Clin Oncol.* 1994; 17:97–102.

151. Kris MG, Grunberg SM, Gralla RJ, et al. Dose-ranging evaluation of the serotonin antagonist dolasetron mesylate in patients receiving high-dose cisplatin. *J Clin Oncol.* 1994; 12:1045–9.

152. Harman GS, Omura GA, Ryan K, et al. A randomized, double-blind comparison of single-dose and divided multiple-dose dolasetron for cisplatin-induced emesis. *Cancer Chemother Pharmacol.* 1996; 38:323–8.

153. Pendergrass K, Audhuy B, Hesketh P, et al. Analysis of optimal dose from eight pooled clinical trials assessing the acute antiemetic efficacy of iv dolasetron mesylate after emetogenic chemotherapy. *Proc Am Soc Clin Oncol.* 1996; 15:547. Abstract.

154. Rubenstein E, Fauser A, Grote J, et al. Determination of optimal dolasetron mesylate dose in prevention of acute nausea and vomiting after moderately emetogenic chemotherapy using pooled data from three pivotal trials. *Proc Am Soc Clin Oncol.* 1996; 15:532. Abstract.

155. Thant M, Pendergrass K, Harman G, et al. Double-blind, randomized study of the dose-response relationship across five single doses of iv dolasetron mesylate for prevention of acute nausea and vomiting after cisplatin chemotherapy. *Proc Am Soc Clin Oncol.* 1996; 15:533. Abstract.

156. Yeilding A, Bertoli L, Eisenberg P, et al. Antiemetic efficacy of two different single intravenous doses of dolasetron in patients receiving high-dose cisplatin-containing chemotherapy. *Am J Clin Oncol.* 1996; 19:619–23.

157. Grote TH, Pineda LF, Figlin RA, et al. Oral dolasetron mesylate in patients receiving moderately emetogenic platinum-containing chemotherapy. *Cancer J Sci Am.* 1997; 3:45–51.

158. Rubenstein EB, Gralla RJ, Hainsworth JD, et al. Randomized, double blind, dose-response trial across four oral doses of dolasetron for the prevention of acute emesis after moderately emetogenic chemotherapy. *Cancer.* 1997; 79:1216–24.

159. Roila F, Tonato M, Cognetti F, et al. Prevention of cisplatin-induced emesis: a double-blind multicenter randomized crossover study comparing ondansetron and ondansetron plus dexamethasone. *J Clin Oncol.* 1991; 9:675–8.

160. Smith DB, Newlands ES, Rustin GJS, et al. Comparison of ondansetron and ondansetron plus dexamethasone as antiemetic prophylaxis during cisplatin-containing chemotherapy. *Lancet.* 1991; 338:487–90.

161. Smyth JF, Coleman RE, Nicolson M, et al. Does dexamethasone enhance control of acute cisplatin induced emesis by ondansetron? *Br Med J.* 1991; 303:1423–6.

162. Italian Group for Antiemetic Research. Dexamethasone, granisetron, or both for the prevention of nausea and vomiting during chemotherapy for cancer. *N Engl J Med.* 1995; 332:1–5.

163. Italian Group for Antiemetic Research. Persistence of efficacy of three antiemetic regimens and prognostic factors in patients undergoing moderately emetogenic chemotherapy. *J Clin Oncol.* 1995; 13:2417–26.

164. Latreille J, Stewart D, Laberge F, et al. Dexamethasone improves the efficacy of granisetron in the first 24 hours following high-dose cisplatin chemotherapy. *Support Care Cancer.* 1995; 3:307–12.

165. Nukariya N, Nakarai I, Kobayaski H, et al. A comparative study of the effect of granisetron and a combination of granisetron plus steroids on cancer chemotherapy induced emesis. *Gan To Kagaku Ryoho.* 1995; 22:1821–9.

166. Tsukuda M, Kohno H, Enomoto H, et al. Comparison of granisetron alone and granisetron plus dexamethasone or hydroxyzine hydrochloride for the prevention of nausea and vomiting during chemotherapy including cisplatin. *Gan To Kagaku Ryoho.* 1995; 22:1377–82.

167. Olver I, Paska W, Depierre A, et al. A multicentre, double-blind study comparing placebo, ondansetron, and ondansetron plus dexamethasone for the control of cisplatin-induced delayed emesis. *Ann Oncol.* 1996; 7:945–52.

168. Ozono S, Okajima E, Hirao YK, et al. A comparative study of the effects of granisetron alone and a combination of granisetron plus steroids on CDDP-based combination chemotherapy-induced emesis—outcomes of a multicenter randomized comparative study using the Central Registration Method. *Gan To Kagaku Ryoho.* 1997; 24:349–56.

169. Joss RA, Bacchi M, Buser K, et al. Ondansetron plus dexamethasone is superior to ondansetron alone in the prevention of emesis in chemotherapy-naïve and previously treated patients. *Ann Oncol.* 1994; 5:253–8.

170. Proleukin package insert. Emeryville, CA: Chiron Corp; 1994.

171. Smith KA. T cell growth factor and glucocorticoids: opposing regulatory hormones in neoplastic T-cell growth. *Immunobiology.* 1982; 161:157–73.

172. Arya SK, Wong-Staal F, Gallo RC. Dexamethasone-mediated inhibition of human T cell growth factor and gamma-interferon messenger RNA. *J Immunol.* 1984; 133:273–6.

173. Schleimer RP, Jacques A, Shin HS, et al. Inhibition of T cell-mediated cytotoxicity by anti-inflammatory steroids. *J Immunol.* 1984; 132:266–71.

174. Roman AD, Gandara DR, Perez EA, et al. Evaluation of an oral three drug regimen in the control of acute and delayed emesis after cisplatin. *Proc Am Soc Clin Oncol.* 1998; 23:68a.

175. Cassileth PA, Lusk EJ, Torri S, et al. Antiemetic efficacy of high-dose dexamethasone in induction therapy in acute nonlymphocytic leukemia. *Ann Intern Med.* 1984; 100;701–2.

176. Zaglama NE, Rosenblum SL, Sartiano GP, et al. Single high-dose intravenous dexamethasone as an anti-emetic in cancer chemotherapy. *Oncology.* 1986; 43:27–32.

177. Chiara S, Campora E, Lionetto R, et al. Methylprednisolone for the control of CMF-induced emesis. *Am J Clin Oncol.* 1987; 10:264–7.

178. Markman M, Sheidler V, Ettinger DS, et al. Randomized, double-blind, crossover study with prochlorperazine in patients receiving cancer chemotherapy. *N Engl J Med.* 1984; 311:549–52.

179. Goldstein D, Levi JA, Woods RL. Double-blind randomized cross-over trial of dexamethasone and prochlorperazine as anti-emetics for cancer chemotherapy. *Oncology.* 1989; 46:105–8.

180. Moertel CG, Reitemeier RJ, Gage RP, et al. A con-

trolled clinical evaluation of antiemetic drugs. *JAMA.* 1963; 186:116–8.

181. Jurgens H, McQuade B. Ondansetron as prophylaxis for chemotherapy and radiotherapy-induced emesis in children. *Oncology.* 1992; 49:279–85.

182. Sullivan MJ, Abbott GD, Robinson BA. Ondansetron antiemetic therapy for chemotherapy and radiotherapy induced vomiting in children. *N Z Med J.* 1992; 105:369–71.

183. Hewitt M, McQuade B, Stevens R. The efficacy and safety of ondansetron in the prophylaxis of cancer chemotherapy induced nausea and vomiting in children. *Clin Oncol.* 1993; 5:11–4.

184. Kolecki P, Wachowiak J, Beshari SE. Ondansetron as an effective drug in prophylaxis of chemotherapy-induced emesis in children. *Actas Haematol Pol.* 1993; 24:115–22.

185. Mayron D, Gennaro AR. Stability and compatibility of granisetron hydrochloride in i.v. solutions and oral liquids and during simulated Y-site injection with selected drugs. *Am J Health-Syst Pharm.* 1996; 53:294–304.

186. Quercia RA, Zhang J, Fan C, et al. Stability of granisetron hydrochloride in an extemporaneously prepared oral liquid. *Am J Health-Syst Pharm.* 1997; 54:1404–6.

187. Mehta P, Gross S, Graham-Pole J, et al. Methylprednisolone for chemotherapy-induced emesis: a double-blind randomized trial in children. *J Pediatr.* 1986; 108:774–v6.

188. Graham-Pole J, Weare J, Engel S, et al. Antiemetics in children receiving cancer chemotherapy: a double-blind prospective randomized study comparing metoclopramide with chlorpromazine. *J Clin Oncol.* 1986; 4:1110–3.

189. Van Hoff J, Olszewski D. Lorazepam for the control of chemotherapy-related nausea and vomiting in children. *J Pediatr.* 1988; 113:146–9.

190. Marshall G, Kerr S, Vowels M, et al. Antiemetic therapy for chemotherapy-induced vomiting: metoclopramide, benztropine, dexamethasone, and lorazepam regimen compared with chlorpromazine alone. *J Pediatr.* 1989; 115:156–60.

191. Relling MV, Mulhern RK, Fairclough D, et al. Chlorpromazine with and without lorazepam as antiemetic therapy in children receiving uniform chemotherapy. *J Pediatr.* 1993; 123:811–6.

192. Buxton MJ, O'Brien BJ. Economic evaluation of ondansetron, preliminary analysis using clinical trial data prior to price setting. *Br J Cancer.* 1992; 66(suppl 19):S64–7.

193. Johnson NE, Nash DB, Carpenter CE, et al. Ondansetron: costs and resource utilization in a U.S. teaching hospital setting. *Pharmacoeconomics.* 1993; 3:471–81.

194. Tanneberger S, Lelli G, Martoni A, et al. The antiemetic efficacy and the cost-benefit ratio of ondansetron calculated with a new approach to health technology assessment (real cost benefit index). *J Chemother.* 1992; 4:326–31.

195. Cox F, Hirsch J. Ondansetron: a cost-effective advance in antiemetic therapy. *Oncology.* 1993; 50:186–90.

196. Cunningham D, Gore M, Davidson N, et al. The real costs of emesis—an economic analysis of ondansetron vs metoclopramide in controlling emesis in patients receiving chemotherapy for cancer. *Eur J Cancer.* 1993; 29A:303–6.

197. Zammit-Lucia J. Modeling budgetary impact from decision makers. *Anticancer Drugs.* 1993; 4(suppl 3):21–5.

198. Bleiberg HH, Spielmann M, Falkson G, et al. Antiemetic treatment with oral granisetron in patients receiving moderately emetogenic chemotherapy: a dose-ranging study. *Clin Ther.* 1995; 17:38–51.

199. Johnson N, Bosanquet N. Cost effectiveness of 5-hydroxytryptamine-3 receptor antagonists: a retrospective comparison of ondansetron and granisetron. *Anticancer Drugs.* 1995; 6:243–9.

200. Dranitsaris G, De Angelis C, Warr D, et al. Pharmacoeconomic analysis of prophylactic treatments for emesis secondary to breast cancer chemotherapy. *Can J Hosp Pharm.* 1995; 48:266–75.

201. Zbrozek AS, Cantor SB, Cardenas MP, et al. Pharmacoeconomic analysis of ondansetron versus metoclopramide for cisplatin-induced nausea and vomiting. *Am J Hosp Pharm.* 1994; 51:1555–63.

202. Casteels-Van Daele M, Jaeken J, Van Der Schueren P, et al. Dystonic reactions in children caused by metoclopramide. *Arch Dis Child.* 1970; 45:130–3.

203. Cousin J, Katende G, Pauli A, et al. L'intoxication par metoclopramide chez l'enfant. *J Sci Med Lille.* 1973; 91:1.

204. Low LC, Goel KM. Metoclopramide poisoning in children. *Arch Dis Child.* 1980; 55:310–1.

205. Bateman DN, Craft AW, Nicholson E, et al. Dystonic reactions and the pharmacokinetics of metoclopramide in children. *Br J Clin Pharmacol.* 1983; 15:557–9.

206. Terrin BN, McWilliams NB, Maurer HM. Side effects of metoclopramide as an antiemetic in childhood cancer chemotherapy. *J Pediatr.* 1984; 104:138–40.

207. Allen JC, Gralla R, Reilly L, et al. Metoclopramide: dose-related toxicity and preliminary antiemetic studies in children receiving cancer chemotherapy. *J Clin Oncol.* 1985; 3:1136–41.

208. Howrie DL, Felix C, Wollman M, et al. Metoclopramide as an antiemetic agent in pediatric oncology patients. *Drug Intell Clin Pharm.* 1986; 20:122–4.

209. Campora E, Vidili G, Oliva C, et al. Control of refractory, chemotherapy-induced emesis with the serotonin antagonist ondansetron (GR 38032F). *Oncology.* 1991; 48:403–5.

210. Seynaeve C, de Mulder PHM, Lane-Allman E, et al. The 5-HT$_3$ receptor antagonist ondansetron re-establishes control in refractory emesis induced by non-cisplatin chemotherapy. *Clin Oncol.* 1991; 3:199–203.

211. Du Bois A, Meerpohl HG, Vach W, et al. Course, patterns, and risk-factors for chemotherapy-induced emesis in cisplatin-pretreated patients: a study with ondansetron. *Eur J Cancer.* 1992; 28:450–7.

212. Voth EA, Schwartz RH. Medicinal applications of delta-9-tetrahydrocannabinoid and marijuana. *Ann Intern Med.* 1997; 126:791–8.

213. Navari RM, Gandara D, Hesketh P, et al. Comparative clinical trial of granisetron and ondansetron in the prophylaxis of cisplatin-induced emesis. *J Clin Oncol.* 1995; 13:1242–8.

214. The Italian Group for Antiemetic Research. Ondansetron versus metoclopramide, both combined with dexamethasone, in the prevention of cisplatin-induced delayed emesis. *J Clin Onc.* 1997; 15:124–30.

215. Strum D, McDermed J, Abrahono-Umcli R, et al. Management of cisplatin-induced delayed onset nausea and vomiting: preliminary results and 2 drug regimens. *Proc Am Soc Clin Oncol.* 1985; 4:263. Abstract.

216. Clark RA, Kris MG, Tyson LB, et al. Antiemetic trials to control delayed vomiting following high-dose cisplatin. *Proc Am Soc Clin Oncol.* 1986; 5:257. Abstract.

217. Sridhar KS, Donnelly E. Combination antiemetics for cisplatin chemotherapy. *Cancer.* 1988; 61:1508–17.

218. Scarantino CW, Ornitz RD, Hoffman LG, et al. On the mechanism of radiation-induced emesis: the role of serotonin. *Int J Radiat Oncol Biol Phys.* 1994; 30:825–30.

219. Roberts JT, Priestman JT. A review of ondansetron in the management of radiotherapy-induced emesis. *Oncology.* 1993; 50:173–9.

220. Coia LR, Moylan DJ. Introduction to clinical radiation oncology. Madison, WI: Medical Physics Publishing; 1991.

221. Tyers MB, Bunce KT, Humphrey PP. Pharmacological and anti-emetic properties of ondansetron. *Eur J Cancer Clin Oncol.* 1989; 25(suppl 1):S515–9.

222. Lucraft HH, Palmer MK. Randomised clinical trial of levonantradol and chlorpromazine in the prevention of radiotherapy-induced vomiting. *Clin Radiol.* 1982; 33:621–2.

223. Priestman TJ, Priestman SG. An initial evaluation of nabilone in the control of radiotherapy-induced nausea and vomiting. *Clin Radiol.* 1984; 35:265–6.

224. Priestman TJ. Clinical studies with ondansetron in the control of radiation-induced emesis. *Eur J Cancer Clin Oncol.* 1989; 25(suppl 1):S29–33.

225. Priestman TJ, Roberts JT, Lucraft H, et al. Results of a randomized, double-blind comparative study of ondansetron and metoclopramide in the prevention of nausea and vomiting following high-dose upper abdominal irradiation. *Clin Oncol.* 1990; 2:71–5.

226. Collis CH, Priestman TJ, Priestman S, et al. The final assessment of a randomized double-blind comparative study of ondansetron vs. metoclopramide in the prevention of nausea and vomiting following high-dose upper abdominal irradiation. *Clin Oncol.* 1991; 3:241–3.

227. Franzen L, Nyman I, Hagberg H, et al. A randomized placebo-controlled study with ondansetron in patients undergoing fractionated chemotherapy. *Am Aniol.* 1996; 7:587–92.

228. Hewitt M, Cornish J, Pamphilon D, et al. Effective emetic control during conditioning of children for bone marrow transplantation using ondansetron, a 5-HT$_3$ antagonist. *Bone Marrow Transplant.* 1991; 7:431–3.

229. Hunter AE, Prentice HG, Pothecary K, et al. Granisetron, a selective 5-HT$_3$ receptor antagonist, for the prevention of radiation induced emesis during total body irradiation. *Bone Marrow Transplant.* 1991; 7:439–41.

230. Logue JP, Magee B, Hunter RD, et al. The antiemetic effect of granisetron in lower hemibody radiotherapy. *Clin Oncol.* 1991; 247–9.

231. Jurgens H, McQuade B. Ondansetron as prophylaxis for chemotherapy and radiotherapy-induced emesis in children. *Oncology.* 1992; 49:279–85.

232. Rosenthal SA, Marquez CM, Hourigan HP, et al. Ondansetron for patients given abdominal radiotherapy. *Lancet.* 1992; 339:490.

233. Sullivan MJ, Abbott GD, Robinson BA. Ondansetron antiemetic therapy for chemotherapy and radiotherapy induced vomiting in children. *NZ Med J.* 1992; 105:369–71.

234. Tiley C, Powles R, Catalano J, et al. Results of a double blind placebo controlled study of ondansetron as an antiemetic during total body irradiation in patients undergoing bone marrow transplantation. *Leuk Lymphoma.* 1992; 7:317–21.

235. Priestman TJ, Roberts JT, Upadhyaya BK. A prospective randomized double-blind trial comparing ondansetron versus prochlorperazine for the prevention of nausea and vomiting in patients undergoing fractionated radiotherapy. *Clin Oncol.* 1993; 5:358–63.

236. Spitzer TR, Bryson JC, Cirenza E, et al. Randomized double-blind, placebo-controlled evaluation of oral ondansetron in the prevention of nausea and vomiting associated with fractionated total-body irradiation. *Clin Oncol.* 1994; 12:2432–8.

237. Prentice HG, Cunningham S, Gandhi L, et al. Granisetron in the prevention of irradiation-induced emesis. *Bone Marrow Transplant.* 1995; 15:445–8.

238. Bey P, Wilkinson P, Resbeut M, et al. A double-blind, placebo-controlled trial of iv dolasetron mesilate in the prevention of radiotherapy-induced nausea and vomiting in cancer patients. *Support Care Cancer.* 1996; 4:378–83.

239. Hewitt M, Cornish J, Pamphilon P, et al. Effective antiemetic control during conditioning of children for bone marrow transplantation using ondansetron, a 5-HT$_3$ antagonist. *Bone Marrow Transplant.* 1991; 7:431–3.

240. Lippens RJ, Broeders GC. Ondansetron in radiation therapy of brain tumor in children. *Pediatr Hematol Oncol.* 1996; 13:247–52.

241. Holt JAG. A trial of thiethylperazine (Torecan) in patients suffering from radiation sickness. *Med J Austr.* 1965; 279–81.

242. Burnette PK, Perkins J. Parenteral ondansetron for the treatment of chemotherapy- and radiation-induced nausea and vomiting. *Pharmacotherapy.* 1992; 12:120–31.

243. Tami JA, Waite WW. Metoclopramide suppository considerations. *Drug Intell Clin Pharm.* 1988; 22:268–9. Letter.

244. Vance JP, Neill RS, Norris W. The incidence and aetiology of post-operative nausea and vomiting in a plastic surgical unit. *Br J Plast Surg.* 1973; 26:336–9.

245. King MJ, Milazkiewicz R, Carli F, et al. Influence of neostigmine on postoperative vomiting. *Br J Anaesth.* 1988; 61:403–6.

246. Cohen MM, Cameron CB, Duncan PG. Pediatric anesthesia morbidity and mortality in the perioperative period. *Anesth Analg.* 1990; 70:160–7.

247. Kamath B, Curran J, Hawkey C, et al. Anaesthesia, movement and emesis. *Br J Anaesth.* 1990; 64:728–30.

248. Parnass SM, McCarthy RJ, Ivankovich AD. The role of pain as a cause of postoperative nausea/vomiting after outpatient anesthesia. *Anesth Analg.* 1992; 74:S233. Abstract.

249. Lerman J. Surgical and patient factors involved in postoperative nausea and vomiting. *Br J Anaesth.* 1992; 69(suppl 1):24S–32S.

250. Watcha MF, Simeon RM, White PF, et al. Effect of propofol on the incidence of postoperative vomiting after strabismus surgery in pediatric outpatients. *Anesthesiology.* 1991; 75:204–9.

251. Gan TJ, Ginsberg B, Grant AP, et al. Double-blind, randomized comparison of ondansetron and intraoperative propofol to prevent postoperative nausea and vomiting. *Anesthesiology.* 1996; 85:1036–42.

252. Tramer M, Moore A, McQuay H. Propofol anaesthesia and postoperative nausea and vomiting: quantitative systematic review of randomized controlled studies. *Br J Anaesth.* 1997; 78:247–55.

253. Morrison JD, Clarke RSJ, Dundee JW. Studies of drugs given before anesthesia XXI: droperidol. *Br J Anaesth.* 1970; 42:730–5.

254. Patton CM, Moon MR, Dannemiller FJ. The prophylactic antiemetic effect of droperidol. *Anesth Analg.* 1974; 53:361–4.

255. Winning TJ, Brock-Utne JG, Downing JW. Nausea and vomiting after anesthesia and minor surgery. *Anesth Analg.* 1977; 56:674–7.

256. Korttila K, Kauste A, Auvinen J. Comparison of domperidone, droperidol and metoclopramide in the prevention and treatment of nausea and vomiting after balanced general anesthesia. *Anesth Analg.* 1979; 58:396–400.

257. Loeser EA, Bennett G, Stanley TH, et al. Comparison of droperidol, haloperidol and prochlorperazine as postoperative anti-emetics. *Can Anaesth Soc J.* 1979; 26:125–7.

258. Rita L, Goodarzi M, Seleny F. Effect of low dose droperidol on postoperative vomiting in children. *Can Anaesth Soc J.* 1981; 28:259–62.

259. McKenzie R, Wadhwa RK, Uy NTL, et al. Antiemetic effectiveness of intramuscular hydroxyzine compared to intramuscular droperidol. *Anesth Analg.* 1981; 60:783–8.

260. Mortensen PT. Droperidol (Dehydrobenzperidol): postoperative anti-emetic effect when given intravenously to gynaecological patients. *Acta Anaesthesiol Scand.* 1982; 26:48–52.

261. Abramowitz MD, Oh TH, Epstein BS, et al. The antiemetic effect of droperidol following outpatient strabismus surgery in children. *Anesthesiology.* 1983; 59:579–83.

262. Cohen SE, Woods WA, Wyner J. Antiemetic efficacy of droperidol and metoclopramide. *Anesthesiology.* 1984; 60:67–9.

263. Layfield DJ, Walker AKY. Premedication for children with oral trimeprazine and droperidol. *Anaesthesia.* 1984; 39:32–4.

264. O'Donovan N, Shaw J. Nausea and vomiting in daycase dental surgery: the use of low dose droperidol. *Anaesthesia.* 1984; 39:1172–6.

265. Santos A, Datta S. Prophylactic use of droperidol for control of nausea and vomiting during spinal anesthesia for cesarean section. *Anesth Analg.* 1984; 63:85–7.

266. Korttila K, Kauste A, Tuominen M, et al. Droperidol prevents and treats nausea and vomiting after enflurane anaesthesia. *Eur J Anaesthesiol.* 1985; 2:379–85.

267. Valanne J, Korttila K. Effect of a small dose of droperidol on nausea, vomiting and recovery after outpatient enflurane anaesthesia. *Acta Anaesthesiol Scand.* 1985; 29:359–62.

268. Hardy JF, Charest J, Girouard G, et al. Nausea and vomiting after strabismus surgery in preschool children. *Can Anaesth Soc J.* 1986; 33:57–62.

269. Kauste A, Tuominen M, Heikkinen H, et al. Droperidol, alizapride and metoclopramide in the prevention and treatment of post-operative emetic sequelae. *Eur J Anaesthesiol.* 1986; 3:1–9.

270. Lerman J, Eustis S, Smith DR. Effect of droperidol pretreatment on postanesthetic vomiting in children undergoing strabismus surgery. *Anesthesiology.* 1986; 65:322–5.

271. Madej TH, Simpson KH. Comparison of the use of domperidone, droperidol and metoclopramide in the prevention of nausea and vomiting following major gynaecological surgery. *Br J Anaesth.* 1986; 58:884–7.

272. Van Den Berg AA, Lambourne A, Yazji NS, et al. Vomiting after ophthalmic surgery. Effects of intraoperative antiemetics and postoperative oral fluid restriction. *Anesthesia.* 1987; 42:270–6.

273. Tigerstedt I, Salmela L, Aromaa U. Double-blind comparison of transdermal scopolamine, droperidol and placebo against postoperative nausea and vomiting. *Acta Anaesthesiol Scand.* 1988; 32:454–7.

274. Chestnut DH, Owen CL, Geiger M, et al. Metoclopramide versus droperidol for prevention of nausea and vomiting during epidural anesthesia for cesarean section. *South Med J.* 1989; 82:1224–7.

275. Christensen S, Farrow-Gillespie A, Lerman J. Incidence of emesis and postanesthetic recovery after strabismus surgery in children: a comparison of droperidol and lidocaine. *Anesthesiology.* 1989; 70:251–4.

276. Pandit SK, Kothary SP, Pandit UA, et al. Dose-response study of droperidol and metoclopramide as antiemetics for outpatient anesthesia. *Anesth Analg.* 1989; 68:798–802.

277. Melnick B, Sawyer R, Karambelkar D, et al. Delayed side effects of droperidol after ambulatory general anesthesia. *Anesth Analg.* 1989; 69:748–51.

278. Jorgensen NH, Coyle JP. Intravenous droperidol decreases nausea and vomiting after alfentanil anesthesia without increasing recovery time. *J Clin Anesth.* 1990; 2:312–6.

279. Larsson S, Jonmarker C. Postoperative emesis after pediatric strabismus surgery: the effect of dixyrazine compared to droperidol. *Acta Anaesthesiol Scand.* 1990; 34:227–30.

280. Brown RE, James DJ, Weaver RG, et al. Low-dose droperidol versus standard-dose droperidol for prevention of postoperative vomiting after pediatric strabismus surgery. *J Clin Anesth.* 1991; 3:306–9.

281. Blanc VF, Ruest P, Milot J, et al. Antiemetic prophylaxis with promethazine or droperidol in paediatric outpatient strabismus surgery. *Can J Anesth.* 1991; 38:54–60.

282. Alon E, Himmelseher S. Ondansetron in the treatment of postoperative vomiting: a randomized, double-blind comparison with droperidol and metoclopramide. *Anesth Analg.* 1992; 75:561–5.

283. Liu YC, Kang HM, Liou CM, et al. Comparison of antiemetic effect among ephedrine, droperidol, and metoclopramide in pediatric inguinal hernioplasty. *Acta Anaesthesiol Sin.* 1992; 30:37–41.

284. Fujii Y, Tanaka H. Postoperative anti-emetic effects of low dose droperidol. *Masui.* 1993; 42:694–7.

285. Klockgether-Radke A, Demmel C, Braun U, et al. Emesis and the oculocardiac reflex. Drug prophylaxis with droperidol and atropine in children undergoing strabismus surgery. *Anaesthesist.* 1993; 42:356–60.

286. Lawhorn CD, Brown RE, Schmitz ML, et al. Preven-

tion of postoperative vomiting in pediatric outpatient strabismus surgery. *Anesthesiology.* 1993; 79:A1196. Abstract.

287. Pendeville PE, Veyckemans F, Van Boven MJ, et al. Open placebo controlled comparison of the antiemetic effect of droperidol, metoclopramide, or a combination of both in pediatric strabismus surgery. *Acta Anaesthesiol Belg.* 1993; 44:3–10.

288. Peterson MD, Bishop J, Tanner K. Comparison of droperidol and ondansetron for prevention of vomiting after strabismus surgery in children. *Anesth Analg.* 1993; 76:S329. Abstract.

289. Furst SR, Rodarte A. Prophylactic antiemetic treatment with ondansetron in children undergoing tonsillectomy. *Anesthesiology.* 1994; 81:799–803.

290. Heim C, Munzer T, Listyo R. Ondansetron versus droperidol: treatment of postoperative nausea and vomiting. Comparison of efficiency, side-effects and acceptance by gynaecological inpatients. *Anaesthesist.* 1994; 43:504–9.

291. Ummenhofer W, Frei FJ, Urwyler A, et al. Effects of ondansetron in the prevention of postoperative nausea and vomiting in children. *Anesthesiology.* 1994; 81: 804–10.

292. Davis PJ, McGowan FX, Landsman I, et al. Effect of antiemetic therapy on recovery and hospital discharge time. A double-blind assessment of ondansetron, droperidol, and placebo in pediatric patients undergoing ambulatory surgery. *Anesthesiology.* 1995; 83:956–60.

293. Desilva PHDP, Darvish AH, McDonald SM, et al. The efficacy of prophylactic ondansetron, droperidol, perphenazine, and metoclopramide in the prevention of nausea and vomiting after major gynecologic surgery. *Anesth Analg.* 1995; 81:139–43.

294. Grond S, Lynch J, Diefenback C, et al. Comparison of ondansetron and droperidol in the prevention of nausea and vomiting after inpatient minor gynecologic surgery. *Anesth Analg.* 1995; 81:603–7.

295. Kymer PJ, Brown RE, Lawhorn CD, et al. The effects of oral droperidol versus oral metoclopramide versus both oral droperidol and metoclopramide on postoperative vomiting when used as a premedicant for strabismus surgery. *J Clin Anesth.* 1995; 7:35–9.

296. Fortney JT, Gan TJ, Graczyk S, et al. A comparison of the efficacy, safety and patient satisfaction of ondansetron versus droperidol as antiemetics for elective outpatient surgical procedures. *Anesth Analg.* 1998; 86:731–8.

297. Handley AJ. Metoclopramide in the prevention of post-operative nausea and vomiting. *Br J Clin Pract.* 1967; 21:460–2.

298. Dobkin AB. Perphenazine in clinical anesthesia. *Can Anaesth Soc J.* 1968; 15:80–91.

299. Clark MM, Storrs JA. The prevention of postoperative vomiting after abortion: metoclopramide. *Br J Anaesth.* 1969; 41:890–3.

300. Ellis FR, Spence AA. Clinical trials of metoclopramide (Maxolon) as an antiemetic in anaesthesia. *Anaesthesia.* 1970; 25:368–71.

301. Shah ZP, Wilson J. An evaluation of metoclopramide (Maxolon) as an anti-emetic in minor gynaecological surgery. *Br J Anaesth.* 1972; 44:865–8.

302. Dundee JW, Clarke RSJ. The premedicant and antiemetic action of metoclopramide. *Postgrad Med J.* 1973; 49(suppl):34–7.

303. Assaf RAE, Clarke RSJ, Dundee JW, et al. Studies of drugs given before anaesthesia XXIV: metoclopramide with morphine and pethidine. *Br J Anaesth.* 1974; 46:514–9.

304. Dundee JW, Clarke RSJ, Howard PJ. Studies of drugs given before anesthesia XXIII: metoclopramide. *Br J Anaesth.* 1974; 46:509–13.

305. Cooke RD, Comyn DJ, Ball RW. Prevention of postoperative nausea and vomiting by domperidone. A double-blind randomised study using domperidone, metoclopramide and a placebo. *S Afr Med J.* 1979; 56:827–9.

306. Diamond MJ, Keeri-Szanto M. Reduction of postoperative vomiting by preoperative administration of oral metoclopramide. *Can Anaesth Soc J.* 1980; 27:36–9.

307. Rao TL, Madhavareddy S, Chinthagada M, et al. Metoclopramide and cimetidine to reduce gastric fluid pH and volume. *Anesth Analg.* 1984; 63:1014–6.

308. Spelina KR, Gerber HR, Pagels IL. Nausea and vomiting during spinal anesthesia. Effect of metoclopramide and domperidone: a double-blind trial. *Anaesthesia.* 1984; 39:132–7.

309. Waldmann CS, Verghese C, Short SM, et al. The evaluation of domperidone and metoclopramide as antiemetics in day care abortion patients. *Br J Clin Pharmacol.* 1985; 19:307–10.

310. Chestnut DH, Vandewalker GE, Owen CL, et al. Administration of metoclopramide for prevention of nausea and vomiting during epidural anesthesia for elective cesarean section. *Anesthesiology.* 1987; 66:563–6.

311. Miller CD. Silent regurgitation in day case gynaecological patients. *Anaesthesia.* 1988; 43:321–3.

312. Williams JJ, Goldberg ME, Boerner TF, et al. A comparison of three methods to reduce nausea and vomiting after alfentanil anesthesia in outpatients. *Anesth Analg.* 1989; 68:S311.

313. Broadman LM, Ceruzzi W, Patane PS, et al. Metoclopramide reduces the incidence of vomiting following strabismus surgery in children. *Anesthesiology.* 1990; 72:245–8.

314. Bone ME, Wilkinson DJ, Young JR, et al. Ginger root—a new antiemetic; the effect of ginger root on postoperative nausea and vomiting after major gynaecological surgery. *Anaesthesia.* 1990; 45:669–71.

315. Kraynack BJ, Bates MF, Gintautas J. Antiemetic efficacy of ranitidine, metoclopramide and gastric suctioning in outpatient laparoscopy. *Anesth Analg.* 1990; 70:S218. Abstract.

316. Raphael JH, Norton AC. Antiemetic efficacy of prophylactic ondansetron in laparoscopic surgery: randomized, double-blind comparison with metoclopramide. *Br J Anaesth.* 1993; 71:845–8.

317. DeVries PM. A double-blind cross-over clinical evaluation of metoclopramide and a combination of haloperidol and isopropamide iodide in gastroenterology. *Arzneimittelforschung.* 1969; 19:1766–7.

318. Tornetta FJ. Double-blind evaluation of haloperidol for antiemetic activity. *Anesth Analg.* 1972; 51:964–7.

319. Lind B, Breivik H. Metoclopramide and perphenazine in the prevention of postoperative nausea and vomiting. *Br J Anaesth.* 1970; 42:614–7.

320. McGarry JM. A double-blind comparison of the antiemetic effect during labour of metoclopramide and perphenazine. *Br J Anaesth.* 1971; 43:613–5.

321. Shaklai M, Pinkhas J, De Vries A. Metoclopramide

and cardiac arrhythmia. *Br Med J.* 1974; 1:385.

322. Park GR. Hypotension following metoclopramide administration during hypotensive anaesthesia for intracranial aneurysm. *Br J Anaesth.* 1978; 50:1268–9. Letter.

323. Pegg MS. Hypotension following metoclopramide injection. *Anaesthesia.* 1980; 35:615. Letter.

324. Withington DE. Dysrhythmias following intravenous metoclopramide. *Intens Care Med.* 1986; 12:378–9.

325. Bevacqua BK. Supraventricular tachycardia associated with postpartum metoclopramide administration. *Anesthesiology.* 1988; 68:124–5.

326. Friedman LS, Weinrauch LA, D'Elia JA. Metoclopramide-induced neuroleptic malignant syndrome. *Arch Intern Med.* 1987; 147:1495–7.

327. Wetchler BV, Sung YF, Duncalf D. Ondansetron decreases emetic symptoms following outpatient laparoscopy. *Anesthesiology.* 1990; 73:A36. Abstract.

328. Bodner M, White PF. Antiemetic efficacy of ondansetron after outpatient laparoscopy. *Anesth Analg.* 1991; 73:250–4.

329. Larijani GE, Gratz I, Afshar M, et al. Treatment of postoperative nausea and vomiting with ondansetron: a randomized, double-blind comparison with placebo. *Anesth Analg.* 1991; 73:246–9.

330. Leeser J, Lip H. Prevention of postoperative nausea and vomiting using ondansetron, a new, selective, 5-HT$_3$ receptor antagonist. *Anesth Analg.* 1991; 72:751–5.

331. Lessin JB, Azad SS, Rosenblum F, et al. Does antiemetic prophylaxis with ondansetron prolong recovery time? *Anesth Analg.* 1991; 72:S162. Abstract.

332. Rosenblum F, Azad SS, Bartkowski R, et al. Ondansetron: a new, effective anti-emetic prevents postoperative nausea and vomiting. *Anesth Analg.* 1991; 72:S230. Abstract.

333. Bouly A, Nathan N, Feiss P. Prevention of postoperative nausea and vomiting by ondansetron. *Ann Fr Anesth Reanim.* 1992; 11:496–501.

334. Dershwitz M, Rosow CE, Di Biase PM, et al. Ondansetron is effective in decreasing postoperative nausea and vomiting. *Clin Pharmacol Ther.* 1992; 52:96–101.

335. Helmers JHJH. Oral ondansetron in the prevention of postoperative nausea and vomiting. *Eur J Anaesthesiol.* 1992; 9(suppl 6):49–54.

336. Kenny GN, Oates JD, Leeser J, et al. Efficacy of orally administered ondansetron in the prevention of postoperative nausea and vomiting: a dose ranging study. *Br J Anaesth.* 1992; 68:466–70.

337. Kovac A, McKenzie R, O'Connor T, et al. Prophylactic intravenous ondansetron in female outpatients undergoing gynaecological surgery: a multicentre dose-comparison study. *Eur J Anaesth.* 1992; 9(suppl 6):37–47.

338. Dupeyron JP, Conseiller C, Levarlet M, et al. The effect of oral ondansetron in the prevention of postoperative nausea and vomiting after major gynaecological surgery performed under general anaesthesia. *Anaesthesia.* 1993; 48:214–8.

339. Helmers JHJH, Briggs L, Abrahamsson J, et al. A single iv dose of ondansetron 8mg prior to induction of anaesthesea reduces postoperative nausea and vomiting in gynaecological patients. *Can J Anaesth.* 1993; 40:1155–61.

340. Khalil SN, Kataria B, Pearson K, et al. Ondansetron prevents postoperative nausea and vomiting in women outpatients. *Anesth Analg.* 1994; 79:845–51.

341. Sung YF, Wetchler BV, Duncalf D, et al. A double-blind placebo-controlled pilot study examining the effectiveness of intravenous ondansetron in the prevention of postoperative nausea and emesis. *J Clin Anesth.* 1993; 5:22–9.

342. McKenzie R, Kovac A, O'Connor T, et al. Comparison of ondansetron versus placebo to prevent postoperative nausea and vomiting in women undergoing ambulatory gynecologic surgery. *Anesthesiology.* 1993; 78:21–8.

343. McKenzie R, Sharifi-Azad S, Dershwitz M, et al. A randomized, double-blind pilot study examining the use of intravenous ondansetron in the prevention of postoperative nausea and vomiting in female inpatients. *J Clin Anesth.* 1993; 5:30–6.

344. Scuderi P, Wetchler B, Sung YF, et al. Treatment of postoperative nausea and vomiting after outpatient surgery with the 5-HT$_3$ antagonist ondansetron. *Anesthesiology.* 1993; 78:15–20.

345. Claybon L. Single dose intravenous ondansetron for the 24-hour treatment of postoperative nausea and vomiting. *Anaesthesia.* 1994; 49(suppl):24–9.

346. Gan TJ, Collis R, Hetreed M. Double-blind comparison of ondansetron, droperidol and saline in the prevention of postoperative nausea and vomiting. *Br J Anaesth.* 1994; 72:544–7.

347. Malins AF, Field JM, Nesling PM, et al. Nausea and vomiting after gynaecological laparoscopy: comparison of premedication with oral ondansetron, metoclopramide and placebo. *Br J Anaesth.* 1994; 72:231–3.

348. Pearman MH. Single dose intravenous ondansetron in the prevention of postoperative nausea and vomiting. *Anaesthesia.* 1994; 49(suppl):11–5.

349. Rodrigo MR, Campbell RC, Chow J, et al. Ondansetron for prevention of postoperative nausea and vomiting following minor oral surgery: a double-blind randomized study. *Anaesth Intens Care.* 1994; 22:576–9.

350. Rust M, Cohen LA. Single oral dose ondansetron in the prevention of postoperative nausea and emesis. *Anaesthesia.* 1994; 49(suppl):16–23.

351. Suen TK, Gin TA, Chen PP, et al. Ondansetron 4 mg for the prevention of nausea and vomiting after minor laparoscopic gynaecological surgery. *Anaesth Intens Care.* 1994; 22:142–6.

352. Paxton LD, McKay AC, Mirakhur RK. Prevention of nausea and vomiting after day case gynaecological laparoscopy: a comparison of ondansetron, droperidol, metoclopramide, and placebo. *Anaesthesia.* 1995; 50:403–6.

353. Polati E, Finco G, Bartoloni A, et al. Prevention of postoperative nausea and vomiting with ondansetron: a prospective, randomized, double-blind study in 90 patients. *Minerva Anestesiol.* 1995; 61:373–9.

354. Honkavaara P. Effect of ondansetron on nausea and vomiting after middle ear surgery during general anaesthesia. *Br J Anaesth.* 1996; 76:316–8.

355. Koivuranta MK, Laara E, Ryhanen PT. Antiemetic efficacy of prophylactic ondansetron in laparoscopic cholecystectomy: a randomized, double-blind, placebo-controlled trial. *Anaesthesia.* 1996; 51:52–5.

356. Rose JB, Martin TM, Corddry DH, et al. Ondansetron reduces the incidence and severity of poststrabismus repair vomiting in children. *Anesth Analg.* 1994; 79:486–9.

357. Watcha MF, Bras PJ, Ceislak GD, et al. The dose-response relationship of ondansetron in preventing postoperative emesis in pediatric patients undergoing ambulatory surgery. *Anesthesiology.* 1995; 82:47–52.

358. Litman RS, Wu CL, Catanzaro FA. Ondansetron decreases emesis after tonsillectomy in children. *Anesth Analg.* 1994; 78:478–81.

359. Splinter WM, Baxter MR, Gould HM, et al. Oral ondansetron decreases vomiting after tonsillectomy in children. *Can J Anaesth.* 1995; 42:277–80.

360. Khalil S, Rodarte A, Weldon BC, et al. Intravenous ondansetron in established postoperative emesis in children. S3A-381 Study Group. *Anesthesiology.* 1996; 85:270–6.

361. Ulusoy HO, Akturk G, Luleci N, et al. Prophylactic administration of ondansetron in emergency intraabdominal operations. *Middle East J Anesthesiol.* 1996; 13:513–26.

362. Kovac AL, Pearman MH, Khali SN, et al. Ondansetron prevents postoperative emesis in male outpatients. *J Clin Anesth.* 1996; 8:644–51.

363. Rose JB, Brenn BR, Corddry DH, et al. Preoperative oral ondansetron for pediatric tonsillectomy. *Anesth Analg.* 1996; 82:558–62.

364. Fujji Y, Tanaka H, Toyooka H. Optimal anti-emetic dose of granisetron for preventing postoperative nausea and vomiting. *Can J Anaesth.* 1994; 41:794–7.

365. Fujii Y, Tanaka H, Toyooka H. Reduction of postoperative nausea and vomiting with granisetron. *Can J Anaesth.* 1994; 41:291–4.

366. Fujii Y, Tanaka H, Toyooka H. Granisetron reduces vomiting after strabismus surgery and tonsillectomy in children. *Can J Anaesth.* 1996; 43:35–8.

367. Fujii Y, Toyooka H, Tanaka H. Antiemetic effects of granisetron on postoperative nausea and vomiting in patients with and without motion sickness. *Can J Anaesth.* 1996; 43:110–4.

368. Fujii Y, Toyooka H. Antiemetic efficacy of granisetron and metoclopramide in children undergoing ophthalmic or ENT surgery. *Can J Anaesth.* 1996; 43:1095–9.

369. Cieslak GD, Watcha MF, Phillips MB, et al. The dose-response relation and cost-effectiveness of granisetron for the prophylaxis of pediatric emesis. *Anesthesiology.* 1996; 85:1076–85.

370. Naguib M, el Bakry AK, Khoshim MH, et al. Prophylactic antiemetic therapy with ondansetron, tropisetron, granisetron and metoclopramide in patients undergoing laparoscopic cholecystectomy: a randomized, double-blind comparison with placebo. *Can J Anaesth.* 1996; 43:226–31.

371. Wilson AJ, Diemunsch P, Lindeque BG, et al. Single-dose IV granisetron in the prevention of postoperative nausea and vomiting. *Br J Anaesth.* 1996; 76:515–8.

372. Fujii Y, Tanaka H, Toyooka H. Granisetron-dexamethasone combination reduces postoperative nausea and vomiting. *Can J Anaesth.* 1995; 42:387–90.

373. Mikawa K, Takao Y, Nishina K, et al. The antiemetic efficacy of prophylactic granisetron in gynecologic surgery. *Anesth Analg.* 1995; 80:970–4.

374. Graczyk SG, McKenzie R, Kallar S, et al. Intravenous dolasetron for the prevention of postoperative nausea and vomiting after outpatient laparoscopic gynecologic surgery. *Anesth Analg.* 1997; 84:325–30.

375. Korttila K, Maillet M, Diemunsch P, et al. IV dolasetron mesylate (DM) vs IV ondansetron (OND) for prevention of post operative nausea and vomiting (PONV). *Anesthesiology.* 1996; 86(3A suppl):A35. Abstract.

376. Diemunsch P, Leeser J, Feiss P, et al. Intravenous dolasetron mesilate ameliorates postoperative nausea and vomiting. *Can J Anaesth.* 1997; 44:173–81.

377. Diemunsch P, D'Hollander A, Paxton L, et al. Intravenous dolasetron mesylate in the prevention of postoperative nausea and vomiting in females undergoing gynecological surgery. *J Clin Anesth.* 1997; 9:365–73.

378. Kovac A, Melson T, Graczyk S, et al. Treatment of postoperative nausea and vomiting with single doses of IV dolasetron: a multicenter trial. *Anesthesiology.* 1995; 83(3A suppl):A6. Abstract.

379. Watkins WD, Kovac A, Hickok C, et al. Evaluation of optimally effective IV dose of dolasetron mesylate (DM) for treating established post operative nausea and vomiting (PONV). *Anesthesiology.* 1996; 85(3A suppl):A17. Abstract.

380. Diemunsch P, Leeser J, Helmers JH, et al. Oral dolasetron mesylate for prevention of postoperative nausea and vomiting (PONV). *Anesthesiology.* 1996; 85(3A suppl):A3. Abstract.

381. Warriner CB, Knox D, Belo S, et al. Prophylactic oral dolasetron mesylate reduces postoperative nausea and vomiting following abdominal hysterectomy. *Anesthesiology.* 1995; 83(3A):A312. Abstract.

382. Pan PH, Moore CH. Intraoperative antiemetic efficacy of prophylactic ondansetron versus droperidol for cesarean section patients under epidural anesthesia. *Anesth Analg.* 1996; 83:982–6.

383. Alon E, Biro P, Lenzlinger PM, et al. Ondansetron as prophylaxis for postoperative nausea and vomiting. A prospective randomized double-blind comparative trial with droperidol. *Anaesthestist.* 1994; 43:500–3.

384. Tang J, Watcha MF, White PF. A comparison of costs and efficacy of ondansetron and droperidol as prophylactic antiemetic therapy for elective outpatient gynecologic procedures. *Anesth Analg.* 1996; 83:304–13.

385. Watcha MF, Smith I. Cost-effectiveness analysis of antiemetic therapy for ambulatory surgery. *J Clin Anesth.* 1994; 6:370–7.

386. Litman RS, Wu CL, Lee A, et al. Prevention of emesis after strabismus repair in children: a prospective, double-blinded, randomized comparison of droperidol versus ondansetron. *J Clin Anesth.* 1995; 7:58–62.

387. Fujii Y, Tanaka H, Toyooka H. Granisetron reduces the incidence and severity of nausea and vomiting after laparoscopic cholecystectomy. *Can J Anaesth.* 1997; 44:396–400.

388. Howat DDC. Anti-emetic drugs in anaesthesia: a double blind trial of two phenothiazine derivatives. *Anaesthesia.* 1960; 15:289–97.

389. Cramb R, Fargas-Babjak A, Hirano G. Intraoperative prochlorperazine for prevention of postoperative nausea and vomiting. *Can J Anaesth.* 1989; 36:565–7.

390. Patterson KW, Armstrong C, Timon D, et al. The value of buccal prochlorperazine in the prevention of postoperative nausea and vomiting. *J Ir Coll Physic Surg.* 1991; 20:200–2.

391. Moore DC, Bridenbaugh LD, Piccioni VF, et al. Control of postoperative vomiting with marezine: a double-blind study. *Anesthesiology.* 1956; 17:690–5.

392. Tillman WW, Wise GF, Crawford OB. Evaluation of Marezine and Bonamine in lowering the incidence of

postoperative nausea and vomiting. *Anesthesiology.* 1956; 17:112–5.

393. Bonica JJ, Crepps W, Monk B, et al. Postanesthetic nausea, retching and vomiting: evaluation of cyclizine (Marezine) suppositories for treatment. *Anesthesiology.* 1958; 19:532-40.

394. Bellville JW, Bross ID, Howland WS. The antiemetic efficacy of cyclizine (Marezine) and triflupromazine (Vesprin). *Anesthesiology.* 1959; 20:761–6.

395. Dundee JW, Assaf RAE, Loan WB, et al. A comparison of the efficacy of cyclizine and perphenazine in reducing the emetic effects of morphine and pethidine. *Br J Clin Pharm.* 1975; 2:81–5.

396. Larrauri RM. Benzquinamide parenteral for the treatment of post-operative nausea and vomiting. *Curr Ther Res Clin Exp.* 1969; 11:118–20.

397. Klein RL, Graves CL, Kim Y, et al. Inhibition of apomorphine-induced vomiting by benzquinamide. *Clin Pharmacol Ther.* 1970; 11:530–7.

398. Finn H, Urban BJ, Thomas JS, et al. Antiemetic efficacy of benzquinamide. *N Y State J Med.* 1971; 71:651–3.

399. Lutz H, Immich H. Antiemetic effect of benzquinamide in post-operative vomiting. *Curr Ther Res Clin Exp.* 1972; 14:178–84.

400. Taylor E, Monk TG, White PF. Use of dronabinol for preanesthetic medication. *Anesthesiology.* 1990; 73:A386. Abstract.

401. Purkis IE. The action of thiethylperazine (Torecan), a new anti-emetic, compared with perphenazine (Trilafon), trimethabenzamide (Tigan) and a placebo in the suppression of postanaesthetic nausea and vomiting. *Can Anaesth Soc J.* 1965; 12:595–607.

402. Dobkin AB, Evers W, Israel JS. Double-blind evaluation of metoclopramide (MK 745, Sinemet), trimethobenzamide (Tigan) and a placebo as postanaesthetic anti-emetics following methoxyflurane anaesthesia. *Can Anaesth Soc J.* 1968; 15:80–91.

403. Knapp MR, Beecher HK. Postanesthetic nausea, vomiting and retching: evaluation of the antiemetic drugs dimenhydrinate (Dramamine), chlorpromazine, and pentobarbital sodium. *JAMA.* 1956; 160:376–85.

404. Battersby C. A clinical trial of thiethylperazine (Torecan) suppositories in postoperative nausea and vomiting. *Med J Aust.* 1965; 2:450–2.

405. Khanna SK, Anand SS, Saini VK. Control of postoperative vomiting by thiethylperazine. *J Indian Med Assoc.* 1965; 45:5958.

406. Albert SN, Coakley CS. The use of chlorpromazine to control postanaesthetic vomiting. *Curr Res Anesth Analg.* 1954; 33:285–8.

407. Boulton TB. Oral chlorpromazine hydrochloride: a clinical trial in thoracic surgery. *Anaesthesia.* 1955; 10:233–46.

408. Caplin D, Smith C. A comparison of the anti-emetic effects of dimenhydrinate, promethazine hydrochloride and chlorpromazine following anaesthesia. *Can Anaesth Soc J.* 1955; 2:191–7.

409. Dyrberg V, Johansen SH. Pre-anesthetic medication with chlorpromazine: a comparison with morphine. *Acta Anaesthesiol Scand.* 1958; 2:133–47.

410. Kvisselgaard N. Chlorpromazine and chlorcyclizine I in the prevention of postoperative nausea and vomiting. *Acta Anaesthesiol Scand.* 1958; 2:153–62.

411. Barton MD, Libonati M, Cohen PJ. The use of haloperidol for treatment of postoperative nausea and vom-

iting—a double-blind placebo-controlled trial. *Anesthesiology.* 1975; 42:508–12.

412. Rothenberg DM, Parnass SM, Litwack K, et al. Efficacy of ephedrine in the prevention of postoperative nausea and vomiting. *Anesth Analg.* 1991; 72:58–61.

413. Snow JC. Hydroxyzine for postoperative nausea and vomiting following ophthalmologic surgery. *Anesth Analg.* 1965; 44:487–91.

414. Moore DC, Bridenbaugh LD, Van Ackeren EG, et al. Control of postoperative vomiting with perphenazine (Trilafon): a double-blind study. *Anesthesiology.* 1958; 19:72–4.

415. Scurr CF, Robbie DS. Trials of perphenazine in the prevention of post-operative vomiting. *Br Med J.* 1958; 1:922–3.

416. Braly BB, Moore DC. The use of intramuscular perphenazine control for postoperative vomiting following strabismus surgery in children. *Anesthesiology.* 1990; 77:245–8.

417. Splinter WM, Roberts DJ. Perphenazine decreases vomiting by children after tonsillectomy. *Can J Anaesth.* 1997; 44:1308–10.

418. Splinter W, Noel LP, Roberts D, et al. Antiemetic prophylaxis for strabismus surgery. *Can J Ophthalmol.* 1994; 29:224–6.

419. Transderm Scop package insert. East Hanover, NJ: Novartis; 1996 Aug.

420. Rung GW, Claybon L, Hord A, et al. Intravenous ondansetron for postsurgical opioid-induced nausea and vomiting. S3A-255 Study Group. *Anesth Analg.* 1997; 84:832–8.

421. DuPen S, Scuderi P, Wetchler B, et al. Ondansetron in the treatment of postoperative nausea and vomiting in ambulatory outpatients: a dose-comparative, stratified, multicentre study. *Eur J Anaesthesiol.* 1992; 9(suppl 6):55–62.

422. Diemunsch P, Leeser J, Feiss P, et al. Dolasetron mesylate treats established nausea and vomiting after general surgery. *Anesthesiology.* 1995; 83(3A):A1109. Abstract.

423. Goldberg ME, Vekeman D, Torjman M. Intravenous dolasetron (D) versus placebo (P) for the treatment of post operative nausea and vomiting (PONV). *Anesth Analg.* 1996; 82(2 suppl):S133. Abstract.

This official ASHP practice standard was developed through the ASHP Commission on Therapeutics and approved by the ASHP Board of Directors on November 14, 1998.

Members of the 1998–1999 ASHP Commission on Therapeutics are Austin J. Lee, Pharm.D., BCPS, FASHP, Chair; C. Wayne Weart, Pharm.D., FASHP, Vice Chair; G. Dennis Clifton, Pharm.D.; Matthew A. Fuller, Pharm.D., BCPS, BCPP; Kent M. Nelson, Pharm.D., BCPS; William L. Green, Pharm.D., BCPS, FASHP; Mary Beth Gross, Pharm.D.; Michael D. Katz, Pharm.D.; Shirley J. Reitz, Pharm.D.; Jane E. DeWitt, Student Member; Donald T. Kishi, Pharm.D., Board Liaison; and Leslie Dotson Jaggers, Pharm.D., BCPS, Secretary.

Project Coordinator: Mary Lea Gora-Harper, Pharm.D., Director, Drug Information Center, Associate Professor, Division of Pharmacy Practice and Science, College of Pharmacy and Hospital, University of Kentucky.

Expert Panel: Carol Balmer, Pharm.D., Clinical Oncology Pharmacist, University of Colorado Health Sciences Center, Associate Professor, School of Pharmacy, University of Colorado; Frank C. Castellano, R.Ph., M.S.[a], Oncology Sales Specialist, Alza Pharmaceuticals; Lorraine Baltzer Cleri, R.N., M.S.N., Quality Control Manager, Parexel Research Operations, Clinical Data Services; Terri Graves Davidson, Pharm.D., FCCP, FASHP, BCOP[b], Vice President, Medical Information and Editorial Services, Cortex Communications, Inc., Chief Executive Officer, Clinical Pharmacy Associates, Inc., Adjunct Assistant Professor, College of Pharmacy, University of Georgia; Mark T. Holdsworth, Pharm.D., BCPS, Associate Professor, College of Pharmacy, Clinical Pharmacist, Pediatric Oncology, University of New Mexico; Mark G. Kris, M.D., Chief, Thoracic Oncology Service, Division of Solid Tumor Oncology, Memorial Sloan Kettering Cancer Center; Amy Wells Valley, Pharm.D., BCOP, Oncology Pharmacy Specialist, Audie L. Murphy Division, South Texas Veterans Health Care System, Clinical Assistant Professor, University of Texas Health Science Center at San Antonio.

[a]During development of the guidelines, Mr. Castellano was Pharmacy Manager, Operating Room Pharmacy, Tampa General Health Care.

[b]Formerly, Dr. Davidson was Clinical Associate, Hematology/Oncology, Department of Pharmaceutical Services, Emory University Hospital.

The recommendations in this document do not indicate an exclusive course of treatment to be followed. Variations, taking into account individual circumstances, may be appropriate.

The recommended bibliographic citation for this document is as follows: American Society of Health-System Pharmacists. ASHP Therapeutic Guidelines on the Pharmacologic Management of Nausea and Vomiting in Adult and Pediatric Patients Receiving Chemotherapy or Radiation Therapy or Undergoing Surgery. *Am J Health-Syst Pharm.* 1999; 56:729–64.

ASHP Therapeutic Guidelines on Stress Ulcer Prophylaxis

Despite the publication of more than 100 studies of the frequency, risk factors, and prophylaxis of stress ulcer bleeding, these subjects continue to generate controversy. Several meta-analyses pertaining to stress ulcer bleeding have been published, including one designed to resolve the discordant results of the others. Given the sheer volume of published information, it is understandable that health care providers experience frustration when confronting this topic.

Stress ulcers are superficial lesions commonly (but not exclusively) involving the mucosal layer of the stomach that appear after major stressful events such as surgery and trauma.[1] Endoscopic studies have found gastroduodenal erosions (shallow ulcers) to be common in patients who have had such stressful events, and these may lead to ulceration and bleeding.[1] Microscopic bleeding associated with gastroduodenal lesions can be detected by occult blood testing (e.g., guaiac test) in patients with gastric tubes.[2] However, other factors may influence the results of occult testing. Simply placing tubes in the upper respiratory or GI tract may injure the mucosa and result in microscopic or macroscopic (i.e., overt) bleeding. Because not all episodes of microscopic bleeding are clinically relevant, studies using only microscopic bleeding as an endpoint artificially inflate the reported frequency of GI bleeding. Making clinical use of these inflated estimates has patient care implications and cost implications, because stress ulcer prophylaxis adds to the number of medications given and increases the risk and cost of adverse reactions.[3,4]

It is important to determine the frequency of clinically important bleeding due to stress-induced erosions or ulcerations. Although endoscopy is a specific and sensitive test for GI bleeding, it is an invasive and expensive procedure. For endoscopy to be used as a diagnostic tool, it would need to be repeated during the period the patient remains at risk for clinically important bleeding. Gastroduodenal bleeding associated with clinically important complications, such as hemodynamic compromise and the need for blood transfusions or surgery, has been suggested in the literature as a useful definition for clinically important bleeding. This definition was used to evaluate the clinical trials in order to develop these guidelines.[5] The reported frequency of clinically important bleeding has varied widely, although the general perception is that the frequency of stress-related bleeding has been decreasing in recent years.[6] Whether this decrease is related to the use of stress ulcer prophylaxis medications, improvements in technology, or improvements in patient care is not known, because a variety of factors (e.g., type of resuscitative technique) may contribute to clinically important stress-related bleeding.[7]

The presence of patient risk factors for clinically important bleeding, not just admission to an intensive care unit (ICU), should determine the need for stress ulcer prophylaxis. The purpose of this document is to help health care professionals to identify appropriate candidates for stress ulcer prophylaxis and select cost-effective modalities for prophylaxis when prophylaxis is indicated. An economic evaluation has been provided that can be adapted to individual practice sites.

Scope

These guidelines pertain to stress-induced bleeding associated with events such as trauma, surgery, and acute organ failure. In general, they apply to the days immediately after the stressful event, when endogenous healing processes or exogenous manipulations by health care professionals have yet to substantially improve the underlying disease process. However, a patient may have resolution of the initial problem but then have reactivation or initiation of a stressful event that could precipitate stress-induced bleeding. These are not unexpected occurrences in patients with ICU stays of more than a few days and could lead to periodic institution of prophylaxis to prevent bleeding.

The guidelines focus on agents that are used for stress ulcer prophylaxis in the United States, whether or not the agents have FDA-approved labeling for this indication. A majority of studies have involved histamine H_2-receptor antagonists, antacids, or sucralfate, and these agents are discussed in detail. Few controlled, comparative studies have been conducted to assess the efficacy of misoprostol or proton-pump inhibitors (e.g., lansoprazole, omeprazole) in preventing clinically important bleeding. The potential advantages and disadvantages of the latter medications for stress ulcer prophylaxis are discussed.

The guidelines include information for patients in all age groups for which there is literature. When age groups are not specifically cited, the discussion refers to the adult patient population. Few prospective, randomized studies in the pediatric population have been published, particularly with regard to clinically important bleeding. Where appropriate, the lack of age-specific data is specified. It is hoped that the guidelines will stimulate research in these areas.

The guidelines are not intended to apply to the prevention of bleeding associated with chronic diseases or long-term medication use. However, the contribution of pre-existing diseases and the use of ulcerogenic medications as aggravating risk factors for stress-induced bleeding are considered appropriate issues for review.

Guideline Development and Use

The ASHP Therapeutic Guidelines on Stress Ulcer Prophylaxis were prepared by the University of Arizona under contract to ASHP. The project was coordinated by two pharmacy specialists, one with expertise in critical care and the other with expertise in drug information, who consulted with two physicians and a nurse specialist from the Arizona Health Sciences Center. The project coordinators worked in conjunction with an independent multidisciplinary panel of seven clinical specialists (a surgeon, a nurse, and five pharmacists) representing adult or pediatric critical care. The panel was appointed by ASHP. Panel members and contractors were required to disclose any possible conflicts of interest before their appointment. The guidelines underwent multidisciplinary field review in order to evaluate their validity, reliability, and utility in clinical practice. The final document was approved by the ASHP Commission on Therapeutics and the ASHP Board of Directors.

The recommendations in this document may not be appropriate for use in all clinical situations.[8] Decisions to follow these recommendations must be based on the professional judgment of the clinician and must take into account individual patient circumstances and available resources. These guidelines reflect current knowledge (at the time of publication) on the use of stress ulcer prophylaxis in critically ill patients. Given the dynamic nature of scientific information and technology, periodic review, updating, and revision are to be expected.

Literature Search

Detailed and exhaustive literature searches of MEDLINE from 1966 to 1997 and International Pharmaceutical Abstracts (IPA) from 1970 to 1997 were performed. The searches of the two databases were compared to check for duplicates and were subsequently compared with the references listed in a recent meta-analysis by Cook, et al.[5] for completeness.

Ten key articles pertinent to stress ulcer prophylaxis were identified and entered into MEDLINE to capture appropriate MeSH headings. Applicable MeSH headings were combined with relevant text words into five sets. Set A1 combined terms for the condition to be avoided in broad terms (e.g., peptic ulcer) by using the subheadings *prevention and control* and *complications*. Set A2 covered terms more specific to the condition being treated (e.g., peptic ulcer hemorrhage) by using the same subheadings. Set B included terms describing patient location (e.g., intensive care) or condition (e.g., critical illness). Set C covered terms related to the treatments to be considered (e.g., H$_2$-receptor antagonists) with the subheadings *adverse effects* and *therapeutic use,* and set D was the free-text term *stress ulcer prophylaxis.* The sets were combined as [(A1 and B) or (A2 and C) or D]. The search was limited to reports on humans published in the English language. The search in IPA differed in that combining set A2 and C decreased the retrieval. The sets were combined in IPA as {[(A1 or A2) and B] or D}. All relevant citations were printed and reviewed for pertinent articles, which were subsequently retrieved and copied. The reference lists of the retrieved articles were studied for investigations that may have been missed through the computerized search.

Periodic literature searches using the same method were conducted during the compilation of the guidelines. The reference lists of review articles were examined for potentially pertinent references. Unpublished abstracts (e.g., those presented at meetings) and abstracts in foreign languages were not included in the evaluation.

Although all relevant articles were reviewed, they are not necessarily referenced in this document. In particular, isolated case reports or case series involving fewer than 25 patients were not routinely included unless they provided unique information that would substantially affect the recommendations. Similarly, pharmacokinetic and pharmacodynamic studies of medications were not included unless there was some applicability to stress ulcer prophylaxis.

Level of Evidence for Recommendations

There are several methods for assessing the literature by using evidence tables.[9–12] The methods of Guyatt, et al.[9] and the American College of Chest Physicians (1995 revision)[10] were determined to be the most applicable to the literature to be reviewed because they involved meta-analysis and distinctions based on confidence intervals, homogeneity, and

heterogeneity. These methods were modified slightly and expanded to include a category D that represents a panel consensus based on the clinical experience of the panel members and a paucity of quality supporting literature. Before reviewing the literature, the panel of experts agreed that a meta-analysis carried more weight than a randomized, controlled trial (RCT) in determining a recommendation unless at least two RCTs had similar results or one RCT was designed with a sample large enough to detect a difference of 50% or less in bleeding rates (considered the primary outcome) between the treatment and control groups with a power of ≥80% and an α of ≤0.05.

The recommendations in this document were categorized according to the strength of the evidence. Category A corresponds to levels of evidence I+, I, and I–; category B to levels II+, II, and II–; and category C to levels III+, III, IV+, IV, and V. Table 1 includes definitions for each level of evidence. The level of evidence was evaluated for each trial. When there were multiple RCTs of comparable power pertaining to a particular recommendation and their levels of evidence differed, the level of evidence for the least stringent trial was used in determining the strength of evidence for a recommendation. Recommendations were assigned to category D if they represented the expert opinion of panel members. For a recommendation based on RCTs to be assigned to category A, there had to be at least two RCTs or one RCT with a sample size sufficient for detecting a difference of 50% or less in rates of clinically important bleeding with a power of ≥0.8 and an α of ≤0.05.

One problem with both the grading systems[9,10] on which this system was based is the relative inability to distinguish the quality of individual investigations. Two RCTs may each be ranked similarly, but one may have been better designed and reported than the other. Therefore, in addition to listing levels of evidence for the various trials, the superscript *wd* was used to signify a well-designed and well-reported trial when the guidelines were sent to the panel of experts and other reviewers to aid them in evaluating the literature presented. More than 30 criteria, some of which have been published, were used in the analysis of the investigations.[13,14] The criteria represented a nonnumerical assessment and were not used as a scoring system for the formal statistical analysis.[15]

The levels of evidence were used to evaluate those studies that assessed the frequency of clinically important bleeding (i.e., gastroduodenal bleeding associated with hemodynamic compromise or the need for blood transfusion or surgery) and nosocomial pneumonia. Analysis of the number and type of risk factors associated with bleeding by a rigid evidence-based evaluation may be misleading for a number of reasons, including the following: studies used various definitions of bleeding and risk factors associated with bleeding, various risk factors were studied, various risk factors were used as inclusion criteria, the analysis of risk factors often was not a study objective, and, in many studies, multivariate analysis was not used to determine which risk factors might be independent predictors of bleeding. Observational trials with large numbers of patients are often used appropriately to assess risk factors for bleeding, although the strength of evidence would never be higher than C.

Pathophysiology of Stress-Induced Lesions

Stress ulceration is a form of hemorrhagic gastritis that may occur in patients who have had a major stressful event such as trauma, surgery, organ failure, sepsis, or thermal injury. In general, the histological and macroscopic appearance of stress-induced fundal lesions are similar to those associated with nonsteroidal anti-inflammatory drugs (NSAIDs) seen in the antrum and the body of the stomach. However, in contrast to NSAID-induced lesions, stress-induced lesions often cause more congestion and bleeding, and they eventually involve multiple sites in the upper GI tract.[16] Cushing's ulcer, which is associated with CNS injury, often presents as a single deep lesion in the duodenum or in the stomach.[16] Curling's ulcer, which is associated with thermal injury, is morphologically similar to other stress-induced lesions but may appear in the esophagus, the stomach, the small intestine, or the colon.[16]

The pathogenesis of stress-induced lesions is probably multifactorial.[17] Acid hypersecretion is often stated as being particularly important in the formation of ulcers associated with head and thermal injuries.[18] However, acid hypersecretion is not a universal finding in such patients, and higher pH values (>4.5) do not ensure avoidance of lesions.[19-21] During stressful events, normal protective mechanisms are altered, including epithelial turnover in the gastric mucosa and secretions of mucus and bicarbonate. These events, combined with the release of various mediators (e.g., arachidonic acid metabolites, cytokines, oxygen free radicals), result in erosions that may progress to ulceration and bleeding.[22] Reductions in mucosal blood flow may also be important in ulcer formation. Alterations in blood flow at the microcirculatory level may initiate a series of changes resulting in erosions that could progress to ulceration and bleeding. Necrosis and erosions of the gastric membrane have occurred within 45 minutes of hemorrhagic shock in experiments in rats.[23] In adult humans, erosions may occur very quickly (i.e., during the first 24 hours of hospital admission) in association with a stressful event, although the time from the inciting event to the diagnosis of bleeding may be much longer (e.g., >10–14 days).

Other less well-studied factors may be involved in the pathogenesis of stress-related lesions. For example, elevated concentrations of anti-*Helicobacter pylori* immunoglobulin A have been found in the serum of critically ill patients.[24] Although the association between *H. pylori* and chronic ulceration has been established, few studies have been performed in acute care settings.

It is not known whether differences in basal or maximal gastric acid production seen in various age groups affect the frequency of ulceration and clinically important bleeding. For example, premature infants typically produce less gastric acid than full-term infants, albeit with substantial interinfant variability.[25,26] Newborns often have slightly acidic gastric pH values that become more acidic within a few hours of birth.[27] Gastric pH values in infants begin to approach those of healthy adults during the first six months of life. However, stress ulcer lesions may occur at any age, including in preterm infants, lending additional support to a multifactorial process.[28]

The frequency of ulceration, the number of ulcers, and the sites of ulceration may be different between children and adults, depending on the stress-related event. In one retrospective study involving 93 children less than 10 years of age and 178 adults who died of burn-related injuries, 13 (14.0%) of the children had duodenal ulceration on postmortem examination compared with 13 (7.3%) of the adults. In addition, 21 (22.6%) of the children had gastric ulceration compared with 20 (11.2%) of the adults.[29] No relationship between sex and ulceration was found. Another review of infants less than one year of age with stress ulceration found that single duodenal ulcers were common, in contrast to the multiple gastric erosions usually found in adults.[30]

Frequency of Bleeding, Efficacy of Prophylaxis, and Risk Factors for Bleeding in General (Medical, Surgical, Respiratory, Pediatric) ICU Populations

Acute bleeding in critically ill patients has been described in the medical literature since the 1800s. To determine the true frequency of, and risk factors associated with, stress-induced

Table 1.
System Used for Defining Levels of Evidence in Stress Ulcer Prophylaxis Guidelines[a]

Level of Evidence	Definition
I+	Meta-analysis of randomized, controlled trials (RCTs) with homogeneity[b] of results and a 95% confidence interval (CI) that lies entirely on one side of the numerical threshold for clinically important benefit
I	Meta-analysis of RCTs with homogeneity of results but with a 95% CI that includes the threshold for clinically important benefit
I–	RCT in which the entire 95% CI lies on one side of the threshold for clinically important benefit
II+	Meta-analysis of RCTs with heterogeneity of results and a 95% CI that lies entirely on one side of the threshold for clinically important benefit
II	Meta-analysis of RCTs with heterogeneity of results and a 95% CI that includes the threshold for clinically important benefit
II–	RCT in which the 95% CI includes the threshold for clinically important benefit
III+	Nonrandomized concurrent cohort study in which the entire 95% CI lies on one side of the threshold for clinically important benefit[c]
III	Nonrandomized concurrent cohort study in which the 95% CI includes the threshold for clinically important benefit
IV+	Nonrandomized historic cohort study in which the entire 95% CI lies on one side of the threshold for clinically important benefit
IV	Nonrandomized historic cohort study in which the 95% CI includes the threshold for clinically important benefit
V	Case series suggesting clinically important benefit

[a]Adapted from references 9 and 10.
[b]Various definitions of homogeneity were used in the literature (e.g., the difference between the risk reductions or odds ratios between the two most disparate trials is less than 20% and the difference between 95% confidence intervals for the two most disparate trials is less than 5%); the fact that homogeneity was tested for is more important than the precise method used.
[c]This assumes the availability of comparative data for calculating 95% CIs.

bleeding in general ICU populations, studies that contained at least one defined group of patients who did not receive prophylaxis were evaluated.[31-63] As will be seen in the following discussion, determining a true frequency of clinically important bleeding is complicated by the difficulty in measuring endpoints, the variability in endpoints used, the variability in definitions of endpoints, and the heterogeneity of the patient populations.

In general, the studies included in this section of the document on general ICU populations determined the frequency of stress ulcer lesions and the risk factors associated with clinically important bleeding in patients in medical, surgical, or respiratory ICUs. Only two of the studies involved a relatively homogeneous sample of patients with a single-system disease or surgery. One study was conducted in patients with respiratory disease, and the other involved patients undergoing abdominal surgery.[36,44] These studies were included because the patient populations were similar to those enrolled in other investigations. Studies enrolling patients with single-system injuries (e.g., head or spinal cord surgery), patients with thermal injuries, or patients undergoing transplantation were not included (see the section on special populations) because of presumed differences in the pathophysiology or frequency of stress-induced bleeding.

Frequency of Bleeding. In all studies conducted before 1978, the frequency of clinically important bleeding and related complications ranged from 5.3% to 33%. From 1978 on, substantial differences in the frequency of stress-induced bleeding have been recorded among trials. For example, in an RCT published by Pinilla, et al.[42] in 1985, the frequency of bleeding was 1.6% (1 of 61 patients), and it was not clear whether this patient had clinically important bleeding. In contrast, an RCT published by Peura and Johnson[43] in the same year, involving adult patients in a medical ICU, found a 39% frequency (7 of 18 patients) of endoscopically confirmed, clinically important, stress-induced bleeding in patients not receiving prophylaxis. Articles published from 1984 to 1994 on the frequency of clinically important bleeding in patients not receiving prophylaxis indicate that the average frequency of bleeding is 6% (0.1–39%).[64]

With regard to the pediatric population, it is difficult to estimate the frequency of clinically important bleeding because of the small numbers of patients enrolled in published investigations and the use of endpoints other than clinically important bleeding (e.g., endoscopic evidence of bleeding or overt bleeding). There are important exceptions, albeit with differing results. In one study involving 140 children from birth to 20 years of age, the frequency of clinically important bleeding was 20% in a control group and 5.7% in a combined treatment group.[65] In contrast, the frequency of clinically important bleeding (not defined in the published abstract) was 1.6% in a study of 1006 admissions to a pediatric ICU, although it was not stated whether the children received any form of stress ulcer prophylaxis.[66]

Efficacy. *Prophylaxis versus no prophylaxis.* Two studies conducted in the 1990s can be used to illustrate the disparate results of the more than 20 RCTs of prophylaxis conducted in general ICU populations. The first trial, conducted in 1993 by Martin, et al.,[58] was a multicenter, double-blind, placebo-controlled study involving general medical and surgical ICU patients with an expected length of stay of at least 36 hours

and at least one risk factor (of eight studied) for bleeding. The study had 90% power to detect a 75% difference in bleeding between placebo and pH-adjusted cimetidine therapy. The study was terminated early when an interim analysis revealed a significant difference in bleeding rates between the control and cimetidine groups. In the control group, 16 (24.2%) of 66 patients had overt and clinically important bleeding (some bleeding was not cleared by lavage, but the patients did not require transfusion), compared with 5 (7.7%) of 65 patients in the treatment group ($p = 0.009$). Six (10.0%) of 66 patients in the control group and 4 (6.2%) of 65 in the treatment group had clinically important bleeding. Statistical testing of this endpoint was not performed.

The second study, a single-blind RCT, was conducted in 1994 by Ben-Menachem, et al.[59] In that trial, only medical ICU patients who were expected to have a length of ICU stay of at least 24 hours were enrolled. The study was designed to have 80% power to detect a 75% treatment-related reduction in bleeding. Patients could be randomly assigned to a control (no placebo) group, a pH-adjusted cimetidine group, or a sucralfate group. There were no significant differences between groups with respect to clinically important bleeding episodes (including some patients whose bleeding did not clear by lavage): 6 of 100 patients in the control group, 5 of 100 patients in the cimetidine group, and 5 of 100 patients in the sucralfate group. In addition, there were no significant differences between groups when respiratory failure and coagulopathy were studied as risk factors. If the different findings between this trial and that of Martin, et al. can be attributed to differences in the populations being studied, it might be reasonable to consider withholding prophylaxis in general medical ICU patients. However, it should be stressed that the trial by Ben-Menachem, et al. was not designed to detect a difference of less than 75% in bleeding between groups, even though a smaller difference might be clinically important.

Another study enrolled 90 intensive care patients with septic shock, severe head injury, and trauma.[67] The patients were randomly assigned to receive pirenzepine 30 mg/day, omeprazole 80 mg/day, or no prophylaxis. A rating scale of zero (normal mucosa) to four (>25 hemorrhages, erosions, or invasive ulcers) was used to evaluate all patients at baseline and after five days of prophylaxis. Although all patients were at high risk for stress ulcer hemorrhage, no patients developed severe bleeding from stress lesions, and no difference in endoscopic evaluations was noted at baseline or at five days among the three groups.

Because individual trials have demonstrated conflicting results with respect to the frequency of bleeding with or without prophylaxis, several meta-analyses have sought to resolve this issue (Table 2).[5,68-71] Abstracts and non-English-language articles were frequently included in the data sets of these analyses, as were reports of studies involving populations that other studies specifically excluded (e.g., patients with head or thermal injuries). One meta-analysis was published in 1989, and three were published in 1991, so the number of trials combined for each analysis was limited.[68-71] Despite this difference in time frame, there was definite overlap among the meta-analyses in the studies that were included. Only one of the meta-analyses investigated the difference in bleeding rates with sucralfate compared with no prophylaxis.[5]

The meta-analysis conducted by Lacroix, et al.[68] included randomized studies only. The frequency of bleeding in patients receiving no prophylaxis (or placebo) ranged from 3.4% to 52.7%. Use of cimetidine and antacids was associated with a significantly lower frequency of bleeding compared with no prophylaxis. Among the limitations of this meta-analysis were that the evaluated studies had methodological problems, demonstrated heterogeneous effects, and investigated the frequency of occult or overt—but not necessarily clinically important—bleeding, defined as hemodynamic instability or the need for blood transfusion.

In a meta-analysis published by Tryba[69] in 1991, overt and clinically important bleeding (i.e., need for blood transfusion) were combined in the definition of upper GI bleeding. Randomized and nonrandomized studies were included. The odds ratios (ORs) and 95% confidence intervals (CIs) calculated for H_2-receptor antagonists or antacids compared with no prophylaxis were all less than one (i.e., treatment was effective in preventing bleeding). The data were presented only in the form of figures, so the exact ORs and CIs are not available. However, the frequency of bleeding was 5.3% in the group receiving H_2-receptor antagonists versus 16.1% with no prophylaxis and 5.6% in the group receiving antacids versus 14.9% with no prophylaxis. A second meta-analysis by Tryba[71] in 1991 included only studies with clinically important bleeding. The results were similar to those of Tryba's previous meta-analysis.

Two meta-analyses published by Cook, et al.[5,70] in 1991 and 1996 included only randomized, controlled trials. The investigations looked at clinically important bleeding, defined as overt bleeding with hemodynamic changes (a 20-mm Hg decrease in blood pressure within 24 hours or a 10-mm Hg decrease plus a 20-beat/min increase in heart rate on standing) or the need for transfusion (a decrease in hemoglobin of 2 g/dL plus transfusion of two units of blood in 24 hours). In the 1991 analysis, H_2-receptor antagonists were found to be more efficacious in preventing clinically important bleeding than no prophylaxis.

The 1996 meta-analysis was performed to resolve some of the inconsistencies associated with the previously conducted meta-analyses and to incorporate more recent studies.[5] The methodology was similar to that of the earlier meta-analysis. Only H_2-receptor antagonists were found to have a 95% CI of <1 for preventing clinically important bleeding compared with no prophylaxis. However, only three trials with an antacid group and one with a sucralfate group were available for comparison with no prophylaxis. Because the

Table 2.
Meta-analyses Investigating the Risk of Bleeding with and without Stress Ulcer Prophylaxis

Reference	Comparison[a]	No. Trials	Endpoint	Results[b]
68	Cimetidine versus control	7	Overt bleeding	OR = 0.32, CI = 0.21–0.49 (lower rate of bleeding with cimetidine)
	Antacids versus control	9	Overt bleeding	OR = 0.12, CI = 0.08–0.19 (lower rate of bleeding with antacids)
	Cimetidine versus antacids	10	Overt bleeding	OR = 1.61, CI = 0.97–2.65
69	Antacids versus control	6	Overt or clinically important bleeding	OR and CI <1 (lower rate of bleeding with antacids)
	H_2-RAs versus control	14	Overt or clinically important bleeding	OR and CI <1 (lower rate of bleeding with H_2-RAs)
	H_2-RAs versus antacids	14	Overt or clinically important bleeding	CI included 1
	Sucralfate versus H_2-RAs	6	Overt or clinically important bleeding	OR and CI <1 (lower rate of bleeding with sucralfate)
	Sucralfate versus antacids	10	Overt or clinically important bleeding	CI included 1
71	Sucralfate versus H_2-RAs	9	Clinically important bleeding	OR = 0.532, CI = 0.303–0.933 (lower rate of bleeding with sucralfate)
	Sucralfate versus antacids	10	Clinically important bleeding	OR = 0.868, CI = 0.452–1.667
70	Antacids versus control	3	Clinically important bleeding	OR = 0.35, CI = 0.08–1.33
	H_2-RAs versus control	6	Clinically important bleeding	OR = 0.35, CI = 0.15–0.76 (lower rate of bleeding with H_2-RAs)
	H_2-RAs versus antacids	9	Clinically important bleeding	OR = 0.84, CI = 0.45–1.56
	Antacids versus sucralfate	5	Clinically important bleeding	OR = 0.65, CI = 0.16–2.49
	H_2-RAs versus sucralfate	1	Clinically important bleeding	OR = 0.95, CI = 0.06–15.40
5	Antacids versus control	3	Clinically important bleeding	OR = 0.35, CI = 0.09–1.41
	H_2-RAs versus control	10	Clinically important bleeding	OR = 0.44, CI = 0.22–0.88 (lower rate of bleeding with H_2-RAs)
	H_2-RAs versus antacids	10	Clinically important bleeding	OR = 0.86, CI = 0.46–1.59
	Sucralfate versus control	1	Clinically important bleeding	OR = 1.26, CI = 0.12–12.87
	Sucralfate versus antacids	5	Clinically important bleeding	OR = 1.49, CI = 0.43–5.27
	Sucralfate versus H_2-RAs	4	Clinically important bleeding	OR = 1.28, CI = 0.27–6.11

[a]H_2-RAs = histamine H_2-receptor antagonists.
[b]OR = odds ratio, CI = 95% confidence interval. Exact values provided when available; some values were extrapolated from figures.

1996 meta-analysis was the most recent and comprehensive, its results are used in this document whenever the findings from previous meta-analyses are conflicting.

To date, the study with the largest number of prospectively enrolled patients was published by Cook, et al. in 1994.[61] This multicenter follow-up trial enrolled 2252 patients older than 16 years of age who were admitted to medical and surgical ICUs. Approximately half of the enrolled patients were admitted for cardiovascular surgery. Some subgroups (head or spinal cord injuries, multiple trauma or thermal injuries, and transplantation) had few patients. This limits the generalizability of the results to these populations. Lack of resources at three of the four hospitals prohibited enrollment of consecutive patients as intended, and physicians were not required to withhold prophylaxis. Various prophylactic medications were used, and the dosage and duration of prophylaxis were not controlled. Clinically important bleeding occurred in 10 (0.6%) of 1578 patients not receiving prophylaxis and 23 (3.4%) of 674 patients receiving prophylaxis (22 of the 33 bleeding episodes were confirmed). This suggests that, in this observational design, physicians were probably able to predict who was at risk for bleeding and administer prophylaxis; it does not necessarily represent failure of prophylaxis.

Prophylaxis in pediatric patients. The number of stress-induced lesions progressing to clinically important bleeding with or without prophylaxis is not well studied in pediatric patients. Lacroix, et al.[48] compared prophylaxis with no prophylaxis in 40 patients from birth to 18 years of age. When the results were reported, overt bleeding was not distinguished from clinically important bleeding, and no differences in upper GI bleeding were noted between the cimetidine group (9 of 19 patients) and the placebo group (8 of 21 patients). Six patients had massive bleeding, defined as the presence of nasogastric blood with changes in blood pressure or hemoglobin levels. It was not stated which groups these patients were in, and it was noted that five of these patients had bleeding at other sites due to disseminated intravascular coagulation. The researchers concluded that routine prophylaxis in medical pediatric patients is not warranted.

In another study, 165 pediatric patients admitted to an ICU were randomly assigned to one of three active-treatment groups or a no-treatment group.[65] The investigators used clinically important bleeding as an outcome. A significant (p < 0.05) difference between the active-treatment groups and the no-treatment group was achieved only if the results for the three active-treatment groups were combined. Two studies focused on a neonatal population but did not use clinically important bleeding as an endpoint.[49,63] In one of these studies that had a control group, the risk of endoscopically diagnosed gastric lesions in mechanically ventilated infants was found to be lower with ranitidine prophylaxis (OR = 0.03; 95% CI, 0.003–0.178). Surfactant therapy, which was used to treat infants with respiratory distress syndrome, was also associated with a lower rate of formation of lesions (OR = 0.083; 95% CI, 0.009–0.788).[63] The mechanism for the apparent protective effect of surfactant on the GI tract remains to be elucidated. No RCT conducted to date in pediatric patients has conclusively demonstrated a significant difference in clinically important bleeding when prophylaxis was compared with no prophylaxis.

Risk Factors. In Cook's prospective observational study, two risk factors were found to be significant predictors of

stress-induced bleeding: respiratory failure, as defined by mechanical ventilation for at least 48 hours (OR = 15.6; CI not reported, p < 0.001), and coagulopathy, defined as a platelet count of <50,000 mm³, an International Normalized Ratio of >1.5, or a partial thromboplastin time of >2 times the control value (OR = 4.3; CI not reported, p < 0.001).[61] The frequency of bleeding was 3.7% (95% CI, 2.5–5.2%) if one or both of these risk factors were present and 0.1% (95% CI, 0.02–0.5%) if neither factor was present. Patients who had received prophylaxis and those who had not were included. Simple regression analysis showed that sepsis, renal insufficiency, hepatic failure, enteral feeding, and the use of glucocorticoids, heparin, and warfarin were risk factors for bleeding; multiple regression analysis showed that only mechanical ventilation and coagulopathy were independently predictive of clinically important bleeding.

The finding that enteral feeding was a risk factor for bleeding (OR = 3.8, p < 0.001) is of interest because previous retrospective studies in adults have found various effects of enteral feedings on pH and the frequency of bleeding.[72–75] These differences may be due to differences in location of the enteral feeding tubes. For example, feedings placed into the stomach may alkalinize stomach contents, and jejunal feedings may stimulate gastric acid secretion. The fact that patients are able to tolerate tube feedings may mean they are less ill than patients who cannot tolerate such feedings, and this may determine the differences noted. Other factors may be specific to certain types of injury, such as the development of GI edema after thermal injury.

Conflicting associations with total parenteral nutrition (TPN) and bleeding have been noted. Ben-Menachem, et al.[59] found that the frequency of bleeding was not related to the use of TPN. Ruiz-Santana, et al.[52] concluded that TPN was protective, but their sample size was small, and their findings require confirmation in larger randomized trials.

The most recently published large-sample retrospective study of risk factors in ICU trauma patients involved 2574 patients.[76] The only patients receiving prophylaxis (antacids) were those with a history of gastroduodenal ulcerations. The published abstract does not reveal how many of the 2574 patients received antacids. Clinically important bleeding was not analyzed separately from GI bleeding. GI bleeding was noted in 60 (2.3%) of the patients. The risk factors associated with a higher risk of bleeding included male sex, spinal cord injury, respiratory failure, acute renal failure, and severe sepsis.

Of the other trials in which risk factors were studied, a majority of those conducted in adults showed a higher risk of bleeding as the number of risk factors increased.[37–39,42,45–47,54,55,58] The results of most trials are consistent with those of the 1994 study by Cook, et al.[61] in that mechanical ventilation (as a measure for respiratory failure)[36,41,59] and coagulopathy[36,41,53] are the primary risk factors for bleeding. Other risk factors associated with bleeding in adult patients in some studies include sepsis,[35] length of ICU stay greater than one week,[41] presence of occult bleeding for at least six days,[53] and administration of high doses of corticosteroids (>250 mg/day of hydrocortisone or equivalent).[54,59] However, the studies by Cook, et al. did not find use of cortico-steroids, heparin, warfarin, or NSAIDs to be independent risk factors for bleeding when respiratory failure and coagulopathy were considered.[53,61]

Prophylaxis does not necessarily prevent bleeding in patients with documented risk factors, and the effectiveness of prophylaxis varies in different populations.[59] Some potential risk factors for bleeding have not been adequately studied, and it is unclear whether they are independent predictors of bleeding. A majority of investigations excluded patients with a history of GI disease, particularly ulcers and bleeding. It is unknown whether a history of ulceration or bleeding increases the risk of acute, stress-induced bleeding. Similarly, ulcerogenic medications with well-documented associations with bleeding problems, such as long-term use of NSAIDs, have not been adequately studied as risk factors for stress-induced bleeding. Typically, patients receiving such medications either were not discussed in the methods section of study reports or were prohibited from enrolling in the studies.

In pediatric patients (birth to 19 years of age), coagulopathy,[48,57] shock,[56] surgery lasting for longer than three hours,[56] trauma,[56,57] and pneumonia[57] were associated with an increased risk of bleeding, while the use of enteral nutrition reduced the risk of bleeding.[57] The results were not stratified by age. One study in pediatric patients (median age, 34.9 months) found that a Pediatric Risk of Mortality Score greater than 10 was associated with a greater risk of bleeding.[57] Another study in mechanically ventilated preterm and full-term infants found that 20 (80%) of 25 patients had stress-induced lesions as determined by endoscopic evaluation when no prophylaxis was administered.[63] That study and others demonstrated that gastric lesions due to stress may occur in the very young despite their possible physiological differences from adults.[29,63]

The rate of progression of these lesions to clinically important bleeding is not known. In a study in 881 pediatric ICU patients (1006 admissions), 16 (1.6%) clinically important bleeding episodes occurred.[66] Because this was an observational investigation, physicians were not hindered from prescribing medications for stress ulcer prophylaxis. Among the 110 patients who received prophylaxis, there were 10 clinically important bleeding episodes. The authors noted that the three strongest independent risk factors for clinically important bleeding were respiratory failure (OR = 10.2), coagulopathy (OR = 9.3), and a Pediatric Risk of Mortality Score of ≥ 10 (OR = 4.0). Of the 16 patients with clinically significant bleeding, 9 (56%) had all three risk factors and 14 (88%) had at least two.

Summary. The reported frequency of stress-induced bleeding has varied substantially since approximately 1978 and depends on the number and type of risk factors. Data from large prospective, observational investigations in children and adults have found that general medical and surgical ICU patients who have either coagulopathy or respiratory failure requiring mechanical ventilation have a substantially higher risk of clinically important bleeding. The studies often excluded neurosurgery, burn, and transplant patients. Another risk factor for children is a Pediatric Risk of Mortality Score of ≥ 10. A number of other risk factors have been associated with overt bleeding in isolated studies (prolonged ICU stay or occult bleeding and administration of high-dose corticosteroids in adults; prolonged shock or surgery and trauma in children), but it is unknown whether these are independent predictors of clinically important bleeding, except in the case of coagulopathy or respiratory failure. Several studies that included both medical and surgical ICU patients suggest that, as the number of risk factors increases, the frequency of clinically important bleeding increases. It has been proposed that adult medical ICU patients may not necessarily need stress ulcer prophylaxis, even if they have

respiratory failure or coagulopathy. However, there are concerns related to inadequate sample sizes in the studies that resulted in this conclusion. Overall, according to RCTs, about 6% (range, 0.1–39%) of adult medical and surgical patients at risk for stress ulcers who do not receive prophylaxis have clinically important bleeding.[64] Observational studies involving large numbers of pediatric or adult patients suggest that the risk may be substantially lower.[61,66]

Recommendation (adults). Risk factors for ICU patients have been delineated in trials comparing prophylaxis with no prophylaxis by using clinically important bleeding as an endpoint. Prophylaxis is recommended in patients with coagulopathy or patients requiring mechanical ventilation for more than 48 hours. (Strength of evidence = C) Prophylaxis is also recommended in patients with a history of GI ulceration or bleeding within one year before admission and in patients with at least two of the following risk factors: sepsis, ICU stay of more than one week, occult bleeding lasting six days or more, and use of high-dose corticosteroids (>250 mg per day of hydrocortisone or the equivalent). (Strength of evidence = D) (Table 3) Recommendations for specific prophylactic medications can be found in the Medications used for prophylaxis section.

Recommendation (pediatrics). Although various risk factors have been associated with bleeding in pediatric patients, published RCTs have either not used clinically important bleeding as an outcome or had insufficient power to enable a definitive conclusion that prophylaxis provides protection. Risk factors that have been associated with clinically important bleeding include respiratory failure, coagulopathy, and a Pediatric Risk of Mortality Score of ≥ 10. (Strength of evidence = C)

Frequency of Bleeding, Efficacy of Prophylaxis, and Risk Factors for Bleeding in Special Populations (Single-System Injuries, Thermal Injuries, Transplantation, Miscellaneous)

Patients with head or spinal cord injuries or patients undergoing surgical exploration for suspected disease have usually been studied as defined groups rather than as part of general ICU populations.[77–84] A majority of these studies in special populations were conducted in adults, although two studies included younger patients (mean age, 28 years, range, 2–74; mean age, 35 years, range 13–76) who were not discussed separately when the results were reported.[77,79] Five of the trials were RCTs.[78,81–84] Three of these trials found significantly lower rates of clinically important bleeding with H$_2$-receptor antagonist prophylaxis than with no prophylaxis.[78,83,84] However, in the RCT with the largest number of patients ($n = 167$), the number of patients with clinically important bleeding was not reported.[82] Only two of the studies looked at a possible association between the number of risk factors and the frequency of bleeding. In both studies, the frequency of bleeding increased with the number of risk factors.[82,84]

In general, the studies demonstrate an increasing frequency of bleeding as the severity of injury increases. Two RCTs demonstrated substantial increases in clinically important bleeding (27.8–45.8%) with severe head injury (inability to obey simple commands in one trial and Glasgow

Table 3.
Strength of Evidence for Prophylaxis for Adult ICU Patients According to Risk Factor[a]

Risk Factor	Strength of Evidence
General (medical, surgical, respiratory) ICU populations[b]	A (for H$_2$-RAs, antacids), B (for sucralfate)
Head injury with Glasgow Coma Score of ≤10 or inability to obey simple commands	B (for H$_2$-RAs), D (for antacids, sucralfate)
Thermal injury involving >35% of body surface area	B (for antacids), D (for H$_2$-RAs, sucralfate)
Partial hepatectomy	C (for H$_2$-RAs), D (for antacids, sucralfate)
Hepatic or renal transplantation	D (for H$_2$-RAs, antacids, sucralfate)
Multiple trauma with Injury Severity Score of ≥16	D (for H$_2$-RAs, antacids, sucralfate)
Spinal cord injury	D (for H$_2$-RAs, antacids, sucralfate)
Hepatic failure	D (for H$_2$-RAs, antacids, sucralfate)
History of gastric ulceration or bleeding during year before admission	D (for H$_2$-RAs, antacids, sucralfate)
Presence of at least two of the following: sepsis, ICU stay of >1 wk, occult or overt bleeding for ≥6 days, corticosteroid therapy (>250 mg of hydrocortisone or equivalent daily)	D (for H$_2$-RAs, antacids, sucralfate)

[a]H$_2$-RAs = histamine H$_2$-receptor antagonists, INR = International Normalized Ratio, PTT = partial thromboplastin time. Refer to the text for discussion of the risk factors and the economic analysis behind the recommendation.

[b]There is evidence to suggest that patients in general ICU populations who have respiratory failure or coagulopathies (as defined in the text) are at higher risk for clinically important bleeding.

Coma Score of ≤10 in the other), irrespective of corticosteroid administration.[78,84] In another RCT involving patients with head injuries, no association was found among 12 specific risk factors and bleeding, although bleeding rates were significantly higher when more than five risk factors were present.[82] In patients undergoing surgery for nontraumatic cerebral disease, cimetidine prophylaxis was more likely to fail when the preoperative Glasgow Coma Score was <15 (impaired consciousness) or when the syndrome of inappropriate antidiuretic hormone secretion was present.[80]

Patients with thermal injuries represent another population that has usually been studied separately with regard to stress ulcer prophylaxis and bleeding.[85–91] In the only trial that appeared to be randomized (48 patients), the frequency of clinically important bleeding was 29.2% in patients who received no prophylaxis and 4.2% in patients given antacids (p <0.02).[90] Only patients with thermal injury to >35% of their body surface area (BSA) were included in this trial. In other published investigations, the number and types of risk factors (other than the thermal injury that may have contributed to bleeding) were not studied, except for a possible association between sepsis and ulceration. The retrospective study by Solem, et al.[91] was one of the first to suggest that enteral feedings might be effective prophylaxis for stress-induced bleeding, but the feedings were administered only if ulcers were unlikely to develop, a situation that was not defined. In addition, some patients received both antacids and enteral feedings.

While many of the thermal injury studies included

injuries in children (35 days to 13 years of age), only one study investigated the effect of no prophylaxis in pediatric patients only.[88] All 477 children had thermal injuries involving 13% or more of their BSA. Thirty-six (7.5%) of the children had clinically important bleeding when no prophylaxis was given (or at least was not mentioned). Some 32 of the 36 children (89%) with clinically important bleeding required blood transfusions, and 5 patients (14%) required surgery; 1 death (2.8%) was associated with GI bleeding.

Another defined population studied for stress ulcer prophylaxis includes patients (at least 14 years of age in published studies) undergoing renal or hepatic transplantation or hepatic surgery.[92–97] Cimetidine or antacids were used for prophylaxis in all the trials except one investigation that used ranitidine.[97] Of the studies evaluated, one was randomized. In all the investigations, both randomized and nonrandomized, overt and clinically important bleeding were combined. The frequency of bleeding was lower with cimetidine prophylaxis in one study involving renal transplant patients but not in the other.[93,94]

Prophylaxis with ranitidine was associated with a significantly lower frequency of endoscopically confirmed stress ulceration in the one available study of hepatic transplant patients, but the frequency of clinically important bleeding was not delineated.[97] One RCT involved patients with hepatic failure,[95] and one prospective trial enrolled patients undergoing partial hepatectomy.[96] The frequency of bleeding was lower with prophylaxis in both studies, but only the hepatectomy study contained adequate information about clinically important bleeding to be able to conclude that it was significantly lower with prophylaxis. None of the studies looking at renal or hepatic surgery or disease investigated the number or type of other risk factors potentially associated with bleeding. Thus, direct evidence that concomitant organ disease or surgery increases the risk of clinically important bleeding is lacking.

Several studies have included defined patient populations other than those previously mentioned.[98–102] Only one of these investigations was randomized. That study involved patients with tetanus who had tracheostomies, a majority of whom were not mechanically ventilated.[100] The frequency of overt bleeding was similar between the patients who did and did not receive prophylaxis, and there were no episodes of clinically important bleeding. The frequency of bleeding and risk factors associated with bleeding were evaluated in one retrospective study of 33,637 trauma patients, most of them adults.[101] It is unknown how many of these patients received prophylaxis, and overt and clinically important bleeding episodes were combined (18 of 33,367 patients bled). Risk factors associated with bleeding included an Injury Severity Score of ≥16, a Glasgow Coma Score of <8, and spinal cord injury. Elderly patients and patients with infections and organ failure were also more likely to bleed.

The frequency of, and risk factors for, clinically important bleeding in patients with single-system injuries such as head trauma, spinal cord injury, and thermal injuries; patients undergoing transplantation; and patients with multiple trauma have not been well studied. These populations were usually excluded from studies in which patients might be randomly assigned to receive no prophylaxis. It is not known whether respiratory failure or coagulopathy would serve as independent predictors of bleeding in these populations.

Recommendation (adults). Prophylaxis is recommended for ICU patients with a Glasgow Coma Score of ≤10 (or the inability to obey simple commands) or thermal injuries to

>35% of their BSA. (Strength of evidence = B) ICU patients with partial hepatectomy may also benefit from prophylaxis. (Strength of evidence = C) Prophylaxis may also be indicated in ICU patients with multiple trauma (e.g., Injury Severity Score of ≥16), transplantation patients in the ICU perioperatively, ICU patients with hepatic failure, and ICU patients with spinal cord injuries. (Strength of evidence = D) (Table 3)

Recommendation (pediatrics). For pediatric patients (one month of age or older) with thermal injuries, prophylaxis is recommended, but there is insufficient evidence to recommend prophylaxis based on any given percentage of BSA. (Strength of evidence = D) For other pediatric surgery or trauma patients, insufficient evidence is available to allow recommendations about prophylaxis to be made.

Medications Used for Prophylaxis

In general, medications used for preventing stress-induced bleeding exert their pharmacologic effect through one of the following mechanisms: inhibition of gastric acid secretion, neutralization of gastric acid secretions, and protective mechanisms unrelated to acid secretion or neutralization.[103] The H_2-receptor antagonists, prostaglandin analogues, and proton-pump inhibitors act primarily as antisecretory agents by inhibiting gastric acid secretion. But, other explanations for the beneficial actions of these agents have been proposed. For example, H_2-receptor antagonists have immuno- modulatory actions at the cellular and mediator levels.[104] However, mediation of cytokine concentrations is a complex process, and the cytokine concentrations fluctuate widely in critically ill patients, often not correlating with more global physiological derangements.[105] Similarly, the prostaglandin analogue misoprostol prevents gastric mucosal damage by irritants that do not appear to depend on acid or acid secretion and is sometimes referred to as a cytoprotective agent.[106] There is no convincing evidence to establish that "cytoprotection" with misoprostol plays an important role in preventing stress-induced lesions.[107] Although alternative explanations for the effectiveness of antacids in preventing stress-induced bleeding have been proposed (e.g., stimulation of prostaglandin release), neutralization of gastric acid is the primary mechanism of action.[108] In contrast, sucralfate has multiple actions on the GI tract besides providing a direct protective barrier, including modulation of pepsin and mucus activity, arachidonic acid metabolism, bicarbonate secretion, and tissue growth or repair.[109] Which, if any, of these mechanisms is of primary importance for stress ulcer prophylaxis is not clear.

The H_2-receptor antagonists that are available commercially in the United States are cimetidine, famotidine, nizatidine, and ranitidine. Only cimetidine administered as a continuous intravenous infusion has FDA-approved labeling for the prevention of bleeding in critically ill patients, although there is no reason to suspect any substantial difference in prophylactic efficacy when other H_2-receptor antagonists are given in equipotent doses.[110] However, other reasons may preclude their use, such as the lack of an i.v. dosage form (as with nizatidine). No RCTs of adequate sample size have compared dosage regimens (e.g., intermittent versus continuous i.v. administration) or routes (e.g., i.v. versus oral) of H_2-receptor antagonists by using clinically important bleeding as a study endpoint.

One concern with using oral H_2-receptor antagonists and proton-pump inhibitors in critically ill patients is the potential for malabsorption. Because these agents must be absorbed to exert their effects, the patient must have a functioning GI tract. A functioning GI tract is usually presumed when tube feedings are tolerated without nausea, vomiting, abdominal distention, or diarrhea. In patients with nasogastric tubes, the clinician may monitor the gastric residual volume when feeding formulas are administered into the stomach. Residuals refer to the feedings and gastric secretions that accumulate with GI dysfunction. A volume of more than 200 mL or an amount greater than the volume infused over a two-hour period is usually indicative of dysfunction.[111]

Although widely used for stress ulcer prophylaxis, sucralfate is not labeled for this indication. Because sucralfate appears to exert its predominant effects locally, it must be administered either orally or by a nasogastric, orogastric, or gastrostomy tube. Sucralfate should not be administered with nasogastric tube feedings (see Adverse Effects of Prophylactic Agents). Neither should it be administered by feeding duodenal or jejunostomy tubes because the medication will miss the site of action.

Similar to sucralfate, antacids have local actions and must be administered directly into the stomach. A number of antacid products have been routinely used for stress ulcer prophylaxis. Several formulations carry FDA-approved labeling for this indication.

Misoprostol is available in tablet form, while proton-pump inhibitors such as omeprazole and lansoprazole are available in delayed-release capsules. These medications have not been well studied for stress ulcer prophylaxis and are not labeled for this indication. The delayed-release dosage forms of the proton-pump inhibitors create administration problems when oral intake is not possible, although some interesting compounding techniques for omeprazole have been reported.[112–115] In addition, lansoprazole has FDA-approved labeling for administration by nasogastric tube with some fruit juices.[116] One open-label study involving 75 mechanically ventilated surgery patients found a compounded omeprazole suspension effective in preventing stress- induced bleeding.[114] Larger comparative studies are needed to determine efficacy and assess the potential for adverse effects such as pneumonia (from increased gastric pH, as postulated for the H_2-receptor antagonists) and other unanticipated problems.

Although medications may have different mechanisms for their protective effects, there is no evidence that combination therapy is more effective than a single agent for initial prophylaxis, but the potential risk of adverse effects would increase with combination therapy. Therefore, combination therapy for initial prophylaxis cannot be recommended. Combination therapy for the prevention of recurrent bleeding is discussed further in this document (see Prevention of Recurrent Bleeding).

Efficacy of Prophylactic Agents: Prevention of Bleeding

A substantial number of clinical trials, a majority of which were randomized, have involved comparisons of medications used for stress ulcer prophylaxis.[117–174] In general, no significant differences between medications used for the prophylaxis of clinically important bleeding have been found.

However, in a majority of studies, the sample size needed to detect a difference between treatment groups in clinically important bleeding was not calculated. Therefore, the number of patients enrolled in any given study was often insufficient to preclude a Type II statistical error. Other studies have found substantial differences in bleeding between groups, but the frequency of bleeding was unexpectedly high for one of the groups. For example, Phillips, et al.[175] reported clinically important bleeding (the definition of clinically important was different than the definition used in these guidelines) in 4 (16%) of 25 patients receiving ranitidine by continuous i.v. infusion and 1 (3%) of 33 patients receiving omeprazole suspension. Compared with the results of other studies, 16% is a high rate of bleeding with ranitidine.[64,176]

In the largest RCT published to date, 1200 patients who required mechanical ventilation for at least 48 hours were assigned to receive either nasogastric sucralfate slurry (1 g every 6 hours) and i.v. placebo or i.v. ranitidine (50 mg every 8 hours) and nasogastric placebo.[176] The patients in this multicenter study were admitted to medical and surgical services (approximately 60% and 40%, respectively). There were relatively few patients from special populations: CNS surgery, 49 patients; trauma, 158; burns, 12; and transplantation, 19. These special populations were not discussed separately. Although the estimated sample size was based on the power to detect differences in rates of pneumonia (power, or $1-\beta = 75\%$), the rates of clinically important bleeding and mortality were additional study objectives, and the trial's power to detect a difference in bleeding rate was 90%. A significant difference in favor of the H_2-receptor antagonist (ranitidine) compared with sucralfate was noted. Ten (1.7%) of the 596 patients in the ranitidine group and 23 (3.8%) of 604 patients in the sucralfate group had clinically important bleeding (relative risk, 0.44; 95% CI, 0.21–0.92; $p = 0.02$). Endoscopic confirmation of an upper GI source of bleeding was obtained for 3 patients in the ranitidine group and 10 in the sucralfate group. An additional patient in the ranitidine group had an upper GI source of bleeding confirmed by angiography and red blood cell scanning. Because invasive diagnostic testing was left to the discretion of participating physicians, the source of bleeding was not found for 19 patients. In addition, no differences were noted in the overall length of stay or mortality. Therefore, the largest RCT conducted to date has not definitively determined the agent of choice for the prevention of clinically important GI bleeding.

Five meta-analyses have been conducted to resolve some of the discrepancies noted between RCTs, including the issue of inadequate sample size.[5,68–71] None of these meta-analyses included the recently published RCT by Cook, et al. (1998) and the Canadian Critical Care Trials Group (Table 2).[176] The other major limitations of these analyses have been discussed previously. In general, the meta-analyses found H_2-receptor antagonists and antacids to be more effective than no prophylaxis, but in some cases the 95% CIs were wide, indicating substantial variation in the data. Only one trial compared sucralfate with no prophylaxis, and this trial was included in the 1996 meta-analysis by Cook, et al.[5] The results of these meta-analyses were conflicting when medications were compared. In the meta-analyses by Lacroix, et al.[68] and Tryba,[69] H_2-receptor antagonists were compared with antacids, but the 95% CIs included 1, indicating that the two regimens did not differ significantly. In the 1991 meta-analysis by Cook, et al.,[70] H_2-receptor antagonists were significantly more effective than antacids for preventing overt bleeding, but the therapies were similar in preventing

clinically important bleeding.

Tryba[71] found sucralfate to be significantly more effective than H_2-receptor antagonists and similar in efficacy to antacids (OR = 0.532; 95% CI, 0.303–0.933). Cook, et al.[70] (1991) found sucralfate to be similar to H_2-receptor antagonists or antacids for preventing overt and clinically important bleeding.

Given the disparities noted in the previous meta-analyses, Cook, et al.[5] (1996) conducted a meta-analysis to resolve the apparent discrepancies. This meta-analysis included studies that were not available when the initial meta-analyses were completed. In addition to being significantly more effective than no prophylaxis, H_2-receptor antagonists were found to be significantly more effective than antacids in preventing overt bleeding but not clinically important bleeding. Sucralfate was similar to antacids or H_2-receptor antagonists for prophylaxis of both overt bleeding and clinically important bleeding.

While useful, this meta-analysis raises some important questions.[5] For example, the definitions for overt and clinically important bleeding are very explicit, which contrasts to the definitions used in many of the randomized investigations that were analyzed. It is not possible to derive rates of clinically important bleeding from many of the trials, particularly if a rigid definition is used. The meta-analysis also included RCTs from a variety of populations that have usually been studied as distinct populations (e.g., patients with head and thermal injuries). Even if one assumes that the pathogenesis of bleeding is similar, there may be differences in the frequencies of bleeding compared with populations studied more frequently (e.g., general medical and surgical ICU patients). If the frequency of bleeding has decreased over time as a result of improvements in the care of the ICU patient (which is difficult to verify because many recent studies have not included a no-treatment group), this could have also influenced the results of the meta-analysis. Finally, the results of this meta-analysis are somewhat inconsistent with the findings of the large RCT recently published by the same lead authors with regard to possible differences in medication efficacy.[176]

Recommendation (adults). Given the conflicting results of several meta-analyses and a recent RCT (both with strengths of evidence = A), the choice among antacids, H_2-receptor antagonists, and sucralfate for use as prophylactic agents to prevent clinically important bleeding associated with stress in adult patients admitted to general medical and surgical ICUs should be made on an institution-specific basis. This choice should take into account concerns regarding administration (e.g., functioning GI tract), adverse-effect profile, and total costs. (Strength of evidence = D) Insufficient data on misoprostol or the proton-pump inhibitors are available to allow any recommendation about these agents to be made.

Recommendation (pediatrics and special populations). The lack of comparative trials of these agents in pediatric and special populations (e.g., patients with burns, trauma patients, patients undergoing neurosurgical procedures or with neurologic disorders, and transplantation patients) precludes definitive recommendations as to the agent of choice in these situations. The choice of agent should be made on an institution-specific basis and should take into account concerns about administration (e.g., functioning GI tract), adverse-effect profile, and total costs.

Efficacy of Prophylactic Agents: Mortality

Many of the available studies did not include mortality outcomes, and still fewer specifically associated mortality with bleeding. In the largest RCT to date, there was not a significant difference in mortality between ranitidine recipients and sucralfate recipients despite the finding of a lower frequency of clinically important bleeding with ranitidine.[176] This may be partially explained by the relatively low frequency of bleeding in both groups. Any attempt to attribute differences in mortality to any single intervention in ICU patients must be interpreted with caution given the problems with controlling multiple confounding variables. Furthermore, the limitations associated with the extraction and interpretation of this information from the original trials must be appreciated during consideration of the results of published meta-analyses that have investigated the mortality associated with various forms of prophylaxis.

In a meta-analysis by Tryba[69] in 1991, sucralfate was associated with a lower mortality rate than use of either a H$_2$-receptor antagonist or an antacid. No significant differences in mortality were found between any of the groups in the 1991 meta-analysis by Cook, et al.[70] (Table 4). In contrast to the finding of the 1991 meta-analysis, sucralfate was associated with a lower rate of mortality than antacids in two other meta-analyses conducted by Cook, et al.[5,177] (1994 and 1996). When medications were compared with no prophylaxis, all the CIs in the published meta-analyses included 1, the threshold of importance, suggesting no substantial differences in mortality.

Adverse Effects of Prophylactic Agents

Most adverse effects attributable to antacids, H$_2$-receptor antagonists, and sucralfate are uncommon and occur in less than 1% of adult patients, particularly when given on a short-term basis (e.g., for less than two weeks).[178] The frequency of adverse effects may increase if certain diseases are present, such as renal failure, when electrolyte accumulation secondary to antacid administration or CNS disturbances secondary to administration of H$_2$-receptor antagonists may occur. Sucralfate may cause substantial elevations in serum aluminum concentrations in adult patients with chronic renal insufficiency or in the elderly,[179] although this does not appear to be a problem when the drug is used for less than two weeks in critically ill patients.[180,181] Elevated aluminum concentrations and resultant toxicity are more of a concern in children with renal dysfunction, particularly given that well-defined dosage guidelines have not been established.[182] Although aluminum hydroxide-containing antacids and sucralfate may be used to lower phosphate levels in patients with uremia, they may cause unwanted hypophosphatemia in patients with normal renal function.[183]

Some products given by oral, nasogastric, or enteral administration may result in local adverse effects. For example, constipation may occur with aluminum-containing antacids and sucralfate and diarrhea may occur with magnesium-containing antacids at frequencies higher than 1%.[184] Sucralfate and antacids may occlude feeding tubes. If the occlusion cannot be removed, the tube may have to be replaced, potentially causing patient discomfort and resulting in complications from placement of a new tube (e.g., esophageal perforation, aspiration, inappropriate placement in the trachea).[185]

Table 4.

Meta-analyses Investigating the Risk of Mortality with and without Stress Ulcer Prophylaxis

Reference	Comparison[a]	No. Trials	Results[b]
69	H$_2$-RAs or antacids (combined group) versus control	11	CI included 1
	Sucralfate versus H$_2$-RAs or antacids (combined group)	9	OR and CI <1 (lower rate of mortality with sucralfate)
70	Antacids versus control	6	OR = 1.06, CI = 0.67–1.66
	H$_2$-RAs versus control	9	OR = 0.80, CI = 0.54–1.18
	H$_2$-RAs versus antacids	14	OR = 1.16, CI = 0.83–1.61
	Antacids versus sucralfate	8	OR = 1.22, CI = 0.83–1.79
	H$_2$-RAs versus sucralfate	3	OR = 1.25, CI = 0.61–2.58
177	Antacids versus control	5	OR = 1.36, CI = 0.83–2.24
	H$_2$-RAs versus control	11	OR = 1.03, CI = 0.73–1.48
	H$_2$-RAs versus antacids	15	OR = 1.06, CI = 0.78–1.46
	Sucralfate versus antacids	11	OR = 0.70, CI = 0.52–0.94 (lower rate of mortality with sucralfate)
	Sucralfate versus H$_2$-RAs	7	OR = 0.71, CI = 0.49–1.04
5	Antacids versus control	3	OR = 1.42, CI = 0.82–2.47
	H$_2$-RAs versus control	15	OR = 1.15, CI = 0.86–1.53
	H$_2$-RAs versus antacids	14	OR = 0.89, CI = 0.66–1.21
	Sucralfate versus control	4	OR = 1.06, CI = 0.67–1.67
	Sucralfate versus antacids	11	OR = 0.73, CI = 0.54–0.97 (lower rate of mortality with sucralfate)
	Sucralfate versus H$_2$-RAs	11	OR = 0.83,

[a]H$_2$-RAs = histamine H$_2$-receptor antagonists.
[b]OR = odds ratio, CI = 95% confidence interval. Exact values provided when available; some values were extrapolated from figures.

Although not well studied, there are potential interactions between enteral feeding products and medications administered enterally for prophylaxis. Such interactions could result in clogged feeding tubes or diminished medication efficacy (e.g., by inhibiting the local actions of sucralfate or interfering with the absorption of other medications). When intermittent feedings are used, interactions can be minimized by giving the feedings and medications at different times. When continuous feedings are used in conjunction with any medications, the feedings should be temporarily stopped. The tube should be flushed with water before the medication is administered. After the medication is administered, the tube should again be flushed with water to ensure passage through the tube. It is probably unnecessary to discontinue postpyloric (jejunal) feedings for administration of sucralfate, because sucralfate binds to the stomach mucosa. For more details about enteral feeding–medication interactions and methods to prevent them, the reader is referred to published reviews.[111,186]

Case reports suggest that sucralfate may contribute to esophageal and GI bezoar formation, especially when given in conjunction with enteral feedings in patients with motility disorders.[187–190] In addition to technical problems related to the removal of bezoars, complications such as intestinal obstruction and perforation have been reported in pediatric patients. For example, intestinal obstruction and perforation were reported with sucralfate in a low-birth-weight infant who was given 250 mg every eight hours by nasogastric tube.[191] Also, bezoars, hypermagnesemia, and intestinal perforation have been reported with liquid antacids used in premature infants and newborns.[192,193] Therefore, sucralfate and antacids should be used with caution, particularly in premature infants.

The H$_2$-receptor antagonists are associated with a number of adverse effects that occur infrequently but may lead to a consultation with a specialist, a diagnostic test, a new medication to treat the adverse effect, or a switch to another medication for prophylaxis. Potential adverse effects include hepatitis, cytopenia, and cardiovascular and CNS toxicities. The exact frequency of each of these problems is difficult to determine, but estimates range from 0.0023% for cytopenia to 1.9% for CNS toxicity.[194–199] The low rate of these adverse effects in adults and limitations associated with postmarketing surveillance studies prohibit accurate comparisons of the frequencies of such effects among medications in this class. The lack of studies in the pediatric population precludes an accurate assessment of the frequency of particular adverse effects. There is a possibility that pediatric patients may be more susceptible to some adverse effects (e.g., thrombocytopenia associated with cimetidine[49]) than adults. Similarly, the lack of information related to pediatric dosing could result in either underdosing with diminished efficacy or overdosing with increased adverse effects.

H$_2$-receptor antagonists and proton-pump inhibitors have the potential for drug–drug, drug–nutrient, and drug–test interactions through a variety of mechanisms. For example, some drug–drug interactions are mediated through effects on the cytochrome P-450 systems in the liver. Although a number of interactions with some of these acid-suppressing agents are of potential concern (e.g., warfarin, ketoconazole, phenytoin, theophylline), few are clinically important when patients are adequately monitored.[200] However, there may be other reasons for avoiding particular medications. For example, cimetidine may increase serum creatinine concentrations without affecting the glomerular filtration rate by competition for tubular secretion in the kidneys.[201] This could be interpreted as renal dysfunction in patients receiving nephrotoxic medications, leading to inappropriate reductions in the dosage of the suspected medication. Other interactions may occur as a result of the acid-suppressing properties of these two classes of agents.

Sucralfate and antacids can affect the absorption of other medications. Although most problems can be avoided if doses of sucralfate and antacids are separated from doses of potentially interacting substances, this practice is often not used.[202] Potentially interacting medications should be administered one to two hours before the sucralfate dose. Furthermore, medications may interact with sucralfate and antacids despite separation (e.g., the bioavailability of quinolone antimicrobials has been substantially reduced by sucralfate even when the two products were separated by two or more hours).[203,204]

Test interference is a cause for concern with all medications used for stress ulcer prophylaxis. This concern also applies to agents that do not alter pH (e.g., sucralfate interferes with at least one method of occult blood testing).[205]

A full discussion of all potential drug–drug interactions with these agents is beyond the scope of these guidelines; however, comprehensive reviews have been published.[206]

The proton-pump inhibitors have few clinically important adverse effects. The most common concerns are mild GI or CNS toxicities.[207] The prostaglandin analogue misoprostol is rarely used clinically for prophylaxis and is associated with substantial adverse effects compared with placebo (nausea, abdominal pain, diarrhea).[208]

Lansoprazole (pregnancy risk category B) and omeprazole (FDA pregnancy risk category C) should be used in pregnant or nursing mothers only when the potential benefits exceed the potential risks.[116,209] Similar caution is advised for the H$_2$-receptor antagonists (pregnancy risk category B for cimetidine, famotidine, and ranitidine; pregnancy risk category C for nizatidine) and sucralfate (pregnancy risk category B).[110,210–213] Misoprostol is an abortifacient, may result in miscarriage (pregnancy risk category X), and is generally contraindicated in pregnant women, women of childbearing age, and nursing mothers.[214]

Pneumonia. The frequency of nosocomial pneumonia associated with stress ulcer prophylaxis has been widely debated. In addition to patient morbidity and economic concerns, mortality rates associated with pneumonia may be as high as 70%.[215] There are multiple mechanisms by which bacteria may enter the lungs, including inhalation, hematogenous spread, contiguous spread, direct inoculation, aspiration of secretions, and translocation from the GI tract.[216] The vast majority of studies investigating a possible connection between pneumonia and stress ulcer prophylaxis have been conducted in adults. In the few studies involving pediatric patients receiving stress ulcer prophylaxis, pneumonia was usually not studied. When pneumonia was reported, it was typically not a primary endpoint.[65]

Early reports of adult patients receiving antacids and cimetidine demonstrated that the stomach and upper airways had similar bacterial flora, suggesting retrograde transmission from the stomach.[217] Gastric colonization was uniformly seen in patients with alkalinized stomach contents.[218] However, a positive correlation between increased gastric pH and colonization with bacteria does not mean there is a linear relationship between acid-suppressing drugs and pneumonia.

It is also important to keep in mind that the techniques used to diagnose pneumonia have continued to evolve. Bronchoscopy, which is now a widely used and accepted diagnostic tool in research, was not performed in older studies of medication-associated pneumonia. Although the sensitivity and specificity of bronchoscopy for diagnosis of infection have been improved by newer techniques such as use of a protected-specimen brush, morbidity and economic concerns have been expressed about its widespread clinical use.[219] Other methods are less invasive but often have lower sensitivity and specificity, particularly when not performed appropriately.

Agents that do not alter gastric pH, such as sucralfate, may be less likely to result in pneumonia through retrograde transmission or translocation of bacteria.[220,221] When protected specimens, bronchoalveolar lavage, or both were used, one prospective randomized, double-blind study involving 141 patients showed no difference in the effect of antacids or sucralfate on gastric acidity or rates of bacterial colonization or ventilator-associated pneumonia.[145] Decreased gastric acidity was observed in conjunction with greater colonization of the stomach but not of the upper respiratory tract. In another prospective investigation in which samples were obtained by bronchoscopy, mechanically ventilated patients were randomly assigned to receive either antacids or sucralfate and then studied for risk factors associated with colonization and pneumonia.[222] As in the previous study, gastric colonization was not associated with the development of pneumonia, but duration of mechanical ventilation and upper-respiratory-tract colonization were found to be risk factors. A more recent study on this issue had a double-blind, double-dummy design and compared the growth of gastric pathogens in 140 patients undergoing elective surgery who were randomly assigned to receive either sucralfate or antacids.[223] Patients' gastric and respiratory tract contents were cultured for routine aerobic bacteria and fungi before surgery and daily throughout the hospitalization until the patient was discharged or died. Clinical endpoints included upper GI tract bleeding (grossly bloody fluid in nasogastric aspirate that failed to clear with saline lavage), pneumonia, wound infection, and urinary tract infection. New gastric microorganisms appeared in 24% of the patients receiving sucralfate and 51% of the patients receiving antacids. The rates of gastric bleeding, pneumonia, and nosocomial infection were not significantly different.

Other risk factors for nosocomial pneumonia have been identified and ranked according to supporting evidence.[224] In addition to host factors (e.g., gastric hypoacidity) and environmental factors, the use of a nasogastric tube to administer medications (with the attendant risks of aspiration and guaiac-positive stools from nasogastric manipulation), along with the volume and pH of medications and feedings administered, determines the frequency of pneumonia. However, despite these other risk factors, a committee associated with the Centers for Disease Control and Prevention has recommended that non-pH-altering medications (e.g., sucralfate) be used for prophylaxis in mechanically ventilated patients (ages not specified).[225] The recommendation was "suggested for implementation in many hospitals." While sucralfate may not contribute to translocation or colonization of the airways by bacteria, animal models of aspiration pneumonia have demonstrated that the volume of fluid administered with sucralfate and the drug's minimal buffering activity may increase the risk of acid aspiration and pulmonary edema.[226]

In the RCT by Cook, et al.[176] that involved 1200 patients, the determination of ventilator-associated pneumonia was based on criteria modified from the Centers for Disease Control and Prevention. The study had sufficient power to detect a 25% difference in rates of pneumonia (power = 75%). Bronchoalveolar lavage or protected specimen brush sampling was used for diagnostic confirmation in patients with pneumonia suspected by clinical criteria. One potentially confounding variable was the use of enteral feedings by a majority (approximately 70%) of patients in each group. Pneumonia was diagnosed in 114 (19.1%) of 596 patients in the ranitidine group and 98 (16.3%) of 604 patients in the sucralfate group, a difference that was not significant (relative risk, 1.18; 95% CI, 0.92–1.51; $p = 0.19$). It is possible that a significant, albeit small, difference in favor of sucralfate

would be found if a larger trial were conducted. There were five patients with "definite" pneumonia in the ranitidine group (0.8%) but none in the sucralfate group (95% CI, 0.1–1.6; $p = 0.03$).

Five meta-analyses of the frequency of nosocomial pneumonia associated with stress ulcer prophylaxis have also been conducted (Table 5). Two of the investigations published in 1991 were conducted by Tryba and included many of the studies previously mentioned. One meta-analysis found a lower rate of pneumonia with sucralfate use than with use of either an H_2-receptor antagonist or an antacid.[69] The second meta-analysis showed a lower rate of pneumonia with sucralfate than with H_2-receptor antagonists and for sucralfate than with antacids.[71] The other three meta-analyses were conducted by Cook, et al. and were published in the 1990s. In the 1994 meta-analysis by Cook, et al.[177] involving six investigations, sucralfate-treated patients had a lower rate of pneumonia than patients who received an antacid or an H_2-receptor antagonist. However, in the other two meta-analyses, no significant differences among any of the treatments were found.[5,227] However, these findings should be interpreted with caution given the methodological differences (e.g., diagnostic criteria for pneumonia) among the trials being evaluated, the trials not included in the meta-analyses, and the tendency to combine the results for acid-suppressive therapies together (i.e., H_2-receptor antagonists and antacids).[228]

Summary. Antacids, H_2-receptor antagonists, and sucralfate have been used for many years and have well-delineated adverse-effect profiles, with the one notable exception of nosocomial pneumonia associated with pH-altering agents in critically ill patients. Although data from RCTs or large surveillance studies are lacking for pediatric patients, all these agents have been used in various age groups for multiple GI disorders with relatively few adverse effects. Experience with the proton-pump inhibitors for stress ulcer prophylaxis is limited, but experience treating peptic ulcers suggests that these agents have a low rate of serious adverse effects in adults when used on a short-term basis. When compared with that of other agents, the adverse-effect profile of misoprostol, as well as the fact that there are limited studies of efficacy, precludes its use for stress ulcer prophylaxis.

Recommendation (adults and pediatrics). It is recommended that patients with a history of serious reactions to antacids, H_2-receptor antagonists, proton-pump inhibitors, or sucralfate avoid future use of the offending agent. There are no other absolute contraindications that would preclude the short-term use of any of these medications for stress ulcer prophylaxis. However, unless the benefits clearly exceed the risks, it is recommended that sucralfate and antacids be avoided in neonates (particularly premature neonates) because of the possibility of adverse effects (e.g., bezoar formation, accumulation of aluminum and magnesium). Also, it is recommended that aluminum-containing products such as sucralfate be avoided in children with renal failure because dosing information has not been well established. Whether acid-suppressing agents are associated with a higher rate of pneumonia than sucralfate is unresolved, although any difference between these medications would appear to be small. It is recommended that potential adverse effects be considered as part of the economic analysis when an agent is chosen (see Economic Analysis). (Strength of evidence = D)

Table 5.
Meta-analyses Investigating the Risk of Pneumonia with Medications Used for Stress Ulcer Prophylaxis

Reference	Comparison[a]	No. Trials	Results[b]
69	Sucralfate versus H$_2$-RAs or antacids (combined group)	6	OR and CI <1 (lower rate of pneumonia with sucralfate)
71	Sucralfate versus H$_2$-RAs	5	OR = 0.498, CI = 0.316–0.783 (lower rate of pneumonia with sucralfate)
	Sucralfate versus antacids	4	OR = 0.402, CI = 0.235–0.687 (lower rate of pneumonia with sucralfate)
227	Prophylaxis adjusted according to gastic pH versus no adjustment	3	OR = 0.63, CI = 0.24–1.62
	Antacids or H$_2$-RAs versus placebo versus control (combined group)	4	OR = 0.42, CI = 0.61–1.10
	Sucralfate versus antacids or H$_2$-RAs (combined group)	4	OR = 0.55, CI = 0.28–1.06
177	Sucralfate versus antacids or H$_2$-RAs (combined group)	6	OR = 0.50, CI = 0.21–0.79 (lower rate of pneumonia with sucralfate)
5	H$_2$-RAs versus control	8	OR = 1.25, CI = 0.78–2.00
	H$_2$-RAs versus antacids	3	OR = 1.01, CI = 0.65–1.57
	Sucralfate versus control	2	OR = 2.11, CI = 0.82–5.44
	Sucralfate versus antacids	6	OR = 0.80, CI = 0.56–1.15
	Sucralfate versus H$_2$-RAs	11	OR = 0.78, CI = 0.62–1.09

[a]H$_2$-RAs = histamine H$_2$-receptor antagonists.
[b]OR = odds ratio, CI = 95% confidence interval. Exact values provided when available; some values were extrapolated from figures.

Initial Dosage

Some of the dosages listed in Table 6 had to be extracted from the literature because stress ulcer prophylaxis is not an FDA-approved indication for most of the medications used for this purpose.[110,209–211,213] The dosages included in Table 6 have been commonly used for initiating prophylaxis against stress-induced bleeding in adults. In some of the studies, dosages were subsequently adjusted according to gastric pH measurements. Dosages for patients with renal dysfunction were mostly taken from published guidelines.[110,209–211,213] No well-documented maximum dosage for each agent has been reported, although studies involving

pH determinations often set an arbitrary upper limit. Antacids were not included in Table 6 because of the large number of commercially available products with differing acid-neutralizing capacities and the large number of regimens used in the literature (many adjusted on the basis of gastric pH determinations); the reader is encouraged to consult available studies.[36–40,42,54,90–92] The dosage guidelines in Table 6 are based on limited clinical data and may need to be adjusted according to adverse effects or clinical response.[229]

Dosages for pediatric patients can be estimated from the few studies that have been published on stress ulcer prophylaxis (Table 7), extrapolated from pediatric handbooks that describe dosing for related conditions (e.g., GI bleeding), or extrapolated from pharmacokinetic studies.[48,49,56,57,63,65,88,168,230–235] In published studies, i.v. ranitidine was given in dosages of 2–6 mg/kg/day (in three or four divided doses) to preterm newborns and children up to 18 years of age.[63,65,232,233,235] Cimetidine was given i.v. in dosages of 15–24 mg/kg/day (in four divided doses) in two studies involving newborns and another study involving patients from birth to 18 years of age (maximum dosage, 1000 mg/day).[48,49,231]

Pharmacokinetic or dosage studies in pediatric patients have been published, but these are not necessarily related to the prevention of stress-induced bleeding. For example, Martyn, et al.[236] determined the pharmacokinetics of cimetidine in children with burn injuries. Twenty-one

Table 6.
Initial Adult Dosage Regimens for Agents Used for Prophylaxis of Stress-Induced Bleeding[a]

Medication	Normal Renal Function	Reduced Renal Function
Cimetidine[110,178]	300 mg four times a day p.o., NG, or i.v. or 50 mg/hr by continuous i.v. infusion	If CL$_{cr}$ <30 mL/min: 300 mg twice a day p.o., NG, or i.v. or 25 mg/hr by continuous i.v. infusion
Famotidine[178,210]	20 mg twice daily p.o., NG, or i.v. or 1.7 mg/hr by continuous i.v. infusion	If CL$_{cr}$ <30 mL/min: 20 mg once daily p.o., NG, or i.v. or 0.85 mg/hr by continuous i.v. infusion
Ranitidine[178,211]	150 mg twice daily p.o. or NG, 50 mg every 6–8 hr i.v., or 6.25 mg/hr by continuous i.v. infusion	If CL$_{cr}$ <50 mL/min: 150 mg once or twice daily p.o. or NG, 50 mg every 12–24 hr i.v., or 2–4 mg/hr by continuous i.v. infusion
Omeprazole[112–115,209]	40-mg loading dose, then 20–40 mg daily p.o. or NG	No adjustment necessary
Sucralfate[178,213]	1 g four times daily p.o. or NG	No adjustment necessary

[a]NG = by nasogastric tube, CL$_{cr}$ = creatinine clearance. Dosages can be modified on the basis of response or adverse effects.

Table 7.
Studies of Stress Ulcer Prophylaxis in Pediatric Populations[a]

Reference	Study Design and Population (No. Patients or Admissions)	Age	Medication	No. with Clinically Important Bleeding
88	Retrospective; thermal injury to 13–93% (mean, 29%) BSA; (477)	35 days to 13 yr; mean, 4.3 yr	None stated	36
230	Retrospective; thermal injury to 5–92% BSA (582)	4 wk to 15 yr	Milk or feeding formula plus diazepam	2
48	Prospective, randomized; general ICU (40)	Birth to 18 yr; mean, 1.85 yr	Cimetidine 5 mg/kg i.v. every 6 hr (1 g/day maximum)	NA
231	Prospective, randomized; general ICU (33)	30–41.5 wk	Cimetidine 6 mg/kg i.v. every 6 hr	NA
232	Prospective, randomized; general ICU (40)	Birth to 18 yr; mean, 2.6–4.3 yr (varied by group)	Ranitidine 2–4 mg/kg NG every 12 hr or 0.75–1.5 mg/kg i.v. every 6 hr	NA
49	Prospective, randomized; general ICU (100)	Full-term neonates	Cimetidine 3.75–5 mg/kg i.v. every 6 hr	NA
65	Prospective, randomized; general ICU (140)	Birth to 20 yr; mean, 4.6 yr	Ranitidine 1.5 mg/kg i.v. every 6 hr, sucralfate 0.5 g (<10 kg) or 1 g (>10 kg) every 6 hr, antacid (almagate) 0.25–0.5 mL/kg every 2 hr	7/35 in control group versus 6/105 in combined medication groups (p <0.05); no significant differences for any single medication versus control group
56	Prospective, observational; general ICU (208)	Mean ± S.D., 38 ± 53.5 mo	None	None
57	Prospective, observational; general ICU (984)	Mean ± S.E., 62.6 ± 2.1 mo	Various (per discretion of physician)	2/698 with no prophylaxis versus 2/286 with prophylaxis
168	Prospective, randomized; cardiac surgery (79)	35 days to 9.85 yr; mean, 2.62 yr	Famotidine or pirenzepine 1 mg/kg/day i.v. (3 doses if <10 kg), 0.5 mg/kg/day if serum creatinine >3 mg/dL	NA
63	Prospective, randomized; general ICU (53)	Neonates, mostly preterm; mean, 32 wk gestation	Ranitidine 1.67 mg/kg i.v. every 8 hr	NA
233	Prospective, observational; general ICU (45)	2 wk to 264 mo; median, 36 mo	Ranitidine 2–6 mg/kg/day i.v. (mean, 3.3 mg/kg/day) given at intervals of 6, 8, or 12 hr[b]	None
66	Prospective, observational; general ICU (1006)	3 days to 18 yr; mean, 61.5 mo	Various (per discretion of physician)	6/990 with no prophylaxis versus 10/110 with prophylaxis

[a]Only studies with at least 25 patients were included. BSA = body surface area, ICU = intensive care unit, NA = not available, NG = by nasogastric tube.
[b]Administered every eight hours in 89% of patients.

children ranging in age from 0.3 to 17.5 years were administered cimetidine in doses of 10–15 mg/kg. These children had higher cimetidine clearances and shorter elimination half-lives than healthy or burned adults (primarily because of greater renal clearance). The authors suggested that in order to maintain a gastric pH of ≥4, continuous infusions of cimetidine would be required.

Another study looked at the pharmacokinetics of cimetidine in 30 critically ill children age 4.5 to 15 years.[237] The patients received a mean dosage of 26 mg/kg/day administered in four doses infused over 15 minutes. Patients receiving ≥20 mg/kg/day maintained plasma cimetidine concentrations at ≥0.5 µg/mL for longer periods. The investigators found a significant (p <0.001) inverse correlation between age and total body clearance ($r = 0.75$, p <0.001) and age and apparent volume of distribution ($r = 0.76$, p <0.001). They concluded that a dosage of cimetidine of 20–30 mg/kg/day given in six divided doses would provide more optimal steady-state plasma cimetidine concentrations.

Ranitidine was studied in 12 children ranging in age from 3.5 to 16 years with peptic ulcer disease.[238] Each child

received ranitidine by continuous i.v. infusion, with the rate adjusted to achieve at least 90% inhibition of gastric acid secretion. The dosage and response data were used to design intermittent dosage regimens, consisting of i.v. bolus doses given every 6 hours and then oral doses given every 12 hours. The i.v. dose ranged from 0.13 to 0.8 mg/kg. Another study involving ranitidine for neonates with documented gastric bleeding used a loading dose of 0.6 mg/kg followed by a continuous infusion of 0.15 mg/kg/hr.[239] No adverse effects from the ranitidine were noted.

Treem and colleagues[240] studied i.v. famotidine in 18 children ranging in age from 0.16 to 5.7 years who were admitted to a pediatric ICU after major elective orthopedic or cardiac surgery. Doses required to keep the gastric pH above 4 for at least six hours ranged from 0.4 to 0.8 mg/kg. Famotidine was pharmacokinetically evaluated in 14 children ranging in age from 1.25 to 15.5 years who were diagnosed with gastric or duodenal ulcers.[241] Although famotidine effectively treated the ulcers, 0.5 mg/kg i.v. or orally twice daily failed to keep the pH above 5 for the dosage interval. These two studies suggest that, for children, famotidine should be given every six hours or, at least, every eight hours.

In summary, pharmacokinetic studies suggest that children clear H_2-receptor antagonists faster and have larger volumes of distribution than adults and that doses should be given either by continuous infusion or more frequently than those recommended for adults. Studies addressing the proper dosing of agents for stress ulcer prophylaxis in pediatrics are needed.

In general, there is little dosing information for the neonatal population, in particular, premature neonates. Dosing in premature neonates is further complicated by decreased renal function secondary to disease or lack of maturation. Caution should be exercised when H_2-receptor antagonists are used in combination with tolazoline. Tolazoline may still be used in some institutions to treat pulmonary hypertension in neonates and has been associated with gastric bleeding. Case reports have implicated both cimetidine and ranitidine with reversal of tolazoline's histamine-mediated effects on pulmonary vasculature.[242] In general, the use of antacids and sucralfate should be avoided in premature infants because of the possibility of complications (see Adverse Effects of Prophylactic Agents).

Doses of H_2-receptor antagonists are often reduced (or the intervals extended) for patients with renal dysfunction, because all these medications have slower clearances and longer half-lives in this population.[243] These alterations in dose or interval have been based on expected serum drug concentrations, because well-controlled studies have not investigated various dosage regimens in preventing stress-induced bleeding. Whether doses or intervals of H_2-receptor antagonists need to be adjusted in patients with severe hepatic dysfunction or other diseases that might affect the pharmacokinetic properties of the agents is not known. There are no adequate dosage guidelines for children with renal dysfunction. Many practitioners recommend estimation of renal function by established methods for children. Most methods yield creatinine clearances normalized to an average BSA (mL/min/1.73 m²). Adjustments are then made by using adult guidelines for impaired renal function. Still other practitioners may not make adjustments, believing that the risks of excessive dosing would not outweigh the risk of underdosing in children.

Gastric pH monitoring may help in developing dosage regimens, especially in patients with renal dysfunction or immaturity (preterm infants). On days a patient is being dialyzed, it is advisable to administer the medications after dialysis to avoid rapid clearance during the dialysis procedure.

Table 6 lists dosage regimens for commonly used agents in adult patients. Some of the oral dosage regimens are equivalent to the i.v. regimens in terms of total daily dosage (e.g., cimetidine, famotidine), although an argument could be made for larger oral dosages on the basis of bioavailability differences between the two routes of administration. Table 8 provides pediatric doses for the H_2-receptor antagonists and sucralfate. The recommendations were derived from limited data from published studies and were based on toxicity as well as efficacy considerations.

Monitoring

For agents that do not affect gastric pH, such as sucralfate, monitoring is limited to potential adverse events and GI bleeding. However, for agents that neutralize gastric acid, particularly antacids, monitoring has frequently included pH determinations. No large, controlled studies have been published that document a benefit to pH monitoring in association with stress ulcer prophylaxis. The issue is further complicated by differences in the validity and reliability of methods used to measure gastric pH. Although monitoring with pH paper is simple and is considered by many clinicians to be a standard of practice for agents that raise gastric pH, this method lacks accuracy.[246] One study found that 33% of gastric pH determinations were not ≥4, despite pH paper testing demonstrating evidence to the contrary.[247]

A number of studies have concluded from gastric pH determinations that continuous infusions of H_2-receptor antagonists are more effective than intermittent dosage schedules.[248–253] Many factors must be considered in the interpretation of these studies, beginning with the role of gastric acidity in the pathogenesis of stress ulceration. Although gastric acidity may have a role in stress-induced damage, gastric acid is unlikely to be the main cause of bleeding.[254] Not only do many ICU patients have hyposecretion of gastric acid,[255] but gastric pH fluctuates rapidly and may not be controlled even if dosages of antisecretory agents are individualized.[256,257] Gastric pH can also be increased by the presence of blood and bile in the GI tract. Although newer methods of pH monitoring, such as noninvasive, intramucosal pH measurements, may prove useful for predicting stress-induced bleeding, such measurements have been studied primarily as indicators of systemic tissue oxygenation and hence of overall mortality rates in critically ill patients.[258]

Checking for microscopic bleeding by occult blood testing techniques has similar limitations. Most important, there is no proven relationship between microscopic bleeding and outcomes such as clinically important bleeding, although the results of one prospective study suggest that occult bleeding for at least six days increases the risk for overt bleeding.[53] Overt bleeding is defined as the presence of blood or "coffee-ground" material in nasogastric aspirates, hematemesis, hematochezia, or melena. Overt bleeding that results in hemodynamic compromise or the need for blood transfusions or surgery is clinically important. Therefore, patients at risk for stress-related complications should be routinely followed for overt bleeding.

When overt bleeding occurs, the patient should be closely monitored for decreases in blood pressure (e.g., a decrease of 20 mm Hg or more in the diastolic pressure during a 24-hour period), hemoglobin (e.g., ≥3 g/dL during a 24-hour period), and hematocrit (e.g., ≥9% during a 24-hour period), all of which suggest clinically important GI bleeding in the absence of other causes. When overt bleeding, with or without hemodynamic compromise, continues despite conservative therapies such as saline lavage, endoscopy is usually indicated. Endoscopy can be used to confirm a GI source of bleeding.

Recommendation (adults and pediatrics). It is recommended that all patients receiving medications for stress ulcer prophylaxis be monitored for bleeding and adverse drug effects (see Adverse Effects of Prophylactic Agents). Paper techniques for measuring gastric pH have questionable validity and reliability, and there is no evidence that adjusting the dosage of pH-altering medications (antacids, H_2-receptor antagonists, proton-pump inhibitors) on the basis of these measurements influences patient morbidity or mortality. Despite the lack of supporting data, pH monitoring for antacids may be appropriate (goal pH of >3.5–4). Such monitoring may also be useful for H_2-receptor antagonists

Table 8.
Pediatric Dosage Recommendations for H$_2$-Receptor Antagonists and Sucralfate

Medication	Dosage[a]		
	Neonates	Infants	Children
Cimetidine[48,49,231,236,237]	10 (5–20) mg/kg/day i.v. in 2 or 3 divided doses[b]	20–40 mg/kg/day i.v. in 3 or 4 divided doses	30–40 mg/kg/day i.v. (1200 mg/day maximum) in 6 divided doses
Famotidine[168,240,241]	Inadequate information available to make dosage recommendations	1.2 (1–2) mg/kg/day i.v. in 2 or 3 divided doses	1.6 (1–2) mg/kg/day i.v. (40 mg/day maximum) in 3 divided doses
Raniti-dine[63,65,232,233,235,238,239,244,245]	Continuous i.v. infusion: 0.0625–0.2 mg/kg/hr Intermittent i.v. doses: If full term, 1.5–3 mg/kg/day in 3 divided doses; if premature, 0.5 mg/kg/day in 2 divided doses	4.5 (3–6) mg/kg/day i.v. in 3 divided doses	6 (3–6) mg/kg/day i.v. (200 mg/day maximum) in 4 divided doses
Sucralfate[65,234]	Not recommended[c]	40 mg/kg/day p.o. or NG in 4 divided doses[d]	40–80 mg/kg/day p.o. or NG (lower end of range for younger children, 4000 mg/day maximum) in 4 divided doses[d]

[a]Dosages are for patients with normal renal function. NG = by nasogastric tube. There is a lack of data to make definitive dosage adjustments in pediatric patients for renal dysfunction, but decreases in the total daily dosage of cimetidine, famotidine, and ranitidine would be logical. This could be done either by decreasing individual doses while keeping the dosage interval the same as for patients with normal renal function or by extending the dosage interval and keeping individual doses the same as for patients with normal renal function. No adjustment in the dosage of sucralfate is required for patients with renal dysfunction.

[b]In general, half-lives were longer in neonates (2–3.4 hours), more than likely because of immature renal function. There is inadequate dosage information on premature neonates with respect to stratification by birth weight or gestational age. Thus, a wide range of dosages have been reported in the literature. Many dosage handbooks and institutions use 5–10 mg/kg/day divided every 12 hours in premature neonates.

[c]Inadequate information is available. Not recommended because of reports of bezoar formation in neonates (particularly premature neonates). Amount of aluminum in adult doses of sucralfate may contribute to hypophosphatemia in neonates.

[d]Dosage not well established. Bezoar formation with obstruction has been reported. Caution is advised when sucralfate is administered to any pediatric patient, especially in cases of impaired gastric motility and dehydration.

when standard dosage regimens might not be appropriate (e.g., in cases of renal dysfunction, for increased dosages due to perceived failure of therapy, in pediatric patients). (Strength of evidence = D)

Other Options for Prophylaxis

Similar to the principles involved in preventing global ischemia, a primary intervention for reducing the frequency of stress-induced bleeding should be the prevention of GI hypoperfusion and attendant ischemic complications.[259,260] If ischemia is prevented during the early stages of injury, stress ulcer prophylaxis may be unnecessary. In fact, acid inhibitors or neutralizers may be harmful. In the case of acid neutralizers, increasing gastric pH allows for bacterial overgrowth, with subsequent spread to other organs.[261]

As discussed previously, the effect of enteral feedings on the frequency of stress-induced bleeding and pneumonia has not been established through controlled trials. Although gastric acid appears to play a role in stress-induced bleeding, and while it is clear that microbial growth is inhibited at low gastric pH, it has not been conclusively demonstrated that continuous or intermittent enteral feedings consistently raise gastric pH.[262] The site of enteral feeding administration (stomach or sites distal to the pylorus) varied in published studies, and potential site-specific effects remain to be elucidated. The possibility that enteral feedings offer protection against bleeding and pneumonia through other mechanisms (e.g., maintenance of a positive nitrogen balance that is important for normal reparative functions of the gastric mucosa) should be explored.

Appropriate supportive care, such as administration of fluids and blood products, nutritional support, ventilatory support, and timely definitive surgery, may preclude the need for stress ulcer prophylaxis in many patients.[263,264] Before the widespread use of H$_2$-receptor antagonists for stress ulcer prophylaxis, a number of regimens were used to prevent acute upper GI bleeding in burn patients, including milk and diazepam given to children and vitamin A injection given to adults.[230,264] Although corticosteroids have been studied as inciting factors for GI bleeding, other evidence suggests that corticosteroids may protect against bleeding in some populations, including patients with shock.[265]

Combinations of allopurinol and dimethyl sulfoxide have been studied in two RCTs in patients with leg or pelvic fractures who had clinical evidence of shock.[166,266] These agents were studied because of their ability to decrease free-radical formation and, therefore, potentially prevent gastric mucosal injury. Both trials showed significant (p <0.01) decreases in endoscopically confirmed lesions. Both of these studies are promising but require confirmation in different populations. Comparisons with existing agents that include economic evaluations of the options are also needed.

Recommendation (adults and pediatrics). It is premature to recommend the use of novel therapies (e.g., free-radical scavengers) in place of conventional agents for stress ulcer prophylaxis, although the limited number of studies have had promising results. (Strength of evidence = D)

Prevention of Recurrent Bleeding

The efficacy of nonsurgical therapies such as antacids and H_2-receptor antagonists in preventing recurrent bleeding has varied considerably from study to study.[267-269] The number of patients requiring surgery for continued or recurring stress-induced bleeding has steadily decreased since approximately 1978. In a number of published studies, bleeding stopped spontaneously without intervention. In others, the patients' bleeding often stopped and did not recur when conservative measures were instituted, usually an increase in the dosage of the current medication, a switch to a different medication, or the addition of another agent, plus gastric lavage. No large controlled trials have compared the various medication options for preventing a recurrence of stress-induced bleeding. However, when combination therapy for prophylaxis is being considered in a patient who bled while receiving single-agent prophylaxis, use of drugs with different mechanisms of action would seem logical. Potential interactions between prophylactic agents from different classes have not been well studied but could occur (e.g., reduced activity of sucralfate with neutral or alkaline gastric pH, binding of agents by sucralfate). Providing any definitive recommendation regarding this issue is difficult. The assumption is, of course, that *any* medication is of benefit in preventing recurrent bleeding.

Recommendation (adults and pediatrics). The lack of available trials prohibits definitive recommendations for preventing recurrent bleeding after an episode of stress-induced GI bleeding, although consideration could be given to increasing the dosage of the prophylactic agent, adding another medication, or switching to a different agent. (Strength of evidence = D)

Prophylaxis in Non-ICU Settings

It is possible that patients in non-ICU settings could have coagulopathy or other conditions that have been identified as risk factors for bleeding (e.g., transplantation). Only one RCT has addressed stress ulcer prophylaxis in non-ICU settings.[54] The study involved 100 adults and was conducted on a general medical and surgical hospital ward in Spain. Bleeding was significantly (p <0.001) less frequent with antacid prophylaxis than with placebo. However, bleeding was defined broadly to include patients who had a decrease in hematocrit, regardless of whether they required transfusion. Three patients required transfusion in the placebo group and none in the antacid group. Upon institution of antacid and H_2-receptor antagonist therapy, the bleeding stopped in the three patients in the placebo group without subsequent complications. The frequency of all types of bleeding (e.g., overt, clinically important) was significantly lower with prophylaxis only if two or more risk factors for bleeding were present before prophylaxis was initiated.

Discontinuation of Prophylaxis

An increase in the number of risk factors has been associated with a higher risk of bleeding in multiple studies conducted in the ICU setting and one study conducted on a hospital ward. The risk of clinically important bleeding would probably diminish as the number of risk factors is reduced. In most clinical trials, prophylaxis was discontinued without evidence of clinically important bleeding upon extubation or the patient's discharge from the ICU. Thus, it is reasonable to assume that prophylaxis can be stopped once risk factors have resolved.

Recommendation (adults). Stress ulcer prophylaxis is not recommended for adult patients in non-ICU settings. (Strength of evidence = B for general medical and surgical patients with fewer than two risk factors for clinically important bleeding; strength of evidence = D for patients with two or more risk factors) (Table 3)

Recommendation (pediatrics). Stress ulcer prophylaxis is not recommended for pediatric general medical and surgical patients or special populations (e.g., transplantation) in non-ICU settings if fewer than two risk factors for bleeding are present. (Strength of evidence = D). Data are insufficient to allow recommendations to be made about the use of prophylaxis in pediatric patients with two or more risk factors. If prophylaxis is given, it should be discontinued once risk factors have resolved. (Strength of evidence = D)

Economic Analysis

Inappropriate stress ulcer prophylaxis can be costly, but implementing guidelines may decrease the inappropriateness and the expense.[270,271] Published economic analyses can be useful for developing institution-specific guidelines for prophylaxis. Two cost-effectiveness analyses have been completed concerning prophylaxis for stress-induced bleeding. In the first investigation, by Schumock, et al.,[272] an antacid regimen of 30 mL given every 4 hours was compared with sucralfate 1 g given four times daily and three H_2-receptor antagonists (ranitidine 50 mg i.v. every 8 hours, cimetidine 300 mg i.v. every 6 hours, and famotidine 20 mg i.v. every 12 hours), all of which were based on a seven-day course of therapy. The study was conducted from the viewpoint of the payer, with hospital charges measured in 1994 dollars. The authors assumed that the frequency of bleeding would be approximately 70%, 80%, and 36% lower with the use of sucralfate, antacids, and H_2-receptor antagonists, respectively, and that it cost $6128 to treat an episode of bleeding. The frequency of pneumonia was assumed to be unchanged with sucralfate but increased by approximately 7% with antacids and 13% with H_2-receptor antagonists. The net saving associated with prevention of one case of acute upper GI bleeding was $7373 for sucralfate and $4321 for antacids. In contrast, therapy with an H_2-receptor antagonist would cost between $6655 and $7986 to prevent one episode of acute upper GI bleeding. The difference in costs between sucralfate or antacids and H_2-receptor antagonists was related to the assumed higher rates of bleeding and nosocomial pneumonia with H_2-receptor antagonists. One-way sensitivity analysis showed that sucralfate remained the preferred agent regardless of the cost of prophylaxis, the cost of treatment for pneumonia or bleeding, or the presumed frequency of bleeding or nosocomial pneumonia.

The second cost-effectiveness study, by Ben-Menachem, et al.,[64] was based on the perspective of the health care provider. Cimetidine (300 mg i.v. every six hours) was compared with sucralfate (1 g every six hours), both given for seven days. One notable difference from the previous analysis was the assumption that it would cost $595 to treat a GI bleed. It was presumed that both therapies would decrease the frequency of bleeding by 50%; in the sensitivity analysis, the percent reduction was varied over the range of 10–90%. Despite different assumptions from the investigation by Schumock, et al., the results were similar in that sucralfate (cost of $1144 per bleeding event averted) was more cost-effective than cimetidine ($7538 per bleeding event averted), even when rates of pneumonia were presumed to be equal.

In one study involving a small number of patients, the costs of enteral and i.v. ranitidine administration were compared, although only enteral administration was used.[273] Ten patients were assigned to receive ranitidine 150 mg every 12 hours and eight patients to receive 300 mg every 12 hours; both dosages were given by nasogastric tube. Both therapies reduced stimulated acid secretion by at least 50%. Drug costs were calculated to be at least 48% less with the enteral administration than with i.v. administration.

A formal economic analysis from an institutional perspective was conducted as part of the guideline development process. The general steps of acceptable cost-effectiveness analysis were followed: identification of clinical choices, determination of costs and benefits, statement of time frame, determination of cost-effectiveness ratio, and performance of a sensitivity analysis.[274] Readers are encouraged to make institution-specific decisions and to use the template to construct their own institution-specific economic analysis.

The medications were assumed to have equal prophylactic efficacy on the basis of the most recent meta-analysis.[5] Although both the meta-analysis and the recent large RCT met our criteria for a grade of A, the meta-analysis had a level of evidence of I and the RCT a level of evidence of I– (see Table 1 for definitions).

Drug and administration costs[9,64] and adverse event costs[9,185,275,276] and frequency[61,64,176,194–199,277,278] were extrapolated from the literature (Table 9). Ranitidine was chosen as the representative H$_2$-receptor antagonist; i.v. administration was assumed. Because of the cost of commercial sucralfate suspension, the cost analysis was done under the assumption that nursing staff would administer sucralfate tablets as a slurry through a nasogastric tube. The medication cost figures were based on a five-day course of prophylaxis. Costs and benefits were assumed to occur within the same period, making discounting unnecessary. Any estimates not based on the literature were mentioned. The cost estimates for many of the adverse effects were small (e.g., $500), because it was assumed that the effects would be readily reversible or found to have a different cause. The costs reflect laboratory or consultation estimates that would be incurred even if the problem were eventually found to be unrelated to the medication. One hundred patients were assumed to be in each treatment group in our decision model because of the small probabilities of some of the events. It was assumed that the number of events would not vary with the number of patients.

Figure 1 is the decision tree used for the economic analysis associated with these guidelines. The overall results are consistent with those of other published cost-effectiveness analyses that concluded that sucralfate is the most cost-effective agent for prophylaxis, with a saving of $4913 for each episode of bleeding averted. The cost-effectiveness ratio for ranitidine was lower, with a cost saving of $1766. Antacids were nearly cost neutral. The differences are particularly notable if the pH-altering medications are assumed to cause a higher rate of nosocomial pneumonia (0.8% for acid suppressants and 0 for sucralfate); this is true regardless of the route of administration for the H$_2$-receptor antagonists.

Table 9.
Cost Assumptions [9,64,185,275,276]

Variable	Cost Assumptions per Episode or Course of Therapy ($)[a]
Pneumonia	10,062
Bleeding	7,000
Hepatitis	500
CNS toxicity	500
Cytopenia	500
Cardiovascular toxicity	500
Clogged tubes	160
Antacids every two hours	78.00
Histamine H$_2$-receptor antagonist three times daily[b]	61.50
Sucralfate four times daily	33.80

[a]A course of therapy was assumed to be five days. Drug acquisition costs are average wholesale costs.
[b]Ranitidine used as the example.

If it is assumed that none of the medications cause adverse effects (including pneumonia) and that they are similar in efficacy, sucralfate and orally administered H$_2$-receptor antagonists would have similar costs.

The following is a template for evaluating the cost-effectiveness of stress ulcer prophylaxis regimens on the basis of institution-specific data.

Step 1. Estimate the risk of clinically important bleeding events without prophylaxis (baseline rate stated as a percentage).

Step 2. Estimate the reduction in clinically important bleeding events associated with prophylaxis.

Step 3. Estimate the cost per patient of treating GI bleeding at the institution.

Step 4. Estimate the cost of using sucralfate prophylaxis in 100 patients.

Step 5. Estimate the cost of adverse events per 100 patients if all 100 are given prophylaxis.

Step 6. Estimate the cost of treating bleeding per 100 patients treated [(risk of bleeding without prophylaxis) × (estimated cost of treating GI bleed per patient)].

Step 7. Estimate the savings with stress ulcer prophylaxis per 100 patients treated {[(risk of bleeding without prophylaxis) (risk reduction with prophylaxis expressed as a decimal)] × (cost of treating GI bleed per patient)}.

Step 8. Determine the marginal cost of prophylaxis per 100 patients treated {[(cost of medication per 100 patients) + (cost of adverse drug events per 100 patients)] – (savings with stress ulcer prophylaxis in 100 patients)}. Note that positive numbers represent a cost liability, negative numbers a cost saving.

Step 9. Determine the cost-effectiveness ratio [(marginal cost of prophylaxis in 100 patients)/(risk of

Figure 1. Decision tree for stress ulcer prophylaxis. H$_2$-RAs = histamine H$_2$-receptor antagonists, CV = cardiovascular.

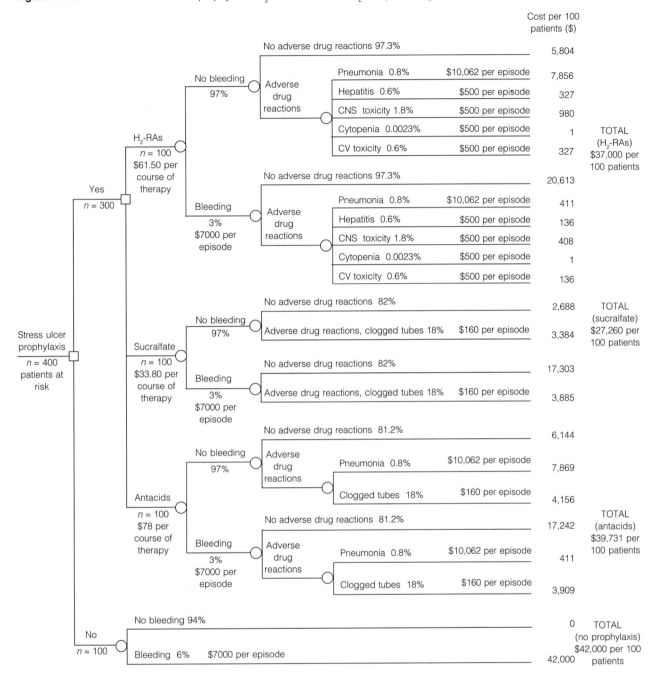

bleeding)(risk reduction with prophylaxis expressed as a decimal)]. A negative value indicates a saving.

Table 10 provides an example of how the cost-effectiveness calculation for sucralfate was performed. The cost-effectiveness ratios for the various therapies can be compared in order to choose the appropriate agent. As with any guidelines, patient-specific information should always be used for determining prophylaxis for the individual patient. To perform a sensitivity analysis for various rates of bleeding and reductions in bleeding associated with prophylaxis, simply vary the values in step 9. Table 11 shows the results of the sensitivity analysis for sucralfate.

Figure 2 is an algorithm for stress ulcer prophylaxis in adult patients that is based on the recommendations contained in this document. The lack of pediatric RCTs involv-

ing medications and the age stratification in those studies that did include pediatric patients preclude development of a separate pediatric algorithm. Because the number (≥2) and type (coagulopathy, respiratory failure, and Pediatric Risk of Mortality Score of ≥10) of risk factors for clinically important bleeding have been elucidated,[66] the reader is referred to the discussion in the section titled "Adverse effects of prophylactic agents" for help in deciding which medication, if any, should be used for prophylaxis.

The adult algorithm is intended to serve as a template that can be modified according to institution-specific data. The strength of the evidence for prophylaxis varies substantially from one risk factor to the next (Table 3). ICU patients with a history of recent GI pathology are deemed appropriate candidates for prophylaxis, but the recommendation must be graded D because patients with recent histories of GI pathol-

Table 10.
Cost-effectiveness Calculations for Sucralfate

Variable	Value
Risk of bleeding without prophylaxis (%)	6.0 (0.1–39)[61,64]
Risk reduction with prophylaxis (%)	50 (10–90)[64]
Cost of treating episode of GI bleeding per patient ($)	7000
Cost of sucralfate per 100 patients ($)	3380
Cost of adverse drug events per 100 patients treated ($)	2880
Cost of treating GI bleeding in 100 patients ($) [(Six episodes of bleeding) × ($7000 cost of treatment)]	42,000
Savings with stress ulcer prophylaxis in 100 patients ($) [(Three episodes of bleeding) × ($7000 cost of treatment)]	21,000
Marginal cost of prophylaxis in 100 patients ($) [($3380 + $2880) – ($21,000)]	–14,740
Cost-effectiveness ratio	4913 for each bleeding episode averted

ogy were often excluded from the published investigations, and thus it is unknown whether these patients are at increased risk for clinically important bleeding. The recommendation for use of oral H_2-receptor antagonists in patients with functioning GI tracts (Figure 2) is based on presumptive efficacy, because no RCTs are available that have compared i.v. with oral H_2-receptor antagonists administration for preventing clinically important bleeding.

Recommendation (adults). Given some of the unresolved issues regarding stress ulcer prophylaxis, it is recommended that institution-specific guidelines be developed on the basis of economic models such as the one included in this document. For institutions willing to accept the assumption that H_2-receptor antagonists and sucralfate have equal efficacy, the accompanying economic analysis found sucralfate to be the most cost-effective agent. Exceptions to the use of sucralfate include lack of oral or other gastric access for administration and, potentially, documented failure of prophylaxis with sucralfate. If ranitidine is assumed to be more effective than sucralfate without increasing the risk of pneumonia, ranitidine (and presumably other H_2-receptor antagonists) would be the drug of choice and would also result

in a cost saving, although less than that achieved with sucralfate.

Recommendation (pediatrics). There are also unresolved issues for pediatric patients. Institution-specific guidelines can be developed by using the economic models included in this document, but the percentages and costs need to be tailored to this population on the basis of institution-specific data. There is supporting evidence in the literature that the risk of stress-induced bleeding is greater in pediatric patients with respiratory failure, coagulopathy, a Pediatric Risk of Mortality Score of ≥ 10, and thermal injuries. Whether prophylaxis will reduce the risk of bleeding is yet to be proven in this population, so there is no clear agent of choice at this time.

Conclusion

Although medications such as antacids have been used for at least two decades to prevent stress-induced bleeding, many issues remain unresolved. While prophylactic agents have demonstrated efficacy in preventing clinically important bleeding in randomized, controlled trials (and meta-analyses), the frequency of stress-induced bleeding has varied substantially from study to study since approximately 1978. This has led some experts to suggest that prophylactic agents are very effective if used appropriately; other experts conclude that the frequency of clinically important stress-induced bleeding has been decreasing as a result of advances in technology and patient care, not medication prophylaxis. The collection of institution-specific data should help clinicians to resolve this issue, at least for their particular patient populations.

When institution-specific rates of stress-induced bleeding are not available, the recommendations contained in these guidelines can serve as a model for adaptation by the institution. Although the recommendations were made on the basis of data published up to the final guideline review process, changes may be needed as information evolves. The reader is encouraged to consider such changes as they occur rather than wait for revised guidelines.

References

1. Anderberg B, Sjodahl R. Prophylaxis and management of stress ulcers. *Scand J Gastroenterol.* 1985; 20(suppl 110):101–4.
2. Shuman RB, Schuster DP, Zuckerman GR. Prophylactic therapy for stress ulcer bleeding: a reappraisal. *Ann Intern Med. 1987;* 106:562–7.

Table 11.
Cost-effectiveness Ratio for Sucralfate Prophylaxis: Results of Sensitivity Analysis[a]

% Reduction in Risk with Prophylaxis	Risk of Bleeding (%)							
	0.1	1	2	4	6	10	20	39
10	619,000	55,600	24,300	8,650	3,433	(740)	(3,870)	(5,395)
30	201,667	13,867	3,433	(1,783)	(3,522)	(4,913)	(5,957)	(6,465)
50	118,200	5,520	(740)	(3,870)	(4,913)	(5,748)	(6,374)	(6,679)
70	82,429	1,943	(2,528)	(4,764)	(5,509)	(6,106)	(6,553)	(6,771)
90	62,556	(44)	(3,522)	(5,261)	(5,841)	(6,304)	(6,652)	(6,822)

[a]Assumptions about the risk of bleeding and the effectiveness of prophylaxis were varied from 0.1% to 39% and from 10% to 90%, respectively. The values represent the cost or saving (in parentheses) for each bleeding episode averted. Costs and benefits were presumed to occur within a similar period, making discounting unnecessary.

Figure 2. Algorithm for stress ulcer prophylaxis in adult patients.

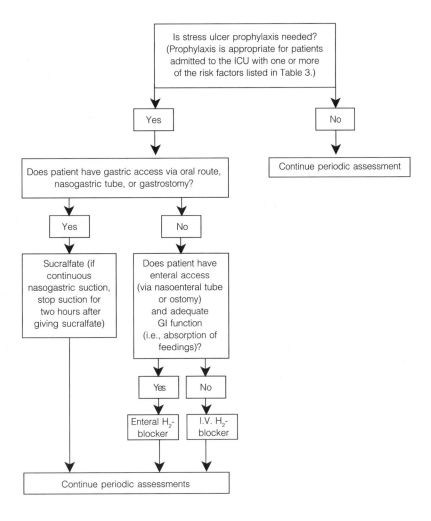

3. Halpern NA, Bettes L, Greenstein R. Federal and nationwide intensive care units and healthcare costs: 1986-1992. *Crit Care Med.* 1994; 22:2001–7.

4. Dasta JF. Drug prescribing issues in the intensive care unit: finding answers to common questions. *Crit Care Med.* 1994; 22:909–12.

5. Cook DJ, Reeve BK, Guyatt GH, et al. Stress ulcer prophylaxis in critically ill patients: resolving discordant meta-analyses. *JAMA.* 1996; 275:308–14.

6. Peura DA. Prophylactic therapy of stress-related mucosal damage: why, which, who, and so what? *Am J Gastroenterol.* 1990; 85:935–7.

7. Tryba M. Stress ulcer prophylaxis—quo vadis? *Intensive Care Med.* 1994; 20:311–3.

8. Berger JT, Rosner F. The ethics of practice guidelines. *Arch Intern Med.* 1996; 156:2051–6.

9. Guyatt GH, Sackett DL, Sinclair JC, et al. User's guide to the medical literature: IX. A method for grading health care recommendations. *JAMA.* 1995; 274:1800–4.

10. Cook DJ, Guyatt GH, Laupacis A, et al. Clinical recommendations using levels of evidence for antithrombotic agents. *Chest.* 1995; 108(4 suppl):227S–30S.

11. Spitzer WO, chair. The periodic health examination. *CMA J.* 1979; 121:1193–254.

12. Gross PA, Barrett TL, Dellinger EP, et al. Purpose of quality standards for infectious diseases. *Clin Infect Dis.* 1994; 18:421.

13. D'Agostino RB, Weintraub M. Meta-analysis: a method for synthesizing research. *Clin Pharmacol Ther.* 1995; 58:605–16.

14. Begg C, Cho M, Eastwood S, et al. Improving the quality of reporting of randomized controlled trials: the CONSORT statement. *JAMA.* 1996; 276:637–9.

15. Greenland S. Quality scores are useless and potentially misleading. *Am J Epidemiol.* 1994; 140:300–1.

16. Sloan JM, Correa P, Lindeman J, et al. The stomach: part I. Acute haemorrhagic gastritis and acute infective gastritis; gastritis caused by physical agents and corrosives; uraemic gastritis. In: Whitehead R, ed. Gastrointestinal and oesophageal pathology. New York: Churchill Livingstone; 1995:461–85.

17. Cho CH, Koo MWL, Garg GP, et al. Stress-induced gastric ulceration: its aetiology and clinical implications. *Scand J Gastroenterol.* 1992; 27:257–62.

18. Navab F, Steingrub J. Stress ulcer: is routine prophylaxis necessary? *Am J Gastroenterol.* 1995; 90:708–12.

19. O'Neill JA. The influence of thermal burns on gastric acid secretion. *Surgery.* 1970; 67:267–71.

20. Gudeman SK, Wheeler CB, Miller JD, et al. Gastric secretory and mucosal injury response to severe head trauma. *Neurosurgery.* 1983; 12:175–9.

21. Larson GM, West G, McGraw P. Intracranial pressure, gastrin, and acid secretion in severe head injury. *Surg Forum.* 1982; 33:175–7.

22. Eastwood GL. Prevention of gastrointestinal bleeding. In: Rippe JM, Irwin RS, Alpert JS, et al., eds. Intensive care medicine. Boston: Little, Brown; 1985:743–4.

23. Menguy R, Desbaillets L, Masters YF. Mechanism of stress ulcer: influence of hypovolemic shock on energy metabolism in the gastric mucosa. *Gastroenterology.* 1974; 66:46–55.

24. Ellison RT, Perez-Perez G, Welsh CH, et al. Risk factors for upper gastrointestinal bleeding in intensive care unit patients: role of *Helicobacter pylori. Crit Care Med.* 1996; 24:1974–81.

25. Hyman PE, Clarke DD, Everett SL, et al. Gastric acid secretory function in preterm infants. *J Pediatr.* 1985; 106:467–71.

26. Kelly EJ, Newell SJ, Brownless KG, et al. Gastric acid secretion in preterm infants. *Early Hum Dev.* 1993; 35:215–20.

27. Euler AR, Byrne WJ, Cousins LM, et al. Increased serum gastrin concentrations and gastric acid hyposecretion in the immediate newborn period. *Gastroenterology.* 1977; 72:1271–3.

28. Maki M, Ruuska T, Kuusela AL, et al. High prevalence of asymptomatic esophageal and gastric lesions in preterm infants in intensive care. *Crit Care Med.* 1993; 21:1863–7.

29. Sevitt S. Duodenal and gastric ulceration after burning. *Br J Surg.* 1967; 54:32–41.

30. Bell MJ, Keating JP, Ternberg JL, et al. Perforated stress ulcers in infants. *J Pediatr Surg.* 1981; 16:998–1002.

31. Skillman JJ, Bushnell LS, Goldman H, et al. Respiratory failure, hypotension, sepsis, and jaundice: a clinical syndrome associated with lethal hemorrhage from acute stress ulceration of the stomach. *Am J Surg.* 1969; 117:523–30.

32. Fischer RP, Stremple JF. Stress ulcers in post-traumatic renal insufficiency in patients from Vietnam. *Surg Gynecol Obstet.* 1972; 134:790–4.

33. Glass GBJ, Stremple JF. Stress ulcers. *Lancet.* 1973; 1:1506–7. Letter.

34. Bowen JC, Fleming WH. A prospective study of stress ulceration in Vietnam. *South Med J.* 1974; 67:156–60.

35. Le Gall JR, Mignon FC, Rapin M, et al. Acute gastroduodenal lesions related to severe sepsis. *Surg Gynecol Obstet.* 1976; 142:377–80.

36. Harris SK, Bone RC, Ruth WE. Gastrointestinal hemorrhage in patients in a respiratory intensive care unit. *Chest.* 1988; 72:301–4.

37. Hastings PR, Skillman JJ, Bushnell LS, et al. Antacid titration in the prevention of acute gastrointestinal bleeding. *N Engl J Med.* 1978; 298:1041–5.

38. Zinner MJ, Zuidema GD, Smith PL, et al. The prevention of upper gastrointestinal tract bleeding in patients in an intensive care unit. *Surg Gynecol Obstet.* 1981; 153:214–20.

39. Basso N, Baragani M, Materia A, et al. Cimetidine and antacid prophylaxis of acute upper gastrointestinal bleeding in high risk patients. *Am J Surg.* 1981; 141:339–41.

40. Friedman CJ, Oblinger MJ, Surratt PM, et al. Prophylaxis of upper gastrointestinal hemorrhage in patients requiring mechanical ventilation. *Crit Care Med.* 1982; 10:316–9.

41. Schuster DP, Rowley H, Feinstein S, et al. Prospective evaluation of the risk of upper gastrointestinal bleeding after admission to a medical intensive care unit. *Am J Med.* 1984; 76:623–30.

42. Pinilla JC, Oleniuk H, Reed D, et al. Does antacid prophylaxis prevent upper gastrointestinal bleeding in critically ill patients? *Crit Care Med.* 1985; 13:646–50.

43. Peura DA, Johnson LF. Cimetidine for prevention and treatment of gastroduodenal mucosal lesions in patients in an intensive care unit. *Ann Intern Med.* 1985; 103:173–7.

44. Cheadle WG, Vitale GC, Mackie CR, et al. Prophylactic postoperative nasogastric decompression. *Ann Surg.* 1985; 202:361–6.

45. Van den Berg B, van Blankenstein M. Prevention of stress-induced gastrointestinal bleeding by cimetidine in patients on assisted ventilation. *Digestion.* 1985; 31:1–8.

46. Van Essen HA, van Blankenstein M, Wilson JHP, et al. Intragastric prostaglandin E and the prevention of gastrointestinal hemorrhage in ICU patients. *Crit Care Med.* 1985; 13:957–60.

47. Groll A, Simon JB, Wigle RD, et al. Cimetidine prophylaxis for gastrointestinal bleeding in an intensive care unit. *Gut.* 1986; 27:135–40.

48. Lacroix J, Infante-Rivard C, Gauthier M, et al. Upper gastrointestinal tract bleeding acquired in a pediatric intensive care unit: prophylaxis trial with cimetidine. *J Pediatr.* 1986; 108:1015–8.

49. Agarwal AK, Saili A, Pandey KK, et al. Role of cimetidine in prevention and treatment of stress induced gastric bleeding in neonates. *Indian Pediatr.* 1990; 27:465–9.

50. Karlstadt RG, Iberti TJ, Silverstein J, et al. Comparison of cimetidine and placebo for the prophylaxis of upper gastrointestinal bleeding due to stress-related gastric mucosal damage in the intensive care unit. *J Intensive Care Med.* 1990; 5:26–32.

51. Knight George AB, Bihari DJ. Gastric intramural pH and stress ulcer prophylaxis in critically ill patients. *Clin Intensive Care.* 1990; 1:249–55.

52. Ruiz-Santana S, Ortiz E, Gonzalez B, et al. Stress-induced gastroduodenal lesions and total parenteral nutrition in critically ill patients: frequency, complications, and the value of prophylactic treatment: a prospective, randomized study. *Crit Care Med.* 1991; 19:887–91.

53. Cook DJ, Pearl RG, Cook RJ, et al. Incidence of clinically important bleeding in mechanically ventilated patients. *J Intensive Care Med.* 1991; 6:167–74.

54. Estruch R, Pedrol E, Castells A, et al. Prophylaxis of gastrointestinal tract bleeding with magaldrate in patients admitted to a general hospital ward. *Scand J Gastroenterol.* 1991; 26:819–26.

55. Labattut AG, Santolalla PM, De Andres AP, et al. Efficacy of sucralfate in the prevention of upper gastrointestinal stress bleeding in intensive care patients: comparison vs a control group. *Clin Intensive Care.* 1992; 3:S19–25.

56. Cochran EB, Phelps SJ, Tolley EA, et al. Prevalence of, and risk factors for, upper gastrointestinal tract bleeding in critically ill pediatric patients. *Crit Care Med.* 1992; 20:1519–23.

57. Lacroix J, Nadeau D, Laberge S, et al. Frequency of upper gastrointestinal bleeding in a pediatric intensive care unit. *Crit Care Med.* 1992; 20:35–42.

58. Martin LF, Booth FVM, Karlstadt RG, et al. Continuous intravenous cimeditine decreases stress-related upper gastrointestinal hemorrhage without promoting

pneumonia. *Crit Care Med.* 1993; 21:19–30.

59. Ben-Menachem T, Fogel R, Patel RV, et al. Prophylaxis for stress-related gastric hemorrhage in the medical intensive care unit: a randomized, controlled, single-blind study. *Ann Intern Med.* 1994; 121:568–75.

60. Eddleston JM, Pearson RC, Holland J, et al. Prospective endoscopic study of stress erosions and ulcers in critically ill adult patients treated with either sucralfate or placebo. *Crit Care Med.* 1994; 22:1949–54.

61. Cook DJ, Fuller HD, Guyatt GH, et al. Risk factors for gastrointestinal bleeding in critically ill patients. *N Engl J Med.* 1994; 330:377–81.

62. Zandstra DF, Stoutenbeek CP. The virtual absence of stress-ulceration related bleeding in ICU patients receiving prolonged mechanical ventilation without any prophylaxis. *Intensive Care Med.* 1994; 20:335–40.

63. Kuuscla AL, Ruuska T, Karikoski R, et al. A randomized, controlled study of prophylactic ranitidine in preventing stress-induced gastric mucosal lesions in neonatal intensive care unit patients. *Crit Care Med.* 1997; 25:346–51.

64. Ben-Menachem T, McCarthy BD, Fogel R, et al. Prophylaxis for stress-related gastrointestinal hemorrhage: a cost-effectiveness analysis. *Crit Care Med.* 1996; 24:338–45.

65. Lopez-Herce J, Dorao P, Elola P, et al., for the Gastrointestinal Hemorrhage Study Group. Frequency and prophylaxis of upper gastrointestinal hemorrhage in critically ill children: a prospective study comparing the efficacy of almagate, ranitidine, and sucralfate. *Crit Care Med.* 1992; 20:1082–9.

66. Chaibou M, Tucci M, Dugas MA, et al. Clinically significant upper gastrointestinal bleeding acquired in a pediatric intensive care unit. *Pediatrics.* 1998; 102:933-8. Abstract.

67. Wiedeck H, Stanescu A, Reinelt H, et al. Evaluation of stress ulcer prophylaxis in high risk intensive care patients. *Intensive Care Med.* 1997; 23(suppl 1):S139.

68. Lacroix J, Infante-Rivarde C, Jenicek M, et al. Prophylaxis of upper gastrointestinal bleeding in intensive care units: a meta-analysis. *Crit Care Med.* 1989; 17:862–9.

69. Tryba M. Prophylaxis of stress ulcer bleeding: a meta-analysis. *J Clin Gastroenterol.* 1991; 13(suppl 2):S44–55.

70. Cook DJ, Witt LG, Cook RJ, et al. Stress ulcer prophylaxis in the critically ill: a meta-analysis. *Am J Med.* 1991; 91:519–27.

71. Tryba M. Sucralfate versus antacids or H$_2$-antagonists for stress ulcer prophylaxis: a meta-analysis on efficacy and pneumonia rate. *Crit Care Med.* 1991; 19:942–9.

72. Layon AJ, Florete O, Day AL, et al. The effect of duodenojejunal alimentation on gastric pH and hormones in intensive care unit patients. *Chest.* 1991; 99:695–702.

73. Choctaw WT, Fujita C, Zawacki BE. Prevention of upper gastrointestinal bleeding in burn patients. *Arch Surg.* 1980; 115:1073–6.

74. Pingleton SK, Hadzima SK. Enteral alimentation and gastrointestinal bleeding in mechanically ventilated patients. *Crit Care Med.* 1983; 11:13–6.

75. Gurman G, Samri M, Sarov B, et al. The rate of gastrointestinal bleeding in a general ICU population: a retrospective study. *Intensive Care Med.* 1990; 16:44–9.

76. Cochard JF, Leger A, Pinaquy C, et al. Gastrointestinal bleeding in trauma ICU patients: incidence and risk factors. *Intensive Care Med.* 1997; 23(suppl 1):S140. Abstract.

77. Kamada T, Fusamoto H, Kawano S, et al. Gastrointestinal bleeding following head injury: a clinical study of 433 cases. *J Trauma.* 1977; 17:44–7.

78. Halloran LG, Zlass AM, Gayle WE, et al. Prevention of acute gastrointestinal complications after severe head injury: a controlled trial of cimetidine prophylaxis. *Am J Surg.* 1980; 139:44–8.

79. Mouawad E, Deloof T, Genette F, et al. Open trial of cimetidine in the prevention of upper gastro-intestinal haemorrhage in patients with severe intracranial injury. *Acta Neurochir.* 1983; 67:239–44.

80. Chan K, Mann KS. Failure of cimetidine prophylaxis in neurosurgery. *Aust N Z J Surg.* 1989; 59:133–6.

81. Reusser P, Gyr K, Scheidegger D, et al. Prospective endoscopic study of stress erosions and ulcers in critically ill neurosurgical patients: current incidence and effect of acid-reducing prophylaxis. *Crit Care Med.* 1990; 18:270–4.

82. Metz CA, Livingston DH, Smith JS, et al. Impact of multiple risk factors and ranitidine prophylaxis on the development of stress-related upper gastrointestinal bleeding: a prospective, multicenter, double-blind, randomized trial. *Crit Care Med.* 1993; 21:1844–9.

83. Chan K, Lai ECS, Tuen H, et al. Prospective double-blind placebo-controlled randomized trial on the use of ranitidine in preventing postoperative gastroduodenal complications in high-risk neurosurgical patients. *J Neurosurg.* 1995; 82:413–7.

84. Burgess P, Larson GM, Davidson P, et al. Effect of ranitidine on intragastric pH and stress-related upper gastrointestinal bleeding in patients with severe head injury. *Dig Dis Sci.* 1995; 40:645–50.

85. O'Neill JA, Bash MC, Pruitt BA, et al. Studies related to the pathogenesis of Curling's ulcer. *J Trauma.* 1967; 7:275–87.

86. Stone HH. Stress ulcers in patients with major burns. *Am Surg.* 1972; 38:107–10.

87. Pruitt BA, Foley FD, Moncrief JA. Curling's ulcer: a clinical-pathology study of 323 cases. *Ann Surg.* 1970; 172:523–39.

88. Bruck HM, Pruitt BA. Curling's ulcer in children: a 12-year review of 63 cases. *J Trauma.* 1972; 12:490–6.

89. Czaja AJ, McAlhany JC, Pruitt BA. Acute gastroduodenal disease after thermal injury: an endoscopic evaluation of incidence and natural history. *N Engl J Med.* 1974; 291:925–9.

90. McAlhany JC, Czaja AJ, Pruitt BA. Antacid control of complications from acute gastroduodenal disease after burns. *J Trauma.* 1976; 16:645–9.

91. Solem LD, Strate RG, Fischer RP. Antacid therapy and nutritional supplementation in the prevention of Curling's ulcer. *Surg Gynecol Obstet.* 1979; 148:367–70.

92. Jones RH, Rudge CJ, Bewick M, et al. Cimetidine: prophylaxis against upper gastrointestinal haemorrhage after renal transplantation. *Br Med J.* 1978; 1 (Feb 18):398–400.

93. Schiessel R, Starlinger M, Wolf A, et al. Failure of cimetidine to prevent gastroduodenal ulceration and bleeding after renal transplantation. *Surgery.* 1981; 90:456–8.

94. Walter S, Andersen JT, Christensen U, et al. Effect of cimetidine on upper gastrointestinal bleeding after renal transplantation: a prospective study. *Br Med J.*

1984; 289:1175–6.

95. MacDougall BRD, Bailey RJ, Williams R. H₂-receptor antagonists and antacids in the prevention of acute gastrointestinal hemorrhage in fulminant hepatic failure: two controlled trials. *Lancet.* 1977; 1:617–9.

96. Nagasue N, Yukaya H, Ogawa Y, et al. Prophylaxis of upper gastrointestinal bleeding with cimetidine in patients undergoing partial hepatectomy. *Ann Chir Gynaecol.* 1984; 73:6–10.

97. Klompmaker IJ, Slooff MJH, de Bruijn KM, et al. Prophylaxis with ranitidine against peptic ulcer disease after liver transplantation. *Transpl Int.* 1988; 1:209–12.

98. Fusamoto H, Hagiwara H, Meren H, et al. A clinical study of acute gastrointestinal hemorrhage associated with various shock states. *Am J Gastroenterol.* 1991; 86:429–33.

99. Rosen HR, Vlahakes GJ, Rattner DW. Fulminant peptic ulcer disease in cardiac surgical patients: pathogenesis, prevention, and management. *Crit Care Med.* 1992; 20:354–9.

100. Apte NM, Karnad PR, Medhekar TP, et al. Gastric colonization and pneumonia in intubated critically ill patients receiving stress ulcer prophylaxis: a randomized, controlled trial. *Crit Care Med.* 1992; 20:590–3.

101. Simons RK, Hoyt DB, Winchell RJ, et al. A risk analysis of stress ulceration after trauma. *J Trauma Inj Infect Crit Care.* 1995; 39:289–94.

102. Faigel DO, Metz DC. Prevalence, etiology, and prognostic significance of upper gastrointestinal hemorrhage in diabetic ketoacidosis. *Dig Dis Sci.* 1996; 41:1–8.

103. Schepp W. Stress ulcer prophylaxis: still a valid option in the 1990s? *Digestion.* 1993; 54:189–99.

104. Rixen D, Livingston DH, Loder P, et al. Ranitidine improves lymphocyte function after severe head injury: results of a randomized, double-blind study. *Crit Care Med.* 1996; 24:1787–92.

105. Friedland JS, Porter JC, Daryanani S, et al. Plasma proinflammatory cytokine concentrations, Acute Physiology and Chronic Health Evaluation (APACHE) III scores and survival in patients in an intensive care unit. *Crit Care Med.* 1996; 24:1775–81.

106. Walt RP. Misoprostol for the treatment of peptic ulcer and antiinflammatory-drug-induced gastroduodenal ulceration. *N Engl J Med.* 1992; 327:1575–80.

107. Guth PH. Mucosal coating agents and other nonantisecretory agents: are they cytoprotective? *Dig Dis Sci.* 1987; 32:647–54.

108. Walt RP, Langman MJS. Antacids and ulcer healing: a review of the evidence. *Drugs.* 1991; 42:205-12.

109. McCarthy DM. Sucralfate. *N Engl J Med.* 1991; 325:1017–25.

110. Tagamet product information. Philadelphia, PA. SmithKline Beecham; 1998.

111. Rollins CJ. Adult enteral nutrition. In: Young LY, Koda-Kimble MA. Applied therapeutics. Vancouver, WA: Applied Therapeutics; 1995:1–28.

112. Sharma VK, Heinzelmann EJ, Steinberg EN, et al. Nonencapsulated, intact omeprazole granules effectively suppress intragastric acidity when administered via a gastrostomy. *Am J Gastroenterol.* 1997; 92:848–51.

113. Balaban DH, Duckworth CW, Peura DA. Nasogastric omeprazole: effects on gastric pH in critically ill patients. *Crit Care Med.* 1997; 92:79–83.

114. Phillips JO, Metzler MH, Palmieri TL, et al. A prospective study of simplified omeprazole suspension for the prophylaxis of stress-related mucosal damage. *Crit Care Med.* 1996; 24:1793–800.

115. Lasky MR, Metzler MH, Phillips JO. A prospective study of omeprazole suspension to prevent clinically significant gastrointestinal bleeding from stress ulcers in mechanically ventilated trauma patients. *J Trauma Inj Infect Crit Care.* 1998; 44:527–33.

116. Prevacid product information. North Chicago, IL. Abbott; 1998.

117. Tryba M, Zevounou F, Torok M, et al. Prevention of acute stress bleeding with sucralfate, antacid or cimetidine. *Am J Med.* 1985; 79(suppl 2C):55-61.

118. Cannon LA, Heiselman D, Gardner W, et al. Prophylaxis of upper gastrointestinal tract bleeding in mechanically ventilated patients. *Arch Intern Med.* 1987; 147:2101–6.

119. Driks MR, Craven DE, Bartolome RC, et al. Nosocomial pneumonia in intubated patients given sucralfate as compared with antacids or histamine type 2 blockers. *N Engl J Med.* 1987; 317:1376–82.

120. Rath T, Walzer LR, Meissl G. Preventative measures for stress ulcers in burn patients. *Burns.* 1988; 14:504–7.

121. Laggner AN, Lenz K, Graninger W, et al. Stress-blutungsprophylaxe auf einer internen intensivstation: sucralfat versus ranitidin. *Anaesthesist.* 1988; 37:704–10.

122. Laggner AN, Lenz K, Base W, et al. Prevention of upper gastrointestinal bleeding in long-term ventilated patients. *Am J Med.* 1989; 86(suppl 6A):81–4.

123. Colardyn F, Vogelaers D, Verschraegen G, et al. Cimetidine versus sucralfate for stress ulcer prophylaxis in medical intensive care unit patients. *Intensive Care Med.* 1990; 16:S18. Abstract.

124. Kappstein I, Schulgen G, Friedrich T, et al. Incidence of pneumonia in mechanically ventilated patients treated with sucralfate or cimetidine as prophylaxis for stress bleeding: bacterial colonization of the stomach. *Am J Med.* 1991; 91(suppl 2A):125S–31S.

125. Simms HH, DeMaria E, McDonald L, et al. Role of gastric colonization in the development of pneumonia in critically ill trauma patients: results of a prospective randomized trial. *J Trauma.* 1991; 31:531–7.

126. Eddleston JM, Vohra A, Scott P, et al. A comparison of the frequency of stress ulceration and secondary pneumonia in sucralfate- or ranitidine-treated intensive care unit patients. *Crit Care Med.* 1991; 19:1491–6.

127. Sirvent JM, Verdaguer R, Ferrer MJ, et al. Nosocomial pneumonia and stress ulcer prophylaxis in intubated patients: comparative study of antacids and ranitidine versus sucralfate. *Intensive Care Med.* 1992; 18:S186. Abstract.

128. Ryan P, Dawson J, Teres D, et al. Nosocomial pneumonia during stress ulcer prophylaxis with cimetidine and sucralfate. *Arch Surg.* 1993; 128:1353–7.

129. Grau JM, Casademont J, Fernandez-Sola J, et al. Prophylaxis of gastrointestinal tract bleeding in patients admitted to a general hospital ward. *Scand J Gastroenterol.* 1993; 28:244–8.

130. Levy MM, Carson R, Miyasaki A, et al. Randomized trial: continuous infusion H₂ blockers, bolus H₂ blockers or Carafate bid for the prophylaxis of stress ulcers in the ICU. *Crit Care Med.* 1993; 21(suppl):S181.

131. Fabian TC, Boucher BA, Croce MA, et al. Pneumonia and stress ulceration in severely injured patients. *Arch Surg.* 1993; 128:185–92.

132. Pickworth KK, Falcone RE, Hoogeboom JE, et al. Occurrence of nosocomial pneumonia in mechanically ventilated trauma patients: a comparison of sucralfate and ranitidine. *Crit Care Med.* 1993; 21:1856–62.

133. Prod'hom G, Leuenberger P, Koerfer J, et al. Nosocomial pneumonia in mechanically ventilated patients receiving antacid, ranitidine, or sucralfate as prophylaxis for stress ulcer: a randomized controlled trial. *Ann Intern Med.* 1994; 120:653–62.

134. Maier RV, Mitchell D, Gentilello L. Optimal therapy for stress gastritis. *Ann Surg.* 1994; 220:353–63.

135. Cioffi WG, McMannus AT, Rue LW, et al. Comparison of acid neutralizing and non-acid neutralizing stress ulcer prophylaxis in thermally injured patients. *J Trauma.* 1994; 36:541–7.

136. Thomason M, Payscur ES, Hakancwerth AM, ct al. Nosocomial pneumonia in ventilated patients during stress ulcer prophylaxis with sucralfate, antacid and ranitidine. *J Trauma Inj Infect Crit Care.* 1996; 4:503–8.

137. Borrero E, Margolis IB, Bank S. Antacid versus sucralfate in preventing acute gastrointestinal bleeding. *Am J Surg.* 1984; 148:809–12.

138. Borrero E, Bank S, Margolis I, et al. Comparison of antacid and sucralfate in the prevention of gastrointestinal bleeding in patients who are critically ill. *Am J Med.* 1985; 79(suppl 2C):62–4.

139. Borerro E, Ciervo J, Chang JB. Antacid versus sucralfate in preventing acute gastrointestinal tract bleeding in abdominal-aortic surgery. *Arch Surg.* 1986; 121:810–2.

140. Bresalier RS, Grendell JH, Cello JP, et al. Sucralfate suspension versus titrated antacid for the prevention of acute stress-related gastrointestinal hemorrhage in critically ill patients. *Am J Med.* 1987; 83(suppl 3B):110–6.

141. Tryba M. Risk of acute stress bleeding and nosocomial pneumonia in ventilated intensive care unit patients: sucralfate versus antacids. *Am J Med.* 1987; 83(suppl 3B):117–24.

142. Israsena S, Kladcharoen N, Limthongkul S, et al. Sucralfate versus antacid in the prevention of stress ulcer bleeding in patients on mechanical ventilation. *J Med Assoc Thai.* 1987; 70:678–82.

143. Mundinger GH, Hays A, Allo M, et al. Effect of meciadanol and sucralfate as compared with antacid titration regimen on prevention of acute gastrointestinal hemorrhage in post-operative intensive care patients. *Surg Forum.* 1985; 36:121–3.

144. Kitler ME, Hay A, Enterline JP, et al. Preventing postoperative acute bleeding of the upper part of the gastrointestinal tract. *Surg Gynecol Obstet.* 1990; 171:366–72.

145. Bonten MM, Gaillard CA, van der Geest S, et al. The role of intragastric acidity and stress ulcer prophylaxis on colonization and infection in mechanically ventilated ICU patients. *Am J Respir Crit Care Med.* 1995; 152:1825–34.

146. McElwee HP, Sirinek KR, Levine BA. Cimetidine affords protection equal to antacids in prevention of stress ulceration following thermal injury. *Surgery.* 1979; 86:620–6.

147. Martin LF, Max MH, Polk HC. Failure of gastric pH control by antacids or cimetidine in the critically ill: a valid sign of sepsis. *Surgery.* 1980; 88:59–68.

148. Priebe HJ, Skillman JJ, Bushnell LS, et al. Antacid versus cimetidine in preventing acute gastrointestinal bleeding. *N Engl J Med.* 1980; 302:426–30.

149. Stothert JC, Siminowitz DA, Dellinger EP, et al. Randomized prospective evaluation of cimetidine and antacid control of gastric pH in the critically ill. *Ann Surg.* 1981; 192:169–74.

150. Kahn F, Parekh A, Patel S, et al. Results of gastric neutralization with hourly antacids and cimetidine in 320 intubated patients with respiratory failure. *Chest.* 1981; 79:409–12.

151. Weigelt LA, Aurbakken CM, Geweritz BL, et al. Cimetidine versus antacid in prophylaxis for stress ulceration. *Arch Surg.* 1981; 115:597–601.

152. Luk GD, Summer WR, Messersmith JF, et al. Cimetidine and antacid in prophylaxis of acute gastrointestinal bleeding: a randomized, double-blind, controlled study. *Gastroenterology.* 1982; 82:1121. Abstract.

153. Zach GA, Gyr KE, von Alvensleben E, et al. A double-blind randomized, controlled study to investigate the efficacy of cimetidine given in addition to conventional therapy in the prevention of stress ulceration and haemorrhage in patients with acute spinal injury. *Digestion.* 1984; 29:214–22.

154. Kingsley AN. Prophylaxis for acute stress ulcers: antacids or cimetidine. *Am Surg.* 1985; 51:545–7.

155. Moscona R, Kaufman T, Jacobs R, et al. Prevention of gastrointestinal bleeding in burns: the effects of cimetidine or antacids combined with early enteral feeding. *Burns.* 1985; 12:65–7.

156. Polesky MH, Spanier AH. Cimetidine versus antacids in the prevention of stress erosions in critically ill patients. *Am J Gastroenterol.* 1986; 81:107–11.

157. Noseworthy TW, Shustack A, Johnston RG, et al. A randomized clinical trial comparing ranitidine and antacids in critically ill patients. *Crit Care Med.* 1987; 15:817–9.

158. LaMothe PH, Rao E, Serra AJ, et al. Comparative efficacy of cimetidine, famotidine, ranitidine, and Mylanta in postoperative stress ulcers: gastric pH control and ulcer prevention in patients undergoing coronary artery bypass graft surgery. *Gastroenterology.* 1991; 100:1515–20.

159. Martin LF. Stress ulcers are common after aortic surgery: endoscopic evaluation of prophylactic therapy. *Am Surg.* 1994; 60:169-74.

160. Cloud ML, Offen W, and the Nizatidine Intensive Care Unit Study Group. Continuous infusions of nizatidine are safe and effective in the treatment of intensive care unit patients at risk for stress gastritis. *Scand J Gastroenterol.* 1994; 29(suppl 206):29–34.

161. Skillman JJ, Lisbon A, Long PC, et al. 15R-15-methyl prostaglandin E2 does not prevent gastrointestinal bleeding in seriously ill patients. *Am J Surg.* 1984; 147:451–5.

162. More DG, Raper RF, Munro IA, et al. Randomized, prospective trial of cimetidine and ranitidine for control of intragastric pH in the critically ill. *Surgery.* 1985; 87:215–24.

163. Jmelnitzky AC, Moday MC, Gallardo EA, et al. Prophylaxis of acute gastric hemorrhage from stress-induced lesions: comparison of pirenzepine and cimetidine in intensive care units. *Dig Dis Sci.* 1986; 31:206. Abstract.

164. Tryba M. Prevention of stress bleeding with ranitidine or pirenzepine and the risk of pneumonia. *J Clin*

Anesth. 1988; 1:12–20.

165. Zinner MJ, Rypins EB, Martin LK, et al. Misoprostol versus antacid titration for preventing stress ulcers in postoperative surgical ICU patients. *Ann Surg.* 1989; 210:590–5.

166. Salim AS. Protection against stress-induced acute gastric mucosal injury by free radical scavengers. *Intensive Care Med.* 1991; 17:455–60.

167. Martin LF, Booth FVM, Reines HD, et al. Stress ulcers and organ failure in intubated patients in surgical intensive care units. *Ann Surg.* 1992; 215:332–7.

168. Behrens R, Hofbeck M, Singer H, et al. Frequency of stress lesions of the upper gastrointestinal tract in pediatric patients after cardiac surgery: effects of prophylaxis. *Br Heart J.* 1994; 72:186–9.

169. Mustafa NA, Akturk G, Ozen I, et al. Acute stress bleeding prophylaxis with sucralfate versus ranitidine and incidence of secondary pneumonia in intensive care unit patients. *Intensive Care Med.* 1995; 21:287. Letter.

170. Reusser P, Zimmerli W, Scheidegger D, et al. Role of gastric colonization in nosocomial infections and endotoxemia: a prospective study in neurosurgical patients on mechanical ventilation. *J Infect Dis.* 1989; 160:414–21.

171. Mahul P, Auboyer C, Jospe R, et al. Prevention of nosocomial pneumonia in intubated patients: respective role of mechanical subglottic secretions drainage and stress ulcer prophylaxis. *Intensive Care Med.* 1992; 18:20–5.

172. Thomasen M, Reeves R, Payseur E, et al. Nosocomial pneumonia in ventilated trauma patients during stress ulcer prophylaxis with sucralfate, ranitidine and antacid. *Crit Care Med.* 1995; 23:A93. Abstract.

173. Fiddian-Green RG, McGough E, Pittenger G, et al. Predictive value of intramural pH and other risk factors for massive bleeding from stress ulceration. *Gastroenterology.* 1983; 85:613–20.

174. Levy MJ, Seelig CB, Robinson NJ, et al. Comparison of omeprazole and ranitidine for stress ulcer prophylaxis. *Dig Dis Sci.* 1997; 42:1255–9.

175. Phillips JO, Metzler MH, Huckfeldt RE, et al. A multicenter, prospective, randomized clinical trial of continuous infusion IV ranitidine versus omeprazole suspension in the prophylaxis of stress ulcers. *Crit Care Med.* 1998; 26(suppl):A101. Abstract.

176. Cook D, Guyatt G, Marshall J, et al. A comparison of sucralfate and ranitidine for the prevention of upper gastrointestinal bleeding in patients requiring mechanical ventilation. *N Engl J Med.* 1998; 338:791–7.

177. Cook DJ, Reeve BK, Scholes LC. Histamine-2-receptor antagonists and antacids in the critically ill population: stress ulceration versus nosocomial pneumonia. *Infect Control Hosp Epidemiol.* 1994; 15:437–42.

178. McEvoy GK, ed. AHFS drug information 98. Bethesda, MD: American Society of Health-System Pharmacists; 1998.

179. Moore JG, Coburn JW, Sanders MC, et al. Effects of sucralfate and ranitidine on aluminum concentrations in elderly volunteers. *Pharmacotherapy.* 1995; 15:742–6.

180. Burgess E, Muruve D, Audette R. Aluminum absorption and excretion following sucralfate therapy in chronic renal insufficiency. *Am J Med.* 1992; 92:471–5.

181. Tryba M, Kurz-Muller K, Donner B. Plasma aluminum concentrations in long-term mechanically ventilated patients receiving stress ulcer prophylaxis with sucralfate. *Crit Care Med.* 1994; 22:1769–73.

182. Baines PB, Ratcliffe J, Petros A. Aluminum concentrations in critically ill children with renal impairment. *Crit Care Med.* 1995; 23:1931.

183. Leung ACT, Henderson IS, Halls DJ, et al. Aluminum hydroxide versus sucralfate as a phosphate binder in uraemia. *Br Med J.* 1983; 286:1379–81.

184. Brogden RN, Heel RC, Speight TM, et al. Sucralfate: a review of its pharmacodynamic properties and therapeutic use in peptic ulcer disease. *Drugs.* 1984; 27:194–209.

185. Marcuarad SP, Perkins AM. Clogging of feeding tubes. *J Parenter Enteral Nutr.* 1988; 12:403–5.

186. Beckwith MC, Barton RG, Graves C. A guide to drug therapy in patients with enteral feeding tubes: dosage form selection and administration methods. *Hosp Pharm.* 1997; 32:57–64.

187. Algozzine GJ, Hill G, Scoggins WG, et al. Sucralfate bezoar. *N Engl J Med.* 1983; 309:1387. Letter.

188. Anderson W, Weatherstone G. Esophageal medication bezoar in a patient receiving enteral feedings and sucralfate. *Am J Gastroenterol.* 1989; 84:205–6.

189. Quigley MA, Flicker M, Caldwell EG. Sucralfate bezoar—theory or fact? *Am J Gastroenterol.* 1986; 81:724–5. Letter.

190. Strozik KS, Walele AH, Hoffman H. Bezoar in a preterm baby associated with sucralfate. *Clin Pediatr.* 1996; 35:423–4.

191. Tang TS, Yeung CY. Intestinal obstruction and perforation following sucralfate administration in a very low birth weight infant. *J Perinat Med.* 1992; 20:317–21.

192. Portuzguez-Malavasi A, Aranda JV. Antacid bezoar in a newborn. *Pediatrics.* 1979; 63:679–80.

193. Brand JM, Greer FR. Hypermagnesemia and intestinal perforation following antacid administration in a premature infant. *Pediatrics.* 1990; 85:121–4.

194. Dobbs JH, Muir JG, Smith RN. H_2-antagonists and hepatitis. *Ann Intern Med.* 1986; 105:803. Letter.

195. Lewis JH. Hepatic effects of drugs used in the treatment of peptic ulcer disease. *Am J Gastroenterol.* 1987; 82:987–1003.

196. Davis TG, Pickett DL, Schlosser JH. Evaluation of a worldwide spontaneous reporting system with cimetidine. *JAMA.* 1980; 243:1912–4.

197. Aymard J-P, Aymard B, Netter P, et al. Haematological adverse effects of histamine H_2-receptor antagonists. *Med Toxicol.* 1988; 3:430–48.

198. Hinrichsen H, Halabi A, Kirch W. Clinical aspects of cardiovascular effects of H_2-receptor antagonists. *Eur J Clin Invest.* 1995; 25(suppl 1):47–56.

199. Cantu TG, Korek JS. Central nervous system reactions to histamine-2 receptor blockers. *Ann Intern Med.* 1991; 114:1027–34.

200. Smallwood RA, Berlin RG, Castagnoli N, et al. Safety of acid-suppressing drugs. *Dig Dis Sci.* 1995; 40(suppl): 63S–80S.

201. Puff MR, Carey WD. The effect of cimetidine on cyclosporine A levels in liver transplant recipients: a preliminary report. *Am J Gastroenterol.* 1992; 87:287–91.

202. Berardi RR, Kirking DM, Townsend KA, et al. Identifying potential interactions of sucralfate with other drugs in hospitalized patients. *Am J Hosp Pharm.* 1992; 49:1488–90.

203. Guay DRP. The role of fluoroquinolones. *Pharmaco-*

therapy. 1992; 12:71S–85S.

204. Just PM. Overview of fluoroquinolone antibiotics. *Pharmacotherapy.* 1993; 13:4S–17S.

205. Holman JS, Shwed JA. Influence of sucralfate on the detection of occult blood in simulated gastric fluid by two screening tests. *Clin Pharm.* 1992; 11:625–7.

206. Dal Negro R. Pharmacokinetic drug interactions with anti-ulcer drugs. *Clin Pharmacokinet.* 1998; 35:135–50.

207. Blum RA. Lansoprazole and omeprazole in the treatment of acid peptic disorders. *Am J Health-Syst Pharm.* 1996; 53:1401–15.

208. Hausken T, Stene-Larsen G, Aronsen O, et al. Misoprostol treatment exacerbates abdominal discomfort in patients with non-ulcer dyspepsia and erosive prepyloric changes. *Scand J Gastroenterol.* 1990; 25:1028–33.

209. Prilosec product information. Wayne, PA: Astra Merck; 1997.

210. Pepcid product information. West Point, PA: Merck; 1996.

211. Zantac product information. Research Triangle Park, NC: Glaxo Wellcome; 1996.

212. Axid product information. Indianapolis, IN: Lilly; 1997.

213. Carafate product information. Kansas City, MO: Hoechst Marion Roussel; 1996.

214. Garris RE, Kirkwood CF. Misoprostol: a prostaglandin E1 analogue. *Clin Pharm.* 1989; 8:627–44.

215. Pittet D. Predicting nosocomial pneumonia in the ICU . . . an ongoing challenge. *Intensive Care Med.* 1996; 22:1139–40.

216. Official statement of the American Thoracic Society. Hospital-acquired pneumonia in adults: diagnosis, assessment of severity, initial antimicrobial therapy, and preventative strategies. *Am J Respir Crit Care Med.* 1995; 153:1711–25.

217. Du Moulin GC, Paterson DG, Hedley-Whyte J, et al. Aspiration of gastric bacteria in antacid-treated patients: a frequent cause of postoperative colonization of the airway. *Lancet.* 1982; 1:242–5.

218. Garvey BM, McCambley JA, Tuxen DV. Effects of gastric alkalinization on bacterial colonization in critically ill patients. *Crit Care Med.* 1989; 17:211–6.

219. Garrard CS, A'Court CD. The diagnosis of pneumonia in the critically ill. *Chest.* 1995; 108(suppl):17S–25S.

220. Tryba M. Side effects of stress bleeding prophylaxis. *Am J Med.* 1989; 86(suppl 6A):85–93.

221. Daschner F, Kappstein I, Engels I, et al. Stress ulcer prophylaxis and ventilation pneumonia: prevention by antibacterial cytoprotective agents? *Infect Control Hosp Epidemiol.* 1988; 9:59–65.

222. Bonten MJ, Bergmans DJ, Ambergen AW, et al. Risk factors for pneumonia, and colonization of respiratory tract and stomach in mechanically ventilated ICU patients. *Am J Respir Crit Care Med.* 1996; 154:1339–46.

223. Ephgrave KS, Kleiman-Wexler R, Pfaller M, et al. Effects of sucralfate vs antacids on gastric pathogens: results of a double-blind clinical trial. *Arch Surg.* 1998; 133:251–7.

224. Craven DE, Steger KA. Epidemiology of nosocomial pneumonia: new perspectives on an old disease. *Chest.* 1995; 108(suppl):1S–16S.

225. The Hospital Infection Control Practices Advisory Committee. Part II: recommendations for prevention of nosocomial pneumonia. *MMWR.* 1997; 46:45–79.

226. Toung TK, Rosenfeld BA, Yoshiki A, et al. Sucralfate does not reduce the risk of acid aspiration pneumonitis. *Crit Care Med.* 1993; 21:1359–64.

227. Cook DJ, Laine LA, Guyatt GH, et al. Nosocomial pneumonia and the role of gastric pH. *Chest.* 1991; 100:7–13.

228. Bonten MJM, Guillard CA, de Leeuw PW, et al. Role of colonization of the upper intestinal tract in the pathogenesis of ventilator-associated pneumonia. *Clin Infect Dis.* 1997; 24:309–19.

229. Hardman JG, Limbird LE, Molinoff PB, et al., eds. Goodman and Gilman's the pharmacological basis of therapeutics. 9th ed. New York: McGraw-Hill Health Professions Division; 1996.

230. Watson LC, Abston S. Prevention of upper gastrointestinal hemorrhage in 582 burned children. *Am J Surg.* 1976; 132:790–3.

231. Vandenplas Y, Sacre L. The use of cimetidine in newborns. *Am J Perinatol.* 1987; 4:131–3.

232. Lopez-Herce J, Velasco LA, Codoceo R, et al. Ranitidine prophylaxis in acute gastric mucosal damage in critically ill patients. *Crit Care Med.* 1988; 16:591–3.

233. Harrison AM, Lugo RA, Vernon DD. Gastric pH control in critically ill children receiving intravenous ranitidine. *Crit Care Med.* 1998; 26:1433–6.

234. Taketomo CK, Hodding JH, Kraus DM. Pediatric dosage handbook. 4th ed. Hudson, OH: Lexi-Comp; 1997–98.

235. Osteyee JL, Banner W. Effects of two dosing regimens of intravenous ranitidine on gastric pH in critically ill children. *Am J Crit Care.* 1994; 3:267–72.

236. Martyn JAJ, Greenblatt DJ, Hagen J, et al. Alteration by burn injury of the pharmacokinetics and pharmacodynamics of cimetidine in children. *Eur J Clin Pharmacol.* 1989; 36:361–7.

237. Lloyd CW, Martin WJ, Taylor BD, et al. Pharmacokinetics and pharmacodynamics of cimetidine and metabolites in critically ill children. *J Pediatr.* 1985; 107:295–300.

238. Blumer JL, Rothstein FC, Kaplan BS, et al. Pharmacokinetic determination of ranitidine pharmacodynamics in pediatric ulcer disease. *J Pediatr.* 1985; 107:301–6.

239. Sarna MJ, Saili A, Dutta AK, et al. Stress associated gastric bleeding in newborns: role of ranitidine. *Indian Pediatr.* 1991; 28:1305–8.

240. Treem WR, Davis PM, Hyams JS. Suppression of gastric acid secretion by intravenous administration of famotidine in children. *J Pediatr.* 1991; 118:812–6.

241. Nagita A, Manago M, Aoki S, et al. Pharmacokinetics and pharmacodynamics of famotidine in children with gastroduodenal ulcers. *Ther Drug Monit.* 1994; 16:444–9.

242. Bush A, Busst CM, Knight WB, et al. Cardiovascular effects of tolazoline and ranitidine. *Arch Dis Child.* 1987; 62:241–6.

243. Feldman M, Burton ME. Histamine$_2$-receptor antagonists. *N Engl J Med.* 1990; 323:1672–80.

244. Kuusela AL. Long term gastric pH monitoring for determining optimal dose of ranitidine for critically ill preterm and term neonates. *Arch Dis Child Fetal Neonatal Ed.* 1998; 78:F151–3.

245. Kelly EJ, Chatfield SL, Brownlee KG, et al. The effect of intravenous ranitidine on the intragastric pH of preterm infants receiving dexamethasone. *Arch Dis Child.* 1993; 69:37–9.

246. Smythe MA, Zarowitz BJ. Changing perspectives of stress gastritis prophylaxis. *Ann Pharmacother.* 1994; 28:1073–85.

247. Dobkin ED, Valcour A, McCloskey CR, et al. Does pH paper accurately reflect gastric pH? *Crit Care Med.* 1990; 18:985–8.

248. Ostro MJ, Russell JA, Soldin SJ, et al. Control of gastric pH with cimetidine: boluses versus primed infusions. *Gastroenterology.* 1985; 89:532–7.

249. Heiselman DE, Hulisz DT, Fricker R, et al. Randomized comparison of gastric pH control with intermittent and continuous intravenous infusion of famotidine in ICU patients. *Am J Gastroenterol.* 1995; 90:277–9.

250. Jones LA, Gonzalez ER, Reines HD, et al. Assessment of 24-hour gastric pH measurements in trauma patients receiving intravenous famotidine by intermittent bolus versus continuous infusion administration. *Ann Pharmacother.* 1994; 28:841–4.

251. Baghaie AA, Mojtahedzadeh M, Levine RL, et al. Comparison of the effect of intermittent administration and continuous infusion of famotidine on gastric pH in critically ill patients: results of a prospective, randomized, crossover study. *Crit Care Med.* 1995; 23:687–91.

252. Ballesteros MA, Hogan DL, Koss MA, et al. Bolus or intravenous infusion of ranitidine: effects on gastric pH and acid secretion. *Ann Intern Med.* 1990; 112:334–9.

253. Gedeit RG, Weigle CGM, Havens PL, et al. Control and variability of gastric pH in critically ill children. *Crit Care Med.* 1993; 21:1850–5.

254. Tryba M. Stress ulcer prophylaxis and gastric alkalinization—death of a myth? *Intensive Care Med.* 1992; 18:1–3.

255. Moore JG, Clemmer TP, Taylor S, et al. Twenty-four-hour intragastric pH patterns in ICU patients on ranitidine. *Dig Dis Sci.* 1992; 37:1802–9.

256. Mela GS, Savarino V. Inaccuracy of hourly sampled pH measurements in describing the effect of antisecretory drugs on circadian gastric acidity. *J Clin Pharmacol.* 1990; 30:45–9.

257. Wilder-Smith CH, Halter F, Hackl W, et al. pH feedback controlled infusions of ranitidine are no more effective than fixed-dose infusions in reducing gastric acidity and variability in antisecretory responses. *Br J Clin Pharmacol.* 1992; 33:487–93.

258. Doglio GR, Pusajo JF, Egurrola MA, et al. Gastric mucosal pH as a prognostic index of mortality in critically ill patients. *Crit Care Med.* 1991; 19:1037–40.

259. Levine JH, Durham RM, Moran J, et al. Multiple organ failure: is it disappearing? *World J Surg.* 1996; 20:471–3.

260. Vincent JL. Prevention and therapy of multiple organ failure. *World J Surg.* 1996; 20:465–70.

261. Chernov MS, Hale HW, Wood M. Prevention of stress ulcers. *Am J Surg.* 1971; 122:674–7.

262. Spilker CA, Hinthorn DR, Pingleton SK. Intermittent enteral feeding in mechanically ventilated patients: the effect on gastric pH and gastric cultures. *Chest.* 1996; 110:243–8.

263. Bengmark S, Gianotti L. Nutritional support to prevent and treat multiple organ failure. *World J Surg.* 1996; 20:474–81.

264. Baue AE, Durham RM, Mazuski JE. Clinical trials of new and novel therapeutic agents. *World J Surg.* 1996; 20:493–8.

265. Matsumoto T, Kaibara N, Sugimachi K, et al. Pathophysiology and management of acute gastric mucosal hemorrhage. *Jpn J Surg.* 1978; 8:261–9.

266. Salim AS. Scavenging free radicals to prevent stress-induced gastric mucosal injury. *Lancet.* 1989; 2:1390.

267. Curtis LE, Simonian S, Buerk CA, et al. Evaluation of the effectiveness of controlled pH in management of massive upper gastrointestinal bleeding. *Am J Surg.* 1973; 125:474–6.

268. Taylor PC, Loop FD, Hermann RE. Management of acute stress ulcer after cardiac surgery. *Ann Surg.* 1973; 178:1–5.

269. MacDonald AS, Pyne DA, Freeman ANG, et al. Upper gastrointestinal bleeding in the intensive care unit. *Can J Surg.* 1978; 21:81–4.

270. Wadibia EC, Lucas BD, Hilleman DE, et al. Economic impact of inappropriate histamine$_2$-receptor antagonist use. *Clin Ther.* 1997; 19:1085–91.

271. Erstad BL, Camamo JM, Miller MJ, et al. Impacting cost and appropriateness of stress ulcer prophylaxis at a university medical center. *Crit Care Med.* 1997; 25:1678–84.

272. Schumock GT, Lam NP, Winkler SR, et al. Pharmacoeconomic analysis of stress ulcer prophylaxis for critically ill patients. *PharmacoEconomics.* 1996; 5:455–65.

273. Pemberton LB, Schaefer N, Goehring L, et al. Oral ranitidine as prophylaxis for gastric stress ulcers in intensive care unit patients: serum concentrations and cost comparisons. *Crit Care Med.* 1992; 21:339–42.

274. Chalfin DB, Cohen IL, Lambrinos J. The economics and cost-effectiveness of critical care medicine. *Intensive Care Med.* 1995; 21:952–6.

275. Jiranek GC, Kozarek RA. A cost-effective approach to the patient with peptic ulcer bleeding. *Surg Clin North Am.* 1996; 76:83–103.

276. Roberts MS. Gastrointestinal bleeding in critically ill patients. *N Engl J Med.* 1994; 331:52. Letter.

277. Hofstetter J, Allen LV Jr. Causes of non-medication-induced nasogastric tube occlusion. *Am J Hosp Pharm.* 1992; 49:603–7.

278. Nicholson LJ. Declogging small-bore feeding tubes. *JPEN.* 1987; 11:594–7.

Recommendations

Indications for Prophylaxis

For adults: Risk factors for ICU patients have been delineated in trials comparing prophylaxis with no prophylaxis by using clinically important bleeding as an endpoint. Prophylaxis is recommended in patients with coagulopathy or patients requiring mechanical ventilation for more than 48 hours. (Strength of evidence = C) Prophylaxis is also recommended in patients with a history of GI ulceration or bleeding within one year before admission and in patients with at least two of the following risk factors: sepsis, ICU stay of more than one week, occult bleeding lasting six days or more, and use of high-dose corticosteroids (>250 mg per day of hydrocortisone or the equivalent). (Strength of evidence = D) (Table 3) Recommendations for specific prophylactic medications can be found in the Medications used for prophylaxis section.

For pediatrics: Although various risk factors have been associated with bleeding in pediatric patients, published randomized, controlled trials (RCTs) have either not used clinically important bleeding as an outcome or had insufficient power to enable a definitive conclusion that prophylaxis provides protection. Risk factors that have been associated with clinically important bleeding include respiratory failure, coagulopathy, and a Pediatric Risk of Mortality Score of ≥10. (Strength of evidence = C)

Indications in Special Populations

For adults: Prophylaxis is recommended for ICU patients with a Glasgow Coma Score of ≤10 (or the inability to obey simple commands) or thermal injuries to >35% of their body surface area (BSA). (Strength of evidence = B) ICU patients with partial hepatectomy may also benefit from prophylaxis. (Strength of evidence = C) Prophylaxis may also be indicated in ICU patients with multiple trauma (e.g., Injury Severity Score of ≥16), transplantation patients in the ICU perioperatively, ICU patients with hepatic failure, and ICU patients with spinal cord injuries. (Strength of evidence = D) (Table 3)

For pediatrics: For pediatric patients (one month of age or older) with thermal injuries, prophylaxis is recommended, but there is insufficient evidence to recommend prophylaxis based on any given percentage of BSA. (Strength of evidence = D) For other pediatric surgery or trauma patients, insufficient evidence is available to allow recommendations about prophylaxis to be made.

Agent of Choice

For adults: Given the conflicting results of several meta-analyses and a recent RCT (both with strengths of evidence = A), the choice among antacids, H_2-receptor antagonists, and sucralfate for use as prophylactic agents to prevent clinically important bleeding associated with stress in adult patients admitted to general medical and surgical ICUs should be made on an institution-specific basis. This choice should take into account concerns regarding administration (e.g., functioning GI tract), adverse-effect profile, and total costs. (Strength of evidence = D) Insufficient data on misoprostol or the proton-pump inhibitors are available to allow any recommendation about these agents to be made.

For pediatrics and special populations: The lack of comparative trials of these agents in pediatric and special populations (e.g., patients with burns, trauma patients, patients undergoing neurosurgical procedures or with neurologic disorders, and transplantation patients) precludes definitive recommendations as to the agent of choice in these situations. The choice of agent should be made on an institution-specific basis and should take into account concerns about administration (e.g., functioning GI tract), adverse-effect profile, and total costs.

Adverse Effects

For adults and pediatrics: It is recommended that patients with a history of serious reactions to antacids, H_2-receptor antagonists, proton-pump inhibitors, or sucralfate avoid future use of the offending agent. There are no other absolute contraindications that would preclude the short-term use of any of these medications for stress ulcer prophylaxis. However, unless the benefits clearly exceed the

risks, it is recommended that sucralfate and antacids be avoided in neonates (particularly premature neonates) because of the possibility of adverse effects (e.g., bezoar formation, accumulation of aluminum and magnesium). Also, it is recommended that aluminum-containing products such as sucralfate be avoided in children with renal failure because dosing information has not been well established. Whether acid-suppressing agents are associated with a higher rate of pneumonia than sucralfate is unresolved, although any difference between these medications would appear to be small. It is recommended that potential adverse effects be considered as part of the economic analysis when an agent is chosen (see Economic Analysis). (Strength of evidence = D)

Monitoring

For adults and pediatrics: It is recommended that all patients receiving medications for stress ulcer prophylaxis be monitored for bleeding and adverse drug effects (see Adverse Effects of Prophylactic Agents). Paper techniques for measuring gastric pH have questionable validity and reliability, and there is no evidence that adjusting the dosage of pH-altering medications (antacids, H_2-receptor antagonists, proton-pump inhibitors) on the basis of these measurements influences patient morbidity or mortality. Despite the lack of supporting data, pH monitoring for antacids may be appropriate (goal pH of >3.5–4). Such monitoring may also be useful for H_2-receptor antagonists when standard dosage regimens might not be appropriate (e.g., in cases of renal dysfunction, for increased dosages due to perceived failure of therapy, in pediatric patients). (Strength of evidence = D)

Other Options

For adults and pediatrics: It is premature to recommend the use of novel therapies (e.g., free-radical scavengers) in place of conventional agents for stress ulcer prophylaxis, although the limited number of studies have had promising results. (Strength of evidence = D)

Prevention of Recurrent Bleeding

For adults and pediatrics: The lack of available trials prohibits definitive recommendations for preventing recurrent bleeding after an episode of stress-induced GI bleeding, although consideration could be given to increasing the dosage of the prophylactic agent, adding another medication, or switching to a different agent. (Strength of evidence = D)

Non-ICU Patients

For adults: Stress ulcer prophylaxis is not recommended for adult patients in non-ICU settings. (Strength of evidence = B for general medical and surgical patients with fewer than two risk factors for clinically important bleeding; strength of evidence = D for patients with two or more risk factors) (Table 3)

For pediatrics: Stress ulcer prophylaxis is not recommended for pediatric general medical and surgical patients or special populations (e.g., transplantation) in non-ICU settings if fewer than two risk factors for bleeding are present. (Strength of evidence = D) Data are insufficient to allow recommendations to be made about the use of prophylaxis in pediatric patients with two or more risk factors. If prophylaxis is given, it should be discontinued once risk factors have resolved. (Strength of evidence = D)

Institution-Specific Guidelines

For adults: Given some of the unresolved issues regarding stress ulcer prophylaxis, it is recommended that institution-specific guidelines be developed on the basis of economic models such as the one included in this document. For institutions willing to accept the assumption that H_2-receptor antagonists and sucralfate have equal efficacy, the accompanying economic analysis found sucralfate to be the most cost-effective agent. Exceptions to the use of sucralfate include lack of oral or other gastric access for administration and, potentially, documented failure of prophylaxis with sucralfate. If ranitidine is assumed to be more effective than sucralfate without increasing the risk of pneumonia, ranitidine (and presumably other H_2-receptor antagonists) would be the drug of choice and would also result in a cost saving, although less than that achieved with sucralfate.

For pediatrics: There are also unresolved issues for pediatric patients. Institution-specific guidelines can be developed by using the economic models included in this document, but the percentages and costs need to be tailored to this population on the basis of institution-specific data. There is supporting evidence in the literature that the risk of stress-induced bleeding is greater in pediatric patients with respiratory failure, coagulopathy, a Pediatric Risk of Mortality Score of ≥ 10, and thermal injuries. Whether prophylaxis will reduce the risk of bleeding is yet to be proven in this population, so there is no clear agent of choice at this time.

This official ASHP practice standard was developed through the ASHP Commission on Therapeutics and approved by the ASHP Board of Directors on November 14, 1998.

Members of the 1998–1999 ASHP Commission on Therapeutics are Austin J. Lee, Pharm.D., BCPS, FASHP, Chair; C. Wayne Weart, Pharm.D., FASHP, Vice Chair; G. Dennis Clifton, Pharm.D.; Matthew A. Fuller, Pharm.D., BCPS, BCPP; Kent M. Nelson, Pharm.D., BCPS; William L. Green, Pharm.D., BCPS, FASHP; Mary Beth Gross, Pharm.D.; Michael D. Katz, Pharm.D.; Shirley J. Reitz, Pharm.D.; Jane E. DeWitt, Student Member; Donald T. Kishi, Pharm.D., Board Liaison; and Leslie Dotson Jaggers, Pharm.D., BCPS, Secretary.

Project Coordinators: Brian L. Erstad, Pharm.D., FCCM, FASHP, BCPS, Associate Professor/Assistant, Department Head, Department of Pharmacy Practice and Science, College of Pharmacy, University of Arizona, Tucson; Kathryn L. Grant, Pharm.D., FASHP, Assistant Professor, Department of Pharmacy Practice and Science, College of Pharmacy, University of Arizona,Tucson.

Expert Panel: Bradley A. Boucher, Pharm.D., BCPS, Associate Professor and Director of Research, Department of Clinical Pharmacy, The University of Tennessee, Memphis; Jimmi Hatton, Pharm.D., BCNSP, Associate Professor of Pharmacy and Surgery, University of Kentucky Medical Center, Lexington; Judith Jacobi, Pharm.D., BCPS, Critical Care Clinical Pharmacist, Department of Pharmacy Services, Methodist Hospital of Indiana, Indianapolis; Rick Jones, Jr., Manager, Strategic Development, Pharmacy Department, Orlando Regional Healthcare System, Florida; Keith M. Olsen, Pharm.D., FCCP, Associate Professor of Pharmacy, College of Pharmacy, University of Nebraska Medical Center, Omaha; H. David Reines, M.D., Professor of Surgery, Tufts University School of Medicine, Newton, MA; and Andrea Quinn Wilson, APRN, CETN, CS, Clinical Nurse Specialist, Yale New Haven Hospital, New Haven, CT.

The recommendations in this document do not indicate an exclusive course of treatment to be followed. Variations, taking into account individual circumstances, may be appropriate.

The bibliographic citation for this document is as follows: American Society of Health-System Pharmacists. ASHP Therapeutic Guidelines on Stress Ulcer Prophylaxis. *Am J Health-Syst Pharm.* 1999; 56:347–79.

Index

Index

━━━C